2023

CU00922641

## The Cambridge Handbook of Pragmatics

Pragmatics is the study of human communication: the choices speakers make to express their intended meaning and the kinds of inferences that hearers draw from an utterance in the context of its use. This Handbook surveys pragmatics from different perspectives, presenting the main theories in pragmatic research, incorporating seminal research as well as cutting-edge solutions. It addresses questions of rational and empirical research methods, what counts as an adequate and successful pragmatic theory, and how to go about answering problems raised in pragmatic theory. In the fast-developing field of pragmatics, this Handbook fills the gap in the market for a one-stop resource on the wide scope of today's research and the intricacy of the many theoretical debates. It is an authoritative guide for graduate students and researchers with its focus on the areas and theories that will mark progress in pragmatic research in the future.

KEITH ALLAN is Emeritus Professor in Linguistics at Monash University, Australia.

KASIA M. JASZCZOLT is Professor of Linguistics and Philosophy of Language at the University of Cambridge, and fellow of Newnham College, Cambridge.

CAMBRIDGE HANDBOOKS IN LANGUAGE AND LINGUISTICS

Genuinely broad in scope, each handbook in this series provides a complete state-of-the-field overview of a major sub-discipline within language study and research. Grouped into broad thematic areas, the chapters in each volume encompass the most important issues and topics within each subject, offering a coherent picture of the latest theories and findings. Together, the volumes will build into an integrated overview of the discipline in its entirety.

## Published titles

*The Cambridge Handbook of Phonology*, edited by Paul de Lacy
*The Cambridge Handbook of Linguistic Code-switching*, edited by
    Barbara E. Bullock and Almeida Jacqueline Toribio
*The Cambridge Handbook of Child Language*, edited by Edith L. Bavin
*The Cambridge Handbook of Endangered Languages*, edited by Peter K. Austin
    and Julia Sallabank
*The Cambridge Handbook of Sociolinguistics*, edited by Rajend Mesthrie
*The Cambridge Handbook of Pragmatics*, edited by Keith Allan
    and Kasia M. Jaszczolt

## Further titles planned for the series

*The Cambridge Handbook of Language Policy*, edited by Bernard Spolsky
*The Cambridge Handbook of Biolinguistics*, edited by Cedric Boeckx and
    Kleanthes K. Grohmann
*The Cambridge Handbook of Second Language Acquisition*, edited by Julia Herschensohn
    and Martha Young-Scholten
*The Cambridge Handbook of Generative Syntax*, edited by Marcel Den Dikken
*The Cambridge Handbook of Communication Disorders*, edited by Louise Cummings

# The Cambridge Handbook of Pragmatics

Edited by
**Keith Allan**
and
**Kasia M. Jaszczolt**

CAMBRIDGE
UNIVERSITY PRESS

# CAMBRIDGE
## UNIVERSITY PRESS

University Printing House, Cambridge CB2 8BS, United Kingdom

Published in the United States of America by Cambridge University Press, New York

Cambridge University Press is part of the University of Cambridge.

It furthers the University's mission by disseminating knowledge in the pursuit of education, learning and research at the highest international levels of excellence.

www.cambridge.org
Information on this title: www.cambridge.org/9780521192071

© Cambridge University Press 2012

This publication is in copyright. Subject to statutory exception and to the provisions of relevant collective licensing agreements, no reproduction of any part may take place without the written permission of Cambridge University Press.

First published 2012
3rd printing 2013

Printed in the United Kingdom by the CPI Group Ltd, CR0 4YY

*A catalogue record for this publication is available from the British Library*

*Library of Congress Cataloguing in Publication data*
The Cambridge handbook of pragmatics / edited by Keith Allan and Kasia M. Jaszczolt.
p.   cm. – (Cambridge handbooks in language and linguistics)
Includes bibliographical references and index.
ISBN 978-0-521-19207-1 (hardback)
1. Pragmatics.   I. Allan, Keith, 1943–   II. Jaszczolt, Katarzyna.   III. Title.
P99.4.P72C365   2012
401'.45 – dc23      2011041740

ISBN 978-0-521-19207-1 Hardback

Cambridge University Press has no responsibility for the persistence or accuracy of URLs for external or third-party internet websites referred to in this publication, and does not guarantee that any content on such websites is, or will remain, accurate or appropriate.

# Contents

# Figures

# Contributors

**Keith Allan,** Professor Emeritus in Linguistics, Monash University, Australia

**Mira Ariel,** Professor of Linguistics, Tel Aviv University, Israel

**Jay David Atlas,** Peter W. Stanley Professor of Linguistics and Philosophy, Pomona College, Claremont, USA

**Johan van der Auwera,** Professor of Linguistics, Universiteit Antwerpen, Belgium

**Kent Bach,** Professor of Philosophy, Emeritus, San Francisco State University, USA

**Emma Borg,** Professor of Philosophy, University of Reading, UK

**Berit (Brit) Brogaard,** Associate Professor of Philosophy and Psychology, University of Missouri St Louis, USA

**Robyn Carston,** Professor of Linguistics, University College London, UK, and Centre for the Study of Mind in Nature, Oslo, Norway

**Anita Fetzer,** Professor of English Linguistics, Universität Würzburg, Germany

**Luna Filipović,** Research Fellow, University of Cambridge, UK

**Rachel Giora,** Professor of Linguistics, Tel Aviv University, Israel

**Jeanette K. Gundel,** Professor of Linguistics, University of Minnesota, Minneapolis, USA

**Michael Haugh,** Senior Lecturer in Linguistics, Griffith University, Nathan, Australia

**Laurence R. Horn,** Professor of Linguistics, Yale University, New Haven, USA

**Kasia M. Jaszczolt,** Professor of Linguistics and Philosophy of Language, University of Cambridge, UK

**Andreas H. Jucker,** Professor of English, University of Zurich, Switzerland

**Napoleon Katsos,** Lecturer, University of Cambridge, UK

**Istvan Kecskes,** Professor of Linguistics and Education, State University of New York at Albany, USA

**Ruth Kempson,** Professor of Linguistics, King's College London, UK

**Mikhail Kissine,** Post-doctoral Researcher, Université Libre de Bruxelles, Belgium

**Caterina Mauri,** Research Fellow, Dipartimento di Linguistica Teorica e Applicata, Università degli Studi di Pavia, Italy

**Jaroslav Peregrin,** Professor of Logic, Institute of Philosophy, Academy of Sciences of the Czech Republic, Prague, Czech Republic

**François Recanati,** Research Fellow, Institut Jean Nicod, Ecole Normale Supérieure, Paris, France

**Rob van der Sandt,** Professor of Philosophy of Language and Logic, Radboud University of Nijmegen, The Netherlands

**Louis de Saussure,** Professor of Linguistics and Discourse Analysis, Université de Neuchâtel, Switzerland

**Arthur Sullivan,** Associate Professor of Philosophy, Memorial University, St. John's, Canada

**Marina Terkourafi,** Assistant Professor of Linguistics, University of Illinois Urbana-Champaign, USA

**Elizabeth Closs Traugott,** Professor Emeritus of Linguistics and English, Stanford University, USA

**Tim Wharton,** Lecturer in English Language and Communication, Kingston University, London

**Henk Zeevat,** Senior Lecturer in Computational Linguistics, University of Amsterdam, The Netherlands

# Acknowledgements

First and foremost we want to thank all the contributors for their reliability, hard work, enthusiasm and words of encouragement during the process of collating this volume; it has been a pleasure to work with you. Next, we owe thanks to our editorial assistant Jos Tellings for collating the bibliography for the volume and standardising the final drafts. We also thank Andrew Winnard from Cambridge University Press for keeping a careful eye on the timing of this project, imprinting in us the belief that Press deadlines mustn't be flouted, or at least not excessively. Next, our gratitude goes to Malcolm Todd for his efficient, dedicated and thoughtful copy-editing and to Kim Birchall for the professionally and comprehensively compiled index. Kasia Jaszczolt would like to thank her little helper Lidia Berthon for eagerly, enthusiastically and competently performing various office tasks to do with the preparation of this book under some unusual conditions. Finally, thank you to our bright and enthusiastic students in Melbourne, Australia and Cambridge, United Kingdom for helping us maintain a lively interest in the intricacies of meaning for all those years we spent in joint discussions, formal and informal.

# 1

# Introduction
## Pragmatic objects and pragmatic methods

### Kasia M. Jaszczolt and Keith Allan

*The Cambridge Handbook of Pragmatics* defines pragmatics from different points of view, presenting the main orientations in pragmatic research of both wide and narrow scope, incorporating seminal research as well as cutting-edge state-of-the-art solutions. It addresses the question of rational and empirical research methods, the question of what counts as an adequate and successful pragmatic theory, and how to go about answering the questions that pragmatic theory identifies. *The Cambridge Handbook of Pragmatics* aims to offer accessible introductions that present the many different problems and approaches to be found in the current literature on pragmatics.

There is no doubt that acts of communication deserve methodologically sound pragmatic theories. The state-of-the-art studies of discourse practices, utterance interpretation and processing, and acts of speech demonstrate that a lot of progress has been achieved since the times of programmatic slogans of ordinary language philosophers, urging philosophers and linguists to focus on language use rather than on fitting natural languages into the mould of formal languages of logic. First, we have progressed as far as the unit of analysis is concerned; while Grice (e.g. 1975) talked about pragmatic inferences from an utterance, a pragmatic equivalent of the syntactic unit of a sentence (albeit not necessarily a linguistic equivalent: showing to one's interlocutor a picture or a clear gesture would do just as well), now we are equipped with sophisticated theories that take discourses as units of study. Second, we have progressed beyond observations that assertives are not the centre of pragmatics, which we owe to Austin (1962), Searle (1969) and other speech act theorists, to sophisticated analyses of non-assertive acts of communication. Next, and arguably most importantly, we have leaped forward to incorporate pragmatic theory into linguistics as a legitimate and even potentially formalisable level of analysis of language. At the same time, pragmatics remains the level that makes most use of rich and bidirectionally equally invaluable interfaces. The 'pragmatic turn' (Mey 2001: 4) is now definable not only as a manifesto that proclaims a shift from the focus on sentence structure to the uses we make of sentences in communication as initiated by Peirce, Morris or Carnap, and nowadays generally associated with Wittgenstein's *Investigations* (1953). Instead, it is implemented as powerful pragmatic theories.

The message this collection sends out is that pragmatics is a well-established subdiscipline of linguistics and at the same time a progressive branch of philosophy of language. When Jacob Mey published his first edition of the *Concise Encyclopedia of Pragmatics* in 1998, he talked of pragmatics as a 'relatively young science', 'a truly catholic discipline' in view of being a descendant of philosophy and linguistics (Mey 1998a: xxvii). Judging from textbooks such as Levinson's seminal *Pragmatics* (1983), it was indeed so; notwithstanding its depth of argumentation, that textbook is still sometimes described by professionals as a collection of articles that define the scope of a new discipline. We hope the current *Handbook* will testify to the enormous progress on this front. We also hope to have demonstrated progress in pragmatic methods as well as a slight shift of emphasis since that presented in the excellent handbook by Horn and Ward (2004) several years ago. Cutting-edge research on the semantics/pragmatics interface led to the pragmatic turn orientation in the domains of the conceptualisation of syntax (Kempson), dynamic semantics and pragmatics (Zeevat), two-dimensional semantics and pragmatics (Brogaard), the study of presupposition (van der Sandt), meaning and truth conditions (Recanati), compositionality and intentional contexts (Jaszczolt), literal/nonliteral distinction (Carston), to name only a few conspicuous examples. In another dimension, the volume also engages with the progress in experimental methods for testing theories of discourse interpretation, and notably inference and automatic construal of intended meaning (Katsos, Giora, Allan, Haugh and Jaszczolt).

Yet another welcome area of change in the general orientation of pragmatics is the increasing integration of the Anglo-American and continental European pragmatics. While the first has always been firmly based on the philosophical foundations of ordinary language philosophy on the one hand, and the interface with grammar on the other, and has remained close to the philosophical outlook on conversation,[1] European researchers put more emphasis on the domains collectively called macropragmatics (see e.g. Verschueren 1999), including notably the domain of sociopragmatics and topics such as cross-cultural and intercultural communication and ideology. This integration is evident in several chapters in the volume (Kecskes, Haugh, and Terkourafi). Yet another dimension of integration is that of post-Gricean semantics/pragmatics disputes that adhere to the tool of truth conditions as for example in truth-conditional pragmatics (see Recanati 2004a, 2010 and this volume) and cognitive linguistics. Non-literal meanings can be understood as part of truth-conditional content (see also Carston, this volume, and Jaszczolt 2005, 2010c and this volume), at the same time exemplifying human tendencies toward certain kinds of conceptualisations.[2]

The *Handbook* is divided thematically into three parts. The first introduces problems and objects of study for pragmatics as well as the main current pragmatic theories. In accordance with the editors' assessment of the current progress in pragmatics, more attention has been given to the problems and methods identified and followed by post-Griceans, such as the role of inference and intentions. Part II focuses on applications of pragmatic approaches to selected phenomena that present a particular challenge for this subdiscipline and that produced cutting-edge analyses in the literature. Part III follows with the most seminal interfaces into which pragmatic theory enters, reviewing, among others, the semantics/pragmatics and syntax/pragmatics boundary disputes.

The content of the chapters is as follows. The current chapter introduces readers to the aims, objectives, and objects of study of pragmatics, pointing out seminal discussions in the literature concerning the focus, scope and methods of pragmatic analysis largely through a discussion of the contributing chapters. Next, Mira Ariel's 'Research paradigms in pragmatics' introduces the main orientations of Gricean inferential pragmatics, form/function pragmatics, and historical and typological pragmatics, also discussing the division of labour among them. For the most part, theories from different research paradigms complement each other, despite being in competition when they address the same linguistic phenomenon (e.g. the neo-Gricean versus Relevance-theoretic analyses of scalars and *and*). Ariel outlines three prominent research paradigms under the assumption that grammar is encoded and pragmatics is inferred. Grice's insight about the crucial role of inferencing for conveying the speaker's intended message has been adopted by all *inferential pragmatics* theories as a major ingredient in utterance interpretation. *Form/function pragmatics* uses naturally occurring examples to investigate a small subset of pragmatic meanings associated with constructions and discourse markers. Much *historical and typological pragmatics* research analyses the current grammar as pragmatically motivated. All newly formed form/function correlations are crucially context-bound as interlocutors exploit grammar to fulfil interactional goals. Once grammaticalised (conventionalised) cancellability no longer applies, nor is contextual support needed. Each of these approaches amends the classical code model of language. For inferential pragmatists truth-conditional codes cannot exhaust speakers' intended on-line meanings, because ad hoc contextual inferences are generated in addition. For form/function pragmatists, also, not all codes are truth-conditional. Finally, *contra* generative grammarians, historical/typological pragmatists argue that classical codes cannot account for possible versus impossible natural language grammars. Since each approach finds different flaws in the classical code model, they each enrich it, but differently. This is demonstrated in their different approaches to referring expressions. The conclusion is that all three paradigms are necessary for a complete picture of grammatical forms, and for what should be assigned pragmatic status.

In Chapter 3, 'Saying, meaning, and implicating', Kent Bach addresses Grice's notion of saying and the post-Gricean concepts of *what is said*, *explicature*, and *implicature*, remarking on some deplorable confusions in the literature such as conflating implicated and inferred meaning or endowing linguistic expressions, rather than speakers, with implicatures. It serves as an introduction to Grice's intention-based view of communication, his intention-based theory of meaning and his notion of implicature. A speaker can say something without meaning it or she can mean something without saying it, by merely implicating or impliciting it. This is possible because we rely on recourse to common ground (including the conversational maxims) when communicating and on the very fact that the utterance is made under that condition. Bach therefore distinguishes linguistic and speaker's meaning. He points out that Grice could usefully have invoked the Austinian differentiation of locutionary, illocutionary and perlocutionary acts rather than requiring that to say something entails meaning it. This would have clarified his account of the speaker saying, meaning, and the resulting communicative effect. Implicature is explained with the help of the concepts of intention, inference in communication and a comparison with logical implication and is presented in the critical perspective of post-Gricean developments, including the disputes concerning the speaker's vs the addressee's perspective and the classification of implicit meanings. Like relevance theorists, Bach finds that the distinction between saying and implicating needs supplementing with *impliciture* (which overlaps RT *explicature*) for that part of meaning that is located between what is said and what is implicated. In brief, implicitures are cancellable expansions of what is said (such as *and* expanded to 'and then', *It's raining* to 'it is raining here and now'). Conversational maxims or what Bach prefers to call *presumptions* do not directly generate implicatures and implicitures but raise possibilities that the hearer should take into account when figuring out the speaker's message. A hearer does not necessarily have to infer the thing the speaker implicates but merely that the speaker implicates (means) it.

The confusions surrounding implicature are further discussed and relevant issues are clarified in the next chapter, in which Larry Horn, like Kent Bach, emphasises that *speakers implicate*, while *hearers infer*. The chapter 'Implying and inferring' offers a thoughtful analysis of the foundations of the Gricean programme and of the term *implicature*, with references to the history of relevant concepts such as Frege's defence of conventional implicatures ('andeuten'). Horn discusses the various meanings and uses of *infer*, *imply* and *implicate*, as well as the nouns *explicature* and *implicature*. He points out that so-called Gricean scalar implicature from *some* to *not all* was recognised by Mill as early as 1867, who pointed out that the use of the word 'some' is normally associated with the denial of the possibility of the use of a stronger word 'all'. This is an early refutation of those who contend that *some* simply means 'not all'. Horn discusses and compares the original Gricean maxims, his own Q and R principles, Levinson's three-way Q, I and M principles, and the single Relevance theory principle of relevance. He holds to the Gricean view that conversational implicature arises from the shared presumption that speaker and hearer interact to reach a shared goal. He criticises Levinson for defining generalised conversational implicatures as default inferences, arguing that an implicature is an aspect of speaker's meaning, not hearer's interpretation – although many others too fail to make such a distinction. There are, of course, many who dispute that GCIs are defaults. Pragmatic enrichments that supply the conditions necessary to build truth-evaluable propositions involve what Recanati has called *saturation* and Bach *completion*. Horn argues that Bach's impliciture – constructed from what is said – such that *some* N (= what is said) implicitly communicates 'not all N' (= what is meant), but on a Gricean account this combines with what is said to yield 'Some but not all' such that impliciture includes scalar implicature and does not supplant it. Such scalar implicatures are challenged by Relevance theorists and relegated to pragmatically derived components of propositional content known as explicatures. As a confirmed Gricean, Horn finds explicature an unnecessary category of analysis.

In 'Speaker intentions and intentionality', Michael Haugh and Kasia Jaszczolt focus on the role of intentions in communication. They assess the link between intentions and the property of intentionality exhibited by relevant mental states and continue by discussing the explanatory function of various types of intentions identified in the literature, pointing out strengths and weaknesses of utilising intentions as well as the question of where intentions are located, contrasting cognitive, interactional and discursive perspectives. They put the intention-based theory of utterance meaning into a philosophical perspective of the intentionality of mental states which underlie communication (although allowing that cognitive pragmatics assumes that the recognition and attribution of communicative intentions underlies communication). They raise the question of how pragmatic theory can be soundly founded on the imprecise and empirically untestable notions of intentions and intentionality defined as the act of consciousness directed at an object. Haugh and Jaszczolt counter that the advantages outweigh this shortcoming, claiming for instance that intentionality better predicts speaker meaning as the means used to convey the speaker's intention than alternatives such as default rules of inference and the semanticised pragmatic relations between sentences postulated in dynamic approaches to meaning. Intentions in communication derive their theoretical status from the intentionality of consciousness, which is hopefully to be revealed by experiments in neuroscience. Speech acts have basic intentionality as externalisations of mental states, and also derived intentionality as linguistic objects, thus the same conditions of satisfaction pertain to the mental intention and to the linguistic intention. There is speaker intention as envisaged by Grice, but is this a private goal of the speaker or is it also the intention to achieve a social goal? Furthermore the intention in some cooperative endeavours is a *we*-intention and even an emergent co-constructed intention. Thus the notions of intention and intentionality are productively deployed in many different ways in pragmatics.

Chapter 6, 'Context and content: Pragmatics in two-dimensional semantics', moves into the domain of context as understood and approached in two-dimensional semantics. Berit Brogaard explains the utility of David Kaplan's *content-character* distinction in accounting for indexical expressions, as well as the advantages of a formal notion of context, where context cannot be simply identified with a speech situation. She also discusses links between context-sensitivity and cognitive informativeness. Context figures in the interpretation of utterances in many different ways. In the tradition of possible-worlds semantics, the seminal account of context-sensitive expressions such as indexicals and demonstratives is that of Kaplan's two-dimensional semantics (the content-character distinction), further pursued in various directions by Stalnaker, Chalmers, and others. The two dimensions are (1) narrow content, which can take the form of linguistic meanings (e.g. functions from context to content) or descriptive Fregean contents, and (2) wide content, which is a set of possible worlds or a structured Russellian proposition consisting of properties and/or physical objects. This chapter introduces and assesses the notion of context-sensitivity presented by the various two-dimensional frameworks, with a special focus on how it relates to the notion of cognitive significance and whether it includes an intuitively plausible range of expressions within its scope. Three types of two-dimensional semantic frameworks are assessed in terms of how well they account for the connection between cognitive significance and the broader notion of context-sensitivity. It is argued that context-sensitivity and cognitive significance are, to some extent, inseparable. For example, linguistic strings have twin tokens with a different content that David Chalmers calls 'twin-earthable expressions'. When an earthling uses *water*, the term picks out $H_2O$; when this earthling's counterpart on Twin-Earth uses *water*, it picks out XYZ (to exploit a notion of Putnam's). Thus *water* has a variable character and is broadly context-sensitive, which helps explain the cognitive significance of sentences such as *water is $H_2O$*: the earthling may not know what determines the character of *water*, so being told that the character of *water* determines $H_2O$ is informative. The chapter concludes with a discussion of the prospects of using epistemic two-dimensional semantics to account for context-sensitive expressions in dynamic discourse.

In Chapter 7 François Recanati introduces the orientation of contextualism in the theory of meaning and defends it against some competing views. Among others, he addresses the issue of compositionality, context-dependent meanings in lexical pragmatics, and the contextualist concept of content modulation. His 'Contextualism: some varieties' reviews several different positions with respect to contextualism. In the modular position, to determine *what the speaker means*, pragmatics takes as input the output of semantics, but they do not mix, and in particular, pragmatic processes do not interfere with the process of semantic composition, which, based on *what is said*, outputs the truth-conditions and ignores the speaker's beliefs and intentions. But some contextualists hold that pragmatic competence is involved in the determination of truth-conditional content because the semantic value of a context-sensitive expression varies from occurrence to occurrence as a function of what the speaker means. In addition, the content of an expression may depend on the speaker's context, e.g. whether *water* is $H_2O$ or XYZ; therefore every expression is context-sensitive. So Recanati concludes that, at least for a contextualist, context-sensitivity is pervasive in natural language and that, rather than an algorithmic, grammar-driven process, semantic interpretation is a matter of holistic guesswork that seeks to make sense of what the speaker is saying. Nonetheless, the adjusted (called here *modulated*) sense of an expression *e* in a context *c* is the result of applying a so-called modulation function *mod (e, c)* that is appropriate for this context to its semantic interpretation *I(e)* – which is a moderate form of contextualism.

Next, in 'The psychology of utterance processing: context vs salience', Rachel Giora focuses on the process of utterance interpretation, considering the salience of the lexicon vis-à-vis context-dependent meaning and introducing her influential *graded salience hypothesis*, according to which contextually irrelevant lexical meanings are activated to a certain degree. She discusses a number of factors that shape utterance interpretation: salient/coded meanings, contextual information, and their unfolding interaction (or lack of it). Experiments show that salient meanings cannot be blocked, not even by a strong context. Such contexts do not facilitate non-coded, inferred or novel interpretations such as irony, but they do slow down ironic targets compared to more salient literal counterparts. Novel metaphoric items in supportive contexts take longer to read compared to their salient (normally literal) interpretation. Non-coded ironic utterances are always processed according to their most salient (often literal) meaning first, despite a strongly supportive context. The graded salience hypothesis posits that salient meanings are activated faster than less salient ones. In addition, suppression of contextually incompatible meanings is sensitive to discourse goals and requirements, allowing for contextually incompatible meanings and interpretations to be retained if they are invited, supportive or non-intrusive. Salience is a matter of degree: regardless of its degree of literality, a meaning is salient if it is coded in the mental lexicon and enjoys prominence due to cognitive priority, experiential familiarity, frequency or conventionality. *Contra* Grice, non-literal interpretations may be the default, even when innovative, free of semantic anomaly and context-less; for example, statements such as *He is not exceptionally bright* are assigned an ironic interpretation even outside a specific context. The psychology of utterance processing is a multi-faceted phenomenon, whose products may be surprisingly creative and even amusing.

In Chapter 9, 'Sentences, utterances, and speech acts', Mikhail Kissine revives Speech Act Theory, revisiting the concept of illocutionary force and the sentence–utterance–speech act links. He seeks to sort out the interrelationships among sentences, utterances and illocutionary contents. He disputes Searle's view that any illocutionary act type IA can be matched with a certain sentence type $s$ in such a way that IA corresponds to the literal meaning of $s$; i.e. that illocutionary force is directly derivable from sentence meaning. Kissine demonstrates that imperative mood does not necessarily signal directive illocutionary force and that entreaties such as *Have a nice day* are not indirect or non-literal speech acts. He argues convincingly that non-directive uses of the imperative mood are as literal and direct as the directive ones. Kissine takes up Grice's point that uttering a sentence amounts to its acquiring an illocutionary force. If the speaker wishes to express the belief that $p$, the utterance will be an assertive speech act; if it is that the speaker intends to bring about the truth of $p$, the utterance will be a directive. A speaker who is sarcastic does not say anything, but just makes (acts) as if to say something – which is counter-intuitive. A sarcastic utterance of *Of course, John is ready* is a full-fledged, contextually determined proposition and not just a propositional radical. The semantics of sentence-types constrains which locutionary-act types the utterance of sentences can potentially constitute and the locutionary act performed in turn constrains the range of direct illocutionary forces. Although a rational reconstruction of the steps leading to the recognition of the illocutionary point can be proposed, according to Bach and Harnish's standardisation thesis the illocutionary point of a conventionalised indirect speech act is automatically derived without going through the derivation of the primary, literal speech act. This is a good reason for not taking rational reconstructions of indirect speech-act interpretation as reflecting actual interpretive processes; especially since, well before the age of seven, children respond adequately to indirectness and produce conventionalised indirect requests, but have not yet mastered second-order mental state attribution such as is required for understanding irony and for lying efficiently. The hypothesis also allows that explicit performatives *can* be interpreted as assertions, notwithstanding the fact that, in most cases, explicit performatives *are not* interpreted as assertions.

Next, in 'Pragmatics in update semantics', Henk Zeevat introduces a group of formal approaches to meaning known under the umbrella term of *update semantics* and suggests looking at them as a way of formalising pragmatics. This is a natural way of approaching them because they stress the importance of the dynamism of discourse in that information states are regularly updated by new information. He focuses in this chapter on presupposition, implicature, speech acts and disambiguation, and concludes by emphasising the methodological advantage of the orientation in its power to test predictions. He regards update semantics as central to any theory of interpretation because it is a technical tool for being precise about what utterances do to information states involved in communication. A new utterance updates an existing information state and the basic formula is simple: the update of $\phi$, written $[\phi]$ on an information state $\sigma$ (written $\sigma[\phi]$) could be given as $\sigma$ restricted to those worlds M such that $[[\phi]](M) =$ true. Update semantics is shown to be central to accounts of pronouns and presupposition. Update semantics is also useful in resolving issues with the communicative effect of, for example, *John has two pigs*: resolving whether this answers such questions as *How many pigs does John have?* or *What animals does John have?* or *Who has pigs?*. It can also seek to establish the relevance of an utterance and suggest that surprising information be questioned, doubtful information should be justified, and the background clarified if there is ambiguity. Update semantics offers a rigorous account of slow and continuous shifts in the meaning such as that from root to epistemic modality. Finally, Zeevat claims that the changes in information states captured in update semantics can be evaluated experimentally.

Jaroslav Peregrin's contribution 'The normative dimension of discourse' concerns an interesting but often neglected topic of pragmatism and normativity. He addresses the issue of a model of discourse as a rule-governed enterprise and discusses the, largely implicit, rules that allow people to engage in discursive practices. He introduces the latter following the views of Wilfrid Sellars and Robert Brandom, starting with rules of material inference and ending with a normative use-theory of meaning, seeing the meaning of expressions as their *inferential roles*. He argues that discourse interacts with normative relationships among people, relationships such as *obligations* or *entitlements*. He explores the possibility that normativity is crucial for language: a certain kind of normativity is actively constitutive of our distinctively human mind (reason), founding our concepts and infiltrating the semantics of our language. If this is true, then normativity is a key ingredient of our speech acts. An underlying assumption is that language is not merely for transfer of information but foremost a means of achieving practical ends. His concept of meaning is distinctly pragmatic: an expression means something when it is correct to use it in this way, which gives rise to a set of rules. Such rules are social facts, a collective awareness of corresponding behavioural regularities in both compliance and deviation. A boundless number of meanings are acquired in the achievement of practical aims of communicating, such that lexical items are tools rather than 'codes'. For example, *This is a dog* means that 'this is a dog' because normally the speaker is *disposed* to use the word *dog* when referring to a dog. More often than not, this disposition does not provoke overt utterance. The link between referent and utterance is normative rather than causal: it is correct to utter *This is a dog* when a dog is in focus. It is for this reason that a rule is said to be a matter of a collective awareness of what is correct where something else is incorrect, leading to the appropriate behaviour. The correlation between *This is a dog* and its referent identifies a convention that identifies a kind of habit, but also a habit that is a norm because it identifies what is taken to be correct and appropriate behaviour. Applications to artificial intelligence are also discussed.

Chapter 12 moves to the domain of the lexicon. In 'Pragmatics in the (English) lexicon', Keith Allan focuses on the interaction of semantics and pragmatics in the lexicon, accounting for frequency, familiarity and speakers' assumptions. He examines ways in which pragmatics intrudes on the lexicon, which is largely an addition to the semantic specifications; for instance, it is useful to identify the default meanings and connotations of listemes. Default meanings are those that are applied more frequently by more people and normally with greater certitude than any alternatives. Pragmatic components include encyclopaedic data such as the euphemistic status and the origin of *jeepers*, and non-monotonic inferences (NMI): in addition to the lexicon entry specifying the necessary components of meaning in the semantics for an entry, it should also specify the most probable additional components of meaning, which are accepted or cancelled as a function of contextual constraints (such as that *bull* typically denotes a bovine but when used of, say, a whale, this meaning is cancelled). A credibility metric is proposed for propositions and used to calibrate NMIs in the lexicon to correspond with the degree of confidence one might have in the truth of the inference (e.g. that *bull* will denote a bovine in an estimated percentage of cases). A review of collective and collectivisable nouns (denoting mostly game animals) reveals that whereas different interpretations for collective nouns arise from their morphosyntactic context (a fact that needs to be captured in the lexicon), nouns that are collectivisable occur under the pragmatic constraint that they are restricted to a defined set of contexts. Discussion of the much disputed semantics of *and* postulates a uniform semantics by which English *and* has the semantics of logical conjunction but there is a graded salience captured in an algorithm that assigns one of a set of non-monotonic inferences as supplementary meaning on the basis of context. A minimalist semantics is proposed for *sorites* terms; e.g. if baldness is defined as lack of a full complement of hair, two speakers, or the same speaker on different occasions, may differ as to what counts as 'not a full complement of hair' such that there is no single state of hair-loss for which it is invariably true of x that *x is bald* for all occasions and all speakers.

Next, in 'Conversational interaction', Michael Haugh introduces approaches to conversation, focusing on Conversation Analysis and stressing its view of conversation as emergent and non-summative, all of which is amply illustrated with insightfully analysed excerpts from dialogues. He emphasises that pragmatic phenomena cannot all be subsumed under emergent phenomena of the 'here and now': social and cultural factors also have to be given their due attention. Therefore, he supplements the discussion with *situatedness* in sociocognitive worlds of interlocutors. The framework for analysing pragmatic phenomena in conversational interaction is based on a tripartite distinction among pragmatic meaning, action, and evaluation, which along with investigations of the interactional machinery and the sociocognitive engine underpinning conversation, forms the basis of a programme for investigating the pragmatics of conversational interaction. A wide range of methodologies are used to elicit the properties of emergence and situatedness that characterise conversational interaction. While face-to-face conversation dominates our use of language, different types of computer-mediated communication are increasingly frequent in our daily lives (instant messaging, asynchronous forms such as email exchanges, blogs, discussion boards and social networks). These need to be accommodated within dyadic as well as multipartite theories of conversational interaction in pragmatics. They also tend to refute the assumption that talk is inherently fleeting because they often log the conversation, to leave a record that engenders greater metalinguistic and metapragmatic awareness amongst interactants themselves, with such awareness offering a rich analytical vein for future research on conversational interaction.

In the final chapter of this section, 'Experimental investigations and pragmatic theorising', Napoleon Katsos addresses the collaboration of pragmatics and psycholinguistics, viewing pragmatics as a discipline aspiring to cognitive plausibility. In the discussion he draws on recent experimental evidence, in particular in the domain of scalar implicature. He cites experimental evidence from both young children and adults measuring the time-course of the process of meaning derivation and noting the preferences when assessing competing default vs unitary accounts of scalar implicature (SI). Broadly speaking, default accounts stem directly from the work of Grice whereas unitary accounts stem from Relevance theory. Some experimental results favour the unitary account, but others counter it. Neither the default nor the unitary hypothesis is completely vindicated by experimental results. Some discrepancies are explained on the assumption that the richer experience of adults leads them to interpret SI differently from young children. Katsos suggests that minor changes in the details of an experimental design impact on the interpretation of the data. One conclusion is that Gricean maxims, being essentially philosophical heuristics, enjoy some psycholinguistic validity.

Part II opens with arguably the most commonly discussed topic in theories of meaning, namely that of reference and referring in discourse. In Chapter 15, 'Referring in discourse', Arthur Sullivan offers an overview of Russell's approach and Strawson's objections to it, discussing the notions *reference* and *speaker's referring* against the background of, and from the perspective of, current minimalism–contextualism debates. The question that emerges from this perspective is whether reference is a context-dependent or context-independent notion. He defines reference as a relation between a use of an expression and the entity it stands for. He points out that in strict usage within philosophy the term applies only to the relation between singular terms (such as proper names and pronouns) and what they are used to single out. Thus, a sentence such as *The oldest woman in Mongolia* expresses a general proposition and its subject NP does not refer whereas the proper noun in *Brigitte was sexy* does (typically) refer. Strawson challenged this Russellian orthodoxy with his concept of the act of referring by a speaker. Thus reference depends on the speaker's context-specific communicative intentions. This is the more usual interpretation within linguistics. Next, the semantics of an indexical referring expression specifies a relation that is contextually dependent and is not constant across distinct uses, whereas the reference of a non-indexical is constant across different uses. A distinction made between speaker's reference and semantic reference correlates with that between pragmatic context-conditioned speaker's meaning and context-independent semantic meaning or between Kaplan's *content* vs *character* or, on some interpretations of Frege, between his *Bedeutung* and *Sinn*.

The problem of reference is continued in the next chapter 'Propositional attitude reports: Pragmatic aspects', in which Kasia Jaszczolt addresses pragmatic aspects of propositional attitude constructions and attitude ascription. Propositional attitudes have traditionally been discussed in the domains of philosophy of language and formal semantics, where the core issues are truth-preserving substitutivity and semantic compositionality. In this chapter, reference and referring in intensional contexts are approached from the perspective of an act of communication, and compositionality is shifted to the domain of pragmatics. She argues that reports on people's cognitive attitudes (such as believing, doubting, knowing, fearing or hoping) pose a problem for pragmatics as well as for semantics. A belief (e.g. that the author of *Wolf Hall* is visiting Cambridge) may be reported in very many different ways. For instance, the holder of the attitude knows the identity of the subject of the uttered sentence and is able to substitute other expressions to refer to them; does not know the identity of the subject and holds a, so to speak, 'half-digested attitude'; is mistaken as to the identity of the subject. Furthermore, all these also apply to the reporter. Interpersonal differences in background information constitute a pragmatic problem. There is also the semantic problem with substitutivity *salva veritate* of coreferential expressions giving rise to either *de re* or *de dicto* readings. Ideally, if two expressions have the same meaning, then they have all properties in common but, in reality, individuals may have different thoughts associated with the subject of the belief; thus Jaszczolt wants to introduce into the semantic representation a theoretical derivative of the mode of presentation (MoP) under which a belief is held. Normally, the speaker formulates the utterance in such a way that its meaning can be recovered by the addressee without creating ambiguities or mismatches between the intended meaning and the recovered meaning. But an exception arises when the addressee's informational state is misjudged by the speaker. This can be dealt with, says Jaszczolt, when semantics is conceived of as contextualist. MoP is examined in the light of the proposals of Schiffer, contextualists like Recanati, intensionalists like Chalmers and mentalists like Fodor. Jaszczolt also asks whether belief reports should be analysed in terms of the way they are assessed by a hearer rather than, or as well as, in terms of speaker intention. All in all, in the contextualist spirit, she argues that the pragmatics of attitude reports is crucial to discussions concerning their meaning.

In 'Presupposition and accommodation in discourse', Rob van der Sandt introduces the concept of presupposition and asks pertinent questions concerning the behaviour of presupposed information in discourse. He discusses the semantic and pragmatic roles of presupposition and employs the concept of accommodation as a solution to bridging the gaps between information content in a sequence of sentences/utterances. The main part of the paper is devoted to the presentation of accommodation in the dynamic framework of Discourse Representation Theory, demonstrating thereby the interaction of semantic and pragmatic content. Van der Sandt defines presupposition as information that is taken for granted by the participants in a conversation; the non-presuppositional remainder is asserted, questioned, or requested and so forth. There is a general condition that the presupposition has to be given for the non-presuppositional remainder to be interpretable. If the presuppositional information is not already in common ground (such as prior discourse) but nevertheless uncontroversial, a cooperative hearer will construct the context to include the required information (e.g. *My daughter's husband has just been kidnapped* addressed to someone who did not know the speaker had a daughter, and *a fortiori* not that she was married). Lewis called this 'accommodation', which is here shown to be constrained by conditions on binding (understood as a discourse relation) and the cooperative principle. Accommodation adds presuppositional material to the common ground. Normally sentences are interpreted in context but when uttered in isolation a sentence typically offers clues as to what contexts would qualify for it to be felicitously interpreted: constraints of global and local informativity and consistency suffice as constraints on acceptability. Van der Sandt argues for presuppositional expressions being anaphoric expressions similar to pronouns in that they induce a search through discourse structures in order to find a suitable antecedent to link up with. But they differ from pronouns and other impoverished anaphors in their structure and content. In *If France has a king, the king of France is bald* the antecedent of the conditional implies that France may have a king and this cancels the presupposition that France does have a king. If the addressee cannot find an antecedent for a pronoun, the sentence/utterance cannot be interpreted; the algorithm does not end in completion. Finally, van der Sandt adopts Partee's suggestion that verb tense be treated as a kind of pronoun and encodes the tense morpheme as a presuppositional expression consisting of an anaphoric variable and an associated temporal constraint.

In Chapter 18, 'Negation', Jay David Atlas addresses the phenomenon that gave rise to the semantics/pragmatics boundary disputes of the 1970s, namely the functioning and scope of negation. He introduces what came to be known in some circles as the Atlas–Kempson thesis, saying that negation is semantically underspecified between wide and narrow scope, leaving a role to play for pragmatic inference in further precisification. He assesses this view against other solutions in pragmatic theory. The chapter begins by reviewing Aristotle's account of negation on sentences and terms, and the characterising of contraries, subcontraries and contradictories. Next, he points out that *not* sentences encompass exclusion negations, the exclusion of exclusion negations, choice negations and forms of metalinguistic negations. He answers Horn's criticism of the Atlas-Kempson thesis that *not* sentences are semantically non-specific rather than lexically or scope-ambiguous. Semantical non-specificity makes pragmatic inference essential to every interpretation of utterances of *not* sentences, removes the unmotivated asymmetry in the application of Gricean implicatures to negative sentence-strings, provides a theoretical foundation for research in semantic processing and provides a perspective from which to assess the controversies between the semantical underdeterminists and the minimal semanticists.

Another seminal issue for pragmatics is that of sentential and discourse connectives. In 'Connectives', Caterina Mauri and Johan van der Auwera discuss the phenomena in an impressively broad, cross-linguistic, typological perspective, dispelling the myths of their universality at the syntactic or semantic level, at the same time opening a new ground-breaking perspective for their pragmatic study. They conclude that what is left to inferential mechanisms of interpretation in some languages or at some diachronic stage of a language may be part of the encoded semantics in other languages or at successive diachronic stages. The connection between states of affairs (SoAs) may be encoded by invariable discourse connectives, auxiliaries, clitics, pre- and post-positions, case affixes, adverbial affixes and suprasegmental marking. The authors show that simple juxtaposition may give rise to inferred sequentiality, which becomes established in the semantics of the connection and in turn gives rise to causal and purposive relations. The burden of communication gradually passes from pragmatics to semantics. Disjunctive connectives frequently develop from the overt indication of the potential nature of the linked SoAs: speakers reinterpret irrealis markers, such as dubitative adverbs, hypothetical forms or interrogative markers, as the overt indicators of the notion of an alternative, thus reanalysing them as disjunctive connectives. If only one of the pair of SoAs is irrealis it may invite a conditional reading. Adversative connectives frequently derive from sources denoting temporal values: the co-existence over time of two SoAs comes to be perceived as a surprising one, a consequence of the fact that the differences existing between the two events are foregrounded at the expense of their temporal relation.

In Chapter 20, 'Spatial reference in discourse', Luna Filipović discusses spatial reference in a cross-linguistic perspective focusing on its universal and language-specific aspects. She presents the problem of the conceptualization of the relationship between objects and events, assessing the dispute concerning the trade-off between universalism and relativity. Reviewing discussions on the relation between spatial structures and semantic/conceptual structures by, among others, Jackendoff, Talmy and Levinson, Filipović concludes that the various perceivable characteristics of phenomena such as figure, ground, a point, a line, a plane, a boundary, parallelness, perpendicularity, horizontality, adjacency, contact, support, containment and relative magnitude are universal, but the way in which languages capture them varies greatly. Uncertain is the extent to which Talmy's categories of verb-framed vs satellite-framed languages generalises. When we habitually express certain features, they become entrenched and it seems that languages, cultures and environments make some perceptual, conceptual and linguistic features more or less salient. It seems that languages reflect a culture's dominant perspective, but this does not preclude the registration of other spatial properties that can be used and referred to in discourse.

The next contribution, by Louis de Saussure, follows suit with 'Temporal reference in discourse'. While tense and aspect have enjoyed wide coverage in the linguistic literature, there has been little discussion of pragmatic inferences from temporal and aspectual information where it is not overtly encoded in the lexicon or grammar. De Saussure helps fill this gap by addressing temporality and aspectuality from the perspective of pragmatic, mainly post-Gricean theory. He illustrates the discussion with cross-linguistic comparisons. Temporal reference needs to include the aspectual properties of the represented eventuality and also modality to resolve any conflict between the time indicated by a tense and a salient time stemming from other information (as with epistemic futures). Grammatical tenses and temporal adverbials are often poor guides to the temporality of an event or state intended by the speaker. In languages where tense and aspect are optional, reliance on pragmatic means of conveying temporality is even more pronounced. The chapter shows how aspect, a central conceptual feature of verbs and verb clauses, is changed by pragmatic processing under various contextual conditions. Tense provides only hints about how to construct the pragmatically meaningful temporal reference; it is manipulated to fulfil discursive aims (e.g. through deictic shifting). Pragmatic accommodation of aspect is shown in several languages (e.g. *Al and Kate knew each other at university* is understood inchoatively). Pragmatic implicatures of a pair of sentences like *Mary came in. John stood up* suggest a temporal sequence. *I didn't turn off the stove* can be understood as a deictic present; also pragmatically present is the initial clause in *I wondered if you'd like to come to supper on Saturday*. Finally, de Saussure discusses some pragmatic issues relating to the temporal interpretation of connectives and indexicals.

Chapter 22 pertains to 'Textual coherence as a pragmatic phenomenon'. Anita Fetzer addresses the question of what makes a text coherent and discusses aspects of context that are relevant for that purpose. The core importance of this topic lies in the fact, too often ignored by pragmatists, that patterns can be found also in units larger than a sentence or a speech act. Fetzer points to the difficulty in accounting for textual coherence because of its inherent dynamism and complex, multi-faceted nature and the fact that the whole is more than the sum of its parts: it is simultaneously process and product, co-constructed with heavy reliance on deductive and abductive reasoning, inference and implicature. In discourse, common ground for the individual and the collective common ground are continuously updated: ratified discourse units and their ratified presuppositions being allocated to the collective discourse common ground. Coherence arises from a proper narrative structure and proper interplay between given and new information, theme and rheme, the sequential organisation of communicative action (e.g. adjacency pairs), preference organisation, and observation of the cooperative maxims. Fetzer examines thematic structure, discourse relations and discourse connectives, and ends by analysing the links between textual coherence, cooperation, common ground and the many aspects of context.

In Chapter 23 we move to the topic of literal vs non-literal discourse. In 'Metaphor and the literal/non-literal distinction', Robyn Carston presents the phenomenon of non-literalness, concentrating on various approaches to metaphor and on the comparison between metaphor and other tropes and, in particular, irony. Grice treated all instances of non-literal language use (metaphor, metonymy, hyperbole, understatement, irony etc.) as cases where a speaker says something so blatantly false, uninformative or irrelevant that the hearer is prompted to undertake an inferential process to recover what the speaker really means. Thus non-literal language is indirect communication, with the figurative meaning derived through conversational implicature. Carston critically assesses Grice's pragmatic account: one objection is that to deliberately produce a blatantly false utterance is a pointless irrational act since the speaker could express her intended meaning by producing a literal utterance which would be easily grasped by the hearer. Carston cites psycholinguistic experiments that claim metaphorical interpretations are derived automatically whenever the context makes them accessible. She further argues for a categorical distinction between metaphor and irony; the latter echoically metarepresents someone else's thought and expresses a negative attitude toward it. Carston moves on to introducing the idea of ad hoc concepts pursued in recent lexical pragmatics (e.g. describing someone as a chameleon to indicate their frequently changing opinions, which picks only one aspect of the lizard – and partially at that). These contribute the *explicature* of the utterance. This is in line with developments in cognitive linguistics wherein metaphorically used language is fundamental within thought. The chapter concludes by revisiting the literal/non-literal distinction against the background of some recent discussions in the literature.

Part III opens with a historical perspective on pragmatics. In 'Pragmatics in the history of linguistic thought', Andreas H. Jucker traces the development of pragmatics as a subdiscipline of linguistics, pointing to an unprecedented diversification of subfields of pragmatics, especially in the continental European tradition. At the same time other fields of linguistics have extended to encompass a pragmatic perspective as well. There are paradigm shifts such as that in historical pragmatics from a study of native speaker competence to a study of language use, with a concomitant shift to reliance on corpus-based methods. Such investigations focus much more on the heterogeneity and variability of the data than on the homogeneity. Jucker begins by outlining the roots of pragmatics in the academic traditions of the nineteenth and early twentieth century and assesses the contributions of many relevant philosophers and linguists in the Anglo-American and continental European orientations, including Peirce, Morris, Carnap, Wittgenstein, moving on to Austin and Grice. He distinguishes the Anglo-American tradition as focusing on the study of meaning arising from the use of language, whereas the continental European tradition is more sociolinguistically and culturally oriented to a general account of language in use. Contrastive pragmatics sets out to compare interactive patterns in different cultures, while intercultural pragmatics focuses on the interactions between members of different cultures. The latter began by looking at the factors that prevent understanding but has progressed to analyse the processes that lead to mutual understanding. Experimental pragmatics uses elicitation techniques. The chapter concludes with a prospective on the future of pragmatics.

Next, we move to a series of papers on interfaces. In Chapter 25, 'Semantics without pragmatics?', Emma Borg addresses the semantics/pragmatics boundary, defending the concept of minimal semantics through cautious but powerful arguments and juxtaposing it with the contextualist construal and with a radical non-propositional minimalism. Borg argues against a strong version of the view that semantics deals with decontextualised meaning and pragmatics with meaning that varies according to context. She argues that sentences with demonstratives and (other) indexicals must appeal to context, thus context-sensitivity is an all-pervasive, core feature of linguistic meaning requiring contextual contribution to the conditions under which a proposition is evaluated for truth. Borg defends a minimal (radical) semantics that strictly constrains the input of pragmatics to semantics and which is, to a large extent, free from contextual input: sentences express minimal propositions or minimal truth conditions that are recoverable via a grasp of word meaning and sentence structure alone and which do not require significant appeal to a context of utterance prior to their recovery. That leaves pragmatics to deal with context-dependent speaker meaning. She carefully assesses the compatibility of this view with other main approaches in the boundary dispute, concluding that the compatibility is greater than it is usually thought to be. However she does admit certain unresolved problems for minimal semantics.

In Chapter 26, Ruth Kempson pursues the topic of 'The syntax/pragmatics interface', taking syntax to operate on discourses rather than sentences. Syntax is viewed as a set of mechanisms that pertain to utterances and their logical forms. As a result, the syntax/pragmatics interaction persists throughout any derivation. Kempson begins by reviewing the legacy of a distinction made between syntactic and semantic components of a grammar, with pragmatics outside the grammarian's remit. Recently, though, not only have semanticists sought to incorporate contextual considerations but have increasingly incorporated pragmatic properties such as generalized conversational implicatures. Contextualists agree that, due to interaction between information supplied by the grammar and pragmatic processes, there is more to utterance understanding than a narrow concept of sentence meaning provides. Furthermore, there is evidence of overlap between syntax and pragmatics, which is particularly evident with respect to ellipsis (gapping, stripping, sluicing, etc.) that has both sentence-internal properties and some properties extending across sentences (anaphora and tense construal likewise). Lots of evidence is given for the grammatical, semantic and pragmatic properties inherent in elliptical expressions. Kempson demonstrates how a dynamic syntax can account for the underspecification of structure and content by logging the updating of context represented in tree structures, including those linked in discourse structures, using a modal logic of finite trees (LOFT). Thus, syntax is defined as the dynamics whereby interpretation is built up. Although the trees represent parses, Kempson claims that sentence generation follows the same process, such that parsers and producers alike use strategies for building up representations of content, either to establish interpretation for a sequence of words, or to find words which match the content to be conveyed. Thus texts (discourses) are seen as the growth of semantic representations with pragmatics as the articulation of constraints determining natural language syntax.

Next, in 'Pragmatics and language change', Elizabeth Closs Traugott puts pragmatics to use in addressing questions in historical linguistics. Although there is a view that meaning change derives from syntactic change, a more realistic hypothesis is that people contribute to language change throughout their lives. Interlocutors are active partners in the communicative dyad and may be invited to make novel inferences (as in the case of Carston's 'ad hoc concepts'). Change is both internal and driven by social factors. Where an expression $p$ implicates $q$ (there is an invited inference from $p$ that $q$) there may come a time when $p$ means $q$ (is ambiguous between 'p' and 'q') and eventually the 'p' sense disappears leaving only the 'q' sense. Traugott associates semantic narrowing with Horn's Q-principle and semantic broadening with his R-principle. Discussing Levinson's Q, I and M heuristics (wherein Q > M > I) Q accounts for conservatism, M for change. The semanticisation of implicatures requires them to first be salient within a community. An important cognitive mechanism underlying change is metonymy, i.e. the co-presence of elements within the same conceptual framework. Shifts from temporal to causal, concessive or conditional, or from deontic to epistemic modality all involve increase in subjectivity (revealing speaker point of view) over time within and across semantic domains. Traugott discusses many examples of change and emphasises the persistent significance of context. She also points to some other sources of semantic change than invited inference.

Chapter 28, 'Pragmatics and prosody', concerns the relationship between prosody and intentional communication. It is widely acknowledged that voice quality, pitch variation, the length of syllables and other pragmatic factors affect utterance meaning. However, the ways of incorporating this information into pragmatic theory are not yet well researched. Focusing on an example of a post-Gricean account, the theory of Relevance, Tim Wharton addresses this pragmatic role of prosody, discussing in particular the relationship between prosody and intentions in communication. Prosody encodes both linguistic and paralinguistic meaning. Subtle changes in the tone and quality of voice, and the range of pitch variation we use, the location of disjuncture (pause), the tempo of delivery, all convey attitudinal information and information about our physical, mental or emotional state. Some are natural signs over which the speaker has little or no control, others (such as interjections) are natural signals which imply deliberate communicative intention. Prosodic signals such as lexical stress, lexical tone and nuclear tones facilitate the retrieval of certain types of syntactic, semantic or conceptual representation. Wharton discusses gesture as prosodic because gestures almost always accompany spoken language and they are part of a speaker's communicative repertoire.

'Pragmatics and information structure' are taken up in Chapter 29. Jeanette Gundel discusses the fact that natural languages offer speakers a variety of morphological, syntactic and prosodic means to express the same basic informational content in different contexts. She traces the history of the concept of information structure, progresses to an in-depth analysis of givenness, and reviews ways that information structure is formally expressed. She distinguishes 'referential' from 'relational' givenness/newness and demonstrates their independence. There is a hierarchy of referential givenness (in focus > activated > familiar > uniquely identifiable > referential > type-identifiable) typically signalled by determiners and pronouns. This hierarchy gives rise to scalar implicatures (e.g. in English the implicature that the interpretation of an indefinite article phrase is at most referential but not uniquely identifiable and familiar, etc.). Relational givenness involves a partition into two complementary parts determined by the assumed knowledge and attention state of the addressee at that point in the discourse: what the sentence is about (given/topic/theme/background) and what is predicated of this (new/comment/rheme/focus). The components of relational givenness are pragmatically relevant categories with clear pragmatic effects such as the (in)appropriateness of sentences with different possibilities for information-structural interpretation in different discourse contexts. Referential givenness, on the other hand, is grammatical in the sense that different lexical items encode it as part of their conventional meaning. The topic of prosody and meaning, addressed in the previous chapter, reappears here because its contribution to differences in information structure can have truth-conditional effects.

Next, in the chapter 'Sociopragmatics and cross-cultural and intercultural studies', Istvan Kecskes discusses the closely interrelated topics of communication and society, cross-cultural communication, cross-dialectal and cross-sociolectal communication, as well as the acquisition of communicative skills of a newly encountered culture. When people communicate, they craft what they need to express to fit the context (presumed common ground); at the same time, the way people speak or write the words, expressions and utterances they use create the very situation, context and sociocultural frame in which the communication occurs. Meaning emerges from recalled fragments that are reiterated, reshaped and manipulated at the same time; new meaning arises as a more or less radical alternation of something familiar and recognisable. Rather than focusing on conditions and rules for an individual speech act it is more appropriate to characterise acts of speech in a situation because the individual is situated in a social context that empowers and constrains them. Pragmatic competence is the ability to comprehend and produce a communicative act conditioned by awareness of social distance, speakers' social status, cultural knowledge (including politeness) and linguistic knowledge. One needs to recognise the cultural relativity of definitions of sincerity, relevance and the ranking of imposition. Attention should be paid to communication breakdown, misunderstanding and language-based aggression as well as cooperation and politeness. Kecskes also examines intercultural and cross-cultural pragmatics in the light of his sociocognitive approach.

The final yet essential contribution addresses the issue of linguistic politeness. In Chapter 31, 'Politeness and pragmatics', Marina Terkourafi presents the main current approaches to that phenomenon in (socio)pragmatics, focusing on the questions of intentionality of politeness, the notion of face, and the mechanisms for conveying recognition of politeness and impoliteness in discourse. She reviews applications of post-Gricean pragmatics, speaker's intention, implicatures, perlocutionary effects and the Relevance-Theoretic notion of communication to the analysis of im/politeness. She distinguishes first-order explicitly normative politeness (the way polite behaviour is perceived by members of sociocultural groups) from second-order politeness (as perceived within a theory of social behaviour and language usage). Terkourafi writes about impoliteness (rudeness, incivility) in adversarial encounters and notions of face – which she also divides into first-order face (in culturally defined contexts and settings) vs second-order face (a schematic theoretical notion pertaining to the image of the other in social-interactive behaviour). Importantly she recognises that face pervades all instances of communication and that it depends on an interlocutor's assumptions about the (relevant) intentions of other interlocutors. Nevertheless, cross-language data reveal that politeness is routinely achieved by means of conventionalised expressions that Terkourafi refers to as providing 'cognitive frames'.

*The Cambridge Handbook of Pragmatics* is a comprehensive review of pragmatics that reflects the editors' judgement concerning current cutting-edge research at the beginning of the second decade of the twenty-first century as well as the editors' assessment concerning the areas and theories that will mark progress in pragmatic research in the future. We hope it stands the test of time.

# Part I

## Problems and Theories

# 2

# Research paradigms in pragmatics

Mira Ariel

There is no shortage of definitions for pragmatics. Many have proposed a division of labor between grammatical phenomena with their dedicated accounts and pragmatic phenomena with their dedicated accounts. Few succeeded. The majority failed, because they were aiming too high (see Ariel, 2010: Part I; Levinson, 1983: Chapters 1, 7; Turner, 1999). Two major obstacles blocked the attempts to come up with a coherent definition for pragmatics. First, there was the hope that a multiplicity of criteria simultaneously converge to distinguish between all of grammar (including semantics) and all of pragmatics, e.g., context sensitivity, non-truth-conditionality, implicitness, discourse scope (and many others), all characterizing pragmatics, and context invariability, truth-conditionality, explicitness, sentential scope (and many others), all characterizing grammar. Naturally, the more criteria we can mobilize for drawing the grammar/pragmatics division of labor, the more contentful each of the defined domains is made out to be, and the more significant the distinction between them. The second high hope was that complete topics, such as speech acts, implicatures, politeness, functional syntax, deixis, presupposition, agreement, and argument structure each, en bloc, belongs either in grammar or in pragmatics. Indeed, this would guarantee a very neat division of labor between grammar and pragmatics. Thus, speech acts, implicatures, politeness, and functional syntax should wholly belong on the pragmatics turf, agreement and argument structure should wholly belong on the grammatical turf, and semanticists and pragmatists should do battle over, e.g., presupposition and deixis.

Unfortunately, neither one of these worthy goals can be achieved. Multiple criteria for distinguishing grammar and pragmatics resulted in multiple contradictions between the various criteria, which render the definitions of both grammar and pragmatics incoherent. And aiming for a single-domain account (either pragmatics or grammar) for each topic on the canonical

Funding for this research was received from THE ISRAEL SCIENCE FOUNDATION, grant # 161–09.

list of pragmatic topics (such as speech acts and implicatures) is a mission impossible, because almost all linguistic expressions require both a grammatical account and a pragmatic account. Therefore, for a division of labor between grammar and pragmatics to work, we have to lower our expectations. We must do with just a single dichotomy, and we must concede that only aspects of phenomena can receive uniform grammatical or pragmatic analyses: Labeled topics (such as presupposition, reference, politeness, functional syntax) typically straddle both sides of the grammar/pragmatics divide. Whereas the issue of a uniform domain analysis for each topic is hardly ever explicitly addressed (but see Ariel, 2010: Part III; Wilson and Sperber, 1993a), the multiple definitional problem has been widely recognized, and one criterion has emerged as a clear, even if not exclusive, winner.

On this criterion, grammar is taken to comprise conventional codes pertaining to linguistic forms, and pragmatics comprises plausible (not necessarily logical) inferences based partly on that code. Now, some have advocated this criterion as the single criterion to be used (Ariel, 1999, 2008b, 2010; Prince, 1988, Sperber and Wilson, 1986). Others believe that the code/inference criterion converges with some other criterion, (non-)truth-conditionality being the favorite (Grice, 1989; Recanati, 2004b). Be that as it may, there is at least some consensus in the field: grammar minimally analyses conventional codes whereby specific linguistic expressions are associated with their semantic interpretations and/or use conditions; pragmatics complements grammar in that it is responsible for speaker-intended meanings or use conditions she complies with, which are rationally derivable when we take into consideration the linguistic meaning, relevant contextual assumptions, and some discourse or cognitive principle(s). This division of labor is the starting point for this chapter.

Assuming we define grammar as a set of codes associating linguistic forms with their interpretations and use conditions and pragmatics as a set of inferences rationally, but only plausibly, derived on the basis of the explicit utterance, a more practical set of questions arises: What are the research questions linguists pose when they do pragmatics? What kind of answers can they give when analyzing pragmatic phenomena? I will briefly outline three prominent research paradigms adopted by pragmatists who set out from the assumption that grammar is encoded and pragmatics is inferred (sections 2.1, 2.2, 2.3 respectively).[1] My goal is to offer a bird's eye view of how these approaches go about doing pragmatic research.[2] As will become evident below, however, agreeing on a set of research questions, and even on methodology, does not mean that each research paradigm reduces to a single theoretical approach, nor to uniform linguistic analyses for specific phenomena. Quite the contrary. Typically, the theories and analyses grouped under the same paradigm compete with each other, so that within-paradigm disagreements are quite common. Surprisingly, perhaps, cross-paradigmatic theories and analyses typically (though not invariably) actually complement each other, since they each shine the light on different aspects of linguistic phenomena.

In order to facilitate comparisons between the different accounts within, and more importantly, across the three research paradigms, some common denominator is needed. I have chosen one issue, discourse reference, which I exemplify for all the theories discussed in this chapter. Different analyses of the same issue, each falling within one of the three research paradigms, can be readily compared and contrasted (section 2.4). In the end, the argument I will make is that even if some or even all current pragmatic theories, as well as specific analyses of discourse reference, turn out to be wrong, all three research paradigms are necessary for a complete picture of grammar, of pragmatics, and of the grammar/pragmatics interface (section 2.5).

## 2.1 Grammar is grammar and pragmatics is pragmatics: Inferential pragmatics

Inferential pragmatics theories are all traceable to Grice (1989).[3] The main protagonists within this pragmatics research paradigm are Griceans, neo-Griceans, and Relevance theoreticians. Their goals are: (a) to provide an inferential pragmatic theory to account for speaker-intended implicit interpretations; (b) based on this theory, to establish the division of labor between grammar, specifically semantics, and pragmatics, concentrating on difficult cases, often those termed generalized conversational implicature cases (GCIs); (c) to distinguish between different implicit interpretations: particularized conversational implicatures (PCIs), versus GCIs, implicatures versus inferences that form part of the truth conditions of the proposition expressed (the explicature), conventional implicatures versus conversational implicatures. Naturally, both codes and inferences are here discussed, the goal being a complementary distribution between the two.

### 2.1.1 The inferential pragmatics research paradigm

Grice's original insight about the crucial role of inferencing for conveying the speaker's intended message (at the expense of encoding) has been adopted by all inferential pragmatics theories, and inferencing is now seen as a major ingredient in utterance interpretation. In fact, whenever the linguist is debating whether to assign semantic or pragmatic status to some interpretation, the default preference is to treat it as pragmatically inferred. Following Grice's (1989: Chapter 3) Modified Occam's Razor Principle, it is more economical to assign a given interpretation to pragmatics than to semantics, since the former comes "for free", speakers performing pragmatic inferences anyway. The latter requires grammatical stipulation, which is supposed to burden native speakers.

Inferential pragmatists leave formal grammar mostly intact, except for some "territory seizures", where some potentially semantic accounts are relegated to pragmatics. As empirical basis for the analyses offered, inferential pragmatists traditionally, and very often even today, rely on their own intuitions, although recently, some corpus studies (Ariel, 2004) and some experimentation (Gibbs and Moise, 1997; Noveck, 2001; Noveck and Chevaux, 2002; Papafragou and Musolino, 2003) have been adduced in support of researchers' positions. The three variant inferential pragmatics theories proposed by Grice, neo-Griceans, and Relevance theoreticians are quite well known. Given the commonalities outlined above, emphasis will here be laid on the differences between them.

We start with Grice. Grice's theory simultaneously addresses two fundamental problems about linguistic interactions. The first one is, how can we distinguish between a natural and an unnatural discourse? In other words, what characterizes coherent discourse progression? Grice's answer is that interlocutors first and foremost abide by the Cooperative Principle, which dictates to them to "[m]ake your conversational contribution such as is required, at the stage at which it occurs, by the accepted purpose or direction of the talk exchange in which you are engaged" (Grice, 1975: 45). Presuming that this agreement is adhered to, the interlocutors can further assume that four maxims and eight sub-maxims inform speakers' utterances, and hence, addressees' interpretations: Quantity (informativity), Quality (truth and reliability), Relation (relevance), and Manner (optimal choice of linguistic form).

The second question is, how can speakers convey more than they explicitly encode? Grice proposed that interlocutors need not always straightforwardly obey the maxims in order to be cooperative. He offered the mechanism of conversational implicature generation to account for such cases. The idea is that speakers guide their addressees to extract more meaning out of their utterances than they actually encode. Taking into consideration the encoded message, the maxims, as well as relevant contextual background, addressees must "read between the lines" in order to process the additional inferred meanings intended by the speaker. These conversational implicatures may be generated in order to make sure that some maxim is abided by, or in order to justify an apparent maxim violation.

The neo-Griceans (most notably, Horn, 1984b, 1989; Levinson, 1987, 2000) accept the Gricean picture for the most part, but they don't have use for so many maxims and sub-maxims. They leave Quality intact, Relation is kept by Levinson but rejected by Horn. The neo-Griceans' attention is mainly focused on reducing the six sub-maxims subsumed under Quantity and Manner. Horn proposes two principles instead, based on Grice's Quantity. Whereas Grice saw no particular problem in balancing between his $Q_1$ and $Q_2$, Horn and Levinson see the two as clashing, one instructing the speaker to be maximally informative, thereby blocking potentially inferable enrichments, the other instructing the speaker to be minimally informative, thereby encouraging the addressee to enrich the speaker's linguistic meaning with pragmatic inferences. They then explain how interlocutors resolve this clash, by reference to markedness: "The use of a marked expression when a corresponding unmarked alternate expression is available tends to be interpreted as a marked message (one which the unmarked alternative would not or could not have conveyed)" (Horn, 1984b: 22). In other words, enrichment to the stereotype (a derivative of $Q_2$) applies when unmarked forms are involved, and anti-enrichment (a derivative of $Q_1$) applies when marked forms are used.

Sperber and Wilson (1986) are even more reductive than the neo-Griceans. They have suggested that a single principle of optimal relevance can account for discourse coherence, as well as for how addressees go about reading more into speakers' utterances. According to this theory, Relevant information necessarily hooks up with addressees' contextual assumptions, yielding contextual implications based on the two computed together. Speakers aim for an adequate quantity of contextual implications (pragmatic inferences), which must be conveyed in a way that requires the least processing cost from the addressee.

In this way all three theories account for how discourse is coherent, and what triggers addressees' inferences. Interestingly, while the theories are quite different, for the most part there is agreement between them on where to draw the grammar/pragmatics division of labor for specific linguistic phenomena. For example, they all agree that, e.g., *and*'s semantic meaning is equivalent to its logical counterpart ∧, and that the additional interpretations often associated with it (e.g., 'and then', 'and therefore', etc.) are pragmatically derived. The same is true for (*either*) *or* and for scalar expressions (such as *some, good*). The semantic meanings of the latter are lower-bounded only (e.g., 'at least some/good'), the upper bound ('not all'/'not excellent') pragmatically provided. However, there can, theoretically, be disagreements within this inferential pragmatics research paradigm regarding the grammar/pragmatics division of labor.[4] Moreover, the fact that we mostly find agreement regarding the semantics/pragmatics division of labor does not mean that the analyses are otherwise identical. Quite the contrary. (Neo-)Gricean and Relevance-theoretic theories classify pragmatic interpretations somewhat differently.

While there is universal agreement that PCIs play a major role in natural discourse, Sperber and Wilson have proposed an additional distinction between implicated assumptions and implicated conclusions. The former are assumptions the speaker intends the addressee to draw on because they are needed for deriving the implicated conclusions. Only the latter are actually a speaker's point in the discourse. Next, (neo-)Griceans assume a special status for conventional implicatures. These are like conversational implicatures in that they don't affect the truth conditions of the proposition they are in, but like semantic meanings, they are conventionally encoded for specific expressions. (Neo-)Griceans here prefer truth-conditionality as the criterion for the grammar/pragmatics divide. Since Relevance theoreticians (see

Blakemore, 1987 and onwards about *but*) take the code/inference distinction alone as the criterion distinguishing semantics from pragmatics, conventional implicatures fall squarely on the semantics side of the divide. In other words, there is no place for conventional implicatures as a distinct species of pragmatic interpretation under Relevance theory, since no inference is involved.

Last, neo-Griceans, much more than Grice himself, focus their attention on generalized conversational implicatures (GCIs). These are conversational implicatures, except that they are generated under normal circumstances (as a default, according to Levinson). It is these implicatures which under some contextual circumstances "intrude" on semantics, in that they contribute to the truth-conditional meaning of the relevant proposition, despite the fact that they are pragmatic implicatures. Relevance theoreticians have argued against assuming this additional type of conversational implicature. According to Carston (1990 and onwards), for example, to the extent that GCIs are conversational implicatures, they should be seen as PCIs (which happen to be generated rather often). But for many inferences treated as GCIs by the neo-Griceans, Relevance theoreticians have proposed a different status, that of explicated inferences, i.e., inferences which form part of the Relevance-theoretic concept of explicature.[5]

Relevance theoreticians are not surprised that pragmatics intrudes on semantics. They take it as given that pragmatic inferences contribute to the truth-conditional content of the proposition. While semanticists and pragmatists are in agreement these days that the linguistically encoded meaning falls short of the meaning actually communicated by the speaker, Griceans have more or less adhered to Grice's original "what is said," which includes only a minimal quantity of pragmatically inferred interpretations, and they are happy to call this level truth-conditional semantics. Sperber and Wilson disagree. Any pragmatically inferred interpretation is a full-fledged pragmatic inference, which should count as one. The fact that many of these are needed to develop the encoded Logical Form of the speaker's utterance into a complete proposition doesn't alter their pragmatic status. Instead of the minimally enriched "what is said," Sperber and Wilson offer the pragmatically richer explicature (the idea being that the pragmatic inferences needed to complete the speaker's encoded meaning into a full proposition count as part of the explicit message). Now, these differences mean that pragmatic interpretations associated with the same linguistic expressions may well receive different analyses by proponents of different inferential pragmatics theories. Indeed, whereas for (neo-)Griceans the pragmatic interpretations commonly associated with *and* are GCIs, they are explicated inferences for Relevance theory. And whereas the upper bound on, e.g., *some* is a GCI under the neo-Gricean analysis, it is sometimes a PCI, and sometimes part of the explicature for Relevance theoreticians.[6]

In sum, all three inferential pragmatics theories propose some overarching principle(s) in order to account for discourse coherence and for how pragmatic inferences are routinely drawn over and above the speaker's linguistically encoded message. Differences between the theories are found in the number of principles, and in the types of pragmatic interpretations researchers assume in general and for specific cases (*and*, *some*). But these don't alter the common focus within this research paradigm: drawing a grammar/pragmatics division of labor between semantic codes and pragmatic inferences.[7]

## 2.1.2 Inferential pragmatics and reference

Reference, just like any other speaker-intended interpretation, requires both a code and a set of inferences. The common goal shared by inferential pragmatics theories is the attempt to relegate as much as possible to pragmatics. In other words, preference is given to analyses involving small codes and big inferences. The role of the specific referential forms tends to be downplayed, while the role of the contextual inferences is upgraded.

Kempson (1988) is a typical Relevance-based proposal. Referring expressions, Kempson reminds us, have quite a variety of uses. For example, only some are referential. Some are impersonal, some involve bound variable anaphora, others require bridging. Kempson proposes a very "thin" code for all definite noun phrases: "Presumed accessibility." It is then up to the addressee to determine both the type of reading and the referent intended by the speaker, based on Relevance theory (making sure there are sufficient contextual effects for a minimal processing cost). Wilson (1992) emphasizes that reference assignment forms part of the overall process of utterance interpretation, which is Relevance-guided. She focuses on cases where more than one NP can serve as antecedent (e.g., **Sean Penn**$_i$ attacked **a photographer**$_j$. **The man**$_{i/j}$ was badly hurt). While both interpretations are conceivable, Relevance theory, she proposes, does not force the addressee to consider all options before he can choose the one intended by the speaker (a costly processing procedure). Interlocutors are tuned to specific coherence patterns, and can immediately choose the appropriate overall interpretation (the state here described in the second utterance is the consequence of the event in the first) based on the content of the utterances. This effortlessly points them to the appropriate reference.

Assuming that coreferential readings are more informative than disjoint readings, Levinson (2000) constructs a Horn scale of the prototypical referring expressions: Lexical NP < Pronoun < Ø (see also Huang, 2000). The idea is that less informative forms (on the right) trigger stronger (coreferential) readings (via Q$_2$ – enrichment to the stereotype). If so, using an informative expression when the grammar would allow for a coreferent reading with a less informative expression triggers a disjoint reading (via Q$_1$ – the anti-enrichment principle, e.g., **He**$_i$ *went over there and approached* **the man**$_j$).

As can be seen, inferential pragmatic analyses naturally assign a primary role to pragmatic inferencing in determining the use and interpretation of referring expressions. While Levinson does draw some formal distinctions between referring expressions, a much finer set of distinctions will be offered by form/function pragmatics theories (see section 2.2.2).

## 2.2 (Some) pragmatics is grammar: Form/function pragmatics

Form/function pragmatics, as I propose to call the second research paradigm, has altogether different intellectual roots from inferential pragmatics. Whereas the inspiring figure in the first tradition is Paul Grice, form/function pragmatics emerged as a reaction to Chomsky's generative syntax. Hence, researchers within this paradigm focused on syntax initially, where, they argued, not all conditions (on transformations, in those days) could be grammatically specified, because they often pertained to information structure, a pragmatic concept. The thought behind most research within this paradigm is that grammar is at least partly geared towards communication. Hence, it is only natural for factors relevant to communication to play a role in it. Pioneering research was conducted by Susumu Kuno, Ellen Prince, Wallace Chafe, Sandra Thompson, and various generative semanticists (see Chafe, 1976, 1994; Green, G. M., 1975, 1976; Hooper and Thompson, 1973; Kuno, 1972, 1987; Prince, 1978, 1988; Thompson, S. A., 1990). In time, linguistic analyses were no longer restricted to syntactic structures, discourse markers too receiving prime attention (following Schiffrin, 1987). And some current approaches actually advocate the replacement of formal syntax by form/function theories (most notably, Goldberg, 1995).

### 2.2.1 The form/function pragmatics research paradigm

Form/function pragmatics is concerned with a small subset of pragmatic meanings, those conventionally associated with specific linguistic expressions (constructions and discourse markers for the most part). Since these meanings are conventional, the pragmatic meanings offered are claimed to belong in grammar. Most, though not all, researchers use naturally occurring examples, but hardly any experimentation has been used to support pragmatic form/function claims.[8]

Here is one example. Originally, the generative account needed to stipulate that the subject (X) "removed" from sentence initial position in existential sentences (*there is an X . . .*) had to be an indefinite NP. This grammatical condition, however, is lacking in both descriptive and explanatory adequacies, it was argued, in the jargon of the period. The missing explanatory generalization is that existential constructions serve a specific discourse function, to introduce new entities into the discourse. Since indefinite NPs stand for new entities, no wonder this restriction applies to existential sentences. Hence, what seems to be an arbitrary grammatical stipulation turns out to be pragmatically motivated. Moreover, once the grammatical restriction (against definites) was replaced with a functional restriction (against Given entities), formally definite NPs no longer constitute counterexamples to the account, provided they are not Given (Rando and Napoli, 1978).

Now, grammar is responsible for form/function correlations, and the analyses here concerned clearly associate specific forms with specific functions. Why should this research be considered pragmatics then? Different researchers provide different reasons. The dilemma here is identical to the one concerning conventional implicatures – in fact, there is no reason not to view the form/function correlations here concerned as conventional implicatures. For some form/function pragmatists, their research is pragmatic, because the functions associated with the syntactic constructions and discourse markers all concern interpretations that do not contribute truth-conditional elements to the proposition expressed. In other words, if we were to present new information where old information is called for, or vice versa, the resulting sentence is not taken to convey a false proposition, nor is it an ungrammatical sentence. Since, especially early on, many pragmatists subscribed to the truth-conditionality criterion as distinguishing semantics from pragmatics, the functions associated with syntactic constructions were automatically classified as pragmatic (see Brinton, 2008 for a similar assumption). Later on, in view of the inner contradictions between various definitions for pragmatics, pragmatists tended to give up on a coherent definition for the field, and such research was seen as part of pragmatics, simply because a canonical list of pragmatics topics had been established, and functional syntax formed a (marginal) member on this list. Thus, for the most part, functional syntax, and certainly research on discourse markers, is considered pragmatic, rather than semantic.

At the same time, some researchers insisted that the form/function correlations they were analyzing were conventional, and hence part of grammar. Prince (most explicitly in 1988) treated the non-truth-conditional interpretations she was analyzing as grammatical, because they directly and conventionally associated specific linguistic forms with specific interpretations and/or use conditions.[9] Now, although for Prince form/function pragmatics forms part of grammar, she assigns it to a special, discourse component within grammar. Blakemore took one step further, and treated conventional implicatures as part of semantics proper (see Ariel, 2010: Chapter 8 for arguments for and against this position). So, while the status of form/function pragmatic meanings within grammar is not settled, there is no doubt that the conventions involved (or at least a subset of these) are encoded for specific forms, and hence fall on the grammar side of the grammar/pragmatics divide.

Most classical form/function pragmatic analyses leave formal grammar intact. Rarely do they appropriate a grammatical phenomenon as pragmatic (as in the case of the definiteness restriction in existential constructions).

Traditionally, attention was focused on so-called optional choices between variant forms (paraphrastic utterances). The argument made was that speakers' preference for one rather than another of these syntactic paraphrases (or for using or not using some discourse marker) was not random: "every contrast a language permits to survive is relevant, some time or other" (Bolinger, 1972: 71). Formal grammar cannot offer an account for such choices between semantic paraphrases (nor between zero discourse markers and explicit discourse markers), but form/function pragmatics can. In fact, what seems an "optional" choice between "free variants" in terms of grammar turns out to be a choice informed by form/function conventions pertaining to non-truth-conditional meanings and/or use conditions. Recently, there is a new line of research which incorporates many of the insights introduced by form/function pragmatists, but sees no reason whatsoever to (a) distinguish between + and – truth-conditional meanings and (b) accept formal syntactic analyses: Cognitive Linguistics (Lakoff, G., 1987; Langacker, 1987, 1991) and Construction Grammar (Goldberg, 1995). On these approaches, form/function correlations are part of grammar, no matter what their nature is.

A typical form/function pragmatics analysis is Prince (1978), where she not only distinguishes between unmarked non-clefted constructions and cleft sentences, she also points to the different discourse functions associated with the two cleft sentences in English. The presupposed component in *it*-clefts, she argued, introduces Given information in general. But the presupposed component in *wh*-clefts refers to a subset of the information Given to the addressee, that which can cooperatively be assumed to be currently accessible to him. In Ariel (1983) I analyzed a specific appositive in Hebrew, which is dedicated to the introduction of (very) important persons, and Ward (1990) argued that English VP preposing is restricted to cases where the speaker intends to affirm her commitment to a proposition which has recently been evoked in the discourse. In each of these cases a specific discourse function is associated with a specific syntactic construction.

But these are marked constructions. Most constructions do not manifest a one-to-one form/function correspondence. In fact, even Prince analyzed a few functions for *it*-clefts, as did Ziv (1982) for existential constructions (and see especially Kuzar, 2009; Lakoff, G., 1987). The idea is that each construction has multiple features, each of which is potentially appropriate for a certain discourse function. For example, Prince found that in addition to stressed-focus *it*-clefts as characterized above, there are also informative *it*-clefts, where the presupposed information is not actually Given to the addressee. Rather, it is presented as a fact known to some, knowledgeable people. It is not surprising that *it*-clefts, rather than *wh*-clefts, are used for this non-Given function. Note that unlike for *wh*-clefts, the presupposed information in *it*-clefts is presented in final sentence position, a position more appropriate for non-Given information. Different sentential positions for certain syntactic roles (non-initial position for subjects for existential constructions), different degrees of verb transitivity and semantic content (existential *there* takes low-transitivity and low-content verbs), different optional components in the construction (is there or is there not an additional embedded clause attached to the subject NP in the existential clause?) are all potentially mobilized for conveying various discourse functions. Hence the realization that syntactic constructions are not invariably reducible to single pragmatic "sign" functions. Rather, they constitute structure functions which allow for a variety of sign functions to be realized in them (Du Bois, 2003).

Summing up, form/function pragmatic research associates discourse functions and/or use conditions with linguistically specified forms (morphemes, phrases, or whole syntactic constructions). The difference between classical semantic functions and these mostly information-status conditions is that although they are equally grammaticized, they involve extralinguistic factors which normally do not contribute to the truth-conditions of the proposition expressed. Since researchers within this paradigm are committed to the code/inference division of labor between grammar and pragmatics, these form/function correlations are considered grammatical. The result is that they see the pragmatic interpretations they analyze as separate in nature from other pragmatic interpretations, most notably, from conversational implicatures, analyzed by inferential pragmatics theories. But at the same time, many of these researchers also uphold the conviction that being non-truth-conditional, the interpretations at hand are pragmatic. Hence their self-classification as pragmatists.

## 2.2.2 Form/function pragmatics and reference

Although form/function pragmatists do appreciate the role of inferencing in referential acts, they see a larger role for the specific referring expressions. Both Ariel (1990) and Gundel *et al.* (1993) have proposed much richer scales of referring expressions than Levinson's, the idea being that there is a conventional form/function association between forms and referential interpretations.[10] I have proposed that referring expressions each specialize for a different degree of accessibility for the mental representation the addressee is to retrieve. The form/function associations are far from arbitrary. Less informative expressions (*she* vs *the woman*), less rigid (uniquely referring) expressions (*the woman* vs *Dana*), and more phonetically attenuated forms (Ø vs *she*, *USA* vs *the United States*) are used to access relatively highly accessible referents. Conversely, the more informative, rigid, and phonetically large the form (e.g., *June, the woman who just walked out*, SBC: 008), the less accessible the mental representation is assumed to be.[11] Infinitely many referring expressions indicate various intermediate degrees of mental accessibility (e.g., *June*, *the woman*, demonstratives, pronouns, cliticized pronouns, etc.), all arranged on a scale of degrees of accessibility. Gundel *et al.* (1993) are more ambitious and propose that each referring expression encodes a specific cognitive status (such as 'in focus', 'activated', 'familiar' etc . . . ). For example, *it* is chosen in (1), because the colander is extremely accessible according to Ariel, and similarly, it is 'in focus' for Gundel *et al.* (1993). *That*, on the other hand, is used in (2) because the propositional 'reading you some' is not highly accessible to justify the use of a pronoun according to Ariel (it is 'activated', not 'in focus' for Gundel *et al.*, 1993):

(1)    MARILYN: . . . There's a colander$_i$ – . . . Oh. **It**$_i$'s gone. Oh here **it**$_i$
       is. (SBC: 003)

(2)    PAMELA: . . . I could read you some . . . I mean is **that** allowed?
       (SBC: 005)

As can be seen, a much more central role is assigned to specific linguistic forms under this approach, although both theories fully appreciate the need for pragmatic inferencing on top of decoding for proper reference resolutions (see section 2.5.1). Referring expressions are each directly associated with some cognitive concept in a grammatical manner.

## 2.3  Grammar is (yesterday's) pragmatics: Historical and typological pragmatics

The pragmatists so far considered may infringe on the grammarian's territory, pushing some borders around, but they do not challenge deeply ingrained generative grammar assumptions. The functionalists discussed here do. Most importantly, many reject the innateness hypothesis, arguing that typological universals are better accounted for by reference to extralinguistic factors. Grammar is neither innate nor arbitrary. It evolves in real-time through discourse use. Since communicative needs are relatively similar across different speech communities, it's not surprising that similar grammatical constructions and semantic meanings evolve in a similar fashion from similar sources in unrelated languages. Now, not all extragrammatical forces are pragmatic in the sense being discussed, but we here focus specifically on the role of recurrent pragmatic inferences in shaping grammar.[12] Prominent practitioners within this research paradigm include Givón (1979 and onwards), Traugott (1982 and onwards), Traugott and Heine (1991), Traugott and Dasher (2002), Heine (1993), Bybee *et al.* (1994), Comrie (1994), Du Bois (1987), Haspelmath (2004), and Croft (2000). Note that these researchers do not actually consider themselves pragmatists. Rather, they see themselves as historical linguists, as functionalists, and/or as typologists. Nonetheless, I insist that this research count as a relevant pragmatics research paradigm, because a crucial grammar/pragmatics interface is analyzed: the process by which recurrent pragmatic inferences turn into grammatical codes.[13] The majority of the research in grammaticization (the creation of some grammatical form) and semanticization (the evolution of new meanings for old forms) is corpus-based, and so is some recent functional typological research (Haspelmath, 2008).[14]

## 2.3.1  The historical and typological pragmatics research paradigm

Much historical (grammaticization) and typological pragmatics research ana-
lyzes the current grammar as pragmatically motivated. As in inferential
pragmatics thinking, the assumption here is that in order to best use their
grammar to fulfill their interactional goals, interlocutors make heavy use of
context. All newly formed form/function correlations are crucially context-
bound, and hence the clear role of pragmatics in their initiation. Gradually, a
consistent use of some form in some context, which contributes to the derivation of some extralinguistic reading, may bring about the entrenchment of
the pragmatically derived form/function correlation into conventional codes.
Once conventional, cancelability no longer applies, nor is contextual support
needed. A piece of grammar has emerged.

   We start with innovations. When meanings are intended, which are not
straightforwardly codable in the current grammar, speakers must improvise.
Uttering ungrammatical utterances is not an option. But speakers can mobilize current lexemes and constructions to convey their innovative messages
relying on pragmatic inferencing as mediators. A wealth of relevant examples, universally attested, are provided by Heine and Kuteva (2002): 'Alone'
can be mobilized to express 'only', body parts (e.g. 'back') can be mobilized to
express spatial relations ('in back of'), demonstratives can indicate a relative
clause construction (*that* anaphorically referring to the head) or definiteness
in general (*that* > *the*), 'or' can help mark (alternative) questions, 'ability' can
trigger an interpretation of 'possibility', 'all' or 'people' can indicate 'plurality', possessive + 'head' or 'body' can help indicate an action performed
on the self, etc. In all these cases, the assumption is that initially, the inno-
vated meaning was only a conversational implicature derived with the help
of a richly supportive context. But, as Grice (1989) originally noted, what is
initially generated as a PCI may end up a semantic meaning.

   Note that speakers rely on pragmatic implicatures not only when their
grammar is incapable of expressing their intended meaning. We often prefer
to convey our messages only implicitly. For example, instead of explicitly
stating that x is the reason for y (using some *because* expression), speakers can
implicate it. Now, we're here interested in the eventual development of a
specialized form for expressing reasons. One form speakers can use in order
to implicate a causal relation is a temporal adverbial such as *after*, because
events preceding other events are easily construed as causing or explaining
them (Hopper and Traugott, 2003). Interestingly, cross-linguistically, many
reason conjunctions are either ambiguous (*since*) or etymologically derived
from temporal expressions (Hebrew *ekev* derived from *be=ikvot* 'following'):

(3)   And there's a lot of moves that we just know. **After** being ... there for
      so long (LSAC).

Clearly, "being there for so long" is intended as an explanation for how
it is that "there's a lot of moves that we just know." But the speaker in (3)
chose not to use an explicit 'because' adverbial, although quite a few of those

are available in English: *because, since, for, as, on account of.* The reason is that speakers sometimes wish to convey their message indirectly. This can account for the fact that many languages possess multiple causal/reason adverbials, most of which are motivated diachronically since they can easily be seen as having originally triggered a causal implicature. Clearly grammatical constructions too can be similarly motivated, the creation of what are now called reflexive pronouns, for example. Initially, speakers mobilized an emphatic (complex: pronoun + *self*) referring expression to indicate what they rightly considered an unexpected/marked coreference relation (see section 2.3.2 below).

Finally, even an (initially) unintended meaning may become associated with some form, given our encyclopedic knowledge, which is automatically brought in when we interpret messages. Consider the reflexive construction, which often turns into a low transitivity construction (e.g., French *se laver*, 'wash oneself' = 'wash' – Kemmer, 1993). It so happens that self-inflicted actions tend to be associated with a low degree of transitivity (as defined by Hopper and Thompson, 1980). They are often unintended (Cf. *I hit/cut myself* with *I hit/cut it*), internal, rather than external (*blame/consider oneself*), etc. If that's the case, then even in the absence of an initial intention to convey a low degree of transitivity, interlocutors may come to associate the construction with low-transitivity activities.

The idea is that all contextual enrichments, no matter their source, may penetrate the grammar. The processes here briefly mentioned have one thing in common. Once many speakers start using the same explicit forms (e.g., *back, after*) as a basis for the same pragmatic inferences (a spatial relationship, a causal interpretation, respectively) a conventional code may be established between these forms and functions. The pragmatically derived meaning semanticizes, and becomes a coded meaning. Similarly, once the syntactic contexts in which reflexive forms tended to recur became a discourse pattern salient to speakers, a grammatical convention could set in, and in fact did set in in many languages. Since reflexive pronouns were very often used for a coreferent co-argument, this could very well explain the nature of Binding Condition A. And once the low transitivity often attributed to reflexive-marked actions becomes salient to speakers (not necessarily consciously) the construction may be reanalyzed as a low-transitivity or even an intransitive construction (cf. French *se*).

Researchers within this paradigm feel they can offer substantive explanations not only for why grammars of unrelated languages are so similar. They can also account for differences between languages, which the innateness assumption cannot (parametric variation is not enough to account for the rich, fine-grained variety found in the world's languages). The idea is that for the most part what we have are near universals, rather than precisely identical codes (Evans and Levinson, 2009). If grammar evolves when specific forms gradually come to be associated with specific functions, then differences between languages can be found where some language has already grammaticized some form/function correlation, but another hasn't (yet). Supporting evidence for this claim is the common finding that what is grammatically stipulated in one language is a possible, or sometimes even very common, discourse pattern in another (English *after* possibly triggers a 'because' interpretation, as in (3), but in Hebrew it has grammaticized). And if the Binding Conditions are setting in, they may only be optionally applied in some language (e.g., Old English, where personal pronouns regularly received bound readings), but be obligatory in another (Modern English). Another source of (slight) variation is the somewhat different translation of a pragmatic motivation into grammatical dress. For example, if speakers are indirectly conveying the 'behind' spatial relation using a body part, they may choose 'back' for triggering this initially pragmatic interpretation, but they may equally plausibly choose 'buttocks' for this purpose (this is the source of Hebrew 'behind'). Such is also the variation between languages which use resumptive pronouns, as analyzed in Keenan and Comrie (1977).

Summing up, researchers within the historical and typological pragmatics paradigm deal with both codes and inferences, although their main interest lies in providing what they consider natural explanations for the universal tendencies in the typology and grammaticization of natural languages. The interest in pragmatic inferences is restricted to explaining the why and how of grammatical codes: the processes leading from inferences and represented discourse patterns to grammatical codes and the principles restricting typological variability. Core grammatical phenomena are here pragmatically motivated, and not only optional choices among equally acceptable forms (cf. form/function pragmatics).

## 2.3.2 Historical/typological pragmatics and reference

Binding relations are taken as a universal, in fact innate, linguistic concept by generative grammarians. However, not all languages have use for a dedicated marking of these relations. Historical/typological research seeks to explain how it is that such marking can evolve in real discourse. The assumption is that the pragmatic inference at work here is that co-arguments of the same verbs tend to stand for disjoint referents (e.g., Faltz, 1985, and see Ariel 2008a: 6.1.1 for supporting corpus statistics). If so, co-argument personal pronouns should preferably be interpreted as disjoint. However, since speakers do sometimes need to refer to coreferent co-arguments (e.g., *Am I killing myself?*, SBC: 015), more marked pronouns (what we now call reflexive pronouns) gradually evolved to indicate the marked coreference. Since it is co-argument coreference that is consistently marked, the resulting binding conditions grammaticized specifically around co-arguments (Reinhart and Reuland, 1993). Such an account can explain why the application of the binding rules was slow and gradual. Reflexive forms first appeared for more marked cases, where self actions (i.e., coreference) are less expected, as when destruction events are described (e.g., *X destroyed herself*). They appeared later for self actions which are more expected (e.g., *X dressed her(self*). Keenan, 2003).

Ariel (2000) has argued that the evolution of verbal person agreement markers out of personal pronouns (e.g., Hebrew *shavar=t* 'broke=2nd pers. fem.' from *shavar at* 'broke you-fem.') can be accounted for by Accessibility theory. Recall that Accessibility theory predicts that highly accessible mental representations are retrieved using highly accessible referring expressions, which are phonetically attenuated. It stands to reason that the speaker and the addressee, both highly accessible referents in face-to-face interactions, would frequently be referred to by high-accessibility markers, cliticized pronouns quite often. A consistent pattern whereby first and second person pronouns are reduced may lead to their cliticization to the verb. This may pave the way for a reanalysis whereby the original pronouns are taken as first/second person verbal bound morphemes. This pragmatic explanation can also account for why typologists have found a cross-linguistic difference between first/second person verbal agreements and third person verbal agreement. The latter are far less commonly marked on verbs. Accessibility theory can account for this asymmetric paradigm by noting that unlike the speaker and the addressee, third person referents are not consistently highly accessible in discourse (see the statistics in Ariel, 2000). Hence, third person pronouns do not get reduced consistently enough to trigger a gradual process of cliticization.

In sum, typological/historical analyses set out from pragmatically motivated pressures (the need to mark a marked coreference, the tendency to reduce referring expressions denoting highly accessible referents) and explain the grammaticized pattern as resulting from an unintended series of small and gradual changes, starting with optional choices, going through preferred discourse patterns, and ending with an entrenchment whereby the discourse pattern is translated into an obligatory grammatical convention. The focus for this research paradigm is on the crossing from pragmatics to grammar.

## 2.4   Competition within and across paradigms

We have now briefly surveyed three paradigms of pragmatics research. Inferential pragmatics focuses on drawing the grammar/pragmatics divide at the synchronic level, distinguishing between predominantly truth-conditional codes and pragmatic inferences. Form/function pragmatics focuses on extralinguistic factors, which nonetheless play a grammatical role, because they manifest a coded association with specific linguistic forms. And typological/historical pragmatics focuses on explaining the diachronic relationship between pragmatic inferences and evolving grammatical codes. To give the flavor of the three research paradigms we briefly mentioned a few proposals within each paradigm, mainly ones pertaining to discourse reference. But what is the relationship between these theories? Are all of them needed? Indeed, some theories within and across paradigms stand in conflict. For lack of space, this section again focuses on reference.

### 2.4.1  Competition within paradigms

The different accounts for discourse reference by the two inferential pragmatics theories mentioned above (the Relevance and neo-Gricean accounts) follow straightforwardly from the general differences between the theories. Typically, the Relevance accounts assign a more significant role to the overall interpretation of the utterance, governed by the single Principle of Relevance. They naturally emphasize how reference resolution is a by-product of this interpretative process. Levinson focuses more on (some) actual forms, and relies on the interaction between the various neo-Gricean Principles (I, Q) to explain referential patterns. The specific context plays less of a role for him, the interpretations seen as GCIs.

Next, recall that both Ariel and Gundel *et al.* offer form/function accounts for the use and interpretation of referring expressions. While Ariel views referring expressions as arranged on a scale, each indicating a relatively higher (or lower) degree of mental accessibility, Gundel *et al.*'s theory is much more precise in that it associates each referring expression with a specific cognitive status. I have elsewhere argued that when we examine the definitions given by Gundel *et al.* (1993) for each cognitive status, it's no longer clear that they are indeed distinct (Ariel, 2001). But a major problem with the Givenness hierarchy is that there simply aren't enough cognitive statuses to go around. Here's one such case:

(4)  REBECCA:  .. put **the newspaper**$_i$ on his lap,
     RICKIE:   Y[eah],
     REBECCA:  Ø [mas]turbated,
               and then lifted **the paper**$_i$ up, (SBC: 008)

It is no coincidence that the first mention of the newspaper is phonetically larger than the second one (this is a consistent finding). But under a six-category Givenness scale (Gundel *et al.*'s) there is no way to account for such delicate differences (between a full and a reduced definite NP, as well as between full and cliticized pronouns, etc.). An additional theory is needed, which could arguably be Accessibility theory. In fact, this is the point of Gundel *et al.* (forthcoming), where their Givenness hierarchy is shown to be orthogonal to Accessibility accounts (for the main part). If so, the fact that both theories offer form/function pragmatics accounts for referential forms does not automatically render either one of them redundant. It may well be that referential forms must meet both requirements, for example, that a referent marked by a demonstrative NP must be 'familiar', as well as relatively (but not maximally) accessible.

## 2.4.2  Competition across paradigms

I here cite two cases where the grammar/pragmatics division of labor is under debate. Both form/function pragmatic theories and historical/typological accounts compete with inferential pragmatics as to what to relegate to pragmatics and what to grammar. What is viewed as currently pragmatically inferable under an inferential pragmatics approach may be taken as a form/function code (Hebrew cliticized pronouns). Similarly, a distributional pattern may be analyzed as grammaticized by historical/typological theories, although it seems straightforwardly derivable by inferential pragmatic theories (some reflexive pronouns).

Consider the following Hebrew discourse, where the same entity (the press$_i$), is already very highly accessible (the first mention here is the sixteenth reference to it):

(5)  ...$\mathbf{h}_i$ [=hem] =  mociim    et     ze     kaxa...
     They                  publish   ACC    this   like-this...

     aval  $\mathbf{hem}_i$   madgishim...   $\mathbf{h}_i$   notnim   kama...
     But   they    emphasize...    they    give     some...

     od          davar she=  $\mathbf{hem}_i$  asu...
     Another   thing that   they    did... (Ariel 1990).

Given the availability of cliticized pronouns for Hebrew *hem* 'they', it is the avoidance of the shorter forms in the second and fourth references that is puzzling on any inferential pragmatic theory. Minimizing processing cost should have prompted the speaker to use the reduced pronouns throughout according to Relevance theory, for the same interpretation is made available by the two forms (see especially Reboul, 1997). Levinson actually predicts a disjoint reading here, because the speaker avoided the most minimal form. Form/functionalists Ariel and Gundel *et al.*, however, can account for the alternating uses of full and cliticized pronouns by noting the points at which the speaker switches from one to the other. Discourse connectives, such as 'but' and 'another thing' here, signal that a potential topic change may occur, thus reducing the accessibility of the current topic. Gundel *et al.* can similarly explain the data as a change from 'in focus' to 'activated'.[15] Hence, the differential preference for full and for cliticized pronouns in different contexts. In this case, it looks like the form/function approach is superior to the inferential approach.

Next, what is the status of the binding conditions regarding the use of reflexives? Levinson (2000: Chapter 4), König and Siemund (2000) and Ariel (2008b: Chapter 6) are all in agreement that a pragmatic interpretative pattern lies behind these grammaticized conventions (see again sections 2.3.1, 2.3.2). As an inferential pragmatist, Levinson points out that reflexives in different languages don't necessarily share the same grammatical/pragmatic status. For example, in some languages co-arguments can, but need not always be reflexive-marked. Obviously, the pattern is only pragmatic in these languages. But the picture is more complicated than that. Even for a single language, sub-patterns may be either pragmatic or grammatical. For example, according to Ariel's (2008b: 6.3) grammaticization analysis, some adjuncts obligatorily take reflexive forms (*despite herself, with himself*) when coreferential with a clause-mate antecedent, although other adjuncts only manifest a pragmatic preference for the extension of the Binding convention beyond co-arguments (*except for him(self), picture of her(self), jokes about him(self)*). Other sub-constructions obligatorily take a pronoun, even though an obligatorily coreferential co-argument is involved (*He didn't have any spots on him(*self/*her)*). Although this pattern is an exception to the general Binding principle, and although it is clearly pragmatically motivated (according to the pragmatic motivation here, unmarked coreference is not in need of special marking), a grammatical convention is nonetheless involved (note the unacceptable reflexive form above). In other words, a competition between pragmatic and grammatical analyses is at work not just for the general distributional pattern applicable to the language as a whole, but also at much lower-level generalizations within the same language.

Different pragmatic theories certainly compete for the best account, whether within (2.4.1) or across (2.4.2) research paradigms. While researchers have mainly engaged in intra-paradigm debates, it's time for cross-paradigmatic debates and collaborations to take the stage in pragmatic research.

## 2.5 Inferential, form/function, and historical/typological pragmatics too

Surprisingly perhaps, there is not much interaction between researchers subscribing to different research paradigms. The goal of this section is to prompt all researchers to open up to the idea that their research must take into consideration questions addressed by other research paradigms. The three paradigms, I argue, complement each other in crucial ways.

### 2.5.1 Reference in three keys

We've briefly looked at a number of competing pragmatic accounts for the use and interpretation of referring expressions. Although some accounts will ultimately have to be rejected, reality is that we need all three approaches in order to fully account for natural language reference systems. Each approach provides some of the relevant pieces needed to complete the great grammar/pragmatics puzzle. Form/function pragmatics codes (which may turn out to be neither Gundel *et al*'s nor Ariel's) are needed to account for the basic conventions informing reference marking and resolution. But, of course, codes never exhaust actual use. This is true for classical semantic codes, and it is equally true for grammatical pragmatic codes. This is where inferential pragmatic accounts must come in. For example, *those two idiots* (in (6)) seems to be too low an accessibility marker for an entity just now mentioned by pronominal *they*. The violation of Accessibility theory can, then, be explained as a special inferred use (epithet), where the speaker's goal is not just to refer, but at the same time to also predicate on the referent:

(6)    .. So **they**$_i$ go barging in on ~Mar.
       .. So Mom felt obligated,
          to ask **those two idiots**$_i$ to lunch (SBC: 006).

The same applies to the reference resolution cases analyzed by Kempson (1988) and Wilson (1992) (see section 2.1.2). Finally, we need an account for why and how the pragmatics/grammar divide is crossed (e.g., how pronouns evolve into verbal person agreement markers). It is the discourse profiles analyzed by historical and typological pragmatists that constitute potential grammaticization paths. Such theories bridge the gap between temporary integrations between inferred and coded meanings (on-line conveyed meanings) and permanent (grammaticized) form/function correlations. To account for the full range of use and interpretation of referring expressions we therefore need the three different pragmatic approaches, even if some (or possibly all) current theories are factually incorrect. Different research paradigms are needed for handling the different aspects of the grammar and pragmatics of reference. The same applies to all other linguistic phenomena.

## 2.5.2   Conclusion: The value of multiple paradigms in pragmatics

Each of the pragmatic approaches here surveyed has offered a significant amendment to the limited classical code model of language. The main point of the (originally Gricean) inferential pragmatics critique of the code model was that truth-conditional codes cannot exhaust speakers' intended on-line meanings, because ad-hoc contextual inferences are generated in addition. According to form/function pragmatists, the classical codes fall short of exhausting all grammatically specified conventions, because not all codes are truth-conditional. Finally, *contra* generative grammarians, historical/typological pragmatists argue that classical codes cannot account for possible versus impossible natural language grammars. Since each approach finds different flaws in the classical code model, no wonder they each enrich it in a different direction. But it cannot be emphasized enough that these different research directions are not at all contradictory. Quite the contrary. They complement each other. Here are some thoughts on how they could each gain from interactions with the other approaches.

The most basic pragmatic approach, inferential pragmatics, has a strong preference for maximizing pragmatics and minimizing grammar. Anything that can be analyzed as pragmatic inference must so be analyzed. However, once researchers consider form/function pragmatics findings regarding potentially conventional associations between constructions and non-truth-conditional meanings, some analyses in terms of inferences may be relegated to form/function pragmatics within the grammar. Why shouldn't perfectly plausible inferences get entrenched in an automatic, subconscious process? For example, perfectly general inferential pragmatics attempts to explain the use and interpretation of cleft constructions by reference to their compositional meaning accompanied by pragmatic inferences (Wilson and Sperber, 1979) must give way to a form/function pragmatic analysis, where a conventional interpretation is associated with each of the constructions (see section 2.2.1 above). Indeed, Blakemore (2002) is a clear example of a Relevance theoretician who has consistently used form/function (procedural) analyses for discourse connectives (and see Ariel, 2010: Part III).

The same is true for the relevance of historical/typological pragmatics findings for inferential pragmatics, specifically, the recognition that inferences may gradually turn into grammatical codes. For example, if GCIs are normal or default inferences associated with specific forms, they are potential semanticization cases (Traugott and Dasher, 2002). Indeed, Levinson's (2000: Chapter 4) is an analysis in this spirit (and see Ariel, 2008b: Part II). At the same time, the fact that the GCIs most discussed in the field (e.g., scalar implicatures, *and*-associated implicatures) do not seem to semanticize in any language might mean that the inferences are not after all as "normal" or default. Why is that? Such questions will naturally arise once cross-paradigmatic discussion (and debate) become more commonplace.

Next, form/function pragmatists tend to automatically assume that the correlations they find between specific linguistic forms and non-truth-conditional meanings or use conditions are conventional, and hence, grammatical. But it's not clear that this is invariably the case. Such pragmatists would do well to integrate the code/inference division of labor with form/function analyses. While, no doubt, many of the correlations they discussed are encoded for specific constructions and forms, others may be better accounted for as further inferences (see Ariel, 2010: Chapter 7 for such analyses). Du Bois' (2003) distinction between sign functions (codes) and structure functions, which only allow for certain functions to be fulfilled in them (with the help of inferencing), should then be useful. Especially now that less marked constructions are increasingly analyzed for their functions (following Construction Grammar), it is becoming rather clear that there is no one-to-one relationship between the added meaning of syntactic constructions and discourse functions. Often, a few functions are associated with a single construction, only some of which are encoded. Form/function pragmatists tend not to problematize such questions of code/inference division of labor (Goldberg, 2006: Chapter 8).

Finally, historical/typological pragmatics research too could benefit from integrating inferential pragmatics theories and questions. Proponents must ascertain that they only assume very small steps of grammaticization, each of which is analyzable as depending on a reasonable on-line pragmatic inference. Etymological analyses can serve as excellent pointers to potential paths of grammaticization, but they cannot replace detailed analyses of the actual inferential steps, leading from one stage to the next. There is a danger in only noting common source-target pairs (Heine and Kuteva, 2002), because these are more often than not connected by a whole series of very small changes. For example, it's a bit misleading to claim that expressions denoting small quantities, such as French *pas* 'step', Hebrew *klum* 'something', evolve into negators or negative polarity items, because the change never involves the initial and the endpoint directly. Indeed, this is why some of Sweetser's (1990) analyses of metaphoric changes have been reanalyzed by Bybee *et al.* (1994) and Traugott and Dasher (2002) as processes where enrichment inferences have been semanticized. The same applies to the very valuable typological clines and semantic maps (Croft, 2001; Haspelmath, 2003; Kemmer, 1993). Semantic changes must be shown to have evolved out of theoretically justified on-line pragmatic inferences.

We can also envision further sophistication in explaining the processes leading from pragmatics to grammar by reference to inferential pragmatics theories. Ever since Grice proposed that conversational implicatures can semanticize, the assumption has been that implicatures sometimes turn semantic. Traugott has argued that it is specifically generalized invited inferences (she prefers this term over GCIs), rather than particularized inferences, that are potential semanticization cases. But what about the Relevance-theoretic explicated inferences (see the definition in section 2.1.1 above)? Given that explicated inferences are closer to semantic meanings than PCIs and GCIs (explicated inferences contribute truth-conditional aspects; they are inseparable from the linguistic meaning – Recanati, 1989), I have suggested that it may be explicated rather than implicated inferences that directly semanticize. PCIs must go through an explicated stage before they semanticize (Ariel, 2008a, 2008b).[16] Last, some historical pragmatists have relied on the form/function pragmatics practice of distinguishing truth-conditional from non-truth-conditional meanings. Since some historical changes evolve non-truth-conditional functions (for many discourse markers), they have defined these as pragmaticization, rather than semanticization (Erman and Kostinas, 1993). Given that the processes here concerned make a pragmatic pattern evolve into grammatical convention, the distinction is probably not justified. Greater attention should then be paid to the role of inferential pragmatics theories.

Summing up, while theories within the same research paradigm addressing the same linguistic phenomenon are in competition with each other (e.g., neo-Gricean and Relevance-theoretic analyses of scalars and *and*), theories from different research paradigms complement each other for the most part. Just because they each focus on a different aspect of linguistic form and use, all three paradigms are necessary for a complete picture of grammatical forms, and for what should be assigned pragmatic status. Our main (but all too brief) test cases were competing, as well as complementary, referential theories. I've argued that form/function pragmatic theories (e.g., Gundel *et al.*,

Ariel) should account for the conventional interpretations associated with various referring expressions, inferential pragmatic theories (e.g., Relevance, neo-Gricean theories) account for the many referential interpretations mediated by inference (e.g., bridged coreference, type versus token readings), and historical/typological pragmatic theories account for dominant discourse tendencies regarding the actual use of referring expressions (e.g., marked coreference by marked forms), some of which turn grammatical, at least in some languages.

What the field of pragmatics, indeed of linguistics, needs now is not so much, or not only, inter-paradigmatic debates about who got it right and who got it wrong. More fruitful and exciting insights will be gained from cross-fertilization and cooperative research between proponents of different paradigms. It takes all pragmatic keys to fine-tune the grammar/pragmatics division of labor.[17]

# 3

# Saying, meaning, and implicating

Kent Bach

> You make a few distinctions. You clarify a few concepts. It's a living.
>
> Sydney Morgenbesser, on being a philosopher.

A speaker can say something without meaning it, by meaning something else or perhaps nothing at all. A speaker can mean something without saying it, by merely implicating it. These two truisms are reason enough to distinguish saying, meaning, and implicating. And that's what we'll do here, looking into what each involves and how they interconnect. The aim of this chapter is to clarify the notions of saying, meaning, and implicating and, with the help of some other distinctions, to dispel certain common misunderstandings.

Paul Grice famously developed accounts of what it is for a speaker to mean something and to implicate something. His basic idea was not new, as this oft-quoted passage from Mill illustrates:

> If I say to any one, "I saw some of your children today", he might be justified in inferring that I did not see them all, not because the words mean it, but because, if I had seen them all, it is most likely that I should have said so: even though this cannot be presumed unless it is presupposed that I must have known whether the children I saw were all or not. (Mill 1867: 501)

Not only did Mill appreciate the phenomenon of what, thanks to Grice, has come to be known as *conversational implicature*, in this passage Mill points to the importance of distinguishing what is meant by the words a speaker utters and what a speaker means in uttering them. This is perhaps the distinction most basic to pragmatics.

So we have the distinction between linguistic and speaker's meaning, as well as the three-part distinction between saying, meaning, and implicating, as done by a speaker. Why fuss over these distinctions? The main reason is to identify the sorts of information that speakers (or writers) make available to their listeners (or readers), the sorts of intentions that speakers have in so doing, and the means by which this information is made available to or is inferable by the hearer from the fact that the speaker did what she did. We do not use psychokinesis to make ourselves understood or telepathy to figure out what others mean. We rely primarily on the meanings of the words we utter or hear. They carry information and we, as speakers of the same language, share this information and mutually presume that we share it. But we do not rely solely on linguistically encoded information. In communicating to and understanding one another, we rely also on general background information and on specific information about the situation in which the utterance is taking place. Importantly, this includes the very fact that the utterance, *that* utterance, is being made. As speakers aiming to communicate things, we choose to utter bits of language that make our communicative intentions evident to our hearers. We do so with the tacit expectation that the package of linguistic and extralinguistic information associated with our utterance will enable our listeners to figure out what we mean. Correlatively, as hearers, we rely on what we presume to be the very same information, both linguistic and extralinguistic, to figure out what the speaker means.

In the first three sections we will take up saying, meaning, and implicating, respectively. Our initial discussion of saying will be brief, serving mainly to explain how saying, in the sense tied to linguistic meaning, contrasts with (speaker) meaning and implicating. The discussion of speaker meaning will focus on its two main features, one due to Grice and one due to his critics. Grice's ingenious idea was that in meaning something a speaker has a special sort of hearer-directed intention, which he sometimes called a *reflexive* intention, because part of its content is that the hearer recognize this very intention. She succeeds in communicating if he does recognize it (from now on, when using pronouns for a pair of interlocutors, I will use "she" for the speaker and "he" for the hearer). As for implicating, it is a case of meaning something without saying it. Grice proposed an extraordinarily influential account of how this works, at least when communication succeeds and the conversational implicature is recognized, by proposing a *Cooperative Principle* and certain *conversational maxims* subordinate to it.

Grice's account, as influential as it has been, has also been widely misunderstood and even misrepresented. In section 3.4 we will identify the main misconceptions and thereby clarify just what he was claiming or, in some cases, should have claimed. In section 3.5 we will consider several complications to the distinction between saying, meaning, and implicating, including the phenomena of conventional implicature and conversational impliciture (as opposed to implicature), and, in light of these phenomena and in the face of certain popular objections, modify our notion of saying.

## 3.1  Saying and what is said

The verb "say" has a variety of everyday uses. We speak not only of speakers saying things but also of sentences, signs, and even clocks saying things.

Even limited to acts by speakers, "say" has a range of common uses. On one end of that range, it denotes the act of uttering (a sentence, typically) and, on the other end, acts of stating or asserting (a proposition). Acts of the former sort are reported by direct quotation, of the form "S said '...'," and acts of the latter sort by reports of the form "S stated/asserted that p," where "p" denotes a proposition. Given that we have these other verbs and given that stating or asserting something entails meaning it (not that this in turn entails believing it), it makes sense to reserve the term "say" for the in-between act that is reported by indirect quotation, with sentences of the form "S said that p," assuming that what is said is a proposition.

The notion of saying, along with the correlative notion of what is said, comes into the picture for a very simple reason: a speaker can say one thing while meaning something else. She could mean something instead of what she says, or she could mean something in addition to what she says. Indeed, a speaker can say something without meaning anything at all, as in recitation or translation. Acts of saying, in the sense in which we will be using the term, correspond to Austin's (1962) notion of *locutionary* act. Performing a locutionary act goes beyond merely producing certain sounds, even as belonging to a certain language. On the other hand, it must be distinguished from both the *illocutionary* act of doing something *in* saying something and the *perlocutionary* act of doing something *by* saying something. To perform a locutionary act is to utter a sentence "with a more or less definite sense and a more or less definite reference" (Austin 1962: 93). To be sure, these different categories of speech are abstractions from the total speech act. It is not as though in uttering a sentence a speaker is performing a series of acts. Rather, in uttering, say, "I love turnips," a speaker would be saying that she loves turnips, probably asserting that she loves turnips, and perhaps wanting and maybe even getting her audience to want to try some.

Grice's stipulated sense of "say" is not quite the same as Austin's. He writes, "I intend what someone has said to be closely related to the conventional meaning of the words (the sentence) he has uttered" (Grice 1975/1989: 25). Assuming that what is said must be a unique proposition, he required further that any semantic ambiguities be resolved and references be fixed. So far this sounds like Austin's notion of locutionary act, although, curiously, Grice did not connect his notion with his former teacher's (indeed, as we will see in the next section, Grice's analysis of speaker meaning could have benefited by taking into account Austin's distinction between illocutionary and perlocutionary acts). However, unlike Austin, Grice required that saying something entails meaning it. Otherwise, one merely "makes as if to say" it. This requirement seems odd (it conflicts with the first of our opening truisms), since if one can't say something without meaning it, one doesn't say anything unless one means it. There is a sense in which that is true, the sense in which "say" is synonymous with "state." Indeed, in Grice's (1961) preliminary account of implicature, the preferred verb was "state," not "say." In my opinion, Grice's main reason for insisting on this stronger sense of "say" was that it supported his controversial view (proposed in Grice 1968), not to be discussed here, that what expressions mean in a language ultimately comes down to what speakers mean in using them. In any case, surely there's a perfectly good sense in which one can say something without meaning it.

What is the rationale for adopting a locutionary notion of saying and the correlative notion of what is said? The point of tying what is said closely to the conventional meaning of the uttered sentence is to limit it to information carried by that sentence. We can think of what is said as, in effect, the interpreted logical form of the sentence. Grice's reason for requiring resolution of ambiguity is to further limit what is said to the sense of the sentence that is operative in the speaker's act of uttering it. Otherwise, whenever there is ambiguity (often!), multiple things would be said. Presumably it is the speaker's semantic intention that does the disambiguating. This intention determines what she takes her words to mean as she is using them, and is distinct from her communicative intention, which determines how she intends her audience to take her act of uttering those words.

As for fixing reference, in cases involving indexicals (including pronouns, certain temporal and locational adverbs, and tense), the point is more subtle. With them we need to distinguish their meaning from their reference and take into account the fact that it is the reference, not the meaning, that figures in what is said. The meaning helps pin down the reference but is not itself part of what is said. So, for example, if I utter the sentence "I love turnips," I thereby say that I love turnips. I do not say that the current utterer of this sentence loves turnips. After all, what I said, that I love turnips, could be true (not that it is true) even if I hadn't uttered the sentence. The meaning rule, that "I" as used by a given speaker on a given occasion refers to that speaker, is not part of what I say, or would say, if I were to utter "I love turnips." An analogous point applies to the use of the present tense. The general idea here was developed by Kaplan (1989a), who proposed that the *character* of an expression determines the *content* of the expression relative to a given context of use. The character is a meaning rule that provides for how this content, the expression's reference, is determined in the context. Obviously the rule for "I" is different from, for example, the rule for "you" and the one for "yesterday."

There is an ongoing debate in philosophy regarding the range of expressions whose reference is literally determined, according to a meaning rule, as a function of their context of use. The primary question at issue is whether it is really the context of use, as opposed to the speaker's referential intention, that determines the reference. We will not pursue this issue here. Suffice it to say that there seems to be a basic difference between what determines the reference of terms like "she" and "that" as opposed to the reference of terms like "I" and "today." Arguably, the difference is great enough to justify Strawson's (1950) contention that speakers, not expressions, refer (see Bach 2006d for discussion of the question "What does it take to refer?").

The above niceties aside, both ambiguity and indexicality are different ways in which linguistic meaning does not determine speaker meaning even if the speaker is being completely literal. The meaning of an ambiguous sentence underdetermines what a speaker could mean in using it literally, obviously because the sentence has too many meanings, i.e. more than one (a speaker can mean more than one thing by trading on an ambiguity, as with puns, but this is an exceptional case). The case of indexicality is different. When we use an expression like "I," "tomorrow," "she," or "that," the meaning of the expression merely constrains what we can mean in using it literally. Indexicality is like ambiguity insofar as in both cases linguistic meaning limits but does not fully determine what one can mean in speaking literally. They differ, however, in that with ambiguity there is too much linguistic meaning and with indexicality there is too little.

As we will see later on, following our discussions of meaning and implicature, ambiguity and indexicality are not the only ways in which linguistic meaning can underdetermine literal speaker meaning. It will emerge that finding a suitable notion of saying, together with the correlative notion of what is said, is not as straightforward as Grice supposed, and not just because he needlessly required that to say something entails meaning it. But what is it for a speaker to mean something?

## 3.2  Speaker meaning

Grice (1957) contrasted "natural" meaning with the sort of meaning ("non-natural," he called it) involved in language and communication. Smoke means fire because it is naturally correlated with fire, but the word "smoke" means smoke by virtue of being conventionally correlated with smoke. Smoke means fire in the sense of indicating the presence of fire, and that is because it is correlated with fire. However, the word "smoke" is not correlated with the presence of smoke. It is a conventional means for talking about smoke, whether or not smoke is present. Its meaning is a matter of convention, since it could just as well have meant something else (and some other word could just as well have meant smoke). It means smoke because, and only because, speakers normally use it to mean that and expect others who use it to mean that as well.

So within the category of non-natural meaning there is both linguistic meaning, in this case what "smoke" means, and speaker meaning, here what a speaker means in using that word. Take an example. Suppose a speaker utters the sentence, "I smell smoke," using the pronoun "I" to refer to herself, the verb "smell" (in the present tense) for olfactory sensing, and the noun "smoke" to refer to smoke, presumably some that is nearby. Given what these words mean and how, as syntactically determined, these combine to comprise the (linguistic) meaning of the entire sentence, the semantic content of the sentence, relative to that context, is that she (the speaker) smells smoke. This could well be what she means in uttering that sentence, but it might not be. For she could have been speaking figuratively, in which case she would have meant something else. She could have meant, regarding something her interlocutor had just said, that he was trying to divert her attention from what was at issue. On the other hand, she could have been speaking perfectly literally. Even then, it is one thing for the sentence to mean something and another for a speaker to mean that in uttering it.

### 3.2.1 Meaning intentions

We will not delve into the long-debated meta-semantic question of what it is for an expression to have meaning, except to note one aspect of that question: which is more basic, expression meaning or speaker meaning? This question was important to Grice, who held not only that speaker meaning is more basic but that expression meaning ultimately reduces to speaker meaning (Grice 1968). His was a controversial version of the relatively uncontroversial view that semantics reduces to psychology.

Our question is what is it for a speaker to mean something, whether in using language or in doing something else. It is not merely to produce some effect in one's audience. There are lots of ways of doing that. At the very least it must be intentional. Besides, there are different ways in which one can intend to produce some effect on others, and most of them are not just matters of successful communication. In communicating something, one has a special sort of intention and intends to produce a special sort of effect.

What is special about the intention? Part of it is that one intends one's audience to recognize the very effect one is trying to produce in them. Moreover, as Grice (1957) argued, one intends to produce that effect precisely *by way of* their recognizing that intention. This is the gist of Grice's ingenious idea that the special sort of intention involved in meaning something, in trying to communicate something, is in a certain sense *reflexive*.

Think about what is involved in communicating. You have a certain thought and you wish to "get it across" to someone. So your intention to convey it must not be hidden. Your intention will not be communicative if you intend the hearer to think a certain thing without thinking you intend them to think it. For example, if you yawningly say "I am sleepy," your intention that they think you are sleepy is not essential to their coming to think that you are sleepy – your yawning manner of speech will do. Of course, they will recognize that you intend them to think that you are sleepy. However, because of how you said it, their recognizing this would not have been necessary. Indeed, they would think that you are sleepy even if you had said something completely different, provided you said it yawningly. In some cases, recognizing your intention may vitiate it, for example, if you make some self-deprecating remarks in order to get your listener to think you are modest. Your intention that they think this won't be fulfilled if they recognize your intention that they think this. But even in our first example, in which recognizing the speaker's intention doesn't interfere with its fulfillment, the hearer's recognition of it is not needed for its fulfillment.

Such examples suggested to Grice that for an intention to be communicative, it must be overt in a specific sort of way. It must be intentionally overt and this feature must play a special role in its fulfillment. That is, in trying to communicate something to others by saying something, a speaker intends the audience to recognize that intention partly by taking into account *that* they are intended to recognize it. Because this is part of what the speaker intends, communicative intentions are distinctively self-referential or reflexive. A speaker means something by her utterance only if she intends her utterance "to produce some effect in an audience by means of the recognition of this intention" (Grice 1957/1989: 220). However, not just any sort of effect will do.

## 3.2.2 The intended "effect"

If you are communicating something to someone, *communicative* success does not require that they respond as you wish, such as to believe you, obey you, or forgive you. As Searle pointed out, these are perlocutionary effects, the production of which goes beyond merely communicating (1969: 47). It is enough, as Strawson similarly argued, for the hearer to understand the utterance (1964b: 459), that is, for the speaker to achieve uptake (Grice later (1989: 351–2) objected to this, but did not make clear why). For that the hearer must identify the attitude the speaker is expressing – believing, intending, regretting, etc. – and its content, but the speaker can succeed in communicating even if she does not actually possess that attitude. For example, she can convey an apology without actually having the regret she expresses and without the hearer believing she possesses it. If the speaker says, "I'm sorry I broke your vase," to succeed in communicating the apology it is enough that the hearer take her to be expressing her regret. This is clear from the fact that the hearer might understand the apology as such even if he doubts that the speaker regrets breaking the vase.

So, it seems, the intended "effect" required for meaning something, for communicating, is for the hearer (or reader) to recognize one's communicative intention. Achieving any further effect, such as being believed or being obeyed, goes beyond communicating successfully. The purely communicative effect is just having one's utterance understood. Bach and Harnish distinguish expressing an attitude (a belief, desire, regret, or whatever) from actually possessing it or at least intending the hearer to think one possesses it. According to their definition, "to express an attitude is reflexively to intend the hearer to take one's utterance as reason to think one has that attitude" (Bach and Harnish 1979: 15). Accordingly, communicating successfully, being understood, consists simply in having the expressed attitude recognized. It does not require the hearer to respond in any further way, not even to think one actually possesses attitude. As they say, "the fulfillment of a communicative intention consists simply in its recognition" (*ibid.*). By isolating the purely communicative effect of an act of utterance, this formulation makes sense of Grice's idea that speaker meaning essentially involves a reflexive intention.

### 3.2.3 Reflexive paradox?

Now that we have identified the intended effect specific to communication, we can return to Grice's original characterization of the intention itself. After describing it as the intention "to produce an effect in an audience by means of the recognition of this intention," Grice comments, "this seems to involve a reflexive paradox, but it does not really do so" (1957/1989: 219). It seems to because the intention is self-referential. Moreover, there seems to be something circular about the hearer's inference. After all, the hearer is to identify the speaker's intention partly on the supposition that he is intended to. But is there anything really paradoxical about this?

A reflexive intention is not a series of intentions, each referring to the previous one. Not appreciating this has led to considerable confusion, even on Grice's part. Indeed, earlier in the very paragraph just quoted from, he gives an alternate formulation that requires that a speaker "must also intend his utterance to be recognized as so intended" (1957/1989: 219). Grice (1969), in trying to improve upon his earlier formulation, explicitly abandons reflexive intentions in favor of iterative intentions. So had his critic Strawson (1964b), and so would his defender Schiffer (1972). Their ever more complex formulations, each prompted by counterexamples to the previous formulation, start with an intention to convey something and a further intention that the first be recognized, itself accompanied by a still further intention that it in turn be recognized, and potentially so on *ad infinitum*. No wonder Grice was eventually led to reject the whole idea and suggest that what is needed instead is the absence of a "sneaky intention" (1989: 302). Sticking with self-referential intentions avoids this complexity and the threat of an infinite regress. For there was nothing wrong with Grice's original idea, assuming the intended effect is properly characterized, as above. It does not lead to the reflexive paradox that worried Grice.

The semblance of reflexive paradox in Grice's original formulation arises from the key phrase "by means of the recognition of this intention." This might suggest (and has suggested to some) that to understand the speaker the hearer must engage in some sort of circular reasoning. It sounds as though the hearer must already know what the speaker's communicative intention is in order to recognize it. But that misconstrues what the hearer has to take into account in order to recognize the speaker's intention. The hearer does not infer that the speaker means a certain thing from the premise that the speaker intends to convey that very thing. Rather, he operates on the presumption that the speaker, like any speaker, intends to communicate something or other. The hearer takes into account this general fact, not the content of the specific intention, in order to identify that intention.

## 3.3 Conversational implicature

Grice is best known, in both linguistics and philosophy, for his theory of conversational implicature. It was sketched in a section (III) of his 1961 paper, and developed in his William James Lectures at Harvard in 1967, which were subsequently published individually in disparate places and eventually collected as Part I of the posthumous Grice 1989. The main ideas are laid out in "Logic and Conversation" (Grice 1975/1989), which, from what I have been able to ascertain from Google Scholar, is the most cited philosophy paper ever published. Grice's basic idea was not new, although his name for it was. What distinguished his work from previous work on "contextual" or "pragmatic" implication (see Hungerland 1960) was his ingenious account of how it works (it also served as an antidote to the excesses of ordinary language philosophy, in ways chronicled in Chapman 2005). This account was essentially an extension of his theory of speaker meaning, but what made it original, as we will see, was the role of his "Cooperative Principle" and the various "maxims of conversation" that fall under it.

In Grice's view one can mean something either by saying it or by saying (or "making as if to say") something else. What one implicates by saying something is generally not implied by what one says. That is why Grice used the verb "implicate" rather than "imply" and the neologism "implicature" rather than "implication." For example, suppose you are asked about a dinner you had at an expensive restaurant, and you reply, "It didn't make me sick." Your saying this implicates that it was not very good. However, what you said obviously does not *imply* this. After all, a dinner that does not make you sick can still be excellent. However, it is possible for what is implicated to be implied. If you are asked whether you have more than two children and you reply that you have three girls and a boy, what you say implies the very thing that you implicate, namely, that you have more than two children. That is because you also mean, albeit indirectly, that you have more than two children. There are many other things implied by what you say that you do not mean, hence do not implicate, for example that you have more than one child and that you have more than two girls (much of Davis's (1998) and other critiques of Grice assume that he did not require that implicatures be things speakers mean).

The mediocre meal example illustrates Grice's observation that conversational implicatures are *cancelable* – you could have added, "I don't mean to suggest that the meal wasn't great," without taking back your assertion that it didn't make you sick. In fact, there are circumstances in which the implicature (that the dinner was not very good) would not have been in the offing in the first place. Suppose that you and your interlocutor had just learned that there had been an outbreak of food poisoning at the restaurant in question. In that case, your saying that the meal didn't make you sick would not implicate anything about its culinary quality.

How can a speaker implicate something that is not implied by what she says and still manage to convey it? She can do this by exploiting the fact that the hearer presumes her to be cooperative, in particular, to be speaking truthfully, informatively, relevantly, and otherwise appropriately. If taking the utterance at face value is incompatible with this presumption, the hearer, still relying on this presumption, must find some plausible candidate for what else the speaker could have meant. And, crucially, the speaker must intend him to do this. In the case of the speaker asked about dinner, the hearer must figure out what she meant, relying on the presumption that she intended it to be an accurate, informative, and appropriate answer to the question. In effect what the hearer does is, on the presumption that the speaker is being cooperative, to find a plausible explanation for why she said what she said.

### 3.3.1 The Cooperative Principle and the maxims of conversation

Grice systematized these ideas by formulating an overarching *Cooperative Principle* and four sets of subordinate *maxims of conversation* (Grice, 1975/1989: 26–7):

COOPERATIVE PRINCIPLE: Make your conversational contribution such as is required, at the stage at which it occurs, by the accepted purpose or direction of the talk exchange.

QUALITY: Try to make your contribution one that is true.

1. Do not say what you believe to be false.
2. Do not say that for which you lack evidence.

QUANTITY:

1. Make your contribution as informative as is required (for the current purposes of the exchange).
2. Do not make your contribution more informative than is required.

RELATION: Be relevant.

MANNER: Be perspicuous.

1. Avoid obscurity of expression.
2. Avoid ambiguity.
3. Be brief. (Avoid unnecessary prolixity.)
4. Be orderly.

We will not fuss over the precise meanings of these maxims, except to note one quirk about the wording of the sub-maxims of Quality. Like the

Cooperative Principle itself, most of the maxims and sub-maxims concern a speaker's "conversational contribution." However, the sub-maxims of Quality specifically concern what (not) to *say*. This was probably just a slip on Grice's part, since if these two sub-maxims do not constrain what the hearer can plausibly take the speaker to be implicating, they won't motivate an inferential strategy aimed to correct the appearance, due to what the speaker says, that what she means is false or unwarranted.

There are questions one could ask about the precise formulation of Grice's maxims and about whether the list is incomplete or, for that matter, overly elaborate (for discussion see Harnish 1976 and Grice 1989: 368–72). One might wonder, for example, about what happens when maxims clash, that is, when applying different maxims gives different candidates for what a speaker might be implicating. A common objection to Grice's account is that it is not adequately predictive and, indeed, that different social situations or cultural norms call for different formulations. Such worries presuppose that Grice intended his account to explain precisely how a hearer figures out what the speaker is implicating and, for that matter, how a speaker manages to come up with something to say that will make evident what she means in saying it. These are psychological questions, far beyond the capacity of current psychology to answer.

Philosophically, the important point is that, whatever the particulars, even though what we mean cannot in general be read off of what we say, we as speakers are pretty good at making our communicative intentions evident and that as hearers we are pretty good at identifying such intentions. Grice's primary insight was that unless communication were a kind of telepathy, there must be rational constraints on speakers' communicative intentions and corresponding constraints on hearers' inferences about them. As the examples below will illustrate, Grice's maxims point to the sorts of considerations that speakers intend hearers to take into account, and hearers do take into account, if communication is to succeed, not that it always does. With this in mind Bach and Harnish suggest that the maxims are better viewed as *presumptions* (1979: 62–5), which hearers rely on to guide their inferences as to what speakers mean. So, when a presumption seems not to be in force, a hearer seeks an interpretation of the speaker's utterance such that it does apply after all, and interprets it partly on the supposition that she intends him to. Bach and Harnish propose to replace Grice's CP, the vague and rather unrealistic Cooperative Principle, with a *Communicative Presumption*: when people speak, presumably they do so with identifiable communicative intentions (1979: 12–15). After all, conversations need not be cooperative – people often argue or have conflicting aims – but successful communication is still generally necessary for whatever else takes place.

## 3.3.2 Examples

The following examples illustrate how hearers compensate for apparent violations of the different maxims (or, if you prefer, apparent suspensions of different presumptions). If a speaker says something that is obviously false, thereby flouting the first maxim of quality, she could well mean something else. For example, with (1) she would probably mean the opposite of what she says, with (2) something less extreme, and with (3) something more down to earth.

(1)    George W. Bush was the most intellectual president in American history.

(2)    I could have eaten a million of those chips.

(3)    He bungee-jumped from 85% approval down to 40%, up to 60%, and down to 15%.

In these cases, respectively, of irony, hyperbole, and metaphor, it should be evident what a speaker is likely to mean, even though it is not what she says. Notice that it is possible, however unlikely, that the speaker *does* mean what she says, but then her communicative intention would be unreasonable, since she could not reasonably expect the hearer to figure this out. It is important to remember that it is one thing for a speaker to mean/implicate something and another thing for the hearer to figure out what she means/implicates, that is, for the utterance to be communicatively successful.

   With quantity implicatures a speaker typically means not just what she says but also that she does not mean something stronger. It is her not saying the stronger thing that conveys that she is not in a position to assert it (note that the speaker may implicate instead that she is unwilling to assert something stronger). Consider these examples:

(4)    Barry tried hard to lift the 300-lb barbell.

(5)    He thought he was strong enough to lift it.

(6)    He had lifted the 250-lb barbell three times.

(7)    Barry finished his workout with a swim or a run.

Keeping in mind that speakers, not sentences, implicate things, we have to imagine uttering such sentences or hearing them uttered in particular contexts in order to get clear cases of implicature, quantity implicature in this case. In uttering (4) you would likely implicate that Barry failed to lift the 300-lb barbell. Otherwise, you would have said that he succeeded. Similarly, with (5) you might implicate that he wasn't sure that he could lift it. With (6) you would probably implicate that he didn't lift the 250-lb barbell more than three times. And, finally, in uttering (7) you would implicate that Barry went for either a swim or a run and not both and that you do not know which. In the case of (4) and (5), what the speaker implicates can be figured out on the presumption that if she was in a position to give stronger or more specific information, she would have. With (6), the presumption is that the speaker is in a position to know how many times Barry lifted the 250-lb barbell, whereas with (7) the presumption is just the opposite, since if she knew whether Barry went for a swim or a run (or both), she would have said so.

Relevance implicatures can also be cases of conveying information by saying one thing and leaving something else out. Grice's two best-known examples are of this type:

(8)   There is a garage around the corner. [said in response to "I am out of petrol"]

(9)    He is punctual, and his handwriting is excellent. [the entire body of a letter of recommendation]

An utterance of (8) is relevant, and a rational speaker would intend it as such, only if the speaker means also that the garage is open and has petrol for sale. So the hearer is to reason accordingly. (9) is rather different, on account of the speaker's reason for not being more explicit. In this case, the writer intends the reader to figure out that if she had anything more positive to say about the candidate, she would have said it.

If it seems that quantity implicatures are special cases of relevance implicatures, that is because, generally speaking, they are. What makes them special is that they involve the exploitation of a scale. As Horn (1972) first spelled out, conveying a "scalar implicature" takes advantage of the existence of a naturally stronger alternative along a scale, e.g. "some" rather than "all" and "or" rather than "and." So using "some" typically conveys "not all" and using "or" typically conveys "not both."

Manner implicatures are probably the least common. They exploit not just the speaker's saying a certain thing but her saying it in a certain way. For that reason, they are exceptions to Grice's nondetachability test, according to which what a speaker implicates would have been implicated even if the speaker had said the same thing in a different way (Grice 1975/1989: 39). With manner implicatures, the way matters. It could be the wording, such as using an elaborate phrase when a single word is obviously available to say the same thing, or perhaps the pronunciation, such as by uttering a certain word in a conspicuously odd way. Obviously, if there are different ways of saying the same thing and how the speaker says it affects what the hearer is likely to take into account in figuring out what the speaker means, the implicature *is* detachable. The following examples illustrate this.

(10)   You have prepared what closely resembles a meal of outstanding quality.

(11)    I would like to see more of you.

Imagine a culinary instructor uttering the long-winded (10). Her intention would likely be to convey that the meal is not nearly as good as it appears. A speaker of (11) could exploit its ambiguity (compare "I would like to see you again") to convey something besides wanting to spend more time with the hearer.

It should be understood that Grice does not suppose that speakers consciously exploit the maxims or that hearers consciously take them into account. However, this raises the interesting question of just what is involved psychologically in the process of communication when the speaker does not mean exactly what she says. There is not only the commonly addressed question of how hearers manage to figure out what speakers mean given that they say what they say (and say it in the way they say it), but also the rarely addressed question of how speakers choose what to say so as to make evident what they mean, even when they do not make it explicit. Grice did not address the latter question, and his account of implicature is commonly misconstrued as an answer to the former question. Being clear on what Grice was up to and what he was not avoids a number of misunderstandings.

## 3.4 Common misunderstandings about conversational implicature

There are two common misconceptions about the role of the maxims (or presumptions). First, they do not *determine* implicatures (even Grice (1989: 372) occasionally suggested that they do) but, rather, help explain how they get conveyed. They are considerations that speakers implicitly intend hearers to, and hearers do, take into account to figure out ("determine" in the sense of ascertain) what the speaker is implicating. Since that is a matter of speaker meaning, it is the speaker's communicative intention that determines (in the sense of constitute) what is implicated. Also, it should not be supposed, as it often is, that the maxims apply only to implicatures. This misconception is understandable insofar as the maxims play a key role in Grice's account of how implicatures get conveyed, but in fact they apply equally to completely literal utterances, where the speaker means just what she says. After all, the hearer still has to infer this. It is thus wrong to suppose that the maxims come into play only where linguistic meaning leaves off and speaker meaning and extralinguistic, contextual information take over (for more on context and what it does and doesn't determine, see Bach 2005).

Another misunderstanding concerns what, when a speaker says one thing but means something else, the hearer is to infer. Contrary to what philosophers and linguists seem commonly to suppose (perhaps because of the ambiguous phrase "infer what the speaker implicates"), the hearer does not have to infer the thing the speaker implicates. He merely has to infer that the speaker implicates (means) it. So, for example, if the speaker says and means that a certain new book has a beautiful cover and implicates that it is not worth reading, the hearer needs to infer that the speaker means that it is not worth reading. He does not need to infer that it is in fact not worth reading. The speaker might want him to believe that, but this is not necessary as far as communication is concerned. Indeed, he could even doubt that *she* believes it (he might think she resents the author's success).

A remarkably widespread misconception is that implicatures are inferences, or at least are determined (and not merely ascertained) by inferences rather than by the speaker. It is based on confusing what is implicated (by a speaker) with what is involved in figuring out what is implicated. Implicatures are things speakers mean, not what hearers, even rational ones, think they mean. Accordingly, if a speaker is to succeed in communicating something, the hearer must figure out that it is meant. That requires inference. Yet some of the most brilliant researchers, including Levinson (2000), Geurts (2010), and Chierchia *et al.* (forthcoming), write as if implicatures themselves are inferences.[1]

A further misconception is that linguistic expressions can implicate things. Speakers do. To be sure, there are certain expressions that are *characteristically* used (by speakers) to implicate things (Davis (1998) regards this as a reason to say that sentences themselves implicate things, but he does so in the course of arguing that what is implicated is generally a matter of convention, not speaker intention). When this occurs we have what Grice calls *generalized* conversational implicatures (as opposed to *particularized* ones). These have been investigated in great depth by Levinson (2000), who thinks they give rise to an intermediate level of meaning. In fact, they give rise to an intermediate kind of inference, but inferences are not meanings.

A related misunderstanding leads to Levinson's objection that Grice's approach cannot account for the (alleged) phenomenon of "pragmatic intrusion," which he thinks is exemplified by so-called embedded implicatures. As Levinson puts it,

> Grice's account makes implicature dependent on a prior *determination* of 'the said'. The said in turn depends on disambiguation, indexical resolution, reference fixing, not to mention ellipsis unpacking and generality narrowing. But each of these processes, which are prerequisites to *determining* the proposition expressed, may themselves depend crucially on processes that look indistinguishable from implicatures. Thus what is said seems both to *determine* and to be *determined* by implicature. Let us call this Grice's circle. (Levinson 2000: 186; my italics)

This objection is based on confusing the two sorts of determination mentioned above. The first two highlighted words are forms of "determine" in the sense of ascertain, but the last two, where Levinson draws his conclusion, are in the constitutive sense. In that sense, what is said neither determines nor is determined by what is implicated. This is a matter of the speaker's intention.

Levinson and many others misconstrue Grice's account as a psychological model of the hearer's inference, indeed one according to which the hearer must ascertain what the speaker says before figuring out what the speaker is implicating (see Bach 2001: 24–5, and Saul 2002b). But that is not how Grice intended his account. He required that "the presence of a conversational implicature be capable of being worked out" (1975/1989: 31), but he did not require that it must be.

This last misconception (for still more see Bach 2006c) leads to the widespread misconception, evident from an extensive literature, that some implicatures are "embedded," "pre-propositional" (Recanati 2003), or "pre-compositional" (Chierchia *et al.* forthcoming). This is thought to arise with utterances of sentences like these:

(12)  It is better to get married and get pregnant than to get pregnant and get married.

(13)  Bill thinks that there were four boys at the party.

Since the two infinitival clauses of (12) are semantically equivalent, a speaker is likely to implicate that what is better is getting married and *then* getting pregnant. With (13) the implicature is not that there were exactly four boys at the party but that Bill thinks that. In fact, such examples illustrate merely that the process of figuring out what is implicated does not require first ascertaining what is said. They do not show that the implicature is embedded in anything. Indeed, since speakers implicate, it does not even make sense to say that some implicatures are embedded. It is irrelevant that the hearer figures out what is implicated without having first to figure out what is said. Recanati supposes that Grice's account requires (conversational) implicatures to have a "global, post-propositional character," on the grounds that for Grice "implicatures are generated via an inference *whose input is the fact that the speaker has said that* p" (Recanati 2003: 300). Recanati's point is that certain implicatures get "computed" before what is said is ascertained. However, this does not show that the implicature itself is somehow embedded. In the case of (13), one of Recanati's examples, the implicature is supposed to be that Bill believes that there were not more than four boys at the party in question. But the implicature is not literally embedded. What the speaker says is the proposition expressed by (13), and what the speaker implicates is this other proposition. How the hearer figures this out is another matter.

Not only that, it seems that the speaker does not really mean two things, the proposition that Bill believes that there were four boys at the party and the proposition that Bill believes that there were not more than four boys at the party in question. It seems, rather, that the speaker means but one thing, that Bill believes that there were exactly four boys at the party in question. This example illustrates that some apparent instances of implicature are really cases of something else.

## 3.5  Between saying and implicating

A speaker can say something and mean just that. The contrast between saying and implicating allows both for cases in which the speaker means what she says and something else as well and for ones in which the speaker says one thing and means something else instead. Grice counted both as kinds of implicature, although the latter might better be described as speaking figuratively (recall, though, that Grice described this as a case of merely "making as if to say" something, since for him saying entails meaning). Grice seems to have overlooked a phenomenon intermediate between saying and implicating, one that has been investigated by many others (Sperber and Wilson 1986, Bach 1994a, Carston 2002, and Recanati 2004a). As they have observed, there are many sentence forms whose typical uses go beyond their meanings, even with references fixed and ambiguities resolved, but are not cases of implicating (or speaking figuratively). The reason is that what the speaker means, although distinct from what is said (strictly speaking), is too closely tied to what is said to be a case of merely implicating.

### 3.5.1 Two kinds of impliciture

In homage to Grice I call these in-between cases conversational *impliciture* (Bach 1994a). That's with an "i" rather than an "a." It comes in two forms, depending on whether or not what is said fully comprises a proposition. In the first case what the speaker means is a more elaborate proposition than what is expressly said, as with a likely utterance of (14):

(14)   Jack and Jill are married.

The speaker is likely to mean that they are married *to each other*, even though she does not make the last part explicit. Clearly that element is cancelable, since she could have added 'but not to each other' without contradicting herself. Even so, she is not implicating that Jack and Jill are married to each other, since she does not mean *both* that Jack and Jill are married *and* that they are married to each other. She means one thing, not two. What she means is an embellished version of what she says. Similarly, someone uttering (15),

(15)   Harry took two aspirin and got rid of his headache.

would likely mean that Harry took two aspirin and *then, as a result*, got rid of his headache. Again, the inexplicit part is cancelable, for a speaker uttering (15) could have added, "but not because of the aspirin." In both cases it is not the linguistic meaning of the uttered sentences but the fact that the speaker said what she said, presumably with maximal relevant informativeness, as per the first maxim of quantity, that provides the hearer with reason to think that the speaker intended to convey something more expansive.

   Then there are cases in which what the speaker says is not merely less expansive than what she means but falls short of comprising a proposition (even with references fixed and ambiguities resolved). Suppose you are meeting some friends at a restaurant. You arrive at the appointed time, and all but one of the others are there. After a few minutes, you remark,

(16)   Larry is late.

You cannot mean merely that Larry is late, full stop. Presumably you mean that Larry is late for the dinner in question. And if the *maître d'* announces,

(17)   Your table is ready.

presumably he means that your table is ready for your party to be seated there. In both cases the sentence falls short of fully expressing a proposition – it is *semantically incomplete*. Yet in each case what the speaker means *is* a complete proposition. Sentences like (16) and (17) appear to violate the grammar school dictum that a sentence, unlike a mere word, phrase, or "sentence fragment," must express a "complete thought." As with (14) and (15), though for a different reason (semantic incompleteness), what the speaker means is more specific than what the sentence means. We might say that whereas what a user of (14) or (15) means is an *expansion* of the sentence meaning, what a user of (16) or (17) means is a *completion* of it. These terms are meant to suggest, on the assumption that what a speaker means must be propositional, that in the first case what the speaker said is something that she could have meant (expansion is in a sense optional), whereas in the second case what was said is insufficient to have been meant (it requires completion into a proposition).

Regarding examples like (16) and (17) and many others like them (for numerous examples see Sperber and Wilson 1986 and Bach 1994a), it might be objected that the lexical semantics of "late" or of "ready" requires a complement (or, as it is sometimes put, includes a variable that must be given a value or an argument slot that must be filled), hence that (16) and (17) are not really semantically incomplete but more akin to sentences containing indexicals. Properly replying to this objection would require going through the variety of different lexical items that seem to give rise to semantic incompleteness, but the general idea is very simple. Consider examples like (18) and (19):

(18)   It is 9 in the morning.

(19)   The earth rotates at more than 1,000 mph.

Time of day is relative to a time zone, but (18), as it stands, that is, without any specification of time zone, is neither true nor false and does not express a proposition. Many speakers, particularly very young ones, are ignorant of time zones, and it would be charitable to attribute to them implicit reference to a time zone or even to their location. It is a fact about time of day, not about lexical semantics, that time of day is relative to a time zone. Similarly, as it stands (19) is neither true nor false and does not express a proposition. Even leaving aside the fact that the earth's rotation is relative to other objects, the sun in particular, its speed of rotation is relative to latitude. If the intended location is at or near the equator, a speaker of (19) would be asserting something true but not if it were at the North or South Pole. However, there seems to be no basis for supposing that the requirement of relativization to latitude is lexically or otherwise linguistically imposed. So, even if it is arguable that some terms that seem to give rise to semantic incompleteness lexically require complements, this is not the case in general.

Now some have contended that semantic incompleteness is the norm, not the exception. Recanati, for example, denies "that semantic interpretation can deliver something as determinate as a proposition. On my view, semantic interpretation, characterized by its deductive character, does not deliver complete propositions: it delivers only semantic schemata" (2004a: 56). Sperber and Wilson (1986) and Carston (2002) have taken a similar stance. However, it seems to me that while it is true that much is left implicit in ordinary speech, they have seriously overgeneralized from this fact and relied on a skewed sample of relatively short sentences. If they were right, then all of the things we mean would be ineffable. For their view entails that no proposition is semantically expressible, even by a sentence too verbose to use in casual conversation. However, the most they can hope to have shown is that the propositions people convey when using short, idiomatic sentences are not semantically expressed by *those* sentences. They haven't begun to show that there aren't other, less semantically impoverished sentences that speakers could have used to make what they meant fully explicit.

### 3.5.2 Saying and impliciture

These same critics of Grice have pointed out that expansions and completions are not related closely enough to conventional meaning to fall under Grice's notion of what is said but are too closely related to count as implicatures. Sperber and Wilson (1986: 182) coined the word *explicature* for this in-between category, since part of what is meant explicates what is said (sometimes they describe it as a "development of the logical form" of the uttered sentence). However, their neologism trades on an association with "explicit," as in their pet phrase "explicit content" and Carston's (2002) "explicit communication" (this term occurs in the book's subtitle). "Impliciture" seems like a better term for this phenomenon, since it suggests that part of what is meant, the implicit content, is communicated implicitly, whether by expansion or completion (however, the issue here is not merely terminological, for, as explained in Bach 2010, there are some subtle but real differences between impliciture and explicature). David Braun (p.c.) has invented the verb "implicite" for what a speaker does when what she means is an enrichment of what she 'locutes' (says in the locutionary sense).

Rather than adopt the term "explicature," Recanati (2004a) proposes to extend the notion of what is said, hence of saying itself, to cover the above cases. In fact, he offers a series of progressively more liberal notions of saying. It is hard to see that what we mean by "say," hence by "what is said," can be anything more than a terminological question, albeit one whose answer depends on theoretical utility. Grice's preferred notion had the constituents of what is said "corresponding to the meanings of the constituents of the sentence and mirroring its syntactic structure" (Grice 1969/1989: 87), but he also insisted that what is said be meant (by the speaker). The latter requirement seems arbitrary, for reasons discussed in section 3.1. Worse than that, it obscures the distinction between saying in the locutionary sense, for which we have independent need, and the illocutionary notion of saying, i.e. stating or asserting. Keeping this distinction in mind allows for a notion, saying in the illocutionary sense of stating, whereby what is said is "enriched" by "pragmatic processes" (Recanati 2004a). Notice, moreover, that this does not result in what Levinson calls "pragmatic intrusion" (2000: 189ff.), since the illocutionary level is inherently pragmatic.

Recanati does not deny that we can notionally draw this distinction, but he has argued, on both intuitive and psychological grounds, against the theoretical utility of adopting the locutionary notion of saying (for fuller discussion of the following issues see Bach 2001: 21–8). He contends that people's intuitions about what is said (and about the truth or falsity of what is said) tend to be responsive to the presence of implicit elements. However, all this goes to show, assuming that Recanati is right about people's intuitions (he has not conducted actual studies), is that people tend to conflate saying with meaning, specifically stating or asserting. Imagining themselves in real-life conversational situations, they would imagine what speakers are likely to mean in making their utterances. It seems likely that subjects would make stereotypical assumptions about the situations in which target sentences are uttered and that their intuitions would be colored accordingly. So of course their intuitions would be responsive to embellishments of the content of the sentence actually uttered.

Recanati also appeals to claims about psychological processes to debunk the locutionary notion of saying/what is said, and Carston has argued similarly (2002: 170–81). The gist of their argument is that what is said in the strict, locutionary sense generally does not get mentally represented in the process of understanding an utterance. They claim, quite plausibly, that hearers figure out what is "implicited" on the fly, not after and without the benefit of ascertaining what is strictly said. However, this is irrelevant to what speakers do when they produce utterances. What is said (again, in the sense at issue) is the content of the locutionary act performed by the *speaker*. It has nothing to do with what goes on in the mind of the *hearer*.

This is not to deny the importance of investigating the cognitive processes involved in hearers' understanding of what speakers mean. Like Recanati, Sperber and Wilson (1986), Carston (2002), and many others have concerned themselves with these processes, but that does not justify equivocating on the term "determination" as it occurs in the phrase "determination of what is said." As we have seen, this phrase can designate either the process of ascertaining what a speaker says in uttering a certain sentence or whatever it is that makes it the case that the speaker says a certain thing. Obviously ascertaining what a speaker says in uttering something presupposes that there is something that the speaker does say. It plays no role in making it the case that the speaker says what she says.

## 3.6  Summing up

Clarifying the distinction between saying, meaning, and implicating has required refining Grice's notions of each by way of introducing further distinctions. Borrowing from speech act theory, we invoked the distinction between locutionary and illocutionary acts to drop Grice's counter-intuitive requirement that to say something entails meaning it. In order to make sense of Grice's ingenious idea that speaker meaning involves a kind of self-referential yet audience-directed intention, we needed to distinguish the specifically communicative "effect" of understanding from other, perlocutionary effects on an audience. Next we clarified Grice's notion of conversational implicature, mainly by identifying various misconceptions about it. Many of these can be avoided by heeding the distinction between a speaker's meaning something and the hearer's figuring out that the speaker means it. Also, the conversational maxims or presumptions do not generate or even determine implicitures but, rather, provide considerations that the hearer may be intended to take into account to figure out what a speaker means/implicates. We then pointed out that the distinction between saying and implicating is not exhaustive and defended the use of the term "impliciture" for what falls between what is said (and meant) and what is implicated. Finally, by distinguishing the speaker's semantic intention from her communicative intention and both from what may be intuitive, evident to, or otherwise go on in the mind of the hearer, we defended the notion of a speaker's purely locutionary, or semantic, act of saying. The aim of all this has been to distinguish the linguistic from the extralinguistic information that speakers try to make available to their listeners, to identify the sorts of intentions they have in so doing, and to describe the means by which this information is made available to or is inferable by the hearer from the fact that the speaker did what she did.

We have not covered the many debates that Grice's notions have provoked, the radical alternatives to his approach, the range and variety of implicatures (never mind presuppositions) that philosophers and linguists have discussed, or how all this fits into speech act theory and pragmatics in general. Whereas we have focused on issues raised by Grice's most important and influential ideas, speaker meaning and conversational implicature, Neale (1992) presents a much fuller discussion of these and related ideas, Levinson (2000) offers an in-depth study of generalized conversational implicature, Bach (1999a, 2006a) and Potts (2005, 2007a) address Grice's controversial notion of conventional implicature, Chapman (2005) provides a full-length intellectual biography of Grice, Horn (2009b) gives a forty-year retrospective on implicature, Geurts (2010) offers in-depth study of quantity implicatures, the most thoroughly studied kind, and the papers collected in Petrus 2010 present some of the most recent developments.

# 4

# Implying and inferring

Laurence R. Horn

> To draw inferences has been said to be the great business of life.
> John Stuart Mill, *Logic* (1843), Intro. §5

## 4.1 A "vulgar conflation"

In Bach's short manifesto unveiling his list of the top ten misconceptions about implicature (2006c: 23), #2 is the thesis "Implicatures are inferences." For Bach, such a claim – whether explicit (as in the subtitle of Levinson 2000, "Generalized conversational implicatures as default inferences") or implicit – is a "misnomer" amounting to a "slight variation on the vulgar conflation of implying with inferring." The distinction in each case is seen as a straightforward one: implying (or, more specifically, implicating) is something the producer or sender of a message (speaker or writer) does, while inferring pertains to the cognitive effort of the receiver. Bach submits the entry from the *American Heritage Book of English Usage*:[1]

> When we say that a speaker or sentence implies something, we mean that information is conveyed or suggested without being stated out-right ... Inference, on the other hand, is the activity performed by a reader or interpreter in drawing conclusions that are not explicit in what is said.

The distinction is vital for pragmatic theory because an interpreter may "recover" an implication (presupposition, implicature) that was not intended by the utterer, and a speaker may imply (presuppose, implicate) something that the interpreter does not grasp. In I. A. Richards's words (MWDEU 1994: 541), "An utterer may imply things which his hearers cannot reasonably

I am grateful to Barbara Abbott, Keith Allan, Kent Bach, Betty Birner, Bart Geurts, Kasia Jaszczolt, Nicole Palffy-Muhoray, and Gregory Ward for their helpful comments and pointers; the usual disclaimers apply.

infer from what he says"; in other cases, the expectation of inference may be reasonable but nevertheless unfulfilled, whether through inattention or a mismatch of shared beliefs. But what of the straightforward distinction between implying and inferring itself?

Most usage manuals endorse the distinction, but a closer look shows that it's not that simple. *WDS* (1942), for example, begins with this prescription, complete with pointy finger:

☞Do not confuse *infer* with *imply*.

But then the rockier landscape of actual usage is surveyed (*WDS* 1942: 449–50):

> The use of *infer* in the sense of to hint at or to intimate (as, by his remarks he *infers* [correctly *implies*]) is still regarded as erroneous. However, in the past *infer* sometimes meant, and still to some extent means, to give grounds for believing (something that is stated) or to permit (something) to be inferred. In such use, a personal subject is to be avoided, for in precise English only that which gives the grounds for or permits an inference, or which leads to a given conclusion, can rightly be the subject; as "This doth *infer* the zeal I had to see him" (*Shak.*); "Consider first that great Or bright *infers* not excellence" (*Milton*); "Matters were by no means so far advanced between the young people as Henchard's jealous grief *inferred*" (*Hardy*).

So, in effect, "Don't use *infer* to mean *imply* – but if you do, make sure your subject is inanimate." The secure footing appears to have become a bit slippery, presumably because a misstep with impersonal subjects yields no ambiguity.

In *Merriam Webster's Dictionary of English Usage*, the linguistically best informed usage compendium, the extensive entry for **infer, imply** (MWDEU 1994: 541–4) disentangles three uses of *infer*, eloquently illustrating that "Real life is not as simple as commentators would like it to be" (541). Besides the universally accepted 'deduce, conclude' sense for *infer*, MWDEU differentiates the impersonal-subject *infer-for-imply* illustrated in the Shakespeare, Milton, and Hardy examples above[2] from the "personal *infer*" attested in an Ellen Terry letter from 1896: "I should think you *did* miss my letters. I know it! but . . . you missed them in another way than you infer, you little minx!" The *MWDEU* suggests that this latter use, the specific target of twentieth-century prescriptive opprobrium, has always been largely restricted to informal spoken language.

Similarly, the *OED*'s sense 4 for *infer* reads as follows:

> To lead to (something) as a conclusion; to involve as a consequence; to imply. (Said of a fact or statement; sometimes, of the person who makes the statement.)

> This use is widely considered to be incorrect, esp. with a person as the subject.

But even if incorrect, not inexistent; cites range from the sixteenth century to the nineteenth ("Socrates argued that a statue inferred the existence of a sculptor") and the twentieth ("I can't stand fellers who infer things about good clean-living Australian sheilahs").

It should be noted that the direct target of objections like that of Bach (or Horn 2004) is the nominal form (*inference*) rather than the verbal (*infer*), as in Levinson's implicatures as default inferences. But the speaker-oriented sense here boasts its own distinguished pedigree: the relevant *OED* sense 2 for *inference* is glossed as

> That which is inferred, a conclusion drawn from data or premises. Also an implication; the conclusion that one is intended to draw. Cf. INFER *v*. 4.

– with no disparagement of the latter usage and with attestations back to a 1612 essay by Francis Bacon on judicial practice warning that "Judges must beware of hard constructions and strained inferences."

What does not seem to be noted in any of the dictionaries and manuals is the asymmetry exhibited in these purportedly erroneous uses. While *infer* has been used for almost five centuries in the sense of 'imply, convey' (whether with impersonal or personal subjects), *imply* is always sender-, not receiver-oriented; it is never used for 'infer', to refer to the cognitive processes of the hearer or reader. Although this asymmetry may be seen as betokening the primary status of the speaker or producer of the message, we can find other cases in which a predicate exhibits an analogous ambiguity but where the direction of the meaning shift is less clear.[3] Thus *entendre* exhibits a range of meanings in French from the speaker-oriented 'mean, intend' to the hearer-oriented 'understand, hear'. This is especially significant for pragmatic theory because, as we shall see, conversational implicature first appeared in Mill's invocation of the SOUS-ENTENDU, that which is literally under-meant or under-understood.

## 4.2 Implication and implicature

Since classical rhetoricians first described figures in which we say less and mean more (*minus dicimus et plus significamus*),[4] semanticists and pragmaticists have explored the boundaries between what is said and what is meant-but-not-said. The latter is the realm of the implied. Recognition of the distinction between the said and the (merely) implied is not, however, limited to philosophers, linguists, and rhetoricians. Consider this exchange between Elinor and Marianne Dashwood, Austen's eponymous Sense and Sensibility, respectively (1811: Chapter 29), concerning the reprehensible but not actionable misbehavior of the latter's erstwhile beau Willoughby:

'But he told you that he loved you?'

'Yes – no – never absolutely. It was every day implied, but never professedly declared. Sometimes I thought it had been, but it never was.'

This is a distinction vital to lawyers as well as cads, as seen in the myriad devices for exploiting the difference between what is said and what is implied under oath. An important precedent in this domain is *Bronston v. United States*. Samuel Bronston, president of a film production company, responded as follows to a cross-examining prosecutor in his 1973 trial (409 U.S. 352–354, cited in Solan and Tiersma 2005: 213):

Q: Do you have any bank accounts in Swiss banks?
A: No, sir.
Q: Have you ever?
A: The company had an account there for about six months, in Zurich.

In fact, besides the company account, Bronston had actively maintained a large personal account in a Swiss bank. Thus, while his first response was truthful (depending, as President Clinton might have said, on the meaning of the word *do*), his second answer was at the very least misleading or "non-responsive." But was it false? Bronston was convicted of perjury, on the grounds that his last response, while literally true, "falsely implied that he had never had a personal Swiss bank account," but the judgment was reversed by a unanimous US Supreme Court. The particulars of this and related cases are illuminated by Solan and Tiersma (2005: 212–35), who point out that Bronston's violation concerned what is implicated (via the quantity and relation maxims) rather than what is literally said and endorse the *Bronston* "literal truth" defense against perjury charges, whether for sleazy movie producers or jesuitical presidents.

The difference between lying (based on the falsity of what is said) and misleading (based on the falsity of what is implied), as instantiated above and in a variety of other fictional and all too real settings over the last two millennia from the Oval Office to everyday conversation, can be taken to support an orthodox Gricean conception of what is said that hugs the syntactic ground of the spoken or written sentence as opposed to an "inflationary" view that incorporates pragmatically derived aspects of the intended communication; see Horn 2009b for elaboration.

But not just any (non-logical) implication is an implicature. In particular, conversational implicature in the Gricean model typically arises from what the speaker didn't say but (given rationality and cooperation) would have been expected to say if she had been in a different epistemic position. This point, rightly associated with Grice's William James lectures, was actually made exactly a century earlier.

In the locus classicus, a speaker uttering *Some F are G* implies that (for all she knows) not all F are G because she would have been expected by the hearer to have expressed the stronger proposition if she had been in a position to do so. The key insight is provided in this passage in which John Stuart Mill rejects Sir William Hamilton's (1860) treatment of *some* as logically expressing 'some only, some but not all':

> No shadow of justification is shown ... for adopting into logic a mere *sous-entendu* of common conversation in its most unprecise form. If I say to any one, "I saw some of your children today", he might be justified in inferring that I did not see them all, not because the words mean it, but because, if I had seen them all, it is most likely that I should have said so: though even this cannot be presumed unless it is presupposed that I must have known whether the children I saw were all or not. (Mill 1867: 501)

Mill invokes here the two-stage process allowing the hearer's move from the weaker recovered implication ('for all the speaker knows, not all ... ') to the stronger ('the speaker knows that not all ... ') when epistemically licensed. These are the primary and secondary implicatures of Sauerland (2004), built into the rationality-driven Gricean model (cf. Horn 1989, 2009b: §2; Geurts 2009) but not captured in current alternative grammatical theories of "blind mandatory scalar implicature" (Chierchia *et al.* forthcoming; Magri 2009; see Geurts 2010 for discussion).

Mill's allusion to a tacit principle requiring the speaker's choice of the stronger *all* over the weaker *some* when possible, and inviting the hearer to draw the corresponding inference when the stronger term is eschewed, is echoed by others in his own time –

> Whenever we think of the class as a whole, we should employ the term All; and therefore when we employ the term Some, **it is implied** that we are not thinking of the whole, but of a part as distinguished from the whole – that is, of a part only. (Monck 1881: 156, emphasis added)

– and in Grice's (e.g. Nowell-Smith 1954, Fogelin 1967: 20–22; see Horn 1990, Chapman 2005 for discussion).[5]

The principle tacitly invoked by Mill and Monck for generating such implications (or sous-entendus) is formulated by Strawson (1952: 178–9) as a "general rule of linguistic conduct" he attributes to "Mr H P Grice": "One should not make the (logically) lesser, when one could truthfully (and with greater or equal clarity) make the greater claim." The implicational relation between the subcontraries *some* and *some not* is captured independently in this overlooked passage that stresses the role of cancelability in distinguishing what is said from "what can be understood without being said" while also touching on the roles of relevance, economy, and epistemic insecurity:

> What can be understood without being said is usually, in the interest of economy, not said ... A person making a statement in the form, "Some S is P", generally wishes to suggest that some S also is not P. For, in the majority of cases, if he knew that all S is P, he would say so ... If a person says, "Some grocers are honest", or "Some books are interesting", meaning to suggest that some grocers are not honest or that some textbooks are

not interesting, he is really giving voice to a conjunctive proposition in an elliptical way.

Though this is the usual manner of speech, there are circumstances, nevertheless, in which the particular proposition should be understood to mean just what it says and not something else over and above what it says. One such circumstance is that in which the speaker does not know whether the subcontrary proposition is also true; another is that in which the truth of the subcontrary is not of any moment. (Doyle 1951: 382)

Grice's contribution, beyond securing the naming rights to the relation in question, was to ground the operation of Mill's "sous-entendu of common conversation"[6] within an overall account of speaker meaning and the exploitation of conversational principles based on assumptions of the interlocutors' rationality and mutual goals. In fact, like presupposition, implicature was (re)introduced into the philosophical literature and thence into the consciousness of linguists not with a specialized label but as a species of implication distinct from logical implication or entailment:

To say, "The king of France is wise" is, in some sense of "imply" to *imply* that there is a king of France. But this is a very special and odd sense of "imply". "Implies" in this sense is certainly not equivalent to "entails" (or "logically implies"). (Strawson 1950: III)

If someone says "My wife is either in the kitchen or in the bedroom" it would normally be implied that he did not know in *which* of the two rooms she was. (Grice 1961: 130)

Just as Strawson (1952) carved out a dedicated relation of presupposition two years after his first broadside at the non-existent French king,[7] so too Grice ([1967]1989) advances specialized labels – conventional and non-conventional (specifically conversational) implicature – for what he had earlier (1961: §3) described as varieties of (non-logical) implication delineated by the diagnostics of cancelability and detachability.

Conversational implicature arises from the shared presumption that S and H interact to reach a shared goal. A speaker S saying $p$ and implicating $q$ counts on her interlocutor's ability to compute what was meant from what was said, based on the assumption that both S and H are rational agents. On Grice's view, speakers implicate, hearers infer; such inferences may or may not succeed in recovering the speaker's intended implicature(s), if any. Nevertheless, it is S's assumption that H will draw the appropriate inference that makes implicature a rational possibility.[8]

The governing dictum is the Cooperative Principle: "Make your conversational contribution such as is required, at the stage at which it occurs, by the accepted purpose or direction of the talk exchange" (Grice 1989: 26). This principle is instantiated by a set of general maxims of conversation whose exploitation potentially yields implicatures:

(1)   QUALITY: Try to make your contribution one that is true.
              1. Do not say what you believe to be false.
              2. Do not say that for which you lack evidence.
      QUANTITY:
              1. Make your contribution as informative as is required
                 (for the current purposes of the exchange).
              2. Do not make your contribution more informative than
                 is required.
      RELATION: Be relevant.
      MANNER: Be perspicuous.
              1. Avoid obscurity of expression.
              2. Avoid ambiguity.
              3. Be brief. (Avoid unnecessary prolixity.)
              4. Be orderly.

A year after introducing the notion (or, more precisely, the label) of implicature in the William James lectures, Paul Grice published Lecture 6 as Grice
1968, situating his take on linguistic semantics within his broader project
for speaker meaning (Grice 1968: 225; cf. also Grice 1989: 118):

> The wider programme . . . arises out of a distinction I wish to make within
> the total signification of a remark, a distinction between what the speaker
> has *said* (in a certain favored and maybe in some degree artificial, sense of
> "said"), and what he has "implicated" (e.g., implied, indicated, suggested,
> etc.), taking into account the fact that what he has implicated may be
> either *conventionally* implicated (implicated by virtue of the meaning of
> some word or phrase which he has used) or *non-conventionally* implicated (in
> which case the specification of implicature falls outside the specification
> of the conventional meaning of the words used).

The characterization of implicature as an aspect of speaker meaning – what
is meant without being said – was set forth at a time when similar notions
were in the air, especially that of Oxford and its ordinary-language sphere of
influence. A case in point is "contextual implication" as invoked by Nowell-
Smith (1954: 80–82) and revisited by Hungerland (1960) in her eponymous
paper: "A statement *p* contextually implies *q* if anyone who knew the normal
conventions of the language would be entitled to infer *q* from *p* in the
context in which they occur." The *locus classicus* for contextual implication is
the context familiar from Moore: "When a speaker uses a sentence to make
a statement, it is contextually implied that he believes it to be true" (Nowell-
Smith 1954: 81). But the relation between (my saying) *He has gone out* and
my believing that he has gone out cannot be assimilated to conversational
implicature, for reasons Grice himself would later provide:[9]

> On my account, it will not be true that when I say that *p*, I conversationally
> implicate that I believe that *p*; for to suppose that I believe that *p* (or rather

think of myself as believing that *p*) is just to suppose that I am observing the first maxim of Quality on this occasion. I think this consequence is intuitively acceptable; it is not a natural use of language to describe one who has said that *p* as having, for example, "implied", "indicated", or "suggested" that he believes that *p*. The natural thing to say is that he has expressed (or at least purported to express) the belief that *p*. (Grice 1989: 42)

The difficulty of canceling such a (putative) implicature without epistemic or doxastic anomaly also argues against such an analysis. This applies as well to other cases of sincerity conditions Hungerland cites, e.g. the relation between *I promise to p* and *I intend to p*. Another of Nowell-Smith's examples of contextual implication does qualify as prefiguring Grice on the maxims, specifically Relation, although not on implicature as such: "What a speaker says may be assumed to be relevant to the interests of the audience." This maxim may indeed be overridden, as Nowell-Smith and Hungerland both observe. But Hungerland (1960: 212) is properly skeptical of the heterogeneity of a construct that extends from this relevance injunction to the sincerity condition on assertions and promises. Nowell-Smith himself concedes that the violation of the latter leads to "logical oddity" – "It's raining, but I don't believe it is" – while the non-observance of the relevance rule, according to him (and Hungerland), runs the mere risk of boredom. Even when relevance violations produce confusion or a recognition of the different conversational goals of speaker and hearer, such consequences do not rise to the level of the "logical oddity" of Moore's paradox.

## 4.3  Scalar implicature and the maxim map

Conversational implicature differs from contextual implication, and non-demonstrative implication more generally, in being defined as a relation between a speaker (not a sentence!) and a proposition that typically arises from the exploitation of the maxims (Grice 1989: 26ff.; cf. Horn 2004); in the case of scalar implicature in particular, what is implicated depends on what isn't (but could have been) said. The crucial principle of informative strength or quantity – whether formulated à la Strawson 1952 channeling Grice ("One should not make the (logically) lesser, when one could truthfully (and with greater or equal clarity) make the greater claim"), à la Grice 1961 ("One should not make a weaker statement rather than a stronger one unless there is a good reason for so doing") or à la Grice [1967]1989 ("Make your contribution as informative as is required (for the current purposes of the exchange)") – balances what the speaker can and does say with what she doesn't and hence presumably can't (or shouldn't) say. A speaker may opt for a weaker utterance from a belief that to utter its stronger counterpart might violate considerations of relevance, brevity, clarity, or politeness (note the codicils and parentheticals in each of the formulations above[10]), but especially – as Mill and Doyle foresaw – from a lack of certainty that the stronger counterpart holds.

This reasoning, exploiting Grice's first quantity maxim, is systematically exploited to yield upper-bounding SCALAR IMPLICATURES associated with relatively weak scalar operators, those configurable on a scale defined by unilateral entailment as in <*all, most, many, some*>. What is **said** in the use of a weak scalar value like those boldfaced in (2) is the lower bound ( . . . *at least* . . . ); what is **implicated**, in the absence of contextual or linguistic cancellation, is the upper bound ( . . . *at most* . . . ). What is **communicated** is the "two-sided reading" that combines what is said with what is implicated. Thus in (2c), to quote Mill (1867: 512), "If we assert that a man who has acted in a particular way must be either a knave or a fool, we by no means assert . . . that he cannot be both" – but we do typically communicate this "exclusive" understanding of the disjunction.

(2)                         1-SIDED READING     2-SIDED READING

     a. You ate **some** of the cake.     'some if not all'     'some but not all'

     b. It's **possible** she'll win.     'at least possible'     'possible but not certain'

     c. He's a knave **or** a fool.     ' . . . and perhaps both'     ' . . . but not both'

     d. It's **warm**.     'at least warm'     'warm but not hot'

The alternative view on which each scalar predication in (2) is lexically ambiguous between one-sided and two-sided readings contravenes Grice's (1989: 47) Modified Occam's Razor: "Senses are not to be multiplied beyond necessity." Scalar implicature was introduced and formalized in work by Horn (1972, 1989), Gazdar (1979), Hirschberg (1991), and Levinson (2000); cf. also Matsumoto (1995), Katzir (2007), and Geurts (2010) for insightful discussions of certain problems arising in the implementation of the central notions involved and Bontly (2005) for a defense of Modified Occam's Razor based on its role as a heuristic in acquisition.

The implicature-based approach to scalar predications has been vigorously challenged by relevance theorists (see Carston 1988, 2002, 2004a and work reviewed therein), who take such sentences to involve propositional ambiguity, with the pragmatically enriched two-sided meanings constituting not implicatures but EXPLICATURES, pragmatically derived components of propositional content.[11]

Two major challenges to the Gricean picture of implicatures involve the number and status of the maxims and the relationship between implicature and propositional content. To begin with the former issue, Grice himself later acknowledged (1989: 371ff.) that the four macroprinciples (inspired by Kant) and nine actual maxims in his inventory are somewhat overlapping and non-coordinate. The number of maxims has been revised both upward (Leech 1983) and downward. The dualistic program of Horn (1984b, 1989,

2007a) follows Grice (1989: 371) in ascribing a privileged status to Quality, on the grounds that without the observation of Quality, or Lewis's (1969) convention of truthfulness, any question of the observance of the other maxims fails to arise (though relevance theorists, beginning with Sperber and Wilson 1986, offer a dissenting view). The remaining maxims are subsumed under two countervailing functional principles governing the economy of communication. On Horn's Manichaean model, implicatures may be generated by either the Q Principle (essentially 'Say enough', generalizing Grice's first sub-maxim of Quantity and collecting the first two 'clarity' sub-maxims of Manner) or the R Principle ('Don't say too much', subsuming Relation, the second Quantity sub-maxim, and brevity).

The hearer-oriented Q Principle is a lower-bounding guarantee of the sufficiency of informative content, exploited to generate upper-bounding (typically scalar) implicata. The speaker-oriented R Principle reflects Zipf's principle of least effort dictating minimization of form, exploited to induce strengthening implicata; it is responsible for euphemism, indirect speech acts, neg-raising, and meaning change (Horn 2007a). Opposition and equilibria between speaker's and hearer's communicative economies have been posited since Paul (1889: 351ff.) and Zipf (1949: 20ff.). According to the division of pragmatic labor (Horn 1984b), a relatively unmarked form – briefer and/or more lexicalized – will tend to become R-associated with a particular unmarked, stereotypical meaning, use, or situation, while its periphrastic or less lexicalized counterpart, typically more complex or prolix, will tend to be Q-restricted by implicature to those situations outside the stereotype, for which the unmarked expression could not have been used appropriately (as in *kill* vs *cause to die*, or *mother* vs *father's wife*). Formalizations of the division of pragmatic labor have been undertaken within bidirectional optimality theory and game-theoretic pragmatics; cf. e.g. Blutner 2004, van Rooij 2009, and references cited therein.

Levinson's (2000) framework posits an interaction of three heuristics: Q, I (for Informativeness, ≈ Horn's R), and M (Manner). Levinson's reconstruction of the division of pragmatic labor involves not Q but the M heuristic, given that *some* differs from *all* in informative content whereas *kill* differs from *cause to die* in complexity of production or processing. As Levinson acknowledges, however, the Q and M patterns are closely related, since each is negatively defined and linguistically motivated: S tacitly knows that H will infer from S's failure to use a more informative and/or briefer form that S was not in a position to have used that form. Unlike Q implicature, R/I-based implicature is not negative in character and is socially rather than linguistically motivated, typically yielding a culturally salient stereotype (cf. Huang 2007 for a useful overview).

Relevance theorists (e.g. Sperber and Wilson 1986, Carston 2002) posit one pragmatic principle, that of Relevance, defined in non-Gricean terms. It may be argued, however, that the RT program is itself covertly Manichaean, given that Relevance itself is calibrated as a minimax of effort and effect. In the words of Carston (1990: 231), "Human cognitive activity is driven by the goal of maximizing relevance: that is . . . to derive as great a range of contextual effects as possible for the least expenditure of effort."

## 4.4  What is meant and what is said: the -plicature family

We now return to the perennial dispute over the shape of the landscape of implied meaning. In recent years a partial consensus has formed as to semantic underspecification and pragmatic enrichment, one that transgresses the view inherited from Grice that the pragmatics can be simply "read off" the semantics. When we turn from the relatively straightforward cases of reference fixing and ambiguity resolution acknowledged by Grice himself to the more problematic phenomena of completion, saturation, and free enrichment (cf. Bach 2001; Recanati 2001, 2002; Carston 2002; and references therein, as well as the relevant chapters in Horn and Ward 2004), it is clear we must grant what Bach (2005) terms the "contextualist platitude":

> Linguistic meaning generally underdetermines speaker meaning. That is, generally what a speaker means in uttering a sentence, even if the sentence is devoid of ambiguity, vagueness or indexicality, goes beyond what the sentence means.

Thus, the speaker uttering the non-bracketed material in each example in (3) may well communicate the full sentences indicated, enriched by the bracketed addenda. As seen from the cancelability evidence in (4), however, this process, resulting in truth-conditionally relevant propositions not directly expressed, is pragmatic in character.

(3)  a.  I haven't had breakfast {today}.
    b.  John and Mary are married {to each other}.
    c.  They had a baby and they got married {in that order}.
    d.  Dana is ready {for the exam}.

(4)  a.  John and Mary are married, but not to each other.
    b.  They had a baby and got married, but not necessarily in that order.

Those enrichments constituting necessary conditions for the expression of truth-evaluable propositions involve what Recanati has called saturation and Bach completion. Recanati (2002) distinguishes the bottom-up processes linguistically triggered by indexicals (*I*, *today*) and other expressions requiring saturation from those top-down modulation and free enrichment processes motivated on purely pragmatic grounds. At issue here are, for example, the underspecification of genitives (*John's car* – the one he owns? is driving? is following? is painting? is repairing?), unspecified comparison sets (*Chris is tall* – for an adult? for an adult American of the relevant sex?), and various expressions with apparent free variable slots: *You are late* (for what?), *Robin is too short* (for what?). For Recanati – *contra* Stanley 2000 and King and Stanley 2005 – "unarticulated constituents" are real and cannot be reduced to independently motivated elements in abstract syntax or logical form.

Since Grice, the pragmatic landscape has exploded with aspects of meaning variously identified as conversational implicatures, conventional implicatures, presuppositions, implicitures, and explicatures. These are not simply diverse labels for given subclasses of implication but different ways of mapping the territory between the said and the meant. Situating "what is said" along this spectrum is itself controversial; what is said for Recanati (2001), Ariel (2008b), and the relevance theorists is enriched by pragmatically derived material (hence constituting an explicature). Levinson (2000), on the other hand, responds to the apparent need to allow "pragmatic intrusion" into what is said by allowing conversational implicatures to have truth-conditional consequences for the propositions in question, *contra* Grice; in cases like (3c) or Deirdre Wilson's aperçu *It's better to meet the love of your life and get married than to get married and meet the love of your life*, an implicature ("P precedes Q") can feed into (rather than just being read off) what is said. (See Carston 2002 and Russell, Benjamin 2006 for illuminating discussions of the complexity of conjunction buttressing.)

For orthodox Griceans, the pragmatically enriched proposition in such cases – what is communicated – is distinct from what is said. As we saw in §4.2, an "austere" conception of what is said (to borrow Jenny Saul's phrase; cf. Borg 2004, Horn 2009b), corresponding closely to the syntax of the sentence uttered and excluding pragmatically derived material, may have more to recommend it than first appears. Further, as Bach (2001) observes, once we abandon "OSOP" (the One Sentence, One Proposition assumption) we can recognize that a sentence may express not only more than one proposition but fewer than one. What is said in *Dana is ready* constitutes not a truth-evaluable proposition but a propositional radical. Completing such a radical within a given context to yield e.g. *Dana is ready to write a dissertation* yields not what is said (which is tightly constrained by the actual syntax) or an explicature (since there is nothing explicit about it), but rather an IMPLICITURE, a proposition implicit in what is said in a given context as opposed to a true implicature, a proposition read off what is said (or the way it is said). What Grice failed to recognize, argues Bach, is the non-exhaustive nature of the opposition between what is said and what is implicated.

"Scalar 'implicatures' are implicatures" is #9 in Bach's hit parade of misconceptions (2006c: 28–9): since a speaker uttering "Some of the boys went to the party" means not two separate things but just one, i.e. that some but not all of them went, this enriched proposition is an implic-i-ture (built up from what is said), not an implicature. But on the Gricean account (Horn 1972, 1989; Gazdar 1979; Hirschberg 1991), the strong scalar implicature here is "Not all of the boys went to the party"; this combines with what is said ("Some . . . ") to yield what is communicated ("Some but not all . . . "). Thus the implicature includes the scalar implicature rather than supplanting it.[12]

While Levinson (2000) defines generalized conversational implicatures as default inferences, others argue that they are neither inferences – an implicature is an aspect of speaker's meaning, not hearer's interpretation[13] – nor true defaults. This last point is especially worth stressing in the light of much recent work in experimental pragmatics (see e.g. Noveck and Posada 2003; Bott and Noveck 2004; Breheny *et al.* 2006; Katsos 2008) suggesting that children and adults do not first automatically construct implicature-based enriched meanings for scalar predications and then, when the "default" interpretation is seen to be inconsistent with the local context, undo such meanings and revert to the minimal implicature-free meaning. To the extent that this empirical work on the processing of implicature recovery can be substantiated and extended, this is a very interesting result, but not (contrary to some claims) one that threatens the actual Gricean tradition, which predicts no automatic enrichment or default interpretation. This is clear from the passage distinguishing generalized and particularized implicature (Grice 1989: 37, emphases added):

> I have so far considered only cases of what I might call 'particularized conversational implicature' . . . in which an implicature is carried by saying that p **on a particular occasion in virtue of special features of the context**, cases in which there is no room for the idea that an implicature of this sort is normally carried by saying that p. But there are cases of generalized conversational implicature. Sometimes one can say that the use of a certain form of words in an utterance would **normally (in the absence of special circumstances)** carry such-and-such an implicature or type of implicature.

The classic contrast here dates back to Grice 1961: §3 – the particularized implicature with the "Gricean letter of recommendation" for a philosophy job candidate (*Jones has beautiful handwriting and his English is grammatical*) vs the generalized implicature with logical disjunction (*My wife is in Oxford or in London*, implicating I don't know which). Crucially, an implicature may arise in an unmarked or default context without thereby constituting a default or automatic inference. (See Bezuidenhout 2002a; Jaszczolt 2005; and Geurts 2009 for different views on defaults and their relation to implicature.)

Despite their substantial differences (from each other and from Grice) as to the role of implicature and the relation between what is implicated and what is said, the proponents of the approaches touched on above share Grice's commitment to situating implicature within a rationality-based pragmatics. On a competing view that has recently been elaborated by Chierchia (2004) and his colleagues, scalar implicatures in particular are generated locally as part of the grammar and/or the conventional lexical semantics of weak scalar operators. Support for this variety of defaultism involves an appeal to cases in which the Gricean model appears to yield the wrong results, thus arguing for local computation of "embedded implicatures." Others (e.g. Sauerland 2004; Russell, Benjamin 2006; Horn 2006) have challenged these conclusions and defended a global account of implicature along Gricean lines. In particular,

Geurts (2009, 2010) provides a broad survey of the landscape. Drawing a distinction between marked L[evinson]-type cases and unmarked C[herchia]-type cases of putative locality effects, Geurts (2009) argues that unlike the latter type, the Levinsonian contrast-induced narrowings represent true problems for a classical Gricean (or neo-Gricean) theory of implicature but shows that these can be handled by allowing upper-bounding to enter into the reinterpretation of what scalar operators express, a reinterpretation that is itself pragmatic in nature. In his treatise on Q-implicatures, Geurts (2010) argues that the conventionalist alternative to a Gricean approach is not only stipulative but also empirically flawed in predicting the full range of implicature-related results.

## 4.5 Conventional implicature from Frege to Grice (and beyond)

Alongside the successful conversational implicature model, Grice's category of CONVENTIONAL IMPLICATURE – a non-cancelable but truth-conditionally transparent component of encoded content – plays the role of ugly stepsister. The coherence of this category has evoked much skepticism: Bach (1999a) consigns it to the dustbin of mythology, Carston (2002: 134) remarks that "there simply is no such thing as 'conventional' implicature in relevance theory (or, we would argue, in reality)," while Potts (2005, 2007b) rehabilitates it in a different guise. But Grice's account of conventional content that does not affect the truth conditions of the asserted proposition has a rich lineage. Frege (1892, 1897, 1918) delineates a class of meanings that, while of linguistic interest, do not "affect the thought":

> With the sentence "Alfred has still not come" one really says "Alfred has not come" and, at the same time **hints** [*andeutet*] that his arrival is expected, but it is only hinted. It cannot be said that, since Alfred's arrival is not expected, the sense of the sentence is therefore false. The word 'but' differs from 'and' in that with it one **intimates** [*andeutet*] that what follows it is in contrast with what would be expected from what preceded it. Such suggestions in speech make no difference to the thought. A sentence can be transformed by changing the verb from active to passive and making the object the subject at the same time . . . Naturally such transformations are not indifferent in every respect but they do not touch the thought, they do not touch what is true or false. (Frege 1918: 295–6)

While recent scholarship largely follows Dummett (1973) in dismissing Frege's positive proposals in this area as representing a confused and subjective notion of "tone," this mischaracterizes Frege's actual account of the relevant phenomena. The two verbs in Geach's rendering highlighted above – *hint* and *intimate* – both translate Frege's *andeuten*, i.e. 'conventionally implicate'; no subjectivity or confusion is involved.

For a range of constructions including discourse particles (*but*, *even*, Ger. *ja*, *doch*), subject-oriented adverbs, epithets, and other "loaded" words, a version of the approach proposed by Frege and Grice remains eminently plausible (Barker 2003; Horn 2007b, 2008; Gutzmann 2008; Williamson 2009). Such an approach extends naturally to a range of other linguistic phenomena, including the familiar vs formal second person singular ("T/V") pronouns of many modern European languages, evidential markers, and arguably the uniqueness/maximality condition on definite descriptions. In addition, certain syntactic constructions can be profitably analyzed along these lines such as the southern US English "personal dative," a non-argument pronominal appearing in transitive clauses that obligatorily coindexes the subject as exemplified in *I love me some squid*, truth-conditionally equivalent to, but not fully synonymous with, 'I love squid' (Horn 2008). In each case, we find aspects of conventional content that are not entailed and do not fall inside the scope of logical operators.

The category of conventional implicatures poses a complication for the distinction between what is said and what is meant. Such expressions present a recalcitrant residue for Grice (who was concerned with delineating what is said and what is conversationally, and hence calculably, implicated) as they did for Frege (who was concerned with the thought, i.e. with sense and potential reference); for both, detecting a conventional implicature facilitates the real work by clearing away the brush. But Grice did undertake to situate this relation within what we refer to (though he did not) as the semantics/pragmatics divide. His contributions in this area, if not always accepted, are widely recognized, as in this passage from Davidson (1986: 161–2):

> It does not seem plausible that there is a strict rule fixing the occasions on which we should attach significance to the order in which conjoined sentences appear in a conjunction: the difference between "They got married and had a child" and "They had a child and got married." Interpreters certainly can make these distinctions. But part of the burden of this paper is that much that they can do should not count as part of their *linguistic* competence. The contrast in what is meant or implied by the use of "but" instead of "and" seems to me another matter, since no amount of common sense unaccompanied by linguistic lore would enable an interpreter to figure it out. Paul Grice has done more than anyone else to bring these problems to our attention and help to sort them out.

But how, exactly, does this sorting work? If descriptive content, reflecting what is said, is clearly semantic and if what is conversationally implicated (e.g. the "for all I know, not both p and q" upper-bounding implicatum associated with the utterance of the disjunction *p or q* or the negative effect of the Gricean letter of recommendation) is pragmatic (*pace* Chierchia 2004, among others), where is conventional implicature located? One standard view is that by falling outside what is said, the conventionally implicated

must be pragmatic (see e.g. Gutzmann 2008: 59). One argument on this side
is terminological; in Kaplan's words (1999: 20–21):

> According to Grice's quite plausible analysis of such logical particles as
> "but", "nevertheless", "although", and "in spite of the fact", they all have
> the same descriptive content as "and" and differ only in expressive con-
> tent . . . The arguments I will present are meant to show that even accepting
> Grice's analysis, the logic is affected by the choice of particle . . . If this is
> correct, then generations of logic teachers, including myself, have been
> misleading the youth. Grice sides with the logic teachers, and though
> he regards the expressive content as *conventional* and hence (I would say)
> semantic (as opposed to being a consequence of his conversational max-
> ims), he categorizes it with the maxim-generated *implicatures*.

To be sure, conventional implicatures are implicatures. But then again, they
are conventional; we are indeed dealing here, unlike in the maxim-based
cases, with aspects of content.

Two decades after the William James lectures, Grice revisited these categories in his Retrospective Epilogue (1989: 359–65), where he sought to
establish central and non-central modes of meaning through the criteria
of FORMALITY ("whether or not the relevant signification is part of the conventional meaning of the signifying expression") and DICTIVENESS ("whether
or not the relevant signification is part of what the signifying expression
*says*"). Thus, when a speaker says "*p; on the other hand, q*" in the absence of any
intended contrast of any kind between *p* and *q*, "one would be inclined to say
that a condition conventionally signified by the presence of the phrase 'on
the other hand' was in fact not realized and so that the speaker had done vio-
lence to the conventional meaning of, indeed had misused, the phrase 'on the
other hand'." Crucially, however, "the nonrealization of this condition would
also be regarded as insufficient to falsify the speaker's statement" (Grice 1989:
361). Thus, formality without dictiveness yields conventional implicature. (As
for dictiveness without formality, a plausible candidate is the pragmatically
enriched content of relevance theorists, the TRUTH-CONDITIONAL PRAGMATICS
of Recanati 2001.)

In uttering a given sentence in a given context, the speaker may intentionally communicate more than one truth-evaluable proposition, but these
communicated propositions do not necessarily have equal status; in *They
are poor but happy*, the conjunctive content is truth-conditionally relevant
while the contrastive content is not. Yet *but* and *and* are not synonyms. Conventional implicatures constitute part of encoded content but not part of
truth-conditional content per se; their falsity does not project as falsity of
the expression to which they contribute (cf. Barker 2003). What they contribute is use-conditional meaning (Kaplan 1999, Gutzmann 2008).

Besides detachability and non-cancelability (Grice 1961, 1989), additional
diagnostics for conventional implicatures include their tendency to project
out of embedded contexts, their immunity to certain kinds of objection,

and their contextual variability or DESCRIPTIVE INEFFABILITY (Potts 2007b, Horn 2008). The last property is the difficulty of pinning down the precise contribution of *but* (contrast? unexpectedness?) or *even* (relative or absolute? unlikelihood or noteworthiness?) and in the intention prompting the use of a second person "familiar" (**T**[u]) or "formal" (**V**[ous]) pronoun (**T** can be affectionate, presumptuous, comradely, or condescending; **V** can be polite, aloof, diplomatic, or hostile). Ineffability has a plausible source: modulo the well-known problems associated with vagueness, it is plausible that the edges of truth-conditional meaning should for the most part remain discrete, while inconsistency in the mental representation of non-truth-conditionally relevant content is less pernicious. If you know that my use of *vous* rather than *tu* signals some aspect of formal respect, distancing, or lack of intimacy, my precise motives can be left underdetermined, but if you don't know whether I'm using a second person or third person pronoun, the indeterminacy is more costly.

For Frege and Grice, identifying the class of conventional implicature-licensing constructions – scalar particles, speaker-oriented sentence adverbs, epithets and slurs, prosodic features, evidential markers, "affected" pronom-inals, word order effects – serves to characterize them in terms of what they are not: they do not affect the thought or the truth-conditionally relevant meaning of a given expression, and at the same time they are not derivable from general principles of rationality. While they share the former prop-erty with conversational implicatures, they differ crucially from them in the latter respect.

## 4.6  Implication and speaker meaning

Whether conversationally or conventionally triggered, implicatures are gen-erally understood to constitute a proper subset of speaker-meant implica-tions. As we have seen, the assimilation of implicature to inference has been deplored as an instance of the *imply/infer* confusion. But just as the latter turns out to be more complex than meets the eye, so too the subsumption of conversational implicature within the category of speaker meaning is not entirely straightforward. Saul (2002a) has argued that the full range of Grice's remarks on the topic suggests that we need to allow for a category of AUDIENCE-IMPLICATURE along with the traditional UTTERER-IMPLICATURE. Others (e.g. Bach 2001, 2006c), while acknowledging the role of the speaker's expectations about the inferences that the hearer can reasonably be expected to draw, defend the classical view that implicatures constitute part of speaker meaning.

In this respect, it is worth touching on evidence that *imply* in ordinary language use is not always definable in terms of speaker intention. A Google search on the string *didn't mean to imply* returns 929 valid hits (retrieved 16 June 2010) – "The President didn't mean to imply that AARP supports current health care legislation", "Bolivian President Evo Morales Didn't Mean to Imply Straight Guys Go Gay Over Chicken", etc. – with the sense of 'x didn't intend in saying p that y should infer q'. So we can unintentionally imply propositions, whether or not we can unintentionally implicate them. This is reinforced by the 785 googla instantiating *unintentionally imply/implied* – "I'm sorry if I unintentionally implied here anything that touched your feelings", "I realized that I might have unintentionally implied that no Christian would feel right about attending a pagan ceremony" – and the 705 hits for *accidentally imply/implied*, including "When you accidentally imply she's fat – send chocolates instead" and "Did you know you're supposed to say 'best wishes' to the bride instead of 'congratulations', lest you accidentally imply that the bride won her groom through trickery or deceit? Like she most likely did. But still."[14]

Ideally, *imply* and *infer* would map respectively into what the speaker intends and what the hearer grasps. Most likely, that would make for a simpler pragmatics. But still.

# 5

# Speaker intentions and intentionality

Michael Haugh and Kasia M. Jaszczolt

## 5.1 Introduction

Speaker intentions made their way into contemporary pragmatics through three different but interrelated routes. One of them dates back at least to medieval philosophy and the inquiries into the logic of modal contexts, leading to the study of intentionality. Another begins with ordinary language philosophy of the mid-1950s and the attempts to define meaning through language use, which in turn led to the employment of the concept of speaker's intended effect of an act of communication. The third, and arguably the most influential route, was that of the attempts to rescue formal semantic analyses by employing a concept of meaning that would incorporate not only the truth-conditional content but also the intended implicated messages, forming the overall concept of communicated content. This introduction to intentionality and intentions is structured as follows. In section 5.2, we present the philosophical idea of intentionality and explain the relation between intentionality of mental states and linguistic intentionality conveyed through acts of communication. In section 5.3 we move to the role of intentions in communication, focusing on the second and third routes mentioned above, starting with Grice's and Searle's views, attempting also a typology, explanation and exemplification of various kinds of speaker intentions distinguished in the literature. Finally, we discuss the question as to where intentions are located, contrasting cognitive, interactional and discursive perspectives on this issue, and conclude in section 5.4 with a brief assessment of the advantages and weaknesses of utilising intentions and intentionality in pragmatic theory.

The first question to ask is why linguists would want to appeal to a concept as murky as intentions and award it the status of an explanandum in pragmatic theory. The main reason is that the possession of the concept of intentional action is crucial for understanding human behaviour. As Anscombe (1957: 83) says in her seminal book *Intention*, there are many descriptions of happenings which are directly dependent on our possessing the *form* of description of intentional actions. It is easy not to notice this, because it is perfectly possible for some of these descriptions to be of what is done unintentionally. For example 'offending someone'; one can do this unintentionally, but there would be no such thing if it were never the description of an intentional action.

The notions of intention and intentionality have since been deployed in a multitude of ways in explaining speaker meaning (Grice 1957, 1989), speech acts (Searle 1969, 1983), the development of language (Searle 2007), social development (Tomasello *et al.* 2005), and the cognitive processes underlying action and meaning interpretation (Bara 2010; Pacherie 2006, 2008), to name just a few. However, this proliferation has generated challenges for the conceptual and theoretical status of intentionality and intention in pragmatics, as we will discuss.

## 5.2  Intentionality

Intentionality has a long and celebrated tradition in philosophy. Coming from the Latin term *intendere*, meaning aiming in a certain direction, directing thoughts to something, on the analogy to drawing a bow at a target, it has been used to name the property of minds of having content, *aboutness*, being *about* something (Duranti 1999; Harland 1993; Lyons 1995; Jacob 2003; Nuyts 2000; Smith, D. W. 2008; Jaszczolt 1999; Woodfield 1994). In other words, it means the ability of minds to *represent* objects, properties or states of affairs. In medieval philosophy, forms of beings consisted of so-called *esse naturale*, or natural objects, and *esse intentionale*, or concepts, mental images or thoughts. It is the latter that we are interested in here.

The very idea of intentionality dates back to ancient philosophy, as far back as the fifth century BCE and Parmenides of Elea. It was taken up by Aristotle and the Stoics (Caston 2007), and was subsequently extensively used in medieval doctrines of knowledge and revived in nineteenth-century phenomenology by Brentano (1874) and Husserl (1900–1901), and later by Meinong, Twardowski, Heidegger, Sartre, Merleau-Ponty and many others. By phenomenology we mean the study of the way in which things (*phenomena*) are presented in consciousness, or generally the study of forms of conscious experience from the first-person point of view. Mental attitudes such as belief, desire or want are intentional in that they are *about* something, they have an object. For phenomenologists, things exist as physical objects, but they also have an *intentional* existence, so to speak, in acts of consciousness. Their intentional existence is revealed in our mental states or acts, as for example in (1) or (2).

(1)   I am thinking *about my holiday in Australia.*

(2)   I hope *to meet Peter Carey one day.*

In the case of hallucinations, the existence is only intentional.

Brentano and Husserl developed intricate arguments concerning the meaning of such mental existence, in particular the question as to whether there are intentional objects that are internal to the thinker's mind. This discussion, albeit fundamental in the study of phenomenology, can only be sketched here. For Brentano, objects of conscious mental acts had the status of mental entities. On this view, the act does not consist of a relation between its subject and an intersubjectively identifiable object but rather can be spelled out in a so-called *adverbial theory*: 'Tom sees a horse' amounts to a property of Tom's 'seeing horsely', so to speak (see Smith and Smith 1995). However, the adverbial theory comes with a considerable limitation. It does not provide for the fact that our acts of consciousness are about things in the world, real world properties, or states of affairs. It was therefore subsequently replaced with the relational theory by Twardowski and Meinong. In the next logical step, Husserl rejected mental objects *tout court*. Current theories of intentionality adopt such a relational view.

Now, this is not to say that where the real object does not exist, 'made-up' substitutes are never needed in a theory of natural language meaning. To give one pertinent example, Clapp (2009) discusses so-called negative existentials, i.e. sentences of the type in (3) and (4) (from Clapp (2009: 1422)).

(3)   The Loch Ness monster does not exist.

(4)   Nessie does not exist.

As he puts it, the problem with negative existentials is that they presuppose existence and immediately deny it. We can, of course, stipulate that there is something real to which one refers in (3) and (4), à la Meinong, or say that there is no existential presupposition there, à la Russell. On the modern version of the classical phenomenology, mental objects are intentional, mind-independent entities; following McGinn (2000), we can introduce the theoretical construct of representation-dependent, intentional objects. Then we replace the dichotomy 'existent – non-existent' with a new dichotomy 'existent – intentional' and thereby vindicate the latter as a theoretical construct.

Intentional content has been the subject of discussions between so-called neo-Fregeans and neo-Russellians (Recanati 1993; Siewert 2006). In the Anglo-American tradition in semantics and pragmatics we often think of the analytic tradition as separate from continental European psychologism with its emphasis on consciousness, mental states, first-person psychology and the like. However, it is worth remembering that the most ground-breaking achievements in phenomenology and in analytic philosophy took place at the same time, at the end of the nineteenth century and the beginning of the twentieth century, and that they are much more interrelated than they are usually taken to be. Frege's (1892) notion of sense, whose offshoots have been so influential in current semantic theory of the Anglo-American tradition, is a direct predecessor of Husserl's phenomenological theory of meaning and object. We briefly attend to this interrelation in what follows.

Husserl held various consecutive ideas of meaning, culminating in his view from *Ideen* (1913) according to which meaning is contained in the objective content of consciousness, called *noema*. An act of consciousness is directed at an object determined by noemata. Here Frege's concept of sense can be seen as a clear precursor for Husserl's idea of meaning as distinguished from objects, and hence subsequently also his notion of noema. However, their respective distinctions between meaning and object, and sense and reference, led them in very different directions. Whereas Husserl and other phenomenologists concentrated on experience, Frege and analytic philosophers concentrated on developing a theory of meaning making use of intersubjective generalisations over 'meaning-giving mental acts' such as Frege's sense.

But this departure from psychologism does not reflect a sudden split. It happened gradually through various reanalyses of intentionality and subsequently ascribing intentionality to linguistic acts. So, the question to ask is how the theory of meaning became dissociated from Husserlian meaning as noema, that is from meaning attached to mental acts, discussed above. First of all, for Husserl from his *Ideen* period (1913), it was language, rather than a particular mental act of a language user as it was claimed in earlier phenomenological accounts, that was a carrier of meaning. Already in Husserl's work of this period meaning acquires the status of an abstraction, noematic meaning, attached to relevant mental acts. There is one step from there to freeing theory of meaning from the constraints of psychology. And this step was taken by Frege and his battle against the 'corrupting intrusion' of psychology in logic and mathematics, and thereby subsequently in natural language meaning.

Frege's *sense* (*Sinn*), as contrasted with *reference* (*Bedeutung*), saved formal semantics from the problem of substitutivity of coreferential expressions. For example, since it is true that Hilary Mantel is the author of *Wolf Hall*, it should be possible to substitute 'Hilary Mantel' for 'the author of *Wolf Hall*' as in (6), preserving the truth of the sentence.

(5)   The author of *Wolf Hall* is visiting Cambridge this spring.

(6)   Hilary Mantel is visiting Cambridge this spring.

However, although Hilary Mantel is identical to the author of *Wolf Hall*, sentence (7) differs substantially from (8); (7) is informative while (8) is not.

(7)   Hilary Mantel is the author of *Wolf Hall*.

(8)   Hilary Mantel is Hilary Mantel.

These two ways of referring to the winner of the 2009 Man Booker Prize come with different ways of thinking, ways of understanding or, to use the celebrated phrase, different *modes of presentation* of the referent. The senses we grasp when we understand these two expressions are different. Now, when we embed (7) and (8) in the contexts expressing mental attitudes, using intentional verbs such as 'believe' or 'doubt', Frege's concept of sense acquires a new importance for semantic theory. In (9) and (10), using Frege's own explanation, the *sense* of 'Hilary Mantel' plays the role of the *referent*.

(9)     Harry believes that Hilary Mantel is the author of *Wolf Hall*.

(10)    Harry believes that Hilary Mantel is Hilary Mantel.

Analogously, in (11), the sense of the definite description 'the author of *Wolf Hall*' plays the role of the referent. The description refers not to its customary reference, but instead to the sense. Sense, however, is more than the speaker's way of thinking; it is an intersubjective way of thinking. It can function as the speaker's own mode of presentation of the referent, but equally it can function as someone else's way of thinking about this referent.

(11)    Harry believes that the author of *Wolf Hall* is a man.

This objectivity of sense shifted intentionality from the domain of the individual and the mental to the domain of the external. For Kripke (1972) and Putnam (1975), proper names and natural kind words acquire reference through the causal link with the world. The topic of the externalist/internalist debate, albeit very important, is tangential to the present discussion of intentionality vis-à-vis intentions and will not be pursued here. Instead, we will now focus on one aspect of the debate, namely the role of intentionality in the theory of meaning.

   Let us now return to the topic of the 'antipsychologism' of analytic philosophy. Frege can be credited with developing a new concept of logic. In his *Begriffsschrift* (Frege 1879), he developed an analysis of the logical form of sentences in terms of predicates and arguments, where the reference of a predicate is a function from objects to truth values. This development marked the end of the era of psychological logic that studied thought processes and subjective mental representations. According to Frege, the object of study of logic is not the agent who uses the rules of inference, but the rules of logical inference themselves, and thereby the languages of logic themselves. In *Grundlagen der Arithmetik*, Frege (1884) offers a new, depersonalised stance on truth, definitions, logic, mathematics and indirectly on natural language semantics. He says that '[t]here must be a sharp separation of the psychological from the logical, the subjective from the objective' (p. 90). The ways of thinking about objects must not be confused with the objects themselves. Instead of focusing on someone's 'thinking that something is true or valid', we now focus on truth and validity as such. To give further examples, in his *Grundgesetze der Arithmetik* (Frege 1893: 202), he calls the effect of psychology on logic a 'corrupting intrusion' because it has to be emphasised that '*being true* is quite different from *being held as true*'. In *Logic*, he stresses that 'Logic is concerned with the laws of truth, not with the laws of holding something to be true, not with the question of how people think, but with the question of how they must think if they are not to miss the truth' (Frege 1897: 250).

   This ban on psychologism has never been lifted since.[1] Frege's function/argument analysis, juxtaposed with Tarski's semantic definition of truth, led to the development of formal semantics of natural languages. Now, this rejection of psychology can easily be taken to suggest that the very idea of intentionality had to be poured out with the bath water as well. After all, what we have here is Frege's forceful rebuttal of Husserl's stance on logic as a study of mental processes.[2] As can be seen from the following section, however, intentionality need not necessarily pertain to mental states and proves to be a useful theoretical tool that can easily be dissociated from 'psychologising'.

The follow-up question to ask is whether intentionality is a property of mental states only, or whether it can also be construed as a property of other objects. The answer gleaned from subsequent theorising is definitely positive. For the current purpose, however, we will not be concerned with the intentionality of human organs and limbs, or intentionality of information-processing systems discussed by Millikan and Dretske (see e.g. Lyons 1995; Jacob 2003). Neither will we be interested in Fodor's (e.g. 1975, 1981) discussion of intentionality as a feature of the brain. What we will focus on is the intentionality of linguistic expressions.

For Searle (1983, 1992b), our beliefs and intentions have intrinsic, basic intentionality, while linguistic expressions have derived intentionality in the sense that the meaning of acts of speech can be analysed in terms of intentional states, such as belief or intention. In other words, Searle says that the mind 'imposes' intentionality, so to speak, on linguistic expressions in that the basic intention to represent is responsible for the derived intention to communicate. The intentionality of the mental state that underlies the act of communication bestows on that act so-called *conditions of satisfaction*. In brief, beliefs have intrinsic intentionality, while utterances have derived intentionality (Searle 1991: 84), or 'I impose Intentionality on my utterances by intentionally conferring on them certain conditions of satisfaction which are the conditions of satisfaction of certain psychological states' (Searle 1983: 28).

What Searle proposes here is a so-called *double level of intentionality*. Mental states such as beliefs, wishes or hopes impose conditions of satisfaction on the expressions of these states. These conditions, in turn, play a major role in determining the meaning of the linguistic expressions. For example, a request may inherit conditions of satisfaction from the speaker's wish or desire. An important question arises at this point, namely what exactly does it mean to impose, or confer, conditions of satisfaction by one object on another? How can one transfer them from a wish, a mental state, to a request, a linguistic object? Harnish (1990: 189) points out that an *intention to confer* them does not suffice because there must be a constraint that one cannot intend and fail. Furthermore, there must be a restriction on types of objects from and to which intentionality can be transferred. As was proposed in Jaszczolt (1999: 106), we should divert our attention from the conferment as such and direct it instead to the fact that *the same* conditions of satisfaction pertain to the mental and to the linguistic. Once we pose the problem in this way, what remains is to take a stance on the relation between the mental and the linguistic, perhaps arguing as follows. Since the double level is supposed to characterise speech acts themselves rather than the relation between a speech act on the one hand and a mental state on the other, then we should think that speech acts have both basic intentionality, *qua* externalisations of mental states, and derived intentionality, *qua* linguistic objects. Since language is one of the vehicles of mental states, this seems to be a natural way of explaining the mysterious and rather unfortunately named 'double level' of intentionality.[3] By this reasoning, intentionality is always an intrinsic rather than a 'conferred' property.

Next, just as intentionality is a property of linguistic acts, so having intentions is a property of their owners. The latter is the topic to which we now turn.

## 5.3   Intentions in communication

### 5.3.1   Intentions and inferences

Intentions and the study of language communication have long and intertwined traditions. For John Locke, language is there to fulfil the intention of expressing the thoughts of their holders. In a similar vein, for Grice, the concept of meaning is founded on what is communicated, intentionally, by the speaker. Analysing sentence meaning takes us only part of the way; without employing the communicative intention the analysis is incomplete. In order to present the principles on which his theory of meaning is founded, we have to begin with Grice's seminal paper 'Meaning' (Grice 1957). Firstly, he points out the difference between the so-called *natural meaning* and *non-natural meaning*. When meaning that *p* entails that it is the fact that *p*, we have an instance of natural meaning. (12) is an example of natural meaning in that the symptom and the disease are linked through a natural connection.

(12)   These red spots mean meningitis.

This kind of meaning is of no interest to a linguist. Instead, linguists should focus on *speaker's meaning* or *non-natural meaning*, also known as meaning$_{nn}$. Meaning$_{nn}$ is conventional, not characterised by the relation of entailment discussed above, and it is this kind of meaning that is the object of study in Gricean and post-Gricean pragmatics. Speaker's intentions are crucial for defining meaning$_{nn}$, and so is, to a greater or lesser degree depending on the approach, the recognition of speaker's intentions by the addressee. Grice utilises intentions in the definition as follows:

> 'A meant$_{nn}$ something by *x*' is roughly equivalent to 'A uttered *x* with the intention of inducing a belief by means of the recognition of this intention'. (Grice 1957 [1989]: 219)

and elaborates further in 'Utterer's Meaning and Intentions' (Grice 1969 [1989]: 92):

'U meant something by uttering *x*' is true iff [if and only if], for some audience A, U uttered *x* intending:

[1] A to produce a particular response *r*

[2] A to think (recognize) that U intends [1]

[3] A to fulfill [1] on the basis of his fulfillment of [2].

This definitional role of intention was also essential in the speech-act literature of that period (cf. Austin 1962; Searle 1969).

The reliance of pragmatic theory on intentions does not mean, however, a return to the psychologism addressed in section 5.2. Making a definitional use of them need not lead to the inclusion of a theory of mental processes in pragmatics. Further developments in the post-Gricean tradition testify to a free choice here: some pragmaticists stayed close to Grice's spirit and upheld the antipsychological stance (e.g. Levinson 2000), focusing on general principles of rational action, but as a matter of methodological assumption, without an investigation of the psychological processes underlying linguistic communication,[4] while others ventured into cognitive science and discussions of inferential processes that lead to the intended or recovered utterance meaning (Sperber and Wilson 1986; Recanati 2004a; Jaszczolt 2005). It has to be remembered at this juncture that for Grice the recognition of the speaker's intentions need not always mean conscious and laborious processing. The recovery of the intention can be 'short-circuited', so to speak, when the meaning is conventionalised in a language and the conventions create a 'shortcut' through the recognition of the intentions. It can also be short-circuited when the intended content can be presumed in the particular context. Default meanings of the first type originated in Grice's concept of the generalised conversational implicature and have been developed further in the theory of presumptive meanings (Levinson 2000). Default Semantics (Jaszczolt 2005, 2010c) accounts for both types.[5] Some examples are given in (13)–(17), with the convention-driven or context-driven defaults in (13a)–(17a).

(13)     Some people like jazz.
(13a)   Not all people like jazz.

(14)     It is possible that soon all cars will run on electricity.
(14a)   It is not certain that soon all cars will run on electricity.

(15)     A secretary brought us coffee.
(15a)   A female secretary brought us coffee.

(16)     A Botticelli was stolen from the Uffizi.
(16a)   A painting by Botticelli was stolen from the Uffizi Gallery in Florence.

(17)     Kate and Leonardo performed superbly in *Revolutionary Road*.
(17a)   Kate Winslett and Leonardo diCaprio performed superbly in the film *Revolutionary Road*.

All in all, the possibility of such a non-inferential uptake notwithstanding, it is evident that Gricean accounts explain communication in terms of *intentions* and *inferences*. An intention to inform the addressee is fulfilled simply by the recognition of this intention by the addressee. We devote more attention to the types of intentions in communication in section 5.3.2, and the range of inferences underlying communication in section 5.3.3.

Meaning$_{nn}$, explained in terms of intentions and inferences, provided the foundations for Grice's theory of cooperative conversational behaviour and thereby his theory of implicature. According to this theory, interlocutors are rational agents whose behaviour is governed by the Cooperative Principle: 'Make your conversational contribution such as is required, at the stage at which it occurs, by the accepted purpose or direction of the talk exchange in which you are engaged' (Grice 1975 [1989]: 26).[6] Implicatures are normally considered to be meanings intended by the speaker and recovered thanks to this rationality assumption. To use Horn's (2004: 6) apt dictum, 'Speakers implicate, hearers infer' (but see Horn, this volume). However, in literary texts, for example in poetry, the writer may intentionally leave the choice of possible implicatures open for the reader. And even in interaction, speakers may be taken to be implying something that is contrary to their intention (so-called 'unintended implicature') (Cummings 2005: 20–21; Haugh 2008b), or may intentionally leave the interpretation of what has been said or implied open to the hearer (Clark, H. 1997; Jaszczolt 1999: 85; Haugh 2011). It has to be pointed out that originally, in Grice's writings, the term 'implicature' referred to the process of intentionally conveying some meaning in addition to what is said (and thus was restricted to the speaker), whilst the product of this process was called an 'implicatum' (based on inferences by either the speaker or the hearer). Gradually, however, the term 'implicature' took over to serve both functions, obscuring the distinction between 'utterer-implicature' and 'audience-implicature' (Saul 2002a; see also Bach, this volume, and Horn, this volume).

It is evident that implicatures are pragmatic constructs through and through. They pertain to communicated thoughts and need not, or according to some post-Griceans must not, have direct counterparts in uttered sentences. They stand for inferred meanings and one of their most interesting characteristics is their cancellability. For example, we can always cancel the implicature in (15a) as in (15b).

(15b)   A secretary brought us coffee. He was smartly dressed and moved swiftly.

This property is particularly interesting in that it clearly allows for gradation. In post-Gricean pragmatics, one of the main bones of contention has been the delimitation of what is said: contextualists, such as Sperber and Wilson (e.g. 1995b) or Recanati (e.g. 1989, 2004a) provide for the development of the logical form of the sentence until it represents the content understood to be the main message communicated by this utterance. Such an extended unit is not, however, dubbed an implicature; it is an *explicature* or *what is said*, respectively for these authors. Implicatures have to pertain to separate, additional thoughts with their own pragmatic force (Haugh 2002: 128–30). Default Semantics, a more radical contextualist post-Gricean approach, lifts this restriction on what is said by the utterance and allows for the main intended message, or primary meaning, to be independent from the logical form of the uttered sentence. This is where the interesting property of cancellability comes into the picture. When we try to define implicatures *qua* separate thoughts as cancellable meanings, while what is said *qua* enriched, modulated, extended sentence meaning, we soon realise we are barking up a wrong tree and are forced to retreat all the way to Grice (1978). Implicatures can be dubbed cancellable only if we maintain Grice's original all-encompassing definition of conversational implicature,[7] also pertaining to the cases of the development of the sentence meaning such as (18a).

(18)      Sue took a sharp knife and chopped the onions.
(18a)     Sue took a sharp knife *and then* chopped the onions.

When we allow for such cases of sentence embellishment to be classified as *what is said* or *what is explicit*, leaving the term *implicature* only for instances of separate thoughts communicated by means of the uttered sentence, then the property of cancellability becomes much less clear-cut than it was on Grice's original account. In theory, what we would want in order to strengthen the rationale for the *what is said/what is implicit* distinction drawn in this way is the property of cancellability to apply to implicatures but not to what is said. This, however, is not the case. It is not the 'enriched said' vs implicit distinction that marks the boundary between the cancellable and non-cancellable meanings, but rather, when our aim remains Gricean meaning$_{nn}$, we have to acknowledge that cancellability is a gradable property, dependent on the speaker's intentions. When the explicit content corresponds to the main speaker intention, cancellability is unlikely; likewise, when one of the implicit contents corresponds to the main intended meaning, this implicature is also entrenched. All in all, we have to either remain minimalist about semantics and construe what is said as sentence meaning *tout court* (Borg 2004; Cappelen and Lepore 2005a) and deny it the property of cancellability, or we should be contextualist about meaning and tie cancellability to the strength of intending, disregarding the explicit/implicit distinction.[8]

## 5.3.2  Types of intentions

The intention on which Grice's theory of meaning$_{nn}$ is founded can be called *communicative* intention: an intention to communicate certain content to the audience. It is fulfilled by its recognition. Bach and Harnish (1979: 7) call it an *illocutionary-communicative* intention and founded it on the so-called *communicative presumption*: an assumption that when the speaker utters something to the addressee, the speaker is doing so with an illocutionary intention. Potentially ambiguous utterances result in unambiguous acts of communication thanks to the recognition of the speaker's intentions. Analogously, sentences with indexical terms result in referentially complete utterances because of the recognition of the speaker's referential intention. Referential intention is understood here as part of the overall communicative intention.

The inherent reflexivity of the communicative intention is what, according to Levinson (2006a: 87), 'makes open-ended communication, communication beyond a small fixed repertoire of signals'. There is some debate, however, around whether the communicative intention involves one or two degrees of reflexivity.[9] Grice's original formulation of communicative intention involved two levels of reflexivity: a first-order intention (to intend to inform or represent something) embedded in a second-order intention (to intend that this first-order intention be recognised by the hearer), which was further embedded in a third-order intention (to intend that the recognition of the first-order intention be based on the hearer recognising the speaker's second-order intention). The utility of this third-order intention, however, has been disputed (Bara 2010: 82–3). Searle (2007: 14), for instance, argues that Grice's third-order intention ties meaning$_{nn}$ to perlocutionary effects thereby confounding meaning with 'successful' communication.

Subsequently, communicative intention has thus been reanalysed as only involving two kinds of intentions, the latter embedded in the first: the communicative intention and the informative intention. Communicative intention in this view consists of making it obvious to the addressee that the speaker has an intention to inform him/her about something (Sperber and Wilson 1986: 61). An informative intention can remain covert when it is not issued as part of the communicative intention. In other words, A may let B know something without letting B know that A wants B to know that. Puzzles carried by examples of situations contrived to demonstrate communication through hidden intentions, and implications for the definition of meaning$_{nn}$, have exercised many philosophers, and it has been proposed that "manipulative intentions" may underlie informative and communicative language use in some instances (Németh 2008).

Searle's (1983) work on intentionality introduced a further distinction between prior intentions and intention-in-action, the latter referring to 'the proximal cause of the physiological chain leading to overt behaviour' (Ciaramidaro *et al.* 2007: 3106; see also Pacherie 2000: 403). The different types of intention said to underlie communication have subsequently proliferated as intention has been variously used to refer to "action planning and representation, goal-directedness and action control" (Becchio and Bertone 2010: 226), thereby encompassing a continuum from states of mind to actions (Pacherie 2003: 599). In the remainder of this section we concentrate on exploring different types of prior intentions, rather than action intentions, as it is the former that are arguably the most relevant to the analysis of (speaker) meaning in pragmatics.

The notion of prior intention was initially proposed by Searle (1983: 165–6) to encompass the communicative intention (or what he prefers to call meaning intention, encompassing a first-order representation intention and a second-order communication intention). However, subsequent work has indicated that there are a range of different types of prior intentions, including not only communicative and informative/representation intentions, but also future-directed/higher-order intentions, private intentions and we-intentions. The latter are ontologically ambiguous, however, as to whether they are actually, in practice, prior intentions, or better characterised as (post-facto) 'emergent' intentions.

The first distinction made in relation to prior intentions is between those which are present-directed (or proximal) and those which are future-directed (or distal) (Bratman 1987, 1999; Ciaramidaro et al. 2007: 3106).[10] While the communicative intention is essentially present-directed, being used to account for speaker meanings at the utterance level, it has become apparent that higher-order intentions, controlling 'whole segments of dialogue' (Tirassa 1999) or the planning of activity types, including long-term goals (Bratman 1999), may also be relevant to speaker meaning.

The analytical import of considering higher-order intentions is underscored in Ruhi's (2007) analysis of compliment responses. In the excerpt below, a compliment (you're a good cook) is deployed by one family member to another in order to imply a request (that the receiver of the compliment cook again for guests).

(19a)
    1   Aysun:   Ayhan! I didn't know you were so skilled [at cooking]
                 darling
    2   Ayhan:   Go on canım! You continue thinking I'm inept
                                            (Ruhi 2007: 138)[11]

Ayhan responds to Aysun's positive assessment of his cooking in line 1 by questioning the sincerity condition (line 2), thereby displaying uptake of Aysun's communicative intention to compliment him. However, Ayhan's response to the compliment also 'metarepresents the higher-order intention of the C[ompliment] as a request' (Ruhi 2007: 139), as by disputing Aysun's claim that she thinks Ayhan is skilled in cooking, Ayhan forestalls the implication that Aysun wants Ayhan to cook for the guests (ibid: 138–9). In other words, Ayhan undermines the legitimacy of Aysun's implied request that he cook for guests by challenging one of its preparatory conditions (i.e. he can cook well).

This analysis is confirmed in the subsequent turns, reproduced below, where it becomes obvious that Ayhan was attempting to pre-empt any future requests for him to cook again.

(19b)

 3 Aysun: How can that be! From now on we'll discover your
       talents every time we have guests for dinner
 4 Ayhan: Don't exaggerate Aysun! This was just a one-off

                (Ruhi 2007: 138).

Ruhi goes on to argue that such an example challenges the view that meanings can be analysed solely in terms of (communicative) intentions, and suggests that meanings and actions are 'hierarchically controlled by higher-order intentions that affect single speech act production and the unfolding of discourse' (Ruhi 2007: 139).

 A second distinction made is that between private intentions (involving the representation of a goal that involves only the speaker) and social intentions (involving the representation of a social goal, where the speaker's goal involves at least one other person in addition to the speaker). While it might be assumed at first glance that only prior intentions involving the representation of social goals could be relevant to communication, it is evident that private intentions may also become salient in some cases, for example, when inferences about private intentions (e.g. the hearer reaching into her purse to pay for her coffee) may enter into a context salient to formulating a social intention (e.g. the speaker offering to pay for the hearer's coffee).

 Finally, the argument that certain joint, cooperative activities, including communication, cannot be straightforwardly reduced to individual intentions has led to the introduction of the notion of we-intention into this increasingly complex landscape (Searle 1990). One key question around the notion of we-intentions (sometimes also called shared or joint intentions) is whether they can be reduced to individual intentions supplemented with mutual beliefs (Bratman 1992, 1993, 1999; Pacherie 2007; Tuomela and Miller 1988), or whether they constitute a primitive form of intentionality that cannot be reduced to individual intentions (Becchio and Bertone 2004: 126; Searle 1990; Tuomela 2005).

 According to Bratman's (1992, 1993) account, which is defended by Pacherie (2007), shared intention can be explicated in terms of individual intentions in the following way:

> Where J is a cooperatively neutral joint-act type, our J-ing is a shared
> cooperative activity only if:
>
> (1)(a)(i) I intend that we J.
> (1)(a)(ii) I intend that we J in accordance with and because of meshing
>      subplans of (1) (a) (i) and (1) (b) (i).
> (1)(b)(i) You intend that we J.
> (1)(b)(ii) You intend that we J in accordance with and because of meshing
>      subplans of (1) (a) (i) and (1) (b) (i).
>  (1)(c) The intentions in (1) (a) and (1) (b) are minimally cooperatively
>     stable.

> (2)    It is common knowledge between us that (1)

(Bratman 1992: 338)

While Pacherie (2007) argues that this formulation of shared intention captures the commitment of the participants to a joint activity (conditions (1) (a) (i) and (1) (b) (i)) the mutual responsiveness of each participant to the other (conditions (1) (a) (ii) and (1) (b) (ii)) and commitment to mutual support (condition (1) (c)), Becchio and Bertone (2004: 127–8) argue that a formulation of shared intention building on mutual belief about individual intentions is 'cognitively implausible' as the requirement for sharedness is too strenuous.

Searle (1990: 407), on the other hand, defines a we-intention as simply 'we intend that we perform act A', which in turn presupposes *cooperation* on the part of the we-intenders. He argues that 'we-intentions cannot be analyzed into sets of I[ndividual]-intentions, even I-intentions supplemented with beliefs' (ibid.: 404), giving the example of playing football to illustrate his point:

> Suppose we are on a football team and we are trying to execute a pass play. That is, the team intention, we suppose, is in part expressed by 'We are executing a pass play.' But now notice: no individual member of the team has this as the entire content of his intention, for no one can execute a pass play by himself. Each player must make a specific contribution to the overall goal . . . Each member of the team will share in the collective intention, but will have an individual assignment that is derived from the collective but has a different content from the collective. Where the collective's is 'We are doing A,' the individual's will be 'I am doing B,' 'I am doing C,' and so on. (Searle 1990: 403)

The essence of Searle's argument, then, is that each member of the football team I-intending different parts of the action of pass play does not simply add up (i.e. summatively) to the collective action of a pass play, because a level of cooperation is presupposed that goes beyond each person 'doing their part' (ibid.: 405). Cooperation implies, we would suggest, that each team member's I-intentions are responsive to their perceptions of the I-intentions of other team members, meaning, in other words, that the I-intentions of team members are both afforded and constrained by the I-intentions of others in making the pass play. In order for these I-intentions to be responsive in this manner, it is claimed that the team members must be we-intending to engage in this collective activity.

This description of a particular collective action bears remarkable similarities to the cooperative nature of communication assumed by Grice, with a number of scholars noting, in passing, the potential importance of we-intentions for the analysis of communication (Becchio and Bertone 2004: 132; Clark H. 1996, 1997; Gibbs 1999, 2001; Searle 1990: 415). The place of we-intentions in analysing speaker meaning and communication, however, has received only passing attention in pragmatics to date. This is perhaps due to the inherent ontological ambiguity of we-intentions (Haugh 2008c: 53–4): while they are characterised as prior intentions in the minds of speakers and hearers, there is equivocality about how such an a priori mental state comes to be shared between two or more people in the first place (Fitzpatrick 2003; Velleman 1997), even in models which argue for their importance (Tomasello and Rakoczy 2003; Tomasello *et al.* 2005).

Consider, for instance, Levinson's (1983: 358) example of a 'transparent pre-request' in line 1 in the excerpt below:

(20)
1  A:  Hullo I was wondering whether you were intending to go to
       Popper's talk this afternoon
2  B:  Not today I'm afraid I can't make it to this one
3  A:  Ah okay
4  B:  You wanted me to record it didn't you heh!
5  A:  Yeah heheh
6  B:  Heheh no I'm sorry about that . . .

                                        (Levinson 1983: 358)

While it is not entirely clear from B's response in line 2 whether B was in fact treating A's utterance in line 1 as a pre-request or simply as a request for information, it is evident by line 4 that B has understood A's initial question as a pre-request through his topicalisation of A's intentions ('*wanted* me to record it') (Haugh 2009: 95). However, in order for B to infer the communicative intention underpinning A's question in line 1 (i.e. the intention to check the preparatory conditions for a forthcoming request that B record Popper's talk), it appears an inference about A's higher-order intention (to launch a request sequence) is also required. This, in turn, presupposes that A and B are we-intending engagement in a particular activity, namely, conversational interaction. The issue is, however, and this proves crucial to the interpretation of A's communicative intention underlying his utterance in line 1, whether they are we-intending the joint activity of phatic/relational talk (consistent with an interpretation of A's communicative intention simply being a request for information about B's intentions in relation to Popper's talk), or they are we-intending the joint activity of goal-oriented talk (consistent with A's higher-order intention of negotiating a request that B record the talk for him).[12] In other words, the communicative intention of A is embedded within his higher-order intention, with both intentions arguably being further embedded within a we-intention.

This requirement for multiple types of prior intentions embedded within each other, however, leads to analytical equivocality on two counts. First, the requirement for inferences directed at both A's communicative intention (which is present-directed) and his higher-order intention (which is future-directed) leads to trouble in ascertaining when exactly this implied request arises. Second, there is equivocality about how this we-intention is shared in the first place. It is not until line 4 in this interaction that A and B could plausibly be taken to be we-intending the joint activity of goal-oriented talk (in the context of which a request sequence makes sense). Searle's characterisation of a we-intention as a prior intention thus strikes very real problems when applied to the analysis of joint activities such as conversation. It appears, then, that what underpins the request implicature here might be better characterised as a kind of 'emergent' intention (Clark H. 1997; Gibbs 1999: 38, 2001; Haugh 2007c: 95, 2008c, 2009; Kecskes 2010a: 60–61).

Finally, it is also worth noting in passing that in example (20) above, A also makes reference to B's (higher-order) intentions ('*intending* to go') in line 1, while A ratifies in line 5 ('yeah') B's preceding topicalisation of his intentions. It appears, then, that the folk notion of *intending*, encompassing (1) the expression of future plans for self, (2) ascribing to or asking of others their future plans, (3) describing what oneself or others want to achieve by doing or saying something and (4) classifying actions as being done with the speaker's awareness of the implications of them (Gibbs 1999: 22–3), may also be sometimes relevant to the analysis of speaker meaning. The notion of higher-order intention appears to overlap with senses (1) through to (3) of the folk notion of *intention* while the last two senses of *intention* appear consistent with the claim in ethnomethodological conversation analysis that speakers are held (morally) accountable for their meanings (Garfinkel 1967; Heritage 1988); Sacks [1992:1964 4–5].[13] While there has been work focusing on intuitive, folk understandings of *intention* (Breheny 2006; Gibbs 1999, 2001; Knobe 2003; Knobe and Burra 2006; Malle 2004, 2006; Malle *et al.* 2001),[14] there remains considerable work to be done in comparing folk understandings of intention with the various analytical concepts of intention developed in philosophical pragmatics. Drawing a clear distinction between folk and theoretical/analytical notions of intention is clearly important, as it is through their common link to the folk notion of *intentional* actions that intentionality (encompassing the directedness/aboutness of linguistic acts) and speaker intentions (encompassing the a priori goal-directedness and deliberateness of speaker actions) are often confounded. It is only by making such comparisons that we will better understand the relationship between the intuitive notions of *intention/intending* and the more technical notions we have reviewed here.

### 5.3.3 From mental acts to communicative acts and types of inference

The detailed work on different types of (prior) intention and their relationship to speaker meaning has been expanded upon in two quite different ways in pragmatics, as noted in section 5.3.1. Those more closely aligned with the spirit of Grice's original programme have focused on moving from mental acts to communicative acts. This includes both the so-called neo-Griceans and speech act theorists. Those taking a more psychological or cognitive stance, in contrast, have focused on explicating the inferential processes leading from communicative acts to intended or recovered speaker meaning.

In Searle's (1983, 2007) work on the relationship between speech acts, speaker meaning and intention(ality), he claims that for a speech act to be communicated a double level of intentionality is required, as noted in section 5.2. This double level of intentionality builds on the notion of direction of fit. Word-to-world direction of fit encompasses the assertive class of speech acts (e.g. statements, assertions etc.), which are 'expressions of beliefs and are supposed, like beliefs, to represent how the world is' (Searle, e.g. 2007: 14), while world-to-word direction of fit encompasses both the directive class of speech acts (e.g. requests, orders, commands etc.), which are expressions of desires, and the commissive class (e.g. promises, offers etc.), which are expressions of intention (ibid.). Declaratives have a double direction of fit, while expressives (e.g. apologies, thanks etc.) have no direction of fit (ibid.: 14–15). To illustrate this double level of intentionality he gives the example of a speaker wishing to communicate the belief 'It is raining':

> When the speaker intentionally utters a token of the symbol [It is raining], the production of the token is the condition of satisfaction of his intention to utter it. And when he utters it *meaningfully* he is imposing a further condition of satisfaction on the token uttered. The condition of satisfaction is: That it is raining. The imposition of conditions of satisfaction on conditions of satisfaction is the essence of speaker meaning. (Searle 2007: 23, original emphasis)

According to Searle, then, the first level of intentionality arises from the prior intention of the speaker, namely, that uttering 'It is raining' is a goal-directed and deliberate action. The second level of intentionality arises from the intrinsic aboutness of beliefs. It is by imposing conditions of satisfaction of the belief in question (i.e. that it is indeed raining) upon the conditions of satisfaction of the intention in question (i.e. to utter the token 'it is raining') that a speaker can be taken to be meaning this particular assertion. Further work modelling the link between prior intentions (i.e. intentions as mental states) and intention-in-action (i.e. uttering something) has been undertaken (Bara 2010; Pacherie 2006, 2008), in an attempt to move Searle's analytical work into an empirical, testable reality. But such work, albeit very important, is largely tangential to the current discussion since it focuses on investigating neural mechanisms.[15]

While Searle makes little reference to inferential work in his analysis,[16] Levinson's (2000) account of implicature is grounded in default logics (for generalised implicatures) and practical reasoning (for particularised implicatures). Default logics aim to capture the notion of reasonable presumption, a *ceteris paribus* assumption. Levinson (2000: 46) argues that default logics capture two important features of generalised implicatures: their defeasibility and the way in which they involve preferred presumptions. While a number of models of default logics are discussed by Levinson (2000: 46–9), he does not offer a definitive answer to the question of how to formally model the inferences underlying generalised implicatures.

Practical reasoning systems, first mentioned by Aristotle, aim to explicate how speakers reason from a particular goal (i.e. a prior intention) to the means by which this goal is achieved (e.g. an utterance). Levinson argues that a modified 'Kenny logic', building on Kenny's (1966) work on practical reasoning, captures two important features of desirability reasoning: its defeasibility and its ampliativeness (see Brown P. and Levinson 1987: 89). The system formalises inferences that are valid when propositions are 'satisfactory' relative to goal wants: 'A fiat F(a) is satisfactory relative to a set G of desires $\{F(g_1), F(g_2), \ldots F(g_n)\}$ if and only if, whenever $a$ is true, ($g_1$ and $g_2 \ldots$ and $g_n$) is true' (ibid.: 87). In other words, practical reasoning accounts for how speakers move from formulating intentions (ends) to what is uttered (means). However, it has to be acknowledged that a logic-based reasoning system such as this cannot account for how hearers understand speakers' communicative intentions (ibid.: 8).

In moving from communicative acts to mental acts, in contrast, a number of different types of inference have been claimed to underlie speaker meaning, including the recovery of (intended) implicatures. According to some, an implicature is recovered through inductive inference on Grice's account, and thus constitutes 'a probabilistic conclusion derived from a set of premises that include the utterance and such contextual information as appears relevant' (Grundy 2008: 102). It is argued that the probabilistic nature of inductive inferences accounts for mismatches between what the speaker intends and how this is interpreted by the hearer (ibid.). Others have claimed that the recovery of conversational implicatures by hearers is better explicated with reference to abductive reasoning (i.e. inference to best explanation) (Allot 2007), or its formal analogue, inference to best interpretation (Atlas 2005; Atlas and Levinson 1981). The key difference between induction and abduction is that the former involves reasoning 'from particular instances to a general hypothesis', while the latter involves reasoning where 'the conclusions are based on a best guess' (Allan 2006c: 652).

Somewhat controversially, in their *Relevance* book, relevance theorists Sperber and Wilson have proposed that deductive reasoning is central to utterance interpretation (Sperber and Wilson 1995b: 69; see also Wilson and Sperber 1986: 45). In the following example, Mary implies that she wouldn't drive a Mercedes in response to Peter's question.

(21)   Peter:   Would you drive a Mercedes?
        Mary:   I wouldn't drive *any* expensive car.
                 (Sperber and Wilson 1995b: 194)

It is claimed by Sperber and Wilson that this implication can be deduced through the addition of encyclopaedic information about expensive cars ('a Mercedes is an expensive car') as an additional premise together with Mary's assertion that she 'wouldn't drive *any* expensive car' (ibid.).

One key problem with a reliance on deductive reasoning in explicating how hearers recover speaker meaning, however, as Cummings (1998, 2005) points out, is how to establish the closed set of propositions required for strict deduction (Allan 2006c: 553; Allot 2007: 60). As she argues,

> no set of deductive premises is ever fully circumscribed in the sense of containing all the information that is relevant to the comprehension of that utterance – for every set of such premises, some factor that is not part of the set can nonetheless be shown to be integral to the comprehension of that utterance. (Cummings 2005: 130)

In other words, there is no solution given in Relevance theory as to how the hearer decides which premises to include and those to be excluded, except by the arguably circular argument that the premises selected are determined by calculations of relevance,[17] which in turn determines what the hearer understands to have been implied by the speaker. The circularity of their approach as presented in that book lies in the fact that calculations of the relevance of the contextual premises are determined by the hearer's calculations of the relevance of what is implied.[18]

As Cummings (2005: 108) has argued, there remains considerable work to be done to clarify the types of inference that underlie the recovery of speaker meaning. In line with the emphasis on non-deductive inference present in the pragmatic literature in the last decade (see e.g. Levinson 2000, or, in a different paradigm, Asher and Lascarides 2003), she discusses two further types of inference that are crucial to this process: elaborative inferences and presumptive reasoning. Elaborative inferences are knowledge-based inferences used to 'establish causal connections between events and construct intentional relations between actions within reasoning' (Cummings 2005: 91), with this knowledge often being of 'behaviour tendencies and everyday routines' that serve 'to specify normality or typicality conditions on inference' (ibid.: 93). She claims that the implicature arising in the example below, for instance, cannot be recovered without elaborative inference.

(22)  A:  I'm out of milk.
      B:  There's a shop at the end of the street.
                (Cummings 2005: 102)

In order for A to understand that B is implying that A can get milk from the shop at the end of the street, real-world knowledge is required: that corner shops stock commonly used groceries, including milk (ibid.: 103). She goes on to claim that 'knowledge provides a cohesive link between the utterances of the above exchange – it is through our knowledge of corner shops and their merchandise that we are able to establish the relevance of B's utterance to A's utterance in this exchange' (ibid.). Such elaborative inferences allow hearers to go from 'abstract communication norms and principles' to particular communicated meanings (ibid.: 104).

Cummings (2005) also suggests that presumptive reasoning is crucial to the recovery of implicatures, since although potential implicatures are always subject to revision based on the addition of further contextual information, they are nevertheless held by hearers to be communicated, at least provisionally. One kind of presumptive reasoning system proposed by Cummings is 'argument from ignorance', where a proposition is accepted as true because there is no evidence that it is not true (or vice versa) (ibid.: 109). Thus, while earlier attempts to model the move from communicative acts (utterances) to mental acts (intentions) have tended to rely on traditional forms of inference, both monotonic and non-monotonic (deductive, inductive, abductive), strong arguments have been mounted for more attention to be paid to other non-monotonic forms of inference as well (Cummings 2005: 242; Levinson 2000: 46).[19]

One problem facing current models of inference that privilege the speaker's intention in determining whether communication has occurred (whether in moving from speaker intentions to communicative acts or vice versa), is the failure to 'address how the participants themselves could come to know whether the recipient's inference and attribution regarding that intention is to any extent consistent with it' (Arundale 2008: 241). In other words, there is no account in current intention-based models given as to how speakers and hearers determine something has indeed been communicated. Approaches that conceptualise the inferential work underlying meaning and communication as contingent and non-summative (Arundale and Good 2002; see also Haugh 2009) thus arguably deserve further consideration as well.

In the next subsection we consider the question of where intentions (and inferences about them) can be located, in particular, whether or not they should be analysed as a purely cognitive phenomenon. While the emphasis in the discussion thus far has largely been on speaker intentions underlying utterances, in broadening our scope to consider their place in interaction and broader society, it is further emphasised that intentions are not only traceable to the mind, but also to interaction, and to broader societal norms and discourses.

### 5.3.4  Locating intentions

According to the received view of meaning as the intended expression of thoughts, intentions pertain to the mental states of speakers. Recent work in social neuroscience has begun exploring the neural correlates of our ability to attribute mental states, including intentions, to others (Walter et al. 2004: 1854). This capacity to attribute mental states is termed theory of mind (ToM), with it being assumed that without ToM 'other people's behaviour would be meaningless from a third-person perspective: behaviour would be observed, but the meaning of actions would not be understood' (Ciaramidaro et al. 2007: 3111). Experiments combining brain imaging with various kinds of language use prompts have found that a distributed neural system underlies the ToM mechanism, including the right and left temporo-parietal junctions (right TPJ and left TPJ), the precuneus, and the medial prefrontal cortex (MPFC) (Ciaramidaro *et al.* 2007: 3105; Enrici *et al.* 2011; Walter *et al.* 2004: 1854). The detection of agency, for instance, has been tied to neural activity in the superior temporal sulcus (STS) (Frith and Frith 2003), while the representation of our own and other people's mental states (including intentions) has been tied to activity in the medial prefrontal cortex (MPFC) (Walter *et al.* 2004: 1854).

Further work on intentions specifically has established that different parts of this distributed neural network are activated depending on the kind of prior intention involved. This lends some empirical support to the hitherto conceptual distinctions discussed in section 5.3.2, including that between private and social intentions, and within the category of social intentions, between communicative intentions and prospective social intentions, the latter being a form of higher-order intention (Ciaramidaro *et al.* 2007: 3105; see also Saxe 2006; Walter *et al.* 2004), and also between the representation of individual and we-intentions (Becchio and Bertone 2004: 132).

Attempts to model the understanding of intentions (Bara 2010; Pacherie 2006, 2008) have also been given empirical support. Becchio *et al.* (2006), for instance, have argued that the recognition, attribution and representation of action intentions can be traced to different forms of neural activity. They hypothesise that the recognition of the intentions of others is partly based on the same areas of the brain that are activated when one (intentionally) per-forms actions oneself. The neural basis of this has been argued to be 'mirror neurons' (i.e. neurons that fire during action execution and action observa-tion) in the premotor cortex (Fogassi *et al.* 2005; Rizzolatti and Craighero 2004; Rizzolatti and Fabbri Destro 2007), although mirror neurons do not in themselves provide the basis for different forms of agentive understanding and shared intentionality (Pacherie and Dokic 2006).[20] The attribution of intention to a particular agent is traced in Becchio *et al.*'s (2006) experiments to another area of the brain, the inferior parietal lobe, while the representa-tion of prior intentions, particularly those which are social, has been traced to the anterior paracingulate cortex (Walter *et al.* 2004). Recent work has also shown that a common neural network is employed when subjects are com-prehending communicative intentions, no matter whether the prompt is linguistic or gestural (Enrici *et al.* 2011). Although the area of study is in its rel-ative infancy, then, social neuroscientists have begun tracing hypothesised mental states (i.e. intentions and inferences about intentions) to specific neu-ral activity, lending support to the kinds of distinctions made in pragmatics between different kinds of intentions.

However, work in psycholinguistics on the comprehension and attribution of intentions suggests that while these may indeed have neural correlates, speakers consistently over-estimate their ability to project intended mean-ings onto addressees (Keysar 1994b, 2000; Keysar and Henly 2002). Moreover, hearers often do not routinely consider what the speaker knows (i.e. common ground) or other mental states in interpreting what has been said (Keysar 2007, 2008). This fundamental egocentrism in the early stages of processing language suggests that due caution should be given to interpreting results of experiments attesting to neural correlates of intentions. While no one would suggest that speakers do not at times have intentions motivating them to say things, or that hearers do not at times make conscious inferences about such intentions, the question is the extent to which such an explanation is sufficient to account for speaker meaning and communication (Haugh 2008c: 52; 2009: 93). The evidence from psycholinguistics suggests that while a (prior) intention-based account of speaker meaning may be necessary, it may not be sufficient.

Work from an interactional perspective also attests to the difficulty of locating intentions relative to meanings in discourse (rather than simply relative to utterances). Haugh (2008c, 2009), for instance, argues that the intentions hypothesised to underlie implicatures are temporally, ontologically and epistemologically ambiguous when the analyst attempts to trace them in actual interactional data. In more closely tracing intentions in conversational interaction it becomes apparent that intentions can be characterised as being 'emergent', as both the speaker and the hearer jointly co-construct understandings of what is meant (Clark H. 1997; Gibbs 1999: 38, 2001; Haugh 2007c: 95, 2008c, 2009; Kecskes 2010a: 60–61). Kecskes (2010a), for instance, argues that John's initial intention to give Peter a chance to talk about his trip is not realised in the excerpt below.

(23)  John:    Want to talk about your trip?
      Peter:   I don't know. If you have questions . . .
      John:    OK, but you should tell me . . .
      Peter:   Wait, you want to hear about Irene?
      John:    Well, what about her?
      Peter:   She is fine. She has . . . well . . . put on some weight, though
                                                          (Kecskes 2010a: 60).

Kecskes suggests that John's original intention is sidelined by Peter talking about Irene, perhaps because he thinks John might want to know about her (being his former girlfriend). He argues that 'it was the conversational flow that led to this point, at which there appears a kind of *emergent, co-constructed intention*' (Kecskes 2010a: 61, original emphasis).

These 'emergent' intentions have interesting parallels with the notion of we-intention discussed in section 5.3.2. However, Haugh (2008c) argues that the relatively static characterisation of we-intentions does not do full justice to the contingent and emergent nature of the inferential work underlying joint, cooperative activities, including conversational interaction. The key difference between the notions of we-intention and emergent intention is that the former assumes a monadic view of cognition, involving 'the summative sequence of individual cognitive activities' (Arundale and Good 2002: 124), while the latter builds upon a dyadic view of cognition:

> Each participant's cognitive processes in using language involve concurrent operations temporally extended both forward in time in anticipation or projection, and backwards in time in hindsight or retroactive assessing of what has already transpired. As participants interact, these concurrent cognitive activities become fully interdependent or dyadic. (Arundale and Good 2002: 122)

Yet while there are differences in their underlying frameworks, the view in philosophical and cognitive pragmatics that we-intentions cannot be reduced to individual intentions due to the sharedness requirement being cognitively implausible (Becchio and Bertone 2004: 127–8), and the complementary view in interactional pragmatics that models of individual intentions are 'formally incapable of explaining the non-summative effects or emergent properties observable when individuals are engaged in interaction' (Arundale 2008: 243), both strongly suggest that meaning cannot necessarily always be traced analytically to prior intentions of individual speakers (including their communicative intentions). Instead, the interpretation of meaning is 'doubly-dynamic' in the sense that it is 'created in-between the interlocutors and the hearer may also be given freedom to create assumptions rather than recover them' (Jaszczolt 1999: 76; see also Hirsch 2010). Gauker (2001, 2003, 2008) has also argued that the role of situational inferences has been vastly underplayed in communicative intention-based models of meaning and communication.

However, such views should not be simplistically interpreted as constituting an anti-intentionalism stance as some have recently assumed (Åkerman 2009; Montminy 2010). Instead, there is growing evidence that we need to make clearer distinctions between speaker (intended) meaning, which pertains to the subjective processing domain at the utterance level, and 'joint meaning', which pertains to the interpersonal domain at the discourse level (Carassa and Colombetti 2009; Kasper 2006; Kecskes 2008, 2010a; Kriempardis 2009: 186). Different types of intentions arguably have different roles to play relative to these different types of meaning. Instead of remaining committed to a hardline intentionalist or anti-intentionalist stance, greater dialogue between those with different views on intention lies at the heart of advancing our understanding of meaning and communication (Haugh 2008a).

We have discussed thus far how intentions can be located both in the minds of individuals, as well as more diffusely in interaction, where they emerge '*between* the mind and the world' (Jaszczolt 1999: 117). There is, however, an additional level at which intentions can be productively located, namely, the social (or societal) level of analysis. The focus here is on deontological aspects of intention and intentionality. Philosophers have conceptualised this as commitment to undertake we-intended actions (Gilbert 2009), for instance, or commitment to the truth conditions of utterances (Searle 2007: 33–4). The notion of speaker accountability in ethnomethodological conversation analysis (Garfinkel 1967; Sacks 1992 [1964]: 4–5), where interlocutors hold themselves and others normatively accountable for the meanings that arise from what is said (Heritage 1984), can also be productively explored in regards to both speaker intentions and intentionality (Arundale 2008; Edwards 2006, 2008; Haugh 2008c, 2009). For instance, the ways in which speakers are held accountable to meanings through topicalising intentions, and how this intersects with interpretative and socio-cultural norms can be explored (Haugh 2008b, 2008c).

Holding speakers accountable for what they are understood by others to have implied can also enter into broader societal debates, as argued by Haugh (2008b) in an analysis of the discursive dispute arising in the Australian media as to what was intended by comments in regards to the status of women made by a Muslim cleric.[21] In the following excerpt, the cleric is being interviewed in the controversial wake of the publication of his sermon.

(24)      ('Defending the faith: Sheik Taj Aldin Alhilali', Australian *60 Minutes*, Channel 9, broadcast 12 November 2006)
1  M:  But you're the grand mufti, you're the grand mufti. Why would
2       you say something like that which is going to offend everybody?
3  H:  ((translated)) I say straightaway what is in my heart. I say it.
4  M:  I hear what you are saying Sheik Alhilali. But, but, you can't
5       say these things, and then say I was misunderstood,
6       misinterpreted, I meant something else. If you say them they
7       exist. If you say these things about rape, about Jews, about
8       militants and bombers if you say them people believe you.
9  H:  ((translated)) My words, as correctly understood, I stand behind.

(Haugh 2008b: 213)

Martin (the interviewer) first asks in lines 1–2 why Hilali would say something offensive when he holds a position of responsibility in the Australian Muslim community (the grand mufti), to which Hilali responds by claiming he always speaks honestly, implying that he does not necessarily always say what others want him to say (line 3). Martin then invokes the folk view of meaning as residing in words (Bilmes 1986), in arguing that Hilali is responsible for how people understand him (lines 6–8), and that one cannot be absolved from this responsibility by claiming one was 'misunderstood' or 'misinterpreted' (lines 4–6). This stance, however, is implicitly rejected by Hilali in line 9, when he claims he stands behind the 'correct' interpretation of what he implied, in this case, what he intended by his comments. The deontological dimensions of speaker meaning were thus clearly topicalised in this particular interview.

In considering the question of where intentions can be located, then, it has become apparent that this concept is deployed in pragmatics for a number of different analytical purposes. In philosophical pragmatics it is used in accounting for how speakers mean things (communicative intentions) or undertake joint activities (we-intentions), although there are varying levels of commitment to the psychological reality of those intentions (Jaszczolt 1999). In cognitive pragmatics there is a clearer commitment to the assumption that the recognition and attribution of (communicative) intentions underlies communication, but there is also consideration of a much more fine-grained range of different types of intentions (including the distinction between prior intentions versus intentions-in-action), with work attempting to correlate neural activity with such distinctions. Here, intentions tend to be conceptualised as being firmly located in the minds of speakers. In contrast, in interactional pragmatics the focus is on examining the relationship between speaker (intended) meaning and joint or interactionally achieved meanings, with the notion of 'emergent intention' (Kecskes 2010a) or 'emergent intentionality' (Haugh 2008c, 2009) sometimes being deployed to account for the latter. Here, intentions and inferences are treated as contingent (and non-summative), arising in the course of interaction, and thus better traced with reference to dyadic views of cognition (Arundale and Good 2002) rather than individual minds. Finally, in more discursive approaches to pragmatics, the analytical focus is on the normative work intention does when deployed in discourse or interaction, with a particular emphasis on how speaker commitment or accountability can be disputed. In these approaches, intentions can be found to be diffused across social networks, ranging from dyadic units through to larger social groups.

## 5.4 Concluding remarks: intentions as 'creatures of darkness' or a useful tool?

We are now in a position to address the methodological question as to how pragmatic theory, aspiring to high predictive power, can be founded on intentions and intentionality – theoretical notions which are inherently so imprecise and, moreover, possibly not directly empirically testable. In other words, this lack of testability may prove not to be a fleeting state of affairs but an inherent property of intentions. In answering this question one has to point out that the advantages seem to outweigh the shortcomings. We attempt to list here a few arguments in favour of an outlook that maintains the importance of intentions for theorising in pragmatics.

(1) If we ban intentions from pragmatics, we have to use a substitute theoretical tool such as default rules of inference, semanticised pragmatic relations between sentences as in dynamic approaches to meaning, or other similar solutions, e.g. constraints of optimality-theory pragmatics. None of these alternative tools has comparable predictive power as far as speaker meaning is concerned. Instead, we are forced to change the object of study of pragmatics from, so to speak, speaker meaning

'whatever means the speaker may have used to convey it' to speaker meaning 'modelled on the fairly probable semantic patterns'.[22]

(2)  In the current state of experimenting in neuroscience, it seems very unlikely that intentions can remain creatures of darkness. Instead, they are being correlated with neural activity as discussed in the preceding section. Intentions in communication derive their theoretical status from intentionality of consciousness. The more we know about intentionality in the brain, the more will we know about intentions. The structure of the explanation is already there in the form of Gricean pragmatics; the scientific flesh is being provided as cognitive science progresses.

(3)  Language is a vehicle of thought and pragmatic theory of its use in communication should derive from theories of thought. In order to theorise expression meaning (word/sentence meaning), the basic intentionality of thought needs to be taken into account. In this way, the extent to which expression meaning can be productively defined in terms of speaker meaning (intentions), as originally proposed by Grice, may be further explored.[23]

(4)  The notion of intention (and indeed intentionality) is already being productively deployed in many different ways in pragmatics. While this proliferation can at times create analytical confusion, it is also no doubt reflective of the metaphorical power of intentions and intentionality in advancing our understanding of how speakers mean things through the use of language.

We suggest, therefore, that while intentions may be difficult to pin down, it is clear that disciplines do not advance by avoiding slippery questions, particularly when they lie at their very foundations, as do the concepts of intention and intentionality in pragmatics. Ultimately, it is only through refining or even discarding certain views and developing alternatives that we will continue to advance in our theorisation and analysis of meaning and communication.

# 6

# Context and content
## Pragmatics in two-dimensional semantics

## 6.1 Introduction

Two-dimensional semantics in its most general characterization is a semantics that recognizes two kinds of content: narrow content and wide content.[1] Narrow contents can take the form of linguistic meanings (e.g., functions from context to content) or descriptive Fregean contents. Wide content is a set of possible worlds or a structured Russellian proposition consisting of properties and/or physical objects. On some approaches (for instance, Kaplan's and Stalnaker's), "narrow content" is not semantic content (it is not what is shared in communication) but belongs to what Stalnaker calls "the metasemantics." On other approaches (e.g., Chalmers and Jackson), the narrow content is (part of) the semantic content.

Kaplan (1989a) originally introduced two-dimensional semantics in order to account for the semantics of context-sensitive expressions, primarily indexicals and demonstratives. Names, indexicals, and demonstratives have often been treated as having as their semantic content the individuals to which they refer. But indexicals and demonstratives do not acquire their content in the same way as names. Unlike names, as traditionally construed, their content varies across worlds, times, speakers, and locations. This difference between names and indexicals prompted Kaplan to introduce a further layer of meaning, viz. a function that takes an expression from worlds, times, speakers, or locations to its content. This function can then be either constant (names) or variable (indexicals and demonstratives).

Two-dimensional semantics has subsequently been employed by Robert Stalnaker (e.g. 1978), David Chalmers (e.g. 1996, 2006), Frank Jackson (e.g., Chalmers and Jackson 2001), and others as a tool for explaining how sentences that have necessary contents can be cognitively informative and how

I am grateful to Keith Allan, David Chalmers, Melissa Ebbers, and Kasia Jaszczolt for helpful comments on an earlier version of this paper.

sentences that are cognitively uninformative can be contingent, and David Chalmers and Frank Jackson have developed the approach further in debates about the role of conceptual analysis and reductive explanation.

Here I will introduce and assess the notion of context-sensitivity presented by the various two-dimensional frameworks, with a special focus on how it relates to the notion of cognitive significance and whether it includes an intuitively plausible range of expressions within its scope. I will argue that the two phenomena (viz. context-sensitivity and cognitive significance) are, to some extent, inseparable. I will conclude with a discussion of the prospects of using epistemic two-dimensional semantics to account for context-sensitive expressions in dynamic discourse.

## 6.2  Kaplan

### 6.2.1  Kaplan's two-stage theory

In "Demonstratives" (1989a) David Kaplan introduced a two-stage semantic theory of indexicals and demonstratives. In Kaplan's framework, disambiguated expression types have a linguistic meaning or what Kaplan calls a "character." A character is a function from context to content. The context is a sequence of parameters which include (at least) a world, a speaker, a time, and a location. In the extended (1989a) version of the previously unpublished text Kaplan included an addressee among the contextual parameters. A demonstration is not directly included in the context as a contextual parameter. Instead demonstratives associated with different demonstrations are treated as different lexical items.[2] The character of 'I am speaking now' is a function from a world $w$, a speaker $s$, and a time $t$ of the context to a content that is true just in case $s$ is speaking at $t$ in $w$. The content of a sentence is the proposition expressed and also what is said by the sentence in context. Context together with a disambiguated sentence type with a determinate character thus yields a proposition.

In Kaplan's original framework, only pure indexicals (e.g., 'I', 'now', and 'here'), true demonstratives (e.g., 'this', 'that') and perhaps a few other types of expression (including complex demonstratives) are context-sensitive expressions. They are the only expressions that have variable character. Noun phrases have constant character.[3] So, the word type 'water' used by Oscar on Earth where the clear potable liquid that comes out of faucets is $H_2O$ and the word type 'water' used by Oscar's physical and phenomenal duplicate Twin-Oscar on Twin-Earth where the clear potable liquid that comes out of faucets is XYZ are different lexical items with different constant characters.

For Kaplan, contexts need not be real speech situations. Strictly speaking, they need not be possible either. A sequence of the actual world, the present author, 3 PM Canberra time, 1535, and The Lounge in Melbourne forms an improper context. However, the sorts of contexts that are relevant for determining contents are possible contexts.

There are two main reasons that contexts, for Kaplan, need not comprise real speech situations. First, this notion of context allows that sentence types that are necessarily true or necessarily false relative to real speech situations can be assigned a different truth-value relative to different contexts. These include sentence types such as 'I am not speaking now', 'I do not exist now', and 'I am not here now'. Since there are contexts relative to which these sentence types express true propositions and contexts relative to which these sentence types express false propositions, these sentence types are not logical truths but contingent truths.

Second, if contexts were real speech situations, intuitively valid arguments would come out as invalid. Consider the following argument:

> If John is hungry now, then he is grumpy now.
> John is hungry now.
> So, John is grumpy now.

Utterances take time. So, if contexts were real speech situations, then there would be contexts in which it is true that if John is hungry now, then he is grumpy now, and true that John is hungry now, but false that John is grumpy now because he eats something before we have a chance to utter the conclusion. Below I will sketch a way to deal with dynamic discourses in a two-dimensional framework.

## 6.2.2  Kaplan and cognitive significance

Kaplan's theory was intended to give an account of context-sensitive expressions. It was not intended as an account of cognitively informative necessities (Kripke's a posteriori necessities) or cognitively uninformative contingencies (Kripke's a priori contingencies). But Kaplan's framework provides a reasonably good explanation of the phenomenon when indexicals and demonstratives are implicated. For example, 'I am Brit (if I exist)' expresses, relative to my context, a necessary truth of the form 'a = a (if a exists)'. Yet it can be cognitively significant. We can explain its cognitive significance by noting that 'I' and 'Brit' have different characters. The character of 'I' is a function from a context to the speaker of the context, the character of 'Brit' is a function from a context to Brit. The identity claim, it may be said, is cognitively significant, because the expressions flanking the identity sign have different characters. If we discover that the different characters determine the same content in a context, our overall knowledge state has been enriched. Kaplan's original example of cognitive significance runs as follows:

> If I see, reflected in a window, the image of a man whose pants appear to be on fire, my behavior is sensitive to whether I think, "His pants are on fire" or "My pants are on fire", though the object of thought may be the same. (1989a: 533)

Thinking "his pants are on fire" (referring to myself) and thinking "my pants are on fire" will elicit different behavioral responses. For Kaplan, what explains the difference and hence what explains cognitive significance is the character of the sentence (the way the proposition expressed is presented), not the proposition expressed.

Kaplan's theory does not by itself offer a general explanation of cognitive significance. 'Hesperus is Phosphorus' is ordinarily cognitively significant, yet if 'Hesperus' and 'Phosphorus' are genuine names rather than disguised descriptions, then the character of 'Hesperus' is identical to the character of 'Phosphorus'. It is a constant one-place function mapping contexts to Venus.

Noting that Kaplan's theory does not offer a general explanation of cognitive significance is not a criticism of his framework thought of as a theory of indexicals and demonstratives. However, there is some reason to think that the correct story of indexicals and demonstratives ought to be generalizable to noun phrases. To see this it may be helpful to introduce the notion of 'twin-earthability'. David Chalmers defines the notion as follows:

> We can say that two possible individuals (at times) are twins if they are physical and phenomenal duplicates; we can say that two possible expression tokens are twins if they are produced by corresponding acts of twin speakers. Then a token is Twin-Earthable if it has a twin with a different 2-intension [Russellian intension]. (Chalmers 2006: section 3.5)

A twin-earthable expression is one which has a twin token with a different 2-intension (or Kaplan content). For example, 'water' is twin-earthable. 'Water' has the same 2-intension as '$H_2O$' when I use the word, and it has the same 2-intension as 'XYZ', when my phenomenal and physical twin uses the word on Twin-Earth, where the clear potable liquid that flows in oceans, rivers, and lakes has the chemical composition XYZ. Note that, on Chalmers' definition, it is not required that the word tokens spoken by the twin-speakers be tokens of the same lexical item.

Twin-earthability plays a crucial role in testing whether an expression is semantically neutral. Semantically neutral expressions, roughly, are the non-twin-earthable expressions (e.g. 'phenomenally conscious', 'cause', and 'friend'). To a first approximation, they are expressions that do not have wide content (Kaplan content) that does not supervene on the physical-phenomenal make-up of the particular speakers (deferential uses aside). Twin-earthable expressions are required to generate (ideally) cognitively significant sentences.[4] Semantically neutral expressions cannot be used to generate (ideally) cognitively significant sentences.

Note that in order for twin-earthability and semantic neutrality to be relevantly connected, it must be true that narrow content (1-intension) supervenes on the physical-phenomenal make-up of particular speakers.[5] If it does not, then almost any expression (semantically neutral or not) comes out as twin-earthable. Take 'phenomenally conscious'. There is a scenario in which people speak the language Schmenglish. In Schmenglish 'phenomenally conscious' has a somewhat different 1-intension (and hence 2-intension). It means, roughly, *alert*. So, when twins on Earth and Schmenglish Earth make corresponding acts and say "I am conscious," their tokens pick out different properties. So 'phenomenally conscious' comes out as twin-earthable, which was not the result we wanted.

Assuming Kaplan's original framework, indexical and demonstrative expressions are both twin-earthable and context-sensitive. If Oscar and Twin-Oscar both say "I am human," the twin tokens of 'I' have different 2-intensions (Kaplan contents). One picks out Oscar at every world, the other picks out Twin-Oscar at every world. Likewise, if Oscar and Twin-Oscar demonstrate the clear potable liquid in their drinking glasses and say "that is water," the twin occurrences of 'that' have different 2-intensions. One picks out $H_2O$ at every world, the other picks out XYZ at every world.

Given Kaplan's original framework, most noun phrases are twin-earthable but not context-sensitive. 'Water' is twin-earthable, because in Kaplan's framework, Oscar and Twin-Oscar's tokens of 'water' pick out different chemical substances. 'Water' is not context-sensitive because its character is a constant function from contexts to contents.

There is some reason to think that the characters of noun phrases like 'water' ought not to be considered constant functions. Here is one argument. Chalmers' definition of twin-earthability does not require that the twins use tokens of the same lexical item. However, as it stands, it does not rule it out either. But whether we consider Oscar's and Twin-Oscar's uses of the string of letters 'water' tokens of one word type or different lexical items seems somewhat of a methodological choice (I say "somewhat" because treating Oscar and Twin-Oscar as speaking the same language allows us to reject the requirement that narrow content supervenes on the intrinsic make-up of particular speakers). Suppose, then, that we consider Oscar's and Twin-Oscar's uses of tokens of a single lexical item. Oscar and Twin-Oscar then use twin tokens to pick out different chemical substances. So, the lexical item 'water' then must have a variable character yielding different contents relative to different contexts. Relative to Oscar's context the character of 'water' yields $H_2O$, and relative to Twin-Oscar's context it yields XYZ. So, the character of 'water' is variable. But if the character of 'water' is variable, then it may reasonably be thought to be in the range of broadly context-sensitive expressions. The same sort of argument applies to other noun phrases typically thought to be twin-earthable.

Granting this point, we can account for the cognitive significance of informative necessities in the following way. Being less than omniscient with respect to empirical matters we may not know whether we are on Earth or Twin-Earth (or some other exotic planet). If we are on Earth, then the character of 'water' determines $H_2O$. If we are at Twin-Earth, then it determines XYZ. Discovering that water is $H_2O$ here thus amounts to discovering that 'water' determines $H_2O$ here, and hence amounts to discovering what the character of 'water' is in our context.

Of course, someone fond of Kaplan's original semantics might reasonably baulk at this move. Strings of letters forming lexical entries with a constant character, it might be said, simply form different lexical entries with a different constant character when used elsewhere. The phenomenon, they will continue, is akin to that of homonymy. The English word 'red' and the Danish word 'red' (meaning: 'rode') are not one lexical item with variable character but two distinct lexical entries spelled in the same way but with distinct characters. Likewise, given Kaplan semantics, the Earth word 'water' and the Twin-Earth word 'water' are distinct lexical items spelled the same way with distinct characters.

Personally I find this sort of response somewhat ad hoc. But granting it, we may reasonably ask whether there is a different way of accounting for cognitive significance within the original Kaplan framework. I think there is a way of partially accounting for the phenomenon. This involves introducing the notion of a diagonalized character. To a first approximation, a diagonalized character is a meaning content that picks out different referents at different contexts. It's similar to a linguistic contextual intension. For example, the diagonalized character of 'I' picks out the speaker of the context, and the diagonalized character of 'now' picks out the time of speech. For Kaplan, the linguistic contextual intension of names picks out the same referent in all contexts. However, as we will see below, we can define a diagonalized character in the following way. Though the characters of names are constant, the strings of letters forming English expressions could have had different characters. For example, 'water' could have been a function from context to XYZ rather than a function from context to $H_2O$. So, if we take sentence types to be associated with different functions from contexts to characters at different worlds, we can take the diagonal character to be a set of functions from contexts to propositions that are true relative to parameters of the context. For example, the diagonal character of 'water is $H_2O$' yields the proposition that (1) $H_2O$ is $H_2O$ at a context that contains the actual world as a parameter and yields the proposition that (2) the clear liquid that fills oceans, rivers, and lakes is XYZ at a context relative to which the character of 'water' is a function from context to the descriptive content 'the clear liquid that fills rivers, oceans, and lakes', and relative to which the character of '$H_2O$' is a function from context to XYZ. So, it might seem that we can account for the intuitive cognitive significance of 'water is $H_2O$' by noting that the diagonal character yields different propositions at different contexts, and so says different things, relative to different contexts. It is plausible that further investigation into our use of the language is needed in order to discover which linguistic contextual intension (or what Kaplan simply calls "character") sentences actually have and which propositions they actually express.

Despite their virtues, however, the variable-character approach and the diagonal approach to cognitive significance have at least two shortcomings. Both approaches trade on the idea that we are less than competent speakers and hence are not sure about what the characters of our expressions are. But this then has the consequence that 'water is water' might be cognitively significant. If we are not certain what the character of 'water' is, then we are not certain what the character of 'water is water' is. So, while we know that the sentence expresses necessary propositions relative to contexts, we do not know which proposition it expresses relative to our context.

Furthermore, 'Hesperus is bright at night' is contingent because Venus (which 'Hesperus' actually refers to) might not have been the brightest object in the evening sky, but if the name 'Hesperus' is introduced as a disguised description that stands for 'the brightest object in the evening sky', then the sentence is uninformative. Yet both its variable character and its diagonal character yield different propositions relative to different contexts. So, 'Hesperus is bright at night' comes out as cognitively informative when it should have come out as cognitively uninformative. So, neither the variable-character approach nor the diagonalization approach provides a good account of cognitive informativeness.

There is independent reason to think that even when limited to sentences containing context-sensitive expressions neither one of the attempted Kaplan explanations of cognitive significance is within the spirit of Kaplan's framework. In Kaplan's framework, the proposition determined by a sentence in a context is evaluated relative to a circumstance of evaluation. The parameters of the default circumstance of evaluation are parameters of the context. But circumstance-shifting operators can shift the parameters of the circumstance of evaluation. For example, in the case of 'it was the case that John visited Mary', 'it was the case that' functions as a circumstance-shifting operator which shifts the time parameter of the default circumstance of evaluation to some time prior to it. 'It was the case that John visited Mary' is true iff (if and only if) John visited Mary at some time prior to the time of speech. However, according to Kaplan, English contains no corresponding operators that operate on character. There are no Kaplanian monsters or context-shifting operators in English (1989a: 510). For example, 'John believes that I am hungry' cannot be used to express the proposition that John believes that he is hungry. 'John believes' does not operate on character and so cannot shift the speaker's context to John's context to produce a John-content for 'I'. If, however, Kaplan's framework could explain informative necessities involving indexicals and demonstratives, then we need to allow that some sentential operators operate on character. To see this, consider (1).

(1)   For all I can rule out from the armchair, I am not Brit.

(1) is a plausible specification of the cognitive significance of 'I am Brit'. In the actual context, of course, 'I' and 'Brit' yield the same propositional contents. So, for (1) to be true, the operator 'for all I can rule out from the armchair' must take us to a context that yields different propositional contents for 'I' and 'Brit'. The English operator 'for all I can rule out from the armchair' must function as a monster. So, if we extend Kaplan's framework in the ways suggested above, then there are monsters after all, contrary to what Kaplan claimed.

## 6.3  Stalnaker

### 6.3.1  Assertion

In "Assertion" Robert Stalnaker (1978, see also 1999) offers a theory of content that is similar in some respects to Kaplan's. However, where Kaplan opts for structured propositions, Stalnaker takes a proposition to be a set of possible worlds that are the way the world is said to be. Stalnaker thinks of possible worlds as the conditions that must obtain for the proposition to be true, hence they are truth conditions. This idea is motivated by the thought that when one asserts a proposition, one seeks to eliminate the set of possible situations at which what one says is false. Unlike Kaplan, Stalnaker seeks to account for cognitive significance or *the information that a statement conveys* in those cases in which what one says is informative despite being necessarily true. Necessarily true statements do not exclude any possibilities, yet if one utters an informative necessity, then it seems that one is seeking to rule out possibilities.

In "Assertion" Stalnaker's account of cognitive significance is similar to the diagonalization approach I imaginatively outlined above on behalf of Kaplan. For Stalnaker, utterances are associated with propositional concepts, functions from possible worlds containing the utterance to propositions. The diagonal proposition is the set of worlds at which the utterance's propositional concept yields a true proposition. If, for example, context maps 'water' to the descriptive material 'the clear liquid that fills oceans, rivers, and lakes' and maps 'H$_2$O' to XYZ, then the diagonal proposition of 'water is H$_2$O' is the proposition that the clear liquid that fills oceans, rivers, and lakes is XYZ. Cognitive informativeness is explained by our uncertainty about which context we occupy and hence which proposition is in fact expressed by our assertions.

This approach generates the same problems as diagonalizing on character does. We might be uncertain about which proposition is in fact expressed by the a priori necessity 'water is water' and the a priori contingency 'Hesperus is bright at night', in which case these sentences are cognitively informative despite being a priori.

Of course, our uncertainty might be limited in various ways. We might know 'water' does not refer to tigers but refers to a chemical substance. Likewise, we might know that 'water = water' expresses a necessary proposition even if we don't know what. Still, the approach is bound to yield some intuitively mistaken results.

The early Stalnaker approach has other virtues. It can explain communication failure. If A is identical to B, but I lack competence, I may fail to grasp that 'A is F' and 'B is F' express the same proposition. If you are competent and believe I am too, communication failure might ensue. Stalnaker's early account can explain why. However, the early Stalnaker account does not yield a good account of informative necessity and uninformative contingency.

## 6.3.2 Assertion revisited

In "Assertion revisited" Stalnaker (2004) proposes to treat Kaplanian character as a kind of narrow content but understood metasemantically (i.e., not as content proper). He also proposes to treat a wider class of expressions as context-sensitive. Nearly all names and descriptive expressions are treated as having a generalized variable character. For example, 'Socrates' and 'water' are treated on the model of indexicals. So, their character is a variable function mapping context to individuals. The generalized character of 'Socrates lived in Athens' is a variable function mapping context to propositions (or sets of worlds). In this new framework, it is the variability of the character of 'water is $H_2O$' that explains its cognitive informativeness. Stalnaker furthermore assumes that there may be cases in which speakers know what a sentence says. So, a sentence may be informative relative to one speaker but not relative to another.

Stalnaker's new approach, of course, is similar in a number of ways to the first approach I outlined above on behalf of Kaplan. However, it differs from this approach in treating some expressions which intuitively are not twin-earthable as context-sensitive. Like the variable-character approach we considered above on behalf of Kaplan, Stalnaker's new approach has difficulties distinguishing between the differences in the cognitive value of 'water is water' and 'water is $H_2O$', and 'Venus is bright at night' and 'Hesperus is bright at night'. If 'water is $H_2O$' is informative in virtue of the fact that we don't know which content its variable character determines in our context, then so is 'water is water'. Likewise, if 'Venus is bright at night' is informative because we don't know what content its variable character determines in our context, then so is 'Hesperus is bright at night'.

Stalnaker's proposal has further problems. One potential problem is overgeneration. If the expression 'The Mayor of Boston' is treated on a par with 'I' and 'now', which the framework seems to allow, then it has a variable character which maps the expression from context to an individual. So, 'the Mayor of Boston is rich' and 'Thomas M. Menino is rich' have the same content (though different characters). This is not a super-controversial proposal. It familiarly goes against Bertrand Russell's (1905) theory of descriptions, according to which descriptions are incomplete symbols which do not denote. But it is in broad agreement with Peter Strawson's (1950) proposal that descriptions are referential and Keith Donnellan's (1966) proposal that descriptions have attributive and referential uses. Elsewhere both Stalnaker and Kaplan have welcomed this consequence of an extended two-stage approach to semantics.[6]

Furthermore, starting with Strawson many have thought that incomplete descriptions must be treated as context-sensitive. Stanley and Szabó (2000), for example, introduce nominal restriction to account for the context-sensitivity of quantifiers. If I were to say that every bottle is on the table, I would not ordinarily mean that every bottle in the universe is on the table.

What I would mean in the envisaged circumstance is that every <bottle, i> is on the table, where 'i' is contextually completed. So, '<bottle, i>' denotes, say, the set of bottles in the kitchen. The problem of incomplete descriptions can possibly be resolved in the same way (see e.g. Stanley 2002b). 'The book is on the table' can be treated as being of the form 'the <book, i> is on the <table, j>', where '<book, i>' and ' <table, j>', once the indexical variables are contextually completed, denote, say, the set of books I have in mind and the set of tables in the living room, respectively.

However, granting that incomplete descriptions are context-sensitive does not vindicate a treatment of characters as generalized. Nominal restriction, for example, does not require treating characters as generalized. It does admittedly require treating the restrictor-plus-hidden variable as having a variable character that returns a property or an extension relative to context (e.g., the property of being a bottle in my kitchen or the set of bottles in my kitchen). But this character variability is arguably just of the sort postulated in the original Kaplan text. Nominal restriction does not indicate a need for a more generalized treatment of character.

Moreover, without further constraints on which expressions can have variable character, it would seem that the generalized proposal extends to other quantificational expressions. For example, 'every rich person from Boston' might have a variable character that takes the expression from a context to a set of people. A referential treatment of universally quantified expressions seems less attractive than a referential treatment of definite descriptions.

The generalized character proposal also threatens to turn intuitively non-twin-earthable (or semantically neutral) expressions like 'consciousness', 'friend', and 'cause' into context-sensitive expressions with variable characters. For example, it might be thought that, given some functional description of consciousness, we can define a variable character that yields different properties relative to different contexts. So, relative to the actual world, 'is conscious' and 'is phenomenally conscious' might have the same content, whereas at a zombie world 'is conscious' and 'is able to report part of the content of their computational states' might have the same content. Without further constraints in place, Stalnaker's new proposal seems to threaten to make too many expressions context-sensitive. In response to this sort of worry Stalnaker suggests treating fundamental, natural properties and relations as context-insensitive (and hence as having a constant character).

It might be thought that a limited extension of the variable-character approach would be a good way to account for context-sensitivity more generally. For example, it might be thought that expressions such as 'local', 'nearby', 'tall', 'big', and so on, which beg to be treated as context-sensitive, could be treated as having themselves variable characters rather than as being associated with a hidden constituent with a variable character.[7] But the motivation for this approach is somewhat meager, given that these expressions can be treated, on the model of nominal restriction, as containing a hidden indexical variable (see, e.g. Stanley 2002b).

Philosophers have in recent years argued that the range of context-sensitive expressions must be widened to include epistemic expressions (e.g., 'know' and 'might'), moral expressions (e.g., 'decent' and 'appropriate'), predicates of personal taste (e.g., 'fun' and 'tasty') and vague expressions (e.g., 'bald' and 'heap'). If they are right about this, then these expressions may well be best treated on the more generalized variable-character model, though it is possible that the less explored options in these areas of philosophy, viz. the hidden-indexical-variable approach or the epistemic two-dimensional approach, ultimately can provide a better account of the contextual nature of these expressions.

## 6.4 Chalmers

### 6.4.1 Epistemic two-dimensionalism

David Chalmers (1996, 2002, 2006, forthcoming a) and Frank Jackson (Chalmers and Jackson 2001) have proposed a different two-dimensional framework, according to which epistemic variability and cognitive significance are to be explained at least partially in terms of a basic notion of apriority ("partially" because they recognize that a priori sentences may be cognitively informative to non-ideal reasoners). If 'Hesperus' is introduced as shorthand for 'the brightest object in the evening sky', it is a priori that Hesperus is the brightest object in the evening sky. That is, we can figure out that this is true without engaging in empirical investigations of what the world is like. It is also a priori that Hesperus is Hesperus. But it is not a priori that Hesperus is Phosphorus or that water is $H_2O$. Even though 'Hesperus is Phosphorus' and 'water is $H_2O$' are necessarily true, it wasn't possible for us to just see that this was so. To figure it out, we needed to examine whether the same planet, namely Venus, appeared both in the morning and at night and whether the chemical composition of water was $H_2O$ or some other chemical structure. Over the years Chalmers and Jackson have appealed to the notion of apriority to formulate a two-dimensional framework that avoids the shortcomings of the linguistic approaches. Roughly, the idea is that because we cannot know a priori that water is $H_2O$, there are scenarios compatible with what can be known a priori in which water is not $H_2O$. So, the sentence is cognitively significant. There are some differences between Chalmers's, and Jackson's approaches. Here I shall focus on Chalmers's (1996, 2002, 2006, forthcoming a) framework.

Chalmers offers two versions of his epistemic two-dimensional framework, one which treats the space of possible worlds as plentiful enough to provide a model for deep epistemic possibility (i.e., possibilities not ruled out a priori), and one which constructs epistemic space out of sentences. Let us look at the former proposal first. On the former proposal, there is a space of possible worlds which allows us to define 2-intensions (Kaplan contents or intensions) as either sets of worlds or as functions from worlds to truth-values.

2-intensions are necessarily true in the standard sense when they yield the truth-value true at every world and necessarily false when they yield the truth-value false at every world. On the plenitude proposal, however, the space of possible worlds is large enough to model deep epistemic possibility. A scenario is a possible world in which certain features are marked: in most cases an individual and a time. A world in which certain features are marked is called 'a centered world'. As a helpful heuristic, we can think of a centered world as an n-tuple of parameters. A centered world in which a speaker and a time is marked can be thought of as a triple containing a world, a speaker, and a time-parameter. For every centered world, there is then a maximal hypothesis about the world in question expressed in a canonical language. A canonical language is a semantically neutral language. To a first approximation, an expression is semantically neutral just in case it is not twin-earthable as defined above.[8] Part of the hypothesis about a centered world might be that some heavenly body called 'Venus' is the brightest object in the evening sky and that some heavenly body called 'Venus' is the brightest object in the morning sky. As 'Venus' is not semantically neutral, it is not part of the description that Venus is the brightest object in the evening sky.

The important principle on the plenitude conception of deep epistemic possibility is what Chalmers calls 'Metaphysical Plenitude':

> Metaphysical Plenitude: For all S, if S is a priori possible, there is a centered metaphysically possible world that verifies S.

Suppose it is not ruled out a priori that Hesperus, the brightest object in the evening sky, is not identical to Phosphorus, the brightest object in the morning sky, despite the fact that it is necessary that Hesperus is identical to Phosphorus. It is then deeply epistemically possible that Hesperus is not identical to Phosphorus. While there is no possible world in which Hesperus is not identical to Phosphorus, there is a canonical description of a centered world which a priori implies that Hesperus is not identical to Phosphorus. This description might, for example, be a description of a centered world in which Jupiter is the brightest object in the evening sky and Mars is the brightest object in the morning sky. As Jupiter is not identical to Mars, the world verifies the sentence 'Hesperus is not identical to Phosphorus'.

On the alternative picture of scenarios, a scenario is an equivalence class of epistemically complete sentences in a canonical language. A specification of a scenario is a sentence in its equivalence class. The rest of the two-dimensional apparatus goes as before. On the constructive treatment of scenarios, one can in principle allow for strong necessities (i.e., deeply epistemically contingent necessities involving semantically neutral terms).

Given either framework, the 1-intension of an expression is defined as a function from scenarios to extensions. A priori (and uninformative) sentences have epistemically necessary 1-intensions, whereas a posteriori sentences have epistemically possible 1-intensions.[9] So, given this framework 'water is $H_2O$' has a necessary 2-intension that yields the truth-value true at every possible world, but it has a contingent 1-intension that yields the truth-value true at some scenarios and the truth-value false at some scenarios. For example, it yields the truth-value false at scenarios that have a canonical description which a priori implies that the clear liquid that flows in rivers, oceans, and lakes is XYZ. All a posteriori necessities, in Kripke's sense, have a 1-intension that comes apart from their 2-intension.

Chalmers's two-dimensional framework does not inherit the problems of the earlier frameworks. But its explanatory power has some limitations. The framework explains cognitive informativeness for ideal reasoners, but as Chalmers recognizes, it does not explain informativeness for non-ideal reasoners. Despite the fact that all mathematical and logical truths are a priori, many true mathematical conjectures are cognitively informative. Moreover, because the space of scenarios is the space of deep epistemic possibilities, the space of scenarios cannot be used as a way to model hyperintensionality more generally, for instance, belief contexts and strict epistemic possibility contexts. For example, 'I believe that p and not-p' might be true, but there is no scenario that verifies p & not-p. However, as Chalmers (forthcoming a) observes, the framework of scenarios can be extended to account for both non-ideal cognitive informativeness and hyperintensionality.

In Chalmers's two-dimensional semantics, scenarios play roughly the role contexts play in Kaplan's framework, narrow contents (1-intensions) play roughly the role that characters play, except that they are part of the semantics proper ("the propositional content"), and wide contents (2-intensions) play roughly the role that Kaplan contents play.

Despite the analogy between these approaches, however, there are significant differences. Chalmers explicitly distinguishes epistemic variability from context-sensitivity. An expression is epistemically variable if it has a non-constant 1-intension, whereas an expression is context-sensitive if it has a non-constant character. Epistemic variability is structurally analogous to standard context-sensitivity in certain respects but is conceptually distinct.

Given Chalmers's framework, standard context-sensitive expressions (e.g. pure indexicals and true demonstratives) have 1-intensions that come apart from their 2-intensions. Their 1-intensions are non-constant functions from the marked individuals and times (or features of the individuals) in the centers of scenarios to extensions. Their 2-intensions are constant functions from the speaker's scenario to extensions. For example, the 1-intension of a token of *I* is a non-constant function from scenarios to the individual in the center. The 2-intension of a token of *I* is a constant function from the speaker's scenario to the speaker. Likewise, the 1-intension of a token of *this* is a non-constant function from scenarios to the object demonstrated by the individual in the center. The 2-intension of 'this' is a constant function from the speaker's scenario to the object demonstrated by the speaker.

Context-sensitive expressions are twin-earthable. Oscar and Twin-Oscar's tokens of *I* have the same 1-intension but different 2-intensions. Other twin-earthable expressions, of course, also have a 1-intension that comes apart from their 2-intension (e.g. 'water', 'Hesperus', etc.). But Chalmers treats these other twin-earthable expressions as epistemically variable, not as context-sensitive. One advantage of doing so is that Kaplan's original division of expressions into context-sensitive and non-context-sensitive is preserved. Indexicals come out as context-sensitive, whereas names come out as non-context-sensitive.

### 6.4.2  Twin-earthability and context-sensitivity broadly speaking

Despite the differences between epistemic variability and context-sensitivity within the original epistemic two-dimensional framework, I believe one could understand epistemic variability as a kind of context-sensitivity. This proposal is similar to the variable-character approach I sketched above on behalf of Kaplan but it avoids some of the most obvious problems with the earlier suggestions. It takes context-sensitivity, broadly construed, to be grounded in twin-earthability. Chalmers, of course, would not endorse this. But here is some motivation for this line of thought. Suppose we have a more localized Twin-Earth phenomenon. Water in and around Australia is XYZ, whereas water in and around America is $H_2O$. It now seems possible to treat the 1-intension of 'water' as a function from locations of individuals in scenarios to chemical substances found on those locations and the 2-intension of 'water' as a function from the speaker's location to the chemical substance found on that location.

Of course, there is still the option of denying that the string of letters 'water' forms is a single lexical item. One could hold that we have here a case of homonymy or polysemy. If this were so, then 'water' as used by speakers in Australia and 'water' as used by speakers in America would be different lexical entries with the same spelling.

But this rejoinder can be empirically falsified. For example, we might discover that competent American and Australian speakers treat the word 'water' in the same way that they treat the word 'I', not as a string of letters spelling different words, but as a single lexical entry, and that they are oblivious to the context-sensitivity of the word. To illustrate consider the following dialogue:

(A)
AMERICAN: I am hungry.
AUSTRALIAN: No, you are wrong, I am not hungry.

Just as competent speakers treat (A) as revealing a failure to recognize that 'I' is context-sensitive rather than a failure to recognize that the speakers use two different homonymous words, so we can imagine that competent speakers would treat the following dialogue as revealing a failure to recognize that 'water' is context-sensitive rather than a failure to recognize that the speakers use two different homonymous words:

(B)
AMERICAN: Water is $H_2O$.
AUSTRALIAN: No, you are wrong, water is XYZ.

To say that context-sensitivity, broadly construed, is grounded in twin-earthability is not to deny that there are important differences between, say, indexicals and noun phrases. There is, for example, a difference in how we normally use these two types of expression. As we normally use 'I', its 1-intension is a function from centered worlds to individuals in the center. As we normally use 'water', its 1-intension is, roughly, a function from scenarios to whichever substance satisfies the description 'the clear potable liquid that comes out of our kitchen faucets'.

But it is not clear how much weight this difference carries. First, like the 1-intension of 'water', the 1-intension of 'I' is, roughly, equivalent to the 1-intension of a description, perhaps, 'dthat [the person who utters this token]' (Kaplan 1989a: 522). For example, the 1-intension of 'I am not here' is plausibly equivalent to the 1-intension of 'dthat [the person who utters this token] is not here'.

Second, it is not difficult to imagine that 'water' could have the 2-intension it actually does and yet have a 1-intension that is definable in much the same way as the 1-intension of 'I'. Suppose water is person-dependent and happens to have a person-specific chemical structure. For example, chemical structures might be causally connected to the individual essences of people. So, when you pour yourself a glass of clear odorless liquid, the chemical structure is $H_2O$, and when I pour myself a glass of clear odorless liquid the chemical structure is XYZ. In the envisaged circumstances we might be using 'water' with a 1-intension that, at each scenario, picks out the chemical substance at the center of the scenario. The fact that this 1-intension, even in this scenario, very well could be (roughly) equivalent to the 1-intension of 'the clear, odorless liquid that comes out of the faucet in my kitchen' only emphasizes my point that there is no obvious reason to treat indexicals as context-sensitive and twin-earthable noun-phrases as context-insensitive.

However, as I mentioned above, Chalmers would not endorse this proposal. Moreover, there is an interesting difference between how indexicals and noun phrases are actually used. Presumably Kaplan was right in thinking that there are no operators in English that can change the context to yield a different content for 'I'. For example, 'John believes I am hungry' cannot be used to say that John believes that John is hungry. However, it is possible that there are some monsters in English that can change the context to yield a different content for noun phrases. Here is how.

If twin-earthable expressions can be treated as a kind of context-sensitive expressions, then whenever we have an expression that has a twin token which yields a different 2-intension elsewhere, we have context-sensitivity. If, now, we can have operators relocating speakers from a place where the expression has one 2-intension to a place where it has a different 2-intension, then we have an operator on context, hence a monster in Kaplan's sense. It might plausibly be thought that there are operators of this kind. Consider a color term like 'redness'. Let's suppose, for simplicity, that its 1-intension picks out a reflectance type in the actual world but some other property in other worlds. For example, in worlds in which colors are purely qualitative properties instantiated by external objects (as color primitivism would have it), the 1-intension of 'red' picks out these purely qualitative properties. Now consider (2).

(2)    In Eden objects instantiate redness in virtue of instantiating a purely qualitative or 'primitive' color property.

If 'redness' as it occurs in (2) picked out a reflectance property, (2) would be false. But (2) looks true. So, it must be that 'In Eden' is capable of changing the scenario (or centered world) from the actual one to an Edenic one. So, to the extent that scenarios are contexts in a broad sense 'In Eden' is a context-shifting operator.

Other cases of context-shifting are more controversial. Consider the following conditional:

(3)    Should this turn out to be Twin-Earth, water is not $H_2O$.

Intuitions seem divided on whether (3) is true or false. I am inclined to think it is true (given the fiction). There are numerous ways to deal with conditionals. But on one plausible account the antecedent 'should this turn out to be Twin-Earth' functions as a context-shifting operator which shifts the speaker's context (i.e., scenario) from Earth to Twin-Earth (either by shifting the world or the location within the world). Given a variable-character approach to names, the character of 'water' is something like a description which, relative to Twin-Earth, determines that the content of 'water' is XYZ, not $H_2O$. Given a version of epistemic two-dimensionalism, it is plausible to think that the antecedent 'Should this turn out to be Twin-Earth' shifts us to a different centered world (or scenario or context) that has a specification that a priori implies that water is XYZ. So, while the 1-intension of 'water' stays the same, the 1-intension now determines a 2-intension that picks out XYZ at every possible world. If Twin-Earth is a planet in our universe, the operator 'On Twin-Earth' shifts the speaker's scenario to a scenario with a different center, viz., a center occupied by Twin-Oscar. The 1-intension of 'water' stays the same, but because we have a new center, the 1-intension determines a different 2-intension that picks out XYZ at every possible world.

So, given a reasonable extension of epistemic two-dimensionalism, some operators in English (in the broad sense of 'operator' that includes antecedents of conditionals) can perhaps be thought of as context-shifting operators which shift context (i.e., the scenario) to determine a new content (2-intension) for broadly context-sensitive expressions (viz., noun phrases).

It may be argued that there are no operators like 'In Eden' or 'Should this turn out to be Twin-Earth' in English. However, I think English is expressively rich, and we can felicitously utter sentences like (2) and (3). Whether they have true readings is an empirical question. If they do, then there are context-shifting operators, in the broad sense, in English.

I also note that while Chalmers does not endorse these considerations and does not propose to treat 1-contingency in terms of context-shift, the foregoing considerations suggest a way for the two-dimensional approach to be understood this way. If (3) is true in my mouth and we evaluate whether (3) is 1-contingent or not, it might reasonably be suggested that we evaluate the sentence within the scope of an envisaged context-shifting operator, for instance, 'should this turn out to be Twin-Earth' or 'given hypothesis H'. On this approach then, an evaluation of a sentence's 1-modal features requires shifting the scenario (i.e., the context) either by shifting the world part of the scenario or by shifting the center of the scenario. We then look to see what content is determined given this context-shift. I believe this way of thinking about two-dimensional semantics is broadly within the spirit of Chalmers's approach.

## 6.5   Dynamic two-dimensional semantics

As it stands, epistemic two-dimensional semantics does not allow for a treatment of dynamic discourse.[10] Consider the following discourse fragment:

(4)   John is now entering the room, and he is now taking off his hat and is therefore not now wearing a hat, but he is now putting the hat back on, and is therefore now again wearing a hat.

If the conjuncts in (4) are thought of as parallel-asserted, then (4) is a contradiction, not so if (4) is asserted at the right sort of pace in non-parallel fashion. Call a non-parallel assertion a 'dynamical assertion'. So, a parallel assertion of (4) and a dynamical assertion of (4) have different intensions.

The fact that discourse fragments like (4) exist in natural language suggests a need for a dynamic two-dimensional semantics. Given length considerations I can only briefly sketch how such an approach might proceed. Consider:

(5)   $John_1$ is $now_1$ spotting $Susan_2$.

Following Irene Heim (1982), let us introduce the notion of a filing system, that is, a system that keeps track of variables, names, and descriptive material introduced by the discourse. Here is an illustration.
  Filing system F1:

  x, y, $t_1$
  Now $t_1$
  John x
  Susan y
  Spot (x, y)

Additions to the discourse give rise to a new system:

(6)   He$_1$ is now$_2$ walking over to her$_2$.

Filing system F2:

| x, y, t$_1$ | x, y, t$_2$ |
| Now t$_1$ | Now t$_2$ |
| John x | |
| Susan y | |
| Spot (x, y) ➜ | Walk over to (x, y) |

(7)   And is now$_3$ starting a conversation with her$_2$

Filing system F3:

| x, y, t$_1$ | x, y, t$_2$ | x, y, t$_3$ |
| Now t$_1$ | Now t$_2$ | Now t$_3$ |
| John x | | |
| Susan y | | |
| Spot (x, y) ➜ | Walk over to (x, y) ➜ | Start a conversation with (x, y) |

(8)   She$_2$ is now$_4$ talking to a man$_3$.

Filing system F4:

| x, y, t$_1$ | x, y, t$_2$ | x, y, t$_3$ | x, y, z, t$_4$ |
| Now t$_1$ | Now t$_2$ | Now t$_3$ | Now t$_4$ |
| John x | | | |
| Susan y | | | |
| Man z | | | |
| Spot (x, y) ➜ | Walk over to (x, y) ➜ | Start a conv with (x, y) ➜ | Talk to (y, z) |

(9)   Now$_5$ he$_1$ is talking to the man$_3$ she$_2$ talked to just a moment ago$_4$

Filing system F5:

| x, y, t$_1$ | x, y, t$_2$ | x, y, t$_3$ | x, y, z, t$_4$ | x, y, z, t$_5$ |
| Now t$_1$ | Now t$_2$ | Now t$_3$ | Now t$_4$ | Now t$_5$ |
| John x | | | | |
| Susan y | | | | |
| Man z | | | | |
| Spot (x, y) ➜ | Walk over to (x, y) ➜ | Start a conv with (x, y) ➜ | Talk to (y, z) ➜ | Talk to (x, z) |

We can introduce a notion of truth of files as follows. Given an understanding of scenarios as centered possible worlds, we can take 1-models to be pairs of a domain D of actual individuals, some of which serve as a center and an interpretation function I.

$$M = <D, I>$$

The 1-interpretation function I maps the non-indexical variables (i.e., discourse referents) of file F to members of D, indexical variables of F to the center of D, and the descriptive material and names (i.e., predicate nominals) of F to properties or relations (or sets of n-tuples) on D. One set of assignments, $i^{@1}$, contains as an element the distinguished interpretations: the actual sets of assignments of extensions to the expressions (or the set of actual centered worlds). Let a 1-assignment A in a model M $=$ <D, I> be a mapping of non-indexical variables onto elements of D, and indexical variables onto the centered elements of D. We can then say that assignment A verifies filing system F in M if there is an extension E of A such that the elements satisfy the descriptive material and names at the scenario. A 1-information state is a space of scenarios (interpretations) with the same filing system. A dynamic 1-intension is a sequence of 1-information states. We can then say that discourse fragments express dynamic 1-intensions which are sequences of spaces of scenarios that share a filing system. If we introduce a designated sequence of scenarios, we can then say that a dynamic 1-intension is true at a designated sequence of scenarios just in case each scenario in the designated sequence of scenarios is in the space of scenarios (or interpretations) with the same filing system as the designated scenario.

A different model is needed to model dynamic 2-intensions. A 2-model is a pair of an uncentered domain of actual individuals and an interpretation function. The 2-interpretation function I maps the indexical and non-indexical variables and the associated names (if any) of file F to members of D, and the descriptive material of file F to properties or relations (or sets of n-tuples) on D. One assignment, $i^{@2}$, is the distinguished interpretation, the actual assignment of extensions to the expressions (or the actual world). Let an assignment A in a model M $=$ <D, I> be a mapping of variables and associated names (if any) onto elements of D. We can then say that assignment A verifies filing system F in M if there is an extension E of A such that the elements satisfy the descriptive material at the scenario.

A 2-information state is a space of worlds with the same filing system. A dynamic 2-intension is a sequence of 2-information states. A dynamic 2-intension is true at a distinguished sequence of worlds just in case each world in the designated sequence of worlds is in the space of worlds with the same filing system as the designated world.

We can give the following validation conditions for universal operators:

$\Box^h$, $\Box^h \Phi$ is true just in case at every h-admissible interpretation i, i assigns true to $\Phi$.

So, 'It is metaphysically necessary that $\Phi$' is true iff at every 2-interpretation i, i assigns **T** to $\Phi$, and 'It is a priori that $\Phi$' is true iff at every 1-interpretation i, i assigns **T** to $\Phi$. To illustrate consider (10) and (11).

(10)  The brightest heavenly object is now$_1$ Hesperus$_1$, and the brightest heavenly object is now$_2$ Phosphorus$_2$, and Hesperus$_1$ is identical to Phosphorus$_2$.

(11)  It is deeply epistemically possible that: the brightest heavenly object is now$_1$ Hesperus$_1$, and that the brightest heavenly object is now$_2$ Phosphorus$_2$, and that Hesperus$_1$ is not identical to Phosphorus$_2$.

(10) is true iff the dynamic 2-intension it expresses has the truth-value true at the designated sequence of worlds. So, (10) is true if the brightest heavenly object is Hesperus at the worlds that assign the utterance time to the variable associated with 'now$_1$', and the brightest heavenly object is Phosphorus at a designated world that assigns the utterance time to the variable associated with 'now$_2$', and Hesperus is identical to Phosphorus. (11) is true iff there is a sequence of scenarios at which the dynamic 1-intension of the embedded clause is true. This is so if the brightest heavenly object is the brightest object in the evening sky at the scenarios that assign the time in the center to the variable associated with 'now$_1$', and the brightest heavenly object is the brightest object in the morning sky at the scenarios that assign the time in the center to the variable associated with 'now$_2$', and the brightest object in the evening sky in scenarios in the first set is not identical to the brightest object in the morning sky in the scenarios in the second set.

## 6.6  Conclusion

As we have seen, in Kaplan's original framework, context-sensitive expressions are expressions with a variable character – a linguistic meaning that determines different contents relative to different contextual parameters. This approach to context-sensitivity has much to recommend it but it fails to capture a plausible connection between context-sensitivity, broadly understood, and cognitive informativeness. The two phenomena are not unrelated. Cognitively informative necessities arguably contain what David Chalmers calls "twin-earthable expressions," linguistic strings that have twin tokens with a different content. Twin-earthable expressions are broadly context-sensitive. When I use 'water', the term picks out $H_2O$. When my twin on Twin-Earth uses 'water', it picks out XYZ. On the assumption that we speak the same language, an assumption which is consistent with the definition of *Twin-Earthability*, 'water' has a variable character and hence is broadly context-sensitive. But if 'water' is context-sensitive, we have a partial explanation of the cognitive significance of sentences such as 'water is $H_2O$'. The sentence, relative to my context, expresses a proposition of the form 'a = a', yet owing to my cognitive limitations I may not know what content is determined by the character of 'water' at my location. Being told that the character of 'water' determines $H_2O$ is informative for me. Thus, if we keep fixed the language spoken, there is a tight connection between twin-earthability and cognitive informativeness.

I have assessed three types of two-dimensional semantic frameworks in terms of how well they account for the connection between cognitive significance and the broader notion of context-sensitivity. One is a diagonalized character approach that takes names and kind terms to have a constant character but allows for the possibility that a diagonal proposition that functions much like a variable character has some explanatory power with respect to the phenomenon of cognitive informativeness. A second approach is to widen the range of expressions that have a variable character to include various noun phrases and descriptions. A third approach is to treat expressions as having epistemic meaning in addition to semantic meaning. I argued that while all three approaches go some way toward explaining the connections between context-sensitivity and cognitive informativeness, the non-epistemic approaches seem to fall short of offering a fully adequate account of cognitively informative necessities and informative contingencies. I concluded by pondering a new problem for the epistemic approaches posed by indexicals in dynamic discourses and sketched a solution.

# 7

# Contextualism
## Some varieties

François Recanati

A number of distinct (though related) issues are raised in the debate over Contextualism. My aim in this chapter is to disentangle them, so as to get a clearer view of the positions available (where a 'position' consists of a particular take on each of the relevant issues simultaneously). The position I defend will be apparent at the end of the chapter.

## 7.1 The modularity issue

According to a view which used to be standard, and which, for reasons that will soon emerge, I call the modular view, knowledge of a language, and especially semantic knowledge or *semantic competence*, enables language users to ascribe truth conditions to arbitrary sentences of that language. To be sure, when a sentence is context-sensitive (as most sentences are), it only carries truth conditions 'with respect to context'; so knowledge of the context is required in addition to knowledge of the language. But (according to the view in question) the context at issue involves only limited aspects of the situation of utterance: who speaks, when, where, to whom and so forth. Given a context thus understood, the rules of the language – e.g. the rule that 'I' refers to the speaker – suffice to determine the truth-conditional contribution of context-sensitive expressions. There is no need to appeal, in addition, to *pragmatic competence*. That is the gist of the modular view.

By 'pragmatic competence', I mean the ability to understand *what the speaker means* by his or her utterance. As Grice emphasised, speaker's meaning is a matter of intentions: what someone means is what he or she overtly intends – or, as Grice says, 'M-intends' – to get across through his or her

The research leading to this paper has received funding from the European Research Council under the European Community's Seventh Framework Programme (FP7/2007–2013) / ERC grant agreement n 229 441 – CCC.

utterance. Communication succeeds when the M-intentions of the speaker are recognised by the hearer. Pragmatic competence is needed to determine *what the speaker means* on the basis of *what she says*; but what the speaker says is supposed to be autonomously determined by the semantics (with respect to context), irrespective of the speaker's beliefs and intentions. So the modular story goes.

On this conception, semantics and pragmatics are insulated from each other. Pragmatics takes as input the output of semantics, but they do not mix, and in particular, pragmatic processes do not interfere with the process of semantic composition which outputs the truth conditions.[1] This makes sense if one construes semantic competence and pragmatic competence as belonging to two distinct 'modules' (Borg 2004: chapter 2) – hence my name for the view.[2] Semantic competence belongs to the language faculty, Borg says; it is an aspect of our 'knowledge of language'. Pragmatic competence has more to do with the so-called 'theory of mind', that faculty in virtue of which human subjects are able to explain other people's behaviour by ascribing intentions to them and reading their mind.

The modular picture I have just described has started to lose grip in recent years. Nearly everybody nowadays acknowledges the fact that the reference of indexicals and, more generally, the semantic value of context-sensitive expressions cannot be determined without appealing to full-fledged pragmatic factors (e.g. speaker's intentions). The semantic value of a context-sensitive expression varies from occurrence to occurrence, yet it often varies not as a function of some objective feature of the context but as a function of *what the speaker means*. Pragmatic competence, therefore, is required not only to determine what the speaker means on the basis of what she says, but also to determine what is said in the first place. That means that we have to give up the modular view, and accept that pragmatics and semantics *do* mix in fixing truth-conditional content.

Of course, if one wants to maintain a semantics pure of pragmatic intrusion, one can, but then one has to construe the goal of semantics differently than it is on the standard conception. Pure semantics will no longer deliver truth conditions, but it will deliver, say, conditional truth conditions, or schemata, or characters, or propositional radicals, or whatever. To get full-blown truth-conditional content, pragmatics will be needed. This non-modular approach to truth-conditional content is one of the key ingredients of contemporary Contextualism.

## 7.2   The 'extent of context-sensitivity' issue

According to most contemporary theorists, context-sensitivity is pervasive in natural language. In addition to the obvious indexicals, many expressions turn out to be context-sensitive in one way or another. This covers two types of case. There are expressions which display hidden indexicality in that, when properly analysed, they turn out to behave very much like standard indexicals, or to contain hidden constituents which do; and there are expressions which display other forms of context-sensitivity. In any case, we don't know in advance whether a given expression is, or is not, context-sensitive: it is an empirical question, to be resolved through linguistic analysis. So we must reject a certain presumption which was still prevalent twenty years ago and which we may call the 'literalist presumption'.

To introduce the literalist presumption, let us start from the following (uncontroversial) premiss:

- There is a 'basic set' of expressions whose content is known to depend upon the context in a systematic manner: the indexicals.

The presumption which the pervasiveness of context-sensitivity leads us to reject can now be stated as follows:

- **Literalist presumption**: expressions *not* in the basic set are (by default) assumed to be context-*in*sensitive.

The literalist presumption is implicitly at work in a number of fallacious arguments using Grice's 'Modified Occam's Razor', or an equivalent principle of parsimony, to demonstrate that a semantic analysis in terms of conversational implicature is preferable to an account in terms of truth-conditional content proper (Recanati 1994, 2004a: 155–8). Classic examples involve the use of Modified Occam's Razor against Strawson's (1952) view of the contextually varying truth-conditional contributions of 'and', or against Donnellan's view of the contextually varying truth-conditional contributions of definite descriptions. In each case, the possibility that the relevant expression (which seems to carry different contents in different contexts) might be context-sensitive even though it does not belong to the basic set is ignored, in virtue of the literalist presumption, and the argument proceeds as if the only options available to account for the data were lexical ambiguity on the one hand and conversational implicature on the other hand (with Modified Occam's Razor being used to rule out the former option).

Rejection of the literalist presumption is another key ingredient in contemporary Contextualism. It corresponds to a stance I dubbed 'Methodological Contextualism' (Recanati 1994). According to Methodological Contextualism, we don't know in advance which expressions are context-sensitive and which aren't. For all we know, *every expression might be context-sensitive*. Here the universal quantifier takes scope over the epistemic modal, so what generalises is the *possibility* of context-sensitivity. For every expression *e* – including 'and' or definite descriptions – it may be that *e* is context-sensitive and contributes different contents in different contexts (even though *e* is not ambiguous). As a result, we need to draw a *general* distinction between the linguistic meaning of an expression and its contribution to propositional content, while allowing for special cases in which they will be identical, instead of doing the opposite (i.e. equating conventional meaning and propositional contribution, while allowing for exceptions – the expressions in the 'basic set').

Methodological Contextualism goes together with the view that context-sensitivity is a pervasive phenomenon in natural language. Not everybody accepts this view, however. The so-called 'semantic minimalists' (e.g. Cappelen and Lepore 2005a) believe that context-sensitivity is a *very limited phenomenon*, corresponding roughly to expressions in the basic set, so they don't feel compelled to reject the literalist presumption.

## 7.3  Does context-sensitivity generalise?

The two contextualist ingredients I have described so far correspond to views that are widely shared among contemporary theorists. Those who still believe in modularity and are faithful to the literalist presumption are a rather small minority (see Chapter 25 for more on their view). But there is another minority, at the other end of the spectrum: the *radical* contextualists. What characterises their view is the *generalisation* of context-sensitivity.[3]

There are several possible arguments for the generalisation of context-sensitivity. First, one should distinguish the claim that context-sensitivity generalises at the sentential level from the much stronger claim that it generalises at the constituent or the lexical level. One generalises context-sensitivity at the sentential level if one holds that *the truth conditions of a sentence* always depend upon the context (so that there are no 'eternal sentences'). Here is an example of an argument for that conclusion:

(a)   A successful sentence (i.e. a sentence that succeeds in expressing a proposition) expresses either a singular proposition or a general proposition.

(b)   If a sentence expresses a singular proposition, it does so in a context-sensitive manner because (i) a sentence expresses a singular proposition only if it contains a successful referring expression (i.e. an expression which succeeds in referring), and (ii) reference is inherently context-sensitive. (That is so because an expression-token only refers to some object in virtue of *contextual relations* between the token and the object.[4])

(c)   If a sentence expresses a general proposition, it does so in a context-sensitive manner because (i) a sentence expresses a general proposition only if it contains a (successful) quantificational expression, and (ii) quantification is inherently context-sensitive. (That is so because the domain of quantification depends upon the context. An expression succeeds in quantifying only if the context supplies an appropriate domain of quantification.)

(d)   Conclusion: Whenever a sentence expresses a proposition, it does so in a context-sensitive manner.

The argument I have just presented relies on many controversial assumptions regarding, *inter alia*, the nature of reference, the semantics/

meta-semantics distinction, the semantic analysis of plurals, proper names and definite descriptions, quantifier domain restriction, and so on and so forth. It is not my intention to go into these thorny issues here, in order to evaluate the argument. Rather, I will focus on arguments for the generalisation of context-sensitivity at the level of sentential constituents, or at the lexical level, rather than at the sentential level. As I already suggested, the claim that context-sensitivity generalises at the constituent or lexical level is much stronger than the claim that it generalises at the sentential level. What we are now considering is the possibility that *every expression* (not just every sentence) might be context-sensitive. This is a very radical form of Contextualism indeed.

We have already encountered the claim that 'every expression might be context-sensitive' in the context of Methodological Contextualism, but then the universal quantifier 'every expression' took scope over the epistemic modal. What Methodological Contextualism meant to generalise to every expression was only the *possibility* of its being context-sensitive. In the context of Radical Contextualism, the claim that 'every expression might be context-sensitive' is understood differently: the modal now scopes over the universal quantifier. The possibility that is being considered is the possibility that, for every expression *e*, *e is* context-sensitive. Here what tentatively generalises is (actual) context-sensitivity, not the possibility of context-sensitivity.

In what follows I will present two types of argument for the generalisation of context-sensitivity at the lexical or constituent level. One such argument involves the phenomenon of pragmatic modulation. It is of special importance and will be discussed in sections 7.5 and 7.6. Other arguments, to which I now turn, are based on considerations from lexical semantics.

## 7.4  Arguments from lexical semantics

What is the meaning of a word? Let us assume that utterances express 'propositions' or 'thoughts', and that these propositions/thoughts are made out of, or can be analysed into, certain building blocks or constituents, to be called *senses*. The standard assumption regarding word meaning is that *the conventions of the language associate expressions with senses*. What an expression contributes, when it is used (together with other expressions) in making a complete utterance, is supposed to be the sense which it independently possesses in virtue of the conventions of the language. Indexicals (and context-sensitive expressions more generally) are considered an exception: *their* sense is not to be equated with their linguistic meaning, but depends upon the context. Now Radical Contextualism rejects the very idea that the conventions of the language associate expressions with full-fledged senses. It generalises the distinction between the lexical meaning of an expression and its sense (or 'content' or 'propositional contribution'), which is said to depend upon the context.

Putnam's ideas about the lexical semantics of nouns can be seen as a fore-runner of Radical Contextualism. Putnam criticises the Fregean idea that the meaning of a noun is a (context-independent) sense which determines the noun's reference (i.e. its extension). In many cases, Putnam points out, we start with the reference: the noun is associated with contextually given exemplars known to fall into the extension of the noun, or, on a more refined picture, with a *stereotype* used to identify the exemplars to be found in one's local environment. What determines the extension of the noun is not the lexically given stereotype, however, but a certain relation $R$ of similarity to the local exemplars. So the extension-determining sense of an expression is context-dependent on two counts: it depends upon the contextually given exemplars (e.g. whether the transparent, thirst-quenching liquid around us is $H_2O$ or XYZ), and it depends upon the relation $R$, which itself may vary according to the interests of the conversational participants (Putnam 1975: 238–9). The sense thus determined in context is utterly different from the lexical meaning of the noun, which Putnam describes as a 'vector' consisting of, *inter alia*, a 'semantic marker' (e.g. *liquid*) and the exemplar-fixing stereotype.

Putnam's story is meant to apply to the nouns that are used to talk about things in the environment, and which we learn by getting acquainted with the things they are used to talk about. Not merely natural-kind terms like 'water', but also, he says, nouns for artefacts like 'pencil'. It could presumably be extended to other categories of lexical items, such as verbs and adjectives. On a Putnamian semantics, context-sensitivity generalises to all the words which have a 'referential' dimension and directly connect up with aspects of the world around us. That is arguably the core of the language.

Another class of expressions which might claim to be 'the core of the language', though for totally different reasons, are the *most frequently used* expressions – light verbs (e.g. *get, have, take*), prepositions and the like. Such expressions exhibit a high degree of polysemy, and this raises a problem for lexical semantics. What do such words mean? A number of scholars believe their meaning is schematic and has to be fleshed out on any particular use. This suggests that, perhaps, their conventional meaning is not a full-fledged sense. Can one argue that they are *ambiguous* between a number of distinct senses? That is not obvious because it does not seem that there is a *discrete* list of such senses available but, rather, a continuum of possible senses to which one can creatively add in an open-ended manner. That is not to say that the meaning of such an expression reduces to an abstract schema: the expression is undoubtedly *also* associated in memory with conventional ways of using it in collocations with (more or less) determinate senses. All this – the abstract schema or schemata, the collocations, the senses – arguably goes into the linguistic meaning of the expression, which starts looking rather messy. On such a view, the meaning of an expression does not have the right 'format' to be what the expression contributes to propositional content.[5] In other words, linguistic meanings are not senses (though they may involve senses, *inter alia*).

The two views of lexical semantics I have just mentioned may well be wrong, of course. When it comes to lexical semantics, nearly everything is up for grabs. That, however, is precisely the point. As theorists, we have an idea what senses are, i.e. what words contribute when we speak. We know, more or less, how to model that. But we know very little about what words themselves mean and what relation there is between word meaning and contributed sense. In view of the limits of our knowledge, it is reasonable to give up the simplifying assumption that linguistic meanings *are* senses, in order at least to start making serious enquiries in that area.

If we give up that simplifying assumption, we are left with the idea that lexical meaning plays some role in determining the sense which is an expression's contribution to the thought expressed. This idea can be expressed by saying that the sense of an expression is a function of the lexical meaning of that expression and some factor *x*, where '*x*' is whatever, in addition to lexical meaning, is needed to determine sense.[6] If, as seems very likely, '*x*' includes the *context* in which the expression is tokened (and in particular the most important among contextual factors: what one is talking about), then we get a radical form of Contextualism that 'generalises indexicality'.

## 7.5 Pragmatic modulation

The arguments from lexical semantics I have just mentioned support Radical Contextualism because they cast doubt on the idea that an expression's contribution to truth-conditional content (its sense) is fixed by the rules of the language independent of context. Most expressions are treated as indexical-like in that their semantic content depends upon the context somehow. But this does not (yet) mean that the semantic contribution of *every* expression is context-dependent. The next argument for Radical Contextualism leads to that stronger conclusion, however. I call it the argument from pragmatic modulation.

The argument from pragmatic modulation is independent of the arguments from lexical semantics, and it can be put forward even if we *grant* the assumption which the arguments from lexical semantics lead us to doubt: that the conventions of the language directly associate expressions with full-fledged senses.[7] Let us, indeed, grant that assumption. One can still deny that the senses which – on this view – are the meanings of expressions are also what these expressions contribute when they are used (together with other expressions) in making a complete utterance. Because of pragmatic modulation, an expression may, but *need not*, contribute its sense – i.e. the sense it independently possesses in virtue of the conventions of the language (assuming for the sake of argument that it possesses such a sense); it may also contribute an indefinite number of *other* senses resulting from modulation operations (e.g. free enrichment, predicate transfer, sense-extension etc.) applied to the proprietary sense.

For example, a sentence like (1) has several readings.

(1)    There is a lion in the middle of the piazza.

On one reading 'lion' is given a non-literal interpretation and means something like 'statue of a lion'. On that reading (1) may be true even if, literally, there is no lion in the middle of the piazza (but only a statue of a lion). Or consider (2).

(2)    The ATM swallowed my credit card.

This can be given a literal reading, if we imagine a context à la Putnam in which ATMs turn out to be living organisms. But the sentence can also and typically will be interpreted non-literally. In an ordinary context, 'swallow' will be given an *extended sense*, corresponding to what ATMs sometimes do with credit cards (something which, indeed, resembles swallowing). The sentence may be true, on such a reading, even though no real swallowing takes place. In a less ordinary context in which there is a person disguised as an ATM, the predicate 'ATM' in the description will be given a non-literal reading: through 'predicate transfer' (Nunberg 1995), it will acquire the meaning '*person disguised as* an ATM' (just as 'lion' acquires the meaning '*statue of* a lion' in the previous example). The sentence may well be true, on that interpretation, even though no real ATM swallows anything, provided the person disguised as an ATM does swallow the credit card.[8]

Accepting pragmatic modulation (here, the process mapping the literal meaning of 'lion' or 'ATM' to the relevant representational reading, or the meaning of 'swallow' to its extended reading) as a possible determinant of truth-conditional content leads to a radical form of Contextualism, because modulation itself is context-sensitive: *whether or not* modulation comes into play, and if it does, *which* modulation operation takes place, is a matter of context. It follows that what an expression actually contributes to the thought expressed by the utterance in which it occurs is *always* a matter of context.

Of course, not everybody accepts that pragmatic modulation affects the truth-conditional content of an utterance. On the currently dominant picture, pragmatics comes into play in the determination of truth-conditional content but does so *only when* the semantic rules of the language prescribe it (as when an indexical demands a contextual value). On this view the only truth-conditional role of pragmatics corresponds to what I have called 'saturation' (in contrast to 'modulation'). Saturation is a pragmatic process of contextual value-assignment that is triggered (and made obligatory) by something in the sentence itself, namely the linguistic expression to which a value is contextually assigned. For example, if the speaker uses a demonstrative pronoun and says 'She is cute', the hearer must determine who the speaker means by 'she' in order to fix the utterance's truth-conditional content. The expression itself acts as a variable in need of contextual instantiation. So pragmatic competence comes into play, but it does so under the guidance of the linguistic material: the pragmatic process of saturation is a 'bottom-up' process in the sense that it is signal-driven, not context-driven. In contrast, pragmatic modulation is a 'top-down' or context-driven process, i.e. a pragmatic process which is not triggered by an expression in the sentence but takes place for purely pragmatic reasons – in order to make sense of what the speaker is saying. In other words, it is a 'free' pragmatic process – free because it is not mandated by the linguistic material but responds to wholly pragmatic considerations. That is clearly the case for the pragmatic processes through which an expression is given a non-literal interpretation: we interpret an expression non-literally in order to make sense of the speech act, not because this is dictated by the linguistic materials in virtue of the rules of the language.

The dominant view is that the only pragmatic process that can affect truth-conditional content is saturation. No 'top-down' or free pragmatic process can affect truth-conditions – such a process can only affect what the speaker means (but not what she says). As Stanley puts it, 'all truth-conditional context-dependence results from fixing the values of contextually sensitive elements in the real structure of natural language sentences' (Stanley 2000: 392). Or, as King and Stanley put it, there can only be 'weak' pragmatic effects on truth-conditional content. They define a weak pragmatic effect as follows:

> A weak pragmatic effect on what is communicated by an utterance is a case in which context (including speaker intentions) determines interpretation of a lexical item *in accord with the standing meaning of that lexical item*. A strong pragmatic effect on what is communicated is a contextual effect on what is communicated that is not merely pragmatic in the weak sense. (King and Stanley 2005: 118–19; emphasis mine)

Radical Contextualism rejects the view that only weak pragmatic effects can affect what is said. It holds that truth-conditional content may be affected not only by saturation (as when an indexical is assigned a contextual value) but also by *free* pragmatic processes of modulation. In (1) the non-literal reading of 'lion' arguably results from a pragmatic operation that is not dictated by the lexical item *lion* in virtue of its standing meaning. There is no slot to be filled, no free variable or context-sensitive element whose value is to be fixed, or anything of the sort. Moreover, nothing (except the desire to make sense of the speaker, in a context in which the literal reading is unlikely) prevents the sentence from being interpreted literally. The pragmatic effect here looks like a strong pragmatic effect, yet it affects truth-conditional content. Since the semantic content of any expression can be pragmatically modulated in this way, what an expression actually contributes depends upon the context.

## 7.6  Why resist Radical Contextualism?

I have presented five distinct issues relevant to the overall debate between Contextualism and Literalism. On each issue there are two sides: the contextualist side and the literalist side.

*Modularity*. Is pragmatic competence involved in the determination of truth-conditional content? Contextualism: Yes. Literalism: No.

*Extent of context-sensitivity*. Is context-sensitivity pervasive in natural language? Contextualism: Yes. Literalism: No.

*Generalisation of context-sensitivity (1)*. Is it true that there are no eternal sentences, i.e. no sentence which expresses a proposition independent of context? Contextualism: Yes. Literalism: No.

*Generalisation of context-sensitivity (2)*. Are all/most expressions like indexicals in that their lexical meaning does not add up to a full-fledged sense? Contextualism: Yes. Literalism: No.

*Generalisation of context-sensitivity (3)*. Does pragmatic modulation affect truth-conditional content? Contextualism: Yes. Literalism: No.

On the first two issues (the modularity issue, and the extent of context-sensitivity issue) Contextualism wins in the sense that it is the dominant position. The role of a speaker's intentions and pragmatic competence in fixing contextual values for indexicals etc. is widely acknowledged, as is the pervasiveness of context-sensitivity in natural language. With respect to the 'generalisation of context-sensivity' issues, however, it is the other way round: Literalism wins, sociologically speaking. There is widespread resistance to the most radical forms of Contextualism – those which generalise context-sensitivity. Why?

In this section, I will discuss some of the reasons one might have for resisting the generalisation of context-sensitivity.[9] I will argue that they do not carry much weight. This will bring a *sixth* issue to the fore – the systematicity issue, to which the final section of this chapter will be devoted.

Let us start with the arguments from lexical semantics. Why not simply accept them? I submit that the main source of resistance to the idea that a word's lexical meaning does not add up to a full-fledged sense is the following. Most semanticists worry more about compositional semantics than about lexical semantics, so they make their lives simpler by uncritically accepting the simplifying assumption (inherited from our elders) that lexical meanings are senses. In this way we don't have to care about how senses are generated – we take them simply as *given*. Admittedly, this is an acceptable idealisation at a certain stage in the development of semantics; but as soon as one gets interested in the foundations of lexical semantics, one should start by lifting the simplifying assumption in order at least to consider the issue with an open mind.

The resistance to pragmatic modulation is a more serious matter. Here it seems that there are substantive reasons to be suspicious of Radical Contextualism. The first reason is this. If free pragmatic processes are allowed to affect semantic content, semantic content leaps out of control – it is no longer determined by the rules of the language but varies freely, à la Humpty Dumpty. But then, how can we account for the success of communication? Communication (content sharing) becomes a miracle since there is nothing to ensure that communicators and their addressees will converge on the same content. Now communication *is* possible (it takes place all the time), and there is no miracle. It follows that we should give up the view that free pragmatic processes play a role in the determination of semantic content (Cappelen and Lepore 2005a: chapter 8).

This argument fails, I believe, because the problem it raises is a problem for everybody, as soon as one gives up the modular view. *Whenever* the semantic value of a linguistic expression must be pragmatically inferred, the question arises, what guarantees that the hearer will be able to latch on to the exact same semantic value as the speaker? Whether the pragmatic process at stake is saturation or modulation is irrelevant as far as this issue is concerned, so the argument fails as an argument specifically intended to cast doubt on pragmatic modulation.[10]

Another argument against pragmatic modulation as a possible determinant of semantic content can be put as follows. 'What is said', the truth-conditional content of an utterance, is what is *literally* said, and that – by definition – has to be determined by the conventions of the language. Pragmatics can enter the picture, provided its role is to assign a contextual value to a lexical item in a bottom-up manner, i.e. in accord with (and under the guidance of) the conventional meaning of that context-sensitive item. In contrast, strong pragmatic effects achieved in order to make sense of the speech act without being linguistically mandated take us into the realm of speaker's meaning, away from literal meaning.

Insofar as this argument is based upon a certain understanding of the phrase 'what is said' (or 'what is literally said'), it is *not* substantive, but verbal. There is no doubt that one can *define* 'what is said' in such a way that only weak pragmatic effects can affect what is said. But what the advocate of pragmatic modulation means by 'what is said' corresponds to the *intuitive truth-conditional content* of the utterance.[11] According to the contextualist side in the debate, the intuitive truth conditions of an utterance of (1) or (2) *are* affected by free pragmatic processes. Assuming this is true, this does not prevent us from defining another notion of what is said, conforming to literalist standards. Let 'what is said$_{min}$' be the proposition expressed by an utterance when strong pragmatic effects have been discounted (the so-called 'minimal proposition'), and let 'what is said$_{int}$' correspond to the intuitive truth conditions of the utterance. According to the contextualist view under discussion, what is said$_{int}$ may be affected by top-down pragmatic processes. This is compatible with the claim that only weak pragmatic effects can affect what is said$_{min}$. So that claim in no way counters the idea that pragmatic modulation affects the (intuitive) truth-conditional content of utterances.

According to yet another argument, if we accept the view that pragmatic modulation affects semantic content, we blur the semantics/pragmatics distinction to the point where there no longer is any difference between what is said and what is meant; so – assuming this distinction is essential – we should reject the view that pragmatic modulation affects truth-conditional content. I find this argument unconvincing, because acknowledging the effects of pragmatic modulation on truth-conditional content (what is said$_{int}$) in no way prevents one from distinguishing what is said$_{int}$ from other things that are conveyed by an utterance without belonging to its intuitive truth-conditional content, e.g. the particularised conversational implicatures (Grice 1989) or the effects achieved through 'staging' (Clark H. 1996). In other words, we can distinguish between 'primary' pragmatic processes, such as modulation, and 'secondary' pragmatic processes that do not contribute to what is said$_{int}$ (Recanati 1989, 2004a). So we do not lose the distinction between what is said and what is meant.

Conclusion: the three arguments against pragmatic modulation I have extracted from the literature and presented in this section are no good.[12] However, the most important argument against pragmatic modulation is, by far, the systematicity argument, which I have not yet introduced. That argument, which I take to be the main source of resistance to Radical Contextualism, deserves separate discussion since it raises a new issue relevant to the overall debate.

## 7.7  The systematicity issue

Many theorists argue as follows. If Radical Contextualism is true, the project of constructing a systematic truth-conditional semantics for natural language is doomed to failure. We should therefore reject Radical Contextualism, since it leads to scepticism. Or rather, we should reject that ingredient which is incompatible with the project of constructing a systematic truth-conditional semantics. That is not the generalisation of indexicality prompted by the lexical semantics considerations; for, if indexicality is compatible with formal semantics, generalised indexicality should be compatible with it, too. The problem, rather, comes from the acceptance of pragmatic modulation as a determinant of semantic content. That is what we should reject.

Of course, one has to say *why* the acceptance of pragmatic modulation as a determinant of semantic content is incompatible with the project of building a systematic semantics. Here is a first sketch of an argument for that conclusion.

In contrast to the contextual assignment of values to indexicals, modulation is not driven by the linguistic meaning of words. Nothing in the linguistic meaning of the words whose sense is modulated tells us that modulation ought to take place. Modulation takes place purely as a matter of context, of 'pragmatics'; what drives it is the urge to make sense of what the speaker is saying. So modulation *is* unsystematic. If we allow it as a determinant of semantic content, we make it impossible to construct a systematic theory of semantic content.

I grant the objector that modulation is unsystematic. Still, I think it is easy to make room for it within a systematic semantics.[13] In general, nothing prevents unsystematic factors from being handled systematically, by being assigned their proper place in the theory. In the case at hand, we can define a function *mod* taking as argument an expression *e* and the context *c* in which it occurs: the value of *mod* is the particular modulation function that is contextually salient/relevant/appropriate for the interpretation of that expression in that context. If no modulation is contextually appropriate and the expression receives its literal interpretation, the value of *mod* will be the identity function. In this framework, we can distinguish between the *literal* sense of a simple expression *e*, namely its semantic interpretation $I(e)$, and the *modulated* sense $M(e)_c$ carried by an occurrence of *e* in context *c*. The modulated sense of an expression *e* (in context *c*) results from applying the contextually appropriate modulation function *mod* $(e, c)$ to its semantic interpretation $I(e)$:

$$M(e)_c = mod\,(e, c)(I(e))$$

So far, this is very standard: in distinguishing $I(e)$ from $M(e)_c$ we are just appealing to the traditional semantics/pragmatics distinction. What is *not* standard is the claim that **the semantic interpretation of a *complex* expression (e.g. a sentence) is a function of the *modulated senses* of its parts and the way they are put together** (Recanati 2010: chapter 1). This is what examples like (1) and (2) suggest if we take at face value the effects of modulation on truth-conditional content which they seem to display. On the resulting view the semantic process of composition and the pragmatic process of sense modulation are intertwined. For simple expressions, their semantic interpretation is their literal sense, but *for complex expressions pragmatic modulation is allowed to enter into the determination of semantic content*. This is non-standard, for sure, but there is nothing unsystematic about this view.

   The systematicity objection can be understood differently, however. What is not systematic enough, according to the objection, is not so much the radical contextualist's *theory* of utterance interpretation, but utterance interpretation itself (what the theory is about) as construed by the radical contextualist. We have seen that, in the contextualist framework with its 'free' pragmatic processes, interpretation (content recovery) is no longer driven by the linguistic material. In introducing modulation (in contrast to saturation), I said that in saturation 'pragmatic competence comes into play, but does so under the guidance of the linguistic material', whereas modulation 'is not triggered by an expression in the sentence but takes place for purely pragmatic reasons – in order to make sense of what the speaker is saying'. This suggests that, for a radical contextualist, utterance interpretation is pragmatic through and through and does not significantly differ from 'the kind [of interpretation] involved in interpreting kicks under the table and taps on the shoulder' (Stanley 2000: 396): it is not the systematic affair which formal semanticists have claimed it to be. In this way, we reach the conclusion that Radical Contextualism is incompatible with the programme of formal semantics.

Thus understood, I think the objection is confused. Even though free pragmatic processes, i.e. pragmatic processes that are not mandated by the standing meaning of any expression in the sentence, are allowed to enter into the determination of truth-conditional content, still, in the framework I have sketched, *they come into the picture as part of the compositional machinery*. Semantic interpretation remains *grammar-driven* even if, in the course of semantic interpretation, pragmatics is appealed to not only to assign contextual values to indexicals and free variables but also to freely modulate the senses of the constituents in a top-down manner. Semantic interpretation is *still* a matter of determining the sense of the whole as a function of the (possibly modulated) senses of the parts and the way they are put together.

If what I have just said is right, the systematicity issue is orthogonal to the other issues I discussed as relevant to the Contextualism/Literalism debate. The systematicity issue can be formulated thus:

> *Systematicity.* Is semantic interpretation a matter of holistic guesswork (like the interpretation of kicks under the table), rather than an algorithmic, grammar-driven process as formal semanticists have claimed? Contextualism: Yes. Literalism: No.

On that issue I am happy to part company with the most radical contextualists – the 'sceptics' who would go for the holistic guesswork answer (assuming they exist, which I doubt). Like Stanley and the formal semanticists, I maintain that semantic interpretation is grammar-driven. But this issue is orthogonal to the others! So, without contradicting what I have just said, I can still hold that a good deal of holistic guesswork comes into play in semantic interpretation, e.g. in order to fix the values of context-sensitive elements or to pick the right modulation functions. Both in the case of saturation and in the case of modulation – the two types of contextual process that play a part in the determination of truth-conditional content – one has to rely heavily on pragmatic competence. Accepting this point means that one endorses a quite radical form of Contextualism; but this is compatible with maintaining that semantic interpretation is grammar-driven and proceeds recursively. I conclude that there is no reason to take one's adherence to the project of building a systematic semantics to prevent one from being a contextualist with respect to any of the issues talked about earlier.

Of course, a radical contextualist will be prone to set *limits* to systematicity in semantics; but that is not the same thing as getting rid of systematicity altogether. As I said, when it comes to fixing the values of context-sensitive elements or to picking the right modulation functions, pragmatic competence takes over: formal semantics has nothing to say regarding the pragmatic mechanisms in play, and the hand-waving word 'salience' which semanticists like to use is only a placeholder. But these limitations put on semantics are nothing but the price to pay for giving up the modular view. We have to admit, once and for all, that (intuitive) truth-conditional content or 'what is said' is not something purely semantic – something that can be retrieved simply by exercising one's semantic competence. Pragmatic competence massively comes into the picture. To reach that conclusion, however, there is no need to consider anything fancier than deictic pronouns. In particular, there is no need to go into the 'generalisation of context-sensitivity' issues which have loomed large in our discussion of Radical Contextualism.

What I have just said shows that there is a continuum of positions with respect to systematicity. The more literalist one is, the stronger the form of systematicity one will be in a position to claim for semantics. This means that even a moderate contextualist – someone who (merely) gives up the modular view and accepts the pervasiveness of context-sensitivity – will have to set limits to systematic semantics. These limitations I think most language theorists currently accept. Radical contextualists who generalise context-sensitivity simply go a bit farther in the same direction, but, I insist, there is only a difference of degree between them and the moderate contextualists. (In this respect I agree with Cappelen and Lepore 2005a.) Radical Contextualism, therefore, is not a revolutionary position which threatens the programme of formal semantics, as many theorists have claimed. If revolution there is, it antedates Radical Contextualism and coincides with the advent of the moderate form of Contextualism which almost everybody embraces.

# 8

# The psychology of utterance processing

## Context vs salience

Rachel Giora

## 8.1 Introduction

Consider the cartoon in Figure 8.1,[1] which is an optimal innovation: it includes a novel stimulus intended to further activate coded, salient meanings, so that both the novel and the salient, though different, may interact and affect pleasurability (Giora, 2003; Giora *et al.*, 2004).

Put differently, this cartoon will be optimally innovative only to those familiar with the coded meanings it echoes (see e.g., the poster in Figure 8.2). The initiated audiences are thus invited to invoke a wide range of coded, salient meanings which might allow an insight into the ironic message of the cartoon. However, those not in the know will only have access to what is literally spelled out, superimposed on the pictorial background (in addition, of course, to the figurative title and the symbol of the crown). Indeed, if taken at face value, the cartoon will encourage people to get terrified and stop doing what they are doing on account of the nasty weather (referred to in the background). But the poster in Figure 8.2, if retrievable from memory, will bring to mind an altogether different meaning which this cartoon must be weighed against: the British mindset on the eve of World War II – the "British restraint and stiff upper lip."[2]

Additionally, one of Lance Corporal Jones's catchphrases in *Dad's Army* – the British sitcom about the Home Guard in the Second World War (Perry and Croft, 1968–1977) – might also spring to mind, echoing, via another irony, the mindset derided here:

(1)  Don't panic![3]

The title of the cartoon – *Spirit of the Blitz 2009* – allows another ironic turn of the screw, reminding us of the spirit of the blitz exercised by the people of

This paper was supported by a grant to the second author by THE ISRAEL SCIENCE FOUNDATION (grant No. 652/07). Thanks also go to Ran Abramson for the cartoons in Figures 8.1 and 8.2 and for example (1), and to Keith Allan and Kasia Jaszczolt for their very valuable comments.

Figure 8.1. *Spirit of the Blitz 2009*

Figure 8.2. *Keep Calm and Carry On*

Britain, who, during the 1940 bombing of London, exhibited stoical courage and endurance.[4]

All these meanings, if coded and available, will be invoked automatically as a direct response to the stimulus in Figure 8.1, despite their apparent irrelevance to the immediate context at hand – the ferocious weather in Britain during December 2009. When weighed against contextual information – the blitz-like storm which forced many in Britain to assume the spirit of the blitz rather than the spirit of Christmas – these meanings strongly deride the panicky spirit of the Brits on Christmas Eve 2009.

The way this cartoon can be interpreted illustrates the need to take various factors into consideration when examining the end-product of utterance interpretation. Indeed, the psychology of utterance processing takes into account a number of factors that shape utterance interpretation, such as (i) salient/coded meanings, (ii) contextual information, and (iii) their unfolding interaction (or lack of it).

Debates within psycholinguistics can, thus, be viewed as divisible into two main approaches (for a review, see Giora, 2003: chapters 1–3). At one end of the spectrum are context-based models which assume that a strong context reigns supreme in that it governs early processes and facilitates contextually compatible meanings only. Consequently, the output of the interpretation processes must be seamless, involving no contextually incompatible meanings and interpretations (the *connectionist model*, e.g., Bates, 1999; Bates and MacWhinney, 1989; MacWhinney, 1987; Small *et al.*, 1988; the *constraint-based model*, e.g., McRae *et al.*, 1998; Pexman *et al.*, 2000; the *direct access view*, e.g., Gibbs, 1979, 1994; Keysar, 1994a; Ortony *et al.*, 1978).

At the other end are lexicon-based models which hold that coded meanings of stimuli are speedy responses, activated automatically, regardless of contextual information. As a result, initially accessed meanings may fail to meet context fit. Consequently, they may induce incompatible interpretations which will either feature in final outputs alongside the appropriate ones or will be subjected to revisitation or suppression processes (the *modular view*, e.g., Fodor, 1983; Swinney, 1979; the *standard pragmatic model*, e.g., Grice, 1975; Searle, 1979a; the *graded salience hypothesis*, e.g., Giora, 1997, 2003; Peleg *et al.*, 2004, 2008). The context-based and the lexicon-based models, then, have different predictions, especially with regard to initial processes, which, in turn, affect later interpretation processes.

Specifically, according to the context-based view, specific and supportive contextual information penetrates lexical access and selects the contextually appropriate meaning only, the consequence of which is contextually compatible interpretations only (section 8.1.1). In contrast, the lexicon-based view predicts that coded meanings cannot be blocked and, therefore, at times, end-product interpretations will also involve contextually incompatible meanings and interpretations (section 8.1.2). To tease apart these two approaches, we need to look at research into utterance interpretation processes.

## 8.1.1  Context-based approaches
Context-based approaches focus on the *facilitative* effects of strong contexts which allow them to select only compatible meanings and interpretations. Thus, according to the *connectionist model*, when words (*bulb*), ambiguous between salient/dominant ('light') and less salient/subordinate ('flower') meanings, are preceded by a context strongly biased toward one of the meanings, their processing will result in selecting the contextually

appropriate meaning exclusively, regardless of degree of salience. For instance, processing *The gardener dug a hole. She inserted the **bulb*** resulted in an exclusive activation of the less-salient, subordinate ('flower') meaning of *bulb* when probed immediately (Vu et al., 1998; Vu et al., 2000).

However, as shown by Peleg and Giora (in press) and Peleg et al. (2001, 2004, 2008), this finding need not attest to selective access; it might just as well be the effect of a predictive context, which guesses the intended meaning without interacting with lexical processes. For instance, Peleg et al. (2001) show that guessing the contextually appropriate meaning in a context biased toward the less salient meaning occurred even before the processor encountered the relevant stimulus (*bulb*). Additionally, as shown by Peleg and Eviatar (2008, 2009), briefly following the encounter of the stimulus in question at 250 ms stimulus onset asynchrony (SOA), the salient incompatible meaning as well as the less salient compatible meaning were both activated. This was further qualified by the type of homograph. In the case of homophonic homographs (*bulb*), both meanings were activated at a short (150 ms SOA) delay and remained active even 100 ms afterwards; in the case of heterophonic homographs (*tear*), the contextually appropriate, less salient meaning was activated exclusively in the left hemisphere at 150 ms SOA, but 100 ms later (at 250 ms SOA), the salient but contextually incompatible meaning also became available (Peleg and Eviatar, 2008, 2009). When probed later, 1000 ms after encountering the homophonic homograph, the left hemisphere selected the contextually appropriate (less salient) meaning, whereas both the salient and less salient meanings were still activated in the right hemisphere. At this long delay, 1000 ms following the onset of the ambiguous word, the left hemisphere was unable to suppress the salient contextually inappropriate meaning of heterophonic homographs, while the right hemisphere could (see Peleg et al., 2008). Such findings demonstrate that salient meanings cannot be blocked, not even by a strong context.

According to the *constraint-based model*, both contextual as well as lexical "constraints" may affect end-product interpretations, depending on their quantitative strength. The greater the number of the constraints favoring a specific meaning/interpretation the greater chance it stands to be selected exclusively (McRae et al., 1998). For instance, if contextual information is biased toward an ironic interpretation of a target, and, in addition, involves other biasing factors (such as a speaker whose profession indicates s/he could be ironic), such a strong context should facilitate the appropriate (ironic) interpretation only, even though its literal meaning may be more salient.

Findings, however, show that such contexts did not facilitate non-coded, inferred or novel interpretations such as irony, but instead slowed down ironic targets compared to more salient literal counterparts (Pexman et al., 2000; but see Ivanko and Pexman, 2003 for similar but also for somewhat different results, argued against in Giora et al., 2007b).

The *direct access view* (Gibbs, 1979, 1986, 1994) argues against the temporal priority of utterance-literal interpretation (posited by Grice, 1975), contending instead that, in a strongly supportive context, interpretations of literal and non-literal utterances should exhibit similar interpretive processes. Indeed, when Ortony *et al.* (1978) embedded statements, ambiguous between literal and novel (metaphoric) interpretations, in poor contexts, literal utterances were faster to read; however, when provided with rich contextual support, both literal and metaphoric statements took similarly long to read, thus testifying to context's facilitative effects on novel metaphors.

Later studies, however, failed to replicate these results. Rather, novel metaphoric items, embedded in supportive contexts, always took longer to read compared to their literal interpretation (Brisard *et al.*, 2001; Giora and Fein, 1999a; Pexman *et al.*, 2000; Tartter *et al.*, 2002; see also Giora, 1997, 1999). Similarly, non-coded ironic utterances were always processed literally first despite a strongly supportive context (Giora *et al.*, 2007b; Giora *et al.*, 2009).

## 8.1.2  Lexicon-based approaches

Lexicon-based approaches focus on the insensitivity of lexical processes to contextual information. According to the *modular view* (Fodor, 1983), cognitive processes are either domain-specific or domain-general. Domain-specific processes (such as lexical access) are modular: they are low-level bottom-up processes, which are sensitive only to relevant stimuli (e.g., lexical items). Among other things, modular processes are informationally encapsulated, that is, impenetrable to processes occurring outside the input system. In contrast, domain-general, central systems, such as contextual information, consist in top-down, integrative, and predictive processes that are receptive to outputs of various domains.

Modular processes such as lexical access, then, are not affected by top-down feedback from higher-level representations such as contextual information or world knowledge. Rather, lexical access is autonomous and, on some views, exhaustive: *all* the meanings of a lexical stimulus are activated once this stimulus is encountered, regardless of either contextual bias or degree of salience. However, once these meanings are activated, contextual, central system processes may influence them. For instance, the central system may either integrate them with contextual information or discard them from the mental representation as contextually incompatible (for a review of other versions of modular and also hybrid models, see Giora, 2003: chapters 1–3).

The *standard pragmatic model* (Grice, 1975; Searle, 1979a) may be viewed as a version of a modular view, attributing properties such as imperviousness to contextual information and, consequently, temporal priority to *literal* meanings. According to the standard pragmatic model, the meanings of a linguistic stimulus to be activated first are literal. On the basis of these literal meanings, utterance-literal interpretations are to be constructed first. However, if literally-based (meanings and) interpretations do not meet contextual fit, suppression of these representations will take place, to be followed by their replacement with contextually appropriate alternatives.

Following the modular view (Fodor, 1983), the *graded salience hypothesis* (Giora 1997, 1999, 2003; Peleg and Giora, in press; Peleg *et al.*, 2001, 2004, 2008) assumes two kinds of mechanisms that run parallel: a bottom-up modular system, which is encapsulated and autonomous in that it is impervious to context effects (e.g., lexical access), and a top-down central system (e.g., contextual information), which is integrative but can also be strong enough to predict a compatible meaning or interpretation. Diverging from the modular view, however, the graded salience hypothesis posits that lexical access is ordered: salient meanings are activated faster than less salient ones. In addition, suppression of contextually incompatible meanings is not unconditional but rather functional; it is sensitive to discourse goals and requirements, allowing for contextually incompatible meanings and interpretations to be retained if invited or if supportive or non-intrusive of the intended interpretation (see also Giora and Fein, 1999a; Giora *et al.*, 2007a).

According to the graded salience hypothesis, salience is a matter of degree: a meaning is *salient* if it is coded in the mental lexicon and enjoys prominence due to cognitive priority (e.g., prototypicality, stereotypicality) or amount of exposure (e.g., experiential familiarity, frequency, or conventionality), regardless of degree of literality; a meaning is *less salient* if it is coded but low on these variables, regardless of degree of literality; a meaning is *non-salient* if it is non-coded – either novel or derivable (e.g., on the basis of contextual information), regardless of degree of literality.

Although salience is a property of words and fixed expressions rather than a property of utterances' compositional meaning and interpretation, utterance interpretation may often rely on the salient meanings of its components. Interpretations that are based on the salient meanings of the utterance components are salience-based interpretations and could be both literal and non-literal (see Giora *et al.*, 2007b).

Rich and specific contextual information can be predictive of an oncoming message, as well as supportive and facilitative. However, even when it is rich enough to activate meanings and interpretations on its own accord, it does not penetrate lexical processes but runs parallel. As a result, often salient but inappropriate meanings and, consequently, salience-based but inappropriate interpretations might be involved in utterance interpretation. Such inappropriate interpretations need not be suppressed; they may be retained, provided they do not interfere with the final contextually compatible interpretation. The result is the involvement of such interpretations in the final outputs of utterance interpretation (e.g., the salience-based, often literal interpretation of ironies and metaphors, see Brisard *et al.*, 2001; Giora and Fein, 1999a; Pexman *et al.*, 2000; Tartter *et al.*, 2002; see also Giora, 1997, 1999).

## 8.2 Salient meanings and salience-based interpretations are not necessarily literal

According to the graded salience hypothesis (Giora, 2003, 2006; Giora and Fein, 1999a), neither salient meanings nor salience-based interpretations need to be literal. Similarly, non-salient interpretation need not be figurative.

### 8.2.1 Salient meanings are not necessarily literal

A number of studies demonstrate that salient meanings need not be literal. For instance, in Gibbs (1980), familiar (English) idioms (*spill the beans*), whose salient meaning is figurative, took less time to read in an idiomatically than in a literally biasing context, the latter inviting a salience-based literal interpretation. In Giora and Fein (1999b), familiar (Hebrew) ironies, whose salient meanings were both ironic and literal, were processed initially (at 150 ms ISI [interstimulus interval]) both ironically and literally, regardless of context bias; in contrast, less familiar ironies, whose salient components were literal, were processed initially only literally, regardless of context bias.

In Colston and Gibbs (2002), familiar (English) metaphors (*This one's really* **sharp** said of a student) were faster to process when embedded in metaphorically than in ironically biasing contexts. Indeed, one of the salient meanings of their keyword (e.g., *sharp*) is metaphorical, which accounts for their metaphorical salience-based interpretation. When embedded in an irony-biasing context, the salience-based interpretation of the ironic use should be metaphorical and will have to be adjusted to the ironically biased contextual information.

Similarly, in Giora *et al.* (forthcoming), (healthy) participants were faster to respond to familiar (Hebrew) metaphors (*flower bed*), whose salient meaning is metaphorical, than to novel ones whose non-salient interpretation is metaphorical (*golden laugh*), even though the individual words that made up the target word-pairs were similarly highly familiar.

### 8.2.2 Salience-based interpretations are not necessarily literal

Given that salient meanings need not be literal (section 8.2.1), it follows that salience-based interpretations need not be sensitive to degree of literality either. After all, they are derived on the basis of the salient meanings of the utterance's components, which may be either literal or non-literal. Recall that the ironic *This one's really sharp*, whose salience-based interpretation is metaphorical (relying on the salient, metaphorical meaning of *sharp*) took longer to process in an ironically than in a metaphorically biased context (see Colston and Gibbs, 2002), since the salience-based (metaphorical) interpretation of the ironic use is contextually incompatible.

Figure 8.3. *Know Hope*

### 8.2.3  Non-salient interpretations are not necessarily non-literal

Consider the example in Figure 8.1, which is literal: its final interpretation includes a number of salient meanings to which it adds a novel twist. Consider further *Know Hope* (in Figure 8.3)[5] which is a literal, non-salient use, harping on the salient, literal "no hope."

In Giora *et al.* (2004) we studied such (Hebrew) innovations, termed "optimal innovations." To be optimally innovative, a stimulus should evoke a novel – less or non-salient – response to a familiar stimulus, alongside a salient one from which it differs (both quantitatively and qualitatively), so that both can interact, regardless of non-literality. Admittedly many optimal innovations may be non-literal (novel metaphors or unfamiliar ironies). However, quite a few are literal (as can be deduced from Figures 8.1 and 8.3). Consider the following examples: *Body and sole* – the name of a shoe shop – which evokes the salient *body and soul*, both of which are literal but only the first is non-salient; *Curl up and dye* (the name of a hair salon) which is non-salient and literal and which evokes the salient but metaphorical *Curl up and die* (see Giora *et al.*, 2004).

Given that optimal innovation involves processing a salient meaning on top of the novel interpretation, it is no wonder that optimal innovations take longer to process than their salient meanings, regardless of metaphoricality (as shown by Giora *et al.*, 2004). Indeed, in Giora *et al.* (forthcoming: Experiment 2), both healthy individuals and individuals diagnosed with Asperger's syndrome took longer to process and more frequently

Everybody is                                    We are celebrating
sad today                                         Memorial Day
                                                         today

Figure 8.4. *This is Memorial Day*

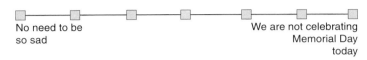

No need to be                                   We are not celebrating
so sad                                              Memorial Day
                                                         today

Figure 8.5. *This is not Memorial Day*

erred on (Hebrew) non-salient interpretations compared to salient ones, regardless of metaphoricality. Thus, literal optimal innovations such as *a Tverian horse* (meaning 'a horse from Tiberias'), reminiscent of a salient, metaphorical collocation – *a Trojan horse*, were slower to induce correct meaningfulness judgments compared to familiar literal collocations, whose meanings are salient. Non-salient interpretations then are not necessarily non-literal.

## 8.3 Opting for the literal interpretation is not necessarily a default strategy

To further test the claim that opting for a non-literal rather than a literal interpretation may be a default strategy, independent of explicit contextual information (including information about the speaker and the addressee), one needs to neutralize factors affecting non-literality such as degree of salience (recall that familiar items may have a lexicalized non-literal meaning; see section 8.2.1), semantic anomaly (known to trigger metaphoricality; see e.g., Beardsley, 1958), and contextual information (since breach of pragmatic maxims or contextual misfit may invite a non-literal interpretation; see e.g., Grice, 1975). It thus follows that for this claim to be experimentally substantiated, testing it should involve novel items susceptible to a literal interpretation and presented outside a specific context.

Indeed, in Giora *et al.* (2010), materials were affirmative statements of the form X is Y (such as *This is Memorial Day*; *I am your doctor*) and their negative versions (*This is not Memorial Day*; *I am not your doctor*), all of which could, potentially, be assigned a literal interpretation in that they were all equally novel, semantically intact, and presented in isolation (see Figures 8.4 and 8.5).

Participants were asked to rate the interpretation of these targets on a seven-point scale ranging between two specific (either literal or non-literal) interpretations presented randomly at the scale's ends.

Results show that the negative statements were rated as significantly more metaphorical than their affirmative counterparts, supporting the claim that opting for the literal interpretation need not be a default strategy.

Indeed, when the negative statements were embedded in contexts equally supportive of either their metaphorical or their literal interpretation, reading times were faster for items embedded in metaphorically than in literally biasing contexts (Giora *et al.*, 2011a), further supporting the claim that a non-literal interpretation may be a default interpretation.

Additional evidence supportive of this claim comes from research into irony interpretation. Giora *et al.* (2005b) show that negating affirmative overstatements results in assigning these statements an ironic interpretation, even though these statements are amenable to literal interpretation as well. Specifically, findings demonstrate that negative overstatements (*He is not exceptionally bright*) come across as ironic even outside a specific context. When presented in isolation, they are rated as more ironic than other alternatives such as affirmative overstatements (*He is exceptionally bright*) or negated non-overstatements (*He is not bright*).

Taken together, findings from various negative statements indicate that it is not the case that, when available, literal interpretation is a default. Instead, our findings demonstrate that even non-conventional utterances, susceptible to literal interpretation, are often perceived as non-literal, even when no supportive information of that interpretation is made manifest.

## 8.4  Context effects – later interpretation processes

Although the various approaches outlined above differ in their predictions with regard to the effects of a "strong context" on early lexical processes (section 8.1), there seems to be an agreement that contextual information should affect later interpretation processes. But what these effects should look like is still a matter of debate. To test the various predictions of the approaches with regard to later processes, I will focus here on late effects of a "strong context" (such that anticipates an ironic utterance) on irony interpretation and on the effects of coherence on later processes of negated information.

### 8.4.1  Irony interpretation
According to context-based approaches, if context is strongly biased in favor of the appropriate (ironic) interpretation, only that interpretation should be activated immediately and feature exclusively in the final product. According to some lexicon-based approaches, inappropriate meanings as well as inappropriate (literal) interpretations (of irony) should be activated immediately even in the presence of a strong context. However, later, they should be discarded from the mental representation so that the final product features

only contextually appropriate (ironic) interpretations (Grice, 1975; Fodor, 1983).

Whereas these two approaches have similar predictions with regard to how contextual information should affect the final (ironic) representation, the *graded salience hypothesis* has different predictions. According to this hypothesis, salience-based yet inappropriate interpretations (the salience-based interpretation of novel metaphors and unfamiliar ironies), which are activated immediately, need not be discarded. They may be retained since they contribute to (or at least do not disrupt) the final interpretation processes (Giora, 2003).

But what makes up a strong context? According to Gibbs (1986, 2002), a context may be strong enough to facilitate the ironic interpretation of an utterance exclusively if it sets up an "ironic situation" through contrast between what is expected and the reality that frustrates it. Inducing an expectation for an ironic utterance should allow ironic interpretation to be tapped directly, with no recourse to contextually inappropriate utterance-level interpretations. According to Gibbs, then, a strong context is one that allows addressees to anticipate an ironic utterance. This expectation should, in turn, render irony interpretation frictionless (the *expectation hypothesis*).

But a close look at "ironic situations" reveals that they need not promote an expectation for an ironic utterance nor do they facilitate irony interpretation (Giora *et al.*, 2009; see also Ivanko and Pexman, 2003). Rather, such contexts encouraged readers to select literal utterances (*This demonstration is a remarkable failure*), which were by far the most preferred option, over ironic ones (*This demonstration is a remarkable success*), whether following a context featuring a frustrated expectation (section 8.4.1.1) or a fulfilled one (section 8.4.1.2) see Giora *et al.* (2009).

### 8.4.1.1  Frustrated expectation

Shirley is a feminist activist. Two weeks ago, she organized a demonstration against the closure of a shelter for victimized women, and invited the press. She hoped that due to her immense efforts many people would show up at the demonstration, and that the media would cover it widely. On the day of the demonstration, twenty activists arrived, and no journalists showed up. In response to the poor turn out, Shirley muttered:

a.   This demonstration is a remarkable success. (Ironic)
b.   This demonstration is a remarkable failure. (Literal)

### 8.4.1.2  Realized expectation

Shirley is a feminist activist. Two weeks ago, she organized a demonstration against the closure of a shelter for victimized women, and invited the press. As always, she prepared herself for the idea that despite the hard work, only a few people would show up at the demonstration and the media would ignore it entirely. On the day of the demonstration, twenty activists arrived, and no journalists showed up. In response to the poor turn out, Shirley muttered:

a.   This demonstration is a remarkable success. (Ironic)
b.   This demonstration is a remarkable failure. (Literal)

In addition, "ironic situations" did not facilitate irony. Rather, ironic statements (*A skiing vacation is recommended for your health*) took as long to read following a context featuring a contrast between what is expected and the reality that frustrates it (section 8.4.1.3) as following a context in which this expectation is met (section 8.4.1.4).

### 8.4.1.3   Frustrated expectation

Sagee went on a skiing vacation abroad. He really likes vacations that include sport activities. A relaxed vacation in a quiet ski-resort place looked like the right thing for him. Before leaving, he made sure he had all the equipment and even took training classes on a ski simulator. But as early as the beginning of the second day he lost his balance, fell, and broke his shoulder. He spent the rest of the time in a local hospital ward feeling bored and missing home. When he got back home, his shoulder still in a cast, he said to his fellow workers:

"A skiing vacation is recommended for your health". (Ironic)
Everyone smiled.

### 8.4.1.4   Realized expectation

Sagee went on a skiing vacation abroad. He doesn't even like skiing. It looks dangerous to him and staying in such a cold place doesn't feel like a vacation at all. But his girlfriend wanted to go and asked him to join her. As early as the beginning of the second day he lost his balance, fell, and broke his shoulder. He spent the rest of the time in a local hospital ward feeling bored and missing home. When he got back home, his shoulder still in a cast, he said to his fellow workers:

"A skiing vacation is recommended for your health". (Ironic)
Everyone smiled.

Importantly, however, both ironic targets took longer to read than a salience-based (literal) interpretation which followed a context featuring no expectation (section 8.4.1.5).

### 8.4.1.5   No-expectation

Sagee went on a skiing vacation abroad. He has never practiced skiing so it was his first time. He wasn't sure whether he would be able to learn to ski and whether he could handle the weather. The minute he got there he understood it was a great thing for him. He learned how to ski in no time and enjoyed it a lot. Besides, the weather was nice and the atmosphere relaxed. When he got back home, he said to his fellow workers:

> "A skiing vacation is recommended for your health". (Salience-based, literal)
> Everyone smiled.

### 8.4.1.6 Will expecting an ironic utterance facilitate it initially?

What, then, can make a strong context, such as would induce an expectation for an ironic utterance? In Giora *et al.* (2007b), we showed that the involvement of an ironic speaker *in vivo* (in context mid-position, in bold for convenience) induced an expectation of another such utterance on the part of that speaker when these contexts were presented without the final utterances and had to be completed by participants. We therefore used these contexts, completed by an utterance which was biased either toward the ironic (2) or toward its salience-based (literal) interpretation (3) in a reading experiment.

(2)   Barak: I finish work early today.
      Sagit: So, do you want to go to the movies?
      Barak: I don't really feel like seeing a movie.
      Sagit: So maybe we could go dancing?
      Barak: No, at the end of the night my feet will hurt and I'll be tired.
      Sagit: **You're a really active guy** . . .
      Barak: Sorry, but I had a rough week.
      Sagit: So what are you going to do tonight?
      Barak: I think I'll stay home, read a magazine, and go to bed early.
      Sagit: **Sounds like you are going to have a really interesting evening**.
      Barak: So we'll talk sometime this week.

(3)   Barak: I was invited to a film and a lecture by Amos Gitai.
      Sagit: That's fun. He is my favorite director.
      Barak: I know, I thought we'll go together.
      Sagit: Great. When is it on?
      Barak: Tomorrow. We will have to be in Metulla in the afternoon.[6]
      Sagit: **I see they found a place that is really close to the center**.
      Barak: I want to leave early in the morning. Do you want to come?
      Sagit: I can't, I'm studying in the morning.
      Barak: Well, I'm going anyway.
      Sagit: **Sounds like you are going to have a really interesting evening**.
      Barak: So we'll talk sometime this week.

Although both contexts raised an expectation for an ironic utterance, identical targets (*Sounds like you are going to have a really interesting evening*) took longer to read following ironically biasing contexts (2) than following salience-based, literally biasing contexts (3). Strong contexts, then, inducing an expectation for an ironic utterance, did not facilitate ironic interpretations nor did they slow down salience-based, literal interpretations.

To further test the expectation hypothesis we attempted to induce an expectation of an ironic utterance by presenting participants only with contexts that ended in an ironic utterance (4) so that they are trained to anticipate an ironic utterance. This (+Expectation) condition was compared to a weaker (–Expectation) condition in which only half the contexts ended in an ironic utterance; the other half ended in a non-ironic utterance (5). Results from lexical decisions to probes related to ironic ("harmful") and salience-based ("healthy") utterance-level interpretations showed facilitation of the salience-based interpretation only, regardless of context bias. This was true when short (250 ms) as well as long (750–1000 ms) processing time was allowed. This pattern of results was not different from the one obtained in the weaker condition. Such results suggest that, *contra* the direct access view, but in keeping with the graded salience hypothesis, inducing an expectation for an ironic utterance does not facilitate ironic interpretation immediately and does not affect a seamless interpretation process.

(4) Yuval and Omry went out for their lunch break after a morning of work. They went to the cafeteria in their office building and each filled a platter with food. They stood in line for a long while and were eager to start the meal. When they had sat down, Yuval saw that his colleague chose fried sausage, chips, a glass of coke for a drink, and a sugar-glazed doughnut for dessert. Then Yuval said: "I see that you picked the *ideal* meal today!"

(5) Yuval and Omry went out for their lunch break after a morning of work. They went to the cafeteria in their office building and each filled a platter with food. They stood in line for a long while and were eager to start the meal. When they had sat down to eat, Yuval saw that his colleague filled his platter with salad, tofu, and sprouts and chose natural carrot juice for a drink. Then Yuval said: "I see that you picked the *ideal* meal today!"

Importantly, in Giora *et al.* (2011b; see Giora 2011), we strengthened the ironically biasing condition used in Giora *et al.* (2007b) by introducing an additional constraint, informing participants that the aim of the experiment was to test irony interpretation. The control group, whose experimental design was mixed, raising no expectation, were not informed about this specific aim of the experiment; their contextual information was therefore weaker compared to that in which expectation of ironic utterances was made more pronounced, both implicitly and explicitly. Still, although contextual information was now more strongly biased in favor of the ironic interpretation, this did not affect the pattern of results which replicated those obtained earlier (in Giora *et al.*, 2007b). Even this multiple constraints condition did not facilitate irony interpretation; only salience-based albeit incompatible interpretations were made available in both the strongly and weakly biasing conditions.

Would allowing extra processing time make a difference? In Giora *et al.* (2011b) we allowed participants longer (1500 ms) processing time. We predicted that even if, at this stage, irony is understood, salience-based but incompatible interpretations would still be available. Indeed, as predicted, even at such a long delay, the pattern of results did not change: the salience-based though incompatible interpretation was never less accessible than the ironic yet compatible interpretation.

Such results demonstrate that understanding utterances in a strong context supportive of and anticipating their non-salient (ironic) interpretation via inducing an expectation of such an interpretation does not unconditionally involve dispensing with the salience-based but incompatible interpretation. Do salience-based interpretations have a role in shaping up utterance-final products?

We have seen that processing utterances in context may involve entertaining meanings and interpretations on account of their salience rather than because of their contextual compatibility. According to the *suppression/retention hypothesis* (Giora, 2003), such meanings and interpretations, when incompatible, will either be retained or discarded from the mental representation depending on the role they might play in shaping the contextually appropriate interpretation. When they might contribute to the final representation they will be retained. For instance, on the *indirect negation view*, the involvement of salience-based interpretation in irony processing allows computing the gap between what is said and the reality referred to (Giora, 1995 and Giora *et al.*, 2009); on the *tinge hypothesis* (Dews and Winner, 1995, 1997, 1999; Dews *et al.*, 1995), the involvement of salience-based interpretations in irony processing is functional in mitigating the negativity of ironic criticism and the positivity of ironic praise. Although salience-based interpretations might not be the intended interpretation, they are instrumental in shaping it up and are therefore retained.

The involvement of salience-based but incompatible interpretations in the late stages of irony interpretation supports the graded salience hypothesis and the suppression/retention hypothesis (Giora, 1997, 1999, 2003). However, it argues against both the *standard pragmatic model* (Grice, 1975)[7] and *the direct access view* (Gibbs, 1986, 2002), which assume that the products of irony processing will not involve incompatible interpretations.

## 8.4.2　Negation interpretation

Consistent with the graded salience hypothesis, results obtained from studies of irony interpretation support the view that salient meanings and salience-based interpretations are activated initially, regardless of a strong contextual bias toward the non-salient interpretation. They further demonstrate that, as predicted by the retention/suppression hypothesis (Giora, 2003; Giora and

Fein, 1999a), suppression of contextually incompatible meanings and inter-pretations is not unconditional. Instead, suppression is attuned to contextual goals and requirements and would not operate if apparently incompatible information may be conducive to the final interpretation.

A great number of studies probing the effect of negation (*no, not*) on pat-terns of activation of negated concepts show that, outside a specific context, negated information ('fast' in *The train to Boston was* **no rocket**) is activated initially (between 100–500 ms) as is non-negated information (Hasson and Glucksberg, 2006; Giora, Balaban, Fein, and Alkabets, 2005a; Kaup *et al.*, 2007; MacDonald and Just, 1989: Experiments 1–2 reading phase). However, later on (between 500–1000 ms) initial levels of activation of negated concepts drop to baseline levels (Hasson and Glucksberg, 2006). When given extra pro-cessing time (1500 ms), negated information is suppressed and replaced by an alternative opposite (Kaup *et al.*, 2006; for conflicting results, however, see Lüdtke *et al.*, 2008). Outside a specific context, then, the suppressive effect of negation is a default strategy.

However, when provided with late coherent vs incoherent context (*The train to Boston was* **no rocket***. The trip to the city was* *fast*, *though*), such negated items did not dispense with the negated, albeit incompatible concept ('fast') even as long as 1000 ms following its mention. Retention of apparently irrelevant, salience-based interpretations, however, allow for late context to resonate with earlier context, despite indication to the contrary invited by the negation marker (Giora *et al.*, 2007a; on discourse resonance, see Du Bois, 1998, 2001; on discourse resonance following negation, see Giora, 2007).

Contextual effects on the retention of negated information were also found in Kaup (2001) and Kaup and Zwaan (2003). Results of these studies show that a concept's accessibility may be affected by its presence in the situation model rather than by negation. In the following (6), the fact that a referent (*photographs*) is not removed from the situation allows its retention despite it being within the scope of negation (Kaup, 2001):

(6)   Elizabeth tidied up her drawers. She burned the old letters but not the photographs. Afterwards she cleaned up.

Similarly, in Kaup and Zwaan (2003), only concepts absent from the situa-tion described lost accessibility, regardless of negation. In contrast, negated concepts present in the situation described retained their accessibility even after being entertained for as long as 1500 ms.

Suppression and retention are functional, then, and conform to global rather than to local coherence considerations (Giora, 2006).

## 8.5 Coda

Is our mind "efficient" enough to engage in processing only contextually appropriate interpretations given that contextual information is strongly supportive of that interpretation, as argued by the contextualist school (e.g., Gibbs, 1994; Vu *et al.*, 2000; see section 8.1.1)? Luckily, it is not. In fact, there is enough evidence now to allow the conclusion that processing utterances, even inside highly biasing contexts, may involve entertaining meanings and interpretations solely on account of their meaning salience and consequently their salience-based interpretation, regardless of contextual fit, as argued by the graded salience hypothesis (see section 8.1.2). Additionally, the activation of such incompatible meanings and interpretations in utterance processing is not unconditionally aborted by suppression processes (as assumed by Fodor, 1983 or Grice, 1975). Rather, such meanings and interpretations are retained because they are deemed functional in shaping up final interpretations (the *suppression/retention hypothesis*, Giora, 2003). Such a functional view of suppression and retention allows for the poetics of linguistic and non-linguistic stimuli such as optimal innovations (whether literal or non-literal; section 8.1), for discourse resonance, and humor (section 8.4).

It has also become clear that, *contra* Grice (1975), non-literal interpretations may be a default interpretation even when innovative, free of semantic anomaly, and context-less (section 8.2.3). Indeed, when affirmative statements of the form *X is Y* are negated (*This is not Memorial Day*), they are assigned a non-literal interpretation even when presented in isolation. Similarly, negative overstatements such as *He is not exceptionally bright* are assigned an ironic interpretation even outside a specific context.

The review of the literature introduced in this chapter reveals that the psychology of utterance processing is a multi-faceted phenomenon; its products may, at times, be surprisingly creative and even amusing.

# 9

# Sentences, utterances, and speech acts

Mikhail Kissine

A gleam pushed through the sleepiness in his grey eyes, and he sat up a little in his chair, asking: 'Leggett's been up to something?'
'Why did you say that?'
'I didn't say it. I asked it.'

Dashiell Hammett, *The Dain Curse*

## 9.1  Introduction

Most of the time, when we speak, we do more than express propositions; we suggest, promise, offer, accept, order, threaten, assert – we perform *speech* (or *illocutionary*) *acts*. The history of the research on this topic – initiated by Austin (1975) – is well-documented, and many textbooks, handbooks and encyclopaedias contain excellent surveys, thus treating speech acts as a major topic (e.g. Levinson 1983: chapter 5; Jaszczolt 2002: chapter 14; Sadock 2004). However, the main contemporary pragmatic theories of utterance interpretation devote little space, if any at all, to the way utterances are interpreted as speech acts, that is to the way they are assigned an *illocutionary force* (see, for instance, Sperber and Wilson 1986; Levinson 2000; Carston 2002; Recanati 2004a; Jaszczolt 2005). One might think that speech acts went out of fashion simply because the topic had been exhausted by the considerable number of publications spanning from Austin's work in the late fifties to the late eighties – when other topics, such as the pragmatic determinants of literal meaning, came to the fore.

I'm grateful to Keith Allan, Philippe De Brabanter, Marc Dominicy and Kasia Jaszczolt for helpful comments on previous versions of this paper. My research is supported by a post-doctoral research grant from the Fonds de la Recherche Scientifique de la Communauté Française de Belgique (F.R.S.-FNRS). The results presented here are also part of the research carried out within the scope of the ARC project 06/11–342 *Culturally modified organisms: 'What it means to be human in the age of culture'*, funded by the Ministère de la Communauté française – Direction générale de l'Enseignement non obligatoire et de la Recherche scientifique.

Yet, contemporary literature is rife with confusions stemming from the lack of careful consideration of the role of illocutionary force attribution in utterance interpretation. In particular, two crucial mistakes must be avoided. The first consists in conceiving of illocutionary forces as determined by sentence meaning; the second equates utterance content and speech act content. Interestingly enough, both confusions can be traced back to the founding fathers of modern pragmatics: the former to Searle, the latter to Grice. I will start this chapter by considering these two problematic legacies in turn. Next, we will see how avoiding the confusion between sentence meanings, utterance meanings and illocutionary contents helps to better grasp the major issues related to the analysis of illocutionary force attribution.

## 9.2   Searle: illocutionary forces as intrinsic to sentence meanings

According to Searle (1969, 1975a, b; Searle and Vanderveken 1985), the meaning of a sentence corresponds to the speech act any literal utterance of this sentence constitutes. In Searle's conception, the study of linguistic meaning amounts to the study of speech acts. It follows that in order to determine the literal illocutionary force of an utterance, it suffices to know its linguistic meaning. Searle's view rests on the assumption (explicitly stated by his Expressibility Principle; cf. Searle 1969: 20–21) that any illocutionary act type IA can be matched with a certain sentence type $s$ in such a way that IA corresponds to the literal meaning of $s$. Detailed criticisms of such a 'literalist' view – which takes literal utterance meaning to be determined by sentence meaning – can be found in Recanati (1987: 219–24), Carston (2002: 30–42, 64–70) and Kissine (2011). The important point for present purposes is that Searle's conception implies that illocutionary forces are located at the level of conventional sentence meaning. In his view, if a sentence is used literally, its illocutionary force is directly derivable from its linguistic meaning.

Sentences with imperative mood might seem to provide the strongest case for such a direct derivation of illocutionary force from sentence meaning. This is the reason why I will use imperative sentences to build up my case against incorporating illocutionary forces within sentence meaning. In languages that have a morphological imperative mood – and we will see in a moment that this qualification is important – directive speech acts such as requests, orders, commands etc. are prototypically realised by uttering grammatically imperative sentences. Of course, this does not entail that the linguistic, conventional meaning of the imperative mood is to be analysed in terms of a directive illocutionary force. Yet, I am not flogging a dead horse here, for such an idea underlies many recent accounts of imperative mood: see, for instance, Han (2000), Barker (2004), Portner (2007) or (Benjamin)

Russell (2007). Without getting into the details, all such theories presuppose that the imperative mood, at the level of sentence meaning, encodes the notion that the speaker (S) is prompting the addressee (A) to bring about the truth of the propositional content (for recent and critical surveys, see Schwager 2006; Iatridou 2009).

As is well known, many imperative sentences may be used to perform non-directive speech acts (e.g. Wilson and Sperber 1988). The most obvious examples include permissions (1), advice (2), good wishes (3), and threats (4):

(1)  A: May I have this piece of cake?
     B: Yes, take it.

(2)  Always cut your fingernails round and your toenails square.
                                             (from Hamblin 1987: 11)

(3)  Have a nice journey.

(4)  Hit me, and I'll hit you back.

Virtually everyone agrees that in (sincerely) performing a directive speech act $F_D(p)$, where $F_D$ stands for the directive force and $p$ for the propositional content, S expresses her intention/desire that A bring about the truth of $p$ with $F_D(p)$ as a reason (e.g. Searle 1975a; Bach and Harnish 1979; Searle and Vanderveken 1985; Alston 2000). Clearly, the examples in (1)–(4) can be felicitously uttered even though it is mutually manifest that S does not intend A to bring about the truth of the propositional content; for instance, because S would prefer H not to (1), because S does not care whether H does so or not (2), because H has no active control on the truth of the propositional content (3) or because H's bringing about the truth of the propositional content is undesirable for S (4).[1]

Those scholars who analyse the meaning encoded by the imperative mood as including some reference to the directive illocutionary force have two options available in order to explain away examples like (1)–(4).[2] The first consists in elaborating a semantic account of the imperative mood that is flexible enough to predict non-directive uses of imperative sentences (e.g. Wilson and Sperber 1988; Clark B. 1993; Allan 2006a; Schwager 2006). This amounts to rejecting the equivalence between the directive illocutionary force and the imperative mood – which is precisely a theoretical recommendation I wish to make in this chapter. The second option is to maintain that the imperative mood encodes the illocutionary directive force, and to claim that (1)–(4) are either indirect or non-literal speech acts.

Let us start by considering the possibility that (1)–(4) are indirect speech acts. Traditionally, a speech act is said to be indirect whenever its performance by means of the utterance $u$ requires $u$ to constitute another, direct speech act. (We will qualify this definition later on, but it is perfectly suited for the needs of the present discussion.) For instance, while (5) is literally a question, it will also constitute a request in many contexts.

(5)   Don't you think you've had enough beer already?

Likewise, (6) is, literally, an assertion; but it can be interpreted as a directive speech act.

(6)   You've had enough beer already.

The important point is that while (5) and (6) often constitute indirect directive speech acts, they still remain a question and an assertion, respectively. In other words, if an illocutionary act $IA_2$ is performed by way of performing another illocutionary $IA_1$, such that both $IA_1$ and $IA_2$ correspond to the same utterance $u$, the interpretation of $u$ as $IA_1$ remains available.

   In sum, the claim under examination holds that (1)–(4) are, *qua* direct speech acts, directives (since the imperative mood encodes the directive illocutionary force), but that, *qua* indirect speech acts, they are interpreted as permission, advice, a good wish and a threat, respectively. However, it is impossible to interpret (1–4) as directive speech acts, except in very specific contexts. And whenever one sets up such a context, it becomes impossible to interpret the examples at hand as permission, advice, a good wish and a threat, respectively. Imagine, for instance, that S and A are involved in some kind of sadomasochistic game, and that S utters (4). To be sure, the imperative in (4) then receives the directive illocutionary force; but in such a context, the example cannot be read as a threat anymore.

   It thus turns out that, if the imperative mood is to be associated with the directive illocutionary force, (1)–(4) cannot mean what would be literally said. So we are led to the idea that, while (1)–(4) are directive speech acts when taken literally, they are not interpreted as such when S is speaking non-literally. In other words, non-directive imperatives should be treated in the same way as sarcastic or ironic declaratives. By uttering (7), S may mean that the party is boring; similarly, by uttering (1)–(4) non-literally, S will give advice, give permission, express a good wish or make a threat.

(7)   This party is great.

The first problem here is that irony may be, and often is, missed. Hearing (7) you can fail to discern the sarcasm, and come to believe that I really love the party. Yet, it seems totally implausible to suppose that, when hearing (1)–(4), we may miss the alleged non-literal meaning and interpret these utterances as plain directive speech acts.

   Perhaps such an argument does not settle the issue, for it may be argued that the difficulty of accessing the (alleged) literal meaning of (1)–(4) – that is, to interpret them as directive speech acts – stems from the fact that the (alleged) non-literal readings – viz. permission, advice, good wish and threat – are so conspicuous that one can hardly miss them. In order to bring home the point that in (1)–(4) the imperative mood is used literally, albeit non-directively, let us consider in more detail the idea that the threat in

(4) means the opposite of what is literally said (cf. Dominicy and Franken 2002). A first possibility would consist in assuming that only the imperative conjunct is non-literal; (4) would then amount to something like (8).

(8)   Don't hit me, and I'll hit you back.

This is clearly not what S means by (4). One can envisage, as a second possibility, that both conjuncts are used non-literally such that (4) amounts to something like (9).

(9)   Don't hit me and I won't hit you back.

Conjunctions of the form *!p and q* (where *!* stands for the imperative mood) entail the corresponding conditionals *if p, q*; thus (4) entails (10).

(10)   If you hit me, I will hit you back.

However, what (9) entails is (11), not (10):

(11)   If you don't hit me, I won't hit you back.

To be sure, (11) can be 'perfected', that is pragmatically enriched, into a biconditional (e.g. Geis and Zwicky 1971; Horn 2000) that would ground the entailment relation between (9) and (10). However, 'conditional perfection' is a pragmatic, hence defeasible interpretive process, so that (9) – which is supposed to be what is meant by (4) – is compatible with the falsity of (10). The examples in (12) are typical instances of cancelled pragmatic enrichment.

(12)  *a.* Don't hit me and I won't hit you. But/actually, even if you hit me, I won't hit you back.
      *b.* If you don't hit me, I won't hit you back. But/actually, even if you hit me, I won't hit you back.

By contrast, the threat in (4) proves infelicitous if the conditional in (10) turns out to be false, and the examples in (13) are sheer contradictions.

(13)  *a.* Hit me, and I'll hit you back. ?But/ ?actually, even if you hit me, I won't hit you back.
      *b.* If you hit me, I'll hit you back. ?But/ ?actually, even if you hit me, I won't hit you back.

It can be concluded from the foregoing that non-directive uses of the imperative mood are as literal and direct as the directive ones. This I take to be a clear case against building the illocutionary force within sentence meaning (for the same point, see Wilson and Sperber 1988).

Scholars eager to pair sentence meanings with illocutionary forces sometimes invoke typological data (e.g. Han 2000: 164). The rationale is along the following lines: 'If natural languages bother to devote a specific form to directive speech acts, then the directive illocutionary force is not a matter of pragmatic processing, but part and parcel of sentence meanings.' Sadock and Zwicky (1985) claim that every language has a specific imperative sentence-type associated with directive speech acts. Yet, the morphosyntactic system of many languages lacks – totally or partially – distinctively imperative linguistic forms (this is the case for 122 languages out of the 552 analysed in van der Auwera and Lejeune 2005). In languages with defective or empty imperative paradigms, various compensatory strategies can be found: aorist (e.g. Georgian), subjunctive mood (e.g. French or Armenian), optative mood (e.g. Eskimo), irrealis mood (e.g. Javanese), indicative mood (e.g. Hebrew) and, perhaps more surprisingly, passive forms (Maori) (see, for instance, Xrakovski 2001; Allan 2006a; König and Siemund 2007). If the directive illocutionary force were encoded within the linguistic meaning, how are we to explain these typological facts? Should we accept that, in languages that lack genuine imperative mood, some sentence-types are linguistically ambiguous?

First, such an 'ambiguity' thesis violates Grice's Modified Occam's Razor (which recommends avoiding the multiplication of linguistic meanings beyond necessity). Second, the ambiguity thesis proves hard to maintain across languages. To see this clearly, contrast the use of future in Nunggubuyu and in French. Nunggubuyu lacks any morphosyntactic imperative; the same construction is used to express future time reference and to perform directive speech acts (Heath 1984, 1986). Out of context, it is impossible to decide whether (14a) should be translated as (14b) or (14c).

(14)  a.  Ba-buraː-v́ (Verstraete 2005; after Heath 1984: 343)
         2SG(CLASS-A)[3]-sit-NONPAST
      b.  'You will sit down.'
      c.  'Sit down.'

In French, an authoritative way to order things is to use the future constructions. However, French has also a morphological second person imperative; accordingly, a literal translation of (15a) can only be (15b) – not (15c).

(15)  a.  Tu partiras demain.
         You.SG leave-IND.FUT.SIMPLE.2SG tomorrow
      b.  'You will leave tomorrow.'
      c.  'Leave tomorrow.'

As far as I can see, there is no principled ground for the following joint claims: (a) that the Nunggubuyu construction 'Class-A prefix + non-past' is ambiguous between two illocutionary forces, each such sentence being either a direct and literal assertion about the future or a direct and literal directive speech act; and (b) that in French requests performed with the future indicative are indirect.

But if future tense constructions are said to be ambiguous between the assertive and the directive forces across languages – thus in French too – why should we refrain from extending this rationale to other morphosyntactic forms? As I have just mentioned, there exists a wide range of linguistic strategies for compensating for defective imperative paradigms. Following the thread, one would have to assume linguistic ambiguity for any such form that happens to be prototypically used to perform directive speech acts in some language. Take Lingala, which has an imperative form for the singular second person only; in directive speech acts with second person plural, subjunctive mood is used instead (van der Auwera and Lejeune 2005). On the one hand, no sensible semantic theory of mood would consider it plausible that, in Lingala, the ambiguity between a directive and some other illocutionary force might characterise the plural second person subjunctive form only, and not extend to the singular second person subjunctive form. On the other hand, data on the distribution of moods militates against the ad hoc hypothesis of a cross-linguistic ambiguity of the subjunctive mood. For instance, French has both second person imperative and subjunctive forms; but the subjunctive proves unacceptable whenever imperative forms are available. To borrow an example from Schlenker (2005), one can advise the Queen to be prudent using either a third person subjunctive (16) or a second person imperative (17); by contrast, the second person subjunctive in (18) is deviant.

(16)  Que  votre  Majesté  soit              prudente!
      Q    your   Majesty   be.SBJV.PRS.3SG  cautious
      (= Let her Majesty be cautious)

(17)  Soyez        prudente!
      be.IMP.2PL   cautious

(18)  ?Que  vous     soyez            prudente!
       Q    you.PL   be.SBJV.PRS.2PL  cautious

In (16), the Queen is addressed as a third person; second person addressed directive speech acts are unacceptable with the subjunctive.

(19)  a.  Sors!
          Get.out.IMP.2SG
      b.  ?Que  tu       sortes.[4]
           Q    you.SG   get-out-SBJV.PR.2SG

Moreover, the acceptability of subjunctive in French is not linked to the presence or the absence of the directive force. For instance, in French equivalents of (4), the surface form of the first verb is unambiguously imperative (20a) (cf. note 2), and the first clause has clearly no directive force. In such environments, second person subjunctives are unacceptable (20b); however, in the third person – for which there is no morphological imperative form – the subjunctive is fine (20c).

(20) a. Sachez        trop        de            choses trop tôt  et
        know.IMP.2PL too.many ART.PARTITIVE things too  early and
        vous    serez                  traumatisé.
        you.PL. be.IND.FUT.SIMPLE.2PL traumatised.
        'Get to know too much too early, and you'll be traumatised.'
     b. ?Que vous      sachiez          trop      de              choses
        Q    you.PL know.SBJV.PR.2PL too-many ART.PARTITIVE things
        trop tôt   et vous   serez                 traumatisé.
        too  early and you.PL be.IND.FUT.SIMPLE.2PL traumatised.
     c. Qu' il    sache          trop     de            choses
        Q   he know.SBJV.PR.3SG too-many ART.PARTITIVE things
        trop tôt et  il  sera                traumatisé.
        too early and he be.IND.FUT.SIMPLE.3SG traumatised.

At this point, I see no justification for arguing that a certain sentence-type –
e.g. future in Nunggubuyu or subjunctive in Lingala – is ambiguous between
several illocutionary forces, rather than admitting that illocutionary forces
belong to the level of utterances rather than to that of sentences.[5]

## 9.3   Grice's heritage: illocutionary forces and utterances

In the previous section, we saw that illocutionary forces do not belong to the
level of sentence meaning. From this, however, one should not conclude that
whenever a sentence is uttered and acquires propositional meaning, a speech
act has been performed *eo ipso*. Yet, a customary – but misguided – shortcut is
precisely to recast the opposition between sentences and utterances in terms
of the contrast between sentence meanings and speech acts. This opposition
plays a major role in a much-discussed issue of contemporary philosophy
of language: that of contextual contributions to the propositional content.
To take a well-worn example, (21) will mean different things in different
contexts – depending on what John is ready for.

(21)   John is ready.

Phenomena of this kind have been taken to show that literal content cannot
be determined by linguistic meaning alone. Yet, opposing this interpretation, so-called 'semantic minimalists' argue (a) that the contents expressed
by (21) on different occasions of utterance are speech act contents; (b) that
these speech act contents do not correspond to the literal, semantic content of the sentence uttered. In other words, while different utterances of
the same sentence correspond to the performance of different speech acts,
with possibly different contents, speech act contents are to be distinguished
from the semantic content proper, which – except a restricted set of indexicals – is entirely determined by sentence structure and remains constant
across contexts of uses (Cappelen and Lepore 2005; Soames 2002). Implicit in

this view is the assumption that any utterance constitutes a speech act, or, in other words, that for a sentence to be uttered amounts to its acquiring an illocutionary force.

Such an assumption can be traced back to Grice's notion of meaning$_{nn}$. Saying, for Grice, is intending to provoke some cognitive response, such that the reason for the cognitive response is the recognition of this very intention (or, at least, cases of saying can always be reconstructed in this way). The nature of the response S intends to provoke by her utterance in the mind of A determines the 'central' speech act the instance of saying corresponds to: if it is the belief that $p$, S's saying will be an assertive speech act; if it is the intention to bring about the truth of $p$, S's saying will be a directive speech act (cf. Grice 1968, 2001: 50–55).

Now take a sarcastic utterance like (7) above: S says that the party is great, but, clearly, she doesn't mean it. To the best of my knowledge, no theory of irony would claim that in such a case S asserts that the party is great. Furthermore, a sarcastic utterance that $p$ is clearly not accompanied by an overt intention (to communicate that $p$) of the kind that, according to Grice, characterises saying. This entails, in Grice's view, that the sarcastic S does not say anything, but just acts as if she was saying something – a very counter-intuitive consequence (see Neale 1992; Carston 2002: 114–16; Kissine 2009).

The existence of cases where S says that $p$ without asserting that $p$ constitutes a strong argument against equating utterances and illocutionary acts. Austin (1975) explicitly distinguished between sentence meaning (phatic act), contextual meaning (locutionary act) and illocutionary act (for a detailed discussion, see Kissine 2008b, 2009). In other words, even though sentence meaning and utterance meaning are not to be confused, illocutionary force attribution constitutes yet another level of interpretation.

In a series of papers, Kent Bach (e.g. 1994a, 2005) argues that what is said by an utterance does not coincide with the content of the illocutionary act performed by this utterance; what is said corresponds to the *locutionary* act performed. However, unlike, for instance, Recanati (2004a and this volume) or Carston (2002 and this volume), Bach defines what is said as the output of the semantic interpretation of the syntactic structure; pragmatic contributions to what is said are limited to determining the reference of a restricted set of indexicals. Moreover, in Bach's view, what is said does not always correspond to a full-blown proposition. Take (21), for instance. As pointed out above, it is impossible to decide what John is ready for in the absence of any contextual information. But such extra-linguistic information does not contribute, according to Bach, to what is said. Illocutionary content is the place where such pragmatic influences come into play. What is said by (21), for Bach, is the sub-propositional radical [*John is ready___*], whose empty slot has to be completed at the illocutionary level.

One of the reasons Bach – rightly – invokes for distinguishing between locutionary and illocutionary acts is that sometimes we do not mean what we say; irony is a case in point. Accordingly, in such cases, the utterance reduces, at the literal level, to a locutionary act that corresponds, in Bach's view, to the semantic interpretation of the syntactic structure and to the indexical resolution, both of which remain blind to the pragmatic, wide context.

Bach's conception does not conform to Austin's original definition of the term *locutionary act* (cf. Kissine 2008b, 2009). More importantly, while the existence of cases where we do not mean what we say justifies the rejection of Grice's equation of saying with performing a speech act, it also shows that 'forceless' saying – the locutionary act – is already endowed with propositional, pragmatically determined meaning. Imagine that John is notoriously bad at preparing his talks on time. Imagine that, a few hours before John's talk, S sarcastically says:

(22)   Of course, John is ready.

Whatever theory of irony one favours, it is clear that in saying (22) S does not mean what she says. But in order to determine what she does mean – something like 'Of course, John is not ready *for his talk*' – one has to know what S does not mean. And at this stage one cannot avoid determining what John is ready for in (22). In other words, S's locutionary act – what she says in (22) – is not, *pace* Bach, a sub-propositional radical: it is a full-fledged, contextually determined proposition.

There is another argument to support this claim. The verb *say*, as used in indirect reports of the 'S said that *p*' kind, is ambiguous, according to Bach (2005), between locutionary and illocutionary meanings. Therefore, Bach must accept that in reporting the ironic utterance in (22) by (23) one transmits S's locutionary act (since her illocutionary act has a different content):

(23)   S said that John was ready.

Some may feel inclined to say that the report in (23) is false in a context where the audience does not have access to the non-literality of S's original utterance. However, no sense could be made of (24) if (23) were not true:

(24)   S said that John was ready, but she didn't mean that/it.

Even though the truth of (23) does not depend on the possibility for the audience of recovering the non-literality of the original utterance, it remains impossible to maintain that the embedded clause in (24) is sub-propositional. The main reason is, of course, that the reference of the demonstrative *that* or of *it* in (24) must be a full-fledged proposition.

## 9.4  Locutionary acts

In section 9.2, we saw that illocutionary forces do not belong to sentence meaning. In the previous section, we saw that some utterances do not have any (direct and literal) illocutionary force, even though they are endowed with propositional and context-dependent meaning. However, until now the discussion was limited to grammatically declarative sentences. A chief reason for introducing the notion of a locutionary level – intermediate between sentence meaning and illocutionary level – is, as we have seen, the existence of cases where what is said differs from what is meant. Parallel cases of non-literality can be found with imperative sentences. In the following example, S does not literally request, order, allow or wish A to ruin her carpet.

(25)   [A spills his glass of wine over the carpet, and clumsily attempts to wipe it off. S says:] Go on! Ruin my carpet!

Exactly as S does not literally assert anything when she sarcastically says that the party is great, the speaker of (25) does not perform any literal directive speech act. But if so, what is the literal content of (25)?

In section 9.2, I have argued that the meaning of the imperative mood should not be analysed in illocutionary terms. Without getting into details, imperative clauses may just be, at the literal level, expressions of propositional contents under a certain attitude or with a certain mode of presentation. Let me just quote two possible accounts, among many. According to the first, the imperative mood presents the utterance content as desirable and potential (Wilson and Sperber 1988; Clark B. 1993; for critical discussions, see Dominicy and Franken 2002; Schwager 2006). According to the second, the imperative mood functions like a necessity operator; roughly, the 'attitude' bearing on the propositional content would be derived from the context-dependent base (i.e. from the domain of quantification) of the modal (Schwager 2006). Independently of the account favoured, locutionary acts must be thought of not only as having propositional content, but also as endowed with a certain mode of presentation of this content (Kissine 2009).

Assessing the semantic accounts of sentence types – e.g. imperative, indicative, subjunctive, interrogative – falls far beyond the scope of this chapter. The important point is that the semantics of sentence types predicts which locutionary-act types the utterances of the sentence can constitute; the nature of the locutionary act performed constrains, in turn, the range of those direct illocutionary acts the locutionary act can constitute.

## 9.5   Forceless meaning and indirect speech acts

Conceiving of illocutionary forces as *optional* properties of utterances allows a fresh perspective on indirect speech acts. Classically, a speech act is said to be indirect whenever its uptake (i.e. A's understanding the utterance as being this speech act) is tied to the uptake of another speech act (Searle 1975b; Bach and Harnish 1979: 70; also Recanati 1987). For instance, if S utters (26) as an answer to A's offer to go to the movies, A can infer, by using various conversational, cooperation-based principles, that in addition to stating that she is tired, by (26) S rejects A's offer.

(26)   I'm very tired.

Some indirect speech acts are highly conventionalised. For instance, although (27) has an interrogative syntactic structure, it constitutes, in English, an extremely conventionalised means to request things.

(27)   Can you pass me the salt?

After Morgan (1978), it is customary to think of such cases as 'short-circuited' implicatures. In a nutshell, Morgan's idea is that the link between (27) taken as a literal question about A's ability to pass the salt and (27) taken as a request to pass the salt can be reconstructed in Gricean terms; however, such an inference generally does not take place. This is so because the link between the *Can you___?* construction and the directive interpretation is highly conventionalised and largely automatic. (Of course, conventionalisation is not arbitrary. In particular, the link between the literal meaning and the indirect force must be easy to grasp. Not every question of the form *Can you___?* will easily receive a directive interpretation. For instance, that S is able to pass the salt is a preparatory condition which must be fulfilled in order for a request to pass the salt to be successful. According to Searle (1975b), this is why a conversationally irrelevant question about a preparatory condition will be readily interpreted as the performance of the corresponding request.)

   A view rival to the 'short-circuited implicature' account is that of Sadock (1974), according to whom each sentence-type is associated with an illocutionary force at the syntactic level. Under such an analysis, (27) is linguistically ambiguous between the interrogative and imperative meanings. As we have seen in section 9.2, the doctrine of a linguistic coupling between sentence types and illocutionary forces is problematic for independent reasons. There is one point of Sadock's analysis that is worth considering here, though. According to him (1974: 97–109), certain grammatical properties distinguish questions used as requests, and conventionalised forms whose meaning is (allegedly) ambiguous between a question and a directive speech act. Take (28) as an instance of the former case, (29) of the latter.

(28)   When will you close the door?

(29)   Will you close the door?

Sadock assumes that only grammatically imperative sentences can be followed by *please* or by an indefinite vocative.

(30)   Close the door, please.

(31)   Close the door, someone.

The unacceptability of (32)–(33) shows, according to Sadock, that (28) is an indirect request performed by means of uttering an unambiguously interrogative sentence.

(32)   ?When will you please close the door?

(33)   ?When will you close the door, someone?

By contrast, the acceptability of (34)–(35) (allegedly) reveals that (29) is linguistically ambiguous between being a grammatically imperative sentence – hence a direct request to close the door – and being a grammatically interrogative sentence – hence a direct question about S's ability to close the door.

(34)   Will you please close the door?

(35)   Will you close the door, someone?

In reaction to Sadock's argument, Bach and Harnish (1979: 200–202) point out that *please* is also acceptable in (36).

(36)   Can you reach the salt, please?

If (27) is, grammatically, a request to bring about the truth of the propositional content, one should expect (36) to be a request to reach the salt. This is counter-intuitive: (36) is a request to pass the salt, not to reach the salt. Likewise, as pointed out by Bach and Harnish, the following example is clearly not ambiguous between an indicative and an imperative underlying structure, despite the acceptability of *please*.

(37)   I'd like some salt, please.

Following Morgan's lead, Bach and Harnish claim that certain questions of the form *Can you___?* or *Will you___?* are standardised means to perform requests. In order to explain away Sadock's grammatical constraints, they argue that (29) is ungrammatical, although pragmatically acceptable.

Both Sadock's and Bach and Harnish's accounts presuppose that the grammatical acceptability of *please* is linked to the imperative mood. However, the acceptability of *please* or of the indefinite vocative does not depend on the utterance's mood, but on whether or not the utterance's (primary) illocutionary force is directive. The following examples are acceptable only if S believes (or pretends to believe) A to have control over his having a nice journey back or getting well soon, that is only if the utterances at hand constitute (pretend) directive speech acts.

(38)   ?Have a nice journey back, please.[6]

(39)   ?Get well soon, please.

Even under such a reading, indefinite vocatives prove unacceptable:

(40)   ?Have a nice journey back, someone.

(41)   ?Get well soon, someone.

When the imperative clauses cannot receive a directive illocutionary force, as in (4) and (42), *please* and the indefinite vocative are clearly ruled out.

(4)    Hit me and I'll hit you back.     [repeated]

(42)   Be tall and people will be respectful.

(43)   ?Hit me, please, and I'll hit you back.

(44)   ?Be tall, please, and people will be respectful.

(45)   ?Hit me, someone, and I'll hit you back.

(46)   ?Be tall, someone, and people will be respectful.

It thus seems that the acceptability of *please* does not depend on grammatical factors – on the sentence mood – but on pragmatic ones – the utterance's illocutionary force. What do we make of the fact that the adjunction of *please* and of *someone* is constrained by the presence of the directive illocutionary force and not of the imperative mood? According to Bach and Harnish's standardisation thesis, when an indirect speech act is conventionalised, hearers automatically derive the secondary indirect force without going through the derivation of the primary, literal speech act. That is, (29) is directly understood as a request to close the door, whereas (28) is interpreted as a question, and it takes supplementary pragmatic reasoning for A to understand it as a request to close the door.

So why not say that (29) has the force of a request only, whereas (28) has the primary force of a question, and, indirectly, constitutes a request? We have seen above that some utterances constitute a locutionary act with a certain content $p$ but do not correspond to any illocutionary act with the content $p$. The same applies here. In (29), the content of the directive illocutionary act – of the request to close the door – differs from that of the locutionary act which the utterance of the interrogative sentence corresponds to.[7] Since the only illocutionary force of (29) is a directive one, it is also, trivially, the primary force. As expected, constructions whose acceptability depends on the primary force being directive are allowed to take *please*. By contrast, the literal force of (28) is that of a question; since the directive force is not primary in this case, *please* is not allowed.

To repeat, (29) is syntactically and semantically an interrogative; however, it is not interpreted – nor intended by S to be interpreted – as a question. Such a rationale presupposes that literal and serious utterances of interrogative sentences are not necessarily associated with the act of requesting information, exactly in the same way as not all utterances of imperative sentences constitute directive speech acts. Interrogatives that are neither requests for information nor expressions of ignorance include the following: rhetorical questions (47), exam questions (48), guess questions (49), and surprise questions (50).

(47)   [Peter, who had made a New Year resolution to give up smoking, lights up. Mary says:] What was your New Year's resolution?
                                   (from Wilson and Sperber 1988)

(48)   Where did Napoleon die?

(49)   Which hand is the marble in?

(50)   A: The President has resigned.
       B: Good heavens. Has he?
                                   (from Wilson and Sperber 1988)

For a careful and illuminating account of the relationship between the interrogative mood and the speech act of questions the reader is referred to Fiengo (2007), who analyses interrogative sentences as expressing incomplete or truth-valueless propositions.

Further arguments in support of the view that conventionalised indirect speech acts like (27) or (29) are, at the literal and direct level, cases of saying without performing an illocutionary act, can be found in Terkourafi (2009c), who provides an interesting discussion of the relevant experimental data.[8] On the one hand, experiments reveal that the putative direct force of a *Could you___* request like (27), namely the illocutionary force of questioning, seems to be ignored in favour of the intended speech act of request. On the other hand, the interrogative *form* of the sentence is processed, as shown by answers such as 'Yes, I can' or by the fact that the interrogative form is recalled (for an extensive discussion and references, see Terkourafi 2009c).

We thus arrive at the following picture of the possible relationships between locutionary and illocutionary acts:

a)   The locutionary content corresponds to the content of the primary, direct speech act. This is the ordinary case.

b)   The locutionary act does not constitute any direct speech act; the only speech act performed by the utterance is indirect. Here, two further subcategories must be distinguished.

   i)   The utterance is non-literal; S does not endorse the locutionary content. For instance, this content 'echoes' an utterance or a thought of another (possibly virtual) person (e.g. Sperber and Wilson 1981; Wilson 2006). The important point is that, in such cases, S's performance of the indirect speech act cannot be reconstructed as an inference taking as one of its premises the performance of a primary speech act that shares its content with the locutionary act.

   ii)   The utterance is literal, but the content of the only illocutionary act the utterance constitutes is distinct from that of the corresponding

locutionary act. However, it is possible to reconstruct the interpretation process as starting from the performance of an illocutionary act
whose content is identical with that of the locutionary act.

The contrast between ironic utterances – point b(i) – and conventionalised
indirect speech acts – point b(ii) – deserves a little more discussion. Morgan's
(1978) idea in treating conventional indirect speech acts as 'short-circuited'
implicatures is precisely that even though the indirect speech act can be
derived from the putative performance of a direct speech act, such an inference does not actually take place: instead, A jumps directly to the indirect
speech act. Take (27).

(27)   Could you pass the salt?        [repeated]

One possible Gricean reconstruction of A's interpretation of (27) runs as
follows (cf. Searle 1975b):

(51)   *Step 1:*   S is asking me whether I have the capacity to pass the salt;
       *Step 2:*   S probably knows that I have this capacity;
       *Step 3:*   S knows that I know that she knows that;
       *Step 4:*   So, S believes that I understand that she does not want to be
                   informed as to my capacity to pass the salt;
       *Step 5:*   We are at a dinner, and it is possible that S needs salt;
       *Step 6:*   Being able to pass the salt is necessary in order to pass the
                   salt;
       *Step 7:*   So, by asking me whether I am able to pass the salt S requests
                   me to pass her the salt.

However, A's exposure to conventions of language use allows him to jump
directly from his recognition of S's utterance of an interrogative sentence
of a certain form – which *does not* amount to a question – to interpreting
S's utterance as a request to pass the salt. The important point about the
rational reconstruction of the interpretation of an indirect speech act like
(27) is that the first step – S's performance of the primary speech act of
questioning – remains compatible with the last step – S's performance of a
request. This reconstruction parallels that of genuinely indirect speech acts
like (28).

(28)   When will you close the door?        [repeated]

The fact that, by uttering (28), S asks A when he will close the door is compatible with the fact that S, by means of this same utterance, requests A to
close the door.

Now, contrast this with the ironic utterance of (7):

(7)   This party is great.        [repeated]

In order to understand what S really means by (7), A has to understand
that S does not assert what she is saying. As in (51), let us try a rational

reconstruction that would start with the premise that S performed a direct and literal speech act.

(52) *Step 1:*  S is asserting that the party is great;
     *Step 2:*  This party is all that S hates;
     *Step 3:*  So, most probably, S does not believe that the party is great;
     *Step 4:*  S is cooperative and would not violate conversational Maxims gratuitously;
     *Step 5:*  S believes that I believe that S does not believe that the party is great;
     *Step 6:*  S does not assert that the party is great;
     *Step 7:*  S means that the party is awful.

Whatever the details, the important point is that, this time, and by contrast with (51), taking the last two steps requires falsifying the first one.

Note also that both rational reconstructions (51) and (52) presuppose that A is capable of making hypotheses about S's beliefs about A's mental states – i.e. that A has the capacity to attribute second-order or third-order mental states. Take first the reconstruction in (51). In order to get to the conclusion that S does not merely want him to say whether he can pass the salt, A must assume that S believes that A knows that S is not interested in (merely) knowing the answer. It would be irrational for S to use a question in order to request something, if she were fairly certain that A would not understand this. That is, A must attribute to S beliefs about A's beliefs about S's beliefs. Things are similar for (52): if A does not understand that S believes that A believes that S does not like the party, A cannot tell the difference between S's telling a lie and S's being sarcastic (for a more detailed discussion see Kissine 2008a).

From the foregoing, we can draw an important empirical reason for not taking rational reconstructions of indirect speech act interpretation as reflecting actual interpretive processes. Children do not master second-order mental state attribution before the age of 7 (Perner and Winner 1985). Importantly, this cognitive ability seems to be required for understanding irony and for lying in an efficient way (Winner and Leekam 1991; Talwar and Gordon 2007). By contrast, it has been repeatedly shown that well before 7, children respond adequately to and produce (conventionalised) indirect requests (e.g. Bates 1976: 275–82; Shatz 1978; Reeder 1978; Carrell 1981; O'Neill 1996), which reveals that this pragmatic ability does not require complex mind-reading skills, contrary to what is implied by rational reconstructions of the kind of (51).

## 9.6  Indirect speech acts and explicit performatives

Explicit performatives constitute one of the oldest and most vexing topics in the history of theorising about speech acts (for recent surveys, see Harnish

2002, 2004). While, again, I will not attempt an exhaustive review here, the fact, discussed in the previous section, that conventionalised indirect speech acts do not have more than one illocutionary force has an implication for the analysis of performatives that is worth considering.

Prototypical performative sentences have the form 'I VP ___', where the VP stands for the illocutionary act the utterances of these sentences constitute under normal conditions. Here are some examples:

(53)    I order you to leave this room.

(54)    I promise that I'll come to your party.

(55)    I name this ship *Queen Elizabeth*.

Utterances of (53)–(55) are generally self-verifying: they constitute the act named by the matrix verb. By uttering (53), S makes it the case that she has ordered A to leave; by uttering (54), S makes it the case that she has promised to come to the party; by uttering (55), S makes it the case that the ship is named *Queen Elizabeth*.

The 'self-verifying' character of performatives like (55) can be explained by extra-linguistic, culture-specific institutions (for a more extensive discussion, see Kissine forthcoming). However, it is highly doubtful that the same treatment can be applied to (53)–(54) (for an attempt, see Searle 1992a; for a cogent criticism, see Bach and Harnish 1992). The challenge consists in explaining how (53) is interpreted as an order and (54) as a promise without, at the same time, giving up commonplace semantics – i.e. by deriving the truth-conditional content of (53)–(54) through the same compositional semantic principles as for other structures of the form 'I VP that___', as in (56), or other present simple forms of *order*, as in (57).

(56)    I hope that you are well.

(57)    He orders you to leave.

That explicit performatives do not involve any extraordinary semantic features is further suggested by the observation that in some circumstances a sentence like (53) does not constitute a directive speech act at all, and has the content predicted by standard truth-conditional interpretation.

(58)    A: Imagine that I light up a cigarette. What is your reaction?
        B: I order you to leave this room.

Another interesting fact is that the following examples (59)–(62) are as well suited as (53)–(54) to performing orders and promises.

(59)    Leave the room, and that's an order.

(60)    I'll come to your party, and that's a promise.

(61)   Leave the room, I order you.

(62)   I'll come to your party, I promise.

The analysis of examples in (59)–(60) is pretty straightforward. The speaker first utters a sentence, and then, with the second conjunct, indicates its illocutionary force, the demonstrative *that* picking up the first conjunct. As for (61)–(62), according to the account developed by Potts (2005; also Bach 1999a), utterances with parentheticals express two propositions. The first is the main one – 'at-issue' – while the second is secondary. This second proposition may have a 'procedural' role (cf. Wilson and Sperber 1993a), in that it facilitates the processing of the at-issue information. Following this widely accepted line of thought, in (61)–(62) the secondary propositions – the parenthetical ones – help attribute the illocutionary force to the main content.

The spirit of Davidson's (1979) 'paratactic' account of explicit performatives is quite similar. In his view, the surface form of, for instance (53), hides the following two utterances, where the first demonstrates the second one: *I order you that. You leave the room.* However, it is pretty clear that the *that* in (53) is not a demonstrative. Compare with French where there is no homophony between demonstratives and complementisers or relative pronouns.

(63)   J'ordonne          **que**          tu          sortes          d'ici.
       I order.IND.PRS.1SG  that.COMP  you.SG  leave.SBJV.PR.2SG from here.
       'I order that you leave.'

(64)   Sors              d'ici          et      **c'**      est          un ordre.
       Leave.IMP. 2SG  from here  and  that.DEM  is-IND.PR.3SG a    order.
       'Leave, and that's an order.'

Although it is not viable, Davidson's account is attractive in that it puts the explicit performatives in (53)–(54) and (59)–(62) on the same footing; the utterance's main informational content is assigned an illocutionary force through a comment on this content.

As for Bach and Harnish (1979: 203–33; 1992), they claim that explicit performatives are standardised (conventionalised) indirect speech acts, exactly in the same way as indirect requests of the kind of (27).

(27)   Could you pass the salt?              [repeated]

Recall from the previous section that, on their view, although at the direct level (27) is a question, standardisation allows one to interpret it as a request without going through the inference from the direct to the indirect force. Likewise, they argue, explicit performatives like (53)–(54) are, at the direct level, 'constative' speech acts. The constative class includes those speech acts that aim at transferring information, assertion being a paradigmatic case. Bach and Harnish thus claim that by uttering (53) S asserts that she orders A to leave the room; this assertion is interpreted as an indirect order. However, because the inference from the direct to the indirect force is 'compressed by the precedent', (53) is a standardised indirect order exactly in the same way as (27). Bach and Harnish thus predict both that the content of (53) is the proposition [S orders that A leaves] and that (53) is an order.

Reimer (1995) objects to Bach and Harnish's account that it does not seem intuitively plausible that S asserts anything by means of (53); the constative part of performatives is introspectively inaccessible. However, it is not obvious that the (alleged) question part of indirect requests like (27) is always accessible either. If, when solving a problem, I ask you 'Can you tell me the square root of 16?', it would be highly counter-intuitive to interpret my utterance as a question (e.g. Clark H. 1979). In any event, nothing implies that conventionalised indirect speech acts have two illocutionary forces. We have seen above that indirect speech acts do not necessarily have a direct illocutionary force; in conventionalised indirect speech acts the content of the locutionary act is different from that of the illocutionary act, but only one illocutionary act is performed. Things are not different with explicit performatives. Recall that locutionary acts are endowed with a full-blown propositional content. Therefore, at the locutionary level explicit performatives have exactly those truth conditions that would be predicted by regular compositional semantics. The propositional content of the locutionary act performed in (53) is [S orders A to leave]. Yet, this does not imply that S asserts this content. The only illocutionary act performed in (53) is the order that A (should) leave. We can reconcile two seemingly conflicting intuitions: on the one hand, an explicit performative has the same propositional content as would an assertion constituted by an utterance of the same sentence; on the other hand, it does not constitute such an assertion.[9]

An interesting example in favour of the account of explicit performatives just sketched can be drawn from Allan (2006a). He points out that (65) is adequately paraphrased by (66):

(65)   In the first place I admit to being wrong; and secondly I promise it will never happen again.

(66)   The first thing I have to say is that I admit to being wrong; and the second thing I have to say is that I promise it will never happen again.

In (66) *the second thing* does not refer to a second act of promising, but to the second act of saying, that is to the explicit performative *I promise it will never happen again*; ditto for *secondly* in (65). That explicit performatives are acts of saying is consonant with the analysing of saying as the performance of a locutionary act. This is not to say that explicit performatives cannot be subject to a rational reconstruction, starting from the premise that S asserted that she, say, ordered A to leave the room. However, to repeat, rational reconstructions do not aim at modelling actual interpretive processes. Note that the fact that the interpretation of explicit performatives can be reconstructed on the basis of primary assertions does tell us something: that S is ready to endorse the content of the locutionary act – that she's not ironic. That is, it tells us that explicit performatives *can* be interpreted as assertions; but it remains that, in most cases, explicit performatives *are not* interpreted as assertions.

## **9.7** By way of conclusion: illocutionary force attribution

A natural question to ask, at this point, is how illocutionary forces are attributed. We have seen that developmental evidence makes it unlikely that illocutionary force attribution is underpinned by Gricean inferences about multi-layered communicative intentions (for a classical version of such an account, see Bach and Harnish 1979). Very young children are good at attributing illocutionary forces to utterances well before being able to attribute complex mental states required by Gricean reconstructions. As for contemporary pragmatic theories, as I said in section 9.1, they are fairly elusive on psychological mechanisms underlying illocutionary force attribution.

In Kissine (2009) I argued that speech acts should be thought of as (not necessarily effective) reasons for S to believe that the propositional content is true (assertives), for A to bring about the truth of the propositional content (directives) or for S to bring about the truth of the propositional content (commissives).[10] An important feature of this analysis is that it does not require advanced mind-reading skills for attributing illocutionary forces, except for complex communicative moves like irony (cf. Kissine 2008a).

Whenever the content of a speech act corresponds to the content of the constitutive locutionary act, this speech act is literal and direct. We have seen that utterances often constitute locutionary acts, that is they express propositional contents under a certain mood of presentation. The type of the mode of presentation constrains the range of the possible direct speech acts the locutionary act may constitute. For instance, if the imperative mood expresses an attitude characteristic of desiderative mental states, the potential direct illocutionary force will be a directive one.

However, there does not necessarily exist a one-to-one correspondence between sentence types and modes of presentation of the propositional content. In particular, it is fairly possible that the indicative mood is neutral in this respect (e.g. Recanati 1987; Allan 2006a). An indicative sentence like (67) can be performed either as an assertion that A leaves the city on Monday or as an order that A leave the city on Monday.

(67)   You leave the city Monday.

Let us assume that the indicative mood does not constrain the locutionary-act type. Illocutionary force attribution and the interpretation of the utterance type as a locutionary act with a certain mode of presentation will thus mutually influence each other. Note also that, in both cases, the propositional content is the same; it thus follows that the order in (67) is as direct as the one in (68); cf. Recanati (1987) for the same conclusion.

(68)    Leave the city tomorrow morning.

This is in tune with the widely acknowledged fact that most interpretive processes operate on-line. The precise ways sentence types, locutionary modes of presentation and illocutionary forces interact constitute a rich matter for future research.

# 10

# Pragmatics in update semantics

Henk Zeevat

## 10.1 Introduction

A person who listens to, understands and accepts the utterance of another acquires new information. There may be new beliefs that are about the main event described in the utterance, but crucially understanding and accepting it entails obtaining new information about the intentions of the other speaker. And if the intention is to inform, it also entails obtaining new information about the world. As long as there is no intention to correct old information, the new information can be described as an update of the beliefs of the hearer (and as a 'downdate' followed by an update if the new information is a correction of existing information). The direct description of the utterance as an update of an existing information state and the claim that this cannot be reduced to more fundamental operations and is the suitable framework for natural language semantics are characteristic of update semantics.

 Probably the most basic way to think of update semantics in relation to pragmatics is as a natural environment for formalising pragmatics. Nearly everything in pragmatics can be described as (partly or completely) determining a change to an information state, the information state of the hearer, of an idealised hearer, of the speaker or the speaker's model of the hearer or of the common ground or the common ground according to one of the speakers. It seems fair to say that a pragmatic theory that cannot be described as characterising aspects of the up- or downdates in a context that models (real or imagined) hearers in a context interpreting the utterance is hard to imagine. On the other hand, many pragmatic approaches are still not theories that make precise and testable predictions and formalisation is very much needed to turn this area of study into proper science. So update semantics and update-semantical approaches to pragmatics are an important field of study even if e.g. one rejects the ideology of update semantics or some of the ideas that have been formalised in it. It still would seem the natural format for formalising any pragmatic ideas, even if one would like to include new mechanisms or reinterpret some of the mechanisms contained in the literature.

In this sense, up- and downdating information states is just a technical tool for being precise about what utterances do to the various information states involved in communication (the common ground between speaker and hearer, the hearer's and the speaker's knowledge and beliefs) and the natural successor of the commitment slates of Hamblin (1971) or the version of those that is employed by Gazdar (1979) or by Karttunen (1973) in the definition of filters. The tool has the advantage that whatever semantic assumptions one needs to make for one's pragmatics can be formulated directly in the same framework and in the same way.

What information states one wants to update depends on one's pragmatics. For semantic applications, it does not seem to matter. It suffices to assume somebody exposed to a series of trustworthy speech acts who is updating her own set of beliefs by accepting all these utterances and who happens to be an ideal hearer perfectly understanding the utterances she is exposed to. For pragmatical applications, the obvious candidate seems to be the common ground between speaker and hearer in a conversation. Both parties can update that and it would be possible to follow the progress of the conversation by taking in the effect of both parties' moves. This would be third-party conversational analysis as proposed by Sacks *et al.* (1974), but it is well known that it does not quite work for real conversations since misunderstandings and deceptions occur frequently. The best choice would be to have two separate versions of the common ground (or more if there are more speakers) and to try to track the evolution of all these common grounds. The common ground according to the speaker seems the most relevant information state from a linguistic point of view, since it can account for the speaker's choices in formulation and for the effect the speaker expects her utterances to have on the hearer. It also accounts for the hearer's choices in interpreting the utterances and for modelling the hearer in making choices in her formulation of those utterances, but in this second role, it does not account for the variation in linguistic form studied in linguistics. But there is no extra problem involved in formalising the third-party perspective: one just takes the model of the common ground of both parties.

Any serious semantic and pragmatic theory makes empirical predictions. Update semantics would be the theory with the shortest distance between the theoretical construct and what can be tested. What people assume after an utterance which they did not assume before is what can be tested almost directly. Much more than a truth-conditional account, update semantics seems to be about the primary function of linguistic utterances: to transfer information from one person to another (this also covers speech acts other than assertion).

Information states can be and have been modelled in many different ways. A simple and effective way is to start from a logical formalism with a proper model theory. Information states are consistent theories (sets of formulas that can be satisfied on at least one model for the theory) and updating is just adding new formulas to the set. Most of the older approaches like Hamblin's or Gazdar's follow this pattern, and Discourse Representation Theory (Kamp and Reyle 1993) can be seen as an instance of this approach with a more sophisticated interface with syntax and maximal decomposition of formulas. It is also not difficult to make connections with tableau-based theorem-proving and to think of information states as sets of open branches with positive and negative literals (a formalism like that of Dekker (1992) comes close to that). Literals are here atomic formulas with constants, variables and skolem constants as the set of allowed terms. This may well be the best road towards implementing update semantics. Updating becomes the closure of those branches that become inconsistent under the new information and the addition of the necessary new literals to the branches that remain. Purely eliminative notions of update semantics are reached if the information state is a set of models, a set of possible worlds or a set of possibilities. Conceptual simplicity is typical for this last group of approaches; concreteness and thereby simple search procedures are typical for the first group, while mixed systems are best for implementational purposes. But it is not difficult to do translations between different formalisms. In this chapter, an elimination approach will be introduced in preference to other approaches because of its inherent simplicity.

### 10.1.1  Basic update semantics

The following gives a basic development of update semantics for a language $L$ (the set of atomic propositions) of propositional logic. The definitions follow the notation of Veltman (1996).

(1)  Models $M$ for $L$:
   Any subset of $L$ is a model $M$. (The subset of true atoms).
   Information states $\sigma \in \Sigma$:
   Any subset $\sigma$ of the set of models for $L$ is an information state. This makes the set of all information states the powerset of the set of models.
   $\Sigma = pow(pow(L))$
   Atomic updates: (the update of an information state $\sigma$ with an atomic proposition $p$)
   $\sigma[p] = \{M \in \sigma : p \in M\}$
   Full updates: (the update of an information state $\sigma$ with a complex formula $\varphi$).
   $\sigma[\varphi \wedge \psi] = \sigma[\varphi][\psi]$
   $\sigma[\neg\varphi] = \sigma \setminus \sigma[\varphi]$
   $\sigma[\varphi \rightarrow \psi] = \sigma[\neg(\varphi \wedge \neg\psi)]$
   $\sigma[\varphi \vee \psi] = \sigma[\neg(\neg\varphi \wedge \neg\psi)]$
   $\sigma[\varphi \leftrightarrow \psi] = \sigma[(\varphi \wedge \psi) \vee (\neg\varphi \wedge \neg\psi)]$

(2)  $\varphi$ is *inconsistent* with $\sigma$ iff $\sigma[\varphi] = \emptyset$

(3)  $\sigma \vDash \varphi$ iff $\sigma[\varphi] = \sigma$

The state of no information (1) is $pow(L)$, the set of all models. The inconsistent information state (0) is Ø.

This basic system can be extended to first-order logic and modal logics. For first-order logic one changes the set of models to first-order models for a language $L$. Variables are treated as extra constants for which the models are either defined or not.

A simple development, designed to capture discourse referents and DRT-style semantics goes as follows. This requires a DRT-like language in which atoms are either variables or atoms as in first-order logic.

> If $\varphi_1$ and ... and $\varphi_n$ are formulas so is $\varphi_1 \wedge \ldots \wedge \varphi_n$
> If $\varphi$ is a formula so is $\neg\varphi$
> If $\varphi$ and $\psi$ are formulas so are $\varphi \rightarrow \psi, \varphi \vee \psi$ and $\varphi \leftrightarrow \psi$

The update semantics below assumes 'normal' formulas: variable atoms are on the left in a conjunction, conjunctions are always maximal and there is at most one occurrence of an atom $x$ in a formula for each variable.

(4)  $\sigma[x] = \{M \in \sigma : Mx \text{ is defined}\}$

This allows the definition of a function $dm(\sigma)$ which finds the discourse referents of $\sigma$

(5)  $dm(\sigma) = \{x : \forall M \in \sigma\, Mx \text{ defined}\}$

Atomic updates are redefined in (6).

(6)  $\sigma[P x_1 \ldots x_n] = \{M \in \sigma :< M x_1, \ldots, M x_n >\in M P$ or $< M x_1, \ldots, M x_n >$ is undefined$\}$

A negation with built-in quantification is given in (7). The two information states $\sigma$ and $\sigma[\varphi]$ together determine the set of discourse referents introduced by $\varphi$. An element of $\sigma$ is eliminated if it has a variant with respect to these discourse referents in $\sigma[\varphi]$.

(7)  $\sigma[\neg\varphi] = \{M \in \sigma : \neg\exists M' M' =_X M M' \in \sigma[\varphi]$ and $X = dm(\sigma[\varphi]\backslash dm(\sigma)\}$

(8) defines $M =_X M'$. Two models $M$ and $M'$ are exactly the same apart from what their interpretation functions may do with the subset $X$ of the language $L$.

(8)  $M' =_X M$ iff for all $\alpha \in L \backslash X\, M\alpha = M'\alpha$

The definition of negation builds in quantification over discourse referents in the usual way: $\sigma[\varphi]$ is existentially closed for its own discourse referents (which are the ones it does not share with $\sigma$) before being subtracted from $\sigma$. The definitions of the other operations are as before.

## 10.1.2  History

Update semantics came into its own in Karttunen (1976), Heim (1982), Heim (1983), Kamp and Reyle (1993) and Stalnaker (1973) with the breakthrough that is now known as dynamic semantics and which was aimed at three problems: pronoun-binding semantics, presupposition satisfaction and the semantics of tense in discourse. The problems in pronoun-binding semantics go back to Geach (1962) (with medieval predecessors) and become acute in Montague (1974b). The update perspective on presupposition starts with the notion of pragmatic presupposition of Stalnaker (1973) reacting to the essentially semantic view of presupposition in a tradition going back to Frege where presupposition is a condition on having a truth value, something that is hard to maintain for a class of presupposition triggers. For Stalnaker (1973), presuppositions become the conditions under which it is appropriate to use presupposition triggers. Karttunen (1974) extends this view with a detailed study of the kind of requirements that triggers impose on their environments (the inheritance conditions). Heim (1983) finally managed to reduce these inheritance conditions to the update conditions of the operations involved (see above). The problems of temporal reference were first noted by Reichenbach (1947), addressed by Kamp and Rohrer (1983) in early DRT, while Partee (1973 and 1984) showed the essential similarity between the problems of pronouns and temporal reference.

The common solution turned out to be to go dynamic. That is, first, to explain the truth of a natural language assertion in terms of both the world of evaluation and the informational component of the context (the 'linguistic context') and, second, to explain how the utterance (or parts of it) changes the informational context for further processing. These two aspects of dynamic semantics can be combined into a theory of information states and an account of how the expressions of a natural language (or of a suitable formalism designed to capture aspects of natural language) update information states.

An important insight is that truth can be defined in terms of updates. A true information state is one that contains the one true model (the model of the actual world) and (9) defines truth of sentences in terms of true information states.

(9) An utterance is *true* iff it updates any true information state into a true information state.

This can be generalised into an account of intensions. Let $M$ be any model.

(10) $\varphi$ is true on $M$ iff it maps any information state containing $M$ onto an information state still containing $M$.

And into an account of logical consequence as in (11):

(11) $\varphi_1 \ldots \varphi_n \vDash \psi$ iff $\psi$ is true on any model on which each of $\varphi_1$ and $\ldots$ and $\varphi_n$ are true.

More natural in the dynamic setting is to have a sequential definition as in (12), though this does not correspond with a classical notion.

(12)   $\varphi_1 \ldots \varphi_n \models \psi$ iff for all $\sigma$, $\sigma[\varphi_1] \ldots [\varphi_n][\psi] = \sigma[\varphi_1] \ldots [\varphi_n]$

This also has a local version, as in (13).

(13)   $\varphi_1 \ldots \varphi_n \models \psi$ on $\sigma$ iff $\sigma[\varphi_1] \ldots [\varphi_n]$ is defined and identical to
       $\sigma[\varphi_1] \ldots [\varphi_n][\psi]$

One is a proper update semanticist iff one holds that the meaning of a natural language expression is its contribution to the updates defined by the complete expressions in which it occurs.[1] This includes, for example, that the setting up of a new discourse referent belongs to the meaning of an indefinite description, that the meaning of a definite description contains its undefinedness in information states in which it does not single out a unique referent, or the variation of referents or undefinedness of pronouns in particular information states. But often the update-semantical version of a meaning is an obvious lift of its traditional meaning.

### 10.1.3  Pragmatics

The interesting aspect of the proposal is that now suddenly many phenomena in the pragmatic waste-bin (which had landed there because they resisted a treatment in terms of truth conditions) can be taken out again and become part of semantics.

The reason is that far more structure is available. If classical semantics treats sentences as functions from possible worlds to truth values, update semantics assigns to the same sentences functions from information states to information states with the additional option of letting the function be undefined for certain options. If classical semantics were correct (i.e. the meaning of sentences is exhaustively characterised by a function from possible worlds to truth values), the intension $[[\varphi]]$ of classical semantics would be sufficient for defining the corresponding updates. The update of $\varphi$, written $[\varphi]$, on an information state $\sigma$ (written $\sigma[\varphi]$) could be given as $\sigma$ restricted to those worlds $M$ such that $[[\varphi]](M) = \mathbf{true}$. If classical truth-conditional semantics is insufficient for giving an account of natural language meanings and update semantics does indeed help, it can be shown that the reverse is not the case. Updates that are not intersective ($\sigma[\varphi] \subseteq \sigma$) and distributive ($\sigma[\varphi] = \{\{M\}[\varphi] : M \in \sigma\}$) are not characterisable by a truth condition $[[\varphi]]$. The interesting updates are therefore the ones that lack one of the two properties. A simple example is the update with $\varphi$ as a version of the partial analysis of assertion in Stalnaker (1978) (an update $[ASSERT(\varphi)]$ which updates with $\varphi$ if $\varphi$ is consistent and informative and the trivial update otherwise):

(14)   if $\varphi$ is consistent with $\sigma$ ($\sigma[\varphi] \neq \emptyset$) and informative $\sigma[\varphi] \neq \sigma$),
       $\sigma[ASSERT(\varphi)] = \sigma[\varphi]$ else $\sigma[ASSERT(\varphi)] = \sigma$).

One cannot see in a single world $w$ whether $\varphi$ is consistent or informative with respect to the whole information state. If $\varphi$ is true in $w$, it may fail to be informative by not eliminating anything in the larger $\sigma$; if it is false, $\varphi$ is informative but it may be inconsistent with $\sigma$ by eliminating all the worlds of $\sigma$.

In many cases, the inhabitants of the pragmatic waste-bin should not have been there in the first place. The specification of what it means that a pronoun has a certain antecedent in a context seems a semantical problem (and was taken e.g. by Montague to be an important part of natural language semantics). An equally semantic question is which antecedents are possible given the linguistic context. Arguably only the question which antecedent is the right one for a given pronoun is a pragmatic question. In presupposition theory, the question whether the presupposition is true in the context of a trigger seems semantic (or the more appropriate question for 'anaphoric presupposition': whether the context of the trigger entails a suitable antecedent for the presupposition) but questions of accommodation (for the case that the presupposition is locally satisfied) would be pragmatic. The meaning of tenses and aspectual operators is also a semantic question, but the anaphoric processes that in many accounts play an important role in characterising their meaning in a particular context are not semantic but pragmatic.

A number of core applications of update semantics are also 'semantic' in this sense of enlarging the horizon beyond truth-conditional semantics. A good example is the semantics of epistemic *may* and *must* and natural language implication in the work of Veltman (1996), or the semantics of imperatives and deontic modality in the work of Mastop (2005) and Nauze (2008). This work adds more structure to information states: an updatable preference ordering in the case of Veltman and 'to do lists' in the case of Mastop and Nauze. Such applications are, however, properly semantic and aim at exploiting update semantics for dealing with semantic phenomena that are not within the reach of truth-conditional semantics.

## **10.2** Semantics and pragmatics

If pragmatics is incorporated in update semantics the distinction between semantics and pragmatics seems largely lost: in both cases one has updating operations. One can do some classification: some update operations are eliminative and distributive and can be called classical, but semantics seems to go further than just that.

For example, the analysis of *may* in Veltman (1996) makes it a test on information states: does the information state have worlds in which its complement holds? If so, [**may** $\varphi$] is the trivial update; otherwise it is inconsistent information and leads to an absurd information state.

This would be half of the minimal analysis of assertion by Stalnaker, which requires assertions to be informative and consistent with the common ground. A variant of the analysis in which bad assertions lead to the absurd information state can be defined using *may* as: $\sigma[\textbf{may } \varphi][\textbf{may } \neg\varphi][\varphi]$.

The same holds for a proposal by Beaver (2001) to analyse a presupposition trigger like *bachelor* as $\sigma[\mathbf{pres}(adult(x) \wedge male(x))][\neg married(x)]$. The semantics for **pres** $\varphi$ proposed is also a test: $\sigma[\mathbf{pres}\,\varphi] = \sigma$ if $\sigma[\varphi] = \sigma$ and undefined otherwise. This is close to the semantics for *must* that is most in line with the semantics for *may*. Being non-classical therefore does not mean being 'pragmatic.' The semantic/pragmatic distinction appealed to in attributing *may* a semantics is the distinction between lexically coded properties and properties that belong to the use of the expression. But it is questionable whether that distinction can be maintained. Conventional implicatures are lexically coded and so are presuppositions. Many particles are best seen as markers of rather unclear semantic features like additivity, formal contrast, denial of expectation etc. Their functional explanation seems related not to the expressive possibilities of the language, but to the difficulties of maintaining complex ranges of facts in memory.

One way to save the distinction would be to revert to a historical picture. An important feature of grammaticalisation processes is the semantics of the grammaticalised items becoming more pragmatical ('semantic bleaching'). The existence of modal operators with 'pragmatic' meaning could then be explained as the outcome of such a process. The 'ability' readings with which 'may' started – as is generally assumed – would be classical updates. The process by which 'ability' became 'epistemic possibility' turned the classical update into a non-classical one. And this holds for the other cases as well. It is a standard assumption in historical linguistics that words start as either deictic elements or as descriptive ('truth-conditional' or property-expressing) elements. The elements that give trouble must therefore have come invariably from elements whose truth-conditional characterisation is unproblematic.

## 10.3 Presupposition

Karttunen's study of presupposition projection starting in the 1960s and carried on into the 1970s can be thought of as the origin of update semantics, but without the name and the slogan 'the meaning of an expression is the change it brings to an information state'. For Karttunen, presuppositions are the prerequisite for using their triggers: a context that does not entail the presupposition cannot accept the use of the trigger that presupposes it. In Karttunen (1973) this leads to a classification of contexts of triggers into plugs, holes and filters. Plugs are sentential operators that do not let any presuppositional requirement out (e.g. verbs like 'x says that p'), holes let all the presuppositional requirements out (*not, maybe, x knows that*) and filters are the ones that let some presuppositions out and not others (*and, or* and *if . . . then* are examples). To understand this properly, one must realise that Karttunen is interested in presuppositional requirements.[2] The requirement of a trigger like 'is glad that' can be fulfilled under 'says that' as in (15), and so it would be wrong to make the truth of the complement a requirement of the whole sentence.

(15)  John said that Mary left and that Bill is glad that she did.

Filters are formalised in Karttunen (1974) in terms of information state, as in (16).

(16)  $X$ allows $A_p$ iff $X \vDash p$
      $X$ allows $\neg A$ iff $X$ allows $A$
      $X$ allows $A \& B$ iff $X$ allows $A$ and $X + A$ allows $B$
      $X$ allows $A \rightarrow B$ iff $X$ allows $A$ and $X + A$ allows $B$
      $X$ allows $A \vee B$ iff $X$ allows $A$ and $X + \neg A$ allows $B$

The last of these has given some trouble, due to examples like

(17)  Either the toilet is in a funny place or this house does not have a toilet.

There is still no fully satisfactory solution.

From the point of view of update semantics, this is an attempt to characterise presupposition in terms of properties of the input context for their triggers: the use of the trigger is inappropriate unless the presupposition holds in the input state. Update semantics can capture this 'allowing' by update restrictions along the lines of (18).

(18)  $\sigma[T]$ is undefined unless $\sigma \vDash p$

The notion is problematic however. For some triggers (*too* and many other particles; definite descriptions) the place where the presupposition is true can be other than the local context of the trigger. In (19), B's parents presumably have no opinion about whether A is in bed, and John can think that Tim likes him, without having any idea that Tim is the hearer's brother.

(19)  A: My parents think I am in bed.
      B: My parents believe I am in bed too.
      John thinks that your brother likes him.

And it ignores accommodation. Often – but not always and not for all triggers – the missing presupposition can be added, but when this happens it is more likely to happen in the global context than in the direct local context of the presupposition trigger. What one can say is that if the presupposition is not just missing but overtly absent (the speaker says 'I do not know whether $p$') or if it holds in the context of the trigger that $p$ is false, the trigger is not acceptable.

Irene Heim realised that this can be stated better as an update semantics.[3] In this way, truth conditions and allowance conditions are captured by one single definition.

Heim brings a second improvement to Karttunen's system, the addition of global accommodation. If a trigger is updated into an auxiliary information state and the presupposition $p$ can be added either locally or globally, it is assumed that either the local state or the global state can be changed to be $X[p]$, with a preference for the global state. This captures the predictions of Gazdar.

While Karttunen uses a concept of update semantics to explain filters, Gazdar's aim was the modern update semantics goal of stating the full change that utterance will bring to an input context. His contribution is flawed, because of an attempt to replace Karttunen's insights with an only seemingly equivalent formulation in which filtering is the effect of clausal implicatures. This does not work, witness (20).

(20)   If John has a son, his child must be happy.

(20) would only produce clausal implicatures that the speaker does not know whether John has a son. This is not inconsistent with the presupposition of the definite description 'his child' which therefore does not get cancelled. So Gazdar predicts – against intuition – that 'John has a child' is projected.

It is, however, not difficult to amend Gazdar's idea with Karttunen-style filtering, as in (21). Here $X$ is the given context (the information state in which the trigger is used).

(21)   (i)    The potential presuppositions of a simplex formula $A$ under $X$ are those given by the triggers in $A$ that are not entailed by $X$.
       (ii)   For $O$ one of $\neg, \Box, \diamond, x$ *Vs that*, the potential presuppositions of $O\,A$ under $X$ are those of $A$ under $X$.
       (iii)  The potential presuppositions of $A \to B$ and $QAB$ (for $Q$ a positive quantifier) under $X$ are the potential presuppositions of $\neg(A \wedge \neg B)$ under $X$ and those of $A \vee B$ under $X$ those of $\neg(\neg A \wedge \neg B)$ under $X$.
       (iv)   The potential presuppositions of $A \wedge B$ under $X$ are the potential presuppositions of $A$ together with those of $B$ that are not entailed by $A$ under $X$.

The exception to the cumulative hypothesis given in Langendoen and Savin (1971) can be fully explained by Gazdar's view of triggers as signs that the speaker accepts the presupposition. Such a sign has no significance if the speaker has locally entailed that she accepts the presupposition in the context. The conversational contribution of utterance $u$ can now be simply stated as

(22)   $X \cup \{u\} \cup !potIMP(u)$

where $potIMP(u)$ collects the potential scalar implicatures of $u$, the potential clausal implicatures of $u$ and the potential presuppositions of $u$ and $\cup!$ is Gazdar's satisfiable incrementation: add an element $x$ of $potIMP$ to $X \cup \{u\}$ unless $x$ makes a set consisting of $X \cup \{u\}$ and other members of $potIMP$ inconsistent. The global projection of presuppositions in this view is treated quite rightly as yet another implicature,[4] nowadays attributed by most who share the view that these projections are implicatures to Grice's maxim of relevance.[5]

While this is an attractive reformulation of Gazdar that improves on Karttunen and Heim by restricting global accommodation in interesting ways (conflicts with implicatures and other presuppositions), it falls short of Heim and Van der Sandt in one point: a cancelled presupposition only stays as a local entailment of the simplex clause in which the trigger occurs.[6] This is probably too inflexible and the theories of van der Sandt (1992) and Heim (1983) offer the full space of auxiliary contexts necessary to put the presupposition in other places.

Van der Sandt's theory assimilates presupposition to the dynamic treatment of anaphora and is formulated in the DRT (a representational version of update semantics, as assumed in this paper). It incorporates the idea that presupposition triggers (just as pronouns) can only update the context if the context contains the presupposition (an antecedent for an anaphoric pronoun). Van der Sandt obtains the effects of Gazdar by allowing the insertion of a missing presupposition in any context to which the presupposition trigger has access and to which the presupposition can be consistently added, with a preference for the highest available one, a stronger assumption than in Heim, who just postulates a preference for the main context.[7]

All the theories treated so far fail on one important presuppositional phenomenon: partial resolution. This is the situation where an antecedent is present but not quite. Spenader (2003) investigated corpora for *too* and Kamp and Rossdeutscher (1994) formalised some specific texts for the German *wieder*, 'again'. In both studies, most antecedents turn out to be incomplete, i.e. one finds material that is intuitively the antecedent, but information needs to be added to it to make it a proper antecedent as required by the trigger. Kamp and Rossdeutscher (1994) have interesting suggestions about how to make the amendments and the treatment of these is more feasible in a representational theory than in an eliminative update semantics. Important is also to prevent it happening. For example, *John is walking in the park. Mary will have dinner in New York too.* does not lead to a repair in which John will have dinner in New York. (The example is due to Nicholas Asher, p.c.) This partial resolution happens with other triggers as well, as in McCawley's famous example (23).

(23)  a.  LBJ dreamt that he was a homosexual and everybody knew that his foreign policy was a failure.
      b.  LBJ dreamt that he was a homosexual and everybody knew that he was waiting for boys in the restroom of the YMCA.

The examples show that (23b) is an example of resolution, since the presupposition does not project out. The processing that a sufficiently informed human interpreter of the sentence seems to go through seems to involve weighing several possibilities against each other, e.g. as in (24).

(24)   Is LBJ waiting for boys in restrooms? Seems rather unlikely. Does
       everybody know this in his dream where he is a homosexual? Quite
       possibly.

This weighing of possibilities is important. (25a) is an example from Beaver
(2001).

(25)   a.   When Spaceman Spiff lands on planet X he will be surprised
            that he weighs more than on Earth.
       b.   When Spaceman Spiff lands on planet X he will notice that he
            weighs more than 200 kilos.

   In the (25b) example, Spaceman Spiff can weigh 200 kilos (in his own
perception of his weight) when he lands on planet X, but this can also
be his normal weight. In the latter case (this is serious overweight of the
kind that happens), it would be extremely unlikely that he would be chosen to be a spaceman. The more local accommodation, that he weighs
200 kilos on planet X, is just as preferred as in the (a) case, but unlike the
(a) case, it depends merely on probabilistic reasoning: the other possibility is
consistent.

## 10.4  Implicature

Gazdar's formalisations of clausal and scalar implicatures are the first in an
update perspective. They consist in the cancellable additions of the negations
of scalar lexical alternatives further up the Horn scale and in the addition of
$\neg K \neg \varphi$ and $\neg K \varphi$ for clauses $\varphi$ whose truth value is left undetermined by the
matrix sentence in which they occur.
   While there are many alternative treatments for the scalar implicatures,
the treatment of clausal implicatures does not seem to have drawn much
discussion. An obvious criticism (Rob van der Sandt, p.c.) is that the proposal
appears to be too strong. It is perfectly possible to believe A or that A is false
and at the same time state that John believes that A. But this is less of a
problem in the context of the revised Gazdar solution from the last section,
where it is easy to get cancellation of these implicatures. The implicatures
can be connected to either quantity (if A is left undecided, while the speaker
knows that A or that not A, he is being economical with the truth) or relevance: using the clause A is raising the question whether A and leaving it
open is a sign that one cannot decide the matter. This also seems relevant
for the example (26) discussed in Karttunen and Peters (1979), where in (26b)
the medical speaker would take into account that there could be a view of
the matter around under which the measles is not a possibility.

(26)   (a) If he has the measles, he would have precisely these symptoms.
       (b) If he had the measles, he would have precisely these symptoms.

There are now many versions of update semantics where questions are used to obtain exhaustivity effects, including scalar implicatures. The idea combines an analysis of the topic/focus distinction in terms of answers to a question (Klein and von Stutterheim 1987; van Kuppevelt 1995) with the exhaustive interpretation of *wh*-questions (Groenendijk and Stokhof 1984). The trouble of course is that very often these questions are not overtly given, while at the same time the scalar implicatures and the exhaustivity effects are intuitively there.

Zeevat (2007) uses question updates to assign an exhaustive value to the *wh*-variable involved. In this way, *John has two pigs* can answer questions like *How many pigs does John have? What animals does John have? Who has pigs? Who has two pigs?* and give exhaustivity entailments like: the number of John's pigs is 2, the animals that John has are pigs, the one who has pigs is John, the one who has two pigs is John. The context should make it clear which of these questions apply.

Another way of going about this problem is to structure the set of possibilities in an information state into partitions (e.g. Jäger 1996) and more recently in inquisitive semantics (an enterprise that goes well beyond just a treatment of these implicatures) by maintaining a possibility structure over the set of indices (Groenendijk 2009).

Another approach (Schulz 2007) integrates another aspect of relevance, utility for action, into the topic question. The treatment of relevance as a dimension of information structure is probably the biggest theme of update semantics.

Inquisitive semantics achieves a breakthrough by addressing the representation of questions in a way which also deals with the natural emergence of questions out of assertions. *John is in Paris or London* will lead to the information state that also represents the question whether John is in Berlin or Paris. And this should be generalisable to a similar mechanism for existentials: not just the information that there is one, but also the question which one.

Theories of topic and focus and many accounts of particles can profit from mechanisms that raise questions as well as give information. One would like to have predictive theories that add questions to the information state, such as a causal question if the information is surprising, a justification question if there is good reason for doubting the information, a background question if the setting is too unclear, more information questions when an object or a concept is not clear etc. This is often not a question of only logic.

## 10.5 Speech acts and discourse relations

There is surprisingly little work on speech acts within update-semantical pragmatics.[8] Yet, the work of Austin (1962) and Searle (1969) fits in remarkably well. First of all, speech acts come with preconditions which can be captured much like other presuppositions, including accommodation. Then they can be seen as manifestations of intentions. The speaker wants to inform that $p$, wants to know who $\varphi$'s or whether $\psi$, wants to commit herself to a course of action $p$, wants the hearer to do $p$, etc. Then the decision to use a speech act indicates a belief in its possible success, which normally can be cashed out as attitudes of the hearer: the hearer does not believe that $\neg p$, the hearer may know whether $p$, the hearer would want the speaker to do $x$, the speaker has the necessary power over the hearer to order that $p$ etc. Finally, the intention may connect to known goals of the speaker and allow further inferences. Especially if the utterance does not stand alone but is connected to an earlier utterance by the same or another speaker.

Then various forms of reaction to the speech act can be characterised in a similar way. The common ground that results from these speech acts may contain shared information, shared goals, shared emotions, contracts, shared questions, shared experience and shared plans.

## 10.6  Probabilities

A problem that has been equally ignored in update semantics as in other dynamic frameworks is the problem of pronoun resolution. It is normally put out of sight by coindexing or by employing the same variable in different updates. Or equally problematic: the choice between different readings of a word, for which – if the problem is noticed – a similar enrichment of the update with subscripts is chosen. What if one tried to integrate it? After all, the context should not just make the antecedents available but also serve as the content that allows a good choice between different antecedents. The context is normally supposed to play a similar role for word senses.

It is not easy to imagine something which is not similar to the picture that comes out of recent psychological investigations: the parallel activation of many readings with elimination of the less likely on the fly. An approximation is to have all the possible readings and a mechanism that computes conditional probabilities based on the probabilities of the predications on types ($hit_{ag}(person, stone)$ vs $hit_{th}(person, stone)$ vs $hit_{th}(stone, person)$) and combines them with information coming from the context. The construction requires a theory of how the information state can influence the probabilities and it is not directly clear how this can be achieved, though quite a number of things can be tried. The principle seems to be that if there is a clear probabilistic winner, it is the update, otherwise the update blocks (and feedback is sought). It is an unusual ingredient of a semantics, but it fits directly into the picture of an update semantics trying to model what happens to a hearer when exposed to utterances. It is also a necessary ingredient of any pragmatics. The process that selects word meanings, parses, antecedents, discourse relations and other unexpressed ingredients of the intended

meaning is pragmatic because it stands under the normal pragmatic constraints. In particular, it stands under a constraint which makes the global
interpretation as probable as possible, among the set of possible global
interpretations.

It can be argued that this entails several operations that have traditionally
been studied as part and parcel of pragmatics. One is a preference for connecting interpretations – formulated in different traditions as 'Do not miss
anaphoric possibilities!' (Hendriks and de Hoop 2001), 'Do not accommodate!' (Blutner and Jäger 2003), '*New' (Zeevat 2009), 'The Inertia Principle'
(Hamm and van Lambalgen 2005), 'Minimal Models' (Schulz 2007) – over
interpretations that are less connected. It can be constructed as consisting
of preferring anaphoric (repeating) referents over bridging referents over
brand-new referents, with a preference for connections to most activated
referents. An anaphoric referent is the referent of some earlier expression,
a bridging referent is a proper part of a given plural referent or a proper
part of a given singular referent, or the cause of a given event. This principle
has a surprising number of applications in the area of presupposition treatment and in the area of pronoun resolution, but also in the area of discourse
structure.

It is not correct that a principle of this kind increases probability on the
level of content. If $p$ and $p'$ only differ in that $p$ makes more contextual
connections, $p$ may well have a lower probability given the context. But on
the level of what speakers are likely to intend with utterances such as $p$,
they have a clear advantage: speakers seem to operate under the principle
that where an identification is not intended, it is overtly marked that the
entities are different. The result is that identifying interpretations are more
probable, since they have been made impossible if unintended.

An explanation for this speaker strategy may lie in the fact that any kind
of perception seems biased to identification and integration with the preceding experience. Natural language interpretation is just a special case of
perception, so that speakers need to work against overidentification and
overintegration.

A second principle is known as 'Relevance' (also as 'Strongest Interpretation' (Blutner and Jäger 2003), 'Maximise Discourse Coherence' (Asher and
Lascarides 2003), 'Minimal Models' (Schulz 2007) in many traditions, though
the different traditions give different accounts and it is not directly clear
that everybody intends the same. The author's favourite formulation is that
interpretations that can be constructed as addressing a raised question win
over minimally different interpretations that do not and lose out to identical
interpretations that are taken as settling that question ('Strongest Interpretation' – there are a number of instances of a strict interpretation of this
principle that are counterexamples, and it should probably not be taken as
a correct characterisation; see Beaver and Lee 2003). 'Maximise Discourse
Coherence' (Asher and Lascarides 2003) seems to work in the same direction
as this principle. Minimal Models either minimises the domain of the model

(new objects are assumed only under *force majeure*, possibly by assuming that the new object is part of an old one), or alse 'minimal' refers to the size (extension) of certain relations.

The effect of the relevance principle is restricted by the conservativity principle: one cannot freely invent answers to a raised question. In the formulation given, it will deal with a wide range of phenomena again: scalar implicatures (27a), a side effect of settling quantity questions; exhaustivity implicatures (27b), a side effect of settling identity questions; presupposition projection (27c), a side effect of settling the question whether the presupposition holds taking into account that the speaker gives a signal with her use of the trigger that it does; certain explicature implicatures (27d); strengthening discourse relations (27e); relevance implicatures in the sense of Grice (27f) and even most of the other effects of relevance in Relevance Theory. (The symbol '+>' in (27) stands for 'conversationally implicates'.)

(27)  a.  John has 2 cats and a canary. +> John does not have three cats.
      b.  John has 2 cats and a canary. +> John does not have other pets.
      c.  John hopes that his niece will visit. +> John has a niece.
      d.  John had a drink. +> John had an alcoholic drink.
      e.  John pushed Bill. He fell. +> Bill fell because of the pushing.
      f.  There is a garage around the corner. +> The garage can help you to get some petrol.

Settling raised questions produces more information than keeping these questions open and so again works against probability. The set of minimal models is also a part of the set of all models, so again, probability can at best go down. But again it holds that speakers who want to avoid such inferences should mark against them, i.e. that not marking against them is sufficient for being taken to intend them. Again, the tendency of interpreters to make them can be reduced to a bias in perception (seeing what you want to see).

The author would conjecture that approximations to content probability together with symbolic implementations of the two principles discussed above would give promising results.

The given information state functions three times in such a programme: as a source of information which determines the relevant conditional probability that would decide between different interpretations of the new contribution; as a source of the objects given in the context and of their activation levels, for the second principle; and as a source of activated questions and their activation levels, for the third.

The last role highlights once again the importance of integrating the other speech acts into update semantics. The information state that is shared between speaker and hearer must meet the functional demands arising from the various roles that it has to play.

## 10.7 Conclusion and prospects

Probably the most important conclusion about update semantics is that it is a central format for any theory of interpretation. Even if one holds that the basic mechanisms of pragmatics are not related to updating, the predictions of any new proposal can only be tested if they are brought into the format of update semantics, since only this will give the predictions of the new proposal.

Second, update semantics seems central to accounts of pronouns, presupposition and speech acts, to the extent that alternative treatments tend to be unnatural and problematic. Whatever is interesting about E-type analyses of pronouns can be easily captured in an update semantics. The view that pronouns refer to an object of their local context is easier and more natural and much closer to the historical origin: deictic pronouns. Presupposition requires a distinction between old and new, a distinction which is the architectural backbone of update semantics. In other frameworks (cf. Schlenker 2008) this distinction has to be carefully reconstructed. While non-controversial accounts of accommodation and partial resolution are not currently available, the formalisation of relevance on which it seems to depend is the focus of study in recent update semantics, since it is a central aspect of pragmatic updating. Relevance seems much further away in classical semantics.

Third, there is another side to our problematic attempts to separate semantics from pragmatics. In the classical picture, the historical shifts from a classical notion such as ability to a pragmatic notion such as epistemic modality would necessarily be something of a *saltus*: one moment there is a truth criterion, the next moment there is only an assertability condition. This does not sit well with an evolutionary account of these changes in which certain numerical parameters would slowly change. Update semantics offers continuity for changes of this kind and would predict in general the possibility of slow and continuous shifts in the meaning of lexical items that can move from descriptive to more and more pragmatic.

Finally, there is a philosophical point akin to the eliminability of a representational level for semantics in Montague's conception of natural language semantics. Update semantics is about changes to information states and these are sufficiently accessible to speakers and hearers to allow for experimental validation. This would be a level of representation that is as robust as the ability to communicate nonsense words through speech and hearing: performance can be tested. This does not apply to any of the intervening levels in standard accounts of language such as syntactic trees, logical forms of various flavours, proto-logical forms without resolution of pronouns, representations of ambiguous words. These levels have been assumed in accounts of grammar or of the interpretation or of the formulation and speaking process but lack any direct evidence of their own. Update semanticists are not committed to any of these intermediate representations, with the exception of phonetic representation, though – of course – they face the burden of explaining how the assumed processes might work just as much as anybody else and may have to adopt some of these levels in their accounts.

Current update semantics falls short of modelling linguistic agents in various ways: they have information (including anything that can be modelled as information, such as perception and desires), defaults, obligations and questions. There is no good reason, it seems, why they should not have other aspects as well, such as emotions, goals, intentions and decisions. It can be surmised that the future update semantics will not be about information states anymore, but about agents that are updated by linguistic communication (or about all the aspects of an agent that can be changed by communication).

Another element that was mentioned above is the need for more probabilities in these models (this is also part and parcel of a shift from information states to agents). Current update-semantical pragmatics is not able to weigh different resolutions of the same pronoun against each other, is not able to decide between accommodating and partly resolving a presupposition, and certainly not capable of the subtle weighing of the literal meaning of an utterance against an ironic interpretation. This last task is difficult. It would be wrong just to proceed with a probabilistic reinterpretation of the bivalent notion. In our perception and in linguistic communication, there is perhaps always an element of doubt, but on the whole our intuitions place us firmly in one single environment.

# 11

# The normative dimension of discourse

Jaroslav Peregrin

## 11.1  Discourse and normativity

It is not too controversial to say that discourse may interact with normative relationships among people, relationships such as *obligations* or *entitlements*. Some speech acts may produce novel normative links: if you promise your friend to return the money he lent you, then your speech act institutes an *obligation* on your part, the obligation to return the money. Some speech acts may presuppose specific already-extant normative relationships: for example, to speak at the banquet of a scientific conference presupposes some entitlement yielded by the speaker's status – such as his being the head of the organizing committee or perhaps the dean of the faculty backing the conference.[1]

In some cases, a speech act may both presuppose and institute normative relationships. A typical case in point is ordering (commanding): this purports to institute an obligation on the part of its addressee; but it succeeds in instituting it only if it meets the condition that the actor's position is in a relevant sense superior to that of the addressee. Moreover, it would seem that ordering can be *completely characterized* in terms of the changes of the normative links it brings about: ordering, we can say, is simply *the* act which, when carried out by an entitled actor, creates a specific obligation on the part of the addressee. However, ordering is not usually thought of as a particularly typical speech act; language, so the usual story goes, is more a matter of something like "encoding and decoding information" or "communicating ideas and feelings", while giving orders, or other ways of building on or establishing normative links, is little more than a by-product of this.

In this chapter I want to explore the possibility that normativity is far more crucial to language than this. An idea flickering in the theories of several twentieth-century philosophers of language (and seen earlier in Immanuel Kant) is that a certain kind of normativity is constitutive of our distinctively

Work on this paper was supported by the research grant No. P401/10/0146 of the Czech Science Foundation.

human mind (aka reason), founding our concepts and infiltrating the semantics of our language. If this is true, then normativity is not only an accidental element of some of our speech acts, but rather their essential ingredient. Here we want to expose the motivations supporting this view and search out its consequences.

In section 11.2, we will reconsider the traditional picture of communication as essentially a matter of transferring information and the related picture of language as a collection of representations (of ideas or things of the outer world); and we will consider, in section 11.3, alternative pictures. This will not only result in giving pragmatics pride of place over semantics in explaining the nature of language, but, moreover, endorsing a peculiar version of pragmatics, which we will call *pragmatist pragmatics* and which will take words to be first and foremost means of achieving practical ends. However, this will be only an intermediate station before our ultimate terminus: inspection of *normative* versions of pragmatics. We will reach it in section 11.4 after we reject the possibility of erecting the pragmatist picture of language on the concept of disposition and thus will be driven to what we will call the *normative turn*. In sections 11.5 and 11.6 we will then consider the consequences of this turn.

To foreshadow this approach to language and discourse, let us take as a basic thesis that meaningfulness is not a (naturalistic) property of a type of sound or an inscription, but rather a *propriety*: saying that an expression means thus and so is saying that it is *correct* to use it thus and so, that it is governed by a certain set of *rules*. The mechanism is supposedly similar to that animating games and sports: saying a piece of rubber is an ice-hockey *puck* is not ascribing the piece a peculiar (naturalistic) property, but citing its role vis-à-vis the rules of ice hockey. Hence from this viewpoint, discourse is like a kind of game: it is governed by rules (though in contrast to ice-hockey, not necessarily *explicit* rules) and meaningfulness is the effect of the rules.

It is crucial to realize that *rules*, as we understand the term here, are something different from what is studied in Chomskyan linguistics. The latter are certain principles implemented in human brains and thus inevitably governing our linguistic behavior; whereas rules in the sense adopted here guide us always "evitably" – it is a hallmark of the rules in our sense that they can be, as a matter of principle, violated. A rule construed thus is a *social fact*, consisting in the collective awareness that something ought to be thus and so, manifested in the corresponding behavioral regularities (not only the more or less regular compliance with the rules, but a more or less regular prosecution of deviations, etc.)

## 11.2  Transferring information?

Consider the received wisdom that language is a matter of *transferring information*. There seems nothing particularly normative about such transfers (aside from the trivialities that it can be exercised, as any other kind of act, correctly or incorrectly, well or badly, appropriately or inappropriately, etc.). What is going on is the moving of something from one head to another – a perfectly naturalistic enterprise.

But is this truly so? Consider the act of "transferring information" accompanying the act of assertion. What happens when I assert something, tell something to somebody, or inform somebody about something? I emit a certain sound (let us disregard the written form of language, for simplicity's sake), and it reaches my audience's ear. What can be effected by a mere *sound*? Seeing it as merely a sound, rather than an expression, we can imagine that its capabilities might include being able to scare the audience or attract its attention; but using the specific kinds of sounds that constitute language enables us to do much more complicated and very specific things: for example, we might cause somebody at a distant place to open a particular door, go into a room and take something from a particular drawer. How do we achieve this?

There is the temptation to have all the explanatory work done by the terms *information* and, indeed, *meaning*. The sounds that constitute language differ from other kinds of sounds, and acquire their almost miraculous abilities, because they have been furnished with meanings. (How? Perhaps – we pull another rabbit out of the hat – by means of a *convention*!) This grants them the ability to transfer information from one head to another, and as potential pieces of information constitute an incredibly large and fine-grained spectrum, we can achieve, by sending them to our audience, a very large and differentiated spectrum of reactions.

However, using such concepts as *information* and *meaning* as unexplained explainers begs the question. Almost everybody would agree that the talk about transferring information by means of words is merely metaphorical, that there are no such things as actual units of *information* literally hanging on the words that flow from my mouth to your ear.[2] But what is it a metaphor of? An immediate answer might be that our brains have the ability of dealing with language in the sense that they discern a vast number of sounds and somehow recognize them as "codes" encoding something. Hence the speaker uses the ability of his brain to "encode" information and the hearer uses it to "decode" it. Thus, nothing must literally hang on the words, it "hangs" on them merely metaphorically in that they *encode* it.

But in what precisely does the encoding/decoding ability of our brains consist? Does the brain contain some huge "code table," which allows it to translate information to and from the linguistic codes? This seems to be precisely the idea put forward by Chomsky, who urges that language is a huge system of pairings of sounds and meanings.[3] But how do such "code tables" materialize in our brains?

Clearly, this must happen during the process of learning the language in question. (It cannot be innate, for the codes, the words, differ from society to society.) A forthright picture of how this happens was described by Augustine: we are shown things and told their names, thereby building the table.[4] This has developed into what can be called a *semiotic* or a *representationalist* picture of language, according to which meaningfulness consists, first and foremost, in *standing for something*. But is this picture plausible? Two problems immediately surface: First, although we can be shown things or people, and perhaps also, less straightforwardly, we can be introduced to qualities such as redness or manhood by being shown red things or male persons, there still remains a plethora of words where it is utterly unclear what we can be shown (think, for example, of adverbs, such as *rapidly* or *always*). Second, to speak a language is to have use of an *unlimited* number of expressions, so inevitably no amount of pointing can furnish them all with their meanings.

These problems are usually not considered insurmountable. As for the first, it is assumed that only some of the words of our language are learned by ostension and thus come to function as proxies for things, whereas the rest of them constitute some kind of auxiliary scaffolding for employing the "core words" (see, e.g., Weinreich, 1962: 36). As for the second, learning a language is seen to consist of learning the meanings of words plus mastering ways of composing meanings of complex expressions out of those of simpler ones.

Note, however, that this essentially compromises the picture of our semantic competence as a matter of the possession of a code table. As for the first problem, the remaining worry concerns *what* it is that is stored in our brains along with words like *rapidly* or *always*. As for the second, we can certainly say that what effects the encoding/decoding should be seen more as an algorithm than as a table, which would account for the potential infinity of meaning–sound pairs; but what about the infinity of meanings themselves? Certainly if we are to encode a potentially infinite number of entities, we need to *have* the entities (if only merely potentially). But how do we generate all the meanings expressible in a language? Of course, we can generate them via generating all the expressions expressing them; but if they are to be *encoded* by the expressions, then it seems they should be available *before* the encoding happens. And if we have an *unlimited* number of meanings, what sense does it make to think that we *have* them as being *assembled* in our brain for a potential encoding?

We may try to meet this challenge by claiming that the meanings are something we are born with – that nature and our genes endow us with a "language of thought" that does not consist of expressions codifying meanings, but rather of expressions that directly *are* meanings. This seems to be the strategy of Fodor (1975; 2008) and his followers. However, if we see a *language* as a collection of sound- or inscription-types that become meaningful via their engagement with our complicated discursive practices, then such a detachment of meanings from expressions is basically problematic: once again it leads to unexplained explainers that stand in essential need of explanation themselves.

## 11.3 The pragmatist turn

At this point, the picture of communication as principally a matter of exchanging encoded information loses its initial plausibility, encouraging us to consider some other approach. And as many philosophers and linguists have recommended, a useful alternative might be to see language not in terms of representing things and encoding/decoding information, but rather in terms of practical ends to which linguistic items can serve as means, to see expressions as *tools* rather than as *codes*. This insight is characteristic of philosophical pragmatism (see Haack and Lane, 2006), but it has found its way into various other philosophical and linguistic conceptions of language in the later twentieth century. It is central to the neopragmatist theories of Quine and Davidson, it animates the later Wittgenstein's theory of *language games* and it is partly also present within the speech act theory initiated by Austin and Grice. I will call this view of language and communication *pragmatist pragmatics*. From this perspective, questions of meaning and information, of course, are radically altered.

Consider a toolbox (the metaphor for language favored by the later Wittgenstein[5]). I may learn various ways of using the tools the toolbox contains; and not only each of them alone, but also in combination: the hammer and a nail, the screwdriver and a screw, a bolt and a nut ... I may accomplish various useful things. The more skillful I am with the tools, the more practical tasks they can help me solve. Moreover, they render it possible for me to do things I would never have even considered before: to build and mend things I would previously have been unable to imagine. Thus, although sometimes I use tools to cope with tasks that would have faced me independently of whether I had a toolbox or not, very often I use them to do things that I would not come to think about were it not for my experience with the toolbox – it is the skill of using the tools that makes many tasks that can be solved by its means visible in the first place. For this reason it would be absurd to think of the tools and their combinations as responses to tasks given beforehand.

Switching to this pragmatist view of language also prompts us to re-evaluate the traditional view of the semantics/pragmatics boundary. Recall that the traditional definition of the boundary between semantics and pragmatics, as given by Morris (1938) and Carnap (1942),[6] was conceived within the representationalist framework. Semantics was considered to address questions central to the framework, namely what things our words stand for, while pragmatics was relegated to the sphere of peripheral, residual questions of how we use words – how the words endowed with meanings get also peripherally endowed with our habits, moods, or fancies.

Given the pragmatist turn that leads us to see language more as the vehicle of an activity, semantics is effectively swallowed up by pragmatics – *everything* is a matter of how we use language. Of course, we can still have a semantics/pragmatics boundary, but now pragmatics will not be an unessential appendage of semantics, but rather semantics will be a slightly artificially demarcated part of pragmatics (such as, for example, the part which deals with truth-conditions, as Stalnaker (1970) suggests).

Hence, the pragmatist turn may help us overcome the obstacles generated by the earlier idea that what we principally do with language is transfer information, which led to the consequent code conception of language.[7] From the pragmatist viewpoint, language is not a mere instrument of dealing with the extralinguistic world: while in some cases it may help us cope with problems we would face independently of us having or not having a language, more often than not we will use it for tasks which only came into being with the birth of language – discussing theoretical questions, reciting poetry, buying a book, and so forth. Hence it seems that the tasks for which expressions are fitted co-evolve with language. For this reason it seems to me to be misleading to imagine expressions as codes of something given independently of them.

Note that, although we claimed that this pragmatist approach to pragmatics is not alien to the speech act theory of Austin and Grice (see their *perlocution* dimension of the speech act), ultimately it is an alternative to the specifically Gricean approach to pragmatics based on the concept of intention, which dominates the current pragmatics scene. Just as this avoids taking either the concept of *information* or that of *meaning* as an unexplained explainer, so it also avoids taking *intention* as such.[8] In this way it is more thoroughly naturalistic.

Hence the impasse into which we were brought by the code conception might be overcome if we take the pragmatist turn; but from the opening comments of this chapter it follows that we want to consider one more turn, namely a *normative* one. Why is this? Why should we not rest content with the pragmatist turn?

## 11.4   What ties an observation report to what it reports?

Consider the sentence *This is a dog*. What does the fact that it means what it does in English consist in? It would seem that whatever else might come into its meaning, what is essential is that English speakers use this sentence when confronted with a dog, and not when confronted with, say, a horse.

However, is this true? For a start, we can think of cases where competent speakers might utter *This is a dog* when confronted with a horse – as a result of bad sight, of jocularity, irony, or poetic inspiration, etc. But perhaps such cases may be dismissed as statistically insignificant, and more substantial is the observation that the majority of English speakers when confronted with a dog would be extremely unlikely to actually utter *This is a dog*. In fact, I suspect the number of positive cases may well be statistically insignificant. (As Chomsky (1975) conjectured, the statistical probability of uttering almost any specific expression in a given situation will not be significantly higher than zero.)

Hence we are back at the conundrum of what establishes the connection between *This is a dog* and dogs. The usual rabbit that philosophers and linguists pull out of their hats here is the concept of *disposition*. *This is a dog* means that this is a dog (and not, say, a horse) because speakers are *disposed* to utter it when confronted with a dog. This disposition sometimes provokes the overt utterance, but more often than not it remains covert.

But this rabbit, I feel, is just a trick to delay clarification. What does it mean that a speaker has a covert disposition to utter *This is a dog*? It amounts to the counterfactual claim that the person would utter it were it not for some hindrance. What would substantiate such a claim? Certainly, it would be well substantiated were we able to identify some mechanism in a person's brain which tends to lead to the utterance, which may be obstructed by certain factors, and which may be shown to be so obstructed in the case in point. But at present we are party to no such mechanisms.

Alternatively, we can interpret the claim as not a claim about an inner mechanism, but rather about empirical regularities. We may report that *This is a dog* is always uttered in the presence of a dog unless certain "hindering" factors occur. But for such a claim to have empirical content (to be, for example, testable) we would have to be able to specify the relevant factors. Otherwise the claim would be empty: *any* evidence would be compatible with it. (We would never be able to object that the claim is at variance with the facts: cases of speakers reacting to dogs with *This is a dog* would be in order, and cases of those not reacting in this way could always be explained away with reference to unspecified hindering factors.)

Are we able to give an exhaustive catalog of things or events that stop one exclaiming *This is a dog* in the presence of a dog? Can we say, for example, that principal factors are unwillingness to talk, preoccupation with other matters, or not noticing the dog in question? Hardly; we can clearly think of any number of others. Hence it seems that invoking the concept of disposition here is a mere illusion of explanation. Does this mean that there is, despite appearances, no intelligible connection between *This is a dog* and dogs after all? I do not think so; but I think that we tend to look at this connection in the wrong way. What I think is the case is that the connection is *normative* rather than causal. This is to say that the link between the occurrence and the utterance is not a matter of any causal mechanism connecting the two, but rather of the fact that to utter *This is a dog* when a dog is in focus is *correct*.[9]

However, without further ado, this would be at most a gesture towards an explanation (if not merely another trick). What is a *non-causal, normative connection*? Should one imagine some kind of supernatural fiber leading from dogs (and other potential objects of reference) to the minds of speakers? It is clear that unless we give a viable clarification, this alleged explanation would not really be useful. Hence it is the clarification to which we now turn our attention.

## 11.5  Correctness

To foreshadow where we expect our normative turn to lead us to, let us consider an activity seemingly very different from using language: the game of football. What is important for us is that playing football amounts to enjoying a spectrum of actions that are not available for us outside of its framework: get into an offside position, foul an opponent, or (joy of joys!) score a goal. How do such actions become available for me? Obviously because I, as well as my team-mates and our opponents, *submit to the rules of football* – it is the *rules*, and in particular the collective submission to them, that open up the space for the new kind of actions. And the thesis I want to put forward and discuss is that *linguistic actions*, actions that we tend to describe as cases of *meaningful talk*, *transfer of information*, or *stating facts* (or whatever else one can do with *meaningful* language), arise analogously: namely as a result of our collective recognition of the rules of language.

This recognition means nothing over and above the fact that we take certain linguistic utterances for correct, and others for incorrect. (This may be the case on several disparate levels – an utterance may be, e.g., *grammatically* correct while being *incorrect* as an assertion.) We know that it is correct to say *This is a dog* when pointing at a dog (whereas that this is incorrect when pointing at a bus); we know that it is incorrect to dissent from *This is an animal* while assenting to *This is a dog*; and we know that it is correct to raise one's hand when assenting to *Will you raise your hand?* Thus, a rule in this sense is a matter of a collective awareness, of an awareness that something is correct and something else is incorrect, leading to the appropriate behavior (praising the correct and trying to do away with the incorrect).

Let us start from the question of how we recognize the presence of a normative link of the kind discussed above. (After all, as Quine reminded us, we all learn to speak by means of observing our elders and peers and as what we can perceive is exclusively behavior – hence, we can say, *there cannot be anything in meaning that was not in behavior before*.) How does a language-learner recognize that *This is a dog* is "normatively linked" to dogs (rather than horses) and so grasp the meaning of the sentence (and especially of the word *dog*)?

When learning a language we may witness a demonstration of using *This is a dog* as accompanying pointing at a dog. However, though this can indicate the existence of a link, it cannot intimate the nature of the link, let alone that it is a *normative* link. Given our genetic tendency to imitate, we may come to utter *This is a dog* when pointing at a dog ourselves; but nothing apparently stops us from uttering it when pointing at things other than dogs – say, all furry things, or even at anything whatsoever.

The decisive step here is that we must learn that using it when pointing at something not a dog is *incorrect*. How do we learn this? By experiencing some kind of "social friction," by facing "corrective reactions" of other speakers to such misuse (our own or somebody else's). What constitutes such a "corrective reaction"? It may be anything from a true punishment to a mild dissatisfaction or puzzlement. Anyway, one of the principal "social skills" anybody must master to be an integral part of his or her society is to recognize which kinds of behavior count as "corrective" (and being able to feel this kind of "friction" appears to be one of the most essential social skills).

Hence the original encounter with the normativity of meaning is in this "must not": We do not learn what we should do, but rather what we should *not* do. This is important, for this may help clarify one of the most frequent misunderstandings regarding the normativity of meaning: the normativity does not rid us of our *freedom* in using language and hence does not contradict the obvious fact that using language is a *spontaneous* activity – it merely *restricts* the freedom, still leaving a vast number of possibilities. (We will return to this later.)

This also indicates that the normativity of meaning is somehow carried by the *corrective*, or as we may say more generally, *normative* attitudes of speakers to other speakers' pronouncements. And this may bring us to a suspicion that we have not done away with the concept of disposition we deemed suspicious above, but merely shifted it one level up: for do we not need the concept for the characterization of the concept of normative attitude? Can we say that normative attitudes *consist* in a "corrective behavior" – or do we have to say that they consist in the *disposition* to corrective behavior? After all, not everybody who uses language incorrectly faces correction by others!

It is true that though the occurrence of a generic "corrective behavior" is more easily predicted than individual pronouncements, it is not, of course, the case that we cannot say that a pronouncement is wrong only if some such behavior occurs. But we may avoid the concept of disposition in the same way as before: instead of saying that an utterance is incorrect either if it faces corrective behavior, or if others would have the disposition to the "corrective behavior" towards it, we can say that it is incorrect if the corrective behavior towards it would be *correct*.

However, this definitely looks like a trick, and in this case a particularly naive one. (Am I criticizing my colleagues for pulling rabbits out of their hats only to end up pulling one out myself?) Is it not merely shifting the whole problem to a third level and thus possibly starting an infinite regress? The attempt to reduce correctness to behavior or to dispositions to behavior would indeed lead us to an infinite regress; but my answer is that this is to be taken as indicating that the reduction is impossible.

But is this, then, not a mere *reductio ad absurdum* of the whole idea of the "normativist turn"? Am I suggesting that behind (or above) human behavior (and the whole network of causal relationships, in which it is embedded) there looms some different, supernatural stratum of reality where we can encounter correctnesses? Of course not, though admittedly it may sometimes be useful to invoke this picture as a metaphor. The point is rather that there are no such *things* as correctnesses. Why they *seem* to be here is that we seem to state facts about them; but what looks like declarative statements about such correctnesses – I will call the statements *normatives* – are not always really declaratives. Hence what is behind the untranslatability of the normative idiom into the declarative one (and hence the reduction of "norms" to "facts") is not the incommensurability of a "normative" and a "factual" stratum of reality, but simply the more mundane fact that many of the normatives are not genuine declarative sentences at all, but rather belong to a different species of speech act. They are, as Wilfrid Sellars (1962: 44) put it, "fraught with ought."

Return to the case of football; and consider the statement *Hands should not touch the ball*. This is a normative. There are two ways of employing a statement of this kind. First, one can state the fact that this kind of rule is in force in some community. This is, as it were, an "outsider" statement; a statement made by a disengaged observer describing the practices of the community in question. Second, one can state this as an "insider", which does not amount to (or *only* to) stating a fact, but also to *upholding* the rule, urging its propriety or at least confirming its legitimacy. And *true* normatives are normatives posed precisely from this perspective. It follows that to say that rules *exist* is strictly speaking a metaphor: they do not exist, of course, in the way rocks, trees, or dolphins do. To say that a rule exists is to take some true normatives people use for ordinary declaratives. It seems to be our human way to do this; but we should be aware of the fact that this is a sense of *existence* different from the one in which we use the word when we talk about the existence of spatiotemporal particulars and their constellations.

And here we come to the mystery of how correctnesses, or proprieties, can exist relatively independently of our attitudes, and yet without being situated in some independent stratum of reality. The point is that any verdict we reach regarding correctness is at best tentative, it belonging to the nature of the concept that the verdict is considered as always amendable by our successors. They can find out that what we hold for correct is in fact not correct – but unlike in the case of *blue*, *indivisible*, or *animate*, we do not always see such cases as errors in the application of the concept, but rather as discovering the true nature of the concept of *correctness*.

Perhaps we can say that a rule or a norm is always an *unfinished and open project* (see Gauker, 2007). Usually it grows out of our current practices, is continuous with them, sometimes to the extent that we can understand its statement as a description of the practices as they, as a matter of fact, are; but the statement of a norm is also usually its prolongation, an urge "And we should go on like this!" Hence a rule is never a completed whole, it is always open to the future, not only to prolongations, but also to modifications and amendments. It is like a track that we must go on extending to ever new horizons.

## 11.6  Norms and convention

I have mentioned the concept of *convention* as a "rabbit" which is usually pulled out of the semanticist's hat when we need to say what ties an observation report to the observation it reports. But at this point someone might want to wonder whether the theory I have been developing in terms of the concepts of *norms* and *normativity* is not about what semanticists have long been referring to by means of the term "convention." Well, in one sense it is. However, this is due to the fact that the term is largely ambiguous; and *some* of its senses do refer to normative phenomena.

As Rescorla (2007) points out in his overview article, "in everyday usage, 'convention' has various meanings, as suggested by the following list: Republican Party Convention; Geneva Convention; terminological conventions; conventional wisdom; flouting societal convention; conventional medicine; conventional weapons; conventions of the horror genre." He offers a useful list of possibilities that the "conventional" may be contrasted with: "the natural; the mind-independent; the objective; the universal; the factual; and the truth-evaluable." This indicates that to deal with the concept of *convention*, we need to start with disambiguation. I think there are at least three senses of the term relevant for the theory of language. In the first sense, "convention" is something like a *habit*; in this sense, "the conventional" is, in the words of Goodman (1989: 80), "the ordinary, the usual, the traditional, the orthodox as against the novel, the deviant, the unexpected, the heterodox". In the second sense, convention is what has been established by man and has not been part of nature all along; in this sense, "the conventional" is, using Goodman's words again, "the artificial, the invented, the optional, as against the natural, the fundamental, the mandatory" (*ibid.*). In the third sense, "the conventional" is what has been explicitly agreed upon.

I think that the attractiveness of the term "convention" stems largely from the conflation of the three senses. When we encounter a problem concerning the way language hooks onto the world, we often invoke the term in the second sense. Surely the sentence – that is, the sound-type – "This is a dog" is not *naturally* connected with dogs, hence the relation is *conventional*. So far so good; but aside from giving the relationship a label nothing has been explained yet. However, the next step often is that we do not really need to explain anything, for the concept of *convention* is more or less self-explanatory. However, whereas this might be true for "convention" in the *third*, or perhaps also in the *first*, sense, it is definitely not true for "convention" in the second sense, for this sense remains blatantly neutral with respect to how conventions come into being and what their nature is. And it is clear that if we use the term to account for how language hooks onto the world, then it cannot be generally convention in the third sense of the word: language cannot be based on this kind of convention, for language is *presupposed* by this kind of convention.[10]

Could it be "convention" in the first sense, convention as a habit, that holds together the sentence and dogs? Habits do not seem to be too unperspicuous; so maybe it is "convention" in this sense that those who use the term as the universal unexplained explainer use it. However, "conventions" in this sense clearly do not overlap with our normative account of language and discourse:

habits as such do not have any normative dimension. If my habit is to go for a walk every evening, it may be surprising that I do not go out today, but it is in no sense *wrong*.

Habits, to be sure, may *evolve* into norms. Once people start to take the habitual as not merely what usually happens, but rather what *should* happen, there emerges a norm – or, you may want to say, the habit becomes a norm. But here the latter step is crucial. For consider chess or football, which we use as our models of our discursive practices. People may acquire the habit not to take the ball into their hands; but the game cannot really get off the ground until this starts to be felt as what *should not* be done and until those who keep doing this start to be penalised. Hence the habitual substrate is surely not everything that makes up norms.

When you look into the writings of Austin (1961; 1962), Grice (1989), Searle (1969) or other speech act theorists, what you find there is that the terms "convention" and "conventional" are among the most frequently used words, but despite this none of the authors pay much explicit attention to the question of what conventions are. Of course there are some hints: Austin (1961: 64), for example, when mentioning a "semantic convention" adds a parenthesis "(implicit, of course)" which indicates that what he has in mind is *not* "convention" in our third sense of the word. Elsewhere he talks of an assertion justified "not merely by convention, nor merely by nature," which in turn indicates that he uses "conventional" in opposition to "natural"; hence that he uses it in the second of our three senses.

There is a flagrant disproportion between the huge explanatory work the concept of *convention* is supposed to do in such writings and the absence – or near absence – of its own explanation. This can be, to a great extent, justified by the fact that these authors use the terms "convention" and "conventional" in a sense that they do not see as being in need of explanation, hence, I would think, mostly in our second sense. But sooner or later, then, we must face the question of how this kind of conventionality comes into being.

The first person who realized that this is a serious problem was David Lewis (1969). He clearly realized that the concepts of *convention* and *conventionality* that occur so frequently in writings about language cannot be generally construed as explicit agreements, and set himself the task of showing how "tacit conventions" can come into being. His solution of this problem is based on two assumptions: conventions come into being to solve *coordination problems*, and the solution of such problems can evolve spontaneously along the lines envisaged by game theory.

I think that despite the fact that Lewis laudably brought the nature and emergence of conventions into the focus of attention and showed how some tacit conventions may emerge spontaneously (thus breaking from the vicious circle into which we would fall if we wanted to base language on explicit conventions), his approach is not general enough. In particular I think that by no means all the norms language is based on can be seen as deriving from conventions solving coordination problems – at least not unless we generalize the concept of *coordination problem* to the extent that it will no longer be explainable in Lewis's simple game-theoretical terms.

Consider chess or football again. Can we say that their rules are a matter of conventions? Obviously, we can; in fact it would seem that the rules of games or sports are prototypes of what we would call *conventional*. (As we saw, there might be some terminological disputes over whether we should say that the rules themselves *are* conventional, or whether they *evolved from* conventions, but this is not important now.) But can we see them as solutions to *coordination problems*? This does not seem to be too plausible.

The fact is that, as I have argued elsewhere (see Peregrin, 2011 from the game-theoretical viewpoint the basic kind of rules relevant for language is more akin to those governing games of the kind of the Prisoner's Dilemma (solving genuine conflicts) than those of coordination.[11] Thus I do not think that the sector of game theory Lewis took into account is general enough to account for the problems standardly addressed under the heading of normativity.

On the other hand, I repeat that I think that it *is* possible to see a large overlap between "normativity" and "conventionality." However, one thing to keep in mind is that this is due to the catholic nature of the concept of *conventionality*. Moreover, if we adhere to the sense of conventionality for which this overlap obtains, this sense of convention is not sufficiently explained and the present considerations may be seen as a contribution to its explanation.[12]

## 11.7   Normative speech acts theory?

The ideas exposed in the previous sections have led to the project of normative pragmatics that was first explicitly formulated – on a very general level – by Brandom (1994: Chapter 1).[13] Brandom's tenet is that

> it is only insofar as it is appealed to in explaining the circumstances under which judgments and inferences are properly made and the proper consequences of doing so that something associated by the theorist with interpreted states or expressions qualifies as a *semantic* interpretant, or deserves to be called a theoretical concept of a *content*. (Brandon, 1994: 144)

In this sense semantics must be "answerable to pragmatics," namely to normative pragmatics.

When Searle (1969), in his classic book about speech acts, elaborated on the Gricean and Austinian speech act theory, his major example, discussed in the third chapter of the book, was the act of promising. His incipient characterization of this act reads as follows (Searle 1969: 57–61):

Given that a speaker S utters a sentence T in the presence of a hearer H, then, in the literal utterance of T, S sincerely and non-defectively promises that p to H if and only if the following conditions 1–9 obtain:

1. Normal input and output conditions obtain.
2. S expresses the proposition that p in the utterance of T.
3. In expressing that p, S predicates a future act A of S.
4. H would prefer S's doing A to his not doing A, and S believes H would prefer his doing A to his not doing A.
5. It is not obvious to both S and H that S will do A in the normal course of events.
6. S intends to do A.
7. S intends that the utterance of T will place him under an obligation to do A.
8. S intends (i-I) to produce in H the knowledge (K) that the utterance of T is to count as placing S under an obligation to do A. S intends to produce K by means of the recognition of i-I, and he intends i-I to be recognised in virtue of (by means of) H's knowledge of the meaning of T.
9. The semantical rules of the dialect spoken by S and H are such that T is correctly and sincerely uttered if and only if conditions 1–8 obtain.

This characterization involves a normative notion, namely the notion of *obligation* (point 7). Then Searle points out that his characterization leaves no room for insincere promises; so he then proposes to replace condition 6 with 6a:

6a. S intends that the utterance of T will make him responsible for intending to do A.

Thus he introduces the normative notion of *responsibility*. (As the concepts of *obligation* and *responsibility* may be interdefinable, maybe it is not *another* normative notion, but merely the reiteration of the original one.)

However, is the list, and especially the role of the normative notions in it, formulated adequately? Does one, making a promise, *intend* to be placed under an obligation? Of course, as we assume that a typical promise is an intentional act, we would tend to consent; but is this inevitable? Suppose that I agree, say in a written form, to return somebody some money he lends me. Then suppose that I do not do so and when my creditor sues me, I tell the court that I did not really intend to have this obligation, hence that my act was not really a promise. (And let us suppose this is all true.) Am I likely to win the trial on the basis of proving that I have not promised anything? (It is hard to imagine how my declaration about my intention – if we understand the term "intention" in the sense of Grice and Searle as a basically *internal* act – could be challenged, for I alone have direct access to it.)

In view of this fact we can consider replacing 7 with 7*:

7*. The utterance of T will place S under an obligation to do A.

Then, it would seem, some of the other entries on the list may become super-fluous. Consider, for that matter, 6 or 6a. Suppose that someone promises me to give me some money, but in fact does not intend to be responsible for it. Does it mean that what he does is not promising?

In fact, it would seem that the rest of the list might also dwindle (if not vanish completely). True, the inflation of the point 7 to 7* results from using a more robust concept of obligation than the one used by Searle: insofar as I understand him, what he has in mind is obligation as a matter of psychology, whereas the one suggested by me is obligation in the sociologico-institutional sense. Hence inflating the normative dimension of the act also involves moving the act "out of the head," into the open. This means that some or all of the differences between Searle's account and the proposal made here may be terminological.

This does not mean, though, that the difference between them is insub-stantial. The normative twist given to speech act theory involves a significant reinterpretation of the whole enterprise – instead of having psychological states as its direct concern, it now concentrates on normative statuses. Unlike its traditional version, it is wholly broken away from psychology of commu-nication, which is the result of the conviction that language, and especially meaning, is more an institution than a psychological reality, and that psy-chology of communication is no more directly connected to communication than psychology of chess to chess.[14]

Moreover, a normative speech act theory must make it plausible that not only speech acts like promising or ordering, which it can handle relatively easily, but also such speech acts as asserting can be characterized in norma-tive terms. This is a much harder nut (see, e.g., Pagin, 2004, for a skeptical viewpoint). The idea here is that making an assertion is nothing over and above assuming the commitment to provide a specific justification; and to entitle anybody else to reassert the sentence in question while deferring its justification to you.

Kukla and Lance (2009) proposed a normative version of speech act theory, according to which speech acts are generally characterized by the normative conditions of their appropriateness and the normative outcomes of their occurrence. Thus, for example, ordering is appropriate if the orderer is in some sense superior to the orderee; and in such a case its normal felicitous outcome is the commitment on the part of the orderee to do what he or she was ordered. Using this unusual key to the classification of speech acts yields an unusual classification: for example, the usual category of assertions divides into declaratives and what Kukla and Lance call *observatives*. The two acts differ in their conditions. Declaratives, assertions like *There is a pig in the yard*, are indiscriminatingly available to anybody; whereas only certain people are entitled to observatives, assertions like *Lo, a pig!*

Another peculiar kind of speech act which has surfaced after Kukla and Lance put our linguistic practices under the normative lens is what they called *vocatives*, acts of the kind of *Hey, you!* While observatives are characterized by having specific normative conditions (not everybody is entitled to make them), but general normative outcomes (they entitle everybody to make use of them), with vocatives it is the other way around: they have general normative outcomes (everybody is entitled to them), but their outcome is specific (they entitle a specific individual to enter the ongoing language game). Kukla and Lance claim that the identification of such speech acts, which do not surface in traditional speech act theory, significantly advances our understanding of language.

All of this, of course, presupposes that we accept that there is no *meaningfulness* without a normative dimension. This is, recall, the result of taking the Wittgensteinian picture of our discursive practices as a cluster of language games at face value, not only in the sense that the practices are heterogenous, but also in the sense that they are essentially underlain by rules. Given this, any speech act is individuated by the way in which it fits into the normative scaffolding that constitutes the space which provides the necessary substrate for such speech acts. And given this, in turn, our perspective on discursive practices shifts significantly, and may illuminate aspects hardly discernible from the perspective of Austin and Grice.

## 11.8  Conclusion

The traditional approach to language was based on the assumption that we must first explain how a word means something (which was, in turn, taken as tantamount to explaining how it can stand for that something), and then we would be able to explain language as a product of the synergic effect of an assembly of meaningful words. The pragmatic turn in the twentieth century (especially in its pragmatist variety) inverted the perspective: we must explain, the credo has come to be, directly how language works, i.e. our linguistic practices, using the concept of meaning at most as an expedient of this enterprise.

What I have been exploring here is the possibility of this pragmatic turn being given a normative twist: of meanings being explained as roles vis-à-vis rules of language. Let us return to football. As I noted above, once you accept its rules, you can do things which you were not capable of doing before. Note that this does not mean: some things you *were* capable of doing before (like kicking a round thing through a gate-like thing) now receive new descriptions ("scoring a goal"). Scoring a goal is not reducible to kicking. I and my team-mates might do precisely the same movements we do now, but without being caught in the normative network constituted by the rules of football they would not be scoring goals and they would not have many of the effects they have now (like making us happy, making our opponents annoyed, bringing money to those who laid bets on us, while causing those who betted against us to lose their money, etc.). In short, the rules of football constitute a new spectrum of actions not available to us before. And likewise, the amazing spectrum of things we can do with words is created analogously – by means of the rules of language.

When Carnap and Morris presented their division of the theory of language into syntax, semantics, and pragmatics, they gave, in effect, pride of place to semantics (relegating syntax to the auxiliary role of honing the vehicles that only semantics discloses as carrying meanings; and relegating pragmatics to the marginal role of sidekick to semantics). Moreover, Carnap then reconstructed semantics as a mostly logico-mathematical, armchair enterprise: the semantic theories he presents in his *Introduction to Semantics* (1942) or *Meaning and Necessity* (1947) do not seem interconnected, in any significant way, with any empirical investigations of natural languages. I think this was an unhappy development (and it justified the revolt of the many theoreticians of language who subsequently made pragmatics, rather than semantics, the centerpoint of the study of language[15]), and I want to ensure that the normative turn discussed here should not lead to a similar consequence.

It is true that *normativity* seems to be a tool that only philosophers have in their philosophical toolbox. Linguistics, one is tempted to say, is a down-to-earth science, and science describes how things are, not how they should be – so what use for *normativity* is there? The present chapter has tried to offer an answer, an answer as down-to-earth as possible. Human activities, be it chess or football or some much more complex and socially important ones, are *governed by rules* – indeed they are *constituted* by the rule-governance. This is clearly nothing mysterious or at odds with science – it is simply an empirical fact. And here I want to suggest that insofar as this applies also to language (which presupposes seeing language as a social institution, rather than, say, a psychological reality), we may come to see that this enterprise has an important normative dimension and that to understand this dimension may be essential for understanding language and discourse.

# 12

# Pragmatics in the (English) lexicon

Keith Allan

## 12.1 Introduction

In this chapter I shall discuss only the lexicon of English, but the general principles seem to apply to many, if not all, other languages even though the minutiae do not. By "lexicon" I mean a rational model of the mental lexicon or dictionary. Although the way a lexicon is organized depends on what it is designed to do, it is minimally necessary for it to have formal (phonological and graphological), morphosyntactic (lexical and morphological categorization), and semantic specifications. Relations are networked such that formal specifications are (bi-directionally) directly linked to morphosyntactic specifications that are directly linked to semantic specifications – which, for the moment, subsumes pragmatic specifications. A lexicon must be accessible from three directions: form, morphosyntax, and meaning; none of which is intrinsically prior. Each of these three access points is, additionally, bi-directionally connected with an encyclopaedia. Haiman (1980: 331) claimed "Dictionaries *are* encyclopaedias" and certainly many desktop dictionaries contain extensive encyclopaedic information (e.g. Hanks 1979; Kernfeld 1994; Pearsall 1998). The position taken here is that a lexicon is a bin for storing listemes,[1] language expressions whose meaning is (normally) not determinable from the meanings (if any) of their constituent forms and which, therefore, a language user must memorize as a combination of form, certain morphosyntactic properties, and meaning. An encyclopaedia is a structured database containing exhaustive information on many (perhaps all) branches of knowledge. It therefore seems more logical that the lexicon forms part of an encyclopaedia than vice versa, but the actual relationship does not significantly affect this chapter. I assume that encyclopaedic information is typically, if not uniquely, pragmatic.

My thanks to Kasia Jaszczolt for making me clarify bits of this chapter. Kasia is not to blame for remaining infelicities; indeed, she heartily disapproves some of my claims.

A lexicon is a bin for storing listemes for use by language speakers in any and all contexts. This is not to deny that new listemes are occasionally created, but the coining of a new listeme is a rare event and the resources of a lexicon are normally adequate for all contexts that a speaker faces. Consequently the meanings of listemes are expected to be adapted by semantic extension or narrowing both concretely and figuratively by speakers in utilizing them and hearers in interpreting them. Such lexical adjustment can be illustrated by the various meanings of the related listemes *cut* in (1).

(1)   cut grass, cut hair, cut steel, cut the thread, cut the cards, cut your losses, cut out the middle man, cut the ties, to cut and run, cut the cackle, cut a class, cut someone socially, be a cut above, she's all cut up by the breakdown in her marriage, be cut to the quick, cut through the obfuscation, cut my finger, cut the tyres, cut the cake, cut a disk, a railway cutting, cut through the back lane, cut a [fine] figure

Most, if not all, of these seem to derive from a basic notion of severing, interpreted in various ways according to what is severed and/or the manner of severing (this could even apply to *cut a figure*). Similarly, it is well known that a color term may extend to shades very far from the focal color (Berlin and Kay 1969; MacLaury 1997) as selected from, say, the Munsell Color Array; we can attribute this to the elasticity that language needs to have in order that it can usefully be applied to the world around us. In certain domains and in certain formulaic expressions color terms are used of hues vastly distant from the focal color. Take the domain of human appearance: terms like *white*, *black*, *yellow*, and *brown* have all been used to characterize the skin pigmentation of people of different races, often dysphemistically. These color terms are descriptively appropriate not so much in relation to the focal colors as in relation to each other: a *white person* is typically paler than the others and a *black person* darker; a *yellow person* is typically yellower than the others. The peoples of southeast Asia and Austronesia are often referred to as *brown*, despite the fact that peoples labeled *black* are often of similar brown skin color. So *brown*, too, functions by contrast with *white*, *black*, and *yellow* in this domain. In the domain of oenology, *red wine* does have a (usually dark) red tinge but *white wine* is only white by virtue of being paler than red wine; white wine is normally pale yellow or pale green. Clearly what determines the meanings of these particular sets of color terms is their comparative function: by means of very rough approximation to the focal color, they distinguish within a semantic field between different species of the kind of entity denoted by the noun they modify.

Pragmatics within the lexicon is largely an addition to the semantic specifications; for instance, it is useful to identify the default meanings and connotations of listemes. Default meanings are those that are applied more frequently by more people and normally with greater certitude than any

alternatives. Bauer (1983: 196) proposed a category of "stylistic specifications" to distinguish between *piss*, *piddle*, and *micturate*, i.e. to reflect the kind
of metalinguistic information found in traditional desk-top dictionary tags
like 'colloquial', 'slang', 'derogatory', 'medicine', 'zoology'; such metalinguistic information is more encyclopaedic than lexical. So too is etymological information. Pustejovsky (1995: 101) specifies *book* as a "physical object"
that "holds" "information" created by someone who "write[s]" it and whose
function is to be "read." Certainly, there is a relation between *book*, *write*,
and *read* that needs to be accounted for either in the semantic specification
or pragmatically – Pustejovsky represents it in terms of a network and networks are also used in frame semantics (Fillmore 1982; 2006; Fillmore and
Atkins 1992; FrameNet at http://framenet.icsi.berkeley.edu) and by Vigliocco
*et al.* (2009). Category terms like *noun*, *verb*, *adjective*, and *feminine* are part
of the meta-language, not the object language; but they also appear in the
lexicon as expressions in the object language and there needs to be a demon-
strable relation from object language to meta-language (and vice versa). It
would seem incontrovertible that encyclopaedic data is called upon to interpret non-literal expressions like *Ella's being a tiger*; likewise, to explain the
extension of a proper name like *Hoover* to denote vacuum cleaners and vacuum cleaning or the formation of the verb *bowdlerize* from the proper name
*Bowdler*. I assume that, because many proper names are shared by different
name-bearers, there must be a stock of proper names located either partially
or wholly in the lexicon, even if they are stored differently in the brain (see
section 12.9). The production and interpretation of statements like those in
(2)–(3) requires pragmatic input.

(2)   Caspar Cazzo is no Pavarotti!

(3)   Harry's boss is a bloody little Hitler!

(2) implies that Caspar is not a great singer; we infer this because Pavarotti's
salient characteristic was that he was a great singer. (3) is abusive because of
the encyclopaedic entry for the name *Hitler* that carries biographical details
of a particular infamous name-bearer. Such comparisons draw on biodata
that are appropriate in an encyclopaedia entry for the person who is the
standard for comparison but not appropriate in a lexicon entry; the latter
should identify the characteristics of the typical name-bearer, such as that
*Aristotle* and *Jim* are normally names for males, but not (*contra* Frege 1892)
the biographical details of any particular name-bearer – any more than the
dictionary entry for *dog* should be restricted to a whippet or poodle rather
than the genus as a whole.

   One of the earliest investigations of lexical pragmatics was McCawley
(1978); McCawley (correctly) argued that a listeme (such as *pink* or *kill*) and
a semantically equivalent paraphrase (such as *pale red* or *cause to die*) are
subject to different pragmatic conditions of appropriateness that give rise
to different interpretations, which he thought could be captured by general conditions of cooperative behavior such as Grice's cooperative maxims.

He did not tackle the question of whether pragmatics intrudes on lexical entries. Nor does Blutner (1998; 2004; 2009). Blutner discusses pragmatic compositionality, blocking (if a listeme already exists to express a meaning, do not construct another one without good reason to do so),[2] and pragmatic anomaly (recognized as early as Apollonius Dyscolus in *Peri Suntaxeōs* III.149; see Uhlig 1883). The closest Blutner comes to pragmatics within the lexicon is discussing the interpretation of certain adjectives and institute-type nouns (Blutner 1998).

Carston (2002: Ch. 5), then Wilson and Carston (2007) discuss lexical narrowing (e.g. *drink* used for 'alcoholic drink'), approximation (e.g. *flat* meaning 'relatively flat'), and metaphorical extension (e.g. *bulldozer* used to mean 'forceful person'). They argue that the same interpretive processes as are employed for literal utterances are used for narrowing, broadening, through to approximation and figurative usage in hyperbole and metaphor. Interpretation is triggered by the search for "relevance" constrained by the principle of least effort: "An input is relevant to an individual when it connects with available contextual assumptions to yield positive cognitive effects (e.g. true contextual implications, warranted strengthenings or revisions of existing assumptions)" (Wilson and Carston 2007: 245). Inferences deriving from "explicature," "implicature," and context-based assumptions satisfy the expectation of relevance, which causes the interpretive process to stop at whatever interpretation a hearer judges satisfactory in the context of utterance.

Huang (2009) also deals with lexical narrowing, lexical blocking, and pragmatic anomaly and, in addition, contrastive focus reduplication. But (despite his title "Neo-Gricean pragmatics and the lexicon") he has very little more to say about pragmatics in the lexicon than is found in Blutner or Wilson and Carston.

Copestake and Lascarides (1997) identified the importance of noting in the lexicon the frequency of particular word senses, in a manner very similar to that independently proposed for a broader range of data by Allan (2000; 2001 and again in this chapter). Copestake and Lascarides (1997: 140) write "For example, in the BNC [British National Corpus] *diet* has probability of about 0.9 of occurring in the food sense and 0.005 in the legislature sense (the remainder are metaphorical extensions, e.g. *diet of crime*)." In section 12.2 below I introduce a credibility metric like that of Copestake and Lascarides which applies to (some) nonmonotonic statements within the lexicon. I argue the case for nonmonotonic statements in the lexicon in entries for nouns in section 12.3 and for verbs in section 12.4. In section 12.5 I discuss the pragmatic intrusions into the interpreting of collectives and collectivized nouns. This leads naturally to a consideration in section 12.6 of the entries for animal nouns that may refer to either the animal's meat or its pelt (after Allan 1981; Nunberg and Zaenen 1992). Section 12.7 takes up the dictionary entry for *and*; 12.8 discusses the pragmatic component of lexicon entries for sorites terms; 12.9 looks at the place of "prefabs" or "formulaic

Table 12.1. *The credibility metric for a proposition*

| cred = 1.0 | Undoubtedly true: | $\Box p$, I know that $p$ |
|---|---|---|
| cred = 0.9 | Most probably true: | I am almost certain that $p$ |
| cred = 0.8 | Probably true: | I believe that $p$ |
| cred = 0.7 | Possibly true: | I think $p$ is probable |
| cred = 0.6 | Just possibly true: | I think that perhaps $p$ |
| cred = 0.5 | Indeterminable: | $(\diamond p \geq 0.5) \veebar (\diamond \neg p \leq 0.5)$ |
| cred = 0.4 | Just possibly false: | It is not impossible that $p$ |
| cred = 0.3 | Possibly false: | It is not necessarily impossible that $p$ |
| cred = 0.2 | Probably false: | It is (very) unlikely that $p$ |
| cred = 0.1 | Most probably false: | It is almost impossible that $p$ |
| cred = 0.0 | Undoubtedly false: | $\Box \neg p$, I know that $\neg p$ |

expressions" in the lexicon and 12.10 tackles ways in which connotation might be incorporated into entries for listemes. Section 12.11 summarizes the chapter.

## 12.2 A credibility metric

In some of what follows it will be helpful to use a credibility metric for a proposition. The truth value of a proposition $p$ hinges on whether or not $p$ is, was, or will be the case. What matters to language users is not so much what is in fact true, but what they believe to be true.[3] The credibility of $p$ is what is believed with respect to the truth of $p$, or believed is known, or is in fact known of its truthfulness. Because most so-called "facts" are propositions about phenomena as interpreted by whomever is speaking, we find that so-called "experts" differ as to what the facts are (for instance, with regard to global warming, or what should be done about narcotics, or what is the best linguistic theory). Whether ordinary language users judge a proposition true or false depends partly on its "pragmatic halo" (Lasersohn 1999): in any normal situation *Sue arrived at three o'clock* is treated as true if she arrived close to three o'clock; the slack afforded by the pragmatic halo is restricted by a pragmatic regulator such as *precisely* or *exactly* in *Sue arrived precisely at three o'clock* or *Sue arrived at exactly three o'clock*.[4] Mostly, though, truth or falsity is assigned by the ordinary language user on the basis of how credible the proposition is, and this is reflected in the way that language is produced and understood. There is a credibility metric such as that in Table 12.1, in which complete confidence that a proposition is true rates 1, represented as CRED = 1.0, and complete confidence that a proposition is false rates CRED = 0.0; indeterminability is midway between these two: CRED = 0.5. Other values lie in between. ($\Box$ is the necessity operator, $\diamond$ is the possibility operator, $\veebar$ symbolizes exclusive disjunction, $\neg p$ means "not-p.")

In reality, one level of the metric overlaps an adjacent level so that the cross-over from one level to another is more often than not entirely subjective; levels 0.1, 0.4, 0.6, 0.9 are as much an artifact of the decimal system as they are independently distinct levels in which I have a great deal of confidence. Nonetheless, I am certain that some variant of the credibility metric exists and is justified by the employment of the adverbials (*very*) *probably*, (*very*) *possibly*, and *perhaps* in everyday speech. This metric is needed in some lexical entries, as we shall see.

## 12.3  Semantic specifications for *bird* and *bull*

Birds are feathered, beaked, and bipedal. Most birds can fly. Applied to an owl this attribute of flight is true; applied to a penguin it is false. Birds are sexed and a normal adult female bird can lay eggs. It is a defining characteristic that members of the female sex carry ova; I'll label this function sxF (which can be glossed 'sexual female'). Where they don't, or the ova are non-viable, the organism can count for our purposes as a gendered female, GENF, but not sxF. Mostly, sexual females are gendered females too; see (4) where → indicates semantic entailment.

(4)    MOST(x)[sxF(x) → GENF(x)]

Although we do speak of human eggs, nonetheless the default egg is from an oviparous genus such as a bird, so I'll assume this characteristic ought to be noted in the lexicon.[5] Based on Allan 2001: 252, I propose that the semantic part of the lexicon entry for *bird* be (5), where ∧ symbolizes logical conjunction, +> indicates (defeasible) nonmonotonic inference (NMI), which could perhaps be referred to as an implicature and which is cancelled for species such as emus and penguins.

(5)    ∀x $\begin{bmatrix} \text{BIRD(x)} \rightarrow \lambda\text{y[FEATHERED(y)} \wedge \text{BEAKED(y)} \wedge\text{BIPEDAL(y)](x)} \\ \text{BIRD(x)} +> \diamond\text{FLY(x), CRED} \geq 0.7 \\ \lambda\text{z[BIRD(z)} \wedge \text{sxF(z)} \wedge \text{ADULT(z)](x)} \rightarrow \text{OVIPAROUS(x)} \end{bmatrix}$

The lambda-operator is useful to identify an individual as having a number of properties jointly, e.g. being a member of the set of creatures that are at the same time feathered and beaked and bipedal. In (5) the line BIRD(x) +> ◇FLY(x) identifies that a bird is most probably capable of flight with a credibility rating of 0.7. In the case of a sparrow, the semantic component of the lexicon entry may look like (6); for a penguin, like (7).

(6)    ∀x $\begin{bmatrix} \text{SPARROW(x)} \rightarrow \text{PASSERINE(x)} \\ \text{PASSERINE(x)} \rightarrow \lambda\text{y[BIRD(y)} \wedge \diamond\text{FLY(y)](x), CRED} \geq 0.99 \end{bmatrix}$

(7)    ∀x $\begin{bmatrix} \text{PENGUIN(x)} \rightarrow \text{SPHENISCIDA(x)} \\ \text{SPHENISCIDA(x)} \rightarrow \lambda\text{y[BIRD(y)} \wedge \neg\text{FLY(y)](x), CRED} = 1 \end{bmatrix}$

For both (6) and (7) the oviparity of sxF sparrows and penguins is an entailment of their being birds. The credibility of a sparrow being able to fly is estimated at CRED ≥ 0.99 (it might be injured), whereas the credibility of a penguin flying is 0 (its not-flying has a credibility of 1).

The first entry under *bull* in the *Oxford English Dictionary* (1989) is "The male of any bovine animal; most commonly applied to the male of the domestic species (*Bos Taurus*); also of the buffalo, etc." Part of this is more formally stated in (8).

(8)   $\forall x[\lambda y[\text{BULL}(y) \wedge \text{ANIMAL}(y)](x) \rightarrow \lambda z[\text{MALE}(z) \wedge \text{BOVINE}(z)](x)]$

I will ignore the facts identified in (9).

(9)   $\text{MALE}(x) \rightarrow \text{GENM}(x) \mathrel{+>} \text{SxM}(x)$

(8) is inaccurate because the noun *bull* is not restricted in application to bovines; it is also properly used of male elephants, male hippos, male whales, male seals, male alligators, and more. The initial plausibility of (8) is due to the fact that it describes the stereotypical bull. The world in which the English language has developed is such that *bull* is much more likely to denote a bovine than any other species of animal. Peripheral uses of *bull* are examples of semantic extension from bovines to certain other kinds of large animals; consequently they require that the context make it abundantly clear that a bovine is not being referred to. This is often achieved by spelling it out in a construction, such as *bull elephant* or *bull whale*, which is of greater complexity than the simple noun *bull* used of bovines – a difference motivated by the principle of least effort (Zipf 1949). There is no regular term for "the class of large animals whose males are called 'bulls', females 'cows', and young 'calves'" so in Allan 2001: 273 I coined the term \**bozine* to label it.[6] The semantics of English *bull* is given in (10) from which the NMI of bovinity will be cancelled where the animal is contextually specified as giraffid, hippopotamid, proboscid, pinniped, cetacean, or crocodilian.

(10)   $\forall x \begin{bmatrix} \lambda y[\text{BULL}(y) \wedge \text{ANIMAL}(y)](x) \rightarrow \lambda z[\text{MALE}(z) \wedge {}^*\text{BOZINE}(z)](x) \\ \lambda y[\text{BULL}(y) \wedge \text{ANIMAL}(y)](x) \mathrel{+>} \text{BOVINE}(x), \text{CRED} \geq 0.9 \end{bmatrix}$

Once again we see a default interpretation being recorded as an NMI in the lexicon because of the salience of this particular characteristic, namely bovinity, of the default reference (i.e. the denotatum) for *bull*. (At first sight a salient meaning should be almost the opposite of a default meaning: something that is salient jumps out at you; by contrast a default is the fall-back state when there is no contextual motivation to prefer any other. On a second look, what qualifies a state to become the default is its salience in the absence of any contextual motivation to prefer another.) The credibility of $\geq 0.9$ is based on my intuition. A search of ten corpora totaling about ten million words (the Australian corpus of English; Australian ICE; the Lancaster–Oslo/Bergen corpus of British texts; the London–Lund corpus; the Freiburg corpus of British texts; the Freiburg corpus of American texts; the Brown corpus of American texts; the Wellington corpus of written New Zealand texts; New Zealand ICE; Kenya–East Africa ICE) revealed no applications of *bull* to animals other than bovines, nor indeed were such searches useful in confirming or disconfirming any of the other credibility ratings in this chapter.

In this section I have shown that a lexicon entry can be constructed to indicate the necessary components of meaning for the entry and also the most probable additional components of meaning that obtain for most occasions of use but which may be canceled as a function of contextual constraints. These can be seen as prototype effects that, for instance, help distinguish *cup* from *mug* and *bowl* (see Labov 1978). Traditional Arab and Turkish coffee cups are small bowls with no handle, very similar in configuration to Chinese porcelain teacups. The typical Western teacup or coffee cup has a handle and is accompanied by a saucer. All these types of cup are bowl-like in shape though they are smaller, usually have higher sides, and serve a different function than most bowls. Cups are intended to be put to the lips to convey liquid to the mouth whereas liquid in food bowls is spooned into the mouth; otherwise a bowl is used for food preparation. These kinds of conditions (that distinguish *cup* from *mug* and *bowl*) are encyclopaedic and pragmatic rather than purely semantic.

For each lexicon entry the semantic identity of the listeme is presented as a meaning postulate – cf. (10); for instance, the noun *bull* is semantically represented by the predicate BULL ranging over a variable for the entity denoted. Predicates like BULL, ANIMAL, MALE, and BOVINE are not decomposed into semantic primitives but give rise to certain inferences some of which are necessary semantic entailments, others are probabilistic nonmonotonic inferences. Similar conditions apply to the verb *climb*, as we see in section 12.4.

## 12.4  Climbing

Jackendoff (1985) identified some interesting characteristics of the verb *climb*. From (11) we understand that Jim climbed up the mountain – contrast (11) with (12). We also understand that he used his legs and feet – contrast (11) and (12) with (13).

(11)  Jim climbed the mountain.

(12)  Jim climbed down the mountain.

(13)  Jim climbed (down) the mountain on his hands and knees.

Snakes, airplanes, and ambient temperature lack legs and feet they can use when climbing (which is presumably a metaphorical extension with these actors), and they can't *climb down*, some other verb must be employed.

(14)  The snake climbed $\begin{cases} \text{the tree.} \\ \text{?? down the tree.} \end{cases}$

(15)  The airplane climbed $\begin{cases} \text{to its cruising altitude.} \\ \text{?? down to land.} \end{cases}$

(16)  The temperature climbed $\begin{cases} \text{to 42.} \\ \text{?? down to minus 10.} \end{cases}$

In (17) the lexicon entry captures the fact that the default interpretation of *climb* presumes both upward movement, symbolized by $\uparrow$[7] **and** the use of feet (and therefore legs, too).

(17) $\forall x \begin{bmatrix} \text{CLIMB}(x) \rightarrow \lambda y[\text{GO}(y)\_\uparrow \vee \text{USE\_FEET}(y)[\text{CAUSE}(y)[\text{MOVE}(y)\_\uparrow]]](x) \\ \text{CLIMB}(x) +> \lambda y[\text{GO}(y)\_\uparrow \wedge \text{USE\_FEET}(y)[\text{CAUSE}(y)[\text{MOVE}(y)\_\uparrow]]](x), \\ \text{CRED} \approx 0.7 \end{bmatrix}$

NMIs apply not just to nouns and verbs but potentially in any lexicon entry.

## 12.5 Collectives and collectivizing

Allan 1976 and 2001 discuss the semantics of collective nouns such as *admiralty, aristocracy, army, assembly, association, audience, board, class, clergy, committee, crowd, flock, government*, and collectivized nouns such as those italicized in (18)–(19).

(18) These three *elephant* my great-grandfather shot in 1920 were good tuskers, such as you never see today.

(19) Four silver *birch* stand sentinel over the driveway entrance.

A definition of collectivizing will be given shortly, but let's begin with familiar collectives.

Collective nouns allow reference to be made to either the set (collection) as a whole or to the set members. In many dialects of English (but not all) the different interpretations are indicated by NP-external number registration; consider (20).[8]

(20) The herd $\begin{Bmatrix} \text{is} \\ \text{are} \end{Bmatrix}$ getting restless and $\begin{Bmatrix} \text{it is} \\ \text{they are} \end{Bmatrix}$ beginning to move away.

Whereas singular NP-external number registration indicates that the set as a holistic unit is being referred to, cf. (21), the plural indicates that the set members are being referred to (22). In these and later examples, X and Y are (possibly null) variables for NP constituents; $\text{NP}_{\text{SG}}$ is a singular NP, and $\text{NP}_{\text{PL}}$ is plural; x, y, z are sets, either unit sets (individuals)[9] or multi-member sets, so one should understand from (21) and (22) that $\forall x[\exists y[y \subseteq x]]$.

(21) $\forall x[\text{NP}_{\text{SG}}[X \ N_{\text{HEAD}}[\lambda y[\text{MANY}(y) \wedge \text{COLLOCATED}(y)](x)] \ Y]$
        $\rightarrow \text{COMBINED\_MEMBERSHIP}(x)]$

(22) $\forall x[\text{NP}_{\text{PL}}[X \ N_{\text{HEAD}}[\lambda y[\text{MANY}(y) \wedge \text{COLLOCATED}(y)](x)] \ Y]$
        $\rightarrow \text{CONSTITUENT\_MEMBERS}(x)]$

Thus, (23) identifies the composition of the committee, while (24) identifies dissension among the membership of the committee.

(23)   The committee $\left\{ \begin{array}{l} \text{is} \\ _{?*} \text{ are} \end{array} \right\}$ composed of many notable scholars.

(24)   The committee $\left\{ \begin{array}{l} _{?*} \text{ is} \\ \text{are} \end{array} \right\}$ at odds with each other over the new plan.

NPs denoting institutions, e.g. *the company I work for*, *the BBC*, *the university* must be singular ($NP_{SG}$ in (27) and (28)) when the institution as a building, location, or single constituent body is referred to, as in (25), but can have plural NP-external registration when referring to the people associated with it (26).

(25)   The library $\left\{ \begin{array}{l} \text{is} \\ _{?*} \text{ are} \end{array} \right\}$ located in the new civic centre.

(26)   The library $\left\{ \begin{array}{l} \text{charges} \\ \text{charge} \end{array} \right\}$ a heavy fine on overdue books.

The facts with respect to such collective nouns are represented in (27)–(29), where $N_0$ is the form of the noun unmarked for number.

(27)   $\forall x \exists z [N_0[\text{LIBRARY}(x)] \rightarrow \lambda y[\text{MANY}(y) \wedge \text{BOOK}(y) \wedge \text{COLLOCATED}(y)](z) \wedge x \supseteq z]$
$+> \exists x[NP_{SG}[X\ N_{0,\text{HEAD}}[\text{LIBRARY}(x)]\ Y] \wedge \text{INSTITUTION}(x)]$

(28)   $\forall x[NP_{SG}[X\ N_{0,\text{HEAD}}[\text{INSTITUTION}(x)]\ Y] \rightarrow \text{CONSTITUENT\_BODY}(x) \vee \text{SITE}(x)]$

(29)   $\forall x[NP_{PL}[X\ N_{0,\text{HEAD}}[\text{INSTITUTION}(x)]\ Y] \rightarrow \text{STAFF\_MEMBERS}(x)]$

There is no evidence in (20)–(29) of probabilistic representation being required in the lexicon. The different interpretations are indicated through morphosyntactic choices.

Allan 1976 and 2001 identify a principle of $N_0$ usage for English, given in (30).

(30)   $N_0$, the form of the noun unmarked for number, is used when the denotation for N is perceived not to consist of a number of significant similar units.

In a plural NP headed by $N_0$, the absence of plural inflexion on the head noun marks "collectivizing." Collectivizing signals hunting, conservation, or farming jargon because $N_0$ is characteristically used of referents that are NOT perceived to be significant as individuals. Early users of the collectivized form were not interested in the individual animals except as a source for food or trophies. Consider the italicized nouns in (18)–(19) and (31)–(34), to which italics have been added.

(31)  A three month shooting trip up the White Nile can offer a very good
      mixed bag, including, with luck, *Elephant, Buffalo, Lion*, and two
      animals not found elsewhere: Nile or Saddle-back (Mrs. Gray's) *Lechwe*
      and White-eared *Kob*. (Maydon 1951: 168)

(32)  On the way back to camp we sighted two *giraffe* on the other side of
      the river, which were coming down to the water's edge to drink.
      (Arkell-Hardwicke 1903: 285)

(33)  These *cucumber* are doing well; it's a good year for them.

(34)  The *cat-fishes*, of which there are about fifty distinct forms arranged
      in four families, constitute the largest group, with probably the
      greatest number of individuals per species. In some parts of the
      country where nets are little used and fishing is mainly done with
      traps and long lines, at least three-quarters of the annual catch is of
      *cat-fish*. (Welman 1948: 8)

The plural NP "cat-fishes" at the beginning of (34) refers to species of cat-fish,
whereas the $N_0$ at the end refers to individuals caught by fishermen. Collectivizing of trees and other plants is much less common than collectivizing
animals – from which, perhaps, it derives. Vermin are never collectivized;
though individual language users may differ over what counts as vermin.
Early uses of the collectivized form were applied to animals hunted for food
or trophies. Today, collectivizing occurs in contexts and jargons of hunting,
zoology, ornithology, conservation, and cultivation, where $N_0$ is characteristically used of referents that, as I've already said, are not perceived to be
significant as individuals. Two possible contributing factors to the establishment of $N_0$ as the mark of collectivizing are (1) the unmarked plural of *deer* –
which once meant 'wild animal, beast', and (2) the fact that meat nouns are
$N_0$ (discussed in the next section). Despite the fact that there is a good deal
of variation in the data (see Allan 1976: 100f.), collectivizable nouns should
be marked as such in the lexicon. Reference will need to be made to the
discourse domain being one of the contexts identified above and vermin will
need to be excluded. The kind of entry I envisage is (35), which uses *giraffe* as
an example.

(35)  IF Domain = conservation THEN $\forall x[NP_{PL}[X\ N_0[\text{GIRAFFE}(x)]\ Y]]$; CRED $\approx$
      0.6

Clearly, more work is needed.

## 12.6  Animals for food and fur

In this section I take up a discussion from Allan 1981. Consider the sentences
in (36)–(37).

(36)   Harry prefers lamb to goat.

(37)   Jacqueline prefers leopard to fox.

Most likely you will interpret the animal product nouns in (36) to refer to meat, such that (36) is paraphrasable by (38), whereas the animal product nouns in (37) refer to animal pelts such that (37) is paraphrasable by (39).

(38)   Harry prefers eating lamb to eating goat.

(39)   Jacqueline prefers leopard skin to fox fur.

The converse interpretations are unlikely, especially *Jacqueline prefers eating leopard to eating fox.*[10] The predicate *prefer* in (36)–(37) offers a neutral context permitting the default animal product to rise to salience. This suggests that the lexicon entries for *lamb* and *goat*, and that for other creatures (such as *whale*, see (40)) should include a specific application of the formula in (41).

(40)   In Tokyo, whale gets ever more expensive!

$$(41) \quad \forall x \left[ \begin{array}{l} \lambda y[NP_{MASS}[N(y) \wedge ANIMAL(y)](x)] \rightarrow PRODUCT\_OF(x) \\ \lambda y[NP_{MASS}[N(y) \wedge ANIMAL(y)](x)] \mathrel{+}> MEAT\_OF(x) \end{array} \right]$$

The lexicon entries for *leopard* and *fox* should include a specific application of the formula in (43); so will all of the italicized animal product nouns in (42).

(42)   a.   Jacqueline was wearing *mink*.
       b.   Elspeth's new handbag is *crocodile*, I think.
       c.   This settee's made of *buffalo*.
       d.   The tannery has loads of *impala* right now.

$$(43) \quad \forall x \left[ \begin{array}{l} \lambda y[NP_{MASS}[N(y) \wedge ANIMAL(y)](x)] \rightarrow PRODUCT\_OF(x) \\ \lambda y[NP_{MASS}[N(y) \wedge ANIMAL(y)](x)] \mathrel{+}> PELT\_OF(x) \end{array} \right]$$

A mass NP headed by an animal noun will refer to the pelt of the animal denoted by that NP when there is in the clause an NP head or clause predicate describing apparel, accessories to apparel, furniture, the creation of an artifact, or any object likely to be made from leather and any place or process that involves pelts, hides, or leather such that these constrain the domain for the interpretation of $N_0$. Thus the nonmonotonic inference in (41) is canceled by the implications of *the lining* in (44); from (43) the NMI is canceled by the predicate *eat* in (45).

(44)   I prefer the lining to be made of lamb, because it's softer.

(45)   All we had to eat was leopard.

More subtle interpretations are required in (46)–(49).

(46)   A plate of lamb can be worn by no-one.

(47)   The girl holding the plate was wearing rabbit.

(48)   The girl who wore mink was eating rabbit.

(49)   Because she decided she preferred the lamb, Hetty put back the pigskin coat.

In (46) "plate of lamb" identifies meat. Although the most likely interpretation of *a plate of steel* is 'a plate made of steel' (CRED $\geq$ 0.99), *a plate of lamb* is, with similar credibility, interpreted as 'a plate bearing food'. The predicate "wearing rabbit" in (47) identifies the rabbit pelts as apparel (again, CRED $\geq$ 0.99) and, likewise, "wore mink" in (48) identifies mink as apparel while the predicate in "eating rabbit" coerces the reference to rabbit meat. In (49) "the lamb" is most likely to be interpreted as meat (CRED $\geq$ 0.8) until this is revealed as a "garden-path" misinterpretation, corrected by the preference for a porcine pelt in the second clause, which cancels the original NMI, replacing it with the coerced interpretation "lambskin coat".

In this section I have claimed that animal nouns in mass NPs which denote a product from the dead animal typically refer to either the animal's flesh or its pelt, but this probabilistic inference can be canceled by certain contextual elements that condition the domain for interpretation. Credibility rankings can be assigned as shown in (50). However, in (50) these rankings are based on my intuition, although they ought to be made on the basis of the frequency of interpretations retrieved from large and diverse corpora.

(50)   $NP_{MASS}$ $[N[\lambda y[LAMB(y) \wedge ANIMAL(y)](x)]]$ $+>$ MEAT_OF(x); CRED $\geq$ 0.8
            IF NOT MEAT_OF(x) THEN PELT_OF(x)
        $NP_{MASS}$ $[N[\lambda y[GOAT(y) \wedge ANIMAL(y)](x)]]$ $+>$ MEAT_OF(x); CRED $\geq$ 0.7
            IF NOT MEAT_OF(x) THEN PELT_OF(x)
        $NP_{MASS}$ $[N[\lambda y[RABBIT(y) \wedge ANIMAL(y)](x)]]$ $+>$ MEAT_OF(x); CRED $\geq$ 0.7
            IF NOT MEAT_OF(x) THEN PELT_OF(x)
        $NP_{MASS}$ $[N[\lambda y[LEOPARD(y) \wedge ANIMAL(y)](x)]]$ $+>$ PELT_OF(x); CRED $\geq$ 0.9
            IF NOT PELT_OF(x) THEN MEAT_OF(x)
        $NP_{MASS}$ $[N[\lambda y[FOX(y) \wedge ANIMAL(y)](x)]]$ $+>$ PELT_OF(x); CRED $\geq$ 0.9
            IF NOT PELT_OF(x) THEN MEAT_OF(x)
        $NP_{MASS}$ $[N[\lambda y[MINK(y) \wedge ANIMAL(y)](x)]]$ $+>$ PELT_OF(x); CRED $\geq$ 0.9
            IF NOT PELT_OF(x) THEN MEAT_OF(x)
        $NP_{MASS}$ $[N[\lambda y[BUFFALO(y) \wedge ANIMAL(y)](x)]]$ $+>$ PELT_OF(x); CRED $\geq$ 0.8
            IF NOT PELT_OF(x) THEN MEAT_OF(x)
        $NP_{MASS}$ $[N[\lambda y[CROCODILE(y) \wedge ANIMAL(y)](x)]]$ $+>$ PELT_OF(x); CRED $\geq$ 0.8
            IF NOT PELT_OF(x) THEN MEAT_OF(x)
        $NP_{MASS}$ $[N[\lambda y[IMPALA(y) \wedge ANIMAL(y)](x)]]$ $+>$ PELT_OF(x); CRED $\geq$ 0.7
            IF NOT PELT_OF(x) THEN MEAT_OF(x)

It would seem obvious that there should be some generalization over nouns that can refer to either meat or pelts; one might refer to the degree of choice between these two alternatives being "graded salience" (Giora 2003: 10 and this volume), but this notion is yet more relevant in the lexicon entry for *and*.

## 12.7 *And*

*And* may conjoin all sorts of sentence constituents and whatever is felicitously conjoined is grouped together such that there is always some plausible reason for the grouping. This "plausibility" valuation is a coherence metric and necessarily pragmatic because it relies on knowledge of whatever world is spoken of; later, I shall question whether it is relevant to the lexicon entry for *and*. With the exception of some conjoined NPs that I will refer to as NP-\*COM-Conjunction (and briefly exemplify in (61)–(65)), the conjoined constituents are synonymous with a conjunction of sentences, e.g. in (51e) 'Two is a number $\wedge$ Three is a number'.

(51)  a.  Sue is tall and slim.
      b.  Eric was driving too fast and hit a tree.
      c.  Elspeth always drove slowly and carefully.
      d.  Joe and Harriet are tall.
      e.  Two and three are numbers.

On the assumption that $\Phi$ and $\Psi$ are well-formed (combinations of) propositions expressed as well-formed conjunctions in English, the semantics of $\Phi$ *and* $\Psi$ is as presented in (52). There is, in addition, a series of nonmonotonic inferences that exemplify Giora's "graded salience" (Giora 2003: 10); they are listed with the strongest contextually possible inference as the first to be considered.

(52)  $\Phi$ *and* $\Psi \leftrightarrow \Phi \wedge \Psi$
    a. IF CRED($\neg\Phi \rightarrow \neg\Psi$) $\geq$ 0.9 $\wedge$ CRED(CAUSE($\Phi,\Psi$)) $\geq$ 0.8
    THEN $\Phi$ *and* $\Psi$ +> $\Phi$ *causes* $\Psi$ (e.g. *Flick the switch **and** the light comes on*; cause $\prec$ effect[11]) ELSE
    b. IF CRED(ENABLE ([DO($\emptyset,\Phi$)],$\Psi$)) $\geq$ 0.9 $\wedge$ CRED($\neg\Phi \rightarrow \neg\Psi$) $\geq$ 0.8
    THEN $\Phi$ *and* $\Psi$ +> $\Phi$ *enables the consequence* $\Psi \vee \Phi$ *is a reason for* $\Psi$ (e.g. *Stop crying **and** I'll buy you an ice-cream*; action $\prec$ consequence) ELSE
    c. IF CRED($\Phi < \Psi$) $\geq$ 0.8
    THEN $\Phi$ *and* $\Psi$ +> $\Phi$ *and then later* $\Psi$ (e.g. *Sue got pregnant **and** married her boyfriend*; $\Phi \prec \Psi$) ELSE
    d. IF CRED(ENABLE($\Phi$,[DO(S,[SAY(S,$\Psi$)])])) $\geq$ 0.8[12]
    THEN $\Phi$ *and* $\Psi$ +> $\Phi$ *is background for* $\Psi$ (e.g. *There was once a young prince, **and** he was very ugly*) ELSE
    e. $\Phi$ *and* $\Psi$ +> $\Phi$ *is probably more topical or more familiar to S than* $\Psi$ (e.g. *On Saturdays my mum cleans the flat **and** Sue washes the clothes*)

Note the conditional relations in (53):

(53)   ($\Phi$ *causes* $\Psi$) $\rightarrow$ ($\Phi$ *is a reason for or enables the consequence* $\Psi$) $\rightarrow$ ($\Phi$
       *temporally precedes* $\Psi$)[13]

Whether the last two discourse-based implicatures of (52) are part of this
sequence remains to be determined. However, it is arguable that if $\Phi$ *is
background for* $\Psi$ then $\Phi$ is prior to $\Psi$; and if $\Phi$ *is more topical or more familiar
than* $\Psi$, then again, it is arguable that $\Phi$ is prior to $\Psi$; and should these rather
tenuous claims be acceptable, then the fact that $\Phi$ precedes $\Psi$ when they are
conjoined is normally iconic. However, the choice of sequence is a matter
of usage (or pragmatics) and is not obligatory, but it does seem to justify a
general statement such as (54):

(54)   $\Phi$ *and* $\Psi$ $\leftrightarrow$ $\Phi \wedge \Psi$
       $\Phi$ *and* $\Psi$ $+>$ $\Phi$ is prior to $\Psi$; CRED $\geq 0.9$

Consider (from (52c)) *Sue got pregnant and married her boyfriend*: it is false
(CRED $= 0$) that Sue's getting pregnant literally causes her to marry her
boyfriend, though it may be her reason for doing so, CRED $\approx 0.4$; but it is quite
probable (CRED $\approx 0.75$) that her marriage to the boyfriend is a consequence
of her being pregnant, whether or not he is the biological father-to-be. It is
almost certain (CRED $\geq 0.9$), even though defeasible, that Sue's pregnancy
precedes her marriage. Out of any natural context of use it is not possible to
determine whether or not saying *Sue got pregnant* is a background for going
on to say that she married her boyfriend. This aside, it has been possible to
propose a (partial) lexicon entry for *and* which includes its implicatures in
grades of salience. There seems to be no good reason to treat *and* as multiply
ambiguous semantically when one core meaning can be identified (logical
conjunction) and all other interpretations can be directly related to that
as a hierarchy of nonmonotonic inferences processed algorithmically. As
Ockham wrote: *Numquam ponenda est pluralitas sine necessitate* 'Plurality should
never be posited without necessity' (Ordinatio Distinctio 27, Quaestio 2,
Ockham 1967–88: I, K)

   Is it possible to define a plausibility measure for $\Phi$ *and* $\Psi$ that is semantically based? I suspect not. At first sight the acceptability of (55) as against
the unacceptability of (56) seems explicable semantically because only living
things eat and if Max is dead he is no longer living and this is a semantic
entailment of *die*.

(55)   Max ate a hearty meal and died.

(56)   *Max died and ate a hearty meal.

However, the situation seems pragmatically determined in (57)–(60): it is a
matter of conventional beliefs about death, going to hospital, and going to
heaven.

(57)   Max went to hospital and died there.

(58)   *Max died and went to hospital.

(59)   Max died and went to heaven.

(60)   *Max went to heaven and died there.

   In NP-*com-Conjunction, *com is a ≥2-place predicate with a sense 'is added to, is mixed or combined with, acts jointly or together with, is acted upon jointly or together with' (Allan 2000: 196). It is found in (61), which is not semantically equivalent to (62) – contrast the latter with (51e).

(61)   Two and three are five.

(62)   *Two is five ∧ Three is five

A revealing recipe-like paraphrase of (61) is (63), which accounts for the fact that (64) is a paraphrase of (61).

(63)   Take two$_x$ and take three$_y$, combine them (*com(x,y)), and you get five$_w$, cf. *Mix flour$_x$ and water$_y$ to make paste$_w$* or just *Flour and water make paste.*

(64)   Two and three make five.

NP-*com-Conjunction is recognized when a conjunction of sentences either cannot apply or is unlikely to apply as in (61) and (65).

(65)   Joe and his wife have a couple of kids.

The subject NP of (65) is most likely NP-*com-Conjunction whereas that of (66) is not. That these judgments are pragmatically rather than semantically plausible is seen by comparing them.

(66)   Joe and his sister have a couple of kids.

(66) is, given social constraints on incest, most likely an infelicitous manner of expression where the conjunction is intended to be Φ *and* Ψ with the weakest of nonmonotonic inferences; preferred would be *Joe and his sister each have a couple of kids.* With respect to (65), although it is true that each of Joe and his wife has two kids, the sentence *Joe and his wife each have a couple of kids* suggests these derive from former relationships such that the married couple has four children altogether.

## 12.8  Sorites

Two horses don't constitute a *herd* nor do ten grains of sand constitute a *heap*. For collections such as these, denoted by sorites nouns,[14] the number of constituents needed to render the description accurate depends on the nature of the constituents; for example, whereas the least lower bound on a herd of horses might be three, that on a heap of sand is probably more than a hundred. There are sorites predicates like *be bald, be tall, be many* and sorites adverbs like *slowly, loudly.* These are invariably gradable and contextually determined as may be seen from the contrasts in (67).

(67)   **tall** *for a Pygmy* VERSUS **tall** *for a North American basket-ball professional*[15]

   **many** *people thought George W Bush was a fool* VERSUS **many** *of my students didn't attend class today*

   *a slug moves* **slowly** VERSUS *the train went through the station* **slowly**

There is a similar contextual relevance for the nouns: a *herd* of horses, ele-phants, or giraffes will typically have fewer members than a herd of wilde-beest, though this is not necessarily the case; moreover, it has no bearing on the lexical meaning of *herd*. The least lower bound on a *heap* of beans is lower than that on a *heap* of sand, probably because of the size of the constituent members. Clearly these are facts about the world referred to but are they facts about the meaning of listemes? No, but they are relevant to the propositions in which the listemes occur: for instance, if speakers wish to report the speed at which a slug is moving they need to apply different criteria than when reporting the speed at which a train is moving. It appears from work reported by Hagoort *et al.* (2004) that the brain is prepared to do exactly that kind of thing and that contextual information is integrated with semantic information from the start; see also Terkourafi (2009b). However, as I've said, although this is relevant to the meaning of propositions, we can dispense with such enriched interpretations in the lexicon because they are instances of lexical adjustment: they count as "ad hoc categories" (Barsalou 1983; Carston 2002; Wilson and Carston 2007) dependent on a particular domain of discourse. What we see in (67) is a context-induced specification of the meaning for the sorites words. The same holds for *bald*: various degrees of baldness are characterized in (68)–(70).

(68)   His hair is thinning / thin ≈ He is balding / going bald / has a bald patch.

(69)   He is bald.

(70)   He is completely bald.

The domain of baldness extends from thinning (head) hair to its almost complete absence. It is arguable that (69) is applicable in situations where (68) or else (70) would also hold true, even though the accuracy of (69) might be disputed in favor of either (68) or (70). So, how sorites words should be specified in a lexicon is highly controversial.

   Although not directly concerned with the lexicon, there is a large number of proposals discussed in Williamson (1994), Beall (2003), and N. J. J. Smith (2008). They include supervaluation, subvaluation, and plurivaluation. Smith suggests "talk of the meanings of some terms must always be relative to a group of speakers, whose dispositions regarding the use of those terms play an essential part in fixing those meanings" (Smith 2008: 314). This is a recasting of Quine's "There is nothing in linguistic meaning beyond what is to be gleaned from overt behavior in observable circumstances" (Quine 1992: 38). To return to (69): what I suggest for the meaning of *bald* is the minimal semantics of (71).

(71)  BALD(x) → ¬[FULL_COMPLEMENT_OF_HAIR(x)]

Two speakers, or the same speaker on different occasions, may differ as to what counts as 'not a full complement of hair' such that *x is bald* has a range of truth values; i.e. there is no single state of hair-loss for which it is invariably true of x that *x is bald* for all occasions and all speakers. A modification like (68) is appropriate to the least lower bound and (70) to the greatest upper bound; (69) applies to both.

Defining sorites terms often invokes alternative points on the relevant scale. For instance *many* implies a contrast with other points on a quantity scale; more precisely, less than *most* and greater than *a few*. In (72), |f∩g| can be glossed 'the number of Fs that (are) G'.

(72)  [MANY(x): Fx](Gx) → |f∩g| > [A_FEW(x): Fx]G(x)
                              +> |f∩g| < [MOST(x): Fx]G(x)

(I assume that *a few x > few x > one x*.) The domain referred to significantly affects the actual numbers, as we saw in (67). It is notable that to establish the truth of (73) we cannot look to a specific number because even if that can ever be known, the precise number that justifies the use of "many" will differ for different speakers and even for the same speaker on different occasions.

(73)  Many US citizens live in poverty.

Although the meaning of (73) falls under the definition in (72) there is also an implication, or perhaps connotation, that (according to the speaker) *the number of US citizens living in poverty is greater than it ideally ought to be*. Similar conditions hold for *Many of my students were absent from class today*, which does not imply that more than half of them weren't there, but that 'more than one might have expected to be absent were in fact absent' – and that could easily be as little as 5 per cent.

For sorites like *tall* and *slowly* it will be necessary to invoke, respectively, the height scale *tall > average height > short* and the speed scale *slow < average speed < fast* on condition that these apply to a particular domain or set of domains as shown in (67).

Sorites like *herd* and *heap* (in the sense of Eubulides' *soros*) involve configurational criteria.

$$(74)\quad \forall x,y \begin{bmatrix} \text{HERD}(x) \text{ of } c \to c = \{y: y \text{ is a member of } x\} \\ \qquad\qquad \wedge \text{ TRAVEL\_TOGETHER}(y) \wedge |c| \geq 3 \\ \text{HERD}(x) \text{ of } c \;+\!\!> |c| \gg 3 \end{bmatrix}$$

$$(75)\quad \forall x,y \begin{bmatrix} \text{HEAP}(x) \text{ of } c \to c = \{y: y \text{ is a constituent of } x\} \\ \qquad\qquad \wedge \text{ COLLOCATED\_INTO\_A\_ROUGH\_CONE}(y) \wedge |c| \geq 3 \\ \text{HEAP}(x) \text{ of } c \;+\!\!> |c| \gg 3 \end{bmatrix}$$

Suppose that three is the least lower bound for a herd or heap and often the number of constituents is many more, often vastly many more. There is no upper bound. A *heap of sand* will typically have many more constituents than a *heap of logs*; though if the domain of discourse is an egg-timer on the one hand and a clear-felled forest on the other, there may not be such a discrepancy. There is no unique quantity that defines a heap, not even a heap of some particular substance; that is, there is no exact number that determines when a quantity of sand constitutes a heap; the roughly conical configuration is a necessary part of the requirement but is insufficient in itself – as is the condition on quantity. However, the semantic extension of *heap(s)* as in *I have a heap of things to do* and *There were heaps of people at the party* has lost all notion of a particular configuration and is roughly synonymous with *lots of* or *many* and must be defined in a manner similar to (72).

## 12.9  Formulaic language in the lexicon

"A formulaic sequence is a sequence, continuous or discontinuous, that appears prefabricated and stored as a chunk, rather than being generated afresh" (Wray 2008: 94). Just as metaphor is pervasive in language, so are "prefabs" – a useful term succinctly defined by Erman and Warren 2000 as "specific conventionalized multiword strings." Especially in the spoken language, people use thousands of them (just look, for example, at www.phrases.org.uk/index.html); but they are also markers of oral literature, religious texts, best-seller scripts, and popular radio and TV shows (see Allan 2001, 2006b; Corrigan *et al.* 2009; Donahue 1991; Goldman 1990; Jackendoff 1995b; Jensen 1980; Kuipers 2009; Paraskevaides 1984; Schmitt 2004; Wray 2002, 2008). Prefabs can be classed into at least three groups.

> *Idioms* are primarily figurative; they include: *a bit of the other*; *Bob's your uncle*; *by and large*; *come a cropper*; *fuck off*; *go the whole hog*; *kick the bucket*; *put a sock in it*; *rain cats and dogs*; *set store by*; *sleep like a log*; *spill the beans*; *sweat blood*; *the key to*.
>
> *Clichés* are primarily nonfigurative; they include: *be heavily compromised*; *be not very well*; *believe you me*; *don't do anything I wouldn't do*; *Good Lord*; *Happy Birthday! Hot-dog!* [= great!]; *ladies and gentlemen*; *out of sight out of mind*; *reading, writing, and (a)rithmetic*; *to make a long story short*; *un je ne sais quoi*; *you can say that again*; *you'd better* [do A].
>
> *Catchphrases* include: *Beam me up, Scotty*; *Computer says 'No'*; *Frankly, my dear, I don't give a damn*; *It doesn't amount to a hill of beans*; *Not that there's anything wrong with it*; *One potato, two potato, three potato, four . . .* ; *Play it again Sam*; *S/he loves me, s/he loves me not*.

Subclassifications of these groups sometimes suggest themselves (e.g. imprecations, proverbs) and a prefab can often be classed into more than one of the three (e.g. *be worth one's weight in gold*).

Prefabs have similar characteristics to compounds and phrasal verbs in that, although they may have a variable slot, they are largely immutable and function as lexical islands phonologically and syntactically (Underwood *et al.* 2004; Van Lancker *et al.* 1981; Wray 2002, 2008). Like proper names and tabooed terms (such as *fuck*) they seem to be stored in a different manner from the normal lexicon, perhaps in the right brain. The evidence for this is that people with left hemisphere trauma often have access to prefabs, proper names, and tabooed terms when they don't have normal access to ordinary language; furthermore, persons with right hemisphere damage use significantly fewer prefabs than normal subjects (Van Lancker 2009: 452). Lexicography has ignored the conclusion that different kinds of vocabulary are stored in different hemispheres of the brain, even though it could be relevant to classifying types of lexical data; I shall maintain this tradition.

A simplified lexicon entry for *kick the bucket* might be something like (76).

(76)    /kɪk ðə bʌkət/ — [VP[V[KICK]] NP[D[THE] N[BUCKET]]] → DIE(x)

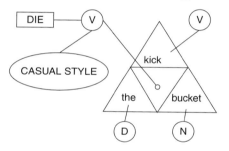

The ellipse in the figure contains encyclopaedic information that is clearly pragmatic yet according to Allan (2001) is outside of the lexicon. Traditionally such information is located in dictionaries, for instance, the *Oxford English Dictionary* (1989) labels *kick the bucket* "slang" and the *Macquarie Dictionary* (2003) describes it as "Colloquial" (it doesn't appear in Webster 2002). Such descriptions, whether assigned to the lexicon or the networked encyclopaedia, are clearly pragmatic. The explanation for the meaning of *kick the bucket* is metonymic: in former times a *bucket* was a 'beam' and when an animal (such as a pig) was tied to the beam by its hind legs to be slaughtered, it would kick the bucket in the throes of death. But information about this source for the idiom is an encyclopaedic datum that is not generally known, and plays no part in the interpretation today of the idiom *kick the bucket*.

Unlike the meaning of the typical idiom, the meaning of a typical cliché is computable from its constituent parts. What marks the cliché is that it occurs frequently as the clichéd chunk (Bannard and Lieven 2009: 300f., 304), and experimental evidence suggests that it is normally processed as a chunk and not according to its constituent parts (Underwood *et al.* 2004; Wray 2002, 2008). I suggest that clichés should therefore be noted in full in a lexicon and (pragmatically) marked as clichés. *Mutatis mutandis*, the same goes for catchphrases: their meaning is almost invariably computable from their parts, but they are recalled and used as chunks – or perhaps as articulated chunks in the case of items of play like *one potato, two potato, three potato, four...*, or the words of a national anthem or of the full version of *Happy Birthday to you*. It is a debatable matter whether these can count as lexical entries rather than encyclopaedia entries. They seem to be evoked by a particular kind of event that triggers a speech act, e.g. *Happy birthday* by the occasion of someone's birthday that the speaker wishes to demonstrably recognize; *Beam me up, Scotty* is triggered by the thought 'Get me out of here'. It seems feasible to propose that the listeme *birthday* is linked to the networked encyclopaedia with a free pragmatic condition like (77):

(77)   If it is X's birthday then it is appropriate to tell X *Happy birthday*.

The situation with respect to *Beam me up, Scotty* is far more constrained: it can perhaps be tagged to the phrasal verb *get NP out* in some thesaurus-like way on condition that the constituent NP refers to the speaker (perhaps, along with others); it can only be used as a jocular expression and to an addressee likely to understand the utterance as a catchphrase. This latter condition does not apply to all catchphrases: for instance, it doesn't apply to *not that there is anything wrong with it*, which functions adequately as a non-prefab; the condition that applies is that "it" refers to a mildly tabooed topic (such as being gay).[16] This illustrates the squishiness[17] of prefabs.

Prefabs are, by definition, multiword expressions. Traditional dictionaries of phrases list them in alphabetical order but the mental lexicon is surely more akin to a database which is searched in a manner similar to a Google search engine operating on key words and combinations of words. The mental lexicon will also be accessed semantically and pragmatically (i.e. via meanings and encyclopaedic information; see Giora, this volume and Katsos, this volume) and not merely through aspects of the form of language expressions.

## 12.10  Connotation in the lexicon

The connotations of a language expression are pragmatic effects that arise from encyclopaedic knowledge about its denotation (or reference) and also from experiences, beliefs, and prejudices about the contexts in which the expression is typically used. Terms like *surgeon, nurse, secretary/receptionist*, and *motor mechanic* evoke connotations of gender from the fact that the typical job-holder in each case is, even today, a gendered stereotype: most surgeons and motor mechanics are male; most nurses and secretary/receptionists are female. These connotations are all, clearly, the pragmatic effects of normative conceptions of typical job-holders.

(78)  *surgeon*  →   a medical practitioner who treats wounds, fractures,
                     deformities, or disorders by manual operation and/or
                     instrumental appliances
               +>    a male medical practitioner who treats wounds,
                     fractures, deformities, or disorders by manual
                     operation and/or instrumental appliances, CRED ≈ 0.85
(79)  *nurse*   →    a person employed or trained to take charge of young
                     children or who cares for the sick or infirm
               +>    a woman employed or trained to take charge of young
                     children or who cares for the sick or infirm, CRED ≈ 0.94

The most common denotations of *bunny* and *rabbit* or *doggie* and *dog* are
the same, but the connotations are different: bearing the diminutive, the
first member of the two pairs connotes endearment or childish language;
see (80).

(80)  *doggie*  →   dog
               +>   the speaker is a child ∨ the speaker is addressing a
                    child with respect to the animal ∨ the speaker is
                    expressing endearment with respect to the animal

To avoid blaspheming (for which the Bible sanctions execution: Leviticus
24:16), people use a variety of euphemistic expletives (see Allan and Burridge
2006: 15ff., 39). For instance, *Jesus* is end-clipped to *Jeeze!* and *Gee!* (which is
also the initial of *God*); *Gee whiz!* is a remodelling of either *jeeze* or *jesus*. More
adventurous remodelings are *By jingo! Jiminy cricket!* [from *Jesus Christ*] *Christmas! Crust! Crumbs! Crikey!* Note that the denotation of *Gee!, Jeepers!,* and *Jesus!*
is identical. All function as exclamations of surprise, dismay, enthusiasm,
or emphasis. From a purely rational viewpoint, if one of them is blasphe-
mous, then all of them are. What is different is that the first two have
connotations that are markedly different from the last. Connotation – or,
more precisely its pragmatic effect, reaction to connotation – is seen to be
a vocabulary generator. But the question here is what goes into the lexicon,
and I suggest (81)–(82) (in which statements introduced by a simple + are
encyclopaedic).

(81)  *Jesus*  →   Proper name for a male
              +>   Jesus Christ of Nazareth, son of Mary (Mariam)
              +    Jesus the Christ or Messiah, central figure of
                   Christianity, which takes him to be the son of God.
      *Jesus*  →   Interjection (expressive idiom). Blasphemous
                   exclamation of surprise, dismay, enthusiasm, or
                   emphasis.
              +>   Often not regarded as literally blasphemous, CRED ≈ 0.8

(82) *Jeepers* → Interjection (expressive idiom). Exclamation of surprise, dismay, enthusiasm, or emphasis.
+ Euphemism based on remodelling of the blasphemy *Jesus*

Whether the encyclopaedic statements should be included within the lexicon is a matter of debate. I personally don't believe they should form a part of the lexicon entry but they must certainly be accessible from and networked with the lexicon.

## 12.11 Conclusion

In this chapter I have looked at ways in which pragmatics intrudes on the lexicon. I count as "pragmatic" encyclopaedic data and nonmonotonic inferences (NMI) – which arguably arise from encyclopaedic data. In section 12.2, I introduced the notion of a credibility metric for a proposition and used it to calibrate NMIs in the lexicon to correspond with the degree of confidence one might have in the truth of the inference: its probability. Sections 12.3 and 12.4 demonstrated that in addition to the lexicon entry specifying the necessary components of meaning in the semantics for an entry, it should also specify the most probable additional components of meaning, which are accepted or canceled as a function of contextual constraints. These same sets of conditions were demonstrated for different kinds of entries throughout the rest of the chapter. Section 12.5 looked at lexicon entries for collective and collectivizable nouns. These differ in that different interpretations for collective nouns arise from their morphosyntactic context and although this needs to be captured in the lexicon it is not a matter of pragmatics; on the other hand, a noun is collectivizable only in some defined set of contexts and these are a pragmatic constraint. Section 12.6 discussed the use of animal nouns in mass NPs to denote either the animal's meat or its pelt. Although there are defined morphosyntactic conditions on such interpretations, the choice of one interpretation or the other is pragmatically determined because it is contextually induced and is open to calibration against a credibility metric. Section 12.7 returned to the much disputed semantics of *and*. The view taken here is for a monosemic semantics which assumes that English *and* has the semantics of logical conjunction but there is a graded salience captured in an algorithm that assigns one of a set of nonmonotonic inferences as supplementary meaning on the basis of context. Section 12.8 discussed the vexed question of how to represent the semantics of sorites terms in the lexicon. A minimalist semantics was proposed. Section 12.9 discussed the matter of prefabs or formulaic expressions. It is only recently that their frequency and ubiquity has been recognized. They pose a challenge to the lexicon principally because they are multiword expressions; many are figurative; many are stylistically marked. These pragmatic characteristics are appropriate to encyclopaedic information linked to the entry. Section 12.10 considered the representation of connotation in the lexicon as a matter of pragmatic intrusion.

In this chapter I have shown different motivations for including pragmatics in the lexicon or linking it to the lexicon, and I have demonstrated how that may be accomplished. This is not to deny that other formalizations are possible.

# 13

# Conversational interaction

Michael Haugh

## 13.1 Introduction

The study of conversational interaction is now approached in a multitude of different ways in pragmatics, reflecting in part the ever increasing diversity of the field. Approaches range from the study of the structure and management of talk as a form of social order itself in conversation analysis, through to the study of a wide variety of pragmatic phenomena that occur in conversational interaction, including formulaic language, discourse/pragmatic markers, reference and deixis, presupposition, implicature, speech and pragmatic acts, humour, im/politeness and beyond to issues of identity and power, to name just a few. The latter study of pragmatic phenomena in conversational interaction draws from a wide range of approaches, including conversations reconstructed through the introspective methods of philosophical pragmatics, the study of naturally occurring conversations through ethnography of speaking, interactional sociolinguistics, philology, (critical) discourse analysis, interactional pragmatics and more recently corpora, and the study of conversation elicited through devices such as discourse completion tests or role plays.[1]

Within this complex analytical landscape two key trends can be discerned in relation to the place of conversational interaction in pragmatics. First, the work of the ordinary language philosophers, Austin, Grice and Searle, who were all focused on analysing meaning (and to a lesser extent action) in language from ordinary conversation, has been enormously influential with regard to the ways in which conversation itself, and language data from conversation, are approached by many in pragmatics, particularly those practising cognitive and philosophical forms of pragmatics (so-called Anglo-American pragmatics). In such approaches, the analyst largely abstracts away from the details of conversation itself in order to formalise the rules and principles by which speakers mean (and to a lesser extent do) things in ordinary discourse. For instance, the constitutive rules for different speech acts developed by Searle (1969), and the conversational logic proposed by Grice (1989) to account for meaning that the speaker intended but did not explicitly express, are both examples of formalised systems of abstract reasoning through which speaker meaning can be analysed. This tradition of drawing from conversational data, albeit often reconstructed through introspection, has been inherited by scholars who focus on the analysis of pragmatic meaning (see Allan, Bach, Carston, de Saussure, Horn, Jaszczolt, Sullivan, this volume), or treat speech acts as a form of speaker meaning (see Kissine, Peregrin, this volume).

The second key trend is the formative influence of the work of sociologists and anthropologists, in particular, that of conversation analysis (Sacks *et al.* 1974) and interactional sociolinguistics (Gumperz 1982), which has changed the ways conversation is approached by many scholars in pragmatics, particularly those practising interactional and socio-cultural forms of pragmatics (so-called European-Continental pragmatics). In conversation analysis (CA), however, the main focus is on understanding the organisational and social structure of conversation itself. The analyst thus closely examines the fine details of conversational interaction, teasing out how participants themselves understand and experience action, and manage the mechanisms through which talk is accomplished. While this approach could not be more different to cognitive-philosophical pragmatics in its underlying ontological and epistemological commitments, and thus in its treatment and analysis of conversational data, both approaches have nevertheless formed the bedrock of much of the work in pragmatics on or using conversation, ever since they were brought together by Levinson's (1983) highly influential textbook.

However, while much of the interest in pragmatics and CA was initially focused on conversation in the folk sense of ordinary or everyday uses of talk between family, friends or acquaintances, conversation has since garnered a more technical definition, encompassing all types of face-to-face or telephone-mediated interaction that use language, including that occurring in institutional settings such as the classroom or workplace. More recently still it has been extended again to include various forms of computer-mediated communication (CMC), particularly those which allow (close to) real-time exchange of messages. The latter more technical notion of conversation is sometimes called talk-in-interaction in CA in order to distinguish this broader, academic notion from the ordinary sense of conversation. In this chapter, however, the term conversational interaction will be retained, in part to emphasise that it is a perspective on mundane and institutional conversation rooted in the analytical concerns of pragmatics, which is the primary focus of discussion here, rather than those of CA proper.

The importance of a pragmatics perspective on conversation is emphasised here because although work in CA has been enormously influential in advancing our understanding that conversational interaction is fundamentally emergent or non-summative in nature, the view that talk is situated not only locally in interaction but also in the sociocognitive worlds of participants does not lie within the purview of CA. In not strictly allowing for 'inferences about what they [participants] are thinking, or why they do what they do, or assumptions about their roles and the wider social context' (Myers 2009: 502), conversation analysts place evaluations, meanings to some extent, as well as the sociocognitive underpinnings of conversational interaction outside of the direct scope of their analytical interests.[2] The point here is not to argue for the superiority of one methodology over another, however, as Jucker (2009) quite rightly points out in regard to the analysis of pragmatic phenomena:

> an assessment of a particular method always depends on the specific research question that the researcher tries to answer because the different methods vary enormously in their suitability for specific research questions. One particular method may provide interesting results for one specific question or set of questions while it is of little value for another set of questions. (Jucker 2009: 1633)

Thus, while it is suggested here that developing an approach informed by research and methods in CA in studying pragmatic phenomena that occur in conversational interaction is likely to be more productive than one which eschews such research, it is important to note that to be informed by such research is one thing, to be unduly constrained by it is another. Consequently, in this chapter, it is proposed that although the emergent nature of pragmatic phenomena in conversational interaction should clearly not be neglected, neither should the way in which such phenomena are inherently situated, not only locally in interaction but also within the sociocognitive worlds of participants. In this respect, it is argued that the properties of both emergence and situatedness should be taken into account in any analysis of pragmatic phenomena in conversational interaction. This entails drawing in a principled manner from a range of other analytical traditions, then, including not only conversation analysis, but those of cognitive, philosophical and socio-cultural pragmatics.

This chapter begins by first briefly outlining the landscape in terms of the different types of conversational interaction that have been studied thus far, including emerging computer-mediated forms of conversational interaction. The interactional engine underpinning these different types of conversational interaction, including the ways in which it is structured and managed, is next briefly described. The two key properties of conversational interaction, namely, emergence and situatedness, are then discussed, with particular emphasis placed on the implications of these properties for the analysis of pragmatic meaning, action and evaluation in conversational interactions. In this section, the sociocognitive engine that underpins conversational interaction is also discussed, based on the specific requirements that conversational interaction places on that system. The chapter concludes by sketching a programme for furthering our understanding of the pragmatics of conversational interaction.

## 13.2  Types of conversational interaction

Conversational interaction defined in the broad sense of all face-to-face or technology-mediated forms of interaction that use language encompasses a wide range of different types of talk. Building on Hakulinen's (2009) analysis of conversation types, conversational interactions can be classified relative to four different dimensions: degree of institutionality, activity type/genre, channel and participation framework.

As previously noted, the main focus of analysis in pragmatics and CA was initially everyday conversations between family, friends and acquaintances, although the scope was soon extended to include other institutional forms of talk in workplaces, classrooms and the like. Mundane or ordinary conversation is thus generally defined in contrast to institutional talk. Levinson (1983), for instance, defines (ordinary) conversation as 'the predominant kind of talk in which two or more participants freely alternate in speaking, which generally occurs outside specific institutional settings' (p. 284). More specifically, such mundane conversation involves 'organization of talk which is *not* subject to functionally specific or context-specific restrictions or specialized practices or conventionalized arrangements' (Schegloff 1999: 407, original emphasis). Yet despite being defined relative to institutional forms of conversational interaction, ordinary conversation is regarded as primordial. Schegloff (1999), for instance, goes on to argue

> [w]hat humans grow up with is an ordinary interaction within the family, within peer groups, neighborhoods, communities, etc. In all of these, it appears most likely that the basic medium of 'interactional exchange' is ordinary conversation – in whatever practices it is embodied in those settings. (Schegloff 1999: 413)

In the sense that everyone engages in it from an early age and constantly throughout their lives, then, ordinary conversation is uncontroversially basic.

However, the claim in CA that institutional forms of conversational interaction are restricted variations of the basic system of ordinary conversation is somewhat more controversial. Schegloff (1999) argues that 'other speech-exchange systems themselves appear to be shaped by the adaptation of the practices and organizations of ordinary conversation to their special functional needs, legal constraints, etc.' (ibid. 415; see also Goodwin and Heritage 1990: 289). Types of institutional conversational interaction examined in this way range from courtroom talk, classrooms and workplace meetings and interactions through to broadcast interviews and debates, police interviews, medical consultations and various forms of counselling, including phone-in help-lines (Heritage 2005). Key differences between ordinary and institutional forms of conversational interaction include their overall structure and turn allocation. While institutional talk generally has particular phases (e.g. a recognisable beginning and end), ordinary talk has no such recognisable phases or formal procedures. Moreover, turns in institutional talk tend to be pre-allocated, while in everyday talk turns are allocated on a local basis (Heritage 2005). However, while the claim that institutional talk involves particular adaptations of the turn-taking and sequential structure of ordinary talk is perhaps intuitively appealing, such a claim still requires further exploration across various institutional settings.

A second, related dimension of conversational interaction is that of activity type (Levinson 1979) or communicative genre (Fairclough 2003). These involve 'practised patterns of language use' that are constitutive of different communicative activity types or genres, such as intimate talk, family dinner-table conversation, troubles telling (or troubles talk), small talk, negotiation talk, consultation, advice giving and so on (Hakulinen 2009). However, while activity types or genres are clearly an important dimension of analysis, there is no principled way of classifying conversational interactions in this way, with such categorisations often being based on commonsense or vernacular terms that inevitably overlap in some respects. The analytical focus is thus generally more on *how* such activity types or genres are accomplished through conversational interaction rather than attempting to enumerate them as such (Auer 2009: 95).

The channel in which conversational interaction takes place was, up until recently, restricted to auditory (e.g. telephone conversations) or audio-visual (e.g. face-to-face conversations) modes of communication. However, in recent years the notion of conversational interaction has been extended to encompass various forms of computer-mediated communication, particularly those that occur in real-time (or near to it). These include instant messaging via various software applications such as Windows Live Messenger or Yahoo Messenger, on-line chat rooms or forums (synchronous conferencing), text messaging (or SMS) via mobile phones, and the use of email in some instances for close to real-time exchange of messages. The increasing use of software such as Skype that supports audio-visual calls over the internet is also an area of interest in that such software often features text messaging and file sharing functions together with the audio(-visual) channel. Early studies of turn-taking systems in various forms of computer-mediated communication (CMC) indicated that the turn-taking system in ordinary face-to-face conversation cannot always be straightforwardly mapped onto that occurring in CMC. A variety of factors relating to the medium of CMC in question can influence how closely it maps onto spoken conversational interaction (Garcia and Jacobs 1999; Georgakopoulou 2005; Herring 1999, 2004, 2007). Key factors include synchronicity, message transmission (i.e. one-way transmission where the receiver cannot see the message until it is sent versus two-way transmission where both the sender and receiver are able to see or hear the message as it is produced), persistence, size of message, channels of communication (including not only text but images, audio and video), degree of anonymity and whether the system enables private or public communication (Herring 2007: 14–17).

Generally speaking, synchronous forms of private CMC are structurally the closest in many respects to spoken conversational interaction, as will be discussed in the following section. Yet while on-line interactions can have similarities with spoken conversational interaction, CMC does not constitute one homogeneous variety of discourse, as it also encompasses asynchronous forms such as blogs (= 'weblogs'), discussion boards and social networks, and also varies in terms of register, style and genre of the forum in question (Georgakopoulou 2005; Herring 2007). The question of which forms of CMC can be legitimately treated as forms of conversational interaction thus remains an empirical one, and an evolving one at that, as emerging technologies continue to afford different configurations of channel and other medium-related factors in communicating.

The fourth dimension influencing the type of conversational interaction in question is the participation framework (Goffman 1979). Multiparty interactions tend to have more complex instantiations of turn allocation practices as opposed to dyadic interactions where turn-taking can be more smoothly (albeit not always) accomplished (Sacks, Schegloff and Jefferson 1974). In addition, multiparty interactions afford different discourse roles for participants ranging from straightforward speakers and addressees through to virtual speakers (who invoke what could have been said by someone at some point) and non-addressed participants, who include side-participants, bystanders and overhearers (Levinson 1988; Verschueren 1999).

## 13.3 The interactional machinery of conversational interaction

While conversational interaction encompasses a diverse range of forms of talk (and more recently text), one of the key contributions of CA has been in explicating the interactional mechanisms underlying these different types of conversational interaction. These are generally taken to include turn-taking, sequence organisation, repair organisation, recipient design, and structural organisation (Schegloff 2006). In this section, the two main features of this interactional machinery relevant to analysing pragmatic phenomena in conversational interaction, namely, turn-taking and sequence organisation, are briefly described in relation to an excerpt from a spoken face-to-face conversation, and then extended to an analysis of a conversation conducted through an on-line messaging service.[3]

The first excerpt, which is from a casual chat between two male under-graduate students who are also friends, can be used to illustrate some of the most salient interactional features of ordinary conversation.[4]

(1)   GCSAusE09: 0:00[5]
    1   B:     >so <u>what</u> did you do on the weekend<
    2          (1.2)
    3   A:     ah::: went and saw a friend and °ah:°
    4          (0.6)
    5   B:     ah ↑o↓kay, (1.8) >was it <u>fun</u>?<
    6          (0.9)
    7   A:     it wa:s okay we went and ate subway °a:nd° (1.2)
    8          yeah just <u>chatted</u> about (0.2) world events
    9          and [the economies]
   10   B:              [just >chilling out<]
   11          (0.3)
   12   A:     yeah
   13          (1.0)
   14   B:     cool (0.2) yeah <u>I</u> ah (1.0) ><u>what</u> did I do I just<
   15          studied (0.2) >spent the whole weekend studying
   16          did semantics on Saturday, (0.6) and <u>di:d</u> (0.2) CA
   17          conversation analysis< on ↑Sun↓day
   18          (1.8)
   19   A:     sounds like fun °there goes° the <u>stu</u>dents life
   20          HA ha [.hh hh.hh hh.hh]
   21   B:              [ah:: yes it was <u>very</u>] interesting

The first thing to note in this conversation is that the two participants take turns in speaking, illustrating the first key principle of the interactional machinery of conversational interaction, namely, composition (Clift *et al.* 2006: 11). Although there are no set institutional rules guiding the alloca-tion of turns, the two participants are able to take the speaking floor in a relatively orderly fashion that reflects the principles of turn-taking first out-lined by Sacks *et al.* (1974: 704). These rules, in turn, rest on the ability of both participants to parse the ongoing speech into what are called turn con-struction units (TCUs) on the basis of grammar, intonational packaging and where it 'constitutes a recognizable action in context' (Schegloff 2007: 3–4). The span of a TCU-in-progress that projects imminent possible completion is termed a transition relevance place (TRP) (Schegloff 2007: 4). Such TRPs are not spans where speaker change has to occur, however, but rather are recognisable places where speaker change can occur. Speaker change may, of course, occur at points other than a TRP, but speakers are held interactionally accountable for such changes.

In the excerpt above, we can see Ben selects Alex as next speaker in lines 1 and 5, while he self-selects as next speaker to continue his speaking turn in line 14. The only point at which there is overlap between semantically meaningful TCUs occurs across lines 9–10, when Ben offers a gloss of Alex's weekend (as 'just >chilling out<'). There are two things to note about this overlapping turn. First, its design closely aligns with the action in the preceding turn, as through it Ben offers a formulation of what it is that Alex is trying to do in the preceding turn, namely, describe his weekend activities (Garfinkel and Sacks 1970: 342). Second, it occurs at a projectable TRP, thus constituting a form of recognitional onset (Jefferson 1986). It can also be observed more generally that turns are designed to accomplish actions in a manner that maintains progressivity in moving from one element (e.g. a turn or TCU) to the next with as little intervening as possible (Heritage 2009: 308; Schegloff 2007: 14–15) and respects minimisation with regard to reference to or formulations of persons, places, times, actions and so on (Schegloff 2006: 80). The second-turn design principle has also been productively applied to the analysis of person reference (or deixis) (Enfield and Stivers 2007; Lerner and Kitzinger 2007).

The second point to note is that the relationship between the turns is orderly, illustrating the second key principle of the interactional machinery, namely, position or sequentiality (Clift et al. 2006: 11). The observation by Sacks that actions in conversational interaction tend to come in pairs was formalised through the notion of adjacency pairs, such as question-answer or invitation-acceptance/declination. Adjacency pairs are not limited to two turns, however, as they can also be expanded in various ways, the main ones being pre-expansion (e.g. pre-request, pre-invitation, pre-offer), insert expansion (e.g. pre-second insert expansion for request) and post-expansion (Schegloff 2007). In the excerpt above, question-answer adjacency pairs and minimal post-expansions are evident in lines 1–12, while Ben's telling in lines 14–17 occasions an assessment on the part of Alex of the upshot of this telling (lines 19–20), with which Ben displays agreement (line 21) (Pomerantz 1984). Notably here, as Alex does not reciprocate Ben's initial question about the weekend's activities (cf. the reciprocal 'how are you' routine noted by Schegloff 1986), Ben occasions this telling through a self-directed question about his own weekend's activities. Ben's telling is treated as a possible complaint by Alex (Schegloff 2005), who responds with an ironic positive assessment (line 19). The non-serious frame here is marked through laughter (Glenn 2003; Jefferson 1979; Schenkein 1972), and Ben's subsequent continuation of the ironic frame in upgrading Alex's preceding positive assessment from 'fun' to 'very interesting' (line 21).

However, it is important to note that while reference has been made to adjacency pairs in explicating the sequential architecture of this particular excerpt, this is not to say that all conversational interaction can be reduced to adjacency pairs or expansions thereof. Instances of extended storytelling (or personal narratives), for instance, involve a different kind of overall sequential structure (Jefferson 1978; Sacks 1986). One of the key findings in CA, however, is that such sequences, whether with respect to adjacency pairs or the overall structural organisation of the interaction, are for the most part organised around actions rather than topics (Schegloff 1997, 2007).

The interactional machinery of turn-taking and sequence organisation can also be applied to some synchronous forms of private CMC, as seen in the following excerpt from a private conversation between two friends conducted through instant messaging.[6]

(2)  (R and B are females in their early twenties using the messenger
      service on Facebook)
1    R (6:18pm):   Hey, Haven't spoken to you in ages, what have you been
2                  up to?
3    B (6.20pm):   hey yea its been a while
4                  just uni and work u no REAL exciting stuff
5                  I cant wait for the holidays
6    R (6.25pm):   Yeah I Know. I've been going to the skatepark a lot lately
7                  and I've gotten really good. I can do a disaster (its when
8                  you come out of the bowl and do a 180 with the front
9                  wheel still over the copeing its so rad
10   B (6:26pm):   o wow cool
11   R (6:27pm):   So yea with that and learning new songs on my guitar
12                 I've kept myself really busy.
13                 Do you have plans for the holidays?
14   B (6:28pm):   well i have to catch up with all my friends that i neglect
15                 during the semester haha and i have to go to nz
16                 for my grandmas 80th
17   R (6:29pm):   that sounds like fun. I'm probs just gonna chill at
18                 skatepark. Learn new tricks you know the usual
19   R (6.30pm):   so how have you been?
20   B (6:34pm):   good hey
21   R (6:36pm):   thats good. ive been good too. well i have to go bye byes

The excerpt above bears a number of striking similarities with the face-to-face conversational interaction discussed in example (1) despite being conducted entirely through a textual channel. Once again there is an orderly taking of turns by the two participants. However, rather than relating to recognition of TRPs, next turns are allocated by the current sender, who holds the floor in three main ways. First, in a manner similar to ordinary spoken conversation, the current sender can select next sender through 'addressing them with a turn whose action requires a responsive action next' (Schegloff 2007: 4). In this interaction these are primarily information-seeking questions (Stivers 2010), as seen in lines 1, 13 and 19. Second, the current sender self-selects by continuing her current turn. For instance, Rachel moves from an expression of solidarity in response to Bronwyn's previous turn (constituting one TCU) to a telling of her recent activities (constituting a second TCU) in the same turn (line 6). Unlike face-to-face conversation, however, interruption or overlap of a current turn is not possible due to limitations of the medium (i.e. the messenger allows only one-way transmission), although a turn can be displaced if another participant sends another message in the meantime. Third, the current sender selects next sender through posting the message, thereby implicitly relinquishing rights to next turn, a practice evident throughout the interaction. However, this implicit relinquishment of next turn can easily be reversed, if that sender goes on to take the next turn. An example of this latter move, which can be seen in lines 17–18, appears to be occasioned by a lack of reciprocation in asking questions on the part of Bronwyn.

There are also similarities with the underlying sequential structure of the face-to-face conversation in example (1), as a clear pattern of adjacency pairs (question-answer-assessment) is apparent. There is, moreover, a striking resemblance with another practice found in example (1), namely, self-talk despite the current speaker's inquiries about the other not being reciprocated. Rachel's inquiries about Bronwyn's recent activities (line 1), her plans for the holidays (line 13) or how Bronwyn has been (line 19), for instance, occasion a telling on Rachel's part about her recent activities (lines 5–8), her plans for the holidays (lines 17–19) and how she has been (line 21). These latter tellings by Rachel occur despite Bronwyn not reciprocating Rachel's questions, which mirrors Ben's telling about his weekend's activities despite his initial inquiry not being reciprocated by Alex in example (1). It appears, then, that the routinely reciprocal nature of such question-answer-assessment sequences can occasion self-initiated tellings in some cases, or what might be glossed as 'occasioning self-talk through inquiring about others'.

## 13.4  Characterising conversational interaction

Conversational interaction can arguably be characterised in terms of two key properties. The first is emergence, where the activities of participants in conversational interaction are reciprocally linked and conditional upon those of others (Arundale 1999, 2006a, 2008, 2010a, 2010b; Arundale and Good 2002). The upshot of this reciprocal conditionality, or non-summativity, is that pragmatic phenomena cannot always be straightforwardly reduced to an analysis of the mental states, including a priori intentions, of individuals (see Haugh and Jaszczolt, this volume). The second key property is that of situatedness, where the activities of participants in conversational interaction are not only interpretable in terms of the local, situated context of that particular interaction (that is, what has come before and what comes afterwards in the interactional sequence to which participants themselves are demonstrably orienting) (Schegloff 1987, 1991, 2005), but also beyond the here-and-now, encompassing the layers of historicity and orders of indexicality (Blommaert 2005, 2007) that afford pragmatic meanings and actions (Mey 2001: 115, 227; 2010: 445–6). The upshot of the inherent situatedness of conversation is that pragmatic phenomena in conversational interaction cannot always be straightforwardly reduced to emergent interactional phenomena in the here-and-now without a proper consideration of their sociocognitive roots.

### 13.4.1  Emergence

The term interaction is used in two quite distinct ways in pragmatics. In the ordinary or 'weak' sense, interaction refers to 'a situation in which people converse' (Arundale 2006a: 196), and thus where talk is 'directed to another person and has potential for affecting that other person' (Schiffrin 1994: 415). In the folk sense, then, interaction is synonymous with talk or contact. This view of interaction assumes a summative view where the 'output of one system . . . serves as an input to a separate, independent system' (Arundale 2006a: 196). The conceptualisation of interaction as the summative pairing of the behavioural and cognitive states of individuals is dependent on the assumption that no reciprocal conditionality can be identified across the activities of those individuals, and thus 'explanations of those activities can be reduced without remainder to the simple sum of the independent individual's behaviour and/or cognitive states' (Arundale 2010a: 2079). The classic view in pragmatics that meaning involves recipients attributing intentions to speakers based on the behaviour, normally an utterance, of that speaker (see Haugh and Jaszczolt, this volume, for further discussion) presupposes a summative conceptualisation of interaction, where speaker meaning is reduced to the speaker's behaviour (output) and the recipient's inferences about intentions underlying the speaker's behaviour (input). It is assumed, therefore, that in cases of successful communication, the recipient's inferences about the speaker's intentions match those of the speaker, while miscommunication is characterised as cases where those inferences do not match the actual intentions of the speaker. While such an approach can account for at least some of what goes on in conversational interaction, especially when language-use data from conversations is abstracted away from its sequential environment, the inadequacy of a summative conceptualisation of interaction for explaining how meanings, actions and evaluations often arise in conversational interaction has been repeatedly emphasised by those examining naturally occurring conversation (see Arundale 2005 for a good summary).

For example, in the following exchange an understanding that Sirl wanted to use the shower first emerged over a number of turns, and was thus only retrospectively attributed to a previous utterance.

(3)    (Michael is staying at Sirl's house on holiday in London and
       Michael is going out sightseeing that day. Sirl and Michael have
       just met outside the bathroom in the morning)
1    S:    What time are you leaving this morning?
2    M:    Oh, in about an hour I suppose. Are you in a hurry to leave?
3    S:    No, no. Just asking.
(2 second pause)
4    M:    Would you like to use the bathroom first?
5    S:    Yeh, sure, if you don't mind.

                                             (Haugh 2007c: 94)

While Sirl's initial inquiry in turn 1 might be interpreted as a pre-request
in that it constitutes a preparatory condition for making a request to use
the bathroom first, and Michael subsequently leaves open the possibility
that Sirl may wish to make such a request in turn 2, Sirl does not go on to
make the request in turn 3. Instead, he treats his first utterance as simply a
request for information, thereby blocking the interpretation of this utterance
as a pre-request. However, the marked pause after Sirl's counter-response
indicates that something has been left unsaid, and so Michael makes an offer
to Sirl in turn 4 that he use the bathroom first, thereby reinterpreting Sirl's
utterance in turn 1 as a pre-request. The subsequent acceptance of this offer
by Sirl in turn 5 ratifies Michael's retrospective interpreting. Crucially, this
interpreting only emerges in this interaction over the course of a number of
turns, and rests on contingent inferences made by Michael that are afforded
and constrained by the inferences made by Sirl, and vice versa.

   According to a summative view of interaction this short conversation is an
instance of miscommunication, as Sirl's utterance in turn 1 (the output) initially failed to elicit the 'correct' inference on the part of Michael (the input).
Yet characterising this interaction as miscommunication neglects the possibility that it was in fact a matter of the two participants 'sounding each
other out' before coming to an agreed interpretation of Sirl's initial utterance. Moreover, an analyst taking a summative view of interaction would
also have to assume that Sirl really did intend to imply that he wanted to
use the shower with his first utterance. Yet it is equally possible that Sirl
decided he wanted to use the shower only after Michael made the offer. Sirl
himself may not have been able to distinguish his own a priori intention and
what eventually emerged as their understanding of his utterance in turn 1
(cf. Haugh 2007c: 94–5)

   The contingent inferencing underlying the emergence of a particular
understanding of Sirl's first utterance in this interaction goes beyond the
traditional monadic account of inference located in the autonomous minds
of individuals. Instead, it is arguably more productively understood in terms
of anticipatory and retroactive inferencing (Arundale 2008; Arundale and
Good 2002; Good 1995).

Each participant's processing in using language involves a set of concur-
rent cognitive operations that are temporally extended, not only forward
in time in recipient design of their own utterances and in anticipation of
other's talk...but also backwards in time in the retroactive assessing of
interpretations of what has already been produced in their own and in
other's utterance. (Arundale and Good 2002: 135)

In other words, implicatures and other interpretings are contingent not
because the inferences are necessarily always defeasible, as various scholars
have pointed out (Carston 2002: 138–9; Haugh 2008d: 445–6; Weiner 2006),
but because such inferences are both anticipatory and retroactive in nature
(Haugh 2009: 97–102).

In another example of the emergent nature of conversational interaction, Chris is asking Emma about her acupuncture business. The utterance-
final disjunction here appears to occasion an instance of 'not saying', where
the speaker partly leaves the interpretation of what is not said up to the
recipient.

(4)    AGA: ERCH[7]
1    C:    how do you go generally with most of your
2           customers °are they happy or°
3           (0.8)
4    E:    ↑YEAH
5    C:    Yeah
6    E:    Yeah I've been getting (0.6) most of my
7           business actually <u>now</u>(0.2)<u>now</u> that it's
8           gaining (0.2) momentum is um word of mouth
9    C:    Mmm
10   E:    From (.) patients telling other patients
11   C:    Right
                        (Haugh 2008c: 59–60)

In this excerpt, Chris begins by asking about Emma's customers' level of
satisfaction with her work (lines 1–2). Emma responds in the affirmative
(line 4) after a brief pause (line 3), before going on to give a justification for
her assertion that her customers are happy, namely that she is getting business through word of mouth (lines 6–8, 10), which presupposes they must
be happy. Careful examination of Chris's utterance in lines 1–2, however,
indicates that his question could have been legitimately interpreted both as
a polar question ('or not'), or as an alternative question ('or something', for
example 'unhappy', 'dissatisfied' etc.). Chris leaves it open to Emma as to
which one of these interpretations is meant. In this way, a default implicature of epistemic optionality arises, whereby Chris not only claims a lack of
knowledge about the level of satisfaction experience by Emma's customers,

a claim standardly associated with questions (Heritage and Raymond forth-coming; Raymond 2003), but increases the epistemic cline between them in implicitly claiming that he is unable or unwilling to even guess by offering a complete candidate answer (Pomerantz 1988).[8] Emma opts for an interpreta-tion of his question as a polar question in responding with 'YEAH' in the next turn (Raymond 2003), which is subsequently accepted by Chris (line 5), who also simultaneously prompts her to give an account of her answer through repeating her affirmative response.

Crucially, then, the interpretation of Chris's question in lines 1–2 as a polar question rather than an alternative question emerges over the course of a number of turns, that is, the initial question from Chris, Emma's response and Chris's subsequent response. This interpretation cannot be reduced to a summative explanation based on Chris's intentions at this point as Chris's intentions were left opaque through his not saying. Thus, while a default implicature of epistemic optionality is interactionally achieved here, this arguably follows from a general presumption of intentionality (Haugh and Jaszczolt, this volume), and an understanding of the practice of not saying through utterance-final disjunctive type questions, rather than from the ascription of specific a priori intentions to Chris (cf. Haugh 2008c: 59–60). It also draws from inferencing on the part of Chris and Emma which is mutually affording and constraining, or what Arundale and Good (2002) term more broadly 'dyadic cognizing':

> Each participant's cognitive processes in using language involve concur-rent operations temporally extended both forward in time in anticipation or projection, and backwards in time in hindsight or retroactive assessing of what has already transpired. As participants interact, these concurrent cognitive activities become fully interdependent or dyadic. (Arundale and Good 2002: 122)

Such a view precludes a monadic explanation of the inferencing under-pinning this interaction, where each individual participant's inferences arise independently of the other, but instead suggests that these cog-nitive processes are fully interdependent (Arundale and Good 2002: 127).

In both these examples, then, another sense of interaction appears more apt, namely, a technical conceptualisation of interaction as 'the conjoint, non-summative outcome of two or more factors' (Arundale 2006a: 196). In these instances, the factors involved are the inferences made by the two participants about what is being meant, done and evaluated through these conversations. The definition of interaction in the technical sense of emer-gence assumes conversational interaction is 'a non-summative phenomenon involving two or more cognitively autonomous persons engaged in afford-ing and constraining one another's designing and interpreting of utter-ances and/or observable behaviours in sequence' (Arundale 2010a: 2079; cf.

Arundale 1999: 125–6, 129; Kidwell and Zimmerman 2006: 7; Krippen-dorff 2009: 43). Treating conversational interaction as emergent assumes that it is a system that can be treated as fundamentally non-summative in nature.

Arundale (2010b) explains this property of non-summativity by appealing to analogies with statistical inference, systems theory and chemical reactions. In mathematical terms, summativity refers to instances where the effect of one factor depends on the levels of another factor in statistical inference, while non-summativity encompasses instances where there are interaction effects between variables that go beyond that main effect when conducting analysis of variance. In systems theory, a formal system arises when

> [t]he state of each unit is constrained by, conditioned by, or dependent on the state of other units. The units are coupled. Moreover, there is at least one measure of the sum of its units which is larger [or less] than the sum of that measure of its units. (Miller 1965: 200–201)

In other words, the emergent property is characteristic of the system as a whole, not its individual parts (Georgiou 2003: 241). In chemistry, non-summativity refers to the properties of a compound (e.g. sodium chloride, NaCl, or common salt) being qualitatively different from the properties of the two elements (sodium and chlorine) that constitute it. More generally, non-summativity refers to cases where 'the state(s) of one component become reciprocally linked to and conditional upon those of other component(s) in space and/or time' (Arundale 2010b: 139).

In relation to conversation, then, non-summativity is a property of conversational interaction as a system, which is framed by Arundale as involving 'two [or more] persons' evolving, reciprocal co-creating of meanings and actions in on-going address and uptake' (Arundale 2010a: 2079; see also Arundale and Good 2002; Krippendorff 2009: 37–47). This view is developed in considerable detail in Arundale's Co-Constituting Model of Communication (CCM) (Arundale 1999, 2005, 2006a, 2008, 2010a, 2010b; Arundale and Good 2002),[9] and to some extent in other interactional achievement models of communication (Clark H. 1996; Sanders 1987). It also underpins the analysis of social actions in CA (Schegloff 1996, 2007). The key idea is that participants reciprocally afford and constrain interpretations of meanings, actions and evaluations in interaction through the adjacent placement of subsequent utterances, through which they display their understandings of the interactional import of prior and forthcoming utterances (Arundale 2006a: 196). In examples (1) and (2) above, the response of the recipient helps constrain what is implicated amongst the potential interpretings initially afforded by the speaker's first utterance, an interpretation which is subsequently ratified, qualified or rejected by the first speaker.

While a non-summative model of conversational interaction is necessarily complex, it is arguably essential for the analysis of pragmatic phenomena, as summative models are 'formally incapable of explaining the non-summative effects or emergent properties observable when individuals are engaged in interaction' (Arundale 2008: 243; see also Krippendorff 1970). The advantage of an approach that accounts for the emergent properties of conversational interaction is that it can also accommodate particular instances of pragmatic phenomena which do not necessarily need to be treated as formally emergent. In other words, a summative explanation of certain pragmatic phenomena is possible within a non-summative approach. The reverse, however, is not true. One implication of treating pragmatic phenomena in conversational interaction as emergent or non-summative phenomena is that while the sociocognitive engine (cf. Levinson 2006a: 86) underlying conversational interaction clearly encompasses monadic (i.e. individual) cognitive processes and states of attention, (individual) intentions, inference and agency, it also needs to go beyond explanations rooted at the level of individual psychological processing into forms of dyadic cognising (Arundale 2008; Arundale and Good 2002; Haugh 2009; see also Haugh and Jaszczolt, this volume).

## 13.4.2  Situatedness

While CA is primarily concerned with the local situated context, a stance that is understandable given the analytical concerns of conversation analysts, it is commonly argued in pragmatics that we also need to consider the historical, social and cultural circumstances in which conversational interaction occurs (Grundy 2008: 223). Mey (2001), for instance, argues that language, which lies at the heart of conversational interaction, 'transcends the historical boundaries of the "here and now", as well as the subjective limitations of the individual's knowledge and experience' (115), as it 'functions both as a repository of earlier experience and as a tool-box for future changes' (227). Such a stance points to a potential issue for the CA approach to analysing actions (and to a lesser extent meanings) in conversational interaction: while it is claimed 'analysis requires demonstrating that the action in question was *understood and experienced as such by the participants*' (Schegloff 1996: 172, original emphasis), the identification (and labelling) of actions by the analyst itself is treated as unproblematic. For example, recognising a 'possible complaint' as an action is argued to be 'a matter of position and composition – how the talk is constructed and where it is' and thus 'it is not a matter of divining intentions' (Schegloff 2006: 88). However, it is never made clear how the analyst (or participants) know this constitutes a (possible) complaint in the first place.

In the previous analysis of example (1), the relevant section of which is reproduced below, for instance, the recognition of a "complainable" (namely, having to spend all weekend studying) was claimed to be evident from Alex's subsequent ironic assessment of Ben's weekend spent studying.

(1′)     GCSAusE09: 0:17
14   B:   cool (0.2) yeah I ah (1.0) >what did I do I just<
15        studied (0.2) >spent the whole weekend studying
16        did semantics on Saturday, (0.6) and di:d (0.2) CA
17        > conversation analysis< on ↑Sun↓day
18        (1.8)
19   A:   sounds like fun °there goes° the students life
20        HA ha [.hh hh.hh hh.hh]
21   B:              [ah:: yes it was very] interesting

In lines 15–17, Ben describes how he spent the whole weekend studying. This is treated as a complainable by Alex, who responds with an ironic assessment in line 19 ('sounds like fun °there goes° the students life'). It is interpretable as ironic since evidently Alex does not mean studying all weekend is really a fun thing to be doing, but rather that having to study all weekend can be assessed as being exactly the opposite (that is, not fun), and thus something about which making a complaint is understandable. However, such an analysis begs the question of just how it is we can conclude a possible complaint is at issue here, and how we recognise Alex's assessment as ironic.[10] Evidently we are drawing from some kind of interactional competence or intuition that lies outside of this particular interaction.

Mey (2010) argues that what makes speech acts possible, including 'possible complaints', are particular conditions or what he terms 'affordances':

> for any activity to be successful, it has to be 'expected', not just in the sense that somebody is waiting for the act to be performed, but rather in a general sense: this particular kind of act is apposite in this particular discursive interaction. (Mey 2010: 445)

In other words, social actions are dependent on the 'situation being able to "carry" them' (Mey 2010: 445). In the case of possible complaints and ironic assessments this involves a general understanding of what students do (i.e. not only study, but also recreation, and sometimes part-time work), how much time they normally spend doing study as opposed to those activities, and thus what would constitute a reasonable, as opposed to unreasonable, balance between less desirable activities (i.e. study) and more desirable activities (i.e. recreation).

It appears, then, that attempts to formalise such conditions in philosophical pragmatics perhaps have a more important role to play than generally acknowledged by those preferring empirical analyses of naturally occurring data, since without some 'precise reflections on what constitutes the nature' of the speech act in question (Jucker 2009: 1620), analysts may inadvertently reify their own intuitions to the level of theory. Such a problem is admittedly less likely to arise in CA, where such theorising is normally eschewed. However, in pragmatics, where theorising about pragmatic phenomena is one of its primary goals, the reification of informal intuitions can lead to an endless proliferation of categories, internally contradictory schemas, and ultimately, incoherence in theorising about pragmatic phenomena. The potential for such problems suggests that we need to take not only the local, situated context of a particular interaction into account in our analyses of conversational interactions, but also the sociocognitive world that underpins them.

The notion of situatedness proposed here encompasses both the local, here-and-now of conversational interaction, as well as the 'layered simultaneity' and horizontal and vertical distribution of 'orders of indexicality' charac-terising that which lies beyond the here-and-now (Blommaert 2005, 2007). As Blommaert (2005) argues, various forms of discourse, including conversa-tional interaction, are subject to what he describes as 'layered simultaneity'.

> It occurs in real-time, synchronic event, but it is simultaneously encapsu-lated in several layers of historicity, some of which are within the grasp of participants while others remain invisible but are nevertheless present. (Blommaert 2005: 130)

Such a view of interaction goes beyond the locally observable to encompass 'a polycentric and stratified' environment where 'people continuously need to observe "norms" – orders of indexicality – that are attached to a multitude of centres of authority, local as well as translocal, momentary as well as lasting' (Blommaert 2007: 2). These orders of indexicality are spread horizontally across social networks, as well as vertically in the sense that they belong to different scales of operation and degrees of validity (Blommaert 2007: 1).

Norms (see Peregrin, this volume) are often conceptualised as external forces that drive (or cause) particular actions, interpretations or evaluations by individuals, a perspective that is sometimes labelled Parsonian, as it was most famously advanced in the work of Parsons ([1937]1968). The treatment of norms as external forces was critiqued by Garfinkel (1967) among others,[11] and the view has since emerged that norms, or 'orders of indexicality', can be understood more productively as distributed and emergent properties that are enabled across networks of speakers, including those broader networks of which conversational interactions constitute an important part. Arundale argues that

> we co-constitute anew in each inter-action patterns that we have likely co-constituted in similar form in the past, and it is the continual re-co-constituting or co-maintaining of these patterns that observers attempt to explain using abstractions like 'ideologies' or 'social institutions.' But from the perspective of the co-constituting model of communication, *an ideology or social institution does not exist except as a continual renewing of patterns in inter-action*. (Arundale 1999: 141–2, original emphasis)

In other words, the ongoing renewal of inter-action[12] patterns across social networks is the mechanism by which orders of indexicality are sustained (and thus evolve). Instances where such inter-action patterns are not renewed thus constitute challenges to orders of indexicality, although the impact of such challenges depends very much on their place of occurrence within the wider social network. A similar view of 'norms' is advanced by Eelen (2001), who suggests they constitute a kind of 'working consensus', a set of practices rather than beliefs. Indeed, this view of broader socio-cultural norms reflects a perspective that has long been argued for by ethnomethodologists (Garfinkel 1967; Heritage 1984), with Mey (2006b) succinctly representing this perspective in arguing that the 'social context not only constrains language use, but is itself constructed through the use of appropriate language: social norms are (re)-instituted through the use of language' (53). These orders of indexicality, then, form part of a 'shared memory' that arises as 'inter-action within a network across time and space creates a structural form of social memory, independent of the memories of individuals' (Arundale 1999: 141). Krippendorff (2009) argues that such social memory cannot be reduced, at least not without remainder, to the psychological processes of individuals. Instead, it should be modelled as a system in its own right distributed across social networks. Work on different kinds of knowledge schemata, such as frames and scripts, for instance, represent an attempt to do just that, albeit within a largely structuralist framework.[13]

Such a perspective clearly has implications for those attempting to characterise the conditions (or affordances) that make particular pragmatic meanings, actions and evaluations possible. It also has implications for the way in which we approach the analysis of various pragmatic phenomena in conversational interaction. In particular, the situatedness of conversational inter-action needs to be taken into account, especially in cases where speakers in local, situated interaction also invoke particular schemata and orders of indexicality that are variously distributed across social networks. In the following excerpt, for instance, from a conversation between two friends talking about Chris's recent visit to the dentist, the way in which scripts and orders of indexicality associated with dentists are invoked is illustrated.

(5)    ICE-AUS: S1A-024: 3:58[14]
1    M:   bet he gets <u>you</u> if he has to do any work.
2          (2.3)
3    C:   ye::ah but he- (.) he's the sort of guy
4          who <u>w:on</u>'t do <u>work</u> unless there's
5          work to be done.
6    M:   mm.
7    C:   you know how with some they'll give you
8          a <u>fluori:</u>de an[d um
9    M:                      [chip your teeth away (.)
10         and then tell you they've gotta cap 'em.
11   C:   Ha ha [ha ha ha °he he he°
12   M:         [Ha HA ha ha ha

Up until this point in the conversation, Chris has been telling Mark about his dentist, and how impressed he is with him. Mark responds to this over-extolling by teasing Chris that he is probably charged a lot for the dentist's services (line 1). While Chris initially agrees, he goes on to account for his previous extolling by claiming that his dentist only does work that needs to be done (lines 3–5). This presupposes that dentists sometimes do unnecessary dental work, thereby inflating what they can charge. This presupposition is made explicit in a subsequent turn, when Chris begins talking about what some dentists do, namely, offering a fluoride treatment (apparently perceived by Chris as unnecessary) (lines 7–8), before Mark co-constructs a humorous completion to Chris's utterance, where it is suggested that dentists make money by first deliberately causing damage to their patient's teeth (lines 9–10). While it is not clear what Chris might have said had he finished what he was saying in line 8, Mark was able to anticipate what *could* have been said.[15] In this way, Mark co-constructs a common stance about dentists who do unnecessary work with Chris (cf. Haugh 2009: 101–2). This stance is recognisably humorous not only because of the incongruity between the action attributed to such dentists (i.e., deliberately damaging the patient's teeth), and the assumption that dentists are there to help people, but also because it draws upon stereotypical views of dentists as overcharging their patients. In other words, in order to fully appreciate the humour here, we arguably need to go beyond the local, situated interaction to include a consideration of views of dentists that reside in our shared memories or schemata.

In another example, taken from an interaction occurring in an institutional setting (a television broadcast), the way in which multiple layers of historicity can be invoked becomes even more apparent. The following excerpt is from a debate between Sanna Trad, daughter of a prominent leader in the Australian Muslim community in Sydney, and Bronwyn Bishop, a conservative senator, about Australian Muslims wearing the hijab.

(6)     ('Good Muslim/bad Aussie?', *Sunday*, Channel 9, 12
         November 2006)
1    T:   So for- so I don't- I'm <u>sick</u> of <u>everybody</u> thinking
2         that Muslim women (.) are <u>prisoners</u>, we're
3         <u>lib</u>erated. I GET TO CHOOSE who looks at ↑me
4         ((gestures at herself))
5         [a lot of people don't
6    B:   [If you if YOU beli<u>:</u>eve tha:t, in a <u>sla</u>:ve society a
7         <u>slave</u> can believe they're [↑free
8    T:                                    [So you're calling me
9         a slave now?
10   B:   [( )]
11        [((voices in background arguing))]
12   T:   I LIVE IN A DEMOCRATIC SOCIETY. I LIVE IN A

13        DEMOCRATIC SOCIETY. I was BORN here, I was
14        rai:sed here. went to an Austra:lian school=
15   B:   =But you [choose to limit your freedom
16   T:              [<I LIVE IN A DEMOcratic> socie↑ty.
17        My BEST friends are from Anglo-Christian-
18        European backgrounds.

This excerpt begins with Trad expressing her frustration that wearing the hijab is interpreted (by many Australians) as a sign of a lack of freedom on the part of Muslim women, and then going on to claim that she is actually exercising her agency in choosing to wear a hijab (lines 1–4). However, she is interrupted by Bishop, who implies that Trad is unaware of the limits placed on her freedom by her Islamic beliefs, by drawing an analogy with slaves who in never having experienced freedom do not understand its meaning (lines 6–7). Trad's subsequent response is very heated. In particular, she tries to counter the implication that she is *not* part of Australian society (which is a negative evaluation of Trad displayed by Bishop, which thus constitutes a potential challenge to her identity), by claiming she was 'born and raised' in Australia (lines 13–14) and has Australian friends who are, importantly, from Anglo-Christian backgrounds (lines 16–18). The way in which this face threat involves multiple layers of historicity is made evident in Trad's response to Bishop's implied accusation, namely, that Trad (and all those who wear hijabs) are not legitimate members of Australian society. In other words, the discourse of 'Muslims as un-Australian' as a broader underlying concern is invoked in this interaction. It also draws from a shared understanding that there are supposedly 'real' Australians who are born and raised in the country and are stereotypically from Anglo-Christian backgrounds. The point here is not to endorse such understandings, but simply to point out that such understandings are evidently presupposed by both Bishop and Trad.

While conversation analysts often eschew the need for invoking shared knowledge (see the recent debate in McHoul *et al.* 2008), it has been argued here that pragmatic phenomena in conversational interaction cannot always be reduced to emergent interactional phenomena in the here-and-now. More serious consideration of their sociocognitive roots, and consequently acknowledgement of the inherent situatedness of conversation interaction, has thus been advocated here.

## **13.5** Towards a pragmatics of conversational interaction

Conversational interaction is an important concern for any theory of pragmatics. While there are clearly many forms of language use apart from conversational interaction that are also deserving of analytical attention, conversational interaction remains important due to its enduring ubiquity in social life. In this chapter, it has been argued that pragmatic phenomena in conversational interaction should be recognised as emergent and situated in nature. This has implications for the ways in which we might approach the analysis of pragmatic phenomena that occur in conversational interaction.

A basic framework for analysing pragmatic phenomena in conversational interaction has also been assumed in this discussion. This framework is based on a tripartite distinction between pragmatic meaning, action and evaluation, which, along with investigations of the interactional machinery and sociocognitive engine underlying conversation, arguably forms the basis of a programme for investigating the pragmatics of conversational interaction. In advancing this programme, a wide range of methodologies can legitimately be called upon. It has been argued here, however, that this should occur in a principled manner, bearing in mind the properties of emergence and situatedness that characterise conversational interaction.

It is also apparent that more work on conversational types of computer-mediated communication is necessary. While face-to-face conversation remains at the core of much of our language use, variant forms of conversational interaction are emerging as different types of computer-mediated communication are increasingly becoming a part of our daily lives. These emergent forms of conversational interaction need to be accommodated within dyadic as well as multiparty theories of conversational interaction in pragmatics. The assumption that talk is inherently fleeting also needs revisiting in light of the increasing prevalence of conversational forms of computer-mediated communication where the conversational record remains there for all to inspect. The advantage of such a record is that it engenders greater metalinguistic and metapragmatic awareness amongst interactants themselves, with such awareness offering a rich analytical vein for future research on conversational interaction. It appears, then, that there still remains much to explore in better understanding the pragmatics of conversational interaction.

## Appendix: Transcription conventions (following Jefferson 2004)

| | |
|---|---|
| [ ] | overlapping speech |
| (0.5) | numbers in brackets indicate pause length |
| (.) | micropause |
| : | elongation of previous vowel or consonant sound |
| - | word cut-off |
| . | falling or final intonation |
| ? | rising intonation |

| , | 'continuing' intonation |
| = | latched utterances |
| underlining | contrastive stress or emphasis |
| CAPS | markedly louder |
| ° ° | markedly softer |
| ↓ ↑ | sharp falling/rising intonation |
| £ £ | perceptibly smiling voice |
| < | talk is compressed or rushed |
| < > | talk is markedly slowed or drawn out |
| ( ) | blank space in parentheses indicates uncertainty about the transcription |

# 14

# Experimental investigations and pragmatic theorising

Napoleon Katsos

## 14.1 Introduction: pragmatics in the mind

Paul Grice's (1975) seminal proposal on the Cooperative Principle and max-ims can be seen as a philosophical reconstruction of the conventions that interlocutors assume each other to adhere to. Bach (2001 and this volume), Horn (2004, 2005 and this volume), Saul (2002b) and other researchers con-strue the study of pragmatics at such a normative level, subscribing to a view whereby Grice and neo-Gricean accounts are concerned with what inter-locutors ought to do, and which implications ought to arise given a set of pragmatic principles and what has been said. Yet a great and still growing part of the pragmatic community sees pragmatics (and semantics) as a sub-set of the science that investigates human communicative competence (see Carston and Powell, 2006; Chierchia, 2004; Levinson, 2000; Sperber and Wil-son, 1986; among others). Such theorists consider that the object of descrip-tion for semantics and pragmatics is the implicit knowledge that competent speakers have which enables them to produce and understand meaningful utterances. The cognitively oriented pragmatician considers that pragmatics, just like syntax or phonology, is related to cognitive psychology and to dis-ciplines that investigate knowledge representation (Marantz, 2005; Ferreira F., 2005). Under this light, whether Grice himself actually thought about the representation of pragmatic norms in the mind is a question that is per-haps more relevant to the historian of pragmatics rather than the modern linguist.

It follows from the difference in the object of description that the two traditions also differ in the kind of data that they admit as relevant evidence. For example, in the cognitive tradition it is important to document the dominant interpretation of an utterance as well as any other possible but less preferred ones, and to account for the processes through which these interpretations are derived. As such, the cognitive turn brings pragmatics much closer to the discipline that studies how language is processed in the minds of speakers and listeners, namely psycholinguistics. Recently, the collaboration of theoretical pragmaticians and psychologists of language has been of benefit to all parties. Linguistic phenomena have been a fruitful domain for psychological study, and the empirical data gathered in connection with these phenomena have provided theory-critical evidence beyond the reach of conceptual argumentation and reflective intuition.

In this review, I focus in particular on quantity implicature, and I outline three theory-critical questions that are best addressed through empirical methodologies. These concern (i) the role of context in the derivation of implicature; (ii) differences between generalised and particularised implicatures; and (iii) the post- or sub-propositional nature of the process of implicature derivation. I discuss how these questions can be addressed through experimental methodologies that study the time-course of the process of meaning derivation as well as subtle differences between the degree to which certain interpretations are preferred.

Quantity implicature is but one of the topics that have recently been approached from this interdisciplinary perspective: other topics include reference, speech act, metaphor and figurative language (see the contributions in Noveck and Sperber, 2004). Recent studies on these aspects of language, initially motivated by theoretical linguistic considerations, have generated plentiful psycholinguistic data. In many cases, these data not only have enabled researchers to settle linguistic debates but also contribute to more general models of human cognition. However, quantity implicature is a particularly good case to exemplify the contribution of experimental methods to pragmatics on three grounds. First, for most cases, there is widespread agreement among theoretical accounts about the eventual interpretation of scalar terms. Consequently the predictions that discriminate between these accounts are subtle and fine-grained and concern the process through which the interpretation is derived. Chierchia (2004), Levinson (2000) and Sperber and Wilson (1986) concur that this renders empirical investigation a more appropriate means of evaluating these predictions than using the traditional tools of the theoretical linguist, introspection and intuition. Their theoretical accounts of implicature are tailored to this form of investigation, exhibiting a conceptual clarity and precision which makes it possible to draw testable predictions from the theories. These cases are reviewed in section 14.2.1. Second, for the cases where there is disagreement about the preferred interpretation of an utterance, or the relative preference for a certain interpretation, it is once again advantageous to turn to empirical methods in order to document which interpretation is favoured by linguistically naïve competent speakers. These cases are reviewed in sections 14.2.2–3. Third, the theories of implicature that will be put to the test make claims that have implications for the organisation of the entire meaning system and how the semantics/pragmatics distinction is to be conceptualised. As such, it is possible to draw conclusions whose implications are wider than the actual phenomenon under study. Let us briefly review the linguistic phenomena.

## 14.2  Quantity implicature

It is a commonplace observation that interlocutors may communicate and infer more information than what is explicitly said. Take for example the discourses in (1) and (2).

(1)  a.  Mary: Did you dance with John and Bill?
     b.  Jane: I danced with John.
     c.  Implicature: Jane did not dance with Bill.

(2)  a.  Mary: Did all your class fail the test?
     b.  Jane: Some of my class failed.
     c.  Implicature: Not all Jane's class failed.

   Given questions (1a) and (2a), the speaker of (1b) and (2b) can be understood as conveying their literal meaning as well as (1c) and (2c) respectively. However, the latter inferences are not part of what is explicitly said. Grice's Cooperative Principle and maxims (1975) have been seminal in providing a framework of how information is communicated in this implicit fashion. Grice proposed that interlocutors should assume each other to be cooperative, and moreover to be informative, truthful, concise and relevant. If it would appear that the information that is explicitly communicated by the speaker would violate any one of these assumptions, listeners are enjoined to infer that some additional information that would repair such a violation is implicitly communicated. These reparatory pragmatic inferences are known as *implicatures*. (See Horn, this volume; Ariel, this volume; Jucker, this volume.)

   Specifically, with regard to (1), according to the Gricean proposal (Grice, 1975; see also Atlas and Levinson, 1981; Horn, 1972, 1984b; Levinson, 1983) the implicature in (1c) is derived if interlocutors assume each other to adhere to the first maxim of Quantity, which enjoins them not to provide less information than what would be required bearing in mind what is relevant for the purpose of the conversation. The inference would be derived by the following reasoning: Jane said that she danced with John, but there is a more informative statement that she could have made, namely that she danced with John and Bill (the fact that the latter statement is more informative can be easily demonstrated by the observation that 'Jane danced with John and Bill' entails 'Jane danced with John' – but not the other way round). Given question (1a), it would be relevant to know whether the more informative statement is the case. By virtue of the Cooperative Principle and the first maxim of quantity of information, Mary is licensed to assume that Jane would not be underinformative. Therefore, the most likely reason why Jane did not mention that she danced with Bill as well as John would be that this is not the case, and so Jane could be understood to be communicating this implicitly through an implicature. Since this implicature is derived in order to observe the first maxim of Quantity, it could further be called a quantity implicature.

In a similar fashion for the discourse in (2), there exists a proposition, 'all of Jane's class failed', that would have been relevant and more informative than what was explicitly said. The fact that Jane did not say so enjoins Mary to infer that Jane is communicating that this is not the case, to the effect of deriving the implicature in (2c). Because (2b) is part of a scale of informativeness formed by propositions with the quantifiers 'some', 'many', 'most', 'all', it could further be called a scalar implicature.

While both (1c) and (2c) are instances of quantity implicatures, they differ on the grounds that the alternative more informative proposition that could have been used in the case of (1c) can't be independently established outside of a specific context. By contrast, the scale of informativeness for quantifiers, sentence connectives ('or', 'and'), modals ('might', 'must') and other expressions can be known without reference to a specific communicative situation. Grice, and subsequent pragmatic theorists, acknowledged this difference. The terms *generalised* and *particularised* conversational implicatures captured the difference between implicatures that are usually associated with a certain form of words as opposed to implicatures that are not. In this spirit, (2c) is a *scalar* implicature (because 'some' belongs to a scale which is context-independent) and it can be classified as a generalised quantity implicature. (1c) on the other hand relies on a contrast that is only available in an ad hoc fashion, depending on the context and it can be classified as a particularised quantity implicature. However, both cases satisfy criteria for pragmatic rather than logical meaning (for a discussion on criteria for implicature-hood see Horn, 1984b; Levinson, 1983; Sadock, 1978). For example, neither of these implicatures will be generated if the speaker is not in position to make the stronger proposition (because for example she doesn't have complete knowledge of the situation), or if she is opting out of the maxim of Quantity for reasons of diffidence, deceit or politeness (for empirical evidence for the latter see Bonnefon *et al.*, 2009). Moreover, the explicit contradiction of such implicatures is considered less infelicitous than contradictions of logical entailment (for empirical evidence see Katsos, 2007).

Recently, certain pragmatic theories have strengthened the distinction between generalised and particularised implicatures, to the effect that the former are considered to be triggered by virtue of the tokening of the lexical expressions that they are associated with. This is done by a short-circuited process that does not employ all the steps of the Gricean derivation. Specifically, Levinson (2000) and Chierchia (2004, 2006) propose that scalar implicatures are derived just as long as they lead to an informationally stronger interpretation. Other considerations, such as whether the implicature is relevant to the context of the conversation, whether the interlocutor is cooperative and whether she is in a position to know whether the stronger statement is true, are important steps in the derivation, but they come into play at a later stage and may call for the cancellation of an implicature that has already been derived. The system that derives these short-circuited but defeasible implicatures is either a specialised default-pragmatic system (according to

Levinson, 2000), dedicated to generalised implicatures, or a subcomponent of the grammatical system which has incorporated a mechanism for evaluating the informativeness of a proposition (according to Chierchia, 2004). Both these alternatives call for a distinction between a Gricean-like pragmatic system which deals with the derivation of particularised implicatures (like the ad hoc quantity ones) and a short-circuited system that derives default (lexically associated and defeasible) generalised implicatures. One of the main perceived advantages of these default accounts is that they make use of the intuitive difference between two types of implicatures in a systematic way. (It is worth noting from the beginning that these accounts are not the only ones that make use of defaultness as a theoretically and empirically relevant notion in the study of meaning. See Jaszczolt (2005) for various uses of the term with distinct content. Thus, when referring to 'the default account' I shall always be referring to the specific proposals put forward by Levinson (2000) and Chierchia (2004)).

However, according to other neo-Gricean and post-Gricean theorists, the distinction between generalised and particularised implicatures does not entail the postulation of two separate pragmatic systems. Unitary accounts such as the ones put forth by Carston (1998), Geurts (2010), Hirschberg (1991), Horn (1984b) and Sperber and Wilson (1986) among others interpret the distinction as an empirical generalisation on the degree of association of a certain form of words with a certain implication. However, regardless of whether a certain form of words tends to be associated with a certain implicature more than others do, all conversational implicatures are derived by a common set of pragmatic principles, which takes into account cooperativity, epistemic state and relevance to the discourse context among others.

The predictions of the default, two-systems accounts, and the unitary accounts respectively can be clustered as follows with regard to quantity implicatures. First, according to default accounts, scalar implicatures are generated upon the tokening of a scalar expression and as long as the interpretation with the scalar implicature is informationally stronger than the interpretation without. Should the implicature not be relevant to the context of the conversation, or should the interlocutor not be cooperative or in a position to know whether the stronger statement is true, the implicature which has been generated by default is subsequently cancelled. On the contrary, unitary accounts predict that the implicature is simply not generated in the first place if any of the licensing conditions are not met. This prediction is best tested by looking at the time-course of the interpretation of scalar expressions in conditions where one of these licensing factors is not met.

Second, according to default accounts, scalar implicatures are more strongly associated with their triggering expressions than ad hoc ones. It follows that young children who are still in the process of acquiring adult-like pragmatic competence should find more evidence in the input to guide their acquisition of default implicatures than ad hoc ones. (A second prediction is that the contradiction of a default implicature should be more infelicitous than the contradiction of a non-default one.) By contrast, unitary accounts predict that children acquire competence with all quantity implicatures across the board. (Moreover, the contradiction of either kind of implicature is equally infelicitous.)

A third topic that will be discussed is whether the locus of implicature generation is sub- or post-propositional. This issue is conceptually distinct from the topic of the defaultness of scalar implicatures. It is relevant to review it here as default theories such as Levinson's and Chierchia's also tend to take a sub-propositional, localist position, on the grounds that this explains why sometimes scalar implicatures seem to intrude into truth conditions. This issue will be reviewed in section 14.2.3. Let us now turn to the debate on the role of context.

## 14.2.1  The role of context

Unitary and default accounts agree that scalar implicatures (henceforth SIs) are ultimately available when relevant to the discourse goal and not available otherwise; however, they differ as to how this interpretation arises. Default accounts predict that the SI is first generated, regardless of relevance to the context, and then cancelled if it is contextually irrelevant, whereas context-driven accounts predict that the SI is not generated at all if it would not be relevant. Clearly intuition alone cannot settle this question, as we are concerned not with the ultimate interpretation but with the process through which it is derived. However, psycholinguistic investigations of the time-course of scalar implicature can shed light on this.

More generally, a central debate in the area of sentence processing concerns whether there is an initial, encapsulated stage of structure assignment, or whether different categories of information (syntax, semantics, context, co-occurrence frequencies etc.) interact and coordinate from the earliest possible stage (Spivey-Knowlton and Sedivy, 1995; Tanenhaus et al., 1995). The question of how SIs are generated could be seen as part of this debate. According to the default approach, more processing time should be required when participants are processing scalar terms in so-called *lower-bound* contexts (where all that is relevant is the semantic meaning of the scalar expression and the SI is irrelevant) than in upper-bound contexts (where the SI is relevant), because in the latter the inference must be generated and then cancelled. This additional processing should manifest itself as a delay in reading time, in self-paced reading studies. Unitary accounts do not share this prediction, as no cancellation is required in lower-bound contexts; in fact, accounts based on Relevance theory (see Bott and Noveck, 2004) predict that reading time will be slower in upper-bound contexts, because an additional inference is generated in these contexts. Thus, by investigating the reading times of scalar expressions in upper- and lower-bound contexts, we can gather evidence about the role of context as well as the automaticity of the inference.

To exemplify this, let us return to examples (1) and (2) and look at the effect of manipulating the question that is asked:

(1)  a.    Mary: Did you dance with John and Bill?
     a′.    Mary: Why are you upset?
     b.    Jane: I danced with John.
     c.    Implicature: Jane did not dance with Bill.

(2)  a.    Mary: Did all your class fail the test?
     a′.    Mary: Why are you disappointed?
     b.    Jane: Some of my class failed.
     c.    Implicature: Not all Jane's class failed.

Both unitary and default accounts predict that if Mary were to ask (1a) and (2a) then she would be licensed to infer that her interlocutor is also communicating (1c) and (2c) in addition to the literal meaning of (1b) and (2b). This is because the specific question she asked raises the issue of whether the stronger proposition, the one with the conjunction ('John and Bill') or the one containing 'all', is the case. Moreover, no implicature would have been inferred had Mary asked (1a′) and (2a′) as in this context it is not relevant to consider the stronger proposition. The semantic meaning of the utterances in (1b) and (2b) suffice to answer the question that she asked. However, while the unitary account predicts that given (1a′) and (2a′) no implicature is generated in the first place, the default account predicts that in the case of (2a′) the implicature is first generated by virtue of being associated with the lexical expression which creates a scale ('some') and then cancelled. This contrasts with (1a′) where the implicature is simply not generated.

In a series of self-paced reading experiments, Breheny, Katsos and Williams (2006; see also Katsos, 2008; Katsos *et al.*, 2005) investigated the reading time of scalar expressions in so-called upper- and lower-bound contexts where the implicature is and isn't relevant to the context respectively. For example, for the existential quantifier 'some of the Fs', Breheny *et al.* (2006) constructed upper-bound (UB) and lower-bound (LB) conditions by manipulating whether 'all of the Fs' was relevant to the discourse. Using the examples employed so far, a UB context for the utterance 'some of my class failed' can be created by a preceding question which explicitly raises the importance of 'whether all of the class failed' as in (2a). An LB context can be created by a preceding question which is fully answered by the utterance 'some of my class failed' regardless of whether some or all did, such as (2a′). Moreover, Breheny *et al.* (2006) included a control condition with 'only' (e.g. 'only some of my class failed') that explicitly encoded the SI. The reading time was measured on the scalar term itself ('some of the students...') and on a dependent phrase that followed (e.g. 'The rest passed the test') whose interpretation is facilitated by the SI. If the participants interpret 'some' as 'some but not all', then the reference set for 'the rest' is already available when they read the dependent phrase; if they do not, then extra processing time is required to interpret who 'the rest' refers to.

As predicted by all accounts, the dependent phrase was read faster in the UB and control conditions than in the LB. This indicates that the SI was ultimately generated in UB and not in LB, indicating that the conditions were appropriately constructed. To answer the theory-critical question – whether the SI is generated and then cancelled in the LB condition – we have to look to the scalar expression itself. In this study (and in Katsos *et al.*, 2005 for English), the trigger phrase 'some of the Fs' was read more slowly in UB than in LB contexts. This is hard to reconcile with the default account, since no reading-time delay was evident in the LB condition. Thus, these findings show that contextual factors have a primary role in the process that generates SIs, not merely in cancelling them at a later stage. (For experimental studies that reach different conclusions, see Bezuidenhout and Cutting, 2002; but see also the discussion of that paper in Breheny *et al.*, 2006). Further evidence that interpreting a scalar expression with an SI is more time-consuming than interpreting it without are presented by Bott and Noveck (2004), Noveck and Posada (2003), de Neys and Schaeken (2007). Again, these findings pose a challenge to the default account's prediction that in cases where the scalar term is interpreted without an implicature the implicature has nevertheless been generated and then cancelled.

## 14.2.2   Implicatures drawn from generalised and ad hoc scales

Accounts of quantity implicature differ in the extent to which they posit a difference between generalised and particularised conversational implicatures. In the previous section I reviewed evidence that suggests that scalar implicatures, a subclass of generalised implicatures, are not generated by default. If this is on the right track, then generalised and particularised implicatures must be generated by the same mechanism. However, the evidence for this is only indirect so far. It is therefore desirable to directly test whether the two types of implicatures are generated in the same way.

The comparison between scalar and ad hoc quantity implicature was studied by Papafragou and Tantalou (2004). To study whether a participant generated an implicature they used the under-informative utterance paradigm. In this paradigm participants are presented with a situation where a certain proposition is true (e.g. the dolls painted all the stars or the mouse ate the cheese and the ham). However, a puppet describes the situation using an informationally weaker proposition which triggers a quantity implicature (e.g. she would say that 'the doll painted some of the stars', 'the mouse ate the cheese'). Participants who interpret the utterance with a quantity implicature should reject it as a description of the situation.

Specifically, Papafragou and Tantalou examined whether Greek participants reject underinformative utterances with three types of scales / contrasts: the generalised lexical quantifier scale <some, all>, contrasts that rely on encyclopaedic world-knowledge such as <cheese, sandwich>, and so-called ad hoc contrasts that are evoked only in specific conversational contexts and could not in any sense generalise across situations (e.g. <{parrot}, {doll}, {parrot and doll}>). The critical utterances in these cases are those which are strictly speaking true but which have the potential to give rise to false implicatures to the effect that the stronger term of the scale does not hold. The task was oriented towards young children, addressing in particular the claim (typical of default accounts) that children acquire the implicatures of context-independent generalised scales sooner than the truly Gricean particularised implicatures of context-dependent contrasts.

In their experiment, adults and 5-year-old children were presented with act-out scenarios in which a puppet would receive a reward if (s)he performed a task which involved achieving the stronger term of the scale, e.g. if (s)he managed to colour all of the stars, to eat the sandwich, or to wrap up the presents (the parrot and the doll). The puppet went away and performed the action hidden from the participant's view, and then came back to report that (s)he had achieved something less than the goal that was set, by saying e.g. 'I coloured some of the stars', 'I ate the cheese', 'I wrapped the parrot'. The participants were then asked to decide whether or not the puppet should receive the reward.

For each critical underinformative condition, the adults always withheld the reward. The children withheld the reward in over 70 per cent of the trials, and they were able to justify their response on the grounds that the puppet did not complete the task. Numerically, children were more sensitive to violations with contrasts that are specific to some context, than with logical or encyclopaedic ones (withholding the reward in 90%, 77.5% and 70% of cases respectively), but this difference did not reach statistical significance. The authors interpreted their data as supportive of unitary models of pragmatics, in that the reward is withheld at comparable levels regardless of whether or not the critical term entered a generalised scale.

However, in interpreting these findings, it is necessary to sound notes of caution. The experimental design is atypical within the literature (for other applications of this paradigm see Noveck, 2001, experiment 3; Guasti *et al.*, 2005, all experiments; Pouscoulous *et al.*, 2007, experiment 1). In a typical task involving underinformative utterances, participants who do not detect that an utterance is underinformative should be able straightforwardly to accept the utterance, while participants who detect the underinformativeness should be able to reject the utterance. In Papafragou and Tantalou's task, the picture is less clear. If the puppet is taken to be informative, participants should withhold the reward, because they can infer that the task has not been completed. However, if the puppet is understood to be underinformative (e.g. 'I wrapped the parrot' is interpreted as 'I wrapped the parrot, and it is possible that I also wrapped the doll'), then participants are again entitled to withhold reward, as they have no way of knowing with certainty whether the task actually has been completed. Therefore the grounds for withholding reward are potentially ambiguous, which undermines the results of the study. It must be noted however that the justifications given by participants are consistent with the informative interpretation of the utterances, which suggests that the findings are at least indicative.

Based on this study, Katsos and Smith (2010) investigated the same question using the standard paradigm for underinformative utterance tasks. In this paradigm, participants watch the situation unfold, and can therefore tell whether or not an utterance is underinformative for the actual situation. Katsos and Smith looked at 7-year-old English-speaking children as well as adults. Corroborating the findings of Papafragou and Tantalou (2004), they demonstrated no advantage for generalised scales in the child groups. Indeed, the numerical tendency of Papafragou and Tantalou's study attained significance in this study: underinformative utterances with ad hoc contrasts were rejected at higher rates than underinformative utterances with generalised scales. This result is clearly not predicted by the default account, but nor is it straightforwardly supported by unitary accounts, which predict a uniform pattern of development for all scales.

Relevant data are also reported by Katsos and Bishop (2011), who tested a group of 5-year-old English-speaking children and a group of adults as well. In this study, which has younger children than the one reported in Katsos and Smith (2010), the difference between generalised and ad hoc contrasts was numerically in favour of ad hoc contrasts but it did not reach statistical significance. However, a novel pattern emerged with the adults. While adults always objected to underinformative utterances with generalised and ad hoc contrasts at ceiling rates, an indirect, qualitative advantage for generalised expressions over ad hoc ones was obtained. That is, rejections of underinformative utterances were of two different types: first, straightforward rejections, and second, indirect rejections, phrased as revisions, hedging remarks, ambivalent judgements or metalinguistic comments ('Yes, but he painted the heart as well'; 'This was half right, half wrong'; 'It's not false, but he missed something'; 'This one is tricky!'; 'This is technically correct'). While roughly 15 per cent of the adult objections to underinformative utterances with scalar contrasts were indirect, over 40 per cent of the adult objections to underinformative utterances with ad hoc contrasts were indirect. If we were to take the straightforwardness of the response as an index of how participants treat underinformativeness, we could interpret this as evidence that adults treat violations of informativeness with generalised scales as graver than violations with ad hoc contrasts.

To summarise, all three studies, Papafragou and Tantalou (2004), Katsos and Smith (2010) and Katsos and Bishop (2011) administered a version of the underinformative utterances task and reported differences between context-independent generalised expressions and context-dependent ad hoc expressions. Children's performance on ad hoc expressions proved better than that with generalised expressions (it was always numerically higher, and in Katsos and Smith it reached statistical significance as well). Moreover,

Katsos and Bishop demonstrated a qualitative advantage for generalised expressions over ad hoc ones in the adult data. Thus, we arrive at a picture that is not predicted by any of the existing theories.

One suggestion to explain the child data is to focus on the kind of violations that were evoked for the specific generalised and ad hoc contrasts tested. In this methodology, when a speaker is underinformative with regard to the generalised quantifier scale, they are correct about the type of object acted upon (e.g. carrots rather than pumpkins), but miss out information on the quantity of objects (some rather than all). Thus, the speaker has met some of the informativity requirements (kind of objects) but failed others (quantity of objects). However, when a speaker is underinformative with regard to the ad hoc scale, they miss out information both on how many objects were acted upon and on the identity of one of the objects. A child who considers it important to give information first and foremost about the kind of objects that were acted upon might plausibly tolerate the former kind of underinformativeness while rejecting the latter. The difference between scales that was obtained may be due to the fact that younger children seem first and foremost to be focused on avoiding and objecting to violations about the kind of objects.

Turning to the adult group, we note that the pattern of privileged treatment is reversed. The indirect privilege of the generalised scale (in terms of how categorically they were rejected) can be interpreted in two ways: either this reflects the special status of generalised scales in the linguistic system (as per default accounts), or this is due to some other factor. As the default account was not upheld for the child groups, and they are not upheld by the studies on the role of context reviewed in section 14.2.1, one would need to postulate some non-obvious reason why these accounts should in any case apply for adults. Other factors might include an effect of frequency of contrast: in actual language use, 'some' is clearly far more often contrasted with 'all' than, for instance, 'the triangle' is contrasted with 'the triangle and the heart'. This may explain why the privileged status of generalised scales is manifest only in the adults, this being the group with the greatest exposure to language. Horn's (1984b; see also 2004) non-default account of implicature and informativeness might be compatible with this explanation. He proposes that the contexts in which terms of a generalised scale are contrasted with one another are quantitatively more numerous than the contexts in which the terms of an ad hoc scale are contrasted. Thus, context-independent generalised scales are associated not with default implicatures, but with default contexts of occurrence. This account is compatible with the data presented here, if we assume that the adults' far richer experience with language and contexts of use makes them, unlike the children, sensitive to this special property that the terms of a generalised scale possess. In summary, the differences between generalised and ad hoc expressions that are reported do not conform with the predictions of the default account.

### 14.2.3  Scalar implicature and the localist–globalist distinction

Another point of contention between competing theories of quantity implicature concerns the locus of the inference. In the traditional neo-Gricean understanding of implicature, the input to the pragmatics is the output of the semantic system, which is nothing less than a full proposition. For quantity implicature specifically, this means that the linguistic unit that is evaluated for whether it was informative or not is the whole proposition that is expressed by a speech act. To turn to the examples in (3a) and (4a), the standard neo-Gricean process can derive the (c) implicature: these statements are simply the negations of the stronger alternatives to (a), 'George believes that all of his advisors are crooks' and 'Every student passed all of the tests' respectively. However, in these widely discussed examples, cited here from Benjamin Russell (2006), it has been argued that it is also possible to interpret these utterances as conveying the (b) implicatures. These implicatures can only be generated if the input to the quantity maxim is a unit which is different to the full proposition expressed by (3a) and (4a). In fact, the input has to be a sub-propositional expression, the complement of the belief clause and the object of the verb respectively. In the terminology used, the implicatures in (c) are called *global* or post-propositional, while the ones in (b) are called *local* or sub-propositional.

(3)  a.   George believes that some of his advisors are crooks.
    b.   George believes that not all of his advisors are crooks.
    c.   George does not believe that all of his advisors are crooks.

(4)  a.   Every student passed some of the tests.
    b.   Every student passed some but not all of the tests.
    c.   Not every student passed all of the tests.

On the strength of the observation that the (b) implicatures are possible, some accounts of scalar implicature take a localist stance, and predict that (3a) and (4a) should be interpreted with the local implicature. Such accounts typically also commit to a default view of scalar implicature, although these are in principle independent considerations. In a similar vein, it has been observed (by Levinson and others) that implicatures appear in some cases to enter into the truth conditions of the proposition which gives rise to them. This is also impossible on the traditional Gricean account. Establishing the presence of these aspects of meaning in the truth conditions of the proposition is a sensitive issue. However, one commonly accepted criterion is passing the scope test, according to which only aspects of meaning that can be part of what is denied or supposed, or generally fall within the scope of logical operators, are truth-conditional. Carston (2004b) discusses the history of this approach. Under this criterion, widely cited examples such as (5a–c) have convinced Levinson (2000: 198ff.), M. Green (1998) and others that scalar implicatures can intrude into truth conditions.

(5)  a.   It is better to eat some of the cake than it is to eat all of it.

      b.   You shouldn't be too upset about failing some of your exams; it's much better than failing the whole lot.

      c.   Because the police have recovered some of the gold, they will no doubt recover the lot.

According to these analyses, the scalar implicature (that 'some' implies 'some but not all') must fall within the scope of logical operators in the above examples in order for the constructions to be felicitous. Since this is not compatible with the classical neo-Gricean account, it appears that some kind of encapsulated default-pragmatic system must be involved in generating these inferences, which are neither semantic nor fully pragmatic.

However, Chierchia (2004) and Horn (2004), among others, doubt that these examples show intrusion into truth conditions per se. They argue that what is involved is post-propositional accommodation of the inference, which is triggered retrospectively once the sentences following the scalar terms are processed in order to avoid a contradiction. Horn (2004) further suggests that the extraordinary nature of this process is indicated by the requirement for focus intonation on the scalar term (an observation which is also part of King and Stanley's (2005) account; and see Geurts, 2009).

Localism does not necessarily take a position on whether SIs can intrude upon truth conditions: it only makes predictions with regard to the domain (sub- or post-propositional) in which pragmatic principles may operate. It is also conceivable to detach localism from defaultism: a local but non-default theory, in which SIs are generated locally but are context-dependent, is in principle coherent. However, these two claims have tended to go hand-in-hand for Levinson, and perhaps even for Chierchia.

Localist accounts argue that the occurrence of local implicatures is a grave challenge for global accounts. Globalists have addressed this challenge in three ways. According to Benjamin Russell (2006) and Geurts (2009), one can consider the instances brought forward by the localists one by one, and argue in each case whether these involve true implicature generation or some other process. (This is similar to Chierchia's and Horn's responses to cases cited in Levinson such as (5) above.) For instance, the global account can derive local SIs if some non-arbitrary assumptions are taken into account. In the case of examples such as (3a) Russell (2006) provides a globalist account of the derivation of the 'local' implicature, by adding the assumption that George is epistemically adept, or at least biased towards his beliefs. That is, George could be supposed to take a stance and either believe that something is the case or believe that it is not the case; that is, we exclude the possibility that he simply does not believe it to be the case. With regard to the proposition that all George's advisors are crooks, the global implicature (3c) is compatible with two situations, one in which George simply does not hold the belief that all his advisors are crooks; and one where he believes that it is not the case that all his advisors are crooks (this latter equating to the situation in (3b)). The addition of the assumption that George is opinionated about his beliefs rules out the situation in which George does not have the belief that all his advisors are crooks. This allows only the situation in which George believes it is not the case that all his advisors are crooks. Ergo, a global implicature augmented with assumptions about the interlocutor's epistemic stance can generate what looks like a local implicature. The process that generates the SI, however, is fully Gricean.

Besides these responses, it is possible to cast doubt upon the very foundations of the localist challenge. Geurts and Pouscoulous (2009a, 2009b) have been asking whether local implicatures are actually as readily available as has been assumed. To investigate this, they presented participants with embedded and unembedded instances of propositions with the existential quantifier, as in (6a) and (6b). They then asked participants to respond to the corresponding questions (6a′) and (6b′).

(6)  a.   Fred heard some of the Verdi operas.
     b.   Betty thinks that Fred heard some of the Verdi operas.
     a′.  Would you infer from this that Fred didn't hear all the Verdi operas?
     b′.  Would you infer from this that Betty thinks that Fred didn't hear all the Verdi operas?

While the localist account predicts equal rates of acceptance for (6a′) and (6b′), the global account predicts that participants will be much more prone to accept (6a′) than (6b′). This is indeed documented by Geurts and Pouscoulous, for whom participants show evidence of unembedded SIs at rates of 93 per cent but embedded SIs only at 50 per cent. Moreover, they found that the rates of local implicatures vary substantially between conditions: while the rates of generation are as high as 50 per cent for embedding under 'think', they are as low as 3 per cent for embedding under the universal quantifier (as in example 4a). These findings seem clearly to indicate that local implicatures are not derived with the consistency expected by local accounts. In fact, bearing in mind that the local implicature under 'think' can be derived using a global process of inference, as proposed by Russell (2006), the evidence from embedding under 'every' suggests that there may be no truly local SIs, as predicted by global accounts.

Of course, it should further be remarked that these investigations are disconfirming the local account without necessarily providing positive evidence for the global one. They do not investigate whether participants are generating the global implicature associated with (6b) (which is also predicted by the global account, just as much as it is predicted that there should not be local implicatures), nor do they show that the apparent instances of local implicature do not arise through authentic scalar implicatures. While the former can easily be tested with the existing paradigm, simply by asking participants whether the global SI follows from (6b), addressing the latter question is perhaps less straightforward.

## 14.3   Overview and outlook

In the previous sections we reviewed empirical investigations on quantity implicature that have been motivated by debates in the theoretical pragmatics literature. The evidence that is accumulating on the role of context (section 14.2.1) suggests that scalar implicatures, which are an instance of generalised implicatures, are generated only when relevant to the contextual purpose (which is considered a *sine qua non* condition for particularised implicatures as well). Further direct comparisons between scalar and non-scalar, ad hoc quantity implicatures in child language acquisition (section 14.2.2) document that scalar implicatures are not privileged in development. When we look at these two strands of research in combination, the emerging pattern strongly disconfirms the predictions of the default account, which postulates a special pragmatic system dedicated to the generation of generalised implicatures. Instead, they are in line with the predictions of unitary accounts. However, the evidence from the adult experiment reported by Katsos and Smith (2010) on the comparison of scalar and non-scalar implicatures calls for a careful treatment of the distinction between generalised and particularised implicatures: rather than completely dismissing it, it can be interpreted as a frequency-based observation about contexts of occurrence rather than theory-critical mechanisms of derivation.

Finally, with respect to the locus of SI generation, in section 14.2.3 we reviewed empirical evidence that the 'local' embedded SIs are inferred with much less frequency than the 'global' non-embedded SIs, and that in many cases the former are apparently not available to participants at all. All in all, these experimental investigations are contributing evidence against default and local accounts of scalar implicature. It is worth reiterating that not all unitary or default accounts take (or need to take) a position with regard to all these issues. It is possible to have a local account without assuming defaultness (in the sense of independence from discourse context), or vice versa. However, the emerging picture favours accounts which take a more-or-less orthodox Gricean position, where a single pragmatic system is responsible for deriving both generalised and particularised implicatures in a post-propositional process. Crucially, from the perspective of the cognitively oriented pragmaticians, these investigations contribute towards constructing a model of language processing and acquisition where Gricean maxims are not just philosophical norms but psycholinguistically valid principles as well.

Although we have seen how various different methodologies may be gainfully employed when we come to operationalise competing theoretical proposals, we must remain vigilant that the responses of participants are in fact conditioned by the variables that we wish to test. Moreover, I sounded caution on how minor changes in the details of an experimental design can impact upon the interpretation of the data (section 14.2.2). It is also important to highlight potential terminological pitfalls, such as the use of the term 'default' to refer to accounts which associate inferences with lexical expressions. The evidence we reviewed disconfirmed the predictions of these 'lexical-default' accounts, without bearing on other accounts which employ the concept of defaultness in different ways and at different levels (e.g. see Jaszczolt's 2005 conceptual-default account).

Notwithstanding these difficulties, we see that the relationship between concept and experiment is a productive one, as far as quantity implicature is concerned. Clear predictions at a theoretical level motivate empirical study, and the drive towards empirical investigation motivates clarity at a theoretical level. Moreover, critical evaluation of the nature of responses to experimental stimuli can broaden our theoretical base by suggesting the relevance of additional factors in actual linguistic contexts, and thus rendering these additional factors amenable to theoretical formalisation. For quantity implicature, as for many topics in semantics and pragmatics, the collaboration of theorist and experimentalist appears set to pave the way for future progress at both levels.

# Part II

## Phenomena and applications

# 15

# Referring in discourse

Arthur Sullivan

## 15.1  Introduction

*Reference* is the relation that obtains between a use of a linguistic expression and what it stands for or denotes.[1] (For example, when I write "London is a massive city," I use the first word to *refer* to a certain city.) Inquiry into the nature of reference stretches back over millennia, and it is evident why: insofar as language is to play a role in tracking the states and doings of the specific individuals, events, and phenomena which are of interest to us, then referring expressions (such as "London") have a core, central job to do. Indeed, many take reference to be the simplest, most basic case of a language–world connection; and so, for example, revolutionary moments within the theory of reference are often integrally linked to distinctive conceptions of the nature of language itself.[2] The aim of this chapter is to shed light on some core issues and questions about reference, with a view to how they relate to the semantics/pragmatics interface.

The notion of reference is closely tied to the distinction between singular and general propositions (in at least one canonical sense of those terms, defined immediately below). Let us call a proposition "singular" if its truth condition essentially involves a specific individual, and "general" if its truth condition does not essentially involve any specific individual. To illustrate, compare (1) with (2).

(1)   Aristotle is fond of dogs.
(2)   Some cats are fond of dogs.

The proposition expressed by (1) is essentially about a certain, specific individual. In contrast, in the case of (2), the proposition expressed essentially concerns only certain concepts, not any specific individuals – i.e., the content of the proposition stays constant, regardless of which cats are or are not fond of dogs in the relevant domain of discourse. Thus, (1) expresses a singular proposition, while (2) expresses a general proposition. (Alternatively, according to another prevalent way of speaking, the truth conditions of a singular proposition are *object-dependent*, but the truth conditions of a general proposition are *object-independent*.)

Following seminal work in philosophical logic by Frege (1879) and Bertrand Russell (1905), general propositions are taken to consist of quantificational relations among concepts or properties. In contrast, it seems that one cannot have an account of the content of singular propositions which does not essentially involve the notion of reference. As such, the question of exactly what it takes to express a singular proposition (in this above sense) is a central and contested one in some of the debates described below.

## 15.2   The classical background, an initial refinement

It will be useful to take as our point of departure the following classical conception of the semantics/pragmatics interface, and to make adjustments and refinements to it as they become necessary. Semantics is the study of linguistic meaning, and pragmatics is the study of speech acts. In general, the information communicated with a use of a sentence may include as distinct proper parts what is semantically expressed (or encoded in the sentence) and what is pragmatically conveyed (or generated by the act of uttering that particular sentence in that particular context). For example, imagine that A says to B: "The cops are around the corner." From a semantic point of view, that sentence semantically expresses one unambiguous proposition; every token of that sentence-type semantically expresses the same proposition; and all competent speakers of English grasp exactly that proposition when they encounter a token of the sentence. From a pragmatic point of view, there are an indefinite number of things that A might be conveying to B, by uttering this sentence at a certain time and place: say, "let's split," or "we're about to be rescued," or "yell HELP," or "be quiet," etc. What is semantically expressed is one of the factors which play a role in determining what is pragmatically conveyed; but, in general, what is pragmatically conveyed with a use of an expression is a heavily context-dependent matter. Semantic competence and pragmatic competence are thus conceived as related but distinct subcomponents of our ability to use language to communicate.[3]

To crystallize this rough-and-ready working conception of the semantics/pragmatics interface: semantic properties of a linguistic expression are shared in common by all tokens of the type; whereas any information communicated with a token of an expression that is not shared in common by all tokens of the type should be classified as pragmatic – i.e., as conveyed by the act of using that expression in a certain context, not as expressed by virtue of its linguistic meaning.

Traditionally, reference has often been conceived as a two-place semantic relation between certain kinds of expression and what they conventionally stand for or denote. The guiding intuition here is that there is a special sub-category of terms which should be classified as referring expressions, because their semantic role is to single out a specific referent as the subject of discourse. (Hence, again, the link between reference and singular propositions.) Proper names are thus taken to be the very paradigm of a referring expression, as names are explicitly introduced to refer to specific individuals.[4] Similarly, this is how individual constants are treated in most simple, standard formal languages – once a referent has been assigned, that is all there is to say about the term's literal semantic meaning. If a singular term is a referring expression, then its having a certain specific individual as its referent is a context-independent semantic property of the term, and competence with such a term is simply a matter of associating it with the correct referent.

Few today would deny that this traditional picture of semantic reference involves some drastic oversimplifications. Even in the relatively straightforward case of proper names, there is the issue of homonymy – i.e., there are many thousands of people named "John," and I myself know personally about fifteen or twenty of them; but nonetheless I seem to be able to refer to exactly one of them when I write "John loves to snowboard."[5] Another immediate complication for this traditional view concerns some other much-discussed, basic cases of reference, including referential uses of demonstratives (such as *this*) and personal pronouns (*she*). While it is plausible that their literal semantic role is to single out a specific referent as the subject of discourse, these referring expressions are *indexical*, in the sense that different uses of them single out different referents. The traditional approach gets amended for such cases: here the context-independent semantic property is a certain character or role, and these characters or roles can be viewed as a function from a context of utterance to a referent. (For example, the character of *she* is something along the lines of 'the contextually salient female'; and so if I say in a certain context "She is tall," the value of that function might be (say) my niece Erin.)[6]

With this amendment to the traditional picture, two distinct sub-types of referring expression are distinguished. Indexical referring expressions (such as *this* or *she*) single out a referent via its current place within the context of utterance that is shared in common among speaker and audience; whereas, in contrast, non-indexical referring expressions (here the paradigm cases are proper names) single out a referent via a context-independent stipulative convention. The semantics of a non-indexical referring expression specifies a referent that is constant across distinct uses; but the semantics of an indexical referring expression specifies a relation between speaker and referent that is constant across distinct uses.[7]

## 15.3   Referring vs denoting: the Russellian orthodoxy

All of the referring expressions discussed so far (*John*, *this*, *she*, etc.) are semantically atomic, in that they lack meaningful proper parts. In contrast, "the oldest woman in Mongolia," for example, is a molecular expression, in that it has meaningful sub-parts and compositional structure. The question of whether referring expressions must be semantically atomic (in this sense) is controversial; disputed cases include definite descriptions (e.g., "the old-est woman in Mongolia"), indefinite descriptions (e.g., "a man I met on my way here today"), and complex demonstratives (e.g., "that big green-headed duck").[8]

I will use the expression "the Russellian orthodoxy" to designate the view that referring expressions must be semantically atomic. The core idea here is that reference is essentially a stipulative, conventional connection between an expression and either a referent or a role; to be a referring expression is to be conventionally used as a tag or label. I name this view after Bertrand Russell, since he did seminal work in elaborating this conception of reference (see especially Russell 1905, 1911, 1918).

Some such distinction as Russell's (1905) distinction between "referring" and "denoting" is crucial to all variants of the Russellian orthodoxy. While referring is a conventional or stipulative relation between certain kinds of expression and what they are used to designate (paradigm cases include "Aristotle", "this", "she"),[9] denoting is a distinct sort of connection that holds between certain kinds of expressions (such as "the oldest woman in Mongo-lia" or "a man I met on my way here today") and that, if anything, which satisfies the compositionally determined condition semantically expressed.[10] The distinctive Russellian claim is that sentences containing denoting expres-sions in the subject position semantically express general propositions, not singular propositions, and hence this referring/denoting distinction is of paramount importance for the theory of reference.

To illustrate, first compare two possible situations: (i) Alf was the only person I met on my way here today, and he said "Guten Tag" to me, vs (ii) Bert was the only person I met on my way here today, and he said "Guten Tag" to me. Russell's guiding intuition is that (3) would semantically express exactly the same proposition in either of these contexts:

(3)   A man I met on my way here today said "Guten Tag" to me.

Hence, the proposition semantically expressed with an utterance of (3) is general, not singular, in the sense defined in section 15.1 above – i.e., its truth conditions are not essentially tied to anyone in particular. Next, compare these two situations: (i) Alice is the oldest woman in Mongolia, and she is 117 years old, vs (ii) Betty is the oldest woman in Mongolia, and she is 117 years old. The Russellian orthodoxy has it that, as above, (4) would semantically express exactly the same proposition in either of these contexts:

(4)   The oldest woman in Mongolia is 117 years old.

Again, according to Russell, the truth conditions of (4) are object-independent – i.e., not essentially tied to anyone in particular. Hence, the propositions semantically expressed by sentences containing definite descriptions, too, are general, not singular. Semantically speaking, they specifically concern only concepts or properties, and so do not instance reference to any particular individuals.

According to the Russellian orthodoxy, then: Denoting is a quantificational relation, having to do with the satisfaction of compositionally determined, semantically specified properties. Reference, in contrast, is simple, basic, semantically atomic, and conventional or stipulative. For example, Neale (1993: 104) contains a relatively recent elaboration and defense of this point of view:

> [Reference] is an arbitrary relation that holds between a symbol and an individual, and as soon as one invokes a constructive or compositional procedure for determining the semantical value of an expression, one is no longer engaged in trying to establish reference. If an NP has any internal structure it is to be accorded a nonreferential treatment (though of course some of its parts may be referential).[11]

As alluded to in note 9, many specific details of Russell's theory of reference have come to be widely rejected – particularly the respects in which epistemology and semantics are irredeemably conflated in some corners of Russell's thought. Two important refinements to the Russellian orthodoxy occurred in the later twentieth century. One was the coupling of Russell's referring/denoting distinction with a more sophisticated theory of reference, the causal-historical theory of reference, in the 1960s and 1970s;[12] but a discussion of that refinement lies beyond the scope of this chapter. The second was Grice's (1989) recognition of the importance of the semantics/pragmatics distinction for issues in the theory of reference (and elsewhere throughout the philosophy of language), and his application of this refinement to Strawson's important challenge to the Russellian orthodoxy. Let us now turn to Strawson's challenge.

## 15.4  Speaker's reference: Strawson's challenge

Strawson (1950: 328) is a seminal statement of a central challenge to the Russellian orthodoxy, in which he argues that: "Referring is not something that an expression does; it is something that someone can use an expression to do." The allegation has it that the homonymy of names and the prevalence of indexicality (as catalogued above in section 15.2) are just the thin end of the wedge, when it comes to drastic oversimplifications inherent within the Russellian orthodoxy. All manner of terms are routinely used to refer to things which no semantic theory would classify as their literal semantic referent, as the terms italicized in the following sentence might be thought to illustrate:

(5)   *The book* is on *the table*.

In such cases, the speaker may well be intending to use the italicized molecular expressions to single out a specific referent, and to express a proposition whose truth conditions essentially involve that specific individual; but in no such case is there any tight constitutive relation between the literal semantic meaning of the term and the particular intended referent. Here we have instances of terms which do not obviously belong in the traditional category that includes the likes of "John" and "she", but which seem to be used referentially, in the course of expressing singular propositions.

And note well that Strawson's point is not merely a technical one, fussing over particular details of Russell's theory of the semantics of definite descriptions. Rather, Strawson's challenge has the potential to be a drastic blow to traditional conceptions of semantic reference, and to related conceptions of the semantics/pragmatics interface, outlined in section 15.2 above. Whether a proposition should be classified as singular or general, according to Strawson, is simply not determined by any context-independent semantic properties of the linguistic expressions involved. It entirely depends on the speaker's context-specific communicative intentions.[13] Relatedly, Strawson calls into question the very idea that there exists some privileged subclass of singular terms, the referring expressions, with some kind of exclusive hold on the expression of singular propositions.

Proponents of Strawson's challenge conclude that it is a hopeless oversimplification to view reference as a two-place semantic relation between an expression and a referent. Instead, reference is irreducibly a four-place, context-dependent relation: a speaker (i) uses an expression (ii) to refer an audience (iii) to a referent (iv). Speaker's reference is the fundamental notion, when it comes to providing a theoretical account of linguistic communication; any plausible theory can only define "reference" or "referring expression" in terms of regularities over such individual referential intentions. To the extent that any theorists run afoul of this, they are spending too much time thinking about formal languages, and their theories do not apply to natural languages.

To sum up, then: Strawson (as well as many others, who are sometimes called "ordinary language" or "communication-intention" theorists) holds that it is the use, not the expression, which is the primary bearer of semantic properties. Hence, the very idea of reference as a context-independent semantic property is drastically wrong-headed, and much of what traditionally had been classified under the theory of reference belongs within the study of pragmatics, not semantics.

## 15.5  Defending the Russellian orthodoxy

It can hardly be contested that speakers often intend to express singular propositions about the subject of discourse, when employing various kinds of molecular designators – such as definite descriptions (e.g., "the oldest woman in Mongolia"), indefinite descriptions (e.g., "a man I met on my way here today"), and complex demonstratives (e.g., "that big green-headed duck"). What is controversial is the question of exactly what relevance that phenomenon should be taken to have for the theory of reference. One factor which complicates the controversy is that it is interwoven with related controversies regarding contrasting theoretical accounts of the semantics/pragmatics interface.

Following especially Grice (1989) and Kripke (1977), the orthodox Russellian response to Strawson's challenge is not to conclude that speaker's reference replaces semantic reference, or that there is no such thing as semantic reference; but rather, to conclude that it is crucial to attend carefully to the distinction between speaker's reference and semantic reference. Rather than junking the traditional semantics/pragmatics interface, to the contrary, the orthodox Russellian strategy begins from a refinement to the traditional conception of it – i.e., the distinction between speaker's meaning and semantic meaning.

The idea is that we can build a coherent and plausible account of the data entirely from what Kripke (1977: 263) calls "a general theory of speech acts," without committing to anything to which we were not already committed before we noticed the phenomenon of referential uses of molecular expressions. The need for the distinction between speaker's meaning and semantic meaning has long been evident (cf, Grice (1957)); and it suffices to ground an ample explanation for how one might not need to employ a referring expression to express a singular proposition. Consider again (5), *The book is on the table*. The Russellians' claim is that what an utterance of (5) semantically expresses is the general proposition that there is exactly one book and exactly one table (in the relevant restricted domain of discourse[14]) and that the former is on the latter. To use this sentence literally, strictly speaking, is to use it to express this general proposition. In such cases, the speaker's meaning is identical to the semantic meaning.

Now, a speaker may well utter (5) with the intention to express a singular proposition, essentially involving a specific book (and/or table), as opposed to merely denoting whichever book happens to be about (across modal and/or temporal contexts); but speech act theory affords the means to accommodate this phenomenon. Like any sentence, (5) can be used to speaker-mean (i.e., communicate in a one-off, context-dependent fashion) something distinct from its semantic meaning.[15] Additionally, of course, unlike any sentence, sentences like (5) especially lend themselves to referential uses, precisely because definite descriptions denote exactly one individual. When one wants to express a singular proposition about some unnamed individual, or about an individual whose name is not mutually known among present interlocutors, definite descriptions are often the best means available. Nonetheless, the definite description's one univocal, quantificational semantics is still evident and operative on referential uses.[16] These denoting phrases (along with many others, such as "a man I met yesterday" or "three thugs") are especially suited to the distinctive kind of non-literal speaker meaning that Kripke (1977) calls "speaker reference."[17]

Hence, for another example, the semantics of (4), *The oldest woman in Mongolia is 117 years old*, is constant, whether the speaker has in mind Alice, Betty, or no one in particular. In context, such constructions may be used to communicate a singular proposition, but they do not semantically express singular propositions, nor do they undermine the entire theoretical basis for such traditional semantic distinctions.

So, then: as Grice and Kripke develop, the distinction between speaker's reference and semantic reference is a specific instance of the more general distinction between speaker's meaning and semantic meaning, and it affords a way to accommodate Strawson's challenge with only minimal refinements to traditional conceptions of reference and the semantics/pragmatics interface. Semantic reference should still be viewed as an atomic, context-independent semantic property; but when speakers use molecular expressions with the intention of singling out a specific topic of discourse and expressing a singular proposition, here we have a case of speaker reference, not semantic reference. Hence, refinements in the course of the development of pragmatics might be brought to bear in saving a recognizably traditional conception of the division of labor between semantics and pragmatics.[18]

## 15.6 Extending Strawson's challenge

Despite those developments, though, dissatisfaction with the Russellian orthodoxy lives on, and has evolved into various sub-varieties. Strawson (1971) himself flamboyantly described a central fissure in twentieth-century philosophy of language as a great "Homeric struggle." On the one hand, there is what Strawson calls the "formal-semantics tradition," which conceives of the semantic enterprise as a matter of pairing well-formed sentences with (context-independent) truth conditions, and among whose ranks one tends to find the upholders of the Russellian orthodoxy. On the other hand, there is what Strawson calls the "communication-intention tradition," whose proponents hold that truth conditions, in general, are simply not determined by any context-independent semantic properties of the linguistic expressions involved. (Relatedly, they hold that, along with the pernicious myth of semantic reference, so crumbles the very idea of a clean split between semantics and pragmatics.) While in many respects these traditions have been synthesized (cf. Grice 1989; Kaplan 2004), still many such disputes in lexical semantics, pragmatics, and more generally throughout the philosophy of language might be profitably viewed as flare-ups within this classic overarching debate concerning whether semantic meaning determines, or underdetermines, truth conditions.

Approached down this avenue, the varieties of semantic contextualism are a noteworthy descendent of Strawson's challenge.[19] Contextualists, akin to the communication-intention theorists, attach great significance to the complex, dynamic adaptability of our linguistic behavior, and tend to hold that formal semantic theories are not terribly relevant to our unreflective, everyday communicative exchanges. Among the many strands of contextualist lines of argument against traditional conceptions of the semantic enterprise, *semantic underdetermination* arguments are particularly pertinent to this general discussion.

Contextualists' underdetermination arguments are built upon mundane, ubiquitous cases in which semantic meaning falls well short of what we would intuitively characterize as the proposition expressed (with a use of a sentence). In some cases, semantic meaning does not seem to suffice to constitute truth-evaluable content (e.g., "Jill is ready"); in other cases, literal semantic meaning seems to inappropriately specify the proposition expressed (e.g., "I have had nothing to eat"). A formal semanticist might dismiss such cases as loose talk – as merely leaving the obvious unsaid, for the sake of convenience – but it seems that even an otherwise completed, neither vague nor ambiguous sentence (e.g., "John finished Sally's book") can be used to express an indefinite number of distinct propositions (e.g., John finished binding the book that Sally wrote; John finished reading the book that Sally recommended for their book club; John finished writing the book that he dedicated to Sally; etc. etc.). Contextualists take the kind of creative, supplementary interpretive process which Recanati (2004a) calls "free enrichment" to be the norm, not a peripheral and circumscribed oddball. (E.g., when we hear "She took out her key and opened the door," we take the sentence to assert that she opened the door *with* the key.) And then there is the wealth of convergent data cataloguing the extent to which the lexicon is adaptable, malleable – that linguistic interpretation requires constantly shrinking or expanding the senses of words to fit the context at hand.[20]

The general upshot, according to contextualists, is that traditional conceptions of the semantics/pragmatics interface are simply untenable, because all linguistic communication is thoroughly permeated by pragmatic interpretive processes. The common further *ad hominem* point has it that widespread blindness to this evident fact is attributable to theoreticians tending to spend too much time thinking about formal languages, and not enough time talking to people.

So, there has also been considerable growth and development, when it comes to Strawson's challenge to the very idea of reference as a two-place (context-independent) relation, and its attendant conception of the semantics/pragmatics interface. Indeed, the contextualists' challenges to the very idea of semantic meaning would also go some way toward undercutting the Grice–Kripke–Russellian orthodox response to Strawson, as the orthodox response clearly seems to presuppose a (more or less) determinate notion of semantic meaning. On many particular fronts, Strawson's Homeric struggles still endure, over the extent to which literal semantic meaning determines truth conditions, and over what effects any specific resolution of that battle would have on such things as semantic reference.

## 15.7  Summing up: Context and reference

One central, general question, then, is: Is reference a two-place, context-independent relation? Until well into the twentieth century, anyone who cared about the question had assumed so – and so the most divisive debates in the theory of reference had to do with Millian (1843) direct reference theories vs Fregean (1892) indirect reference theories (which are now generally acknowledged to have a lot more to do with *content* than with reference, per se).[21] However, for decades now it has been evident that there are various and varied ways in which context affects reference, and this recognition forces a thorough re-evaluation of such traditional presumptions.

For one thing (section 15.2), there is the phenomenon of indexicality, which necessitates the recognition of a distinct class of indexical or perspectival referring expressions (e.g., "this", "she"). For these sorts of cases, some such distinction as Kaplan's (1989b) character/content distinction is essential for understanding the ways in which context affects reference. Then (section 15.4) there is the phenomenon of speaker's reference – i.e., uses of terms which do not obviously belong in the traditional category of referring expressions, but which seem to be referential, in that they are used to single out the subject of discourse and express a singular proposition. At a minimum, recognizing the prevalence of speaker's reference necessitates some further refinements to classical notions of semantic reference, and to traditional conceptions of the division of labor between semantics and pragmatics. When it comes to the more ominous challenge of semantic underdetermination (section 15.6) – more ominous because it is so pervasive – here the floodgates may well spill open, one result being that context-specific pragmatic interpretive processes are taken as essential ingredients constitutive of any instance of reference in natural language.

Semantic reference is a significant battleground in that general, theoretical debate; and the Russellian orthodoxy is working hard toward resisting that latter challenge. So, on the one hand, there are those who think that the two-place relation of semantic reference is the most fundamental notion of reference in a systematic theory of linguistic communication, and that it provides the necessary intentional language–world content, upon which all more sophisticated speech acts depend. For these theorists – whom I have been calling "orthodox," and whom Strawson calls "formal semanticists" – context-dependent pragmatic considerations have no relevance to the drawing of meaning distinctions. On the other hand, there are those who find that line of thought commits a hopeless theoretical abstraction, resulting in theories of linguistic communication which are of limited scope and questionable relevance. This camp runs from the ordinary language philosophers to the semantic contextualists, and they hold that unless pragmatic considerations are taken to play a constitutive role in the drawing of meaning distinctions, then we have a theory that only applies to toy formal languages, not to human natural language.

Referring in discourse is thoroughly context-dependent, in that all parties concede that what Kripke (1977) calls "speaker's reference" is a prevalent phenomenon. Virtually any linguistic expression could be used as a device of speaker-reference. However, the exact sense in which referring in discourse is context-dependent is deeply contested. As we have seen, that question is integrally tied, in complex ways, with contrasting theoretical stances on the semantics/pragmatics distinction, i.e., the very idea that we can cleanly distinguish between what is encoded in the sentence vs what is generated by the act of uttering that particular sentence in that particular context.

# 16

# Propositional attitude reports
## Pragmatic aspects

Kasia M. Jaszczolt

## 16.1  Propositional attitudes and propositional attitude reports

Believing, doubting, knowing, fearing, hoping and so forth, that something is the case are all examples of a propositional attitude: a cognitive attitude to a certain content (proposition) expressed by a sentence. Reports on people's cognitive attitudes pose a particularly challenging problem for semantics and pragmatics for a variety of reasons. First, the sentence uttered by the holder of the attitude may not give sufficient information about the intended proposition because the information states of the holder of the attitude and the reporter on the attitude differ more than the utterer of the attitude predicted. For example, uttering (1), Lidia may not know who the author of *Wolf Hall* is and therefore dissent from the report made by Charles in (2).

(1)   The author of *Wolf Hall* is visiting Cambridge this spring.

(2)   Lidia believes that Hilary Mantel is visiting Cambridge this spring.

Second, Charles, who reports on Lidia's attitude, may not know who wrote *Wolf Hall* and simply 'echo' Lidia's statement of belief as in (3).

(3)   Lidia believes that the author of *Wolf Hall* is visiting Cambridge this
      spring.

Third, either Lidia or Charles may be under the misapprehension that *Wolf Hall* was written by, say, Michael Morpurgo, producing (1) or (3), respectively, with a referential mistake, associating the description with an incorrect referent. This gives various combinations in which we include the scenarios where the holder of the attitude (i) knows the identity of the subject of the uttered sentence and is able to substitute other expressions to refer to it/him/her; (ii) does not know the identity of the subject and holds a, so to speak, 'half-digested attitude' (a *semi-propositional belief*, see Sperber 1985; 1996); (iii) is mistaken as to the identity of the subject. Next, (i)–(iii) also apply to the reporter. Allowing for the misjudgement of the background information (say, in (2), Charles thinks that Lidia knows that Hilary Mantel wrote *Wolf Hall*), presents us with the full spectrum of the conversational problem with attitude reports.

Moreover, a report can be produced on the basis of non-linguistic evidence. Suppose Lidia is reading *Wolf Hall*, showing clear signs of involvement in the story and reluctance to put the book down when Charles arrives. Charles utters (4).

(4)   Lidia thinks *Wolf Hall* is a very captivating novel.

In this chapter I focus on this conversational problem and hence address the *pragmatics* of propositional attitude reports. But, as will become clear in what follows, the pragmatic problems and the semantic problems with attitude reports are closely related. I shall also argue that the semantics and the pragmatics of attitude reports are closely related in that the most satisfactory semantic solutions are also at the same time the most satisfactory pragmatic solutions because semantics benefits from the contextualist outlook and from assigning truth conditions *not* to minimal content of sentences but rather to the intended speaker's meaning, thereby taking Grice's programme further into new, compositional, pragmatics-rich truth-conditional semantics. Let us therefore begin with some selected problems and some semantic and pragmatic solutions.

## 16.2   Attitudes at the semantics/pragmatics interface: An overview

Standard approaches in philosophy of language consider propositional attitudes to be ambiguous between the *transparent* and the *opaque* reading. The transparent reading asserts the existence of the subject of the attitude, giving it a wide scope as in (5a), while the opaque reading puts the referent in the scope of the attitude verb as in (5b). 'Bel$_L$' stands for 'Lidia believes that', 'AoWH' for 'the author of *Wolf Hall*', and 'VC' for 'is visiting Cambridge this spring'.

(5)   Lidia believes that the author of *Wolf Hall* is visiting Cambridge this spring.

(5a)   $\exists x\,(\text{AoWH}(x) \wedge \forall y\,(\text{AoWH}(y) \rightarrow y = x) \wedge \text{Bel}_L\,\text{VC}\,(x))$

(5b)   $\text{Bel}_L\,\exists x\,(\text{AoWH}(x)\,\forall y\,(\text{AoWH}(y) \rightarrow y = x) \wedge \text{VC}\,(x))$

(See Bertrand Russell 1905, 1919a; Quine 1956; Neale 1990; Jaszczolt 2010b.) 'Transparent' and 'opaque' refer here to the characteristics of the definite description in the subject position of the *that*-clause, namely transparency and opacity to the substitution of coreferential expressions in place of the extant one, say, 'Hilary Mantel' or 'the winner of the 2009 Man Booker Prize' for 'the author of *Wolf Hall*'.

Now, Quine (1956) focused on the problem of 'quantifying into' such constructions, hence emphasising their structural ambiguity, which Quine referred to as the ambiguity between the *relational* sense (where substitutivity holds) and the *notional* sense (where it does not). His tentative solution pertained to 'degrees of intensions' for quantifying into such contexts. On a distinction that is more relevant for our cognitive and pragmatic interests, we have the reading in (5a) according to which Charles ascribes to Lidia a belief in a particular, known individual, and the reading in (5b) on which the reporter says that the holder of the belief believes that there is someone to whom the description 'the author of *Wolf Hall*' correctly applies and about whom she predicates an upcoming visit to Cambridge. The latter report pertains to a belief about the proposition, *dictum*, and is called *de dicto*. (5a) reports on a belief about an intersubjectively identifiable individual or object (*res*) and is called *de re*.

It is immediately evident at this point that (5a) and (5b) fall short of presenting the pragmatic problem with reporting on cognitive attitudes. The mistaken identity scenario is not accounted for. In fact, it is not normally accounted for in the semantics of attitude reports because traditionally semantics has been understood as pertaining to the meaning of the sentence rather than utterance. In short, (5c) is not offered as a potential reading, where 'm' stands for a proper name (and hence a directly referring expression) Michael Morpurgo.

(5c)   $\text{Bel}_L \text{ VC (m)}$

Neither are the mistakes and information deficiencies of the believer and the reporter accounted for. The semantic problems of the ambiguities *de re/de dicto* or transparent/opaque require considerable fine-tuning to reflect the complexity of the pragmatic problem. In brief, as far as utterance interpretation is concerned, we are not dealing here with the ambiguity of scope but with a much more complicated picture. If we wish to retain the concepts of *de re* and *de dicto* beliefs and *de re* and *de dicto* reports, the latter also making use of the transparent/opaque distinction, we have to add *res₁* pertaining to correct referring and *res₂* pertaining to incorrect referring, as well as the higher-level distinction into correct/incorrect referring by the holder of the belief vis-à-vis correct/incorrect referring by the reporter. This amounts to a great deal of pragmatic information and a hefty dose of Gricean intention-based theory of utterance meaning (see Haugh and Jaszczolt, this volume).

Next, in addition to the *de re/de dicto* distinction, we also have to point out the distinction between *factive* and *non-factive* attitudes and the corresponding distinction between factive and non-factive attitude verbs. Factive verbs engender the entailment (or presupposition, depending on the theoretical assumptions) that the proposition expressed by the *that*-clause is true. 'A knows that *p*' entails (or presupposes) that the proposition *p* is true. Non-factive verbs, on the other hand, such as 'believe' or 'think', do not give rise to such a relation. For example, (6) reports on a factive attitude and (7) on a non-factive one.

(6)    George knows that the Conservatives won the election.

(7)    George believes that the Conservatives will win the election.

In addition, a third category of so-called *counterfactives* (or *contrafactives*) is sometimes distinguished whereby verbs belonging to this category entail the falsity of the embedded proposition. 'Wish' or 'imagine' are good examples of counterfactives, as in (8).

(8)    George wishes that the Liberal Democrats had won the election.

It goes without saying that it is the category of non-factives that poses a particular difficulty for semantics and therefore examples belonging to this category, and in particular the verb *believe* and the corresponding attitude of belief, are the most widely studied ones.

   Attitude reports are an example of so-called *intensional contexts*. In intensional contexts (as contrasted with extensional contexts), two expressions that refer to the same individual (*coreferential expressions*) are not always substitutable for each other in that such a substitution may lead to altering the truth value of the sentence. From the point of view of pragmatic analysis, we therefore say that such a substitution cannot guarantee that the meaning of the attitude report will be preserved. From the traditional semantic point of view, the problem is that the law of substitutivity does not hold. In particular, the law of truth-preserving substitutivity (referred to in the literature as substitutivity *salva veritate*), attributed to Leibniz, does not hold. Leibniz's Law says that two things are identical with each other if they are substitutable where this substitution preserves the truth of the resulting sentence. Or, after Frege, *Eadem sunt, quae sibi mutuo substitui possunt, salva veritate*. The law is also referred to as the *identity of indiscernibles*.

   In short, belief reports are an example of an intensional context and intensional contexts are characterised by the lack of applicability of Leibniz's Law. But there is a further distinction worth mentioning, namely that between two types of non-extensional contexts: intensional and hyperintensional. Belief constructions are also sometimes called *hyperintensional* in that referring expressions that are substitutable for one another in other types of intensional contexts, such as modal constructions, cannot always be substituted in belief (and other attitude) constructions. Hyperintensional constructions involve an added level of difficulty for a theory of meaning in that expressions that are used to refer to the subject of the attitude may have the same intension, and yet not be substitutable. Directly referring expressions, for example, behave differently in these two types of contexts. Coreferential proper names are substitutable *salva veritate* in modal contexts, while their substitution in an attitude context is not always truth-preserving. In what follows, however, we shall not make use of intensional/hyperintensional as a qualitative distinction but instead we are going to discuss a scalar approach to this opacity to substitution. We will consider the possibility that there are different degrees to which the human concept pertaining to the referent 'obscures' the semantics and makes these constructions non-extensional. This option is preferred in a pragmatic approach to attitude reports for one very important reason: in analysing utterance meaning and speaker intentions, we want to emphasise the fact that substitution can *sometimes* go through rather than the fact that substitution cannot be guaranteed. It is a well-researched fact of conversation that unless the interlocutors have indication to the contrary, they assume that they use referring expressions with compatible and mutually correctly assumed background information and thereby there are no obstacles to substitutions. In other words again,

> From the pragmatic point of view, all constructions are 'extensional' unless the context indicates otherwise.

On the contrary, traditional minimal, pragmatically uncontaminated semantic theory, as assumed in the analytic tradition, focuses on the fact that substitutivity in such a context is not reliable and therefore, so to speak, does not hold *tout court*.

A word of warning is needed at this juncture in that when one browses through the more than century-long tradition in analytic philosophy of discussions on substitutivity, one can observe that the law has become somewhat distorted. Leibniz's Law states that things (in our case: terms, or expressions) are identical if they have all properties in common. Meaning-preserving substitutivity is one such property. So, one can infer that since such substitution does not guarantee that the meaning is preserved, coreferring terms cannot be deemed identical. However, what is commonly invoked in philosophical discussion is not the *identity of indiscernibles* but rather the so-called *indiscernibility of identicals*: if two things are identical, then they have all properties in common. We owe this rather different implication to Quine and it should be properly referred to as Quine's Law. Again, in the context of the discussion of belief reports, we rephrase it as: if two expressions have the same meaning, then they have all properties in common. In other words again, if two expressions have the same meaning, then all that can be predicated of an object referred to by one term can also be predicated of an object referred to by the other term. Anything that is true of one is also true of the other as is summarised formally in (9):

(9)  $\forall x \forall y (x = y \rightarrow (F(x) \rightarrow F(y)))$

The problem is, of course, that when we want our theory of meaning to stay close to speakers' intuitions, then no two terms will ever fulfil this criterion: as soon as we have a different way of presenting an individual, we have a different way of thinking associated with it. Equally, as soon as we consider two different people, or even one person on two different occasions, holding a belief expressed by one and the same sentence, we may have different thoughts associated with the subject of the belief. While some semantic theories find ingenious ways of ignoring these complications, the pragmatic problem with attitude report retains them as its core. Equally, any semantic theory of a contextualist orientation, that is a semantic theory that allows for a substantial intrusion of pragmatic inference into the truth-conditional content, will have them as its core. In what follows, I shall be making use of the law of the indiscernibility of identicals, remembering that this is not the same as the original Leibniz's Law.

## 16.3  Attitude reports and pragmatics-rich semantics

Reporting on people's beliefs and various other mental states has generated a plethora of philosophical and formal semantic solutions. However, more and more frequently philosophers turn to the practice of conversation and to commonsense intuitions on the matter of substitutivity of coreferential expressions and on the content of the semantic representation of intensional constructions. In this section I briefly present some approaches which are associated with, or compatible with, the pragmatic problem with proposi-tional attitudes, that is the approaches which do not shun complicating semantics and attempt to account for 'intuitive meaning', intended speaker meaning, at the cost of making the boundary between semantics and prag-matics less sharp.

Let us return to example (5), repeated below.

(5)    Lidia believes that the author of *Wolf Hall* is visiting Cambridge this spring.

(5a)    $\exists x\ (\text{AoWH}(x) \land \forall y\ (\text{AoWH}(y) \rightarrow y = x) \land \text{Bel}_L\ \text{VC}\ (x))$

(5b)    $\text{Bel}_L\ \exists x\ (\text{AoWH}(x) \land \forall y\ (\text{AoWH}(y) \rightarrow y = x) \land \text{VC}\ (x))$

To repeat, (5a) is transparent to substitution of coreferential terms such as 'Hilary Mantel' or 'the winner of the 2009 Man Booker Prize', while (5b) is opaque. When one's theoretical objective is to develop a semantic theory that takes the possibility of this opacity into account, one may want to try to incorporate this difference in the *way of thinking about x* into that semantics. In more familiar terms, one may want to introduce the *mode of presentation* or *sense* (*guise* under which the belief is held) into the semantic representation. Before we proceed, we have to assume that whatever kind of semantic theory we formulate in the end, it has to fulfil the criterion of compositionality. I shall assume that a theory of meaning which does not observe this principle for some relevant unit of analysis or at some relevant level is inherently flawed. We will leave aside for the moment the essential question as to whether this unit has to mean a sentence, or perhaps an entire act of communication which relies not only on the uttered sentence but also on other channels of conveying information.

The received argumentation is this. The failure of truth-preserving sub-stitutivity suggests that we have two options in semantics: we can either (i) abandon the assumption that semantics has to be compositional, or (ii) incorporate contextual information in semantic theory. We have just rejected the first option as it pours the semantics out with the bath water of compositionality. We will briefly review some ideas pertaining to this rejected solution later on in this section and explain why they are of no interest to a pragmaticist. Within the domain of the second option, various solutions have been proposed, beginning with Frege (1892), who suggests that in intensional contexts the role of *reference* (*Bedeutung*) is taken by sense (*Sinn*). *Sinn* is an interesting theoretical construct in that it is not the same as the individual guise or private idea or concept under which the referent is thought about but rather pertains to an intersubjective way of construing the referent that can be shared by different individuals. In other words, it is a mode of presentation of the object and this mode can (i) affect the truth value of the sentence and (ii) be shared, intersubjectively.

It has to be pointed out that Fregean solutions, albeit suitably 'pragmaticky' in spirit, are not without problems. In (10), it would be difficult to incorporate information from the mode of presentation of the referent (henceforth MoP) into the semantics in that the quantifier is insensitive to the individual MoPs.

(10)   Many people believe that the author of *Wolf Hall* has many more novels up her sleeve.

It seems that in order to preserve the Fregean outlook, one would have to have a concept of a, so to speak, 'second-order sense' that would ensure some pragmatic/contextual/cognitive compatibility of the individual senses – or perhaps just a non-committal concept of sense which is not as rich as the intersubjective, albeit psychological, MoP. We will leave the proposed solutions and speculations aside.

The anti-Fregean solutions start with the premise of so-called *semantic innocence* (see Davidson 1968). Assuming that the category of attitude verbs includes the construction with 'say + *that*-clause', attitude constructions should succumb to Davidson's *paratactic account* according to which the demonstrative 'that' takes the utterance following it as its referent. The essence of Davidson's semantic innocence view is that an expression embedded in an attitude report contributes exactly the same content as it does in an ordinary extensional context. Next, the main block of solutions that is standardly (although arguably no longer legitimately, as I point out in the next paragraph) contrasted with neo-Fregeans is that of neo-Russellians in that both, unlike Davidson, assume a structured proposition but differ in their assumptions concerning the semantic content. Russell's theory gave the name to the latter direction in that he proposed that beliefs can be directly about individuals. Logically proper names contribute only the individual to the meaning of the sentence. Approaches advocating semantic innocence ignore truth-value judgements made by participants in the discourse, and in particular they would ignore the subject's dissent from the report about his/her attitude, but focus instead on the sentence itself. In other words, the identity of reference suffices for the identity of meaning. In more theoretical terms, neo-Russellians deny that sense or MoP could contribute to the semantics of such constructions (see e.g. Salmon 1986; Soames 1987, 1995). The semantic content of a sentence is a so-called *singular proposition* (after Kaplan 1989a). Neo-Russellians can therefore be naturally associated with the current orientation of semantic minimalism in that the semantic content on this account allows for only minimal admixture of pragmatics in the form of resolving the reference of indexical terms – or perhaps not even that much. (On the debate between semantic minimalism and contextualism and on different orientations within minimalism see e.g. Borg 2004, 2007 and this volume; Cappelen and Lepore 2005a, 2005b; Recanati 2005).

More pragmatics-driven developments include Richard's (1990, 1995) proposal that the verb 'believe' is context-sensitive and therefore indexical. On this view a sentence expresses a so-called Russellian annotated matrix (RAM) which, while growing out of the Russellian outlook, becomes quite Fregean and 'pragmaticky'; linguistic expressions pair up with interpretations to form the so-called annotations and matrices to serve as the semantic content as well as the content of the attitude. In a somewhat related argumentation, Pelczar (2004, 2007) argues as follows. The fact that a speaker holds a belief about water expressed in (11) but at the same time does not hold the belief in (12) is not a problem with the *objects* of belief but instead a problem with the properties we assign to the *attitude* of belief.

(11)   Water is in short supply.

(12)   $H_2O$ is in short supply.

What this means is that instead of following Kaplan, Perry or Schiffer in attempts to explain the objects of believing, we should assume one single object of belief that can be referred to by a variety of suitable expressions and 'complicate' the belief relation instead. Belief is on this account a context-dependent, indexical predicate. 'Context' includes here the beliefs and knowledge of the interlocutors, the topic of the conversation, and co-text. It is clear from this crude summary that the account helps itself to a great deal of pragmatics in proposing the solution: compositionality of attitude reports is preserved but at the expense of bringing in heavy context-dependence and indexicality of attitude expressions.

There are also more lexicon- and grammar-driven solutions to choose from. Larson and Ludlow (1993) suggest so-called *interpreted logical forms* (ILFs) which are composed of linguistic forms and extra-linguistic objects named by these forms. By proposing ILFs they embrace *sentential ism*: they assign theoretical importance to the expression that was actually used to perform the referring function in the sentence. For Stanley (2002a), the contextual factors that affect truth conditions are traceable to elements of the syntactic structure, the so-called *unarticulated constituents*. The origin of the latter orientation is the topic to which I now turn.

There have been various attempts to incorporate the MoP in the logical form of attitude reports, to mention only the hidden-indexical theory (see e.g. Schiffer 1992, 1996). Let us begin with John Perry. In his early work, Perry (1977), focusing on demonstratives, distinguishes between the *content* of an attitude and the *role*, the latter understood as being akin to Fregean sense but taking the addressee from the context to the content. My belief 'I am in Cambridge' and Keith's belief 'I am in Cambridge' have different belief content because the indexicals are resolved differently, but the belief states are the same for me and for Keith: each of us holds a first-person belief about being in Cambridge at the time when the belief is held. Our beliefs then have the same *role*. This distinction parallels the one between content and character of demonstratives proposed by Kaplan (1989a), where the content of the pronoun *I* is the referent and its character is the linguistic meaning: the speaker or the writer of the utterance. Within this orientation, Crimmins and Perry (1989) and Crimmins (1992) proposed a so-called 'notion', an unarticulated constituent of the proposition (see also objections by Clapp (1995), among others).

From the perspective of current debates we can say that their insistence that all this conceptual content is not part of the proposition makes these approaches difficult to classify. While they are standardly categorised as neo-Russellian (e.g. by McKay and Nelson 2005), when we assume a slightly different approach to the semantics/pragmatics interface, the solutions can equally fall under the Fregean label. For example, in his later work, Perry (2001) acknowledges the following:

> If there is some aspect of meaning, by which an utterance *u* of *S* and an utterance *u'* of *S'* differ, so that a rational person who understood both *S* and *S'* might accept *u* but not *u'*, then a fully adequate *semantics* should say what it is. (Perry 2001: 9; my emphasis)

He does so by complicating the notion of content and distinguishing different types of it, notably the referential ('official') content and the reflexive one, where the latter accounts for the linguistic expression, linguistic MoP.

In short, the unarticulated constituents view of Crimmins and Perry (1989) and Crimmins (1992), seems to sit mid-way. While often dubbed neo-Russellian, it can easily be reanalysed and domiciled as contextualist. Although sentences with coreferring terms such as (5a) and (5b) express the same singular proposition, the Fregean ways of thinking about the referents do have their input and this input can be construed as the 'semantic' input when we adopt the contextualist view of semantic content. Perry's (2001) distinction between different types of content make the possibility of such a (somewhat subversive) reanalysis even more diaphanous. In other words, semantics can easily be enriched by the MoP of the referent conceptualised as an unarticulated constituent, irrespective of the author's original intent because an unarticulated constituent can be regarded as an orientation-independent tool. To give an analogous example, truth conditions are now considered as a tool for a contextualist, leading to what is sometimes called truth-conditional pragmatics (Recanati 2002, 2010). Approached from this angle, the debate reduces from the semantics/pragmatics boundary dispute to the debate internal to contextualism and concerning the provenance of disambiguating/enriching information, with the two stances represented by (i) syntax-driven, bottom-up enrichment and (ii) syntax-independent, top-down, 'free' enrichment.

Now, what neo-Russellians say in effect is that although our conversational experience tells us that substituting other terms for an individual may alter the meaning of the sentence, for the purpose of semantic theory substitution does not alter the meaning: the truth value of the sentence after a substitution of a coreferential expression remains the same. Neo-Fregeans opt for a more psychologically immersed semantics and endorse the fact that substitutions may intuitively change the meaning of the sentence as a *semantic fact*. But then, how does one represent the logical form of the sentence?

Let us now move to Schiffer's proposal and the debate it gave rise to and see how it can be reinterpreted in the light of the current cutting-edge question of 'How much pragmatics is there in semantics?' For Schiffer, the attitude of belief is a three-place relation holding among the believer, the proposition, and an MoP under which the person believes this proposition. In (14), $\Phi^*m$ stands for a contextually determined *type of mode of presentation*. $< >$ mark the content of the intension.

(13)    Ralph believes that Fido is a dog.
(14)    $(\exists m)(\Phi^*m \wedge Bel(Ralph, <Fido, doghood>, m))$
                                   (from Schiffer 1992: 503)

$\Phi^*m$ seems to be a useful and malleable unit. It is a *type* of MoP, is 'pragmaticky' through and through, and yet when we adopt the contextualist semantic outlook, we can easily domesticate it as a pragmatic intrusion, enrichment, modulation of the semantic representation (see Recanati 1994, 2004a; Carston 2002; Jaszczolt 2005). If $\Phi^*m$ is conceived of as 'pragmaticky', then the need to answer the question as to what kind of information falls under it becomes relaxed; pragmatic enrichment is free and often situation-driven.

Hidden-indexical theory tries to give a role to the MoP but giving it a *semantic* role would mean giving up compositionality. Hidden indices don't correspond to any grammatical units; they are added somewhat ad hoc. They are also added post hoc: having encountered the difference in interpretation we try to build it into the logical form. Now, looking at this problem from the perspective of the contextualism/minimalism debate in respect of the semantics/pragmatics interface that has flared up with new strength since around 2004 (e.g. Borg 2004; Cappelen and Lepore 2005a; Recanati 2005), a more constructive reinterpretation becomes available. As was briefly remarked above, either the hidden indices can belong to semantic representation understood in contextualist terms, or they are banned from it but pop up in pragmatics instead when semantics is kept minimal.

A less radical form of free enrichment has also been proposed. Jaszczolt (1999, 2000) suggests clear-cut degrees of semantic significance of the mode of presentation, depending on the default or non-default status of the interpretation of the attitude report. Instead of accepting that the relevant conceptual content, or psychological mode of presentation, always enriches the semantic representation of attitude reports 'top-down' (i.e. non-indexically, without regard to syntactic slots), we distinguish (i) situations where the mode of presentation is relevant; (ii) situations where semantics does not need it, so to speak, because substitution can go through thanks to the well-tuned background information of the participants; and (iii) situations in which all we need is that part of the mode of presentation that will allow the representation to distinguish between correct and incorrect reference in the case of a referential mistake as in (5c). In (i), $\Phi^*m$ makes use of any background beliefs of the interlocutors that are relevant. In (ii), the value of $\Phi^*m$ is nil, or, alternatively, the logical form does not include a slot for it. In (iii), it normally reduces to the linguistic representation in that a correct or intended but mistaken referent is selected. A similar line of criticism is present in Ludlow's (1995: 105) discussion of Schiffer's $\Phi^*m$, where he points out that the reporter on an attitude is often in a position to make only general claims such as (15) and (16).

(15)    Ralph believes, *in a sense*, that Fido is a dog.

(16)    Ralph believes, *so to speak*, that Fido is a dog.

The objection also bears some affinities with Forbes's (1990, 1997) so-called *modes of self-presentation*, or logophors, as in (17), where, to cut a Superman story short, Superman known to Lois under his other identity as Clark Kent is *not* believed to be able to fly.

(17)    Lois has always believed that Superman can fly, *so-labelled*.
                    (from Forbes 1997: 109; my emphasis)

Extending this line of analysis further, this mystical constituent *in a sense, so to speak* or *so-labelled* need not necessarily be understood as a description held in the mind. Let us look at example (18).

(18)    The Iron Lady was so called because of her cold-blooded political decisions.

Since 'Iron Lady' is a popular nickname identifying the referent uniquely as Margaret Thatcher, a former Prime Minister of Britain, we should be able to substitute the name as in (19).

(19)    Margaret Thatcher was so called because of her cold-blooded political decisions.

Substitution fails, and the argument, Fregean in spirit, says that we have a complex concept here to the effect 'A so-believes that…' or 'A believes that B, so-labelled, Φs' (cf. Forbes 1990, 1997). In a similar vein, in his later work Forbes (2006) suggests an opacity-inducing expression 'as such' whose role is to invoke the appropriate MoP and thereby adjust the extension of 'seeks' in (20), as represented in (21).

(20)   Lois seeks Superman.

(21)   ((as(such))(seeks(superman)))(lois)

(adapted from Forbes 2006: 159)

What is interesting for our discussion of pragmatic and semantic aspects of attitude reports is that Forbes seems to subscribe here to the contextualist view on the interface. When one draws the boundary between semantics and pragmatics in the contextualist way and allows for the output of pragmatics to contribute to the truth-conditional representation, it is the semantics of attitude reports that contains a covert constituent *as(such)* – irrespective of its provenance. Forbes also points out that a more 'syntacticky' explanation would be possible, according to which covert 'as such' is explained by ellipsis and thereby by the presence of a slot in the representation à la Stanley's (2002a) bottom-up enrichment, i.e. enrichment triggered by the logical form of the sentence.

Schiffer's $\Phi^*m$ engendered a debate on the adicity of belief reports (see Ludlow 1996, 1996; Schiffer 1996). Schiffer ends his seminal paper (1992) with a rejection of the logical form in (14) on the grounds that it lacks compositionality. Viewed from a current contextualist orientation, however, (14) can be rescued. Pragmatic compositionality, embraced in Recanati (2004a) and subsequently further developed in the theory of Default Semantics (Jaszczolt 2005, 2010c), is a view according to which interaction of information coming from various sources produces a compositional representation. Recanati calls it the representation of *what is said* in truth-conditional pragmatics; Jaszczolt calls it *merger representation* or a merged proposition pertaining to primary meaning in Default Semantics. The stance on compositionality is similar though: compositionality is not to be sought in the syntactic representation of the sentence uttered in discourse, but rather on the level of the intended primary meaning. What these two views mean by primary meaning differs substantially but this issue is tangential to the current purpose. Contextualist views on belief reports are also aptly discussed in Recanati 1993 and Bezuidenhout 1997, the latter engaging with Devitt's (1996) ambiguity view.

The two-dimensional account of attitude ascription proposed by Chalmers (e.g. 1996, 2006, forthcoming b) belongs broadly in the same Fregean orientation. For him, what sentences express is well represented by Fregean thoughts. The two dimensions of intensions work broadly similarly to Kaplan's and Stalnaker's construals: a primary intension is a function from scenarios to extensions, and a secondary intension is a function from possible worlds to extensions. The first one is epistemic, for example taking the meaning from the linguistic meaning of an indexical (Kaplan's 'character') to a referent in a world, and the second is modal, taking the meaning from possible worlds to referents. For example, 'Snowdon' and 'Yr Wyddfa' (which is the Welsh name for that mountain) have the same secondary intensions, leading to the highest mountain in Wales. The substitutivity problem can be ascribed to the primary intension. 'Scenarios' are here formal equivalents of context but it is important to emphasise that context is understood very differently from Gricean context: scenarios, also called 'centred worlds' – 'centred' on an individual and a time; they are ordered triples of (i) worlds, (ii) individuals and (iii) times (see Chalmers forthcoming b; also Brogaard, this volume) – are very different from the Gricean construals of situations of discourse triggered by the recognition of the speaker's intentions, be it inferential or conventional.

Now, the importance of the primary intension as well as the extension for substitutivity leads to the reanalysis of the notion of a proposition. Chalmers proposes here a so-called 'enriched proposition' (or 'enriched intension') which is an ordered pair of the primary intension and the extension of an expression. The question arises at this point as to whether this enriched proposition, which happens to share the term 'enrichment' with Gricean pragmatics, also shares with the latter the *concept* of enrichment. It can be said with certainty that it will not share the procedure of enrichment in that post-Gricean enrichment is intention- and inference-driven (see Haugh and Jaszczolt, this volume). But it is very likely that it shares with it the output, the consequence of making the proposition sensitive to the individual's epistemic state, familiarity with modes of presentation, suitability of these modes in a situation and so forth (captured by Chalmers's idea of *appropriateness*, founded on the individual's *endorsement* of a proposition that is *coordinated* with the expressed proposition in a given context – where all three emphasised concepts are technical terms used to capture the intricate and varied sensitivity to the primary intension in addition to the sensitivity to the singular (Russellian) content).

Next, if this role of context permeates into semantics, that is, if Chalmers-enriched propositions, just as post-Gricean, say, Recanati-enriched propositions, are the semantic content and are, say, the input to the truth-conditional analysis, then we can classify Chalmers's account as a contextualist account in the same sense as the contextualist accounts discussed above. Differences of assumptions and methods notwithstanding, it seems justified, and advantageous, to do so. Truth and falsity for Chalmers are the domain of intuitive judgements (forthcoming b). Like modes of presentation in hidden-indexical theory (e.g. Schiffer 1992, discussed above), primary intensions collect those aspects of the meaning of the sentence that are indispensable for substitutivity *salva veritate* to work. As for a hidden-indexicalist, so here we have a problem of what to do with these aspects of meaning when we want to adhere to the assumption that semantics is compositional. Here, just as in post-Gricean accounts, we adopt so-called pragmatic compositionality (Recanati 2004a, 2010; Jaszczolt 2005, 2010c). In the two-dimensional account Chalmers proposes a version of the 'composition of senses', that is the composition of his enriched propositions. The compatibility of this suggestion with the post-Gricean theory of Default Semantics, where compositionality is sought on the level of the merger of information about meaning coming from different sources, will become apparent in section 16.5.

## 16.4   Beyond substitutions

It has been famously pointed out that puzzles with beliefs arise even when substitution does not take place. Moreover, they arise equally with proper names and with definite descriptions, although the first, unlike the latter, arguably refer directly. Kripke's (1979) puzzle challenges the *principle of translation* which says that if a sentence in one language is true, its translation into another language is also true. It also undermines the *principle of disquotation* which says that if a speaker assents to 'p', then he believes that *p*. On Kripke's scenario, Pierre, who lives in France and speaks French, holds a belief about a city called Londres, but otherwise unknown to him, that it is pretty, as in (22).

(22)    Londres est jolie.

We should be able to report on (22) in English as in (23):

(23)    Pierre believes that London is pretty.

But Pierre subsequently moves to London, finds it unattractive, and acquires a belief, now expressed in English, as in (24).

(24)    London is not pretty.

He does, however, still earnestly hold his belief expressed in (22) without engendering a contradiction. By means of this example Kripke points out the fact that the problem of attitude reports arises independently of substitutivity. Pierre can hold both beliefs, and even associate identical sets of identifying properties with the proper names London and Londres, and yet not succumb to a contradiction.

Kripke's other example is even more striking: even when we consider only one language and only one proper name, the puzzle may still arise. (25) can be regarded as true and false at the same time by someone who does not realise that the Polish politician Ignacy Paderewski was the same person as the famous pianist Ignacy Paderewski.

(25)    Ignacy Paderewski had musical talent.

Kripke comes very close to the core of the pragmatic problem with attitude reports: the real puzzle is not about the lack of substitutivity *salva veritate* in intensional contexts, neither is it about the relative scopes of the referring term and the belief operator. It concerns instead the question as to how to capture the truth-makers for such sentences when uttered by speakers. Kripke modestly says that he does not offer a solution. However, in a sense, he *is* pointing us towards one, and this solution is not incompatible with contextualism: in order to provide a solution to the 'puzzle' with belief reports we have to look at speaker meaning. Sentence meaning only stops posing problems when we reconcile it with speaker meaning. Needless to say, this is where the theoretical problem with attitude reports meets the folk explanations of 'what really happens there'.[1]

## 16.5  Representation of attitude reports

On many accounts discussed in the previous sections, in order to avoid con-tradictions, we dress proper names with an MoP or its functional equivalent which has a semantic role to play either in virtue of Frege's stipulation or in virtue of the subsequent contextualist stipulation that pragmatically derived information contributes, on occasions (or according to some authors always), to the semantic representation (see Recanati 2004a; Jaszczolt 2005). Pragmatic components of this kind have also been accounted for in formal, dynamic approaches to meaning. In Discourse Representation Theory (DRT; see e.g. Kamp and Reyle 1993), proper names are 'anchored', so to speak, to objects (Asher 1986; Kamp 1990). These objects can be real or conceptual, which accounts for the *de re/de dicto* distinction.[2]

This is, in brief, how beliefs and other attitudinal states can be represented in DRT. First, the language of DRT makes use of discourse referents and discourse conditions which make up discourse representation structures (DRSs, represented formally as K). Next, there are mode indicators (MOD), such as for example belief (BEL), desire (DES) or intention (INT). Discourse referents can be anchored and an anchor is represented as [ANCH, x]. Finally, an attitude description is a pair <MOD,K>. There can be two types of anchors: external and internal. <[ANCH, x], K> is an internal anchor for $x$, while an external anchor (EA) is a function whose domain is given by the set of internally anchored discourse referents in the DRS K, and the range by a set of referents that do not occur in K. External anchors are important in that a DRS has to be 'affixed to' entities of the conversational domain in order to stand for a singular proposition (see also Kamp 1990, 1996, 2003).

The language of DRT contains a predicate *Att* ('attitude') in order to repre-sent attitudinal states $s$: Att($x$, K, EA) (adapted from Kamp 2003). Using this language, sentence (3), repeated below as (26), can be represented by the DRS in Figure 16.1.[3]

(26)  Lidia believes that the author of *Wolf Hall* is visiting Cambridge this spring.

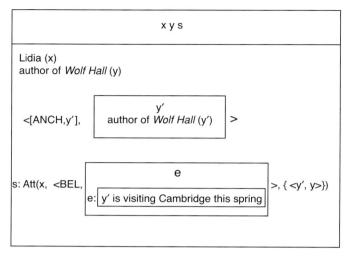

Figure 16.1. *Partial DRS for example (26)*

In Figure 16.1, y′, standing for 'the author of *Wolf Hall*', is both internally and externally anchored. In other words, there is both a concept and an intersubjectively identifiable individual that correspond to the discourse referent y′. What it means is that on this representation 'the author of *Wolf Hall*' is used referentially and the reading can be called *de re*.[4]

Next, Default Semantics (henceforth DS: Jaszczolt, e.g. 2005, 2010c) amends and extends the language of DRT and uses it for a more pragmatics-rich object. Classified as a post-Gricean, radical contextualist approach, its aim is to represent the meaning intended by the Model Speaker and recovered by the Model Addressee. It represents the result of the interaction of meaning-giving information that comes from the sources identified in the theory and yielding the following components in processing (on the revised 2009 version):

(i)   combination of word meaning and sentence structure (WS)
(ii)  conscious pragmatic inference from situation of discourse, social and cultural assumptions, and world knowledge (CPI)
(iii) cognitive defaults pertaining to the universal operations of the human brain (CD)
(iv)  social, cultural and world-knowledge defaults (SCWD).

The processes operate on an equal footing, which means that the resulting representation may on some occasions depart from the structure of the uttered sentence that is processed through WS. The resulting representation is called a *merger representation* (Σ) in that it merges information coming from a set of identified sources and produced through an interaction of some or all of the above processes.[5] Σ is assumed to be compositional, where compositionality is understood as a methodological principle. It applies not to the level of structure and word meanings (WS) but rather on the higher

*Primary meaning:*

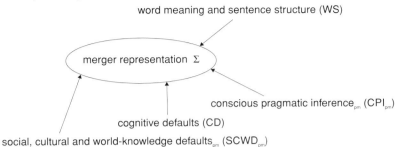

Figure 16.2. *Primary meaning according to the* processing model *of the revised version of Default Semantics*

level of utterance meaning, the level of the merged proposition represented as $\Sigma$.[6] The processing model for $\Sigma$s is given in Figure 16.2.

Using example (26) again, we can now make use of discourse referents to represent not only sentence meaning and the ambiguities associated with the definite description, but also any other aspect of utterance meaning which, on the contextualist view, appears in the semantic representation through a pragmatic route – via pragmatic inference or via speaker's and addressee's default assumptions. Asher (1986: 129) uses an apt metaphor, saying that discourse referents are 'pegs' on which the addressee 'hangs' the properties given by DRS conditions. Analogously, in DS, discourse referents are 'pegs' whose properties are given by a variety of linguistic and non-linguistic sources, and are collected through the interacting processes specified in Figure 16.2. We are now in the Gricean domain of intended meanings and therefore we also want to represent mistaken reference and the situation where a referent cannot be assigned by the speaker. Assuming, as can be recalled from the readings (5a)–(5c) of sentence (5) in section 16.2, that 'the author of *Wolf Hall*' can refer correctly, incorrectly, or not refer at all, we obtain the discourse conditions in (27). For this purpose, the scenario for (26) is that, according to the speaker, Lidia (a) may hold a belief about the actual author of the novel, Hilary Mantel; (b) may use the description attributively; or (c) may be mistaken and thinking about, say, Michael Morpurgo.[7] Square brackets stand for the content on which the process operates and the subscripts for the name of the process.

(27)  (i)  [Hilary Mantel]$_{\text{CD}}$ (y)
      (ii)  [the author of *Wolf Hall*]$_{\text{CPI}}$ (y)
      (iii)  [Michael Morpurgo]$_{\text{CPI}}$ (y)

Next, DS proposes that a belief report is represented as Bel (x, $\tau$), standing for '*x* believes that $\tau$', meaning that on a particular interpretation the individual *x* has the cognitive state $\tau$. The $\Sigma$s for the three readings of (26) incorporating

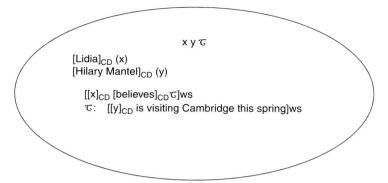

Figure 16.3. *The correct referential reading of the definite description in (26).*
*Partial* Σ

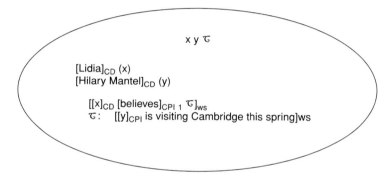

Figure 16.4. *The attributive reading of the definite description in (26). Partial* Σ

the senses in (27) are presented in Figures 16.3–5 respectively. The sources
CD and CPI are responsible for the difference in reading.

These two types of analysis, in DRT and in DS, demonstrate that pragmatic
information is essential for an adequate representation of attitude reports,
but at the same time it can be incorporated in it and constitute an integral
part of the semantic theory. DRT subsumes anchoring under the dynamic
semantics of discourses; DS, on the other hand, seeks compositionality on a
more pragmatics-rich level where even information provided by the lexicon
and grammar can alter without constraints other than those imposed by
speaker's intention and addressee's intention recognition. In other words, Σ
may end up modelling an indirect speech act when the primary intended
meaning happens to be expressed indirectly.

In brief, the semantics of attitude reports in the framework of DS is compositional but to be compositional it has to be radically contextualist. The
question arises at this point as to whether we can still call it a semantics
of English in that Σs draw not only on the processing of English sentences

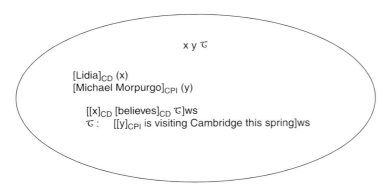

Figure 16.5. *The mistaken referential reading of the definite description in (26).*
*Partial Σ*

but also on the output of other sources. It is possible that the answer to this
question is Fodorian. This is the topic of section 16.6.

## 16.6 Mentalese, compositionality and attitudes

Fodor (e.g. 2008: 14–15) uses the logical form of attitude reports 'A believes
*that p*' to vindicate Cartesian priority of thought to action. He uses it in two
different ways. Firstly, knowing *that p* has to precede knowing how to change
*p*. Secondly, if we distinguish the content of mental states, i.e. objects of *that*-
clauses, we can pinpoint the relations between them. For example, desiring
*p*, combined with the premise that *p* if and only if *q*, leads to an action that
brings about *q*.

For Fodor, semantics has to be kept simple. It has to be the semantics
of Mentalese, the language of thought. As he says, '[t]here may be no good
reason for supposing that English has a semantics at all; perhaps the only
thing that does is Mentalese' (Fodor 2008: 219). He argues that Frege was
wrong to say that semantics requires the notion of sense; it is precisely
because we introduced murky concepts such as senses into the semantics
that propositional attitudes continue being a puzzle. Instead, he says, we
have to adopt the assumption that compositionality holds only on the level
of referring properties. Semantics has to be referential, and look for a solution
to the substitutivity problem elsewhere. For referentialists, (28) and (29) stand
for the same belief and they differ only in *causal powers* (cf. Fodor 2008: 69).

(28)   Cicero is tall.

(29)   Tully is tall.

The way it works is this. Whenever people have different mental representations, the causal powers of their mental states also differ. So, although the
semantics of the English sentences (28) and (29) is the same because semantic
theory is referential, the substitutivity problem in attitude reports obtains

a solution from causal powers. Causal powers are the domain of the computational theory of mind, not the representational, semantic one. They are sensitive to the syntax of Mentalese. But, as Fodor surmises, it may be the case that Mentalese is compositional, while English is not.

Next, if Fodor's theory is on the right track, it also has to deal with cases of missing modes of presentation. In other words, since a person may have a concept of Ignacy Paderewski as a famous Polish politician but lack a concept of Ignacy Paderewski as a famous pianist, the substitutivity problem turns up in spite of an analytical truth and the identity of reference. Here again the solution comes from the claim that it is Mentalese, not English, that has a compositional semantics – indeed, any semantics at all. In Mentalese, the story goes (Fodor 2008: 72), there are two names that are translated into English as 'Paderewski'. This is how semantics is kept simple and referential, by kicking the problem up to computational states, or even higher into the physics of the brain.

> Intentional states and processes are multiply realized by computational states; computational states and processes are multiply realized by neurological states (or whatever), and, for all I know, neurological states are multiply realized by biochemical states; and so on down to (but not including) basic physics. (Fodor 2008: 91)

Pragmatic compositionality of merger representations in DS introduced in the previous section is not incompatible with Frege's account. In DS, the question as to whether the composition of $\Sigma$ takes place in Mentalese is an open question and therefore the compositionality of Mentalese offers a very plausible route to pursue. However, DS would not separate the levels of the semantics of English and the semantics of Mentalese in the Fodorian way. For a contextualist, elements of processing that do not bear directly on language as a closed system may bear directly on the use of the system, and it is the use of the language that calls for a compositional account. This is the route pursued in DS and this is how merger representations are to be understood: they draw on the lexicon and grammar of a natural language in which the utterance was expressed, but also on other sources of information about meaning, without commitment to the language of processing used there. In other words, whether we think and perform our inferences in English or in Mentalese will not change the fact that for a contextualist such a pragmatics-rich semantics is still a semantics of natural language.

To sum up, Fodor's proposal offers a captivating view on processing but what remains is to show that it indeed constitutes a solution to our problem. Even if we adopt the compositionality of the language of thought, whatever Mentalese turns out to be, what do we do with the semantic problem of substitutivity of coreferential expressions in propositional attitude constructions *in English*? Fodor's answer seems to be that we do nothing. English may not have a semantics, it may not be compositional. Suppose we adopt this view and assume that English does not have a compositional semantics (and hence, it becomes fair to say it has no semantics whatsoever). Then the translation of sentences of Mentalese into English would have to be independently motivated.

By this token, Mentalese for (30) is very different from (30) itself.

(30)   Paderewski is Paderewski.

The big problem with Fodor's solution is that in rejecting compositional semantics of English it shuns pragmatics, while it is by now widely accepted that semantics must not stray from pragmatics. Meaning in language must not be taken in isolation from meaning in communication. Otherwise we obtain a semantics that is psychologically implausible.[8] We stipulate that (30) does not pose a problem because it is not an analytical truth for any rational agent who is prepared to think or say it. We follow with the stipulation that propositional attitude reports in (31) and (32) have the same semantics because semantics is referential, but different syntax and different computational properties – or, better, that they do not have any semantics at all, only their Mentalese equivalents do.

(31)   Paul believes that Cicero is tall.

(32)   Paul believes that Tully is tall.

All is well when one focuses on the syntax and semantics of *sentences* and on mental states with their representational and computational properties. But in the study of communication the problem is that the impacts of (31) and (32) may differ. The fact that there is no one-to-one correspondence between an expression in Mentalese and an expression of English constitutes an explanation and part of the solution for Fodor's problems. At the same time, it is *the* problem itself for a pragmaticist. It is an assessment of this pragmatic problem to which I now turn in the final section.

## 16.7   Concluding remarks: The pragmatic perspective

To come back to example (1), Lidia's belief that the author of *Wolf Hall* is visiting Cambridge may be reported in the three different ways represented in (5a)–(5c), and in fact in an infinite number of different ways. Some of the reports would produce Lidia's consent but others would make her object. This fact of conversation has nothing to do with correct or incorrect referring: Lidia may be convinced that Michael Morpurgo, her favourite author, wrote *Wolf Hall*, but equally well she may simply not know who wrote the novel and dissent from the report in (2), just as she may not know that the author of *Wolf Hall* won the Man Booker Prize for 2009 and therefore dissent from (33).

(33)   Lidia believes that the winner of the Man Booker Prize for 2009 is
        visiting Cambridge this spring.

We will call this interpersonal difference in background information corresponding to the referent *the pragmatic problem*. To begin with, it is necessary to observe that while the semantic problem with substitutivity *salva veritate* of coreferential expressions is a genuine theoretic issue, the pragmatic problem is much less diaphanous. Normally, all goes well in communication and the speaker formulates the utterance in such a way that its meaning can be recovered by the addressee without creating ambiguities or mismatches between the intended meaning and the recovered meaning. In other words, on normal scenarios, rational communication does not fail. Moreover, rational communication is well accounted for in various Gricean approaches that emphasise the role of intentions in a theory of utterance meaning or speaker meaning (see Haugh and Jaszczolt, this volume). So, what is left to explain is only exceptions caused by misjudging of the addressee's informational state on the part of the speaker. This is a much more modest task than having to develop the entire pragmatics of propositional attitude reports. One may object here that the situation is analogous in semantics in that substitutivity *sometimes*, and even quite often, goes through and only *sometimes* is problematic. But this would be mixing the inner-theoretic problem that has exercised a Parnassus of minds at least since the Middle Ages, namely the *de re/de dicto* ambiguity, with a practical problem found, albeit rarely, in conversation. So, are these problems interrelated?

To recapitulate, the semantics of attitude reports can be repaired by the aid of a neo-Fregean device such as an MoP or its derivative, or it can be left simple and counter-intuitive. Or, Schiffer's rejection of $\Phi^*m$ can be put more strongly and natural languages can be denied a semantics à la Fodor. To repeat, what we called 'the pragmatic problem' is the fact that interlocutors' background knowledge may on occasion differ and that they may have different kinds of assumptions, or different sets of assumptions, at their disposal when using the same description or name. Now, to repeat, it is still a hotly debated issue as to whether semantics should be kept minimal and pertain just to sentence meaning as semantic minimalists claim (e.g. Borg 2004, 2007; Cappelen and Lepore 2005a, 2005b; or even more radically Bach 2006b), or to pertain to the meaning that reflects the speaker or writer's intended content as contextualists have it (e.g. Sperber and Wilson 1986; Carston 1988, 2002; Recanati 1989, 2004a; Jaszczolt 2005, 2010a; Travis 2008).[9]

Additional fuel is provided by the question 'Whose perspective?', namely the question as to whether semantics should model speaker's intended meaning or the addressee's recovered meaning. At this point we enter the debate between contextualists and relativists. According to the latter, newly reignited orientation, belief reports should be subjected to an analysis *not* from the position of the intended meaning but rather from the position from which the belief is *assessed* (see e.g. MacFarlane 2005; forthcoming). This perspective alters the conception of context; it allows for different truth values of a belief report, depending not only on the context of use but also on the context of assessment. This is not a place to pursue this debate;

suffice it to say that the pragmatics of propositional attitude reports should acknowledge relativism but at the same time utilise it with caution. Norms of rational conversational behaviour guarantee that in most cases discourse progresses smoothly; the meaning intended by the speaker and the meaning recovered by the addressee coincide, at least to the degree that is relevant for the purpose at hand. Seen in this light, relativism offers a dimension that is useful for deviations from the norms but the contextualism/relativism debate as such remains tangential to the problem of constructing a theory of meaning of utterances expressing propositional attitude reports. In contrast, the minimalism/contextualism debate is at the heart of the problem and as long as it continues, the *pragmatics* of attitude reports will be at the heart of the discussions concerning their *meaning*.

# 17

# Presupposition and accommodation in discourse

Rob van der Sandt

## 17.1   Presupposition and context

A general, intuitive and language-independent way to characterise presup-positions is as information that is taken for granted by the participants in a conversation.[1] Such information has a different status from the information that the participants intend to convey as new or relevant. Borrowing the terminology from speech act theory, the latter information is often said to be asserted.[2] Thus, by his utterance of (1a), a speaker typically presupposes that the Netherlands has a queen and conveys as new information that she wears a wig. By his utterance (1b) a speaker typically presupposes that Lydia failed the exam and conveys as new information that she regrets that.

(1)   a.   The Queen of the Netherlands wears a wig.
      b.   Lydia regrets that she failed the exam.

This distinction between presupposed and asserted information is encoded in the linguistic structure of sentences. (1a) contains the definite phrase *the Queen of the Netherlands* and such a phrase is said to induce or trigger the pre-supposition that there is some entity that satisfies the descriptive material, in the present example that the Netherlands has a queen. (1b) contains the factive verb *regret*. By the use of such a sentence, the speaker indicates that he takes the information of the complement for granted. By an utterance of (1b), the speaker thus presupposes Lydia failed the exam. Natural lan-guage contains many more lexical items or syntactic constructions that have been identified as presupposition inducers. Paradigmatic examples are cleft-constructions, quantifiers, verbs of transition (*begin, stop, continue*), temporal clauses and a variety of particles like *again, still* and *too.*

There are standard diagnostics to determine whether an expression or syntactic construction is a presupposition inducer and thus to dis-tinguish between the presuppositional information induced and the non-presuppositional remainder, i.e. the information that is conveyed as assertoric. The diagnostics are based on the fact that presuppositional information tends to emerge as intuitive inferences in environments where standard entailments don't survive. The traditional test is constancy under negation. Other tests are embedding under epistemic modals, embedding in the antecedent of a conditional construction, and questioning.[3] In the examples under (3), we see that the presuppositional information that is triggered in (2) is preserved as an inference from the full sentence in which (2) occurs embedded.

Applying these tests to the possessive construction *John's children* identifies it as a presupposition inducer.

(2)   John's children are playing in the garden.

(3)   a.   John's children are not playing in the garden.
      b.   Maybe (It is possible that) John's children are playing in the garden.
      c.   If John's children are playing in the garden, they'll be having a good time.
      d.   Are John's children playing in the garden?

From each of these sentences, we infer that John has children. This is the presupposition induced. We thus perceive in (2) two meaning components, the presupposition (4a) and the non-presuppositional contribution (4b).

(4)   a.   John has children.
      b.   They are playing in the garden.

The presupposition is not affected by the embedding operators. It 'projects out', to use the classic terminology. The non-presuppositional remainder remains in the scope of the embedding operators, follows the standard rules of semantic composition and is thus negated, modalized or (in (3d)) questioned. From a discourse perspective, 'projecting out' simply means projecting to the main context. The interpretation of the examples in (3) thus corresponds to mini-discourses as the following.

(5)   a.   [John has children...] They are not playing in the garden.
      b.   [John has children...] Maybe (It is possible that) they are playing in the garden.
      c.   [John has children...] If they are playing in the garden, they will be having a good time.
      d.   [John has children...] Are they playing in the garden?

Viewed as a whole these discourses don't presuppose that John has children. The speaker explicitly asserts it. We will call such representations the non-presuppositional expansions of the examples in (3).

Note that the pronouns in the second sentences in (5) are contextually bound by the presuppositional expressions that precede them. The presupposition binds into the non-presuppositional remainder. And note, furthermore, that the order is crucial. The presupposition has to be given for the non-presuppositional remainder to be interpretable.[4]

The phenomenon is general for most types of presuppositions as shown by the following sentences, where the factive and cleft-induced presuppositions are anaphorically linked in the discourse expansion.

(6) a. Mary regrets that John failed the exam.
  b. [John failed the exam...] Mary regrets that.

(7) a. It was John who failed the exam.
  b. [Someone failed the exam...] It was John who did.

In general, if the presuppositional information is given in the preceding discourse, we may refer back to the information which is already given. If not (e.g. when a sentence is offered in isolation), presuppositional expressions indicate in what class of context this sentence can be felicitously interpreted. However, if the presuppositional information is not already there but nevertheless uncontroversial, a cooperative hearer will construct (part of) the intended context as one that contains the required information. The idea goes back to the work of Stalnaker in the early seventies (see in particular Stalnaker 1970, 1974 and 1978). Karttunen discusses the phenomenon in his (1974). Van der Sandt (1982/1988) called it contextualization. Lewis (1979) coined the term 'accommodation'.

## 17.2 Accommodation

According to semantic theories of presupposition, sentences containing presuppositional expressions require that the presupposition is satisfied for the inducing sentence to have a truth value. According to pragmatic accounts, the presuppositions of a sentence have to be satisfied for the inducing sentence to be uttered felicitously. However, this idealised picture does not fit the facts. Karttunen (1974: 191) gives the following examples of sentences which may be quite felicitous if uttered out of the blue.

(8) a. We *regret* that children cannot accompany their parents to commencement exercises.
  b. I would like to introduce you to *my wife*.
  c. John lives in *the third brick house down the street from the post office*.

The italicised items induce the presuppositions. Consider the last. It presupposes that there is a post office, a street going down from it and at least three brick houses there. And the speaker asserts that John lives in the third of them. Clearly the non-presuppositional expansion (*There is a post office, a street going down to it, at least three brick houses there and John lives in the third one*) would be a rather redundant way of conveying the message. Karttunen remarks:

> ordinary conversation does not always proceed in the ideal orderly fashion described [above] . . . People do make leaps and shortcuts by using sentences whose presuppositions are not satisfied in the conversational context. This is the rule rather than the exception . . . If the current conversational context does not suffice, the listener is entitled and expected to extend it as required. He must determine for himself what context he is supposed to be in on the basis of what was said and, if he is willing to go along with it, make the same tacit extension that his interlocutor appears to have made. (Karttunen (1974: 191))

Stalnaker comments in similar vein and sees it as a kind of pretence on the part of the speaker.

> [A] speaker may act as if certain propositions are part of the common background when he knows that they are not. He may want to communicate a proposition indirectly, and do this by presupposing it in such a way that the auditor will be able to infer that it is presupposed. In such a case, a speaker tells his auditor something in part by pretending that this auditor already knows it. (Stalnaker (1974: 202))

Lewis famously coined the term accommodation for the phenomenon.

> Some things that might be said require suitable presuppositions. They are acceptable if the required presuppositions are present; not otherwise. 'The King of France is bald' requires the presupposition that France has one king and only one . . .
>
> Be that as it may, it's not as easy as you might think to say something that will be unacceptable for lack of required presuppositions. Say something that requires a missing presupposition, and straightway that presupposition springs into existence, making what you said acceptable after all. (Lewis (1979: 339))

This brings him to the following 'rule of accommodation for presupposition':

> If at time *t* something is said that requires presupposition *P* to be acceptable, and if *P* is not presupposed just before *t*, then – *ceteris paribus* and within certain limits – presupposition *P* comes into existence at *t*. (Lewis (1979: 340))

The phrase 'is not presupposed just before *t* ' should of course be interpreted as 'not part of the common ground' or to use Lewis' terminology 'not already part of the conversational scoreboard'.

And Heim states:

> Suppose [a sentence] $S$ is uttered in a context $c$ which does not admit it ... [People] simply amend the context $c$ to a richer context $c'$ one which admits $S$ and is otherwise like $c$, and then proceed to compute $c' + S$ instead of $c + S$. (Heim (1983: 119))

While the formulations of Karttunen and Stalnaker are quite agnostic as to the conditions under which accommodation can take place, the latter two formulations may suggest that accommodation is a rather unconstrained mechanism which applies blindly to restore felicity or definedness if the interpretation of a presuppositional sentence requires it.[5] So we should be a bit clearer as to the phrase 'presuppositional requirement' or 'admittance' and specify the constraints that are left implicit in Lewis's '*ceteris paribus* and within certain limits' clause.

In the next sections, we will see that accommodation is, in fact, a highly constrained process, subject to conditions on binding and principles of a Gricean nature. We will also see that depending on the theory of presupposition adopted, different views on accommodation emerge.

## 17.3  Projection and cancellation

Following the standard terminology, we say that (1a) and (1b) presuppose respectively that the Netherlands has a queen and that Lydia failed the exam. In the terminology of the previous section, we may say that this information is – if not already there – accommodated in the main context. In these cases, sentence presupposition and accommodation thus coincide. We observe the same in the embedded cases given in (3a)–(3d). The subclause (*John's children are playing in the garden*) induces the presupposition that John has children, the full sentence retains this presupposition ('it is projected') and the presuppositional information is – again adopting the terminology of the previous section – accommodated.

Presuppositions thus have a strong tendency to escape from embedding operators. However, as well known from the literature on presupposition, this is not always the case. Consider the classic pairs below.

(9)  a.  John's children are not bald.
     b.  John does not have any children, so his children are not bald.

(10) a.  Baldness is hereditary and John's children are bald.
     b.  John has children and his children are bald.

(11) a.  It is possible that baldness is hereditary and John's children are bald.
     b.  It is possible that John has children and his children are bald.

(12)  a.   If baldness is hereditary, John's children are bald.
      b.   If John has children, his children are bald.

(13)  a.   Either baldness is not hereditary or John's children are bald.
      b.   Either John does not have any children or John's children are bald.

All of the a-sentences intuitively presuppose that John has children, none of the b-sentences does. This is of course the well-known projection problem for presuppositions. Under what conditions do the presuppositions triggered by components of a compound sentence survive as a presupposition of the full sentence?

Various answers were given in the 1970s and 1980s. The answer of Gazdar's pragmatic theory of presupposition (Gazdar 1979) is – put informally – that the material that is presuppositionally triggered (proto-presuppositions or pre-suppositions, as he calls them) projects to the main context unless it clashes with material that is implicated. For example, in (13b) the first disjunct – not being entailed by the full sentence – invokes the implicature that the speaker is uncertain as to the truth value of this disjunct, or put otherwise it invokes the implicature that it is possible that John has children and the implicature that it is possible that John does not have children. This clashes with the presupposition triggered (i.e. that John has children).[6] Now it is said that implicated material cancels presuppositional material. Thus the presupposition of the second clause does not survive as a presupposition of the full sentence. The same mechanism works for the other b-sentences.[7] What about the a-sentences? They don't conflict with the implicatures evoked, are inherited as presuppositions of the full sentence and added to the context.

Lewis might say that they don't violate the conditions left implicit in his 'ceteris paribus and within certain limits' clause. So 'straight away [the] presupposition springs into existence'. Is this theory of projection a theory of accommodation? If we take a theory of accommodation simply as a theory which adds presuppositional material to the common ground (Gazdar's commitment slate) we could simply relabel Gazdar's theory as a theory of cancellation and accommodation. But given the way Gazdar's theory is set up this gives an uncomfortable feeling. His mechanism conflicts with the notion of presuppositions as information taken for granted. On Gazdar's account, conversational implicatures constitute a stronger kind of information than presupposition: presuppositional information may be defeated by implicatures. This is at odds with the intuitive notion and the way we characterised it in section 17.1. Presuppositional information is (in some sense to be made explicit) required for the inducing sentence to be interpretable. The standard characterisation of conversational implicatures is a very different one. On the Gricean view, a conversational implicature is not a semantic requirement for interpretation, but instead an inference that is computed on the basis of the interpretation of a sentence, contextual information and conversational principles. The question then arises how such inferences, which are dependent for their existence on a previous interpretation of the utterance that invokes them, can possibly defeat information which should already be part of the linguistic or non-linguistic context for the inducing sentence to have an interpretation. If there is any direct interaction between presupposition and conversational implicature, one would expect the former to override the latter and not the other way around.

Van der Sandt (1982/1988) took the picture sketched in Karttunen (1974) and Stalnaker (1970, 1974, 1978) as a starting point and presented a theory that has the feel of accommodation and is in empirical predictions very close to Gazdar's. In normal conversation, sentences are interpreted in context.[8] When a sentence is offered in isolation, the intended context is as yet undetermined. However, a sentence may contain clues as to what contexts would qualify. The presuppositions invoked are the foremost indicators (intonation is another one) and thus delimit the class of contexts in which the sentence can felicitously be interpreted. The presuppositions of a sentence determine the class of contexts that qualify and that contribute to interpretation.

This account agrees with the intuition of Stalnaker and other theorists that presuppositional expressions contain information that is ideally part of the incoming context. In the absence of further information, a cooperative hearer will thus try to interpret such a sentence over contexts that already contain the information invoked. In the default case, this will give us the presupposition as a contextual entailment; we would nowadays call it accommodation. Thus

(14)   Either baldness is not hereditary or John's children are bald.

is predicted to presuppose that John has children. The reason is that (14) can be felicitously interpreted in a context which contains this information as the acceptability of (15) shows:

(15)   John has children. [ . . . ] If baldness is hereditary, his children are
        bald.

This mimics the behaviour of a cooperative interpreter. If he succeeds in contextualising the inducing sentence, this sentence is predicted to be presupposing. But contextualisation is a default process. For, clearly, not every sentence is interpretable in any context. It may be that a sentence is not felicitous in a context which already contains the presuppositional information. This happens if the result of contextualisation would violate Gricean principles. For example,

(16)   Either John does not have any children or all his children are in
        hiding.

is not acceptable in a context which contains the information that John has children, as (17) shows:

(17)   *John has children. [ . . . ] Either he has no children or they are all in
        hiding.

The reason is that in the given context (16) is equivalent to its second disjunct:

(18)   John's children are in hiding.

This is certainly a shorter, less redundant and more efficient way to convey the information that John's children are in hiding, as the unacceptability of (17) shows. The original sentence cannot be interpreted in any context which contains the presuppositional material of the second disjunct and this information will consequently be interpreted locally.[9] Put otherwise, the full sentence is not presupposing for the simple reason that the information cannot be accommodated. This is captured in the following simple definition:

(19)   A sentence $\varphi$ presupposes a sentence $\psi$ in a context $c$ just in case
       (i)    one of the component sentences of $\varphi$ induces the presuppositional information that $\psi$; and
       (ii)   $\varphi$ is acceptable in $c + \psi$.[10]

It turns out that constraints of global and local informativity and consistency suffice as constraints on acceptability.[11]

This account has a conceptual and some empirical advantages over Gazdar's. The acceptability conditions perform the same task as Gazdar's clausals. But by interpreting them as conditions on the felicitous or acceptable utterance of sentences, they act as constraints on accommodation. If a sentential part induces a presupposition, the presuppositional material will be accommodated by default unless this would make the resulting discourse incoherent. It also has some empirical advantages. It accounts for example (as Karttunen and Stalnaker do) for the asymmetric behaviour of presuppositions in conjunctions.[12] However it also shares two major vices. As in Gazdar (1979) it remains unclear what happens to presuppositions in case they don't survive (and why then this information should be invoked to begin with) and it runs into binding problems.[13]

A solution to the last problem had to wait until Kamp (1981) and Heim (1982) presented their versions of dynamic semantics, recaptured meanings as relations between input and output contexts and showed how to handle anaphoricity inter- and intrasententially in a uniform way.[14] But the current dynamic theories have a second advantage. They give an answer to the question what happens to presuppositions in those cases where they cannot be accommodated in the main context.

## 17.4  Accommodation in a dynamic framework

Currently there are two major paradigms in presupposition theory. The first derives from Karttunen's (1974) and Heim's (1983) work and was developed further by Beaver (1995/2001). It is closely related to Stalnaker's ideas. It is known as the satisfaction account. The second derives from the work of van der Sandt (1992) and Geurts (1995/1999) and is known as anaphoric binding theory.[15] I will discuss their respective merits with respect to accommodation in turn.

## 17.4.1  The satisfaction account

The satisfaction account derives from Karttunen (1974) and Stalnaker's papers in the early 1970s. It was set in a dynamic framework by Heim (1983). The theory relies on a very simple idea. A context $c$ acts as a pool of information, and the utterance of a sentence $\varphi$ changes this information pool by adding the content of this sentence to the context, thus yielding a new context $c'$ consisting of the information of the incoming context plus the information contained in $\varphi$. That is, the sentence maps the incoming context $c$ to $c + \varphi$. Presuppositions act as constraints on this update operation. Suppose that a simple sentence $\varphi$ induces the presupposition $\psi$, which I will write as $\varphi_{\langle\psi\rangle}$. The basic requirement is that $\psi$, the presupposition induced, should be entailed by the context for $\varphi$ to be admissible in this context or put otherwise for this context to admit $\varphi$. Heim reinterprets this requirement as a definedness condition on the contextual update. In her account no contextual update will take place unless the presuppositions of a sentence are satisfied, i.e. unless their descriptive content is entailed by the incoming context. Now suppose that (1a) and (1b) are uttered out of the blue, this does not mean – as I pointed out in section 17.2 – that the conversation blocks. A cooperative hearer will *ceteris paribus* accommodate the presupposition, i.e. add it to $c$, so as to make the update defined after all. Let us call the list of basic presuppositions associated with a sentence $\varphi$ Pres($\varphi$). The presuppositional requirement that a simple sentence imposes on a context is then the following:

(20)   A context $c$ admits a simple sentence $\varphi$ just in case $c$ entails Pres($\varphi$).

So much for simple sentences. What about complex sentences? In these cases the subsentences can be viewed as context change devices as well. If $\varphi$ is complex, presuppositional admittance is defined recursively by associating with each constituent sentence of $\varphi$ its own so-called 'local' contexts and by requiring that each of the constituent sentences is admitted by the local context.

(21)   A context $c$ admits a complex sentence $\varphi$ iff each of $\varphi$'s constituent sentences is admitted by its local context.

The incoming context is the global context. For a negated sentence, the local context is the global context. A context will thus admit the negation of a sentence just in case it admits its non-negated counterpart. Or, put in the definedness terminology, $c + \neg\varphi$ will be defined just in case $c + \varphi$ is defined. This predicts that negation sentences preserve their presuppositions under negation (i.e. negation is a hole in the sense of Karttunen 1973). In case $\varphi$ is a conjunction or conditional the local contexts for the constituent sentences are defined as follows.

(22)   In case $\varphi$ is of the form $\psi \wedge \chi$ or $\psi \to \chi$, $c$ is the local context for $\psi$ and $c + \psi$ is the local context for $\chi$.

In the terminology of definedness conditions this means that $c + \psi \to \chi$ is defined just in case $c + \psi$ and $(c + \psi) + \chi$ is defined. This predicts that the presuppositions of the first conjunct of a conjunction or of the antecedent of an implicative sentence always emerge as presuppositions of the full sentence. The presuppositions associated with the second conjunct or with the consequent of a conditional are weakened, though. The requirement that the local context for the first conjunct or the consequent (i.e. $c + \psi$) should entail the presuppositions of $\chi$ simply means that the global context $c$ should entail $\psi \to \text{Pres}(\chi)$.[16] The presuppositions of conjunctions and conditionals thus always surface as implicative constructs.

Let's look at a few examples. Assuming that the modal operator is a hole, i.e. $\diamond\varphi$ is – just like negation – defined just in case $\varphi$ is defined, the theory predicts that the presupposition that *John has children* associated with (2) is preserved as a presupposition of the full sentence in the embedded cases I gave in (3a)–(3d). The theory also correctly predicts that none of (23a)–(23c) presupposes that France has a king.

(23)   a.   France has a king and the king of France is bald.
       b.   It is not true that France has a king and the king of
            France is bald.
       c.   If France has a king, the king of France is bald.

In (23a), (23b) and (23c) the subsentences containing the trigger *the king of France* induce the presupposition that there is a king of France. The clauses given above require that this presupposition should be entailed by the local context for the update to be defined, i.e. they should be entailed by $c +$ *France has a king*. Since *France has a king* is part of the local context, this condition is trivially fulfilled and puts no constraint whatsoever on the incoming context. Definedness is guaranteed and the sentence is predicted to be non-presupposing. No accommodation is required.

So far the predictions are fine. However, when we look at more complicated cases, problems arise. It turns out that the predictions of the satisfaction theory are both too weak and too strong. They are too strong since the theory in its basic form predicts substantial presuppositions that are intuitively not there.[17] And they are too weak since in embedded cases presuppositions tend to be weakened at each embedding. As Geurts pointed out, the basic problem is not that many predictions are too strong. These cases can be handled by the mechanism of so-called local accommodation. I will discuss the mechanism of local (or more precisely non-global) accommodation in the next section. Here I will deal with the problem of 'weakening', which has been extensively discussed in Geurts (1996; 1999) and dubbed the *proviso problem*.

Consider the following sentences:

(24)  a.  If baldness is hereditary, the king of France is bald.
      b.  If baldness is hereditary and the king of France is bald,
          he wears a wig.
      c.  It is not true that baldness is hereditary and that the
          king of France is bald.
      d.  It is possible that baldness is hereditary and that the
          king of France is bald.

In all these sentences, the local context for the subsentence *the king of France
is bald* is $c+$ *Baldness is hereditary*. In order to satisfy the presupposition, the
local context thus should entail that France has a king. As I just pointed
out, this does not require that the global context entails that France has a
king but only that France has a king provided that baldness is hereditary. The
prediction is thus that none of (24a)–(24d) presupposes that France has a king
but instead that they have the conditionalised (25) as their presupposition.

(25)  If baldness is hereditary, there is a king of France.

This does not capture the fact that we intuitively perceive the *France has a king*
instead of the conditionalised version as the presupposition. A proponent of
the satisfaction theory has then two options. He may either argue that such
'semantic' presuppositions are strengthened by Gricean reasoning or some
other pragmatic device. Or he may take the notion of 'semantic' or 'sentential' presupposition as a theoretical construct, appeal to a separate theory
of accommodation and argue that it is not the semantic presupposition but
something else that is accommodated (and then satisfies the 'semantic presuppositions' after all). Karttunen and Peters (1979) took the first option and
presented a Gricean argument purporting to show that presuppositions of
an implicative form are strengthened to the unconditionalised consequent.
I refer to the elaborate discussion in Geurts (1996; 1999: § 3.3). Here I just
present his argument that any account that achieves this for the cases discussed above will deliver false predictions for analogous cases where the
satisfaction account equally predicts such weakened presuppositions. Consider (26a) and (26b).

(26)  a.  If Julius had canard à l'orange, then what his wife ate
          was potato chips.
      b.  Fred knows that if Julius had canard à l'orange, then his
          wife ate something (too).
      c.  If Julius had canard à l'orange, then his wife ate
          something.

The cleft-construction in the consequent of (26a) induces the presupposition that Julius' wife ate something. The full sentence is a conditional. The
satisfaction account predicts that the presupposition that Julius' wife ate
something will be transformed to the conditional (26c). This is too weak and

asks for strengthening. Consider then (26b). The factive verb having *If Julius had canard à l'orange, then his wife ate something* as its complement induces this conditional presupposition straight away. And since this presupposition is not embedded, it is predicted to be a presupposition of the full sentence. But here, this implicative construct emerges as an intuitive presupposition. The question thus arises why we perceive the stronger presupposition in the first case but not in the latter. This is puzzling to say the least. One would expect that any (pragmatic) theory that correctly predicts strengthening of the presupposition in the first case would equally do so in the latter. And, if it does not in the latter, it is hard to see how it could do so in the former. Note that the argument is independent of the way pragmatic strengthening is argued for and note furthermore that it is equally independent of the type of presupposition inducer. The argument can easily be replicated for e.g. definite descriptions, aspectual verbs, factives, etc.

Beaver (2001), building on earlier work, adopts the second strategy, appeals to a separate theory of accommodation and argues that it is not the semantic presupposition but something else that is accommodated. The idea is that what is accommodated depends on world knowledge and involves bridging inferences. Just like Heim he takes presuppositions as the minimal conditions for the update to be defined, but – so he adds – the presupposition computed need not be the material that is accommodated. According to Beaver, we don't just accommodate the presupposition computed. Instead we accommodate whole theories. Now I won't dispute the claim that in the process of accommodation we make additional inferences which will end up as information in the resulting context. This is abundantly clear from the work of e.g. Kamp and Rossdeutscher (1994) and Kamp (2001). Nor will I dispute the claim that a presuppositional mechanism may make use of world knowledge or bridging inferences as in (27):[18]

(27)   If I go to a wedding, the rabbi will get drunk.

I am, however, rather pessimistic about the prospects of explanations that – in the course of the compositional process – transform the material triggered to a new construct and then have to save the phenomenon by adding an independent (and presumably pragmatic) theory which reinterprets the semantic transform of the triggered information to the presupposition we intuitively perceive. Anyway, such a theory has to be quite complicated. For, firstly, the problem is not confined to simple conjunctions and conditionals. And note that if we consider multiple embeddings with conditionals or conjunctions, the presupposition induced gets weakened at each further embedding. Thus (28a) is predicted to presuppose (28b).

(28)   a.   If baldness is not hereditary, then Pfizer will develop a
             cure and the king of France will sell his wig.
       b.   If baldness is not hereditary, then if Pfizer will develop a
             cure, there is a king of France.

The pragmatic theory envisaged has to explain not just the main condition-alisation but also the embedded one which conditionalises the implicative presupposition further with the proviso that Pfizer will develop a cure.

The problem gets worse if we adopt the thesis of Karttunen (1974) and Heim (1992) that attitude verbs relativise presuppositions to the beliefs of the subject of the attitude, i.e. that the sentence in (29a) does not presuppose that France has a king but (29b) i.e. that the speaker believes France has a king.

(29)  a.  John believes that the king of France is bald.
      b.  John believes that France has a king.

For when we substitute (28a) in the context of *John believes that* – (i.e. (30a)), it predicts (30b) as its sentential presupposition:

(30)  a.  John believes that if baldness is not hereditary, then
          Pfizer will develop a cure and the king of France will sell
          his wig.
      b.  John believes that if baldness is not hereditary and Pfizer
          will develop a cure, there is a king of France.

The situation thus gets worse at each further embedding and it is clearly a non-trivial task to develop a pragmatic theory which accounts for the fact that we infer from this weakened presupposition that there is a king of France or that John believes that there is a king of France.[19]

There is a further problem with weakening or conditionalisation though. Note that we may continue (31a) with e.g. 'He is a proud man.'

(31)  a.  If baldness is hereditary, the king of France wears a wig.
      b.  [France has a king . . . ] If baldness is hereditary, the king
          of France wears a wig. He is a proud man.

This is readily explained if we assume that we accommodate the unmodi-fied presupposition in the main context, thereby establishing an accessible discourse referent which allows for pronominal take-up. It is a problem for theories of pragmatic strengthening, however, for the simple reason that inferred discourse referents are not normally available as antecedents for pronouns.

Consider finally (32), which has a presuppositional reading. Again we may pick up the presupposition in subsequent sentences.

(32)  If John has grandchildren, his children will be happy. They wanted
      to have offspring long ago.

Again this is easily explained if we assume accommodation of (32) creates a discourse referent for *John's children*, i.e. that the non-presuppositional expan-sion of the first sentence in (32) would look like (33):

(33)  [John has children . . . ] If he has grandchildren, his children will be
      happy.

It is highly problematic for the satisfaction account, though. For since the presupposition computed is the tautologous *If John has grandchildren, he has children*, no pragmatic strengthening mechanism will be able to establish the stronger construct by some process of inferential reasoning.

## 17.4.2  Anaphoric binding and accommodation

The anaphoric account of presupposition is implemented in an extension of Discourse Representation Theory and has it that presuppositional expressions are anaphoric expressions on a par with pronouns. Such anaphors will search through discourse structures in order to find a suitable antecedent to link up with. But they differ from pronouns and other impoverished anaphors in a crucial respect. They have structure and carry content. It is the latter fact that accounts for their capacity to accommodate. If no proper antecedent is found, the resolution mechanism will establish a discourse marker and attach the descriptive content of the presupposition induced to it, thereby establishing a suitable antecedent after all. The account differs from the satisfaction approach in two crucial respects. Firstly, presuppositions are never transformed to weaker semantic constructs but act as entities in their own right. And these entities either hook up to some given discourse marker or create one to act as an antecedent. Secondly, the resolution algorithm treats accommodation and binding not as separate mechanisms but as two sides of the same coin.

Let me introduce the basic idea by means of two simple examples and contrast it with the accounts I discussed in the previous sections. As discussed before, in the following conditional the apodosis invokes the presuppositional information that there is a king of France, but the whole sentence makes no suggestion whatsoever as to the existence of such an individual.

(34)  If France has a king, the king of France is bald.

Nor does (35).

(35)  It is possible that France has a king and that the king of France is bald.

In the above two cases, the information that France has a king is introduced – in a non-presuppositional way – in respectively the antecedent of the conditional and the first conjunct of the modalized sentence. As to (34) Gazdar (1979) would say that the protasis invokes the implicature that there may not be a king of France, which conflicts with the potential presupposition (his proto- or pre-supposition) that there is. And, since implicatures have priority over (potential) presuppositions, the implicature cancels the latter, which will thus not be established as an actual presupposition in the main context. The same explanation goes through for (35), where we find the information that there is a king of France explicitly and non-presuppositionally encoded.

Van der Sandt (1982/1988) would say that these sentences cannot be felicitously uttered in a context which already contains the information that there is a king of France. That is, their non-presuppositional expansions are not acceptable for Gricean reasons, as (36a) and (36b) illustrate.

(36) a. *[France has a king...] If France has a king, he is bald.
    b. *[France has a king...] It is possible that France has a
       king and that he is bald.

These sentences thus cannot be interpreted over contexts that contain the information that there is a king of France. Put otherwise, this information cannot be accommodated.

Karttunen and Heim would say that the presupposition induced in the apodosis of (34) is entailed by its antecedent. It is thus satisfied by the antecedent and accommodation either does not ensue or is otiose.[20]

According to the anaphoric account of presupposition, the protasis of the conditional establishes a discourse marker for the king of France. The presupposition triggered by the apodosis will search for a suitable antecedent and link up to the information thus introduced. Presuppositions have the same function as pronouns. Pronominalising the descriptions in (34) and (35) yields more idiomatic rephrasings (37a) and (37b) in which the pronouns are bound to the indefinites that serve as their antecedent.

(37) a. If France has a king, he is bald.
    b. It is possible that France has a king and that he is bald.

The phenomenon that presuppositions can be bound by established antecedents is not limited to descriptive phrases but turns out to be quite general. If we find a presuppositional expression that depends on some previously introduced entity, there is normally a more idiomatic counterpart that features anaphoric expressions that are more scantily dressed. The following illustrates this for two other types of presupposition inducers: factive verbs and verbs of transition.

(38) a. If the king of France is bald, his wife will regret *that/that*
      *he is bald*.
    b. If John used to smoke, he stopped *doing so/smoking*.

Just as in (34) and (37), the relevant information is introduced at a subordinate (and accessible) level of discourse structure. The presuppositional information links up to this information, just as pronouns do.

Let us come back to the explanation. Presupposition inducers are regular anaphoric expressions on a par with pronouns and other descriptively impoverished anaphors. This comprises simple and composite descriptions like 'the king of France', 'the boy who kissed all girls' and 'the minder of my neighbour's dog'; it also comprises cleft constructions, verbs of transition (*begin*, *stop*, *continue*), adverbs like *too* and *again*, factive verbs (*regret*, *be surprised*, *discover*) and many others. All these expressions induce information that has to be resolved in context. More specifically, they search for an accessible antecedent. This antecedent may be given at the main level (which is always accessible) or at some subordinate accessible position. In the cases just given, they find their antecedents at a subordinate level, where they resolve just like regular pronouns.

In the examples (34) and (35) the accessible context contains an explicit antecedent. The question arises, what happens if this is not the case, e.g. when we utter (39a) or (39b) or the pronominalized (40a) or (40b).

(39)  a.  If baldness is hereditary, the king of France will wear a
          wig.
      b.  It is possible that baldness is hereditary and that the
          king of France wears a wig.

(40)  a.  If baldness is hereditary, he will wear a wig.
      b.  It is possible that baldness is hereditary and that he
          wears a wig.

In neither case does the anaphoric expression find a suitable antecedent. But here we see a crucial difference. (40a) and (40b) will not get a determinate interpretation, but (39a) and (39b) will be truth-evaluable. The reason is that presuppositions differ from pronouns in that they have semantic content of their own. This accounts for their capacity to accommodate. In case a pronoun does not succeed in finding an antecedent, discourse will come to a halt. However, presuppositional expressions will normally contain enough descriptive content to establish an antecedent if discourse does not already provide one. A discourse referent will be accommodated, and the information triggered will be attached to this entity, which can thus serve as a suitable antecedent after all. Sentences (41a) and (41b) show the (non-presuppositional) expansions of (39a) and (39b).

(41)  a.  [France has a king ... ] If baldness is hereditary, he will
          wear a wig.
      b.  [France has a king ... ] It is possible that baldness is
          hereditary and that he wears a wig.

This illustrates the main difference between presuppositional expressions and pronouns. If a pronoun cannot find an antecedent, the sentence will not get an interpretation for the simple reason that the resolution algorithm does not complete. However, sentences containing presupposition inducers will, under the same condition, normally get a determinate value.

The account given below is formulated in a presuppositional extension of Discourse Representation Theory. I will limit myself to a rough outline and refer the reader for detailed expositions to the work of Kamp (1981) and Kamp and Reyle (1993), and for the presuppositional extension to van der Sandt and Geurts (1991), van der Sandt (1992) and Geurts (1999). Presuppositional DRT differs from standard DRT in three crucial respects. Firstly, anaphoric expressions are not resolved on-line. Instead the construction algorithm yields a structure that is not yet truth-evaluable but is provisional in the sense that anaphoric expressions wait for resolution. Secondly, resolution of anaphoric expressions is taken care of by a separate mechanism, the resolution algorithm. Finally, both pronouns and presuppositional expressions, being anaphoric expressions with internal structure and semantic content, are encoded as complex conditions which are marked by means of a $\partial$ operator to indicate their anaphoric nature. The presuppositional frame of a pronoun is simply $[x \mid \ ]$;[21] the information invoked by regular presupposition inducers carries additional constraints. For example, the presuppositional frame for 'the queen of the Netherlands' comes with an extra condition $[x|\textbf{queen\_of\_the\_netherlands}(x)]$.[22] Thus, if the incoming discourse lacks an accessible antecedent, the descriptive content associated with the presuppositional expression will allow a cooperative recipient to establish a discourse marker and attach the associated constraints to it; the resulting entity may then function as an antecedent for the presuppositional anaphor. This process also captures our intuition that (42a) is presupposing: the sentence requires the presuppositional information for its interpretation. For (42b) there is no such requirement. The first clause introduces, explicitly and non-presuppositionally, the information that France has a king and thus provides an antecedent – just as it happens in the discourse (42c).

(42)  a.  The king of France is bald.
      b.  France has a king and the *king of France/he* is bald.
      c.  France has a king. The *king of France/he* is bald.

The resolution of (43), the provisional DRS for (42a), illustrates the accommodation mechanism.

$$(43) \quad \left[ \ \left| \begin{array}{l} \textbf{bald}(x) \\ \partial \left[ x \mid \textbf{kf}(x) \right] \end{array} \right. \right]$$

This structure resolves to (44):

$$(44) \quad \left[ x \mid \textbf{kf}(x), \textbf{bald}(x) \right]$$

Note that the universe of the provisional DRS (43) is empty – just as in the case of the provisional DRS for its pronominalised counterpart. But (43) differs from the pronominalised version in that the anaphoric condition does not just consist of a bare variable, but comes with the information that this variable should satisfy the condition $\textbf{kf}(x)$. The discourse referent comes about by accommodation and during this process the associated conditions are transferred to the level where the discourse referent is entered in the DRS, thus establishing a proper antecedent for future anaphors to bind to. Note, moreover, that the DRS so obtained is identical to the DRS that would result from processing (42b) or the discourse (42c). The output is the same, but (42a), which is intuitively presupposing, differs from the other examples in that this sentence requires for its interpretation the information that there is a king of France, whereas in the non-presupposing variants no accommodation is called for since the relevant information is explicitly given.

The examples just given illustrate the phenomenon of global accommodation, i.e. accommodation of the presupposition in the main context. However, when logical operators intervene, we perceive a succession of context. Accommodation may then take place in each of the contexts that are accessible from the site of the trigger. Non-global accommodation comes in two variants. The material may be locally accommodated, i.e. the triggered material will be accommodated in the (sub)-DRS where it is triggered. Or it may find a landing site somewhere along the accessibility line between the main context and the site where it originates.

I illustrate these two options in turn. Consider the negation of (42a). The provisional DRS is (45):

$$(45) \quad \left[\ \middle|\ \neg \left[\ \middle|\ \begin{array}{l} \mathsf{bald}(x) \\ \partial\,[x\ |\ \mathsf{kf}(x)] \end{array} \right]\ \right]$$

The negation operator creates a sub-DRS, which contains the presuppositional anaphor. This anaphor will search along its accessibility path for an antecedent to bind to, but just as in (43) it will not find one. The discourse thus has to be saved by accommodation. The first option is the main context. Entering the discourse marker with the presuppositional constraint at top level gives (46):

$$(46) \quad [x\ |\ \mathsf{kf}(x),\ \neg\,[\ |\ \mathsf{bald}(x)]\,]$$

The description has primary occurrence, to put it in the Russellian way. In present-day discourse, this reading will be blocked, however, since it is in conflict with background knowledge. But, given the fact that the description is at a subordinate level, there is a second option: accommodation in the – equally accessible – subordinate structure, i.e. within the scope of the negation operator. This yields the structure where the description has secondary occurrence:

$$(47) \quad [\ |\ \neg\,[x\ |\ \mathsf{kf}(x),\ \mathsf{bald}(x)]\,]$$

In short, the resolution mechanism produces the two readings a Russellian gets – in a purely syntactic way – by the interaction of quantifiers and operators.[23] But in the current framework, we get an additional prediction: on the reading where we accommodate the descriptive phrase in the main context, the sentence is predicted to presuppose that France has a king, just as Frege and Strawson would have it.

Let us turn to some examples of intermediate accommodation. When operators are iterated, we find many uncontroversial examples of intermediate readings as Kripke's (48) shows:

(48)   The number of planets might have been necessarily even.

The classical account by means of Russellian scope gives three possible read-ings. The description may outscope both modal operators. This yields a read-ing according to which the sentence is false. Narrow scope of the description also gives a false reading. The true reading (49) shows intermediate scope and yields truth:[24]

(49)  $\Diamond \exists! x [\text{number\_planets}(x) \land \Box \, \text{even}(x)]$

At the end of the previous section I pointed out that the account of presup-position which views presuppositions as regular anaphors gives us Russellian scope as a bonus.[25] It encodes the descriptive phrase as a standard presup-position inducer,

(50)  $\partial [x \mid \text{number\_planets}(x)]$

which yields (51) as the pre-structure for (48):

(51)  $\left[ \mid \Diamond \left[ \mid \Box \left[ \mid \genfrac{}{}{0pt}{}{\text{even}(x),}{\partial [x \mid \text{number\_planets}(x)]} \right] \right] \right]$

The anaphoric expression will look upwards along its accessibility path and search for an antecedent to bind to. Since no such antecedent will be found, the presuppositional information has to be accommodated. The accommo-dation mechanism gives us – in principle – the option of projecting the presuppositional structure to any of the three Russellian positions (all of which are accessible). The first option is accommodation at the top level of discourse structure (the main context). This yields the reading according to which the description has scope over both embedding operators:

(52)  $[x \mid \text{number\_planets}(x), \Diamond [ \mid \Box [ \mid \text{even}(x)]]]$

But since background knowledge tells us that this reading is false, it will be blocked. Background knowledge will also block the narrow-scope reading of the description. This leaves us with intermediate scope. Put more suc-cinctly, the syntactic base generates (51) and the resolution algorithm maps it to (53):

(53)  $[ \mid \Diamond [x \mid \text{number\_planets}(x), \Box [ \mid \text{even}(x)]]]$

Though non-controversial examples which show intermediate scope are ubiquitous (iteration of attitude verbs, modal operators, logical connectives and various mixtures), there has been some opposition to the idea of inter-mediate accommodation.[26] Accommodation – so the alternative story goes – is not a structural operation at the level of logical form, it is a global process which is handled by pragmatics at a metalevel. It is a process which, in the face of threatening infelicity, forces a cooperative recipient to revise his view on the incoming context and thus modifies the global incoming context by inserting missing material in order to guarantee felicity after all. This view has a number of serious drawbacks, some of which I discussed in section

17.4.1. There is a technical problem as well. It turns out to be very difficult to explain this view in non-metaphorical terms.[27] Then, there is a methodological problem. Rejection of intermediate (and local) accommodation forces the analyst to supplement his (global) accommodation mechanism with an additional Russellian scope mechanism to account for cases which could be handled by the projection mechanism straight away. Ockham certainly would object.

There is a third problem, though. On the account of presupposition I just sketched, presuppositional binding and accommodation are two sides of the same coin. Presuppositional expressions can be bound by a suitable antecedent provided that they occur in an accessible position. And, going in the other direction, they may accommodate an antecedent in any position from where this antecedent can access and thus bind the presuppositional anaphor. Since this account is implemented in a dynamic theory of meaning, it gives an extra option. As I pointed out in the previous section, dynamic theories allow for semantic binding from the antecedent of a conditional into its consequent, and from the restrictor of a quantifier into its nuclear scope. This gives an additional accommodation possibility, the restrictor of a quantifier (or the antecedent of a conditional), an option which was not available on Russell's account.[28]

Examples of restrictor accommodation abound. Quine noted as early as 1941 that (54) is not to be construed as meaning that Tai is always eating and using chopsticks when doing so. It is more likely to mean that whenever Tai eats he does so with chopsticks.

(54)   Tai always eats with chopsticks.

As Quine puts it: the unwanted representation suggests gluttony, the proper representation daintiness (Quine 1965: 91).

Many more examples are found in the literature on generics, focus and presupposition projection. Presuppositional – and in general backgrounded – information tends to be interpreted in the restrictor of quantified structures, as Schubert and Pelletier's (1989) work on generics amply testifies. In (55a), the relevant cats quantified over are cats that are somehow in the air; the proper interpretation of (55b) does not pertain to the majority of Californians but only to the voting ones; and (55c), finally, suggests in no way that each visitor carries a cell phone but only applies to visitors who carry one.

(55)   a.   Cats always land on their feet.
       b.   Most Californians voted for Schwarzenegger.
       c.   All visitors should leave their cell phone with the
            security officers.

Since (55a) and (55b) involve some additional complications relating to tense and focus, I illustrate the mechanism with respect to (55c).[29] The syntactic base generates (56):

$$(56) \quad \left[ \left| \left[x \mid \mathsf{visitor}(x)\right] \binom{\forall}{x} \right. \left[ \left| \partial \left[ y \middle| \begin{matrix} \mathsf{leave}(x, y) \\ \mathsf{phone}(y) \\ \mathsf{poss}(z, y) \\ \partial\,[z\,|\,] \end{matrix} \right] \right] \right] \right]$$

Note that the presuppositional frame for the descriptive phrase embeds the representation of the pronoun. The full structure resolves in two phases. Resolution starts with the most deeply embedded anaphoric expression, i.e. $\partial[z\,|\,]$, which equates $z$ with the quantified referent $x$ in the restrictor, yielding:

$$(57) \quad \left[ \left| \left[x \mid \mathsf{visitor}(x)\right] \binom{\forall}{x} \right. \left[ \left| \partial \left[ y \middle| \begin{matrix} \mathsf{leave}(x, y) \\ \mathsf{phone}(y) \\ \mathsf{poss}(x, y) \end{matrix} \right] \right] \right] \right]$$

The pronoun is thus bound, but the anaphoric variable of its embedder will not find a proper antecedent and thus has to be accommodated. The general rule is that accommodation takes place as high as possible, i.e. preferably in the main DRS. In the present case, this possibility is blocked since $x$ is entered in the restrictor and accommodating $\mathsf{poss}(x, y)$ at top level would leave $x$ free in this condition.[30] We thus accommodate one level lower along its accessibility path, entering the information in the restrictor. This gives (58) as output:

$$(58) \quad \left[ \left| \left[ x, y \middle| \begin{matrix} \mathsf{visitor}(x) \\ \mathsf{phone}(y), \mathsf{poss}(x, y) \end{matrix} \right] \binom{\forall}{x} \left[ \left| \mathsf{leave}(x, y) \right] \right] \right]$$

In the last example, I illustrated the presuppositional mechanism with respect to a dependent possessive phrase – a species of open descriptive phrases. But, as I said before, the mechanism is generally applicable to any kind of anaphoric expression. So let me conclude with a perhaps unexpected example – tense. In (59) the temporal information, which is syntactically induced in the nuclear scope of the quantificational adverb, ends up in the restrictor.[31]

(59)   Floppy was always on the run.

Again, this is readily explained if we adopt Partee's (1973) suggestion that verb tenses should be treated as a kind of pronoun. In the present framework, this comes down to encoding the tense morpheme as a presuppositional expression consisting of an anaphoric variable and an associated temporal constraint. Assuming that the main DRS contains an indexical constant $n$ for the moment of utterance, the past tense is represented as follows:

(60)   $\partial \left[ t \mid t < n \right]$

The syntax thus generates (61b) for (61a):

(61)   a.   Floppy was on the run.

     b.   $\left[ \; \left| \begin{array}{l} \textbf{flop\_run}(t), \\ \partial[t \mid t<n] \end{array} \right. \right]$

Combining this with $[t \mid] \binom{\forall}{t}[\,|\,]$, the frame for the presuppositional adverb yields (62) as the pre-structure for (60):

(62)   $\left[ n \; \left| \; [t \mid]\binom{\forall}{t} \left[ \; \left| \begin{array}{l} \textbf{flop\_run}(t'), \\ \partial[t' \mid t' < n] \end{array} \right. \right] \right. \right]$

Note that the temporal information is encoded in the place where it syntactically originates. However, in the course of the resolution process the temporal information percolates upwards along its accessibility path. But, after being bound by the quantified variable, it is intercepted in the restrictor, resulting in (63):

(63)   $[n \mid [t \mid t < n]\binom{\forall}{t}[\,| \, \textbf{flop\_run}(t)]\,]$

This keeps syntax as simple as possible. For just like other presuppositional information, temporal information is generated in situ, i.e. the place where we syntactically find it (normally the morphology of the verb). The phenomenon that verb tenses tend to link up to contextually given temporal locations and the tendency to take wide scope in case no prior temporal information is given are accounted for by their anaphoric nature.

Let us take stock. Presuppositional expressions are anaphoric expressions on a par with pronouns and other attenuated anaphors and thus need to be resolved in context. This can happen in either of two ways. Firstly, the anaphoric variable of a presuppositional frame may be equated with some discourse marker that it can reach along its accessibility path. If it links up to such a marker (which will thereby serve as its antecedent), the associated conditions will be attached to the binding site and the antecedent will thus inherit all descriptive material the presuppositional expression carries. If no such antecedent can be found, the presuppositional information will (normally) be accommodated at some accessible level, thus creating an accessible antecedent after all.[32]

# 18

# Negation

Jay David Atlas

## 18.1 Introduction

1. The moral of the semantical non-specificity of negative "not" sentences in ordinary language is that their indeterminate univocality permits the realization in utterers' meanings of a range of meanings, including exclusion (sentence) negations and even exclusion negations of exclusion negations, choice negations, and forms of meta-linguistic negations, however syntactically encoded.

2. Only in the last few years has it been possible to answer adequately Horn's (1989) criticism of the Atlas–Kempson Thesis, viz. the thesis that "not" sentences are semantically non-specific rather than lexically or scope ambiguous. Horn's (1989) criticism was dependent on the evidence of negative polarity item (NPI) data discussed in sections 18.5 and 18.6 below. Horn's (2002, 2009a) recent discussions of NPI licensing by "downward assertion" rather than "downward entailment" obviates his earlier syntactico-semantic criticism of the Atlas–Kempson thesis and leaves the thesis a viable even if still controversial analysis of "not" sentences in a natural language.

3. Semantical non-specificity is not the only alternative to the ambiguity of "not" sentences. In order to defend its viability, a comparison with Horn's (1989) alternative to the Atlas–Kempson thesis, his account of an Aristotelian extended term logic, needs to be considered.

4. This essay takes the view that the semantical non-specificity thesis is the only view of "not" sentences that makes pragmatic inference essential to every interpretation of utterances of "not" sentences, removes the unmotivated asymmetry in the application of Gricean implicatures to negative sentence-strings (Atlas 1979), offers a perspective on the "logic" of natural language – the topic is negation, after all – that is not found elsewhere among devotees of semantical underdeterminacy, provides a theoretical foundation for new research in the cognitive science of visual

illusions and semantic processing of sentences,[1] as well as provides a novel perspective from which to assess the controversies between the semantical underdeterminists and the minimal semanticists.[2]

## 18.2  What is a negation statement? The inheritance from the Aristotelian logical tradition

We owe to the tradition from Aristotle a number of crucial assumptions about negative words and phrases in natural languages. Aristotle's (1963) *De Interpretatione*, in the Ackrill translation, begins, "First we must settle what a name is and what a verb is, and then what a negation, an affirmation, a statement [a sentence that is true or false] and a sentence are." And at 17a25: "An *affirmation* is a statement affirming something of something, a *negation* is a statement denying something of something." Then he introduces the notions of contradictory and contrary statements – a pair of statements, if their English translations have no indefinite-subject noun phrases (there is no indefinite article in Greek), are *contradictory* if and only if they have opposite truth values from the set {TRUE, FALSE}, and a pair of statements are *contrary* if and only if they cannot both be true but can both be false. He gives examples like the contraries "every man is just" and "no man is just," the non-contraries "a man is just" and "a man is not just," the contradictories "every man is just" and "not every man is just," the contradictories "some man is just" and "no man is just," and the contradictories "Socrates is just" and "Socrates is not just."

Combinations of "not" with a common noun like "man" in "Not man" is not a name, a phrase, or a negation; it is an "indefinite name." Negative verb phrases like "does not recover" or "does not ail," translated by Ross as "ails-not," are not called "verbs" but "indefinite verbs" because they hold of things whether those things exist or not. (For Aristotle a verb is a verbal expression that signifies the present time when uttered.) The terminology of "indefinite verb" is also misleading in that Aristotle usually intends to indicate that a statement containing an indefinite verb denies something definite rather than affirms something indefinite. Similarly Aristotle creates negative adjectives, e.g. "not-just." This creates a problem of interpretation, as in *Prior Analytics* he treats the negative adjective *not-F* as the same as the privative adjective *unF*, but in *Categories* he treats *not-F* as sometimes *un-F* and sometimes *some property between F and unF*, which he thinks is true of "not-just." In some passages in *De Interpretatione* he is clear that "is not just," the denial of "just," does not entail "is not-just," but in other passages he seems unclear. We will return to discuss this kind of *Term Negation* later in this chapter.

In *De Interpretatione* Aristotle has introduced the notion of a statement being true or being false, distinguished between ambiguities of the scope of the adverb "necessarily" so that a statement that is necessarily either true or false differs from a statement that is necessarily true or necessarily false, and recognized semantic distinctions arising from the syntactical distinctions in the scope of the free negative morpheme 'not' ['$ov$' in Greek].

In *Metaphysics* Γ Aristotle states a version of what we know as the classical law of non-contradiction. In its formal, linguistic version: that a sentence containing "and" and "not" in the example *Paul is wise and Paul is not wise*, having the logical form $\ulcorner \Phi \wedge \neg \Phi \urcorner$, must be false. (That assumes the classical principle of bivalence, that each sentence $\Phi$ has exactly one of the two truth values TRUE, FALSE.) Hence, $\ulcorner \neg(\Phi \wedge \neg \Phi) \urcorner$ must be a semantically valid (logically true) schema, i.e. $\vDash \neg(\Phi \wedge \neg \Phi)$, where $\vDash$ stands for "it is true that."

Let us suppose that we have a set of sentences Γ and sentence A such that Γ ∪ {A} (the union of Γ [gamma] and {A}) entails the negation of B, i.e. Γ, A $\vDash \neg$ B. Then the set of sentences Γ ∪ {A,B} will entail a contradictory sentence and, on Aristotle's view of non-contradiction, the sentence is a logical falsehood $\ulcorner (B \wedge \neg B) \urcorner$. Since that means that the set of sentences Γ ∪ {A,B} is not satisfiable (i.e. its sentences cannot all be true), if we assume as premises the sentences of Γ, and B, then the negation of A must be true, i.e. Γ, B $\vDash \neg$A. What I have just described is a form of reasoning that was essential to classical Greek mathematics, known as *reductio ad absurdum*. If one reasons correctly to a contradiction, which is a necessary falsehood, at least one of the premises must be untrue (and in a bivalent language, false). *Reductio* reasoning allows the introduction of a negative sentence as the conclusion of the reasoning. So, assuming non-contradiction – that a sentence contradictory in form cannot be true – and *reductio* reasoning, we have a form of contraposition that is classically valid; the symbolism below is read 'if the sentences in set Γ and the sentence A together logically imply ¬B, then Γ,B will logically imply ¬A':

$$\frac{\Gamma, A \vDash \neg B}{\Gamma, B \vDash \neg A} \quad (Cp)$$

This is the form of "contraposition," as this kind of reasoning was known to the Stoic logicians (and earlier noted by Aristotle in *Topics*), that I adopted in Atlas (2001) in order to generalize from the logic of statements to a logical typology of negative quantifier noun phrases.[3] From the reflexivity of the logical consequence relation $\vDash$, viz. for any A, A $\vDash$ A, and from contraposition (Cp), it is immediate that Modest (i.e. *constructive*) double negation obtains:

A $\vDash \neg\neg$A. (MDN)

This corresponds to an introduction rule for double negation in natural deduction systems; Gentzen took introduction rules to characterize essentially the meaning of a sentential connective. (Notice that both classical logicians and Brouwerian intuitionists (mathematical constructivists) would accept this form of double negation. What is controversial between them is

the converse principle corresponding to a rule of double negation elimination.) The more traditional statement of contraposition in elementary logic
would be:

$$\frac{A \vDash B}{\neg B \vDash \neg A}$$   (Cp traditional)

This meta-argument characterizes what A. Hazen in 1994 – see Dunn (1996) –
called "subminimal negation." The reflexivity of the logical consequence
relation is obviously not sufficient to produce from the traditional form of
contraposition even the modest double negation. I chose a form of contraposition (Cp) – a *constructive contraposition* – that implied the introduction rule
for double negation, thereby being a sufficiently "negative" form of negation. Assuming Aristotle's view of the basic character of non-contradiction,
and the *reductio* reasoning canonized by Pythagoras and Euclid, the negation of a statement is essentially characterized by contraposition (Cp). If
contraposition does not hold, the statement involved is not, in my view,
a negation.[4]

## 18.3 Negation and presupposition: Gottlob Frege, Bertrand Russell, and Peter Strawson

Frege (1970: 69) claims that:

> If anything is asserted there is always an obvious presupposition that the
> simple or compound proper names used have reference. If one therefore
> asserts "Kepler died in misery," there is a presupposition that the name
> "Kepler" designates something; but it does not follow that the sense of
> the sentence "Kepler died in misery" contains the thought that the name
> "Kepler" designates something. If this were the case the negation would
> have to run not:
>
> Kepler did not die in misery
>
> But:
>
> Kepler did not die in misery, or the name "Kepler" has no reference.
>
> That the name "Kepler" designates something is just as much a presupposi-
> tion for the assertion:
>
> Kepler died in misery
>
> as for the contrary assertion.

In this passage Frege claims that the presupposition of an assertion and of
its main-verb negation are the same, and he offers an argument to support
the claim. It is evident from his argument that the notion of "P contains

a thought Q" was assumed by Frege to be representable by "P contains a conjunct Q" or by "P directly entails Q." (The notion of "direct entailment" is, roughly, the entailment of a sub-formula.) In the case of the negative assertion "Not P," it was obvious to him that the Fregean senses (the truth conditions) of "Not P" and "Not P ∨ Not Q" were not the same, so long as "Not Q" did not entail "Not P." That condition would be guaranteed if " 'Kepler' has no reference" did not entail "Kepler did not die in misery." But what insures that the non-entailment obtains?

If the negative sentence "Kepler did not die in misery" is interpreted as an exclusion negation (van Fraassen 1971), paraphrased in English by "It is not the case that Kepler died in misery," a vacuous singular term in the complement clause might be thought to yield for the negative statement the value TRUE (rather than no truth value at all as Frege might have thought, were "Kepler" to lack a reference). Since the exclusion negation $\ulcorner\neg\Phi\urcorner$ of a statement $\Phi$ is true in a valuation if and only if $\Phi$ is not true, even if $\Phi$ is not true because it is neither true nor false, $\ulcorner\neg\Phi\urcorner$ will be true. But then there is an entailment of "Kepler did not die in misery" by "'Kepler' has no reference," and Frege's argument, which supports the claim that statements and their main-verb negations that contain singular terms share the presupposition that the terms are referentially non-vacuous, fails!

Thus Frege's argument requires that the main-verb negation not be an exclusion negation but a choice negation (van Fraassen 1971). The choice negation $\ulcorner\sim\Phi\urcorner$ of a statement $\Phi$ is true (false) in a valuation if and only if $\Phi$ is false (true). If the choice negation is paraphrased in English by "Kepler did not die in misery," and were "Kepler" to have no reference, one's intuition would be that the choice negation is not true. So Frege's argument survives. But it survives on the assumption that the negative, ordinary-language sentence expresses a choice negation, typically a narrow-scope negation, not an exclusion negation, typically a wide-scope negation. The choice negation permits a failure of truth-value for a statement with a false (not-true) presupposition, but an exclusion negation will be true even though a presupposition is not true, as we have seen. For these reasons van Fraassen (1971) formalizes the semantical notion of presupposition, viz. that A semantically presupposes B if and only if the falsity of B entails that A is neither true nor false, by the claim that A implies (in some sense) B and ∼A implies (in the same sense) B. The formalization uses choice negation, but it commits a theorist of semantical presupposition to the lexical or scope ambiguity of "not" in ordinary language. Bertrand Russell (1905, 1919b) and Whitehead and Russell (1910) also assume that "not" (or "nicht") sentences are ambiguous.

In the theory of definite descriptions, Russell parses "The most famous student of Tycho Brahe did not die in misery" in two ways in classical logical forms, one in which the Boolean complement negation applies to the predicate, so that it has a narrow scope, and one in which the negation applies to the sentence, so that it has wide scope, as in (1) and (2) respectively.

(1) a. The most famous student of Tycho Brahe did not die in misery.
    b. $\exists x ( (Sx \land \forall y(Sy \to y{=}x)) \land \neg Dx)$
    c. There is at least and at most one individual who is a famous student of Tycho Brahe and he/she/it is a non-dier in misery.
(2) a. The most famous student of Tycho Brahe did not die in misery.
    b. $\neg \exists x ( (Sx \land \forall y(Sy \to y{=}x)) \land Dx)$
    c. It is not the case that there is at least and at most one individual who is a famous student of Tycho Brahe and he/she/it is a dier in misery.

For the linguist there are two assumptions in the above reasoning that are worth emphasizing. The first assumption is that a sentence like "It is not the case that Kepler died in misery" expresses univocally in English the exclusion negation interpretation of the sentence. It was pointed out by Atlas (1974) and Kuroda (1977: 105) that this is an incorrect description of the English sentence, which may express the choice negation or the exclusion negation. It is not a presupposition-free sentence by virtue of its meaning; for discussion see Horn (1989: 365). The second assumption is that the negative English sentence is ambiguous between the two negations in (1) and (2).

## 18.4 The Atlas–Kempson thesis (1975): 'Not' is semantically univocal and non-specific for scope

It was first argued, at roughly the same time, in Atlas (1974) and in Ruth Kempson's University of London Ph.D. dissertation, and published in Atlas (1975a, 1977) and Kempson (1975, 1988), that the negative English sentence with the free morpheme "not" was semantically non-specific rather than semantically ambiguous. Both Atlas and Kempson employed ambiguity tests, canonically discussed in Zwicky and Sadock (1975), to argue in support of this novel, indeed, radical linguistic conclusion. Its radical character was discussed in a Colloquium Lecture "Presupposition and Grice's Pragmatics," given in the Department of Phonetics and Linguistics, University College London, in May 1978 and published in Atlas (1979).[5] Its radical implication for semantical theories of presupposition was easy, if people were not always eager, to see. Frege's account of presupposition had required, as had van Fraassen's (1971) formalization of Strawson's (1950) account, that there be an ambiguity in the negative sentence between exclusion and choice negation. If there was no such ambiguity in the English sentence, the accounts were incorrect as explanations of sentence-meanings. In Strawson's (1950) original paper "On Referring," he had committed himself to the view that a negative English sentence like "The king of France is not bald" was univocal, but he took it that it expressed only the choice negation, narrow-scope meaning, by which he would have meant at the time that its rule of use allowed only the expression of a narrow-scope negation statement. That, too, was an incorrect account of negative sentences.

## 18.5   Implications of the Atlas–Kempson Thesis for pragmatics

Atlas and Kempson's 1975 semantic arguments made it clear – as did the arguments of Boër and Lycan (1976) – that only pragmatic theories of presupposition would be adequate explanations, and only if they recognized as part of the theories the semantical univocality and non-specificity of the negative, definite description sentences. The pragmatic theory of Robert Stalnaker (1974) and others was argued to be inadequate (Atlas 1975a; 1975b; 2004a), so only Gricean and related theories were viable, e.g. Sperber and Wilson's (1986) Relevance Theory and ancillary work by Blakemore (1987, 1992), Carston (2002), and Iten (2005), and most recently Philipp Koralus' (2010) "Open Instruction Theory," which utilizes views of sentence-processing and mental representation from Johnson-Laird's (1983) mental models.

The Atlas–Kempson thesis remains controversial. Some of the linguistic judgments are subtle, but despite various critiques over the years, including questions about the formulation of the ambiguity tests, I have not encountered criticism that avoided various errors of understanding or would not succumb to trivial reformulations of the arguments offered by Atlas and Kempson.

The criticisms by Pieter Seuren (1985: 260–6) are among the most discerning of the lot – he does catch his opponents, even Kempson (1975), in ill-considered claims against the ambiguity of "not," but his complaints were against the classical Griceans' attempt to make exclusion negation the only semantic account of "not." I was then and remain a critic of such a position, even though, as a methodological principle of classical Gricean pragmatics I held the position in Atlas (1974, 1975a) and abandoned it even as a plausible methodological principle in Atlas (1975b, 1979) – the latter noted by Seuren (1985: 263). The point is that agreeing with Seuren that "not" is not identical with exclusion negation does not commit one to his view that the "best explanation" of different presupposition-preserving and presupposition-canceling *uses* of "not" is a trivalent logic! There is a tendency in Seuren to dismiss intuitive grammaticality or acceptability judgments generated by Chomskyan ambiguity tests (Zwicky and Sadock 1975) and a tendency to accept intuitive judgments of truth and falsity of utterances instead. Then he uncritically employs the Fregean principle that differences of reference entail differences of sense to yield ambiguities from judgments about truth values (Seuren 1985: 261). One might as well argue that "we" is ambiguous in sense because Queen Victoria could have said truly of herself in a situation "We are amused" but in the same situation said falsely of herself and Prince Albert "We are amused." Seuren evidently believes that judgments of truth value are more reliable than judgments of acceptability or grammaticality, reversing the Fregean view that a grasp of the sense of a sentence precedes a judgment of its truth value.

The linguistic motivation for Seuren's three-valued logic for presuppositional sentences, with two negation truth-functions, as contrasted with a Gricean approach, is dependent on his review of data on "un-", "not all," factive sentences, cleft and pseudo-cleft sentences, contrastive stress, and "not" within lower clauses (Seuren 1985: 230–5). All these data have been given Gricean analyses by Atlas (1975a), Atlas and Levinson (1981), and Horn (1989). The remaining class of data contains sentences with polarity items, but crucial examples are simply incorrectly described as having presuppositions.

Many of Seuren's data are not relevant, since the dispute is over the free negative morpheme "not." Seuren puts emphasis on his linguistic intuitions for two example-types of contrastive stress, his claim that "Joe does NOT mind that his boss is an alcoholic: the man ISN'T an alcoholic" is a logical contradiction, and his claim that "She was NOT delighted that Jim had been saved: Jim had NOT been saved" is a logically consistent utterance; the implication of the data is supposed to be that some negatives irreducibly preserve presuppositions while other negatives allow their cancellation. He claims that Gricean pragmatics cannot plausibly explain the alleged differences in the data. If it is *obvious* to you that the first utterance is self-contradictory, and that the unstressed "Joe does not mind that his boss is an alcoholic" necessarily entails "Joe's boss is an alcoholic" (by contrast with the contraction "Joe doesn't mind that his boss is an alcoholic," a different case), then I suppose you would be sympathetic with Seuren's intuitions about truth values, agree with Seuren that different "ways of using" a negative exist, and that those ways *should be explained by two truth-functionally distinct connectives* in a three-valued logic, "on grounds of simplicity and because no reasonable alternative has been presented so far" (Seuren 1985: 234)!

As a native speaker of American English, it is just as "obvious" to me that the two examples can both be consistent utterances; they do not need different explanations. Moreover, it is a consequence of my non-specificity theory, combined with Gricean pragmatics, that with the same stress on "not" but with a different intonation, one could also understand the first example to be inconsistent (as Seuren thinks). What Seuren (1985) cannot explain is precisely that range of uses and that range of judgments of truth value. One might think that it is a bit anachronistic to comment on Seuren's 1985 book, but in his recent book Seuren (2010: 334–41) appeals to exactly the same data with exactly the same arguments and conclusions.

But the 1985 book contains a brilliantly perceptive passage that I must quote (Seuren 1985: 264):

> If *not* is ambiguous in English or in any other language, it is so between two closely related logico-semantic operators and not between a random pair of meanings, as in the case of *board* or *bank*. As ambiguities go, therefore, the ambiguity of *not*, if real, is highly idiosyncratic. Then, it must not be forgotten that we do not really claim that *not* is ambiguous

or homonymous, for what is to be regarded as Radical *not* [Seuren's truth-function for presupposition-cancelling negation and meta-linguistic negation, which is only a speech-act negation, unembedded] is invariably marked by a special intonation on itself as well as on the surrounding verbal material. Thirdly, and this is the crucial part of the defence, given the principles and structure involved in the discourse-bound semantic processing of utterances of natural language, there is no need for any natural language to distinguish the two negations formally. The discourse is always such that it does the disambiguating for you, so to speak.

Seuren (1985: 263) accuses the classical Griceans of being inconsistent. One could be excused for wondering just what Seuren was claiming here. Is "not" ambiguous or isn't it? But I think the tension in the passage is just right. The resolution, like the resolution of whether Schrödinger's cat is alive or dead, whether the physical state is "ambiguous" between the two, is to say, as in the quantum-mechanical case, that "not" is not ambiguous but is instead semantically non-specific between the two interpretations, the non-specificity being thought of as a superposition of several semantic "wave functions." That is one way to conceive of what its semantic non-specificity consists in. Such is the resolution that I would recommend for the apparent contradictions expressed in this perceptive passage.

The semantic non-specificity of the negative sentence gave Gricean pragmatics something to do; it produced both the choice negation and the exclusion negation interpretations of the uttered sentences from collateral information in the context of utterance and from the semantically non-specific sentence-type meaning (Atlas 1979, 2004a, 2005). If the sentence were ambiguous, the circumstances of utterance – the context – would dictate a *choice* (or perhaps not) of one of the senses for an appropriate, literal, interpretation of the utterance. If the sentence were semantically non-specific with respect to the scope of negation, the circumstances of utterance – the context – would dictate (or perhaps merely permit) a *construction* of one of the utterance interpretations for an appropriate literal interpretation of the utterance. The construction of the utterance interpretation was explained by inferences of a familiar Gricean sort (Grice 1975, Atlas and Levinson 1981, Horn 1984b, Grice 1989, Horn 1989, Levinson 2000, Atlas 2005). There were the constraints of the syntax of negative sentences, of course, but these were merely constraints on a range of literal interpretations. The utterance interpretation depended on the syntax of the sentence, on its semantically non-specific sentence-type meaning, and on the rules of use that delimited a range of literal utterance interpretations for utterance-types and tokens.

Another implication, this one familiar to speech-act theorists, was that the negative sentence-type did not, of itself, express a proposition (truth conditions). It did not contain enough information to do so. Utterance-types and tokens of the sentence-type would express propositions. The surprising aspect of the claim was that simple negative sentences in English and in other natural languages had this property (Horn 1989: 370; Atlas 1989, 2005; Chomsky 1996; Levinson 2000).

## 18.6   An objection to the monoguist non-specificity view of negation

One classic objection that is made to this picture – aside from denying the evidence or the cogency of the ambiguity tests or denying the linguistic judgments – is that the monoguist view "offers no ready explanation for the intuition shared by ambiguists of all camps that negative sentences like [(3) and (4a)] may be used in two radically different ways, with (as Karttunen and Peters (1979) observe) distinct linguistic correlates in each case" (Horn 1989: 370). The two ways are the presupposition-preserving choice negation and a special, linguistically marked, "contradictory" negation, illustrated in (5), (6), and (7). This negation is not, it is said, merely a pragmatic use of the semantically non-specific, unambiguous negative free morpheme in the sentence, as the sentence seems to have special grammatical features. It has a special intonation and cannot trigger an NPI, e.g. "any," as illustrated in (8a,b). If this is not ambiguity, it is something very close to it, or so it is said, and was said by Horn (1989: 370). It is a "pragmatic ambiguity." Not all "not"s are created equal.

(3)      The king of France is not bald.

(4)   a.   Chris didn't manage to solve the problem.
      b.   (4a) presupposes "It was difficult for Chris to solve the problem." (Horn 1989: 368)

(5)   a.   Chris didn't˘*manage* to solve the problem – it was quite easy for him. (Horn 1989: 368)
      b.   (5a) does not presuppose "It was difficult for Chris to solve the problem."

(6)   a.   Chris didn't manage to solve *some* of the problems – he managed to solve *all* of them.
      b.   The negative in (6a) negates a generalized conversational implicatum of "some" in an assertion of the affirmative form of the sentence, viz. "not all." (Horn 1989: 370)

(7)      The king of France is not˘bald – there is no king of France. (Horn 1989: 362)

(8)   a.   Chris didn't *manage* to solve {some/*any} problems – he solved them easily. (Karttunen and Peters 1979: 46–7; Horn 1989: 368)
      b.   The negative in (8a) seems to negate the "presupposition" of the affirmative; cf. (4).
      c.   *Chris didn't *manage* to solve any of the problems – he managed to solve *all* of them.
      d.   Chris managed to solve some of the problems.
      e.   Chris didn't manage to solve any of the problems.

## 18.7  A new reply to the NPI objection to the monoguist view of negation

The NPI objection of the previous section had some weight when it was offered in 1989. The view of licensing NPIs then made it seem that one had to explain a syntactico-semantic feature of negative sentences. Mere "pragmatics" did not seem a good candidate for an explanatory theory. But that was 1989.

In 2002 in the context of a discussion of the licensing of NPIs by non-monotonic quantifier noun phrases "Only *Proper Name*", e.g. "Only Larry" in sentences like (9a–c) that license NPIs like "any," "ever," and the minimizers (e.g. "give a damn"), consistent with previous theoretical predictions only if "Only *Proper Name*" were downwards monotonic, Horn (2002) announced his agreement with Atlas (1991b, 1993, 1996, 1997) that "Only Larry Fs" entails the positive "Larry Fs" as well as the negative quantifier sentence "No one other than Larry Fs." So a non-monotonic rather than a downwards monotonic quantifier did license NPIs! Licensing was no longer explicable by a purely syntactico-semantic theory of negative contexts.

(9)  a.  Only Larry liked any of Jay's counterexamples.
     b.  Only Larry ever went to philosophy of language talks.
     c.  Only Larry gave a damn about logical entailments.

But, as he had done in 1989 with "not" sentences, Horn was now inclined to say that not all entailments are created equal. Semantically entailed material that falls outside of the asserted aspect of utterance meaning (Stalnaker 1978) is "assertorically inert" and transparent to NPI licensing (Horn 2002 (28); 2009a). If only the "No one other than Larry Fs" is asserted when one states "Only Larry Fs," the former's negativity licenses the NPIs. So what licenses NPIs is "downward assertion" not downward entailment. Horn (2002) has advanced a pragmatic theory of NPI licensing.

What puzzled me (Atlas 2007a) about this view was how the assertoric bits did all this licensing of NPIs. Why was it the difference between the allegedly asserted and unasserted entailments of the sentence that explained why an NPI occurred grammatically or acceptably in the original sentence or in an utterance of the original sentence? By what mechanism did the entailed but allegedly asserted negative proposition influence the original non-negative sentence to accept an NPI? Horn's account has not yet been able to address these questions, nor has he made it clear how this notion of assertion is compatible with other notions of assertion. For example, in a theory of Indirect Speech Acts, there is a notion of an indirect assertion, an assertion that is performed successfully by uttering a sentence that is not declarative, etc. Is that the notion being employed here, or a related but distinct notion? Also, I had raised doubts about the adequacy of Horn's criteria distinguishing asserted from non-asserted propositions, which he had adapted from Karttunen and Peters' (1979) criteria distinguishing non-presupposed from presupposed propositions in an utterance. As of yet we have no clear answers to these questions.

But even if Horn had answered these questions, for our purposes here the theoretical importance of his view is that his new theory of NPI licensing is a pragmatic, speech-act one. His 1989 objection to the Atlas–Kempson thesis about "not" was that it could not explain the "ambiguity" tilt rather than the "pragmatic" tilt to the linguistic intuitions distinguishing marked "not" statements that failed to license NPIs from ordinary negative statements that did license them. Since his account of the licensing of NPIs is now pragmatic and depends on what is asserted in asserting the sentence, is he going to claim, in order to explain the unacceptable occurrences of the NPIs in marked negative sentences, that what is asserted in utterances like (8a) are not negative propositions? No, *that* would be absurd! But on his new theory of NPI licensing, that is what he would have to say about Karttunen and Peters' "meta-linguistic" denial sentences, so long as he thinks that "downward assertion" is a necessary condition for the grammatical/acceptable occurrence of an NPI.

The problem is this: Horn's new "pragmatic" theory of NPI licensing is not consistent with his own acceptance of Karttunen and Peters' syntactico-semantic observations about the ungrammatical/unacceptable occurrence of NPIs in marked negative sentences. Here is the dilemma: either Horn gives up his new "pragmatic" theory of NPI licensing in the face of the absurdity that I mentioned in the preceding paragraph that what is asserted in (8a) would not be a negative proposition, or he gives up the observation of Karttunen and Peters that the failure of an NPI to occur acceptably/grammatically in a marked negative sentence is a consequence of a different meaning for "not" in the sentence. If he gives up the second limb of the dilemma, he gives up the "ambiguity" tilt to the linguistic intuitions about the use of negative sentences that was essential to his 1989 objection to the Atlas–Kempson monoguist view of negation. On Horn's (2002, 2009a) new theory of NPI licensing, there is now no objection to the Atlas–Kempson thesis.

There would still be a semantic "ambiguity" tilt to the linguistic intuitions, were the intuitions about the "meta-linguistic" use of the negative sentence failing to license an NPI to be explicable by the semantic account of these sentences suggested by Karttunen and Peters (1979) – their contradictory negation. But their contradictory negation is a wide-scope, logical negation whose content is a conjunction of the asserted and presupposed parts of the original utterance. That wide-scope proposition licenses NPIs perfectly well. So Karttunen and Peters' contradictory negation does not explain the NPI licensing data. It seems that Karttunen and Peters were mistaken to model their marked negative sentences by their contradictory negation. You will get no semantic "tilt" from Karttunen and Peters' account of marked, negative sentences. So what kind of "tilt" do you get, if any?

On Horn's view of the "meta-linguistic" character of these marked negative sentences, he could say that (8a) is a meta-linguistic denial of an "at-issue" affirmative sentence "Chris managed to solve some problems." In light of the discussion of quotation marks in Atlas (1980), in formalizing Horn's semantic intuitions, I would employ semi-quotation marks "$\Delta$", suggested to me by David Kaplan's (1969) "meaning quotes," as follows: Chris didn't $^\Delta$*manage* to solve some problems$^\Delta$. The exact interpretation of the semi-quotation marks is up for debate, but the idea is to create neither an opaque nor a transparent context (in Quine's (1960) senses) but a "translucent" one: language that is mentioned and whose meaning is used, as is often the case with literary use of quotation marks. Horn should not say that there is a special negation in the sentence, though the negative sentence is marked with a special intonation and stress on "manage." What is special is not the negation; what is special is the echoic, weirdly semi-quotational character of the expression in the predicate in the negative sentence. You do not replace "some" with its NPI counterpart "any" in the negative sentence, because "some" does not occur transparently in the predicate; "some" is within a translucently quoted expression in the predicate. On Horn's own view of meta-linguistic denial, he could have said in 1989 that there was no "ambiguity" tilt to his linguistic intuitions about the different uses of a negative sentence.

But Horn in 1989 wanted it both ways. He agreed with Atlas and Kempson that "not" was semantically unambiguous (though he was not prepared to agree that it was semantically non-specific), but he disagreed with Atlas and Kempson when he (1989: 370, 377) said that "not" sentences were "effectively ambiguous" between a truth-functional sentence operator and a meta-linguistic operator "I object to U," where U is an utterance-type or token. By contrast the Atlas–Kempson view claims that the truth-functional mapping from propositions and predicate concepts to propositions and predicate concepts is as much a *construction* from the contribution of an underlying negative lexical item to the meaning of a phrase as the construction to "I object to U" would be.

Since I believe that Horn misdiagnosed the locus of meta-linguistic denial and put it into the "not" of the sentence when it belonged in the "translucent" predicate instead, "not" is just the same old small word with its same old sketchy and schematic, non-specific meaning-contribution, as it always was and is and has been. That is not to say that I have a precise account of that sketchy, non-specific meaning, or why it is so peculiarly adapted to the range of different uses that it has – though I have tried to give some suggestions of that account elsewhere – but neither did Horn (1989) have answers to those questions for his word-meaning.[6] (I will discuss his semantic account below.) In 1989 Horn was no better off than Atlas and Kempson when he worried about explaining the non-occurrence of NPIs in marked, grammatical, negative sentences, and in 2010 he is faced with the even more painful theoretician's dilemma described above. The real issue between us, as he understood, was how to understand ordinary negation (Horn 1989: 423).

## 18.8   Ordinary negation: Aristotle's, Sommers', and Horn's term logic

*Predicate denial*, it is typically asserted, is a *mode of predication* that denies a positive term of a subject (Horn 1989: 464) in forming a sentence, e.g. *Socrates is not happy*. Predicate denial is a way to express a contradictory of the corresponding predicate affirmation, e.g. of *Socrates is happy*. *Term negation* is a way to negate a term or predicate, e.g. prefixing *un* to *happy*. It is typically a way to express a contrary term or predicate. By *contrary* I mean, as usual, that the contrary predicate Ũx (or contrary sentence Ã) to the predicate Ux (or to the sentence A) cannot be true of an individual *x* (or in the case of the sentence, true) if the predicate Ux (or sentence A) is true of *x* (or in the case of the sentence, true); but both predicates can be false of *x* (or in the case of the sentences, both false). By *contradictory* I mean that the contradictory predicate Ūx (or sentence Ā) cannot be true of an individual *x* (or in the case of the sentence, true) if the predicate Ux (or sentence A) is true of the individual *x* (or in the case of the sentence, true); and, that the contradictory predicate Ūx (or sentence Ā) cannot be false of an individual *x* (or in the case of the sentence, false) if the predicate Ux (or sentence A) is false of the individual *x* (or in the case of the sentence, false).

In the last chapter "Negative Form and Negative Function" of his treatise *A Natural History of Negation* Horn (1989: 465) makes two interesting claims, among others: (a) that neither predicate denial nor term negation is "reducible" to a syntactically external, one-place, sentential-connective negation; (b) that there is no genuine, object-level, sentential negation in English. In what follows I wish to examine these claims.

### 18.8.1   What does it mean to say that neither predicate denial nor term negation is "reducible" to a sentential connective?

The non-reducibility claim, put in the words of (a) above, seems a bit imprecise. Before I say what Horn actually meant by that claim, let us consider what someone might possibly mean by it, for in doing so we shall be able to survey some of the semantical puzzles that philosophers and linguists have posed about negation and that particularly concerned Horn. Since Horn (1989: 464, 472) himself observes that predicate denials express denials that are semantical contradictories, he surely does not mean that the set of "translations" of these sentences into formulae of classical First-Order Quantification Theory – the equivalence class of logically equivalent representations of the truth conditions of these sentences – does not contain at least one element that has a syntactically external, one-place sentential connective; formulae that express contradictory denials patently do contain such connectives.

Could one mean by the "non-reducibility" claim that there is no synonymy between the two English sentences (10) and (11)?

(10)   Socrates is not happy.
(11)   It is not the case that Socrates is happy.

Non-synonymy would be one form of the non-reducibility of (10) to (11). If, instead, one thinks that (10) and (11) are synonymous, one agrees with Atlas (1974), Kuroda (1977: 105), and, on the evidence of several passages from *A Natural History of Negation* with Horn (1989: 365) as well, that both sentences, by virtue of the semantical non-specificity of the negative sentences, and the correlative absence of scope ambiguity, can equally well express the same literal interpretations. Therefore on the synonymy account of reducibility, one should not make the "non-reducibility" claim. The sentence (10) is reducible to (11).

Could one mean by the "non-reducibility" claim that there is no necessary equivalence between the English sentences (10) and (11)?[7] No, surely, for the same reasons as just mentioned, one does not mean that either.

Of course not even (11) is a syntactically external negation if by "external" one excludes the case of a "not" following the auxiliary verb in a verb phrase. If the only string that counts as a syntactically external negation is (12a), which is ungrammatical in English, the non-reducibility claim is trivially true. Horn does not intend that, surely.

(12)   a.   *Not Socrates is happy.

But then the criterion for a sentence $P$ in a language $L$ being a sentential negation must be at least partly semantic, namely that $P$ is synonymous with, or necessarily equivalent to, a sentence $Q$ of the form $\ulcorner \mathbf{N} P \urcorner$ in language $L^*$, where $\mathbf{N}$ is a sentential operator belonging to the vocabulary of $L^*$, or at least to a sentence $R$ of the language $L^*$ whose truth conditions are a function of the truth conditions of the translation of $P$ into $L^*$.[8]

## 18.8.2   The Aristotelian term logic of Fred Sommers (1982): How to convert sentence negation to term negation

Unlike Horn and Atlas, Sommers (1982: 355), one of the most sophisticated of defenders of Aristotelian term logic in the twentieth century, thinks that the sentences (10) *Socrates is not happy* and (11) *It is not the case that Socrates is happy* are not synonymous. Sommers takes sentence (10) to be ambiguous, either expressing a contradictory denial of *Socrates is happy*, which Sommers (1982: 317) notates by an external, one-place sentential connective in (12b),

(12)   b.   not: Socrates is happy.

or expressing a contrary of *Socrates is happy*, which Sommers (1982: 317–18) represents by either the contracted negation (13) or the hyphenated predicate neologisms (14 a,b):

(13)        Socrates isn't happy.

(14)    a.    *Socrates is not-happy.[9]
        b.    Socrates is un-happy.

Sommers (1982: 354–5) accepts that in pre-Fregean logic there are contradictory denials not merely of a predicate but of a proposition, expressed e.g. in English in (15b), (16 b,c):

(15)    a.    A creature was stirring.
        b.    Not a creature was stirring.
        c.    *Not: a creature was stirring.

(16)    a.    Socrates is happy.
        b.    It is not the case that Socrates is happy.
        c.    That Socrates is happy is not the case.
        d.    *Not: Socrates is happy.

(17)        "Socrates is happy" is not true.

(18)        It is not true that Socrates is happy.

(19)        That Socrates is happy is not true.

For Sommers (1982: 357) sentences (16b) and (16c) are in the object-language, unlike (17), which is in the meta-language. Like Sommers I wish to distinguish the meta-linguistic sentence of (17) from the sentences in (16 b,c). I (Atlas 1989) have elsewhere provided arguments to demonstrate that the English sentences (16b) and (18) are each semantically non-specific between a contradictory and a contrary object-language interpretation. I have argued that the English sentence (19) is semantically non-specific between (a) a *de re* object-language interpretation and (b) *de dicto* object-language and meta-language interpretations! On the *de re* object-language interpretation (19) has the paraphrase *As for Socrates, that he is happy is not true*. On the *de dicto* object-language interpretation "That Socrates is happy" denotes an abstract object (viz. a proposition), and on the meta-language interpretation "That Socrates is happy" autonymously denotes a different abstract entity (viz. a clause). Finally, I have argued that the sentences (10) *Socrates is not happy*, (16b) *It is not the case that Socrates is happy*, and (18) *It is not true that Socrates is happy* are paraphrases, with (10) semantically non-specific rather than ambiguous between contrary and contradictory interpretations. None of (10), (16b), and (18) is a paraphrase of the explicitly meta-linguistic (17) *"Socrates is happy" is not true*.

    Interestingly Sommers (1982: 358) claimed that the sentence negation (16b) and the sentence (18) are paraphrases, that (16b) is an object language sentence, hence that (18), unlike (17), is also an object-language sentence. Statement (10) is about Socrates, but so are statements (16b) and (18), as the paraphrases that follow show:[10]

(20)    a.    As for Socrates, he is not happy.
        b.    As for Socrates, it is not the case that he is happy.
        c.    As for Socrates, it is not true that he is happy.

About the sentence that expresses the truth-conditions for (16b) *It is not the case that Socrates is happy*, (18) *It is not true that Socrates is happy*, and the object-language interpretation of (19) *That Socrates is happy is not true*, Sommers (1982: 358) is muddled. That sentence, for Sommers, is (21):

(21)    The state of affairs in which it is not true that Socrates is happy exists/obtains.

For Sommers a statement of (21) is about states of affairs.[11] Notice that Sommers has now converted a sentential negation (16b) into a sentence that contains a negative term "not true".

### 18.8.3   Sommers' ontic levels vs linguistic levels

Sommers (1982: 360) construes statements about Socrates as "ground level" propositions, so that statements about states of affairs are "first level" propositions and statements about propositions are also "first level" propositions. The distinction Sommers has in mind is an intuitive metaphysical distinction of ontological levels of entities, not a logical distinction of linguistic levels of expressions. This is not a Tarskian hierarchy of languages. For example, a proposition and a sentence-type are both abstract entities, but their abstractness, like the abstractness of the integer 17, does not make them any less individuals than is the concrete (i.e. not abstract) particular Socrates. And whatever a state of affairs is, so long as it is not a set of individuals, or a set of sets of individuals, etc., it too is an individual (Goodman 1964). Furthermore, since one can give a formalization of elementary set theory in a first-order language, from the mere fact that one's sentences are about sets it does not even follow that one's sentences about sets are not in a first-order language. On Sommers' conception of an individual, quarks, which are not independent Aristotelian substances, are not individuals. It would follow that the statements of elementary particle physics are not at ground level but at some $n^{\text{th}}$ basement level, $n = -1, -2, \ldots$. Such a notion of negative ontological levels is not, I believe, coherent on Sommers' conception of levels.

The incoherence of Sommers' (1982: 290, 360) notion of levels of propositions is also clear from the following considerations. Sommers (1982: 290) believes that *Every S is P* is underlain, i.e. defined, by *No S is not-P*. He (1982: 61, 360) also believes that *No S is not-P* expresses the denial of the truth of *Some S is not-P*. It is thus about the proposition *Some S is not-P*, predicating of it that it is not true (i.e. for Sommers (1982: 295, 357–8), false). So *No S is not-P* is an ontically first-level proposition. It follows that *Every S is P* is an ontically first-level proposition. But Sommers (1982: 51, 360) also appeals to an "aboutness" intuition by virtue of which *Every S is P* is about each of the Ss. So it is also a "ground level" proposition about Ss. In describing this situation Sommers (1982: 360) says that "the definition [of *Every S is P*] achieves, as it were, a semantic descent to ground level amounting to an equivalence between a first-level and a zero-level proposition." Unfortunately, not only

has Sommers not provided a theory of equivalence between differently lev-
eled propositions, his own account entails that a first-level proposition is not
merely equivalent to a zero-level proposition, but, incoherently, identical to
it. This is merely another symptom of the unsatisfactoriness of Sommers'
metaphysical notion of the levels of propositions.

### 18.8.4  Horn's alliance with Sommers on the conversion of sentence negation

In commenting on Sommers, Horn (1989: 474) remarks of the relationship
between a sentential negation "not P" and the Sommersian paraphrase in
terms of states of affairs "The [P] does not obtain"[12] that he (Horn) "would
endorse the conversion of the sentential negation . . . into the second-order
(meta-situational [Barwise and Perry 1983: 138] or meta-linguistic) statement" – using Sommers in the service of the Horn program to rid language
of sentential negation.

But Horn misconstrues Sommers' intention, I believe. Sommers' intention
was that the conversion would not be into a Tarskian second-order statement
but, dubiously even on Sommers' own premises, into an ontically first-level
proposition. Unfortunately, on Sommers' own premises, the statement about
the state of affairs could still be on the "ground level," since Sommers has
notably failed to explain why states of affairs are not complex "ground level"
entities rather than first-level entities.

Furthermore, Sommers does not want to "convert" the sentential negation
statement into a second-order statement, even though he believes that the
truth conditions are given by an ontically first-level proposition. He explicitly holds the view that the sentence (16b) *It is not the case that Socrates is happy*
and the sentence (18) *It is not true that Socrates is happy* are object-language,
though ontically first-level, statements. Since Sommers (1982: 356) also holds
that (18) is synonymous with (19) *That Socrates is happy is not true*, by Sommers' own reasoning (19) is an object-language, though ontically first-level,
statement.

Horn's enlisting the aid of the twentieth century's pre-eminent Aristotelian
term logician in his linguistic program to show the dispensability of sentence
negation carries with it a commitment to a number of linguistic theses
and metaphysical assumptions, not all of which he may have wished to
accept. For semantical reasons, entirely distinct from Sommers' muddled
metaphysical ones, I agree with Sommers that one interpretation of sentence
(19) *That Socrates is happy is not true* is in the object-language. Thus sentence
(19) contrasts with the Tarskian version of sentence (17) *"Socrates is happy" is
not true*$_{OL}$. This sentence is in the meta-language. The semantical comparison
of (19) and (17) tells us something about the vernacular English word "true";
it needs to be distinguished from the Tarskian meta-linguistic predicate of
*ML* "true$_L$" ("true in language *L*").[13]

## 18.8.5 Horn's non-reducibility of predicate denial or term negation to an external negation sentence connective

We began this section asking what Horn (1989: 465) meant when he claimed that neither predicate denial nor term negation is "reducible" to an external, one-place sentential connective. He (1989: 469) states:

> What is crucial for our purposes is that ordinary (auxiliary) negation is treated as a mode of predication, a recipe for combining subject (a **T** or term phrase) and predicate (an *IV* phrase) to form a proposition or sentence (an expression of category **t**), rather than an operation on a fully formed proposition or sentence. But the Intensional Logic translation of syncategorematic negation is the external propositional connective, with the semantics of the contradictory operator (taking scope over the subject phrase, as in Aristotle). Thus we get the semantic effect of Fregean negation without the syntactic commitment to an external pre-sentential operator.

Thus Horn's primary objection to syntactically external, sentential negation is a syntactic one (Horn 1989: 472):

> My rejection of external negation as a sentential operator is motivated by many of the same factors that lead Bach (1980) and Enç (1981: Ch. 3) to challenge traditional analyses of tense . . . as a sentential operator whose scope varies with that of other operators. Enç points out that tense in natural language tends to surface as a bound morpheme on the verb, a free morpheme immediately preceding the verb, an element morphophonemically incorporated into the verb (via ablaut, etc.), or as a marker on an auxiliary verb. On the basis of this distribution and of other considerations indicating scopal analyses are simultaneously too strong and too weak, she concludes that any adequate treatment of natural language syntax and semantics must treat tense, not as a one-place sentential connective, but rather as an operator on VPs (as in Bach 1980) or on the predicate itself. As tense goes, so (I argue) goes sentential negation.

I should not wish to tie an argument about the syntax and semantics of negation to the fate of 1980 arguments about the syntax of tense. Even so, if as tense goes, so goes negation, why not as negation goes, so goes tense?[14] That is, why isn't asserting of Socrates that he *was* happy a different mode of predication from asserting of Socrates that he *is* happy or that he *will be* happy? Somehow tense differences have never seemed to theorists to be a case of different modes of predication, yet Horn's suggestion would seem to lead to just such a claim.

## 18.8.6 A Reductio argument for the existence of sentential negation in English

As we have already seen, Horn endorses Fred Sommers' account of sentential negation, as Horn believes that it is a meta-linguistic, second-order account

compatible with his (1985, 1989) own account of "metalinguistic negation."
But, as I have been at pains to show, Sommers' account is not meta-linguistic
in this sense! Horn (1989: 477) elaborates his position as follows:

> In endorsing binary sentential connectives [extended term logic] differs
> crucially from orthodox term logic in which, as Englebretsen (1981: 51)
> recognizes, all sentences are categorical and there can be no external oper-
> ators: all operators (including modality and the binary connectives) must
> be internalized. But my position on negation is essentially Englebretsen's
> (1981: 49ff): "[So-called] sentential negation is either predicate denial or
> the metalinguistic predication of 'untrue'. . . . There is no genuine, object
> level, external, sentential negation". What there is is predicate denial, term
> (constituent) negation, and metalinguistic negation.

The argument leading up to this summary of Horn's (1989: 476–7) position
explicitly considers the problem that:

> If predicate denial is a mode of predication, a means for mapping a sub-
> ject and predicate into a proposition, there is no way to apply it to a
> non-categorical sentence of the form p and q, p or q, if p then q. Thus, any
> negation which takes scope over a conjunction, disjunction or conditional
> must be metalinguistic. A true sentential disjunction can only be metalin-
> guistically rejected (It's not {true/the case}that Chris won or (that) Sandy lost),
> not descriptively negated.

I have already explained that on Fred Sommers' view, and incidentally my
own, the statement schema It's not {true/the case}that P, containing the statement operator **It's not {true/the case}that** is not meta-linguistic; the meta-
linguistic schema is rather $\ulcorner P \urcorner$ is not true, which contains a truth predicate
preceded by a Quine (1981) quasi-quotation name. To confuse these two formulae is to make the same mistake as confusing the statement operator **It is
necessary that**, viz.□, in the object language of a modal logic (e.g. in □(2 + 2
= 4)) with the meta-linguistic predicate is necessarily true applied to formulae
(e.g. '2 + 2 = 4' is necessarily true). Unlike the necessity operator, the truth
operator is extensional, like the negation operator ¬, which, like the inten-
sional necessity operator, is given a semantical value $\|\neg\|$ in an interpretation
$\vartheta$ of the formal language $L$ that is of the same logical type as the semanti-
cal value $\|\Box\|$ of the necessity operator, viz. a mapping from propositional
concepts to propositional concepts. The semantical definitions for the truth
operator **T**, sentential negation operator ¬, and necessity operator □ would
be as follows:[15]

(22)  a.   $\|\neg\Phi\|_i = 1$ iff $\|\Phi\|_i = 0$ at point of reference $i$.
      b.   $\|T\Phi\|_i = 1$ iff $\|\Phi\|_i = 1$ at point of reference $i$.
      c.   $\|\Box\Phi\|_i = 1$ iff $\|\Phi\|_j = 1$ for all points of reference $j \in \mathbf{I}$ (where $\mathbf{I}$ is
           the set of points of reference, including possible worlds).

It is obvious that ¬ and **T** are dual operators, just as ∧ and ∨ are in sentential logic. The biconditional (¬T*P* ↔ **T**¬*P*) is valid, as is its dual (**T**¬*P* ↔ ¬T*P*), in a bivalent language. Since the linguistic evidence supports the claim that English and other natural languages contain truth operators *It is {true/the case}that*, translated by **T** in our formal language, the attempt by semantical theorists to deny the existence in English of the dual of **T** in a bivalent language, the sentential negation¬, seems as odd as would be the attempt, in the face of the presence of *and* in English, to deny the existence of the inclusive disjunction interpretation of the word *or* in English.

Indeed, a theorist who holds that the only interpretation of *or* in English is the exclusive disjunction is a co-conspirator of the theorist who holds that (the semantically defined) exclusion negation does not have a translation into English.

The preceding amounts to a *reductio* argument for the existence of a translation of exclusion negation into English. I shall now turn to a constructive proof of the existence of a clause-external negation in English.

### 18.8.7   A constructive argument for the existence of clause-external negation in English

Recall that Horn (1989: 476), unlike the Aristotelian term logicians, admits the existence of the two-place sentential connectives in ordinary language: disjunctions, conjunctions, and conditionals. In particular, Horn (1989: 477) allows that English can express a negated disjunction, though he points out that normally it does so via term negation or via the denial of a predicate that incorporates a disjunction, as in the following examples (23) and (24).

(23)   *Neither* Aristotle *nor* Montague allowed iterating negation.

(24)   Aristotle did*n't* allow *either* sentential disjunction *or* propositional negation.

And Horn claims that a sentential disjunction can only be meta-linguistically rejected.

I shall now exhibit a syntactically clause-external negation of a disjunction, expressed in ordinary English without a Hornian "metalinguistic" *It's not true that*, the grammatical acceptability of which demonstrates the existence of a syntactically clause-external negation in English. Consider the sentence in (25):

(25)   Neither did Chris win or Sandy lose, nor did Chris win or Sandy lose.

Sentence (25) seems as much a sentence of English as does the rhetorically more natural and implicaturally laden (26):

(26)   Neither did Chris win or Sandy lose, nor did Sandy lose or Chris win.

Sentence (25) exemplifies the schema *Neither* P ∨ Q, *nor* P ∨ Q, which is a binary sentential negation of the disjunction P ∨ Q. And since Horn has accepted binary connectives in ordinary language, he should not cavil at this one. Thus the binary, clause-external negation of *Chris won* is (27):

(27)   Neither did Chris win, nor did Chris win,

where *neither* and *nor* are perfectly good English conjunctions (in the linguistic sense of the word).[16] Notice that (27) is perfectly grammatical English, while Sommers' neologism

(28)   *Not: Chris won

is not a grammatical sentence of English at all. My binary sentential connective *neither ... nor* is, of course, just one of the two Sheffer "strokes," the one known as Quine's (1981: 47) dagger $\downarrow$, the binary truth-functional connective that is expressively adequate for the definition of all the truth-functional connectives in classical sentential logic, including sentential negation. Recall the truth-table for the dagger, called *joint denial*, in (29):

(29)   P   Q   P$\downarrow$Q
       t   t   f
       t   f   f
       f   t   f
       f   f   t

We can then define the sentential negation as follows:

(30)   $\neg\Phi =_{df} \Phi\downarrow\Phi$ .

### 18.8.8   A review of my arguments' conclusions

To sum up my remarks so far, firstly I have tried to show that there is an object-language understanding of sentence (31):

(31)   It's true that Chris won.

– an interpretation that is about Chris, not about the proposition that Chris won, corresponding to which there is a sentential truth operator in a formal sentential language, the dual of which is a sentential negation operator. To abandon the sentential negation operator is to leave the formal counterpart to *It's true that* dual-less, a situation that would be paralleled by denying the existence of the inclusive disjunction of *or* while accepting the existence of the logical conjunction interpretation of *and*. An obvious representation in English of the semantically defined exclusion negation operator $\neg$ is the object-language operator expression *It is not true that*. (I do not mean that sentences containing this English expression are synonymous with, or necessarily equivalent to, the exclusion negation operator formulae. I am not rejecting the view of Atlas (1974) and Kuroda (1977). I mean merely that the expression is one representation in English of exclusion negation.) Secondly, I have demonstrated the existence in English of a binary connective that expresses a descriptive, sentential negation of atomic sentences as well as disjunctive sentences. This demonstration refutes Englebretsen's and Horn's claims that sentential negation does not exist in English.

### 18.8.9 Some linguistic speculations on the derivability of exclusion negation in a language of extended term logic

I conclude this section of my essay with some science fiction in the spirit of Atlas (1991a: 190) and of Quine's speculations in his Carus Lectures *The Roots of Reference* (1973: 65–8). I have argued elsewhere that English "not" is semantically non-specific with respect to scope distinctions and with respect to object-language/meta-language distinctions. This explains, *inter alia*, the failure of English sentences *It is not true that P* to possess only non-presuppositional interpretations, a datum first pointed out in Atlas (1974) – see Horn (1978, 1985, 1989). But, I believe, exclusion negation interpretations of utterances do arise in natural language. How? Here is one Quinean possibility.

Suppose that I begin with a Hornian language in which there is predicate denial, term negation, and meta-linguistic negation. Let us assume that the speakers of this language have no linguistic difficulty with meta-linguistic claims like "'The king of France is bald' is not true," which they naturally take to be true. Let me contextually define an expression "NOT" that I introduce into this language, which is such that when it occurs in "The king of France is NOT bald," the containing sentence abbreviates "'The king of France is bald' is not true." Since English is not naturally regimented into a Tarskian hierarchy, and it is its own meta-language, so to speak, the meta-linguistic predication "'The king of France is bald' is not true" is paraphrasable by the statement-operator sentence "It is not true that the king of France is bald" (transforming a truth predicate into a sentence operator, thereby confusing use and mention), and then by semantic descent to "It is not the case that the king of France is bald," and then by elision to "It is not that the king of France is bald," and then to "The king of France is not bald." Thus "not" in a token of the sentence "The king of France is not bald" can go proxy for the abbreviation "NOT" of a meta-linguistic negation in "The king of France is NOT bald." That, I suggest, is a possible Quinean explanation for the ability of object-language "not" to represent an exclusion negation proposition, even when one begins with a Hornian Language whose resources are restricted to predicate denial, term negation, and meta-linguistic negation.[17] In fact, with those resources, it seems to me that an ordinary language, for the reasons just suggested, will confuse use and mention, collapsing the Tarskian hierarchy, and will therefore manifest an exclusion negation interpretation of "The king of France is not bald" whether or not "not" is syntactically internal to the verb phrase and whether or not the correct syntactical description of "neither" in (27) *Neither did Chris win, nor did Chris win* turns out, as at least it appears, to be a syntactically external negation. Horn's resources will generate, willy-nilly and by some use/mention confusion that is part of our psychology of language, an exclusion negation interpretation of "The F is not G". You could not get rid of exclusion negation even if you tried. Exclusion negation will arise naturally, and I believe inevitably, from a Hornian language.

## 18.9 Double negation, term logic, and semantical non-specificity

I began this essay with a consideration of what, from a logical point of view, made a statement connective a negation. I suggested that a negation statement would have to satisfy certain deductive relations among statements, primarily contraposition:

$$\frac{\Gamma, A \models \neg B}{\Gamma, B \models \neg A} \quad (Cp)$$

From contraposition, and a fundamental property of logical consequence, viz. reflexivity, a principle of modest double negation follows:

$$A \models \neg\neg A. \quad (MDN)$$

In the previous section I have argued that a syntactically external, semantically exclusion negation exists in English. Thus the discussion of the first section of this essay was not about nothing at all, even if it was about sentential negation. Horn (1989: 479) completes his discussion of Aristotle's and Sommers' term logic with the following remark:

> I have offered here a programmatic sketch of Extended Term Logic, my proposal for coming to terms with term logic. In this way, I have suggested ... a motivated distinction can be drawn between one-place truth-functional operators (which are excluded, ruling out any iterative syntactic external negation) and two-place truth-functional operators (which are permitted). I see this approach as a means for capturing the insight of Aristotle and Montague in taking surface form seriously as a mirror of, and guide to, logical form.

There are two points to consider: (a) the alleged exclusion of a one-place truth-functional operator, and (b) the iteration of negation to give double negation. Horn (1989: 464–5) correctly observes of the traditional term logic of Aristotle and Sommers (1982) that, on its assumptions, predicate denial, which denies a positive term of a subject, since it does not apply to a complete sentence, does not iterate. I have just argued that permitting two-place truth-functional operators allows the definition of a sentential negation operator, that the relevant two-place truth-function through which a sentential negation can be defined does exist in ordinary language, so that one cannot exclude the sentential negation operator, though one might on grounds of syntactical theory exclude a structural description of negative sentences that makes negation a clause-peripheral syntactic object. In any case a good theory should explain why the following are intuitively acceptable arguments:

(32)    Chris won.
        _____
        Chris didn't not win.

(33)    Chris won.
        _____
        It's not the case that Chris did not win.

(34)    Chris won.
        _____
        It's not the case that it's not the case that Chris won.

Sommers (1982: 360) allows such "second level" propositions as the conclusion of the argument (34) as well as "zero level" propositions such as (35):

(35)    Socrates is not un-F.

– which for Sommers (1982: 318) is the contradictory of a contrary to "Socrates is F." Since the conclusion of (32), viz. "Chris didn't not win," certainly looks like the contradictory of a contradictory, a predicate denial of a predicate denial, which is supposed by the term logician to be impossible, the term logician owes us some explanation of the nature of the sentence in (32). Horn's (1989: 296–308) systematic discussion of double negation treats none of (32), (33), (34) explicitly but focuses almost entirely on the linguistic phenomenology of (35) *Socrates is not un-F*. Horn's discussion is relevant to (32) for the following reason.

 Sommers (1982: 317–18) would regiment the English in (32) so that *Chris didn't not win* would express only the contrary of *Chris did not win*, the latter being the contradictory of the affirmative *Chris won*. There seems to me no linguistic evidence in support of Sommers' regimentation. But if the reader shares Sommers' intuition, then change the sentence from *Chris didn't not win* to *Chris did not not win*. Sommers would claim that that sentence would express only the contradictory of the contrary *Chris did not-win* of the affirmative *Chris won*, i.e. something like (35). It strikes me as odd to suppose that what I mean by *Chris did not not win* is the denial of Chris's doing a lot of un-winning, e.g. denying that he's coming in second in the 100 meters while shaving with a dull razor-blade. But Horn's discussion takes Sommers' position for granted. Arguments (32), (33), and (34) still need an account.

## 18.10  Conclusions

As I mentioned in Atlas (1981, 1989, 2001), and in the first section of this essay, a minimal condition on a negation statement is that the following form of the law of double negation holds:

(36)   $A \models \neg\neg A$.  (MDN)

Even the mathematical intuitionist will accept the principle in (36); what he rejects is the converse classical *reductio* principle:

(37)   $\neg\neg A \models A$.

One can abandon, as the intuitionist does, the necessary component (37) of *reductio* arguments, but if one rules out the iteration of (36), one has ruled out mathematical reasoning with negation entirely.

The moral of the semantical non-specificity of negative sentences in ordinary language is that their indeterminate univocality permits the realization in utterer's meaning of a range of meanings, including exclusion negations and even exclusion negations of exclusion negations, however syntactically encoded. The arguments (32), (33), and (34) have meanings not dreamt of in Fred Sommers' philosophy.

Finally, only in the last few years has it been possible to answer adequately Horn's (1989) criticism of the Atlas–Kempson thesis, criticism dependent on the evidence of NPI data discussed in sections 18.5 and 18.6 above. Horn's (2009a) recent discussion of NPI licensing by "downward assertion" rather than "downward entailment" obviates his earlier syntactico-semantic criticism of the Atlas–Kempson thesis and leaves the thesis a viable even if still controversial analysis of "not" sentences in a natural language.

# 19

# Connectives

Caterina Mauri and Johan van der Auwera

## 19.1  Introduction

In this chapter we examine the division of labor between semantics and pragmatics in connectives, integrating considerations on the inferential mechanisms of interpretation with typological and diachronic data, and supporting
a dynamic perspective in which what is left to pragmatics in some languages,
or at some diachronic stage, may be part of the encoded semantics in other
languages, or at successive diachronic stages (cf. Traugott 2004).

By connective we mean a linking device establishing a given relation
between two clauses or phrases. In this work we will mainly focus on interclausal connectives, even though some examples of nominal conjunction
and disjunction will also be provided. Given the typological perspective that
will be adopted, we will take into account clause linkage devices that show
considerable differences from English *and*, *or*, *if* markers. Also, even though
most of the examples will feature syntactically free-standing elements, i.e.
conjunctions in the Standard Average European sense, the notion of connective is not defined in formal terms. A given interclausal relation may indeed
be encoded by an array of morphosyntactic structures, ranging from invariable discourse connectives to auxiliaries, clitics, pre- and post-positions, case
affixes, adverbial affixes, and even suprasegmental marking (e.g. Schmidtke-
Bode 2009: 73 for purposive clause linkage devices).

### 19.1.1  Connectives between semantics and pragmatics

Connectives can be argued to play a central role in the elaboration of Grice's
theory of conversational maxims, and, more generally, in the theoretical
debate on the identification of the borderline between semantics and
pragmatics. Grice's discussion of the Cooperative Principle and of the
maxims governing conversation indeed starts from the comparison between
certain basic logical operators, such as $\supset$, $\wedge$, and $\vee$, and the corresponding

connectives in natural languages, namely *if*, *and*, and *or* (Grice 1989: 22). His aim is to preserve the semantic parallelism commonly established between Boolean logic and natural languages, by explaining the attested divergences on the basis of principles of conversation. In particular, he dedicates several pages to the interpretation of natural language *or* (1989: 44–8) and conditional implications with *if* (1989: 58–85), showing that the apparent deviations from their truth-functional semantics can be accounted for in terms of pragmatic implications.

Since then, many scholars have focused their attention on connectives with the purpose of identifying and separating the inherent semantic properties (frequently equated to truth-functional meaning) from the "extra" meaning that derives from the communicative situation. We can identify two major interests in pragmatic approaches to connectives. On the one hand, great attention has been paid to those connectives that look like the direct linguistic counterparts to Boolean operators, focusing on the mechanisms governing their interpretation and deriving non-truth-functional values from truth-functional ones (Horn 1972, Levinson 1983, Noveck *et al.* 2002, for *or* and *if*; Blakemore and Carston 2005 for *and*). On the other hand, research has also focused on connectives such as *but* and *nevertheless*, which are at best only indirectly related to Boolean operators and which cannot be characterized in terms of truth-functional semantics and have been examined as test-beds for pragmatic theories, with the aim of explaining their meaning in terms of pragmatic implications and principles (Anscombre and Ducrot 1976 and 1977, Blakemore 2000, Iten 2000, Blakemore and Carston 2005).

The central role played by connectives in pragmatic theories is basically motivated by their intrinsic procedural nature, which makes them crucial devices constraining and inviting inferential processes. Within Relevance theory (RT), the term "procedural" is employed in a technical sense, and a distinction is drawn between "conceptual" and "procedural" meanings (Wilson and Sperber 1993a, Carston 1999). Concepts constitute the mental representations that undergo inferential computations, so conceptual meaning in an utterance makes up its logical form. Procedures instead are not constituents of conceptual representations: they signal and constrain aspects of the inferential process of message interpretation. A further crucial claim within this framework is that a given linguistic form may have either conceptual or procedural meaning, but not both (Carston 2002: 164). Connectives have been argued to belong to both categories, with truth-functional connectives such as *and*, *or*, and *if* having conceptual meaning, and non-truth-functional connectives, such as *so*, *but*, *nevertheless*, and discourse markers, having a purely procedural value (Carston 2002: 255–6). In other words, *so* signals that the clause following should be read as a conclusion from the preceding clause, *nevertheless* signals that the following clause bears a message conflicting with some implication or expectation generated by the preceding clause.

However, this dichotomist view of conceptual and procedural meaning has been challenged (cf. Fraser 2006, Hussein 2008). Fraser (2006) argues that most, if not all, discourse connectives have some conceptual content, besides a procedural value. A similar position is held by Hussein (2008), who coins the "conceptuo-procedural" label to denote entities such as *if*, which may be analyzed both in truth-functional and in metalinguistic terms (see a more detailed discussion in section 19.4). In this chapter, we will not strictly follow the RT approach, and will rather go along with Fraser in considering connectives as provided with both an internal conceptual semantics and a procedural component, signaling to the hearer how to integrate the linked states of affairs.[1]

In the next section, definitions of what we mean by semantics and pragmatics will be provided and the basic assumptions underlying our approach will be described. In section 19.1.3 a brief overview of the chapter will be sketched.

## 19.1.2   The dynamic balance of coding and inferencing: a typological-diachronic perspective

Although in classical works on pragmatics semantic analyses usually start from logical abstractions, as briefly illustrated in the preceding section, this is not a universally shared assumption, especially not in comparative research. As far as connectives are concerned, Dik (1968: 274–7) and Lakoff (1971: 142) have argued that there are two major problems with projecting Boolean semantics into natural language (see also Ohori 2004). First, truth values cannot be assigned to expressions such as questions, wishes, and hypotheses, since these cannot be evaluated in terms of their truth value. Nonetheless, questions, wishes, and hypotheses are frequently conjoined, disjoined, or contrasted in natural language (e.g. *Are you vegetarian or do you simply avoid eating meat?*). Secondly, there is a discrepancy between the semantic distinctions identified in Boolean logic and those actually coded by natural languages. For instance, the distinction between inclusive and exclusive disjunction appears to be only marginally relevant to natural language. Actually, languages do not seem to encode the distinction between inclusive and exclusive disjunction at all, since no dedicated connectives for the two types of disjunction are attested (Dik 1968: 275; see also Mauri 2008a: ch. 5). By contrast, languages encode semantic distinctions which are not identified within logic, reserving dedicated connectives to e.g. sequential and non-sequential conjunction (cf. Serbo-Croatian *pa* 'and then', Tukang Besi *kene* 'and at the same time': Mauri 2008a: 90, 94), declarative and interrogative disjunction (cf. Albanian *ose* 'or, listing equivalent alternatives' and *apo* 'or, asking for a choice between alternatives'; "simple" and "choice-aimed" disjunction according to Mauri 2008a: 157–61 and Mauri 2008b). In such cases, it would be difficult to maintain a semantic analysis in terms of truth-functional values, leaving the rest to pragmatics, because the notions of temporal (non-)sequentiality and necessity for a choice are part of the encoded meaning in these connectives.

Furthermore, it is not rare to find languages without any connective meaning 'or' (e.g. Wari', a Chapacura Wanham language spoken in South America; Mauri 2008a: 167) and even without any connective meaning 'and' (e.g. Maricopa, a Hokan Yuman language spoken in Arizona; Gil 1991). Such a discrepancy strongly challenges the plausibility of a direct equivalence between logical connectives and connectives in natural languages, and suggests that a more promising direction of research would be to understand what strategies such languages employ to express conjunction and disjunction: should we assume that in such cases it is all left to pragmatics?

What seems to be more interesting is to examine the division of labor between the part of meaning that is encoded in the connective and the part of meaning that is inferred through pragmatic processes, looking at this borderline as a flexible notch, moving along both a diachronic and a synchronic continuum. In this perspective, we consider as semantics of a connective the portion of meaning that is part of the linguistic form, independent of its possible truth-functionality or logical formalizability, whereas we attribute to pragmatics the portion of meaning that depends on speakers' inferential processes.

The borderline between semantics and pragmatics in connectives is dynamic in two senses, a diachronic and a synchronic one, and we will consider both. As far as diachrony is concerned, Grice (1989: 39) himself remarks that "it may not be impossible for what starts life, so to speak, as a conversational implicature to become conventionalized", thus pointing to a diachronic dimension of pragmatics. The role of pragmatics in diachronic change is indeed widely recognized (see Hopper and Traugott 2003, Traugott 2004 and this volume, Bybee 2006 among others), and it is well known that pragmatic inferences may conventionalize, becoming part of the semantics of the changing form, and they may trigger processes of form/function reanalysis. Concerning connectives, one of the most studied examples is the development of the causal value of *since* out of a purely temporal one, as a result of the conventionalization of an invited inference of causality (according to the frequent logic fallacy characterized as *post hoc propter hoc* 'after this, therefore because of this'; Hopper and Traugott 2003: 80–83). In the next sections, we will provide further examples of connectives undergoing semantic (and in some case also syntactic) change, with pragmatic inferences becoming part of the semantics of the connective.

In synchronic terms, the delimitation between the two levels can be argued to be dynamic both on the basis of the attested crosslinguistic variation and on the basis of the available intra-linguistic options. The same interclausal relations (combination, contrast, cause, alternative, etc.) can indeed be expressed through different *degrees* of coding: they may either be fully encoded (one connective for one interclausal relation, such as *although* for concessive relations), with little or no room for ambiguity and inferential enrichment, or they may be undercoded, by means of general connectives that can be employed for a number of further relations (cf. Prandi 2004: 297–302; Mauri 2008a: 76). In the latter case, the part of meaning provided by the connective has to be enriched in order to derive the intended message. The higher the degree of coding of the relation, the less is left to inference. In case of juxtaposition, i.e. absence of coding, Prandi (2004: 299–302) talks about "inferential bridging", meaning the process whereby the conceptual relation existing between two SoAs is built up completely through inference. Example (1) provides an instance of intra-linguistic variation from English:

(1)  a.  The plane broke down, he decided to take the train to Berlin.
     b.  The plane broke down **and** he decided to take the train to Berlin.
     c.  **After** the plane broke down, he decided to take the train to Berlin.
     d.  **Since** the plane broke down, he decided to take the train to Berlin.

In (1a) the two clauses are juxtaposed and on the basis of their semantics it is possible to infer a number of relations between them: co-occurrence, sequentiality, and causality. In (1b) the connective *and* only encodes the co-occurrence of the linked SoAs, and its semantics is further enriched by an implicature of temporal sequentiality, following the Gricean Maxim of Quality "Be orderly." In (1c) the temporal sequentiality is encoded by the connective *after*, which is however further enriched by a causal invited inference. In (1d), finally, the causal relation is fully encoded by *since*, which does not leave much to pragmatics.

A clear example of crosslinguistic variation is provided by Ohori (2004: 56–9), who argues that in Upriver Halkomelem, a Salish language spoken in northwestern United States, conjunction and disjunction are underdifferentiated, that is, they are expressed by means of the same connective qə. This connective only encodes a link between two entities, leaving further specifications on the nature of the link to inferential enrichments (ex. (2)). As shown in (2a), declarative contexts allow for a conjunctive reading, while interrogative constructions tend to associate with a disjunctive reading (2b). Therefore, it can be argued that in this language the degree of coding of the two relations of combination and alternative is very low, and their disambiguation is left to inferential enrichment deriving from the context (cf. also van der Auwera and Bultinck 2001: 180). An assumption of epistemic uncertainty, such as the ones characterizing interrogative speech acts, induces a disjunctive interpretation, while an assumption of epistemic certainty, such as the one characterizing declaratives, induces a conjunctive reading (more will be said on this topic in section 19.3).

(2)  Upriver Halkomelem (Salish, Ohori 2004: 57)
     a.  Lə́  ləmə́lstəxʷəs  tə    Bill  tə    sqʼə́mə́l  xʷəlɛ́m  tə
         3   throw.3        DEM   Bill  DEM   paddle    to       DEM
         Jim  **qə**  Bob.
         Jim  and     Bob

         'Bill threw the paddle to Jim and Bob.'
     b.  Lí  lɛ́m  kʷə  Bill  **qə**  Bob?
         Q   go   DEM  Bill  or      Bob
         'Did Bill or Bob go?'

To sum up, we will argue for a dynamic perspective in which connectives are examined in their procedural function, and we will focus on the one hand on what is left to pragmatics (and absent from coding) and on the other hand on what is subtracted from pragmatics because it becomes part of coding. We will focus on conjunctive, disjunctive, and conditional connectives, broadening the discussion to include, at least marginally, also temporal, causal, purposive, adversative, and concessive connectives. We will integrate general remarks on the main pragmatic features characterizing the connectives under examination with both data on the attested typological variation and data on frequently recurring diachronic paths, in order to analyze (i) how the world's languages put the borderline between coding and inferencing at different points along the continuum, and (ii) how this borderline may move across time, so that dedicated connectives may arise from undercoded constructions, through pragmatic processes.

### 19.1.3 Overview of the analysis

We will classify connectives on the basis of two major semantic parameters: (i) the co-occurrence vs non-co-occurrence of the linked SoAs and (ii) in case of co-occurrence, its potential or conflicting nature (cf. Mauri 2008a: 48, 80–83, 155–9). Therefore, section 19.2 will be devoted to the discussion of connectives encoding *at least* the co-occurrence of two SoAs, like conjunctives, with some remarks on temporal, causal, and purposive connectives too, which add to the encoded part of meaning the notions of sequentiality and causality, otherwise left to inference. Section 19.3 takes into account disjunctive connectives, encoding the non-co-occurrence of the linked SoAs, which are presented as equivalent and replaceable possibilities. In section 19.4 we will discuss conditional connectives, linking potentially co-occurrent SoAs, and in section 19.5 we will briefly consider adversative and concessive connectives, encoding a conflicting co-occurrence of SoAs. As already mentioned, these types of connectives will be examined both under the lens of traditional pragmatic approaches and from a typological-diachronic perspective.

The discussion will follow a non-random order, along a hypothetical scale going from "less coding/more pragmatics" to "more coding/less pragmatics." Along this continuum, conjunction is considered as the basis for any clause linkage being very underspecified, leaving a lot to inferential enrichment, and subordinating connectives such as concessives are considered as highly specified devices which leave almost nothing to pragmatics (cf. also Prandi 2004: 297–302).

## 19.2  Co-occurrence: conjunctive, temporal, causal connectives

The pragmatic accounts of conjunctive connectives often start from the analysis of English *and* as having the truth-functional value 'p $\wedge$ q', focusing on the inferential mechanisms generating the set of further values and relations that *and* may express (Carston 2002: 222–4, Blakemore and Carston 2005, Jaszczolt 2005, Allan, this volume). Let us start with some examples:

(3)   a.   He took off his boots and got into bed.
      b.   He got into bed and took off his boots.
      c.   She shot him in the head and he died instantly.
      d.   It's summer in England and it's winter in New Zealand.
      e.   He is very tall AND he cannot play basketball.

If one wants to keep the semantic analysis of *and* to a minimum, without postulating any polysemy, it is necessary to account for the different interpretations of sentences (3a–e) in pragmatic terms. In the first two sentences (3a,b) an inference of temporal sequentiality is generated, leading to two different readings if the respective order of the clauses is inverted. Grice's suggestion is that the inference of sequentiality is a conversational implicature generated by the manner Maxim of Orderliness. The same account is provided for (3c), where an inversion of the two clauses would lead to a strange sequence of events, whereby death precedes shooting. In (3c) the conjunction is further enriched by a causal invited inference, interpreting the instant death as a consequence of the shooting. The last two sentences may instead be interpreted as somehow conflicting: (3d) conveys a symmetric opposition, while (3e) conjoins two SoAs that are not expected to co-occur, since the second clause denies some expectation generated by the first one (in this case, *and* has to be heavily stressed, as underlined by the use of capital letters, and the sentence has to be characterized by a special intonational pattern, in order for the contrast to be conveyed). Basically, we may argue that *and* only encodes the co-occurrence of the linked SoAs, leaving room for all possible inferential enrichments compatible with its semantics. We will discuss cases like (3d) and (3e) in more detail in section 19.5, and in the following discussion we will focus on the temporal and causal readings of conjunctive constructions.

A temporal sequence relation is very often inferred from the conjunction of two SoAs, and this recurrent inferencing process has been the object of several analyses after Grice. According to Levinson (2000), this instantiates a generalized conversational implicature, which has to be kept distinct from particularized implicatures. The former type of implicature normally arises across contexts unless they are blocked by specific salient assumptions, whereas a particularized implicature is dependent on specific contextual assumptions. Therefore, in Levinson's view, unless the sequential inference is blocked, it is activated by default in the interpretation of two conjoined SoAs. A different analysis is provided by Carston (2002: ch. 3), within the Relevance theory framework, who explains the sequential and causal reading of cases like (3a–c) in terms of inferential enrichments, rather than implicatures.

Carston's analysis relies on the activation of highly accessible narrative scripts, in which these sequential relations are represented. In her approach, the temporal sequence inference is supported by the accessing of contextual assumptions, which increases the ease of processing and provides a script representing events as occurring sequentially (Carston 2002: 378–9). It is indeed widely assumed in cognitive studies that frequently experienced processes and sequences of events are stored as frames or scripts. Such scripts may be highly specific stereotypical scenarios acquired through experience, such as going to a restaurant for a meal, going to the cinema, or two people getting married, or they may be more abstract. In the latter case, we are dealing with frames deeply rooted in the human cognitive ability, such as the fact that events in the world are usually causally connected to other events or that actions are usually made with a purpose (Carston 2002: 226). In either case, inferential enrichment characterizing the occurrences of *and* in (3) is to be connected to narrative chunks readily accessible for the hearer, and not to conversational implicatures.

Blakemore and Carston (1999, 2005) also take into account the non-narrative instances of *and*, i.e. cases in which the linked SoAs are not parts of a temporal sequence, and compare them to the corresponding juxtapositive constructions, highlighting a number of restrictions that *and* imposes on the set of possible inferences. In particular, they show that in a case like (4), the sentence in (4a) can be interpreted as presenting a fact and its explanation, while such an interpretation is not available for (4b) (Blakemore and Carston 2005: 572).

(4)   a.   Max fell asleep; he was tired.
      b.   Max fell asleep and he was tired.

Further relations that may be inferred from the juxtaposition of clauses, but which are precluded by the presence of *and*, are evidence, reformulation, and certain sorts of elaboration. Blakemore and Carston argue that such restrictions are a consequence of the fact that in explicit conjunction, it is the complex conjoined sentence that carries the presumption of optimal relevance and is therefore elaborated and processed by hearers, not the linked clauses individually (cf. also Mauri 2008a: 37–44). Therefore, relations that imply separate processing for the two clauses, e.g. if the second clause is interpreted as an explanation or elaboration of the first one, are not inferable if an overt conjunctive connective is present. In other words, in the interpretative process, hearers directly look for complex scripts, where the two clauses are relevant together, rather than for individual scenarios for each clause.

If we take a comparative perspective, we see that the behavior of English *and* is but a particular case within a rather complex picture. The world's languages indeed show a great amount of crosslinguistic variation in how they distribute the labor between semantics and pragmatics in conjunctive connectives. First of all, as pointed out by Mithun (1988), in many languages the most common strategy to conjoin two clauses is simply to juxtapose them. The use of simple juxtaposition is especially widespread in languages with a mostly spoken tradition, where the conceptual closeness vs separateness of the SoAs is conveyed by means of different intonational patterns. However, juxtaposition is a frequent alternative option also for languages in which there is some structural device signaling the combination of two SoAs, but this device is not obligatory and in some cases it is at the very beginning of a grammaticalization process, or consists of clause-chaining lacking any structural differentiation between coordinating and subordinating constructions (Mauri 2008a: 91–6). In such cases, the burden of communication is all on inferential enrichment.

Maricopa, for instance, has no overt conjunctive connective, and this is what made Gil title his paper "Aristotle goes to Arizona and finds a language without And" (Gil 1991), highlighting the non-universality of connectives equivalent to *and*. As exemplified in (5), the two linked clauses are simply juxtaposed. The verb form of the first clause bears a switch-reference marker (Different Subject marker), signaling non-identity of the subject of the second clause (i.e. the first couple of people, denoted by the dual marker, is different from the second couple), but there is no way for such a marker to encode any additional interclausal relation.

(5)    Maricopa, Yuman, Hokan (Gordon 1986: 285)
       kafe    sish-m        pastel  mash-k
       coffee  drink:DU-DS   pie     eat:DU-R
       'They-2 drank coffee and they-2 ate pie' (They ≠ they)

Besides radical cases such as Maricopa, it is not rare to find languages with some overt conjunctive marker which is more specific than English *and*, and is restricted to the expression of either sequential or non-sequential conjunction. Hdi (Afro-Asiatic, Chadic, spoken in Nigeria and Cameroon) and Lango (Nilo-Saharan, Nilotic, spoken in Uganda), for instance, use simple juxtaposition as the main strategy for the expression of clausal conjunction, but they also have the possibility to employ an overt connective for the expression of a sequential combination. In both cases, the connectives derive from verbs and are not fully grammaticalized. In Lango *tê*, roughly meaning 'and then', is still conjugated in the habitual and takes infinitive complements (Noonan 1992: 193). In Hdi the verb *lá*, originally meaning 'depart, go', is used in its nominalized form to indicate separation and temporal sequentiality of the SoAs it links. As Frajzyngier and Shay (2002: 428–31) argue, the verb *lá* has entered a process of grammaticalization, whereby it has developed a purely conjunctive sequential function which still synchronically co-exists with its original lexical meaning. In the intermediate stage, during which the conjunctive function arose, the verb 'to go' worked as a bridge between two events, in which a subject had to move to another location in order to continue his action or to begin a new one there. Then, given the high frequency of occurrence in such narrative contexts, speakers reinterpreted the form as signaling a sequential relation.

Example (6) shows the original lexical meaning 'to go' together with the new conjunctive function of *lá*. The original meaning can be observed in *lá-b-ì* 'went away', whereas the following *lá-ghà* has a conjunctive function, which is proved by the fact that its subject (Hyena) does not move.

(6)    Hdi, Chadic, Afro-Asiatic (Frajzyngier and Shay 2002: 429–30)
       mbàɗ   ká      krì    kà    lá-b-ì        **lá-ghà**      pákáwghúvì
       then   COMP    dog    SEQ   go.out-REF    go-D:PVG        hyena
       kà     mná-n-tá     krì
       SEQ    tell-3SG-REF  dog
       'Then Dog went away and Hyena said to Dog . . .'

In other words, in Lango and Hdi what is encoded in the connective is not only the co-occurrence of linked SoAs, but also their temporal sequentiality. On the other hand, there are also languages, such as Tuvaluan (Austronesian, Malayo-Polynesian, spoken in the island of Tuvalu: Besnier 2000) and Koromfe (Niger-Congo, Volta Congo, spoken in Burkina Faso and Mali), where the only overt conjunctive connective attested can only be used in non-sequential combination. In these languages, we observe a demarcation line separating sequential (and causal) combination from all the other co-occurrence relations, in that two SoAs linked within a temporal sequence can only be juxtaposed, while any kind of absence or interruption of sequentiality is overtly signaled by *kae* in Tuvaluan and by *la* in Koromfe. The non-sequentiality encoded in these connectives then frequently activates contrastive inferences, as will be discussed in detail in section 19.5, so that these markers are commonly employed also in adversative contexts.

Finally, there are also languages employing two different dedicated connectives for sequential and non-sequential conjunction, lacking a general undercoded connective comparable to English *and*. Tukang Besi provides a case in point, with the connective *kene* encoding non-sequential conjunction and the connective *maka* encoding temporal sequentiality, as exemplified in (7).

(7)    Tukang Besi, Malayo-Polynesian, Austronesian, spoken in Indonesia
       (Donohue 1993: 427)
    a. Te     mia       no-rato    **kene**    no-ganta-'e      na      uwe
       CORE   person    3r-arrive  and        3r-scoop-3OBJ    NOM     water
       '. . . people keep coming and fetching water . . .'
    b. Jari,   sa-rato-no                i       umbu    na       Ndokendoke
       so      when-arrive-3POSS         OBL     edge    NOM      monkey
       o-sampi-'e-mo           a        loka     iso    **maka**      o-manga
       3R-peel-3OBJ-PRF        NOM      banana   yon    and.then     3r-eat
       'So when Monkey arrived at the top he peeled the bananas and then ate them.'

Cases like Tukang Besi exemplify a division of labor between semantics and pragmatics with a heavier semantics, as compared to English, at least as far as temporal sequentiality is concerned. Of course, sequential and non-sequential connectives may in turn generate a number of further inferential enrichments in particular contexts, such as inferences of causality in sequential contexts or adversative inferences in non-sequential contexts (cf. (3d,e)).

Typological data thus reveal a picture in which conjunctive connectives do not necessarily correspond to English *and*, but may be completely absent, leaving everything to bridging inferences, or they may encode much more than the truth-functional 'p ∧ q' formula, including into the semantics of the connective temporal indications concerning the sequentiality of the SoAs.[2] Let us now have a look at diachronic paths involving conjunctive connectives and see how the borderline between semantics and pragmatics moves across time.

As we have already argued, the main inferential enrichments generated by the co-occurrence of two SoAs are temporal and causal, whereby the two events are interpreted as being parts of a sequence and as being related as cause and consequence. Such pragmatic inferences may become part of the semantics of the connective, which thus develops a sequential meaning out of a purely conjunctive one or a causal meaning out of a temporal one (cf. the case with *since*, section 19.1.2). Heine and Kuteva (2002: 43) cite the case of Min-grelian *do* 'and' developing a temporal value 'as soon as', but this kind of path does not seem to be very frequent across languages. What can be observed in several unrelated languages is instead the second diachronic change, namely the one deriving causal functions out of temporal ones. Heine and Kuteva (2002: 291) list a number of examples from Indo-European and non-Indo-European languages: Old High German *dia wila so* 'so long as' > German *weil* 'because'; Latin *posteaquam* 'after', 'ever since' > French *puisque* 'since', causal marker; Finnish *kun* 'when', 'while', 'as', 'since', 'because'; Estonian *paräst* 'after', 'because of'. In all these cases an invited inference plausibly became part of the semantics of the connective (cf. Geis and Zwicky 1971: 565–6).

It is to be noted that temporal connectives may be the source for other connectives as well, such as conditionals and adversatives, and these paths will be discussed in sections 19.4 and 19.5. The reason why temporal connectives are the source for recurrent diachronic processes is probably rooted in those abstract cognitive scripts described by Carston (2002; see discussion above), which make narrative and causal scenarios easily available during the interpretative process. The frequent activation of causal inferences then determines their systematic association to the connective at issue, determining in turn its functional reinterpretation.

Finally, let us briefly mention purposive connectives, which encode the intentional co-occurrence of two SoAs. Purposive connectives, such as *so that* and *for*, link one SoA, that of the matrix clause, to another SoA, so that the former is performed with the intention of bringing about the latter. The latter SoA is described in the purpose clause (cf. Schmidtke-Bode 2009: 20). Purpose clauses are frequently encoded by means of juxtapositive strategies, in which no explicit connective is used and the purposive relation is expressed through a conjunction of clauses, a serial-verb or quotative construction. As we already argued, two SoAs in immediate succession are indeed likely to be interpreted as being linked in a causal relation, and it is frequently the case that the causal relation is motivated by an intention to bring about the second SoA. Such pragmatic inferences of causality and purpose may eventually become part of the conventionalized meaning of a construction (cf. Schmidtke-Bode 2009: 201).

To sum up, we can see a cline in the degree of coding of co-occurrence relations, going from simple juxtaposition towards the overt coding of causal and purposive relations. In between, we find overt underspecified conjunctions (as in English *and*) and temporal (sequential and non-sequential) conjunctions. Along the cline, the burden of communication gradually passes from pragmatics to semantics. In diachrony this continuum can be examined as successive stages of change.

## 19.3   Non-co-occurrence: disjunctive connectives

Pragmatic accounts of disjunction mainly focus on the distinction between inclusive and exclusive *or* and examine the inferential processes through which one of the two readings is selected over the other in specific contexts. The inclusive reading of disjunction parallels the value of the Boolean operator $\vee$, so that $p \vee q$ is true if $p$, or $q$, or both are true (8a). The exclusive reading on the other hand requires that either $p$ or $q$ is true, but not both (8b). There are contexts, such as (8c), in which both readings are possible.

(8)   a.   To play Bardot the actress needs to be sensuous or seductive.[3]
           (having them both would not be a problem)
      b.   At the moment, Jack is waiting at the airport or he is flying over the Alps.
           (he can't be in both places)
      c.   The ideal candidate should have a law degree or a keen awareness of the legal system.
           (both inclusive and exclusive readings are possible)

The crucial question at issue in most theoretical studies on disjunction is under what conditions the exclusive interpretation is preferred over the inclusive one, and vice versa. The most widespread neo-Gricean view is that the inclusive interpretation of *or* is the basic one and the exclusive one is derived through a scalar implicature (Horn 1973; Gazdar 1979; Levinson 1983). The two connectives *or* and *and* may indeed be analyzed as forming a scale $<$ *and, or* $>$, in which *and* is the more informative element of the scale, since it provides information on the existence of both $p$ and $q$, and *or* is the less informative one, in that it provides information only on the *potential* existence of *p* and *q*. According to this view, *p and q* entails *p or q*. As a consequence, if the speaker utters a disjunctive sentence *p or q*, the hearer will infer that (s)he either has no evidence to argue that *p and q*, i.e. to use the stronger element in the scale, or that (s)he positively knows that *p and q* does not hold. If the speaker had evidence for *p and q* but chose to utter *p or q*, his/her behavior would violate the general Cooperative Principle. Thus, presuming that the speaker is cooperative, the hearer will infer that it is not the case that *p* and *q* both hold, thereby interpreting the disjunction as exclusive. Even if the exclusive reading is derived from the inclusive one, which can therefore be considered as more basic, it is the default interpretation in unembedded contexts (i.e. contexts in which the disjunction is not in the scope of modals or negation, and is not in the protasis of conditional construction; see further discussion below). In case both readings are to be preserved, a formula such as *and/or* is often used.

Slightly different accounts are provided within the RT framework by Sperber and Wilson (1986), and in generative approaches, such as the ones by Chierchia *et al.* (2001) and Crain (2008). Sperber and Wilson argue that scalar implicatures are generated when a weak statement fails to meet the hearer's expectations of relevance. Therefore, in their view the exclusive reading of *or* does not arise as the default, but is rather generated as an effect of the hearer's attempt to identify the most relevant interpretation with the least effort. In the generative approach, the difference is more significant, since scalar implicatures are viewed as grammatical phenomena rather than pragmatic processes. First, an account in terms of informativeness of the two readings in specific contexts is provided (Chierchia *et al.* 2001, Noveck *et al.* 2002), with reference to the distinction between upward and downward entailing contexts; then, it is argued that the ability to recognize the inclusive value of *or* is innate (cf. also Crain 2008: 151).

Chierchia *et al.* (2001: 161–3) start from remarking on a clear parallelism between contexts licensing negative polarity items such as *any* and contexts licensing an inclusive interpretation of *or*, exemplified in (9).

(9)　a.　There aren't people who like John or Bill.
　　　b.　Did John or Bill arrive?
　　　c.　I forbid you to smoke or drink.
　　　d.　If John or Bill go to the gym, Mary is happy.
　　　e.　John or Bill could lift this.

These contexts have been characterized as having a downward entailing semantics. An upward entailing semantics characterizes ordinary declarative sentences, where inferences from subsets to sets are licensed, as in (10a). By contrast, a downward entailing context is characterized by licensing inferences from sets to their subsets, as exemplified by sentential negation (10b).

(10)　a.　Noam bought an Italian car. $\Rightarrow$ Noam bought a car.
　　　b.　Noam didn't buy a car. $\Rightarrow$ Noam didn't buy an Italian car.

According to Chierchia *et al.* (2001; cf. also Noveck *et al.* 2002: 304–5), there is a systematic correspondence between upward entailing contexts and an exclusive interpretation of *or* on the one hand, and downward entailing contexts and an inclusive reading of *or* on the other hand. In their view this distribution is based on the potential informativeness of disjunction, whereby the interpretation having the smallest number of true conditions is considered most informative. In the cases listed in (9), inclusive interpretations make for a more restricted set of possibilities than exclusive ones. Take for instance (9a): an inclusive interpretation in *There aren't people who like John or Bill* allows for one possibility, i.e. nobody likes John and Bill, while an exclusive interpretation would lead to two, i.e. either they like neither or they like them both. Therefore, it can be argued that in downward entailing contexts, an inclusive reading of *or* is more informative than the exclusive one, and the reverse holds for exclusive disjunction in upward entailing contexts. In Chierchia's view, however, such informational computations pertain to grammar, and not to pragmatics. As a consequence, the principles governing the correct interpretation of a disjunctive relation are argued to be *innate* and to be *part of the UG* (Crain 2008: 151).

To sum up, the debate on disjunction and on the mechanisms underlying its interpretation has never challenged two basic assumptions, namely that the exclusive vs inclusive distinction is relevant to natural languages and that the notion of inclusive-or is basic and universal. Actually, if we look at the variation attested in the world's languages, the picture is once again much more complex and these two assumptions are strongly challenged. Although Payne (1985: 40) argues that "on the whole [...] it is rare to find anything unusual in disjunction" and that "the majority of languages appear to possess at least one unequivocal strategy and this is invariably permitted at sentential and at phrasal levels," our data show the opposite.

There are indeed languages without any overt disjunctive marker and in such languages the elicitation of disjunctive constructions can be highly problematic. Kibrik (2004: 547–8), for instance, argues that there does not seem to exist any native way to express disjunction in Kuskokwim (Athabaskan, Alaska), and he reports that one of the consultants, after many attempts to get him to translate a sentence such as *Do you want tea or coffee?*, answered "They did not offer you a choice in the old days," thus highlighting the non-truth-functional meaning perceived by speakers and the close connection with the notion of choice. A further example of language without *or* is provided by Wari' in (11), which exemplifies the two juxtapositive strategies to express the notion of alternative.

(11)   Wari', Chapacura-Wanam, spoken in Brazil (Everett and Kern 1997: 162)

    a.  **mo**    ta      pa' ta'    hwam  ca,    **mo**
         COND  R.future  kill  1SG:R.FUT  fish    3SG.M  COND

|     |     |     |        |     |
|-----|-----|-----|--------|-----|
| ta  | pa' ta' | carawa | ca |     |
| realis.future | kill 1SG:R.FUT | animal | 3SG.M |     |

'Either he will fish or he will hunt.' (lit. 'if he (says) "I will kill fish", if he (says) "I will kill animals".')

b.
|     |     |     |      |     |          |     |
|-----|-----|-----|------|-----|----------|-----|
| **'am** | 'e' | ca | **'am** | mi' | pin | ca |
| perhaps | live | 3SG.M | perhaps | give | complete | 3SG.M |

'Either he will live or he will die.' (lit.'perhaps he will live, perhaps he will die')

It may appear that in cases such as (11), the interpretative burden is fully left to pragmatics, in that no explicit connective is employed. However, if we consider the construction as a whole, we may observe that both strategies are characterized by some overt indication of the potential, rather than truth-functional, status of the linked SoAs: in (11a) each clause is introduced by the conditional marker *mo*, while in (11b) each clause contains the dubitative adverb *'am* 'perhaps' (cf. Mauri 2008a: ch.5 and Mauri 2008b). Such indications are necessary for a disjunctive relation to be inferable, because the simple juxtaposition of two SoAs marked (or unmarked) as realis could not generate a disjunctive inference. In other words, the labor is actually divided between coding and inferencing, but the encoded part of meaning does not refer to the interclausal relation, but to a necessary condition for the relation to be inferable. The notion of an alternative relation indeed implies that the linked SoAs are replaceable *possibilities*, and not facts, because if the speaker had some sort of evidence for at least one of them, there would be no need for establishing an alternative (*Tonight I will certainly go to the cinema or I will certainly stay at home*).

In a cross-linguistic survey on coordination, Mauri (2008a: 170–82 and 2008b) identifies what she calls the 'alternative irreality implication':

(12)   Absence of a disjunctive marker ➜ Presence of some irrealis marker

According to the implicational pattern in (12), in a language where no overt disjunctive marker is present, each state of affairs must display an irrealis marker[4] presenting the event as possible rather than occurring or realized. Therefore, in order for an alternative relation to be conveyed, either a disjunctive marker is present (13b) or an underspecified construction is employed, where a contextual inference based on the irrealis nature of the two juxtaposed SoAs gives rise to the alternative reading (13a). They may also occur together (as (13c)). If neither of the two occurs (13d), however, it is difficult to infer an alternative reading and the construction fails to fulfill an alternative function.

(13)   a.   Perhaps the hawk clawed it, maybe the dog bit it.
             (irrealis coded, alternative implied)
       b.   The hawk clawed it or the dog bit it.
             (alternative coded, irrealis implied)

c.   Perhaps the hawk clawed it or maybe the dog bit it.
     (alternative coded, irrealis coded)
d.   The hawk clawed it, the dog bit it.
     (irrealis and alternative not coded) ➔ possible interpretations:
     sequence of actions, simultaneous actions, opposition,
     ?alternative?

Thus, what seem to be relevant for natural languages are not truth vs false values of the propositions, but rather their status as *possibilities* rather than as facts and non-facts. Interestingly, in the field of logic, too, increasing attention has been paid to the connection between modality and disjunction (cf. also Ohori 2004 on ex. (2)). In the analyses of Zimmermann (2001) and Geurts (2005), the concept of possibility plays a major role in the definition of disjunction, to the point that they equate disjunction to a list of *epistemic possibilities*, naturally rendered as a conjunction of irrealis propositions. The parallelism between their account of disjunction in modal logic and the crosslinguistic pattern described in (12) is striking.

The key innovation in Zimmermann's and Geurts's work is that natural language *or* is argued to express a *modal* concept, rather than a truth-functional one: someone who utters a sentence of the form 'S1 or ... or Sn' presents his audience with a list of alternatives which are modal propositions (Geurts 2005: 385–90), namely irrealis ones. To say that "Brown is either in Lagos or in Harare" is to assert that, as far as the speaker knows, "Brown may be in Lagos, or Brown may be in Harare, and there are no other places where Brown might be." The corresponding formalism is reported in (14):

(14)   $p \vee q \vDash \diamond p \wedge \diamond q$

Before moving on to some diachronic considerations, let us briefly consider a further crucial datum that a typological survey on disjunction reveals: there do not seem to be any languages showing distinct strategies for inclusive vs exclusive disjunction.[5] Since distinctions that are relevant to human communication normally tend to receive overt coding, the fact that no overt marker for inclusive and exclusive disjunction is attested leads us to wonder to what extent this distinction is really relevant to natural languages (cf. also Dik 1968: 274–6, Haspelmath 2007: 25–7). By contrast, a different distinction appears to be frequently encoded in the world's languages, based on the *aim* with which the disjunction is established (see Mauri 2008b: 155–61 for a detailed discussion on the semantic parameter of "aim"): a disjunction may be established in order to present two SoAs as equivalent possibilities, without the need for any choice (simple disjunction, typically occurring in declarative sentences, e.g. *Tonight I will read a book or watch a movie, I don't know yet*), or it may be established in order to elicit a choice (choice-aimed disjunction, typically occurring in interrogative sentences, e.g. *Are we going to the cinema or are we staying at home?*). This distinction rests upon the highly intersubjective dimension of speaker's expectations regarding the hearer's reaction to his/her utterance (cf. also Dik 1968: 276 and Haspelmath 2007: 25–7).

As can be observed in (15), Marathi employs different connectives for simple disjunction (15a) and choice-aimed disjunction (15b), whereas English only has *or* for both relation types. We can say that in English the types of disjunction are undercoded, in that the semantics of the connective only conveys a set of mutually replaceable possibilities, leaving the eventual need for a choice to inference. The pattern of Marathi is rather frequent across languages and it is attested, among others, in Finnish (choice-aimed disjunction: *vai*, simple disjunction: *tai*), Georgian (choice-aimed disjunction: *tu*, simple disjunction: *an*), Polish (choice-aimed disjunction: *czy*, simple disjunction: *lub/albo*), Somali (choice-aimed disjunction: *misé*, simple disjunction: *ama*), Albanian (choice-aimed disjunction: *a/apo*, simple disjunction: *o/ose*), and Vietnamese (choice-aimed disjunction: *hay(là)*, simple disjunction: *hoặ*). If we wanted to employ the traditional lenses in examining the two sentences in (15), we would end up classifying them as two cases of exclusive disjunction, without grasping the difference motivating the use of two distinct markers (for further data and discussion, see Mauri 2008a: ch. 5).

(15) Marathi, Indo-Iranian, Indo-European, spoken in India
     (Pandharipande 1997: 162–3)
     a. madhū āītSyā    śuśruṣesāṭhī    suṭṭī gheīl    **kīmwā/*kī**
        Madhu mother.GEN looking.after.for leave take.FUT.3SG DISJC

        tilā      hɔspiṭalmadhe ṭṭhewīl
        3SG.ACC hospital.in      keep.FUT.3SG
        'Madhu will leave to take care of his mother or keep her in the hospital.'
     b. to   bādzārāt   gelā      **kī/*kīmwā** gharī     gelā?
        3SG market.LOC go.PST.3SG.M DISJC      home.LOC go.PST.3SG.M
        'Did he go to the market or did he go home?'

The typological picture just described underlines two major phenomena: (i) there are languages completely lacking an *or* connective and showing some overt indication of the irrealis status of the SoAs, and in such cases the part of meaning that is encoded concerns the non-factuality implied by the notion of disjunction, while their mutual replaceability is left to inferential enrichment; (ii) languages having two different disjunctive connectives employ them to encode the distinction between choice-aimed and simple disjunction, not that between inclusive and exclusive. Therefore, besides confirming the fact that different languages put the borderline between coding and inferencing at different points, this picture also highlights the crucial anchorage of disjunction on the one hand in the modal dimension of epistemic possibility, and on the other hand in the discourse dimension of speakers' expectations regarding hearers' reactions to their utterance, which may or may not result in a choice. These two poles implied in the notion of disjunction nicely emerge also from a diachronic analysis of disjunctive connectives (see also Giacalone and Mauri, forthcoming).

Disjunctive connectives frequently develop from underspecified constructions, where the disjunctive relation was originally inferred from the overt indication of the potential nature of the linked SoAs, like the one exemplified in (11). Such pragmatic inferences then trigger a form/function reanalysis (cf. Croft 2000: 120ff.), through which speakers reinterpret irrealis markers, such as dubitative adverbs, hypothetical forms, or interrogative markers, as the overt indicators of the notion of alternative, thus reanalyzing them as disjunctive connectives. Interrogative markers typically develop into disjunctive connectives in contexts where the speaker asks for a choice between two equivalent possibilities, i.e. in questions (instrumental form of Common Slavic *ch'to* 'what' > Czech, Polish: *czy*, Belorussian *ci* 'choice-aimed or'). Free choice constructions, on the other hand, grammaticalize as connectives in declarative sentences, where each alternative is overtly stated as a possible choice for the hearer. Examples of this path are provided by Latin *vel* 'want' > 'simple or', and French *soit... soit* 'be it' > 'either... or'. Dubitative epistemic markers and conditional constructions encode the speaker's doubt over the actual occurrence of the two alternatives and are typically reanalyzed as connectives of simple disjunction. Examples are attested both in Indo-European languages (Russian, Bulgarian, Serbo-Croatian: *i* 'and' + *li* (dubitative particle) > *ili* 'or'; Italian *sennò* 'otherwise' < *se* 'if' + *no*) and non-Indo-European languages. Two still transparent instances of these two latter paths are attested in Cavineña (a Tacanan language spoken in Bolivia), where the construction *jadya=ama ju-atsu* 'thus=NEG be-ss' (lit. 'being not thus, if it is not so') is reinterpreted as being a disjunctive connective meaning 'or' (Guillaume 2004: 114), and in Lezgian, where *taχajt'a* 'or' derives from the conditional form of the negated aorist participle of *χun* 'be', meaning 'if it is not' (Haspelmath 1993: 332).

## 19.4  Potential co-occurrence: conditional connectives

Let us now come to potentially co-occurring SoAs, linked by conditional connectives. Part of the debate has focused on tracing the borderline between the part of meaning that is encoded in *if* and the part of meaning that is left to inference, mainly discussing whether *if* is truth-functional or not. A good deal of pragmatic work has also revolved around the explanation of the recurrent interpretation of conditional *if... (then)* as a biconditional *if and only if*, i.e. so-called "conditional perfection" (Geis and Zwicky 1971). Let us address the two issues separately, starting from the identification of the semantic value of *if*.

As Grice (1989) puts it, natural language *if* can be considered semantically identical to material implication in logic '⊃', which is a truth-functional connective according to which $p \supset q$ is true on all possible combinations except when $p$ is true and $q$ is false. However, this assumption is not universally shared and has been discussed widely in the literature. Scholars working in the RT framework tend to maintain such a truth-functional characterization of *if* (Sperber and Wilson 1986, Carston 2002), arguing that the connective has a conceptual meaning, thus contributing to the truth-functional representation of the sentence (see section 19.1.1). By contrast, there is another view, followed among others by van der Auwera (1986) and Sweetser (1990), according to which *if* is not translatable into truth tables, but rather encodes non-truth-functional relations such as causal and consequential ones. For instance, a sentence such as (16) semantically encodes that the president's resignation is the cause for the vice president to assume the presidency.

(16)    If the President resigns, the Vice President shall immediately assume the presidency.

In his analysis of conditionals, van der Auwera (1986: 200; 1997a) proposes a sufficiency hypothesis, according to which *if p then q* means that $p$ is a sufficient condition for $q$. For instance, in (16), the President's resignation is a sufficient condition for the Vice President to assume the Presidency. The sufficiency hypothesis is also retained by Sweetser (1990), in her account of conditionals at the three levels of content, epistemic, and speech-act domains. Content conditionals are established between SoAs, indicating that the reality of one SoA is a sufficient condition (or cause) for the reality of a second SoA, as in (16). In the epistemic domain, conditionals link epistemic states, giving rise to a relation that may be paraphrased as "If I know $p$, I conclude that $q$," as in (17). If the hearer knows that the windows are all closed, (s)he will process this as a sufficient condition for concluding that they are out for dinner. In the speech-act domain, conditionals link a SoA to a speech act, so that the truth of the antecedent is a sufficient condition for the speaker's uttering the consequent speech act. Example (18) is thus equivalent to "if it is true that $p$, then I utter $q$."

(17)    If the windows are all closed, they are out for the evening.

(18)    If you are hungry, there are some biscuits on the table.

Hussein (2008: 77–8) proposes a different account, which looks like a compromise between the two approaches described so far, employing the distinction between conceptual and procedural elaborated in the RT framework. According to his analysis, conditionals can be classified as hybrid cases, having what he calls 'conceptuo-procedural' semantics. In the conceptual use, *if* has a truth-functional value and contributes to the semantic representation of the sentence. By contrast, in the procedural use, *if* is not truth-functional and plays a role in the inferential part of the conditional interpretation. In this perspective, example (16) would be classified as conceptual, while examples (17) and (18) would be classified as procedural. In this work, however, we will follow the approach proposed by van der Auwera and Sweetser, providing typological and diachronic data in support.

The second issue, "conditional perfection," is illustrated in (19), the example originally due to Geis and Zwicky (1971) (see van der Auwera 1997b for an overview of the literature). The pragmatic phenomenon under examination generates from (19a) the invited inferences in (19b,c,d), so that hearers infer a biconditional reading from simple conditional constructions. This inferential process has been explained by van der Auwera (1997a) in terms of scalar implicatures (Horn 1972; Gazdar 1979).

(19)   a.   If you mow the lawn, I'll give you five dollars.
       b.   If and only if you mow the lawn will I give you five dollars.
       c.   I'll give you five dollars just in case/only if you mow the lawn.
       d.   If you don't mow the lawn, I won't give you five dollars.

Jaszczolt (2005: 217) challenges the undisputed step from conditional to biconditional, and instead interprets the invited inferences illustrated in (19) as "a restriction of the domain of discourse, or, alternatively, a restriction (specification) of the topic of discourse." In other words, in her view "mowing the lawn" is established as the *topic* of the discourse and issuing a conditional request is the purpose of the speech act. What Jaszczolt suggests is to limit the analysis to such a topic restriction, without translating it into an equivalence to biconditional relations. She argues that "conditional perfection is just too strong a tool to account for the restriction of the domain of discourse that takes place when the conditional is used," because it is not demonstrated that mowing the lawn and obtaining five dollars are bi-uniquely linked, although the latter is a strong incentive for the former. As will be argued below, crosslinguistic data seem to confirm Jaszczolt's account of conditional protases in terms of topics.

If we have a look at the crosslinguistic variation attested in the coding of conditionals, the picture we are faced with is similar to that of disjunction, and at the end of this section we will argue for purely semantic explanations of such a similarity. Two issues are in focus. On the one hand, the question is how languages lacking an overt *if*-connective express the conditional relation, with special attention to the conditions of inferability, i.e. what elements are necessary in order for the relation to be inferable. On the other hand, we will consider cases in which conditionals are marked in the same way as other relations or notions, resulting in underspecified constructions.

As pointed out by Mauri and Sansò (2009), it is not infrequent to find languages lacking an overt conditional connective and expressing conditional relations by means of juxtapositive or highly underspecified strategies. However, as we saw for disjunction, in such cases not all is left to inferential processes; rather, coding and inferencing divide their labor, with the latter carrying more of the burden than the former. We can indeed identify the following restriction on inferability: if no conditional connective is present, *at least* one of the linked SoAs has to be marked as *potential* (irrealis) in order for the conditional relation to be inferable. Let us examine the two cases in (20) and (21). Example (20) from Nyulnyul shows a construction with an extremely general connective, *ikarr*, whose function is to signal subordination, and in which the verb forms in both protasis and apodosis (condition and conclusion of the conditional reasoning, respectively) are overtly marked as irrealis. Given the underspecification of the subordinator (which is employed for all subordination relations), in (20) the conditional relation can be argued not to be overtly coded. However, in order for it to be inferable, it is necessary that the two verb forms are overtly marked as irrealis, otherwise the hearer could interpret the construction [verb–subordinator–verb] as a purely temporal or causal relation (according to the inferential mechanisms already described in section 19.2).

(20)   Nyulnyul (Australian, Nyulnyulan, spoken in Australia; McGregor and Wagner 2006: 360–61)
Mi-li-jid-ikarr              kinyingk-ung    bur
2.MIN.NOM-IRR-go-SUB    this-ALL         camp
i-li-rr-ar-juy
3.NOM-IRR-AUG-spear-2.MIN.NOM
'If you go into that country, they might spear you.' ➔ irrealis markers in each clause, no conditional connective

Example (21) from Caodeng rGyalrong shows a similar situation, in which however the overt irrealis marker only occurs in the protasis. Here again, the absence of such a marker would easily lead to temporal or causal interpretations.

(21)   Caodeng rGyalrong (Sino-Tibetan, Tibeto-Burman, rGyalrong, spoken in China; Sun 2007: 805)
nɐɟiʔ təciʔ-naŋ      ɐ-nɐ-tə-nə́mder-nəʔ          ɐɟiʔ-ntʃʰon   nəmder-aŋ
2SG   water-inside   IRR1-IRR2.DOWN-2-jump-SUB 1SG-also     jump-1SG
'If you jump into the water, I will jump too.' ➔ irrealis marker in the protasis only, no conditional connective

What distinguishes conditional relations from temporal and, especially, causal ones is indeed the uncertainty of the condition, which makes the whole co-occurrence of the two SoAs a possibility, rather than a fact (or a non-fact). If we thus analyze conditionals as conveying a potential causal relation, we may easily understand why many languages basically employ the same underspecified strategy both for conditional and causal clause linkage, crucially distinguishing the two by means of modal operators. A co-occurence that is overtly marked as irrealis invites the inference of a conditional reading, while a co-occurrence that is unmarked with respect to reality status invites an inference of temporal and causal sequence.[6]

The pattern just discussed recalls the typological implication described in (12) for disjunction, with a small, but crucial, difference, namely for disjunction, if no connective is attested, both clauses have to be explicitly marked as irrealis, while for conditionals it is sufficient that either the protasis or the apodosis be irrealis (by means of irrealis, dubitative, or hypothetical elements). Two SoAs linked in a disjunctive relation indeed typically stand in a symmetric semantic contrast, whereas two SoAs linked in a conditional relation do not stand in a semantic contrast and are typically conceivable as different stages within a causal sequence. As a consequence, in *disjunction*, both SoAs have to be internally marked as irrealis: the juxtaposition of two SoAs that are presented as possibilities, rather than facts, and stand in a semantic contrast invites the inference of their equivalence and reciprocal replaceability as alternatives, leading to a disjunctive interpretation. If only one of the SoAs was overtly presented as a possibility (irrealis), it would be harder to infer their equivalence and hence their alternative status. In *conditional* relations, on the other hand, it is sufficient that at least one SoA be marked as irrealis: the juxtaposition of two SoAs that do not stand in a semantic contrast invites the inference of temporal/causal sequentiality between two SoAs, and a causal sequence in which one of the linked SoAs is marked as irrealis may easily be interpreted as a conditional relation, because, within a conceived sequence of events, if one of two SoAs is irrealis it is highly probable that the other one is irrealis too (see Mauri and Sansò 2009).

The attested crosslinguistic variation further reveals another interesting phenomenon, first analyzed by Haiman (1978). In case the strategy employed for conditionals may also be used for other functions, such functions frequently include polar interrogatives and topics. For instance, in example (22) from Hua, a Trans New Guinea language spoken in Papua New Guinea, the protasis of a conditional relation is conveyed by means of a polar interrogative construction.

(22)   Hua (Haiman 1978:)
        E-si-ve                baigu-e.
        Come-3SG.FUT-INT    will.stay-1SG.
        'Will he come? I will stay'; 'If he will come, I will stay.'

The same tendency is attested in a number of unrelated languages, such as Russian, Turkish, Mayan languages, and Germanic languages (e.g. English *Should you need any help, let me know*, where the subject inversion in the protasis is the same as in polar questions). The complex account provided by Haiman for such crosslinguistic patterns cannot be examined in detail here, for reasons of space. However, the crucial argument he brings forward is that polar questions and conditionals share the topical status of the antecedent, with respect to the consequent (in polar questions, the antecedent is the question, and the consequent is the answer), which motivates the multifunctionality patterns he describes. In his view (Haiman 1978: 586), at the NP level, the topic presupposes the existence of its referent, while at the sentence level, it is the truth of the described proposition (in particular, the existence of the SoA described in the conditional proposition) which is presupposed.

The data and arguments discussed by Haiman seem to provide evidence for Jaszczolt's (2005: 217) account of conditionals, in that both argue that speakers tend to interpret the protasis as the topic of the discourse and the apodosis as conveying the purpose of the speech act (see above). The recurrent interpretation of the condition as the topic of discourse indeed plausibly motivates the crosslinguistic tendency to express the two functions (conditionals and topics) by means of the same strategies.

Diachronic data on the origin of conditional constructions further support the synchronic picture just discussed, starting from underspecified strategies in which the conditional relation is inferred through pragmatic processes and ending in the form/function reanalysis of pivotal elements of the sentence as conditional connectives. As Heine and Kuteva (2002: 94) point out, conditional markers frequently develop from copula constructions, which originally indicate the presupposition of existence of a SoA and then get reanalyzed as conditions, in full accordance with Haiman's and Jaszczolt's argument on the topical status of protases (e.g. Swahili *i-ki-wa* 'it being that' > 'if', Japanese *nara* 'be' > 'if'). Another frequent source for conditional connectives is interrogative markers (Heine and Kuteva 2002: 249), as exemplified by Russian *est' li* 'is it?' > *esli* 'if' and by subject inversion strategies employed in questions and then extended to conditional protasis in Germanic languages. Again, the development of interrogative strategies into conditional connectives goes in the direction of Haiman's analysis. The third main set of diachronic sources for conditionals are temporal markers expressing duration (Heine and Kuteva 2002: 293), which in sequences of events may invite conditional inferences of the type "when $p$, then $q$" > "if $p$, then $q$" (see section 19.2), thus confirming analyses of conditionals giving pride of place to non-truth-functional notions such as sufficiency and cause. Examples of this path are provided by Tagalog (Austronesian, Malayo-Polynesian, spoken in Philippines) *(ka)pag(ka)*, *kung* 'if', 'then', 'while'; Indonesian *djika* 'if', 'when'; and *kalau* 'if', 'when', 'as for' (topic).

## 19.5  Conflicting co-occurrence: adversatives, concessives

In this final section, we will briefly address some issues concerning the semantics and pragmatics of adversative and concessive connectives. Adversatives (e.g. English *but*) and concessives (e.g. English *nonetheless*) have received great attention in the pragmatic literature, since Grice's analysis of *but* as characterized by a $p \wedge q$ semantics, together with a conventional implicature of conflict. In the RT framework, adversatives and concessives are taken to represent prototypical procedural elements (Blakemore 2000 and 2002), in that they do not contribute to the truth-functional representation of the sentence, but constrain the inferential processes underlying its interpretation. The borderline and, at the same time, the division of labor between semantics and pragmatics in adversative connectives have been nicely described by Lang (2000), with special focus on the "denial of expectation" value (cf. German *aber*, Spanish *pero*, English *but*, although *but* may have a number of further contrastive functions, see Mauri 2008a: 120–26).

In Lang's view, "adversative (and probably also concessive) connectors inherently contain pointers to previous information available from the context" (Lang 2000: 245). Adversative connectives thus link two SoAs on the basis of a common topic, or in Lang's terms, a 'common integrator' (Lang 1984: 69–79), i.e. the ground on which the two SoAs are pertinently combined, and further signal that the assertion rendered by the second clause is in contrast to an assumption that either may be read off, or must be inferred, from previous information (cf. (23)).

(23)    Paul is very tall, but he does not play basketball.
          → assumption: very tall people often play basketball.

However, Lang argues that linking the two SoAs to an assumption is not completely dependent on pragmatic mechanisms, but rather involves both a part of meaning that is encoded (semantics) and a part that has to be inferred (pragmatics). The part of meaning functioning as a pointer and indicating a contrast between the assertion of the second clause and some assumption is part of the semantics of *but*. On the other hand, the identification of the assumption in the sentence or in the context is left to pragmatics. Yet, for a correct interpretation of an adversative connective, both dimensions necessarily come into play and complement each other.

If we look at the crosslinguistic variation we see a lot of variation in the degree of coding of adversative and concessive relations. A connective like *although* fully encodes the notion of concessivity and does not leave anything to pragmatics, to the point that in a contradictory context, the relation encoded by the connective forces a concessive reading. However, in many languages contrast is conveyed by means of conjunctive strategies, leaving to inference the identification of a conflict between the linked clauses (see Mauri 2008a: ch. 4 for a survey). It is to be noted, though, that in languages lacking overt adversative connectives, these are very easily borrowed.

In general, connectives tend to be borrowed along a specific order. Matras (1998: 301–5) has identified the following borrowing cline: "but" > "or" > "and". According to this cline, in bilingual contexts languages replacing conjunctive connectives also replace disjunctives, and languages replacing disjunctive connectives also replace adversative connectives. According to Matras (1998: 305–25), this implication mirrors the different degrees of "intensity with which the speaker is required to intervene with hearer-sided mental processing activities" in establishing the relations of combination, alternative, and contrast. The more the relation implies a contrast, the more the speaker has to maintain assertive authority despite the denial of the addressee's expectations. To do so, bilingual speakers tend to adopt connectives of the pragmatically dominant language.

In diachronic terms, there is one recurrent source for adversative connectives that further confirms the cline along which the burden of communication gradually passes from pragmatics to semantics. Adversative connectives frequently derive from sources denoting temporal values, such as the relation of simultaneity "while" and the meaning of continuity "always" (e.g. English *while* 'temporal' > 'concessive'; French *alors que* 'when' > 'whereas'; Italian *tuttavia* and French *toutefois* 'always, continuously' > 'nonetheless'; see Giacalone and Mauri, forthcoming). In both cases, the co-existence over time of two events comes to be perceived as a surprising one, as a consequence of the fact that the differences existing between the two events are foregrounded at the expense of their temporal relation.

## 19.6 Conclusion

In this chapter we reviewed analyses of conjunctive, disjunctive, and implicative connectives, and more briefly temporal, causative, purposive, adversative, and concessive connectives. We focused on the dynamic balance between semantics understood as coded meaning and pragmatics as the meaning that is left to be inferred from context, and we demonstrated what crosslinguistic as well as diachronic studies can reveal about what is universal and language-particular and we compared this perspective to the logico-philosophical one.

# 20

# Spatial reference in discourse

Luna Filipović

## 20.1  Introduction

The relationship between reference and grammar has been a major topic in pragmatics, though it is not unique to the field of pragmatics. There are numerous theoretical and empirical research programmes devoted to it within a number of linguistic frameworks. The very nature of the multi-faceted relationship between reference and grammar has formed the basis for more general discussions of the interaction between universal and language-specific features in language and cognition. The notion of reference, both spatial and temporal, has played a prominent role most notably in philosophy and philosophically grounded semantics and pragmatics. In some approaches certain specific items are grouped and studied together (e.g. proper nouns, pronouns, demonstrative phrases and definite descriptions) as *expressions used to refer* (Jaszczolt 2002: 125). The focus in the present chapter is on spatial reference in a more general sense. I shall discuss critically different approaches to the relationship between objects and events in space on the one hand, and their linguistic description and conceptualisation on the other.

Many approaches to meaning in language address the dynamics of the relationship between a referent in the world and its expression in language (see Sullivan, this volume). In formal frameworks, the relationship between referents and the linguistic means used to refer to them has been represented using formal logic. Successful reference to objects and to events in space and time has been discussed as both a semantic and a pragmatic phenomenon. For example, the difference between *de re* and *de dicto* in propositional attitude reports can be viewed as a duality of use and hence as a matter of pragmatic interpretation. At the same time, the difference in interpretation is truth-conditionally relevant and so its semantic relevance cannot be denied (cf. Jaszczolt 2002 and this volume). Picking out a referent and evaluating the truth of the proposition are only a part of the overall interpretation of an utterance. Semantic and pragmatic theories from philosophically oriented linguistic camps have also been trying to capture contextual and dynamic aspects of meaning, appealing to different mechanisms of contextual enrichment or to processing preferences such as default inferences (cf. Levinson 2000, Jaszczolt 2005). On the other hand, other traditions in linguistics have been tackling the same or similar problems under the auspices of cognitively rather than philosophically oriented programmes.

The two approaches to the study of meaning and language use, namely the philosophical and the cognitive, may seem quite disparate at first glance and they certainly differ in important ways. As Jackendoff (1999, 2003) argues on the cognitive side, meaning in language should be studied from the point of view of the *conceptualiser*, or the language processor, in this case the human mind rather than the external world. In other words, language as a phenomenon can be investigated from the perspective of psychologically plausible explanations for its functioning rather than specifying what is logically required in order to make it correspond to reality. The focus on internal language as opposed to its relationship to the external world appears to be an insuperable conceptual difference between philosophical and cognitive approaches in linguistics. However, to view the distinction in these terms is rather simplistic and the two sides may be seen as approaching a complex phenomenon, namely language, from two different angles: (a) language as an internal, individual and flexible system of representation and (b) language as an external, shared and conventionalised system of communication. These two aspects of language as a phenomenon may overlap in some respects, but they also have independent spheres of influence.

Jackendoff, in the spirit of Chomsky, emphasises that he is not interested in language as an external, objective system (E-language) and in what the world has to be like for an expression referring to it to be true. He argues that the true subject of study in linguistics is I-language, namely trying to answer the question of what one has to know in order to be able to understand what an expression means. Whether the expression 'A tiger has stripes' is true or false is of no concern for the understanding of what a sentence means. Jackendoff says that the position that information conveyed by language is about the *real world* is 'naïve' (1995a: 29). He contends that the information conveyed by language must be about the *projected world* because our conscious access is only to the projected world and 'we can talk about things only insofar as they have achieved mental representation' (*ibid.*). Thus Jackendoff rejects any direct relation of world to language (1995a, 1997, 1999, 2003), which is precisely what philosophical semantics is interested in. Other cognitive approaches to meaning are similarly interested in how language relates to the mind rather than to the external world (e.g. Langacker 1987, 1991).

In spite of this apparent chasm between philosophical and cognitive approaches to meaning, both have a common interest in developing formally precise and cognitively plausible representations of objects and events as construed by language and the mind. Researchers from these two strands in the study of linguistic meaning seem to share more than they credit themselves with since numerous philosophically driven theories are also centrally concerned with language processing, e.g. DRT (Kamp and Reyle 1993), Relevance theory (Sperber and Wilson 1986) and Default Semantics (Jaszczolt 2005), while followers of cognitively driven approaches are recognising the advantages of a more rigorous and formal representation (cf. Jackendoff 1995a, 1997, 2003; Michaelis 2004). Furthermore, Jackendoff (2003: 394), for example, tries to incorporate one of the major concerns of formal semantics (the existential and referential claims a sentence makes about the entities named in it) while at the same time not discarding the truth-conditions-based approaches like DRT (Kamp and Reyle 1993).

In this chapter I discuss the relationship(s) between spatial reference and lexical and grammatical features in different languages as well as the ways in which cognitively oriented theories deal with universal and language-specific factors that impact spatial reference in discourse. The domain of space is particularly relevant in this context since this cognitive domain forms a part of our universal human experience and is also an area of convergence for the language-specific, culture-specific and environment-specific factors that affect how we refer to, and possibly think of, objects and events in space.

## 20.2  Cognitive approaches to reference and grammar

In order to understand the multiple factors that affect spatial reference in discourse we need to study the ways in which spatial information is represented in language. However, views on how many different levels of representation there are and the nature of the interaction between them vary among different scholars.

For instance, Jackendoff argues that semantic/conceptual structure does not *have* semantics, it *is* semantics and it is fully non-intentional. The combinatorial structures that constitute meaning/thoughts are not representations or information *about* something. They are pure non-intentional structures like phonology and syntax. He has replaced his earlier term (e.g. Jackendoff 1995a) 'spatial representation' (SpR) with 'spatial structure' (SpS) in order to eliminate any hint of intentionality (Jackendoff 2003: 346). He distinguishes conceptual structure (CS) and spatial structure (SpS). CS encodes *propositional* representations and SpS is the locus of *mental model* representations. Conceptual structure is an encoding of linguistic meaning that is independent of the particular language in which it is expressed. It is built up out of discrete primitive features and functions. However, 'propositional' in this case does not mean the same as it does in standard logic but rather the term refers to the *underlying composition of concepts*. Jackendoff is only interested in reference to the world *as speakers conceptualise it* and not in any kind of conceptualiser-independent propositional meaning (Jackendoff 1999: 5).

The crucial question for Jackendoff is how to define the link between the two levels, namely the mapping between CS and SpS. In other words, what do the levels of the spatial structure (i.e. the features of the world around us) and conceptual structure (the way we think about the world around us) share in order for it to be possible for them to interface and communicate with each other? Some of the central shared notions are *physical object*, *location*, *path* and *physical motion*. In other words, referents in space, which belong to SpS, and referents in the mind, which belong to CS, have these notions in common, which facilitates the interaction between the two levels involved in thought and language. For Jackendoff (2003: 309) the world is a product of human perception and conception and a 'more ultimate reality' beyond human cognition does not seem to be a valid enterprise. We should think of the perceptual world not as absolute reality but as the reality constructed by our perceptual systems in response to whatever is really out there. Nevertheless, the perceptual world is in sync with the 'real world'. Our perceptual systems are such that they are not concerned with a 'true model of the world' in the logical sense but with a 'world model' that is adequate to support the planning of actions that yield long-term benefits (e.g. to enable a better propagation of our genes; Jackendoff 2003: 308). The perceived world **is** reality for Jackendoff (2003: 308).

A central hypothesis is that the grammatical aspects of language make reference only to CS, not to SpS, and that nothing in grammar depends on, for example, detailed shapes of objects (Jackendoff 2003: 348). On the other hand, SpS is language's connection to perception and it is through this connection that we can talk about what we see (*ibid.*). He adds in a footnote, however, that some examples to the contrary can be found, such as languages that have classifier systems that depend on coarse object shapes (e.g. the Japanese classifier *hon* which is used for skinny objects). Jackendoff asserts that this might or might not be encoded in CS and that it is 'an interesting and as yet unaddressed empirical issue' (*ibid.*). However, following the logic of Landau and Jackendoff (1993), if we can talk about it, then surely we should be able to represent it or encode it in CS. Numerous empirical studies do indeed exist and they provide evidence that there is a persistent reliance on lexicalised language-specific concepts even in tasks that are not explicitly linguistic (cf. Levinson 2003b, 2003c; Lucy 1992; Lucy and Gaskins 2003). For instance, Lucy (1992) explained how Yucatec Mayan speakers classify objects according to material, rather than to shape as preferred by English speakers, as a consequence of categories of grammatical number and of numeral classifiers available in that language. The precise nature and strength of such effects are still under debate and the answers are not conclusive at this point but currently available empirical data and future experimental research should enable us to unveil the precise mechanics behind reported language-specific effects (see section 20.3).

Some aspects of the conceptualised world are formulated solely in terms of CS, such as category membership or abstract concepts (cf. Jackendoff 2003:

347–8), while judgements about exact shapes, locations and forces are for-mulated only in terms of SpS (*ibid.*). For instance, abstract concepts such as *fairness* or *value* and logical concepts such as *and*, *if* and *not* have only CS components (Jackendoff 2003: 348). One the other hand, there is over-lap between the two levels, and notions such as part–whole relationships and causation 'have reflexes in both systems' (Jackendoff 2003: 347). This overlap is of particular interest because language, perception and concep-tualisation of space (and other domains) do interact, but the question is how. In an earlier seminal paper, Landau and Jackendoff (1993) hypothesise that most of the rich range of spatial relations are not visible to the lan-guage faculty and are thus levelled out in the translation into a linguistic format. For example, dimensional adjectives such as *big/small*, *thick/thin* and *tall/short* refer to continuous dimensions of size but linguistic terms "bifur-cate" these dimensions into pairs of relative contrasting terms (Landau and Jackendoff 1993). By the same token, spatial representation recruited by motor navigation must be richer than that appearing in language (*ibid.*: 233). Similarly, a precise metric representation of space emerges early in life, and this is normally the kind of information that is not encoded in language (cf. Talmy 2000). Clearly, spatial representation in other cognitive subsystems and spatial representation in language do not completely overlap. Landau and Jackendoff (1993: 13) reason that it is not economical to have what is encoded in one system also encoded in the other. Linguistic categories are treated as direct projections of universal concepts in this account and a cor-relation is made between a property of grammar (e.g. the kinds of things count nouns and prepositions standardly express) and descriptions of non-linguistic systems represented in particular areas of the brain (Landau and Jackendoff 1993: 237). They emphasise that even without this correlation language would still provide rich and systematic evidence about the charac-ter of spatial cognition, for anything we talk about we must also be able to represent.

However, we do not go around representing everything that is potentially representable. Levinson's position is that linguistic representation cannot be identical to the representation in which we do our conceptual thinking. Rather, they have to be similar in some respects since the language of thought must directly or indirectly support linguistic distinctions. Moreover, there are factors that limit our choice as to what aspects of a spatial scene we habitually refer to, and one of those factors is the language we speak. There is still much debate about whether human conceptual structure is relatively constant in its core features across cultures (cf. Levinson 2003c).

Before we turn to cross-linguistic variation in spatial reference in the next section, we have to explore some more suggestions that have been made for universal factors that may lie in the essence of the mechanisms we rely on for both reference to and conceptualization of space.

One of the first scholars to discuss these mechanisms as *lexicalisation pat-terns* was Len Talmy, who studied a number of cognitive domains as well as the linguistic means used to refer to them across languages. The regularities in these lexicalisations formed the basis for the typology of languages he proposed (Talmy 1985). Talmy's typology of the world's languages is based on the way in which they map *schemas* (cognitive notions) onto surface (linguistic) expressions. He focused on *spatial schemas* in particular because of their ubiquity in human language and human cognition. He begins by assuming that one can isolate elements separately within the domain of meaning and within the domain of surface expression. He then examines which semantic (which for Talmy means *conceptual*) elements are expressed by which surface elements. This relationship is largely not one-to-one. A combination of semantic elements can be expressed by a single surface element, or a single semantic element by a combination of surface elements. For example, we can study how perception, cognition and language are interrelated in the reference to dynamic spatial relations that constitute *motion events*. Talmy specified the range of surface participants (grammatical categories such as nominal, prepositional and verb constituents) and their universal semantic (i.e. conceptual) equivalents (Figure, Ground, Path, and Motion). According to Talmy, we can identify four basic semantic components in a motion event:

Motion:  Presence of motion
Figure:  The moving object
Ground:  The reference-point object with respect to which the Figure moves
Path:    The course followed by the Figure with respect to the Ground

A typical example of an expression for a motion event would be: 'The man ran up the hill'. In this sentence, 'the man' expresses the Figure, 'the hill' refers to the Ground, and the Path is expressed by the particle 'up'. The verb root ('run') itself conflates manner and motion. Lexicalised manner of motion seems to be an additional component in motion expressions, since a description of motion events can appear without it (e.g. 'The man went up the hill'). In perception and conceptualisation, on the other hand, Manner is an indispensable experiential component of a motion event, because every change of location from A to B must have been carried out in a certain manner. Speakers of all languages refer to these event components in different ways, but the different ways of referring to motion events do not vary to such a great extent. In fact, all the languages of the world can be seen as belonging to one of two typological groups depending on where they express the central component of motion, i.e. Path. Talmy shows that languages like the Romance typically express Path in the verb and thus they are termed *verb-framed*. For example, in Spanish one cannot say the equivalent of the English *Jim limped out of the house* but rather it has to be *Jim exited the house limping* (i.e. *Jim salió de la casa cojeando*). On the other hand, Germanic languages express Path outside of the verb, in elements that Talmy terms 'satellites' (e.g. particles of different kinds, prefixes, adverbials, etc.) and such languages belong to the *satellite-framed* group. These typological differences result in numerous consequences for narrative preferences and the habitual provision/omission of information in both spoken and written communication, directly conditioned by this typological dimension (cf. Filipović 2007a, 2008; Slobin 2000, 2006).

For example, the typological preferences result in different pieces of information in a motion expression having different degrees of *salience*. Salience is a cognitive notion that refers to the degree of prominence that individual elements have in a spatial scene and/or in its linguistic expression. Differences in salience can be achieved even within a single language because the grammatical and lexical rules of a language may provide a certain flexibility as to which aspect of a scene will receive more prominence. If we use a less typical or a less usual pattern in our reference to a spatial scene, this gives more salience to one particular aspect of it. In order to make a piece of information more prominent, it has to be placed in a position that is different from its usual one.

For instance, in English, it is typical to have the manner of motion in the verb (as in *fly across* or *sail across*). If we put it outside the verb, we are making the manner more salient, for example, referring to a less typical situation. Therefore, if we say *Jim crossed the Atlantic by boat* we can infer that this is a less common way to cross the Atlantic since the typical way would be by plane, as in *Jim flew across the Atlantic* (cf. Talmy 1996). Similar examples can be found in a variety of motion expressions in English. The manner of motion is made more salient in *Running really fast, he entered the train station* than in the more common pattern *He ran into the train station very fast*. Different languages allow for different degrees of flexibility when it comes to these lexicalisation patterns. Romance languages (e.g. French, Italian or Spanish) have less flexibility with regard to when they use manner verbs. If we want to refer to the event of running into a house, we cannot express the manner of motion in the verb. The only way to lexicalise this event in these languages is by means of a path verb, e.g. *enter*, with manner expressed outside the verb, e.g. in a gerund, as in the following example from Spanish: *Entró en la casa corriendo* ('He entered the house running').

Even though there are many shared features in the way languages deal with spatial reference (which is not surprising since basic spatial relations are ubiquitous in human experience), when speakers use language-specific devices to refer to objects and events in space, some additional meanings can be habitually conveyed while others are habitually excluded. The potential and actual consequences of these habitual preferences in referring may affect not just the *form* of an expression but also its *content* (cf. Filipović 2007a, 2007b, 2008; Slobin 2000, 2006). The extent to which any effects of lexicalisation preferences can be found beyond the frequency and kind of information that is included in spatial reference is currently a vibrant area of research in both linguistics and psychology. According to Slobin (2000, 2006), the habitual/preferred ways of referring to different situations are claimed to impact thinking-for-speaking, translating, listening and possibly remembering. Thinking-for-speaking involves conceptualisation on-line, so language-specific effects may not run deep, i.e. off-line, when we are not engaged in communication, but we cannot exclude the possibility that language may strongly encourage us to forge certain preferred representations of relationships among objects and events in space when we refer to them. Speakers may resort to their habitual lexicalisation patterns in order to organise and store information even when they are not engaged in explicit communication. Spatial categories, given the universality of human spatial abilities, should provide a source for many universals in language and conceptualisation. The cognitive domain of space should be full of prime examples for conceptual/semantic universality. However, the linguistic variation in this area is immense, and some would argue that the conceptualisation as well as the lexicalisation of space is also affected. Why isn't spatial reference more uniform across languages, even in closely related ones? Why are the grammars of space so different?

Some would say that they just appear to be different on the surface but that essentially and underlyingly, they are not very different from one another. For example, Jackendoff has proposed a universal annotation paradigm to 'translate' natural language expressions into the underlying conceptual representations of the situations referred to by these expressions. He observes that one of the central distinctions in spatial cognition and spatial discourse is that between PLACES and PATHS. PLACES are the simpler of the two, they project into a point or a region while PATHS are more varied with respect to their structure and roles in states and events. For instance, the conceptual structure of *The lamp is standing on the floor* (Jackendoff 1995a: 163) is [THING] occupies [PLACE], while *The dog went into the room* will be construed as [Event GO ([Thing DOG], [Path TO ([Place IN ([Thing ROOM])])])] (Jackendoff 1995a: 183). This is how universal conceptual structures can be represented according to Jackendoff and he proposes a set of ontological categories that feature in universal concept formation, such as THING, PLACE, DIRECTION, EVENT, MANNER, PATH, AMOUNT. In this case, linguistic diversity is merely a matter of complex packaging at a higher level, and of universal conceptual primitives at lower level (Jackendoff 1995a, 1997).

Another proposal for unravelling the universal mechanisms responsible for concept formation and spatial cognition in general comes from Talmy (2000, 2006) who talks about *universal spatial prompts* for lexicalisation. He argues that there is a relatively closed and universally available inventory of fundamental conceptual elements that recombine in various patterns to constitute spatial schemas. Spoken languages have two systems of meaning-bearing forms, the open class or lexical subsystem and the closed class, or grammatical subsystem. They perform two different functions, with the open class largely contributing to the *conceptual content* while closed-class forms determine *conceptual structure*. He focuses on the spatial schemas represented by the closed-class forms in order to examine the concepts used by languages (Talmy 2006: 209).

Talmy begins by selecting one closed-class spatial morpheme in a language and providing the full schema and spatial scene that it can apply to. For example, the schema for *across* in *The board lay across the road* contains a Figure (the board) and the Ground (the road). The Ground is 'ribbonal' – a plane with two parallel edges and distance between them. The Figure is linear and bounded at both edges. Another Figure (e.g. a planar object like a wall siding) would not be used with the preposition *across* but with *over* instead as in *The wall siding lay over the road*. Similarly, if the board was lying in another position, e.g. aligned with the road and not perpendicular, then *The board lay along the road* would be a more appropriate reference. Another element of the scene is that the board is in contact with the surface of the road, and if it was lowered or raised from the surface we would need to say *The board lay (buried) in the road* and *The board was (suspended) above the road* respectively (Talmy 2006: 210–11). In this way, we can see that on the basis of this single example we can determine which elements figure in the closed-class spatial schemas: a figure, a ground, a point, a line, a plane, a boundary, parallelness, perpendicularity, horizontality, adjacency (contact) and relative magnitude. Therefore a spatial schema like that for *The board lay across the road* consists of all the individual elements of the scene, their qualities and their relations to one another.

Talmy further observes that one of the properties of spatial schemas is that they 'exhibit a topological or a topology-like neutrality to certain factors of Euclidian geometry' (*ibid*.: 220). For example, they are magnitude-neutral, as seen in the fact that the *across* schema can apply to a situation of any size (e.g. *The ant crawled across my palm* or *The bus drove across the country*). Talmy also argues that they are largely shape-neutral and that this apparent neutrality to shape or magnitude means in turn that the cognitive structure underlying spatial morphemes is largely topological rather than absolute or Euclean (*ibid*.). In contrast, Levinson (2003b, 2003c) argues against putting forward such universalist claims and generalising so broadly across languages. He says that axial and angular properties are expressed in adpositions quite typically (Levinson 2003c: 72), but so are horizontal and vertical axes. For example, the English preposition *in* is a topological notion based on the properties of a Ground object, while *under* combines topological, intrinsic (under-surface, bottom) and absolute (vertical) information (*ibid*.). While shape discriminations are rarer, they turn up often enough, as in the Karuk postposition 'though a tube' or the Nishga locative proclitics encoding 'on something horizontal' (Levinson 2003c: 72–3). Some locative verbs make contrastive pairs based on shape, as in the Tzeltal contrast between 'be in a hemispherical container' and 'be in a cylindrical container' (cf. Brown, P. 1994). In other words, IN cannot be a universal concept and should not be annotated as such. Japanese conflates OVER and ON, Tzeltal has just one preposition to cover the scenes of OVER, UNDER, ON, IN and THROUGH, while some languages have no adpositions at all (Jaminjung or Arrernte). Yélî Dnye has two IN concepts (i.e. forms dedicated to containment) and six forms to cover the semantic space subsumed by the English ON or ABOVE (Levinson 2006b: 167). Levinson insists (2003b: 31) that there is basically 'no agreement as to what constitutes an IN spatial scene, a spatial relation of containment or any other basic topological relation'. In fact, the most recent results of extensive empirical cross-linguistic research indicate that diversity pervades every level of linguistic organisation and 'there are vanishingly few universals of language in the direct sense that all languages exhibit them' (Evans and Levinson 2009: 429).

Even closely related languages like Dutch and German show important differences in the ways they organise semantic space. As Bowerman and Pederson (1992) point out, the particular concern in German is whether the ground object is vertical or horizontal, whereas in Dutch it matters more whether the attachment is at a particular point or over a more extended area. As we shall see in the next section, these linguistic differences may have further consequences that are not limited to surface differences in the ways we refer to the same spatial non-linguistic categories.

## 20.3  Cross-linguistic evidence in spatial language and thought

It has been observed that without the decoupling of semantic and conceptual content we would find it difficult to argue strongly in favour of conceptual universality in humans. In other words, if we do not posit a semantic level of representation, we could conclude that speakers of different languages conceptualise spatial relations differently because they refer to them in conspicuously different ways (cf. Levinson 1997). There are different views with regard to which differences in semantic structure map onto differences in conceptual structure. Theories also differ when it comes to the nature and the content of the universal conceptual core. Some authors limit the possible effects of differences in semantic structures to those domains of cognitive functioning that are explicitly language-driven, for example in categorisation after verbal encoding (Malt et al. 2003), thus allowing for a greater degree of universality in conceptual structure. Other authors propose that the semantic representations of a particular language leave a far more pervasive imprint on cognition, for example in spatial cognition (Levinson 2003b, 2003c; Bowerman and Choi 2003) or in the appreciation of object properties (Lucy and Gaskins 2003).

The intriguing possibility that the same spatial scenes may not only be expressed differently, even by speakers of the same language, but that spatial cognition may be affected as a consequence has been present in linguistic and philosophical thinking for a very long time and has been most commonly known as the linguistic relativity hypothesis or Sapir–Whorf hypothesis. Once a derided theory, linguistic relativity has been given significant empirical support more recently. Pederson et al. (1998) found that cognitive frame of reference correlates with the linguistic frame of reference within the same referential domain. Levinson (1999, 2003c, 2006b) has discussed spatial reference in detail with a particular focus on the frames of reference. He distinguishes three frames: intrinsic (*The ball is on the chair's left side*), relative (*The ball is on the left of the chair from my viewpoint*) and absolute (*The ball is north of the chair*). Levinson (2003b) observes that it has been a tradition to focus on the 'exclusive centrality of egocentric, anthropomorphic, relativistic spatial concepts and abilities, as opposed to allocentric, abstract, absolute spatial information' (Levinson 2003c: 9). He contends that this tradition is deeply flawed because it is based on an exclusively Indo-European perspective. There are many languages that do not use bodily coordinates to construct a relative frame of reference and many other features in those languages indicate that the body may not be the central source for spatial concepts (Levinson 2003c: 14). Levinson pays particular attention to the fact that the semantic and the conceptual levels of representation have to be explicitly decoupled, which is not done in some other frameworks (e.g. Jackendoff's or Talmy's).

For Jackendoff (1995a: 105) the semantic structure is responsible for a formal account of semantic properties of utterances. He goes on to say that 'semantic and conceptual structure collapse into a unified level, and syntactic form is mapped by correspondence rules directly into conceptual structure, without an intermediate level that accounts for purely linguistic inference' (*ibid.*) His Conceptual Structure Hypothesis is a theory that proposes a single universal level of mental representations (Jackendoff 1995a: 19). What follows directly from this isomorphism between the semantic and the conceptual level of representation is that if languages differ in crucial aspects of lexicalisation in a cognitive domain (e.g. space), then so does the corresponding conceptualisation of relations within that domain. This is certainly not something that Jackendoff advocates, but it is a possible consequence of such an isomorphism between the two levels of representation. In essence, the role of semantics as a language-specific intermediate level is something that is of no consequence for conceptualisation, which is universal.

On the contrary, Levinson (2003c) and Levinson and Wilkins (2006) argue that the ways in which languages organise spatial notions are based on atomic concepts such as contact, vertical relation, adhesion, containment, not molar (complex) concepts like ON or IN. Simple conflation of semantics and conceptual structure is not defensible, but if we assume a kind of *partial isomorphism*, decompositional theories can explain how it is possible to learn a language by building up complex constructs from more elementary concepts. However, it need not be an either-or issue and Levinson argues along these lines that there are two levels of representation: decompositional and non-compositional.

At one level, the level of routine language processing, we map lexemes onto unitary molar concepts, and these in turn onto another level where the unitary molar concepts are broken down into formulae of composed atomic concepts. The generative capacity and the universals (if any) lie at the atomic level, while 'all advantages that accrue to us by virtue of thinking in high level "chunks" are reaped on the molar level' (Levinson 2003c: 298). Such a dual-level theory allows us to consider seriously the possibility of Whorfian effects of language on cognition while simultaneously 'buying into the "psychic" unity of mankind' (*ibid.*: 300). By the same token, Landau (2010) has suggested that both universal and language-specific factors are at play and it is a task for cognitive science to unravel the complexity of their interaction. For example, the preference for Source focus in a spatial scene and not Goal may be one example of a universal (cf. also Lakusta *et al.* 2007). Lakusta *et al.* (2007) have shown that there is a universally present asymmetry in Source vs. Goal representation whereby Goal Paths are regularly and systematically encoded, but Source Paths often omitted. This pattern is observed among a variety of populations and across a broad range of domains including manner of motion, change of possession, change of state and attachment/detachment events. Their results indicate that there are universal non-linguistic foundations of spatial language and the biases that arise when we use language to describe what we see.

Furthermore, it is extremely difficult to strip the entrenchment of molar concepts off in order to study the atomic ones. The relativity effects are the result of this difficulty and the quest for universal primitive concepts is not over yet. So if we detect language-specific effects on spatial cognition, we do not necessarily deny that there are strong universal tendencies as well. Levinson and Wilkins (2006) suggest that some concepts (e.g. 'contact' or 'horizontal support') are stronger candidates for universal status than some others (e.g. 'on') (Levinson and Wilkins 2006: 522). In the same vein, Vandeloise (2006: 421) points out that 'the indisputable role of language in the acquisition of spatial terms does not preclude the existence of a universal set of pre-linguistic concepts'. Vandeloise (2003: 421) argues that those spatial concepts are complex primitives and that they are organised in a hierarchy headed by the concept of 'control', which branches into 'containment', 'tight fit', 'support' and 'attachment'. He explains how the spatial relationships in different languages develop from the hierarchy based on the features of 'control' (direction of control, effective versus virtual control, direct versus indirect control) and their combinations.

According to Vandeloise (2003) 'support' and 'containment' are primitive complex concepts. Primitive because they are pre-linguistic and complex because several characteristics acting like family resemblance features are necessary to describe the relationships involved in their formation, namely Bearer/Burden and Container/Content (Vandeloise 2003: 400). They are globally understood before their perceptual characteristics such as form or dimensionality. Since many configurations are in the scope of several complex concepts, the semantics of each language must make a choice among the candidates and this introduces further relativity into the linguistic description of space (*ibid.*: 421). He argues that the set of pre-linguistic concepts anchoring language to conceptualisation of the world might be more universal even though the end result of semantic systems need not be the same for all languages (Vandeloise 2006: 152–3). Control in many directions corresponding to English *in* (and corresponding to Spanish *en*) and control in many directions with contact corresponding to Korean *kitta* are only embedded concepts moving from the more general to the more specific (*ibid*.: 153). The child's pre-linguistic concepts at different levels of generality must be adjusted to each language (*ibid*.: 153). Crucially, the conceptualisation of space involved in language is not a static topological or geometric representation but rather a dynamic representation linked to the use of space that hosts our daily experience of the world.

Another point to debate is where to draw the semantics/pragmatics boundary in this context. Jackendoff (1995a: 105) suggests that the distinction between 'semantic' rules of linguistic inference and 'pragmatic' rules of linguistic interaction with general knowledge is less marked than often assumed. They do not involve different kinds of mental representations but deal with the same primitives and principles of combination. According to Jackendoff, the difference lies in the formal manipulations that the rules perform on conceptual structure. He is against the proposal that linguistic semantics should be concerned only with properties that lead to logical entailments and the establishment of analyticity while all the non-logical semantic properties belong in pragmatics. For instance, a condition may result in logical entailment in one word and a defeasible ('pragmatic') assumption in another. Both *rise* and *climb* carry content pertaining to movement in an upward direction. However, we can say *climb downwards* but not *rise downwards*. The very same piece of information can belong to either pragmatics or semantics depending on the word. For the truth validity of a sentence we must access extra-linguistic information as well as information within the sentence itself and thus for Jackendoff 'true' is a pragmatic notion. In contrast, the judgement that a sentence is analytic involves only information available within the sentence itself plus rules of (semantic) inference, which make the notion of analytic a purely semantic one.

Levinson on the other hand explains why a pragmatic theory is necessary in order to explain the way spatial terms, as well as other aspects of language, are manifested in use. For example, in Yélî Dnye, *nedê* ('attachment by spike/hook') and *p:uu* ('attachment by any means') are two postpositions in privative oppositions. That is, if his pragmatic theory is correct, every time where *nedê* is used *p:uu* should be possible but speakers are expected to hesitate still when describing a scene with a less informative item *p:uu* when a more informative one *nedê* is available (Levinson 2006b: 167). The stronger, more specific conditions (*nedê*) entail the weaker (*p:uu*) while the choice of the stronger form is a pragmatic preference (Levinson 2006b: 169). This is exactly what the empirical results have shown and Levinson concludes that the two postpositions overlap in extensions but that a pragmatic principle (Grice's Maxim of Quantity or Levinson's I-Principle; Levinson 2000) 'induces a division of labour', whereby Saussurean semantic oppositions are better accounted for pragmatically (*ibid*.). The same mechanism may be involved in processing these differences in the extensions of the postpositions (semantic information) and in preferences of use (pragmatic information), but information conveyed by the sentence itself need not tell us about conceptual structure because the two different postpositions would then indicate a difference in conceptualisation of the same spatial scene.

Interestingly, Levinson's insistence on the impact of linguistic diversity is not irreconcilably far from Jackendoff's view in all respects. When it comes to the implications of his theory, Jackendoff is aware of the possibility that since it is only the projected world we can deal with and not the real world, 'people could differ in the interpretation they put on the environmental input and hence it could be impossible in principle to be sure that any two people are talking about the same things' (Jackendoff 1995a: 30). The answer is a dual-levelled one. The processes involved in constructing the projected world are universal, part of our genetic inheritance, and the same for everybody. However, some aspects of the constructed projected world are underdetermined both by universals of human heredity and by common environment and this is where we find 'wide interpersonal and/or intercultural differences' (*ibid*.). Consequently, people's construals of experience are incompatible to the extent that they cannot convey information to each other and language must, indeed, be subjective (*ibid*.: 31).

What is important to observe is that most scholars would agree that both universal and language-specific features co-exist but the details with regard to the relationship between them vary. Both Jackendoff and Levinson apparently acknowledge, though in different terms, that language is a phenomenon with both universal and non-universal facets. However, the role that universal and language-specific factors play in conceptualisation and the strength of their respective influences is a source of major disagreement. Jackendoff's level of conceptualisation is universal, unaffected by the superficial level of linguistic semantics. He does not even recognise semantics as a separate level since syntax and correspondence rules are said to be enough to account for the mapping between language and conceptualisation. Levinson's position is that linguistic representation cannot be identical to the representation in which we do our conceptual thinking; but it has to be similar in some respects at least, since the language of thought must directly or indirectly support linguistic distinctions.

Levinson (2003c), however, argues that while the universals lie on the level of atomic concepts, it is the molar, language-specific concepts that we habitually evoke and use in both linguistic and non-linguistic cognitive activities. We may find a model (e.g. Jackendoff's Conceptual Semantics or DRT) that would adequately represent how we conceptualise what we talk about but the fact that *we tend to talk and think about some aspects of objects and events more often than others depending on our language* seems hard to deny in the light of growing cross-linguistic and experimental evidence.

Language and spatial cognition, though not completely isomorphic, have to be in synch when it comes to both lexicalising and conceptualising spatial relations. For instance, if a spatial scene is referred to in relative or intrinsic terms (e.g. *to the left of X*) it is not possible to deduce absolute coordinates for that scene (e.g. *to the north of X*). The crucial fact is that the *translatability* of the frames of reference is limited and it drives the uniformity of frame of reference through the entire spatial system within the speaking community (Levinson 2003c: 60–61). The frame of reference dominant in a given language 'infiltrates' other modalities, presumably to ensure that speakers can talk about what they see and feel and so on. Frames of reference cannot freely translate into one another, e.g. if we memorise a scene in intrinsic terms we cannot have access to absolute frame information. Language, as a modality most adaptive to external influences, adopts a frame of reference and other modalities must follow suit (Levinson 1999: 157), and in order to make this happen, all modalities must have all frames available. The mystery remains how this cross-modal transfer is achieved. The standardisation of frames of reference across modalities becomes inevitable (*ibid.*). For example, Tenejapans, who speak Tzeltal, employ the absolute frame of spatial reference in language, memory, inference and gesture, whereas people in another community (e.g. Holland) use a different frame for all these functions (i.e. relative). The fact is that language is acquired within a community and within a certain environmental set-up. This set-up may then be schematised in order to provide the templates for drawing the relevant distinctions in a number of cognitive domains (e.g. proper nouns such as place names, landscape motion verbs, locative/property verbs; cf. Levinson and Burenhult 2009: 162). Levinson and Burenhult (2009) have recently proposed that those large cross-category abstracted configurations termed *semplates* (schematisations of a primary domain, e.g. geographical configuration) pervade the organisation of the lexicon in general.

Frames of spatial reference in particular have been studied extensively in order to find support for different positions, in favour or against relativist claims. For example, Levelt discusses the pragmatics of different perspective systems, focusing in particular on the question of whether this perspectival thinking is just for speaking or more generally whether it permeates our spatial thinking in some Whorfian way. Levelt (1999: 102) argues that perspective is linguistically free. There is no hard-wired mapping, as it were, from spatial to semantic representations. What we pick out from a scene is not subject to fixed laws. There are preferences, such as gestalt properties of the scene, human interest, etc. but they are no more than preferences (*ibid.*). The capacities to refer to space are unlimited even for speakers of Guugu Yimithirr, an absolute-only language: they may still choose to say A is in the neighbourhood of B rather than A is north of B (*ibid.*: 103), and choose which referents, relata and spatial relations to express. All speakers attend to what they deem relevant in communicatively efficient and effective ways, thus the isomorphisms between the spatial and the semantic cannot be hard-wired.

Support for more profound language effects can arguably be found in the fact that absolute speakers are better at orienting in space and dead reckoning which, according to Levinson (2003c), is due to their language, not the environment alone, because the languages force this constant attention to the directional attributes of every scene. Crucially, the use of an absolute frame of reference is not tied to environmental factors, as one could have thought, since the populations that typically use it are indigenous people. Three Mayan languages, Tzeltal, Mopan and Yucatec, have a different distribution of the frames: Tzeltal is predominantly absolute, Mopan predominantly intrinsic, and 'Yucatec speakers use all three frames of reference but with heavy use of the intrinsic' (Levinson 2003c: 189). This further indicates that language patterns (not the environmental features) are the key determinant of the non-linguistic ones.

It would be interesting to investigate how good Mopan or Yucatec speakers are in orienting themselves in space, since they do not have a dominant absolute frame. There is a possibility that their cultural and life-style practices would still make them better 'orienters' than the Dutch or the English. It may also be argued that cultural and environmental practices affect habitual thinking about spatial configurations, which are then reflected in language rather than being crucially motivated by language. One could argue that it was probably the particular environmental and cultural needs initially that drove the emergence of linguistic means in order to respond to these needs. For example, Tenejapan Tzeltal speakers abstract a north–south axis from the mountain incline of the local environment, but the axis remains constant outside the territory (Levinson 2003c). The directions of seasonal winds, mountain inclines, river drainage directions etc. served for this purpose in the speakers' natural habitat. Once the linguistic system was in place and became entrenched in the social and cultural practices of the community (e.g. by habitually referring to some aspects of the scene and not some others), it could have taken the role of the driving force behind the understanding of spatial scenes hand in hand with the language acquisition process. Thus, language acquisition, involving the selection of topological relations labelled in a particular language out of a pool of numerous other possibilities, could have become the source of habitual evocation of lexicalised concepts regarding space among speakers of a particular language.

How is one to tease apart the effects on conceptualisation that the language might have on the one hand, and other factors on the other, such as natural environment or cultural practices? One way of doing it would be to displace 'absolute community' speakers in such a way that they cannot use dead reckoning. Another would be to displace absolute speakers out of their natural habitat. In the former case, the experiment would be costly while in the latter case it is simply inhumane. Moreover, in novel circumstances, like the rotation experiments (cf. Levinson 2003b, 2003c), effects of language may be more noticeable because when speakers try to make sense of a new situation they may organise the new input according to the frame of reference that dominates their language. The performance of Tzeltal speakers in a variety of experimental tasks suggests that they 'conceptualize spatial categories and relations in ways which contrast radically with those familiar to us through Indo-European languages and cultures' (Brown, P. 2006: 231). Spatial reference in Tzeltal is based on absolute orientation driven by a geocentric system, described by nouns such as *aik'ol*-'uphill' and *alan*-'downhill'. There is no distinction of left and right (*ibid*.: 232). Spatial descriptions of static scenes rely on predicates incorporating features of configuration, positions, etc. to indicate properties of the figure and/or the precise spatial relation to some ground object. The lack of a left/right distinction and symmetry are present in Tenejapan life, demonstrated in gesture, weaving patterns, architecture, ritual practices and psychological tasks and they 'reveal a tendency to "mirror-image blindness" (that is to treat left/right mirror image reversed images as identical)' (*ibid*.: 272). Further cognitive consequences (such as performance in non-linguistic tasks and early acquisition of this particular absolute system) are suggestive of a different conceptualisation of spatial relations in the Tzeltal language and culture from frequently posited universal systems based on an egocentrically abstract space (*ibid*.).

Numerous other languages show intriguing characteristics in spatial discourse. For instance, Bohnemeyer and Stolz (2006) studied spatial reference in the Yucatec Maya language. In Indo-European languages speakers explicitly refer to the whole path of motion or portions of it, as in *Jack ran out of the garden into the house*. In Yucatec the expression of the same event would involve a series of static scenes, something to the effect of *Jack was in the garden. Jack was in the house*. Translational motion along an extended trajectory from source to goal is left to pragmatic inference (Bohnemeyer and Stolz 2006: 295). A similar restriction is found by Levinson (2006b) in Yélî Dnye. The situation in Yucatec is more extreme in this sense, because motion verbs 'do not entail translational motion along an extended spatial trajectory, but only location with respect to individual grounds' (Bohnemeyer and Stolz 2006: 300). Therefore, what is lexicalised is a state-change event with motion entailed. In Arrernte (Wilkins 2006), an Aboriginal language spoken in central Australia, the conceptualisation of space is driven by 'the nature of Dreamtime geography, which includes visible records of the travels, actions and existence of the dreamtime ancestors' (*ibid*.: 61). Those practices as well as natural environments in which the cultures exist affect the preferred 'packaging' of information into complex, molar concepts for everyday use and efficient communication.

Perhaps we can say that, historically, it was initially a culture's dominant perspective (perhaps centrally affected by the environment) that made speakers attend to spatial properties relevant to that perspective because it would facilitate (later) discourse about the scene. Language provided the means to ensure that the relevant information can be communicated. A speaker may tend to register spatial features that are perspective-specific in memory, e.g. an absolute orientation of the scene whereby the perspective-relevant spatial features do not prevent the registration of other spatial properties that can be referred to or used in discourse. Nevertheless, speakers are habitually more likely to adhere to mentioning absolutely necessary pieces of information that are required by the structures preferred in their language, thus making sure that they fill in the slots of the sentence structure with the required information. It is true that there is no reason why other information, not favoured by the habitual syntactic patterns, may not be retained in memory or referred to using more complex constructions. However, it is more likely that under normal everyday circumstances, this will not be the case because of *communicative efficiency*. Namely, speakers 'weigh' the cost and effect in communication and are more likely to provide shorter forms and typical patterns so as to minimise processing effort (cf. Hawkins 2004 or the Gricean tradition in pragmatics) while achieving satisfactory results (i.e. getting the message across). Cross-linguistic evidence is crucial in the assessment of the various factors that motivate the relationship between, on the one hand, efficient reference to spatial features and relations in discourse which all languages provide and, on the other hand, the language-specific grammatical and lexical categories that make this reference possible.

## 20.4  Conclusion

Spatial reference has been a fertile research area for testing different hypotheses about language and cognition. We can conclude that the relationship between spatial language and spatial cognition is evidently a multi-faceted one. We have discussed numerous language-specific features as well as universal aspects of spatial reference. The interaction between them affects the choices that are made in the expressions that are used to refer. As we saw, the possible ways of structuring space in discourse are not endless – they seem to be typologically definable to a certain extent. The precise nature of these universals is still a matter of vibrant debate, but there is general agreement that they do exist. We all interact with the world around us, thinking and talking about it. However, during that interaction, some environments, cultures and languages may make some perceptual, conceptual and linguistic features more or less salient. When we habitually express certain features, they become entrenched and, according to some scholars, may be used in other non-linguistic cognitive activities (see also Giora, this volume). An opposing view is that the reported effects are not non-linguistic since language is always present, if not explicitly then tacitly, when those effects were observed. Of central importance is the fact that spatial reference in language and conceptualisation reflects both universal and language-specific features. Determining the precise nature of their interaction and the relative contribution of each offers exciting prospects for future research in semantics and pragmatics.

# 21

# Temporal reference in discourse

Louis de Saussure

## 21.1 Introduction

Given that an utterance conveys information about a situation, or "eventuality", holding at some time and possibly having a duration, virtually any utterance has a *temporal reference* and *aspectual* properties. Temporal reference is about some moment or interval of time where the situation is holding. Aspectual properties concern its duration (either as a semantic property of the verb clause or indicated by grammatical markers) and its representation as a "global" whole or as an ongoing process, as happening once or frequently, etc. Furthermore, the temporal reference of an eventuality is obtained through the access to information that resides also outside the sentence, such as a previously mentioned event or pragmatic knowledge. All these linguistic and contextual data are dealt with in order to achieve an interpretation consistent with the speaker's intention.

In Indo-European languages, verbs are tensed, with the consequence that temporal information is morphologically joined to the verb root. But obviously many other linguistic indicators, in particular adverbials and connectives, may contribute when it comes to expressing temporal and aspectual information such as duration, temporal ordering of eventualities in discourse, frequency, and so forth. Yet, despite the grammatical marking of time, many utterances would remain temporally ambiguous, vague, or otherwise unsolved without pragmatic inferencing.

This chapter is dedicated to pragmatic inference in the recovery of temporal and aspectual information. After recalling the basics of the semantics of temporal reference and aspect (section 21.2), we address a series of specific cases where either aspectual properties or temporal reference are established with recourse to pragmatic inference in discourse. The pragmatic modification of the aspectual class, coded by the verb clause, because of conflicting information is addressed in section 21.3. Section 21.4 is dedicated to pragmatic processes that take place in relation to temporal reference and temporal ordering, through a number of typical cases. A shorter last section (section 21.5) discusses some pragmatic features related to temporal connectives.

Data from a variety of languages are discussed, with a focus on the contrast between English and Romance, in particular French.

## 21.2  Semantic notions and pragmatic issues

### 21.2.1  Temporal reference

A classical representation of time in the literature is a left-to-right arrow on which moments such as the present time, the past time (on its left), and the future time (on its right) are positioned. Hence the typical representation of time by scholars involves points and intervals on a line, each bearing a relation to the present deictic time or "speech point". As we recall below (section 21.4.2), in a number of cases the deictic present gets shifted in order to match the writer's, the reader's, or even a character's present. But it remains constant that conceiving a fact as present, past, or future requires at least a representation of some present time, be it actual or shifted.

*Past, present,* and *future* are only three general types of relations that can hold between the two basic *speech* and *event* times. Languages often overtly represent lots of different temporal relations. In order to account for them, a third coordinate is brought into the system as a "reference point" from which the event is considered, so that combinations such as 'past from past' can be represented, typically to handle pluperfect and other perfect tenses. Reichenbach (1947) established the standard notation for the three coordinates: S for *speech point,* E for *point of the event,* and R for *reference point.* He provided a seminal formalization of tenses. For example, the simple past expresses that E is considered from a simultaneous reference point R, both anterior to S, whereas the present perfect expresses that a past E is considered from a present reference point R. The semantics of the present tense is E,R,S, where all are simultaneous; that of the simple future is R and E simultaneous and both posterior to S. The pluperfect is represented as E anterior to R anterior to S, and so forth.[1]

Notably, *Mary read the newspaper* indicates, in the absence of other information, that the reading has been completed: it is a "global" event. On the contrary, the past progressive version, *Mary was reading the newspaper,* simply indicates that at some point R in the past, Mary was in the course of reading the newspaper: the reading began before R and continued after R, but no indication is provided that it has been completed (a consequence which however may be pragmatically inferred). In other words, progressive tenses, and a number of other tenses across languages, trigger unbounded representations which provide the background for global events. In *Mary was reading the newspaper when the doorbell rang,* the progressive clause sets up the unbounded background scene for the ringing event. This property is shared by *imperfective tenses*, a class to which English progressive tenses belong. Since the works of Partee (1984) and Kamp and Reyle (1993), the literature usually assumes that progressive and other imperfective tenses are *anaphoric* in the sense that they cannot refer to a time without anchoring on some time contextually provided (the event of ringing, in the example above). In order to account for imperfectivity, Reichenbach introduces a notion of "extended E," conceiving that in such cases E should not be a point but an interval.

Reichenbach's R point bears also a pragmatic, or discursive, function. It establishes the anaphoric temporal relation with other eventualities denoted by utterances in the context. Reichenbach's discursive rules are *R-permanence* and *R-positional use*. *R-permanence* stipulates that unless there is contrary evidence, R stays in its place. This explains why a simple past~pluperfect sequence leads to the pluperfect utterance denoting an eventuality that happened prior to the one denoted by the simple past utterance: R remains in its original position and E gets positioned before R. The *R-positional use* rule stipulates that R is primarily positioned by adverbials. Hence an adverbial expression such as *at three o'clock* or *ten minutes later* concerns the position of R, not directly the position of E. *Ten minutes later, the car stopped* indicates that *the car stopped* is represented from an R-point, contemporary to the event, but ten minutes later than the previously positioned R-point. That E occupies the same position as R is a mechanical consequence of the semantics of the simple past which encodes "simultaneity of E and R". Hence, *Ten minutes later, the car had stopped* does not convey that the car stopped ten minutes later but that it had *already* stopped at the R-point situated ten minutes later.

## 21.2.2 Temporal ordering: a pragmatic issue

Since the works of Reichenbach on time, a considerable literature has tried to account for the semantics of tenses through various lenses and with (much needed) refinements. However, only pragmatic inference leads to the specification of often ambiguous semantic information. For example, the three following sequences of utterances are constructed in the same way, but some are temporally more ambiguous than others. At first sight, (1) can be interpreted as maintaining the initial position of R, while (2) favors a progressive interpretation, and (3) almost enforces it.

(1) Paul ironed his shirts and listened to the radio.

(2) Paul ironed his shirts and drank a coke.

(3) Paul ironed his shirts and went for a walk in the garden.

The temporal connections here are indeed pragmatically established. Even the fact that going for *a walk in the garden* occurs later than *ironing the shirts* relies on external information: in a world where there are rolling automatic ironing boards, absurd as it is, (3) may convey simultaneity. Moreover,

(3) may be temporally unordered, if both actions are embedded as two actions that made Paul's day, whatever their actual order.

There are several possible relationships among eventualities: besides simultaneity, anteriority and posteriority, utterances can show a relation of *background* (one eventuality holds while the other happens), as in (4), or of *elaboration* (or *encapsulation*) (one eventuality includes a number of others), as in (5).

(4)   Paul walked in the garden. The weather was great.

(5)   Paul walked in the garden. He smelled the flowers and admired the trees.

A number of pragmatic issues are raised by the numerous sources of information contributing to temporal reference. But before we can turn to them systematically, a short introduction to the notion of aspect is necessary.

### 21.2.3  Aspect

The notion of *aspect* concerns (i) the intrinsic conceptual structure of types of eventualities, and (ii) grammatical indications about how the eventuality has to be envisaged in the precise case: global (i.e. bounded), lasting, dynamic, repetitive, etc. The first issue is known as *lexical* or *semantic* aspect, or as *modes of action* (*Aktionsarten* in the terminology of Vendler 1967[2]). The second notion is generally called *grammatical* or *verbal* aspect, and is usually seen as concerning also other indications about the occurrence of a particular eventuality: frequency, beginning, end, repetition, etc. The two categories have often been confused by scholars who addressed only English, since English tenses are in principle unmarked for aspect, thus the aspect of English sentences largely relies on semantic aspect, except when the tense is in the progressive form. But many languages, typically Slavic and Romance, provide two clear paradigms of grammatical aspect that do not match semantic aspect.

Semantic aspect traditionally distinguishes between four classes of eventualities denoted by verb phrases as such.[3] *Accomplishments* have an intrinsic end: they are *telic*. They also require some duration, as *build a house* or *run a hundred meters*. *Achievements* are construed as instantaneous, as *reach the finish line* or *wake up*, thus they can't be said to have an intrinsic end in the proper sense. However, they induce a new state of the world when they occur, just like accomplishments; for this reason both types are often considered *events*. Accomplishments like *build a house* allow for encompassing several kinds of actions: the process of building a house keeps being true when the workers are asleep, provided that they get back to work later. Similarly, if a person falls during a hundred-meter run but gets back on her feet and finishes the run, it will be true that she has run a hundred meters. Hence accomplishments have a property of being *dynamic*, i.e. subject to possible changes or some other kind of evolution through time, and their truth allows for moments inside their interval when they are not happening (for example, when the workers sleep, in the above example). They are *heterogeneous* and therefore compatible with progressive tenses. On the contrary, achievements are not dynamic and cannot be combined with a progressive form without prompting for pragmatic accommodation.

On the other hand, *activities* and *states* potentially do not entail an end to the situation they represent. Their actual duration has to be specified by an adverbial clause or through pragmatic knowledge or inference. Activities, just like accomplishments, are dynamic and have the properties of being true of an interval but possibly false in a minority of sub-intervals: if Mary *walks* during the whole afternoon, she may have stopped in order to admire the scenery every now and then without falsifying the fact that she walked the whole afternoon. On the contrary, states are stable and homogeneous: if a state is true during an interval, then it is true of all its possible sub-intervals. If Paul knows Mary in some interval of time, there is no possible sub-interval at which Paul doesn't know Mary (see Dowty 1986 for the analysis of semantic aspect in these terms).

It is also evident that the classes established by semantic aspect are poor guides to the analysis of time in language, except if talking about languages where aspect is as little grammaticized as English. In English, non-progressive forms are aspectually underdetermined, so that only the semantic properties of the verb select the right aspectual representation. (6), denoting a state, (7), denoting an activity, (8), denoting an accomplishment, and (9), denoting an achievement, are all compatible with the simple past tense form.

(6)   Margaret Thatcher and Ronald Reagan knew each other.

(7)   Mary ran the whole afternoon.

(8)   Mary fixed the chair.

(9)   Mary reached the summit.

That the eventuality is global – it has started and finished – is even not a mandatory effect of English simple tenses. If it were so, (10) would be incompatible with Paul being still alive, and (11) would not allow for the inference that it's still raining today.

(10)   I remember when I met Paul. He had those beautiful blue eyes.

(11)   It rained (already) yesterday.

Only in the case of a progressive form is the representation necessarily unbounded or "ongoing"; this happens naturally with accomplishments (12) and activities (13).

(12)   Paul is building a house.

(13)   Paul is sleeping.

Progressive forms don't normally combine with states (14) nor with achievements (15):

(14)   *Obama is knowing the answer.

(15)   *John is noticing the new statue in the garden.

However, such combinations are only impossible unless a pragmatic reinterpretation is involved, as discussed in the next section.

Only accomplishments are *literally* compatible with *in*-adverbial clauses, as
in *Paul built the house in 36 months*, since only accomplishments are telic and
have a duration. Only states and activities are compatible with *for*-adverbials,
as in (16) or (17).

(16)   They have loved each other for 40 years.

(17)   Paul has slept for 10 hours.

Similarly, some constructions are considered possible only with specific
aspectual categories: pseudo-clefts such as (18) are fine with accomplishments but not with states (19) or activities (20) unless pragmatic accommodation takes place.

(18)   It took Mary ten seconds to draw a circle.

(19)   ?It took Mary ten minutes to be tired.

(20)   ?It took Mary two hours to run.

Certainly, (19) can be fine in English if an inference allows an escape from
semantic constraints. Here, the temporal complement (*ten minutes*) does not
modify temporally the situation expressed by the verb (*be tired*) but another,
inferred, situation, directly preceding it (and certainly leading to it in some
way). Hence it did not literally take Mary ten minutes to *be tired* but rather
to *become* tired, which is quite different. The same holds for example (20): in
that case, it took Mary two hours to finally *start* running.[4] Semantics usually
considers these sentences odd.

Their compatibility with achievements raises other problems we address
further down. Such tests raise many questions about the interplay of information from various sources, the constraints brought by grammatical expressions, and pragmatic reinterpretation and enrichment of semantic meaning. Notably, surprising pragmatic accommodation may be invited by specific combinations of types of eventualities under the pressure of conflicting
aspectual grammatical marking.

## 21.3   The pragmatics of aspect

The semantic categories of aspect can be pragmatically overridden. For example, semantics would predict that the utterance *Paul has known Mary since they
were students in Cambridge ten years ago* implies that there isn't a single instant
within these ten years when Paul did not know Mary. Yet, Paul may have
suffered from amnesia for a few days, forgetting about Mary, without the
utterance being intuitively considered false, or a lie, in actual conversation.

Similarly, if *to love* is also a state, as it clearly seems to be, its representation as an activity remains pragmatically possible as in *I'm loving it*,[5] a process known as *coercion* or *accommodation. Coercion* is, from a semantic point of view, a mechanical modification of the semantic meaning of an expression under the pressure of another linguistic item: it is triggered by a particular clash or mismatch between the semantics of expressions appearing together in a sentence.[6] *Accommodation* is the process of a semantic modification under the pressure of pragmatic knowledge or inference. But taking a closer look at these processes, we notice that from the pragmatic point of view, purely semantic coercion is rare: most meaning constructions rely on pragmatic knowledge and inference.

Pragmatic accommodation of conceptual information occurs under the pressure of either contextual or grammatical information that conflicts with the literal reading of the utterance. A grammatical marker such as the progressive in *I'm loving it* (the slogan of a well-known chain of fast-food restaurants) imposes the dynamicity in the representation, hence the hearer has to build up a representation which is not stative (as it would have been otherwise). Utterances like *I'm totally seeing your point* or *I'm not having any of that* are rather ordinary in English despite the "violation" of aspectual categories predicted by traditional grammars and semantic theory.[7] However, there must be intuitive inferential grounds for the pragmatic modification of semantic aspect under the pressure of grammatical aspect. English's only grammatical marking of aspect is very specific since it implies dynamicity. As a (trivial) consequence, only states that allow for reinterpretation as dynamic situations can be accommodated with a progressive tense. If there is no imaginable reason to apply such a conceptual transfer, the progressive utterance will remain odd or call for a temporalized interpretation, as in (21) if implying that the sky will soon turn red. Example (22), if slightly awkward, still makes sense as an activity.

(21)   The sky is being blue (at the moment).

(22)   I'm loving it.

In principle, an activity of *loving* is easily reconstructed on the basis of the conceptual stative status of *love*; the gerund *loving* is readily found in corpora (think of Scorpions' *Still loving you*). Such a transfer supposes access to encyclopaedic knowledge about what actions and feelings are involved or caused by love. However, (22) is the motto of a fast-food restaurant, and loving a chain of restaurants certainly involves a metaphorical sense since one hardly infers the actual activities involved in such a relationship. But still the slogan is effective precisely because it imposes such a kind of "active loving" representation through grammatical markers. In any case, the process of understanding leads to the formation of the concept so that a representation is made compatible with the dynamicity of an activity at the cost of a conceptual loosening – a metaphor or an approximation – of the original verb. An activity doesn't need to be agentive, but states with agents who are living creatures are in principle pragmatically reinterpretable as activities, as in (22). Some other cases include reinterpretation on the basis of types of behavior, as in (23), or mental states, as in (24).

(23)   You're being old fashioned here.

(24)   I'm not having any of that.

Similarly, *Paul is waking up* is certainly not an odd utterance. In this case, an achievement, abstractly punctual, is reinterpreted as a more complex process which only includes the actual waking. The scheme of pragmatic reinterpretation makes *wake up* an economical shortcut in lieu of a complex phrasing meaning that Paul has started a process of getting awake (typically with some irony, unless uttered in very special circumstances like in a hospital after a surgery). When an achievement is represented with a past progressive, its pragmatic reinterpretation leads in principle not to a variant having some duration, but to the inference of a state of affairs leading to the achievement proper. Hence, (25) is interpreted as implicating that Mary was actually *not* (yet) on the summit at the reference point R.

(25)   Mary was reaching the summit (when she fell).

Noticeably, semantic categories of aspect are too imprecise to allow for clear predictions on pragmatic interpretations. If *reach the summit* is actually conceived of as an instantaneous event, other achievements, like *cross the finish line*, allow for some conceptual pragmatic modification towards some duration. Hence *Mary was crossing the finish line* allows for a reading in which Mary has indeed one foot before and the other after the line. This might be due to semantics: the concept relating to the action of *crossing* can indeed involve some duration, as in *cross the river*, whereas *reach* doesn't seem to allow for such combinations.[8]

Similarly, the pressure of adverb clauses may trigger a pragmatic accommodation of verbal concepts. Hence (26) is not odd if taken to mean that the beers remained out for ten minutes.[9]

(26)   Paul took the beers out of the fridge for ten minutes.

However, it needs to be emphasized that such a pragmatic inference is clearly an implicature, since if it is manifest that the fridge is actually the cold room of a store, it may actually take ten minutes to take them all out – unlikely as the example and the scenario may seem.

Conversely, a marker of boundedness, such as *in n time*, or *it took Mary x minutes to P*, can be expected to force a bounded, event-like, understanding of utterances even with states and activities. Therefore an utterance like *Paul slept in ten minutes* should get accommodated into a bounded eventuality. In such cases, typically, the inchoative reading occurs. In English, *Paul slept in ten minutes* looks odd, but it may actually happen with the meaning of "fell asleep", as in (27), probably slightly archaic:

(27)   Midshipmen always sleep under every variety of disturbance, either
       of body or mind; so William Thornton slept in ten minutes as if he
       had not had a night's rest for twelve months. (F. C. Armstrong, *The
       Frigate and the Lugger, a Nautical Romance*).

In other languages, given the right context, such interpretations are very
natural. The French equivalent, *Paul dormit en dix minutes*, gets accommodated
as such automatically. The pseudo-cleft case is much clearer, as (28), (29), and
(30) show: here the temporal indication concerns some causal process leading
to the actual occurrence of the eventuality.

(28)   It took Paul ten minutes to walk / run.[10]

(29)   It took Paul ten minutes to know Mary.

(30)   It took Mary ten minutes to reach the summit.

These cases have to be compared to similar structures with accomplishments,
where the adverb clause quantifies the duration of the eventuality rather
than of some preliminary situation as in (31).

(31)   It took Mary ten minutes to fix the chair.

In all cases above, a grammatical marker of aspect (a tense or an adverbial
clause), imposes its representational structure on the concept encoded by
the verbal phrase. A pragmatic reinterpretation of the concept is in such
cases achieved by either changing some of its properties or inferring another
situation, so that the utterance becomes likely to fit the expectations of
meaningfulness in actual communication. This overall process is similar
across languages as long as they have explicit aspectual markers in their
lexicon, except if the morphological paradigm of verbs precisely encodes
these nuances, as in Russian.

As in other languages, Russian imperfectives (IMP) are unbounded and
anaphoric, so that (32) only entails that Marija read some part of a
book.

(32)   Marija   čitala      knigu.
       Marija   read-IMP    book.

Russian does not allow systematically for pragmatic accommodation of concepts encoded by verb roots under the pressure of aspectual marking, because
perfective and imperfective verbs are coded in that language, usually with
nuances of meaning. Depending on the verb, Russian has either different
verbal roots for the imperfective and the perfective, or it adds an aspectual
affix with a nuance of meaning – and they are not encoding the same concept
exactly, or even they encode quite different concepts. In the example above,
the verb used (*čitat'*) is the imperfective for *read*, but the perfective counterpart (*pročitat'*) would better translate as *read entirely*; stronger differences arise
with verbs like *pisat'* ('write', imperfective) and *opisat'* ('describe', perfective).

Numerous prefixes can be used in order to achieve the aspectual transformation, so that arguably, these transformations usually go with a conceptual change. Such changes are not pragmatic but semantically attached to verb roots. Perfective verbs are usually translated by accomplishment or achievement verbs. For example, *uznat'*, a perfective verb built on the basis of *znat'* ('know'), can mean both achievements like 'recognize' and accomplishments like 'get to know'.[11]

Romance languages have various ways of indicating the progressive, such as gerund phrases and adverbs (Bertinetto 2000), but they have truly imperfective (past) tenses which allow not only for progressivity but also stativity, as in (33) (French) or (34) (Spanish), which translate in English with the simple past but not with a progressive:

(33)    Margaret Thatcher et Ronald Reagan se connaissaient.
        'Margaret Thatcher and Ronald Reagan knew / *were knowing each other.'

(34)    Margaret Thatcher y Ronald Reagan se conocían.

The observations made above concerning achievements also apply to French: *Mary atteignait le sommet* ('Mary was reaching the summit') typically entails a reading similar to (25), 'Mary was approaching the summit'.

However, French allows strange combinations where the imperfective applies on achievements and accomplishments but still conveys the completion of the eventuality as well as forward temporal ordering, as in (35) or (36), which appear temporally similar to simple past narrative utterances.

(35)    Le lendemain, il partait.
        'The next day, he leave-IMP (left /*was leaving).'

(36)    La clé tourna dans la serrure. Monsieur Chabot entrait, posait son pardessus et s'asseyait dans son fauteuil d'osier.[12]
        'The key turned in the lock. Mr. Chabot come-IMP in (came in /*was coming in), hang-IMP (hanged /*was hanging) his coat and sit-IMP (sat /*was sitting) in his wicker armchair.'

Here, either an adverb or pragmatic knowledge forces the inference that the eventuality has been completed. The combination with the imperfect doesn't end up in an odd utterance but in an accommodation of the unbounded representation so that it is made compatible with a notion of event completion, pragmatically necessary in the circumstances. Hence a very specific pragmatic effect of liveliness or "witnessing" in French that used to be described only through metaphoric terms, such as "camera effect". It has been established that even in such imperfective utterances, the eventuality is represented through an inner viewpoint, therefore compatible with the imperfective type, but without the "background" entailments. In particular, only the *imparfait* is compatible with subjective adverbs such as *déjà* ('already') in such combinations:

(37)　Le train quitta Genève. Une heure plus tard, il entrait /*entra déjà en gare de Lyon.
　　　'The train left Geneva. One hour later, it enter-IMP /*PER already in Lyons station.'[13]

That an imperfective grammatical marker combines meaningfully with event completion or forward temporal ordering is the result of a complex pragmatic process where the instantiation of an inner viewpoint provides a compensation for the clash of aspectual information. Somehow, the eventuality is represented as unbounded by the tense but is bounded by pragmatic necessity. The inference that some character in the story, or some other real or imaginary person, witnesses and directly reports the eventualities seems to be a typical pragmatic effect of these combinations (although this is a debated point). Hence there is a similarity between these "narrative *imparfaits*" and free indirect speech, where *imparfait* is supposed optimal (as well as the conditional) in order to represent the thoughts and feelings occurring to a character without explicit indications of reported thought or speech, as in (38).

(38)　Il　fallait　　　　faire　vite.　Dans　une　heure, la　　ronde
　　　It　was. necessary　to. be　quick.　In　　an　hour,　the　patrol
　　　　　passait　sur　le　　pont.
　　　　　pass-IMP　on　the　bridge.
　　　'We had to be quick. The patrol was to pass over the bridge in an hour.'

The French *imparfait* raises a number of other strange pragmatic non-background effects, all related to pragmatic instantiation of viewpoints consistent with its imperfective semantics. Counterfactual readings instantiate a point of view in a possible world, as in (39), which would better translate with a conditional in other languages.

(39)　Un　kilo　de moins　et　　j'entrais　　dans　cette　robe.
　　　One　kilo　less　　　and　I enter-IMP　in　　this　dress.
　　　'One kilo less and this dress would fit me.'

A plausible assumption is that the speaker represents the state of affairs as true in a possible world as if witnessed by herself, hence a clear flavor of regret concerning the desirable situation which almost occurred. Comparable effects arise when children project a game setting so that they agree to act as if it were true, as in (40), with a pragmatic effect of vividness typical of these utterances.

(40)　J'étais le gendarme et tu volais un vélo.
　　　I be-IMP the policeman and you steal-IMP a bicycle.

Pragmatic accommodation of semantic aspect also occurs when a marker of boundedness appears in otherwise stative utterances. The typical scheme of pragmatic enrichment is then the selection of a bounded sub-part of the concerned eventuality. Hence an utterance such as *And there was light* gets typically interpreted as *light began to be*; and *Margaret and Ronald knew each other in London* is typically understood inchoatively (i.e. beginning) as *met* ('began to know each other'). Similar effects arise in Romance. However, since the simple past in English is not strictly dedicated to boundedness, an utterance like (41) can still be understood as unbounded, meaning something like (41′), which is impossible in French, where the simple past is *necessarily* bounded. Therefore, (42) gets necessarily a bounded reading, typically the inchoative interpretation (42′). In English, such an interpretation is of course very common, but it is only optional.

(41)    Margaret Thatcher knew Ronald Reagan.

(41′)   Margaret Thatcher knows Ronald Reagan at the considered past reference point.

(42)    Margaret Thatcher connut Ronald Reagan.

(42′)   Margaret Thatcher met / began to know Ronald Reagan.

Other typical accommodations of semantic aspectual features are *iterative* (repetitive) interpretations of imperfective utterances combining with activities, accomplishments, and achievements. Here again Romance behaves very differently from English, which marks iteration either by means of the dedicated expression "used to" or the conditional. An English utterance such as *When the weather was fine, he used to / would come over and we used to / would talk for hours on the patio* would translate with the imperfective in Romance, but as a result, Romance is (generally) ambiguous with respect to the choice between iteration and unbounded singular eventuality. Therefore in that case, Romance, not English, requires the recourse to pragmatic ambiguity-solving procedures.

Aspectual accommodation is an issue residing precisely in the area of research shared by semantics and pragmatics and thus concerns very much the semantics/pragmatics interface, in particular those parts of meaning that are categorized as truth-conditional yet pragmatically completed in context.[14] We turn now to the pragmatics of temporal reference proper.

## 21.4  Pragmatics of time

### 21.4.1  Pragmatic determination of temporal reference

Some languages are *tenseless*: they don't have marking of time comparable to tenses or/and temporal connectives present in some other languages. Yucatec Maya, Navajo, Mandarin Chinese, West Greenlandic, Igbo are examples of such tenseless languages. Yucatec Maya, for instance, lacks both tenses and temporal connectives, so that speakers rely entirely on pragmatic inference in order to establish temporal reference in the absence of adverbs. Bohnemeyer (2002 and 2009), taking the example of Yucatec Maya but referring also to other languages, argues that the inferential paths followed by hearers in these languages are in fact similar to what is achieved by speakers of tensed languages: basically, in tenseless languages as in tensed languages, default inferences are obtained on the basis of markers of aspect, so that, unless there is evidence to the contrary, a perfective marker entails temporal forward ordering while an imperfective marker entails a background descriptive representation. A number of adverbial morphemes are available in these languages to specify temporal reference when needed. A similar point is made by C. Smith *et al.* (2007) and C. Smith and Erbaugh (2009) regarding Navajo and Mandarin Chinese. In the classical Whorfian literature, Hopi was once considered as not only tenseless but timeless, with the implication that speakers of Hopi don't have a notion of time, at least not comparable with speakers of other languages. However, this claim has been proven to be based on erroneous data.[15]

In tensed and tenseless languages, grammatical and semantic aspect form one of the crucial bases for the computational calculus of temporal relations holding in discourses, together with pragmatic knowledge and adverbs. Regularities have been observed within discourse semantics, suggesting that perfectivity or boundedness favors forward temporal ordering.[16] However, as was argued by Bohnemeyer (2002), the inference of temporal ordering, if in effect triggered by aspect, often relies on pragmatic inference. That a perfective form involves temporal progression, and that an anaphoric tense imposes background or state overlap, is arguably a defeasible inference, thus an implicature in the Gricean sense. Indeed, in *John entered. Mary stood up*, the inference that Mary stood up after John's entrance is defeasible, since both eventualities can be well conceived of as happening at the same time. However, this is not true as a law, since tenses do impose various restrictions on such inferences across languages. French simple past, for example, forbids backward readings in the absence of connectives or adverbs, and the progressive is hardly able to trigger forward ordering inferences. In a number of cases, pragmatic inference proves indeed to be stronger than tenses in establishing discursive relations, as when a pluperfect (PP) has to be interpreted as posterior to a simple past. (43) is a pertinent example from French.

(43)  Jean entra brusquement. Marie s'était levée, pâle comme une morte.
      'Jean entered suddenly. Marie stand-PP up, pale as a corpse.'

Here, a new R-point is constructed so that Marie's standing up was conceived of as happening later than Jean's entrance but still observed resultatively (Marie is standing up). However this is purely a pragmatic process since (43) may well raise a natural interpretation where the eventuality expressed by pluperfect happens before the one expressed by simple past. Needless to say, a causal relation is saliently activated between the sudden entrance and the standing up so that, *ceteris paribus*, (43) gets indeed pragmatically adapted to fit this conceptual connection.

Besides imperfectives and perfectives, a distinction also holds between simple and compound tenses, the latter expressing "perfection" (not to be confused with "perfective"), that is, the fact that the event has given rise to a new resulting state of affairs. Hence present perfect is as much a present as a past tense.[17] However, not only perfect forms give rise to pragmatic inferences that concern the present time of interaction.

A classical observation by Partee (1973) is that an utterance like (44) does not convey the temporal reference normally provided by the tense but is indeed about the deictic present.

(44)    I didn't turn off the stove. (Partee 1973 602)[18]

This example raises a very complex issue. Negative sentences have a particular temporal-aspectual behavior, either denoting states corresponding to non-occurrences of eventualities, as in (45), or conveying a pragmatically reconstructed positive event, known as "negative event," when a stative reading is not informative enough, as in Horn's (1989) classical case in (46), interpreted as an event of refusal.

(45)    No earthquake (ever) occurred here.

(46)    What happened next is that the consulate didn't give us our visas.

A number of other cases are discussed in the literature. Stockwell *et al.* (1973) suggest that, again, the explanation is pragmatic: according to them, a negative sentence can be interpreted as a negative event when its occurrence doesn't match assumptions about a usual or expected scheme of actions, as with *not pay one's taxes* or *not go to church*. They observe that such phrases combine well with frequency adverbs. De Saussure (1998) studied examples in French and suggests a pragmatic explanation based on schemes of inference, for which the positive counterpart is inferred on the basis of the search for relevance in the circumstances. It is suggested that such a negative sentence makes an underinformative utterance if understood literally as "nothing happened of type P". That such utterances behave actually just like "positive" utterances denoting events (they accept temporal connectives, punctual adverbs, etc.) makes it pragmatically necessary to posit that they lead to the inference that some other event, incompatible with the one explicitly negated, is implicitly communicated: given sentence *not-P*, an event *Q* is inferred, being the most plausible one fitting with the condition that *Q* implies *not-P*. The reason for such utterances to appear is that they are, again, pragmatically far more efficient than a complex literal positive substitute often much more complicated to state (and process) explicitly.

But here the fact is that not only the negative utterance but also the positive version of the utterance is relevant to the present: *I turned off the stove* doesn't mean "there is a specific and identifiable past time t at which the action of turning off the stove is true," but rather "the stove is off now" (so that we can go on peacefully driving away from home). This case raises also complex issues regarding the necessity to distinguish between definite and indefinite past: (44) would be indefinite in the sense that its actual meaning doesn't require the hearer to posit a precise temporal reference other than "past". That an utterance bears a definite or indefinite past reference is actually not due to necessary principles of semantics (as Kuhn 1988 suggests), but clearly to pragmatics.

An example like *Oswald killed Kennedy* (Kuhn 1988: 533) is differently narrowed down as pointing to a definite or indefinite past depending on contextual assumptions and expectations. The fact that the utterance can be an answer to *Who killed Kennedy?* or to *What happened on 22 November 1963?* modifies the relevant temporal reference (see Smith, N. 1990). As many authors have noticed (e.g. Carston 1988), definiteness and indefiniteness is indeed mostly a matter of pragmatics. Since the representation of events – like "turn off the stove" or "kill Kennedy" – entails causal changes in the state of the world, typical pragmatic conclusions are drawn about the relevant state of affairs induced by the event, in turn allowing for very *pragmatic* consequences. If uttered "half way down the turnpike" as in Partee's case, the implicature is about the necessity of going back home immediately, and the interpretation here is of an indefinite past temporal reference.

Wilson and Sperber (1993b) address a similar issue with English present perfect utterances. It is quite clear that the English present perfect does convey the invitation of a resulting state true at S. It is thus not the triggering of such a resulting state which is pragmatic but clearly the nature of it on each occasion. Consider (47) as an answer to an invitation to join the speaker for lunch.

(47)   I've eaten.

Sperber and Wilson surmise that the conclusion *The speaker declines the invitation* is entirely pragmatic. Clearly, in order for the inference to be drawn, the triggering of the appropriate resulting state has first to be derived (*the speaker is not hungry*) on the basis of the present perfect, calling for reference to the present. In English, the observation would however hold also for non-perfect tenses, as in *I had lunch*, but things are slightly different in other languages. In French, the present perfect is ambiguous as for the utterance's relevance in the present or in the past; as a consequence, *Paul est arrivé à cinq heures* focuses simultaneously on the present situation and on the past event, but is translatable in English only with a simple past (*Paul arrived /*has arrived at five*), raising a paradox named "present perfect paradox" by Klein (1992).

## 21.4.2  Deictic shift

Tenses call for a temporal relation with S, hence they are deictic in some way. Various situations induce a shifting of this deictic anchoring. In some cases, linguistic features directly operate the shifting, as in reported speech of thought utterances such as *John thought that Mary is in the kitchen* (Klein 2009: 47): the present tense represents a situation which is not present at S but at some projection of the deictic centre in the past, namely the R-point of the main clause. It is not by chance that these typically occur with reported speech and thought, since it is in the nature of deictic markers that they anchor on some individual's notion of presentness.

There are three main kinds of deictic shifting pragmatically induced. The first case is well known and not worth discussing. It concerns narrative present and future utterances like (48), and equivalents are found in many languages, with the pragmatic effect of raising representations of future (or present) simulation.

(48)   By the overthrow of Louis Philippe and the Republic, two bastard governments, Louis Napoleon will now succeed to the throne, a nephew by blood of Napoleon.
       (www.sacred-texts.com/nos/oon/oon21.htm)

The second case happens outside narratives. Some are again obvious as *I'm leaving tomorrow*, expressing the future eventuality of *leave* as if it were actually present. For example, (49) and (49') mean *I will shortly arrive*:

(49)   J'arrive.
(49')  I'm coming.

Interestingly, (49) and (49') are natural when it is mutually manifest that the speaker is not in the course of arriving. Typically a waiter may catch your call and utter (49) while going first to the kitchen, meaning he will be there in a minute.

Much more interesting are cases in Romance where the present perfect can be used to represent a future state of affairs. The English present perfect is unavailable for such effects, rendered only in some cases with adjectival participles as in *I am done in a minute*. Italian or French can use present perfect in order to represent future states of affairs construed from a further future point of view, although French allows virtually any sort of combinations whereas Italian accepts only a limited number of cases.

(50)   Tra poco ho finito. (Italian)
       Shortly I finish-PP (*I have finished shortly)
       'I am soon done.'

(50')  J'ai bientôt terminé. (French)
       I shortly finish-PP

(51)   Dans un an je suis parti pour l'Amérique. (French)
       In one year I go-PP to America (*In one year I have gone to America)[19]

(52)   ?Demain il a plu. (French)
       Tomorrow it rain-PP (*Tomorrow it has rained)

The anterior future does this normally by placing R in a later future than E, whereas the present perfect achieves this through a projection of S in the future, of course with other pragmatic effects. It's true that these combinations occur mostly with aspectual verbs like *finir* ('finish') but (52) is natural as soon as a pragmatic effect of a particular kind is reachable, namely that a specific attitude or course of actions has to be undertaken in the perspective of the future state of affairs. Hence (52) is all right in the appropriate context, for example if discussing the necessity of watering the vegetable garden. The representation thus keeps the temporal arrangement of coordinates of the present perfect but shifts the whole set to anchor on a future S′ instead of the deictic S.

The third case of deictic shifting occurs in represented thought or speech. In the absence of a verb of reported speech or thought, that is in free indirect speech, the deictic shifting occurs only on pragmatic grounds. However, in such cases, indexical expressions are shifted, not tenses, which refer to the past moment of thought. Hence unexpected combinations of deictic adverbs like *now* with past tenses, as in (53) and (53′):

(53)    What would he do now?

(53′)   Qu'allait-il faire maintenant? (French)

A free indirect speech interpretation is often invited by indicators such as exclamatives, oral speech register, and third-person questions. These, when combined with third-person indications such as the pronoun in the examples above, cannot be interpreted as expressing the speaker's meaning, as expected, but the character's. The discussion of free indirect speech would lead us too far; nonetheless, it is noticeable that a free indirect speech interpretation can well arise in the absence of a deictic or other marker of either presentness or orality, as in (54), again taken from French.

(54)    Il fallait faire vite.
         We had to be quick.

Utterance (54) is ambiguous as regards the free indirect speech. It may be a completely descriptive use of language by the speaker expressing that he, and others with him, had to be quick at that particular moment of the past. But if it's mutually manifest that attributing the responsibility of this thought to the speaker/writer leads to nonsensical interpretations, the hearer pragmatically attributes it to the thought of a character in the story.

Interestingly, free indirect speech is typically activated by utterances with imperfective aspect. In some cases, it has been argued that imperfectivity is not mandatory. However, the French *imparfait* seems to play a particular role in free indirect speech, together with the conditional with which it shares the *-ait* desinence. This may have to do with the fact that imperfective tenses represent eventualities as unbounded, so that the character's thought is represented as if being in the course of its conception, hence a strong effect of identification. In Russian, free indirect speech is rendered with a present (which is imperfectively marked in Slavic languages).

Deictic shifting occurs also in a classical case extensively discussed by the literature in philosophy, when *now* cannot be interpreted as the speaker's present time but the hearer's, thus raising a paradox. Suppose a message recorded on an answering machine says *I am not here now*.[20] Ignoring the possible humorous touch in such utterances, it remains that *now* is interpreted as deictically shifted so that it is made relevant for the hearer's present time. Let us simply note that, strangely enough, such an utterance would be clearly impossible in a number of languages including French (*Je ne suis pas ici maintenant*). This is particularly puzzling since French in principle allows deictic shiftings of a similar kind when the utterance is about the hearer's temporality, which we also find in English utterances like *We will now see that our hero was right*. But there is more: while *I am not here now* can plausibly be uttered in English while pointing on a map (Predelli 1998a), this is still not the case in French, which prefers demonstratives (*Je ne suis pas là en ce moment*), unless a clearly metalinguistic use of the negation.[21]

### 21.4.3  A note on past as indirect speech act conventional trigger
Past tenses are commonly used to perform indirect speech acts:

(55)  I had a question. (at the end of a lecture)

(56)  I wanted a pound of beef. (at the butcher's)

(57)  Excuse me, I was wondering where I could find a grocery in the neighborhood.

These predicates are states and activities, so that English uses either the simple past or the progressive, but Romance languages allow only imperfective tenses, like the French *imparfait* (*J'avais une question*; *Je voulais une livre de boeuf*; *Excusez-moi, je me demandais où je pourrais trouver une épicerie dans le quartier*).

Such utterances represent a state of affairs as past while it's mutually manifest that its relevance is to be found at S. Hence these utterances would normally not be interpreted as, respectively, *there is a moment of the past when I had a question* or *when I wanted a pound of beef* but definitely as *I have a question*, *I want a pound of beef* now. Representing a state of affairs as past when it is mutually manifest that it has to be presently relevant ends up in an indirect speech act – usually of request. This happens because the state of affairs is not explicitly but only implicitly meant to be true in the present, leaving its truth at S at the level of cancelable implicature derivation (the asker may not have a question). Hence some liberty for the addressee – albeit perhaps only apparent liberty – to reject the implicit request without being face-threatening, and, in turn, the speech act of request is itself less face-threatening.

### 21.4.4  Futurity and modality

That temporality and modality are deeply interconnected is a very well-known fact.[22] The discussion about the modal flavor of futurity, primarily based on the observation of Germanic languages, was fed by the description of numerous other languages. Srioutai (2004) showed that the Thai marker $c^{1}a$ ('$^{1}$' indicates a tonality), which serves to indicate futurity, might well have a basic modal meaning. Again, the selection between modal and temporal meanings (or both) is primarily a matter of pragmatic enrichment, and numerous positions within the scale of modality can be associated with future-time utterances. The modal flavor of utterances otherwise indicating future-time reference is also obvious in a number of cases in Romance languages; however, the modal flavor is arguably a pragmatic reconstruction of speaker's intentional meaning and not a necessary semantic feature of future-time utterances. In Germanic languages verbal indicators of futurity bear a connection with volition, which clearly appears in utterances such as *We will never surrender*. Interestingly, the same link with volition happens to be established in a number of languages. Arabic "future volitional negatives" (Holes 2004: 224) show a similar combination with *lan*: *Lan nataslima* ('We will never surrender'). Some German dialects often use the volitional verb *wollen* instead of standard *werden* as an auxiliary for futurity, and a similar case is found in some Swiss French dialects.

The reason for a generalizing assumption about an intrinsic link between future time and epistemic modality is that future states of affairs are by nature uncertain. However, this line of thought may miss the point that language can easily represent unreal situations as real facts, and thus futurity may in principle be represented by individuals as certain. Whatever the right answer to this question, it remains that in a number of cases, future-time indicators, typically tenses, are used to convey a modal meaning *about the present*. These utterances are called *epistemic future utterances*. Since they lead to a modal inference, and since the epistemic reading is context-dependent, they call for a pragmatic analysis. English allows this with *will* and *be going to* but also with a form usually understood as marking anterior futurity as in (58) (the very particular way of indicating the future in English makes it unclear whether it's a tense or a mood).

(58)  He will have missed his train.

Hindi allows similar interpretations with its marker *-gaa* (Kush 2010), and French uses interchangeably the simple future, the proximal future, or the anterior future tenses. Italian standardly communicates epistemic modality with a future tense. Typical examples of epistemic future in English and French are (59) and (60).

(59)  [The doorbell rings] That will be the postman.

(60)  Ce sera le facteur.

That a future-time utterance gets interpreted as having present-time reference, at the cost of a modal meaning, can be explained as the result of a true future representation in the first place. Actually, the conclusion *this is probably the postman at the door* has to be derived from a semantic starting point together with contextual information. The contextual information required in such interpretations is obvious: the considered fact is mutually manifest as holding now – although with some uncertainty concerning some of its properties. In (59) or (60), someone who is likely to be the postman just rang – and will be behind the door for a while. Since there is still a notion of futurity, it seems commonsensical to propose that the semantic meaning of these utterances remains that of a future state of affairs. A typical line of explanation since Damourette and Pichon (1911–1936) assumes that the future utterance represents the future moment when the state of affairs will be verified. Hence (59) and (60) mean something to the effect *it will be the postman at the door at the time when I verify it* (by seeing, by opening the door, and so forth). Hence the conclusion that the state of affairs is not verified in the present, hence again the modal interpretation of probability (since the prediction of future verifiability implies more than mere possibility). However, not all states of affairs seem possible in epistemic future utterances: (61) looks intuitively bizarre as an epistemic modal utterance.

(61)   The Universe will be expanding.

Therefore it is likely that another pragmatic parameter comes into play, having to do with the *present* consequences of the represented situation being probably true. That the postman will be at the door seems to entail a kind of attitude or behavior: we have to hurry up in order to get the awaited letter for example. Predictably, (61) will have a modal interpretation only if the probability of the Universe being in expansion entails in the context a necessary course of actions or attitude such as an expectation of reaching this conclusion through theoretical enquiry or observations. It is the unlikelihood of such a context that makes the utterance intuitively odd. Noticeably, if this analysis is correct, an epistemic interpretation of a future tense utterance triggers an epistemic modality about what is likely to be the case, which is pragmatically enriched as a deontic modality about what should be done.[23] Clearly, such interpretations are not produced by other expressions indicating probability.

  Furthermore, tenses often convey evidentiality (i.e. a specific information about the origin of the communicated assumption, typically hearsay, direct perception, or inference). An epistemic future interpretation seems indeed to communicate evidentiality, according to the analysis above: for what I will have seen, heard, or inferred, it's probably the postman standing at the door. The present perfect, or forms derived from the present perfect, in an array of languages of various families, such as Turkish, Bulgarian, or Norwegian, are reported to trigger evidentiality of "indirect evidence", according to Izvorsky (1997). She explains that in such languages, a sentence like (62) communicates pragmatically something to the effect of (63).

(62)    John has arrived.

(63)    John has apparently arrived.

Noticeably, such interpretations also involve epistemic modality, as expected with indirect evidence.

## 21.5  Connectives and indexicals

To repeat, tense is in fact not the only way to indicate temporal reference and ordering in discourse, since the grammatical tenses are more vague as time indicators than event names and, most of all, adverbs and connectives. There isn't much to say about event names, a class of nouns which refer to events and thus bear a temporal reference, such as *the Russian revolution*, except that they trigger pragmatic reinterpretations of the tense when it clashes with their temporal reference. This happens when a name of a past event occurs in a present- or future-tensed utterance, so that the tense is interpreted as deictically shifted. Some nouns also refer to individuals whose existence is true only in some temporal interval, such as *Julius Caesar* or *druids*; they are temporalized names, at least in the proper context (since druids do still exist in small communities). What is noticeable about them is that since they bear a (more or less vague) temporal reference, they allow anaphoric tenses to temporally anchor onto them, so that imperfective tense forms (for example the progressive in English) can occur without being bound to another eventuality or to an adverbial, as in (64).

(64)    Druids were celebrating the shortest day of the year at the
        mysterious monument with traditional ceremonies.
        (http://findarticles.com/p/news-articles/evening-times-glasgow-uk/
        mi_8052/is_20091222/winter-solstice-gathering/ai_n48725662/).

Some connectives trigger curious pragmatic enrichments. *And*-connectives call for some pragmatic elaboration with regard to their role in temporal reference and ordering. *And* – as well as its equivalents across languages – does not trigger a forward temporal ordering: it can in fact be removed from utterances without affecting their temporal meaning. However, *and*-connectives do forbid reverse temporal ordering (Bar-Lev and Palacas 1980), which is unpredictable on the sole basis of logical connection.[24] Hence (65) normally gets interpreted in such a way that the event of Bill falling happens first, despite a salient causal connection suggesting the opposite order.

(65)    Bill fell and Max pushed him.

As Blakemore and Carston (1999) have shown, reverse order is possible through a meta-linguistic interpretation (favored by specific intonation). As a consequence, in such cases, *and* doesn't connect representations of events but speech acts. Their example is (66):

(66)    Bill went to bed and he took off his shoes.
            (Blakemore and Carston 1999: 11)

This observation allows for assuming that (66) may actually be backward-interpreted if meaning a metalinguistic connection such as "let me say first that Bill went to bed and only then that he took off his shoes", but only as a pragmatically, context-dependent, enriched meaning.

   According to Levinson (2000), *and* invites a path of conventional pragmatic enrichment which goes as follows: from conjunction, infer temporal ordering, and then, if necessary, a causal relation of result. Wilson and Sperber (1993b) argue that causal relations do not imply temporal ones, as in (67).

(67)    It was dark and I couldn't see.
            (Wilson and Sperber 1993b: 282)

Therefore, according to them, *and*-conjunctions get pragmatically enriched through a selection of either temporal or causal or both relationships holding among conjoined utterances and giving relevance to them. It remains however controversial that there can be plainly simultaneous causalities: either there is intuitively a truly causal connection, as in (67), or the fact that one cannot see seems at least to follow temporally from a pre-existing condition (the darkness). However, it remains also true that, from the pragmatic point of view, there is no need to access that particular temporality in order to represent two facts which are simultaneously true and still bearing a continuous causal connection of some sort, as in (67).

   Numerous connectives are dedicated to temporal ordering proper, such as *then*, *afterwards*, *before*, etc. Some of them add various other elements of meaning, such as French *puis* (roughly: 'then'), which doesn't allow for adjacent causal connection (Reyle 1998), but this is a semantic feature of the connective. The meaning of temporal connectives is in itself a very broad topic. Let us simply say that they can be contrasted with *serial* connectives, which bear initially a non-temporal meaning, indicating whatever kind of order, such as *to begin with*, *firstly*, or *finally*, as in example (68), which explains why they are very often found in contexts where they provide indications about how the utterances are to be connected within the discursive structure.

(68)    To begin with, I am not hungry; second, I wouldn't know where to
            find an acceptable restaurant around here; finally I have no
            intention of having dinner with you.

They are, however, able to establish temporal ordering in the appropriate context.

   Now, it has to be pointed out that temporal expressions, in particular temporal connectives, can bear "discursive" functions. In some cases, indeed, a temporal interpretation fails to prove relevant and a rhetorical interpretation is obtained instead – that is, an interpretation in which the connective indicates the organization of the discourse, or the argumentative relations between utterances or spans of discourse. *Then*, for example, can be either used as a temporal marker or as an argumentative marker introducing a conclusion, typically in *if-then* structures.

An interesting case to contrast across languages is given by the class of *now*-indexicals (and related expressions), which may allow pragmatic reinterpretation as markers of a discursive relation, typically an argumentative relation of contrast. It is a very puzzling fact that some languages have more than one *now*-indexical expression, and only some among them allow a pragmatic contrastive interpretation. *Now* can be used to indicate focus or topic change, which is clearly compatible with its temporal meaning, but another deictic expression is preferred when it comes to indicating contrast in English (*yet*). French quite standardly indicates contrast with *maintenant*, but Italian only triggers contrast (and only under some conditions; see Baranzini and de Saussure 2009) with *ora*, while *adesso* is unavailable:

(69)    I know you're an adult. *Yet* / *?Now*, I forbid you to do this anyway.

(69′)   Je sais que tu es une adulte. *Maintenant*, je t'interdis quand-même de le faire. (after Nef 1978)

(70)    Questo studio presenta numerose lacune di ordine teorico; *ora* /\**adesso*, non è certo per questo che smetteremo di farlo leggere agli studenti.
        'This study presents numerous lacunae of theoretical order; ora /\*adesso, this is certainly not a reason for not giving it to the students as a reading.'

Interestingly, when languages allow contrastive interpretations of *now*-indexicals, demonstratives are odd as contrast markers even though they indicate S, which leads to the conclusion that there is more in the pragmatic contrastive interpretation than a simple transfer from referential temporal indexicality to "discursive" indexicality: expressions such as *en ce moment* or *in questo momento* ('at this time') will be discarded. Contrastive examination thus leads to the possibility that there might be a different path of pragmatic understanding with these expressions across languages, since the notion of deictic presentness doesn't seem sufficient to lead conceptually to the inference of a contrast. There might well be a flavor of contrast already in non-pragmatically enriched readings of these expressions in languages allowing for contrast marking; for instance, the idea of a temporal contrast with what precedes might well be the grounds for pure contrastive interpretation, obtained as the hearer eschews to make full sense of a literal, uninformative, temporal interpretation *stricto sensu*.

## 21.6  Concluding remarks

Establishing temporal reference, in a broader sense, includes establishing the aspectual properties of the represented eventuality, so that time and aspect are always conveyed together. Providing temporal reference is also linked with modality, both in the classical cases where there is a conflict between the time indicated by a tense and a salient time stemming from other information, which happens with epistemic futures, but also in a wider sense that they may obey similar basic principles linked to, in fact, fundamental spatial notions of distance (see Chilton 2007, Jaszczolt 2009) in human cognition. Experimental pragmatics is only at the beginning of this exploration, but it's likely that the future of our understanding of the pragmatics of time resides very much in cognitive psychology.

In this chapter, we reviewed the many ways in which pragmatic processing modifies what is usually considered the semantic meaning of temporal expressions *in abstracto*. In particular, we reviewed how aspect, a central conceptual feature of verbs and verb clauses, is changed by pragmatic processing under various contextual conditions. We also reviewed how tenses provide only limited hints about how to construct the pragmatically meaningful temporal reference, and how the typical denotation of tense, again, can be adapted in order to fulfill discursive aims, in particular through deictic shifting, but also how tenses can lead to modal representations, and how negative utterances can get temporalized event-like readings. Finally, we discussed a number of pragmatic issues relating to the temporal interpretation of connectives and indexicals.

# 22

# Textual coherence as a pragmatic phenomenon

Anita Fetzer

## 22.1   Introduction

In its ordinary-language reading, coherence refers to the act or state of being logically consistent and connected, while cohesion denotes the act or state of cohering. In its technical sense, coherence refers to the unity in a text or discourse, which makes sense because its elements do not contradict each other's presuppositions: *surface coherence* refers to the logical relations between clauses and segments of a text (such as time sequence and cause and effect), and *situational coherence* refers to consistency in the structure of the information, its relation to general knowledge and the appropriateness of a text. Cohesion refers to the use of language forms to indicate semantic relations between elements of discourse: *grammatical cohesion* concerns matters such as reference, ellipsis, substitution and conjunction, *lexical cohesion* concerns such features as synonymy, antonymy, metonymy, collocation, repetition etc. and *instantial cohesion* concerns ties that are valid for only a particular text. Together cohesion and register contribute to *textuality*, the sense that something is a text and not a random collection of sentences (cf. Oxford Companion to the English Language 1992). Cohesion is thus an overt (or explicit) linguistic-surface phenomenon, while coherence is a covert (or implicit) deep-structure phenomenon, metaphorically speaking.

   In the research domains of language studies in general and in linguistics and pragmatics in particular, coherence is connected intrinsically with the production and comprehension of text. Texts are not produced and interpreted in some kind of nothingness but rather in local and global contexts. That is to say, local utterances are connected with their directly adjacent neighbours, which are connected with directly adjacent utterances as well as with more global utterances, discourse topics and story-lines.

I am deeply grateful to the editors, especially to Keith Allan and Kasia Jaszczolt, for helpful comments on the first version of this chapter.

The production and interpretation of text in context assigns text the status of discourse, which is produced and interpreted with a certain intention and with a certain goal. In the process of producing and interpreting text, particular information is selected and encoded and at the same time categorised. Adopting a pragmatic perspective, text producers select and categorise information in a speaker-intended manner and the recipients of text interpret them accordingly. Hand in hand with the selection and categorisation of information goes the coupling and decoupling of information. Construing textual coherence thus depends on both linguistic and extra-linguistic information. Moreover, the construal of coherence is a cognitive operation which is based on diverse logical operations, such as inference, and deductive and abductive reasoning (Givón 1989).

In linguistics and pragmatics, language patterns and communicative-action patterns anchored to the sentence and utterance as units of analysis have been investigated in different types of grammar and in speech act theory, postulating necessary and sufficient conditions for an utterance to count as a speech act, and for a sentence to count as a grammatical sentence. While sentence grammar does not generally need to accommodate the linguistic and social context of a sentence to account for its grammaticality, speech act theory needs to integrate context in an explicit manner to account for the felicity of a speech act. That is why felicity conditions have been classified as context conditions (Sbisà 2002; see also Kissine, this volume). However, sentences do not only need to be grammatical to count as good sentences, they also need to be meaningful. To account for the latter, it generally suffices to compose the meaning of the whole sentence by connecting the meanings of the sentence's constitutive parts in an additive manner. For instance, the meaning of the sentence '[[Peter] [bought a house]]' is construed of the meaning of the subject NP realised by the definite description 'Peter' denoting one and only one male person, of the meaning of the VP 'bought a house' denoting an event anchored to the past and the object NP 'a house', denoting a particular kind of building, thus composing the meaning of the whole.

An analysis of speech acts, by contrast, needs to go beyond the analysis of the meaning of its parts to account for their felicity. Speech act theory's basic unit of investigation is the speech act, and depending on the frameworks employed, speech acts divide into locutionary, illocutionary and perlocutionary acts (Austin 1975), or propositional and illocutionary acts (Searle 1969), and their respective sub-acts. In discourse, these acts are performed simultaneously and may be represented linguistically in both direct and indirect modes, i.e. as direct and indirect speech acts. Direct speech acts are more explicit and therefore less context-dependent. They still require speech-act-specific felicity conditions, i.e. specified contexts, in order to be felicitous. Indirect speech acts, on the other hand, are less explicit and therefore more context-dependent. They generally refer to one specific felicity condition and query or state its validity, thereby triggering a process of inferencing in order to retrieve the speaker's communicative intention. The speech act of rejection may, for instance, be represented directly by 'I hereby reject your offer' or it may be represented indirectly by saying 'your offer seems very generous, but it will be difficult to meet all the requirements'. With regard to the explicitly represented rejection, the hearer needs to retrieve further information from context, such as the content of the offer in question and the speaker's identity, i.e. whether the speaker refers to herself as an individual or speaks on behalf of some institution. The implicitly represented rejection requires the hearer to do even more inferential work as she is confronted with a positive evaluation and with a negative evaluation: there is the intensified positive evaluation 'very generous', which seems to indicate that the offer in question was received favourably, and there is the connective 'but' with the function of a contrastive discourse marker, which signifies some kind of non-acceptance. This is confirmed by the directly adjacent part 'it will be difficult to meet all the requirements'. It is the hearer's task to come to terms with this local inconsistency, i.e. the intensified positive evaluation and the negative discourse marker, thus searching for further evidence in context to bridge the gap between these local inconsistencies. More specifically, the predication 'seems very generous' does not only consist of the positive evaluation 'very generous', but also the modality marker 'seems' which reduces the degree of certainty about the positive evaluation. Against this background, the positive evaluation 'very generous' is reinterpreted and the whole utterance 'your offer seems very generous, but it will be difficult to meet all the requirements' is assigned the status of a local rejection.

To conclude, an analysis of utterances and speech acts does not only require the explicit accommodation of context but also that of coherence. This is particularly true if the hearer's perspective is adopted. It is her/his process of inferencing in and through which s/he needs to construe and calculate the speaker's communicative intention, which is no longer an isolated phenomenon anchored to one and only one speech act, but rather needs to cohere with the speech act's local and global contexts.

The goal of this chapter is to examine textual coherence from pragmatic and discourse-analytic perspectives, identifying necessary conditions which make "language patterns above the sentence" (Widdowson 2004: 3) and above the speech act count as a coherent text. The following section examines structural coherence, considering thematic structure, theme and rheme, and thematic progression. Section 22.3 investigates discourse relations and discourse connectives, paying particular attention to their function in the construal of context, and section 22.4 revisits textual coherence, considering its status as process and product, its connectedness with the pragmatic principle of cooperation and with discourse common ground and context. The final section provides an outlook.

## 22.2  Structural coherence

Coherence has been examined thoroughly in the fields of cognitive semantics, discourse semantics, discourse analysis and pragmatics, and it has been assigned a key role in functional grammar (e.g. Hengeveld and Mackenzie 2008; Givón 1993). At first sight, coherence seems to be concerned with semantics only, i.e. with meaning but not with form or structure. This is, however, an oversimplification. Coherence is also intrinsic to the structured interplay of given and new information, as is reflected in the pragmatic phenomenon of information structure (e.g. Lambrecht 1994) and in the systemic-functional-grammar concept of thematic structure (e.g. Gómez-González 2001). Furthermore, coherence is also a basic premise in the sequential organisation of communicative action, as is reflected in the conversation-analytic unit of investigation of paired communicative action, viz. adjacency pair represented by e.g. the first part of offer with the second parts of acceptance or rejection, or the first part of greeting with the second part of greeting. Coherence is also manifest in the context-dependent specification of adjacency pair in the domain of preference organisation in preferred and dispreferred second parts with acceptance being the preferred second part for the first part offer, and rejection being its dispreferred second part. Preference in that context is not a psychological notion but rather depends on distribution, frequency and structural complexity (cf. Levinson 1983; Pomerantz 1984).

In the research paradigm of systemic functional grammar (SFG), meaning and function of language are key concepts, and 'language is interpreted as a system of meanings, accompanied by forms through which the meanings can be realized' (Halliday 1994: xiv). One of those 'forms through which different meanings' are 'realized' is the initial position of a clause which is also referred to as *theme* (Halliday 1994) or *theme zone* (Hannay 1994).

## 22.2.1   Thematic structure: theme and rheme

The concepts of theme and rheme are connected closely with the functional approaches to language fostered by the Prague School and by systemic functional linguistics. Thematic structure refers to the structured interplay of the constitutive parts of a clause: a thematic part (or theme) and a rhematic part (or rheme).

Unlike most traditional grammars, which base their analyses on written language and on the sentence as a unit of investigation, SFG transcends that frame of reference by examining spoken and written language within discourse-semantic perspectives based on the principle of paradigmatic choice. To account for the extended frame of reference, SFG is based on a tripartite system of experiential, interpersonal and textual metafunctions. The *experiential metafunction* looks upon the clause as representation and is based on its semantic representation within a system of transitivity. The *interpersonal metafunction* is concerned with the clause as exchange and is based on its modal representation within a system of mood, and the *textual metafunction* considers the clause as message and is based on its bipolar conception as theme and rheme within a system of thematic structure. While the experiential and interpersonal metafunctions are primarily discourse-semantic in nature, the textual metafunction considers continuative, structural and conjunctive phenomena and thus is syntactic and discourse-semantic.

In all of the three metafunctions, the subject occupies the initial position of a clause or sentence in their unmarked configurations, yet its status differs. In the clause as representation, the subject is conceived of along semantic lines as the agent that performs an action in an intentional manner. In the clause as exchange, the grammatical subject displays concord or agreement with the finite verb, and in the textual metafunction, the psychological subject is the first constituent of the clause with experiential meaning. For example, in the clause '[[the prime minister][is going to resign]]', the psychological subject or theme conflates with the logical subject of the experiential metafunction and with the grammatical subject of the interpersonal metafunction, and is realized by the NP 'the prime minister': the subject intentionally performs the action of resigning and therefore is the logical subject, it displays agreement with the finite verb and therefore is the grammatical subject, and it is the first constituent in the clause with an experiential function and therefore is the theme. As SFG is a discourse grammar, it also needs to account for discourse connectives or conjuncts as well as for the expression of interpersonal meaning. In line with the three metafunctions, theme is subcategorised into topical themes anchored to the experiential metafunction, interpersonal themes anchored to the interpersonal metafunction and textual themes anchored to the textual metafunction.

Theme is hence represented more appropriately as *multiple themes*, which are composed of more than one element. Generally they consist of one element with an experiential function, that is topical theme, and of other themes, that is textual and interpersonal themes (cf. Halliday 1994: 52). To capture the concept of multiple themes, the textual metafunction's constitutive part of theme is referred to as theme zone in the following. *Theme zone* denotes 'the initial zone which codes relational-semantic "aboutness" (the speaker's point of departure setting her / his angle on the experience being constructed) syntactically across different languages, although the relevance of this position varies in accordance with the morpho-syntactic structure of specific languages' (Gómez-González 2001: 132). Looked upon from a cognitive perspective, 'the Theme Zone provides a (re-)orientation or a grounding for what is to follow' (Gómez-González 2001: 351), and is, for this reason, intrinsically connected with the sociocognitive concept of *discourse common ground* (Fetzer 2007). Thus, theme zones are of great importance to the investigation of discourse in general and to the construal of textual coherence in particular. This is due to the fact that they have both a forward-looking (or cataphoric) and a backward-pointing (or anaphoric) function. They connect what has *just* been said, what is being said *now* and what is going to be said *next*.

Analogously to the structured interplay of theme and rheme, the theme can be realised in marked and unmarked formats. A marked configuration of the initial position of a clause or of the theme zone brings the structured interplay of the processing of themes and rhemes or of processing the unmarked sequence of [[textual theme] [interpersonal theme] [topical theme]] to a – temporary – halt, signifying the speaker's local or particularised attitude towards a local stretch of discourse which differs from her/his prevailing one, such as the intention not to accept a particular argument or a particular line of argumentation; it may also indicate a change in the story line. While unmarked topical 'themes do not contrast with an earlier one; that is, they are entirely given or background' (Steedman 2000 :657), marked configurations signify an alternative set, thus instructing the hearer how the speaker intends it to be taken up and accordingly processed. In that particular context, Ji (2002) refers to Givón's (1993) claim that 'all these pre-posed structures . . . have their coherence links in two directions, anaphoric and cataphoric. Their anaphoric links can reach back to thematic information anywhere in the preceding episode. Their cataphoric links anchor themselves nicely to the main clause, which then launches the new episode' (Ji 2002: 1265).

Because of its forward- and backward-pointing potential, the theme zone is of key importance to the construal of textual coherence. This does not only apply to the topical and textual planes of discourse, but also to the interpersonal plane, as has been pointed out by Thompson and Zhou: 'We have argued . . . that coherence in text can only be adequately understood if the concept of propositional coherence is complemented by that of evaluative coherence, and that, amongst other things, this involves recognition of the conjunctive function of disjuncts' (Thompson, G. and Zhou 2000: 139). Consequently, textual coherence is a pragmatic phenomenon par excellence, feeding on propositional coherence and communicative-action-based coherence. To use Halliday's words, '[t]he choice of Theme, clause by clause, is what carries forward the development of the text as a whole' (Halliday 1994: 336).

To summarise, thematic structure, that is the structured interplay between theme and rheme, is of great importance for the construal of textual coherence, jointly constructed discourse coherence and jointly negotiated discourse common ground (Fetzer 2007; Givón 1993).

## 22.2.2  Thematic progression

Theme is represented by an inherently dual concept and therefore is a relational notion par excellence: on the one hand, it is anchored to the initial syntactic slot of a clause, and on the other hand, it is the 'point of departure of the message' (Halliday 1994: 38). From a discourse-semantic perspective (van Dijk 1981, Givón 2005) as well as from a thematic-progression viewpoint (Bloor and Bloor 1995, Ravelli 2003), this means that the theme of clause$_n$ is connected with the rheme of clause$_{n-1}$, expressing a connectedness amongst what is 'here' (theme$_n$) with what has just been said 'there' (rheme$_{n-1}$) and what is going to be said 'next' (rheme$_n$). Against this background, the theme and the theme zone can be assigned the status of some sort of contextual-isation device (Fetzer 2008) and need to be conceptualised accordingly. In Halliday's terms, the theme 'set[s] up a contextualization relationship with some other (typically preceding) portion of the text. The semantic basis of this contextualizing function is that of the logical-semantic relationships of "expansion"' (Halliday 1994: 83). Adapting the concept of markedness, which has been discussed above, to the contextualisation function of theme and theme zone, unmarked configurations of the initial position of a clause, viz. conflated subjects, or unmarked configurations of the theme zone, i.e. [[textual theme] [interpersonal theme] [topical theme]], signify the logical-semantic relationship of expansion, while marked configurations signify a different type of sequential organisation. The type of continuation of the discourse in progress indicated by a marked configuration depends strongly on the semantics of the theme zone as a whole, particularly on the semantics of the textual theme and interpersonal theme.

To encode a particular type of connectedness (from the speaker's perspec-tive), and to infer or decode that type of connectedness (from the hearer's per-spective) are basic cognitive context-based operations, e.g. pragmatic enrich-ment, generalised and particularised implicature and grounding. Against this background, themes and theme zones are assigned the function of a 'coherence *bridge* grounding the chain of the preceding discourse' (Givón 2005: 180). At the same time, they play an important role in the organisation of sociocognitive discourse common ground.

Based on the structured interplay of themes and rhemes, thematic pro-gression has been further refined with respect to more linear and more hier-archical orderings of discourse, viz. constant theme patterns, linear theme patterns, split rheme patterns and derived themes (Bloor and Bloor 1995). While constant-theme-patterned discourse and linear-theme-patterned dis-course are straightforward unfolding types of text with chronological and logically ordered story lines, split-rheme-patterned discourse and derived-theme-patterned discourse are more complex types of text and may display non-chronological and non-logically-ordered story lines. Furthermore, the-matic progression has been examined from a semantic perspective, account-ing for the nature of connectedness between different topical themes dis-tinguishing between the superordinate–subordinate relation of theme and hypertheme (Ravelli 2003). That kind of connectedness is also reflected in the differentiation between topic and more global discourse topic anchored to the units of sequence or episode, and discourse (Cornish 2004).

Thematic progression is also inherent in the Gricean *Cooperative Principle* (Grice 1975), which has been extended to cover the domain of discourse (Fet-zer 2004). This is particularly true of the *maxim of manner*, the supermaxim *be perspicuous* and the sub-maxim *be orderly*. Clauses, sentences, sequences and discourses which are produced in accordance with that maxim, super-maxim and sub-maxim display a chronological and logical order of objects and events and thus a straightforward story line, while clauses, sentences, sequences and discourses which are produced in discordance with the maxim and sub-maxim may trigger a generalised or particularised conversational implicature to infer and calculate the speaker-intended story line, as is the case with cleft-constructions and implicated contrastive sets. Another example is the genteel-tea-party scenario with the contribution 'Mrs. X is an old bag' and the response 'The weather has been quite delightful this summer' (Grice 1975: 54). To construe textual coherence for the discourse as a whole, the nature of the connectedness amongst topical themes needs to be considered by the producers and recipients of discourse, as well as the nature of connectedness amongst interpersonal themes, and the nature of the connectedness amongst textual themes and interpersonal and topical themes. While topical themes are indispensable for the construal of propositional coherence concerning the factual story line, interpersonal themes are indispensable for the construal of interpersonal coherence concerning modality, stance, evaluation and communicative action. Textual themes are relevant to the construal of local coherence, signifying the nature of the connectedness with prior and succeeding clauses, sentences and sequences.

In the following, themes and theme zones are examined more closely, refining the results obtained by comparing and contrasting them with discourse connectives and discourse relations.

## 22.3 Discourse relations and discourse connectives

Discourse is fundamentally concerned with the nature of the connectedness between parts and wholes, and therefore requires the accommodation of both bottom-up and top-down, and process- and product-oriented perspectives. Approaching discourse from a bottom-up perspective tends to focus on the micro domain and proceed from there, examining clauses and their constitutive parts, sentences or utterances (and their constitutive parts), and their discursive status with respect to discourse constraints, such as sequence and sequentiality, adjacency and dovetailedness, discourse relations and textual coherence, paying in general more attention to the discursive processes involved than to the discursive product (as a whole).[1]

Approaching discourse in a top-down manner tends to focus on the discourse-as-a-whole and proceed from there, decomposing the whole into its constitutive parts, such as connectives,[2] clauses and sentences in discourse semantics, and utterances, pragmatic markers and sequences in the field of discourse analysis; or turn-constructional units, discourse markers, turns and opening, closing and topical sequences in conversation analysis (cf. Meierkord and Fetzer 2002). From a discourse-internal perspective, these more generalised constraints are considered as discursive universals, e.g. initial positions, the right frontier, adjacency or rhetorical distance; discursive moves, e.g. request for information and compliance or rejection; and rhetorical relations, e.g. continuation, narration or elaboration (Asher and Lascarides 2003, Kühnlein et al. 2010).

Pragmatics-, sociology- and applied-linguistics-based analyses of discourse investigate the specification of those constraints in order to accommodate the contextual constraints and requirements of an activity type (Levinson 1979) or discourse genre (Luckmann 1995), refining, for instance, the constraint of adjacency with conditional relevance, viz. adjacency position, adjacency relation and adjacency expectation (Levinson 1983). It needs to be pointed out, however, that only very few analyses address explicitly the important methodological issue of whether discourse is a semantic concept concerned with text, or whether it is pragmatic in nature and therefore concerned with communicative action and the performance of speech acts in context (Mey 2001; Sbisà 1991, 2002; Kissine, this volume). In this frame of reference, discourse relations are examined on both the locutionary and illocutionary planes of discourse, considering not only their local impact on the construal of textual coherence and their context-change potentials, but also their perlocutionary effects and perlocutionary intentions. Implicit in this outlook on discourse is the question whether discourse connectives are some kind of peripheral speech act.

The previous section has focused on the examination of structural coherence, while this section is going to examine the nature of the connectedness between the constitutive parts of discourse referred to as discourse relations, and the semantics and pragmatics of discourse connectives.[3] Naturally, the differentiation between structural coherence and pragmatic coherence adopted in this chapter is an analytic one. In practice, the two sides of the coin are constitutive parts of one holistic unit.

### 22.3.1 Discourse relations

Discourse relations are of key importance for the construal of local textual coherence. They may be realised non-overtly through the position of an utterance (or sentence) within a sequence of utterances, e.g. direct adjacency, or they may be realised overtly by discourse connectives. Discourse semantics distinguishes between coordinating discourse relations, e.g. *Narration*, *Background*, *Result*, *Continuation*, *Parallel* and *Contrast*, and subordinating relations, such as *Elaboration*, *Instance*, *Explanation*, *Precondition* and *Commentary*, which are defined by $S_2$ picking up $S_1$ as the topic (Asher and Lascarides 2003). In SFG this relation is referred to as a linear theme pattern (Halliday 1994). Adopting a more global perspective on textual coherence, the semantics-anchored discourse relations need to be supplemented with the pragmatic constraints of adjacency and dovetailedness.

### 22.3.1.1 Adjacency

Adjacency is one of the most fundamental discursive relations in a pragmatics-based theory of discourse, which aims to account for the processing of local discourse units and for the processing of discourse as a whole. At first sight, adjacency seems to be a fairly straightforward notion. From a context-based perspective, however, it is rather complex, comprising adjacency position, adjacency relation and adjacency expectation (cf. Levinson 1983, Schegloff 1995).

Discourse relations, which are anchored to two directly adjacent discourse units and in which adjacency position and adjacency relation conflate, tend to be a straightforward matter with respect to production and processing. They can generally be processed without the accommodation of extra contextual information, and the information contained in them and communicated through them can be attributed directly to discourse common ground. In that scenario, the type of discourse relation is usually implicit in the semantics of the lexical units and in the syntactic configuration of the discourse unit.

In discourse, adjacency position may neither conflate with adjacency relation nor with adjacency expectation. In that kind of scenario, discourse relations tend to be represented overtly to facilitate discourse production and discourse processing. Looked upon from this perspective, discourse connectives may be assigned the status of some kind of indirect directive, requesting the hearer/reader to perform inference operations of a certain kind. For instance, the discourse connective 'but' may signify an upcoming contrastive context and request the hearer to perform corresponding inferences to accommodate the information introduced by 'but', or the discourse connective 'in addition' may signify another argument in a line of arguments with a stronger force, requesting the hearer to perform the corresponding processes of inferencing.

Adjacency, in particular adjacency position, is connected intrinsically with linearity, which is not only of great importance to natural- and non-natural-language reasoning but also to natural-language communication (Grice 1975). The sequential status of two propositions $p$ and $q$ realised with the additive connector '&' leads to different outcomes in natural- and non-natural-language sequences. Contrary to formal logic, the meaning of [p & q] in natural-language communication is usually not identical to the meaning of [q & p]: the 'key$_1$' referred to in the utterance *she picked up the key$_1$ and she opened the door* is generally interpreted as the door-opener, that is the one and only one key with which a female person opened the door. There seems to be general agreement that there is no identity between key$_1$ and key$_2$ referred to in the utterance *she opened the door and she picked up the key$_2$*, which is generally interpreted as the non-door-opener, that is key$_2$ may open other doors, or may be attributed to another class of keys, such as car keys. Thus, logical linearity and temporal linearity do not necessarily conflate.

## 22.3.1.2 Dovetailedness

Grice specifies the discursive constraint of 'such as is required' from his cooperative principle 'Make your conversational contribution such as is required, at the stage at which it occurs, by the accepted purpose or direction of the talk exchange in which you are engaged' (Grice 1975: 45) by the notion of *dovetailed*, i.e. conversational contributions are linked by one or more common goals manifest in prior and succeeding talk (see Grice 1975: 48). Dovetailedness is intrinsically linked to the conversation-analytic conception of conditional relevance and to the sequence of adjacency pair, which, following Mey, 'is a case of coherent sequencing, but not all sequencing needs to be defined strictly in terms of adjacency' (Mey 2001: 249). This is due to the fact that textual coherence and dovetailedness are not only related to the felicity conditions of a speech act in context regarding illocutionary force and illocutionary point, but also to the discourse topic of the discourse as a whole and to its subtopics. Yet coherence and dovetailedness are not only of relevance to the research paradigm of pragmatics. They are also of importance to the field of semantics, in which sequentiality is a constitutive part of coherence, and coherence ties are manifest in coreference, conjunctive relation, substitution, ellipsis, reiteration and lexical cohesion.

Discourse relations are an important requirement for the construal of textual coherence, which is connected intrinsically with the parts–whole configuration of discourse. It is not only the domain of discourse semantics that is important at that stage, but also that of illocutionary force and reasoning, as is argued for by Levinson:

> What makes some utterances after a question constitute an answer is not only the nature of the utterance itself but also the fact that it occurs after a question with a particular content – 'answerhood' is a complex property composed of sequential location and topical coherence across two utterances, amongst other things; significantly there is no proposed illocutionary force of answering. (Levinson 1983: 193)

In a similar vein, Sbisà (1991, 2002) argues for speech acts in discourse to be conceived of as 'attempts' along the lines of Austin's notion of uptake and its consequences (Sbisà 1991). Speech acts in discourse can be looked upon as social acts, which have conventional effects and perlocutionary consequences (Sbisà 2002). For instance, a promise puts the speaker under the obligation to perform the future action s/he referred to in the proposition used, and it entitles the addressee to expect the future action to be undertaken.

### 22.3.2 Discourse connectives

Discourse connectives are indispensable to a theory of discourse in general and to textual coherence in particular. Being processed bottom-up, they fulfil an important indexical function, connecting local domains of discourse with global ones (Gernsbacher and Givón 1995, Schiffrin 1987). They may connect utterances locally, they may connect local utterances with the more global unit of a sequence, they may connect local utterances with the global unit of activity type or discourse genre, and they may specify the nature of the connectedness between utterance and discourse topic or subtopic.

Because of their important metacommunicative function they may signal the nature of connectedness amongst various coherence strands, e.g. referential continuity, temporal continuity, spatial continuity and action continuity (Givón 1993), and amongst various planes of discourse, e.g. topical coherence, illocutionary coherence and other types of interpersonal coherence.

In discourse analysis, discourse connectives signal the nature of the connectedness between utterances, between utterances and discourse, between utterances and interlocutors, and between utterances, discourse and context. They are seen as non-propositional linguistic items, connecting various planes of discourse into a coherent mental picture of discourse. They are crucial for the negotiation of meaning, indicating the speaker's position vis-à-vis the preceding context or hearer, and the mental movement from speaker to hearer. The communicative meaning of discourse connectives can be frequently paraphrased by a performative verb or by a hedged performative, e.g. *as a result* with the value of 'I conclude', *but* with the values of 'I contrast' or 'I do not quite agree', and *like* with the value of 'I quote'. Another type of discourse connective with an overt metacommunicative status are metacommunicative comments, such as *in a nutshell*. They do not simply signal the nature of the connectedness between discursive parts but also comment on them.

Metacommunicative comments refer to the Gricean cooperative principle and the maxims (Grice 1975), particularly the maxim of manner. Prototypical examples are *briefly* with the value of 'I formulate my utterance in accordance with the Gricean maxim of manner, especially with the third maxim "be brief"', *bluntly* with the value of 'I formulate my utterance in accordance with the Gricean maxim of manner, especially with the second one "avoid obscurity of expression"', or *I mean* with the value of 'I formulate my utterance in accordance with the Gricean maxim of manner, especially with the second one "avoid obscurity of expression"'. In discourse, metacommunicative comments may trigger a generalised conversational implicature, indicating what intersubjective positioning the speaker is taking: *I mean* generally introduces a speaker-initiated self-reformulation, implicating that previous utterances may not have been in accordance with the maxim of manner, and *bluntly* implicitly warns the addressee that the formulation of the forthcoming utterance may be a threat to their face (Brown, P. and Levinson 1987).

Discourse connectives have been classified as coherence-building devices, signifying how two or more discursive parts are to be connected (Gernsbacher and Givón 1995), while metacommunicative comments refer to the Gricean maxims, signalling the speaker's attitude towards the formulation of her/his utterance, which may trigger a generalised conversational implicature. Discourse connectives are not employed in an arbitrary fashion in discourse. Rather, they are used in a strategic manner. In spoken dyadic discourse, they may even occupy a full turn (Smith, S. and Jucker 2002). Because of the complex and multi-faceted relationship between discursive parts and discourse as a whole, the connecting parts or discursive joints require particular attention.

In the framework of discourse, discourse connectives instruct the hearer how a particular discursive unit is to be connected with the local linguistic context and how the speaker intends it to be interpreted. In that respect, discourse connectives may be assigned the function of some kind of indirect directive, informing the hearer about local discourse expectations and requesting her/him to perform the corresponding processes of inferencing: 'Many implicatures are generated by such *discourse expectations*' (Thomason 1992: 355) and are necessary to administer their accommodation in the discourse common ground. However, discourse connectives are not 'proper speech acts'. Having undergone a process of semantic bleaching, discourse connectives are seen as non-propositional, lexically marginal forms (Thompson, S. and Mulac 1991; Traugott 1995; Traugott and Heine 1991). They express procedural meaning and are polyfunctional (Brinton 1996, Jucker and Ziv 1998).

### 22.3.3  Discourse relations in context

In discourse, a part, viz. speech act, utterance or clause, needs to be assigned the dual status of a speech act, utterance or clause in its own right, and one which is conditionally relevant to its immediate linguistic context composed of directly preceding and succeeding discourse units. In ethnomethodological terms, discourse units can be seen as *doubly contextual* (Heritage 1984: 242). That is to say, a discourse unit relies upon the existing context, viz. a prior discourse unit, for its production and appropriate interpretation, as regards anaphora resolution, for instance, and it is, in its own right, an event that shapes a new context for the discourse unit that will follow. Consequently, discourse units have a local purpose at a particular stage in discourse and they have a global purpose in the discourse as a whole. Because of the latter, assumptions about the local purpose at a particular stage in discourse may need to undergo a process of modification and recontextualisation at a later stage (cf. Fetzer 2002).

Discourse units do not only contain information related to the contents of the speech acts, utterances or clauses but also to their illocutionary force. Illocutions manifest themselves in the speaker's intention to achieve a certain effect: 'An effect must be achieved on the audience if the illocutionary act is to be carried out... Generally the effect amounts to bringing about the understanding of the meaning and of the force of the locution' (Austin 1975: 116–17). Thus, speech acts are intended to achieve and secure uptake: in a dialogic (micro) frame of reference, they are intended to achieve the interlocutor's uptake. In a discursive (macro) frame of reference, they are also intended to achieve the interlocutor's uptake with respect to the discourse as a whole, and they are intended to achieve the interlocutor's uptake with respect to the speech act as a constitutive part of the discourse: 'Moreover, communicative (illocutionary) intentions generally are accompanied by perlocutionary intentions, and individual utterances are usually parts of larger plans. So it is plausible to suppose that identifying a speaker's perlocutionary intentions and broader plans is often relevant to identifying his communicative intention' (Bach 1992: 397). It is at the stage from discursive parts to the discursive whole that the perlocutionary act becomes a necessary requirement to bridge the gap between the parts of discourse and discourse as a whole (see also Haugh and Jaszczolt, this volume).

The perlocutionary act manifests itself in the 'achievement of a perlocutionary object (convince, persuade) or the production of a perlocutionary sequel' (Austin 1975: 181). This reference to a series or sequence can be interpreted as a requirement to connect a *situated speech act* (Mey 2009b) with its adjacent discursive parts composed of speech acts, and possibly with other more remote ones, bringing about the understanding of the meaning and of the force of the locution, thus construing textual coherence, as is made explicit in the *coherence principle*, which goes beyond textual coherence, including coherence with respect to pragmatic presuppositions and illocutionary intention (Mey 2001). Against this background, Austin's inherently dynamic and dialogic conception of speech acts and his differentiation between intended effects and unintended effects, and attempt and achievement (Fetzer 2002), provides the necessary requirements for a pragmatics-based analysis of textual coherence and thus of discourse.

## 22.4  Textual coherence revisited

Textual coherence is the product of interlocutors construing meaning in discourse by connecting individual parts through inferencing processes feeding on their co-text (or linguistic context), on the nature of their structural and semantic connectedness, and on social context and encyclopaedic knowledge. It is a dynamic construct, which requires the accommodation of local input provided by adjacent discourse units, and at the same time it is the temporary product of local inferencing processes, which may be modified to accommodate the semantics and pragmatics of further input.

Textual coherence is a process insofar as it needs to accommodate information communicated by subsequent discourse units, which may support the participants' construal of a story line. But the units may also conflict with the prevailing story line. If that is the case, the type of textual coherence construed needs to undergo a process of reconstrual in order to accommodate the piece of conflicting information. Should that be evaluated as irrelevant, however, it may simply be ignored. Textual coherence is a product insofar as it represents the result of a process of inferencing by interlocutors which makes a bounded sequence of discourse units meaningful.

Analogous to pragmatic meaning, textual coherence goes beyond the meaning of the strings of words composing a discourse unit which composes text. Textual coherence feeds on the semantics of discourse relations and discourse connectives, but it also feeds on their pragmatics. It is the latter which is indispensable to making a text meaningful at a local stage, and to making the meaningful local stage cohere with the more global stage of discourse and with the discourse as a whole.

Discourse relations tend to be implicit and need to be inferred, signalling the nature of the connectedness between more or less adjacent parts with a higher degree of implicitness, while discourse connectives tend to be less implicit, signalling the nature of their connectedness with a higher degree of explicitness. This holds for the connectedness between discourse units with their directly adjacent counterparts and with their less local counterparts. If the semantics of a discourse connective and discourse relation of directly adjacent parts is considered to be congruent, their discursive processing is straightforward and does not require the accommodation of extra contextual information. This also holds for directly adjacent discourse relations without the overt realisation of a discourse connective. If the semantics of a discourse connective and discourse relation is considered to be incongruent, or if the discourse relation between two directly adjacent discourse relations is considered to be incongruent, their discursive processing and the respective mapping operations require the accommodation of extra contextual information, triggering further processes of inferencing to make the stretch of discourse meaningful. Hence, the construal of textual coherence in monologic settings and its joint co-construction in discourse require the explicit accommodation of context and discourse common ground.

### 22.4.1  Contexts in discourse

Context is one of those concepts, which is indispensable to pragmatic and discursive theories, but almost impossible to define. This is because context is multi-faceted and almost impossible to delimit. Discourse contains context and context contains discourse. Context is imported into discourse, it is invoked in discourse, and it is necessary to construe textual coherence. Consequently, an analysis of discourse is connected intrinsically with an analysis of context: context is a constitutive part of discourse, and discourse is embedded in context. In pragmatics-based terminology, context is presupposed or imported, and co-constructed or invocated (Levinson 2003a), and in interactional-sociolinguistic terms, context is brought into discourse, and context is brought out in discourse (Gumperz 1992). Because of their multi-faceted nature and complexity, and their inherent interdependence, both discourse and context can no longer be considered analytic primes but rather need to be seen from a parts–whole perspective as entities containing sub-entities and as entities contained in super-entities.

In a dynamic outlook on context, context and contextualisation are connected intrinsically and that is why both are indispensable to the construal of textual coherence. Contextualisation has been assigned the status of a basic premise in natural-language communication (Gumperz 1992, 1996; Levinson

2003a), enriching inexplicit forms and contents by assigning values to index-ical tokens. This is usually done through conversational inference (Grice 1975). Discourse analysis differentiates between the (socio)cognitive opera-tion of global inference anchored to discourse genre or activity type (Levin-son 1979, Prevignano and di Luzio 2003) and local inference as described by Gricean conversational implicature.

The multi-layered outlook on context requires an analytic frame of refer-ence based on methodological compositionality (Jaszczolt 2005). Against this background, the most appropriate delimitation is a functional one: context is conceived of as a frame of reference, whose job it is to frame content by delimiting the content while at the same time being framed and delimited by less immediate adjacent frames. This also holds for discourse, whose job it is to frame content by delimiting the content while at the same time being framed and delimited by less immediate discourse.

A further classification of context is anchored to a holistic conception of context embedding its constitutive parts of model user, conversational contribution, surroundings and their presuppositions, viz. cognitive context, linguistic context and social context (Fetzer 2004; see also van der Sandt, this volume and Brogaard, this volume).

### 22.4.1.1 Linguistic context

Linguistic context comprises the actual language used within discourse. Lan-guage is composed of linguistic constructions embedded in adjacent linguis-tic constructions composing a whole clause, sentence, utterance, turn or text. Thus, linguistic context or co-text (de Beaugrande and Dressler 1981) denotes a relational construct composed of local and global adjacency rela-tions. In the viewpoint adopted here, the connectedness between a 'textual part' and other 'textual parts' constituting a text (the whole) is looked upon analogously to Searle's conception of regulative rules and constitutive rules (Searle 1969). That is to say, the rule-governed realisation of 'textual parts' in context constitutes an utterance act, thus counting as a move within the game of producing and interpreting discourse units composed of utterance acts and illocutionary acts.

The production and interpretation of discourse units is based on lan-guage's constitutive parts of syntax, morphology, phonology, semantics and pragmatics. While syntax is composed of structural units, for instance con-stituents and phrases, it is the linear ordering of the parts within a sequence which constitutes their grammatical function. The adverb *really*, for instance, realises the grammatical function of a sentence adverbial with wide scope in the utterance *really, that man is weird*, while it is assigned the grammatical function of the adverbial of a subjunct with narrow scope in *that man is really weird*. Or, the proper noun *Peter* can realise the grammatical function of an object in *Mary called Peter* and it can realise the grammatical function of a subject in *Peter called Mary*. Thus, it is not the linguistic part as such that is assigned a grammatical function. Rather, it is the positioning of a part within a sequence that assigns it a grammatical function.

The relational nature of linguistic context is also reflected in a sentence's topological units of pre-field, middle-field and post-field, and their respective subfields, which are also conceived of in relational terms, thus counting as further constitutive parts in the construction of a discourse unit. For instance, a change in the canonical word order SVO in English in the utterance *Alex hugged Joyce* to a non-canonical OSV *Joyce Alex hugged* with stress on initial O does not change the propositional meaning of the utterance. From a discursive viewpoint, however, the fronting of the object signifies a contrastive set. That is, the speaker intends the message that Alex hugged Joyce while at the same time implicating that Alex did not hug other not-named, but presupposed members of the contrastive set, for instance Joe, Sarah or Lisa. It is that pragmatically implicated meaning that is of relevance to the construal of textual coherence.

## 22.4.1.2 Cognitive context

Cognitive context is not only of relevance to cognitive linguistics and cognitive pragmatics, but also to the field of psychology, and here in particular to the psychology of communication. Bateson (1972) conceives context along the lines of the gestalt-psychological distinction between figure and ground and the related concepts of frame and framing. A frame is seen as a delimiting device which 'is (or delimits) a class or set of messages (or meaningful actions)' (Bateson 1972: 187). Because of its delimiting function, 'psychological frames are exclusive, i.e. by including certain messages (or meaningful actions) within a frame, certain other messages are excluded' and they are 'inclusive, i.e. by excluding certain messages certain others are included' (Bateson 1972: 187). The apparent contradiction is eradicated by the introduction of set theory's differentiation between set and non-set, which – like figure and ground – are not symmetrically related. To use Bateson's own words: 'Perception of the ground must be positively inhibited and perception of the figure ... must be positively enhanced" (Bateson 1972: 187). This leads him to the conclusion that the concept of frame is metacommunicative, which also holds for context. Or in his own words: 'the hypothesis depends upon the idea that this structured context also occurs within a wider context – a metacontext if you will – and that this sequence of contexts is an open, and conceivably infinite, series' (Bateson 1972: 245).

Bateson explicitly connects set and non-set, frame and meta-frame, and context and meta-context with a parts–whole perspective: "whenever this contrast appears in the realm of communication, is simply a contrast in logical typing. The whole is always in a metarelationship with its parts. As in logic the proposition can never determine the meta proposition, so also in matters of control the smaller context can never determine the larger' (Bateson 1972: 267; see also Giora, this volume).

In *frame analysis*, Goffman (1986) uses 'frame' as a metaphor for context, background and setting, thus referring to the relational dimension of meaning: 'I am not addressing the structure of social life but the structure of experience individuals have at any moment of their social lives' (Goffman 1986: 13). The relational conception of frame is reflected in Goffman's differentiation between primary framework, key and fabrication. A primary framework provides a way of describing the event to which it is applied. 'Key' denotes 'the set of conventions by which a given activity, one already meaningful in terms of some primary framework, is transformed into something patterned on this activity but seen by the participants to be something quite else' (Goffman 1986: 44). The concept of frame is fundamental to the construction of meaning, and thus to the construal of textual coherence: 'In general, then, the assumptions that cut an activity off from the external surround also mark the ways in which this activity is inevitably bound to the surrounding world' (Goffman 1986: 249). While the connectedness between frame and framing and among keying, upkeying, downkeying and rekeying needs to be based on metarepresentation, framing also needs to be recursive: 'Frame, however, organizes more than meaning; it also organizes involvement' (Goffman 1986: 345).

Cognitive context is a structured, multi-layered construct which is indispensable for language processing and inferencing. The nature of the connectedness between its constitutive layers and subsystems is metacommunicative and meta-systemic.

### 22.4.1.3 Social context

Social context is often considered to comprise the context of a communicative exchange and is defined by deducting linguistic context and cognitive context from a holistic conception of context. Constituents of social context are, for instance, participants, the immediate concrete, physical surroundings including time and location, and the macro contextual institutional and non-institutional domains.

In discourse, social context is imported through conventional means and through particularised context-dependent means. Prototypical representatives of the former are deictic devices, such as person deixis, concerned with discourse-internal and discourse-external participants; time deixis, dealing with discourse-internal and discourse-external time, for instance coding time and receiving time, and metalinguistic tense and language tense; place deixis, concerned with discourse-internal and discourse-external location and the corresponding personal, social and cultural attitudes connected with location; discourse deixis, considering the structure and sequential organisation of discourse as well as textual coherence, e.g. discourse connectives and other cohesive devices; and social deixis, concerned with social relations, e.g., terms of endearment and honorifics. Naturally, these deictic devices are context-dependent and dynamic, and that is why the domains of reference for time, location and person change in accordance with their local and global contexts of use.

The research paradigm of ethnomethodology investigates the interactional organisation of society. It represents a micro sociological perspective par excellence, in which the indexicality of social action is of key importance. Ethnomethodology focuses on intersubjectivity and examines the questions of how separate individuals are able to know or act within a common world, and of how members (or participants) negotiate or achieve a common context: 'in an interaction's moment-to-moment development, the parties, singly and together, select and display in their conduct which of the indefinitely many aspects of context they are making relevant, or are invoking, for the immediate moment' (Schegloff 1987: 219). Here, common context is synonymous with social context, which, like linguistic context, classifies into micro social context and macro social context.

Construing textual coherence in context is interdependent on the interlocutors' construction of the context-dependent conception of common ground, viz. discourse common ground.

### 22.4.2 Discourse common ground

The construal of textual coherence is intrinsically connected with discourse topics, which are developed through more or less linearly sequenced contributions. Looked upon from a reception-based perspective, a discourse unit in context can be seen as ratifying a prior discourse unit, thus building up a chain of arguments. On the one hand, the arguments may extend the discourse topic's domain of validity by adding further evidence in support of that discourse topic. On the other hand, the arguments may narrow down the discourse topic's domain of validity, for instance, by supplying counterevidence. While in monologue-based genres the construal of textual coherence is performed through a process of internal argumentation, it is anchored to a process of negotiation of meaning in dialogue-based genres. In communication, interlocutors simultaneously construct two context-dependent models of discourse common ground: individual discourse common ground and collective discourse common ground. The former is personal and subjective, and may contain idiosyncratic information, which is not of immediate relevance to the ongoing discourse, while the latter is ratified by the interlocutors and jointly co-constructed.

### 22.4.2.1 Individual discourse common ground

Discourse common ground is a dynamic sociocognitive construct, which administers different types of information exchanged in a communicative encounter. Individual discourse common ground contains and administers the information of one individual's 'MODEL OF THE WORLD AND TIME SPOKEN OR WRITTEN OF in the text' (Allan 2001: 20), comprising force, content, formulation, context, background information and its propositions, beliefs and interpersonal and interactional presuppositions, thus capturing an individual's processing and interpretation of information. The information processed is connected with an individual's possible side activities and may interact with the processing of that type of information. For this reason, the interlocutors' models of their individual discourse common grounds may differ, sometimes even to a large extent. In addition to each interlocutor's subjective construction of their individual discourse common ground, they also construct a ratified collective common ground, which serves as the foundation for their particular communicative encounter.

### 22.4.2.2  Collective discourse common ground

The collective discourse common ground is anchored to the set of interlocutors and to the set of their ratified discourse units. The collective discourse common ground contains and administers set-specific information, such as collective we-intentions, collective communicative goals, collective inferencing strategies and collective textual coherence (Fetzer 2004). In communication, the set-specific values function as a filter that constrains and channels what has been said accordingly by guiding the interpretation and production of intersubjective meaning and of textual coherence in the pre-specified manner. Collective discourse common ground intersects with individual discourse common ground, with other individual discourse common grounds and with cultural common ground.

   In natural-language communication, the individual discourse common ground and the collective discourse common ground are continuously updated, and all of the postulated discourse units and their presuppositions are allocated to the individual discourse common grounds, and all of the ratified discourse units and their ratified presuppositions are allocated to the collective discourse common grounds. The latter are expected to be almost identical for the interlocutors because of the necessary condition of ratification. Naturally, the collective discourse common grounds are continuously updated. In the case of a ratified but negotiated discourse unit, they are revised. Furthermore, the collective discourse common grounds serve as a foundation for the interlocutors' inferencing processes for both assertional implicatures and background implicatures (Thomason 1992: 352).

   What makes the construal of textual coherence such a complex and multi-faceted endeavour is the inherent open-endedness of discourse, which is not functionally equivalent to discourse being unpredictable. While written discourse is delimited by more or less clear-cut beginnings and ends, spoken discourse is more open-ended. As regards contents, however, both modes of discourse realisation are prone to diverging degrees of topic drift and topic shift, and to different degrees of inexplicitness manifest in ellipsis and substitution, deixis and reference, discourse connectives and other cohesive devices playing an important role in the construal of textual coherence.

While discourse as a theoretical construct may be bounded, discourse use 'creates formal hybrids, because it juggles a variety of motivations, which it may package together even in the absence of cognitive coherence behind the packaging' (Ariel 2008b: 173).

## 22.5 Outlook

A conceptualisation of textual coherence within a clearly delimited frame of reference seems to be an almost impossible endeavour. This is not only because of its inherent dynamism and complex, multi-faceted nature. It is also due to its parts–whole configuration and the often-repeated truism that a whole is more than the sum of its parts. For textual coherence this means that it is both process and product. Construing textual coherence requires interlocutors to connect its parts in order to compose a meaningful whole, and it is the meaningful whole which is construed by the interlocutors. This is generally performed through inference and inference triggers, through conventional implicatures and generalised and particularised conversational implicatures, and through encoding and decoding processes, assigning interlocutors the roles of sense-making and sense-attributing agents who employ their cognitive and linguistic systems accordingly, as is formulated succinctly by Ariel (2008b: 60): 'Being a cooperative speaker involves more than following grammatical rules and pragmatic maxims. One also needs to abide by recurrent discourse patterns.'

# 23

# Metaphor and the literal/non-literal distinction

Robyn Carston

## 23.1  Introduction: Gricean pragmatics and non-literalness

A fascination with non-literal language, how it works and what effects it has on hearers and readers, goes a very long way back. In the time of the ancient Greeks and Romans, it was associated with the study of rhetoric; in particular, with figures of speech (or tropes), including metaphor, hyperbole, metonymy and irony, and how they can be used to make a text or a public speech more effective, attractive and convincing to its recipients. The emphasis in this tradition was on the unusual and ornamental nature of these tropes, the assumption being that the *content* they convey (their 'figurative meaning') can be captured by a literal paraphrase. Referring to a person as a 'lion' or a 'mouse', describing a marriage as a 'sunlit garden' or a 'bloody battleground' are simply vivid, lively ways of expressing a more sober literal counterpart, e.g. 'brave man' for 'lion', 'unhappy, acrimonious relationship' for 'bloody battleground'. Similarly, describing someone who has just made a series of blunders as a 'brilliant fellow' is a humorous or striking way of expressing the opinion that he is a 'stupid fellow'.

This view of tropes was vigorously criticised by the Romantics, who insisted that metaphorical language is normal and frequent, and that non-literal uses quite generally express meanings and have effects that cannot be captured by any literal paraphrase (see Sperber and Wilson 1990). However, the classical view resurfaced in modern pragmatics, albeit in a different guise, in the inferential account of linguistic communication pioneered by Paul Grice (1967). The components of Grice's general framework that are crucial to his treatment of non-literal language use are his system of communicative norms ('conversational maxims', in his terms), which enjoin speakers to be truthful,

Many thanks to Catherine Wearing, Deirdre Wilson and Vladimir Žegarac for helpful comments on a first draft of this chapter, and to the editors of this volume, Keith Allan and Kasia Jaszczolt, for sound advice and considerable patience. I am grateful to the Centre for the Study of Mind in Nature, Oslo, for its ongoing funding of my research.

informative, relevant and clear, and his distinction between what a speaker says and what she (merely) implicates. What a speaker says by the words she utters is determined by the semantic conventions of the language and the contextually relevant referents for any indexical expressions. Inevitably, then, non-literal uses of language are seen as in some sense abnormal or at least as employing an indirect means of communication: the speaker is not saying what she means. Grice treated all instances of non-literal language use (metaphor, metonymy, hyperbole, understatement, irony etc.) as cases where a speaker says something so blatantly false, uninformative or irrelevant that her hearer is prompted to undertake an inferential process to recover what she really means (and so is indirectly communicating):

(1)   A:   Mary's new boyfriend is a robot.
      B:   No, he's not. (He's just a bit shy.)

A's utterance flouts (i.e. blatantly violates) Grice's maxim of literal truthfulness ('Say only that which you believe to be true'), while an utterance of its negative counterpart is such an obvious truth (we all know that human beings are not robots) that it flouts his first maxim of informativeness ('Make your contribution as informative as is required'). In order to maintain the prevailing presumption of speaker rationality and cooperativeness (Grice's Cooperative Principle), the addressee, B, is led to infer a related proposition that could well be true, and is relevant and informative, perhaps that Mary's boyfriend lacks feeling and sociability.[1] The same broad picture applies to verbal irony. The sentence 'John is a brilliant fellow', uttered in a context in which speaker and hearer have just witnessed John making some elementary mistakes, is likely to be (and to be recognised as) an overt violation of the maxim of truthfulness, on the basis of which, in order to preserve the presumption of speaker cooperativeness, the hearer infers that the speaker meant (implicated) that John is very incompetent.

   This approach is a version of the classical rhetorical view mentioned above, whereby tropes have a 'figurative meaning' which replaces their literal meaning: using 'robot' is a more vivid way of expressing what could be literally expressed by 'lacks social skills'; saying that John is a brilliant fellow is a humorous way of expressing what could be literally expressed by 'John is an incompetent fellow'. However, Grice's account goes beyond the descriptive taxonomy provided by the classical rhetoricians, in that he provides an explanation of how figurative meanings are produced and understood. He explains the other traditional categories of non-literal language use (e.g. metonymy, hyperbole, litotes) in essentially the same way, that is, as instances of maxim flouting at the level of what the speaker said, which prompt the hearer to undergo a reasoning process to recover the intended figurative meaning. On this account, then, all instances of non-literal language use are cases of indirect communication, with the speaker-meant content (the figurative meaning) arising entirely at the level of conversational implicature.

Of course, the nature of the meaning implicated in each case must be different, but Grice says little about what it is that distinguishes a metaphorical use from an ironical use, an ironical use from a metonymical use, and so on, or how a hearer, having recognised that a maxim is being flouted, goes on to infer the right kind of implicature for the particular trope (the contradictory of what the speaker said in the case of irony, a proposition with a particular resemblance relation to what was said in the case of metaphor, and so on). Furthermore, he doesn't consider what is achieved by the speaker's choice of the more vivid non-literal expression rather than the content-equivalent but duller literal expression, what cognitive effects it has on the hearer/reader, hence why a speaker chooses to use a figurative expression instead of the (allegedly) readily available literal equivalent.[2] In fact, despite its initially appealing systematicity, there are so many problems with Grice's treatment of non-literal language use that, within the field of cognitively oriented pragmatics at least, it has been largely abandoned.

The rest of this chapter is structured as follows. In the next section, I set out some of the problems with Grice's account in more detail and indicate the resulting new directions taken in the pragmatic study of non-literal language. Then sections 23.3 and 23.4 focus squarely on metaphor, though comparisons with other kinds of non-literalness are made in passing. In section 23.3, recent work in the field of lexical pragmatics is discussed, in particular the idea that metaphorical uses of words are instances of ad hoc concepts which contribute to the proposition directly communicated (the explicature of the utterance). In section 23.4, this approach is compared with work in cognitive linguistics which takes metaphorically used language to be a surface reflection of a more fundamental location of metaphor within thought. Finally, in section 23.5, the intuitive literal/non-literal distinction is reconsidered in the light of the theoretical discussions in the preceding sections.

## 23.2 Figurative language – what is said, what is implicated, and how?

Most of the problems with the Gricean account of non-literal language use fall into one or other of the following two groups: (a) internal tensions between that account and his wider 'logic of conversation'; (b) inconsistencies of the account with newer perspectives on communication coming from empirical work in the cognitive sciences.[3] Let's start with a theory-internal problem. In ordinary (non-figurative) cases of implicature, what the speaker meant (intended her hearer to believe) includes both what she said and what she implicated:

(2)  A:  Is Mary's boyfriend good-looking and well-mannered?
     B:  He's good-looking.

Here B conversationally implicates that Mary's boyfriend is not well-mannered, and what she communicates (i.e. what she means and endorses) includes both what she said (that Mary's boyfriend is good-looking) and what she implicated. This is just what the notion of 'what is said', as Grice defined it, requires: it is both the (context-relative) semantic content of the utterance and it is speaker-meant (communicated). So when Grice comes to discuss cases of irony and metaphor, he does not talk of what the speaker has said but rather of what she has 'made as if to say' (Grice 1975: 51) – he has to do this because the speaker patently doesn't mean (endorse, communicate) the proposition that is the semantic content of her utterance (e.g. John is a robot). But now this leads to a worry about the maxim of truthfulness, which is supposed to play the key triggering role in the understanding of many figurative language uses: 'Do not say what you believe to be false.' It seems that this maxim is not, after all, flouted by metaphorical utterances like 'John is a robot/lion/mouse' or by verbal irony, because in these cases the speaker doesn't, in fact, say anything – she merely makes as if (pretends) to say something, and that kind of act doesn't fall under the maxim.

It might seem then that for the maxim of truthfulness to do the work required of it in accounting for non-literal uses, what's needed is a reinterpretation of 'saying' so that to say that P is merely to express the proposition P, without any presumption that the speaker is committed to its content. Then the maxim of truthfulness would become 'Do not express a proposition that you believe to be false' and there would be no need for a shift to the speaker merely 'making as if to say' in cases of figurative use: the speaker has expressed a proposition that she overtly believes to be false, thus flouted the maxim, and the hearer must infer an implicature as the intended meaning. However, this does not seem to be the right way to go.[4] First, it is clearly not what Grice had in mind with his speaker-meant notion of 'what is said' (see Recanati 2004a: ch. 1) and his explicit shift to 'making as if to say' for the non-literal cases. Second, and more important here, this weaker construal of 'what is said' does not save the truthfulness maxim-flouting treatment of non-literalness from its biggest problem, which is that it undermines the whole Gricean account of conversational implicatures. According to this account, attribution of an implicature to a speaker is made in order to maintain or restore the hearer's assumption that the maxims have been observed: 'A man who, by saying (or making as if to say) that P has implicated Q, provided that (i) he is to be presumed to be observing the conversational maxims, or at least the cooperative principle; (ii) the supposition that he thinks that Q is required in order to make his saying or making as if to say P ... consistent with this presumption' (Grice 1975: 49–50). While this is the case with the example above in (2) (and with 'ordinary,' non-figurative implicature cases quite generally), it is clearly not so for (1) or for other figurative uses of language, where the maxim of truthfulness is irretrievably violated at the level of what is said.[5]

More generally, an account that rests on a presumption of literal truth-fulness, which is patently violated in the case of non-literal uses, is beset by myriad problems. To deliberately produce a blatantly false utterance seems a strange and irrational act (at odds with Grice's view of conversation as an achievement of rational agents), and also a pointless one, given that the speaker could express her intended meaning by producing a literal utterance, which would meet the truthfulness maxim and would be easily grasped by the hearer (on the basis of the semantic conventions of the language). Furthermore, it seems that the requirement on implicatures that they be recoverable by a process of reasoning from premises, which include a description of the speaker's having said (or made as if to say) that P – the calculability requirement – simply cannot be met in these cases (see Hugly and Sayward 1979).[6]

Moving now beyond theory-internal issues, Grice's account of non-literal meaning has been further undermined by recent work on utterance comprehension within more cognitively oriented frameworks. Again, the target under fire is Grice's pivotal notion of 'what is said'. The big problem with this construct is that it is required to play two distinct roles which no single level of meaning can, in fact, encompass; it is required to be both sentence semantics and a component of speaker-meant content. Here is just one of the many examples (due to Bach 1994a) that illustrate the problem:

(3)  Mother (to young Billy crying over a cut on his knee): You're not going to die.
   a.  YOU (BILLY) ARE NOT GOING TO DIE FROM THAT CUT
   b.  YOU (BILLY) SHOULD STOP MAKING SUCH A FUSS ABOUT IT

What the mother means (what she intends to communicate to the child) is given in (a) and (b), where (b) is clearly an implicature and (a) seems to be what she has said (explicitly communicated). But the proposition delivered by conventional linguistic meaning and the assignment of a referent to the pronoun 'you' (hence the Gricean 'what is said') is *Billy is not going to die*, which seems to entail that Billy is immortal, something that the mother has no intention of conveying. For other examples of this problem and more detailed discussion, see Carston 1988, 2002; Bach 1994a; Recanati 1993, 2004a.

In recent years, this has led to a clear split between sentence semantics (or a semantic notion of 'what is said'), on the one hand, and the primary level of speaker-meant content (a pragmatic notion of 'what is said', known as 'explicature' in Relevance theory), on the other. The key point is that typically the semantic content provided by the linguistic system greatly underdetermines the speaker-meant propositional content of an utterance and a hearer must, therefore, not only linguistically decode the sentence uttered and perhaps fix some referents, but also perform various pragmatic tasks of meaning adjustment in figuring out the speaker-meant content. So, for instance, in grasping the content of Amy's response in (4) to his question, Max's pragmatic capacity has to augment the linguistic meaning of her utterance by supplying at least the components of meaning highlighted in (5a). This is the explicature (the speaker-meant enriched 'what is said'), on the basis of which he can infer the implicated answer to his question, given in (5b):

(4)  Max:   How was the party? Did it go well?
     Amy:   There wasn't enough drink and everyone left early.

(5)  a.  THERE WASN'T ENOUGH **ALCOHOLIC** DRINK **TO SATISFY THE PEOPLE AT THE PARTY**$_1$ AND **SO** EVERYONE **WHO CAME TO THE PARTY**$_1$ LEFT **IT**$_1$ EARLY
     b.  THE PARTY DID NOT GO WELL

Without spelling out all the details of the example (see Carston 2009), I hope that (5a) indicates clearly the important and extensive part played by pragmatics in the derivation of the speaker's primary meaning (the explicature of the utterance). One result of this 'contextualist' or 'pragmaticist' (Carston 2010a) view of utterance content is that some elements of pragmatically inferred speaker meaning that Grice treated as conversational implicatures have been reanalysed as instances of pragmatic enrichment that affect the primary speaker meaning.[7] A case in point is the cause–consequence enrichment of the 'and'-conjunction sentence uttered by Amy in (4) above: the pragmatic move from the decoded 'P & Q' to the more specific proposition 'P & as a result Q', which Grice considered a (generalised) implicature, is now fairly widely agreed to be contributing to the primary utterance content (explicature) (for extensive supporting argument, see Carston 2002). The importance of this shift is that it opens up a new possibility for accounting for tropes like metaphor, hyperbole and metonymy. Rather than simply assuming that when a speaker uses language non-literally what she means must inevitably be seen as conversationally implicated, it could be that her non-literal meaning contributes to, even constitutes, the content that she directly 'says' or asserts. Such a move is obviously controversial and, prima facie, has problematic consequences for the literal/non-literal distinction; it is explored in some detail in section 23.3.

Grice intended his account as a reconstruction in wholly rational analytical terms of whatever subpersonal processes actually go on in comprehension. However, in the early days of experimental investigation of the online processing of non-literal language, Grice's work was the dominant pragmatic account, so experimental psychologists took it as the starting point for constructing a processing model. As such, it predicts that the interpretation of a metaphorical utterance (or, indeed, the interpretation of any of the other tropes) is a three-step process: the hearer (a) expecting literal truthfulness (as required by the maxim of truthfulness), tries the literal interpretation first; (b) then rejects it on the basis of its blatant falsehood (or blatant uninformativeness or irrelevance); and (c) then proceeds to infer the intended non-literal interpretation. On some variants of this model, the third step involves converting the false categorical form of the metaphor (X is Y) into the corresponding true simile form (X is like Y) and deriving implicatures on that basis. The prediction, then, is that a metaphorical use of language should take longer to process and understand than a comparable literal use. This hypothesis has been extensively tested and has repeatedly been found to be false.

Utterances like those in (6) can be meant literally or metaphorically: for (6b), the predicate could be used to express being a member of the military or being brave, obedient and dutiful; in (6c), 'the lacy blanket' might be an actual blanket, perhaps hanging outside on a clothes-line, or a light layer of snow covering the ground:

(6)   a.   That lecture put me to sleep.
      b.   David is a soldier.
      c.   The winter wind gently tossed the lacy blanket.

The widespread finding with such cases is that people take no longer to read and understand the metaphorical use than the literal use, provided, of course, that they are properly contextualised. The conclusion of extensive work by Ray Gibbs and colleagues (see overview in Gibbs 1994: ch. 3) and Sam Glucksberg and colleagues (summarised in Glucksberg 2001) is that literal interpretation does not have priority over metaphorical interpretation and, even stronger, that metaphorical interpretations are derived automatically whenever the context makes them accessible. So, construed as a comprehension model, Grice's account of metaphor fares badly and it's not clear that its construal as (merely) a rational reconstruction stands up against evidence of this sort either.

With regard to verbal irony, the experimental results are less clear-cut. While Gibbs (1986, 1994) reports experiments in which processing times for ironies and equivalent literal interpretations seem to be very similar, Rachel Giora and colleagues report contrary results: grasping an ironically intended utterance (e.g. 'How clever John is!') often takes significantly longer than grasping an equivalent literally meant utterance (e.g. 'How stupid John is!'). Giora presents strong evidence that the literal interpretation of an ironical utterance is accessed first, even when it is incompatible with the context (Giora and Fein 1999b; Giora 2003, and this volume). On the basis of her findings, she concludes that irony interpretation is both a complex and an error-prone process (hearers sometimes take the literal content to be speaker-meant). Assuming that these results are robust, it might seem that the three-step processing model based on Grice's account of non-literal language use is vindicated in the case of irony.

However, post-Gricean theoretical work on irony indicates that the source of its complexity and the particular demands it makes on hearers/readers are quite different from anything envisaged by Grice. Many theorists working within distinct frameworks and different disciplines (linguistics, psychology, philosophy) have converged on the view that verbal irony is intrinsically metarepresentational, that is, it involves the representation of a representation (rather than of a state of affairs), and an attitude of dissociation towards this representation is implicitly expressed by the speaker. According to Sperber and Wilson (1981, 1986, 1998a) and Wilson and Sperber (1992), irony involves a particular kind of metarepresentational use of language, which they call 'echoic use': the speaker in irony is not expressing her own thoughts, but is echoing a thought she attributes to some source other than herself at that moment, and expressing a mocking, sceptical or derisive attitude to that thought. Consider an example of irony that is clearly echoic in this way:

(7)  *Scenario:* John has declared to Sally that he's giving up smoking and that he's sure it'll be easy now that he's completely resolved. A few weeks later she notices smoke wafted out from under the bathroom door. Later, she confronts him:
Sally: So giving up smoking is no problem at all – just takes a bit of resolve.

Sally is not asserting the proposition that giving up smoking is not a problem but is metarepresenting John's earlier thoughts on the matter and expressing a mocking attitude toward them (and, thereby, toward him).

But there are many cases of ironical utterances where it is much less obvious that anyone has expressed or entertained the thought that is allegedly echoed. Consider the following:

(8)  *Scenario:* Mary has had a particularly bad day: she received a letter saying her application for promotion has been rejected, she tripped on an escalator and twisted her ankle, and when she got home she found her house had been burgled:
Mary: What a wonderful day!

Sperber and Wilson respond to this sort of case by pointing out that echoed thoughts need not be tied to particular individuals at particular times and places, but can be thoughts that are widely entertained or expressed by certain groups of people or by people in general. The thought which Mary echoes in (8) is of this latter sort: that one will have a happy, productive and/or fulfilling day is a common human hope and so is quite generally available to be echoed. An observation which supports this broad notion of echoic use is the widely noted positive–negative asymmetry of ironical utterances: when someone has had a bad day, it's always possible to say ironically how great it was, but when someone has had a wonderful day, it is not always possible to say ironically how awful it was. In fact, such negative ironical comments are only appropriate when some pessimistic thought about the day has been expressed or entertained by someone earlier on and so is available to be echoed (see Wilson 2009b).

The main rival to Sperber and Wilson's echoic account is the view that the key to verbal irony is pretence: the ironical speaker is not performing a genuine speech act (of, say, assertion) but is pretending to do so, in order to convey a mocking, sceptical or contemptuous attitude to the speech act itself, or to anyone who would perform it or take it seriously (Clark, H. and Gerrig 1984; Kumon-Nakamura *et al.* 1995; Recanati 2000; Currie 2006).[8] I won't try to assess the relative merits of the two kinds of theory here but simply note that they have important features in common:[9] both recognise that irony is essentially metarepresentational and dissociative, that is, whether the speaker is echoing a thought or is pretending to perform a certain speech act, her utterance represents, not a state of affairs, but a thought or proposition, which she openly, albeit tacitly, distances herself from. This is quite different from the classical Gricean account according to which a speaker says one thing in order to implicate its contrary and, most important, it makes for a striking distinction between irony and other non-literal uses such as hyperbole, metaphor and metonymy, which are not metarepresentational in this way. That there is this representational difference between metaphorical language use and ironical use has been noted for some time by independent groups of investigators. For instance, Sperber and Wilson (1986) make a distinction between descriptive and interpretive uses of language, with both literal uses and metaphor being descriptive, and reported speech/thought and irony being interpretive (metarepresentational). Somewhat similarly, Winner and Gardner (1993) distinguish the understanding of irony from the understanding of metaphor on the grounds that irony requires an ability to infer other people's beliefs, which is not necessary for metaphor understanding, a difference in complexity that is reflected in the different stages at which young children produce and understand these two kinds of non-literal use (Winner 1988).

There is strong experimental support for this representational distinction between metaphor and irony, starting from Happé's (1993) study of whether people with varying degrees of autism are able to comprehend these tropes. She found a correlation between levels of theory of mind (specifically, the ability to attribute beliefs to other people) and different kinds of non-literal language understanding: irony understanding required a higher order level of belief attribution (beliefs about beliefs) than metaphor. Although some details of this study have been criticised, the basic difference in representational complexity between metaphor and irony emphasised by Happé (who was testing predictions of Sperber and Wilson's (1986) work on the pragmatics of non-literal language) has been corroborated by extensive subsequent experimentation. This includes the testing of different populations of language users, including normally developing children, people with autism, with Asperger's syndrome, with schizophrenia and with right-hemisphere damage (see, for instance, Smith, N. and Tsimpli 1995; Giora *et al.* 2000; Langdon *et al.* 2002; Martin and McDonald 2004; Norbury 2005; Mo *et al.* 2008).[10]

In the next section, the focus will be on metaphor and its relation to other tropes such as hyperbole and simile, all of which, unlike irony, appear to function at the same (descriptive) level of representation. In recent years, there has been a remarkable convergence among psychologists, linguists, pragmaticists and philosophers on a view of metaphor which differs significantly from Grice's maxim-flouting, implicature account. The majority view now is that metaphorical language use contributes not just to what a speaker implicates but also to what she directly communicates (even asserts).[11] I will present this view as it has been developed within relevance-theoretic work on lexical pragmatics (e.g. Carston 1997, 2002, 2010a, 2010b; Sperber and Wilson 1998b, 2008; Wilson and Carston 2006, 2007), drawing also on closely related work from the psychology of metaphor processing (e.g. Glucksberg and Keysar 1993; Glucksberg 2001, 2008) and the philosophy of language (Recanati 1995, 2004a; Bezuidenhout 2001; Wearing 2006).

## 23.3   Lexical pragmatics, ad hoc concepts and metaphor

It is widely recognised that the meanings of words are often pragmatically adjusted and fine-tuned in context, so that their contribution to the proposition expressed is different from their lexically encoded sense. Word meanings may be narrowed in context: e.g. 'money' when it is used to mean 'a large amount of money' as in 'You need money to buy a house in London', or 'man' used to mean 'ideal man' or 'typical man' as in 'Churchill was a man'. Or they may be broadened (loosened): e.g. 'hexagonal' used to mean 'having roughly six sides that are similar in length', as in 'France is hexagonal', or 'raw' used to mean 'too undercooked to be edible' as in 'This steak is raw'. And there are cases where the adjustment made is both a narrowing and a broadening: e.g. when a long-suffering wife says of her husband 'He'll always be a bachelor', her use of the word 'bachelor' means 'behave according to the stereotype of an irresponsible bachelor', which would include certain married men and exclude certain bachelors (those who do not behave in the stereotypical way).

According to the unitary approach to lexical pragmatics developed within Relevance theory (RT), in each of these cases, an ad hoc concept is pragmatically constructed, on the basis of the input provided by the lexically encoded concept and contextual information, and constrained by the addressee's search for an optimally relevant interpretation of the utterance. These ad hoc concepts are marked with an asterisk (MAN*, RAW*, BACHELOR* etc.) to distinguish them from the context-independent lexically encoded concepts (MAN, RAW, BACHELOR etc.) and they are constituents of the proposition the speaker explicitly communicates (for detail and argument, see Wilson and Carston 2007).

The key claim for present purposes is that metaphorically used words and phrases are cases of pragmatic broadening of the linguistically encoded concepts and so, like other loose uses, their interpretation results in an ad hoc concept which is a component of the speaker's explicature. For instance, B's utterance about Sally in (9), in which 'chameleon' is used metaphorically, expresses an ad hoc concept, CHAMELEON*, whose denotation is broader than that of the lexical concept, CHAMELEON, from which it was pragmatically derived, in that it includes not only actual chameleons (a species of lizard that can change its skin colour so as to blend in with its surroundings) but also people with a certain character trait (a tendency to express different views to different people in order to be in apparent agreement with them, thus unreliability):

(9)  A:  Sally told me that she supports our opposition to the
         university's redundancy policy. I think we can rely on
         her to vote with us.
     B:  I'm not at all sure about that. Sally is a chameleon.

The communicated content of B's utterance is as given in (10), where the explicature containing the ad hoc concept CHAMELEON* gives strong inferential warrant to the implicated conclusions:

(10)  Explicature:   SALLY IS A CHAMELEON*
      Implicatures:  SALLY CHANGES HER STATED VIEWS TO MESH WITH
                     WHOEVER SHE IS TALKING TO; SHE IS UNRELIABLE,
                     FICKLE, UNTRUSTWORTHY;
                     WE CANNOT ASSUME SHE WILL GIVE US HER VOTE

So metaphorical use is seen as simply a radical instance of the quite general process of concept broadening, which includes approximations ('hexagonal' above), hyperboles (perhaps 'raw' above) and category extensions (the use of specific names to denote a broader category of entities that share some salient characteristic, e.g. 'Hoover' for the category of vacuum cleaners generally).

On the RT view, then, approximation, category extension, hyperbole and metaphor are not distinct theoretical kinds; rather, they merely occupy different points on a continuum of degrees of broadening with no sharp cut-off points between them. Consider an example which can have a range of loose interpretations:

(11)  The water is boiling.

An utterance of (11) could be intended and understood in any of the following ways: strictly *literally*, communicating that the water is BOILING, so at or above boiling point; as an *approximation*, communicating that it is close enough to BOILING for the differences to be inconsequential for current purposes (e.g. for making a cup of coffee); *hyperbolically*, so not BOILING but closer to it than expected or desired (e.g. too hot to wash one's hands in comfortably); or *metaphorically*, suggesting, for instance, that the water, although not necessarily anywhere near boiling point, is moving agitatedly, bubbling, emitting vapour, and so on. In each case, a different concept is communicated, all of them derived from the literal encoded concept, and on the non-literal interpretations the concept's denotation is broader to varying degrees than that of the lexical concept.

The claim is that all these interpretations are reached in essentially the same way, namely, by an inferential pragmatic process of deriving contextual implications which meets particular standards of cognitive relevance.[12] In the course of that process, an explicature is pragmatically developed on the basis of the decoded linguistic meaning, elements of which, specifically the concept BOILING, may be adjusted by a backwards inference process in response to particular hypothesised implicatures. Consider a context in which the hearer has just run a bath for the speaker, who steps into it and then utters (11); typically, the relevant implications here are that the water is too hot to bathe in, feels unpleasant on the skin, and so on. Much of the information associated with the literal encoded concept BOILING does not enter into the interpretative process at all (information about actual boiling point, the use of boiling water for sterilising instruments, the damage it can do to human skin etc.). The lexically encoded concept is adjusted to an ad hoc concept BOILING* which warrants just these context-specific implications and whose denotation is consequently broader than that of the encoded concept: it includes not only actual instances of boiling point but a range of other, lower temperatures. This is an instance of a hyperbolic use and the idea is that a metaphorical use works in essentially the same way. In an appropriate context, perhaps a violent storm at sea, an utterance of (11) would carry implicatures about the way the sea looks (churning and seething, throwing up foam and vapour) and perhaps about how the speaker experiences it (as overpowering, dangerous, frightening), with quite possibly no implications at all concerning temperature. Again, the encoded concept BOILING would be adjusted so that the explicature as a whole can play its role as a premise grounding these relevance-based implications and, again, the ad hoc concept derived would be considerably broader in denotation than the lexical concept.

Let me draw out some of the features of this account and some of the questions it raises. First, it is strikingly different from Grice's approach: there is no presumption that literal interpretation is the norm and should always be the first option tried; there is no blatant violation of a maxim, resulting in an interpretation consisting just of implicated thought(s), with nothing explicitly or directly communicated. The account follows the Romantic tradition in seeing the metaphorical use of language as natural, normal and pervasive, and as communicating a usually unparaphraseable content rather than functioning as merely a pleasing stylistic adornment.

Second, the claim that there is a loose use continuum, with literal use as the limiting case and metaphorical use as a case of radical loosening, emphasises that, on this view, metaphor is taken to be a descriptive use of language, an employment of words in order to express a thought or impression about some aspect of the external world as experienced by the speaker. This distinguishes it sharply from ironical uses of language, as discussed in the previous section, on which the speaker echoically metarepresents someone else's thought and expresses a negative attitude toward it. Thus, any talk of a continuum from the literal to the non-literal applies to metaphor and hyperbole, which are on the same representational level, but not to irony, which is a quite distinct (meta-level) kind of non-literalness.

Third, this account of metaphor drives a wedge between metaphors (e.g. 'Sally is a chameleon') and their apparently corresponding similes (e.g. 'Sally is like a chameleon') since it is the literal encoded concept CHAMELEON that figures in the explicature of the simile utterance rather than the broadened concept CHAMELEON* (Sally isn't *like* something in that category, she is a member of that category). This might be seen as a shortcoming of the account as, intuitively at least, there is a close relation between these two figures of speech and, on many previous analyses, they have been taken to be versions of each other – metaphors analysed as elliptical similes or similes as hedged metaphors – hence as interchangeable. In fact, there is some psycholinguistic evidence that supports the view that they are distinct tropes with significantly different effects (see Glucksberg and Haught 2006), thus supporting the difference between them that we get on the ad hoc concept account of metaphor. However, this is a more complex issue than it appears to be when we confine our attention to very simple cases of the form 'X is (like) Y', as the experimental work does. On the one hand, there are metaphors that have no obvious simile counterpart (e.g. 'The winter wind gently tossed the lacy blanket', as in (6c) above) and vice versa (e.g. 'Mary sings like an angel', for which 'Mary is an angel' is not the corresponding metaphor and it's not clear what is). On the other hand, both metaphor and simile seem to be based on a process of recognising relevant resemblances between the figurative vehicle and the topic, and, in more extended metaphors, they may work closely together in developing a single idea or conceit, as in the following:

(12)   If they be two, they are two so
          As stiff twin compasses are two;
       Thy soul, the fix'd foot, makes no show
          To move, but doth, if th' other do.

       And though it in the centre sit,
          Yet, when the other far doth roam,
       It leans, and hearkens after it,
          And grows erect, as that comes home.
                    (from John Donne' *A Valediction Forbidding Mourning*)

Here there is an initial simile form, in which the souls of the lovers (the referent of 'they' in the first line) are likened to (are 'so as') a pair of mathematical compasses, which is followed by a series of metaphors that develop the analogy. The difference between the comparative form and the categorical form seems inconsequential here, with both working towards the development of an extended metaphorical conception. For further discussion of similarities and differences between metaphors and similes, and how they may be explained, see Carston and Wearing (2011).

Fourth, on this loose use continuum view, there is claimed to be no clear cut-off point between hyperbolic uses and metaphorical uses – both are simply cases of concept broadening, differing only in the degree and direction of their broadening, and, in some cases, apparently indistinguishable ('John is a saint' may be metaphorical, hyperbolic or both). However, there is a strong intuition that in many cases of metaphor (and simile), the properties of one domain are carried over to a quite different domain (e.g. from animals to human personalities in 'Sally is a *chameleon*'; from physical landscapes to human institutions in 'Their marriage is a *minefield*'). This seems to distinguish metaphors from other kinds of loose use, including hyperboles, whose comprehension simply involves relaxing the encoded property (e.g. 'I'm *starving*', 'It's *boiling* outside'). This 'domain mapping' view of metaphor is fundamental to the approach of the cognitive linguists (e.g. Lakoff, G. and Johnson 1980, Lakoff 1993), who assume that metaphor is a particular phenomenon with distinctive properties and so warrants its own theory, as will be discussed briefly in the next section. However, within the unitary approach to lexical pragmatics set out here, it is worth exploring the possibility that the key property of metaphors (which distinguishes them from hyperboles) is that grasping a metaphorical use requires not only a broadening of encoded content, but also, essentially, a narrowing. In other words, not only is a defining property of the literal concept dropped (e.g. 'lizard' in the case of *chameleon*), thereby broadening the denotation, but some other property, accessed by context-sensitive relevance-based inference, becomes central to the ad hoc concept (e.g. perhaps 'inconsistency' in the case of *chameleon*), and so the denotation is narrowed. On this basis, we may be able to account for the intuition that, for instance, 'John is a *saint*' is both metaphorical and hyperbolic. In brief, on this use of *saint*, a defining property of the literal concept SAINT, namely, 'canonised', is dropped and thus the denotation is broadened, while the property of a self-sacrificial degree of kindness is promoted to central prominence and thus the denotation is narrowed (it excludes cruel saints, like Thomas More, who perpetrated the torture of heretics). It seems that it is this latter property that accounts for the hyperbolic feel of the utterance, as we take it to be an exaggerated expression of John's actual degree of kindness.[13]

Fifth, there is another possible objection to the explicitly 'deflationary'[14] RT ad hoc concept account of metaphor: it might not seem to do justice to what people usually find most striking about metaphors – their sensory, imagistic, phenomenal properties. The ad hoc concepts that the account delivers seem rather general and abstract[15] and, even if this is not what's intended, there is very little said about the apparently non-conceptual (imagistic or affective) effects of metaphors. One line of response to this objection would be that the theory applies only to relatively conventionalised or routinised cases like 'saint', 'angel', 'chameleon', 'boiling', 'block of ice', 'minefield' and 'butcher', for which a second, metaphorical, sense is listed in some dictionaries and whose evocative aspect could be argued to have been lost or greatly diminished as its conceptual content solidified. However, Relevance theorists intend the scope of the account to be considerably wider than this. The interpretive process of ad hoc concept formation is context-sensitive and pragmatic, so applies also to the understanding of relatively novel, unconventional cases, such as the following:

(13)   My garden is a *slum* of bloom.

(14)   *Context:* The protagonist has expressed an opinion that is very much at odds with what her addressee, Sarah, wants to hear.
       *Description:* Sarah's face became a *polished stone*.

(15)   *Context:* A group of young people are discussing older, rather dominant, female members of their families.
       *Utterance:* You should meet my granny, Paul. She's the one would put manners on you. She's a real *paint remover*.[16]

Thus, the account's intended scope requires that it offer some explanation of the imagistic effects of these more creative examples. Further, it is far from obvious that the more familiar metaphorical uses such as 'angel', 'butcher', 'chameleon', 'minefield', etc. are any less imagistic than these more unusual or creative uses, so there does seem to be a further dimension to be accounted for across the board. There are very interesting and challenging questions here concerning how the sensory, imagistic and affective effects of metaphors work; in particular, whether they can be reduced to a cluster of weakly communicated cognitive effects, as Sperber and Wilson (1986, 2008) maintain, or not, as Pilkington (2000) and Carston (2010b) argue.

Finally, while the ad hoc concept account encompasses examples such as those in (13)–(15) where the metaphorical use, although quite original, is limited to a single word or phrase, it is a lot less clear that it carries over to extended metaphorical texts, in which there may be a hierarchy of interacting metaphors developed at some length. These are typical of, but by no means confined to, poetry and other literary texts. The two verses from John Donne in (12) above are a case in point (and the 'compasses' metaphor there is, in fact, developed over several more verses of the poem). Consider also the following passage from a modern novel:

(16)   Depression, in Karla's experience, was a dull, inert thing – a toad that squatted wetly on your head until it finally gathered the energy to slither off. The unhappiness she had been living with for the last ten days was a quite different creature. It was frantic and aggressive. It had fists and fangs and hobnailed boots. It didn't sit, it assailed. It *hurt* her. In the mornings, it slapped her so hard in the face that she reeled as she walked to the bathroom.

                                                    (Zoë Heller, *The Believers*, p. 263)

The question here is whether in interpreting this passage we rapidly construct a lot of distinct ad hoc concepts, one after the other: TOAD*, SQUAT-ON-YOUR-HEAD*, CREATURE*, FRANTIC*, FISTS*, FANGS*, HOB-NAILED-BOOTS* and so on. In my view, the literal meanings of the many metaphorically used words here are so mutually reinforcing that, relative to their high activation, the effort of deriving multiple ad hoc concepts is too great and instead the literal meanings win out temporarily, so that an internally coherent mental scenario is formed representing a somewhat surreal world consisting of repulsive amphibious creatures with different kinds of characteristics (some sitting inertly on human heads, some kicking and biting). Of course, the work of grasping the intended metaphorical interpretation has yet to be done and that requires a further pragmatic inferential process of deriving from the representations comprising the literal interpretation those of its implications that can plausibly apply to the human experiences of depression and grief.[17]

The suggestion, then, is that it may be necessary to supplement the ad hoc concept account with a second kind or mode of metaphor processing, in which the literal meaning of a stretch of metaphorically used language is maintained as a whole and subjected to slower, more reflective interpretive inference, which separates out the implications that are speaker-meant from those that are not. The difference between these two routes to metaphor understanding can be summed up succinctly as follows: on the first one (ad hoc concept formation), word meaning is pragmatically adjusted so as to capture the thought, and, on the second one, the thought or world conception is (albeit temporarily) made to correspond to the (literal) language. The first mode is, as it were, the normal mode – we are adjusting word meanings to a greater or lesser extent all the time in comprehending utterances, in accordance with our occasion-specific expectations of relevance. The switch to the second mode is made only when a certain processing threshold or tipping point is reached, when the effort of local ad hoc concept formation is too great relative to the dominance, the high accessibility, of the literal meaning. For further discussion of this 'two process' account of metaphor comprehension, see Carston (2010b; and Carston and Wearing (2011)).

In the next section, I will consider a different account of metaphor, one which takes its prevalence in language use to be a reflection of its origin in our conceptual system.

## 23.4   Conceptual metaphor and pragmatics

Within the approach to language known as 'cognitive linguistics',[18] metaphor is viewed as, first and foremost, a phenomenon of thought. It consists of conceptual mappings across cognitive domains such that certain abstract domains of thought (e.g. psychological states, time, life, verbal arguments) have the structure of more concrete domains projected onto them (e.g. physical states, space, journeys, wars or physical struggles, respectively).

These domain mappings then surface, derivatively and pervasively, in our use of language:

(17)  a.  After he lost his job, John was *very low* for months, but he seems to be *rising above* it now. <SAD IS DOWN>, <HAPPY IS UP>

   b.  *From* Monday *to* Friday he worked hard, but *in* the weekend he rested.
<TIME IS SPACE>

   c.  I've *reached an impasse* and really don't know *where to go* next.
<LIFE IS A JOURNEY>

   d.  Her *defensive strategy* worked and his objections were *knocked down* one after the other.
<ARGUMENTS ARE WARS>

In their book, aptly entitled *Metaphors We Live By*, Lakoff and Johnson (1980) carried out what can be thought of as a consciousness-raising exercise by comprehensively demonstrating how metaphor-laden our ordinary conventional language use is and how systematically related many of these metaphorical uses are. For example, there are a lot of different terms we use for talking about time which come from the source domain of money (specifically, its property of being a valuable and limited resource): '*spend* time', '*save* many hours', '*waste* several days', '*invest* one's time *profitably*', '*budget* one's time', '*squander* decades', 'live on *borrowed* time', etc. These uses of language, and many others, are claimed to be underpinned by the general metaphor <TIME IS MONEY>, which is part of our conceptual system and structures our thinking about time (the target domain). Another example is the vast array of expressions whose literal meaning concerns spatial location but which are regularly employed for talking about non-spatial domains; for instance, words for being physically up/high or down/low are used to express positive or negative states of health, emotion, morality and social 'standing'. These then are taken as evidence for the conceptual metaphors <GOOD IS UP>, <BAD IS DOWN>. The domain of physical containers is another source domain that figures in a wide range of metaphors with target domains including human minds (e.g. we have thoughts '*in*, *on*, and *at the front/back of* our minds'), visual fields (e.g. things come '*into* and *out of* view'), emotional states and relationships (e.g. 'falling *in* and *out* of love', 'she got more *out of it* than she put *into it*'), activities (e.g. 'get *into* or *out of* 'a particular line of work or business). Again, based on this linguistic evidence, the claim is that our knowledge of the physical domain of containers structures a number of more abstract domains of thought via conceptual metaphors such as <THE MIND IS A CONTAINER>, <RELATIONSHIPS ARE CONTAINERS>, etc.

   The system of conceptual metaphors is claimed to consist of both basic or primary metaphors and more complex ones that are composed out of the simpler ones together with ordinary general knowledge. So, for example, the metaphor <LOVE IS A JOURNEY> is composed of several more basic conceptual metaphors, including <PURPOSES ARE DESTINATIONS>, <DIFFICULTIES ARE IMPEDIMENTS TO MOTION>, <RELATIONSHIPS ARE CONTAINERS>, <INTIMACY IS CLOSENESS> (plus ordinary literal knowledge about, for instance, travelling, containers, motion, etc.). For more detail about the system of primary metaphors and the compositional structures built from them, see Grady (1997), G. Lakoff (1993, 2008).[19] Grady and Lakoff have noted that such primary metaphors are acquired by people all over the world and claim that this is because they are grounded in our shared bodily experience of the world (the 'embodiment' thesis). For example, there is a bodily experiential basis to the (associative) connection between positive/negative experiences and being physically upright/down, hence the primary metaphors <GOOD IS UP> and <BAD IS DOWN>, between knowing something and the experience of seeing it, hence the metaphor <KNOWING IS SEEING>, and between emotional connectedness and physical proximity, hence the metaphor <INTIMACY IS CLOSENESS>. A further, more recent development within conceptual metaphor theory is the idea that there is a neural basis to enduring metaphorical thought (and hence to metaphorical language). Basic metaphorical mappings (e.g. from bodily states and processes to psychological states and processes) are claimed to consist of neural maps that bind sensorimotor information to more abstract ideas so that source domain structures and inferences are carried over to the target domain via neural links (Lakoff, G. 2008).

As this brief outline of the cognitivists' position indicates, their view of metaphor could hardly be more different from that of the classical rhetorical or the Gricean approach, according to which metaphors, along with other tropes, are not natural or normal uses of language (they violate an assumed norm of literalness) and are not essential to the content being communicated, but are merely attractive or attention-grabbing ways of presenting it. Like Relevance theorists, cognitive linguists follow the Romantic tradition, according to which metaphor is an entirely natural and normal phenomenon; it pervades language use and is both contentful and unparaphraseable.[20] However, despite this very basic similarity in outlook, the cognitive linguistic and RT positions are strikingly different in other respects. The most fundamental difference is their distinct views on the origin of metaphors: in thought/conceptualisation, according to the former, and in communication, according to the latter.

A second difference concerns the literal/metaphorical distinction. As discussed in section 23.3, according to the RT view, metaphorical language lies at one end of a literal–non-literal (loose use) continuum, which also includes approximations and hyperbolic uses of language. Nothing of this sort could possibly enter into the cognitivists' account, given that they take the essence of metaphor to be the associative mapping of a concrete conceptual domain onto a more abstract domain.[21] This view of metaphor entails a relatively sharp literal/metaphorical distinction, which applies to both thought and language:

Although I will argue that a great many common concepts like causation and purpose are metaphorical, there is nonetheless an extensive range of non-metaphorical concepts. A sentence like *The balloon went up* is not metaphorical, nor is the old philosopher's favorite *The cat is on the mat*. But as soon as one gets away from concrete physical experience and starts talking about abstractions or emotions, metaphorical understanding is the norm. G. Lakoff (1993: 205)

Given their focus on metaphor and its unique role in conceptualisation, it is not surprising that Lakoff and his colleagues don't discuss hyperbole or approximation. These kinds of language use are not likely to be of much interest to them since they do not involve mappings between conceptual domains and so do not structure our thinking about the world, as metaphor does. The Lakoffians might well find it a reasonable idea that there is a continuum of loose uses of language which includes approximations, category extensions, hyperbole and other intermediate cases, but would take that to be a quite distinct matter from metaphor.

Another question one might have about the cognitivists' position is how they view the relation between a verbal metaphor and its apparently corresponding simile. Given that metaphor is taken to be fundamentally a matter of conceptualisation, it might seem that the verbal metaphor/simile distinction is just a superficial difference in linguistic form with little interpretive import; for example, 'Bill is a bulldozer' and 'Bill is like a bulldozer' would simply be minimally different linguistic manifestations of the <PEOPLE ARE MACHINES> conceptual metaphor. But, while this may be true of some cases, it is only one dimension of what is, in fact, quite a complex issue. First, many of the grammatical forms that manifest prototypical Lakoffian conceptual metaphors cannot be easily recast as similes, e.g. 'The price has *gone up*', 'I'll be home *around* midnight', 'She is *in* danger', 'She looked at him *coldly*', 'Our *paths* will *cross* again one day'. Second, while there is an open-ended mapping between the source and target domains in a metaphor, many similes explicitly specify a single salient resemblance between the two domains at issue, e.g. 'He *followed her around* like a puppy dog', 'The victim had been shot and *dumped* in a field like garbage' (examples from Croft and Cruse 2004: 213). Although there is rather little discussion of similes within the cognitive linguistic paradigm, what there is tends to concur with the view described in section 23.3 that, with the possible exception of a few cases of the 'X is (like) a Y' sort, simile and metaphor are quite distinct uses of language (see Israel *et al.* 2004; Croft and Cruse 2004: 211–16). Of course, the deeper difference for the cognitivists is that while metaphor is fundamentally a matter of conceptualisation, simile is (just) a figure of speech.

It is not one of the aims of the cognitivists' conceptual approach to metaphor to provide an account of how context-specific metaphorical uses of language are understood in on-line communication. That is, the account is not a pragmatic theory and it could, therefore, in principle, be wedded to an independently developed pragmatic theory, such as the relevance-based account of utterance comprehension. What pragmatics provides is an account of how a hearer/reader comes to understand a metaphorical utterance in the way *intended by the speaker*. Consider, for instance, different possible interpretations of the following metaphorical uses:

(18)   a.   My younger brother is a *prince*.
       b.   Elizabeth is *the sun*.
       c.   His feet were *stones* at the end of his legs.

The speaker of (18a) might mean that her brother has a noble character and is destined for greatness, or that he is spoiled and demanding. In some contexts, (18b) might be interpreted as saying that Elizabeth is resplendent and regal; in others, that she is full of warmth and radiantly beautiful. The speaker of (18c) might intend 'stones' to be interpreted as heavy weights or as cold lifeless things.[22] And for each of these, specific contextualisations could yield numerous further, more fine-grained, interpretive possibilities. So, even if there is a stock of conceptual metaphors which make available an array of domain mappings, context-sensitive, relevance-based inferential processes geared to the recovery of the speaker's intended meaning are essential. Furthermore, there are some metaphorical uses of language that cannot be plausibly thought of as grounded in any of the kinds of domain mappings put forward by the cognitivists; for instance, describing one body part in terms of another in (19a) or the human 'heart' in terms of a part of an item of clothing in (19b):

(19)   a.   His face was a *fist* of fury and pain.
       b.   'A man's heart was *a deep pocket he might turn out* and be
            amazed at what he found there.'
                    (from *The Secret River* by Kate Grenville, p. 302)

For these examples, interpreting the metaphor is wholly a matter of pragmatic inference, which takes its premises from non-metaphorical information stored in the encyclopaedic entries associated with the decoded concepts FIST and POCKET. There are probably many cases of this sort, including some of those above (e.g. 'My garden is a *slum* of bloom'), which are the product of a human imaginative capacity to see resemblances and make analogies, and do not depend on established conceptual metaphors.

Recently, Tendahl and Gibbs (2008) have proposed that conceptual metaphor theory and the RT account of metaphor comprehension are complementary and should be brought together into a comprehensive theory of metaphor. They suggest that conceptual metaphors are part of our general encyclopaedic knowledge and may, like other items of such knowledge, be activated when particular concepts are linguistically decoded and so play a role in facilitating the recovery of the speaker's meaning. For instance, in the process of comprehending 'Robert is a bulldozer', the decoded lexical concept BULLDOZER would make available the conceptual metaphors <PEOPLE

ARE MACHINES>, <MINDS ARE MACHINES> and perhaps others, each of which provides a system of mappings between the source and target domains. The idea is that these long-standing, entrenched metaphorical mappings interact with more occasion-specific contextual information resulting in certain components of the domain mappings being more highly activated than others and so more likely to be instrumental in the ad hoc concept formation process. As Tendahl and Gibbs see it, the advantages of conceptual metaphors playing this role in a relevance-based pragmatics are: (a) they would reduce the processing effort involved in metaphor comprehension (thereby increasing the relevance of the metaphorical utterance), and (b) they could account for cases of 'emergent properties' such as, for instance, 'insensitive to the views and feelings of others', which might well be one of the properties understood as meant by the speaker of 'Robert is a bulldozer'. This is not a property of bulldozers (machines) and so does not feature in the encyclopaedic entry for the concept BULLDOZER, but might be made available via the system of associative mappings between the source domain of machines and the target domain of human characteristics.[23] For more detailed discussion, see also Gibbs and Tendahl (2006).

Underpinning the RT account of metaphorical language understanding in terms of ad hoc concepts is the view that the concepts that humans can mentally entertain and manipulate are considerably more numerous and fine-grained than the concepts encoded in public language systems. Thus, the range of concepts we can communicate to each other far outstrips those that are lodged in our linguistic lexicons and it is relevance-based pragmatic processes that make this possible (Sperber and Wilson 1998b). Some of these non-lexicalised concepts may be established in an individual's conceptual repertoire, while others may be formed on the fly, in response to immediate occasion-specific concerns (Barsalou 1987, Carston 2010a). RT doesn't rule out the possibility of metaphorical thought, but, contrary to the cognitivists' stance, takes it that the vast majority of metaphorical language use in communication is a reflection of non-metaphorical thoughts about the world; we can think about mental states, life, love, arguments and other abstract concepts without necessarily having to employ concepts from more concrete domains such as bodily states, journeys, containers and wars in order to do so.

Working within the RT framework, Wilson (2009a) suggests that at least some of the cross-domain correspondences discussed by the cognitivists might be the result of repeated encounters with linguistic metaphors that link the two conceptual domains. Wilson starts by demonstrating how a hearer who encounters a metaphorical use such as 'Bill's marriage is *on the rocks*' for the first time could interpret it successfully via the kind of lexical adjustment process (specifically, lexical broadening) outlined above in section 23.3. That is, without any metaphorical scheme of the type <MARRIAGES ARE JOURNEYS> in his conceptual system, he could, following the usual relevance-driven interpretation process, infer an ad hoc concept <ON THE

ROCKS*> which carries the intended implications about Bill's marriage. Then she points out that, while many ad hoc concepts are a one-off occurrence, others may recur regularly and frequently enough for the inferential route from the lexical concept to the ad hoc concept to become routinised to varying degrees. In very frequently used cases that link two domains (e.g. relationships and journeys, arguments and wars, time and money), the routinisation may go so far as to amount to the kind of systematic cross-domain correspondences that the cognitivists discuss. So, for instance, thoughts about marriage may come to automatically activate aspects of our encyclopaedic information about journeys, and thoughts about arguments may come to automatically activate aspects of our encyclopaedic information about wars. These automatic co-activations would then facilitate the development of further related metaphorical uses of concepts from the same source domains applied to the same target domains, hence the families of related metaphors that the cognitive linguists have highlighted (e.g. 'reached a dead end', 'made a new start', 'sailing along', 'stormy', 'entered calmer waters', etc. used in describing marriages and other relationships). While Lakoffians see these linguistic uses as external manifestations of a prior conceptual metaphor <MARRIAGE IS A JOURNEY>, Wilson's view is, in effect, the opposite, in that she takes the basis of the apparent domain mapping to be communicative rather than cognitive/conceptual. It will be interesting to see how this fundamental difference in the explanation for certain well-established and thematically related clusters of linguistic metaphors is ultimately resolved. One possibility is that there are some primary cognitive mappings, such as the universally instantiated analogy between the physical and the psychological, the body and the mind, while other, more culture-specific cases, such as <MARRIAGE IS A JOURNEY> or <PEOPLE ARE MACHINES>, arise from repeated patterns of linguistic communication.

Finally, whether or not the claim that many metaphors have their origin in our conceptual systems is true, it does seem irrefutable that metaphor abounds in our use of language and has a strong presence in the lexical system itself. This, then, is another difference from ironical uses of language, which are considerably less frequent, apparently less basic among our communicative needs than metaphor, and not a force for semantic change – there aren't ironical sense extensions in the lexicon. Irony is not conceptual in the sense in which the cognitivists believe metaphor to be: no one, as far as I know, has claimed that there are ironical mappings which structure our conceptual systems, and indeed it is difficult to imagine any cognitive utility in such a system.

## 23.5  Conclusion: kinds of non-literalness and the literal/non-literal distinction(s)

Metaphor is usually taken to be the paradigm case of non-literalness. Most ordinary untutored communicators are aware of a distinction between literal and metaphorical uses of words – speakers may, on occasion, preface their utterances with the phrase 'metaphorically speaking' and hearers may question whether someone meant a word literally or metaphorically. Similarly, people are typically alert to the distinction between ironical and literal utterances and may correct someone's apparent misinterpretation of an utterance by saying 'no, she meant it ironically'. In this concluding section, I will briefly consider the extent to which this kind of intuitive folk distinction between the literal and the non-literal is reflected in the kinds of theories discussed in the previous sections.

On the Gricean account of saying and meaning, there is a relatively clear distinction between literal and non-literal language use: a speaker uses language literally when she means what she says (in Grice's semantically oriented sense of 'say'), and she uses language non-literally when she does not mean what she says (or makes as if to say), as in 'Mary is a bulldozer' or 'Bill is a fine friend' (uttered in the appropriate context). The move to a pragmatically enriched conception of what a speaker says (or explicitly communicates), as discussed in section 23.2 above, obliterates this way of drawing the literal/non-literal distinction. On this view, speakers, trading on their hearers' pragmatic capacities, may employ a word to communicate any of a wide range of concepts inferable in context from the encoded lexical concept, and these communicated ad hoc concepts, e.g. MONEY*, BOILING*, BULLDOZER*, ON THE ROCKS*, contribute to what the speaker said (her primary meaning). So, on this account, even in clearly metaphorically used cases the speaker means what she says (a conclusion that the cognitivists would draw too, although basing it on different assumptions).

Relevance theorists maintain that adjustment of lexically encoded meanings is standard practice in communication and that words are seldom used to express just what they encode. So if literal meaning is equated with linguistically encoded meaning, it follows that using words literally is a rarity. However, some cases of pragmatic adjustment of word meanings do not, intuitively at least, seem to count as non-literal uses. Instances of lexical narrowing (or enrichment), e.g. 'money' used to mean 'a lot of money', 'fresh' to mean 'new and bright', 'leave' to mean 'end a relationship', are generally judged to be literal uses of the words. What distinguishes lexical concept narrowing from broadening (loose use) is that while the linguistically encoded meaning is preserved in the former, components of it are dropped in the latter, e.g. a loose use of 'hexagonal' drops the defining feature that the six sides are exactly equal, a broadening of 'saint' to mean 'very kind, unselfish person' drops the 'canonised' component. So we might reasonably suggest that only cases of lexical concept broadening qualify as non-literal uses.

However, although there is a principled distinction here, it does not mesh with ordinary speaker-hearer intuitions because many loose uses, probably including the two just given, are not any more phenomenologically salient as non-literal uses than the enrichment cases are. The folk distinction would include banal loose uses (e.g. 'square' to mean 'squarish', 'flat' to mean 'flat in so far as landscapes can be flat') in the class of literal uses of language and distinguish them from clear cases of metaphor (and irony). If the RT view that there is a loose use continuum, extending from the strictly literal at one extreme to the strikingly metaphorical at the other, is correct, it seems that we should simply abandon any attempt to match the distinctions made by the pragmatic theory with the intuitive folk distinction. What is transparently non-literal to us as ordinary language users would have to be captured in some way that cross-cuts the loose use continuum and explains what property makes it the case that some departures from strict literalness impinge on our conscious awareness while others don't.[24]

Within the class of intuitive non-literal uses, however, metaphor and irony are clearly recognised by speaker-hearers as quite distinct phenomena and, consonant with this, they are given very different explanations within current pragmatic theories, as discussed in sections 23.2 and 23.3 above. While metaphorical uses require hearers to radically broaden or adjust linguistic meanings, ironical uses typically preserve literal word meanings but make it evident that the speaker does not think those literal meanings apply to the situation under discussion. These are very different ways of using language non-literally: metaphorical uses are attempts to describe the world accurately by extending the meaning resources of the linguistic code, while ironical uses are a means of using literal meaning to communicate a dissociative attitude towards particular descriptions of the world. That we can express and communicate thoughts and attitudes that go so far beyond what our languages encode is, of course, entirely due to our powerful pragmatic capacities.

# Part III

## Interfaces and the delimitation of pragmatics

# 24

# Pragmatics in the history of linguistic thought

Andreas H. Jucker

## 24.1 Introduction

Pragmatics is still a relatively young branch of linguistics. It was only in the early 1970s that more and more linguists started to devote their attention to this field. The International Pragmatics Association (IPrA) was founded in 1985. Its early conferences took place in Viareggio (1985), Antwerp (1987), Barcelona (1990), and Kobe, Japan (1993). The international *Journal of Pragmatics* started publication in 1977, and the journal *Pragmatics* in 1991 (Mey 1998b: 720). The *Journal of Pragmatics* started with about 400 pages per year in the seventies and has steadily increased its volume to over 2,500 pages per year by 2009. This increase is mirrored in similar increases in the volume of textbooks, monographs, collected volumes, more specialized journals (*Pragmatics & Cognition* 1993, *Historical Pragmatics* 2000, *Intercultural Pragmatics* 2004, *International Review of Pragmatics* 2009, *Pragmatics and Society* 2010), and in particular in the publication of handbooks in pragmatics (Mey 1998b; Verschueren *et al.* 2003; Horn and Ward 2004; Mey 2009a; Cummings 2010; and Bublitz *et al.* 2010−). Pragmatics is no longer just a small subfield of linguistics but one of the dominant areas, indeed it may be argued to have become a discipline in its own right. It has developed "from a humble beginning at the remote outposts of philosophy and linguistic semantics . . . into a vast realm where often conflicting theories and practices reign" (Mey 2009a: vi).

Given such a large and diverse field of study, it might reasonably be questioned whether it is at all possible to write a coherent history for this field. In 1996, Biletzki still maintained that this was not possible. Pragmatics − according to him − did not have a history.

Its maturity is attested to by both the number of practitioners in the field, and the variety of directions in which its branches grow out to various

My thanks for very useful comments on a draft version of this contribution go to Wolfram Bublitz, Daniela Landert, Irma Taavitsainen and the editors of this handbook. The usual disclaimers apply.

disciplines. Yet sitting on any of the branches of this pragmatic tree – be they philosophical, linguistic, psychological – one wonders if the tree mightn't topple over for lack of roots. For pragmatics seems to have no formal, institutionalized history. (Biletzki 1996: 455)

In the meantime, several (partial) histories of pragmatics have appeared, most notably Nerlich and Clarke (1996) and Nerlich (2009, 2010).

Two issues are at stake. First, where does the history begin and which period does it cover? Does it focus exclusively on the roots of the discipline before it constituted itself as a recognized field of study? Or does it also cover the development of the discipline over the forty or so years of its existence? The introduction of the term "pragmatics" is generally attributed to Charles Sanders Peirce (1839–1914) and to Charles Morris (1901–1979), but the field only constituted itself as such in the 1970s. And second, the historian of pragmatics must decide on the delimitation of the field of pragmatics in order to locate its various roots at a time when the field had not constituted itself (see e.g. Biletzki 1996: 457–9).

I shall take a broad view on both these issues by including not only pragmatics *avant la lettre* but also a brief and necessarily selective account of the development of the discipline itself and by adopting a broad, basically Continental European view of pragmatics (see below). First, I shall briefly outline some of the roots of pragmatics in the academic traditions of the nineteenth and early twentieth century, at a time when the term "pragmatics" had not been introduced and when it was not linguists but scholars in other fields who were interested in studying the use of language. In a second step I shall briefly refer to the work by philosophers such as Peirce, Morris, and Carnap, who in the first half of the twentieth century first introduced and used the term "pragmatics". This leads on to the work by the ordinary language philosophers Austin and Searle, and also to Grice, who in the 1950s and 1960s to a large extent set the agenda for the more widespread work in pragmatics in the 1970s and 1980s, when the field of pragmatics really took off and was taken over by linguists. The second part of this contribution is then devoted to the further development of pragmatics in the context of linguistic thought in general and against the background of some important paradigm shifts that have radically transformed the landscape of linguistics over the last four or five decades.

## 24.2  Pragmatics *avant la lettre*

In a wider sense the roots of pragmatics can be located in all those philosophical traditions that rejected the "descriptive fallacy" (Austin 1962: 3), i.e. the idea that language represents states of affairs that are either true or false. Language is more than just a representation of thoughts, it is used by speakers to communicate with each other, to influence hearers in certain ways, and, indeed, to change the world (see Nerlich 2010: 193). Such a view of language has its roots in antiquity. It was part of the rhetoric in the "liberal arts" or "trivium" of rhetoric, grammar, and logic. From its earliest beginnings rhetoric has been concerned with the art of persuasion, with the different methods by which speakers can influence their audience. In his *Rhetoric* Aristotle distinguished three ways of persuading others: *logos*, the appeal to their reason; *pathos*, the appeal to their emotions; and *ethos*, the appeal to the speaker's personality or character (see Corbett 1990: 37). Aristotle thus focuses on the effect that language has on the audience and how these effects can be achieved (see Dascal and Gross 1999; Tindale 2010).[1]

In the nineteenth century language studies were almost exclusively focused on historical-comparative linguistics, the regularities of sound change, and the reconstruction of earlier languages. Linguists were interested in individual languages and the relationships between them. They compared different languages in order to establish common ancestor languages and in order to reconstruct older languages. Such a perspective did not leave much room for studying language in use, language in its social and communicative context, and the effects of language on the audience. However, there were several neighboring disciplines such as philosophy, psychology, sociology, and semiotics, in which language was seen from an interactive and communicative perspective. What these disciplines had in common was that they saw language not just as an organism growing in more or less predictable ways and not as a system that only serves to represent true or false states of affairs, but as a means to communicate with others, as a means of influencing others in specific ways, and as a means of doing things (see Nerlich 2009: 329; Nerlich and Clarke 1996).

## 24.3   Early uses of the term "pragmatics"

It is the American mathematician and philosopher Charles S. Peirce (1839–1914) who is generally credited with the coining of the term "pragmatism." Parmentier (1997: 3), however, points out that it was the psychologist William James (1842–1910) who introduced it as the "principle of Peirce" into philosophical discourse. But Peirce is the father of pragmatism, a theory of meaning that is based on a theory of signs and the effects which they have on our conduct (see Nöth 1990: 41). The theory also focuses on the connection between thought and action. Later, Peirce changed the term "pragmatism" to "pragmaticism" in order to differentiate it from James's use of the term, taking "pragmaticism" to be a term "so ugly that . . . no one would dare steal it" (Parmentier 1997: 5).

The American philosopher Charles Morris (1901–1979) integrated ideas from Peirce's pragmatism or pragmaticism into his own theory of signs, which he called "semiotic," using a term coined by John Locke (1632–1704).

Today the field is commonly known as "semiotics." The most famous aspect of this theory for linguists and pragmaticists is the semiotic triangle. Morris distinguished three branches of semiotics: syntactics, semantics, and pragmatics, which are devoted to the syntactical, semantical, and pragmatical aspects of signs. Syntactics deals with signs and their relationships towards each other. Semantics deals with the signs and their meanings. And pragmatics deals with the signs in relation to their users. In fact, every sign must always include all three dimensions of semiosis. It is only for analytical purposes that the relation between different signs, the meaning of signs, and the relation of signs to their users can be distinguished (see Petrilli 2000: 6 for details). Morris's conceptualization of pragmatics was very broad. "It is a sufficiently accurate characterization of pragmatics to say that it deals with the biotic aspects of semiosis, that is, with all the psychological, biological, and sociological phenomena which occur in the functioning of signs" (Morris 1938: 108; quoted by Levinson 1983: 2). Such a definition is much broader than the Anglo-American approach to pragmatics and is much closer to the Continental European approach (see below, section 24.5).

The German-born and U.S.-naturalized philosopher Rudolf Carnap (1891–1970), on the other hand, was influential in narrowing down the scope of pragmatics. He conceptualized Morris's semiotic triangle in the following way.

> If in an investigation explicit reference is made to the speaker, or to put it in more general terms, to the user of the language, then we assign it [the investigation] to the field of pragmatics ... If we abstract from the user of the language and analyze only the expressions and their designata, we are in the field of semantics. And, finally, if we abstract from the designata also and analyze only the relations between the expressions, we are in (logical) syntax. (Carnap 1938; quoted by Levinson 1983: 2–3)

This definition of pragmatics focuses on the user of the language. It does not invoke the effects on the audience or the larger social and cultural context in which language is used.

Levinson (1983: 3) points out that Carnap's definition of pragmatics led some scholars to adopt a very restricted scope of pragmatics, which was basically reduced to considerations of deictic elements. Elements, such as *I*, *you*, *this*, *here*, and so on, require for their interpretation reference to the user of these expressions and, therefore, fall squarely under Carnap's definition, for whom the domain of semantics is a proper part of that of pragmatics – opposite to current contextualism.

But at the same time philosophers like Austin, Searle, and Grice had already started to analyze ordinary language. They came to be known as "ordinary language philosophers," had a massive influence on the early development of pragmatics – and they continue to be influential up to the present day.

## 24.4   Philosophers of language

Bertrand Russell (1872–1970) and Ludwig Wittgenstein (1889–1951) in his early writings (often called the Early Wittgenstein) advocated a form of analytical philosophy that relied on an ideal language and on symbolic logic or a quasi-mathematical notation for the analysis of philosophical problems. The ordinary-language philosophers, on the other hand, focused their attention on an analysis of ordinary rather than ideal languages. It was, in fact, Ludwig Wittgenstein in his later writings (known as the Later Wittgenstein), who was one of the earliest proponents of ordinary-language philosophy. It is still a matter of controversy how exactly the Later Wittgenstein differs from the Early Wittgenstein, but it is the Later Wittgenstein's views on the meaning of words that are particularly important for the development of pragmatics. He refutes the position that words in a language name objects and that sentences are combinations of such names. Instead, Wittgenstein proposes that the meaning of a word in a large class of cases is "its use in the language" (Wittgenstein 1953: 18).

The Oxford philosopher J. L. Austin (1911–1960) is best known for his posthumously published book *How to Do Things With Words* (1962). The book was based on the lecture notes of the William James Lectures he delivered at Harvard University in 1955. The book starts with the contrast between performative utterances, i.e. utterances that perform an action, and assertions or constatives that describe a state of affairs and have specific truth conditions. Performatives do not have truth conditions; instead they have felicity conditions, that is to say conditions which must be satisfied in order for the speech act to successfully perform the intended action. In the later part of the book, the theory is extended into a more comprehensive account in which constatives, too, are seen as actions. By using them, speakers perform the action of stating and thus these acts are also subject to felicity conditions (Austin 1962: 136). In his discussion of speech acts, Austin distinguishes three main aspects that pertain to every speech act. The first aspect, the so-called locutionary act, consists in the act of uttering speech sounds, the basic act of talking itself. The second aspect, the illocutionary act of an utterance, describes the conventional nature of an act, such as stating, ordering, asking, promising, warning, or thanking. The third aspect, finally, the perlocutionary act, describes the effect that is achieved by performing the act, for instance in the form of persuading or convincing the addressee or getting him or her to do something (see Sbisà 2006, 2010; also Kissine, this volume).

Austin's theory of speech acts is often conflated with that of John Searle (b. 1932), who has been described as "one of the most influential contributors to speech act theory and pragmatics in the last forty years" (Kirk 2010: 416). Searle studied at Oxford with Peter Strawson, Peter Geach, and J. L. Austin. After his studies he took up a position at the University of California at

Berkeley. On the basis of Austin's pioneering framework Searle developed a more thorough and more detailed theory for the analysis of speech acts. In his consideration of illocutionary acts, to pick out a central aspect of his theory, he explicates a set of conditions that must obtain for the successful performance of particular illocutionary acts, and on that basis he spells out the constitutive rules for that particular speech act. He demonstrates these steps with the example of promising (Searle 1969: 57–64). The propositional content rule specifies that the proposition of a promise must concern a future act A of the speaker S. The preparatory rule specifies that a promise can only be successfully uttered if S has good reasons to believe that H would prefer S's doing A to his or her not doing A, and only if it is not obvious to both S and H that S will do A anyway. The sincerity rule states that a promise can only be felicitously uttered if S intends to do A. And the essential rule, finally, requires that the utterance in question counts as an undertaking of an obligation to do A.

The third philosopher of language who had a major and lasting influence on pragmatics was H. Paul Grice (1913–1988). In pragmatics he is best known for his theory of cooperation and conversational implicatures, which is basically an account of how a hearer can work out aspects of meaning that a speaker intended without explicitly expressing them.[2] He starts by noting that conversations are – generally speaking – cooperative enterprises, which he formulated in his "Cooperative Principle": "Make your conversational contribution such as is required, at the stage at which it occurs, by the accepted purpose or direction of the talk exchange in which you are engaged" (Grice 1975: 45). At a more detailed level and echoing Kant, Grice distinguishes the four categories of Quantity, Quality, Relation, and Manner, and within these categories a number of more detailed maxims. The category of Quantity has to do with the quantity of information provided and its two maxims state that speakers should make their contributions as informative as is required, and they should not make them more informative than is required. The category of Quality has one supermaxim that stipulates that speakers try to make their contribution one that is true, with the more specific maxims not to say what they believe to be false and not to say that for which they lack adequate evidence. The category of Relation contains a single maxim "Be relevant." The category of Manner, finally, relates not to what is said but to how it is said. The supermaxim requires the speaker to be perspicuous, and the specific maxims spell this out by requiring the speaker to avoid obscurity of expression and ambiguity, and to be brief and orderly.

Interlocutors generally assume each other to be cooperative, but speakers may fail to observe one of the maxims. In some cases the requirements of two maxims clash, as for instance, when a speaker cannot give as much information as is required without violating the maxim of truthfulness. The assumption that speakers are generally cooperative even if on occasions they fail to observe all of the maxims provides a systematic account of how hearers can read between the lines of what the speaker says, that is to say how they can work out the implicit meaning or – in Grice's words – the "conversational implicatures" (Grice 1975: 49). Such implicatures may result when the maxims are observed. When a speaker asserts that "most students have handed in their assignments," he or she implicates that some did not because otherwise it would have been more informative to say "all students." Implicatures also derive if maxims are flouted, i.e. if their requirements are not fulfilled in order to achieve a particular effect. In the case of irony, for instance, the maxim of truthfulness is flouted in order to communicate a related proposition. If a speaker says "X is a fine friend," to use Grice's (1975: 53) example, in a situation in which it is clear to the speaker and the hearer that the speaker does not believe this, an implicature derives that states by and large the opposite of what the proposition expresses.

Grice's work, like that of Austin and Searle, has had a lasting influence on the development of pragmatics. It is the work of these three philosophers that has most regularly been referred to in all the textbooks on pragmatics, from the very early ones, e.g. Leech (1983) and Levinson (1983), to the more recent, e.g. Cummings (2005), Huang (2007), and Bublitz (2009).

## 24.5 Anglo-American and Continental European pragmatics

Quite early in the history of pragmatics two different ways of doing pragmatics, or schools of thought as Huang (2007: 4–5; 2010: 341) calls them, established themselves. One of these ways can conveniently be described as the Anglo-American tradition of pragmatics, the other as the Continental European tradition. Levinson (1983: 2, 5–6) had already pointed out the distinction between these two traditions, and it is noteworthy that thirty years later the two traditions can still be clearly delimited in the various textbooks and handbooks. Cruse's (2000: 16) definition of pragmatics is typical for the Anglo-American school of thought:

> [P]ragmatics can be taken to be concerned with aspects of information (in the widest sense) conveyed through language which (a) are not encoded by generally accepted convention in the linguistic forms used, but which (b) none the less arise naturally out of and depend on the meanings conventionally encoded in the linguistic forms used, taken in conjunction with the context in which the forms are used.

Thus, within this school of thought, pragmatics is concerned with the study of meaning that arises through the use of language. This is also called the component view of pragmatics. Pragmatics is seen as one of the core components within linguistics responsible for a clearly delimited set of tasks and clearly distinct from other core components, such as semantics, syntax, morphology, or phonology. On this view, anthropological linguistics,

applied linguistics, and psycholinguistics are considered to be more peripheral components of linguistics (Huang 2007: 4). The set of tasks for which such
a component is responsible includes the study of presuppositions, deixis,
implicatures, and speech acts.

The Continental European school of thought, on the other hand, takes
pragmatics to have a much wider range of tasks. In fact, it is not seen as a
particular component of linguistics on a par with other components, but as
a specific perspective for studying language in general. Verschueren (1999:
1) provides a typical definition:

> [P]ragmatics can be defined as *the study of language use*, or, to employ a
> somewhat more complicated phrasing, *the study of linguistic phenomena from
> the point of view of their usage properties and processes*. [Sic.]

He adds explicitly that "pragmatics does not constitute an additional component of a theory of language, but it offers a different *perspective*" (Verschueren
1999: 2, italics original). This school of thought, therefore, is also called the
perspective view. Mey (2001: 6) proposes an equally wide view of pragmatics:

> Communication in society happens chiefly by means of language. How-
> ever, the users of language, as social beings, communicate and use lan-
> guage on society's premises; society controls their access to linguistic and
> communicative means. Pragmatics, as the study of the way humans use
> their language in communication, bases itself on a study of those premises
> and determines how they affect, and effectualize, human language use.
> Hence: *Pragmatics studies the use of language in human communication as deter-
> mined by the conditions of society*. [Sic.]

Mey's textbook is split into two parts, entitled "micropragmatics" and
"macropragmatics." Micropragmatics deals with context, implicature, reference, pragmatic principles, speech acts, and conversation analysis and thus
coincides more or less with the research interests of Anglo-American pragmatics, while the part entitled macropragmatics adds a range of topics that
are only part of Continental European but not Anglo-American pragmatics,
such as literary pragmatics, intercultural pragmatics, and the social aspects
of pragmatics.

The difference between these two schools of thought is clearly reflected in
the relevant textbooks and handbooks of pragmatics. Horn and Ward (2004),
for instance, explicitly exclude the broader, sociologically based European
view of pragmatics from their *Handbook of Pragmatics* and focus on the "more
narrowly circumscribed, mainly Anglo-American conception of linguistic
and philosophical pragmatics and its applications" (Horn and Ward 2004:
xi). Huang (2007: 5), who also adopts an Anglo-American approach in his
textbook on pragmatics, argues that the Continental European tradition
is too all-inclusive and therefore lacks a clear delimitation and defies any
attempt to establish a coherent research agenda.

The textbooks by Verschueren (1999) and Mey (2001) mentioned above clearly adopt the wider Continental European approach and also include questions about the social and cultural contexts in which language is used. The *Handbook of Pragmatics* edited by Verschueren *et al.* (2003) and the series of handbooks edited by Bublitz *et al.* (2010–) also include many topics that consider the use of language from a cultural and social perspective.

## 24.6  Paradigm shifts and diversification of pragmatics

The beginning of pragmatics as an independent subdiscipline within linguistics constituted a major paradigm shift in linguistics. To repeat, it took place in the 1970s and 1980s and radically changed the landscape of linguistics. "What was marginal in the 1970s has come to be of central interest, above all pragmatics" (Traugott 2008b: 207). It was accompanied and followed by several smaller paradigm shifts. Together they brought with them an unprecedented strengthening and broadening of the field of pragmatics, but they also led to a significant diversification of pragmatics and a split into many subdisciplines of pragmatics. Particularly important in this respect are the following paradigm shifts (based in part on a much longer list in Traugott 2008b: 208–9).

1)  From competence to the use of language. Speakers do not just rely on one homogeneous system of language use. They adopt their use of language to the changing situations in which they find themselves in the course of their daily lives.
2)  From introspective data to empirical investigations of contextualized data of very different kinds. Such data includes both spoken and written instantiations of language ranging from formal to informal, from polite to hostile and aggressive, from casual to academic, and so on.
3)  From homogeneity to heterogeneity. Language is no longer seen as a homogeneous but as a dynamic system subject to spatial, social, and diachronic variation.
4)  From synchrony to diachrony. Language change is seen as an important factor in the description of language and of languages.

These paradigm shifts individually and in combination affected the development not only of linguistics but also of pragmatics. In the following sections, I shall briefly sketch their significance for the current state of research in pragmatics.

### 24.6.1  **From competence to the use of language**
The paradigm shift from an analysis of native speaker competence to the study of the use of language affected linguistics as a whole. It is often called "the pragmatic turn" and as such is the foundation stone of pragmatics in general. Before this shift, there were only few linguists who were interested

in the use of language. But the shift brought a sea change. Pragmatics became mainstream.

The Chomskyan school of linguistics, which dominated the discipline in the 1960s and 1970s saw a theory of syntax as the main theoretical framework and tried to integrate the other levels of linguistic descriptions – phonology, morphology, and semantics – into this framework. Linguistic theory, according to Chomsky (1965: 9), was concerned with "the knowledge of the language by a speaker-hearer," i.e. the language competence of the speaker and the hearer. He explicitly excluded the study of how language was used in actual situations, i.e. the study of performance.

John Robert Ross and George Lakoff were the first linguists who tried to free themselves from the domination of syntax. Lakoff proposed an alternative framework called "generative semantics", in which semantics rather than syntax was the driving force. But later Ross and Lakoff started to work in what came to be known as pragmatic territory.

The American structuralists had treated language with a scientific rigor borrowed from the natural sciences. Meaning had not played a significant role in such an endeavor. Chomsky allowed such semantic notions as synonymy and ambiguity into his theory and thus "opened a door for semantics" (Leech 1983: 2). Ross and Lakoff opened the door even further. Generative semantics, however, which in spite of its name was still mainly a syntactic theory rather than a semantic one, was short-lived. It turned out that some of the problems, such as presuppositions and illocutionary force, could not really be handled in such a framework.

Forty years ago in a paper aptly entitled "Out of the pragmatic wastebasket", the Israeli linguist Yehoshua Bar-Hillel (1915–1975) complained about scholars who ignored the pragmatic nature of certain linguistic problems and tried to force them into syntactic or semantic theories. "Be more careful with forcing bits and pieces you find in the pragmatic wastebasket into your favorite syntactico-semantic theory" (Bar-Hillel 1971: 405). His image of the "pragmatic wastebasket" has often been quoted to refer to problems that resisted a satisfactory analysis at the level of syntax or semantics.

In the end, the wastebasket started to overflow and many linguists started to turn their interests to the contents of the wastebasket itself.

> When linguistic pioneers such as Ross and Lakoff staked a claim in pragmatics in the late 1960s, they encountered there an indigenous breed of philosophers of language who had been quietly cultivating the territory for some time. In fact, the more lasting influences on modern pragmatics have been those of philosophers; notably, in recent years, Austin (1962), Searle (1969), and Grice (1975). (Leech 1983: 2)

As a result, the early work by linguists who turned their attention to the "performance" of language, i.e. the use of language in context, could fall back on the work by these language philosophers. As pointed out in the opening paragraph of this paper, pragmatics constituted itself as a significant subfield of linguistics in the late 1970s and early 1980s with its own journal (*Journal of Pragmatics*) that started publication in 1977, with a series of international conferences in the 1980s and with several relevant textbooks (Levinson 1983; Leech 1983; and Green, G. M. 1989; but see also the very influential monograph by Gazdar 1979). The language problems that previously had been assigned to the wastebasket had become respectable and important objects of research. The focus was no longer on the competence of the native speaker-hearer but on the performance in actual situations. In Mey's (2009a: 796) words,

> [t]he waste basket has served its function – I am not saying it is quite empty yet, but we have managed to upgrade the basket to a more prominent position, and accorded it descriptive and explanatory status as a recognized field of language studies.

### 24.6.2 From introspective data to empirical investigations

The language philosophers Austin, Searle, and Grice had all worked with introspective data. Their reflections on language were based on their intuition and their competence as native speakers of English. In linguistics, dominated by Chomskyan linguistics, too, introspection was the only – and the only acceptable – method of research. The object of study was the internalized language (i-language for short) of the native speaker, i.e. the system of knowledge that underlies the native speaker's ability to use and understand language, rather than the externalized language (or e-language), which manifests itself in observable reality (see Chomsky 1986: 19–24). The only access to i-language was through the native speaker's intuition. Intuition was deemed to be superior to corpus data because corpus data, even if extremely large, may fail to contain a particular construction that any native speaker immediately recognizes as grammatical.

One major branch of linguistics that broke away from this tradition was sociolinguistics, which turned to rigorously empirical methods in order to investigate how actual language use (forms of e-language in Chomsky's terms) correlates with the social class of its speakers (see, for instance, Labov 1972).

Many pragmaticists, too, soon started to employ empirical methods of language investigation. In 1974 a paper appeared in *Language*, which had a lasting influence on pragmatics. In it, Sacks, Schegloff, and Jefferson, three sociologists and ethnomethodologists, used detailed transcriptions of naturally occurring conversations in order to analyze the minutiae of the turn-taking system. In the 1980s, conversation analysis and discourse analysis became important branches within linguistics. Not all of them took their analytical methods from Sacks *et al.* (1974), but they all relied on faithfully transcribed data from more or less naturally occurring conversations and on detailed analyses of the regularities in this type of data. Landmark publications were, for instance, Schiffrin's (1987) seminal analysis of discourse markers or the textbooks by G. Brown and Yule (1983) or Stubbs (1983).

In the 1980s pragmaticists also began to experiment more systematically with elicitation techniques. Blum-Kulka *et al.* (1989), for instance, used discourse completion tasks in order to investigate differences in the ways in which different cultures issue requests or apologies. Requests and apologies are two speech acts that are particularly interesting for such an investigation since requests threaten the addressee's negative face and apologies the speaker's own positive face in the sense of P. Brown and Levinson (1987). In such tasks, an utterance by an interlocutor would be given. This can be a university lecturer, for instance, who reminds the student respondent of a book that should have been returned by today. The respondent's answer is left open for the participant to fill in. A second utterance by the lecturer then indicates that the apology has been accepted. Discourse completion tasks, in spite of the criticism that they have subsequently received, are a useful means for gathering large amounts of data that is comparable across different groups of speakers, and it is a method that is still regularly used by some pragmaticists.

Trosborg (1995) also investigated requests and apologies, to which she added complaints as speech acts that threaten the addressee's positive face. She used role plays and role enactments as a method to elicit these speech acts from Danish learners of English and from native speakers of English. In a role play, the participants impersonate a personality that differs from their own experience, while in a role enactment they perform a role that is part of their normal life or personality. The participants would be asked, for instance, to perform the role of a student who complains to a fellow student living in a flat upstairs about the noise that is preventing him or her from preparing a talk for the next day.

In the 1990s the computer became more and more important as a research tool in linguistics in general. By that time, corpus linguistics had already established itself as a respectable field of linguistic enquiry, but the nineties, with the more widespread availability of computers and personal computers in particular, led to an explosion of computer corpora and of corpus-based work in linguistics. It took somewhat longer for this trend to reach pragmatics. A pioneering example is the work by Aijmer, who used the London–Lund Corpus of Spoken English to describe conversational routines, such as thanking, apologizing, and making requests (Aijmer 1996), and discourse particles, such as *now*, *oh*, *ah*, *just*, and *sort of* (Aijmer 2002). Deutschmann (2003) used corpus-linguistic methods to investigate apologies in the British National Corpus. He argued that apologies in British English are routinized to such a degree that searches for elements such as *sorry*, *excuse*, or *pardon* retrieve most of the apologies in the corpus. Stenström *et al.* (2002) and G. Andersen (2001) provide a detailed pragmatic analysis on the basis of the Corpus of London Teenage Language (COLT).

Corpus pragmatics faces some difficult methodological challenges. While surface forms, such as particular discourse markers or routinized phrases, can relatively easily be retrieved, it is very difficult to retrieve underlying speech functions such as specific speech-act values or expressions of politeness. For some more recent work see, for instance, Adolphs (2008), who investigates a range of utterance functions in large corpora of spoken English, and the papers in the collections of Romero-Trillo (2008), and of Jucker *et al.* (2009).

It has to be stressed that this brief sketch of a development of different types of data in pragmatic research should not be seen as reflecting a linear development leading from one type of research to the next. What happened was rather that new types of data and new research methods became available and added to the research methods that were already there and thus led to an increasing diversification of pragmatics. In fact, there is no research method and no particular type of data that is constitutive of pragmatics in general. Even the introspective methods that stood at the beginning of the development of pragmatics have not disappeared. In certain branches, such as cognitive pragmatics and in particular Relevance theory (Sperber and Wilson 1986; Blakemore 1992; Carston 2002), introspective data is still the chosen method. While many researchers argue for the superiority of a particular method of investigation, others advocate a more eclectic view that appreciates the relative strengths and weaknesses of research methods in relation to the specific analytical task to be undertaken. See for instance Jucker (2009), who discusses a broad range of research methods that have been applied in the research of speech acts and in particular in the research of compliments and compliment responses.

## 24.6.3 From homogeneity to heterogeneity

A further paradigm shift that had major consequences for the landscape of linguistics was the shift from homogeneity to heterogeneity. Chomskyan linguistics tried to describe a homogeneous system of native speaker competence. Such fields as sociolinguistics and text linguistics that started in the 1970s focused on the variability of language and its heterogeneity. The paradigm shift can also be discerned in the monumental descriptive grammars of the English language. Quirk *et al.*'s *Grammar of Contemporary English* (1972) and their *Comprehensive Grammar of the English Language* (1985) acknowledge some dialectal and stylistic variation in English but in general they describe the English language as a more or less homogeneous entity. Biber *et al.* (1999), on the other hand, in their *Longman Grammar of Spoken and Written English* focus centrally on the differences between spoken and written English and between different genres of written English, such as news language, academic discourse, and the language of fiction. English is no longer seen as a homogeneous entity. The heterogeneity is foregrounded and taken seriously.

The early work in pragmatics also depended to a large degree on the (implicit) assumption of a language as a more or less homogeneous entity. Pragmaticists were perhaps not particularly quick to pick up the trend set by sociolinguists to focus on variability and heterogeneity in language. The reason for this may be the fact that sociolinguists largely concentrated on phonological variation, variation that was taken to imply no difference in the meaning of what was said, i.e. on different ways of saying the same thing. Pragmaticists, on the other hand, were explicitly interested in the meanings of what was said, i.e. in elements that were more difficult to contrast. And in fact, it was in contrastive pragmatics that pragmatic units were first compared in different varieties, or rather – at least initially – in different languages. Contrastive pragmatics grew out of a very active research tradition of contrastive linguistics. An early volume was Oleksy (1989), which combined articles that discuss the possibility of contrasting pragmatic entities, e.g. speech acts, across different languages and different cultures. Several papers deal with compliments and investigate the realization of this particular speech act in different cultures. Krzeszowski (1989), one of the papers in that volume, discusses the problem of contrastive studies from a more theoretical angle, viz. the choice and the status of a specific *tertium comparationis* or the notion of equivalence "since only equivalent elements across languages are at all comparable" (Krzeszowski 1989: 59). Some aspect of the construction under investigation has to stay constant across the different contexts in which it is to be compared. Several of the other papers in the same volume focus on praising, complimenting, and responses to compliments and compare these speech acts across different cultures and languages, e.g. Polish and English.

A distinction must be made between contrastive and intercultural pragmatics. Contrastive pragmatics sets out to compare interactive patterns in different cultures, while intercultural pragmatics focuses on the interactions between members of different cultures. In both cases culture is often understood in a very wide sense and can refer to linguistic differences between groups of people, to generational differences, to social differences, or to gender differences. Generalizations across such groups are difficult and tend to lead to stereotyping, but statements about differences between the groups or about interactional problems that occur in conversations between members of different groups depend on generalizations for entire groups.

In fact, earlier work in intercultural pragmatics often set out to identify problem areas in the interaction between members of different cultures and how these could lead to misunderstandings (see, for instance, Scollon and Scollon 2001). In recent years, however, the field has moved on to look "beyond misunderstandings," to use the formulation of the title of a volume edited by Bührig and Ten Thije (2006). The focus has moved away from merely looking at the factors that prevent understanding to a close analysis of the processes that lead to mutual understanding. Moreover, recent work in intercultural pragmatics no longer accepts the essentialist assumptions that speakers belong to or have a particular culture and as such are at the mercy of the peculiarities of this culture. Cultural assumptions are constructions that are jointly created and re-created by large groups of people.

These groups are too large to be "real" groups (i.e. no group member will ever know all the other group members). Therefore, they are best considered as discursive constructions. That means that we do not have culture but that we construct culture discursively. (Piller 2007: 211)

There is also a noticeable body of work on pragmatic differences between different groups of speakers of the same language, most notably on the differences between the genders. The papers in a volume edited by Tannen (1993a), for instance, focus on gender-related patterns in conversational interaction. Holmes (1995) and Mills (2003) investigate the differences in politeness behavior between men and women.[3] Holmes uses data collected in New Zealand and focuses on the ways in which men and women use hedges and boosters, and how they pay compliments or apologize, while Mills develops a model of the complex relation between gender and politeness in order to challenge the stereotype that women are more polite than men. Beeching (2002) focuses on the same stereotype but she uses French data, and she uses four pragmatic particles, *c'est-à-dire (que)*, *enfin*, *hein*, and *quoi* for her argumentation.

Recently, there has been a growing interest in some of the other dimensions of language-internal variation of pragmatic entities. Schneider and Barron (2008a) have given this field of investigation its own name, "variational pragmatics," which they see as a field at the intersection of pragmatics and dialectology. Schneider and Barron (2008b), in the introduction to their volume, develop a framework for variational pragmatics in which they envisage five types of language variation as possible dimensions of investigation: regional, socio-economic, ethnic, gender, and age variation. The articles in their volume provide case studies of regional variation and contrast the realization of requests in corner-shop transactions in Ecuadorian Andean Spanish and Coastal Spanish (Placencia 2008), for instance, or the realizational patterns of small talk in England, Ireland, and the USA (Schneider 2008).

### 24.6.4 From synchrony to diachrony

The last paradigm shift to be briefly outlined is the shift from a strictly synchronic analysis of language to a dynamic and diachronic analysis. In fact, de Saussure's clear-cut distinction between synchronic and diachronic linguistics has given way to an understanding of language as a dynamic system in which older and newer forms co-exist and any description of language has to take its history seriously. As a result historical linguistics has grown in importance, and at the same time it has extended its interests from the confines of the core areas of linguistic investigation, such as phonology, morphology, syntax, and semantics, to wider investigations of the history of the use of language.

The growing interest in language history coincided with the growing interest in the compilation of computerized corpora. This combination led to the Helsinki Corpus, which combines a large selection of historical English texts covering the period from about 750 to 1700 and a broad range of different text genres (see for instance the papers in Rissanen, Kytö and Palander-Collin 1993). This general-purpose diachronic corpus was soon followed by more specialized diachronic corpora, for instance the Corpus of Early English Correspondence (1403–1800) or the Corpus of Early English Medical Writing (1375–1800). The availability of such corpora, at least for the English language, was the basis for an unprecedented proliferation of work in historical linguistics. Much of the work was sociolinguistically inspired, e.g. Nevalainen and Raumolin-Brunberg (2003), Taavitsainen and Pahta (2004), Nevala (2004), and Nurmi and Palander-Collin (2009).

At the same time some pragmaticists started to turn their attention to a larger range of empirical data. They insisted no longer on the native speaker intuitions of language philosophers or on the faithful transcriptions of aurally recorded conversational data. Instead they started to accept various forms of written language as legitimate and useful data for investigation. Thus, the formation of historical pragmatics as a new branch of pragmatics in the 1990s can be seen as the direct result both of the paradigm shifts in linguistics in general and the shifts within pragmatics. Jucker 1995 was an early volume that gave the new field a focus. Since then historical pragmatics has established itself with its own journal (*Journal of Historical Pragmatics*), a large range of monographs, collected volumes, and recently a substantial handbook (Jucker and Taavitsainen 2010).

In the meantime, historical pragmatics has established itself as a vigorous and lively branch of pragmatic research, which sees itself as a field of enquiry that investigates patterns of language use in earlier periods, the diachronic development of such usage patterns, and pragmatic explanations for language change in general (see Taavitsainen and Fitzmaurice 2007 and Taavitsainen and Jucker 2010 for recent overviews).[4]

Patterns of language use in earlier periods have often been studied on the basis of fictional data, for instance the writings of Geoffrey Chaucer (see Pakkala-Weckström 2010 for an overview) or of William Shakespeare (see Busse and Busse 2010 for an overview). Such work often looks at the use of pronominal and nominal terms of address, at other features of politeness, at the use of specific speech acts or interjections. For historical pragmaticists, such data are not imperfect renderings of actual language use but a type of data that warrants a careful pragmatic analysis on its own terms. Courtroom data and personal correspondence have also regularly been used for pragmatic analyses. Culpeper and Kytö (2010) offer a recent account of historical conversational data. Their studies are based on their own *Corpus of English Dialogues 1560–1760*, which comprises data from trial proceedings, witness depositions, plays, fiction, and didactic works.

Historical pragmatics has developed quite considerably from its beginnings in the 1990s and from more incidental earlier work; and this history reflects developments and paradigm shifts in linguistics in general.

## 24.7   Pragmatics of the future

Pragmatic research in the first decade of the twenty-first century has been characterized by an unprecedented diversification of subfields of pragmatics. This is particularly true for the Continental European tradition of pragmatics, and as such it was perhaps inevitable. If pragmatics is seen as a perspective, as a particular way of doing linguistics in general, it is not surprising that it starts to colonize more and more of what used to be subfields of linguistics. Research interests and research methods of earlier subfields of linguistics were extended to encompass a pragmatic perspective as well. And at the same time, pragmatics extended its scope to encompass research questions and research methods that had earlier been used by other fields of linguistics. In many cases relevant pragmatic work in these fields started in the 1990s or even 1980s, but it was often only in the twenty-first century that the fields constituted themselves in a more recognizable and coherent way, as for instance in the case of variational pragmatics or corpus pragmatics.

The paradigm shifts that affected linguistics in general to some extent constituted the field of pragmatics and to some extent shaped it in specific ways. In the previous section I have outlined in separate histories what appear to be the most important of these shifts. In reality, these shifts overlap and converge in the trends that are discernible. To take just one example, historical pragmatics clearly depends on the shift from a study of native speaker competence to a study of language use, as there are no historical speakers whose native language competence could be described. This also necessitates the use of empirical methods of investigation and within the empirical methods a reliance on corpus-based methods. Such investigations focus much more on the heterogeneity and variability of the data than on the homogeneity. And the shift from synchrony to diachrony is just as constitutive of historical pragmatics as the shift from the description of language competence to a description of usage patterns.

But what will the future development of pragmatics look like? What might a gaze into the crystal ball reveal about the pragmatics of the future? It is difficult to extrapolate from current developments into how it might develop in the future. However, a few things can be predicted quite confidently. Pragmatics is a very strong field of scientific enquiry, and as such it will continue to grow. At the moment, the distinction between the narrower conceptualization of Anglo-American pragmatics and the broader, socially and culturally informed variety of Continental European pragmatics is still clearly discernible. This was already pointed out some thirty years ago by Levinson (1983: 2). It does not seem likely, therefore, that this difference will be given up in the foreseeable future.

Over the last two decades, personal computers, the internet, and the mobile phone have radically changed the way many people communicate with each other. These technical innovations have added new forms of spoken and written communication from email messages, short text messages, and written chat to skype conversations, tweets, weblogs, and various forms of communication in virtual worlds and internet-based social networks. In recent years the flood of pragmatic analyses of these new forms of communication has grown steadily (see, for instance, Crystal 2001, 2008; Barnes 2003; Locher 2006; Heyd 2008). It is to be expected that the pragmatics of computer-mediated communication has an enormous potential for future growth.

There is very likely to be a continuing and perhaps accelerating diversification of approaches within pragmatics. Cooperation between traditional fields of linguistics and pragmatics will continue. Historical pragmatics, which combines historical linguistics and pragmatics, and variational pragmatics, which combines dialectology and pragmatics, have been mentioned above. Both of them are very promising fields with a vast range of research opportunities. Corpus pragmatics is another such field that has only recently constituted itself and that has enriched pragmatics with a new set of research tools that offer exciting perspectives for exploring new and as yet uncharted pragmatic territory.

# 25

# Semantics without pragmatics?

Emma Borg

Philosophers of language (following the seminal work of Paul Grice) often distinguish two types of linguistic content: literal or semantic content (usually discussed in the context of sentences) and pragmatic content or speaker meaning (usually discussed in the context of utterances). For instance, imagine I come to tea at your house and, on entering the kitchen, utter the following sentence:

(1)   The cake on the table looks delicious.

Traditionally, since (1) is a well-formed sentence of a natural language, many theorists have been inclined to think that there is a proposition expressed by the sentence which gives its literal meaning. So, at least at a first approximation, (1) might be held to literally express the proposition that

(2)   *the cake on the table looks delicious.*

However it also seems that, by uttering this sentence in this specific context, I may well succeed in conveying an alternative or additional proposition (or propositions). So, for instance, in this situation I may succeed in conveying a further proposition like:

(3)   I would like to have a slice of that cake.

It might initially be tempting here to think that what we have is one kind of content – the literal meaning in (2) – which is entirely *independent* of a context of utterance and another – the pragmatic speaker meaning – which is entirely *dependent* on the context of utterance. If this were right, we could construe semantic content as context-invariant content and speaker meaning as that which covaries with changes in the context of utterance, and we could expect a semantic theory to be freed from any appeal to pragmatics.

Holding that semantic content is context-invariant might seem to be worthwhile for a number of reasons. First, there might be negative reasons concerning the complex, holistic and perhaps rather nebulous nature of pragmatics itself: it might be thought, as Chomsky has suggested, that the search for a theory of pragmatics is a search for 'a theory of everything' and this might speak in favour of isolating a context-invariant kind of content as that which stands a chance of being theoretically tractable. Second, on the positive side it seems that aspects of our linguistic competence point to a need for context-independent content. For instance, it seems we need there to be a stable, invariant core to linguistic meaning to ensure the learnability of natural languages. If *all* aspects of linguistic meaning are in constant contextual flux it is entirely unclear how anyone could ever come to acquire a language in the first place. Furthermore, we might think that we need a context-invariant element to capture the apparently normative dimension to linguistic meaning: the fact that there is such a thing as using a sentence correctly or incorrectly.[1]

Finally, and perhaps most compellingly, context-invariant content seems to be needed to explain features of our linguistic ability like productivity and systematicity.[2] Respectively, these are the ideas that an ordinary subject is capable of understanding an indefinite number of novel sentences and that our patterns of linguistic understanding have a systematic character (so that, for instance, a subject who understands 'Bill loves Jill' will also, *ceteris paribus*, understand 'Jill loves Bill'). This ability to understand sentences we have never encountered before and to manipulate and reconstruct words to form novel yet meaningful arrangements would be explained if the semantic content of sentences was fully determined by the meanings of words and their modes of syntactic composition. This is the constraint of compositionality and although exactly how it should be spelt out is a tendentious matter, still it seems to point to a need for a discrete, recursively definable and essentially context-independent level of semantic content.[3] There are, then, it seems, reasons to think that a semantics free from pragmatics could be explanatorily worthwhile and this view of semantics (as essentially a rule-driven, recursive, context-independent level of content, required to explain features of our understanding like productivity and systematicity) has formed a starting point for so-called formal semantics.[4]

However a moment's reflection shows us that there are significant issues with carving things up in exactly this way, for at least part of what we might intuitively think of as the literal content of some sentences apparently depends on the context in which those sentences are uttered. So, for instance, in our imagined case above, I might, instead of uttering (1), have uttered:

(4)     That looks delicious.

(4) contains an overtly context-dependent expression ('that') whose semantic contribution is only fixed relative to a context of utterance (the referent of a token of 'that' can vary from utterance to utterance). Thus sentences like (4) seem to show the initial idea of treating semantic content as entirely context-independent was mistaken. Furthermore both (1) and (4) are tensed sentences and as such will require a context of utterance to relativise the claims they

express to a specific time. Thus even for sentences like (1) the idea of a 'pure', entirely pragmatics-free semantics looks dubious on reflection.[5]

There are, however, two responses available to an advocate of formal semantics in light of this recognition of an essentially context-dependent element within natural languages. One option would be to admit that these elements of meaning, since they depend on a context of utterance, should be classified as falling *outside* the remit of semantics, being treated instead as elements of pragmatic speaker meaning. In this way, one could hang on to the idea of a pure semantics without pragmatics but at the apparent cost of sacrificing the assumption that what semantics trades in is propositional content. For on this model, features like the disambiguation of ambiguous terms or structures, the resolution of reference for demonstratives and indexicals, and the relativisation to a time for tensed sentences, along with genuine implicatures like (3) above, would all fall on the pragmatic side of the divide. Yet if resolution of reference for a term like 'that' is not treated as part of semantics, then it is clear that what semantics delivers for a sentence like (4) ('That looks delicious') will not be something capable of truth evaluation as it stands. Rather it will be a propositional fragment or 'radical', something with a gap which requires filling prior to truth evaluation. As we will see later (with respect to Kent Bach's 'radical minimalism') this is an option at least some have been willing to pursue in the face of certain cases of context-sensitivity. However, it is I think fair to say that this quite drastic response has been the less popular of our two options. The more popular route has been to seek to 'tame' certain aspects of context-sensitivity and attempt to make them suitable for inclusion within formal semantics.

Perhaps the most well-known attempts to tame pragmatics come in the work of David Kaplan, John Perry and Robert Stalnaker, all of whom suggest formal frameworks for capturing at least some of the contributions context makes to linguistic meaning. So, for instance, in Kaplan's 1989a model, context is conceived of simply as an ordered set of relatively objective parameters (things like world of utterance, time of utterance, place of utterance, speaker etc.) and Kaplan specifies rules attaching to demonstratives and indexicals which allow us to supply a referent for any utterance of one of these expressions relative to the parameters set by its context of utterance. So for instance, we might specify a character rule for 'I' which demands that its value is always the speaker of an utterance or a rule for 'that' which specifies that it refers to the object demonstrated by the speaker. In this way, although we need to treat the semantic content of a sentence like (4) as fixed only relative to a context of utterance and thus not as entirely context-insensitive, still the only kind of appeal to a context of utterance from within the semantic domain appears to be a formally respectable one. It looks only to objectively set parameters and rules for operating over those parameters. This circumscribed and constrained notion of context and its place within the semantic domain has thus seemed to many to be non-threatening to the ethos of formal semantics.[6]

However, this idea that formal semantics has a plausible story to tell about the role of pragmatics in determining literal meaning has come under significant pressure from advocates of so-called 'radical pragmatics' (see, for instance, work by Jay Atlas and Ruth Kempson, also their contributions to this volume). What makes radical pragmatics radical, it seems, is the idea that rich pragmatic processes (that is to say, processes which might look to the whole breadth of a context and which are thus potentially open-ended and non-discrete in nature) must be treated as integral to the determination of literal linguistic meaning. On this model, full-blown pragmatics is not an optional add-on that takes one from literal meaning to implied speaker meaning, rather it pervades throughout what is standardly conceived of as the semantic realm. So, why might we think that the 'semantics plus tame pragmatics' model sketched above is inadequate? Why might one think that semantics is systemically infected by rich, open-ended pragmatic processes?

Well, a first point to note is that even for the expressions for which the above account was designed (indexicals and demonstratives) it is not absolutely obvious that the attempt to tame context works. So, as Predelli (1998b) and others have noted, determining the character rules for these expressions looks much more complicated than formal theorists traditionally assumed and in many (perhaps all) cases the rules seem necessarily to appeal to the speaker's intentions. For instance, note that a demonstrative may be used to pick out both objects in the current environment ('That cake looks tasty') and (via what is sometimes called 'deferred reference') objects merely related to those in the current environment (as when one points at a picture and says 'That artist is my favourite'). Or again, that indexicals like 'I' and 'now' may have a range of different referents (consider 'I am not here now' as said on a telephone answering machine, or written by a colleague and stuck on my door). Once we recognise these kinds of uses it becomes very tempting to think that the rule attaching to an expression like 'that' (or any other context-sensitive term) must itself make appeal to rich features of the context of utterance like the speaker's intentions. As Recanati writes:

> It is generally assumed . . . that the demonstrative refers to the object which happens to be demonstrated or which happens to be the most salient, in the context to hand. But the notions of 'demonstration' and 'salience' are pragmatic notions in disguise . . . Ultimately, a demonstrative refers to what the speaker who uses it refers to by using it. (Recanati 2004a: 57)

Yet if this is right then the idea that we have tamed context in the case of overt indexicals seems pretty suspect, for we still have rich, inferential contextual processes (required to work out to what the speaker intends to refer) in play within the semantic domain.[7] Thus the formal semanticists' idea that context be construed as a set of objectively determinable parameters seems mistaken.[8]

Perhaps more fundamentally, however, radical pragmatists have also stressed the idea of *semantic underdetermination*: the idea that the content which is recoverable on the basis of the meanings of words and their mode of composition alone often or always falls short of the content we take speakers to literally express when they utter that sentence. As they argue, if all we have to go on is the meaning of words (where this is construed in an atomic, context-independent way, see below) and the ways they are put together we will never deliver a semantics which is capable of tracking our intuitions of literal linguistic meaning. So for instance, take the following sentences:

(5)   Ted is tall.

(6)   Alfie's car is red.

In both of these cases the content we can recover simply from the lexico-syntactic content of the sentence seems to fall short of the literal content we would ascribe to someone who uttered one of these sentences. For instance, an utterance of (5) seems to literally commit the speaker to Ted's being tall relative to some contextually set standard (tall for a six-year-old, say), while in (6) we need to look to the context of utterance to discover the relationship between Alfie and his car (the car he owns, built, is driving, etc.) and the way in which it is red (on the inside or outside, etc.). In both these cases, then, there seems to be additional material relevant to literal content which is unmarked by anything at the syntactic or lexical level. Such additional elements, apparently provided to the semantic content of the sentences (though unmarked in the syntax or the lexical content) are commonly known as 'unarticulated constituents' and the form of systemic context-sensitivity they represent has been taken by the radical pragmatists to sound the death knell for any semantics which doesn't cede a central role to pragmatics. Context-sensitivity is not, as semantic underdetermination is supposed to show, an isolable, limited feature of a natural language but is instead an all-pervasive, core feature of linguistic meaning which demands proper semantic-level accommodation.

Radical pragmatists have tended to appeal to two main arguments to support the intuitive existence of unarticulated constituents.[9] First, it is argued that we have to posit unarticulated constituents in order to explain ordinary subjects' judgements of truth conditions. For instance, take sentence (5) and a state of affairs where Ted is 3ft tall: here it intuitively seems that an utterance of (5) might be true in a context where six-year-olds are under discussion, but will be false in another context, where Ted remains 3ft tall, but where basketball players are under discussion. Such a shift in truth values in conjunction with shifts in conversational contexts seems to reveal that, although not obvious on the surface, the sentence 'Ted is tall' must be context-sensitive in some more covert way (this kind of argument has been labelled a 'context-shifting argument' by Cappelen and Lepore 2005a).[10] The second argument for unarticulated constituents is that without them some sentences would apparently fail to determine propositions at all. So, consider:

(7)   Alfie is ready.

(8)   Ted has had enough.

In both of these cases it is plausible to think that we do not get a truth-evaluable content until we look to a context of utterance (seeing, respectively, what Alfie is ready for and what Ted has had enough of). So again it seems that we must posit hidden constituents of the propositions these sentences literally express.

Radical pragmatists are united, then, in claiming that the reach of context-sensitivity is much greater than formal semanticists have traditionally allowed. Beyond this, however, we find a fracturing into a myriad of different approaches. One might choose to accommodate an increased role for pragmatics within the semantic realm by being an indexicalist, a contextualist, a semantic relativist or an occasionalist, or adopting some combination of these different views (and note also that beneath these general headings we again find splintering into further distinct varieties). While the role accorded to pragmatics in each of these approaches is greater than in standard formal semantics, the role played by contextual features also differs in each, thus it will be helpful to have a rough sketch of these dominant schools of thought before us when considering the possibility of a semantics without pragmatics.

Indexicalism cleaves fairly closely to standard formal semantics in maintaining that all context-sensitivity is marked at the syntactic or lexical level and that the standard (e.g. Kaplanian) model for context-sensitivity is sufficient for accommodating the more pervasive kind of context-sensitivity highlighted in radical pragmatics. Thus, on this school of thought, 'unarticulated constituents', though potentially unarticulated at the surface level, are nonetheless held to be marked at the syntactic or lexical level. 'Ted is tall' literally means, say, that *Ted is tall for some contextual standard* but this is because a syntactic or lexical element in the sentence demands this contextual contribution. Indexicalism comes in many distinct forms, for instance there is the hidden indexical view of Stanley (2000 and elsewhere), whereby all nouns are taken to cohabit with hidden, context-sensitive variables at the level of logical form. Alternatively there is the predicate indexicality of Rothschild and Segal 2009, which sees all predicate terms as requiring context-sensitive lexical axioms which put them in the same semantic category as obviously context-sensitive terms like 'this' and 'that'. Finally there is the kind of property-indexicality displayed by Hawthorne's (2004) and Stanley's (2005) take on epistemic vocabulary, whereby a term like 'know' is held to pick out a context-sensitive property: a subject may know or fail to know a proposition depending on features of the context such as how much she has riding on the truth of the proposition. According to all these different versions of indexicalism, although there may be *more* context-sensitivity in our language than was dreamed of in traditional formal semantics, still it is essentially just *more of the same kind* of context-sensitivity as dealt with by Kaplan and others.

A second (and perhaps the most popular) variety of radical pragmatics is commonly known as 'contextualism'. What unites positions under this banner is, I'd suggest, the idea that pragmatics can contribute to semantics even when such a contribution is not required by anything in the lexico-syntactic content of the sentence. Thus the elements we above labelled 'unarticulated constituents' really do turn out to be unarticulated: they are delivered not by something in the syntactic form or lexical content of the sentence but are put there purely by the pragmatic demands in play when a speaker utters a given sentence in a given context.[11] So, for instance, the sentence 'Alfie's car is red', as uttered in a context c, might literally express the proposition that *the car which Alfie is driving is red*, even though the additional restriction *which he is driving* is not, apparently, contributed by any word or syntactic element in the sentence. On this new model rich pragmatic processes get to act *twice*: once, in an inherently semantic guise, *prior* to the determination of literal meaning and once in a standard, post-semantic manner to determine the implicatures of an utterance (hence the label of 'dual pragmatics' deployed in Borg 2004 for this kind of approach). Under the contextualist banner, then, it seems we find theorists such as Recanati (2004a), Relevance theorists like Sperber and Wilson (1986) and Carston (2002), and Discourse Representation theorists like Heim (1982) and Kamp (1981).

Though contextualism provides perhaps the most common current response to arguments for increased context-sensitivity, recently an alternative school of thought, that of semantic relativism, has enjoyed a growing popularity.[12] According to semantic relativism, the framework for handling context-sensitivity set up by theorists like Kaplan, Perry and Stalnaker is essentially sufficient for handling the increased context-sensitivity stressed in radical pragmatics (in this respect, then, the approach agrees with the earlier approach of indexicalism). What is required, however, is not an increase in contextual contributions to the propositions sentences literally express (as assumed in both indexicalism and contextualism), rather what is required is an increased contextual contribution to the conditions under which a proposition is evaluated for truth. The move here is easiest to appreciate via a consideration of possible treatments of tense: on one model, that of eternalism, time forms an integral part of the proposition expressed by a tensed sentence. So if I say, at $t_1$, 'Obama is president of America' the proposition I literally express is taken to have three constituents: Obama, the property of being president of America, and the time $t_1$. On the other hand, according to temporalism, there are only two elements of the proposition I literally express in this case, namely Obama and the property of being president. However by uttering the sentence at $t_1$ I make it the case that the proposition I express should be evaluated for truth or falsity only relative to $t_1$. Eternalism and temporalism both yield exactly the same results in practice (a proposition will be true or false in all the same situations whichever model it is analysed under); what differs is simply whether time is treated as making a contribution to the literal proposition expressed or to the parameters required for truth evaluation. Advocates of semantic relativism suggest that temporalism is the correct treatment for tense and they seek to extend this general strategy (of moving contextually determined content out of the proposition expressed and into the parameters for truth evaluation) to the other kinds of context-sensitivity noted above.[13] In this way, an utterance of, say, 'Ted is tall' is taken to express the proposition that *Ted is tall simpliciter* but this proposition is held to be true or false only relative to a contextually determined parameter of tallness.

Finally, perhaps the most radical move in the light of the systemic contribution of context argued for by radical pragmatists is to throw everything (or almost everything) open to the pragmatic winds and adopt the kind of neo-Wittgensteinian approach advocated by Charles Travis (see Travis 2008 amongst other works, also Dancy 2004; ch. 11). On the occasionalist approach, representation itself occurs only within a context of use and for a purpose, determinacy of meaning is thus a property only of an utterance or an act of thinking:

> The point of the discussion of language games, with which [*Philosophical Investigations*] begins, is that naming, or referring . . . underdetermines conditions for correctness of wholes, notably, where relevant, conditions for their truth. Wholes with given referents, embedded in different language games, would be true under any of many very different sets of conditions . . . [T]rue and false are in the first instance evaluations of particular historical events – speakings of words on particular occasions, in particular circumstances – and of the fittingness of the words for those circumstances. (Travis 2008: 254)[14]

For the occasionalist, words essentially require application in a context of use to fix their meaning; though words might possess some kind of open-ended, holistically specified meaning this could at most serve to constrain, rather than determine, the truth conditions of any sentence in which they appear (see Pietroski 2005).

All of these diverse accounts meet the apparent need elaborated by radical pragmatics of treating contextual input to linguistic content as more pervasive and systemic than traditionally assumed. However, I think it is fair to say that all the approaches also face significant difficulties further down the road and it remains an open question as to whether these difficulties can ultimately be overcome.[15] Thus alongside this plethora of positions which embrace the core idea of radical pragmatics (that pragmatic processes must reach well within the semantic domain), there has also emerged an alternative school of thought which we could perhaps characterise as 'radical semantics'. According to the radical semanticist the fundamental move of standard formal semantics to eliminate or strictly constrain the input of pragmatics to semantics is essentially correct and we should fight to maintain clear blue water between literal meaning, on one side, as substantially context-independent, and speaker meaning on the other, as essentially context-dependent. This idea of a return to a semantics which is to a large extent free from contextual input forms the cornerstone of minimal (or sometimes 'invariant' or 'insensitive') semantics.

According to minimal semantics, sentences express minimal contents (say minimal propositions or minimal truth conditions), which are recoverable via a grasp of word meaning and sentence structure alone and which do not require significant appeal to a context of utterance prior to their recovery. The minimalist recognises, as radical pragmatics suggests, that such contents will (often) not match our intuitions about what a speaker uttering a given sentence is likely to convey. So, for instance, a minimalist might claim that the sentence 'Alfie's car is red' literally expresses the proposition that *the car bearing some relation to Alfie is red in some respect*, even though it is clearly the case that what a speaker uttering this sentence conveys will be a much more fine-grained and informative proposition. However, the minimalist argues that a semantic theory need not and indeed should not be required to track our intuitive judgements of what is said. This is because judgements of speech act content are too variable and various to help in isolating a notion of genuinely semantic content (see e.g. Borg 2004: ch. 2; Cappelen and Lepore 2005a). Minimalists suggest that although the process of recovering speaker meaning clearly involves some kind of grasp of genuinely semantic content, this forms only a tiny part of the story about how speech act content is recovered – judgements of speech act content are massive interaction effects which might, in principle, call on anything the hearer knows. Furthermore, the minimalist claims that there is no way to start with rich attributions of what is said by a speaker and somehow move to abstract out an account of semantic content from there. Instead, she suggests, we should start with the central requirements on a semantic theory (for instance, the requirement to accommodate features of our linguistic comprehension like productivity and systematicity) and then allow the theory thus determined to dictate the boundary between semantic and pragmatic content.

As with most of the other positions in this area, minimalism does not have a single canonical form and the approach has been understood in a number of ways in recent works. So, for instance, the minimalism of Cappelen and Lepore (2005a) differs in certain key respects from the minimalism of Borg (2004) (these differences are discussed in Borg 2007 and Borg forthcoming: ch. 3), while the 'radical minimalism' of Kent Bach differs from both of these (we'll return to Bach's position below). However, one way to understand minimalism (as given in Borg forthcoming) is as the conjunction of the following four claims:[16]

(i)   Semantic content for declarative sentences is truth-evaluable content.
(ii)  Semantic content for declarative sentences is fully determined by syntactic structure and lexical content: the meaning of such a sentence is exhausted by the meaning of its parts and their mode of composition.

(iii)   There are only a limited number of context-sensitive expressions in natural language.

(iv)   Recovery of semantic content is possible without access to current speaker intentions (crudely, grasp of semantic content involves 'word reading' not 'mind reading').

This sort of approach seeks to capture the old-fashioned idea that semantic content is that content recovered via lexico-syntactic interpretation alone, with context playing a role only where there are explicit lexico-syntactic items which require such an input. Furthermore, the claim is that there are only a limited number of genuinely (i.e. lexico-syntactically marked) context-sensitive expressions in our natural languages and that the features these context-sensitive elements call into play are themselves pretty limited (specifically, they do not involve substantial appeal to the current mental states of speakers). What we have on the minimal semantics approach then is not semantics without pragmatics (since it allows for some genuinely context-sensitive expressions) but it is semantics with a very constrained role for context at the semantic level: only what we might think of as 'formal pragmatics' can find a home within the semantic domain according to the tenets of (this version of) minimalism.

There are, however, at least three problems which minimalism, with its appeal to the tamest of tame pragmatics, faces. These are, first, the problem of inappropriateness, second incompleteness, and third internalism.[17] According to the challenge of inappropriateness, though there might be such things as minimal propositions, any such entities are explanatorily redundant: they are not psychologically real and play no part in an account of the communicative success of ordinary interlocutors. This challenge emerges, on the one hand, in the kind of context-shifting arguments we looked at above which seek to show an intuitive change of truth value for distinct utterances of a type-identical sentence uttered with respect to a single state of affairs (so that 'Ted is tall' might be true in a conversation about 6-year-olds but false in a conversation about basketball players). Yet this intuition of shifts in truth value is apparently problematic if we take the sentence 'Ted is tall' to express a univocal, context-independent content like *Ted is tall simpliciter*. The minimal content assigned to this sentence thus seems inappropriate given our intuitions about the content speakers express when they utter the sentence. The challenge of inappropriateness also emerges in Recanati's (2004a) 'availability principle', whereby semantic content is required to be consciously accessible by normal interlocutors in a conversational exchange. As Recanati writes:

> What is said [i.e. literal meaning] must be intuitively accessible to the conversational participants (unless something goes wrong and they do not count as 'normal interpreters'). (Recanati 2004a: 20)

It seems that minimal propositions do not meet this availability constraint: the hearer presented with an utterance of 'Alfie's car is red' will certainly not consciously entertain the proposition that *the car related to Alfie in some way is red in some way*; rather they will directly entertain a more fine-grained proposition such as *the car Alfie is holding is red on its roof*. Since minimal propositions apparently have no role to play in explaining successful communicative exchanges, then, Recanati suggests that they are ruled out as the proper subject matter of semantics.

The second challenge to minimal contents is that of incompleteness. This is a potentially more powerful objection to minimalism than inappropriateness; for whereas the inappropriateness objection allows that minimal propositions might exist (though objecting that they have no useful role to play), the incompleteness objection argues against the very existence of minimal contents. The argument from incompleteness is that, for at least some well-formed sentences, there is simply no proposition to be recovered prior to rich pragmatic input. The paradigm examples in play here are sentences like 'Ted is ready' or 'Alfie has had enough', where it seems that we only reach the level of propositional, truth-evaluable content once we know from a context of utterance what Ted is ready to do or what Alfie has had enough of. Cases like these are thus supposed to demonstrate that the minimalist picture, whereby all well-formed declarative sentences are capable of expressing propositional content prior to rich contextual input, is wrong.

The final challenge to minimalism we will consider here comes from arguments against the kind of atomic, context-independent, referential view of word meaning we find inherent in minimalism (and in favour of the kind of radically context-sensitive view of word meanings found in Travis and others). According to the minimalist, word meanings together with appropriate syntactic structure are sufficient to determine a proposition, so whatever word meanings are they must be the kinds of things which, when appropriately plugged together, are sufficient to result in a truth-evaluable claim. So, the working model might be that our lexicon contains axioms of the following kind:

'Barack Obama' refers to Barack Obama

'red' refers to the property of being red/is true of red objects

However, Chomsky and others have argued that these kinds of simplistic, broadly referential axioms are not possible, since the entities supposed on either side of the reference relation either fail to exist or are the wrong kind of entities for a systematic semantics to employ (see Chomsky 2000, Collins 2009). So, for instance, consider polysemous expressions: 'book' can pick out a concrete object ('the book weighs one pound') or an abstract entity ('the book she is planning will revolutionise the subject'), while 'lamb' can refer to an animal or its meat, and 'good' seems to mean different things in 'a good meal' and 'a good friend' (see also Allan, this volume). Even simple referring terms have, on reflection, an apparently wide sphere of reference: 'London' can refer to a location ('London is east of Reading'), a population or area ('London is bigger than Barcelona'), a form of government ('London has ten county councils') and more besides (see Chomsky 2000). So the idea that we can adopt simple lexical entries like 'London' refers to London, then, must be rejected; in all cases, it turns out, words lack the kind of context-invariant, referential meanings that would be required to underpin the claim that sentences are capable of expressing truth-evaluable content prior to rich pragmatic processing. Thus the idea of a semantic theory which makes use of only tame pragmatics must be rejected.

Clearly, then, there is much work for a minimalist to do if she is to sustain her claim that a semantics which utilises only 'tame' pragmatics remains a viable option. In brief, however, we might note that there are responses the minimalist can make to the challenges above. First, in answer to the concerns of inappropriateness, she might argue that minimal propositions *do* have an explanatory role to play, for instance they have a role to play as fallback content (the content which is guaranteed to be recoverable in a communicative exchange even if something goes wrong with a hearer's grasp of context); see Borg 2007. Furthermore, she might contend that minimal propositions *are* psychologically real as they are what a psychologically realised semantic theory is capable of delivering; see Borg 2009a. Finally, with respect to context-shifting arguments, she might deploy a range of manoeuvres, from claiming that some cases do reveal genuine, syntactically marked context-sensitivity, to arguing that the phenomenon in question is purely pragmatic in nature (i.e. concerns judgements of pragmatic speaker meaning, not literal sentence meaning).[18]

Second, in response to arguments for incompleteness, it seems the minimalist has two distinct options: on the one hand, she might simply deny the claim that intuitions of incompleteness demonstrate that a sentence fails to express a proposition. To support this claim she might point out, as Cappelen and Lepore (2005a) have stressed, that the kind of behaviour theorists standardly appeal to to show that a sentence like 'Ted is ready' is incomplete is actually behaviour common to all sentences, including those where we have absolutely no intuitions of semantic incompleteness. If this is right, then whatever discomfort we feel with the sentence 'Ted is ready' can't be due to its semantic incompleteness, at the risk of then having to take all sentences to be semantically incomplete. The second line the minimalist might take in response to arguments of incompleteness is to stress once again (as noted above with respect to inappropriateness arguments) that there are several distinct lines of response open to the minimalist in the face of putatively problematic cases, ranging from accepting some cases as genuine instances of lexico-syntactically marked context-sensitivity through to providing a purely pragmatic solution, and that this range of responses taken together may be able to dissolve the challenge of putatively incomplete sentences.

Finally, with respect to the third challenge (from Chomsky-style semantic internalism), there are two parts to any successful defence of minimalism. First, the minimalist needs to show that the arguments Chomsky and others have given against the kind of simple, atomic, referential lexical axioms the minimalist assumes can be defused.[19] Second, she needs to show that the minimalist approach itself is well equipped to accommodate the kinds of features which Chomsky and others have drawn attention to as motivating their context-sensitive view of word meaning (for instance, properties like synonymy and polysemy, and patterns of apparently semantically dictated syntactic distribution); see Borg forthcoming: ch. 6. These two tasks remain pressing and it is, I think, this debate about the different accounts of word/concept content which underlie the opposing approaches that will form the next key battleground for debates between radical semanticists and radical pragmatists.

In closing, however, let's return to an option we noted at the very start of this chapter, namely the possibility of a semantics totally free from pragmatics. In the face of issues about the apparently all-pervasive nature of context-sensitivity and the difficulty of taming pragmatics so as to make it suitable for formal semantics, perhaps the best option for the advocate of formal semantics here would be to retreat, to claim that all her semantic theories concern is the kernel of (often or always) non-propositional content which lies at the heart of any natural language sentence. This would be to deny the first clause of minimalism above, the idea (labelled 'propositionalism' in Bach 2006b) that all well-formed declarative sentences express propositions and to allow instead that semantic theories often or always trade in non-truth-evaluable content, something sub-propositional. In favour of this move we should note that many of the motivations we gave for wanting a context-free semantics at the start of this chapter (concerns to do with learnability, say, and accounting for productivity and systematicity) seem to require only that there be *some element* of linguistic meaning which is context-insensitive, not that that context-insensitive element take us all the way to a truth-evaluable proposition. Or again, we might think that concerns about needing a context-insensitive, literal content to serve as 'fallback' content points only to the need for *some* context-insensitive content, not necessarily for that something to be as rich as a complete proposition. So perhaps the move to non-propositional views of semantic content is one worth pursuing?

One well-known advocate of non-propositional semantics is Kent Bach (e.g. this volume), who adopts what he calls 'radical minimalism' – radical precisely because it drops the commitment to semantic content being truth-evaluable content. In fact, however, Bach doesn't champion an entirely pragmatics-free semantics, for he holds that context does play some role in determining semantic content for some sentences. He draws a distinction between what he calls 'narrow' and 'wide' context and he maintains that terms which look only to narrow context have their reference fixed as part of semantics, while terms which look to wide context secure a referent only as part of pragmatics.[20] Thus for Bach, though a sentence like 'I am hot' yields a complete proposition via semantic analysis alone, a sentence like 'That is hot' fails to do so.[21] So, although Bach's radical minimalism is more radical than minimalism per se, it is not as radical as it might be since it doesn't offer us an entirely pure semantics, uninfected by pragmatic processes. However, let's leave this specific feature of Bach's approach to one side and concentrate on the more fundamental issue of treating semantic content for sentences as potentially non-propositional.[22]

A first point to note about this proposal is that taking this step is in fact, I think, pretty much equivalent to embracing some kind of contextualist view. For note that, on the contextualist picture there is still held to be an element of linguistic meaning which is entirely free from contextual input: this is the 'incomplete logical form' (in the terminology of Sperber and Wilson 1986) and concentration on, and theorising about, this partial element yields what Kempson (1986) calls 'linguistic semantics'. On both radical minimalism and contextualism, then, it seems we have three kinds of content: first, an incomplete, sub-propositional, context-invariant content (Bach's propositional radical, Sperber and Wilson's incomplete logical form), second, a pragmatically enriched complete proposition which in some sense gives the literal meaning of the speaker's utterance (Bach's *impliciture*, Sperber and Wilson's *explicature*); and, third, the further content a speaker may convey by her utterance (the Gricean implicatures).

Where the accounts differ then is, first, on the labels assigned to each stage: specifically, Bach treats his pragmatically determined implicitures as part of pragmatics, whereas contextualists treat their pragmatically determined explicatures as delivering literal meaning (see Sperber and Wilson 1986, Recanati 2004a). Second, the accounts differ on the range of cases where semantics may fail to yield something truly propositional. For Bach's radical minimalism, semantics in general may still deal with complete propositions, the claim is simply that with respect to a few exceptional cases (like 'Ted is ready') semantics alone will deliver something sub-propositional. Contextualists, on the other hand, as part of the radical pragmatics tradition, hold that context-free content will rarely, if ever, reach the level of the proposition, so that linguistic semantics in general must deal with propositional radicals. Yet these differences in terminology and in degree of application do not, it seems, amount to fundamental theoretical differences between the two approaches (for discussion of this point see Carston 2008).

However, this kind of *ad hominem* argument is clearly no objection to the move to treat semantics as truly context-free but also as sub-propositional. That the approach collapses into contextualism is a problem *only* if we have reason to think that contextualism itself is ill-advised and (although I think that is the case) I haven't argued for that here. Yet, even without opening the lid on contextualism, we can still, I think, raise initial questions for the idea of sub-propositional semantic content. For instance, it is not obvious that a gappy-proposition approach can accommodate the gradations of judgements subjects are apparently willing to make in these cases. So consider the following:

(9)   *Jack devours.

(10)   *Ready to take the exam.

(11)   Jack is ready.

Ordinary speakers judge (9) to be ill-formed. (10), it seems, is also judged ill-formed, at least where it is not heard as a question ('Are you . . . ?'). (11), on the other hand, is perfectly acceptable. Yet if what semantics delivers is gappy versus non-gappy contents we might wonder why the gaps in (9) and (10) lead to judgements of ill-formedness while the alleged gap in (11) leads at most to a judgement of incompleteness. We might also ask, I think, whether propositional radicals could really be sufficient to play the role of fallback content, whether they could capture our practice of giving reasons and explaining actions via declarative sentences, and whether they could underpin our intuitive assessment of arguments (as opposed to merely utterances of arguments) as valid.

Furthermore, we might also wonder how the non-propositional view can accommodate the intuitive distinction with which this chapter opened between literal meaning on one side and pragmatic, speaker meaning, on the other, for it is clear that an indefinite amount of information can be added to any propositional radical. Thus one might hold that the sentence 'Flintoff is ready', as uttered in some context c, expresses the proposition that *Flintoff is ready to bowl*, or that *Flintoff is ready to bowl the next cricket ball to Tendulker*, or that *Andrew Flintoff, the English all-rounder who hit nine sixes and took seven wickets in the Edgbaston test match against Australia in 2005, is ready to bowl the next cricket ball as a bouncer at the man with the highest number of test runs in any first-class cricket career prior to 2010*. If semantics gives us nothing but a gappy proposition we surely still want to ask which of these contextually provided fillings-in the speaker genuinely expresses or commits themselves to. Yet since we have given up the idea that what counts for literal content is what can be found at the lexico-syntactic level, it becomes quite unclear how we can isolate just one (or some) of all the possible expansions of a propositional radical as the one(s) that delivers literal meaning.

There are then, I think, issues still to be faced by someone who advocates sub-propositional semantics and my suspicion is that, ultimately, when we come to consider what we will lose by dropping the idea that semantics trades in proposition-level content it may come to seem that the game is not worth the candle. Jettisoning the traditional idea that sentences are capable of expressing propositions is likely to prove disruptive across a range of philosophical inquiries and the balance between this cost and the demands of radical pragmatists for a greater role for context within the semantic domain will need to be weighed very carefully.

Clearly, then, there remain crucial issues still to be resolved within this debate and the war is far from being won either by the radical pragmatists or by the radical semanticists, or indeed by those who favour some kind of middle road. Yet it is equally clear that the explosion of recent work on the semantics/pragmatics divide has, at least, done much to clarify where and how the battle lines should be drawn.

# 26

# The syntax/pragmatics interface

Ruth Kempson

## 26.1 Linguistic competence: Syntax/semantics/pragmatics

Throughout the last half century since Chomsky 1965, there has been whole-hearted acceptance of the distinction between the linguistic knowledge humans display, their linguistic competence, and the demonstration of their ability in speaking and hearing, viz. performance. Accordingly, concepts of competence have been articulated solely with respect to language *sui generis*, the sentences of any one language being analysable in terms of syntactic and semantic properties that are articulated in formally specified syntactic and semantic rules of grammar. Following a wholly uncontentious formalist methodology that linguistic theories must be expressible as formal models, these rules, together with rules of phonology, constitute that linguistic competence which any speaker is said to possess.

Once this perspective had been set up by Chomsky, it was taken up by semanticists and philosophers, who despite fundamental differences between different positions coincided on the assumption that the semantics of a natural language had to be given in terms of truth conditions for sentences of the language. Many turned to Richard Montague's formal programme for semantics (Montague 1974a) to provide a detailed formal articulation of what it means to attribute truth-conditional content to sentences of natural language. While there was disagreement as to the nature of syntax to be articulated, even amongst those making this move, the rampant display of ambiguity in natural languages led to very general acceptance of the view that syntactic properties of individual sentences had to be distinguished from a characterisation of their meaning. Moreover, early on, there emerged evidence from the so-called island constraints (Ross 1967) confirming the distinction between syntax and semantics, in virtue of the non-reducibility of island-restriction constraints to semantic considerations (Partee 1976: see also 26.2.2 below). And so, despite major exceptions,[1] it became part of the accepted wisdom that there had to be independent syntactic and semantic components of the grammar, with semantics providing an articulation of truth-theoretic content expressible, for example, by a model-theoretic formulation (Montague 1974a). Such a view was adopted by all those working within generalised phrase structure grammars (HPSG as it developed: Pollard and Sag 1994) and within LFG (lexical functional grammar) (Dalrymple 2001). Within these frameworks, all aspects of language that couldn't meet the methodological requirement of formalisability were taken to fall outside its remit. In particular, pragmatics, being dismissed as the wastebasket of non-formalisable aspects of language use (Bar-Hillel 1971, Kamp 1978), was taken at the time to be merely part of some poorly understood concept of linguistic performance.

Right from the early 1970s, with the publication of Lewis 1970 as part of this semantic programme, an additional objective has been to reflect the way in which understanding of words in combination systematically depends on aspects of the context in which they are produced. Nonetheless, it has been assumed that this can be made commensurate with the competence/performance distinction and the retention of the view of grammar as inducing a pairing of well-formed strings of the language with interpretation to be defined in some sense independent of considerations of use. Semanticists have indeed taken it as their task to articulate a formal articulation of context and how meanings of expressions combine to determine context-dependent interpretability (Lewis 1970, Kamp 1981, Kaplan 1989a, Kamp and Reyle 1993 and many others); and, increasingly, they have grappled with the need to invoke pragmatic aspects of content in semantic characterisations of compositionality where these involve articulating truth conditions (Partee 1999, Chierchia 2004). Pragmatists, on the other hand, along with psycholinguists, have had to take on board the restriction upon their own theorising that the input to performance models has to be whatever some defined grammar defines as output; and, for pragmatists, in particular, this is presumed to be some defined characterisation of sentence-meaning.

However, as our understanding of the systematicity of context dependence displayed by natural languages has deepened, this clean division between data which are properly within the remit of grammar to explain and those which fall outside it has become increasingly hard to sustain. The narrative history of pragmatics since the 1980s is indeed a story of the struggle pragmatists have engaged with, in virtue of presuming this to be an assumption which they must retain. Leaving aside the concept of particularised conversational implicature, which is relatively uncontentious in being outside what an utterance explicitly conveys (Grice 1975), the burden of determining the syntax/pragmatics interface concerns how much of what an uttered sentence conveys is determined internally to the grammar. There are, on the one hand, the instances of generalised conversational implicature which convey some putative implicature so standardly that they are said by some to constitute a default meaning of the expression itself (Asher and Lascarides 2003, Jaszczolt 2005). There is also the problem of conventional implicatures which are said to be an encoded aspect of the use of the word even though not part of the truth conditions conveyed by sentences in which it occurs. And since Grice's work (Grice 1989), there have been numerous variants of a broadly Gricean programme (see Horn and Ward 2004). Nonetheless, despite controversies arising from distinct classifications which the various categories have made available, the concept of sentence meaning as some weak specification of truth-conditional content that has to be enhanced in some way in context has remained a core underpinning to nearly all pragmatic theorising (though see Atlas 1988, Recanati 2004a). Even relevance theorists, with their championing of the gulf between what is encoded and what is only inferentially established, sustain as a concept of sentence meaning a concept of logical form for a sentence that constitutes information established by the grammar, such logical forms being taken by hearers as evidence for a process of enrichment (or other modulation) that yields some propositional form (Sperber and Wilson 1986, Carston 2002, Wilson and Carston 2007, Carston forthcoming). This has led to the debate known as contextualism, with Cappelen and Lepore (2005a) arguing against a group they dubbed 'contextualists' and in favour of a very weak concept of meaning corresponding to truth-conditional content for utterance meaning as well as sentence meaning, with advocacy of a much richer speech-act content as the requisite additional broader notion corresponding to everything that utterances can be taken to convey.[2] The ensuing debate between such contextualists and Cappelen and Lepore has led to fierce disagreements; and there isn't agreement between the various protagonists as to what context amounts to. Nevertheless, all contextualists agree (against Cappelen and Lepore) that there is more to utterance understanding than what some concept of sentence meaning can be seen to provide and, furthermore, that the content expressed by an utterance is due to some interaction between information provided by the grammar and pragmatic processes.

What is less commonly noted is that independent evidence is accumulating in syntax and semantics which equally undermines the clean division of labour between what the grammar formalism provides as output and what pragmatic processes determine. The phenomenon of ellipsis illustrates this particularly dramatically. Informally, ellipsis occurs when the required interpretation is recoverable from context without need of any explicit overt expression. Indeed, precisely because of the total lack of explicit verbal expression other than something to trigger the elliptical construal, ellipsis arguably provides direct evidence of what context amounts to. This makes ellipsis directly pertinent to the context-dependency debate, hence also a window on how the grammar/pragmatics interface should be articulated. One might then think that one could use comparative success in explaining ellipsis in an integrated way as a criterion for evaluating accounts of the grammar/pragmatics interface. However, this has not been realisable in practice. Not only do all accounts of ellipsis articulated from orthodox assumptions fail this criterion of evaluation but none even project ellipsis as providing any such yardstick. This is due to restriction on the remit of the grammar to sentence-internal properties only. Any phenomenon which is displayed both sentence-internally and across sentential boundaries will be bifurcated within this methodology; and ellipsis is certainly one such. Accordingly, some aspects of ellipsis are characterised grammar-internally, but others as an unrelated discourse phenomenon, with no unitary characterisation of ellipsis. Moreover, this problem is not an ellipsis-specific phenomenon. It applies equally to all context-dependent phenomena – ellipsis, anaphora, tense construal, domain selection etc. So it is a problem that lies at the core of explaining what it is that natural-language expressions encode that enables them to allow such flexibility in interpretation in context. As we shall see, there is a way to reinstate some reflection of the folk concept of ellipsis as being a window on the concept of context, but it involves redrawing the grammar/pragmatics boundary. And, in this chapter, we sketch the arguments as to why considerations of ellipsis lead to such a conclusion.

## 26.2   Ellipsis: Syntax vs semantics vs pragmatics

Taking a history-of-linguistics perspective, ellipsis is a remarkably accurate barometer of the way linguistic argumentation has developed over the past fifty years. First, ellipsis was presumed to be a syntactic phenomenon (Ross 1967); then a more inclusive semantic basis was identified (Dalrymple *et al.* 1991); and, most recently, pragmatic forms of ellipsis have been identified which resist either syntactic or semantic characterisations (Stainton 2006, Cann *et al.* 2007).

### 26.2.1   The syntactic basis for ellipsis

Ellipsis as an observable natural-language phenomenon was taken from early on in this period to fall within the remit of a competence theory of language. Conjoined sentences were used to display different elliptical forms in the second conjunct, whose interpretation in some sense matched that of the first conjunct; and with evidence that different forms of ellipsis were subject to somewhat different structural constraints, the distinct forms were taken to motivate distinct analyses involving distinct structures. For example, in transformational grammar (Ross 1967), deletion operations were proposed as part of syntax in order to yield the truncated form of the second elliptical conjunct by a process deleting that structure under some condition of identity with the structure of the antecedent conjunct (what has come to be known as PF deletion) (PF = phonological form):

(1)   John saw Mary, and so did Bill. (VP ellipsis)

(2)   John ignored Mary, and Tom Sue. (Gapping)

(3)   John ignored Mary. Tom too. (Stripping)

(4)   John ignored someone, but I don't know who. (Sluicing)

As part of this, there was recognition of a need to have mechanisms keep track of the bases of interpretation that were invoked through coindexing of expressions:

(5)   John$_i$ washed his$_i$ socks. And Bill did too./Bill too.

But problems emerged with the presumption that sentence strings should have indexing as part of the datum indicating mode of interpretation. Under this assumption, elliptical forms need two distinct indexings, even for a single interpretation. In particular, as (5) shows, the first sentence of (5) gives evidence of needing more than one type of indexing even under the indicated interpretation. This is because the elliptical fragment supposedly displaying the structure of the antecedent clause from which its interpretation is based can be construed either as Bill washed his own socks (the so-called 'sloppy' interpretation of ellipsis), or as Bill washed John's socks (the 'strict' form of ellipsis), thereby indicating two discrete indexings of its antecedent string, and hence ambiguity of structure in that antecedent relative to the one interpretation. Thus, on any such grammar-internal indexing, there have to be two distinct structural sources for the single form of interpretation of that antecedent string and hence deletion in the derivation of the second conjunct of distinct structures (Fiengo and May 1994 and many others). And this isn't the end of the problem, as sentences such as these in their turn led to the recognition that ellipsis is not simply a matter of deleting words in a string, even as indexed, as the appropriate construal may need to be grounded in some replacement of words, as in:

(6)   A: You're sitting on my chair. B: No I'm not.

What A and B are disagreeing about is whether B is sitting on A's chair, irrespective of the pronouns each uses to express that. Moreover, since syntax is defined in exclusively hierarchical terms, there is no basis for imposing a restriction of strict parallelism between the structure under deletion and the antecedent: this is granted to require independent stipulation (Fox 2002).

## 26.2.2   The semantic basis for ellipsis

This postulation of multiple ambiguities, and unclarity as to the level of structure over which the required concept of syntactic identity is defined, led semanticists in response to explore the use of formal-semantic tools for the projection of content directly from the surface sequence of the elliptical expressions. Dalrymple *et al.* (1991), in a very influential paper, defined a mechanism of construal which applied directly to the surface syntactic

structure displayed by the fragment expression itself to yield its interpretation, on the basis of the denotational content of the previous conjunct in the
paired coordinate structure. The VP ellipsis site, that is, is seen as projecting
a predicate variable whose value has to be identified with some predicate
constructible from the antecedent conjunct:

(7)   John sneezed and Bill did too.

The core idea is that ellipsis involves a semantic equation involving unification (called 'the higher-order unification account' because it involves
unifying predicates). The mechanism for achieving it is to construct some
appropriate lambda-defined predicate on the basis of the derived content
of the antecedent conjunct, by binding some position or positions within
it. This involves applying an abstraction operation to the content of the
antecedent conjunct, *John sneezed*, to yield a predicate abstract that could be
applied to the parallel subject, Bill, in the second, ellipsis-containing conjunct. A possible solution of the requisite equation for (7) that provides a
predicate to apply to the content assigned to Bill would be as follows:

(8)   $P = \lambda x.Sneeze'(x)$

The abstract $\lambda x.Sneeze'(x)$ is then predicated of Bill, yielding the overall parallel construal of both conjuncts. This process is not unrestricted: all selected
abstracts must involve a presumption of parallelism between first and second conjuncts, and this must involve one 'primary' argument – the subject; and either only that or the subject plus all occurrences of any pronouns construed in that antecedent clause as picking out the subject are
replaced in the construal of the second conjunct. Accordingly, (9) is ambiguous according to whether Bill is thinking of taking John's mother to John's
sister (the *strict reading*) or whether he is thinking of taking his own mother
to see his own sister (the *sloppy reading*), but there are not more readings
than this:

(9)   John is thinking of taking his mother to see his sister, and so is Bill.

(10)   = 'John is thinking of taking John's mother to see John's sister and
          Bill is thinking of taking John's mother to see John's sister'

          OR

(11)   = John is thinking of taking John's mother to see John's sister and
          Bill is thinking of taking Bill's mother to see Bill's sister.

This particular parallelism between conjuncts and the specification that
the subject must be involved are independent stipulations in this account.
Nevertheless, if we grant these stipulations, the result is, as can be seen in the
strict/sloppy interpretations, that we can derive non-identical resolutions for
ellipsis from a single semantic content, a clear advantage over any syntactic
account.

However, there is reason to doubt whether a semantic explanation could ever be complete. Not only are there problems about more complex VP ellipsis cases, but there is evidence that at least some instances of ellipsis must be reconstructed syntactically. This is because some cases display sensitivity to the island constraints that, in holding over structural configurations, are taken to be diagnostic of there being such structure. The most robust of these is the so-called Complex NP constraint (Ross 1967), which precludes co-dependency of some argument position within a relative clause and an expression external to that relative clause; and it is this restriction to which the case of ellipsis called antecedent-contained deletion (antecedent-contained ellipsis on the semantic form of explanation) appears to be subject to. That is, in this type of ellipsis, the ellipsis site itself is part of a relative, appearing to be recoverable from the very predicate within which it is contained, as in (12). However, what it cannot allow is any dependency across an additional intervening relative clause boundary; and this is taken to indicate sensitivity to the Complex NP constraint. This constraint cannot be expressed within a higher-order unification account because the unification operation is defined within lambda calculus terms, hence over denotational contents, and cannot make reference to structure-specific details.

(12)   John interviewed every student that Bill had.

(13)   *John interviewed every student that Bill ignored the teacher who had.

Hence the granting by semanticists that not all syntactic generalisations are reducible to semantic ones.

The sensitivity of some ellipses to such 'strong island' constraints is far from being the only type of syntactic specification to which elliptical construal has to be sensitive. In many languages, the fragment provided may bear a syntactic specification which the antecedent has to match in order to provide a well-formed pairing of fragment and content. For example, German elliptical fragments must bear the case appropriate to the verb and syntactic position that has to be reconstructed in order to resolve the ellipsis:

(14)   *Hat      er          nicht    den Brief      geschrieben?*
       has      he$_{NOM}$   not      the$_{ACC}$ letter   written
       'Didn't he write the letter?'

       *Nein.    Ich/*Mich.*
       no       I$_{NOM}$/I$_{ACC}$
       'No. I did.'

Thus, whatever the basis for ellipsis, it is seen as having to be sensitive at least to syntactic structure, and in languages with rich case morphology, also to morphological form.

### 26.2.3 Pragmatic forms of ellipsis

Finally, there are cases which appear to resist either syntactic or semantic accounts of ellipsis, requiring an independent pragmatic form of explanation. These are fragment expressions which do not fall into the pattern of using some clausal antecedent from which to build up interpretation (as both syntactic and semantic accounts require). Rather, these are freely interpreted from the utterance scenario directly:

(15)  A   (coming out of the lift): McWhirters?
      B:  Second on the left.
(16)  A   (seeing a woman enter): Sue's mother.

On the basis of evidence such as this, it has been argued in detail by Stainton (2006) that fragments of this type have to be seen as subsentential assertions. In consequence these cannot be taken as either syntactically or semantically of the type that corresponds to propositions, and the grammar itself is not sufficient to license them: some form of pragmatic reasoning has to be involved. There have been counter-arguments to this view proposing complex covert syntactic structure (Merchant 2010), but even if the force of Stainton's specific argumentation for such cases is accepted, it should be noticed that Stainton only takes his arguments to apply to these arguably peripheral cases, leaving all centrally argued cases of ellipsis intact as different forms of grammar-internal specifications, hence ambiguity. In sum, the consensus is that ellipsis is not a unitary phenomenon. Indeed the disparate nature of ellipsis construal has been graphically labelled its 'fractal heterogeneity' (Ginzburg and Cooper 2004). Ellipsis apparently makes use of whatever information the grammar may provide, with morphological, syntactic, semantic, even phonological information yielding different bases for ellipsis, a phenomenon suggestive of the need to employ a rich multi-level form of analysis.

The problem for all these accounts is that there is no commitment to an integrated explanation of the phenomenon of ellipsis itself. To the contrary, there is a plethora of ambiguities, apparently discrete structures, and failure to see just how context might be seen as providing input in each case of ellipsis construal. As with other context-dependency phenomena, it would seem that some forms of context-dependency can be characterised within the remit of the sentence-based grammar, while others cannot, so the phenomenon itself is necessarily bifurcated. The net effect is that context-dependency – arguably the core datum to be captured within any account of natural language understanding – continues to lack a principled explanation.

An alternative, more radical view that we now turn to is to take ellipsis and the range of types of construal it gives rise to as the right set of data for exploring context dependency as manipulated by natural languages. With this in mind, we turn back to a descriptive classification of the types of ellipsis construal to see what the range of data are.

### 26.2.4  Ellipsis: towards a unitary account

It is uncontroversial that ellipsis construal can become available through reiteration of content directly, for example, in strict interpretations of VP ellipsis where the construal of the antecedent VP and that of the ellipsis site are identical:

(17)   John saw Mary, and Tom did too.

In such cases, the immediate context for the construal of the fragment provides a predicate content for re-use without modification.

There are, in addition, cases where the fragment is an add-on to what is in the context, building on what has been started in the context. Question–answer pairs might be seen in this light:

(18)   A:   Where are you going?
       B:   To London.

The interpretation of (18) contains the construal of the entire containing structure of the question modulo the replacement of the wh-term by what is proffered as its answer. Question-and-answer exchanges are in fact illustrative of a very broad phenomenon displayed in dialogue, where speakers freely take over from their conversational partner, switching easily between the role of hearer and the role of speaker, with no restriction as to whether or not what is provided in context is a complete sentence in its own right as in (19) or not, as in (20).

(19)   A:   We're going to Casa Plana.
       B:   To show my mother what we've done there.
(20)   A:   We're going to . . .
       B:   (to) Casa Plana.

Just as in wh-question-and-answer pairs, the fragment in such subsentential cases has to be seen as a development of the structure made available in the immediate previous context. Each party is simply extending the structure they have just processed as a speaker/hearer, using that as their point of departure for the other processing mechanism to which they are switching.

Then there are cases where it appears to be only the PROCESS of building up interpretation that is replicated from context, leading to a different content, but established in the very same manner. These are the sloppy construals of VP ellipsis:

(21)   John washed himself. Sue refused to, until I told her she must.

As we have already seen, it is these that appeared to yield the need of ambiguity of structure for the antecedent in structural explanation. To add to the complications, there is interaction between such sloppy and strict ellipsis construals. For example, a single basis for interpretation established as sloppy can also be used to provide a strict construal of what follows as in an interpretation of (22) in which Harry thinks that Harry is a fool but Harry's wife doesn't think that Harry is a fool:

(22)   John thinks he's a fool. Harry does too, although his wife doesn't.

For such an interpretation, the first ellipsis site has to be sloppily construed, and on the syntactic account represented as such; but the second ellipsis site then presumes on that first ellipsis site taking the form of a strict construal. If we are to make sense of this interaction between types of interpretation, and yet retain an integrated perspective on context as providing the wherewithal in each case to establish the content of the fragment, we have to have a concept of context which is rich enough to encompass all of these as an integral part. In particular, such an account has not merely to allow for the attribution of structure to such a context, but also the dynamics of how interpretation is built up. For this, the novel framework of Dynamic Syntax provides a candidate formalism, for the core of the notion of structure it articulates is this very dynamics.

## 26.3   Dynamic Syntax

Dynamic Syntax (DS) is an avowedly representationalist model of inter-pretation and interpretation growth. It is a model of how interpretations, represented as binary tree-structures of predicate–argument form, are built up relative to context, and individual steps in this building process reflect the incrementality with which hearers (and speakers) progressively build up interpretations for strings using information from context as it becomes available. The core concept is that of underspecification and its update, with underspecification of structure as well as of content. Indeed, this process of building up structure is taken to be what constitutes the syntax of natural-language grammar. With the dynamics of structural growth built into the core grammar formalism, natural-language syntax is defined as a set of prin-ciples for articulating growth of such structures. Syntactic mechanisms are thus meta- to the representations themselves: they are procedures that define how parts of representations of content can be incrementally introduced and updated. Furthermore, all procedures for structural growth are defined rela-tive to context; and context is defined to be just as structural and dynamic as the concept of content with which it is twinned. Context, by definition, con-stitutes a record not merely of the (partial) structures built up, with the typed formulae that decorate them, but also the procedures used in constructing them (Cann *et al.* 2007: see also section 26.4 below). The bonus of such explicit adoption of representationalist assumptions and the shift into a perspective in which the grammar reflects key properties of the dynamics of how language processing takes place is, as we shall see, that a natural basis for a novel grammar/pragmatics articulation emerges that is fully commensurate with an integrated account of ellipsis and context-dependency more generally.

### 26.3.1  The tree logic and tree-growth processes

The general process of parsing is taken to involve building as output a tree whose nodes reflect the content of some uttered formula – in the simple case of a sentence uttered in isolation, a complete propositional formula. The input to this task, in such a simple case, is a tree that does nothing more than state at the root node the goal of the interpretation process to be achieved, namely, to establish some propositional formula. For example, in the parse of the string *John upset Mary*, the output tree to the right of the $\mapsto$ in (23) constitutes some final end result: it is a tree in which the propositional formula itself annotates the top node, and its various subterms appear on the dominated nodes in that tree rather like a proof tree in which all the nodes are labelled with a formula and a type (see below). The input to that process is an initial one-node tree (as in the tree representation to the left of the $\mapsto$ in (23)) which simply states the goal as the requirement to a formula of appropriate propositional type (shown by $?Ty(t)$, the '?' indicating that this is a goal not yet achieved):

(23)   John upset Mary.

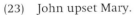

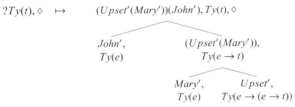

Parsing *John upset Mary*

These DS trees are invariably binary, and, by convention, the argument always appears on the left branch, and the functor on the right branch (a pointer *pointer*, $\diamond$, identifies the node under development). Each node in a complete tree is decorated not with words, but with terms of a logical language, these being subterms of the resulting propositional representation. The parsing task is to use both lexical input and information from context to progressively enrich the input tree to yield such a complete output following general tree-growth actions.

In order to talk explicitly about how such structures grow, trees need to be defined as formal objects; and DS adopts a (modal) logic of finite trees (LOFT: Blackburn and Meyer-Viol 1994).[3] The language of LOFT makes available not only a vocabulary for describing fixed tree relations, but also a basis for defining concepts of structural underspecification. Concepts of *dominate* and *be dominated by* are defined (using Kleene star operators), indicating some possible sequence of mother relations, or conversely a possible sequence of daughter relations; and these can be licensed even before there is some fixed number of such mother or daughter relations. For example, $\langle\uparrow_*\rangle T\,n(a)$ is defined as a decoration on a node indicating that somewhere dominating it is the node $Tn(a)$.[4] All that is determined is that the node in question must always be dominated by the $Tn(a)$ in any future developments of the tree. This structural underspecification is analogous to the more familiar underspecification displayed by anaphoric expressions, which are taken to project place-holding, metavariable formula decorations, to be substituted by pragmatic substitution actions from context. A second core concept in the explanation is that of requirements for update. This is essential to get appropriate reflection of the time-linearity involved in building up trees in stages (partial trees). For every node, in every tree, all aspects of underspecification are twinned with a concept of *requirement*, $?X$, for any annotation $X$ on a node; and these are constraints on how the subsequent parsing steps must progress. Such requirements apply to all types of decoration, so that there may be type requirements, $?Ty(t)$, $?Ty(e)$, $?Ty(e \to t)$ etc.; tree-node requirements, $?\exists x Tn(x)$ (associated with underspecified tree-relations), and formula requirements $?\exists x Fo(x)$ (associated with pronouns and other anaphoric expressions). These requirements drive the subsequent tree-construction process, because unless they are eventually satisfied the parse will be unsuccessful.

Such structural underspecification and update can then be used to define core syntactic notions in a way that follows insights from parsing, and the time-linear dimension of processing in real time. In particular, the long-distance dependency effects which, since the late 1960s, have been taken by most to be diagnostic of a syntactic component independent of semantics are recast in terms of structural underspecification plus update. For example, when first processing the word *Mary* in (24) below, which is initially construed as providing a term whose role isn't yet identified, the parse is taken to involve the application of a computational action which introduces from the initial root node decorated with $?Ty(t)$, a relation to that top node which is UNDERSPECIFIED at this juncture, identifiable solely as dominated by the topnode, and requiring type $e$, i.e. with requirement $?Ty(e)$:

(24)    Mary, John upset.

This enables the expression *Mary* to be taken to decorate this node: this is step (i) of (25).[5] Accompanying the underspecified tree relation is a requirement for a fixed tree-node position: $?\exists\mathbf{x}.Tn(\mathbf{x})$. The update to this relatively weak tree-relation becomes possible only after processing the subject-plus-verb sequence, which jointly yields the two-place predicate structure as in step (ii) of (25). The simultaneous provision of a formula decoration for this node and update of the unfixed node is provided in the *unification* step indicated there, an action which satisfies the update requirements of both nodes to be unified:

(25)    Parsing *Mary, John upset*:

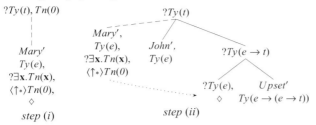

This process feeds into the ongoing development in which, once all terminal nodes are decorated, bottom-up application of labelled type deduction leads to the completed tree indicated in (23). Such an account of structural underspecification and update is not contentious as a parsing strategy; what is innovative is its application within the grammar mechanism as the basic underpinning to syntactic generalisations.

This account might seem in principle skewed by focusing on parsing, but this is only superficial. Production also follows the very same processes, with but one further assumption – that at every step in production, there must be some richer tree, a so-called 'goal tree', which the tree under construction must subsume in the sense of being able to be developed into that goal tree by rules of the system. For the production of both (23) and (24), for example, each selected strategy for update has to be checked for subsumption with respect to the goal tree representing the content to be conveyed. These indeed share such a goal tree, illustrating how more than one sequence of strategies is licensed for any string–content pairing, both in parsing and production (to the advantage of real-time processing: Ferreira, V. 1996). So parsers and producers alike use strategies for building up representations of content, either to establish interpretation for a sequence of words, or to find words which match the content to be conveyed.

To achieve the basis for characterising the full array of compound structures displayed in natural language, DS defines in addition the licence to build paired trees, so-called linked trees, linked together solely by the sharing of terms, established, for example, by encoded anaphoric devices such as relative pronouns. Consider the structure derived by processing the string *John, who smokes, left*:

(26)    Result of parsing *John, who smokes, left*:

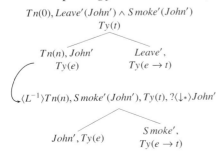

The arrow linking the two trees depicts the so-called link relation. The tree whose node is pointed by the arrow is the *linked* tree (read $\langle L^{-1} \rangle$ as 'linked to'). Within any one such linked tree, the full range of computational, lexical and pragmatic actions remain available;[6] and with this flexibility to allow the incremental projection of arbitrarily rich compound structures, the result is a formal system combining lexical, structural and semantic specifications, all as constraints on the growth of trees. As argued in Kempson *et al.* 2001, Cann *et al.* 2005 and others, this leads to the comprehensive DS claim that the syntax of natural languages does not involve a separate level of representation besides what is needed for semantics, not because there is no level of semantic representation, but because there is no level of syntactic representation other than that of growth of semantic representation.[7]

Despite the assumption that this progressive build up of a semantic representation is a basis for doing syntax, syntax in this model is NOT taken to include a level of representation where there is structure over a string of words. These trees are not inhabited by words and there is no notion of linear ordering expressed on the tree. Furthermore, lexical specifications are defined in exactly the same terms of actions inducing tree growth, and these actions can take place only if the condition triggering these actions matches the decorations on the node at which the pointer has got to in the parse. So all structural restrictions are stated in terms of the interaction of constraints on tree growth.

A consequence of this methodology of incorporating the dynamics of incremental growth into the syntactic formalism itself is the way concepts of structural underspecification and subsequent update replace the need to postulate multiple levels of representation. The building of unfixed nodes and updating them replaces a multi-level account of syntax with progressive growth along a time line towards just one type of representation, hence a single representational level. The characterisation of lexical specifications in the same terms enables seamless integration of lexical and syntactic forms of generalisation, so that discrete vocabularies for lexical and syntactic generalisation are precluded. And constraints that, in other frameworks, are taken to be specific to natural-language syntax and not reducible to semantic generalisations are analysed as constraints on the same growth process. For example, the complex NP constraint associated with a precluding of dependency of some expression outside a relative clause sequence with some site within that relative is analysed in DS via the locality imposed by the licence to build linked-tree pairings. Any expression characterised as decorating an unfixed node, e.g. a relative pronoun,[8] has to be resolved within the tree which that unfixed node construction step initiates. Hence it cannot be resolved in some tree only linked to that tree, and the island constraint is captured, albeit in less familiar terms than is standard.

Such a system might appear to face the challenge of characterising quantification, often thought to constitute a second core case where the syntax of natural languages is disjoint from what is required for the semantics of quantification. Notoriously, no natural language overtly displays quantification following the pattern of predicate logic's propositional quantifying operators. But in this framework, this problem is addressed by grounding the account in the so-called epsilon calculus. This is a logic that provides the formal account of the so-called arbitrary names of natural deduction systems for predicate logic. The heart of such names is that their syntax is simple: they are a naming device like all other individual-denoting expressions of the logic.[9] It is the semantics for such names that is complex, for they are terms denoting witness sets for the entire proposition in which they occur; and this means that a rule of semantic evaluation is defined to determine, as output, that their internal structure reflects the environment in which they occur.[10] There is thus a concept of growth in this aspect too, in growth of the restrictor from what the incremental structural process provides (e.g. that projected by the nominal) and that of the predicate structure within which it is contained (see Kempson *et al.* 2001, Cann *et al.* 2005 for all details). Details aside, the bonus of this account in relation to multiplicity of levels of representation for natural-language grammar-writing is that another supposed dis-symmetry between natural-language syntax and its required semantics dissolves upon analysis, for the account presumes that these are terms of the same type *e* as all other argument expression.[11]

Overall then, the system involves but a single level of representation, the need for multiple levels replaced by the concept of growth of partial representations, these representations themselves being part of a denotationally interpretable system. In particular, the apparent multiplicity confronted by all grammar formalisms which posit independent, statically defined, syntax and semantics is resolved through articulation of the dynamics of how the one type of representation is incrementally built up. An immediate consequence is that the system is unencapsulated. In any one application to yield some derivation, application of general computational actions in interaction with lexical actions as driven by the sequence of words may be interspersed with pragmatic actions of substitution as the carrying out of the lexical actions creates underspecified formula values requiring update; and well-formedness is defined as the availability of at least one possible sequence of actions through from initial goal to some completed propositional output with no requirements outstanding, having used all the words and their actions in order.

## 26.4   Ellipsis as a window on context

With this bringing together of syntax and semantics all reflecting the dynamics of how interpretation is progressively built up, the folk intuition about ellipsis can be modelled directly, opening up a whole new perspective on the syntax/pragmatics interface. For ellipsis can now be seen as making use of the different facets of context which the evolving build-up of interpretation gives rise to. The problem about ellipsis, recall, is that model-theoretic accounts were too weak to handle syntactic constraints, and that syntactic accounts freely posit ambiguity. In DS, though, syntax just is the growth of representations of propositional content as established relative to context, and this together with context is an evolving record of representations of content plus the process of their building. More formally, a DS parse state is a triple of a sequence of words so far parsed, a (partial) structure and actions used to construct that structure. Accordingly, *context*, as a record of how such parsed states have developed, is a sequence of parse states each made up of a sequence of words, a complete or partial tree and the sequence of actions used to develop that structure (see Cann *et al.* 2007 for a formal definition).

Given this notion of context, any aspect of it is expected to be re-usable as a basis for construal of ellipsis, whether representations of content, actions used to induce some structure, or the structure itself. First there is the availability of content annotations as made available in some context tree, re-using a formula just established by a simple substitution process in the manner of anaphora. This direct re-use of a formula from context is illustrated by the strict readings of VP ellipsis, where the content of the ellipsis site matches that assigned to the antecedent predicate (see section 26.2). In the sloppy readings, where there is parallelism of mode of construal but not matching of resultant content, it is the actions that are replicated, applied to the newly introduced subject. (27) provides such a case.

(27)   A:   Who hurt himself?
       B:   John did.

The processing for the question in (27) involves the construction of a two-place predicate as indicated by the verb; the construction of an object argument; and then, because this object contains a reflexive pronoun, it is obligatorily identified with the argument provided as subject. Re-applying these very same actions in the new tree whose subject node has been decorated by the expression John of the elliptical fragment gives rise to the construal of the answer as involving a re-binding of the object argument to this new subject. The effect achieved is the same as the higher-order unification account but without anything beyond what has already been used for the processing of the previous linguistic input. All that has to be assumed is that the metavariable contributed by the anaphoric *did* can be updated by some suitable selection of some action sequence taken from the context. Finally there are the cases where what the context provides is structure, to which the follow-on speaker provides an add-on. Canonical cases of this are question–answer pairs, the answer providing the update to the very structure provided by the question.[12]

(28)   A:   Who did John upset?
       B:   Himself.

Indeed this is the phenomenon so characteristic of dialogue: quite generally, as we saw in section 26.1, one speaker can provide a structure, often one that is in some sense incomplete, to which their interlocutor can provide an extension. So, as expected, the diversity of ellipsis effects matches the richness of dynamically evolving contexts.

With this definition of syntax as the dynamics whereby interpretation is built up, problems that apply to other accounts of ellipsis do not apply to a DS form of analysis (see Cann *et al.* 2005, Purver *et al.* 2006). The ability to shift from sloppy construal to strict (and even back again), as in (22), is predicted to be possible because the context, in evolving along with the content, keeps at each stage a record of content (formula decorations), structure (the emergent tree representation) and actions (the retained record of the growth process). Even the supposed island constraints displayed in antecedent-contained ellipsis turn out to be expressible in view of the fact that the relative pronoun is morphologically present in the initiation of the construal of the expression containing the ellipsis site:

(29)   John interviewed everyone who Bill hadn't.

It is the characterisation of this relativiser as decorating an unfixed node (dominated within the newly emergent structure) which determines that the resolution of this structurally underspecified relation must be satisfied within that individual structure (Cann *et al.* 2005), and not any property of the ellipsis site itself.

Moreover, the account has, as a bonus, the prediction of seamless switching between speaker and hearer roles that is diagnostic of conversational dialogue.

(19)   A:   We're going to Casa Plana.
        B:   To show my mother what we've done there.
(20)   A:   We're going to . . .
        B:   Casa Plana.

Unlike other frameworks, for which such split utterances pose very considerable problems (see Gregoromichelaki *et al.* 2009), on the DS account this phenomenon is predicted to be wholly straightforward, indeed their existence is a consequence of the DS account of production (Purver *et al.* 2006). According to the DS account, the very same mechanisms are used in production as in parsing. Tight coordination between the parties is expected. Each party is building up structure relative to their own context, so at any point, making use of that individually constructed representation whether as parser or producer, they can switch roles and take over the other role, the only difference between the two activities being the greater specificity of the goal to be achieved in production. So, even with a role switch and the first and second person pronouns having to be reinterpreted, the mechanism for processing them remains identical.

(30)   A:   Did you give me back
       B:   your penknife? It's on the table.

(31)   A:   I heard a shout. Did you
       B:   Burn myself? No, luckily.

As these display, the context used by a participant as a producer/hearer is exactly that of the context they use in their shifted role as a hearer/producer. So with the incorporation of the dynamics of structure built in to the grammar itself, a very considerably larger data set becomes characterisable. The split utterances, so signally ignored in accounts of ellipsis that purport to be a sub-part of sentence-based grammar, become core data, relative to which competing grammars can be compared.

## 26.5   Redefining the syntax/pragmatics interface

To see why the ellipsis issue has led to the consequence that natural-language grammars demand a dynamic perspective, we need to look back on the root of the problems posed by ellipsis. The heterogeneity of ellipsis arose because, despite the attempt to see the concept of context as grounded in some operation of lambda-abstraction on some model-theoretically definable concept of content, there appeared to have to be invocation of some independent concept of syntax. This was because restrictions on availability of elliptical forms of construal, in at least some instances, had to be defined in terms of the so-called island constraints. But these constraints were set up in order to explain structural co-dependencies between expressions that are discontinuous within some string, and so were not definable either in terms of the linear sequence of words themselves or in terms of their attributable content. Moreover, these structural co-dependencies across discontinuous sequences and their formulation independent of any level of semantic characterisation have special significance, as, in virtue of not being reducible to any domain-general form of explanation, they were taken as a basis for innately specified, and encapsulated, forms of syntactic architecture as the core of the syntax module. With these being apparently applicable to at least some forms of ellipsis, ellipsis too was taken to fall within the remit of syntactic explanation, hence within the grammar. And with ellipsis being seen as, at least in part, grammar-internal, the phenomenon of ellipsis was presumed to be bifurcated.

    One side effect of this conclusion was that ellipsis played no role in the contextualism debate as driven by Cappelen and Lepore 2005a. However, once we incorporate the concept of growth into the grammar mechanism itself, with its ancillary notion of underspecified structural relations and growth of all aspects of such structure as part of the process defined by the grammar, then the mapping of a linear sequence of words onto some corresponding semantic representation is seen as a property of incremental growth along the timeline of processing such linear sequences. With this move, the supposedly innate uniquely determinative properties of human language are seen in terms of progressive growth of semantic representations, and not some separate domain-specific capacity. Moreover, if syntax is defined to be a system of such procedures, a record of how such representations are built up yields precisely the right degree of richness for the concept of context for such processes of construal. Context simply is a record of previous parse states, hence a record of how progressive transitions from one partial structure to the next yield the current parse state. With this concept of context, an integrated account of ellipsis becomes available, notwithstanding the very considerable diversity in contents for an individual string, and its display both within and across sentence and utterance boundaries. This is a big advance over all sentence-based grammar formalisms, since these cannot do more than list the various forms of ellipsis without further explanation. On the DS characterisation, the range of diversity displayed in forms of ellipsis matches exactly the richness of context to be invoked, viz. building up on the basis of established content, established process of interpretation or established structure. However, with this recognition of what context amounts to, the simple setting aside of phenomena such as ellipsis as of no consequence to the contextualism debate is no longer warranted. To the contrary, ellipsis data have a key role to play in the contextualism debate, as they provide such a clear window on the requisite concept of context. But the account of ellipsis that emerges on the DS perspective demands a dynamic basis to the grammar, for it is this which makes possible the integrated explanation of ellipsis as a grammar-internal mechanism, despite contextual provision of values to be assigned to the ellipsis site.

This account of grammar opens up a radically new perspective on the interface between syntax and pragmatics. With syntax now envisaged as a system of procedures for building up representations of content, the implementation of any such procedures can only take place in interaction with whatever pragmatic, grammar-external constraints there may be that determine how selections from context are made. And, of fundamental significance, the concept of encapsulation associated with any such explanation breaks down. Lack of encapsulation is essential, as the choice mechanism has to pick out some value from the particular context and, whatever the form of this mechanism, it is one that is subject to wholly general constraints that apply to all cognitive processing. Furthermore, on this view, there is no fixed interface at which the system of natural-language syntax stops and pragmatic mechanisms take over. Pragmatics simply is the articulation of constraints that determine how mechanisms definitive of natural-language syntax are implemented. Thus the concept of an interface between syntax and pragmatics as some fixed level of representation constituting the feeding relation into implementation of some pragmatic procedures no longer holds. In its place, we have the articulation of grammar as a set of mechanisms making language processing in context possible, a theory of pragmatics being the articulation of constraints that determine what and how particular choices are made. This interface can take place at any point in the construction of propositional forms from the sequence of expressions provided.

In closing, it is worth noting that core pragmatic phenomena such as conversational implicature do not pose a problem of principle for this account. With grammar defined as providing the architecture in virtue of which humans can build up propositional forms,[13] nothing excludes the characterisation of inference in terms of building further propositional structures leading to additional derived information, both constructed propositional form and additional structures combining through steps of inference defined over the logical formulae which the processing mechanisms license. The mechanisms for such definition are available in the Dynamic Syntax framework in the form of linked tree structures. Moreover, from this perspective, lexical items in language might specifically guide the type or direction of inference to be drawn by enrichment of the minimal context. The result is that the framework retains a competence/performance gap, though radically narrowed; and the grammar specifications may interface with general pragmatic/cognitive constraints at every step of the understanding process.

# 27

# Pragmatics and language change

Elizabeth Closs Traugott

## 27.1 Introduction

Language is always in flux. Over time new patterns can be observed that are either minor modifications to the linguistic system, as when the meaning of a lexical item changes, or major ones, as when word order changes occur. That language change occurs primarily as a result of acquisition is uncontroversial. There are, however, very different theories and discourses about how to interpret this observation. To simplify, one view assumes that change is internal or endogenous, in other words that grammars change (Kiparsky 1968), and focuses mainly on syntactic change (e.g. Lightfoot 1998): meaning change is hypothesized to be derivative of syntactic change. On this view the child is born with a rich innate universal grammar (UG) and passively selects the relevant aspects of this grammar based on input prior to the "critical period" of puberty. A representative statement is: "A grammar grows in a child from some initial state (UG), when she is exposed to primary linguistic data" (Lightfoot 2003: 107). An innovation by one child counts as a change. A competing view is that usage changes and language acquisition occurs throughout life. Change is not only internal but also external, driven by social factors and language users who are active participants in negotiation of linguistic patterning, especially meaning: "languages don't change: people change language" (Croft 2000: 4). On this view, innovation by the individual is not change. "Changes ... are the historical events in a linguistic tradition by which practices of speaking vary over time" (Andersen, H. 2001: 228).

Since pragmatics is largely the study of language in use, the second approach to language change is clearly the most germane. In the study of synchronic pragmatics there is a continuum between approaches that are based in the linguistic system and those based in social factors such as ideology and demographics. Early work on historical pragmatics tended to privilege an "internal" view, even though speakers and addressees involved in communication are regularly invoked. In this work the clause or sentence

|        | Stage 1 | Stage 2     | Stage 3  | Stage 4 |
|--------|---------|-------------|----------|---------|
| Form   | $f$     | $f$         | $f$      | $f$     |
| Meaning| 'p'     | 'p' (+> 'q')| 'p', 'q' | 'q'     |

Figure 27.1. *Stages in semantic change*

is seen as the relevant contextual unit of language. Representative works in this tradition tend to be neo-Gricean (see Traugott 2004 for discussion), though a few are based in Relevance theory (see especially Papafragou 2000; also Groefsema 1995, Nicolle 1997, Koch 2004). More recently there has been a shift toward interactional approaches with discourses and genres as the relevant contextual unit of language (see the *Journal of Historical Pragmatics* and Jucker and Taavitsainen 2010). Here I discuss work in both the more logical and more interactional traditions, with emphasis on the semanticization of pragmatics. In section 27.2 I consider mainly historical neo-Gricean approaches to implicatures and inferences,[1] with particular attention to the question of how pragmatics comes to be semanticized into expressions. In section 27.3 I turn to subjectification and intersubjectification, and in section 27.4 to "pragmaticalization" of expressions. The main unit of analysis in all cases is the "co-text," broadly defined as linguistic context.[2]

## 27.2  Implicatures and inferences

It is generally agreed that if an expression has two meanings A and B, B "often comes into existence because a regularly occurring context supports an inference-driven contextual enrichment of A to B . . . this contextual sense may become lexicalized[3] to the point where it need no longer be supported by a given context" (Evans and Wilkins 2000: 550). Evans and Wilkins call such contexts "bridging contexts." Enfield (2003) modeled them as in Figure 27.1 (simplified).

Stage 2 is regarded as one in which implicating and meaning 'q' become functionally equivalent; "the implicature, usually defeasible, happens to be true in the bridging context, and so *in that context* is non-defeasible" (Enfield 2003: 29, italics original). The bridging context therefore "masks" the difference between pragmatic and semantic interpretation, enabling but not necessarily giving rise to, a new semanticized 'q'; 'p' is left to persist or disappear (*ibid.*).

This view is largely consistent with neo-Gricean approaches to the role of pragmatics in semantic change. In a much-cited brief comment Grice (1989: 39) said: "it may not be impossible for what starts life, so to speak, as a conversational implicature to become conventionalized," and much early work in the neo-Gricean tradition sought to establish how conversational implicatures may become attached to an expression and subsequently become part of its meaning (Brown, P. and Levinson 1987: 261). An example is the development of *since*, derived from *siþ* 'late' (see also German *seit* 'since'). It appears in Old English as *siþþan*, later with an adverbial *-es* as *siþþenes*. In the textual record there are a few examples of its use as a conjunction that suggest the logical fallacy "post hoc ergo propter hoc" was attached to it. However, it occasionally is used in translations of Latin *quia* 'external cause' and *quoniam* 'internal cause' (Molencki 2007).[4] By Middle English it begins to appear in several native-language examples where it cannot be temporal, only causal, indicating that a temporal/causal polysemy had arisen. By contrast, *æfter* 'after', though associated with causal implicatures in relevant contexts, has never become semantically polysemous (Traugott and König 1991). The implicatures can however, be effectively used in slogans and advertisements, for example ABC TV's 1998 advertisement *Before TV, two World Wars. After TV, zero*.[5]

A fundamental assumption of the neo-Gricean approach is that there is a viable distinction to be made between pragmatics and semantics, roughly along the lines of context-dependent meaning (pragmatics) as opposed to context-independent meaning (semantics), and between implicature (what is meant) and what is said (propositional form). One of the challenges for historical linguistics is how to determine what is context-dependent or not, and what is meant beyond what is said. This is because, absent speakers with whom to check intuitions, almost all data other than dictionary entries occurs in linguistic context ("co-text") and we can construe what is meant only from what is said. (For more detailed discussion, see Hansen 2008: 34–40.) The advent of large electronic corpora has helped significantly in overcoming this problem, though it is by no means solved. A further assumption is that there is both pragmatic polysemy (Horn 1984a, Sweetser 1990) and semantic polysemy. Granting that the concept of polysemy is problematic (see Tuggy 1993), without polysemy one cannot account for the fine-grained step-by-step developments that are attested by detailed study of texts and contexts over time.

The neo-Gricean approach draws heavily on Gricean maxims and especially the division of labor that he proposed between Quantity$_1$ and Quantity$_2$ (1989: 26):

(1)   Q1. Make your contribution as informative as is required (for the current purposes of the exchange).
Q2. Do not make your contribution more informative than is required.

Taking a largely truth-conditional approach to meaning, Horn (1984b) proposed two principles grounded in the two types of quantity and in the long-standing hypothesis that language change arises in part from two competing motivations (see e.g. Du Bois 1985): speakers seek to optimize the message for the hearer ("be clear") while at the same time economizing the speech signal ("be quick"). Horn combined the two quantity maxims with the maxim of relation ("be relevant") and the maxim of manner ("be perspicuous," including such maxims as "avoid ambiguity," "be brief") (Horn 1984b: 13):

(2)  a.  The Q principle (Hearer-based):
         MAKE YOUR CONTRIBUTION SUFFICIENT (cf. Quantity$_1$)
         SAY AS MUCH AS YOU CAN (given R)
         Lower-bounding principle, inducing upper-bounding implicata.
     b.  The R principle (Speaker-based):
         MAKE YOUR CONTRIBUTION NECESSARY (cf. Relation,
         Quantity$_2$, Manner)
         SAY NO MORE THAN YOU MUST (given Q)
         Upper-bounding principle, inducing lower-bounding implicata.[6]

The Q principle, being lower-bounding, is an "at least" principle which implies "exactly." The standard example is *John has two children*, which licenses the Q-inference 'exactly two and no more'. But speakers can use the same sentence and license the R-inference 'at least two and possibly more'. Many R-based utterances, such as indirect speech acts like *Can you pass me the salt?*, are understood as meaning more than is said due to relevance in the situation.

   Horn has used these principles to account for semantic changes especially in the contentful lexical domain, most particularly narrowing and broadening, both of which have figured in taxonomies of semantic change at least since Bréal (1964). Horn argues that lexical narrowing may be R-based or Q-based. R-based narrowing usually involves "delimitation of a general term to a sense representing the salient exemplar of the category denoted by the term" (1984b: 35), i.e. set to subset denotation (*ibid*. 32). Examples include *poison*, which was borrowed from French with the meaning 'toxic drink', but derives ultimately from Latin *potio(n)* 'drink'. Another is *deer* from Old English *deor* 'animal' (see the cognate *Tier* in German, which has not narrowed). Several such narrowings involve taboo avoidance, e.g. *smell* (originally the general term, but now often used to mean 'stink'), *undertaker* ('mortician' < 'one who undertakes'), *disease* (< 'discomfort, uneasiness').[7] Q-based narrowing is sporadic and involves the "specialization of a general term triggered by the prior existence of a hyponym of that term" and the development of autohyponyms.[8] Examples of autohyponyms are *dog* understood to include *bitch* and *rectangle* understood to include squares (but still allowing *That's not a dog, it's a bitch; That's not a rectangle, it's a square*: Horn 1984b). In general Q-inferences inhibit change.

   Broadening is said always to involve R-based change: "the generalization of a species to cover the encompassing genus, from genus to phylum, from subset to superset" (Horn 1984b: 35), e.g. Latin *pecunia* 'property/wealth in cattle' (cf. *pecu* 'livestock') > 'money', expansion of place names (*New Yorker*) or trade names (*xerox, thermos*). Such broadening typically involves "semantic impoverishment" or loss of specificity.

   While most of Horn's examples are lexical and involve form-to-function changes in meaning, i.e. "semasiology", one issue of particular interest to him involves the grammatical domain of quantifiers and what constraints on expressions there may be. The issue here is function-to-form relationships, also known as "onomasiology".[9] Horn (1989: ch. 4) noted the absence in most languages of a single word for meanings in the corner of the Aristotelian Square of Oppositions that denotes the negation of the weaker member of a pair on a scale, e.g. the negation of *some* in the scale *some–all*. In English, although we have *all*, *some*, *no*, there is no *nall* ('some X are not Y'), and likewise no *nand*. The generalization is that historically these single-word expressions are Q-blocked by the pre-existence of the positive weak operator on the scale (*some X are Y* implicates both *some X are not Y* and *not all X are Y*, and therefore *nall* would be uninformative). In a typological study of twenty-nine languages of Europe and India, van der Auwera (2001) confirmed the absence of quantifiers and conjunctions like *nall* or *nand* crosslinguistically, but found (as did Horn 1989) that sometimes the negative of the weaker value of a modal scale is expressed as a single word, e.g. *needn't* as in *John needn't eat his soup today* expresses 'not necessary that p'. *Needn't* co-exists with *mustn't* ('necessary that not p') as in *John mustn't eat his soup today*. Van der Auwera cites Russian *nel'zja* 'not possible', which has lost the positive *l'zja*. However, he also notes that in many languages the 'not necessary/possible' expression has come to be understood as 'necessary/possible that not' by R-implication. In French *Il ne faut pas que tu meures* was ambiguous between the two meanings 'It is not necessary that you die' and 'It is necessary that you not die' but came to mean only the latter (Tobler 1921), despite the syntactic mismatch.

Much of the discussion of R- and Q-implicatures rests on privileging expression of several meanings as a single word. This issue underpins Levinson's reinterpretation of Grice's maxims, which involve not two Principles but three Heuristics (Levinson 2000: 35–9):

(3)  i.  The Q heuristic: What isn't said, isn't.
     ii.  The I heuristic: What is expressed simply is
          stereotypically exemplified.
     iii.  The M heuristic: What's said in an abnormal way, isn't
           normal.

Whereas Horn highlights Relation (hence "R principle"), Levinson highlights Informativenss (hence "I heuristic").

Levinson proposes that (synchronically) Q has priority over M and M over I because I-inferences are "based primarily on stereotypical presumptions about the world" (Levinson 2000: 40). Priority of Q can in part account for conservativeness, and M for change. New expressions are always "abnormal", and grammaticalization often involves the choice of periphrastic expressions when shorter ones already exist, e.g. of *cantare habeo* 'sing.INF have.1SG', which eventually became the rV future ending in French, although an inflectional future *cantabo* already existed. This is what Lehmann (1995) has referred to as "expressiveness" and Haspelmath (1999) as "extravagance". However, to the extent that the M heuristic is conceptualized as involving pairs, one more "marked" or longer than the other, it is problematic. New expressions rarely arise or exist in pairs. Rather, lexical and grammatical domains may have several members competing in the same semantic space (Traugott 2004).

Levinson (1995) distinguishes three levels of meaning: (a) coded meaning (semantics); (b) utterance-token meanings that arise in context "on the fly" and may be "one-offs"; and (c) utterance-type meanings, which are implied meanings that may be preferred, but may be also canceled. Utterance-token meanings are similar to Grice's conversational implicatures, utterance-type meanings to Grice's generalized implicatures. Traugott and Dasher (2002) drew on this three-way distinction in developing the Invited Inferencing Theory of Semantic Change (IITSC).[10] The speaker/writer invites the addressee/reader to make inferences, in other words the interlocutors are conceptualized as active partners in the communicative dyad. The speaker/writer may invite one-off interpretations (IINs) or may use ones that have become generalized in the community (GIINs). Focus is almost exclusively on Horn's R principle, to the extent that it accounts for enriching of abstract meaning and for generalization, in part because Traugott and her colleagues were initially concerned primarily with the semanticization of pragmatics in the process of grammaticalization.

While IITSC draws on Grice and Levinson, no exact match with their distinctions should be expected, since it is less concerned with logic and more with interacting partners (although the degree to which interaction is central to the theory has increased substantially over the years), and the maxims are reconceptualized in the way Horn proposed in (2). Hansen and Waltereit (2006) point to an ambiguity in the meaning "generalized" in so far as it is associated with "conventionalized," as in the case of GIINs and GCIs: "conventionalized" can be understood as (a) "arbitrary" or (b) "common, unmarked" (akin to Morgan's 1978 "conventions of usage"). GIINs are to be understood in the second sense. They may be "salient" in the community in that they can be drawn on consciously, cf. the causal implicature of *after*, but for the most part they are used unconsciously (Keller 1994). GIINs may continue to be available and usable over centuries, even millennia, but sometimes they may also be absorbed into the meaning of an expression with which they were formerly only pragmatically associated. In this case semanticization/new coding has occurred.

By "salient" is meant available and recurrent, i.e. frequently used. Salience is likely to be enabled in part by cognitive patterns such as have been identified in the literature on recurrent metaphors and metonymies (see e.g. Cuyckens *et al.* 2003, Koch 2004, Bybee 2007), on cultural scripts (see Evans and Wilkins 2000), and on grammaticalization (see Heine *et al.* 1991, Heine and Kuteva 2002). "Salience" in this sense is not to be identified with "structural weight" as proposed by Geeraerts (1987: 20). Nor is it necessarily to be identified with foregrounding of implicatures as proposed by Heine (2002), since they are largely backgrounded at least initially (Hansen 2008: 29). Salience is essential to the proposal that, if inferences are involved in a particular change, there is a stage when they are generalized. Hansen and Waltereit (2006) and Hansen (2008: 66) question whether GIINs are necessary for the development of coded meaning. To the extent that there is no textual evidence for a "stage" of ambiguity (see section 27.4), this is true, but in many cases textual replication of invited inferences provides evidence that GIINs do play a role in many changes involving semanticization of pragmatic implicatures.

A concept related to invited inferencing is "context-induced reinterpretation" (see e.g. Heine *et al.* 1991). As the term suggests, on this view more attention is paid to outcomes of change (reinterpretation) than to onsets of semantic change, and to the hearer than to the speaker. While the hearer is undoubtedly more likely to reanalyze the pragmatics associated with a construction than is the speaker, it is only when this hearer acts as a speaker that the reinterpretation can be discovered. As Kuteva (2001) points out, context itself is only an enabling factor. The locus of change is to be found in perception of mismatch between speaker intention and hearer interpretation, on the assumption that speakers and addressees are not mirror images of each other, but have different cognitive statuses.

Several domains have been investigated with particular attention to the semanticization of pragmatics. Among them are developments that originate in temporal expressions. Hansen (2008) discusses the polyfunctional development of four French adverbs: *déjà*, *encore*, *toujours*, and *enfin*, roughly 'already', 'yet', 'still', and 'finally'. Another set of changes that has received much attention involves temporals, e.g. *since* 'temporal' > 'causal', *while* 'during the time that' (or rather *þa hwile þe* 'during that time that') > 'concessive' in English, but causal in German. G. Chen (2002) drew attention to the fact that concessives involve contrast, or adversative relationships. Subsequent work on English concessives has found that contrast is a stage prior to the development of concessives in the cases of *while* (Gonzáles-Cruz 2007) and *whereas* (Breul 2007). There is an inference from co-existence in time (*while*) and space (*whereas*) to juxtaposition and contrast, and from contrast to concessive and sometimes other marginal meanings (e.g. *while* has some causal and even additive readings, Breul 2007). These changes have all been shown to arise only in very specific contexts; for one they are clausal, not prepositional, and typically the temporality involved is one of co-extension, not sequence.

In a case of temporal > conditional, Old English *swa lange swa* > *so/as long as*, the temporal clause describes a situation that is or can be construed as temporary, as in (4).

(4)  wring    þurh      linenne   cla∂    on    þæt    eage   swa   *lange*
     wring    through   linen     cloth   on    that   eye    as    long
     *swa*    him       ∂earf     sy
     as       him       need      be

'squeeze (the medication) through a linen cloth into the eye as long as he needs'

(850–950 Lacnunga, p. 100) (Traugott and Dasher 2002: 36)

By hypothesis this medical instruction was meant to be understood as meaning 'for the length of time that he needs'; in addition there is, at least from hindsight, pragmatic strengthening to the concessive 'provided that he needs it'. This concessive meaning can be inferred in some examples for nearly a thousand years of textual history, but appears to become a more salient and plausibly intended meaning, i.e. a GIIN, during the seventeenth century, as in (5).

(5)   They whose words doe most shew forth their wise vnderstanding, and whose lips doe vtter the purest knowledge, *so long as* they vnderstand and speake as men, are they not faine sundry waies to excuse themselves?

'Those whose words most reveal their wise understanding and whose lips utter the purest knowledge, for the length of time/provided that they understand and speak like men, are they not content to excuse themselves in various ways?'
(1614 Hooker, p. 5) (Traugott and Dasher 2002: 37)

It is not until the eighteenth century, however, that we find examples in which the conditional appears to have been semanticized, i.e. is the only plausible reading:

(6)   I heard Ann Wright say ... Chapman had stole Davis's watch; she asked Davis to go and see for it; Davis answered, he did not mind the watch, *so long as* he escaped with his life
(1764 Trial of William Chapman, POB t17641017–18)

Another domain in which invited inferencing has been hypothesized to play a significant role is the development of auxiliaries. The precursors of contemporary future markers *will*, *shall*, *be going to* were *will-* 'intend' (volitional), *scul-* 'owe', and *be going to* 'motion with a purpose'. In relevant contexts all implied later states of affairs that were not realized at time of utterance. The precursors of *may*, *can*, and *must* were *mag-* 'have the (physical) ability', *cunn-* 'have the mental ability', and *mot-* 'be able to' (*must* is a past tense form). From ability there is a societal, if not logical, invited inference to permission or obligation, especially if the subject is a second person, and the speaker is in a position of authority. In (7) God says to Adam:

(7)  Ealra    þæra    þinga         þe      on   neorxna wange
     (of)all  those   things        that    in   Paradise
     syndon   þu      *most*        brucan  ...  buton
     are      you     are able to/may  enjoy  ...  except
     anum     treowe
     one      tree
(c. 1000 ÆCHom I. 12.34) (Warner 1990: 544)

In all the examples of invited inferencing cited here the claim is that the chief cognitive mechanism underlying the changes is metonymy, broadly construed (Traugott and Dasher 2002),[11] i.e. understood as "simultaneous or sequential co-presence of elements within the same conceptual framework (cf. Panther and Thornburg [2003a]: 7)" (Hansen 2008: 71). Semanticization of pragmatics involves a profile shift from pragmatic status to coding status (Koch 2004 identifies it as a foreground–background reversal). This metonymic profile shift may be enabled by metaphors that pre-exist and serve as frames for the shift, and may result in what appear synchronically to be metaphors (see especially Blank 1997: ch. 4).[12]

To the extent that the examples involve grammaticalization (development of expressions conveying grammatical meanings[13]) they also involve the development of procedural meanings: "instructions to hearers on how the conceptual meanings expressed in an utterance should be combined and processed" (Hansen 2008: 20).[14] In the cases discussed so far, there is typically (a) a contentful meaning[15] initially that is associated with abstract procedural implicatures; (b) an intermediary stage in which an expression has both contentful and procedural meanings, e.g. *be going to* understood as both intentional and future; and (c) eventually primarily or exclusively procedural meanings, e.g. *be going to* in raising constructions, e.g. *It's going to rain* (Nicolle 1997). The development of procedural meanings is associable with "bleaching", the loss of lexical meaning, but enrichment of grammatical meaning. As Eckardt (2006: 248) points out, grammatical expressions are relational, "hardly of a kind that would allow ostensive introduction". They are functional elements, the compositional "glue" of clauses (Fintel 1995: 182).

## 27.3  (Inter)subjectification

Among pragmatic factors that come to be semanticized are subjectivity and intersubjectivity as projected by the speaker. Subjectivity and intersubjectivity are ambient in language use because of the dyadic speaker–addressee interaction (Benveniste 1971). The mechanism by which semanticization occurs is a sub-type of semantic reanalysis known as (inter)subjectification. There are two leading approaches to this type of change, one associated with Langacker, one with Traugott. Although the two approaches had much in common in the early stages (see Langacker 1990, Traugott 1989), they have come to be increasingly differentiated (see Langacker 2006, De Smet and Verstraete 2006, Traugott 2010, and López-Couso 2010; extensive examples of the Langacker perspective can be found in Athanasiadou *et al.* 2006, and of Traugott's in Davidse *et al.* 2010).

In Langacker's (2006) view subjectivity concerns construal of vantage-point and how explicitly speaker is referenced in the utterance. Subjectification is a kind of bleaching by which the objectively construed on-stage meaning comes to be construed as off-stage, cf. the change from *be going to* 'agent moves with a purpose' > *be going to* 'future', most clearly with inanimate subjects. Langacker has proposed that "off-stage" subjectivity "was actually there, **immanent**" all along (Langacker 2006: 21, bold original). Intersubjectivity is "apprehension of other minds" and "simulation of the other's experience" in a symmetric speaker–addressee dyad (Langacker 2007); his examples are the use of first and second person pronouns as opposed to third person pronouns. It is not clear how intersubjectification would be conceptualized in this framework.

Whereas Langacker's approach focuses on conceptualization, Traugott's is concerned with changes to linguistic expression (semasiology). Whereas Langacker conceives the speaker–addressee dyad as basically symmetric, with both participants sharing similar experiences, Traugott conceives it as asymmetric in any instance of interaction since speakers' and hearers' (or writers' and readers') intentions may be different, and cognitive statuses usually are (Hansen 2008: 28). On this view subjectification is the new encoding of meanings that express speaker point of view, and includes not only *be going to* and raising constructions, but also such semantic changes as *anyway* 'in any direction' > 'nevertheless' (in clause-final position), 'in any case' (in clause-initial position) and *promise* 'send forward' > 'performative speech act verb'. Intersubjectification, by contrast, is new encoding of meanings that express such types of speaker attention to addressee as consideration of "face" (giving rise to hedged meanings such as are found in pragmatic markers, e.g. *well*, to request forms such as *please* < *if you please* ('if it gives you pleasure'), and to Japanese addressee honorific style-marking; see Traugott and Dasher 2002) and elicitation of a response (e.g. question tags like *right?*). The invited inferences involved in (inter)subjectification enrich meaning beyond what is meant, i.e. are consistent with Horn's R principle, but they are not primarily logical. They are based in interaction and negotiation of meaning between speakers and hearers.

The examples discussed above involving shifts from temporal to causal, concessive, or conditional, or from deontic to epistemic modality all involve subjectification. Generally the textual evidence suggests increase in subjectivity over time within and across semantic domains. For example, epistemic modals may be more subjective in general than deontic modals, but both deontic and epistemic modals show increases in subjectivity over time (Goossens 1999). In English, epistemic *must* originated in generic statements such as (8),

(8)     Ealle   we     *moton*   sweltan.
        All     we     must      die
        'We all must die'
                (?8thC *Exodus*) (Warner 1993: 162)

or in passages of logical reasoning, and only over time come to be used to express clearly personal evaluations as in:

(9)   LADY TOUCHWOOD: Don't ask me my reasons, my lord, for they are
      not fit to be told you.
      LORD TOUCHWOOD: (Aside) I'm amazed; here *must* be something more
      than ordinary in this.
      (1693 Congreve, *Double Dealer* III, p. 154) (Traugott and Dasher 2002:
      129–30)

   A modal domain in which subjectification has recently been identified
is that of modal adjectives like *essential* and *vital* (Van linden 2009). These
originated as non-modal adjectives meaning 'being such by its true nature',
and 'associated with life'; they both came to be used with dynamic modal
meaning (necessity in the situation) and eventually deontic moral meaning.
In the non-modal meaning the adjective is a classifier of the noun as in:

(10)   Those *essentiall* parts of his ('God')
                        (1596 Spencer) (Van linden 2009: 78)

Van linden proposes that the key to the development of dynamic modal
meanings was use with evaluative modification of the noun to which a
particular feature is said to be essential:

(11)   It is an *essentiall* property of man truly wise, not to open all the boxes
       of his bosome.
                        (1618 Raleigh, *Remains*) (OED; Van linden 2009: 82)

The speaker's subjective evaluation of the nominal became associated with
the adjective and gave rise to meanings of potentiality, indeed necessity in
the situation.
   Another domain in which subjectification is a clear factor is the attribution of scalar meanings to an expression, as in the development of modals
(cf. degrees of modal strength from deontic and epistemic *ought to* > *have (got)*
*to* > *must*), of adverbial intensifiers (e.g. *a bit/ lot* < 'a unit of'), and approx-
imators (*sort of* < 'a type of') (see e.g. Denison 2002, Brems 2007, Traugott
2008a). A further domain is the development of evaluative adjectives into
intensifiers. In this meaning they occur to the left of descriptive adjectives
and function as postdeterminers in English, e.g. *pretty* as in *That vase is pretty*
*ugly*; *pure* as in *That's pure nonsense*; *right* in *the right excellent high and mighty*
*prince* (see e.g. Adamson 2000, Nevalainen and Rissanen 2002, Vandewinkel
and Davidse 2008, Méndez-Naya 2008). One of these, *very* 'true' (< Old French
*verrai* 'true') as in *the very God* 'the true God', came in contexts modifying an
indefinite nominal to be used with a scalar implicature (*a very patroness*). Once
interpreted as scalar it came to be used before other adjectives (*very precious*
*stones*), and finally became an adverb; *real*, which is one of its replacements,
is undergoing a similar change (*That's real ugly*). Another set of adjectives that
have been assigned postdeterminer or even quantifier structure includes
adjectives denoting difference (Breban 2008). *Several* is now a quantifier, but
originally it meant 'distinct', as in:

(12)  a.  All men should marke theyr cattell with an open *severall* marke
          upon theyr flanckes
          (1596 Spenser, *State Ireland*) (OED *several* adj I.c; Breban 2008: 299)
      b.  (on learning to distinguish letters of the alphabet) Thus when a
          childe hath got the names of his letters, & their *several* shapes
          withal in a playing manner, he may easily be taught to
          distinguish them in the following leaf
          (HC 1500–1700) (Breban 2008: 299)

In contexts like (12b) there is an invited inference of plurality, presumably
one of the intermediate steps between the original and the present-day meaning. The adjectives discussed here all originate in attributive uses; in their
postdeterminer or quantificational uses they all appear to the left of attributive adjectives. They may be regarded as instances of grammaticalization
since they acquire adverbial properties (see Breban 2010).

Subjectification is independent of grammaticalization, as the example of
*essential* shows. Other lexical examples include the pre-emption for performative use of speech-act verbs like *promise* (derived from the past participle
of a spatial expression, Old French *pro* 'forward' + *mettre-* 'send') (see Traugott and Dasher 2002: ch. 5). However, subjectification is often linked with
grammaticalization because the "glue" that grammatical markers provide
indicates relations selected by the speaker, whether modal assessments of
the factuality of the proposition, establishment of temporal relations to the
time of speaking (tense), or connectivity.

Traugott (1989 and in later work) attempted to unify various types of subjectification as an overarching, dominant type of semantic change, including
the development of evaluative words like *boor* 'crude person' < 'farmer' (see
German *Bauer* 'farmer'). Pejorations of this type, and also ameliorations such
as *knight* < *cniht* 'boy', very often become "objectified" in the sense that they
come to be part of the community norm and are different in kind from
the type of subjectification discussed above, which involves development of
metatextual meanings. There has been some concern that "subjectification"
has as a result become a "catch-all" term. Hence there has been interest in
breaking the concept down again. For example, both Waltereit and Detges
(2007) and De Smet and Verstraete (2006) point to the importance of thinking
about subjectification in terms of the different functions of the subjectified
elements.

Waltereit and Detges contrast the development of French *bien* and Spanish *bien*, both meaning 'well' (adverbial form of 'good'), but functioning in
different ways. In French the adverb of manner develops into a modal that
counters a denial. The modal use is scalar and derives (as is typical of new
epistemic modals) from a dispute about the validity of 'p'. Adopting an interactional and argumentation-based approach to the semanticization of pragmatics which highlights the role of multiple perspectives or "dialogicity"
(see Ducrot 1984, Schwenter 2000), they suggest that French *bien* "emerges

from a stereotyped argumentation which originally is dialogical in nature" (Waltereit and Detges 2007: 77–8), for example (p. 75):

(13)   L1: *p* is not the case.
       L2: *p* is WELL the case.

Such a development is consistent with Horn's R principle, though framed in a more interactional way, and involves negotiation of common ground. Waltereit and Detges contrast Spanish *bien*, which is used not modally, but to initiate a change of topic, and suggest that rather than being a direct extension of the adverb *bien* 'well', it is the result of a rather different strategy: interactional argumentation linking arguments in a discourse. They postulate multiple paths leading to the development of the discourse-marker use of *bien* in the late eighteenth/early nineteenth centuries, including use as response at a turn, and concessive argumentation, and conclude that while both the French and the Spanish *bien* involve subjectification, their different meanings arise in diachrony because speakers have different rhetorical moves in mind.

Somewhat similarly, but with more attention to syntax and outcomes of subjectification, De Smet and Verstraete (2006) show how in Dutch *leuk* 'luke-warm' came to be used to mean 'calm' (of persons) and was eventually ameliorated to 'pleasant, funny'. By contrast *dom* 'dumb' came to be used in the meaning 'unintelligent' and in Belgian Dutch has been pejorated to 'annoying, cursed, bloody'. While both undergo the semantic shift physical > intellectual > evaluative, *leuk* remains a contentful gradable adjective that can be used to define an entity, whereas *dom* has become nongradable and can be used only with a grounding expression. It has undergone intersubjectification.

De Smet and Verstraete (2006) regard what are often called procedural or discourse-marker uses of connectives as interpersonal uses. *Because* and *after* clauses that can serve as the focus of a cleft are distinguished from *as*, *since*, and *for* clauses which cannot (*ibid.*: 380). *As*, *since*, and *for* clauses are considered to involve not only speaker positioning (subjectification) but also "interaction with the interlocutor, because the clause introduced by the conjunction represents a separate speech act in discourse" (*ibid.*: 387). The authors consider subjectification and intersubjectification to be semanticizations; hence this interactive use is presumably a case of coding in their view.

However, many of the examples in which the rise of subjective, and especially intersubjective, meanings is discussed have recently been labeled (conventionalized) "pragmaticalizations", most especially the development of pragmatic enrichments often associated with new uses of more contentful material as "pragmatic markers", "discourse markers", or "comment clauses" in new positions in a clause or intonation unit. The left periphery of the clause or intonation unit in English is often associated with subjective material (e.g. topic marking and epistemic modals), and the right periphery with intersubjective marking (e.g. question tags). Originally meaning 'securely', *surely* became an epistemic modal adverb used in medial and clause-initial position. Like many other epistemic adverbs (e.g. *indeed, actually*), in clause-initial position it came to be used in extended ways. Whereas *in fact* and *actually* came to be used primarily as reformulation markers, *surely* came to be used intersubjectively as a "fighting word" eliciting a response (Downing 2001).[16] It is, however, more intersubjective in right periphery, where, like *no doubt* (Simon-Vandenbergen 2007) and *of course* (Lewis 2003), it can be used to put the addressee down.

In other languages the right periphery may be used for a wider set of functions (see papers on Japanese in Suzuki 2006, Onodera and Suzuki 2007). Yap *et al.* (2004) discuss the development in right periphery of the clause of *no* in Japanese, *de* in Mandarin, *punya* in Malay, all from genitive cases markers to stance markers meaning 'for sure'. This is primarily subjective rather than intersubjective, as is Old Chinese *ye yi yi* 'new realization/resignation on the part of speaker', ultimately derived from *yi* 'finish/perfective aspect' (Yap *et al.* 2008). In some cases, whether the intersubjective meaning is considered to be a GIIN or to have become coded may be a function of the linguist's analysis and the extent to which association with syntactic slots is regarded as determining use. But in others, there appears to be incontrovertible semanticization of intersubjective meanings because the form has changed as well. *Look* (< *look you/thou*, with second person pronoun according to Brinton 2008) and Italian *guarda* 'look' (Waltereit 2006) originate in imperatives, and therefore were originally intersubjective. They have, however, acquired additional intersubjective functions in parenthetical uses when there is nothing to look at. From the eighteenth century on, *look* has been used not only to claim attention but also to express aggression, especially in the phrase *look here*.

The neo-Gricean tradition has little to contribute directly to the study of subjectification and especially intersubjectification since the tradition is primarily "cognitive-inferential" and privileges informativeness (Jucker, forthcoming). As Jucker points out, European researchers have tended to work within a broader "socio-interactional conceptualization." The distinction is readily apparent if one compares Grice's maxims with those of Keller (1994). Although building in part on Grice's maxims, Keller's are maxims of action, including not only "Talk in such a way that the other understands you" (p. 98), but also interactional ones such as "Talk in such a way that you are not recognizable as a member of the [other] group" (*ibid.*: 101), a maxim that is about identity and group dynamics rather than truth or belief. Such an integrated informational and interactional perspective promises to give us a better understanding of (inter)subjectification, and indeed of most issues in pragmatics and language change.[17]

## 27.4  Some special roles attributed to context

Work on ways in which pragmatics comes to be encoded semantically has for the last several decades assumed that change is situated and contextual.

The term "context-induced reinterpretation" used by Heine and his colleagues explicitly calls attention to context (understood as co-text). So does the notion of "context-absorption" (Kuteva 2001: 150), which is essentially the equivalent of the semanticization of pragmatic inferences. There have, however, been debates about how to think about these contexts/co-texts, most especially whether ambiguous contexts are a necessary condition for change.

Heine (2002) and Diewald (2002) both posit a necessary stage between the initial state and grammaticalization. This intermediate stage is a "bridging" stage according to Heine, who focuses on the development of ambiguous contexts in which new interpretations are pragmatically licensed (e.g. the several centuries during which temporal *as/so long as* could be understood in certain contexts to have conditional meaning, but had not yet become semanticized or absorbed). This view is consistent with Stage 2 of Enfield's model in Figure 27.1. Diewald sees this intermediate stage, which she calls a "critical context", as one of not only meaning ambiguity but also morphosyntactic specialization and ambiguity.

Historical data do in many cases attest to an ambiguous intermediate stage. *Be going to* is probably best known for appearing in contexts where it could be understood as literal motion with a purpose or implied future for about a hundred and fifty years (see Eckardt 2006: ch. 4); *as/so long as* appears ambiguously far longer. However, in some cases "context absorption" occurs without ambiguity, at least as far as this can be discovered across different manuscripts and times. A case in point is the development described in Kytö and Romaine (2005) of English *be/have like to* + *V* 'imminently likely to V' into an "avertive" or modal auxiliary marking "action narrowly averted"[18] as in *I had like to have fallen*. In English it was used primarily from the fifteenth to nineteenth centuries, after which it came to be regarded as non-standard. The structural morphosyntactic and semantic contexts for the onset of the avertive construction in later Middle English are past tense (of the verb itself), collocation with infinitive verbs with semantically negative orientation (e.g. *fall*), and with conditional *if*- or *but*- clauses. There is no ambiguity here. Kytö and Romaine regard the development as a case of pragmatic implicatures from context becoming attached to the verb construction, and cueing the addressee about the narrowness of the aversion (i.e. coming to be used in a partly procedural way). This attachment enabled (but clearly did not cause) the use of the construction without explicit counterfactuals in the eighteenth century.

Another example of invited inferencing that became absorbed and semanticized is the development of ALL-pseudo-clefts like *All I want to eat is the peach* (Traugott 2008a). Here *all* means 'the only thing', and the cleft construction picks the peach out as an exhaustive listing. The precursors of constructions of this type were purposive as in *All I did was to honor you*, where *all* means 'everything' and the time of action (doing) preceded that of the intended honoring. The pseudo-cleft constructions originated in contexts of surprise, denial, and discursive contesting/dialogicity generally, as in this excerpt from a letter by the Earl of Leicester, who had fallen from grace at Queen Elizabeth's court:

(14)    For it is more then death unto me, that her majestie should be thus ready to interpret allwayes hardly of my service, specially before it might pleas her to understande my reasons for that I do . . . *All her majestie can laye to my charge ys going a little furder then she gave me commission for*

(1585–6 Leicester: CEEC)

This, the first example of an ALL-pseudo-cleft known to me, is not ambiguous, but derives its meaning from the complaint, the negative orientation of *lay to my charge* 'charge me with', and the situationally dynamic modal *can*. We must conclude that although encoding of pragmatics cannot occur out of context, the context is not necessarily ambiguous.

One of the striking things about contexts that is receiving increased attention as electronic corpora allow for more and more fine-grained analysis is "persistence". Hopper (1991) identified it as a principle of grammaticalization that accounts for the fact that differences between members of a category such as future markers "can be understood as continuations of their original lexical meaning" (Bybee and Pagliuca 1985: 117). An example is the retention of 'oneness' in the various uses of *only* (derived from the numeral *one*). These range from exclusive adverb (*only once*) to focusing adverb (*only Kim left*) to "exceptive" pragmatic marker (*I would have asked you; only my mother told me not to*) (Brinton 2008: 53). Visconti (2006) attributes the difference between Italian *perfino* and *addirittura*, which both mean roughly 'even', to their source meanings. *Perfino* can be an additive marker as well as a scalar focus marker (cf. also in English *even Jane left*, and *I saw Sarah and even Jane*), but *addirittura* cannot. Visconti suggests that the source construction *per fino* 'through to the end' favors an addition reading, but *a dirittura* 'in a straight line' does not.

Since semantic persistence appears to be highly language-specific, it has in some cases been reinterpreted not as an issue of retained elements of meaning, but rather of retained contexts. Since different languages have different structures, crosslinguistic replication of particular contextual types of persistence is less likely to be expected than persistence of meanings. We may note that language-specific pragmatic bridging contexts persist as do the types of morphosyntactic contexts that enable grammaticalization, though of course they are no longer "critical," only harmonic with later uses. For example, Kytö and Romaine (2005) note that contextual cues such as contrastive *but* and reference to events that one could be expected to wish to avoid persisted in the case of avertive auxiliaries. Bonelli (1992) notes that ALL-clefts tend to occur in negative contexts in her later twentieth-century data. Torres Cacoullos and Walker (2009) show that a multivariate analysis of *will* and *be going to* in their Quebec English data reveals almost identical distributions with motion verbs, and little difference in declaratives and main clauses. However, there are significant differences in small "niches", which Torres Cacoullos and Walker correlate with "vestiges of earlier source constructions" (*ibid.*: 327), e.g. *be going to* is favored in interrogatives, *will* with indefinite adverbials like *someday, later* and in main clauses of conditionals.

## 27.5  Conclusion

Not all semantic change arises out of pragmatic implicatures. Some changes are mandated (e.g. definition of *harassment*), some are self-selected and "reclaimed" (e.g. *gay, Yankee*). Others occur because the referent changes (*car, plane*), there are socio-cultural changes (e.g. changes in habits for meal times, in distinguishing kin, and above all politeness) or because a term is borrowed (this will have socially pragmatic effects) (Blank 1999).

   Nevertheless, whether primarily logical or interactional, pragmatic implicatures are always synchronically context-sensitive, and a great many semantic changes do result from the absorption of pragmatic implicatures into the meaning of an expression. Some implicatures can be readily accounted for in terms of a modified neo-Gricean construal of maxims; they are for the most part related to metatextual, modal, and grammatical meanings, although these can also help understand some lexical narrowing and broadenings. Other implicatures tend to be more socially grounded, and can be better accounted for in terms of Keller's maxims of action. These may lead to pejorations and ameliorations as well as to intersubjective interactional meanings. Like other aspects of language change, semantic change is multiply motivated, and forever potentially emergent.

# 28

# Pragmatics and prosody

Tim Wharton

## 28.1 Introduction

The way we say the words we say helps us convey the meanings we intend. In English, for example, the way words are 'chunked' into intonation phrases conveys information about grammatical structure and constituency relations. Within these phrases, differences in the relative amplitude, length and pitch of syllables help direct a listener's attention to the most salient points of a message. Sometimes, using a particular tone of voice indicates that we want to dissociate ourselves entirely from the proposition we are expressing: that we *mean* the opposite of what we are saying. So it is also true that the way we say the words we say is capable of conferring on those words entirely new layers of meaning.

Observations such as these have led phonologists to recognise, in the first instance, three distinct aspects of the prosodic structure of English that contribute to what a speaker means: *tonality* – the chunking of words into groups or phrases; *tonicity* – the location within that phrase of the pitch accent – or *tonic* – a prominent syllable which typically highlights new information; and *tone* – the type of melodic contour on that accent.[1] But commentators on the effects of prosody also acknowledge that it has an 'affective' or *paralinguistic* (Ladd 1996; Gussenhoven 2004, 2006) dimension, which, in contrast to the more language-specific observations above, might be universal across languages. Subtle changes in the tone and quality of voice, and the range of pitch variation we use, convey attitudinal information and information about our physical, mental or emotional state. These variations work closely with facial movements, which often reflect the pitch movements in our voice, and hand gestures and other kinesic behaviours, which often reflect the stress and rhythm of speech (Kendon 2004; McNeill 1992). Even the tempo at which we speak can be meaningful, as can the pauses in our speech.

Over the past forty or so years there has been a huge amount of work into the relationship between prosody and meaning (Halliday 1963, 1967a;

O'Connor and Arnold 1973; Brazil 1975; Ladd 1978, 1996; Bolinger 1983a, 1983b; Ward and Hirschberg 1988; Gussenhoven 1984, 2002, 2006; Pierre-humbert and Hirschberg 1990; Hirschberg and Ward 1995; Chen and Gussenhoven 2003). Various schools and traditions have emerged, and although no one would deny that a number of unanswered questions remain, huge progress has been made. There are sometimes fundamental differences between approaches – compare, for example Cruttenden (1986), Couper-Kuhlen (1986), Ladd (1996) and Gussenhoven (2004) – but we now have detailed formal analyses of prosodic structures and systems in a number of different languages and concrete proposals on how they relate to meaning.

An observation, rather than a criticism, of this body of work is that while much of it talks – to take one example – of 'systems of rich interpretive pragmatics' (Ladd 1996: 39), virtually none of it utilises a recognised theoretical pragmatic framework. Pragmatic theory is appealed to regularly, but rarely rigorously applied.[2] In 1996, D. Robert Ladd – attempting to assess the merits of competing accounts of intonational meaning – wrote: 'There has been very little real debate on this issue. I think this is primarily because we know too little about pragmatic inference for the debate to be conclusive' (Ladd 1996: 101).

In this chapter I want to paint a more positive picture. We know much more about pragmatic inference than we did fifteen years ago. Recent work on reasoning in the cognitive sciences (Gigerenzer *et al.* 1999, Gigerenzer 2000) has developed Herbert Simon's work in the 1940s and 1950s on 'bounded rationality', and proposes that evolution has left humans with economical rules-of-thumb which enable us to make the most of our finite cognitive capacity: 'simple, intelligent heuristics capable of making near optimal inferences' (Gigerenzer 2000: 168). Work within cognitively oriented approaches to pragmatics (Sperber and Wilson 1986, Blakemore 2002, Carston 2002) has allowed us to ask new theoretical questions: What are these fast, frugal pragmatic heuristics? To what extent does the interpretation of prosody rely on them? As well as this, since the early 1990s researchers working within pragmatics have been looking at the kind of issues raised by linguists and phonologists during the previous twenty-five years. There is now a rich literature that considers prosodic contributions to meaning from a 'meaning'-based perspective rather than a phonological one (Vandepitte 1989; Clark and Lindsey 1990; House 1990, 2006; Imai 1998; Escandell-Vidal 1998; Fretheim 2002; Wichmann 2002; Wilson and Wharton 2006; Clark, B. 2007).

The aim of this chapter is to give the reader an idea of the various dimensions along which the debates on the relationship between pragmatics and prosody take place, then go on to suggest ways in which studies in this area might be advanced. It is based around three questions. For ease of presentation, the three questions are dealt with in three separate sections (so question (1) is dealt with in section 28.2, question (2) in section 28.3 and question (3) in section 28.4). The questions are, however, inter-related, and consequently the answers to them are inter-linked:

1) How should the different types of prosody be characterised?
2) What is the relationship between prosody and *intentional* communication?
3) What kind of meaning does prosody encode (if anything)?

In the next section I summarise previous analyses of prosody and meaning and discuss in more detail the distinctions that are generally recognised. I then go on to introduce the idea that 'natural' prosodic inputs fall into two importantly different classes, *natural signs* and *natural signals*. This is a distinction first presented in Wharton 2003a, 2003b and developed in Wilson and Wharton 2006 and Wharton 2009. It suggests how the different types of prosody might be characterised from a pragmatic viewpoint. In section 28.3 I explore the relationship between prosody and intentional communication. Thanks to the work of Paul Grice (1957, 1968, 1969, 1982, 1989) it is increasingly recognised that human communication crucially relies on the expression and recognition of intentions. Utterances do not encode the messages they convey; rather, they are used to provide evidence of the speaker's intentions, which hearers must infer. How prosody fits into a model of communication which characterises human communication as *more* than a simple coding–decoding process is a question that has perhaps been overlooked in the literature so far. In section 28.4 I argue that natural signals and properly linguistic prosodic signals achieve the effects they do by encoding *procedural* rather than *conceptual* information (Blakemore 1987, 2002; Wilson and Sperber 1993a; Fretheim 2002; Wharton 2003a, 2003b). I close the chapter by suggesting that the various distinctions proposed might be useful in developing not only an account of prosody, but also a theoretical model within which we can explore the complex interaction between linguistic, paralinguistic and *non*-linguistic behaviours in utterance interpretation.

## 28.2   Natural prosodic signs, natural prosodic signals and language

One point upon which there is broad agreement is that prosody is not all cut from the same cloth. Sounding happy or sad, or bored or excited, is seen as a natural, and perhaps universal phenomenon (Ladd 1996, Gussenhoven 2004), which is interpreted by non-linguistic systems, while the lexical distinction in English between the verb and the noun 'suspect' – /sʌˈspekt/ and /ˈsʌspekt/, or between the preposition 'below' – /bɪˈləʊ/ – and the verb 'billow' – /ˈbɪləʊ/ – are seen as properly linguistic, as are the tonal lexical contrasts in languages such as Burmese and Thai. Typically, accounts of prosody tend to favour either a predominantly natural view or a predominantly linguistic one.

Bolinger (1983a) is famously of the view that we are better to focus more on the natural, pragmatic side. He focuses on the interaction between intonation and other, parallel natural components of the complex communicative stimulus:

> This kind of working in parallel is easiest to demonstrate with exclamations. An ah! of surprise, with a high fall in pitch, is paralleled by a high fall on the part of the eyebrows... A similar coupling of pitch and head movement can be seen in the normal production of a conciliatory and acquiescent utterance such as 'I will' with the accent at the lowest pitch – we call this a bow when it involves the head, but the intonation bows at the same time. (Bolinger 1983a: 98)

However, he stresses that behaviours may indeed be 'more' or 'less' natural, implicitly suggesting they exist along some kind of continuum. Even though we may feel some aspects of intonation to be properly linguistic, there still is a sense in which they have their roots in natural behaviours:

> Intonation... assists grammar – in some instances may be indispensable to it – but it is not ultimately grammatical... If here and there it has entered the realm of the arbitrary, it has taken the precaution of blazing a trail back to where it came from. (Bolinger 1983a: 106–8)

I return to this continuum in section 28.4.

In direct contrast to Bolinger's natural approach, Halliday's (1963, 1967a) account was based on the idea that a theory of grammar should be rich enough to accommodate intonation patterns and that the notion of language should be extended to incorporate all prosody: that prosody requires a *semantic*, rather than pragmatic, explanation. Indeed, intonation plays an important role in much work in truth-conditional semantics, particularly on considerations of focus (see Bosch and van der Sandt 1999 and Cohen 1999). Other more linguistically oriented accounts of prosody can be found in the works of Sag and Liberman (1975) and Gussenhoven (1984). More recently, it has been proposed that the differences between the various aspects of prosody might be captured by suggesting that prosodic effects range along a continuum from 'more to less linguistic', or from 'natural' to language-specific (Gussenhoven 2002, Pell 2002). According to various phonologists, prosody encodes both *linguistic* and *paralinguistic* meaning.

My aim in this chapter is not to endorse any one approach at the expense of another. Rather, I would like to raise issues and distinctions that have not hitherto received much attention, and which – whilst preserving the insights of the existing literature – might provide a basis for further discussion. Prosody is not all of one type. Some kind of distinction must be made between the natural aspects of prosody and the more 'linguistic' ones. But what kind?

I will begin with the 'natural' end of the natural/language-specific continuum. Chen and Gussenhoven (2003) argue that the interpretation of paralanguage is governed by *biological codes*. An example of one such code is the *effort code*, which links the amount of energy expended in the production of speech to a range of interpretive effects. An increase in effort may, for example, lead to increased articulatory precision, creating an impression of 'helpfulness', or 'obligingness'; or it may result in a wider pitch range, creating an impression of 'forcefulness' or 'certainty' or conveying affective meanings such as 'agitation' or 'surprise'.

There are two problematic issues here. The first concerns the term paralanguage. What is 'paralanguage'? For some, it is seen as including only those vocal aspects of language use that are not, strictly speaking, part of language. On this construal, facial expression, manual and vocal gestures and other kinesic behaviours are *not* part of paralanguage. Yet, others treat the paralinguistic as including most or all of those aspects of linguistic communication that are not part of language per se, but are nonetheless somehow involved with the message or meaning a communicator conveys. The second construal comes closer to how I would want to define paralanguage; rising pitch is so often linked with rising eyebrows, for example, and hand gestures – manual 'beats' – are tied so closely with the *beats* of the rhythm of speech, that it's perhaps not clear why we would want to say that while the former is part of paralanguage, the latter is not. But if this is the case, where does language end and paralanguage begin? At the end of a careful attempt to motivate the distinction, Ladd (1996: 283) concludes: 'But I concede that we must stop short of drawing a clear boundary between language and paralanguage. For now that question remains open.' Ladd's fine-grained autosegmental analyses of intonational phonology shed considerable light on which parts of prosody are universal, and which are language-specific, but if the distinction between language and paralanguage cannot really be sustained, it is hardly a helpful one. Indeed, Seddoh (2002) uses evidence from aphasiology to cast doubt on any perceived dichotomy between linguistic and paralinguistic (or affective) prosody. At some level, a more unified account of prosody is required.

The second problem is more substantive. I will argue that biological communicative systems (as distinct from a linguistic prosodic code) do exist, but not quite in the way Gussenhoven envisages. The main problem with previous characterisations of the natural aspects of prosody is that all such aspects are analysed as codes. Many natural aspects of prosody, however, are not *codes* at all.

In his 1996 study of the evolution of communication, Marc Hauser applies a distinction between signs and signals to cases of information transmission among animals. *Signs* carry information by providing evidence for it. *Signals*, on the other hand, are those behaviours that convey information and have been 'moulded by natural selection to do so' (Seeley 1989: 547): 'if an *adaptation* is a product of the process of evolution by natural selection ... then these things are adaptations. And so, I claim, they have functions. Their *functions* are their effects that make them adaptively superior to the trait variants with which they compete' (Brandon 2005). Put differently, the adaptive function of a behaviour is the effect which is historically responsible for the reproduction and propagation of that behaviour within a species (Millikan 1984, Origgi and Sperber 2000, Sperber 2007).

Whilst a sign may happen to carry information for an observer, it would go on being produced whether or not it carried this information. Hauser (1996: 9–10) provides the following example. As a result of regular travel across dusty soil, predatory species such as lions or pythons might leave traces of their presence. Certain species of prey might learn that such traces indicate the presence of a predator. The traces, however, cannot be said to have a signalling function. One way of describing this is to say that natural signs (e.g. the traces) are not *inherently* communicative. They are, in fact, classic cases of natural meaning (meaning$_N$) in the Gricean (1957, 1989) sense – see (1), (2), (3) – which can be contrasted with Gricean non-natural meaning (meaning$_{NN}$) – see (4) and (5):

(1)   Those black clouds mean$_N$ rain (see Grice 1989: 291).

(2)   Those footprints mean$_N$ a lion has been here.

(3)   That wavy line in the sand means$_N$ a python has been here.

(4)   That remark means$_{NN}$ 'it's going to rain'.

(5)   'Il va pluvoir' means$_{NN}$ 'it's going to rain'.

By contrast, signals have a communicative function. The function of the honeybee's dance is to inform other honeybees about the location of nectar; the function of the bullfrog's call is to alert female frogs to the fact that he is in the vicinity, and looking for a mate. If they did not carry this information, it would be hard to see why these behaviours survived. Most animal communication seems to be based on signalling systems of this type. In many cases, the system is so complex that it is hard to see it as governed by anything but an innately determined code.[3]

In Wharton 2003b I illustrate the distinction between natural signs and signals in the human case by comparing shivering with smiling. Shivering is a natural behaviour whose function is to generate heat by rapid muscle movement. It may provide evidence to an observer that the individual is feeling cold. However, it is not its function to carry this information: it is not a signal but a sign. Smiling, by contrast, appears to have evolved as a signalling activity whose function *is* to convey information to others (van Hooff 1972; Ekman 1989, 1992, 1999; Fridlund 1994). As Ekman puts it, smiling and other spontaneous facial expressions 'have been selected and refined over the course of evolution for their role in social communication' (1999: 51). Like the bee dance and the bullfrog calls, they are signals rather than signs. If some natural behaviours are coded signals, we would predict that they are interpreted by specialised, perhaps dedicated, neural machinery. This prediction appears to be borne out: both non-human primates and humans have neural mechanisms dedicated both to recognising faces and to processing facial expressions (Gazzaniga and Smiley 1991). Moreover, human neonates appear able to distinguish basic facial expressions of emotion, a fact which provides more support for the view that their interpretation is governed by innately determined codes (Field *et al.* 1982, Phillips *et al.* 1990, Nelson and de Haan 1996).

It is not hard to think of prosodic counterparts to shivering and smiling. For instance, a speaker's mental or physical state may affect the prosodic properties of her utterance, enabling a hearer with the appropriate experience or background knowledge to infer whether she is calm or anxious, healthy or ill, tired or alert etc. As with shivering, these prosodic properties carry information about the speaker's mental or physical state, but it is not their function to do so: they are natural signs, interpreted by inference rather than decoding. On the other hand, affective tones of voice, like affective facial expressions, may well be natural signals, interpreted by innately determined codes.

Natural codes are found in animals with no capacity for inferential intention recognition. Honeybees and frogs both lack the ability to infer the intentions of others, but they can still inform each other by means of their dance-based or vocal code. Communication among humans, by contrast, not only requires the capacity for inferential intention recognition, but may be achieved in the absence of any code at all – such as when I nudge my empty glass toward you and you infer that I'd like some more wine. Human linguistic communication exploits the human ability to understand the behaviour of others in terms of the intentions behind it – sometimes known as the 'mindreading' ability. A speaker produces linguistically coded evidence of her intention to convey a certain meaning and the hearer must use this as a starting point from which to infer that intention: linguistic communication therefore involves *both* coding *and* inferential intention recognition.

There is a vast psychological literature on the human ability to express and attribute intentions (Leslie 1987; Astington *et al.* 1988; Happé 1994; Baron-Cohen 1995; Davies and Stone 1995a, 1995b; Carruthers and Smith 1996; Scholl and Leslie 1999), which creates an interesting point of contact between the kind of philosophical concerns Grice raised, intentional accounts of pragmatics based on Grice's work (Atlas 2005; Bach and Harnish 1979; Clark, H. 1996; Gazdar 1979; Horn 1992b, 2000, 2004, 2006; Levinson 1983, 1987, 2000; Recanati 1987, 2004a; Sperber and Wilson 1986) and indeed psychological research on the capacity for mental-state attribution among humans and non-human animals (Allen and Bekoff 1997; Call and Tomasello 2008; Call *et al.* 2003; Cheney and Seyfarth 1990; Hare and Tomasello 2005; Seyfarth and Cheney 1992; Tomasello and Call 1997).

To return to question (1), I suggest that there are three distinct types of prosodic input: natural signs, which are interpreted purely inferentially;

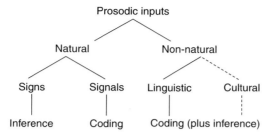

Figure 28.1. *Prosodic inputs*

natural signals, which in some cases are interpreted purely by decoding; and *linguistic signals*, which are part of a *linguistic* signalling system, governed by a *linguistic* code with its own special-purpose principles or mechanisms, and interpreted by a combination of decoding and inference. This position is represented in Figure 28.1.[4]

With the above distinctions in mind, is clear articulation a natural signal, interpreted (as Gussenhoven suggests) by an innately determined biological code? I would suggest that it is better treated as a natural *sign* of the speaker's desire to help the speaker understand, which is interpreted via inference rather than decoding. This particular element of prosody belongs under the leftmost node. A great deal can be communicated by using clear articulation – that you intend to convey helpfulness, or that you are being obliging, or that you want to convey any one of a wide range of other impressions – but nothing is *encoded* by it at all.

In the next section I turn to question (2) – what is the relationship between prosody and *intentional* communication? Then in section 28.4 I return to the question of what kind of information natural *signals*, and linguistic prosody, encode.

## 28.3  Showing and meaning_NN

Although natural prosodic signals have a communicative function, neither they nor, of course, natural signs are intrinsically linked to *intentional* communication. Nonetheless, the sign/signal distinction must be seen in light of the fact that humans have highly developed metapsychological abilities, and hence are continually aware of not only the spontaneous, natural behaviours of others, but also their own.[5] These can therefore be recruited for use in intentional communication. The question of how this takes place is under-explored in studies on pragmatics and prosody.

Sometimes, it may be clear to the audience that an aspect of prosody is being accidentally revealed rather than intentionally conveyed. So a speaker's tone of voice may simply betray the fact that she is anxious or assured, cross or collected. In more sophisticated cases, a speaker may covertly manipulate her tone to suggest to an audience that she is accidentally betraying her feelings rather than wanting them to be recognised as part of her meaning in the full Gricean sense. As well as being used *covertly*, a communicator may also *overtly* show her feelings to an audience. She may do this by deliberately producing, and perhaps exaggerating, a natural sign or signal (e.g. an angry tone of voice); or she may do it by making no attempt to conceal a spontaneously produced natural sign or signal in circumstances where it is obvious to both communicator and audience that she could have taken steps to conceal them. Grice saw an important difference between this kind of deliberate showing and cases of meaning$_{NN}$ and took pains to distinguish between them. He was prepared to treat the *simulation* of a piece of natural behaviour (a frown) as meaning$_{NN}$ and saw its interpretation as crucially involving a process of inferential intention recognition. However, he argued that a spontaneous piece of natural behaviour, even if openly *shown* to an audience, did not amount to a case of meaning$_{NN}$ (Grice 1989: 219).[6]

Grice's distinction has had important consequences for how linguistics and philosophers conceive the domain of pragmatics. According to Grice's framework, a full-fledged speaker's meaning is a type of meaning$_{NN}$. So to deny that the open showing of spontaneously produced natural behaviours is a case of meaning$_{NN}$ has had the effect of excluding it from the domain of pragmatics. This may indeed be why those working within pragmatics have tended to gloss over the prosodic aspects of communication (see note 2). But there seem to be clear cases where the overt showing of spontaneously produced natural signs and signals makes a difference to the speaker's meaning. Suppose that a speaker utters (6), making no attempt to conceal the spontaneous anger in her tone of voice (and facial expression):

(6)  Jack is late.

She would naturally be understood as meaning not only that Jack was late but that she was *angry that he was late*. Implicatures may depend on this: the degree of anger the speaker shows might warrant the hearer inferring that the speaker is going to take a particular course of action against Jack (give him a slight dressing down or fire him, tell him off in a joking manner or end their affair). Supposing a speaker utters (7), and makes no attempt to conceal the spontaneous excitement and happiness in her tone of voice.

(7)  That makes me happy!

The natural tone of voice that the speaker shows to the hearer will not only help him establish the implicit content of her utterance, but will also contribute to the proposition he takes her to be expressing. The truth conditions of her utterance of (7) will vary according to the type or degree of 'happiness' she intends to communicate ('happy' is a degree term), and hence reflects in her natural behaviour.

In my 2009 book I present a detailed defence of an approach which argues that the open showing of spontaneously produced natural signs and signals may be located along a continuum between showing and meaning$_{NN}$. Much of the inspiration for this approach comes from Relevance theory (Sperber and Wilson 1986; Blakemore 2002; Carston 2002). Relevance theorists have consistently argued that there is a continuum of cases between showing and meaning$_{NN}$, *all of which* may fall within the domain of pragmatics and contribute to a speaker's meaning (Sperber and Wilson 1986/1995b). Since aspects of the analysis to follow rely on a little background in Relevance theory, a brief exposition is in order.

According to the theory, utterance interpretation is a two-phase process. The linguistically encoded logical form which is the output of the mental grammar is simply a starting point for rich inferential processes guided by the expectation that speakers will conform to certain standards of communication. In (highly) intuitive terms, an audience faced with a piece of overtly communicative behaviour is entitled to assume that the communicator has a good reason for producing this particular stimulus as evidence not only of their intention to communicate, but of *what* they want to communicate. Thus far, there is no divergence from other post-Gricean and neo-Gricean accounts.

But Relevance theory takes the psychology seriously, and aims to provide an account of *how* pragmatic inference works. It follows recent work in cognitive science which sees the mind as an 'adaptive toolbox', a set of dedicated cognitive mechanisms which have evolved in small steps towards greater *cognitive efficiency* (Hirschfeld and Gelman 1994, Barkow *et al.* 1995, Sperber 2002).

Cognitive efficiency involves making the right choices in selecting which available new information to attend to and which available past information to process it with. The right choices in this respect consist in bringing together inputs and memory information, the joint processing of which will provide as much cognitive effect as possible for as little effort as possible (Sperber 1996: 114).

Seen in this way, cognition and communication rely partly on 'fast and frugal heuristics' (Gigerenzer *et al.* 1999, Gigerenzer 2000), which make it possible to pick out potentially relevant inputs to cognitive processes (e.g. sights, sounds, utterances, memories, conclusions of inferences) and process them in a way that enhances their relevance. Gigerenzer *et al.* could be describing one of the fundamental assumptions of relevance theory when they write (1999: 21): 'Cognition is the art of focusing on the relevant and deliberately ignoring the rest.'

The human cognitive system, then, is geared to look out for relevant information, which will interact with existing mentally represented information and bring about positive *cognitive effects* based on a combination of new and old information. Relevance itself is a property of inputs to cognitive processes, and is defined in terms of cognitive effects gained and processing effort expended: other things being equal, the more cognitive effects gained, and the less processing effort expended in gaining those effects, the greater the relevance of the input to the individual who processes it.

The human disposition to search for relevance is routinely exploited in human communication. Since speakers know that listeners will pay attention only to stimuli that are relevant enough, in order to attract and hold an audience's attention, they should make their communicative stimuli appear at least relevant enough to be worth processing. More precisely, the *Communicative Principle of Relevance* claims that by overtly displaying an intention to inform – producing an utterance or other ostensive stimulus – a communicator creates a presumption that the stimulus is at least relevant enough to be worth processing, and moreover, the most relevant one compatible with her own abilities and preferences. This Communicative Principle motivates the following Relevance-theoretic comprehension procedure – taken from Sperber and Wilson (2002: 13).

Relevance theoretic comprehension procedure:

(a)   Follow a path of least effort in computing cognitive effects:

   Test interpretive hypotheses (disambiguations, reference resolutions, implicatures etc.) in order of accessibility

(b)   Stop when your expectations of relevance are satisfied

The comprehension procedure itself can be seen as one of Gigerenzer *et al.*'s 'fast and frugal heuristics'. In this respect, then, the Relevance-theoretic approach diverges from more traditional Gricean accounts of comprehension (see Grice 1989: 30–31) – indeed, from philosophical characterisations generally – which rationally reconstruct the comprehension process in the form of conscious and reflective inferences about the mental states of others. This, as we shall see, is the first of two important divergences relevant to this chapter.

Consider again utterances of examples (6) and (7). There are many degrees of anger or happiness that that speaker might have intended to convey, and each of these would yield different implications and be relevant in a different way. While a neutral tone of voice would cause the hearer least phonological processing effort, it would give him very little guidance on the type of cognitive effects he was expected to derive. By contrast, any departure from neutral prosody would increase the hearer's phonological processing effort, but would thereby encourage him to look for extra (or different) effects. Which effects should he derive? According to the comprehension procedure above, he should follow a path of least effort, deriving whatever effects are made most accessible in the circumstances by the type of prosodic input used, and stopping when he has enough effects to justify the extra effort caused by the departure from the 'expected' prosody. Thus, the utterance of, say, (7) in an excited, enthusiastic tone of voice, with a wide pitch range and an extremely high melodic contour on 'happy' (or even 'so'), should indicate a degree and type of happiness that would warrant the derivation of a particular range of positive cognitive effects via the automatic working of the Relevance-theoretic comprehension procedure.

Another idea often found in the literature is that contrastive stress, like pointing, is a natural highlighting device, used to draw attention to a particular constituent in an utterance. This idea is explored from a Relevance-theoretic perspective in Sperber and Wilson (1986/1995b, ch. 4). Consider the following brief illustration. It follows from the Communicative Principle of Relevance that if two stress patterns differ in the amounts of processing effort required, the costlier pattern should be used more sparingly, and only in order to create extra, or different, effects. Thus, compare the effects on reference assignment of the neutral stress pattern in (8) and the costlier contrastive pattern in (9):

(8)  Peter insulted John and then he 'hit him.

(9)  Peter insulted John and then 'he hit 'him.

A hearer using the Relevance-theoretic comprehension procedure in interpreting the second conjunct in (8) should follow a path of least effort in assigning reference, and interpret *he* as referring to Peter and *him* to John. This assignment is made easily accessible by syntactic parallelism, on the one hand, and encyclopaedic knowledge, on the other. Use of the costlier contrastive pattern in (9) should divert the hearer from this otherwise preferred interpretation towards the alternative, less accessible interpretation on which *he* refers to John and *him* to Peter. On this account, contrastive stress is a 'natural' highlighting device which achieves its effects via the automatic working of the Relevance-theoretic comprehension procedure.[7] It does not *encode* anything. But some elements *do* convey information by encoding it, and it is to those elements I turn in the next section.

## 28.4  Prosody, coding and procedural meaning

As I said earlier, it is a tacit assumption in much of the literature on prosody (and, indeed, in the literature on human communication) that prosody conveys the information it does by encoding it. So on the one hand *tonality*, *tonicity* and *tone* encode information about grammatical structure and constituency relations, and help direct a listener's attention to the most salient points of a message. On the other, the natural aspects of prosody encode information that creates impressions, conveying evidence of emotional states and attitudes. We have seen that much of what is often treated as governed by either a linguistic or biological code might not be coded at all. Nonetheless, natural codes do exist, as of course does the code of language.

Much of the early work on meaning and prosody – in what might be called the British School – concerned itself with the meanings of English nuclear tones (or *pitch tones* or *melodies*). This is the rising or falling (and rising *and* falling) that occurs on the tonic syllable in an intonation phrase. But assigning meaning to English tones has proved a troublesome business. In general, the more precise one's account, the easier it is to criticise. O'Connor and

Arnold (1973) make highly specific claims about meaning. A low fall, according to them, means that a statement is definite and complete insofar as it is a 'separate item of interest'. In addition it conveys a 'detached, reserved, dispassionate, dull, possibly grim or surly attitude on the part of the speaker'. But so much depends on the words that such accounts are rendered meaningless.

(10)   I \ love you.

It is now recognised that prosody encodes something far less precise, and perhaps hard to pin down in conceptual terms. So rather than a particular tone encoding a concept such as 'detachedness' or 'reservation', the tone encodes information that indicates how the speaker intends the proposition she is expressing to fit in with what she believes the hearer knows or believes at a particular point in the conversation. As House puts it, prosody functions to 'guide the listener in how to proceed: how to access the relevant cognitive context within which to interpret the speaker's contribution, how to evaluate that contribution, and how to construct the interaction itself, to enable the communication to take place' (House 2007: 369). In House's work, part of the job of prosody is to help *create* the context.

Hirschberg and Ward (1995: 407) propose that the high-rise question contour of English encodes 'that the propositional content of the utterance is to be added to the speaker's and hearer's "mutual beliefs" . . . and to question whether the hearer can relate that propositional content to the contents of the hearer's own (unshared) beliefs'. In a recent paper B. Clark (2007), building on the work of Imai (1998), makes proposals about all the tones of Southern 'Estuary' English: a rise, for example, encodes information to the effect that 'an explicature of the utterance is entertained as an interpretation of a thought of someone other than the speaker at the time of utterance'. The Relevance-theoretic term 'explicature' – so-named to parallel Grice's notion of 'implicature' – is an overtly communicated assumption inferentially *developed* from the logical form encoded by the utterance (in the case of a declarative, the intended truth-conditional content of the utterance).[8] Such proposals are vague enough to be worthy of attention, but note that what prosody encodes is often even vaguer: affective prosody communicates moods and vague impressions.

We are led to two apparently incompatible claims: on the one hand, the claim that prosodic signals are naturally or linguistically coded; on the other, that they typically create a diffuse impression rather than conveying a determinate message. A *code* is standardly seen as a set of rules or principles pairing signals with determinate messages. How is it possible to maintain both that prosodic signals are coded and that what they convey may be no more than a wide array of weak non-propositional effects? The answer, I will suggest, is in two parts. In the first place, we need a notion of informative intention that allows for the communication of such vague effects (so we need a second divergence from traditional Gricean accounts); in the second, we need a new notion of coding.

Turning to the first part of the answer, the second divergence from traditional Gricean accounts is that the Relevance-theoretic informative intention is not characterised as an intention to modify the hearer's thoughts directly – 'to produce a particular response r' (Sperber and Wilson 1986, Wharton 2008). Indeed, Relevance theorists argue that this intention is not always reducible to an intention to communicate simply a single proposition and propositional attitude (or even a small set). Instead, the informative intention is characterised as an intention to modify not the hearer's thoughts directly, but his *cognitive environment*: this includes not only all the facts or assumptions that he is aware of, but also all the facts or assumptions he is capable of becoming aware of, in his physical environment – in Relevance-theoretic terms, the set of facts that are manifest to him (i.e. that he is capable of perceiving or inferring). This difference sheds new light on how better to analyse some of the weaker, vaguer aspects of communication, including the communication of impressions, emotions, attitudes, feelings and sensations.

Consider the following example. A man and a woman arrive in a small village in the South of France. Having briefly scanned the square, he smiles at her; then he looks back to the square silently urging her to look too. She follows his gaze. What is he drawing her attention to? Is it the crumbling fountain at the centre of the square? Is it two tall sunflowers growing up the side of the café? Is it the faded pink houses, the group of old men playing *boules*, the general ambience? Is it one, many or all of these things? Is it *none* of these things, but rather the effect they are having on him?

But she does not turn to him and say 'What do you mean?' She acknowledges him and smiles back, because she understands. The sights, sounds and smells perceivable in her physical environment interact with her inferential abilities and her memories to alter her cognitive environment, making it possible for her to have further thoughts, memories and feelings similar to his own. This is all that he intended: to convey an impression. He did not mean any one thing; his intention cannot be pinned down to one specific proposition or small set of propositions; it was simply to make more manifest to her whatever assumptions became manifest to him as he scanned the square.

Such effects can be communicated by a non-coded behaviour, such as an overt gaze, but how is it possible to explain how a diffuse impression or a wide array of weak implicatures – rather than any determinate message – might be the result of a *coded prosodic signal*? In this section of the chapter, I pursue an idea originally proposed by Diane Blakemore (1987, 2002) and applied to different aspects of prosody by Vandepitte (1989), B. Clark and Lindsey (1990), House (1990), Escandell-Vidal (1998, 2002), Imai (1998) and Fretheim (2002). The reason it is hard to pin down what prosody encodes in conceptual terms is that prosody doesn't encode anything conceptual at all.

The idea is this: if linguistic communication typically involves a combination of decoding and inference, then linguistic signals might be expected to encode information of two distinct types. First, there is regular *conceptual* encoding, where a word (e.g. *boy*) encodes a concept (e.g. BOY) which figures as a constituent of the logical form of sentences in which that word occurs. Second, we might expect to find a form of *procedural* encoding, where a word (or other linguistic expression) encodes information specifically geared to guiding the hearer during the inferential phase of comprehension. The function of such 'procedural' expressions would be to facilitate the identification of the speaker's meaning by narrowing the search space for inferential comprehension, increasing the salience of some hypotheses and eliminating others, thus reducing the overall effort required. This distinction draws on the distinction made in cognitive science between the representational and computational aspects of cognition.

Properly linguistic expressions which have been analysed in procedural terms include discourse connectives, mood indicators and discourse particles (cf. Blakemore 1987, 2002; König 1991; Wilson and Sperber 1993a; Hall 2007). So a discourse connective such as *but* encodes a procedure which inhibits a conclusion that might otherwise be drawn; mood indicators – e.g. imperative morphosyntax– encode procedures which facilitate the retrieval of a range of speech-act or propositional-attitude descriptions associated with imperatives; discourse particles such as *please* encode a procedure which facilitates the retrieval of a range of speech-act or propositional-attitude descriptions associated with requests. Properly linguistic prosodic signals (e.g. lexical stress, lexical tone and fully grammaticalised aspects of prosody – perhaps nuclear tones) might be analysed on similar lines, as facilitating the retrieval of certain types of syntactic, semantic or conceptual representation. Thus, the notion of procedural encoding applies straightforwardly to properly linguistic prosodic elements.

Turning to natural signals, there has been some debate about whether interjections such as *oh, ah* and *wow* are properly linguistic. In my 2003a paper I survey the literature and conclude that interjections are best analysed as falling on the natural rather than the properly linguistic side. However, I also argue that interjections are natural signals rather than signs, and that they share with discourse connectives and discourse particles the property of encoding procedural rather than conceptual information. On this approach, the function of an interjection such as *wow* might be to facilitate the retrieval of a range of speech-act or propositional-attitude descriptions associated with expressions of surprise or delight, which might be narrowed in context by information derived from prosody, facial expressions, background assumptions, discourse context etc., and contribute to the speaker's meaning in the regular way, by falling under the Relevance-theoretic comprehension procedure.

The line of argument is taken further in Wharton 2003b, which proposes that natural signals such as smiles and other spontaneous facial expressions should also be analysed as encoding procedural rather than conceptual information. The idea can be extended to natural prosody, such as affective tone of voice. On this approach, the function of affective tone of voice – a natural signal – would be to facilitate the retrieval of similar propositional-attitude descriptions to those activated by interjections. This approach makes it possible, on the one hand, to capture the fact that natural signals, interjections and properly linguistic signals such as mood indicators or discourse particles all have a coded element, and on the other, to explain why what they communicate can sometimes be so nebulous, contextually shaded and hard to pin down in conceptual terms.

If, as Bolinger appears to suggest in the quote in section 28.2, there is a diachronic dimension to the continuum between display and language, then this continuum may turn out to be a useful tool with which to follow the trail back from arbitrary linguistics expressions to their natural origins: perhaps to prosody too. Chen and Gussenhoven (2003) and Wichmann (2002) suggest that since there is considerable cross-linguistic variation in the way paralinguistic meanings are realised, to a point where they may become heavily stereotyped or even fully grammaticalised, they might also become part of language proper. In Wharton 2009 I suggest ways in which vocalisation might be ranged along such a diachronic (and synchronic) continuum, from an entirely natural gag reflex in which the glottis simply closes, to the related *ugh* [ux] through interjections such as *yugh* [jux] and *yuk* [jʌk] to linguistically productive expressions such as *yucky*, *yuckier* and *yuckiest* (see Padilla Cruz 2009a, 2009b for more discussion of interjections). As we will see in the next section, a synchronic version of this continuum is already used in the literature on gesticulation and gesture (McNeill 1992, Kendon 2004).

## 28.5  Mysterious processes

Commenting on an earlier version of Wilson and Wharton 2006, Dan Sperber pointed out to Deirdre Wilson and myself that some prosodic variation may be neither natural (whether coded or not) nor properly linguistic but *cultural* (Sperber 1996, Origgi and Sperber 2000, Sperber 2007). Examples of cultural prosodic inputs might include the stylised intonation patterns or 'calling contours' discussed by Ladd (1978).

While the notion of a cultural, as opposed to linguistic, code has thus far played no role in analyses of prosody, it is widely used in the study of gesture. Communicators have a whole range of gestures at their disposal. At one extreme, there are the entirely natural, non-linguistic gesticulations that are spontaneously used to accompany speech. At the other, there is sign language proper, which is fully linguistic and non-natural in Grice's sense. Between these two extremes lie a range of gestures which, whilst clearly *non-linguistic*, are equally clearly non-natural in Grice's sense. At the beginning of his 1992 book on gesture, David McNeill describes the various types of gesture in terms of a framework that is becoming something of a theme in this book. Gesture, he argues, is best seen as ranging along a

Gesticulation → Language-like gestures → Pantomimes → Emblems → Sign Languages

Figure 28.2. *Kendon's Continuum*

*continuum* between natural display and language proper. The continuum McNeill presents is based on one originally shown by Adam Kendon (1988). 'Kendon's continuum' is reproduced (from McNeill 1992: 37) in Figure 28.2. There are clear parallels with the prosodic continuum discussed earlier in the paper. I would also suggest that the distinctions presented in Figure 28.1 can be applied straightforwardly to the analysis of gestures described here.

As we move from left to right on the continuum, the gestures become less natural, take on more 'language-like' properties and depend less on the co-presence of language itself. Those movements classified as 'gesticulation' in the continuum are the spontaneous movements of the arms and hands that accompany speech: what McNeill describes as 'the unwitting accompaniments of speech' (1992: 72). McNeill 1992 is devoted entirely to these movements, of which communicators are either unaware or, at best, only marginally aware. 'Language-like' gestures are similar to gesticulations but are 'integrated' into a linguistic string in the sense that they must occur at a certain point and contribute to the interpretation of the string as a whole; so Jack might utter 'the dental examination was OK, but when he started [*gesture to represent drilling*] it was agony'. 'Pantomimes' are those movements that depict objects or actions; accompanying speech is no longer obligatory – 'there may be either silence or just inarticulate onomatopoetic [*sic*] sound effects ("whoops!", "click!" etc.)'. 'Emblems' are those cultural-dependent symbolic gestures used to convey a wide range of both positive and negative meanings: the British 'thumbs up' signal and the two-fingered insult are two examples (see McNeill 1992: 57–9 for an overview). Finally, Sign Languages are, of course, languages proper, with their own syntactic, semantic and phonological rules.

I remarked earlier that in the past too little attention has been paid to the question of how prosody fits into a model of communication within which communication is conceived as more than a strict coding–decoding process. The same problem arises in much of the literature on gesture. In general, the overt use of gestures in intentional communication is not acknowledged at all. Kendon (1992: 328) writes:

> If I clear my throat in the midst of an utterance this is not treated as part of what I am 'saying'. If I uncross my legs, take a drag on my cigarette or sip my coffee while another is speaking, such actions are not attended to by other participants as if they are contributions to the conversation. Overt acts of attention to activities of this sort are generally not made at all. Whereas spoken utterances and bodily movements, if perceived as gestures, are regarded as vehicles of explicitly intended messages, directly relevant to the business of the conversation, other aspects of behaviour are not regarded in this light.

But clearing the throat and uncrossing the legs can *certainly* contribute to the overtly intended speaker's meaning, just as bodily movement (and indeed, aspects of the spoken utterance) might convey information accidentally, or even be intended by the communicator to convey information covertly. The distinctions applied to prosody earlier in this paper – between accidental information transmission, covert intentional and overt intentional communication – carry across to the study of gesture too.

Kendon's comments reflect the fact that in accounts of human non-verbal communication generally, discussion of the role of intentions takes a very secondary role. In his account of facial expression Alan Fridlund (1994) abstracts away from it entirely: 'I have circumvented these "levels of intentionality" issues in the interests of space, and use intentionality in a purely functionalist sense' (p. 146). Kendon himself writes: 'the judgement of an action's intentionality is a matter of how it appears to others and not a matter of some *mysterious process by which the intention or intentions themselves that may guide the action may be known*' (2004: 15 – my emphasis).

But the aim of any pragmatic framework is surely to *de*mystify. A spoken utterance is typically a composite of linguistic signals, natural signals and natural signs which interact in complex ways to yield a hypothesis about the speaker's meaning. Only by engaging with these 'mysterious processes' can we hope to better understand the intricate, interwoven relationship between the words we say, *how* we say the words we say, the kinesic movements we make when we say the words we say and how all these factors contribute to our meanings.

# 29

# Pragmatics and information structure

Jeanette K. Gundel

## 29.1 Introduction

Grammars of natural languages offer speakers a variety of options for expressing the same basic informational content. For example, in English, the sentences in (1a)–(1j), among others, can all be used to convey the information that a particular person named Smith won an election.

(1) a.　Smith won that election.
　　 b.　The election, Smith won.
　　 c.　There was an election that Smith won.
　　 d.　This election was won by Smith.
　　 e.　Smith won an election.
　　 f.　It was Smith who won the election.
　　 g.　What Smith won was the election.
　　 h.　(As for) that election, Smith won it.
　　 i.　Smith won it.
　　 j.　He won the election.

The possibilities can be further multiplied by placement of a prominent pitch accent on different constituents of these sentences.

The term 'information structure' has been used to refer to the kinds of distinctions exemplified by the sentences in (1), both at the level of meaning and at the level of morphosyntactic and prosodic form used to express that meaning. It is widely assumed that these different syntactic, morphological, and prosodic options reflect different ways that information expressed in these sentences is conceptualized, depending on (a) what the utterance is primarily about (as distinct from the new information asserted, questioned, etc. about that entity), and (b) what the addressee is assumed to know or believe and/or be attending to. The different forms may also assist the addressee in processing the information in a given context or, in Relevance-theoretic terms (Sperber and Wilson 1986) in identifying the context in which the utterance is to be interpreted. The various factors that determine how information is expressed in the sentences in (1) provide the basis for explaining why the sentences in (1) cannot be used appropriately in the same context, even though they may express the same basic informational content. Thus, while (1a), (1c), and (1e) would be felicitous as the first sentence in a conversation, this is much less likely to be the case for the other sentences in (1). In this sense, information structure is, at least partly, a pragmatic phenomenon.

Work on information structural concepts within the Western grammatical tradition can be traced back to at least the second half of the nineteenth century. The German grammarians von der Gabelenz (1868) and Paul (1880) used the term "psychological subject" for what is now variously called topic, ground, or theme; and "psychological predicate" for what is now commonly called comment, focus, or rheme. Work of the Czech linguist Mathesius in the 1920s (e.g. Mathesius 1928) initiated a rich and highly influential tradition of research in this area within the Prague School that continues to the present day (see Daneš 1974, Firbas 1966, Sgall *et al.* 1973, Sgall *et al.* 1986 *inter alia*). Also influential has been the seminal work of Halliday (1967b), Chafe (1976) and, within the generative tradition, Chomsky (1971), Gundel (1974), Jackendoff (1972), Kuno (1972, 1976), Kuroda (1965, 1972), Prince (1981), Reinhart (1981), Rochemont (1986), *inter alia*. More recent work will be cited below.

## 29.2   What is information structure?

The term "information structure," originally introduced by Halliday (1967b), has been widely associated with the distinction between given and new information expressed in a sentence, the way in which this distinction is formally expressed in a language (through morphology, syntax, and prosody), and the interaction of these factors with more general pragmatics (cognitive and communicative) principles. There continues to be disagreement and confusion, however, regarding the exact nature of information-structural primitives themselves, their relation to one another, and how much of information structure is grammatical and how much is pragmatic. Some of the confusion has resulted from conflating two distinct types of givenness/newness. Following Gundel (1988, 1999a, 1999b) and Gundel and Fretheim (2004) these are described below under the terms "referential givenness/newness" and "relational givenness/newness." The term "information structure" perhaps applies more appropriately to relational givenness/newness, which concerns structural relations on the same level of representation, whereas referential givenness/newness concepts may be better characterized as "information status." However, the terms "information structure" and "information status" have been used interchangeably by many authors for both concepts and both will therefore be discussed here.

## 29.2.1    Referential givenness/newness

Referential givenness/newness involves a relation between a linguistic expression and a corresponding non-linguistic entity in the speaker/hearer's mind, the discourse (model), or some real or possible world, depending on the analyst's assumptions about where the referents or corresponding meanings of these linguistic expressions reside. Some representative examples of referential givenness concepts include existential presupposition (e.g. Strawson 1964a), various senses of referentiality and specificity (e.g. Fodor and Sag 1982), the familiarity condition on definite descriptions (e.g. Heim 1982), the activation and identifiability statuses of Chafe (1994) and Lambrecht (1994), the hearer-old/new and discourse-old/new statuses of Prince (1992), the levels of accessibility of Ariel (1988, 1990), and the cognitive statuses of Gundel *et al.* (1993). For example, the cognitive statuses on the Givenness Hierarchy below represent referential givenness statuses that an entity mentioned in a sentence can be assumed to have in the mind of the addressee.

**The Givenness Hierarchy** (Gundel *et al.* 1993)

| in focus > | activated > | familiar > | uniquely identifiable > | referential > | type identifiable |
|---|---|---|---|---|---|
| it | this N/this/ that/SHE[1] | that N | the N | indefinite *this* N | *a* N |

Gundel *et al.* propose that human languages have individual lexical items (typically determiners and pronouns) which signal such cognitive (memory and attention) statuses as part of their conventional meaning. The relevant English forms are listed here below each status. A speaker's assumptions about the status of some entity in the mind of the addressee thus constrains the linguistic forms that may be appropriately used in referring to that entity and, conversely, the lexical items in question serve to facilitate processing and understanding by providing procedural information to the addressee as to how/where the intended referent can be mentally accessed. Since the statuses are in a relation of unidirectional entailment, forms that encode the various statuses provide increasingly more specified information about cognitive status as one moves up (from right to left) on the hierarchy. For example, in (1e) the indefinite article *a* in *an election* provides the information that the addressee is only expected to access a representation of the type of thing described (type identifiable), which should be possible just in case the addressee understands the meaning of the word *election*; the definite article *the*, as in *the election* in (1b) and (1j), instructs the addressee to associate a unique representation of a specific member of that type with the DP headed by the article (uniquely identifiable) either by association with an entity already in memory or by constructing a new unique representation, if possible; the demonstrative determiner *that*, as in *that election* in (1a), provides the information that the intended referent is to be accessed by selecting a representation that already exists in memory (familiar); the demonstrative determiner *this*, as in *this election* in (1d), provides the information that the intended referent is to be associated with an entity not only in memory, but in current awareness (activated) and the pronoun *it*, as in (1i), provides the information that the intended referent is not only in awareness, but in current focus of attention. The relation of unidirectional entailment that holds between statuses also gives rise to scalar implicatures (Horn 1972), which result from interaction of the Givenness Hierarchy with general pragmatic principles. This includes, for example, the implicature that the interpretation of an indefinite article phrase is at most referential, i.e. not uniquely identifiable, familiar, etc., and the implicature that the referent of a demonstrative determiner is not already in focus, and thus constitutes a focus shift (see Gundel *et al.* 1993, forthcoming, and Gundel 2010 for further discussion).

Since cognitive statuses are assumed to be conventionally encoded by various determiners and pronouns, they are in this sense part of linguistic knowledge, no less so than the conceptual content encoded by other lexical items. However, to the extent that cognitive status meanings are rooted in the interactive, communicative function of language, i.e. a speaker's assumptions about the addressee's knowledge and attention state at a given point in the discourse, they are also pragmatic (though perhaps no more so than the meanings of words like 'I' and 'here').

The Givenness Hierarchy account of referential givenness statuses signaled by different forms allows a principled explanation for why nominal expressions that encode the same conceptual content can have different interpretations and nominal expressions that encode different conceptual content can have the same interpretation. Thus, in (2), the conceptual information directly encoded in the phrase *these primitive reptiles* is that the intended referent is some group of primitive reptiles. However, the content words in the phrase alone do not uniquely determine which primitive reptiles are being referred to.

(2)    A restudy of pareiasaurs reveals that these primitive reptiles are the
       nearest relatives of turtles.
          (M. S. Y. Lee, 'The origin of the Turtle Body Plan.' *Science*, 1993: 1649)

Since the proximal demonstrative determiner *this/these* encodes the cognitive status "activated", it restricts possible interpretations to pareiasaurs, as these are the only activated plural entity at the point when the phrase is encountered, given that (2) is the first sentence in a magazine article. The reference can thus be successfully resolved even without prior knowledge that pareiasaurs are primitive reptiles. If *these primitive reptiles* were replaced with the pronoun *they*, the interpretation would still be pareiasaurs because the personal pronoun *they* signals that the referent is at least activated (also in focus if it is unstressed), and pareiasaurs can be assumed to be in focus, as they were mentioned in a prominent (subject) position earlier in the same sentence and are the only plural entity that can be assumed to be in focus at this point in the discourse. The possible interpretations would change, however, if *these primitive reptiles* were replaced by a phrase headed by the definite article, *the primitive reptiles*. Since the definite article only signals that the addressee is to associate a unique representation with the intended referent, and since anything in focus is necessarily uniquely identifiable, the definite article phrase can also be interpreted as referring to pareiasaurs. However, there is another, for most speakers more likely, interpretation where the phrase refers to the whole class of primitive reptiles, i.e. it is interpreted as generic. This is so because a unique representation of all primitive reptiles can be constructed on the basis of the conceptual content encoded in the phrase alone (at most uniquely identifiable) or can be retrieved from long-term memory (at most familiar). In either case, the conceptual content of the phrase would have to be processed, and since this is all that is necessary for the generic interpretation, this reading is predicted to be the most accessible one (see Gundel 2010 and Gundel *et al.* forthcoming, for further discussion).

Referential givenness concepts have also been shown to play a role in such linguistic phenomena as sentence accent and word order. Greater degrees of referential givenness are associated with weaker stress (cf. Chafe 1976, 1994; Ladd 1978; Lambrecht 1994, *inter alia*) and also with right attachment/dislocation (Grosz and Ziv 1998, Gundel 1988, Vallduví 1992).

## 29.2.2 Relational givenness/newness – topic–focus structure

Relational givenness/newness involves a partition of the semantic-conceptual representation of a sentence into two complementary parts, X and Y, where X is what the sentence is about and Y is what is predicated about X. X is given in relation to Y in the sense that it is independent and outside the scope of what is predicated in Y. Y is new in relation to X in the sense that it is new information asserted, questioned, etc. about X. Relational givenness/newness thus reflects how the informational content of a particular event or state of affairs is conceptualized, represented, and expressed, and how its truth value is to be assessed. For example, (1a) above may be used to describe a particular event of a person named Smith winning an election, from the perspective of Smith, where Smith is what the sentence is about and what is predicated about Smith is that s/he won an election. The same event may be described from the perspective of the election, as in (1d) or (1h), where the election is what the sentence is about and what is predicated about the election is that Smith won it. A somewhat more complex situation exists when, for example, it is taken for granted that Smith won something and the sentence encodes an implicit reference to some entity that fits the description "Smith won x," this entity being what the sentence is about, and the main predication is identification of this entity as the election, as in (1g).

Terms used to denote relational givenness/newness concepts include psychological subject and predicate (e.g. in the works of van der Gabelenz and

Paul mentioned above), presupposition–focus (e.g. Chomsky 1971, Jackend-off 1972), background–focus (e.g. Krifka 2005), topic–comment (e.g. Gundel 1974), theme–rheme (e.g. Steedman 1991, Vallduví 1992, topic–predicate (Erteschik-Shir 1997). The term "topic" will be used here for what has var-iously been called psychological/logical subject, theme, and ground; and "information focus" will be used for what has variously been called psycho-logical/logical predicate, rheme, and comment.[2]

Referential givenness/newness and relational givenness/newness are logically independent, as seen in the following examples.

(3)  A: Who called?
     B: Pat said SHE[3] called.
          (Gundel 1980)

(4)  A: Did you vote for Mary?
     B: Yes. It was MARY I voted for.

If *SHE* in (3) is used to refer to Pat, it is referentially given in virtually every possible sense. The intended referent is presupposed, specific, referential, familiar, activated, in focus, uniquely identifiable, hearer-old, and discourse-old. But the subject of the embedded sentence is at the same time relationally new, and therefore receives a focal accent here. It instantiates the variable in the relationally given, topical part of the sentence, *x called*, thus yielding the new information expressed in (3). Similarly, in (4), Mary is referentially given at the beginning of B's response. Her cognitive status would be at least "activated", as she was mentioned in the immediately preceding sentence; but she is new information in relation to the topic of (4B), who B voted for.

The two kinds of givenness/newness also differ in other respects. Rela-tional givenness/newness concepts such as topic and information focus are necessarily a property of linguistic expressions and the conceptual/semantic representations that are associated with them. As Reinhart (1981) writes in her classic paper on topic, it is "a pragmatic phenomenon which is specif-ically linguistic". Referential givenness/newness, on the other hand, is not specifically linguistic at all. Thus, for example, one can just as easily char-acterize a visual or non-linguistic auditory stimulus, for example a house or a tune, as familiar or not, in focus or not, and even specific or not. By contrast, the topic–focus partition can only apply to linguistic expressions, namely sentences or utterances and their interpretation. Corresponding to this essential difference is the fact that referential givenness statuses, e.g. "familiar" or "in focus", are uniquely determined by what can be assumed to be the knowledge and attention state of the addressee at a given point in the discourse. Thus, in answer to A's question in (4) above, B could have responded *Yes, I voted for HER* or *Yes. SHE's the one I voted for*, because activated referents also allow the use of a stressed personal pronoun or a demonstrative pronoun. The cognitive status of the referent is the same, however, regard-less of whether a pronoun or a full determiner phrase is used. Relational givenness notions like topic, on the other hand, may be constrained or influenced by the discourse context (as all aspects of meaning are in some sense), but they are not uniquely determined by it. As the Czech linguist Peter Sgall pointed out a number of years ago, a sentence like *There was a soccer game last night* could be followed by *Poland beat Sweden* or by *Sweden was beaten by Poland*. The latter two sentences could each have an all-focus interpretation, where the whole sentence is a comment on some topic not overtly expressed in the sentence, possibly established by the preceding utterance. However, it is also possible in exactly the same discourse context to interpret the first of these sentences as a comment about Poland and the second as a comment about Sweden. Which of these possible interpretations is the intended one depends on the interests and perspective of the speaker.

While referential and relational givenness/newness are independent notions, most authors agree that the referential givenness properties of topics are restricted. There continues to be disagreement however about what exactly this restriction is. Some authors (e.g. Gundel 1985, 1988; Gundel and Fretheim 2004) maintain that referents of topics must be familiar, citing the association of topics with definiteness in support of this claim. Others (e.g. Reinhart 1981, Prince 1985) propose that the familiarity condition on topics is too strong, since indefinites can sometimes appear in structural positions typically reserved for topics.[4] It is generally agreed, however, that topics must be at least referential. There must be an individuated entity, or class/group of entities, for the utterance, sentence, or proposition to be about, and in order for truth value to be assessed in relation to that entity.

## 29.3 How is information structure formally expressed across languages?

### 29.3.1 Information structure and prosody

An association between prosody and information structure has been shown to hold in a variety of typologically and genetically diverse languages, where the most consistent way of marking information structure is through placement of a prominent pitch accent within the comment/focus (see Büring 2010 and the papers in Lee *et al.* 2007 for detailed crosslinguistic accounts). In English, for example, information focus is marked by what Bolinger (1961) and Jackendoff (1972) call an A accent (the simplex H* tone of Pierrehumbert 1980). Elements within the prosodic domain of the H* accent are interpreted as part of the information focus and elements outside that domain are interpreted as part of the topic.[5]

Moreover, as illustrated in examples (3) and (4) above, assignment of prominent pitch accent to the relationally new, focal constituent, overrides the weaker stress that is typically assigned to constituents with a high degree of referential givenness, i.e. ones that are in focus or even at most activated (see section 29.2.1).

The crucial role that prosody plays in marking information structure is compellingly illustrated in the following example from Lambrecht (1994).

(5)    Nazis tear down antiwar posters

As Lambrecht notes, most people, when asked to interpret a written sentence like (5) in the absence of any contextual cues, would assign a prominent pitch accent to the direct object (ANTIWAR posters), the default accentual pattern that people normally assume when presented with written sentences in isolation, yielding an interpretation where the topic and focus coincide with the grammatical subject *Nazis* and the grammatical predicate *tear down antiwar posters* respectively. Such an interpretation would be likely, for example, in a context where (5) is uttered during a discussion about Nazis.

Since information focus can be projected to higher constituents (see Chomsky 1971, Selkirk 1995), there are also other possible interpretations of this sentence with pitch accent on the direct object, which Lambrecht doesn't discuss. For example, it could have an interpretation where the topic is items included in the things that Nazis tear down and the information focus is antiwar posters. It can also have an interpretation where the whole sentence is the information focus, what Marty (1918) calls a thetic judgment (see also Kuroda 1972), and what Schmerling (1976) calls an "all-news" sentence and Lambrecht (1994) calls a "sentence focus". This would be the likely interpretation, for example, as a newspaper heading, where the topic is simply what happened today. What is particularly compelling about this example is that, as Lambrecht points out, the interpretation of the sentence, as well as the accentual pattern we assign to it, changes dramatically when we are provided with the context in which he first encountered the sentence. Lambrecht notes that the sentence was "written with a felt pen across a poster protesting the war in Central America. The poster had been partly ripped down from the wall it had been glued onto." Provided with this additional contextual information, the prominent H* pitch accent now shifts to the subject and the resulting interpretation, that people who tear down antiwar posters are Nazis, is truth-conditionally distinct from the one we assign to the sentence when prominent pitch accent is on the direct object.

A new or contrastive topic typically receives some sort of prosodic prominence as well, resulting in sentences with two prosodic peaks, as in (6b).

(6)    a.    What about Fred, what did he do?
       b.    FRED ate the BEANS.

In languages like English and German, the type of pitch accent that marks information focus is distinct from the one that marks a contrastive topic. For example, as an answer to (6a), (6b) would have an H* accent on *beans*, and what Bolinger and Jackendoff call a B accent (Pierrehumbert's complex L + H* tone) on *Fred*. But in response to a question like "What about the beans, who ate them?", *Fred* would have an H* accent and *beans* would have an L + H* accent.[6] However, not all languages distinguish prosodically between information focus and a contrastive or newly introduced topic. Thus, Fretheim (1987, 1992a, 1992b, 2001) argues that the pitch contours that encode contrastive topic and information focus in Norwegian are not distinct. For example, (7), with a prosodically prominent subject as well as a prosodically prominent direct object, could be a statement about Fred or a statement about the beans. There is no intonational phenomenon in Norwegian that enables the hearer to uniquely identify topic and focus in an utterance of (7).

(7)  FRED   spiste   BØNNENE
     Fred    ate       the beans
     'Fred ate the beans'

A speaker's intended topic–focus structure would have to be determined by pragmatic inference alone, based on the context in which the sentence is used (see Gundel and Fretheim 2002 for further discussion).

   Similarly, according to Vallduví and Vilkuna (1998: 89), information focus (their "rheme") and contrast (their "kontrast") are "associated with a single high tone accent" in Finnish; and the distinction between the two is coded syntactically rather than prosodically.[7]

## 29.3.2  Information structure and morphosyntax

All human languages appear to have different syntactic constructions for describing the same event or state of affairs, depending on information-structural concepts such as those discussed above. For example, the structure most widely and consistently associated with syntactic encoding of relational givenness/newness is one where a constituent referring to the topic of the sentence is adjoined to the left or right of a full-sentence comment/focus. Such prototypical topic–comment sentences, exemplified in (1h) above (*That election, Smith won it*), are presumably found in all human languages, and are relatively unmarked structures in so-called topic-prominent languages like Chinese and Japanese (Li and Thompson 1976). In some of these languages, for example Japanese and Korean, topic or focus may also be marked morphologically (see Bak 1977, Gundel 1988, Kuno 1972, Kuroda 1965, Lee 1999, *inter alia*.)

   Languages differ, however, in the consistency with which information structure is directly mapped onto linguistic form. For example, as noted by Chao (1968), the grammatical predicate of a sentence and what he calls the "logical predicate" (our "information focus") do not always coincide in English. Chao illustrates this point with the following exchange between a guide (A) and a tourist (B).

(8)  A: We are now passing the oldest winery in the region.
     B: Why?

The source of the humor here is that the English sentence uttered by the guide has two possible interpretations. On one interpretation, the information focus (Chao's logical predicate) coincides with the grammatical predicate, i.e. *are now passing the oldest winery in the region*. On the other interpretation, the information focus includes only the direct object, *the oldest winery in the region*. The tourist (B) seems to be questioning the first interpretation, but it is the second interpretation that the guide actually intended to convey (what we are passing now is the oldest winery in the region). Chao notes (1968: 78) that the humor would be absent in Chinese because in this case, the guide's intended message would be expressed in Chinese by a structure that more literally translates as "What we are passing now is the oldest winery in the region." Thus, while the different syntactic constructions are available in both languages, Chinese more consistently exploits the syntactic option for directly mapping information structure onto syntactic structure.

Similar differences are found even among very closely related languages. For example, while "it"-clefts such as those in (1f) (*It was Smith who won the election*) exist in all Germanic languages, they are much more frequently used in Norwegian and Swedish than in English (Gundel 2002, 2005; Johansson 2002). Gundel (2002, 2005) proposes that this difference is due to a stronger tendency to map information structure directly onto syntactic structure in Norwegian and Swedish. Specifically, these languages appear to exhibit a much stronger tendency to keep information focus (relationally new information) out of subject position and to encode presupposed (referentially and relationally given) material as a single constituent in the subordinated cleft clause, e.g. *who won the election* in (1f).

Sentence structures like (1b) (*The election, Smith won*), where an argument is displaced from its canonical position and appears sentence-initially, leaving a 'trace' or null argument behind in its original position, are also well suited to syntactic encoding of information structure, as they make the distinction between topic and information focus structurally explicit. But the specific mapping between the information structure and the syntax can vary. Thus, the sentence-initial constituent, *the election*, in (1b) may refer either to the topic (e.g. as an answer to "What about the election?" "Did Smith win the election?") or to the information focus (e.g. as an answer to "What did Smith win?") Corresponding to this distinction, the sentence-initial phrase would also have two different pitch accents in English. As noted above, however, this would not be the case in Finnish or Norwegian, for example, where the pitch accent on the preposed constituent is the same regardless of whether it is the topic or the focus. In either case, non-canonical placement of constituents in sentence-initial position is not in itself uniquely associated with either topic or information focus. Moreover, other information-structural concepts may be marked by such structures as well. For example, Birner and Ward (1998: 95) argue that preposing in English is associated with the more general function of marking the preposed constituent as representing "information standing in a contextually licensed partially ordered set relationship with information invoked in or inferable from the prior context." This contextually determined function is stated solely in terms of referential givenness, and is thus independent of the topic–focus distinction.

Similarly, a clefted constituent, for example *Smith* in (1f), typically marks the information-structural focus, while the open proposition expressed by the cleft clause (*x won the election* in 1f) is presupposed and topical.[8] (1f) would thus be an appropriate response to "Who won the election?". In English, this interpretation would have a prominent H* pitch accent on the clefted constituent. However, "it"-clefts (and their counterparts in other languages) do not always have a single prominent pitch accent on the clefted constituent. The accent associated with information focus may also fall within the cleft clause. Hedberg (1990, 2000) argues that in such cases the information focus is on the whole sentence, i.e. these are "all news" sentences, where the information focus includes both the cleft clause and the clefted constituent, as in (9).

(9)  [Beginning of a newspaper article] **It was just about 50 years ago that Henry Ford gave us the weekend**. On September 25, 1926, in a somewhat shocking move for that time, he decided to establish a 40-hour work week, giving his employees two days off instead of one.

*(Philadelphia Bulletin*, cited in Prince 1978)

## 29.4 Information structure and the grammar/pragmatics interface

As discussed in the previous section, human languages differ in the manner and extent to which information-structural concepts such as topic, focus, and various degrees of referential givenness are directly and unambiguously encoded by linguistic form (syntax, prosody, morphology, or some combination of these). However, it is generally agreed that information structure has important reflexes in the grammars of all human languages, and its expression and interpretation cannot be completely reduced to general pragmatic principles governing human interaction or to other cognitive/pragmatic abilities that are independent of language. In addition, differences in information structure alone sometimes correlate with profound differences in meaning, with corresponding truth-conditional effects, as in the example from Lambrecht (1994) discussed in section 29.3.1. It is not surprising then that many, if not most, accounts of information structure have integrated information-structural concepts into the grammar, as part of the lexicon, the syntax, and/or semantics (interpreted by the phonology in the case of prosody), or as a separate information-structural component (cf. for example, Erteschik-Shir 1997, Lambrecht 1994, and Molnár and Winkler 2005, *inter alia*).

At the same time, however, it is evident that not all the phenomena associated with information structure can be directly attributed to the grammar. Topic and focus are pragmatically relevant categories with clear pragmatic effects, including the appropriateness/inappropriateness of sentences with different possibilities for information-structural interpretation in different discourse contexts. Indeed, the attempt to explain a speaker's ability to choose among various morphosyntactic and prosodic options and the corresponding ability of speakers to judge sentences with different topic–focus structure and forms that encode different referential-givenness status (e.g. definite vs indefinite articles, pronouns vs full DPs) as more or less felicitous in different contexts has been one of the primary motivations for introducing these categories into linguistic analysis and theory. Contrary to what is sometimes assumed, however, the fact that information-structural concepts and the forms that encode them have different pragmatic effects does not in itself make them entirely, or even primarily, pragmatic.

As noted in section 29.2.1, the encoding of referential givenness concepts is grammatical in the sense that different lexical items encode these concepts as part of their conventional meaning. Moreover, while the concepts may be pragmatic in the sense that they encode a speaker's assumptions about the addressee's mental state at a given point in the discourse, the form–meaning associations themselves are not pragmatically determined, and can differ across languages. Thus, for example, the indefinite article in some languages (e.g. Mandarin Chinese) appears to require the interpretation to be referential, whereas in other languages (e.g. English) it only encodes the weaker status "type identifiable." Similarly, the proximal demonstrative determiner in some languages (e.g. English) requires the referent to be activated, whereas in other languages (e.g. Russian) it only requires familiarity (see Gundel *et al.* 1993 for further discussion).

With respect to relational givenness/newness, failure to clearly distinguish between properties of concepts such as topic and focus that are grammar-driven and those that are purely pragmatic is especially evident in attempts at topic and/or focus identification, which typically involve testing the appropriateness of a sentence in a particular discourse context. However, such tests often fail to uniquely identify the information structure of a given sentence, even in the simplest cases. Thus, the fact that the sentence in (10b) would be an appropriate response to the *wh*-question in (10a) shows that (10b) has a possible topic–focus structure where the topic is Jane or what Jane is doing and the focus/comment is that she is dancing.

(10)  a.  What's Jane doing?
      b.  Jane is dancing.
      c.  As for Jane, she's dancing.
      d.  JANE is dancing.
      e.  I love to dance.

The fact that someone could report an utterance of (10b), in any discourse context, as "Someone said about Jane that she's dancing" (see Reinhart 1981) would provide further evidence for this analysis, as would the fact that (10b) is an appropriate response to *What about Jane?* (see Gundel 1974). But none of these tests necessarily show that Jane **must** be analyzed as the topic of (10b). Thus, as an answer to *What's going on?*, *What's happening?*, or *Will there be any entertainment?*, (10b) could have an all-focus (thetic) interpretation as well as an interpretation where Jane is the topic. The failure of such question tests to provide a foolproof procedure for identifying topics has led some authors to question the linguistic relevance of this concept (cf. Prince 1998). But such tests were in fact never intended to serve as necessary conditions for information-structural concepts such as topic or focus. At best, they can help determine when a particular information-structural analysis is possible. Pragmatic tests are not absolute diagnostics for identifying linguistic categories, because pragmatics is not deterministic.

The fact that linguistic context often seems to determine a single topic–focus structure in question–answer pairs no doubt explains why these provide one of the more reliable contextual tests for relational givenness/newness concepts. Thus, (10b) is judged to be an appropriate answer to the question in (10a) because the location of the prominent pitch accent is consistent with an interpretation where the topic is Jane or what Jane is doing and *dancing* is the information focus. But (10d), where the location of prominent pitch accent requires an interpretation where the topic is who is dancing (alternatively, the x who is dancing) is not an appropriate response to (10a). The fact that the judgments here are sensitive to linguistic context has no doubt contributed to the widely held view that topic and focus are pragmatic concepts. However, as argued in Gundel 1999b, questions constrain other aspects of the semantic/conceptual content of an appropriate answer as well. All aspects of the meaning of a sentence have pragmatic effects in the sense that they contribute to a relevant context for interpretation. This much is determined by general principles that govern language production and understanding (Sperber and Wilson 1986). Thus, (10e) is no more appropriate as an answer to (10a) than (10d) would be, though the exact reason for the inappropriateness is different. The fact that location of the prominent pitch accent has pragmatic effects therefore does not itself warrant the conclusion that pitch accent encodes a pragmatic concept, any more so than it would follow that the difference in meaning between (10b) and (10e) is pragmatic (rather than semantic) because the two sentences would be appropriate in different linguistic contexts.

Assuming a Relevance-theoretic pragmatics (Sperber and Wilson 1986), Gundel (1999b) proposes that information structure is an essential component of the semantic/conceptual representation associated with natural-language sentences by the grammar, as it is basic to the information-processing function of language. This representation and the expressed proposition which is an "enrichment" of it, is a topic–focus structure, where the topic is what the sentence is about and the comment/focus is the main predication about the topic. Topic–focus structure is exploited at the grammar/pragmatics interface, where information expressed in the proposition is assessed in order to derive "contextual effects", assessment being carried out relative to the topic. Within this framework, it is possible to reconcile the different positions concerning referential properties of topics noted in section 29.2 above. A semantic/conceptual representation will be semantically well-formed provided that the topic is at least referential, and thus capable of combining with a predicate to form a full proposition. This much is determined by the grammar. It follows from what speakers know about the way sentence forms are paired with possible meanings in their language. Utterances with non-familiar topics may fail to yield adequate contextual effects, since assessment can only be carried out if the processor already has a mental representation of the topic. The result is that such utterances are often pragmatically deviant, even if they are grammatically well-formed. Thus, while the referentiality condition on topics is a semantic, grammar-based restriction, the stronger familiarity condition is pragmatic and relevance-based; it applies at the grammar/pragmatics (conceptual/intentional) interface.

The relevant research question then is not whether information structure is grammatical or pragmatic, but which information-structural concepts and properties are purely linguistic, i.e. grammar-driven, and which are derivable from more general pragmatic principles that govern language use.

# 30

# Sociopragmatics and cross-cultural and intercultural studies

Istvan Kecskes

## 30.1   Introduction

Recent pragmatic theories follow two main lines: the cognitive-philosophical line and the sociocultural-interactional line. In pragmatic interpretation the cognitive-philosophical line of research appears to put more emphasis on the proposition expressed (e.g. Horn 2005; Levinson 2000) while the socio-cultural-interactional line (e.g. Verschueren 1999; Mey 2001) emphasizes the importance of allowing socio-cultural context into linguistic analysis.

*Cognitive-philosophical pragmatics*, often called Anglo-American pragmatics (as represented by neo-Gricean pragmatics, Relevance theory, and speech-act theory), is based on the centrality of intentions in communication. According to this approach, communication is constituted by recipient design and intention recognition (e.g. Arundale 2008; Haugh 2008b). The speaker's knowledge involves constructing a model of the hearer's knowledge relevant to the given situational context; conversely, the hearer's knowledge includes constructing a model of the speaker's knowledge relevant to the given situational context. Communication is expected to be smooth if the speaker's intentions are recognized by the hearer through pragmatic inferences. Consequently, the main task of pragmatics is to explain how exactly the hearer makes these inferences, and to determine what is considered the speaker's meaning. In a recent study, Levinson (2006a) confirmed that (Gricean) intention lies at the heart of communication, and proposes an "interaction engine" that underlies human interaction. Neo-Gricean/formalist scholars base their analysis on the Cooperative Principle and conversational maxims of Grice (e.g. Carston 2002, 2004b; Horn 2006, 2007a; Levinson 2000). They pay particular attention to generalized implicatures. The followers of the relevance-theoretic approach argue that the formalist approach has little to say about "particularized implicatures" (Sperber and Wilson 2005: 358). In spite of several theoretical controversies different trends within cognitive-philosophical pragmatics accept that communication is governed by the expectations about the speaker's intention.

In contrast, the *sociocultural-interactional* paradigm questions the centrality of intention, considers it "problematic," and underlines its equivocality. According to this view, communication is not always dependent on speaker intentions in the Gricean sense (e.g. Verschueren 1999; Nuyts 2000; Mey 2001; Haugh 2008b). In fact, one of the main differences between the cognitive-philosophical approach and the sociocultural-interactional approach is that the former considers intention an a priori mental state of speakers that underpins communication, while the latter regards intention as a *post factum* construct that is achieved jointly through the dynamic emergence of meaning in conversation. In this process socio-cultural factors play the leading role. Since the two approaches represent two different perspectives, it would be difficult to reject either of them *in toto*. The complexity of the issue requires that we consider both the encoded and co-constructed sides of intention when analyzing the communicative process. The *sociocognitive approach* proposed by Kecskes (2008) and Kecskes and Zhang (2009) makes an attempt to unite the two perspectives and emphasizes that there is a dialectical relationship between a priori intention and emergent intention, both of which are motivated by attention.

*Sociopragmatics* was created as a third line of inquiry within pragmatics after Leech (1983) and Thomas (1983) divided pragmatics into two components: pragmalinguistics and sociopragmatics. *Pragmalinguistics* refers to the resources for conveying communicative acts and relational or interpersonal meanings. These resources include pragmatic strategies such as directness and indirectness, routines, and a great variety of linguistic forms which can intensify or soften communicative acts. For example, compare these two versions of a request:

(1)   Police officer to a driver:
      – Can I see your driver's license?

(2)   Alessandro to his American friend, Bill:
      – Would you mind showing me your driver's license?

In both cases, the speaker chooses from among a great variety of available pragmalinguistic resources of the English language which can function as a request.

However, each of these two expressions indexes a very different attitude and social relationship. This is why sociopragmatics is important in speech analysis. Leech (1983: 10) defined sociopragmatics as "the sociological interface of pragmatics." He referred to the social perceptions underlying participants' interpretation and performance of their communicative action. Speech communities differ in their assessment of speakers' and hearers' social distance and social power, their rights and obligations, and the degree of imposition involved in particular communicative acts (Kasper and Rose 2001). According to Thomas (1983), while pragmalinguistics is, in a sense, akin to grammar in that it consists of linguistic forms and their respective functions, sociopragmatics is about appropriate social behavior. Speakers must be aware of the consequences of making pragmatic choices.

Sociopragmatics was further developed, among others, in Gumperz's, Tannen's, and Scollon and Scollon's works. Gumperz (1982) founded interactional sociolinguistics with his work demonstrating that systematically different ways of using language to create and interpret meaning contributed to employment discrimination against London residents who were from Pakistan, India, and the West Indies. Tannen's focus (1985; 2005) is not just on language, but on how communication styles either facilitate or hinder personal interactions. For instance, according to her, men and women are products of different cultures. They possess different, but equally valid, communicative styles. Scollon and Scollon (2001, 2003) locate meaning in the richness and complexity of the lived world rather than just in the language itself. They consider communicative action as a form of selection that positions the interlocutor as a particular kind of person who chooses among different meaning potentials a subset of pathways (Scollon and Scollon 2003: 205).

The sociocultural-interactional line and developments in sociopragmatics have served as basis for the development of several subfields including interlanguage pragmatics, cross-cultural pragmatics, and intercultural pragmatics.

## 30.2 Interlanguage pragmatics and cross-cultural pragmatics

A distinction should be made between *interlanguage pragmatics* and *cross-cultural pragmatics*. Although these terms are often used interchangeably, they do not refer to the same inquiry. *Interlanguage pragmatics* focuses on the acquisition and use of pragmatic norms in L2: how L2 learners produce and comprehend speech acts, and how their pragmatic competence develops over time (e.g. Kasper and Blum-Kulka 1993; Kasper 1998). Boxer (2002) argued that interlanguage pragmatics focuses on the language learner's appropriation and/or acquisition of pragmatic norms represented in the host language community. To date, many cross-sectional, longitudinal, and theoretical studies have been conducted mainly with focus on L2 classroom interactions, which has resulted in a special tie between interlanguage pragmatics and second-language acquisition research.

In a way, interlanguage pragmatics incorporates cross-cultural pragmatics, although there is some difference between the two lines of research. *Cross-cultural pragmatics* "takes the view that individuals from two societies or communities carry out their interactions (whether spoken or written) according to their own rules or norms, often resulting in a clash in expectations and, ultimately, misperceptions about the other group" (Boxer 2002: 151).

Wierzbicka described the fundamental tenet of cross-cultural pragmatics in the following way:

> In different societies and different communities, people speak differently; these differences in ways of speaking are profound and systematic, they reflect different cultural values, or at least different hierarchies of values; different ways of speaking, different communicative styles, can be explained and made sense of in terms of independently established different cultural values and cultural priorities. (Wierzbicka 1991: 69)

Cross-cultural studies focus mainly on speech-act realizations in different cultures, cultural breakdowns, and pragmatic failures, such as the way some linguistic behaviors considered polite in one language may not be polite in another language. A significant number of these studies use a comparative approach to different cultural norms reflected in language use (e.g. House 2000; Spencer-Oatey 2000; Thomas 1983).

Interlanguage pragmatics and cross-cultural pragmatics are based primarily on three theoretical constructs: Gricean pragmatics, Brown and Levinson's politeness theory, the so-called "interlanguage hypothesis" (Selinker 1972), and the understanding of pragmatic competence. Recently, attempts have been made to integrate Relevance theory (e.g. Escandell-Vidal 1996; Jary 1998) and Conversation Analysis (e.g. Markee 2000; Kasper 2004) into interlanguage pragmatics, although the main foci of research have remained pragmatic competence, speech acts, politeness, and pragmatic transfer.

The ability to comprehend and produce a communicative act is referred to as *pragmatic competence* (Paradis 1998; Kasper 1996). This concept usually includes awareness of social distance, speakers' social status, cultural knowledge such as politeness, and linguistic knowledge, both of the explicit and the implicit kind. Bachman (1990: 87) developed a model of communicative ability called "language competence" which is divided into two components, "organizational competence" and "pragmatic competence". Organizational competence includes knowledge of linguistic units and the rules of joining them together at the levels of sentence ("grammatical competence") and discourse ("textual competence"). Pragmatic competence consists of "illocutionary competence" and "sociolinguistic competence". Illocutionary competence is the "knowledge of communicative action and how to carry it out". Sociolinguistic competence refers to the ability to use language appropriately according to context. It includes the ability to select communicative acts and appropriate strategies to implement the selected acts depending on the current status of the communicative process.

Kecskes (2006) argued that the problem with interlanguage pragmatics is that it represents a monolingual and cross-cultural rather than a multilingual and intercultural view, inasmuch as all of its theoretical resources (Gricean theory, politeness theory, and the interlanguage hypothesis) advocate the relative independence rather than interdependence of language systems and cultures, and proclaim the universality of principles such as those of cooperation and politeness.[1] Wierzbicka (1985), Goddard and Wierzbicka (1997), and Meier (1997), among others, have questioned the claims made for the universality of Grice's cooperative principle (Grice 1961), and Brown, and Levinson's theory of politeness (Brown P. and Levinson 1987). For instance, they have made a case for the cultural relativity of definitions of sincerity and relevance in a given speech community, or the ranking of imposition when a request is made.

## 30.3  Sociopragmatics

### 30.3.1  Context-dependency

Recent pragmatic theories including the cognitive-philosophical line, sociocultural-interactional paradigm, and sociopragmatics have two important features in common: an idealistic approach to communication and context-centeredness. According to views dominated by these tendencies, communication is based on the cooperative principle and expected to be a smooth process that is constituted by recipient design and intention recognition. Meaning is socially constructed, context-dependent, and is the result of cooperation in the course of communication. Focus in these paradigms is on the positive features of communication: *cooperation*, *rapport*, *politeness*. The emphasis on the decisive role of *context*, *socio-cultural factors*, and *cooperation* is overwhelming, while the role of the individual's prior experience, existing private knowledge, and egocentrism is almost completely ignored, although these two sides are not mutually exclusive, as we will see later (Kecskes 2010a).

According to the dominant view, context-sensitivity (in various forms) is a pervasive feature of natural language. Nowadays, many pragmaticians seem to be contextualists. Literalism, according to which (many or most) sentences express propositions independent of context, has been extinct for some time; compare Carston's claim which says that "linguistically encoded meaning never fully determines the intended proposition expressed" (Carston 2002: 49). Consequently, linguistic data must be completed by non-linguistic, contextual interpretation processes.

However, as said before, there is some difference in the understanding of context-dependency between the cognitive-philosophical line and sociocultural-interactional line. In pragmatic interpretation the cognitive-philosophical line of research appears to put more emphasis on the proposition expressed (e.g. Horn 2005; Levinson 2000) while the sociocultural-interactional line (e.g. Mey 2001; Verschueren 1999) highlights the importance of allowing socio-cultural context into linguistic analysis. There seems to be a *from-the-inside-out* approach (analytic) in the cognitive-philosophical paradigm while in the sociocultural-interactional line the interpretation goes *from-the-outside-in* (holistic).

The sociocultural-interactional view on pragmatics (e.g. Mey 2001; Verschueren 1999) considers pragmatics as "a general cognitive, social and cultural perspective on linguistic phenomena in relation to their usage in forms of behavior" (Verschueren 1999: 7). This line of thinking was created partly as an opposing view to the component approach (what is said ➔ what is communicated) to pragmatics represented by neo-Gricean pragmatics, Relevance theory, and speech act theory. Following the sociocultural-interactional line, Mey claimed that the explanatory movement in a theory of pragmatic acts should be from the outside in: "the focus is on the environment in which both speaker and hearer find their affordances, such that the entire situation is brought to bear on what can be said in the situation, as well as on what is actually being said" (Mey 2001: 221). This can be considered one of the main claims of sociopragmatics. The claim is unfolded in Mey's pragmatic act theory (PAT).

## 30.3.2  Societal- rather than individual-centered theory

Mey's (2001) PAT originates in the sociocultural-interactional view, emphasizing the priority of socio-cultural and societal factors in meaning construction and comprehension. He argued that the problem with the speech act theory is that it lacks a theory of action, and even if it does have such a theory it is individual- rather than society-centered (Mey 2001: 214). His main criticism against the speech act theory is that in order for speech acts to be effective they have to be situated: "they both rely on, and actively create, the situation in which they are realized" (Mey 2001: 218). In short, "there are no speech acts, but only situated speech acts, or instantiated pragmatic acts". As a consequence, the emphasis is not on conditions and rules for an individual speech act, but on characterizing a general situational prototype (what Mey calls a pragmeme) that can be executed in the situation. A particular pragmeme can be substantiated and realized through individual pragmatic acts. In other words, a pragmatic act is an instance of adapting oneself to a context, as well as adapting the context to oneself. For instance:

(3)  – There is soccer on the telly.
     – *Not interested.*

"Not interested" is a pragmatic act that expresses the pragmeme [I do not care], which can be also substantiated by several other concrete pragmatic acts such as "I do not care", "I do not mind", "whatever . . . ", etc. All these expressions perform the same pragmatic act giving rise to a common illocutionary point.

According to Mey pragmatic acts are situation-derived and situation-constrained. There is no one-to-one relationship between speech acts and pragmatic acts because the latter do not necessarily include specific acts of speech. For instance:

(4)    Mother: Joshua, what are you doing?
       Joshua: Nothing.
       Mother: Will you stop it immediately.
                              (Mey 2001: 216)

The pragmeme represented by the pragmatic act "Nothing" can be described as "trying to get out (opt out) of a conversation."

Mey's pragmatic act approach is right in many respects. It is definitely true that speech acts never come in isolation, they always carry with them several other acts that also contribute to their success in conversation. Some of these other acts are strictly speech-oriented, while others are more general in nature, and may include, besides speech, extralinguistic aspects of communication such as gestures, intonation, facial expression, body posture, head movements, laughter, and so on. The role of context is also inevitable. "No conversational contribution at all can be understood properly unless it is situated within the environment in which it was meant to be understood" (Mey 2001: 217). In Mey's opinion, human activity is not the privilege of the individual. Rather the individual is situated in a social context, which means that s/he is empowered, as well as limited, by the conditions of her/his social life. This is quite a deterministic view that leaves limited space for individual initiatives.

For Mey it is the situation and extralinguistic factors such as gestures and intonation, rather than "wording", that define pragmatic acts. He argued that "*a fortiori*, there are, strictly speaking, no such 'things' as speech acts *per se*, only acts of speech in a situation" (Mey 2006a). Further he claimed that "indirect speech acts derive their force, not from their lexico-semantic build-up, but instead, from the *situation* in which they are appropriately uttered." Mey is right in emphasizing the importance of situation, environment, and extralinguistic factors in meaning construction and comprehension. However, the "wording" of linguistic expressions is as important in shaping meaning as the situation in which they are used and supplemented by extralinguistic factors. Both sides are equally important contributors in meaning construction and comprehension. Words, expressions, and speech acts are tied to the prior experience of the individual with these linguistic elements in social situations (Kecskes 2008). The question is not whether it is the actual situational context or the prior context tied to linguistic expressions that have priority in meaning production and comprehension. Rather, the real questions are (i) *to what extent* the linguistic contextual factors and the actual contextual factors contribute to meaning construction and comprehension and (ii) *at what stages* of the communicative process they do so.

### 30.3.3   Interplay of prior context and actual situational context

A speaker always tries to use those utterances that s/he thinks will convey his/her intention best in the given situation, and vice versa, a hearer will always rely on those prior experiences with linguistic items heard that s/he thinks best match the speaker's utterance in the given situation. Consequently, utterances may not necessarily be underspecified as current pragmatic theories claim. Utterances may not get their full specification from the actual situational context because these linguistic units usually bring as much into the situation as the situation gives them. It is fair to say that they specify each other. What gives specification to utterance meaning is neither the actual situational context nor the prior context encoded in the utterances but both (e.g. Kecskes 2008). The interplay of both sides creates and specifies meaning in a given situation. Mey is right that speech acts should be situated. But this does not mean that their linguistic and/or socio-cultural load encoded in the linguistic units constituting the utterance becomes of secondary importance when they get situated. The real question here is not which side defines the other but "to what extent" each defines the other at particular points of the communicative process. The extent of the contribution of prior context and actual situational context to meaning construction and comprehension keeps changing in the process of communication. At certain stages of this process actual situational context seems to be dominant, while at some other stages prior context encoded in the utterances overrides actual situational context. This constitutes the dynamism of communication.

Situation-bound utterances are ideal means to demonstrate the interplay of actual situational context and prior context in meaning construction and comprehension because they are often linguistically transparent and carry a socio-cultural load at the same time. The following examples demonstrate this.

(5)   Sam: Coming for a drink?
      Andy: Sorry, I can't. *My doctor* won't let me.
      Sam: *What's wrong with you?*

(6)   Sam: Coming for a drink?
      Andy: Sorry, I can't. *My mother-in-law* won't let me.
      Sam: *What's wrong with you?*

The situation-bound utterance "What's wrong with you?" has two different meanings in examples (5) and (6) although the only difference between the two conversations is that "My doctor" was changed to "My mother-in-law". So it is not exactly the actual situational context that creates this difference in meaning. Rather, it is the stigmatic load that is attached to the use of the lexical phrase "My mother-in-law", which has a negative connotation in most contexts. In this particular case the stigma derives from the perception that one's mother-in-law should not constrain one's freedom. If we use a third option "My wife", the meaning of "What's wrong with you?" will depend on the actual situational context, i.e., on how the hearer processes his friend's expression "My wife", based on his knowledge about the relationship between Andy and his wife and some other prior social experience. In this case, because of the "weakness" of the conceptual load tied to the expression "My wife", the dominance of actual situational context becomes obvious. In these two situations the dominant role of prior context or actual situational context seems to be changing and depends on what interpretation the encoded conceptual load of the expression makes possible. If the load is very strong and deeply conventionalized the actual situational context can hardly cancel it.

As the examples above demonstrate, prior experience tied to lexical items is as important in meaning construction and comprehension as actual situational context. The sexual connotation of the sign "Girls wanted for different positions" can hardly be canceled in spite of the fact that the sign was at the entrance to Walmart. Whenever I showed the photo with the sign at Walmart to my students they all laughed because the most salient meaning of the sentence is sexually loaded (for reasons see Allan and Burridge 2006; MacWhinney *et al.* 1982). No actual situational context can cancel it although at Walmart this sign clearly was supposed to serve as a job advertisement.

Mey (2006a) argued that quoting out of context is a well-known means of manipulating a conversational partner. Based on what was said above we have to be careful how we understand "quoting out of context". What it really means is "quoting out of the actual situational context". This manipulation does not mean that there is no context. Yes, there is, because the linguistic expression will create a context of its own. But this context will not necessarily match the original situational context. Actually, we are talking about two different meanings here: actual situational meaning and meaning of an expression without actual situational context. In the first case meaning is created as the result of the interplay of the actual situational context and prior context encapsulated in the expressions used in the actual situational context. In the second case ("out of actual situational context") meaning construction is based only on prior context tied to the linguistic expression (history of use) as interpreted by speaker-hearers. The following example from a sitcom shows this difference.

(7)     Jane: Josh, sorry but I really am bored. You are not a very
        entertaining person. I feel like *I want to sleep with you.*
        Josh: Well, Jane, this is not necessarily my fault.

(8)     Sentence: *I want to sleep with you.*

If we take the expression "I want to sleep with you" out of the original actual situational context (see example 7) it will give way to an entirely different interpretation that is based on the most salient meaning of the expression, which is the figurative rather than the literal meaning of "I want to sleep with you". This happens because context created by an expression without actual situational context relies on the most salient meaning, which is the result of the most familiar and frequent use of the expression.

### 30.3.4  Need for a sociocognitive perspective in sociopragmatics

The idealistic view on communication, the overemphasis placed on context-dependency, and focus either on the analytic (truth conditions and implicatures) or the holistic approach (communicative act, pragmatic act) all give a lopsided perspective on communication by focusing only on the positive features and one side of the process. In fact, communication is more like a trial-and-error, try-and-try-again process that is co-constructed by the participants. It relies on both a priori and emergent factors. The process appears to be a non-summative and emergent interactional achievement (Arundale 1999, 2008; Mey 2001) in which both prior and actual situational experiences are involved (Kecskes 2010a; Kecskes and Mey 2008). Consequently, due attention should be paid to the less positive aspects of communication including breakdowns, misunderstandings, struggles, and language-based aggression – features that seem to be as common in communication as are cooperation and politeness. Similarly, dependency on actual situational context is only one side of the matter, while individuals' prior experience of recurring contexts expressed as content in the interlocutors' utterances likewise plays an important role in meaning construction and comprehension.

This is what Mey says about pragmatic acts:

> The theory of pragmatic acts does not explain human language use starting from the words uttered by a single, idealized speaker. Instead, it focuses on the interactional *situation* in which both speakers and hearers realize their aims. The explanatory movement is from the outside in, one could say, rather than from the inside out: instead of starting with what is said, and looking for what the words could mean, the situation where the words fit is invoked to explain what can be (and is actually being) said. (Mey 2006a: 542)

The problem with this definition is that it emphasizes that the explanatory movement should go from the outside in. I argue that *the explanatory movement in any pragmatic theory should go in both directions: from the outside in (actual situational context* ➔ *prior context encapsulated in utterances used) and from the inside out (prior context encapsulated in utterances used* ➔ *actual situational context)*. This view is based on the sociocognitive approach, which serves as a theoretical framework for intercultural pragmatics.

## 30.4  Intercultural pragmatics

### 30.4.1  Definition

Intercultural Pragmatics is a relatively new field of inquiry that concerns how the language system is put to use in social encounters between human beings who have different first languages, communicate in a common language, and, usually, represent different cultures (Kecskes 2004, 2010a). The communicative process in these encounters is synergistic in the sense that it is a merger in which pragmatic norms of each participant are represented to some extent. Intercultural pragmatics represents a sociocognitive perspective on communication in which individual prior experience and actual situational experience conditioned by socio-cultural factors are equally important in meaning construction and comprehension. Research in intercultural pragmatics has four main foci: (1) interaction between native speakers and non-native speakers of a language, (2) lingua franca communication in which none of the interlocutors has the same L1, (3) multilingual discourse, and (4) language use and development of individuals who speak more than one language. The study of intercultural pragmatics supports a less idealized, more down-to-earth approach to communication than current pragmatic theories usually do. Whilst not denying the decisive role of cooperation, context, and politeness in communication, intercultural pragmatics also gives equal importance to egocentrism, chaos, aggression, trial-and-error, and salience in the analysis of language production.

## 30.4.2 Theoretical framework

Intercultural pragmatics relies on interculturality and adopts a sociocognitive approach (SCA) to pragmatics that takes into account both the societal and individual factors, including cooperation and egocentrism, which, as claimed here, are not antagonistic phenomena in interaction (Kecskes 2008, 2010a).

### 30.4.2.1 The sociocognitive approach (SCA)

Before describing the main tenets of SCA a clear distinction should be made between Kecskes' approach and van Dijk's understanding of the sociocognitive view in language use. Van Dijk (2008: x) said that in his theory it is not the social situation that influences (or is influenced by) discourse, but the way the participants define the situation. He goes further and claims that "contexts are not some kind of objective conditions or direct cause, but rather (inter)subjective constructs designed and ongoingly updated in interaction by participants as members of groups and communities" (*ibid.*). SCA adopts a more dialectical perspective by considering communication a dynamic process in which individuals are not only constrained by societal conditions but also shape them at the same time. Speakers and hearers are equal participants of the communicative process. They both produce and comprehend speech, relying on their most accessible and salient knowledge expressed in their private contexts in both production and comprehension. Consequently, only a holistic interpretation of utterance and discourse from the perspective of both the speaker and hearer can give us an adequate account of language communication. It is very important that we realize that there are social conditions and constraints (contexts) that have some objectivity from the perspective of individuals. Of course, there can always be slight differences in how individuals process those relatively objective societal factors based on their prior experience. But it would be a mistake to deny the presence of any objectivity in social contexts.

When language is used, its unique property is activated in two ways. When people speak or write, they craft what they need to express to fit the situation or context in which they are communicating. But, at the same time, the way people speak or write the words, expressions, and utterances they use create that very situation, context, socio-cultural frame in which the given communication occurs. Consequently, two things seem to happen simultaneously: people attempt to fit their language to a situation or context that their language, in turn, helped to create in the first place (e.g. Gee 1999).

This dynamic behavior of human speech and reciprocal process between language and context basically eliminates the need to ask the ever-returning question: Which comes first – the situation the speakers are in (e.g. faculty meeting, car renting, dinner ordering, etc.) or the particular language that is used in the given situation (expressions and utterances representing ways of talking and interacting)? *Is this a "car rental" because participants are acting and speaking that way, or are they acting and speaking that way because this is a "car rental"?* Acting and speaking in a particular way constitutes social situations, socio-cultural frames, and these frames require the use of a particular language. "Which comes first?" does not seem to be a relevant question synchronically. Social and cultural routines result in recurring activities and institutions (e.g. Schank 1982; Schank and Abelson 1977). However, these institutions and routinized activities have to be rebuilt continuously in the here and now.

The question is whether these cultural models, institutions, and frames exist outside language or not. The social constructivists insist that models and frames have to be rebuilt again and again so it is just our impression that they exist outside language (see van Dijk 2008). However, the sociocognitive approach argues that these cultural mental models have some kind of psychological reality in the individual mind, and when a concrete situation occurs the appropriate model is recalled, which supports the appropriate verbalization of triggered thoughts and activities. Of course, building and rebuilding our world occurs not merely through language but through the interaction of language with other real-life phenomena such as non-linguistic symbol systems, objects, tools, technologies, etc.

The sociocognitive perspective on communication and pragmatics (Kecskes 2002, 2008, 2010a; Kecskes and Zhang 2009) unites the societal and individual features of communication, and considers communication a dynamic process in which individuals are both constrained by and shape societal conditions (see above). In this paradigm, communication is driven by the interplay of *cooperation* required by societal conditions and *egocentrism* that is rooted in prior experience of the individual. Consequently, egocentrism and cooperation are not mutually exclusive phenomena. They are both present in all stages of communication to a different extent because they represent the individual and societal traits of the dynamic process of communication.

On the one hand speakers and hearers are constrained by societal conditions but as individuals they all have their own goals, intention, desire, etc. that are freely expressed and recognized in the flow of interaction.

In the sociocognitive approach framed by the dynamic model of meaning (Kecskes 2008; Kecskes and Zhang 2009) communication is characterized by the interplay of two traits that are inseparable, mutually supportive, and interactive:

| *Individual trait:* | *Social trait:* |
|---|---|
| attention | intention |
| private experience | actual situational experience |
| *egocentrism* | *cooperation* |
| salience | relevance |

*Communication is the result of interplay of intention and attention motivated by socio-cultural background* that is privatized by the individuals. The socio-cultural background is composed of dynamic knowledge of interlocutors deriving from their *prior experience* encapsulated in the linguistic expressions they use, and *current experience* in which those expressions create and convey meaning.

This sociocognitive approach integrates the pragmatic view of cooperation and the cognitive view of egocentrism and emphasizes that both cooperation and egocentrism are manifested in all phases of communication to a varying extent. While cooperation is an intention-directed practice and measured by relevance, egocentrism is an attention-oriented trait and measured by salience. Intention and attention are identified as two measurable forces that affect communication in a systematic way. The measurement of intention and attention by means of relevance and salience is distinct from earlier explanations (e.g. Giora 2003; Sperber and Wilson 1986; Wilson and Sperber 2004).

### 30.4.2.2  Interculturality

Interculturality is a crucial notion for intercultural pragmatics. We should define interculturality in communication and separate it from intraculturality. There have been several attempts (e.g. Gudykunst and Mody 2002; Nishizaka 1995; Samovar and Porter 2001; Ting-Toomey 1999) to explain the difference between the two terms. According to Samovar and Porter (2001) "intracultural communication" is "the type of communication that takes place between members of the same dominant culture, but with slightly different values", as opposed to "intercultural communication", which is the communication between two or more distinct cultures. This approach has led to a common mistake that several researchers have committed. They have considered interculturality as the main reason for miscommunication (e.g. Hinnenkamp 1995; Thomas 1983; Ting-Toomey 1999). In fact, some researchers' findings show the opposite (e.g. House 2003; Kecskes 2008). The use of semantically transparent language by non-native speakers results in fewer misunderstandings and communication breakdowns than expected.

The insecurity experienced by lingua franca speakers make them establish a unique set of rules for interaction which may be referred to as an "interculture," according to Koole and Ten Thije (1994: 69), a "culture constructed in cultural contact".

Blum-Kulka *et al.* (2008: 164) defined interculturality as "a contingent interactional accomplishment" from a discoursive-constructivist perspective. They argued that a growing literature explores interculturality as a participant concern (e.g. Higgins 2007; Markee and Kasper 2004; Mori 2003). Nishizaka (1995) pointed out that interculturality is a situationally emergent rather than a normatively fixed phenomenon. The sociocognitive approach (Kecskes 2008; Kecskes 2010a; Kecskes and Zhang 2009) explained in the previous section goes one step further and defines interculturality as a phenomenon that is not only interactionally and socially constructed in the course of communication but also relies on relatively definable cultural models and norms that represent the speech communities to which the interlocutors belong. Consequently, interculturality has both relatively normative and emergent components. In order for us to understand the dynamism and ever-changing nature of intercultural encounters we need to approach interculturality dialectically. Cultural constructs and models change diachronically, while cultural representation and speech production by individuals changes synchronically. *Interculturality is a situationally emergent and co-constructed phenomenon that relies both on relatively definable cultural norms and models as well as situationally evolving features* (Kecskes 2011). Intercultures are ad hoc creations. They are created in a communicative process in which cultural norms and models brought into the interaction from prior experience of interlocutors blend with features created ad hoc in the interaction in a synergetic way. The result is intercultural discourse, in which there is mutual transformation of knowledge and communicative behavior rather than transmission.

Interculturality has both a *prior side* and an *emergent side*, which occur and act simultaneously in the communicative process. Consequently, *intercultures* are not fixed phenomena but are created in the course of communication in which participants belong to different L1 speech communities, speak a common language, and represent different cultural norms and models that are defined by their respective L1 speech communities. The following conversation (from Albany English Lingua Franca Dataset collected by PhD students) between a Brazilian girl and a Polish woman illustrates this point well.

(9)    Brazilian: And what do you do?
       Pole: I work at the university as a cleaner.
       B: As a janitor?
       P: No, not yet. Janitor is after the cleaner.
       B: You want to be a janitor?
       P: Of course.

In this conversation interlocutors represent two different languages and cultures (Brazilian and Polish), and use English as a lingua franca. This is the prior knowledge that participants bring to the interaction. They create an interculture, which belongs to neither of them but emerges in the course of conversation. Within this interculture the two speakers have a smooth conversation about the job of the Polish woman. Neither of them is sure what the right term is for the job the Polish woman has. There are no misunderstandings in the interaction because each participant is careful to use semantically transparent language in order to be as clear as possible. The Polish woman sets up a "hierarchy" that is non-existing in the target language culture ("cleaner ➜ janitor").[2] However, this is an emergent element of the interculture the interlocutors have been constructing.

Intercultures come and go, so they are neither stable nor permanent. They just occur. They are both synergetic and blended. Interculturality is constituted on the spot by interlocutors who participate in the conversation. But isn't this a phenomenon that also occurs in intracultural communication? Why and how should we distinguish intercultural communication from intracultural communication? Basically the currently dominant approach to this issue is that there is no *principled* difference between intracultural and intercultural communication (e.g. Winch 1997; Wittgenstein 2001). This is true as far as the mechanism of the communicative process is concerned. However, there is a qualitative difference in the nature and content of an intracultural interaction and an intercultural interaction. Speakers in intracultural communication rely on prior knowledge and culture of a relatively definable speech community, which is privatized by individuals belonging to that speech community. No language boundaries are crossed, however subcultures are relied upon and representations are individualized. What is created on the spot enriches the given culture, contributes to it, and remains within the fuzzy but still recognizable confines of that language and culture.

In the case of intercultural communication, however, prior knowledge that is brought into and privatized in the communicative process belongs to different cultures and languages, and what participants create on the spot will disappear and not become an enrichment and/or addition to any particular culture or language. Intercultures are ad hoc creations that may enhance the individual and the globalization process but can hardly be said to contribute to any particular culture. This is exactly what we see in example (9) above. Speakers created a hierarchy between "cleaner" and "janitor" just to create common ground and assure their own mutual private understanding of a given situation. However, this interculture usually disappears when they stop talking. Intercultures can also be recurring for a while in certain cases such as international negotiating teams, international classrooms, international tourist groups, etc. Kasper and Blum-Kulka (1993) talked about "intercultural style", which means that speakers fully competent in two languages may create an intercultural style of speaking that is both related to and distinct from the styles prevalent in the two substrata, a style on which they rely regardless of the language being used. Kasper and Blum-Kulka (1993) claimed that the hypothesis is supported by many studies of cross-cultural communication, especially those focusing on interactional sociolinguistics (e.g. Gumperz 1982; Tannen 1985) and research into the pragmatic behavior of immigrant populations across generations (e.g. Clyne *et al.* 1991).

### 30.4.3  Crossing language boundaries

An example of intracultural communication would be if a dentist in the dominant culture, say, in the United States, spoke about dental issues with a plumber belonging to the same U.S. culture. Their negotiation may not be entirely smooth because the plumber might not be very knowledgeable about dental terms. If, however, the dentist speaks with another dentist about dental issues they would certainly understand each other's language use quite well, although still there might be individual differences. This is what prompts the argument that a U.S. dentist would understand an English-speaking French dentist better than she would understand an English native-speaker plumber. However, we must be very careful with judgments like this. One intercultural situation may differ from another intracultural situation to a great extent. I have argued elsewhere (Kecskes 2010b: 9) that it is impor-tant to make a distinction between a *quantitative change* and a *qualitative change*, and between changes occurring within a culture or across cultures. If a person moves from Albany, New York to New Orleans, Louisiana, and makes adjustments to the new Louisiana subculture, he may start to say things like "I might could do this." This scenario, however, cannot be com-pared *qualitatively* to the case where a person moves from Albany, New York to Lille, France. In the first case we can speak about peripheral rather than core changes in the language use of the person. Louisiana culture and Upstate New York culture can be considered subcultures of American culture, and Louisiana dialect and the Upstate New York dialect are dialects of Ameri-can English. However, the change is different when a person moves from Albany, New York to Lille, France. Upstate New York dialect compares to the Picard dialect of Lille differently than to the Louisiana dialect. In this case we speak about dialects of different languages (English and French) while in the first case we speak about dialects of the same language (English). *There is a qualitative difference between crossing language boundaries and cross-ing dialects* (but staying within the confines of the core of one particular language).

The same is true for cultures. The relationship between American and French cultures qualitatively differs from the relationship between Louisiana subculture and Upstate New York subculture. English–French bilingualism may create qualitatively different changes in the mind and behavior of a per-son than Louisiana–Upstate New York bidialectalism (Kecskes 2010b). I would like to emphasize that this view does not represent a homogenous approach to language and culture. Languages and cultures are never homogenous.

*What is temporarily and relatively homogenous-like is the linguistic faculty (language system) that changes diachronically while language use changes synchronically.*

There is another major difference between intracultural and intercultural communication. Intracultural communication is dominated by preferred ways of saying things (Wray 2002) and preferred ways of organizing thoughts within a particular speech community (Kecskes 2008). This is not the case in intercultural communication because the development of "preferred ways" requires time and conventionalization within a speech community. Human languages are very flexible. They can lexicalize whatever their speakers find important to lexicalize. There are preferred ways of lexicalizing certain actions, phenomena, and things. Americans "shoot a film", "dust the furniture", "make love", "do the dishes", etc. One language has a word for a phenomenon that is important in that culture, and the other does not. In Russian they have the word *spargal'ki* to denote tools for cheating in school. In Hungarian the same phenomenon is denoted by the word *puska*, which can be translated into English as *gun*. However, we have no word for this phenomenon (tools for cheating in school) in American English. (British English has "cribs", "crib notes").

Knowing what expressions to select, what is appropriate or inappropriate in different situations, may be an important sign of *group-inclusiveness*, and "native-likeness" (which is a notion with negative connotations nowadays). In intercultural communication this group-inclusiveness is created on the spot by speakers with different linguistic and cultural backgrounds who can hardly rely on the advantageous use of formulaic and figurative elements of a common language. In an empirical study Kecskes (2008) demonstrated that in lingua franca communication the use of formulaic language by the participants was less than 10 percent. Lingua franca speakers relied on semantically transparent language to make sure that their interlocutor could follow what they said. They also do this because they may not have had enough encounters with the target language and culture to be able to conventionalize the "preferred ways of saying things" and "preferred ways of organizing thoughts".

In sum, it is erroneous to think that intercultural communication differs from intracultural communication because the former is more complicated than the latter, and the former leads to more miscommunication than the other. As we saw above, the dissimilarity is qualitative rather than quantitative, because there is a qualitative difference between crossing language boundaries and crossing dialects.

## 30.5  Conclusion

This chapter discussed research endeavors that focus on social, socio-cultural, intercultural, and sociocognitive features, and their interplay with linguistic elements in meaning production and comprehension in human speech communication. The main point is that language is created by the world and language also creates the world at the same time. This dialectical synergism characterizes the communicative process all the way. Consequently, individual and societal factors play equally important roles in the process, where egocentrism of the individual is not antagonistic to cooperation with other individuals. When language is used, its unique property is activated in two ways. When people speak or write, they craft what they need to express to fit the situation or context in which they are communicating. But, at the same time, the way people speak or write the words, expressions, and utterances they use create that very situation, context, socio-cultural frame in which the given communication occurs. Consequently, two things seem to happen simultaneously: people attempt to fit their language to a situation or context that their language, in turn, helped to create in the first place (Gee 1999).

This dynamic behavior of human speech and reciprocal process requires analysts to develop and apply an explanatory method that goes in both directions: from the outside in (actual situational context ➜ prior context encapsulated in utterances used) and from the inside out (prior context encapsulated in utterances used ➜ actual situational context). New facts of language are grounded in the speakers' memory of previous experiences of using language. Meaning is seen as emerging out of recalled fragments that are reiterated, reshaped, and manipulated at the same time. New meaning is always constituted as a more or less radical alteration of something familiar and recognizable.

This is what pragmatic theories need to recognize and describe.

# 31

# Politeness and pragmatics

Marina Terkourafi

## 31.1 Introduction

Although sociological and social psychological works such as Émile Durkheim's *The Elementary Forms of Religious Life* (1915) and Roger Brown and Albert Gilman's 'The pronouns of power and solidarity' (1960/2003) could be considered early precursors of this line of work, the study of im/politeness within linguistic pragmatics grew more directly out of an interest in the use of indirectness in language, inasmuch as politeness seemed to offer an opportune motivation for indirect speech acts (Searle 1975b) and for departures from Gricean rational efficiency in conversation in general (Lakoff, R. 1973). Brown and Levinson's 1978 essay (republished in 1987) 'Politeness: Universals in language usage' may be said to have officially inaugurated the field by bringing to bear upon each other the tenets of sociology and those of theoretical linguistics (Brown, P. and Levinson 1987). However, as the twin pillars of speech act theory (Searle 1969) and of conversational implicature theory (Grice 1975), on which politeness theory originally developed, were increasingly criticised for their single-utterance orientation and speaker focus, scholarly interest correspondingly shifted toward a broader agenda of explaining the constitution and manipulation of social relationships through language. Under this renewed vision, im/politeness studies are being pursued within – and have borrowed notions from – several neighbouring disciplines, including social psychology, sociology, linguistic anthropology and human communication research.

This chapter focuses on developments in im/politeness research within linguistic pragmatics with a view to identifying the main trends and directions for future research. By way of carving out an area of investigation that does justice to the recent expansion of the field, I begin by introducing two recent developments, namely the distinction between first-order and second-order politeness (section 31.2), and the increasing attention paid to impoliteness/rudeness (section 31.3). These recent developments are also having an impact on how scholars are defining and applying to empirical data central theoretical notions of im/politeness research, to which I turn next. Section 31.4 deals with the notion of face, descended from sociology, while section 31.5 discusses how im/politeness may be accounted for using the notions of the speaker's intentions, implicatures and perlocutionary effects, as these have developed within (post-)Gricean pragmatics. Finally, section 31.6 tackles the question of how im/polite language use relates to extra-linguistic context, and considers some proposed conceptualisations of extra-linguistic context within im/politeness studies. Section 31.7 concludes the chapter. The overall picture that emerges is that of a rich and dynamic field, if also polyphonic and fluid in its boundaries, much like our experience of the everyday enactment of im/politeness itself.

## 31.2  Defining politeness: Politeness1 and Politeness2

The 19 December 2009 holiday double issue of the British weekly *The Economist* featured a three-page article under the rubric of 'Politeness' (*Economist* 2009). About three quarters of the article was devoted to address terms, how they vary from place to place, and how they change over time, with T/V pronominal address, conversational openings and closings, diminutives and the ubiquitous English 'please' also receiving passing mention, alongside non-verbal behaviours such as handshaking and (social) kissing. In short, what were dealt with in the article were behaviours that people tend to associate explicitly with being polite, and to teach and comment on as such. The article ended with a reference to Geoffey Leech's Grand Strategy of Politeness (Leech 2007) and to the recently established *Journal of Politeness Research* (published twice yearly since 2005 by Mouton de Gruyter).

The *Economist* article stands out as the most theoretically informed in a series of press articles dealing with verbal politeness (and, for that matter, impoliteness) that are indicative of the special status of politeness as an area of research sitting midway between lay and academic concerns. In an attempt to untangle this mixture of lay and academic concerns, scholars have distinguished between first-order and second-order politeness (Politeness1 and Politeness2, for short), a distinction that has been receiving increasing attention over the past few years and has served to revive theoretical debate as well as methodological practices in the field. Watts, Ide and Ehlich, who were first to formulate the distinction in these terms, define them as follows:

> We take first-order politeness to correspond to the various ways in which polite behaviour is perceived and talked about by members of socio-cultural groups. It encompasses, in other words, commonsense notions of politeness. Second-order politeness, on the other hand, is a theoretical construct, a term within a theory of social behaviour and language usage. (1992/2005: 3)

While thus explained the distinction between Politeness1 and Politeness2 seems intuitively obvious and applicable also to other terms that have been recruited from everyday usage into specialised, technical uses,[1] in the case of politeness, the distinction between first-order and second-order politeness is itself a matter of theoretical interest and debate that can generate new insights (Terkourafi 2011).

On the one hand, this distinction has far-reaching implications for what one considers to be the object of investigation – the phenomena in need of an explanation. As the definitions above make clear, politeness in a technical sense (Politeness2) is more inclusive than politeness in an everyday sense (Politeness1): roughly, the former encompasses the entire range of behaviours and linguistic forms reflecting and/or affecting people's standing in relation to one another, whereas the latter is restricted to only a subset of these, viz. those that are most salient and positively evaluated. Yet, as Eelen (2001: 48–75) has shown in his extensive and thorough *Critique* of several politeness theories, theorists have typically failed to draw this distinction – or, at least, to do so consistently. It is precisely in a bid to avoid these pitfalls and to embrace more fully the implications of this distinction that scholars have more recently been moving away from the term 'politeness' altogether, opting for alternative labels such as Face Constituting Theory (Arundale 1999, 2010a), 'relational work' (Locher and Watts 2005), or 'X-phemisms', proposed as a cover-term for euphemisms, dysphemisms and 'orthophemisms' alike (Allan and Burridge 2006).

On the other hand, drawing a hard and fast line between the everyday and technical senses of politeness represents a peril all its own, as it risks losing sight of the connection between the two. One aspect that Politeness1 and Politeness2 share is normativity. Contrary to what might appear at first (Eelen 2001: 46–7; Watts 2003: 11), normativity is not the sole purview of Politeness1: Politeness2 is also normative inasmuch as it engenders a comparison with alternative ways of 'doing the same thing'. Such comparison presupposes the categorisation of human behaviour into distinct and recognisable classes – not only into what constitutes polite or less so ways of performing a compliment, a promise or a refusal, but also into what constitutes a compliment, a promise or a refusal in the first place – a categorisation which is in turn enabled only by agreement within a community or group, viz. by shared norms. It is precisely this normative character that enables politeness (in both the everyday and the technical senses) to serve as a socialisation device (cf. Snow *et al.* 1990) – that is, as a device not only for the evaluation of different types of behaviour but also for their delimitation. In other words, if Politeness1 is explicitly normative, Politeness2 is merely implicitly so.[2]

This vital, dialectic link between Politeness1 and Politeness2, whereby one provides the background for the other to emerge, risks being ignored if one focuses on one of the two terms to the exclusion of the other, making it imperative to study them hand in hand rather than in isolation.[3]

Distinguishing between Politeness1 and Politeness2, then, is best interpreted in this light as an opportunity to zoom in on the dynamic trade-off between these two notions, opening the way for more sophisticated understandings of im/politeness in future.

## 31.3  Im/politeness

Another recent development within the field that is indicative of the growing purview of politeness research is the rise of approaches to 'impoliteness' or 'rudeness' (Bousfield 2008, Bousfield and Locher 2008, Bousfield and Culpeper 2008, Culpeper 2011a). Following up on early precursors such as Bolinger (1980), Lachenicht (1980), Tracy (1990), Allan and Burridge (1991) and Culpeper (1996), over the past decade, the use of language to 'cause offense' (Culpeper 2011a) has been increasingly attracting researchers' attention. On the one hand, broader developments in the social sciences – including the questioning of established orthodoxies in the aftermath of large-scale socio-cultural contact that goes under the general rubric of 'globalisation' – have prompted a shift away from homogeneous, 'consensus' views of society toward a renewed appreciation for the explanatory potential of the notion of conflict in pragmatic theorising (e.g. Eelen 2001: 208–9, Haviland 1997: 551–2). On the other hand, a 'first-order' level impression that incivility is becoming increasingly common (e.g. Montry 2002, Truss 2005) has served to reinvigorate academic debate on the matter (see, among others, Blitvich 2010, Cameron, 2006, Lakoff, R. 2005, Mills 2009). An interesting question in this regard concerns the extent to which the object of investigation is, in this case, being shaped by the available scientific paradigms and discourses; in other words, are social actors actually becoming more impolite, or are investigators simply becoming more attuned to perceiving, and better equipped to analyse, such instances?

Some interesting questions arising from the study of impoliteness pertain to its relationship to politeness – is the difference between the two just a matter of degree, or are we dealing, as Mills (2009) has suggested, with two qualitatively different phenomena? – and the theoretical framework best suited to its analysis – briefly, can frameworks proposed for politeness be relatively straightforwardly extended to account for impoliteness as well, as in Culpeper's (1996) extension of Brown and Levinson's (1987) framework in that direction, or must different theoretical and methodological assumptions be made for impoliteness, given the essentially proscribed nature of the latter (Culpeper 2011b)? These are only some of the many fascinating questions currently being explored, making it clear that the recent expansion of the field to encompass the entire range of behaviours from politeness to impoliteness and rudeness – what is increasingly being referred to as 'im/politeness' – is injecting new life into debates about politeness on many levels.

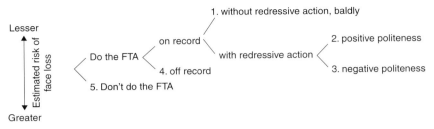

Figure 31.1. *Strategies for performing* FTAs

## 31.4　A sociological motivation: Face

One such level is the study of face. Originally proposed by sociologist Erving Goffman based on his observation of life in two US psychiatric wards in the 1950s (Goffman 1955), the notion of face became current within linguistic circles a couple of decades later, when it was first related to the phenomenon of linguistic politeness by Penny Brown and Steve Levinson in their seminal 1978 essay 'Politeness: universals in language usage' (re-issued in book format under a slightly changed title and with a new introduction in 1987).

Brown and Levinson define face as

> the public self-image that every member wants to claim for himself, consisting in two related aspects: (a) negative face: the basic claim to . . . freedom of action and freedom from imposition [and] (b) positive face: the positive consistent self-image or 'personality' claimed by interactants, crucially including the desire that this self-image be appreciated and approved of (1987: 61).

This notion of face is capitalised upon in Brown and Levinson's work mainly in two ways. First, it serves to define the notion of a face-threatening act (FTA), i.e. a speech act that calls for redress, and to classify FTAs into a four-way grid that includes (i) threats to the hearer's negative face, e.g. requests; (ii) threats to the hearer's positive face, e.g. disagreements; (iii) threats to the speaker's negative face, e.g. responses to thanks; and (iv) threats to the speaker's positive face, e.g. apologies (*ibid*.: 65–8). And, second, it serves to order linguistic strategies along a continuum of least-to-most redress (see Figure 31.1) that ranks negative politeness (i.e. strategies that express concern for negative face) higher than positive politeness (i.e. strategies that express concern for positive face), on the assumption that '[unless you are certain of the contrary], it is safer to assume that [the] H[earer] prefers his peace and self-determination than that he [sic] prefers your expressions of regard' (*ibid*.: 74).

By providing a psycho-social motivation for observed linguistic behaviours, Brown and Levinson's introduction of face into politeness theorising marked a significant step toward a *unified* analysis of behaviours that had up until that point not been systematically treated within existing linguistic frameworks, with the notable exception of Robin Lakoff's ground-breaking 'The logic of politeness, or minding your p's and q's' (Lakoff 1973). In that short article, Lakoff was the first to make good on passing comments by Grice (1975) and Searle (1975b) relating departures from the Cooperative Principle and the attendant maxims with politeness, by outlining three Rules of Politeness, which, combined with the Rules for Clarity (as Lakoff re-dubbed the Gricean maxims), provided a framework for Pragmatic Competence (Lakoff 1973: 298). However, neither she, nor Brown and Gilman before her, in their celebrated analysis of T/V address systems (1960/2003), went so far as to articulate a deeper motivation for polite behaviour, one that not only brought together different types of polite behaviour under a single umbrella, but also helped make specific predictions about their linguistic realisation.

Despite its enormous importance for politeness theorising, Brown and Levinson's notion of face has also been heavily criticised in subsequent applications of the theory, especially cross-linguistically. In attempting to apply their theory to languages/cultures other than the three originally investigated – Tamil, Tzeltal and (British as well as American) English – researchers pointed out that avoidance of face-threat is not the only reason for im/polite behaviour: speech acts may also be designed to boost or enhance face (Matsumoto 1988, Bayraktaroglu 1991, Mao 1994, Kerbrat-Orecchioni 1997, Hernández-Flores 1999), while, at the opposite extreme, deliberate face-attack is also possible, in ways that may be judged reasonable or not (Tracy and Tracy 1998, Tracy 2008; see also Allan and Burridge 2006).

In a separate line of criticism, it is Brown and Levinson's construal of face as individual wants that has been found wanting, especially with respect to interaction in non-Western contexts. Polite behaviour in these contexts is typically thought to reflect one's awareness of one's place in society (Matsumoto 1988: 405–8), prompting researchers to speak of the 'wants of roles and settings' (Ide 1989: 227) and to introduce the notion of 'discernment' (Hill et al. 1986: 348; Ide 1989) in counterpoint to politeness as 'volition' or 'strategic conflict avoidance' (Kasper 1990: 196–7).[4] Other proposals to account for conversational exchanges in non-Western contexts have distinguished between 'group face', 'the individual's desire to behave in conformity with culturally expected forms of behaviour', and 'self-face', 'the individual's desire to attend to his/her personal needs and to place his/her public self-image above those of others' (Nwoye 1992: 313), or proposed the notion of 'relative face orientation', 'an underlying direction of face that emulates...one of two interactional ideals...: the ideal social identity, or the ideal individual autonomy', and which may further be 'centripetal' or 'centrifugal' (Mao 1994: 471–3). In a recent reformulation, Haugh (2007b) talks explicitly of 'the place where one belongs' (uchi) and 'the place where one stands' (tachiba) as two ways of reconceptualising the dynamic of group- vs. individually-based concerns in Japanese society from an emic perspective. As Haugh points out, '[t]his emphasis on the importance of place does not endorse, however, the view that Japanese "(im)politeness" is governed by socio-pragmatic rules, or what Ide (1989) terms *wakimae* (discernment)...[because] place does not exist prior to or independently of interaction, but rather is achieved through social interaction' (Haugh 2007b: 662).

This cross-cultural critique has served to inspire a series of recent reformulations that attempt to capture, above all, the dynamicity of face. Realising that it is not the case that face only comes into play with the performance of particular acts but rather, as Scollon and Scollon put it succinctly, '*there is no faceless communication*' (1995: 38; original emphasis), scholars have been increasingly paying attention to the moment-by-moment constituting of face in interaction, and to its emergent and relational aspects. In an attempt to identify the evolutionary and cognitive underpinnings of face, and inspired by a suggestion by O'Driscoll (1996) to extend the Politeness1/Politeness2 distinction to the domain of face, Terkourafi (2007) proposed a parallel distinction between Face1 and Face2. On this view, Face2 is an underspecified, schematic notion grounded in the emotional dimension of approach vs withdrawal and directed at an Other, which captures what is shared by interlocutors' Face1s, that is, the many observable, fully fleshed-out instantiations of Face2 in different cultural and situational settings. In other words, rather than seeking a single notion that is both universal and psychologically real to participants at the same time, those two attributes are now split between first- and second-order Face, with psychological reality being attributed only to Face1 and universality being claimed only of Face2.[5] Closely related is O'Driscoll's own reconceptualisation of Brown and Levinson's face that preserves the opposition between 'positive' and 'negative' aspects, and further construes them as mutually exclusive and only partly capturing the full content of this notion, since 'there are many aspects of face which have little or nothing to do with togetherness or apartness and are better handled with recourse to some other conceptualisation of face' (O'Driscoll 2007: 480).

On the other hand, the moment-by-moment constituting of face in conversation as uncovered through a conversation-analytic lens is at the heart of Arundale's Face Constituting theory (1999, 2010a), which recruits from the field of communication studies the dialectic of connectedness and separateness (Baxter and Montgomery 1996) as a more appropriate basis on which to reconceptualise face (Arundale 2006a). An ethnomethodological orientation also underlies Ruhi's (2010) conceptualisation of face as 'a Janus-like indexical concept which categorises the self-in-interaction, as it indexes and is indexed by (linguistic) acts' (2010: 2131). Drawing a parallel between face and indexical expressions ('I', 'here', 'now'), Ruhi argues that the content of face is not fixed but rather determined relative to features of the setting/text, in particular, relative to an '"image of other", where the other might be the participant(s) to [sic] an interaction or significant others who may not be present in the interaction' (2010: 2134). Thus, while face is relational in the sense of being grounded in the interactional dyad, it is 'not dualistic in nature in the sense of marking separation or connectedness, as is the case in the relational paradigm. Meanings emerging from the management of face such as pride, embarrassment, solidarity or dissociation are considered to be affective effects, and not a part of self's face value' (Ruhi 2010: 2134).

These recent theoretical proposals draw on different disciplinary backgrounds and consequently differ also in certain aspects of their application to the data. Nevertheless, they all point toward a renewed construal of face that is both more flexible and omnipresent in interaction: in these authors' words, face is something that 'happens anyway' (O'Driscoll 2007: 474), is 'entrenched in features of situated interaction' (Ruhi 2010: 2133), is 'endogenous in talk-in-interaction' (Arundale 2010a: 2087, original emphasis), or 'is continuously and unavoidably brought into existence, constituted, and threatened through language' (Terkourafi 2008: 49). In this way, a common agenda for future research on face is slowly but surely emerging. What is more, this research agenda seems to be increasingly diverging from the study of im/politeness tout court, at least if the latter is limited to the study of first-order notions of politeness and impoliteness – that is, of behaviours that are explicitly perceived and commented on as polite or impolite. For the point of recent work on face is precisely that face pervades all instances of communication, and not only those during which politeness (or impoliteness) is somehow 'at issue'.

Indeed, in view of its wider applicability beyond the realm of first-order politeness and impoliteness, face has been likened to identity and it has been suggested that the two notions can be analysed using the same analytical frameworks (Spencer-Oatey 2005, 2007; Spencer-Oatey and Ruhi 2007). The precise nature of the relationship between the two notions, however, remains a matter of some considerable debate. For one, the two notions seem to be different with regard to the affective underpinnings of face (Spencer-Oatey 2007: 644) and the framing of identity as a person-centred attribute (Arundale 2010a: 2091). Future research on both notions should help elucidate their relationship by revealing further areas of overlap as well as differences between them.

## 31.5 Tools of the trade: Intentions, implicatures and perlocutionary effects

The predication of Brown and Levinson's theory on the notion of face and, more specifically, that of face-threatening acts (FTAs) means that in their model, politeness is conceptualised as a kind of (pre-emptive) remedial action aimed at counteracting the ever-present fiction of the 'virtual offence' – a notion also inherited from Goffman, which refers to the '"worst possible reading" of some action by A that potentially trespasses on B's interests, equanimity or personal preserve' (Brown, P. and Levinson 1987: 1). Politeness, then, for Brown and Levinson, 'presupposes that potential for aggression as it seeks to disarm it, and makes possible communication between potentially aggressive parties' (*ibid.*).[6] In their model, this is achieved by means of linguistic strategies (see Figure 31.1) realising smaller or larger departures from rational efficiency – as this is encapsulated in the Gricean Cooperative Principle and maxims (Grice 1975) – that give rise to contextually dependent inferences about the speaker's intent, that is, to particularised implicatures (Brown and Levinson 1987: 95; cf. Arundale 1999: 144).[7] In other words, for Brown and Levinson, 'politeness must be communicated, and the absence of communicated politeness may, *ceteris paribus*, be taken as absence of the polite attitude' (1987: 5). The importance of the speaker's intention to Brown and Levinson's account is reiterated by Brown (1995: 169), who writes that '[p]oliteness inheres not in forms, but in the attribution of polite intentions, and linguistic forms are only part of the evidence interlocutors use to assess utterances and infer polite intentions. . . . [Interlocutors] must continuously work at inferring each other's intentions, including whether or not politeness is intended.'

Since the appearance of Brown and Levinson's work, however, it has become increasingly clear that politeness does not always have this 'communicated' or 'intended' flavour. Leech's 'tact' (1980: 109), Ide's 'discernment' mentioned above (Hill *et al.* 1986; Ide 1989), or what Kasper has termed 'politeness as social indexing' (1990: 196), Watts's 'politic' behaviour (Watts 1989), and Fraser's 'Conversational Contract' (Fraser 1990) were all early attempts to highlight a parallel, if apparently neglected by Brown and Levinson, kind of socially appropriate behaviour in which the speaker's agency is backgrounded in favour of social structural considerations embodied in local conventions and norms. More recently, the terms 'unmarked' (Terkourafi 2001, 2003), 'default' (Usami 2002), and 'anticipated' (Haugh 2003) politeness have been used to underline the unselfconscious character of most (though not all) use of polite expressions in ordinary discourse. In Brown and Levinson's own work, a distinction is made between strategic exploitations of politeness as 'a kind of social accelerator and social break for decreasing or increasing social distance in relationships' (1987: 93; cf. 228ff.) and politeness simply meeting expectations in discourse (i.e. when the strategy selected by the speaker corresponds to the hearer's own assessment of the situation). However, this difference is not modelled theoretically.

The difference between a 'neutral' kind of politeness that meets social expectations and hence passes unnoticed, and a more 'salient' kind of politeness which is noticed and potentially commented on raises doubts as to whether all of politeness can (or should) be modelled in the same way – specifically, as a kind of particularised implicature. The first to depart from this view and to offer a theoretical account of the difference between these two kinds of politeness within the framework of Relevance theory was Jary (1998). Starting from the Relevance-theoretic viewpoint that, for communication to take place, a change 'in the mutual cognitive environment of the audience and communicator' must occur (Sperber and Wilson 1986:

61), Jary suggested that politeness is communicated (as an implicature of the speaker's utterance) only when it makes mutually manifest a *divergence* in the speaker's and the hearer's assumptions concerning their relative standing for the purposes of an act. The hearer will then infer that the speaker holds him in lower (or higher) esteem than what he had previously assumed and a change in his cognitive environment will occur. Crucially, however, this does not yet amount to politeness being communicated. For that to happen, the hearer must take it that it was the speaker's intention to make manifest such an assumption. This will produce a change in the participants' mutual cognitive environment, fulfilling the preconditions for communication as this is defined within Relevance theory.

Since assumptions regarding the participants' relative standing made manifest by the use of polite forms are relevant – that is, worth the hearer's while to process – *only if they signal a mismatch* between the speaker's and the hearer's perspectives, the strategic use of politeness is now parasitic on its unselfconscious/social-indexing use (Jary 1998: 11). A further step is therefore needed to explain the latter. Taking such a step, Jary suggests that 'in the longer term, [a speaker's] aims will include that of becoming/remaining a liked and respected member of a certain group' (*ibid.*). Social-indexing uses of politeness serve this latter, longer-term aim, while its strategic uses emanate from the manipulation of shorter-term aims without, for that matter, jeopardising the longer-term one.

Although Jary does not discuss it in these terms, his wording suggests that the longer-term aim that he has in mind may be equated with face, especially in its expanded understanding as a notion related to identity (Spencer-Oatey 2007; section 31.4 above). Seen from this perspective, however, the claim that, when the hearer's assumptions about his standing relative to the speaker are in harmony with those of the speaker, no (particularised) implicatures are generated is doubly problematic. For it amounts to claiming that, in such cases, face remains unaffected by the interaction, which would mean that face is either irrelevant or else exists prior to the exchange, both possibilities running counter to the properties of omni-relevance and emergence attributed to face in recent literature on this topic (see section 31.3). The proposed account, then, seems to be unable to explain how assumptions about interlocutors' relative standing (in other words, assumptions about face) come into existence in the *absence* of a mismatch between the speaker's and the hearer's perspectives – such that they can be strategically manipulated later on.

Within the framework of Relevance theory, which provides the background for Jary's account, implicatures are always tied to the speaker's intentions. Social-indexing uses of politeness, however, would seem to have less to do with the speaker's specific intentions vis-à-vis her addressee and more with her own positioning in social space in ways that, following socialisation within a community, she may also be largely unaware of and have little choice over. What would seem to be required to model this, in that case, is a type of meaning that backgrounds the speaker's intention, yet is still sensitive to contextual considerations, since it is clear that im/politeness lies in an evaluative judgement made in relation to context rather than irrespective of it.[8]

It is in view of this last remark that we must also reject the idea that there exists such a thing as 'absolute' or 'semantic' politeness, at least if this is taken to mean that some utterances encode politeness as a non-cancellable part of their meaning that they convey in all contexts (Leech 1983, 2007).[9] This view can be easily conflated with a rather static, one-way interpretation of politeness as indirectness – and hence, one must presume, of impoliteness as directness – when it is well known (and acknowledged by Leech himself) that indirectness itself can constitute a different kind of imposition (Blum-Kulka 1987) and be perceived as impolite (Leech 1983: 171). More importantly, though, to subscribe to the view that

> [s]ome illocutions (e.g. orders) are inherently impolite and others (e.g. offers) are inherently polite. Negative politeness therefore consists in minimising the impoliteness of impolite illocutions and positive politeness consists in maximising the politeness of polite illocutions. (Leech 1983: 83–4; reiterated in Leech 2007: 174)

is to tie up particular types of face (-threatening or -constituting) with particular types of acts (and with particular ways of realising those acts) in a way that may have been prevalent in early thinking about politeness[10] but quickly became untenable as a universalising assumption and has since been superseded by a more flexible understanding of the situated trade-off between interlocutors' faces in current research. In fact, as Turner (1996: 4) has pointed out, '[i]t is not necessary to go to distant parts of the globe to find non-corroborative evidence. The more important issue is a conceptual one and has to do with the possible multifunctionality of all utterances.' As an example of this, Turner considers the utterance 'Could you look after the baby for half an hour?', which, in addition to potentially threatening the addressee's negative face and the speaker's positive face, may also be said to be 'anoint[ing] the addressee's positive face because the speaker is selecting the addressee as a reliable and responsible person to undertake this particular important task' (1996: 4). In view of all this, it is perhaps only the notion of indirectness that can be considered to be assessed on semantic grounds, in terms of its degree of departure from the baseline of rational efficiency set by the Gricean maxims. A similar baseline not being available for im/politeness, the possibility of absolute/semantic politeness must be rejected.

Rejecting the possibility of semantic politeness, however, does not have to mean that we are left with only one option, viz. Leech's 'pragmatic or relative politeness', or what I would call 'micro-level' or nonce im/politeness and, agreeing with Leech (2007: 203 n. 5), I also view as 'an unhelpful restriction'. The middle ground, here, is provided by the notion of generalised conversational implicature (or GCI for short), an implicature or type of implicature carried by the use of a certain form of words in an utterance 'normally (in the absence of special circumstances)' (Grice 1975: 37). Unlike particularised conversational implicatures (or PCIs), which require explicit recourse to the speaker's intentions, GCIs accompany the use of an expression in normal circumstances, yet they remain cancellable in special circumstances – and, in this sense, they are not semantic either. Levinson (2000) makes a compelling case for analysing several phenomena, including scalar implicatures, conventionally indirect speech acts, and even sentential anaphora, in terms of GCIs which are generated ahead of any contextual considerations by three heuristics – Q (for Quantity), I (for Informativeness), and M (for Manner) – but can, crucially, be 'filtered out' when unwarranted by the context. Nevertheless, in the case of im/politeness, a further step would seem to be required. Since intuitions about im/politeness do not arise in a social vacuum but rather against the 'normal circumstances' of one's culture, class, gender, generation or, more likely, all of those combined into a 'frame' or 'minimal context' (Terkourafi 2001, 2009b, forthcoming; see the next section), what is needed is a way of modelling these 'normal circumstances' by reducing the countless actually occurring, nonce contexts to a smaller set of experientially based 'schematic or otherwise "minimal" contexts, consisting of the values of a limited set of contextual parameters ... but with all other specificities removed' (Terkourafi 2009b: 27).

Putting forth such a frame-based account, in Terkourafi 2001, 2003 I proposed that politeness as social indexing ('unmarked politeness') involves using an expression that is conventionalised relative to the minimal context of utterance, giving rise to a special kind of GCI presumed against a minimal context (a $GCI_{mc}$ for short), while strategic ('marked') politeness should be modelled as a PCI arising when the expression used is not conventionalised relative to the minimal context. This scheme can be extended to account for impoliteness/rudeness, by taking into account the existence of adversarial contexts (such as in the military, courthouse, parliament and some media) where rudeness is expected (Terkourafi 2008, forthcoming). Crucially, the relevant notion of conventionalisation is an individually based, experiential one: it refers to 'a relationship holding between utterances and contexts, which is a correlate of the (statistical) frequency with which an expression is used *in one's experience* in a particular context. It is thus a matter of degree, and may well vary for different speakers, as well as for the same speaker over time' (Terkourafi 2001: 130; original emphasis). In this way, the asymmetry between unmarked and marked im/politeness is accounted for by proposing two different, yet related, mechanisms ($GCI_{mc}$s and PCIs), and by introducing the notion of conventionalisation relative to a minimal context (or frame) to signpost the experientially based, shifting boundary between the two.

With the introduction of $GCI_{mc}$s accounting for unmarked im/politeness, in the frame-based approach the onus of explanation is largely – though not wholly, as there is still the possibility of im/politeness PCIs – shifted away from the speaker's intention, which is bypassed or taken for granted so long as the speaker is behaving as expected in the (minimal) context of utterance. In this way, the proposed account both breaks with the Brown and Levinsonian tradition that considers attributions of intention to be necessary for politeness (see above) and is, to some extent at least, impervious to criticisms of the notion of Gricean intention as inadequate to account for human communication (Arundale 2008).

One should nevertheless be careful not to conflate an account of im/politeness in terms of $GCI_{mc}$s and PCIs with the false assumption that im/politeness itself is a kind of implicature. In recent work, Terkourafi (forthcoming) further decouples im/politeness from the speaker's intention by showing that im/politeness can never be a matter of simply recognising the speaker's intention. This is because the kind of reflexive intention that Grice (1969) placed at the heart of human communication through language is directed at *the content of the speaker's belief*:[11] once the hearer recognises that intention, he has recognised what it is that the speaker wants him to believe. But politeness (or impoliteness) is not a belief about what the speaker believes but *about the speaker herself* as a person – namely, that the speaker is polite (or impolite). This further kind of belief cannot be modelled as a reflexive intention since it involves the hearer holding a belief not about what the speaker believes but about the speaker herself directly. Clearly, it is possible for the hearer to recognise that the speaker wants him to think that she is polite, without for that matter concurring with her and actually believing that she is polite. In other words, there is a difference between uptake (the hearer's recognition of the speaker's intention 'on the basis of [having recognised that this is what the speaker intends]'; Grice 1969: 92) and any further perlocutionary effects thereby achieved (other beliefs that the hearer holds at least partly as a result of the speaker's utterance). Im/politeness would seem to be this latter kind of belief. In other words, im/politeness is a kind of perlocutionary effect, or, as Fraser and Nolen (1980: 96) first noted, 'politeness is totally in the hands (or ears) of the hearer'.

However, the fact that im/politeness is 'totally in the hands (or ears) of the hearer' does not mean that it is also entirely out of the hands (or mouth) of the speaker. For, if that were the case, what we ought to be finding in the data is a series of disparate and unrelated attempts by individual speakers at being perceived as polite (or impolite) by a multitude of hearers, some of them familiar, others not, in a multitude of circumstances, some frequently experienced and others novel, with no 'method in their madness'. Contrary to this, data from a variety of genetically unrelated languages (English, Greek, Hebrew, Korean, Ojibwa, Spanish, Tzeltal and many more) collected using several methodologies (questionnaires, role-play, observation of naturally occurring speech) converge on the fact that politeness (and, for that matter, impoliteness; see Culpeper 2011b) is routinely achieved by means of conventionalised expressions, be they conventionally indirect speech acts or else other types of formulaic expressions.[12] What this suggests is that, out of the multitude of linguistic expressions available to speakers, some offer a safer bet (though never a guarantee) of realising im/politeness, and so are preferred by them; in other words, not all expressions are equally good at achieving im/politeness.

This is captured in the frame-based view by proposing the revamped notion of $GCI_{mc}$s attached to particular expressions in particular contexts, which offer a convenient short-cut, for the speaker as much as for the hearer, toward achieving the perlocutionary effect that is im/politeness. On this view, when it passes unnoticed by the hearer, im/politeness relies on a $GCI_{mc}$, i.e. a type of meaning generated inadvertently by the speaker just in case s/he uses an expression that is conventionalised *in the hearer's experience* relative to the minimal context of utterance. All else being equal, in such cases im/politeness 'falls out' effortlessly as a perlocutionary effect of the speaker's utterance. Of course, this analysis would seem to beg the question of just when the speaker is likely to use an expression that is conventionalised in the hearer's experience. In answer to this question, in the frame-based approach it is proposed that frames (or minimal contexts) are instantiations of the interlocutors' Bourdieuan habitus (Terkourafi 2001: 182–4). In Bourdieu's explanation of this notion, habitus develop in response to social conditions of existence and are thus objectively regulated (1990: 53). So long as the interlocutors' social conditions of existence are, then, similar, we should expect them to develop homologous habitus, resulting in comparable ways of perceiving and classifying the social world, i.e. in comparable repertoires of frames.

In addition to the frame-based approach, two other recent approaches offer accounts of im/politeness as a hearer-based phenomenon. In the discursive approach developed by Richard Watts and Miriam Locher (e.g. Watts 2003; Locher 2004; Locher and Watts 2005), a distinction is drawn between 'face-work' or 'relational work', which 'comprises the entire continuum of verbal behavior from direct, impolite, rude or aggressive interaction through to polite interaction, encompassing both appropriate and inappropriate forms of social behavior' (Locher and Watts 2005: 11), and politeness, which 'is only a relatively small part of relational work and must be seen in relation to other types of interpersonal meaning' (*ibid.*: 10). Moreover, within politic/appropriate relational work, one may distinguish between behaviour which is 'unmarked' and goes largely unnoticed ('non-polite') and that which is 'positively marked'– only the latter is deemed to be 'polite' (*ibid.*: 12). What Locher and Watts are trying to zoom in on in this way is Politeness1, that is, participants' own perceptions of politeness, as set against their individual normative expectations about what constitutes politic or appropriate behaviour each time (*ibid.*: 10). Crucially, because such normative expectations are precisely individual, the threshold between what constitutes unmarked politic behaviour ('non-polite') and what constitutes positively marked politic behaviour ('polite') in this approach is also individual; in other words, 'there can be no objectively definable boundaries between these categories' (*ibid.*: 12). In fact, on this view, the point of a theory of politeness is precisely to illustrate what Locher and Watts call 'the discursive struggle over politeness1' (*ibid.*: 29) and so to deconstruct the reified view of politeness sometimes found in earlier work (cf. Haugh 2007a: 296). Perceptions of im/politeness being individual, what the analyst can (and should) do is, at most, to identify in examples of naturally occurring speech those elements which are 'open to a polite interpretation' (Locher and Watts 2005: 26) – however, whether these elements were ultimately perceived as polite by the participants themselves must remain 'debatable' (*ibid.*), since direct access to participants' perceptions during the exchange is impossible and cannot be supplanted by other methods of investigation, such as debriefing interviews or role-play (*ibid.*: 17).[13]

A different stance is taken in the interactional approach developed in ongoing work by Robert Arundale and Michael Haugh (e.g. Arundale 1999, 2006a, 2008, 2010a; Haugh 2007a).[14] Working within the framework of conversation analysis, Arundale and Haugh point out that the equivocality with which scholars working within the discursive paradigm approach the interpretation of the data need not be a foregone conclusion (Haugh 2007a: 304). Rather, close scrutiny of the sequential unfolding of the interaction using the tools of conversation analysis can reveal a lot about participants' ongoing interpretings of im/polite discourse. Attention to the minutiae of interactional speech affords two advantages. First, it shields the analysis from potential analyst bias by providing an empirically verifiable benchmark for the interpretation. Second, and more importantly, it captures all and only the information which is available to participants themselves as they interpret (and reinterpret) each other's speech. In other words, it would be wrong to assume that, as participants converse, they settle on fully formed interpretations of each other's utterances inside their heads that the analyst (or, for that matter, co-participants) will never be able to access – yet, that seems to be precisely the assumption guiding practitioners of the discursive view. On the interactional view, on the other hand, this reified construal of utterance interpretation is rejected in favour of the idea that participant interpretings are 'not fixed, but continually evolving' (Arundale 2010a: 2080–81), naturally leading to the conclusion that the analyst need be no more tentative in his or her analysis than the participants themselves. Using the tools of conversation analysis, the analyst can establish 'procedural relevance', that is, 'demonstrate that his or her analysis is... oriented to the uptake by participants evident in interaction' (Haugh 2007a: 311). However, to make the analysis explanatory of how face is constituted in conversation, a different type of relevance, 'interpretive relevance', must also be established. Interpretive relevance refers to showing that 'the analysis itself is viable with respect to the interactional achievement of (im)politeness1' (Haugh 2007a: 311), and requires taking into account aspects of the wider context beyond the transcript at hand, which may include 'aspects of the currently invoked identity of the participant' and 'the history of their particular relationship, not only within the course of, but also prior to the conversation being examined' (Arundale 2006b: 10, cited in Haugh 2007a: 311).

Clearly, both the discursive approach and the interactional approach share some commonalities with the frame-based approach presented earlier. All three consider im/politeness to be ultimately a matter of the hearer's interpretation of the speaker's utterance rather than of the speaker's intention in making that utterance. They also all acknowledge the importance of normative assumptions about im/politeness which provide the background to participants' evaluative judgements in context. On the frame-based view, these are modelled as 'cognitive frames' (Terkourafi 2001, 2009b), that is, as constellations of observable features of the extra-linguistic context extracted from their experience of similar situations and biasing speech-act interpretation toward specific preferred outcomes, while on the discursive view, such assumptions are discussed under the rubric of 'interactional frames' providing information about participants' roles and obligations in context (Locher and Watts 2005: 11, 23), and on the interactional view as 'moral and empirical norms' (Haugh 2007a: 309) which 'should be based on participants' understandings' (*ibid*.) and are 'shared or constructed across social networks, including so-called "cultures"' (*ibid*.: 308). These similarities between the three approaches point to some emerging methodological trends, some already observed in ongoing research. Specifically, all three approaches emphasise the need for more empirical research that will focus on longer stretches of discourse beyond the isolated speech act, and will take into account the addressee's uptake.

Nevertheless, despite these similarities, differences between these approaches also exist, and these pertain primarily to the different levels of granularity at which they seek to explain im/politeness phenomena (Terkourafi 2005: 254–6). Specifically, by not encompassing a notion of GCIs, that is, 'a level of systematic pragmatic inference based *not* on direct computations about speaker-intentions, but rather on *general expectations about how language is normally used*' (Levinson 1995: 93; original emphasis), the discursive and the interactional approaches are not concerned with the possibility of uncovering regularities of linguistic usage above and beyond the interactional moment. In fact, this possibility would seem to be somewhat programmatically excluded at least on the discursive view, if only through a confounding of the notion of regularity with that of universality (Locher and Watts 2005: 16). However, while this move may be possible to explain as a reaction to what might be viewed as occasionally overzealous attempts at associating linguistic forms directly with im/politeness in earlier work, abandoning efforts to even trace such regularities in the data may be somewhat premature – especially since it is precisely the empirical discovery of such regularities in a bottom-up fashion in a large corpus of naturally occurring speech that led to the insights of the frame-based approach in the first place (see the next section).

In addition to avoiding generalisations about linguistic form, the discursive and the interactional approaches also do not attempt to make any generalisations about the context of im/polite discourse. As a result, although they both acknowledge the importance of normative assumptions as the backdrop against which situated evaluations of im/politeness are made, and moreover state that such assumptions must be 'based on participants' understandings' (Haugh 2007a: 309) or reflect participants' 'past experience' of interaction (Tannen 1993b, cited in Locher and Watts 2005: 11), these approaches have yet to spell out the content of these normative assumptions, or, more to the point, propose an empirical way of verifying their existence.

In focusing on individual encounters *in lieu of* generalisation with regards to both linguistic form and context, the discursive and interactional views are thus displaying an orientation toward the micro level which is not shared by the frame-based view. Rather than analysing im/politeness (solely) as a micro-level phenomenon, the frame-based view also tries to go beyond the specifics of the situation. In this way, it is placed at an intermediate level of granularity between a macro-level, universalising approach (such as that of Brown and Levinson 1987) and the micro-level approaches represented here by the discursive and interactional views (cf. Terkourafi 2005). The tools for this are provided by the notions of $GCI_{mc}$s, discussed above, and of cognitive frames, to which I now turn.

## 31.6  Contexts of im/politeness

Although the claim that im/politeness is a judgement made in context is hardly controversial, there have been very few attempts at modelling this context in an empirically viable way that carries over relatively straightforwardly to new research contexts. Brown and Gilman (1960/2003) were the first to attempt to formalise the relationship between linguistic expressions (cross-linguistic realisations of the pronouns T and V, in their case) and their extra-linguistic contexts of use through their twin notions of 'power' and 'solidarity'. According to Brown and Gilman, power is a non-reciprocal relationship whose potential sources include 'physical strength, wealth, age, sex, institutionalised role in the church, the state, the army or within the family' (*ibid.*: 158), while solidarity is a symmetrical relationship based on similarities in 'political membership, family, religion, profession, sex, and birthplace' (*ibid.*: 160). Both power and solidarity thus have some basis in external attributes. However, they are ultimately behavioural dispositions:

> The T of solidarity can be produced by frequency of contact as well as by objective similarities. However, frequent contact does not necessarily lead to the mutual T. It depends on whether contact results in the discovery or creation of the like-mindedness that seems to be the core of the solidarity semantic. (Brown and Gilman 1960/2003: 160)

And likewise for power: '[o]ne person may be said to have power over another in the degree that he [sic] is able to control the behavior of the other' (*ibid.*: 158). The dimensions of power and solidarity were taken up in later work by Brown and Levinson (1987: 74–83) and by Leech (1983: 126), while Lakoff (1973) speaks of R1, R2 and R3 cultures embodying the interactional ethos of the three rules of politeness that she proposes, namely R1: Formality, R2: Deference, and R3: Camaraderie – without, however, providing further details as to how these three types of cultures may be empirically identified.

As a way of capturing the extra-linguistic context of an act relative to which assessments of im/politeness are made, Brown and Levinson (1987) proposed three sociological variables: social distance between the speaker and hearer (D), relative power of the hearer over the speaker (P), and ranking of the imposition entailed by the act in the culture in question (R). Their definitions of D and P are close to those of Brown and Gilman cited above: D is 'a symmetric social dimension of similarity/difference within which S and H stand for the purposes of this act' (Brown and Levinson 1987: 76) assessed on the basis of frequency of interaction as well as stable social attributes, while P is an asymmetric social dimension based on 'the degree to which H can impose his own plans and his own self-evaluation (face) at the expense of S's plans and self-evaluation' (*ibid.*: 77) emanating from both material and metaphysical control. The last variable, R, 'is a culturally and situationally defined ranking of impositions by the degree to which they are considered to interfere with an agent's wants of self-determination or of approval' (*ibid.*: 77).

These three sociological variables play an important role in Brown and Levinson's scheme, as they determine the choice of strategy from their proposed hierarchy (see Figure 31.1). They do this by providing the input to the following formula, which Brown and Levinson claim guides assessments of the weightiness or seriousness of an act ($W_x$):

$$W_x = D(S, H) + P(H, S) + R_x \text{ (Brown and Levinson 1987: 76)}.$$

Brown and Levinson make several additional claims regarding the calculation of the values of the three sociological variables and the operation of this formula, most importantly: that they are assessed anew for each FTA x (*ibid.*: 78); that they are independent of each other (*ibid.*: 80); that they subsume all other relevant factors (*ibid.*); and that, once combined into the weightiness value of the FTA x according to the proposed formula, their individual values become untraceable 'mak[ing] the sources of the final assessment [of $W_x$] ambiguous' (*ibid.*: 81). Each of these claims has been challenged in subsequent research.[15]

In assessing the values of D, P and R, interlocutors do not always start with a clean slate (Terkourafi 2001: 102, 103) or assess one independently of the other(s) (Holtgraves and Yang 1990: 725; Tannen and Kakava 1992: 13; Watts *et al.* 1992/2005: 9); variables other than these three and not subsumed under them, such as 'affect', have been found to influence politeness judgements

(Slugowski and Turnbull 1988), while sources of W assessment may also be transparent, as when particular linguistic expressions (e.g. address terms) seem to be more closely associated with one of these variables (e.g. power emanating from age) than the other two (Terkourafi 2001, 2004). But probably the most serious weakness of the proposed scheme lies in the fact that it is unfalsifiable: virtually any linguistic form can be construed as an instance of this or that strategy depending on the circumstances in which it is used, making the formula an analytic truth (Terkourafi 2001: 92–3). However, if Brown and Levinson's scheme fails to make the correct predictions when applied to new empirical data, that does not necessarily make it wrong – it may be simply that this is the wrong level of application for their model, and that, on its own, this model is not sufficient to meet the needs of empirical analysis.[16]

Under each politeness strategy shown in Figure 31.1, Brown and Levinson listed several sub-strategies that can realise it linguistically. Their assumption seems to have been that these sub-strategies were interchangeable – in other words, each should be as good as the next in achieving the requisite level of redress. Close analysis of empirical data, however, suggests otherwise. Based on the analysis of a large corpus of naturally occurring conversations, in Terkourafi 2001 I found that, rather than being interchangeable, particular linguistic sub-strategies are preferentially associated with particular extra-linguistic contexts. That is, when faced with a particular arrangement of extra-linguistic features that included the speaker's and the hearer's age, gender and social class, the relationship between them and the setting of the exchange, speakers tended to opt time and again for the same linguistic realisation of a particular act, rather than innovate. This led me to propose that, alongside the quantitative understanding of indirectness prevalent in earlier work, a qualitative notion of indirectness is also needed to help keep apart linguistic sub-strategies otherwise falling under the same politeness strategy from Brown and Levinson's hierarchy. Furthermore, I hypothesised that, through frequent exposure to particular co-instantiations of extra-linguistic features, these combinations tend to be stored together, along with information about the expressions used therein, in the form of 'cognitive frames' or 'minimal contexts' that furnish a baseline (the 'normal circumstances') for the interpretation of these expressions. Through a process of pattern-matching, perceived features of the actual situation activate these frames, resulting in the generation of im/politeness $GCI_{mc}$s as explained above (section 31.5). Frequent exposure to the same situations, as will be the case for members of the same family, local community or, more generally, the same community of practice, will lead to acquiring and storing similar repertories of frames, increasing the chances that im/politeness investments between them will pass unnoticed (i.e. they will be achieved as perlocutionary effects of im/politeness $GCI_{mc}$s). At the same time, an individual's repertory of frames will provide the cognitive 'toolkit' that s/he will draw upon in trying to make sense of a novel (not previously experienced) situation, resulting in frames functioning as prototypical structures of expectations that will also constrain the derivation of im/politeness PCIs.

In recent work, I have elaborated on this notion of cognitive frames, by suggesting the incrementality of interpretation as the reason why it may be advantageous to rely (at least at an initial stage) on a limited set of contextual parameters fixed from the outset upon presumption to infer illocutionary force (Terkourafi 2009b: 35), and by drawing on the notion of the affordances of physical settings as 'the missing link between the limited set of contextual parameters we have been considering (interlocutors' gender, age, and social class, the relationship between them, and the setting of the exchange) and the kinds of goals that the speaker is presumed to be pursuing at any one time' (*ibid.*: 36). I concluded that

> A potentially all-inclusive notion of context is practically unmanageable and of little empirical usefulness. What is needed, in this respect, is a notion of context that is bounded, i.e. that distinguishes context from the totality of the interlocutors' common ground. The emergence of symbolically represented contextual parameters out of perceptual input along the lines proposed by Barsalou (1999) shapes a potentially unlimited body of socio-cultural knowledge into a limited set of contextual parameters available for propositional manipulation. Because of this, the resulting minimal contexts are neither impoverished with respect to the original input, nor reducible to it. At the same time, the contextual parameters jointly constituting a minimal context cannot be further broken down to more abstract ones, such as relative status or power, or social distance. Rather, they are mentally manipulated as primes. (Terkourafi 2009b: 36)

## 31.7    Taking stock and looking ahead

In this chapter, I have tried to provide an overview of the main developments in im/politeness studies since their inception in the 1970s as these relate to research in linguistic pragmatics. We have seen how central notions of Gricean and post-Gricean pragmatics, including the speaker's intention, implicatures, perlocutionary effects, the Relevance-theoretic notion of communication and neo-Gricean notions of defaults have been applied to the analysis of im/politeness leading to a more fine-grained understanding of the relevant phenomena. At the same time, it is clear that the study of im/politeness has a lot to offer to linguistic pragmatic research, by, for instance, clarifying the explanatory purview of the speaker's intention, zooming in on the notion of generalised conversational implicature, and offering new ways of conceptualising extra-linguistic context.

Before closing, I would like to draw attention to one more development which brings im/politeness issues to bear upon research in the burgeoning field of experimental pragmatics. In recent experimental work, Bonnefon and colleagues investigated the impact of face-threatening contexts on the interpretation of scalar implicatures with 'some' (Bonnefon *et al.* 2009). They found that, in such contexts, subjects are less willing to draw the upper-bounding implicature from 'some' to 'not all', adding to our knowledge about the context-variability of scalar implicatures and confirming the importance of face as a factor in implicature derivation all around (cf. Terkourafi 2007: 328–34). Similar results were obtained with conditionals (Demeure *et al.* 2009). These results, along with the other developments overviewed in this chapter, serve to reaffirm the continued relevance of im/politeness studies to research in linguistic pragmatics.

# Notes

## Chapter 1

1 See e.g. Huang 2007 on the interfaces with semantics and syntax.
2 For a discussion of the compatibility of the cognitive and truth-conditional perspectives see also Jaszczolt 2002, chapter 17.7.

## Chapter 2

1 But this chapter does not presume an exhaustive overview of pragmatic theories. See for example pragmatics inside two-dimensional semantics (Brogaard, this volume).
2 While I know no pragmatist who would deny the validity of the code/inference definition for grammar and pragmatics respectively, practically, many pragmatists adopt a much broader ("big-tent") working definition for pragmatics, as is reflected in publications in *Journal of Pragmatics*, for example. These approaches are not here discussed.
3 Most of the chapters in this handbook fall under this research paradigm, e.g., Bach, Horn, Jaszczolt and Haugh, Recanati, Atlas, and Carston.
4 For example, I have argued that the upper bound on *most* and *some* (understood slightly differently than is currently assumed) is linguistically encoded, rather than pragmatically derived, and that 'compatibility with all' is pragmatic, rather than linguistic (Ariel, 2004, 2009). See Chierchia (2004) for a grammatical analysis of GCIs.
5 The term 'explicated inference' is mine.
6 I have proposed the (ad hoc) Privileged Interactional Interpretation (Ariel, 2002), which can be even richer than the explicature (including some PCIs). An even more radical enrichment position is adopted by Jaszczolt (2005). She proposes that we go straight from linguistic meanings to the (model) speaker's primary message. This representation includes not

just pragmatic inferences, but also socio-cultural and cognitive default assumptions.

7 I should point out, however, that there is a dispute as to whose meaning should be presented, the speaker's or the addressee's. See Saul, 2002b.

8 Relevant chapters in this handbook are Allan and Gundel.

9 Prince (1998) even insisted that just like the rest of grammar, form/ function pragmatic conventions can be arbitrary.

10 Chafe (1994) divides up referring expressions into three categories: activated, semiactive, and inactive.

11 SBC is the Santa Barbara Corpus of Spoken American English; see Du Bois *et al.* (2000, 2003). LSAC is the Longman Corpus of Spoken American English.

12 See Ariel (2008b: Chapter 5) for a more general discussion of the extralinguistic pressures involved in grammaticization.

13 Relevant chapters in this handbook are Mauri and van der Auwera, and Traugott.

14 I will not here distinguish between semanticization and grammaticization since from our point of view the same process is involved in both: a pragmatically triggered pattern becomes an entrenched code, be it semantic, morphological, or syntactic.

15 For more comparisons and criticisms of various theories of reference see Ariel (1994, 2001).

16 Griceans too admit now that some PCIs and GCIs contribute truth-conditional aspects to propositions. By PCIs and GCIs above I mean those implicatures which do not contribute truth-conditional meanings in the initial phase. When semanticizing, however, the implicated meaning first becomes truth-conditional, although it is still cancelable (an explicated interpretation), and only at the final stage is cancelability lost, the meaning thus becoming a full-fledged semantic meaning.

17 On the grammar/pragmatics interface see also Kempson, this volume.

## Chapter 3

1 See Horn, this volume, on implying vs inferring, and also Ariel, this volume, on inferential pragmatics.

## Chapter 4

1 Bach cites a link no longer available, but the entry appears in AHBEU 1996.

2 This use, which the *OED* (s.v. **infer**, sense 4) tracks back to a 1533 letter of Sir Thomas More, is also attested in *MWDEU* with additional cites from Jonathan Edwards, James Boswell, Jane Austen, Joshua Whatmough ("the

levels of restricted syntactic relationships infer an individual complication of language") and William Faulkner ("to be a literary man infers a
certain amount of – well, even formal education").

3 Other verbs show a similar sender/receiver duality in their argument
structure, including Fr. *apprendre* = 'teach' or 'learn' or dialectal *learn* in
English.

4 This formula was applied by the fourth-century rhetoricians Servius and
Donatus to characterize litotes or understatement; cf. Hoffmann 1987:
21 and Horn 1991 for elaboration.

5 The implication from the use of *some* to 'not all' cited by Mill and Monck
is a two-way street, as recognized by Sapir (1930: 21; emphasis added):

> "Not everybody came" does not mean "some came", **which is implied**,
> but "some did not come".
>
>   Logically, the negated totalizer [*not every*] should include the totalized
> negative [*none*] as a possibility, but ordinarily this interpretation is
> excluded.

While Chierchia (2004: 58) argues that implications in negative contexts
like Sapir's "appear to be generally somewhat weaker and flimsier than
their positive counterparts," others have disputed the existence of any
such asymmetry (cf. Horn 2006, 2009b).

6 Mill's *sous-entendu* resurfaces as the label for an implicature-like relation invoked by Oswald Ducrot (1972) in his independent formulation
of a Grice-like logic of conversation, which features its own version
of a tacit rule of strength or quantity and of the inferential process
motivated by its exploitation, subject to the now familiar contextual
constraints:

> [The *loi d'exhaustivité*] exige que le locuteur donne, sur le thème dont il
> parle, les renseignments les plus forts qu'il possède, et qui sont suscep-
> tibles d'intéresser le destinataire ... Le destinataire, supposant que le
> locuteur a respecté cette règle, aura tendance, si la réserve du locuteur
> ne peut pas être attribuée à une absence d'information, à interpreter
> toute affirmation restreinte comme l'affirmation d'une restriction (s'il
> ne dit que cela, alors qu'il sait ce qui s'est passé, c'est qu'il n'y a que
> cela). (Ducrot 1972: 134)

7 Strawson's nomenclature was anticipated by the use of *presupposition* in
Land 1876 and the notion of *Voraussetzung* in Sigwart 1873 and Frege 1892
for the existential import associated with the use of quantified expressions and names. For example, Sigwart (1873: 122) notes that "'Socrates
is not ill' presupposes in the first place the existence of Socrates, because
only on the presupposition [*Voraussetzung*] of his existence can there be
any question of his being ill", while Land (1876: 290) observes, "When
we say *no stone is alive*, or *all men are mortal*, we presuppose the existence

of stones or of men." *Implicate* and *implicature*, on the other hand, do not occur in the relevant sense until the publication of Grice 1968.

8 See also Ariel, this volume.

9 It should also be noted that as the relation is defined by Nowell-Smith and Hungerland, we cannot understand contextual implication as a proto-conversational implicature without running afoul of three of the "top ten" (Bach 2006c), misconceptions #1 ("Sentences have implicatures"), #4 ("Gricean maxims apply only to implicatures"), and especially #6 ("All pragmatic implications are implicatures").

10 Like the rationality-based treatments of implication more generally, these codicils too were "in the air" during this period. In his "Implications and meaning", O'Hair (1969: 45) presents his version of the strength rule, complete with his own "unless" codicil: "Unless there are outweighing good reasons to the contrary, one should not make a weaker statement rather than a stronger one if the audience is interested in the extra information that would be conveyed by the latter." (A more Gricean version would read "if **the speaker believes that** the audience is interested . . . ".)

11 Saul (2002b) sees the divergences between Relevance theory and Gricean pragmatics as attributable largely to the focus of the former on inference – the cognitive task of utterance interpretation – as distinguished from the philosophical tradition in which Grice situated his own approach to implicature as a component of speaker meaning.

12 Bach observes (p.c.) that the cases originally motivating the development of the notion of impliciture were those involving completion (or saturation) as in (3), where the distinction between what is implicated and what is communicated does not arise. In any case, this complementary distribution of implicature and impliciture is not limited to instances of scalar predication. On the account of conditional perfection as pragmatic strengthening in Horn 2000, a speaker uttering *If p then q* will (*ceteris paribus*) R-implicate *If not-p then not-q*, the two conditionals combining to yield the biconditional *If and only if p, q*. It is the biconditional that will be communicated, thereby constituting the impliciture.

13 Recall misconception #2 (Bach 2006c: 23), "Implicatures are inferences." But see §4.6.

14 The wedding example (*gratia* Gregory Ward) and its ilk are echoed by a googlum called to my attention by Nicole Palffy-Muhoray: "I hope I did not imply that. What I said was that it's not gasoline. I don't want to be misunderstood." The jury is still out on what to make of this kind of evidence. In response to googled attestations of *unintentionally implied/suggested*, Kent Bach responds as follows (p.c., 19 June 2010):

> Yes, people use such phrases, and their so doing may (unintentionally) suggest that suggesting (or implying) by an agent can be unintentional. But I'm still inclined to think that it shows merely that people can do something that, contrary to or independently of their intention,

suggests (or implies) something. Something is suggested to the listener, but it is not the speaker that does the suggesting. At most the speaker causes something to be suggested.

## Chapter 5

1 However, Travis (2006: 125–6) argues that holding any view on how logical laws apply to thinking subjects constitutes a form of psychologism and thereby dissociating subjects from logical laws à la Frege is a form of psychologism as well.

2 Cf. Frege's letters to Husserl (Frege 1906) and his review of Husserl's *Philosophy of Arithmetic I* (Frege 1894).

3 For a detailed discussion see Jaszczolt (1999, chapters 3 and 6).

4 Cf. Levinson's (2000) word- or phrase-based, and a fortiori language system-based defaults. See Jaszczolt (2010d) on types of defaults in semantics and pragmatics.

5 See also Davis (1998) on the conventionality of sentence implicature.

6 But see also Mill (1872: 517); Ducrot (1972: 134).

7 Conventional implicatures are not included in the discussion as they have been conclusively demonstrated to be redundant in pragmatic theory. See e.g. Bach (1994b).

8 This discussion is developed in detail in Jaszczolt (2008).

9 Although see Recanati (1986), and more recently Davis (2008), who question the necessity for communicative intentions to be reflexive at all (cf. Bach 1987; Witek 2009).

10 Cf. Fetzer's (2002) distinction between macro and micro communicative intentions. The former type appears to be largely analogous with future-directed/higher-order intentions.

11 The original excerpt was in Turkish, but only Ruhi's translation is reproduced here. The term *canım* ('my dear', lit. 'my life/soul') is used here as a mitigator (Ruhi 2007: 113).

12 Although this is not to say there are not relational implications arising in the case of goal-oriented talk.

13 It is this sense of *intention* as a type of moral accountability oriented to by interactants that has been of most interest to those in socio-interactional fields of pragmatics to date (Arundale 2008: 250; Haugh 2008b, 2008c: 69–72; 2009: 108).

14 Malle and others also make reference to *intentionality* as a folk concept, but as Wierzbicka (2006) points out, intentionality is a technical term that has not actually entered into lay talk.

15 But see also Jaszczolt's (1999: 104–11) criticism of the requirement of the double level of intentionality. Searle (1983) says that the intentionality of linguistic expressions is inherited from the intentionality of the corresponding psychological states. However, instead of the transfer of the

conditions from the mental to the linguistic, it is more in line with the intentionality view in philosophy to see language as one of the vehicles of meaning and thereby to regard intentionality pertaining to language as primary rather than derived.

16 Although see Searle (1975b) for an attempt to model inferences underlying indirect speech acts.

17 Relevance is roughly defined as positive cognitive effects relative to processing effort (Sperber and Wilson 1995b: 265–6).

18 But see also later discussions of inference, e.g. Carston (2002, 2007).

19 Non-monotonicity refers to a 'presently reasonable inference whose reasonability may be lost upon the admittance of new information' (Woods 2010: 219).

20 The importance of mirror neurons to action understanding, however, has recently come under challenge (Hickok 2009, 2010), with the view that they may actually constitute a byproduct of sensorimotor learning being forwarded (Heyes 2010; Hickok and Hauser 2010).

21 The comments were reported as follows: 'If you take out uncovered meat and place it outside on the street, or in the garden or in the park, or in the backyard without a cover, and the cats come and eat it ... whose fault is it, the cat's or the uncovered meat? The uncovered meat is the problem. If she was in her room, in her home, in her hijab, no problem would have occurred' ('Muslim leader blames women for sex attacks', Richard Kerbaj, *The Australian*, 26 October 2006).

22 Mid-way solutions are possible though: see Default Semantics (Jaszczolt 2005, 2010c).

23 See Davis (2003, 2008) for further discussion of this issue.

## Chapter 6

1 I am using the terms 'narrow content' and 'wide content' to refer to kinds of contents thought to play different functional roles. For example, narrow content is likely to play a role in accounting for the lack of substitutability in intensional or hyperintensional contexts (see also Jaszczolt, this volume). Some will want to deny that narrow content, so defined, is truly narrow (internal) because they adhere to externalism.

2 Note that this move does not guarantee the context-insensitivity of demonstrative-plus-associated-demonstration, as the same demonstration arguably can demonstrate different objects on different occasions. As Kaplan characterizes 'demonstration', a demonstration is "typically, though not invariably, a (visual) presentation of a local object discriminated by a pointing" (1989a: 490). Arguably, 'this' and a visual presentation might pick out different (visually indistinguishable) objects at different times. Parameters of the context (e.g. the time-parameter) are thus required to determine the content of the demonstrative-plus-associated-demonstration.

3 An expression has a constant character if it has the same semantic value across all contexts.

4 I say "ideally" because we are idealizing away psychological and physiological limitations (e.g., as regards the utterance or comprehension of infinitary sentences) and logical and mathematical non-omniscience.

5 We need some sort of qualification to rule out Eden worlds, i.e., worlds where color properties are primitive or 'purely qualitative' instantiated properties. In Eden worlds the narrow content of color-terms is extrinsic. So, it doesn't supervene on the intrinsic make-up of the perceivers.

6 See Stalnaker (1970) and Kaplan (1978).

7 The literature on tense is too big to deal with in this paper but the issues raised in that literature are obviously relevant to the debate about two-dimensional semantics. In traditional tense logic, the tenses were treated as sentential operators, and that is just how Kaplan treats them. In recent years, however, the tenses have more frequently been treated as indexical referential expressions or as indexical quantificational expressions.

8 Matters are a bit more complicated than this. Semantically neutral concepts are never twin-earthable. But there are some non-twin-earthable concepts that are not semantically neutral. Chalmers offers the following example: Let L be an expression that rigidly designates the speaker's height. Then L is non-twin-earthable because any physical and phenomenal twin of the speaker will have the same height. But L is not semantically neutral because L is a rigidly designating term just like 'President Obama'. '6 ft 1' refers to Obama's actual height in every world in which it is defined, but there are scenarios compatible with what can be known a priori in which 6 ft 1 is not Obama's actual height. There are endless counterexamples of this sort. Any genuine name that rigidly designates a physical or psychological trait of the speaker will be non-twin-earthable but not semantically neutral. The twin-earthability test is nonetheless a good heuristic.

9 Matters are a bit more complicated. An enriched proposition (i.e., a Russellian proposition and a structured primary intension) is a priori at a world w iff the primary intension determined by that proposition is necessary at w, and the proposition is entertainable at w (Chalmers forthcoming b, note 18). An enriched intension is live at a scenario v iff the Russellian component has the same extension as the primary component at v. An enriched proposition is entertainable at a world w iff each of its components is live at a scenario corresponding to w. This additional complication is introduced to avoid that Apriori(P) entails □Apriori(P). For suppose this holds. Then for any a priori truth P, we have □Apriori(P). But by theorem T of system T, Apriori(P). Apriority is factive. So, P. By (restricted) necessitation, necessarily, P. But this result is unfortunate when P is a *contingent* a priori truth.

10 There has been some work done on dynamic two-dimensional semantics (see e.g. Karttunen and Peters 1979 on presupposition and Nouwen 2007

on discourse anaphora and appositives). However, I am not aware of any dynamic semantic approaches to discourse representation that rest on Chalmers's epistemic two-dimensional semantics.

## Chapter 7

1 Pragmatics, of course, is needed for disambiguation; but, on the traditional picture, disambiguation is 'pre-semantic', so it is not a counterexample to the claim that semantics and pragmatics do not mix.

2 Note that Borg herself does not fully endorse the modular view, since she takes semantics and pragmatics to mix in determining 'what is said' (Borg 2004: 128).

3 For example, Charles Travis writes that 'it is intrinsically part of what expressions of (say) English mean that any English (or whatever) sentence may, on one speaking of it or another, have any of indefinitely many truth conditions, and that any English (or whatever) expression may, meaning what it does, make any of many different contributions to truth conditions of wholes in which it figures as a part' (Travis 1997: 87).

4 On this view, contextual relations may be *long-distance* relations, as emphasised in historical-chain accounts of the reference of proper names.

5 This is an instance of the 'wrong format view', described in Recanati 2004a: 140. Putnam's theory is another instance of that view.

6 See also Allan, this volume.

7 It is actually easier to state the argument if one grants the assumption that conventional meanings are senses.

8 We can also imagine mixed readings in which the person disguised as an ATM does not really swallow the card, but does something that resembles swallowing, just as an ATM does.

9 I will only discuss the generalisation of context-sensitivity at the constituent or lexical level. The issue regarding eternal sentences etc. I take to be only of anecdotal interest. (Who cares what the proper analysis of '2 + 2 = 4' exactly is?)

10 Note that one of Stanley's early arguments against radical forms of Contextualism fails for the same reason. In 'Context and Logical Form', Stanley objects that such views make truth-conditional interpretation similar to 'the kind [of interpretation] involved in interpreting kicks under the table and taps on the shoulder' (Stanley 2000: 396). However, Stanley acknowledges that 'each [context-sensitive] element brings with it rules governing what context can and cannot assign to it, *of varying degrees of laxity*' (Stanley 2000: 396; emphasis mine). Presumably, when the degree of laxity of the linguistically encoded constraint is high (as it is for a great deal of context-sensitive expressions), the content of the expression, hence the truth conditions of the utterance containing it, can be determined only by appealing to pragmatic competence and figuring

out what the intentions of the speaker might be. This, in itself, is sufficient to make the interpretation of utterances similar to that of kicks under the table (to some extent), even if we leave free pragmatic processes aside. (I say 'to some extent', because truth-conditional interpretation is grammar-driven, even if it needs to rely on pragmatic competence. This difference – between truth-conditional interpretation and the interpretation of kicks under the table – may be what Stanley has in mind when he objects to pragmatic modulation. See below, §7.7.)

11 See my 'availability principle' (Recanati 1989, 1993, 2004a).

12 But see also Borg, this volume and Bach, this volume.

13 'Acknowledging modulations as primary pragmatic processes isn't in conflict with accepting a central role for compositional semantics', Pagin and Pelletier rightly say (2007: 50). Like Pagin and Pelletier, Westerståhl (forthcoming) sketches a compositional treatment of modulation.

## Chapter 8

1 www.telegraph.co.uk:80/comment/cartoon/?cartoon=6863333&cc=6707029

2 http://news.bbc.co.uk/2/hi/uk_news/magazine/7869458.stm

3 www.youtube.com/watch?v=ZR6wok7g7do&feature=related

4 www.roarsquadron.com/Web/FlashBacks/Ed%2011%20Page%201%20Blitz_1.htm

5 www.flickr.com:80/photos/idanska/247228762/

6 Metulla is a town in the Northern District of Israel.

7 See also Carston, this volume.

## Chapter 9

1 The content of the imperative clauses in (1)–(4) is desirable from S's or H's point of view or from both (for a detailed discussion, see Dominicy and Franken 2002). However this is not always the case:

(i)   Get the flu, and they'll fire you without further ado.

Literature on constructions like (4) and (i) is extensive and intricate, and I will not attempt to review it here (cf. Schwager 2006; Iatridou 2009).

2 Another option is to claim that some non-directive imperatives – for instance, (4) or (i) in note 1 – are not genuine imperatives (e.g. Clark B. 1993; Han 2000; Russell, Benjamin 2007). Such a claim is straightforwardly undermined by cross-linguistic data (Schwager 2006; Iatridou 2009).

3 Verstraete (2005) glosses this 'class-A prefix' as irrealis; nothing in the present discussion hinges on that, since the only way to express future

time reference in Nunggubuyu seems to be combining such class-A prefixes with non-past suffixes.

4 (19b) is acceptable as an expression of surprise; however, under such an interpretation, the corresponding imperative would be strongly deviant. In curses or blessings both imperatives and subjunctives are acceptable.

(i) Sois          maudit!
    be-IMP.2SG.  cursed

(ii) Que  tu       sois          maudit!
    Q     you-SG.  be.SBJV.PRS.2SG.  cursed

However, the subjunctive in (ii) strongly feels like an imprecation addressed to a third party (the gods, fate ... ); when no such third-person addressee is available, as in (iv), the subjunctive becomes unacceptable.

(iii) Va          au  diable!
    go.IMP.2SG.  to   devil

(iv) *Que  tu       ailles        au  diable!
    Q     you.SG.  go.SBJV.PRS.2SG.  to  devil

5 Another theoretical possibility is to claim that in languages that lack a genuine imperative, directive speech acts cannot be performed directly. However, I do not think it is worth considering seriously: it makes no sense to talk about indirectness when no direct alternative is available.

6 Keith Allan pointed out to me that (i) is acceptable:

(i)   Please may you have a safe journey home.

However, (i) is an imploration – a directive act – addressed at some third party (the gods, fate ... ). It is therefore plausible that *please* is acceptable because it is directed at such a virtual addressee.

7 Note that not every utterance of an interrogative sentence constitutes a locutionary act. I can, for instance, utter an interrogative sentence to test a microphone or to practise my English. My utterance – devoid of any contextually determined 'sense and reference' – would then be what Austin calls a phatic act, but not a locutionary one.

8 In opposition to the present chapter, however, Terkourafi endorses Bach's minimal notion of *what is said*.

9 This analysis is unavailable to Bach and Harnish, because in their view, as we have seen, the content of locutionary acts is not necessarily fully propositional, i.e. does not always have truth conditions.

10 Speaking about reasons to believe and reasons to act can also shed a new light on the notion of 'direction of fit'. Searle (1975a) contrasts the word-to-world direction of fit of assertive speech acts with the world-to-word direction of fit of directive and commissive speech acts: the former are

satisfied – true – if, and only if, their propositional content fits the world, the latter are satisfied if, and only if, the world changes in such a way as to fit the propositional content. Searle (1983) claims that the direction of fit of speech acts derives from that of the mental states they express (see Kissine forthcoming for more details on expression and speech acts). Assertive speech acts express beliefs, and beliefs have a mind-to-world direction of fit. Directive speech acts express desires, and commissive speech acts express intentions – both desires and intentions have a world-to-mind direction of fit. However, the parallel is less straightforward than it may seem. Contrast directive speech acts and desires. A desire is satisfied if, and only if, its content is true. My desire to own a car is satisfied as soon as I own a car – how this satisfaction is brought about is irrelevant for the satisfaction of the desire. By contrast, an order is satisfied (obeyed) if, and only if, the content is true *and* the addressee brings about the truth of this content with the order at hand as reason. If I order you to leave the room, and you leave saying that you do so because you need to buy cigarettes, and not because I told you to leave, my order is not obeyed. Saying that directive speech acts are reasons to act explains this causal constraint without appealing to direction of fit: an order is obeyed if, and only if, it becomes a *causally effective* reason to act.

## Chapter 10

1 Somehow it has become less popular to be an update semanticist and I am even not sure anymore whether I still am one. I would say now that both truth-conditional semantics and update semantics are ways of explaining semantic and pragmatic notions that one cannot do without, but I find it much harder now than in the past to claim that update semantics is all that is needed to explain natural language semantics. Obvious limitations of present-day update semantics are basically restrictions on what is in an information state, and one may argue that all that it would take is another dimension. But perhaps it is in the end best to look at meaning as a multi-faceted phenomenon, with classical semantics already being an obvious way of expressing a wide range of notions, and update semantics best suited for yet another theoretical angle, namely those aspects that concern the growth of information, emotional expression or an argumentative dimension.

2 This should be carefully distinguished from another tradition (e.g. Langendoen and Savin 1971; Hamblin 1971; Gazdar 1979; van der Sandt 1988, 1992; Zeevat 1992; Kamp 2001) which wants to predict the effect of a trigger in a context on that same context at a particular occasion. It is the latter version that is formalised in update semantics. The categorisation of Karttunen is important (though his holes seem partially problematic), but the requirement notion is not sufficient until the proviso problem has been solved. Here there are interesting attempts on conditionals (e.g.

Rooij 2007), but no attempts on the full problem that needs to be solved: all filters that properly filter and all plugs come with their own proviso problem. Heim (1992) gives the start of a treatment for *want*.

3 Inspired by Karttunen (1976), which formulates the ideal – building the update machine that can take in information from natural language – and which shows the importance of the machine for understanding pronouns.

4 Even Grice took this line in Grice (1981).

5 The use of a trigger is both a way of raising the question whether the presupposition is true and a sign that the speaker believes the presupposition is true. That combination is enough for a relevance implicature.

6 If the trigger is not an emotional attitude. Also the triggers that do not require local satisfaction are an exception in this respect.

7 There is one other difference with Heim's theory: presuppositions should not just be entailed, they should be overtly given. The question of the correct accommodation site is not easy to resolve. The assumption of the highest non-maximal context as the preferred accommodation site has been shown to be wrong by Beaver (2001) and has been given up by people working in this tradition like Geurts (1999) or Kamp (2001), although none of these authors have told us yet what should come in its stead. Relevance would presumably be a better predictor than DRT geometry, but the details are controversial.

8 But see e.g. Zeevat (1997).


## Chapter 11

1 See also Kissine, this volume.

2 The details of the workings of the metaphor were analyzed by Reddy (1979); see also Lakoff G. and Johnson (1980). See also Carston, this volume.

3 "Each expression is, in this sense, a pairing of sound and meaning. It has been recognized for thousands of years that language is, fundamentally a system of sound-meaning connections," as, e.g., Hauser *et al.* (2002) put it.

4 This is the picture invoked – and criticized – by Wittgenstein (1953: §1): "When they (my elders) named some object, and accordingly moved towards something, I saw this and I grasped that the thing was called by the sound they uttered when they meant to point it out. Their intention was shewn by their bodily movements, as it were the natural language of all peoples: the expression of the face, the play of the eyes, the movement of other parts of the body, and the tone of voice which expresses our state of mind in seeking, having, rejecting, or avoiding something. Thus, as I heard words repeatedly used in their proper places in various sentences, I gradually learnt to understand what objects they signified; and after I had trained my mouth to form these signs, I used them to express my own desires."

5 Wittgenstein (1969: §31) says: "Language is like a collection of very various tools. In the tool box there is a hammer, a saw, a rule, a lead, a glue pot and glue. Many of the tools are akin to each other in form and use, and the tools can be roughly divided into groups according to their relationships; but the boundaries between these groups will often be more or less arbitrary and there are various types of relationship that cut across one another."

6 "In terms of the three correlates (sign vehicle, designatum, interpreter) of the triadic relation of semiosis, a number of other dyadic relations may be abstracted for study. One may study the relations of signs to the objects to which the signs are applicable. This relation will be called the *semantical dimension of semiosis*... The study of this dimension will be called *semantics*. Or the subject of study may be the relation of signs to interpreters. This relation will be called the *pragmatical dimension of semiosis*... and the study of this dimension will be named *pragmatics*... The formal relation of signs to one another... will be called the *syntactical dimension of semiosis*... and the study of this dimension will be named *syntactics*." (Morris, 1938: 6–7).

"If in an investigation explicit reference is made to the speaker, or, to put it in more general terms, to the user of a language, then we assign it to the field of pragmatics... If we abstract from the user of the language and analyze only the expressions and their designata, we are in the field of semantics. And if, finally, we abstract from the designata also and analyze only the relations between the expressions, we are in (logical) syntax." (Carnap, 1942: 9). See Recanati (2004b) for a discussion.

7 As Wittgenstein (1953: §304) puts it: "The paradox disappears only if we make a radical break with the idea that language always functions in one way, always serves the same purpose: to convey thoughts – which may be about houses, pains, good and evil, or anything else you please."

8 See Haugh and Jaszczolt, this volume.

9 On referring see also Sullivan, this volume, Gundel, this volume, and Brogaard, this volume.

10 As Davidson (1984: 280) puts it, "convention is not a condition of language... The truth is rather that language is a condition for having conventions."

11 Game theory was first applied to social sciences by Von Neumann and Morgenstern (1944), who used mathematical methods to model economic behavior. It was subsequently applied to other branches of social sciences and also to evolution theory and anthropology. The Prisoner's Dilemma is the kind of game which is widely believed to model the conflict most characteristic of natural selection: the game portrays the situation where the players can choose between cooperation and defection, where cooperation is generally advantageous in the long run, but in each individual turn of the game taken in isolation the most profitable strategy is defection. See, e.g., Maynard Smith (1982).

12 See Glock (2010) for a defence of a conventional nature of language based on the assumption that *conventionality = normativity*. Glock understands

convention as "a shared, arbitrary rule" and defends the view that conventions thus construed must underlie language.

13 See also Peregrin (2009).

14 But see Giora, this volume, Haugh and Jaszczolt, this volume, and Katsos, this volume.

15 Elsewhere (see Peregrin, 2001: Part III) I indicated that such pragmatization of semantics need not involve discarding all the achievements of the Carnapian formal semantics, but rather merely their reassessment. See Peregrin (2008) for an outline of a normative theory of meaning.

## Chapter 12

1 The term *listeme* is from Di Sciullo and Williams (1987). Listemes may consist of a single morpheme (such as PAST TENSE), a lexeme (such as TAKE), a multiword "prefab" (*put up with*, *shoot the breeze*, *doesn't amount to a hill of beans*; see §12.9) and perhaps potentially productive stems such as –JUVENATE (see Allan 2001). Listemes are (apparently) what Stubbs (2001) calls "lemmas" and Wray (2008) calls "morpheme equivalent units."

2 For discussion of its implementation and exceptions see Allan (2001) and references cited there.

3 Religious conflicts make this very obvious.

4 Lasersohn thinks this erases the slack, but I think the slack is only restricted.

5 One reconstruction of the Proto-Indo-European word for EGG is $*h_a\bar{o}(w)iom$ 'bird-thing' from $*h_ae(w)ei$- 'bird' (I am grateful to Olav Kuhn for this information).

6 The fact that there is no word for *bozines suggests either that English speakers can function with the vague category 'large animals, like bovines are' or that terms such as *bull elephant* and *cow whale* are learned first and *elephant calf* and *bull whale* can be adduced by analogy.

7 This 90° from the horizontal is the prototype for 'upward', but any angle greater than 0 and less than 180° is upward.

8 It is assumed here that countability is characteristic of NPs rather than nouns, as argued in Weinreich (1966), McCawley (1975), and Allan (1980).

9 There is no evidence that natural languages distinguish between individuals and unit sets.

10 I could find no on-line or corpora references to leopard meat or fox meat, but an Illinois butcher does offer lion meat: www.czimers.com/2.html (accessed July 14, 2010).

11 $\Phi \prec \Psi$ means "$\Phi$ precedes $\Psi$ (chronologically)."

12 S identifies the speaker, here and below.

13 Kasia Jaszczolt (p.c.) has questioned whether temporal precedence is applicable with statives such as *She is underage and can't drive*. I don't strongly disagree but I think being underage is prior to inability to drive and this is evident in *She is no longer underage and can now drive*.

14 *Sorites* from Greek σωρείτης 'heaped up'. The earliest discussion of sorites paradoxes is attributed to Eubulides of Miletus, fourth century BCE. A single grain of sand is certainly not a heap. Nor is the addition of a single grain of sand enough to transform a non-heap into a heap. If we keep adding grains, at some point we will have a heap – but there is no agreement on the precise number that constitutes the least lower bound of a heap.

15 The average height for a male Pygmy is less than 5 feet (155 cm): www.physorg.com/|news117456722.html; for a basket-ball player it is 6′6″ (198 cm): http://wiki.answers.com/|Q/|What_is_the_average_height_of_a_basketball_player.

16 *Seinfeld* Season 4, Episode 17 "The Outing" (1993).

17 After Ross (1972).


## Chapter 13

1 See Schiffrin (1994) for a good overview of these various approaches to analysing spoken interaction, and Jucker (2009) for an excellent discussion of the various types of methodologies and their respective value for the study of speech acts in particular.

2 The divide between CA and more interactional forms of pragmatics is becoming increasingly blurred in many respects, however, as conversation analysts increasingly focus on both more 'cognitive' (e.g. epistemics) and 'socio-cultural' (e.g. affiliation) issues in analysing talk-in-interaction (Heinemann and Traverso 2009; Heritage 1984, 2009; Heritage and Raymond 2005; Raymond 2003; Raymond and Heritage 2006; Steensig and Drew 2008; Stivers 2008), while many in pragmatics draw directly from research and methods in CA in so-called interactional pragmatics (Arundale 2010a, 2010b; Haugh 2007a, 2010a).

3 For a more comprehensive overview of the interactional machinery from a CA perspective see Clift *et al.* (2006) or Schegloff (1999, 2006).

4 The symbols used in these excerpts are based on the standard conversation-analytic transcription system (Jefferson 2004). See the list of transcription symbols in the appendix to this chapter for further detail. Pseudonyms are used for all the participants.

5 This excerpt is from the Griffith Corpus of Spoken Australian English, which is being made available through the Australian National Corpus (www.ausnc.org.au/).

6 Thanks to Billie Mertens, a student at Griffith University, for permission to use this excerpt and her observations about it.

7 This excerpt is from the Australians Getting Acquainted corpus held by the author.

8 Notably, in negotiating Emma's epistemic territory in this way, and also avoiding potential impoliteness implications (for example, being

interpreted by Emma as *intending* to imply her business might not be going well), Chris's utterance can be evaluated as 'polite'.

9 For applications of the CCM to explicating various pragmatic phenomena in conversational interaction including implicature, 'miscommunication', co-constructions, humour, im/politeness and face see Haugh (2007a, 2007c, 2008b, 2008c, 2009, 2010a, 2010b, 2011).

10 The analysis of an ironic complaint in Clift *et al.* (2006: 8–9) faces exactly the same difficulties.

11 See Eelen (2001: 188–95) for a detailed summary.

12 The term inter-action is used by Arundale to emphasise the focus of analysis is on actions that are jointly achieved by two or more persons, not simply interaction as commonly understood.

13 Frames are defined as structures of co-occurring components (Minsky 1975; cf. Terkourafi 2005), or, alternatively, interpretive structures that underpin metapragmatic awareness amongst participants about what is going on in interaction (Goffman 1974; Tannen 1993b). Scripts, on the other hand, involve knowledge associated with types of events (Schank and Abelson 1977).

14 This excerpt is from the Australian component of the International Corpus of English, which is also being made available through the Australian National Corpus (www.ausnc.org.au/). Thanks to Pam Peters for access to the sound recordings for transcription.

15 It is worth noting that when making prospective inferences, it is not necessarily the degree of consistency with what a speaker might have 'intended', but rather its degree of plausibility, which can prove crucial (Haugh 2009: 102).

## Chapter 15

1 Note that there are some significant differences of usage when it comes to the range of applicability of the term 'reference'. In its strictest sense, 'reference' applies only to the relation between singular terms (such as proper names and pronouns) and what they are used to single out. On this usage, whatever the semantic relations are, precisely, that are involved in, say, predicates ("is tall") or adverbs ("slowly"), they are distinct from reference. In a broader sense of the term "reference", any expression that makes a difference to the truth conditions of sentences in which it occurs thereby has a referent – and so, for example, predicates refer to properties. In the former, strict sense of the term, the theory of reference is more or less co-extensive with the study of the meaning and use of singular terms, while in the latter, broad sense, the business of the theory of reference is to assign semantic values to all independently meaningful expressions.

2 Here compare the contrastive views of reference developed by Frege (1892) vs Kripke (1972); and see Kaplan (1989b: Part IV) for a discussion of the differing underlying conceptions of language.

3 For different approaches to this boundary see Recanati, this volume and Borg, this volume.

4 The culmination of this line of thought is the Mill (1843) view of the semantics of proper names, according to which names are connotation-less tags. I should point out that Mill's (1843) "connotation" is used in a sense that is much closer to today's "intension".

5 See Kaplan (1990) for discussion of this issue.

6 Kaplan (1989b) and Perry (2001) are seminal discussions of indexical-ity as it pertains to the theory of reference. See also Brogaard, this volume.

7 This explanation of the distinction relies heavily on Perry (2001) and Neale (2008).

8 Space does not permit me to get into the question of whether complex demonstratives should be classified as referring or denoting expressions. See Neale (2008) for a recent discussion.

9 This list constitutes a departure from Russell. (For instance, Russell (1911) argues that one can only refer to the sense data and universals with which one is acquainted.) While I follow Russell in giving central impor-tance to the referring/denoting distinction, I (along with everyone else) reject Russell's strict notion of acquaintance as a necessary condition for reference.

10 Russell's term "denoting" will seem a bit dated, especially to linguists. (Cf. Kaplan (2005: 940): "Linguists call these phrases *determiner phrases* because of their syntactic structure; they are constructed from *determiners*. Russell called them *denoting phrases* because of their semantical property; they are phrases that denote.") I will stick with Russell's term. Suppose I met exactly one man on the way here today, and call him "Alf." *Denoting* is the relation that obtains between, on the one hand, Alf, and, on the other hand, such expressions as "a man I met on the way here today" or "the man I met on the way here today."

11 Cf. Neale (1994) for discussion of the ways in which this conception of reference relates to certain theses in theoretical syntax – e.g., on p. 822, "a phrase can occupy an argument position at LF only if its semantical value is wholly determined by a single axiom, i.e. only if it is semantically atomic" – and Neale (2008) for further general discussion of related issues.

12 Kripke (1972) and Donnellan (1972) are the principal exponents on this front.

13 See also Haugh and Jaszczolt, this volume.

14 Here I scurry past massive and difficult questions in the philosophy of language, which concern the correct theoretical description of contex-tual domain restriction. For example, what exactly determine precise truth conditions for utterances of "*There is* no coffee left" or "*Everyone* has arrived"? For discussion see Stanley and Szabó (2000), and the responses by Bach (2000) and Neale (2000).

15 See also Horn, this volume and Kissine, this volume.

16 See Bach (2004: 201–4). Note especially Bach's discussion at pp. 203, 222 of the exact senses in which referential uses should be categorized as non-literal.

17 Cf. Neale (1990: 88). To borrow a nice parallel case from Bach (2004: 203), the expression "three thugs" may be well-suited to the expression of a singular proposition – e.g., "On my way over here, three thugs attacked me and stole my wallet" – but nonetheless "three thugs" is not semantically ambiguous between its standard quantificational reading and, on the other hand, a referring expression which designates the three specific guys who assaulted me.

18 For further developments and refinements of the Russellian orthodox strategy, cf. Neale (1990; 2004), Bach (2004).

19 Cf. Recanati (2004a and this volume) for discussion and references.

20 Travis (1975) and Searle (1978) are influential sources for this point in philosophy; both acknowledge debts to the ordinary language tradition. For some current research informed by both philosophy and linguistics, see Carston's Lexical Pragmatics Project, on-line at www.phon.ucl.ac.uk/home/lexprag/.

21 Cf. Kaplan (1989b), Bach (2004) and Brogaard (this volume) for discussion.

## Chapter 16

1 Kripke (1977) points out that speaker's reference can evolve historically into semantic reference. He considers this fact to be a plausible candidate for 'one of the facts needed to clear up some puzzles in the theory of reference' (Kripke 1977: 407). See also his 1972.

2 See also Maier 2009 on a DRT account of *de re*, *de dicto* and *de se* belief reports. *De se* refers to beliefs about oneself.

3 In order to capture only relevant aspects of the representation, this is a *partial* DRS in which the representation of the temporality of the event and of the indexicality of 'this spring' are omitted. On representing time in DRT see Kamp and Reyle 1993. On representing time in a more pragmatic offshoot of DRT, Default Semantics, see Jaszczolt 2009. On the foundations for representing indexicals see Kaplan 1989a.

4 N.B., there are ample arguments in the literature that the *de re/de dicto* distinction is misleading at the least. The DR-theoretic semantics of belief reports does not rely on it and is equally compatible with rejecting the dichotomy, as Jaszczolt's approach summarised in this section exemplifies.

5 For a more comprehensive introduction to the theory see Jaszczolt 2010c.

6 See Groenendijk and Stokhof 1991: 93. For a stronger claim that compositionality should be an empirical assumption about the nature of possible human languages see Szabó 2000.

7 This argument is adapted from Jaszczolt 2005: Section 5.3.

8 See the debates between contextualists and semantic minimalists, e.g. in Recanati 2005 and this volume; Borg 2004, 2007 and this volume; and an overview in Jaszczolt 2010a.

9 The topic of the minimalism/contextualism debate is a vast and important one but it cannot be covered here. Suffice to say that Bach is 'even more radical' than other minimalists because his semantics does not require propositions and truth conditions but operates directly on even sub-propositional outputs of syntax, while at the other end of the spectrum Jaszczolt is 'even more radical' than other contextualists because her semantic representations can depart from the logical form of the sentence not only by extending it but also by overriding it. See also Bach, this volume; Horn, this volume; Borg, this volume; Carston, this volume.

## Chapter 17

1 This is basically the Stalnakerian notion. See end of section 17.1.

2 This is not quite right. The proper distinction is between the presuppositional part and the non-presuppositional remainder. Depending on the speech act performed the non-presuppositional remainder can be asserted, or questioned, or requested etc.

3 Of these, the negation test is the least reliable since negative sentences can, in many cases, be interpreted in a metalinguistic way so as to defeat the presuppositional inference. See for metalinguistic negation Horn (1985) and Atlas, this volume.

4 One might try to rephrase the non-presuppositional remainder in e.g. (5c) by means of the full presuppositional expression. This leads to acceptable though unnecessary redundant sequences as *John has children. [...] If John's children are playing in the garden, they will be having a good time.* This works in the present case but breaks down as soon as indefinite expressions are involved. For example, the analysis of *A man saw his children playing in the garden* would amount to *A man has children* (the presupposition induced) and *A man saw his children playing in the garden* (non-presuppositional remainder). This cuts the link between the children introduced and the children in the second sentence. In [*A man has children...*] *A man's children are playing in the garden* the first and the second sentence typically pick a different set of children. This is called the 'binding problem'. See Karttunen and Peters (1979), Heim (1983) and van der Sandt (1992) for discussion.

5 Presumably limited by the requirement of consistency, as Heim suggests when discussing local accommodation. See section 17.4.2.

6 Note that there is no contradiction. To force a logical contradiction, Gazdar modalises the proto-presupposition by means of a necessity operator to be interpreted as 'the speaker knows that ...', which does force a logical contradiction (the set $\{\Box\varphi, \Diamond\neg\varphi\}$ is inconsistent).

7 Except for (10b). See below.

8 This theory is not to be confused with his (1992) anaphoric account.

9 See section 17.4.2.

10 I have simplified the definition for the present purposes. The original definition contained an extra (and awkward) clause intended to account for sentences with conflicting presuppositions. This clause turns out to be superfluous since contradictory presuppositions are already handled by clause (ii). This was pointed out long ago by Henk Zeevat (p.c.).

11 See for details van der Sandt (1982/1988) and Beaver (2001).

12 Gazdar's theory predicts an unfortunate semantic and pragmatic equivalence between (i), (ii) and (iii).

(i)   John's children are on holiday.

(ii)  John has children and John's children are on holiday.

(iii) John's children are on holiday and John has children.

None of these sentences invokes the (proto-)implicature that John may or may not have children and the presupposition that John has children thus passes unharmed. On van der Sandt's account the presupposition that John has children is accommodated in (i). The utterance of (ii) is – in view of the first conjunct – not acceptable in a context which already contains this information. Accommodation is thus blocked and the sentence is predicted to be non-presupposing. Finally, (iii) is predicted to be unacceptable in any context – in view of a Stalnakerian condition which says that a conjunction is acceptable in a context if the first conjunct is acceptable and the second is the enlarged context resulting from the addition of the first conjunct.

13 See note 4 above.

14 See also Zeevat, this volume.

15 See further among others van der Sandt and Geurts (1991), Krahmer (1998), Asher and Lascarides (1998), Kamp (2001), Bos (2003). See Zeevat (1992) for a hybrid account which incorporates ideas from both worlds.

16 Note the equivalence between $c, \varphi \models \psi$ and $c \models \varphi \rightarrow \psi$.

17 Consider

(i)   If I discover later that I have not told the truth, I will confess it to everyone (Karttunen)

(ii)  If the king of France opened the exhibition, ..., but if the president of France opened it, ...

The protasis of (i) induces the presupposition that I have not told the truth and the protasis of (ii) induces the presupposition that France has a king. Neither of these is preserved as presupposition of the whole sentence.

18 See for discussion e.g. Bos *et al.* (1995) and Krahmer and van Deemter (1998).

19 Of course, unless we appeal to the *de re/de dicto* distinction (e.g. Heim 1992). Under a *de re* construal we would get the strong presupposition. However, this offers no comfort for the *de dicto* reading. Such an account has the additional disadvantage of having to assume two different mechanisms for what can be explained as a single phenomenon. I refer to Geurts (1999: ch. 5) and the discussion in the next section, which suggest that it can be done by one and the same mechanism. See on the *de re/de dicto* distinction also Jaszczolt, this volume.

20 Put otherwise the (conditional) sentential presupposition is the tautologous and non-committal *If France has a king, France has a king.* See section 17.4.1.

21 Or, at most, an embellishment with number and gender

22 Or, at a deeper level of analysis: $\partial\left[x \mid \begin{array}{c}\textbf{queen}(x)\,,\,\textbf{of}(x,\,y)\\ \partial\,[\,y\mid \textbf{the\_netherlands}(y)\,]\end{array}\right]$. Note the embedding of a presuppositional condition in another presuppositional condition.

23 See also Beaver (2001: 127–8) for a discussion of the non-trivial correspondence between the projection account outlined here and the Russellian way of assigning scope.

24 Since 2006 Pluto has been demoted to a dwarf. I nevertheless stick to the venerable cultural and philosophical tradition and I thus assume, for the purposes of this paper, that the number of planets is nine. Astronomers who find this offensive may go with the definition of the International Astronomic Union and change in this example and in the following references all occurrences of 'even' to 'uneven'. This does not affect the argument.

25 To prevent misunderstandings, I want to stress that the resolution mechanism regulates the relative scope of presuppositionally induced information with respect to embedding operators. In the case of definite descriptions (and other presuppositional expressions which can be analysed the same way), this information is that there is an object that satisfies the descriptive conditions. The outcome of the resolution process captures what Russell achieves by syntactically generating scope in the description language. This is because every type of presupposition is scope-taking in the following sense: it may – by its capacity to accommodate at different levels of discourse structure – in its final representation represent the presuppositional information within or outside the scope of embedding operators. Of course, this does not capture regular quantifier scope as found in e.g. 'Every boy kissed a girl', where the indefinite phrase may outscope the universal quantifier (though the existential import of the universal quantifier, i.e. the presuppositional information that there is a – contextually given – set of boys, will be scope-taking in the sense explained). Here, I will be totally agnostic as to the issue of how the traditional notion of quantifiers' scope should be regulated in syntax. See Geurts (1999) for a

discussion of the distinction between scope by projection and classic quantifier scope.

26 E.g. Von Fintel (1994) and Beaver (2001).

27 But see Beaver's account in terms of information sets (2001: §9.3).

28 Accommodation in the restrictor of a quantifier has been strongly attacked by several authors, notably by Beaver (1994 and 2001). For a reply and an alternative account in a slightly different formalism see Geurts and van der Sandt (1999).

29 For an account of the focus/background distinction in the present frameworks, see Geurts and van der Sandt (2004).

30 The phenomenon is known as trapping. See van der Sandt (1992) for details.

31 Note that the proper translation in first-order-predicate logic would run as follows $\forall t \left[ t < n \rightarrow \mathbf{flop\_run}\,(t) \right]$.

32 'Normally', since the process of accommodation is constrained by various factors which comprise consistency and various constraints of a Gricean nature. See section 17.3 and van der Sandt (1988) and (1992) for a detailed account.

## Chapter 18

1 See Koralus (2010).

2 See Atlas (2007b), Chomsky (1996), Sperber and Wilson's (1986) Relevance theory and related views of Blakemore (1987), Carston (2002), and Iten (2005), Kent Bach (1982, 1994a, 1994b, 2007), Bezuidenhout (2002b), Recanati (2004a) and other Speech-act Theorists, Borg (2004), and Cappelen and Lepore (2005a). See also Borg, this volume and Recanati, this volume.

3 The introduction of a negation sentence as the conclusion of formal *reductio* reasoning was taken by Dov Gabbay as characterizing what a negation is; see Gabbay (1988). (Cp) characterizes I. Johannson's 1936 *minimal negation* – see Dunn (1996: 6). For my application of these ideas to negative noun phrases, see Atlas (2001). See also Martin (1989).

4 Mine is a "stronger" characterization of negation than some logicians, e.g. A. G. A. Hazen and I. L. Humberstone – again see Dunn (1996) – prefer. Some of them prefer the traditional contraposition, which will not imply the modest double negation, and then they explicitly add modest double negation for the stronger "minimal negation." See Lenzen (1996). Dov Gabbay uses *reductio ad absurdum* reasoning as a criterion for what makes a statement a negation. Mine is merely a variant of Gabbay's idea.

5 For historical remarks see Kempson (1988) and Horn (1989: 433; 1992a).

6 The people with clear accounts were the ambiguity theorists and logical semanticists, e.g. Seuren (1985), and the classical Griceans like Allwood (1972, 1977), Gazdar (1979), and Levinson (of Atlas and Levinson 1981), for whom "not" was univocal but just the exclusion negation. For Atlas'

animadversions about identifying "not" with exclusion negation, see Atlas and Levinson (1981: 55, n. 19).

7  By necessary equivalence I mean, as usual, that it is impossible for one sentence to be true when the other is not true.

8  Alternatively one might seek a slightly more subtle syntactic criterion for sentential negation. I shall return to this below when discussing sentence (25).

9  Though we are used to hyphenated negative "not" expressions from the history of logic and philosophy, (14a) is not actually a sentence of English, so without further explanation it is not obvious what it is supposed to mean in Sommers-ese. Some possible interpretations of the string are (a) *Socrates fails to be happy*, (b) *Socrates is non-happy*, either of which possibly possesses the truth conditions (c) *Socrates is in an emotional state designated by a predicate other than "happy" in the same semantic field as "happy"*, or alternatively, (d) *Socrates has some property other than being happy*.

10  For criteria for Topic Noun Phrases, see Atlas (1988; 1989: 91-119; 2004b).

11  This is incorrect. As I have shown elsewhere, an informative statement of the sentence in (21) is about what exists (Atlas 1988, 1989, 2004b). Likewise in a discourse a newly informative statement of *Pegasus does not exist* is not about Pegasus, not because there is no Pegasus but because "Pegasus" is not a topic noun phrase in the statement.

12  "[p]" means "state of affairs in which p."

13  If one abandons Sommers' conception of ontic levels of propositions, as one ought, the observation also provides the linguistic explanation of the intuitions of those philosophers who hold the "redundancy theory" of truth, i.e. the theory that $\ulcorner$That S is true$\urcorner$ just means $\ulcorner$S$\urcorner$. For the Redundancy theory is plausible only if *That Socrates is happy is true* and *Socrates is happy* are both object-language statements about Socrates. The following paraphrases indicate that both can be about Socrates: (a) *As for Socrates, that he is happy is true*, (b) *As for Socrates, he is happy*. The Redundancy theory has been popular among distinguished philosophers since early in the twentieth century, as it removes the troublesome truth-predicate, the source of the Liar's Paradox, and the difficulty of analyzing the content of a claim that some statement is true in terms, e.g., of the "correspondence" of the statement to "facts" in the world.

14  What is important is Enç's observation of the deficiencies of scopal analyses for tense. Those deficiencies, I have held, are just as great for "not," and on Horn's own view one should be skeptical of scope ambiguities for negation if one is skeptical of them for tense. If Horn had followed his own advice, he would have been skeptical about scope ambiguities for negation too.

15  See Scott (1970).

16  An example from the logic text of Kalish *et al.* (1980: 59), brought to my attention by my former student David Braun, and with apologies to Tarski, Carnap, and Church, is: *Neither Alfred will listen nor Rudolph will*

*listen, if Alonzo is talking to either.* I would expect some speakers to find (27) peculiar, given the way *neither... nor* is typically used, but the question is whether for those speakers the infelicity of utterances of (27) amounts to unacceptability or, worse, to ungrammaticality of the sentence-string. My claim is that the sentence-string is grammatical. There are some reasons why one would believe the string is grammatical. There are even cases where the string would be acceptable when uttered as well. For example, I return from a meeting with a pupil, and I report "Neither did he want to think about his thesis, nor did he want to think about his thesis." The stress and intonation in the utterance-type make this a perfectly acceptable utterance as well as a perfectly grammatical string; I am of course assuming that the stress and intonation do not make it a different sentence-string. There are also logical reasons for the string to be grammatical. Certain entailments follow as the result of general rules. For example, an adolescent son approaches his father with a request to borrow his father's classic Bentley. The indignant father says, "Neither will I lend you my Bentley today or tomorrow, nor will I ever lend you my Bentley." One logical consequence of the sentence is "Neither today or tomorrow will I lend you my Bentley, nor will I lend you my Bentley today or tomorrow." If the latter sentence were ungrammatical, such an obvious logical implication could not be preserved. Similarly for the deductive argument, where the connective is translated into a coordinating NP conjunction: (a) "Neither the evening star nor the morning star interested Frege". (b) The evening start = the morning star. So, (c) "Neither the evening star nor the evening star interested Frege". One finds similar implications from pronoun dependencies, as in "Even though it was Venus, neither the morning star nor the evening star interested Frege." One implication is "Neither Venus nor Venus interested Frege", and, of course, "Venus did not interest Frege". It would be very difficult to systematize these logical consequences of *neither... nor* sentences if the "neither P nor P" string were ungrammatical, and it would be correspondingly hard to explain the intuitive logical knowledge of such implications that speakers possess, despite the infelicity of some of the "neither P nor P" utterances for some speakers.

17 I do not mean to ignore one interesting subtlety in this Quinean argument. Consistently with Atlas (1981) and Atlas (1989: 85–7) the sentence-type "It is not that the king of France is bald" may, by virtue of semantical non-specificity, realize the literal interpretations of the following utterance-types: ($a_1$) the unstressed *It is not the case that the king of France is bald*, ($a_2$) the stressed *It is **not** the case that the king of France is bald* – but $Q$ (where $Q$ is not logically equivalent to *The king of France is bald*), ($a_3$) the stressed *It is **not** the case that the king of France is **bald*** – but he is F (where F $\neq$ *bald*), and the preferred interpretation ($b_1$) *It is **not** that **the king of France** is bald* – but that $x$ is bald (where $x \neq$ *the king of France*), ($b_2$) *It is **not** that the king of France is **bald*** – but that he is F (where F $\neq$ *bald*).

## Chapter 19

1 Henceforth, "state of affairs" will be abbreviated with the acronym SoA.
By state of affairs will be meant here the concept of something that can
be the case in some world, and can be evaluated in terms of its existence.
The term "state of affairs" will be understood as a hyperonym for the
words "situation," "event," "process," and "action" (see Van Valin 2006:
82–9 for detailed definitions).

   In linguistic examples, the following abbreviations are used:

   ACC = accusative; ALL = allative; AUG = augmented number; COMP =
   complementizer; COND = condictional; CORE = core argument; D:PVG =
   distal extension:point of view of goal; DEM = demonstrative; DISJc =
   choice-aimed disjunction; DISJs = simple disjunctions; DS = different
   subject; DU = dual; FUT = future; GEN = genitive; INT = interrogative;
   IRR = irrealis; LOC = locative; M = masculine; MIN = minimal number;
   NEG = negative; NOM = nominative; OBJ = object; OBL = oblique; POSS =
   possessive; PRF = perfective; PST = past; R = realis; REF = referential;
   SEQ = sequential; SG = singular; SS = same subject; SUB = subordinator.

2 It is furthermore to be noted that, as pointed out by Haspelmath (2005), it
is rather common to find distinct constructions for conjunction between
entities (NP conjunction) and conjunction between events, thus reinforcing the discrepancies between logic and natural languages. For NP conjunction, Stassen (2001) distinguishes between "*and*-languages," showing
different strategies for NP combination and accompaniment relations
(frequent in northern and western Eurasia, India, northern Africa, New
Guinea, Australia, and Meso-America), and "*with*-languages," employing
the same asymmetric strategy for accompaniment and conjunctive relations (frequent in sub-Saharan Africa, east Asia, southeast Asia, and the
Pacific Islands, as well as in northern North America and lowland South
America).

3 We thank Keith Allan for suggesting this example.

4 A proposition is said to be realis when it asserts that a SoA is an "actualized
and certain fact of reality" and it is said to be irrealis when "it implies that
a SoA belongs to the realm of the imagined or hypothetical, and as such it
constitutes a potential or possible event but it is not an observable fact of
reality" (Elliot 2000: 66–7). Irrealis propositions belong to the domains of
imagination, possibility, wish, interrogation, necessity, obligation, and so
on, in which a given SoA is presented as not having taken place, or where
the speaker is not sure about its occurrence. An irrealis marker is any
morphosyntactic means (adverbs, sentence particles, verb forms) which
specifically encodes the irrealis value of a given SoA or which encodes
notions that imply the irreality of the relevant SoA within a given clause
(such as interrogative, dubitative, etc.; cf. Mauri 2008a: 171–2).

5 An example employed to illustrate the inclusive vs exclusive distinction
is Latin, where *aut* is argued to have an exclusive value, and *vel* an inclusive one. However, it has been shown by many scholars (see Kühner and

Stegmann 1914: 107–8; Dik 1968: 274–6; Jennings 1994; Jennings and Hartline 2009) that the Latin distinction has to be understood as a pragmatic or stylistic difference, not a logical one. Take for instance the sentence *Tantum superantibus aliis ac mergentibus malis nemo tribunos* **aut** *plebem timebat* 'So greatly did other evils overtop and threaten to engulf them, that no one feared the tribunes or the plebeians' (Livy, Ab urbe condita, III.16): in this occurrence *aut* may only be interpreted inclusively. Likewise, Jennings (1994: 245) quotes the sentence **vel** *dies est* **vel** *nox* 'it is either day or night', where *vel* is used with an exclusive reading. According to Dik (1968: 275), *vel* indicates that the choice between the two alternatives "is left to the interpreter, or is immaterial to the argument," while *aut* indicates more urgency for a choice. A similar proposal had already been made by Kühner and Stegmann (1914: 108), who argue that *vel* is used when the speaker does not decide between the alternatives and leaves the choice open.

6 It is to be noted that characterizing a conditional relation as potential or irrealis is an oversimplification, for languages regularly distinguish between indicative or open conditionals (*If the vase falls, it will break into small pieces*), subjunctive or hypothetical conditionals (*If I could meet him, I would tell him the truth*), and counterfactual ones (*If had met him, I would have told him the truth*). Furthermore, the notion of 'potentiality' characterizing conditionals is not so straightforward. In counterfactuals, for instance, potentiality is located in the past and therefore, in the perspective of the speaker, the chance of the condition being true is zero. Finally, potentiality may relate to a speaker's uncertainty or to a notion of contingency (as expressed by English *whenever*).

## Chapter 21

1 The necessity of an R-point for all tenses has been challenged by some authors (e.g. Comrie 1981), arguing that R is only useful for compound tenses, and that double compound tenses should lead to the introduction of a second R point. That R is mandatory for all tenses, as Reichenbach suggests, has two important consequences. The first one is that each tense is similar in that they all manage a particular relation between three fundamental coordinates, so that there is a common ground for the semantics of all tenses. The other one is that R is very different from both E and S: E is a time attached to a factual eventuality, S is the deictic time, but R has nothing intrinsically mundane. It can certainly anchor on a previously mentioned event or on some time given by an adverb, but it can also be detached from any particular eventuality or fact and be abstractly temporal.

2 Vendler's first work on this topic was actually completed in 1957 but published only in 1967. The first systematic linguistic study on aspect we owe to Jespersen (1924).

3 There is an ongoing debate on the question of whether semantic aspect is attached to the verb itself (as suggested by Vendler 1967) or to the full VP.

4 It has to be noted that the interpretation would have been literal if the verb phrase was not *run* alone but *run from A to B* or *between A to B*. But *run from A to B* is an accomplishment, whereas *run* alone is an activity.

5 "I'm loving it!" is the slogan of *McDonald's* restaurants (www.mcdonalds.com).

6 *Coercion* has also another meaning in syntax.

7 Several theoretical solutions may be envisaged here. Either aspect is a default category which can be overridden according to pragmatic necessity or aspect is not encoded at all and is the result of pragmatic specification alone. What is uncontroversial is that the aspectual category obtained in real communication can be significantly different from what is usually considered encoded by verbs or verb clauses as such.

8 This argument supports a purely verbal notion of semantic aspect, as suggested by Vendler (1967).

9 See Sthioul (2000) for a discussion of such cases in French.

10 Curiously, *It took Paul ten minutes to sleep* is odd. A plausible explanation is, again, pragmatic: for the accommodation to take place with this construction, it might be necessary to figure out a chain of agentive actions leading, finally, to the occurrence of the eventuality, which is fine with *walk* or *run*, but difficult to figure out with *sleep*.

11 Short summaries on Russian aspect are available in Klein (2009: 55) and de Saussure (2003). It is noticeable that one verb root can often combine with several perfective prefixes. For example, *čitat'* can also become *perečitat'* with the meaning of *read again*, or *dočitat'* meaning *read in depth*, and so forth. Some verbs can combine with more prefixes than others. In some cases, even the basic infinitive is perfective itself, and then the prefix brings only a nuance of meaning (*dat'*, 'give', can become *prodat'*, 'sell', both verbal forms being perfective). Because of these nuances, it is often necessary to reconstruct a new imperfective verbal form on the basis of the perfective; this is usually achieved through the insertion of an imperfective affix after the root (*opis-yv-at'*; *prod-av-at'*).

12 This example by Belgian author Georges Simenon was first discussed extensively by Tasmowski-De Ryck (1985).

13 Example discussed in de Saussure and Sthioul (1999). Notably, the perfective version is only impossible if meaning that the train is entering the station at the moment in focus. It can get another interpretation completely, meaning that Lyon station is the first of a series.

14 See Recanati, this volume.

15 The extensive study by Ekkehart Malotki (1983), *Hopi Time*, shows that Hopi has a great number of linguistic resources in order to express various types of temporal information. Not only do Hopis use many spatial metaphors in order to express time, but they also have a wide array of temporal

expressions (in particular a great number of time adverbs, including frequency adverbs and calendar expressions). It is sometimes considered that Hopis have nonetheless a distinct "notion" of time, in particular that they conceive time as cyclic rather than linear, but even if true, it doesn't make Hopi a timeless language or culture, where notions like past, future, now would not exist at all or in any comparable way to other peoples and cultures. Several authors, including E. Malotki, also published volumes of translations of Hopi tales, making it clear that the notion of time necessary to narratives is fully available in that language (see for instance Malotki 2002 or Shaul 2002).

16 Most notably by Kamp and Rohrer (1983), Kamp and Reyle (1993), Lascarides and Asher (1993).

17 This is a classical assumption at least since Damourette and Pichon (1911–1936). See also Benveniste (1966), de Saussure (2003), Portner (2003), Allan (forthcoming). Wilson and Sperber (1993b) also treat the present perfect as making statements relevant in the present. Reichenbach's (1947) formula for the present perfect makes it a perfect in the scope of the present.

18 This example is again extensively discussed in the literature, notably by Dowty (1979). See Smith, N. (1990) for further references.

19 Interestingly, earlier versions of English (but as late as nineteenth-century English) had forms like *In one year I am gone to America* (Keith Allan, personal communication).

20 See Predelli (1998a), who discusses this classical case in much detail from a philosophical point of view.

21 See also section 21.5 below on argumentative uses of *now*-indexicals.

22 See for example Enç (1996), Gosselin (2005), Jaszczolt (2009).

23 See de Saussure and Morency (forthcoming) for a discussion of epistemic future in French.

24 Surprisingly, the French simple past bears exactly that very property, unless a reverse-order temporal connective is present. A sequence like *Bill tomba; Max le poussa* ('Bill fell; Max pushed him') cannot be interpreted as the pushing causing the falling, despite a very accessible causal connection between such event types. Apparent counterexamples, such as *Socrate mourut; il but la ciguë* ('Socrates died; he drank hemlock') are in fact interpreted as loose simultaneity, the French *mourir* ('die') extending potentially to the cause of the death itself. A transformation of the second sentence into a present gerund clause is possible with *mourir* (*Socrate mourut en buvant la ciguë*, lit. 'Socrates died drinking hemlock'), which is not possible with verbs denoting the exact moment of the death (*\*Socrate expira en buvant la ciguë; \*Socrate expira; il but la ciguë*, 'Socrates passed away drinking hemlock'; 'Socrates passed away; he drank hemlock'; a number of other tests are available in de Saussure (2000) in order to see which combinations are in fact interpreted as simultaneous). However a reverse-order temporal connective (typically a causal connective) forces the reverse-order reading, as in *Bill tomba parce que Max le poussa*

('Bill fell because Max pushed him') or *Socrate expira après qu'il but la cigüe* (lit. 'Socrates passed away after he drank hemlock'). This is due to the fact that the connective explicitly states a particular order, which is then semantically mandatory. See de Saussure (2000) for details on this phenomenon.

## Chapter 22

1 See also Zeevat, this volume and Gundel, this volume.
2 Van der Auwera and Mauri, this volume.
3 In this chapter the term 'discourse connective' is used as a cover term to refer to discourse markers, hedges, discourse particles or pragmatic markers, to name but the most prominent ones (Celle and Huart 2007, Jucker and Ziv 1998).

## Chapter 23

1 It's worth considering how B's negative response here is interpreted. According to the Gricean account, she is explicitly denying that Mary's boyfriend is a robot (hence expressing a patently true, hence uninformative, proposition) and is thereby implicating that he doesn't lack feeling or sociability. Intuitively, however, it might seem that B is simply directly denying that the boyfriend lacks feeling or sociability. The account given in section 23.3 captures this intuition.
2 There is one interesting exception to this in Grice's (1978) brief discussion of what's involved in speaking ironically: 'irony is intimately connected with the expression of a feeling, attitude or evaluation. I cannot say something ironically unless what I say is intended to reflect a hostile or derogatory judgment or a feeling such as indignation or contempt' (*ibid.*: 124).
3 However, it needs to be kept in mind that Grice's approach is very much that of a philosopher and his account of non-literal language use falls within his large-scale analysis of the nature of meaning (natural vs non-natural meaning, speaker vs sentence meaning) and was not intended to reflect actual processes of communication or comprehension. With regard to metaphor specifically, the Gricean account has been further developed by Searle (1979b) and Bergmann (1982), both philosophers who are similarly concerned with the nature of metaphorical language use, rather than with the processes of its understanding.
4 A strong advocate of this reconstrual of 'what is said' is Bach (1994a), but he doesn't address its repercussions for the Gricean account of non-literal language use. See also Bach, this volume.
5 See Wilson and Sperber (2002) for a deconstruction of Grice's maxim of truthfulness on various interpretations of his notion of 'saying' and for compelling arguments against there being any maxim or presumption of

literal truthfulness at work in communication and comprehension. On their account, utterance interpretation conforms to a single inviolable principle of relevance, where 'relevance' is defined in such a way that our undeniable orientation toward acquiring true information follows from our relevance-based processing (see, in particular, Sperber and Wilson 1995a).

6 A much smaller, but interesting, issue concerns cases of what are known as 'twice apt' metaphors, that is metaphorical utterances which comply with the maxims at both the level of what is said and what is implicated (see Hills 1997, Camp 2007), e.g. an utterance of 'Jesus was a carpenter' in a context in which both the literal proposition expressed and the metaphorical meaning (Jesus was a crafter of men's souls) are plausibly true, informative and conversationally relevant. Since there is no maxim violation, whether actual or merely apparent, at any level, it is difficult to see how a Gricean account could explain such cases.

7 This is sometimes described as the truth-conditional content *of an utterance* (as opposed to the much more minimal truth-conditional content of the sentence uttered, if indeed sentences can be said to have truth-conditional content at all, an issue I won't pursue here). Thus Recanati (1993, 2004a, 2010) talks of 'truth-conditional pragmatics' and develops an account of the 'primary pragmatic processes' that are instrumental in delivering that content as opposed to the 'secondary pragmatic processes' employed in implicature derivation.

8 Some of these writers mention Grice's talk of an ironical speaker 'making as if to say' as indicative of a pretence account and Grice himself makes the connection explicit in a brief discussion of why it is inappropriate to preface an ironical utterance with the phrase 'to speak ironically': 'To be ironical is, among other things, to pretend (as the etymology suggests), and while one wants the pretense to be recognized as such, to announce it as a pretense would spoil the effect' (Grice 1978: 125).

9 See Wilson (2006, 2009b) for detailed analysis of the differences between the echoic and the pretence accounts and comparison of their adequacy in handling a wide range of examples of verbal irony, both conversational and literary.

10 See Wilson (2009b) for a detailed analysis of this fundamental representational difference between metaphorical and ironical language uses, including an important reassessment of the idea that the ability to interpret irony correlates with a higher order theory of mind ability (i.e. an ability to attribute beliefs about beliefs).

11 There is not a consensus on this point, of course: for example, the philosopher Camp (2006) presents a spirited defence of the Gricean position, and neo-Gricean pragmatists, such as Horn (1988) and Levinson (2000), who have revised the Gricean system of maxims while maintaining his saying/implicating distinction, seem to assume his account of tropes (although they are not explicit about this).

12 For an account of what these standards of relevance are and how they are motivated by the very nature of ostensive communication (against the backdrop of the general cognitive drive toward maximising the benefits and minimising the costs of processing new information), see Sperber and Wilson (1986, 1995b), Wilson and Sperber (2004).

13 Another interesting question here is whether metonymic uses (e.g. 'The handlebar moustache made a stately entrance') are to be accommodated in the unitary lexical pragmatic account and, if so, how, since they constitute neither a narrowing nor a broadening (the concept MAN WITH A HANDLEBAR MOUSTACHE is not a broadening of the concept HANDLEBAR MOUSTACHE). For some preliminary discussion, see Wilson and Carston (2007: 253–4).

14 'There is no mechanism specific to metaphor, no interesting generalisation that applies only to them. In other terms, linguistic metaphors are not a natural kind, and "metaphor" is not a theoretically important notion in the study of verbal communication. Relevance Theory's account of metaphor is on the lean side, and is bound to disappoint those who feel that verbal metaphor deserves a full-fledged theory of its own, or should be at the centre of a wider theory of language, or even of thought.' (Sperber and Wilson 2008: 84–5)

15 This is most marked for accounts that take the ad hoc concept to be superordinate to the literal encoded concept, e.g. analyses on which 'My lawyer is a shark' expresses a concept SHARK*, which includes all actual sharks and certain human beings, and is paraphrased as the category of predatory, aggressive, tenacious entities (Glucksberg 2001).

16 The first example is discussed by Wearing (2006); the second is from Lorrie Moore's novel *A Gate at the Stairs*, p. 79 (Faber and Faber); the third is from Colm Tóibín's novel *The Blackwater Lightship*, p. 37 (Picador).

17 Clearly, this mode of metaphor processing gives a much greater (and more prolonged) role to the literal meaning of the metaphorically used language. In Carston (2010b), where I develop the idea that there is this second processing mode or route for the understanding of certain cases of metaphor, I give some empirical evidence to support the ongoing dominance of the literal meaning. Interestingly, the account meshes quite well with the controversial stance of the philosopher Donald Davidson that 'Metaphors mean what the words, in their most literal interpretation mean, and nothing more' ([1978]1984: 245).

18 The study of language (grammar and semantics) in cognitive linguistics is based on the hypotheses that language is not an autonomous faculty of the mind but arises out of general cognitive capacities and that knowledge of language emerges from language use. The approach was developed in opposition to Chomskyan generative grammar, on the one hand, and truth-conditional semantics, on the other. For a very useful overview and assessment, see Croft and Cruse (2004).

19 Just how simple and general the primary conceptual metaphors are is very unclear and, as they get more and more schematic, they threaten to undermine the notion of domain mapping which is the central plank of the theory. Thus, in discussing Grady's (1997) proposal that the conceptual metaphor <THEORIES ARE BUILDINGS> is composed of more basic metaphors including, for instance, <ORGANIZATION IS PHYSICAL STRUCTURE>, Croft and Cruse (2004: 201) point out that the problem with such highly schematic metaphors as this is that both the alleged source and target domains could be seen as instantiations of this general conceptual schema, making any mapping from source to target redundant. See Jackendoff and Aaron (1991) and McGlone (2001) for more detailed exposition of this particular issue, and see J. Stern (2000: 176–87) for a particularly insightful critique of the conceptual metaphor approach.

20 A further similarity that follows from this basic one is that both approaches predict that metaphorical uses of language need take no longer to understand than literal uses, contrary to the three-step (Gricean-derived) processing model. As mentioned in section 23.2, this prediction has been repeatedly supported experimentally.

21 The cognitivists discuss metonymy as another principle of conceptual organisation. It is distinguished from metaphor in that the source and target concepts exist within a single domain (e.g. 'Nabokov' for the novels of Vladimir Nabokov, or 'Downing Street' for the British prime minister or his spokespeople). For a discussion of the cognitive linguistic account of conceptual (and verbal) metonymy, and its interaction with conceptual metaphor, see Croft and Cruse (2004).

22 Consider: 'In the winter his feet were stones on the end of his legs. At night he and the others lay shivering on the mouldy straw . . . ' from *The Secret River* by Kate Grenville, p. 12 (Canongate).

23 Any fully adequate account of metaphor interpretation will have to confront the issue of emergent properties. A different sort of account is presented by advocates of blending theory, a theory with a broad domain, including both utterance interpretation and more general problem solving, but which, it is claimed, shows how emergent properties can arise from a mental operation of 'blending' two mental spaces (e.g. the space of human traits and the space of bulldozers). For discussion of blending and metaphor, see Grady *et al.* (1999) and for critical assessment of blending theory, see Croft and Cruse (2004), Vega Moreno (2007) and G. Lakoff (2008). Within the RT framework, Vega Moreno (2007) and Wilson and Carston (2006) have attempted to provide a wholly inferential account (i.e. one that employs no special associative mappings) of how hearers recover emergent properties in interpretation.

24 For discussion of at least three different ways in which the literal/non-literal distinction can be drawn on a contextualist (truth-conditional pragmatic) account of utterance meaning and of how the intuitive folk

notion of non-literal use might be reconstructed within such an account, see Recanati (2004a: ch. 5).

## Chapter 24

1 Aristotle distinguished truth-bearing sentences from others (such as prayers) which are not. The Stoics distinguished what today we would call illocutionary types and Apollonius Dyscolus suggested an analysis of clause types or mood in terms that put one in mind of the performative analysis of Ross (1970). See Allan (2010: 50, 61f., 306ff.).
2 See Ariel, this volume and Horn, this volume.
3 See also Terkourafi, this volume.
4 For historical pragmatics in the Anglo-American tradition see Traugott, this volume.

## Chapter 25

1 It is not possible, as Humpty Dumpty claimed in *Through the Looking Glass*, that a word or sentence can mean whatever one wants it to mean; see Lassiter 2008.
2 One further motivation for wanting a semantics free of all but the most limited kinds of appeal to context might come from considerations of modularity: if our semantic competence were held to be modular (in the sense of Fodor 1983) then there would be reason to think that semantics should be pragmatics-free. See Borg 2004: Ch. 2. See also Recanati, this volume and Bach, this volume.
3 For critical discussion see Horwich 2002, Pagin 2006.
4 See, for instance, the work of the early Wittgenstein, Frege, Russell, Carnap, amongst many others.
5 (1) also contains an example of an incomplete definite description, an expression-type many have taken to require contextual completion.
6 See also Brogaard, this volume.
7 For an argument that formal semantics can accommodate demonstratives and indexicals despite the role of speaker intentions in reference determination see Borg (forthcoming: ch. 4).
8 Though we should note that some formal theorists have been unconcerned about the idea of semantically relevant appeals to speaker intentions; for instance, Kaplan (1989c) explicitly takes speaker intentions to settle reference for demonstratives, while more recently Cappelen and Lepore (2005a) have suggested that they see no problem with an appeal to speaker intentions in determining semantic content.
9 Borg (2004: ch. 3 and elsewhere) labels these 'inappropriateness' and 'incompleteness' arguments against context-invariant semantic contents.
10 The paradigm examples of context-shifting arguments are to be found in the work of Charles Travis; see Travis 2008.

11 There is a complication here, for the process I have in mind often goes under the heading of 'free enrichment', a term initially introduced in Recanati 2004a. However, for Recanati something counts as an instance of free enrichment only if it takes one from a proposition to a different proposition. Other kinds of pragmatic enrichment which take one from a propositional fragment (a level of content which is not yet capable of being truth-evaluated) to a complete proposition are, for Recanati, always instances of what he terms 'saturation': the contextual provision of a value for a syntactically marked context-sensitive item. So, for Recanati, one only gets free enrichment (pragmatic contributions to semantic content which are genuinely unmarked at the lexico-syntactic level) when a sentence is capable of expressing a proposition in any context *without* the pragmatic input in question. So, for instance, Recanati (2004a: 9) argues that the sentence 'It is raining' is capable of expressing a proposition without the addition of a location: it expresses simply the proposition that *it is raining*. Nevertheless utterances of this sentence usually convey a richer content like *it is raining here* and in this case the provision of a location is a matter of free pragmatic enrichment. If we take him at his word then there can be no cases for Recanati where the lexico-syntactic content of a sentence fail to deliver a proposition: if it looks like that might happen then there must be something hidden in the lexico-syntactic form which avoids it. I take contextualism in general, however, not to sign up to Recanati's view on what is required for genuine free enrichment, allowing instead that context may contribute to semantic content without being marked at the lexico-syntactic level regardless of whether the elements explicitly marked in the sentence are capable of delivering a complete proposition or not.

12 So, for instance, Recanati moves from a contextualist position in his 2004a to a relativist one in Recanati 2007 and elsewhere.

13 We should note that relativism grew up in response to a distinct set of issues, predominantly the treatment of taste predicates, epistemic vocabulary and future contingents (see e.g. Kölbel 2003, MacFarlane 2003, Lasersohn 2005). However, it does seem that the relativist perspective in general is envisaged, by at least some relativists, as providing a response to the wider issues of context-dependence voiced by radical pragmatics (see Kölbel 2008, Recanati 2008).

14 See also Dancy 2004: 197.

15 See Borg (forthcoming: ch. 1) for discussion; see also pretty much any discussion of one of the approaches for comments on the problems faced by alternative accounts.

16 The following definition of minimalism differs from that advocated in Cappelen and Lepore 2005a in the following ways: C&L reject (i) and (iv), and they take (iii) – understood as the claim that there are no context-sensitive expressions beyond the intuitively obvious ones – to be the

defining feature of minimalism. For further discussion see Borg 2007 and forthcoming.

17 The first of these two problems were touched on above with respect to the motivation for positing unarticulated constituents.

18 See Borg (forthcoming) for the argument that there are a range of different options available to the minimalist in these cases and that allowing some of the problem cases to be treated as genuine instances of lexico-syntactically marked context-sensitivity is compatible with the minimalist approach.

19 See Borg 2009b for one attempt at this.

20 Bach 1999b: 72. For a discussion of how exactly Bach uses the terms 'narrow' and 'wide' context see Stokke 2009.

21 One might think here, it seems, that concerns of uniformity, coupled with the difficulty noted above in providing a truly intention-independent reference rule even for expressions like 'I', would make it more attractive to treat reference assignment for all indexicals and demonstratives on a par, either seeking to incorporate all or none within the semantic realm.

22 An alternative view, which apparently does offer a truly pure semantics, free of all pragmatic taint, then, is Garcia-Carpintero's 2006 proposal that semantic content concerns only character, not content.

## Chapter 26

1 On the one hand, Montague's own methodology was that natural languages were formal languages so that syntactic structure was epiphenomenal and no more than a vehicle for semantic generalisations to be made expressive (a view which is the central core of categorial grammar formalisms, as initiated by Lambek 1958; see also Moortgat 1998, Morrill 1994). On the other hand, Chomsky has consistently denied any status to such a concept of semantics within the grammar (Chomsky 1977 and elsewhere).

2 See also Recanati, this volume, and Borg, this volume.

3 There are two basic modalities, ways of describing node relations: $\langle \downarrow \rangle$ and $\langle \uparrow \rangle$. $\langle \downarrow \rangle \alpha$ holds at a node if $\alpha$ holds at its daughter, and the inverse, $\langle \uparrow \rangle \alpha$, holds at a node if $\alpha$ holds at its mother. There are also LINK ($\langle L \rangle$) relations between trees, with their inverse $\langle L^{-1} \rangle$.

4 This is a standard tree-theoretic characterisation of *dominate*, used in LFG to express *functional uncertainty* (see Dalrymple 2001 and references cited there).

5 $Tn(0)$ decorating the top node of both partial trees is the tree-node identifier of the root node.

6 The only pragmatic action formally defined in this framework is that of *Substitution*, presumed to apply in individual derivations to yield anaphora and ellipsis resolution.

7 Analogous arguments apply to morphological structure but we do not pursue these here.

8 Relative pronouns are lexically defined in English to induce a copy of its head at such an unfixed node (hence its position initiating the structure for relative clause construal).

9 As all students introduced to the natural deduction proof system for predicate logic swiftly find out, it is these arbitrary names which guarantee that the proof rules of predicate logic are notably easier to learn than the rules of semantic evaluation of predicate logic.

10 The core of the calculus is its equivalence to predicate logic:

$$\frac{\exists x \phi(x)}{\phi(\varepsilon, x, \phi(x))}$$

The epsilon term analogue of the existentially quantified formula by definition contains two occurrences of the predicate $\phi$ (the predicate which constitutes the open proposition that the existential quantifier binds), hence its reflection of its containing environment.

11 Idiosyncratic exceptions such as *most* can be individually defined, as there is no requirement of exceptionless parallelism of structural and logical type. Indeed there is independent reason to think determiners are not a homogeneous category.

12 *Wh*-expressions are defined to project a metavariable (Kempson *et al.* 2001).

13 See also Horn, this volume.


## Chapter 27

1 Parts of this section draw on Traugott (2004).

2 For the distinction between linguistic "co-text" and situational "context," see G. Brown and Yule (1983).

3 By "lexicalized" Evans and Wilkins mean what I term "semanticized." I avoid the term "lexicalization" because of its multiple ambiguity.

4 External cause is what Sweetser (1990) calls cause in the socio-physical world (i), and internal cause is inferential cause (ii):

  (i)   *She was late because the bus broke down.*

 (ii)   *She is/must be late because her lights aren't on yet.*

5 Attributed to ABC's executive Alan Cohen in an article entitled "Vince Manze's must see TV is NBC after TV" (exploiting a different use of *after*): www.thefreelibrary.com/|Vince+Manze's+must+see+TV+is+NBC+after+TV.-a053392988 (accessed 12 March 2010).

6 See also Horn, this volume and Ariel, this volume.

7 The symbols "<" and ">" are used to represent "derived from" and "giving rise to" respectively.

8 Autohyponyms (a term that appears to have been coined by Horn) are expressions that serve as hyponyms or superordinate terms for

themselves. They are a highly complex set with different Q-based and R-based properties, depending on conventionalization (Horn 1984a).

9 For the "form-to-function" vs "function-to-form" distinction, see Jacobs and Jucker (1995). Geeraerts (1987) and Grondelaers *et al.* (2007) provide valuable accounts of semasiology and onomasiology.

10 The term invited inferencing is borrowed from Geis and Zwicky (1971), but is not restricted to generalized implicatures, as theirs is.

11 One of the first semanticists to focus on the role of metonymy in semantic change was Stern (1968); he called it "permutation."

12 Discussion of both metaphor and metonymy in terms of semanticization of pragmatics necessarily focuses on their pragmatic rather than mapping properties (see Panther and Thornburg 2003b for the distinction).

13 Many definitions of grammaticalization assume lexical sources only, but recently there has been much interest in the development of grammatical expressions from non-lexical material (see Lehmann 2008, Traugott 2008a); see section 27.4 for some examples.

14 The term "procedural" is due to Blakemore (1987).

15 "Conceptual" in Relevance-theoretic terms.

16 Downing discusses this use in terms of subjectivity, however.

17 See also Kecskes, this volume.

18 This is an auxiliary type identified for Bulgarian in Kuteva (2001).

## Chapter 28

1 The terminology varies: Gussenhoven (2006), for example, calls these three aspects of (what he calls) *linguistic* prosodic structure *prosodic phrasing*, *pitch accent location* and *pitch melody*.

2 It is equally true (and equally an observation rather than a criticism) that many people working in pragmatics, and indeed in linguistics, gloss over the contribution prosody makes to both sentence meaning and speaker meaning. In the next section I will present an argument as to why in the case of pragmatics this is so. In the meantime, it is worth drawing attention to a few notable exceptions: Wichmann and Blakemore (2006) is the result of a conference in 2002 which was a bold attempt to bring people from the two disciplines together. And it should not be forgotten that conversational and discourse analysts (Goodwin 1981; Brown, G. and Yule 1983; Schiffrin 1994) have also considered prosody, as have some of those who look at human interaction and communication from a more sociological or anthropological perspective (Goffmann 1964; Garfinkel 1967; Hymes 1972; Gumperz 1982). Prosody has also been a recurrent theme in the work of Allan (1986, 2006a).

3 Note that there is no evidence that either honeybees or frogs are capable of multi-layered intention expression and attribution required for their communicative behaviours to be characterised as cases of meaning$_{NN}$.

4 In earlier work – see Wilson and Wharton 2006, Wharton 2009 – this 'cultural' node is not present. However, many human communicative codes are non-natural but, crucially, *non-linguistic*. The British two-fingered insult is a good case in point. Whilst I will not discuss this category further in this chapter, there may well be elements of prosody which have previously been analysed as 'language-specific' but which are cultural stylisations rather than properly linguistic; an example might be the British 'calling contour' – 'hell-*aw*-oo'. This is a question to which I hope to return in future work.

5 Of course, we are not aware of *all* such behaviours. Lieberman (2000) provides an account of the *sub-attentive* processes involved in the production and interpretation of unintentional prosodic signs and signals, which may be seen as contributing more to accidental (or covert) than to ostensive communication.

6 For a variety of reasons unrelated to the analysis of deliberately shown natural behaviours being proposed here, some philosophers have questioned Grice's distinction between showing and meaning. Schiffer (1972: 56), for example, argues that cases of overt showing do amount to cases of meaning$_{NN}$; Recanati (1987: 189) argues that while the distinction is well motivated, we should not necessarily limit what he calls 'Gricean communication' to cases of meaning$_{NN}$. Mitch Green's book *Self-Expression* (2007) contains an interesting presentation (and development) of this debate.

7 Contrastive stress patterns do seem to vary across languages, and this may be a possible objection to the 'natural highlighting' account offered here (and in Wilson and Wharton 2006). In that paper, Deirdre Wilson and myself respond: 'this is not a particularly compelling objection unless it can be shown that variations in contrastive stress are not explainable in terms of processing effort. For instance, French has a relatively flat intonation contour and a strongly preferred final placement of focal stress, whereas English has a relatively variable intonation contour and freer placement of focal stress. We might therefore expect the use of non-final contrastive stress in French to be more disruptive, hence costlier in terms of processing effort, and the use of alternative syntactic means (e.g. clefting) to be preferred.'

8 For further discussion see Carston 2002: 116–24.

## Chapter 29

1 *SHE* here represents all stressed personal pronouns.

2 The relational notion of information focus (as complement of topic) should not be confused with the referential notion "in focus", which refers to the cognitive status of a discourse referent. See Gundel (1999a) for further discussion of different senses of the term "focus".

3 Uppercase letters here and elsewhere in the paper indicate location of a prominent pitch accent.

4 See Gundel 1999b for an attempt to resolve this controversy.
5 See Steedman 2000 and Hedberg and Sosa 2007 for more detailed discussion. The identification of topic with material outside the domain of focus only holds if topic and focus are complementary relational categories, as we assume here. This position is not shared by all authors. For example, Büring (1999) considers what he calls S-topic to be only a part of non-focal material. Others define topic positionally, for example as the first element in the sentence (Halliday 1967b), independent of its focal status.
6 See Hetland 2003 for a more thorough overview and discussion of the distinction between contrastive topic and information focus.
7 See Rooth 1985, 1992 for a highly influential account that does not distinguish the semantic/pragmatic properties of the two kinds of focal accent and associates both with the property of contrastiveness, interpreted in terms of "alternative sets". Rooth's account, unlike the others we consider here, does not therefore treat information focus as a relational newness concept, i.e. as a structural complement of topic.
8 The equation of presupposition and topic again depends on an analysis such as the one we are assuming here that views topic and focus as complementary relational categories. The equation does not require that the topic be construed as an open proposition rather than an entity (see Gundel 1985). But see Lambrecht 1994 for a different view of the relation between topic and presupposition.

## Chapter 30

1 For a critical introduction to various approaches to linguistic politeness see Terkourafi, this volume.
2 See also Katsos, this volume on ad hoc scales.

## Chapter 31

1 Take, for instance, the general and technical senses of 'relativity' as defined in the OED s.v. 'relativity'.
2 A similar point is made on different grounds by Haugh (2007a: 308).
3 This point is also made by Locher and Watts (2005: 10, 29), who, however, opt for the alternative label 'relational work' in place of Politeness2.
4 For a recent analysis that emphasises the importance of strategic use of polite devices also in Japanese, see Pizziconi 2003.
5 For a preliminary attempt at fleshing out the link between Face2 and Face1 in contemporary Greek society, see Terkourafi 2009a.
6 It is statements such as this that have likely led to the criticism that their theory represents 'an overly pessimistic, rather paranoid view of human interaction' (Schmidt 1980: 104).

7 See also Ariel, this volume, Horn, this volume and Haugh and Jaszczolt, this volume.

8 Pointing out that im/politeness is a second-order notion that 'evaluates a behaviour but . . . does not constitute it' Terkourafi (2001: 123 n. 19) proposes that this relationship can be formalised 'by construing politeness as a function P that relates behaviours (B) to contexts (C): given that P (B, C), P cannot appear in its own domain, since it is a function and not an argument in the first place'.

9 It is important to note here that what Leech seems to intend by 'semantic politeness' most recently is not this stricter view but one based on the notion of defaults as developed in neo-Gricean pragmatics (2007: 203 n. 5; see also Bousfield 2008: 52–5). As such, Leech's later views are consonant with (though not identical to) the conceptualisation of politeness in terms of generalised conversational implicatures proposed by Terkourafi (2001, 2003, forthcoming; see further in this section).

10 Recall, for instance, Brown and Levinson's notion of intrinsic FTAs and four-way categorisation of FTAs along those lines outlined in section 31.4 above.

11 As a reminder, here is Grice's (1969: 92) definition of r-intention:

'U meant something by uttering x' is true iff, for some audience A, U uttered x intending:

(1) A to produce a particular response r
(2) A to think (recognise) that U intends (1)
(3) A to fulfil (1) on the basis of his fulfilment of (2).

The reflexivity of the intention is captured by the phrase 'on the basis of his fulfilment of (2)' in the third clause.

12 Empirical studies that emphasise the centrality of conventionalisation to achieving im/politeness include, among others, Manes and Wolfson 1981, Blum-Kulka 1987, Rhodes 1989, Holtgraves and Yang 1990, Snow et al. 1990, Holtgraves 1997, Marquez Reiter 2000, Terkourafi 2002 and Culpeper 2011b.

13 For detailed appraisals of the discursive approach, see Terkourafi 2005, 2006; and Haugh 2007a.

14 Since this work is largely conducted within a communication research background, only those parts of it which are directly relevant to the student of linguistic pragmatics are currently discussed. For a comprehensive review, see Terkourafi, forthcoming.

15 For detailed critiques, see, among others, Turner 1996 and Terkourafi 2004.

16 This is the view taken in Terkourafi 2005, where it is argued that '[b]y paying attention to structural aspects of language use, traditional theories [including Brown and Levinson's] are concerned with the "formal" face-constituting potential of an expression x as part of a system and in virtue of x's relation to other expressions in that system' (2005: 254).

# References

Adamson, S. 2000. 'A lovely little example. Word order options and category shift in the premodifying string'. In O. Fischer, A. Rosenbach and D. Stein (eds.) *Pathways of Change: Grammaticalization in English*, pp. 39–66. Amsterdam: John Benjamins.

Adolphs, S. 2008. *Corpus and Context: Investigating Pragmatic Functions in Spoken Discourse*. Studies in Corpus Linguistics 30. Amsterdam/Philadelphia: John Benjamins.

AHBEU 1996. *American Heritage Book of English Usage*. Boston: Houghton-Mifflin.

Aijmer, K. 1996. *Conversational Routines in English: Convention and Creativity*. London: Longman.

　　2002. *English Discourse Particles: Evidence from a Corpus*. Studies in Corpus Linguistics 10. Amsterdam/Philadelphia: John Benjamins.

Åkerman, J. 2009. 'A plea for pragmatics'. *Synthese* 170: 155–67.

Allan, K. 1976. 'Collectivizing'. *Archivum Linguisticum* 7: 99–117.

　　1980. 'Nouns and countability'. *Language* 56: 541–67.

　　1981. 'Interpreting from context'. *Lingua* 53: 151–73.

　　1986. *Linguistic Meaning*. London: Routledge and Kegan Paul.

　　2000. 'Quantity implicatures and the lexicon'. In B. Peeters (ed.) *The Lexicon–Encyclopedia Interface*, pp. 169–218. Amsterdam: Elsevier.

　　2001. *Natural Language Semantics*. Oxford and Malden, MA: Blackwell.

　　2006a. 'Clause-type, primary illocution, and mood-like operators in English'. *Language Sciences* 28: 1–50.

　　2006b. 'Lexicon: structure'. In K. Brown (ed.) *Encyclopedia of Languages and Linguistics*, pp. 148–51. Oxford: Elsevier.

　　2006c. 'Inference: abduction, induction, deduction'. In K. Brown (ed.) *Encyclopedia of Languages and Linguistics*, pp. 651–4. Oxford: Elsevier.

　　2010. *The Western Classical Tradition*. 2nd expanded edition. London: Equinox.

　　(forthcoming). 'The semantics of the perfect progressive in English'. *Proceedings of the conference 'Space and time across languages and cultures'*, Cambridge, April 2010.

Allan, K. and Burridge, K. 1991. *Euphemism and Dysphemism: Language Used as Shield and Weapon.* Oxford University Press.

  2006. *Forbidden Words: Taboo and the Censoring of Language.* Cambridge University Press.

Allen, C. and Bekoff, M. 1997. *Species of Mind.* Cambridge, MA: MIT Press.

Allot, N. 2007. *Pragmatics and Rationality.* Unpublished PhD thesis, University College London.

Allwood, J. 1972. 'Negation and the strength of presupposition'. *Logical Grammar Reports No. 2.* Department of Linguistics, University of Göteborg, Sweden.

  1977. 'Negation and the strength of presupposition'. Revised version in Ö. Dahl (ed.) *Logic, Pragmatics, and Grammar*, pp. 11–52. Department of Linguistics, University of Göteborg.

Alston, W. P. 2000. *Illocutionary Acts and Sentence Meaning.* Ithaca: Cornell University Press.

Andersen, G. 2001. *Pragmatic Markers and Sociolinguistic Variation. A Relevance-theoretic Approach to the Language of Adolescents.* Pragmatics and Beyond New Series 84. Amsterdam/Philadelphia: John Benjamins.

Andersen, H. 2001. 'Actualization and the (uni)directionality of change'. In H. Andersen (ed.) *Actualization: Linguistic Change in Progress*, pp. 225–48. Amsterdam: John Benjamins.

Anscombe, G. E. M. 1957. *Intention.* Oxford: Blackwell.

Anscombre, J.-C. and Ducrot, O. 1976. 'L'argumentation dans la langue'. *Langages* 42: 5–27.

  1977. 'Deux mais en français?' *Lingua* 43: 23–40.

Ariel, M. 1983. 'Linguistic marking of social prominence: The Hebrew *mi she* introducer'. *Journal of Pragmatics* 7: 389–409.

  1988. 'Referring and accessibility'. *Journal of Linguistics* 24: 65–87.

  1990. *Accessing Noun-Phrase Antecedents.* London: Routledge.

  1994. 'Interpreting anaphoric expressions: A cognitive versus a pragmatic approach'. *Journal of Linguistics* 30: 3–42.

  1999. 'Mapping so-called "pragmatic" phenomena according to a "linguistic-extralinguistic" distinction: The case of propositions marked "accessible"'. In M. Darnell, E. A. Moravcsik, F. J. Newmeyer, M. Noonan and K. M. Wheatley (eds.) *Functionalism and Formalism in Linguistics*, vol. II: *Case Studies* (Studies in Language Companion Series 41), pp. 11–38. Amsterdam: John Benjamins.

  2000. 'The development of person agreement markers: From pronouns to higher accessibility markers'. In M. Barlow and S. Kemmer (eds.) *Usage-Based Models of Language*, pp. 197–260. Stanford: CSLI Publications.

  2001. 'Accessibility theory: An overview'. In T. J. M. Sanders, J. Schilperoord and W. Spooren (eds.) *Text Representation: Linguistic and Psycholinguistic Aspects*, pp. 29–87. Amsterdam: John Benjamins.

  2002. 'Privileged interactional interpretations'. *Journal of Pragmatics* 34: 1003–44.

2004. 'Most'. *Language* 80: 658–706.

2008a. 'Xaval al ha-zman ('It's a shame on the time'): In memory of Tanya Reinhart'. Paper presented at a conference in memory of Professor Tanya Reinhart, Tel Aviv University.

2008b. *Pragmatics and Grammar*. Cambridge University Press.

2009. 'Testing the boundaries: Scalarity and the argument from discourse'. Unpublished ms. Tel Aviv University.

2010. *Defining Pragmatics*. Cambridge University Press.

Aristotle. 1963. *Categories and De Interpretatione*. Trans. J. L. Ackrill. Oxford: Clarendon Press.

Arkell-Hardwicke, A. 1903. *An Ivory Trader in North Kenya*. London: Longmans, Green and Co.

Arundale, R. 1999. 'An alternative model and ideology of communication for an alternative to politeness theory', *Pragmatics* 9: 119–53.

2005. 'Pragmatics, conversational implicature, and conversation'. In K. Fitch and R. Sanders (eds.) *Handbook of Language and Social Interaction*, pp. 41–63. Mahwah, NJ: Lawrence Erlbaum.

2006a. 'Face as relational and interactional: A communication framework for research on face, facework, and politeness'. *Journal of Politeness Research* 2: 193–216.

2006b. 'Arguing participants' achieving of relationship in talk: Notes towards an examination'. Unpublished ms. University of Alaska, Fairbanks.

2008. 'Against (Gricean) intentions at the heart of human interaction'. *Intercultural Pragmatics* 5: 231–56.

2010a. 'Constituting face in conversation: Face, facework, and interactional achievement'. *Journal of Pragmatics* 42: 2078–105.

2010b. 'Relating'. In M. Locher and S. Lambert Graham (eds.) *Handbook of Pragmatics*, vol. VI: *Interpersonal Pragmatics*, pp. 137–66. Berlin: Mouton de Gruyter.

Arundale, R. and Good, D. 2002. 'Boundaries and sequences in studying conversation'. In A. Fetzer and C. Meierkord (eds.) *Rethinking Sequentiality: Linguistics Meets Conversational Interaction*, pp. 121–50. Amsterdam: John Benjamins.

Asher, N. 1986. 'Belief in Discourse Representation Theory'. *Journal of Philosophical Logic* 15: 127–89.

Asher, N. and Lascarides, A. 1998. 'The semantics and pragmatics of presupposition'. *Journal of Semantics* 15: 239–99.

2003. *Logics of Conversation*. Cambridge University Press.

Astington, J., Harris, P. and Olson, D. (eds.) 1988. *Developing Theories of Mind*. Cambridge University Press.

Athanasiadou, A., Canakis, C. and Cornillie, B. (eds.) 2006. *Subjectification: Various Paths to Subjectivity*. Berlin: Mouton de Gruyter.

Atlas, J. 1974. 'Presupposition, ambiguity, and generality: A coda to the Russell-Strawson debate on referring'. Unpublished ms. Claremont: Pomona College.

1975a. 'Frege's polymorphous concept of presupposition and its role in a theory of meaning'. *Semantikos* 1: 29–44.

1975b. 'Presupposition: a semantic-pragmatic account'. *Pragmatics Microfiche* 1.4. D13–G9.

1977. 'Negation, ambiguity, and presupposition'. *Linguistics and Philosophy* 1: 321–36.

1979. 'How linguistics matters to philosophy: Presupposition, truth, and meaning'. In D. Dinneen and C. K. Oh (eds.) *Syntax and Semantics 11: Presupposition*, pp. 265–81. New York: Academic Press.

1980. 'Reference, meaning, and translation'. *Philosophical Books* 21: 129–40.

1981. 'Is "not" logical?'. In *Proceedings of the 11th International Symposium on Multiple-Valued Logic*, pp. 124–8. New York: The Institute of Electrical and Electronics Engineers.

1988. 'What are negative existence statements about?'. *Linguistics and Philosophy* 11: 371–93.

1989. *Philosophy without Ambiguity*. Oxford University Press.

1991a. Review of *The Limits to Debate: A Revised Theory of Semantic Presupposition*, Noel Burton-Roberts (Cambridge University Press, 1989). *Mind and Language* 6: 177–92.

1991b. 'Topic/comment, presupposition, logical form, and focus stress implicatures: The case of focal particles *only* and *also*'. *Journal of Semantics* 8: 127–47.

1993. 'The importance of being "only": Testing the neo-Gricean versus neo-entailment paradigms'. *Journal of Semantics* 10: 301–18.

1996. '"Only" noun phrases, pseudo-negative generalized quantifiers, negative polarity items, and monotonicity'. *Journal of Semantics* 13: 265–329.

1997. 'Negative adverbials, prototypical negation, and the de Morgan taxonomy'. *Journal of Semantics* 14: 349–67.

2001. 'Negative quantifier noun phrases: A typology and an acquisition hypothesis'. In J. Hoeksema, H. Rullman, V. Sánchez-Valencia and T. van der Wouden (eds.) *Perspectives on Negation and Polarity Items*, pp. 1–23. Amsterdam: John Benjamins.

2004a. 'Presupposition'. In L. R. Horn and G. Ward (eds.) *The Handbook of Pragmatics*, pp. 29–52. Oxford: Blackwell.

2004b. 'Descriptions, linguistic topic/comment, and negative existentials: A case study in the application of linguistic theory to problems in the philosophy of language'. In M. Reimer and A. Bezuidenhout (eds.) *Descriptions and Beyond*, pp. 342–60. Oxford: Clarendon Press.

2005. *Logic, Meaning, and Conversation: Semantical Underdeterminacy, Implicature, And Their Interface*. New York: Oxford University Press.

2007a. 'On a pragmatic explanation of negative polarity item licensing'. In N. Burton-Roberts (ed.) *Advances in Pragmatics*, pp. 10–23. Houndmills: Palgrave Macmillan.

2007b. 'Meanings, propositions, context, semantical underdeterminacy'. In G. Preyer and G. Peter (eds.) *Context-Sensitivity and Semantic Minimalism*, pp. 217–39. Oxford University Press.

Atlas, J. and Levinson, S. 1981. 'It-clefts, informativeness and logical form'. In P. Cole (ed.) *Radical Pragmatics*, pp. 1–62. New York: Academic Press.

Auer, P. 2009. 'Context and contextualization'. In J. Verschueren and J. O. Östman (eds.) *Key Notions in Pragmatics*, pp. 86–101. Amsterdam: John Benjamins.

Austen, J. 1811. *Sense and Sensibility*. London: T. Egerton.

Austin, J. L. 1961. *Philosophical Papers*. Oxford University Press.

1962. *How to Do Things With Words. The William James Lectures Delivered at Harvard University in 1955*. Oxford University Press.

1975. *How to Do Things With Words*. 2nd edition. Oxford University Press.

Auwera, J. van der. 1986. 'Conditionals and speech-acts'. In E. C. Traugott, A. Meulen, J. S. Reilly and C. A. Ferguson (eds.) *On Conditionals*. Cambridge University Press.

1997a. 'Conditional perfection'. In A. Athanasiadou and R. Dirven (eds.) *On Conditionals Again*, pp. 169–90. Amsterdam: John Benjamins.

1997b. 'Pragmatics in the last quarter century: the case of conditional perfection'. *Journal of Pragmatics* 27: 261–74.

2001. 'On the typology of negative modals'. In J. Hoeksema, H. Rullmann and V. Sánchez-Valencia (eds.) *Perspectives on Negation and Polarity Items*, pp. 23–48. Amsterdam: John Benjamins.

Auwera, J. van der and Bultinck, B. 2001. 'On the lexical typology of modals, quantifiers, and connectives'. In I. Kenesei and R. M. Harnish (eds.) *Perspectives on Semantics, Pragmatics, and Discourse: A Festschrift for Ferenc Kiefer*, pp. 173–86. Amsterdam: John Benjamins.

Auwera, J. van der and Lejeune, L. 2005. 'The morphological imperative'. In M. Haspelmath (ed.) *The World Atlas of Language Structures*, pp. 286–9. Oxford University Press.

Bach, E. 1980. 'Tenses and aspects as functions on verb-phrases'. In C. Rohrer (ed.) *Time, Tense, and Quantifiers*, pp. 19–37. Tübingen: Niemeyer.

Bach, K. 1982. 'Semantic non-specificity and mixed quantifiers'. *Linguistics and Philosophy* 4: 593–605.

1987. 'On communicative intentions: A reply to Recanati'. *Mind and Language* 2: 141–54.

1992. 'Communicative intentions, plan recognition, and pragmatics: comments on Thomason and Littman and Allen'. In P. R. Cohen, J. Morgan and M. E. Pollack (eds.) *Intentions in Communication*, pp. 389–400. Cambridge: MIT Press.

1994a. 'Conversational impliciture'. *Mind and Language* 9: 124–62.

1994b. 'Semantic slack: What is said and more'. In S. L. Tsohatzidis (ed.) *Foundations of Speech Act Theory: Philosophical and Linguistic Perspectives*, pp. 267–91. London: Routledge.

1999a. 'The myth of conventional implicature'. *Linguistics and Philosophy* 22: 327–66.

1999b. 'The semantics-pragmatics distinction: What it is and why it matters'. In K. Turner (ed.) *The Semantics/Pragmatics Interface from Different Points of View*, pp. 65–83. Oxford: Elsevier Science.

2000. 'Reply to Stanley and Szabó'. *Mind and Language* 15: 262–83.

2001. 'You don't say?'. *Synthese* 128: 15–44.

2004. 'Descriptions: Points of reference'. In A. Bezuidenhout and M. Reimer (eds.) *Descriptions and Beyond*, pp. 189–229. Oxford University Press.

2005. 'Context *ex machina*'. In Z. G. Szabó (ed.) *Semantics versus Pragmatics*, pp. 15–44. Oxford: Oxford University Press.

2006a. 'Review of Christopher Potts, *The Logic of Conventional Implicatures*'. *Journal of Linguistics* 42: 490–5.

2006b. 'The excluded middle: Semantic minimalism without minimal propositions'. *Philosophy and Phenomenological Research* 73: 435–42.

2006c. 'The top 10 misconceptions about implicature'. In B. Birner and G. Ward (eds.), *Drawing the Boundaries of Meaning*, pp. 21–30. Amsterdam: John Benjamins.

2006d. 'What does it take to refer?'. In E. Lepore and B. C. Smith (eds.) *The Oxford Handbook of the Philosophy of Language*, pp. 515–54. Oxford University Press.

2007. 'Regressions in pragmatics (and semantics)'. In N. Burton-Roberts (ed.) *Advances in Pragmatics*, pp. 24–44. Houndmills: Palgrave Macmillan.

2010. 'Implicature vs. explicature: What's the difference?'. In B. Soria and E. Romero (eds.) *Explicit Communication: Robyn Carston's Pragmatics*, pp. 126–37. Basingstoke: Palgrave Macmillan.

Bach, K. and Harnish, R. 1979. *Linguistic Communication and Speech Acts*. Cambridge, MA: MIT Press.

1992. 'How performatives really work: a reply to Searle'. *Linguistics and Philosophy* 15: 92–110.

Bachman, L. F. 1990. *Fundamental Considerations in Language Testing*. Oxford University Press.

Bak, S. Y. 1977. 'Topicalization in Korean'. *University of Hawaii Working Papers in Linguistics* 9.2: 63–88.

Bannard, C. and Lieven, E. 2009. 'Repetition and reuse in child language learning'. In R. Corrigan, E. A. Moravcsik, H. Ouali and K. M. Wheatley (eds.) *Formulaic Language*, Vol. ii. *Acquisition, Loss, Psychological Reality, and Functional Explanations*, pp. 299–321. Amsterdam/Philadelphia: John Benjamins.

Bara, B. G. 2010. *Cognitive Pragmatics*. Cambridge, MA: MIT Press.

Baranzini, L. and de Saussure, L. 2009. 'Deixis temporelle argumentative: Remarques sur le français *maintenant* et l'italien *adesso*'. In C. Maas and A. Schrott (eds.), *Wenn Deiktika nicht Zeigen: zeigende und nichtzeigende Funktionen deiktischer Formen in den romanischen Sprachen*, pp. 53–71. Münster and Hamburg: Lit Verlag.

Bar-Hillel, Y. 1971. 'Out of the pragmatic wastebasket'. *Linguistic Inquiry* 2: 401–7.

Barker, S. 2003. 'Truth and conventional implicature'. *Mind* 112: 1–33.

   2004. *Renewing Meaning: A Speech-Act Theoretic Approach*. Oxford: Clarendon Press.

Barkow, J., Cosmides, L. and Tooby, J. 1995. *The Adapted Mind: Evolutionary Psychology and the Generation of Culture*. Oxford University Press.

Bar-Lev, Z. and Palacas, A. 1980. 'Semantic command over pragmatic priority'. *Lingua* 51: 137–46.

Barnes, S. B. 2003. *Computer-Mediated Communication: Human-to-Human Communication Across the Internet*. Boston: Allyn and Bacon.

Baron-Cohen, S. 1995. *Mindblindness: An Essay on Autism and Theory of Mind*. Cambridge, MA: MIT Press.

Barsalou, L. 1983. 'Ad hoc categories'. *Memory and Cognition* 11: 211–27.

   1987. 'The instability of graded structure in concepts'. In N. Neisser (ed.) *Concepts and Conceptual Development*, pp. 101–40. Cambridge University Press.

   1999. 'Perceptual symbol systems'. *Behavioral and Brain Sciences* 22: 577–660.

Barwise, J. and Perry, J. 1983. *Situations and Attitudes*. Cambridge, MA: MIT Press.

Bates, E. 1976. *Language and Context: The Acquisition of Pragmatics*. New York: Academic Press.

   1999. 'On the nature and nurture of language'. In E. Bizzi, P. Calissano and V. Volterra (eds.) *Frontiere della biologia* [Frontiers of biology]. *The brain of homo sapiens*, pp. 241–65. Rome: Giovanni Trecanni.

Bates, E. and MacWhinney, B. J. 1989. 'Functionalism and the competition model'. In B. J. MacWhinney and E. Bates (eds.) *The Crosslinguistic Study of Sentence Processing*, pp. 3–73. Cambridge University Press.

Bateson, G. 1972. *Steps of an Ecology of Mind*. Toronto: Chandler Publishing Company.

Bauer, L. 1983. *English Word-Formation*. Cambridge University Press.

Baxter, L. and Montgomery, B. 1996. *Relating: Dialogues and Dialectics*. New York: Guilford.

Bayraktaroglu, A. 1991. 'Politeness and interactional imbalance'. *International Journal of the Sociology of Language* 92: 5–34.

Beall, J. C. (ed.) 2003. *Liars and Heaps: New Essays on Paradox*. Oxford: Clarendon Press.

Beaney, M. (ed.) 1997. *The Frege Reader*. Oxford: Blackwell.

Beardsley, M. C. 1958. *Aesthetics*. New York: Harcourt, Brace and World.

Beaugrande, R. de and Dressler, W. 1981. *Einführung in die Textlinguistik*. Tübingen: Niemeyer.

Beaver, D. 1994. 'Accommodating topics'. In P. Bosch and R. van der Sandt (eds.) *Focus and Natural Language Processing*, Vol. iii: *Discourse*, pp. 439–48. Heidelberg: IBM Germany, IBM Deutschland, Scientific Centre.

1995. *Presupposition and Assertion in Dynamic Semantics*. PhD thesis, University of Edinburgh.

2001. *Presupposition and Assertion in Dynamic Semantics*. Stanford, CA: CSLI Publications.

Beaver, D. and Lee, H. 2003. 'Input-output mismatches in OT'. In R. Blutner and H. Zeevat (eds.) *Pragmatics and Optimality Theory*. Basingstoke: Palgrave Macmillan.

Becchio, C. and Bertone, C. 2004. 'Wittgenstein running: neural mechanisms of collective intentionality and we-mode'. *Consciousness and Cognition* 13: 123–33.

2010. 'Intention'. In L. Cummings (ed.) *The Pragmatics Encyclopedia*, pp. 226–7. London: Routledge.

Becchio, C., Adenzato, M. and Bara, B. 2006. 'How the brain understands intention: different neural circuits identify the componential features of motor and prior intentions'. *Consciousness and Cognition* 15: 64–74.

Beeching, K. 2002. *Gender, Politeness and Pragmatic Particles in French*. Pragmatics and Beyond New Series 104. Amsterdam/Philadelphia: John Benjamins.

Benveniste, É. 1966. *Problèmes de linguistique générale*. Paris: Gallimard.

1971. 'Subjectivity in language'. In *Problems in General Linguistics*, pp. 223–30, trans. M. E. Meek. Coral Gables, FL: University of Miami Press (first published in French 1958).

Bergmann, M. 1982. 'Metaphorical assertions'. *Philosophical Review* 91: 229–42.

Berlin, B. and Kay, P. 1969. *Basic Color Terms: Their Universality and Evolution*. Berkeley and Los Angeles: University of California Press.

Bertinetto, P. M. 2000. 'The progressive in Romance, as compared to English'. In F. Plank and O. Dahl (eds.) *Tense and Aspect in the Languages of Europe*, pp. 559–604. Berlin/New York: Mouton de Gruyter.

Besnier, N. 2000. *Tuvaluan: A Polynesian Language of Central Pacific*. London/New York: Routledge.

Bezuidenhout, A. 1997. 'How context-dependent are attitude ascriptions?' In D. Jutronic (ed.) *The Maribor Papers in Naturalized Semantics*, pp. 269–84. University of Maribor.

2001. 'Metaphor and what is said: a defense of a direct expression view of metaphor'. *Midwest Studies in Philosophy* 25: 156–86.

2002a. 'Generalized conversational implicatures and default pragmatic inferences'. In J. Campbell, M. O'Rourke and D. Shier (eds.) *Meaning and Truth: Investigations in Philosophical Semantics*, pp. 257–83. New York: Seven Bridges Press.

2002b. 'Truth-conditional pragmatics'. *Philosophical Perspectives* 16: 105–34.

Bezuidenhout, A. and Cutting, J. C. 2002. 'Literal meaning, minimal propositions, and pragmatic processing'. *Journal of Pragmatics* 34: 433–56.

Biber, D., Johansson, S., Leech, G., Conrad, S. and Finegan, E. 1999. *Longman Grammar of Spoken and Written English*. London: Longman.

Biletzki, A. 1996. 'Is there a history of pragmatics?' *Journal of Pragmatics* 25: 455–70.

Bilmes, J. 1986. *Discourse and Behaviour*. New York: Plenum Press.

Birner, B. J. and Ward, G. 1998. *Information Status and Non-Canonical Word Order in English*. Amsterdam: John Benjamins.

Blackburn, P. and Meyer-Viol, G. 1994. 'Linguistics, logic and finite trees'. *Bulletin of Interest Group of Pure and Applied Logics* 2: 2–39.

Blakemore, D. 1987. *Semantic Constraints on Relevance*. Oxford: Blackwell.

1992. *Understanding Utterances: An Introduction to Pragmatics*. Oxford: Blackwell.

2000. 'Procedures and indicators: *nevertheless* and *but*'. *Journal of Linguistics* 36: 463–86.

2002. *Relevance and Linguistic Meaning: The Semantics and Pragmatics of Discourse Markers*. Cambridge University Press.

Blakemore, D. and Carston, R. 1999. 'The pragmatics of and-conjunctions: the non-narrative cases'. *UCL Working Papers in Linguistics* 11: 1–20.

2005. 'The pragmatics of sentential coordination with *and*'. *Lingua* 115: 569–89.

Blank, A. 1997. *Prinzipien des lexikalischen Bedeutungswandels am Beispiel der romanischen Sprachen*. Tübingen: Niemeyer.

1999. 'Why do new meanings occur? A cognitive typology of the motivations for lexical semantic change'. In A. Blank and P. Koch (eds.) *Historical Semantics and Cognition*, pp. 61–89. Berlin: Mouton de Gruyter.

Blitvich, P. G. C. 2010. 'A genre approach to the study of im-politeness'. *International Review of Pragmatics* 2: 46–94.

Blommaert, J. 2005. *Discourse. A Critical Introduction*. Cambridge University Press.

2007. 'Sociolinguistic scales'. *Intercultural Pragmatics* 4: 1–19.

Bloor, T. and Bloor, M. 1995. *The Functional Analysis of English: A Hallidayan Approach*. London: Arnold.

Blum-Kulka, S. 1987. 'Indirectness and politeness in requests: same or different?'. *Journal of Pragmatics* 11: 131–46.

Blum-Kulka, S., House, J. and Kasper, G. (eds.) 1989. *Cross-Cultural Pragmatics: Requests and Apologies*. Norwood, NJ: Ablex.

Blum-Kulka, S., Blondheim, M., House, J., Kasper, G. and Wagner, J. 2008. 'Intercultural pragmatics, language and society'. In P. van Sterkenburg (ed.) *Unity and Diversity of Languages*, pp. 155–73. Amsterdam/Philadelphia: John Benjamins.

Blutner, R. 1998. 'Lexical pragmatics'. *Journal of Semantics* 15: 115–62.

2004. 'Pragmatics and the lexicon'. In L. Horn and G. Ward (eds.) *The Handbook of Pragmatics*, pp. 488–515. Oxford: Blackwell.

2009. 'Lexical pragmatics'. In L. Cummings (ed.) *The Pragmatics Encyclopedia*, pp. 226–7. London: Routledge.

Blutner, R. and Jäger, G. 2003. 'Competition and interpretation: The German adverb wieder ("again")'. In C. Fabricius-Hansen, E. Lang and C.

Maienborn (eds.) *Modifying Adjuncts*, pp. 393–416. Berlin: Mouton de Gruyter.

Boër, S. and Lycan, W. 1976. 'The myth of semantic presupposition'. In *Ohio State Working Papers in Linguistics* 21, pp. 1–90. Department of Linguistics, Ohio State University, Columbus, OH.

Bohnemeyer, J. 2002. *The Grammar of Time Reference in Yucatec Maya*. Munich: Lincom Europa.

2009. 'Temporal anaphora in a tenseless language'. In W. Klein and P. Li (eds.) *The Expression of Time*, pp. 83–128. Berlin/New York: Mouton de Gruyter.

Bohnemeyer, J. and Stolz, C. 2006. 'Spatial reference in Yukatek Maya: A survey'. In S. C. Levinson and D. Wilkins (eds.) *Grammars of Space*, pp. 273–310. Cambridge University Press.

Bolinger, D. 1961. 'Contrastive accent and contrastive stress'. *Language* 37: 87–96.

1972. *That's That*. The Hague: Mouton.

1980. *Language: The Loaded Weapon*. London: Longman.

1983a. 'The inherent iconism of intonation'. In J. Haiman (ed.) *Iconicity in Syntax*, pp. 97–109. Amsterdam: John Benjamins.

1983b. 'Where does intonation belong?'. *Journal of Semantics* 2: 101–20.

Bonelli, E. T. 1992. 'All I'm saying is . . . : The correlation of form and function in pseudo-cleft sentences'. *Literary and Linguistic Computing* 2: 30–41.

Bonnefon, J. F., Feeney, A. and Villejoubert, G. 2009. 'When *some* is actually *all*: Scalar inferences in face-threatening contexts'. *Cognition* 112: 249–58.

Bontly, T. 2005. 'Modified Occam's Razor: Parsimony arguments and pragmatic explanations'. *Mind and Language* 20: 288–312.

Borg, E. 2004. *Minimal Semantics*. Oxford University Press.

2007. 'Minimalism versus contextualism in semantics'. In G. Preyer and G. Peter (eds.) *Context-Sensitivity and Semantic Minimalism*, pp. 339–59. Oxford University Press.

2009a. 'Minimal semantics and the nature of psychological evidence'. In S. Sawyer (ed.) *New Waves in Philosophy of Language*, pp. 24–40. Basingstoke: Palgrave Macmillan.

2009b. 'Must a semantic minimalist be a semantic internalist?'. *Proceedings of the Aristotelian Society, Supplementary Volume* LXXXIII: 31–51.

(forthcoming). *Pursuing Meaning*. Oxford University Press.

Bos, J. 2003. 'Implementing the binding and accommodation theory of anaphora resolution and presupposition projection'. *Computational Linguistics* 29: 179–210.

Bos, J., Buitelaar, P. and Mineur, A. M. 1995. 'Bridging as coercive accommodation'. In W. N. E. Klein, S. Manandhar and J. Siekmann (eds.) *Working Notes on the Edinburgh Conference on Computational Logic and Natural Language Processing (CLNLP-95)*, pp. 1–16: Human Communications Research Centre, University of Edinburgh, South Queensferry, Scotland.

Bosch, P. and van der Sandt, R. (eds.) 1999. *Focus: Linguistic, Cognitive and Computational Perspectives*. Cambridge University Press.

Bott, L. and Noveck, I. A. 2004. 'Some utterances are underinformative: the onset and time course of scalar inferences'. *Journal of Memory and Language* 51: 437–57.

Bourdieu, P. 1990. *The Logic of Practice*. Trans. R. Nice. Cambridge: Polity Press.

Bousfield, D. 2008. *Impoliteness in Interaction*. Amsterdam: John Benjamins.

Bousfield, D. and Culpeper, J. 2008. 'Impoliteness: Eclecticism and diaspora'. *Journal of Politeness Research* 4: 161–337.

Bousfield, D. and Locher, M. (eds.) 2008. *Impoliteness in Language: Studies on its Interplay with Power in Theory and Practice*. Berlin: Mouton de Gruyter.

Bowerman, M. and Choi, S. 2003. 'Space under construction: Language-specific spatial categorization in first language acquisition'. In D. Gentner and S. Goldin-Meadow (eds.) *Language in Mind*, pp. 387–427. Cambridge, MA: MIT Press.

Bowerman, M. and Pederson, E. 1992. 'Crosslinguistic perspectives on topological spatial relationships'. Paper presented to Annual Meeting of the American Anthropological Association, San Francisco.

Boxer, D. 2002. 'Discourse issues in cross-cultural pragmatics'. *Annual Review of Applied Linguistics* 22: 150–67.

Brandom, R. 1994. *Making It Explicit*. Cambridge, MA: Harvard University Press.

Brandon, R. 2005. 'The theory of biological function and adaptation'. Online conference on Adaptation and Representation at www.interdisciplines. org/adaptation/papers/10.

Bratman, M. 1987. *Intention, Plans, and Practical Reason*. Cambridge, MA: Harvard University Press.

   1992. 'Shared cooperative activity'. *The Philosophical Review* 101: 327–41.

   1993. 'Shared intention'. *Ethics* 104: 99–113.

   1999. *Intention, Plans, and Practical Reason*. Stanford, CA: CSLI Publications.

Brazil, D. 1975. *The Communicative Value of Intonation in English*. University of Birmingham Press.

Bréal, M. 1964. *Semantics: Studies in the Science of Meaning*. Trans. Mrs. Henry Cust. New York: Dover (first published in French 1900).

Breban, T. 2008. 'The grammaticalization and subjectification of English adjectives expressing difference into plurality/distributivity markers and quantifiers'. *Folia Linguistica* 42: 259–306.

   2010. *English Adjectives of Comparison: Lexical and Grammaticalized Uses*. Berlin: Mouton de Gruyter.

Breheny, R. 2006. 'Communication and folk psychology'. *Mind and Language* 21: 74–107.

Breheny, R., Katsos, N. and Williams, J. 2006. 'Are generalised scalar implicatures generated by default? An on-line investigation into the role of context in generating pragmatic inferences'. *Cognition* 100: 434–63.

Brems, L. 2007. *The Synchronic Layering of Size Noun and Type Noun Constructions in English*. Doctoral dissertation, University of Leuven.

Brentano, F. 1874. *Psychologie vom empirischen Standpunkt*. Leipzig: Duncker and Humblot. (Trans. as *Psychology from an Empirical Standpoint* by A. C. Rancurello, D. B. Terrell, and L. L. McAlister in 1973. London: Routledge and Kegan Paul.)

Breul, C. 2007. 'A relevance-theoretic view on issues in the history of clausal connectives'. In U. Lenker and A. Meurman-Solin (eds.) *Connectives in the History of English*, pp. 167–92. Amsterdam: John Benjamins.

Brinton, L. 1996. *Pragmatic Markers in English: Grammaticalization and Discourse Function*. Berlin: De Gruyter.

  2008. *The Comment Clause in English*. Cambridge University Press.

Brisard, F., Frisson, S. and Sandra, D. 2001. 'Processing unfamiliar metaphors in a self-paced reading task'. *Metaphor and Symbol* 16: 87–108.

Brown, G. and Yule, G. 1983. *Discourse Analysis*. Cambridge University Press.

Brown, P. 1994. 'The INs and ONs of Tzeltal locative expressions: The semantics of static descriptions of location'. *Linguistics* 32: 743–90.

  1995. 'Politeness strategies and the attribution of intentions: the case of Tzeltal irony'. In E. Goody (ed.) *Social Intelligence and Interaction: Expressions and Implications of the Social Bias in Human Intelligence*, pp. 153–74. Cambridge University Press.

  2006. 'A sketch of the grammar of space in Tzeltzal'. In S. C. Levinson and D. Wilkins (eds.) *Grammars of Space*, pp. 230–72. Cambridge University Press.

Brown, P. and Levinson, S. C. 1987. *Politeness: Some Universals in Language Usage*. Cambridge University Press (first published 1978).

Brown, R. and Gilman, A. 1960/2003. 'The pronouns of power and solidarity'. In T. A. Sebeok (ed.) *Style in Language*, pp. 253–76. Cambridge, MA: MIT. Reprinted in C. B. Paulston and R. Tucker (eds.) *Sociolinguistics: The Essential Readings*, pp. 156–76. Oxford: Blackwell.

Bublitz, W. 2009. *Englische Pragmatik: Eine Einführung*. 2nd edition. Grundlagen der Anglistik und Amerikanistik 21. Berlin: Erich Schmidt.

Bublitz, W., Jucker, A. H. and Schneider, K. P. (eds.) 2010–. *Handbooks of Pragmatics*. 9 vols. Berlin: De Gruyter.

Bührig, K. and Ten Thije, J. D. (eds.) 2006. *Beyond Misunderstanding: Linguistic Analyses of Intercultural Communication*. Pragmatics and Beyond New Series 144. Amsterdam/Philadelphia: John Benjamins.

Büring, D. 1999. 'Topic'. In P. Bosch and R. van der Sandt (eds.) *Focus: Linguistic, Cognitive and Computational Perspectives*, pp. 142–65. Cambridge University Press.

  2010. 'Towards a typology of focus realization'. In M. Zimmermann and C. Féry (eds.) *Information Structure: Theoretical, Typological, and Experimental Perspectives*, pp. 177–205. Oxford University Press.

Busse, U. and Busse, B. 2010. 'Shakespeare'. In A. H. Jucker and I. Taavitsainen (eds.) *Handbook of Historical Pragmatics* (Handbooks of Pragmatics 8), pp. 247–84. Berlin: Mouton de Gruyter.

Bybee, J. 2006. 'From usage to grammar: The mind's response to repetition'. *Language* 82: 711–33.

2007. 'Diachronic linguistics'. In D. Geeraerts and H. Cuyckens (eds.) *The Oxford Handbook of Cognitive Linguistics*, pp. 945–87. Oxford University Press.

Bybee, J. and Pagliuca, W. 1987. 'The evolution of future meaning'. In A. Giacalone Ramat, O. Carruba and G. Bernini (eds.) *Papers from the 7th International Conference on Historical Linguistics*, pp. 108–22. Amsterdam: John Benjamins.

Bybee, J., Perkins, R. D. and Pagliuca, W. 1994. *The Evolution of Grammar: Tense, Aspect, and Modality in the Languages of the World.* University of Chicago Press.

Call, J. and Tomasello, M. 2008. 'Does the chimpanzee have a theory of mind? 30 years later'. *Trends in Cognitive Science* 12: 187–92.

Call, J., Bräuer, J., Kaminski, J. and Tomasello, M. 2003. 'Domestic dogs (Canis familiaris) are sensitive to the attentional state of humans'. *Journal of Comparative Psychology* 117: 257–63.

Cameron, D. 2006. 'LANGUAGE: European you-nity'. *Critical Quarterly* 48: 132–5.

Camp, E. 2006. 'Contextualism, metaphor, and what is said'. *Mind and Language* 21: 280–309.

2007. 'Showing, telling, and seeing: metaphor and "poetic" language'. *The Baltic International Yearbook of Cognition, Logic and Communication*, vol. 3: *A Figure of Speech*, http://thebalticyearbook.org/journals/baltic/issue/view/2.

Cann, R., Kempson, R. and Marten, L. 2005. *The Dynamics of Language.* Dordrecht: Elsevier.

Cann, R., Purver, M. and Kempson, R. 2007. 'Context and wellformedness: the dynamics of ellipsis'. *Research on Language and Computation* 5: 333–58.

Cappelen, H. and Lepore, E. 2005a. *Insensitive Semantics: a Defense of Semantic Minimalism and Speech Act Pluralism.* Oxford: Blackwell.

2005b. 'A tall tale: in defense of semantic minimalism and speech act pluralism'. In G. Preyer and G. Peter (eds.) *Contextualism in Philosophy: Knowledge, Meaning, and Truth*, pp. 197–219. Oxford: Clarendon Press.

Carassa, A. and Colombetti, M. 2009. 'Joint meaning'. *Journal of Pragmatics* 41: 1837–54.

Carnap, R. 1938. 'Foundations of logic and mathematics'. In O. Neurath, R. Carnap and C. Morris (eds.) *International Encyclopedia of Unified Science*, vol. I, pp. 139–214. University of Chicago Press.

1942. *Introduction to Semantics.* Cambridge, MA: Harvard University Press.

1947. *Meaning and Necessity.* University of Chicago Press.

Carrell, P. L. 1981. 'Children's understanding of indirect requests: comparing child and adult comprehension'. *Journal of Child Language* 8: 329–45.

Carruthers, P. and Smith, P. (eds.) 1996. *Theories of Theories of Mind*. Cambridge University Press.

Carston, R. 1988. 'Implicature, explicature and truth-theoretic semantics'. In R. Kempson (ed.) *Mental Representations: The Interface between Language and Reality*, pp. 155–81. Cambridge University Press.

1990. 'Quantity maxims and generalised implicature'. *UCL Working Papers in Linguistics* 2: 1–31. Reprinted in *Lingua* 96: 213–44.

1997. 'Enrichment and loosening: complementary processes in deriving the proposition expressed?'. *Linguistische Berichte* 8, Special Issue on Pragmatics: 103–27.

1998. 'Informativeness, relevance and scalar implicature'. In R. Carston and S. Uchida (eds.) *Relevance Theory: Applications and Implications*, pp. 179–236. Amsterdam: John Benjamins.

1999. 'The semantics/pragmatics distinction: A view from Relevance Theory'. In K. Turner (ed.) *The Semantics/Pragmatics Interface from Different Points of View* (CRiSPI 1), pp. 85–125. Oxford: Elsevier Science.

2002. *Thoughts and Utterances: The Pragmatics of Explicit Communication*. Oxford: Blackwell.

2004a. 'Relevance theory and the saying-implicating distinction'. In L. Horn and G. Ward (eds.) *The Handbook of Pragmatics*, pp. 633–56. Oxford: Blackwell.

2004b. 'Truth-conditional content and conversational implicature'. In C. Bianchi (ed.) *The Semantics/Pragmatics Distinction*, pp. 65–100. Stanford: CSLI Publications.

2007. 'How many pragmatic systems are there?'. In M. J. Frápolli (ed.) *Saying, Meaning and Referring: Essays on François Recanati's Philosophy of Language*, pp. 18–48. Basingstoke: Palgrave Macmillan.

2008. 'Linguistic communication and the semantics-pragmatics distinction'. *Synthese* 165: 321–45.

2009. 'The explicit/implicit distinction in pragmatics and the limits of explicit communication'. *International Review of Pragmatics* 1: 35–62.

2010a. 'Explicit communication and "free" pragmatic enrichment', in B. Soria and E. Romero (eds.), *Explicit Communication: Robyn Carston's Pragmatics*, pp. 217–87. Basingstoke: Palgrave Macmillan.

2010b. 'Metaphor: *ad hoc* concepts, literal meaning and mental images'. *Proceedings of the Aristotelian Society* 110 (3): 297–323.

Carston, R. and Powell, G. 2006. 'Relevance theory – new directions and developments'. In E. Lepore and B. Smith (eds.) *The Oxford Handbook of Philosophy of Language*, pp. 341–60. Oxford University Press.

Carston, R. and Wearing, C. 2011. 'Metaphor, hyperbole and simile: A pragmatic approach'. *Language and Cognition* 3(2): 283–312.

Caston, V. 2007. 'Intentionality in ancient philosophy'. In E. N. Zalta (ed.) *Stanford Encyclopedia of Philosophy*. http://plato.stanford.edu/contents.html.

Celle, A. and Huart, R. (eds.) 2007. *Connectives as Discourse Landmarks*. Amsterdam: John Benjamins.

Chafe, W. 1976. 'Givenness, contrastiveness, definiteness, subjects, topics, and point of view'. In C. N. Li (ed.) *Subject and Topic*, pp. 25–55. New York: Academic Press.

1994. *Discourse, Consciousness, and Time: The Flow and Displacement of Consciousness Experience in Speaking and Writing*. University of Chicago Press.

Chalmers, D. 1996. *The Conscious Mind: In Search of a Fundamental Theory*. Oxford University Press.

2002. 'On Sense and Intension'. *Philosophical Perspectives* 16: 135–82.

2006. 'Foundations of Two-Dimensional Semantics'. In M. Garcia-Carpintero and J. Macia (eds.) *Two-Dimensional Semantics: Foundations and Applications*, pp. 55–140. Oxford University Press.

(forthcoming a). 'The Nature of Epistemic Space'. In A. Egan and B. Weatherson (eds.) *Epistemic Modality*. Oxford University Press.

(forthcoming b). 'Propositions and Attitude Ascriptions'. *Noûs*.

Chalmers, D. and Jackson, F. 2001. 'Conceptual analysis and reductive explanation'. *Philosophical Review* 110: 315–60.

Chao, Y. R. 1968. *A Grammar of Spoken Chinese*. Berkeley: University of California Press.

Chapman, S. 2005. *Paul Grice: Philosopher and Linguist*. Basingstoke: Palgrave Macmillan.

Chen, A. J. and Gussenhoven, C. 2003. 'Language-dependence in the signalling of attitude in speech'. In N. Suzuki and C. Bartneck (eds.) *Subtle Expressivity of Characters and Robots: Proceedings of the Workshop CHI 2003* www.bortneck.de/wp-content/uploads/2009/05/proceedingschi03wrkshp.pdf. pp. 29–32.

Chen, G. 2002. 'The grammaticalization of concessive markers in Early Modern English'. In O. Fischer, A. Rosenbach and D. Stein (eds.), *Pathways of Change: Grammaticalization in English*, pp. 85–110. Amsterdam: John Benjamins.

Cheney D. and Seyfarth, R. 1990. *How Monkeys See the World: Inside the Mind of Another Species*. Chicago University Press.

Chierchia, G. 2004. 'Scalar implicatures, polarity phenomena, and the syntax/pragmatics interface'. In A. Belletti (ed.) *Structures and Beyond*, pp. 39–103. New York: Oxford University Press.

2006. 'Broaden your views: implicatures of domain widening and the "logicality" of language'. *Linguistic Inquiry* 37: 535–90.

Chierchia, G., Crain, S., Guasti, M. T., Gualmini, A. and Meroni, L. 2001. 'The acquisition of disjunction: evidence for a grammatical view of scalar implicatures'. In *Proceedings of the 25th Boston University Conference on Language Development*, pp. 157–68. Somerville, MA: Cascadilla Press.

Chierchia, G., Fox, D. and Spector, B. (forthcoming). 'The grammatical view of scalar implicatures and the relationship between semantics and pragmatics'. In C. Maienborn *et al.* (eds.) *Handbook of Semantics: An International Handbook*. Berlin: Mouton de Gruyter.

Chilton, P. 2007. 'Geometrical concepts at the interface of formal and cognitive models: Aktionsart, aspect, and the English progressive'. *Pragmatics and Cognition* 15: 91–114.

Chomsky, N. 1965. *Aspects of the Theory of Syntax*. Cambridge, MA: MIT Press.

   1971. 'Deep structure, surface structure and semantic interpretation'. In D. Steinberg and L. Jakobovits (eds.) *Semantics: An Interdisciplinary Reader in Linguistics, Philosophy and Psychology*, pp. 183–216. Cambridge University Press.

   1975. 'Quine's empirical assumptions'. In D. Davidson, and J. Hintikka (eds.) *Words and Objections*, pp. 53–68. Dordrecht: Reidel.

   1977. *Essays on Form and Interpretation*. Amsterdam: North Holland.

   1986. *Knowledge of Language: Its Nature, Origin, and Use*. New York: Praeger.

   1996. 'Language and thought: Some reflections on venerable themes'. In N. Chomsky, *Powers and Prospects: Reflections on Human Nature and the Social Order*, pp. 1–30. Boston: South End Press.

   2000. *New Horizons in the Study of Language and Mind*. Cambridge University Press.

Ciaramidaro, A., Adenzato, M., Enrici, I., Erk, S., Pia, L., Bara, B. and Walter, H. 2007. 'The intentional network: how the brain reads varieties of intentions'. *Neuropsychologia* 45: 3105–13.

Clapp, L. 1995. 'How to be direct and innocent: a criticism of Crimmins and Perry's theory of attitude ascriptions'. *Linguistics and Philosophy* 18: 685–711.

   2009. 'The problem of negative existentials does not exist: a case of dynamic semantics'. *Journal of Pragmatics* 41: 1422–34.

Clark, B. 1993. 'Relevance and "pseudo-imperatives"'. *Linguistics and Philosophy* 16: 79–121.

   2007. '"Blazing a trail": Moving from natural to linguistic meaning in accounting for the tones of English'. In R. A. Nilsen, N. A. Appiah Amfo and K. Borthen (eds.) *Interpreting Utterances: Pragmatics and its Interfaces; Essays in Honour of Thorstein Fretheim*, pp. 69–81. Oslo: Novus.

Clark, B. and Lindsey, G. 1990. 'Intonation, grammar and utterance interpretation'. *UCL Working Papers in Linguistics* 2: 32–51.

Clark, H. 1979. 'Responding to indirect speech acts.' *Cognitive Psychology* 11: 430–77.

   1996. *Using Language*. Cambridge University Press.

   1997. 'Dogmas of understanding'. *Discourse Processes* 23: 567–98.

Clark, H. and Gerrig, R. 1984. 'On the pretense theory of irony'. *Journal of Experimental Psychology: General* 113: 121–6. Reprinted in R. Gibbs and H. Colston (eds.) 2007, *Irony in Language and Thought: A Cognitive Science Reader*, pp. 25–33. Hillsdale, NJ: Lawrence Erlbaum.

Clift, R., Drew, P. and Hutchby, I. 2006. 'Conversation analysis'. In J. Verschueren and J. O. Östman (eds.) *Handbook of Pragmatics*. Amsterdam: John Benjamins (loose-leaf publication).

Clyne, M., Ball, M. and Neil, D. 1991. 'Intercultural communication at work in Australia. Complaints and apologies in turns'. *Multilingua*. 10: 251–73.

Cohen, A. 1999. 'How are alternatives computed?' *Journal of Semantics* 16: 43–65.

Collins, J. 2009. 'II—Methodology, not Metaphysics: Against Semantic Externalism'. *Aristotelian Society Supplementary Volume* 83: 53–69.

Colston, H. L. and Gibbs, R. W. 2002. 'Are irony and metaphor understood differently?'. *Metaphor and Symbol* 17: 57–60.

Comrie, B. 1981. 'On Reichenbach's approach to tense'. *CLS* 17: 24–30.

   1994. 'Language universals and linguistic typology: Data-bases and explanations'. *Sprachtypologie und Universalienforschung* 46: 3–14.

Copestake, A. and Lascarides, A. 1997. 'Integrating symbolic and statistical representations: the lexicon pragmatics interface'. In *Proceedings of the 35th Annual Meeting of the Association for Computational Linguistics* (ACL97), Madrid, 7–12 July 1997, pp. 136–43. Madrid: ACL.

Corbett, E. P. J. 1990. *Classical Rhetoric for the Modern Student*. 3rd edition. New York: Oxford University Press.

Cornish, F. 2004. 'Focus of attention in discourse'. In L. J. Mackenzie and M. Gómez- González (eds.) *A New Architecture for Functional Grammar*, pp. 117–50. Berlin: Mouton de Gruyter.

Corrigan, R., Moravcsik, E. A., Ouali, H. and Wheatley, K. M. (eds.) 2009. *Formulaic Language*. 2 vols. Philadelphia: John Benjamins.

Couper-Kuhlen, E. 1986. *English Prosody*. London: Edward Arnold.

Crain, S. 2008. 'The interpretation of disjunction in universal grammar'. *Language and Speech* 51/1–2: 151–69.

Crimmins, M. 1992. *Talk About Beliefs*. Cambridge, MA: MIT Press.

Crimmins, M. and Perry, J. 1989. 'The prince and the phone booth: Reporting puzzling beliefs'. *Journal of Philosophy* 86: 685–711.

Croft, W. 2000. *Explaining Language Change*. Harlow, Essex: Longman, Pearson Education.

   2001. *Radical Construction Grammar: Syntactic Theory in Typological Perspective*. Oxford University Press.

Croft, W. and Cruse, D. 2004. *Cognitive Linguistics*. Cambridge University Press.

Cruse, A. 2000. *Meaning in Language. An Introduction to Semantics and Pragmatics*. Oxford University Press.

Cruttenden, A. 1986. *Intonation*. Cambridge University Press.

Crystal, D. 2001. *Language and the Internet*. Cambridge University Press.

   2008. *Txtng: The Gr8 Db8*. Oxford University Press.

Culpeper, J. 1996. 'Towards an anatomy of impoliteness'. *Journal of Pragmatics* 25: 349–67.

   2011a. *Impoliteness: Using Language to Cause Offence*. Cambridge University Press.

   2011b. 'Conventionalized impoliteness'. *Journal of Pragmatics* 42: 3232–45.

Culpeper, J. and Kytö, M. 2010. *Early Modern English Dialogues: Spoken Interaction as Writing*. Studies in English Language. Cambridge University Press.

Cummings, L. 1998. 'The scientific reductionism of relevance theory: the lesson from logical positivism'. *Journal of Pragmatics* 29: 1–12.

2005. *Pragmatics: A Multidisciplinary Perspective*. Edinburgh University Press.

(ed.) 2010. *The Pragmatics Encyclopedia*. London: Routledge.

Currie, G. 2006. 'Why irony is pretence'. In S. Nichols (ed.) *The Architecture of the Imagination*, pp. 111–33. Oxford University Press.

Cuyckens, H., Dirven, R. and Taylor, J. R. (eds.) 2003. *Cognitive Approaches to Lexical Semantics*. Berlin: Mouton de Gruyter.

Dalrymple, M. 2001. *Lexical Functional Grammar*. Dordrecht: Elsevier.

Dalrymple, M., Shieber, S. and Perreira, F. 1991. 'Ellipsis and higher order unification'. *Linguistics and Philosophy* 14: 399–452.

Damourette, J. and Pichon, E. 1911–1936. *Des mots à la pensée: Essai de grammaire de la langue française*. Paris: D'Artrey, V.

Dancy, J. 2004. *Ethics Without Principles*. Oxford University Press.

Daneš, F. (ed.) 1974. *Papers on Functional Sentence Perspective*. The Hague: Mouton.

Dascal, M. and Gross, A. G. 1999. 'The marriage of pragmatics and rhetoric'. *Philosophy and Rhetoric* 32: 107–30.

Davidse, K., Vandelanotte, L. and Cuyckens, H. (eds.) 2010. *Subjectification, Intersubjectification and Grammaticalization*. Berlin: Mouton de Gruyter.

Davidson, D. 1968. 'On saying that'. *Synthese* 19: 130–46. Reprinted in P. Ludlow (ed.) 1997, *Readings in the Philosophy of Language*, pp. 817–31. Cambridge, MA: MIT Press.

1978. 'What metaphors mean'. *Critical Inquiry* 5: 31–47. Reprinted in D. Davidson 1984, *Inquiries into Truth and Interpretation*, pp. 245–64. Oxford: Clarendon Press.

1979. 'Moods and Performances'. In A. Margalit (ed.) *Meaning and use*, pp. 9–20. Dordrecht: Reidel.

1984. *Inquiries into Truth and Interpretation*. Oxford: Clarendon Press.

1986. 'A nice derangement of epitaphs'. In R. Grandy and R. Warner (eds.) *Philosophical Grounds of Rationality*, pp. 157–74. Oxford University Press.

Davies, M. and Stone, T. (eds.) 1995a. *Mental Simulation: Philosophical and Psychological Essays*. Oxford: Blackwell.

(eds.) 1995b. *Folk Psychology*. Oxford: Blackwell.

Davis, W. 1998. *Implicature: Intention, Convention, and Principle in the Failure of Gricean Theory*. Cambridge University Press.

2003. *Meaning, Expression, and Thought*. Cambridge University Press.

2008. 'Expressing, meaning, showing, and intending to indicate'. *Intercultural Pragmatics* 5: 111–29.

Dekker, P. 1992. 'An update semantics for dynamic predicate logic'. In P. Dekker and M. Stokhof (eds.) *Proceedings of the Eighth Amsterdam Colloquium*. ILLC, University of Amsterdam.

Demeure, V., Bonnefon, J.-F. and Raufaste, E. 2009. 'Politeness and conditional reasoning: Interpersonal cues to the indirect suppression of deductive inferences'. *Journal of Experimental Psychology* 35: 260–66.

Denison, D. 2002. 'History of the sort of construction family'. 2nd International Conference on Construction Grammar (ICCG2), University of Helsinki, Sept. 6–8. www.llc.manchester.ac.uk/subjects/lel/staff/david-denison/papers/thefile,100126,en.pdf.

Deutschmann, M. 2003. *Apologising in British English*. Skrifter från moderna språk 10. Umeå: Institutionen för moderna språk, Umeå University.

Devitt, M. 1996. *Coming to Our Senses: A Naturalistic Program for Semantic Localism*. Cambridge University Press.

Dews, S. and Winner, E. 1995. 'Muting the meaning: a social function of irony'. *Metaphor and symbolic activity* 10: 3–19.

1997. 'Attributing meaning to deliberately false utterances: the case of irony'. In C. Mandell and A. McCabe (eds.) *The Problem of Meaning: Behavioral and Cognitive Perspectives*, pp. 377–414. Amsterdam: Elsevier.

1999. 'Obligatory processing of the literal and the nonliteral meanings of ironic utterances'. *Journal of Pragmatics* 31: 1579–99.

Dews, S., Kaplan, J. and Winner, E. 1995. 'Why not say it directly? The social functions of irony'. *Discourse Processes* 19: 347–67.

Di Sciullo, A.-M. and Williams, E. 1987. *On the Definition of Word*. Cambridge, MA: MIT Press.

Diewald, G. 2002. 'A model for relevant types of contexts in grammaticalization'. In I. Wischer and G. Diewald (eds.) *New Reflections on Grammaticalization*, pp. 103–20. Amsterdam: Benjamins.

Dijk, T. van. 1981. *Studies in the Pragmatics of Discourse*. The Hague: Mouton.

2008. *Discourse and Context: A Sociocognitive Approach*. Cambridge University Press.

Dik, S. 1968. *Coordination: Its Implication for the Theory of General Linguistics*. Amsterdam: North Holland Publishing Company.

Dominicy, M. and Franken, N. 2002. 'Speech acts and relevance theory'. In D. Vanderveken and S. Kubo (eds.) *Essays in Speech Act Theory*, pp. 263–83. Amsterdam: John Benjamins.

Donahue, D. 1991. *Lawman's Brut, An Early Arthurian Poem: A Study of Middle English Formulaic Composition*. Lewiston, NY: Mellen.

Donnellan, K. 1966. 'Reference and definite descriptions'. *Philosophical Review* 75: 281–304.

1972. 'Proper names and identifying descriptions'. *Synthese* 21: 335–58.

Donohue, M. 1993. *A Grammar of Tukang Besi*. Berlin/New York: Mouton de Gruyter.

Downing, A. 2001. '"Surely you knew!" Surely as a marker of evidentiality and stance'. *Functions of Language* 8: 253–85.

Dowty, D. 1979. *Word Meaning and Montague Grammar*. Dordrecht: Reidel.

1986. 'The effects of aspectual class on the temporal structure of discourse: Semantics or pragmatics?'. *Linguistics and Philosophy* 9: 37–61.

Doyle, J. 1951. 'In defense of the square of opposition'. *The New Scholasticism* 25: 367–96.

Du Bois, J. W. 1985. 'Competing motivations'. In J. Haiman (ed.) *Iconicity in Syntax*, pp. 343–65. Amsterdam: Benjamins.

  1987. 'The discourse basis of ergativity'. *Language* 63: 805–55.

  1998. 'Dialogic syntax'. Paper presented at the Cognitive Theories of Intertextuality Meeting, Tel Aviv University.

  2001 'Towards a dialogic syntax'. Unpublished ms. University of California Santa Barbara.

  2003. 'Discourse and grammar'. In M. Tomasello (ed.) *The New Psychology of Language: Cognitive and Functional Approaches to Language Structure*, vol. 2, pp. 47–87. Mahwah, NJ: Lawrence Erlbaum Associates.

Du Bois, J. W., Chafe, W. L., Meyer, C. and Thompson, S. A. 2000. *Santa Barbara Corpus of Spoken American English, Part 1*. Philadelphia: Linguistic Data Consortium, University of Pennsylvania.

Du Bois, J. W., Chafe, W. L., Meyer, C., Thompson, S. A. and Martey, N. 2003. *Santa Barbara Corpus of Spoken American English, Part 2*. Philadelphia: Linguistic Data Consortium, University of Pennsylvania.

Ducrot, O. 1972. *Dire et Ne Pas Dire*. Paris: Hermann.

  1984. *Le Dire et le Dit*. Paris: Minuit.

Dummett, M. 1973. *Frege: Philosophy of Language*. Oxford: Duckworth.

Dunn, J. M. 1996. 'Generalized ortho negation'. In H. Wansing (ed.) *Negation: A Notion in Focus*, pp. 3–26. Berlin: Walter de Gruyter.

Duranti, A. 1999. 'Intentionality'. *Journal of Linguistic Anthropology* 9: 134–6.

Durkheim, É. 1915. *The Elementary Forms of Religious Life*. London: George Allen and Unwin. (Translated from É. Durkheim, 1912, *Les Formes Élémentaires de la Vie Réligieuse*. Paris: Alcan.)

Eckardt, R. 2006. *Meaning Change in Grammaticalization: An Enquiry into Semantic Reanalysis*. Oxford University Press.

Economist 2009. 'Politeness: Hi there'. *Economist* 393 (19 December 2009): 104–6.

Edwards, D. 2006. 'Discourse, cognition and social practices: the rich surface of language and social interaction'. *Discourse Studies* 8: 41–9.

  2008. 'Intentionality and *mens rea* in police interrogations: the production of actions as crimes'. *Intercultural Pragmatics* 5: 177–99.

Eelen, G. 2001. *A Critique of Politeness Theories*. Manchester: St. Jerome.

Ekman, P. 1989. 'The argument and evidence about universals in facial expressions of emotion'. In H. Wagner and A. Manstead (eds.) *Handbook of Social Psychophysiology*, pp. 143–64. New York: Wiley.

  1992. 'An argument for basic emotion'. *Cognition and Emotion* 6 (3/4): 169–200.

  1999. 'Emotional and conversational nonverbal signals'. In L. Messing and R. Campbell (eds.) *Gesture, Speech and Sign*, pp. 45–57. Oxford University Press.

Elliot, J. R. 2000. 'Realis and irrealis: forms and concepts of the grammaticalisation of reality'. *Linguistic Typology* 4–1: 55–90.

Enç, M. 1981. *Tense without Scope: An Analysis of Nouns as Indexicals*. PhD thesis, University of Wisconsin, Madison.

1996. 'Tense and modality'. In S. Lappin (ed.) *The Handbook of Contemporary Semantic Theory*, pp. 345–58. Oxford: Blackwell.

Enfield, N. J. 2003. *Linguistic Epidemiology: Semantics and Grammar of Language Contact in Mainland Southeast Asia*. London: Routledge Curzon.

Enfield, N. J. and Stivers, T. 2007. *Person Reference in Interaction: Linguistic, Cultural and Social Perspectives*. Cambridge University Press.

Englebretsen, G. 1981. *Logical Negation*. Assen: van Gorcum.

Enrici, I., Adenzato, M., Cappa, S., Bara, B. and Tettamanti, M. 2011. 'Intention processing in communication: a common brain network for language and gestures'. *Journal of Cognitive Neuroscience* 23: 2415–31.

Erman, B. and Kostinas, U. B. 1993. 'Pragmaticalization: the case of *ba* and *you know*'. *Studier i Modern Sprakvetenskap* 10: 76–93.

Erman, B. and Warren, B. 2000. 'The idiom principle and the open choice principle'. *Text* 20: 29–62.

Erteschik-Shir, N. 1997. *The Dynamics of Focus Structure*. Cambridge University Press.

Escandell-Vidal, V. 1996. 'Towards a cognitive approach to politeness'. *Language Sciences* 18: 629–50.

1998. 'Intonation and procedural encoding: the case of Spanish interrogatives'. In V. Rouchota and A. Jucker (eds.) *Current Issues in Relevance Theory*, pp. 169–203. Amsterdam: John Benjamins.

2002. 'Echo-syntax and metarepresentations'. *Lingua* 112: 871–900.

Evans, N. and Levinson, S. C. 2009. 'The myth of language universals: language diversity and its importance for cognitive science'. *Behavioral and Brain Sciences* 32: 429–92.

Evans, N. and Wilkins, D. 2000. 'In the mind's ear: the semantic extensions of perception verbs in Australian languages'. *Language* 76: 546–92.

Everett, D. and Kern, B. 1997. *Wari: Descriptive Grammars*. London: Routledge.

Fairclough, N. 2003. *Analysing Discourse: Textual Analysis for Social Research*. London: Routledge.

Faltz, L. M. 1985. *Reflexivization: A Study in Universal Syntax*. New York: Garland.

Ferreira, F. 2005. 'Psycholinguistics, formal grammars, and cognitive science'. *The Linguistic Review* 22: 365–80.

Ferreira, V. 1996. 'Is it better to give than to donate? Syntactic flexibility in language production'. *Journal of Memory and Language* 35: 724–55.

Fetzer, A. 2002. 'Communicative intentions in context'. In A. Fetzer and C. Meierkord (eds.) *Rethinking Sequentiality: Linguistics meets Conversational Interaction*, pp. 37–69. Amsterdam: Benjamins.

2004. *Recontextualizing Context: Grammaticality Meets Appropriateness*. Amsterdam: Benjamins.

2007. 'Reformulation and common grounds'. In A. Fetzer and K. Fischer (eds.) *Lexical Markers of Common Grounds*, pp. 157–79. London: Elsevier.

2008. 'Theme zones in English media discourse. Forms and functions'. *Journal of Pragmatics* 40: 1543–68.

Field, T., Woodson, R., Greenberg, R. and Cohen, D. 1982. 'Discrimination and imitation of facial expressions by neonates'. *Science* 218: 179–81.

Fiengo, R. 2007. *Asking Questions: Using Meaningful Structures to Imply Ignorance*. Oxford University Press.

Fiengo, R. and May, R. 1994. *Indices and Identity*. Cambridge, MA: MIT Press.

Filipović, L. 2007a. 'Language as a witness: insights from cognitive linguistics'. *Speech, Language and the Law* 14: 245–67.

2007b. *Talking about Motion: A Crosslinguistic Investigation of Lexicalization Patterns*. Amsterdam: John Benjamins.

2008. 'Typology in action: applying insights from typological contrasts'. *International Journal of Applied Linguistics* 18: 42–61.

Fillmore, C. J. 1982. 'Frame semantics'. In Linguistic Society of Korea (eds.) *Linguistics in the Morning Calm*, pp. 111–38. Seoul: Hanshin.

2006. 'Frame semantics'. In E. K. Brown (ed.) *Encyclopedia of Languages and Linguistics*, vol. IV, pp. 613–20. 2nd edition. Oxford: Elsevier.

Fillmore, C. J. and Atkins, B. T. 1992. 'Towards a frame-based lexicon: the semantics of RISK and its neighbors'. In A. Lehrer and E. F. Kittay (eds.) *Frames, Fields, and Contrasts*, pp. 75–102. Hillsdale, NJ: Lawrence Erlbaum.

Fintel, K. von. 1994. *Restrictions on Quantifier Domains*. PhD thesis, University of Massachusetts.

1995. 'The formal semantics of grammaticalization'. In J. N. Beckman (ed.) *Proceedings of the Annual Meeting of the North East Linguistic Society 25*, vol. II, pp. 175–89. Department of Linguistics, University of Massachusetts at Amherst.

Firbas, J. 1966. 'On defining the theme in functional sentence analysis'. In F. Daneš (ed.) *Travaux linguistiques de Prague*, vol. I, pp. 267–80. Tuscaloosa, AL: University of Alabama Press.

Fitzpatrick, D. 2003. 'Searle and collective intentionality'. *American Journal of Economics and Sociology* 62: 45–66.

Fodor, J. 1975. *The Language of Thought*. Scranton, PA: Crowell.

1981. *Representations: Philosophical Essays on the Foundations of Cognitive Science*. Brighton: Harvester Press.

1983. *The Modularity of Mind: An Essay on Faculty Psychology*. Cambridge, MA: MIT Press.

2008. *The Language of Thought Revisited*. Oxford: Clarendon Press.

Fodor, J. and Sag, I. 1982. 'Referential and quantificational indefinites'. *Linguistics and Philosophy* 5: 355–98.

Fogassi, L., Ferrari, P. F., Gesierich, B., Rozzi, S., Chersi, F. and Rizzolatti, G. 2005. 'Parietal lobe: from action organization to intention understanding'. *Science* 308: 662–7.

Fogelin, R. 1967. *Evidence and Meaning*. New York: Humanities Press.

Forbes, G. 1990. 'The indispensability of Sinn'. *Philosophical Review* 99: 535–63.

1997. 'How much substitutivity?' *Analysis* 57: 109–13.

2006. *Attitude Problems: An Essay on Linguistic Intensionality*. Oxford: Clarendon Press.

Fox, D. 2002. 'Antecedent contained deletion and the copy theory of movement'. *Linguistic Inquiry* 33(1): 63–96.

Fraassen, B. van 1971. *Formal Semantics and Logic*. New York: Macmillan.

Frajzyngier, Z. and Shay, E. 2002. *A Grammar of Hdi*. Berlin/New York: Mouton de Gruyter.

Fraser, B. 1990. 'Perspectives on politeness'. *Journal of Pragmatics* 14: 219–36.
   2006. 'On the conceptual-procedural distinction'. Style. FindArticles.com. 22 Jul, 2010. http://findarticles.com/p/articles/mi_m2342/is_1-2_40/ai_n17113874/.

Fraser, B. and Nolen, W. 1981. 'The association of deference with linguistic form'. *International Journal of the Sociology of Language* 27: 93–109.

Frege, G. 1879. 'Begriffschrift'. In T. W. Bynum (trans. and ed.) *'Conceptual Notation' and Related Articles*, pp. 101–203. Oxford University Press.
   1884. *Die Grundlagen der Arithmetik, eine logisch-mathematische Untersuchung über den Begriff der Zahl*. Introduction. Breslau: W. Koebner. Trans. M. Beaney in M. Beaney (ed.) 1997, *The Frege Reader*, pp. 84–91. Oxford: Blackwell.
   1892. 'Über Sinn und Bedeutung'. *Zeitschrift für Philosophie und Philosophische Kritik* 100: 25–50. Reprinted in *Translations from the Philosophical Writings of Gottlob Frege*, pp. 56–78, trans. Geach & Black. Blackwell Press, 1953. Translated as 'On sense and reference' in P. T. Geach (ed.) 1960. Reprinted in M. Beaney (ed.) 1997, *The Frege Reader*, pp. 151–71. Oxford: Blackwell.
   1893. *Grundgesetze der Arithmetik*, vol. I. Preface. Jena: H. Pohle. Trans. M. Beaney in M. Beaney (ed.) 1997, *The Frege Reader*, pp. 194–208. Oxford: Blackwell.
   1894. 'Review of E.G. Husserl, *Philosophie der Arithmetik I* [Philosophy of Arithmetic I] '. *Zeitschrift für Philosophie und philosophische Kritik* 103. Trans. H. Kaal in G. Frege 1984, *Collected Papers on Mathematics, Logic, and Philosophy*, pp. 195–209., ed. B. McGuinness. Oxford: Blackwell.
   1897. 'Logic'. Unpublished paper, appearing in H. Hermes *et al.* (eds.) *Nachgelassene Schriften*, pp. 139–61. Hamburg: Felix Meinen. Extract trans. P. Long and R. White, reprinted in M. Beaney (ed.) 1997, *The Frege Reader*, pp. 227–50. Oxford: Blackwell.
   1906. 'Letters to Husserl, 1906'. In G. Frege 1976, *Wissenschaftlicher Briefwechsel*. Hamburg: Felix Meiner. Trans. H. Kaal in G. Frege 1980, *Philosophical and Mathematical Correspondence*, pp. 66–71, ed. by B. McGuinness. Oxford: Blackwell. Reprinted in M. Beaney (ed.) 1997, *The Frege Reader*, pp. 301–7. Oxford: Blackwell.
   1918. 'Thought'. Trans. P. Geach and R. H. Stoothoff. In M. Beaney (ed.) 1997, *The Frege Reader*, pp. 325–45. Oxford: Blackwell.
   1970. *Translations from the Philosophical Writings of Gottlob Frege*. Ed. and trans. P. Geach and M. Black. Oxford: Blackwell.

Fretheim, T. 1987. 'Pragmatics and intonation'. In J. Verschueren and M. Bertuccelli-Papi (eds.) *The Pragmatic Perspective*, pp. 395–420. Amsterdam: John Benjamins.

　1992a. *Grammatically Underdetermined Theme-Rheme Articulation*. ROLIG no. 49. Roskilde University Center, Denmark.

　1992b. 'Themehood, rhemehood and Norwegian focus structure'. *Folia Linguistica* 26(1–2): 111–50.

　2001. 'The interaction of right-dislocated pronominals and intonational phrasing in Norwegian'. In W. van Dommelen and T. Fretheim (eds.) *Nordic Prosody: Proceedings of the VIIIth Conference*. Frankfurt am Main: Peter Lang.

　2002. 'Intonation as a constraint on inferential processing'. In B. Bel and I. Marlien (eds.) *Proceedings of the Speech Prosody 2002 Conference*, pp. 59–64. Denver, CO.

Fridlund, A. 1994. *Human Facial Expression: An Evolutionary View*. San Diego: Academic Press.

Frith, C. D. and Frith, U. 2003. 'The neural basis of mentalizing'. *Neuron* 50: 531–4.

Gabbay, D. 1988. 'What is negation in a system?'. In F. R. Drake and J. K. Truss (eds.) *Logic Colloquium '86*, pp. 95–112. University of Amsterdam.

Gabelenz, G. von der 1868. 'Ideen zur einer vergleichenden Syntax: Wort- und Satzstellung'. *Zeitschrift für Völkerpsychologie und Sprachwissenschaft* 6: 376–84.

Garcia, A. C. and Jacobs, J. B. 1999. 'The eyes of the beholder: understanding the turn-taking system in quasi-synchronous computer-mediated communication'. *Research on Language and Social Interaction* 32: 337–67.

Garcia-Carpintero, M. 2006. 'Recanati on the semantics/pragmatics distinction'. *Critica* 38: 35–68.

Garfinkel, H. 1967. *Studies in Ethnomethodology*. Englewood Cliffs, NJ: Prentice Hall.

Garfinkel, H. and Sacks, H. 1970. 'On formal structures of practical action'. In J. C. McKinney and E. A. Tiraykian (eds.) *Theoretical Sociology*, pp. 338–66. New York: Appleton-Century-Crofts.

Gauker, C. 2001. 'Situated inference versus conversational implicature'. *Nous* 35: 163–89.

　2003. *Words Without Meaning*. Cambridge, MA: MIT Press.

　2007. 'The circle of deference proves the normativity semantics'. *Rivista di Estetica* 47: 181–98.

　2008. 'Zero tolerance for pragmatics'. *Synthese* 165: 359–73.

Gazdar, G. 1979. *Pragmatics: Implicature, Presupposition and Logical Form*. New York: Academic Press.

Gazzaniga, M. and Smiley, C. 1991. 'Hemispheric mechanisms controlling voluntary and spontaneous facial expressions'. *Journal of Cognitive Neuroscience* 2: 239–45.

Geach, P. 1962. *Reference and Generality*. Ithaca, NY: Cornell University Press.

Gee, J. P. 1999. *An Introduction to Discourse Analysis*. London: Routledge.

Geeraerts, D. 1987. *Diachronic Prototype Semantics: A Contribution to Historical Lexicology*. Oxford: Clarendon.

Geis, M. L. and Zwicky, A. 1971. 'On invited inferences'. *Linguistic Inquiry* 2: 561–6.

Georgakopoulou, A. 2005. 'Computer-mediated communication'. In J. Verschueren, J. O. Östman, J. Blommaert and C. Bulcaen (eds.) *Handbook of Pragmatics Online*. Amsterdam: John Benjamins.

Georgiou, I. 2003. 'The idea of emergent property'. *Journal of the Operational Research Society* 54: 239–47.

Gernsbacher, M. A. and Givón, T. (eds.) 1995. *Coherence in Spontaneous Text*. Amsterdam: Benjamins.

  1995. *Presupposing*. Doctoral dissertation, University of Stuttgart.

  1996. 'Local satisfaction guaranteed: a presupposition theory and its problems'. *Linguistics and Philosophy* 19: 259–94.

  1999. *Presuppositions and Pronouns* (CRISPI 3). Oxford: Elsevier.

  2005. 'Entertaining alternatives: disjunctions as modals'. *Natural Language Semantics* 13(4): 383–410.

  2009. 'Scalar implicature and local pragmatics'. *Mind and Language* 24: 51–79.

  2010. *Quantity Implicatures*. Cambridge University Press.

Geurts, B. and Pouscoulous, N. 2009a. 'No scalar inferences under embedding'. *MIT Working Papers in Linguistics*. In P. Egré and G. Magri (eds.), *Presuppositions and Implicatures*. Cambridge, MA: MIT Press.

  2009b. 'Embedded implicatures?!?'. *Semantics and Pragmatics* 2(4): 1–34.

Geurts, B. and van der Sandt, R. 1999. 'Domain restriction'. In P. Bosch and R. van der Sandt (eds.) *Focus: Linguistic, Cognitive, and Computational Perspectives*, pp. 268–92. Cambridge University Press.

  2004. 'Interpreting focus'. *Theoretical Linguistics* 30: 1–44.

Giacalone, A. and Mauri, C. (forthcoming). 'The grammaticalization of coordinating interclausal connectives'. In H. Narrog and B. Heine (eds.) *Oxford Handbook of Grammaticalization*. Oxford University Press.

Gibbs, R. 1979. 'Contextual effects in understanding indirect requests'. *Discourse Processes* 2: 1–10.

  1980. 'Spilling the beans on understanding and memory for idioms in conversation'. *Memory & Cognition* 8: 449–56.

  1986. 'On the psycholinguistics of sarcasm'. *Journal of Experimental Psychology (General)* 115: 3–15.

  1994. *The Poetics of Mind: Figurative Thought, Language, and Understanding*. Cambridge University Press.

  1999. *Intentions in the Experience of Meaning*. Cambridge Unversity Press.

  2001. 'Intentions as emergent products of social interactions'. In B. Malle, L. Moses and D. Baldwin (eds.) *Intentions and Intentionality*, pp. 105–22. Cambridge, MA: MIT Press.

2002. 'A new look at literal meaning in understanding what is said and implicated'. *Journal of Pragmatics* 34: 457–86.

Gibbs, R. and Moise, J. F. 1997. 'Pragmatics in understanding what is said'. *Cognition* 62: 51–74.

Gibbs, R. and Tendahl, M. 2006. 'Cognitive effort and effects in metaphor comprehension: Relevance Theory and psycholinguistics'. *Mind and Language* 21: 379–403.

Gigerenzer, G. 2000. *Adaptive Thinking: Rationality in the Real World*. Oxford University Press.

Gigerenzer, G., Todd, P. and the ABC Research Group 1999. *Simple Heuristics That Make Us Smart*. Oxford University Press.

Gil, D. 1991. 'Aristotle goes to Arizona and finds a language without AND'. In D. Zaefferer (ed.) *Semantic Universals and Universal Semantics*, pp. 96–130. Berlin: Foris.

Gilbert, M. 2009. 'Shared intention and personal intentions'. *Philosophical Studies* 114: 167–87.

Ginzburg, J. and Cooper, R. 2004. 'Clarification, ellipsis, and the nature of contextual updates in dialogue'. *Linguistics and Philosophy* 27: 297–365.

Giora, R. 1995. 'On irony and negation'. *Discourse Processes* 19: 239–64.

1997. 'Understanding figurative and literal language: the graded salience hypothesis'. *Cognitive Linguistics* 8: 183–206.

1999. 'On the priority of salient meanings: studies of literal and figurative language'. *Journal of Pragmatics* 31: 919–29.

2003. *On Our Mind: Salience, Context, and Figurative Language*. New York: Oxford University Press.

2006. 'Anything negatives can do affirmatives can do just as well, except for some metaphors'. *Journal of Pragmatics* 38: 981–1014.

2007. 'A good Arab is not a dead Arab – a racist incitement: on the accessibility of negated concepts'. In L. R. Horn and I. Kecskes (eds.) *Explorations in Pragmatics: Linguistic, Cognitive and Intercultural Aspects*, pp. 129–62. Berlin: Mouton de Gruyter.

2011. 'Will anticipating irony facilitate it immediately?' In M. Dynel (ed.) *The Pragmatics of Humour across Discourse Domains*, pp. 19–31. Amsterdam: John Benjamins.

Giora, R. and Fein, O. 1999a. 'On understanding familiar and less-familiar figurative language'. *Journal of Pragmatics* 31: 1601–18.

1999b. 'Irony: context and salience'. *Metaphor and Symbol* 14: 241–57.

Giora, R., Zaidel, E., Soroker, N., Batori, G. and Kasher, A. 2000. 'Differential effects of right- and left-hemisphere damage on understanding sarcasm and metaphor'. *Metaphor and Symbol* 15: 63–83.

Giora, R., Fein, O., Kronrod, A., Elnatan, I., Shuval, N. and Zur, A. 2004. 'Weapons of mass distraction: optimal innovation and pleasure ratings'. *Metaphor and Symbol* 19: 115–41.

Giora, R., Balaban, N., Fein, O. and Alkabets, I. 2005a. 'Negation as positivity in disguise'. In H. L. Colston and A. Katz (eds.) *Figurative Language*

*Comprehension: Social and Cultural Influences*, pp. 233–58. Hillsdale, NJ: Erlbaum.

Giora, R., Fein, O., Ganzi, J., Alkeslassy Levi, N., and Sabah, H. 2005b. 'On negation as mitigation: The case of irony'. *Discourse Processes* 39: 81–100.

Giora, R., Fein, O., Aschkenazi, K. and Alkabets-Zlozover, I. 2007a. 'Negation in context: a functional approach to suppression'. *Discourse Processes* 43: 153–72.

Giora, R., Fein, O., Laadan, D., Wolfson, J., Zeituny, M., Kidron, R., Kaufman, R. and Shaham, R. 2007b. 'Expecting irony: context vs. salience-based effects'. *Metaphor and Symbol* 22: 119–46.

Giora, R., Fein, O., Kaufman, R., Eisenberg, D. and Erez, S. 2009. 'Does an "ironic situation" favor an ironic interpretation?'. In G. Brône and J. Vandaele (eds.) *Cognitive poetics: Goals, Gains and Gaps* (Applications of Cognitive Linguistics series), pp. 383–99. Berlin/New York: Mouton de Gruyter.

Giora, R., Fein, O., Metuki, N. and Stern, P. 2010. 'Negation as a metaphor-inducing operator'. In L. R. Horn (ed.) *The Expression of Negation*, pp. 225–56. Berlin/New York: Mouton de Gruyter.

Giora, R., Gazal, O., Goldstein, I., Fein, O. and Stringaris, A. (forthcoming). 'Salience and context: interpreting metaphors and literals by young adults diagnosed with Asperger's syndrome'. *Metaphor and Symbol*.

Giora, R., Livnat, E., and Fein, O. 2011a. 'On default nonliteral interpretation'. Unpublished ms.

Giora, R., Fein, O. and Yeari, M. 2011b. 'Interpreting irony: Will expecting it make a difference?' Unpublished ms.

Givón, T. 1979. *On Understanding Grammar*. Perspectives in Neurolinguistics and Psycholinguistics. New York: Academic Press.

1989. *Mind, Code and Context*. Hillsdale, NJ: Laurence Erlbaum.

1993. *English Grammar: A Function-Based Introduction*. Amsterdam: Benjamins.

2005. *Context as Other Minds*. Amsterdam: Benjamins.

Glenn, P. 2003. *Laughter in Interaction*. Cambridge University Press.

Glock, H.-J. (2010). 'Does language require conventions?'. In P. Frascolla, D. Marconi and A. Voltolini (eds.) *Wittgenstein: Mind, Meaning and Metaphilosophy*, pp. 85–112. London: Palgrave Macmillan.

Glucksberg, S. (ed.) 2001. *Understanding Figurative Language: From Metaphors to Idioms*. Oxford University Press.

2008. 'How metaphors create categories – quickly'. In R. Gibbs (ed.) *The Cambridge Handbook of Metaphor and Thought*, pp. 67–83. Cambridge University Press.

Glucksberg, S. and Haught, C. 2006. 'On the relation between metaphor and simile: when comparison fails'. *Mind and Language* 21: 360–78.

Glucksberg, S. and Keysar, B. 1993. 'How metaphors work'. In A. Ortony (ed.) *Metaphors and Thought*, pp. 401–24. Cambridge University Press.

Goddard, C. and Wierzbicka, A. 1997. 'Discourse and culture'. In T. A. van Dijk (ed.) *Discourse as Social Interaction*, pp. 23–57. London: Sage.

Goffman, E. 1955. 'On face-work: an analysis of ritual elements of social interaction'. *Psychiatry: Journal for the Study of Interpersonal Processes* 18: 213–31.

1964. 'The neglected situation'. *American Anthropologist* 66(6/2): 133–6.

1974. *Frame Analysis*. Cambridge, MA: Harvard University Press.

1979. 'Footing'. *Semiotica* 25: 1–29.

1986. *Frame Analysis*. Boston: Northeastern University Press.

Goldberg, A. E. 1995. *Constructions: A Construction Grammar Approach to Argument Structure*. University of Chicago Press.

2006. *Constructions at Work*. Oxford University Press.

Goldman, K. A. 1990. *Formulaic Analysis of Serbo-Croation Oral Epic Songs: Songs of Avdo Avdic*. New York: Garland.

Gómez-González, M. A. 2001. *The Theme-Topic Interface: Evidence from English*. Amsterdam/Philadelphia: John Benjamins.

González-Cruz, A. I. 2007. 'On the subjectification of adverbial clause connectives: semantic and pragmatic considerations in the development of *while*-clauses'. In U. Lenker and A. Meurman-Solin (eds.) *Connectives in the History of English*, pp. 145–66. Amsterdam: Benjamins.

Good, D. 1995. 'Where does foresight end and hindsight begin?'. In E. Goody (ed.) *Social Intelligence and Interaction*, pp. 139–49. Cambridge University Press.

Goodman, N. 1964. 'A world of individuals'. In H. Putnam and P. Benacerraf (eds.) *Philosophy of Mathematics: Selected Readings*, pp. 197–210. Englewood Cliffs, NJ: Prentice-Hall.

1989. '"Just the Facts, Ma'am!"'. In M. Krausz (ed.) *Relativism: Interpretation and Confrontation*, pp. 80–85. Notre Dame, IN: University of Notre Dame Press.

Goodwin, C. 1981. *Conversational Organisation: Interaction Between Speakers and Hearers*. New York: Academic Press.

Goodwin, C. and Heritage, J. 1990. 'Conversation analysis'. *Annual Review of Anthropology* 19: 283–307.

Goossens, L. 1999. 'Metonymic bridges in modal shifts'. In K.-U. Panther and G. Radden (eds.) *Metonymy in Language and Thought*, pp. 193–210. Amsterdam: John Benjamins.

Gordon, L. 1986. *Maricopa Morphology and Syntax*. Berkeley: University of California Press.

Gosselin, L. 2005. *Temporalité et Modalité*. Brussels: De Boeck.

Grady, J. 1997. 'Theories are buildings revisited'. *Cognitive Linguistics* 8: 267–90.

Grady, J., Oakley, T. and Coulson, S. 1999. 'Blending and metaphor'. In G. Steen and R. Gibbs (eds.) *Metaphor in Cognitive Linguistics*, pp. 101–24. Philadelphia: John Benjamins.

Green, G. M. 1975. 'How to get people to do things with words'. In P. Cole and J. L. Morgan (eds.) *Syntax and Semantics, 3: Speech Acts*, pp. 107–41. New York: Academic Press.

1976. 'Main clause phenomena in subordinate clauses'. *Language* 52: 382–97.

1989. *Pragmatics and Natural Language Understanding*. Hillsdale, NJ: Lawrence Erlbaum.

Green, M. 1998. 'Direct reference and implicature'. *Philosophical Studies* 91: 61–90.

2007. *Self-expression*. Oxford University Press.

Gregoromichelaki, E., Sato, Y., Kempson, R., Gargett, A. and Howes, C. 2009. 'Dialogue modelling and the remit of core grammar'. In H. Bunt, V. Petukhova and S. Wubben (eds.) *Proceedings of Eighth International Conference on Computational Semantics*, IWCS-8, pp. 128–39. Tilburg University.

Grice, H. P. 1957. 'Meaning'. *Philosophical Review* 66: 377–88. Reprinted in H. P. Grice 1989, *Studies in the Way of Words*, pp. 213–23. Cambridge, MA: Harvard University Press.

1961. 'The causal theory of perception'. *Proceedings of the Aristotelian Society*, Supplementary Volume 35: 121–52.

1967. 'Logic and conversation'. William James Lectures, Harvard University. Printed in H. P. Grice, *Studies in the Way of Words*, pp. 1–143. Cambridge, MA: Harvard University Press.

1968. 'Utterer's meaning, sentence meaning and word-meaning'. *Foundations of Language* 4: 225–42.

1969. 'Utterer's meaning and intentions'. *Philosophical Review* 78: 147–77. Reprinted in H. P. Grice, *Studies in the Way of Words*, pp. 86–116. Cambridge, MA: Harvard University Press.

1975. 'Logic and conversation'. In P. Cole and J. L. Morgan (eds.), *Syntax and Semantics 3: Speech Acts*. New York: Academic Press, pp. 41–58. Reprinted in H. P. Grice, *Studies in the Way of Words*, pp. 22–40. Cambridge, MA: Harvard University Press.

1978. 'Further notes on logic and conversation'. In P. Cole (ed.) *Syntax and Semantics 9: Pragmatics*, pp. 113–27. New York: Academic Press. Reprinted in H. P. Grice, *Studies in the Way of Words*, pp. 41–57. Cambridge, MA: Harvard University Press.

1981. 'Presupposition and implicature'. In P. Cole (ed.) *Radical Pragmatics*, pp. 183–99. New York: Academic Press.

1982. 'Meaning revisited'. In N. Smith (ed.) *Mutual Knowledge*, pp. 232–43. London: Academic Press.

1989. *Studies in the Way of Words*. Cambridge, MA: Harvard University Press.

2001. *Aspects of Reason*. Oxford: Clarendon Press.

Groefsema, M. 1995. '*Can, may, must*, and *should*: a relevance theoretic account'. *Journal of Linguistics* 31: 53–97.

Groenendijk, J. 2009. 'Inquisitive semantics: two possibilities for disjunction'. In P. Bosch, D. Gabelaia and J. Lang (eds.) *Seventh International Tbilisi Symposium on Language, Logic, and Computation*, pp. 80–94. Berlin: Springer.

Groenendijk, J. and Stokhof, M. 1984. *Studies in the Semantics of Questions and the Pragmatics of Answers*. University of Amsterdam, PhD thesis.

1991. 'Dynamic predicate logic'. *Linguistics and Philosophy* 14: 39–100.

Grondelaers, S., Speelman, D. and Geeraerts, D. 2007. 'Lexical variation and change'. In D. Geeraerts and H. Cuyckens (eds.) *The Oxford Handbook of Cognitive Linguistics*, pp. 988–1011. Oxford University Press.

Grosz, B. and Ziv, Y. 1998. 'Centering, global focus, and right dislocation'. In M. Walker, A. Joshi and E. Prince (eds.) *Centering Theory in Discourse*, pp. 293–307. Oxford University Press.

Grundy, P. 2008. *Doing Pragmatics*. 3rd edition. London: Hodder.

Guasti, M. T., Chierchia, G., Crain, S., Foppolo, F., Gualmini, A. and Meroni, L. 2005. 'Why children and adults sometimes (but not always) compute implicatures'. *Language and Cognitive Processes* 20: 667–96.

Gudykunst, W. B. and Mody, B. 2002. *Handbook of International and Intercultural Communication*, pp. 259–75. Thousand Oaks, CA: Sage Publications.

Guillaume, A. 2004. *A Grammar of Cavineña, an Amazonian Language of Northern Bolivia*. PhD Thesis, RCLT, La Trobe University.

Gumperz, J. 1982. *Discourse Strategies*. Cambridge University Press.

1992. 'Contextualization and understanding'. In A. Duranti and C. Goodwin (eds.) *Rethinking Context: Language as an Interactive Phenomenon*, pp. 229–52. Cambridge University Press.

1996. 'The linguistic and cultural relativity of inference'. In J. Gumperz and S. C. Levinson (eds.) *Rethinking Linguistic Relativity*, pp. 374–406. Cambridge University Press.

Gundel, J. K. 1974. *The Role of Topic and Comment in Linguistic Theory*. Ph.D. Dissertation, University of Texas at Austin. Distributed by Indiana University Linguistic Club, 1977. Also published by Garland, 1988.

1980. 'Zero NP-anaphora in Russian: a case of topic-prominence'. In *Proceedings from the 16th Meeting of the Chicago Linguistic Society. Parasession on Anaphora*, pp. 139–46. Chicago Linguistic Society.

1985. 'Shared knowledge and topicality'. *Journal of Pragmatics* 9: 83–107.

1988. 'Universals of topic-comment structure'. In M. Hammond, E. Moravczik and J. Wirth (eds.) *Studies in Syntactic Typology*, pp. 209–39. Amsterdam: John Benjamins.

1999a. 'On different kinds of focus'. In P. Bosch and R. van der Sandt (eds.) *Focus: Linguistic, Cognitive and Computational Perspectives*, pp. 293–305. Cambridge University Press.

1999b. 'Topic, focus and the grammar pragmatics interface'. In J. Alexander, N. Han and M. Minnick (eds.) *Proceedings of the 23rd Annual Penn Linguistics Colloquium* (Penn Working Papers in Linguistics, vol. 6.1), pp. 185–200. Philadelphia, PA: Penn Linguistics Department.

2002. '*It*-clefts in English and Norwegian'. In B. Behrens, C. Fabricius Hansen, H. Hasselgard and S. Johansson (eds.) *Information Structure in a Cross-Linguistic Perspective*, pp. 113–28. Amsterdam: Rodopi.

2005. 'Clefts in English and Norwegian: implications for the grammar-pragmatics interface'. In V. Molnar and S. Winkler (eds.) *The Architecture of Focus*, pp. 517–48. Berlin: Mouton de Gruyter.

Gundel, J. K. 2010. 'Reference and accessibility from a Givenness Hierarchy perspective'. *International Review of Pragmatics* 2: 141–7.

Gundel, J. K. and Fretheim, T. 2002. 'Information structure'. In J. Verschueren (ed.) *Handbook of Pragmatics*, pp. 1–17. Amsterdam: John Benjamins. (Also published in F. Brisard, J.-O. Östman and J. Verschueren (eds.) *Grammar, Meaning and Pragmatics*, pp. 146–60. Amsterdam: John Benjamins.)

2004. 'Topic and Focus'. In L. Horn and G. Ward (eds.) *The Handbook of Pragmatics*, pp. 175–96. Oxford: Blackwell.

Gundel, J. K., Hedberg, N. and Zacharski, R. 1993. 'Cognitive status and the form of referring expressions in discourse'. *Language* 69: 274–307.

(forthcoming). 'Underspecification of cognitive status in reference production: some empirical predictions'. *Topics in Cognitive Science*, Special issue: *Production of Referring Expressions*.

Gussenhoven, C. 1984. *On the Grammar and Semantics of Sentence Accents*. Dordrecht: Foris.

2002. 'Intonation and interpretation: phonetics and phonology'. In *Speech Prosody 2002: Proceedings of the First International Conference on Speech Prosody*, pp. 47–57. Aix-en-Provence: ProSig and Université de Provence Laboratoire Parole et Language.

2004. *The Phonology of Tone and Intonation*. Cambridge University Press.

2006. 'Semantics of prosody'. In K. Brown (ed.) *Encyclopedia of Language and Linguistics*, 2nd Edition, vol. xi, pp. 170–72. Oxford: Elsevier.

Gutzmann, D. 2008. *On the Interaction Between Modal Particles and Sentence Mood in German*. Mainz: German Institute, Johannes Gutenberg University.

Haack, S. and Lane, R. (eds.) 2006. *Pragmatism Old and New: Selected Writings*. New York: Prometheus Books.

Hagoort, P., Hald, L., Bastiaansen, M. and Petersson, K. M. 2004. 'Integration of word meaning and world knowledge in language comprehension'. *Science* 304: 438–41.

Haiman, J. 1978. 'Conditionals are topics'. *Language* 54: 512–40.

1980a. 'Dictionaries and encyclopedias'. *Lingua* 50: 329–57.

Hakulinen, A. 2009. 'Conversation types'. In S. D'hondt, J. Östman, and J. Verschueren (eds.) *The Pragmatics of Interaction*, pp. 55–65. Amsterdam: John Benjamins.

Hall, A. 2007. 'Do discourse connectives encode concepts or procedures?'. *Lingua* 117(1): 149–74.

Halliday, M. 1963. *Explorations in the Function of Language*. London: Arnold.

1967a. *Intonation and Grammar in British English*. The Hague: Mouton.

1967b. 'Notes on transitivity and theme in English. Part II'. *Journal of Linguistics* 3: 199–244.

1994. *Introduction to Functional Grammar*. London: Arnold.

Hamblin, C. 1971. 'Mathematical models of dialogue'. *Journal of Philosophy* 37: 130–55.

1987. *Imperatives*. Oxford: Blackwell.

Hamilton, Sir William, of Edinburgh 1860. *Lectures on Logic, Volume I*. Edinburgh: Blackwood.

Hamm, F. and van Lambalgen, M. 2005. *The Proper Treatment of Events*. Oxford: Blackwell.

Han, C.-H. 2000. *The Structure and Interpretation of Imperatives: Mood and Force in Universal Grammar*. New York: Garland.

Hanks, P. (ed.) 1979. *Collins Dictionary of the English Language*. London: Collins.

Hannay, M. 1994. 'The theme zone'. In R. Boogart and J. Noordegraaf (eds.) *Nauwe Betrekkingen*, pp. 107–17. Amsterdam: Neerlandistiek; Münster: Nodus Publikationen.

Hansen, M. B. M. 2008. *Particles at the Semantics/Pragmatics Interface: Synchronic and Diachronic Issues; A Study with Special Reference to the French Phrasal Adverbs*. Oxford: Elsevier.

Hansen, M. B. M. and Walterert, R. 2006. 'GCI theory and language change'. *Acta Linguistica Hafniensia* 38: 235–68.

Happé, F. 1993. 'Communicative competence and theory of mind in autism: a test of Relevance Theory'. *Cognition* 48: 101–19.

1994. *Autism: An Introduction to Psychological Theory*. Cambridge, MA: Harvard University Press.

Hare, B. and Tomasello, M. 2005. 'Human-like social skills in dogs?'. *Trends in Cognitive Sciences* 9: 439–44.

Harland, R. 1993. *Beyond Super-Structuralism*. London: Routledge.

Harnish, R. M. 1976. 'Logical form and implicature'. In T. Bever, J. Katz and T. Langendoen (eds.) *An Integrated Theory of Linguistic Ability*, pp. 313–92. New York: Crowell.

1990. 'Speech acts and intentionality'. In A. Burkhardt (ed.) *Speech Acts, Meaning and Intentions: Critical Approaches to the Philosophy of John R. Searle*, pp. 169–93. Berlin: W. de Gruyter.

2002. 'Are performative utterances declarations?'. In G. Grewendorf and G. Meggle (eds.) *Speech Acts, Mind, and Social Reality: Discussions with John R. Searle*, pp. 41–54. Dordrecht: Kluwer.

2004. 'Performatives as constatives vs. declarations'. In F. Brisard, M. Meeuwis and B. Vandenabeele (eds.) *Seduction, Community, Speech: A Festschrift for Herman Parrt*, pp. 43–74. Amsterdam: John Benjamins.

Haspelmath, M. 1993. *A Grammar of Lezgian*. Berlin/New York: Mouton de Gruyter.

1999. 'Why is grammaticalization irreversible?'. *Linguistics* 37: 1043–68.

2003. 'The geometry of grammatical meaning: semantic maps and cross-linguistic comparison'. In M. Tomasello (ed.) *The New Psychology of Language: Cognitive and Functional Approaches to Language Structure*, vol. II, pp. 211–42. Mahwah, NJ: Lawrence Erlbaum Associates.

2004. 'On directionality in language change with particular reference to grammaticalization'. In O. C. M. Fischer, M. Norde and H. Perridon (eds.)

*Up and Down the Cline: The Nature of Grammaticalization* (Typological Studies in Language 59), pp. 17–44. Amsterdam: John Benjamins.

2005. 'Nominal and verbal conjunction'. In M. Haspelmath, M. S. Dryer, D. Gil and B. Comrie (eds.) *The World Atlas of Language Structures*, pp. 262–5. Oxford University Press.

2007. 'Coordination'. In T. Shopen (ed.) *Language Typology and Linguistic Description*, 2nd edition, pp. 1–51. Cambridge University Press.

2008. 'A frequentist explanation of some universals of reflexive marking'. *Linguistic Discovery* 6: 40–63.

Hasson, U. and Glucksberg, S. 2006. 'Does negation entail affirmation? The case of negated metaphors'. *Journal of Pragmatics* 38: 1015–32.

Haugh, M. 2002. 'The intuitive basis of implicature: Relevance theoretic *implicitness* versus Gricean *implying*'. *Pragmatics* 12(2): 117–34.

2003. 'Anticipated versus inferred politeness'. *Multilingua* 22 (4): 397–413.

2007a. 'The discursive challenge to politeness research: An interactional alternative'. *Journal of Politeness Research* 3: 295–317.

2007b. 'Emic conceptualisations of (im)politeness and face in Japanese: implications for the discursive negotiation of second language learner identities'. *Journal of Pragmatics* 39: 657–80.

2007c. 'The co-constitution of politeness implicature in conversation'. *Journal of Pragmatics* 39: 84–110.

2008a. 'Intention in pragmatics'. *Intercultural Pragmatics* 5: 99–110.

2008b. 'Intention and diverging interpretings of implicature in the "uncovered meat" sermon'. *Intercultural Pragmatics* 5: 201–29.

2008c. 'The place of intention in the interactional achievement of implicature'. In I. Kecskes and J. Mey (eds.) *Intention, Common Ground and the Egocentric Speaker-Hearer*, pp. 45–86. Berlin: Mouton de Gruyter.

2008d. 'Utterance-final conjunctive particles and implicature in Japanese conversation'. *Pragmatics* 18: 425–51.

2009. 'Intention(ality) and the conceptualisation of communication in pragmatics'. *Australian Journal of Linguistics* 29: 91–113.

2010a. 'Jocular mockery, (dis)affiliation and face'. *Journal of Pragmatics* 42: 2106–19.

2010b. 'Co-constructing what is said in interaction'. In T. E. Németh and K. Bibok (eds.) *The Role of Data at the Semantics-Pragmatics Interface*, pp. 349–80. Berlin: Mouton de Gruyter.

2011. 'Humour, face and im/politeness in getting acquainted'. In B. Davies, M. Haugh and A. Merrison (eds.) *Situated Politeness*, pp. 165–84. London: Continuum.

Hauser, M. 1996. *The Evolution of Communication*. Cambridge, MA: MIT Press.

Hauser, M., Chomsky, N. and Fitch, W. T. 2002. 'The faculty of language: what is it, who has it, and how did it evolve?'. *Science* 298: 1569–79.

Haviland, J. 1997. 'Shouts, shrieks and shots: unruly political conversations in indigenous Chiapas'. *Pragmatics* 7: 547–73.

Hawkins, J. 2004. *Efficiency and Complexity in Grammars*. Oxford University Press.

Hawthorne, J. 2004. *Knowledge and Lotteries*. Oxford University Press.

Heath, J. 1984. *Functional Grammar of Nunggubuyu*. Canberra: Australian Institute of Aboriginal Studies.

  1986. 'Syntactic and lexical aspects of nonconfigurationality in Nunggubuyu (Australia)'. *Natural Language and Linguistic Theory* 4: 375–408.

Hedberg, N. 1990. *Discourse Pragmatics and Cleft Sentences in English*. Dissertation, University of Minnesota.

  2000. 'The referential status of clefts'. *Language* 76: 891–920.

Hedberg, N. and Sosa, J. M. 2007. 'The prosody of topic and focus in spontaneous English dialogue'. In C. Lee, M. Gordon and D. Büring (eds.) *Topic and Focus: Cross-linguistic Perspectives on Meaning and Intonation*, pp. 101–20. Dordrecht: Springer.

Heim, I. 1982. *The Semantics of Definite and Indefinite Noun Phrases*. Doctoral dissertation, University of Massachusetts, Amherst.

  1983. 'On the projection problem for presuppositions'. In M. Barlow, D. Flickinger and M. Westcoat (eds.) *Second Annual West Coast Conference on Formal Linguistics*, pp. 114–26. Stanford, CA: Stanford University.

  1992. 'Presupposition projection and the semantics of attitude verbs'. *Journal of Semantics* 9: 183–221.

Heine, B. 1993. *Auxiliaries: Cognitive Forces and Grammaticalization*. New York: Oxford University Press.

  2002. 'On the role of context in grammaticalization'. In I. Wischer and G. Diewald (eds.) *New Reflections on Grammaticalization*, pp. 83–101. Amsterdam: John Benjamins.

Heine, B. and Kuteva, T. 2002. *World Lexicon of Grammaticalization*. Cambridge University Press.

Heine, B., Claudi, U. and Hünnemeyer, F. 1991. *Grammaticalization: A Conceptual Framework*. University of Chicago Press.

Heinemann, T. and Traverso, V. 2009. 'Complaining in interaction'. *Journal of Pragmatics* 41: 2381–4.

Hendriks, P. and de Hoop, H. 2001. 'Optimality theoretic semantics'. *Linguistics and Philosophy* 24: 1–32.

Hengeveld, K. and Mackenzie, L. J. 2008. *Functional Discourse Grammar: A Typologically-based Theory of Language Structure*. Oxford University Press.

Heritage, J. 1984. *Garfinkel and Ethnomethodology*. Cambridge: Polity Press.

  1988. 'Explanations as accounts: a conversation analytic perspective'. In C. Antaki (ed.) *Analysing Everyday Explanation: A Casebook of Methods*, pp. 127–44. London: Sage.

  2005. 'Conversation analysis and institutional talk'. In K. Fitch and R. Sanders (eds.) *Handbook of Language and Social Interaction*, pp. 103–47. Mahwah, NJ: Lawrence Erlbaum.

  2009. 'Conversation analysis as social theory'. In B. Turner (ed.) *New Blackwell Companion to Social Theory*, pp. 300–18. Hoboken, NJ: Wiley-Blackwell.

Heritage, J. and Raymond, G. 2005. 'The terms of agreement: indexing epistemic authority and subordination in talk-in-interaction'. *Social Psychology Quarterly* 68: 15–38.

Heritage, J. and Raymond, G. (forthcoming). 'Navigating epistemic landscapes: acquiescence, agency and resistance in responses to polar questions'. In J. P. de Ruiter (ed.) *Questions: Formal, Functional and Interactional Perspectives*. Cambridge University Press.

Hernández-Flores, N. 1999. 'Politeness ideology in Spanish colloquial conversation: the case of advice'. *Pragmatics* 9(1): 37–49.

Herring, S. 1999. 'Interactional coherence in CMC'. *Journal of Computer-Mediated Communication* 4: http://jcmc.indiana.edu.

2004. 'Computer-mediated analysis. An approach to researching online behaviour'. In S. Barab, R. Kling and J. H. Gray (eds.) *Designing for Virtual Communities in the Service of Learning*, pp. 338–76. Cambridge University Press.

2007. 'A faceted classification scheme for computer-mediated discourse'. *Language@Internet* 4: www.languageatinternet.de.

Hetland, J. 2003. 'Contrast, the fall-rise accent and information focus'. In J. Hetland and V. Molnár (eds.) *Structure of Focus and Grammatical Relations* (Linguistische Arbeiten 477), pp. 1–39. Tübingen: Niemeyer.

Heyd, T. 2008. *Email Hoaxes: Form, Function, Genre Ecology*. Pragmatics and Beyond New Series 174. Amsterdam/Philadelphia: John Benjamins.

Heyes, C. 2010. 'Where do mirror neurons come from?'. *Neuroscience and Biobehavioural Reviews* 34: 575–83.

Hickok, G. 2009. 'Eight problems for the mirror neuron theory of action understanding'. *Journal of Cognitive Neuroscience* 21: 1229–43.

2010. 'The role of mirror neurons in speech and language processing'. *Brain and Language* 112: 1–2.

Hickok, G. and Hauser, M. 2010. '(Mis)understanding mirror neurons'. *Current Biology* 20: 593–4.

Higgins, C. (ed.) 2007. 'A closer look at cultural differences. "Interculturality" in talk-in-interaction'. *Journal of Pragmatics* 17: 9–22.

Hill, B., Ide, S., Ikuta, S., Kawasaki, A. and Ogino, T. 1986. 'Universals of linguistic politeness: quantitative evidence from Japanese and American English'. *Journal of Pragmatics* 10: 347–71.

Hills, D. 1997. 'Aptness and truth in verbal metaphor'. *Philosophical Topics* 25: 117–54.

Hinnenkamp, V. 1995. 'Intercultural communication'. In J. Verschueren, J.-O. Östman and J. Blommaert (eds.) *Handbook of Pragmatics 1995*. Amsterdam/Philadelphia: John Benjamins (loose-leaf publication).

Hirsch, R. 2010. 'Making meaning together: a distributed story of speaking and thinking'. *Language Sciences* 32: 528–35.

Hirschberg, J. 1991. *A Theory of Scalar Implicature*. New York: Garland.

Hirschberg, J. and Ward, G. 1995. 'The interpretation of the high-rise question contour in English'. *Journal of Pragmatics* 24: 407–12.

Hirschfeld, L. and Gelman, S. (eds.) 1994. *Mapping the Mind: Domain Specificity in Cognition and Culture*. Cambridge University Press.

Hoffmann, M. 1987. *Negatio Contrarii: A Study of Latin Litotes*. Assen: Van Gorcum.

Holes, C. 2004. *Modern Arabic: Structures, Functions, Varieties*. Washington: Georgetown University Press.

Holmes, J. 1995. *Women, Men and Politeness*. London: Longman.

Holtgraves, T. 1997. 'Politeness and memory for the wording of remarks'. *Memory and Cognition* 25: 106–16.

Holtgraves, T. and Yang, J.-N. 1990. 'Politeness as universal: cross-cultural perceptions of request strategies and inferences based on their use'. *Journal of Personality and Social Psychology* 59: 719–29.

Hooff, J. van 1972. 'A comparative approach to the phylogeny of laughter and smiling'. In R. Hinde (ed.) *Non-verbal Communication*, pp. 209–38. Cambridge University Press.

Hooper, J. B. and Thompson, S. A. 1973. 'On the applicability of root transformations'. *Linguistic Inquiry* 4: 465–97.

Hopper, P. J. 1991. 'On some principles of grammaticization'. In E. Traugott and B. Heine (eds.) *Approaches to Grammaticalization*, vol. I, pp. 17–35. Amsterdam: John Benjamins.

Hopper, P. J. and Thompson, S. A. 1980. 'Transitivity in grammar and discourse'. *Language* 56: 251–99.

Hopper, P. J. and Traugott, E. C. 2003. *Grammaticalization*. 2nd edition. Cambridge University Press.

Horn, L. 1972. *On the Semantic Properties of Logical Operators in English*. UCLA dissertation, distributed by Indiana University Linguistics Club, 1976.

 1973. 'Greek Grice: a brief survey of proto-conversational rules in the history of logic'. *Chicago Linguistic Society* 9: 205–14.

 1978. 'Some aspects of negation'. In J. H. Greenberg (ed.) *Universals of Human Language*, Vol. IV, pp. 127–210. Stanford, CA: Stanford University Press.

 1984a. 'Ambiguity, parsimony, and the London school of parsimony'. *Proceedings of the Annual Meeting of the North East Linguistic Society* 14: 108–31.

 1984b. 'Toward a new taxonomy for pragmatic inference: Q-based and R-based implicature'. In D. Schiffrin (ed.) *Meaning, Form, and Use in Context: Linguistic Applications*, pp. 11–42. Washington, DC: Georgetown University Press.

 1985. 'Metalinguistic negation and pragmatic ambiguity'. *Language* 61: 121–74.

 1988. 'Pragmatic theory'. In F. Newmeyer (ed.) *Linguistics: The Cambridge Survey*, vol. I, pp. 113–45. Cambridge University Press.

 1989. *A Natural History of Negation*. University of Chicago Press.

 1990. 'Hamburgers and truth: why Gricean inference is Gricean'. *BLS* 16: 454–71.

 1991. '*Duplex negatio affirmat . . .*: The economy of double negation'. *CLS* 27(2): 80–106.

1992a. 'Pragmatics, implicature, and presupposition'. In W. Bright (ed.) *International Encyclopaedia of Linguistics*, vol. III, pp. 260–6. New York: Oxford University Press.

1992b. 'The said and the unsaid'. In *SALT II: Proceedings of the Second Conference on Semantics and Linguistic Theory*, pp. 163–202. Columbus, OH: Ohio State University Linguistics Department.

2000. 'From IF to IFF: conditional perfection as pragmatic strengthening'. *Journal of Pragmatics* 32: 289–326.

2002. 'Assertoric inertia and NPI licensing'. *CLS* 38(2): 55–82. Chicago Linguistics Society.

2004. 'Implicature'. In L. Horn and G. Ward (eds.) *The Handbook of Pragmatics*, pp. 3–28. Oxford: Blackwell.

2005. 'Current issues in neo-Gricean pragmatics'. *Intercultural Pragmatics* 2: 191–204.

2006. 'The border wars: a neo-Gricean perspective'. In K. Turner and K. von Heusinger (eds.) *Where Semantics Meets Pragmatics*, pp. 21–48. Oxford: Elsevier.

2007a. 'Neo-Gricean pragmatics: a Manichaean manifesto'. In N. Burton-Roberts (ed.) *Pragmatics*, pp. 158–83. Basingstoke: Palgrave Macmillan.

2007b. 'Toward a Fregean pragmatics: *Voraussetzung, Nebengedanke, Andeutung*'. In I. Kecskes and L. Horn (eds.) *Explorations in Pragmatics: Linguistic, Cognitive, and Intercultural Aspects*, pp. 39–69. Berlin: Mouton de Gruyter.

2008. '"I love me some him": the landscape of non-argument datives'. In O. Bonami and P. Cabredo Hofherr (eds.) *Empirical Issues in Syntax and Semantics* 7, pp. 169–92. Downloadable at www.cssp.cnrs.fr/eiss7.

2009a. '*Only* XL: the assertoric asymmetry of exponibles'. Paper presented at Semantics and Linguistics Theory Conference, Ohio State University, Columbus, OH. May 2009.

2009b. 'WJ-40: Implicature, truth, and meaning'. *International Review of Pragmatics* 1: 3–34.

Horn, L. and Ward, G. (eds.) 2004. *The Handbook of Pragmatics*. Oxford: Blackwell.

Horwich, P. 2002. 'Deflating compositionality'. In E. Borg (ed.) *Meaning and Representation*, pp. 77–93. Oxford: Blackwell.

House, J. 1990. 'Intonation structures and pragmatic interpretation'. In S. Ramsaran (ed.) *Studies in the Pronunciation of English*, pp. 38–57. London: Routledge.

2000. 'Understanding misunderstanding: A pragmatic-discourse approach to analysing mismanaged rapport in talk across cultures'. In H. Spencer-Oatey (ed.) *Culturally Speaking: Managing Rapport Through Talk Across Cultures*, pp. 146–64. London: Continuum.

2003. 'Misunderstanding in intercultural university encounters'. In J. House, G. Kasper and S. Ross (eds.) *Misunderstanding in Social Life, Discourse Approaches to Problematic Talk*, pp. 22–56. London: Longman.

2006. 'Constructing a context with intonation'. *Journal of Pragmatics* 38: 1542–58.

2007. 'The role of prosody in constraining context selection: a procedural approach'. *Nouveaux cahiers de linguistique française* 28: 369–83.

Huang, Y. 2000. *Anaphora: A Cross-linguistic Study*. Oxford University Press.

2007. *Pragmatics*. Oxford University Press.

2009. 'Neo-Gricean pragmatics and the lexicon'. *International Review of Pragmatics* 1: 118–53.

2010. 'Pragmatics'. In L. Cummings (ed.) *The Pragmatics Encyclopedia*, pp. 341–5. London: Routledge.

Hugly, P. and Sayward, C. 1979. 'A problem about conversational implicature'. *Linguistics and Philosophy* 3: 19–25.

Hungerland, I. 1960. 'Contextual implication'. *Inquiry* 3: 211–58.

Hussein, M. 2008. 'The truth-conditional/non-truth-conditional and conceptual/procedural distinctions revisited'. Newcastle Working Papers in Linguistics 14. http://nwplinguistics.ncl.ac.uk/5.Miri_Hussein.pdf.

Husserl, E. 1900–1901. *Logische Untersuchungen*, vol. II. Halle: Max Niemeyer. Trans. as *Logical Investigations* by J. N. Findlay. London: Routledge and Kegan Paul, 1970.

1913. *Ideen zu einer reinen Phänomenologie und phänomenologischen Philosophie*. Book 1: *Allgemeine Einfürung in die reine Phänomenologie*. Halle: Max Niemeyer. Trans. as *Ideas: General Introduction to Pure Phenomenology* by W. R. B. Gibson. London: George Allen and Unwin, 1931. Reprinted 1958.

Hymes, D. 1972. 'On communicative competence'. In J. Pride and J. Holmes (eds.) *Sociolinguistics*, pp. 269–93. Harmondsworth: Penguin.

Iatridou, S. 2009. 'De modo imperativo'. Lecture notes for a course on the syntax and semantics of imperatives at Ealing6, ENS, Paris.

Ide, S. 1989. 'Formal forms and discernment: two neglected aspects of universals of linguistic politeness'. *Multilingua* 8: 223–48.

Imai, K. 1998. 'Intonation and relevance'. In R. Carston and S. Uchida (eds.) *Relevance Theory: Applications and Implications*, pp. 69–86. Amsterdam: John Benjamins.

Israel, M., Harding, J. and Tobin, V. 2004. 'On simile'. In M. Achard and S. Kemmer (eds.) *Language, Culture, and Mind*, pp. 123–35. Stanford, CA: CSLI Publications.

Iten, C. 2000. 'The relevance of Argumentation Theory'. *Lingua* 110: 665–701.

2005. *Linguistic Meaning, Truth Conditions and Relevance*. Houndmills: Palgrave Macmillan.

Ivanko, S. L. and Pexman, P. M. 2003. 'Context incongruity and irony processing'. *Discourse Processes* 35: 241–79.

Izvorski, R. 1997. 'The present perfect as an epistemic modal'. In A. Lawson (ed.) *Semantics and Linguistic Theory* VII, pp. 222–39.

Jackendoff, R. S. 1972. *Semantic Interpretation in Generative Grammar*. Cambridge, MA: MIT Press.

1985. 'Multiple subcategorization and the Θ-criterion: the case of *climb*'. *Natural Language and Linguistic Theory* 3: 271–95.

1995a. *Semantics and Cognition*. Cambridge, MA: MIT Press.

1995b. 'The boundaries of the lexicon'. In M. Everaert, E.-J. van der Linden, A. Schenk and R. Schreuder (eds.) *Idioms: Structural and Psychological Perspectives*, pp. 133–65. Hillsdale, NJ: Erlbaum.

1997. *The Architecture of the Language Faculty*. Cambridge, MA: MIT Press.

1999. 'What is a concept that a person may grasp it?'. In E. Margolis and S. Laurence (eds.) *Concepts: Core Readings*, pp. 305–33. Cambridge, MA: MIT Press.

2003. *Foundations of Language*. Oxford University Press.

Jackendoff, R. S. and Aaron, D. 1991. 'Review of *More than Cool Reason: A Field Guide to Poetic Metaphor* by George Lakoff and Mark Turner'. *Language* 67: 320–38.

Jacob, P. 2003. 'Intentionality'. In E. N. Zalta (ed.) *Stanford Encyclopedia of Philosophy*. http://plato.stanford.edu/contents.html.

Jacobs, A. and Jucker, A. H. 1995. 'The historical perspective in pragmatics'. In A. H. Jucker (ed.) *Historical Pragmatics*, pp. 3–33. Berlin: de Gruyter.

Jäger, G. 1996. 'Only updates. On the dynamics of the focus particle "only"'. In P. Dekker and M. Stokhof (eds.) *Proceedings of the 10th Amsterdam Colloquium*, pp. 387–406. Amsterdam: John Benjamins.

Jary, M. 1998. 'Relevance theory and the communication of politeness'. *Journal of Pragmatics* 30: 1–19.

Jaszczolt, K. M. 1999. *Discourse, Beliefs, and Intentions: Semantic Defaults and Propositional Attitude Ascription*. Oxford: Elsevier Science.

2000. 'The default-based context-dependence of belief reports'. In K. M. Jaszczolt (ed.) *The Pragmatics of Propositional Attitude Reports*, pp. 169–85. Oxford: Elsevier Science.

2002. *Semantics and Pragmatics: Meaning in Language and Discourse*. London: Longman.

2005. *Default Semantics: Foundations of a Compositional Theory of Acts of Communication*. Oxford University Press.

2008. 'Psychological explanations in Gricean pragmatics and Frege's legacy'. In I. Kecskes and J. Mey (eds.) *Intentions, Common Ground, and the Egocentric Speaker-Hearer*, pp. 9–45. Berlin: Mouton de Gruyter.

2009. *Representing Time: An Essay on Temporality as Modality*. Oxford University Press.

2010a. 'Semantics-pragmatics interface'. In L. Cummings (ed.) *The Pragmatics Encyclopedia*, pp. 458–62. London: Routledge.

2010b. 'Propositional attitudes'. In L. Cummings (ed.) *The Pragmatics Encyclopedia*, pp. 388–9. London: Routledge.

2010c. 'Default Semantics'. In B. Heine and H. Narrog (eds.) *The Oxford Handbook of Linguistic Analysis*, pp. 193–221. Oxford University Press.

2010d. 'Defaults in semantics and pragmatics'. In E. N. Zalta (ed.) *Stanford Encyclopedia of Philosophy*. http://plato.stanford.edu/entries/defaults-semantics-pragmatics/ (first published online 30 June 2006).

Jefferson, G. 1978. 'Sequential aspects of storytelling in conversation'. In J. N. Schenkein (ed.) *Studies in the Organization of Conversational Interaction*, pp. 219–48. New York: Academic Press.

　1979. 'A technique for inviting laughter and its subsequent acceptance-declination'. In G. Psathas (ed.) *Everyday Language: Studies in Ethnomethodology*, pp. 79–95. New York: Irvington.

　1986. 'Notes on "latency" in overlap onset'. *Human Studies* 9: 153–83.

　2004. 'Glossary of transcript symbols with an introduction'. In G. Lerner (ed.) *Conversation Analysis: Studies from the First Generation*, pp. 13–23. Amsterdam: John Benjamins.

Jennings, R. 1994. *The Genealogy of Disjunction*. Oxford University Press.

Jennings, R. and Hartline, A. 2009. 'Disjunction'. In E. N. Zalta (ed.) *The Stanford Encyclopedia of Philosophy*. http://plato.stanford.edu/archives/spr2009/entries/disjunction/.

Jensen, M. S. 1980. *The Homeric Question and the Oral-Formulaic Theory*. Copenhagen: Museum Tusculanum Press.

Jespersen, O. 1924. *The Philosophy of Grammar*. London: George Allan and Unwin.

Ji, S. 2002. 'Identifying episode transitions'. *Journal of Pragmatics* 34: 1257–72.

Johansson, M. 2002. *Clefts in English and Swedish: A Contrastive Study of It-Clefts and Wh-Clefts in Original Texts and Translations*. PhD dissertation. Lund University.

Johnson-Laird, P. 1983. *Mental Models*. Cambridge, MA: Harvard University Press.

Jucker, A. H. (ed.) 1995. *Historical Pragmatics: Pragmatic Developments in the History of English*. Pragmatics and Beyond New Series 35. Amsterdam/Philadelphia: John Benjamins.

　2009. 'Speech act research between armchair, field and laboratory: the case of compliments'. *Journal of Pragmatics* 41: 1611–35.

　(forthcoming). 'Pragmatics and discourse'. In L. J. Brinton (ed.) *Historical Linguistics of English*, vol. II. Berlin: Mouton de Gruyter.

Jucker, A. H. and Taavitsainen, I. (eds.) 2010. *Handbook of Historical Pragmatics*: Handbooks of Pragmatics 8. Berlin: Mouton de Gruyter.

Jucker, A. H. and Ziv, Y. (eds.) 1998. *Discourse Markers*. Amsterdam: Benjamins.

Jucker, A. H., Schreier, D. and Hundt, M. (eds.) 2009. 'Corpora: pragmatics and discourse'. In *Papers from the 29th International Conference on English Language Research on Computerized Corpora (ICAME 29), Ascona, Switzerland* (Language and Computers: Studies in Practical Linguistics 68), pp. 14–18. Amsterdam: Rodopi.

Kalish, D., Montague, R. and Mar, G. 1980. *Logic: Techniques of Formal Reasoning*. New York: Harcourt, Brace, Jovanovich.

Kamp, H. 1978. 'Semantics versus pragmatics'. In F. Guenthner and S. Schmidt (eds.) *Formal Semantics and Pragmatics for Natural Languages*, pp. 255–87. Dordrecht: Foris.

1981. 'A theory of truth and semantic representation'. In T. Janssen and M. Stokhof (eds.) *Truth, Interpretation, and Information*, pp. 1–34. Dordrecht: Foris.

1990. 'Prolegomena to a structural account of belief and other attitudes'. In C. A. Anderson and J. Owens (eds.) *Propositional Attitudes: The Role of Content in Logic, Language, and Mind*, pp. 27–90. Stanford, CA: CSLI Publications.

1996. 'Some elements of a DRT-based theory of the representation of mental states and verbal communication'. Unpublished ms.

2001. 'The importance of presupposition'. In C. Rohrer and A. Rossdeutscher (eds.) *Linguistic Form and its Justification: Selected papers from the SFB 340*, 207–254. Stanford, CA: CSLI Publications.

2003. 'Temporal relations inside and outside attitudinal contexts'. Paper presented at the workshop 'Where Semantics Meets Pragmatics', LSA Summer School, University of Michigan, July 2003.

Kamp, H. and Reyle, U. 1993. *From Discourse to Logic: Introduction to Modeltheoretic Semantics of Natural Language, Formal Logic and Discourse Representation Theory*. Dordrecht: Kluwer.

Kamp, H. and Rohrer, C. 1983. 'Tense in texts'. In R. Bauerle, C. Schwarze and A. von Stechow (eds.) *Meaning, Use, and Interpretation of Language*, pp. 250–69. Berlin/New York: Mouton de Gruyter.

Kamp, H. and Rossdeutscher, A. 1994. 'DRS-construction and lexically driven inference'. *Theoretical Linguistics* 20: 165–235.

Kaplan, D. 1969. 'Quantifying in'. In D. Davidson and G. Harman (eds.) *Words and Objections: Essays on the Work of W. V. Quine*, pp. 206–42. Dordrecht: D. Reidel.

1978. 'Dthat'. In P. Cole (ed.) *Syntax and Semantics 9: Pragmatics*, pp. 221–43. New York: Academic Press.

1989a. 'Demonstratives'. In J. Almog, J. Perry and H. K. Wettstein (eds.) *Themes from Kaplan*, pp. 481–563. Oxford University Press.

1989b. *Themes from Kaplan*, ed. J. Almog, J. Perry and H. K. Wettstein. Oxford University Press.

1989c. 'Afterthoughts'. In J. Almog, J. Perry and H. K. Wettstein (eds.) *Themes from Kaplan*, pp. 565–614. Oxford University Press.

1990. 'Words'. *Aristotelian Society, Supplementary Volume* 64: 93–119.

1999. 'The meaning of *ouch* and *oops*: Explorations in the theory of *Meaning as Use*'. Unpublished ms. UCLA.

2004. 'The meaning of "ouch" and "oops"'. Unpublished ms.

2005. 'Reading "On Denoting" on its centenary'. *Mind* 114: 933–1004.

Karttunen, L. 1973. 'Presuppositions of compound sentences'. *Linguistic Inquiry* 4: 167–93.

1974. 'Presuppositions and linguistic context'. *Theoretical Linguistics* 1: 181–94.

1976. 'Discourse referents'. In J. McCawley (ed.) *Syntax and Semantics 2: Notes From the Linguistic Underground*, pp. 363–85. New York: Academic Press.

Karttunen, L. and Peters, S. 1979. 'Conventional implicature'. In C.-K. Oh and D. A. Dinneen (eds.) *Syntax and Semantics 11: Presupposition*, pp. 1–56. New York: Academic Press.

Kasper, G. 1990. 'Linguistic politeness: current research issues'. *Journal of Pragmatics* 14: 193–218.

  1996. 'The development of pragmatic competence'. In E. Kellerman, B. Weltens and T. Bongaerts (eds.) *EUROSLA 6: A Selection of Papers* 55(2), pp. 103–20. Amsterdam: VU Uitgeverij.

  1998. 'Interlanguage pragmatics'. In H. Byrnes (ed.) *Learning Foreign and Second Languages: Perspectives in Research and Scholarship*, pp. 183–208. New York: The Modern Language Association of America.

  2004. 'Speech acts in (inter)action: repeated question'. *Intercultural Pragmatics* 1: 125–35.

  2006. 'Speech acts in interaction: towards discursive pragmatics'. In K. Bardovi-Harlig, C. Felix-Brasdefer and A. S. Omar (eds.) *Pragmatics and Language Learning*, Vol. xi, pp. 281–314. Honolulu: National Foreign Language Resource Center, University of Hawai'i at Manoa.

Kasper, G. and Blum-Kulka, S. 1993. 'Interlanguage pragmatics: An introduction'. In G. Kasper and S. Blum-Kulka (eds.) *Interlanguage Pragmatics*, pp. 3–17. Oxford University Press.

Kasper, G. and Rose, K. R. 2001. 'Pragmatics in language teaching'. In K. Rose and G. Kasper (eds.) *Pragmatics in Language Teaching*, pp. 1–11. Cambridge University Press.

Katsos, N. 2007. *Experimental Investigations on the Effects of Structure and Context on the Generation of Scalar Implicatures*. PhD thesis, University of Cambridge.

  2008. 'The semantics/pragmatics interface from an experimental perspective: the case of scalar implicature'. *Synthese* 165: 358–401.

Katsos, N. and Bishop, D. V. M. 2011. 'Pragmatic tolerance: implications for the acquisition of informativeness and implicature'. *Cognition* 120: 67–81.

Katsos, N. and Smith, N. 2010. 'Pragmatic tolerance and speaker-comprehender asymmetries'. In K. Franich, K. M. Iserman and L. L. Keil (eds.) *Proceedings of the 34th Annual Boston Conference in Language Development*, pp. 221–32. Somerville, MA: Cascadilla Press.

Katsos, N., Breheny, R. and Williams, J. 2005. 'The interaction of structural and contextual constraints during the on-line generation of scalar inferences'. In B. Bara, L. Barsalou and M. Bucciarelli (eds.) *Proceedings of the 27th Annual Conference of the Cognitive Science Society*, pp. 1108–13. Mahwah, NJ: Erlbaum.

Katzir, R. 2007. 'Structurally defined alternatives'. *Linguistics and Philosophy* 30: 669–90.

Kaup, B. 2001. 'Negation and its impact on the accessibility of text information'. *Memory and Cognition* 29: 960–7.

Kaup, B. and Zwaan, R. A. 2003. 'Effects of negation and situational presence on the accessibility of text information'. *Journal of Experimental Psychology (Learning, Memory, and Cognition)* 29(3): 436–9.

Kaup, B., Lüdtke, J. and Zwaan, R. A. 2006. 'Processing negated sentences with contradictory predicates: Is a door that is not open mentally closed?'. *Journal of Pragmatics* 38: 1033–50.

Kaup, B., Yaxley, R. H., Madden, C. J., Zwaan, R. A. and Lüdtke, J. 2007. 'Experiential simulations of negated text information'. *Quarterly Journal of Experimental Psychology* 60: 976–90.

Kecskes, I. 2002. *Situation-Bound Utterances in L1 and L2*. Berlin/New York: Mouton de Gruyter.

2004. 'Lexical merging, conceptual blending, cultural crossing'. *Intercultural Pragmatics* 1: 1–26.

2006. 'Pragmatics aspects of multilingualism'. In K. Brown (ed.) *Encyclopedia of Language and Linguistics*, 2nd edition. Oxford: Elsevier Science.

2008. 'Dueling context: a dynamic model of meaning'. *Journal of Pragmatics* 40: 385–406.

2010a. 'The paradox of communication: socio-cognitive approach to pragmatics'. *Pragmatics and Society* 1: 57–82.

2010b. 'Dual and multilanguage systems'. *International Journal of Multilingualism*. 7: 1–19.

2011. 'Intercultural pragmatics'. In D. Archer and P. Grundy (eds.) *Pragmatic Reader*, pp. 371–87. London: Routledge.

Kecskes, I. and Mey, J. 2008. 'Introduction'. In I. Kecskes and J. Mey (eds.) *Intention, Common Ground and the Egocentric Speaker-Hearer*, pp. 1–8. Berlin/New York: Mouton de Gruyter.

Kecskes, I. and Zhang, F. 2009. 'Activating, seeking and creating common ground: a socio-cognitive approach'. *Pragmatics and Cognition* 17: 331–55.

Keenan, E. L. 2003. 'A historical explanation of some binding theoretic facts in English'. In J. Moore and M. Polinsky (eds.) *The Nature of Explanation in Linguistic Theory*, pp. 212–56. Stanford, CA: CSLI Publications.

Keenan, E. L. and Comrie, B. 1977. 'Noun phrase accessibility and universal grammar'. *Linguistic Inquiry* 8: 63–99.

Keller, R. 1994. *On Language Change: The Invisible Hand in Language*. Trans. B. Nerlich. London: Routledge (first published in German in 1990).

Kemmer, S. 1993. *The Middle Voice*. Typological Studies in Language 23. Amsterdam: John Benjamins.

Kempson, R. 1975. *Presupposition and the Delimitation of Semantics*. Cambridge University Press.

1986. 'Ambiguity and the semantics–pragmatics distinction'. In C. Travis (ed.) *Meaning and Interpretation*, pp. 77–104. Oxford: Blackwell.

1988. 'Grammar and conversational principles'. In F. J. Newmeyer and R. H. Robins (eds.) *Linguistics: The Cambridge Survey*, vol. ii: *Linguistic Theory: Extensions and Implications*, pp. 139–63. Cambridge University Press.

Kempson, R., Meyer-Viol, W. and Gabbay, D. 2001. *Dynamic Syntax: The Flow of Language Understanding.* Oxford: Blackwell.

Kendon, A. 1988. 'How gestures can become like words?'. In F. Poyotas (ed.) *Cross-cultural Perspectives in Nonverbal Communication*, pp. 131–41. Toronto: Hogrefe.

  1992. 'The negotiation of context in face-to-face interaction'. In A. Duranti and C. Goodwin (eds.) *Rethinking Context: Language as an Interactive Phenomenon.* Cambridge University Press.

  2004. *Gesture: Visible Action as Utterance.* Cambridge University Press.

Kenny, A. J. 1966. 'Practical inference'. *Analysis* 26: 65–75.

Kerbrat-Orecchioni, C. 1997. 'A multilevel approach in the study of talk in interaction'. *Pragmatics* 7: 1–20.

Kernfeld, B. 1994. *The New Grove Dictionary of Jazz.* London: Macmillan.

Keysar, B. 1994a. 'Discourse context effects: metaphorical and literal interpretations'. *Discourse Processes* 18: 247–69.

  1994b. 'The illusory transparancy of intention: linguistic perspective taking in text'. *Cognitive Psychology* 26: 165–208.

  2000. 'The illusory transparency of intention: does June understand what Mark means because he means it?'. *Discourse Processes* 29: 161–72.

  2007. 'Communication and miscommunication: the role of egocentric processes'. *Intercultural Pragmatics* 4: 71–84.

  2008. 'Egocentric processes in communication and miscommunication'. In I. Kecskes and J. Mey (eds.) *Intention, Common Ground and the Egocentric Speaker-Hearer*, pp. 277–96. Berlin: Mouton de Gruyter.

Keysar, B. and Henly, A. 2002. 'Speakers' overestimation of their effectiveness'. *Psychological Sciences* 13: 207–12.

Kibrik, A. A. 2004. 'Coordination in Upper Kuskokwim Athabaskan'. In M. Haspelmath (ed.) *Coordinating Constructions*, pp. 537–54. Amsterdam/Philadelphia: John Benjamins.

Kidwell, M. and Zimmerman, D. 2006. '"Observability" in the interactions of very young children'. *Communication Monographs* 73: 1–28.

King, J. and Stanley, J. 2005. 'Semantics, pragmatics, and the role of semantic content'. In Z. Szabó (ed.) *Semantics Versus Pragmatics*, pp. 111–64. Oxford: Clarendon Press.

Kiparsky, P. 1968. 'Linguistic universals and linguistic change'. In E. Bach and R. T. Harms (eds.) *Universals in Linguistic Theory*, pp. 171–202. New York: Holt, Rinehart and Winston.

Kirk, L. 2010. 'Searle, J.'. In L. Cummings (ed.) *The Pragmatics Encyclopedia*, pp. 416–19. London: Routledge.

Kissine, M. 2008a. 'Assertoric commitments'. *Belgian Journal of Linguistics* 22: 155–78.

  2008b. 'Locutionary, illocutionary, perlocutionary'. *Language and Linguistics Compass* 2: 1189–202.

  2009. 'Illocutionary forces and what is said'. *Mind and Language* 24: 122–38.

Kissine, M. 2001. 'Misleading appearances: Searle, assertion, and meaning'. *Erkenntnis* 74(1): 115–29.

(forthcoming). 'Speech act classifications'. In K. Turner and M. Sbisà (eds.) *Speech Actions*. Berlin: Mouton de Gruyter.

Klein, W. 1992. 'The present perfect puzzle'. *Language* 68: 525–52.

2009. 'How time is encoded'. In W. Klein and P. Li (eds.) *The Expression of Time*, pp. 39–81. Berlin/New York: Mouton de Gruyter.

Klein, W. and von Stutterheim, C. 1987. 'Quaestio und referentielle Bewegung in Erzählungen'. *Linguistische Berichte* 109: 163–83.

Knobe, J. 2003. 'Intention action and side effects in ordinary language'. *Analysis* 63: 190–4.

Knobe, J. and Burra, A. 2006. 'The folk concepts of intention and intentional action: a cross-cultural study'. *Journal of Cognition and Culture* 6: 113–32.

Koch, P. 2004. 'Metonymy between pragmatics, reference, and diachrony'. *Metaphorik.de*. www.metaphorik.de/07/preface.htm.

Kölbel, M. 2003. 'Faultless disagreement'. *Proceedings of the Aristotelian Society* 104: 53–73.

2008. 'Motivations for relativism'. In M. Garcia-Carpintero and M. Kölbel (eds.) *Relative Truth*, pp. 1–40. Oxford University Press.

König, E. 1991. *The Meaning of Focus Particles: A Comparative Perspective*. London: Routledge.

König, E. and Siemund, P. 2000. 'Intensifiers and reflexives: a typological perspective'. In Z. Frajzyngier and T. S. Curl (eds.) *Reflexives: Forms and Functions*, pp. 41–74. Amsterdam: John Benjamins.

2007. 'Speech act distinctions in grammar'. In T. Shopen (ed.) *Language Typology and Syntactic Description*, vol. I: *Clause Structure*, pp. 276–324. 2nd edition. Cambridge University Press.

Koole, T. and Ten Thije, J. 1994. *The Construction of Intercultural Discourse: Team Discussions of Educational Advisers*. Amsterdam/Atlanta: Rodopi.

Koralus, P. 2010. *Semantics in Philosophy and Cognitive Neuroscience: The Open Instruction Theory*. Ph.D. thesis, Department of Philosophy, Princeton University.

Krahmer, E. 1998. *Presupposition and Anaphora*. Stanford, CA: CSLI Publications.

Krahmer, E. and van Deemter, K. 1998. 'On the interpretation of anaphoric noun phrases: towards a full understanding of partial matches'. *Journal of Semantics* 15: 355–92.

Kriempardis, E. 2009. 'Shared content as speaker meaning'. *Lodz Papers in Pragmatics* 5: 161–90.

Krifka, M. 2005. 'Association with focus phrases'. In V. Molnár and S. Winkler (eds.) *The Architecture of Focus*, pp. 105–36. Berlin: Mouton de Gruyter.

Kripke, S. 1972. *Naming and Necessity*. Cambridge, MA: Harvard University Press.

1977. 'Speaker's reference and semantic reference'. *Midwest Studies in Philosophy* 2: 255–76. Reprinted in P. Ludlow (ed.) *Readings in the Philosophy of Language*, pp. 383–414. Cambridge, MA: MIT Press.

1979. 'A puzzle about belief'. In A. Margalit (ed.) *Meaning and Use*, pp. 875–920. Dordrecht: D. Reidel. Reprinted in P. Ludlow (ed.) *Readings in the Philosophy of Language*, pp. 239–83. Cambridge, MA: MIT Press.

Krippendorff, K. 1970. 'On generating data in communication research'. *Journal of Communication* 20: 241–69.

2009. *On Communicating: Otherness, Meaning, and Information*. London: Routledge.

Krzeszowski, T. P. 1989. 'Towards a typology of contrastive studies'. In W. Oleksy (ed.) *Contrastive Pragmatics* (Pragmatics and Beyond New Series 3), pp. 55–72. Amsterdam: John Benjamins.

Kuhn, S. T. 1988. 'Tense and time'. In D. Gabbay and F. Guenther (eds.) *Handbook of Philosophical Logic* IV, pp. 513–52. Dordrecht: Kluwer.

Kühner, R. and Stegmann, C. 1914. *Ausführliche Grammatik der lateinischen Sprache*. Part 2: *Satzlehre*, vol. II. Hannover: Hahn. (Reprinted 1992).

Kühnlein, P., Benz, A. and Sidner, C. 2010. *Constraints in Discourse 2*. Amsterdam: Benjamins.

Kuipers, K. 2009. *Formulaic Genres*. Basingstoke: Palgrave Macmillan.

Kukla, R. and Lance, M. 2009. *'Yo!' and 'Lo!': The Pragmatic Topography of the Space of Reasons*. Cambridge, MA: Harvard University Press.

Kumon-Nakamura, S., Glucksberg, S. and Brown, M., 1995. 'How about another piece of pie: the allusional pretense theory of discourse irony'. *Journal of Experimental Psychology (General)* 124: 3–21. Reprinted in R. Gibbs and H. Colston (eds.) *Irony in Language and Thought: A Cognitive Science Reader*, pp. 57–95. Hillsdale, NJ: Lawrence Erlbaum.

Kuno, S. 1972. 'Functional sentence perspective: a case study from Japanese and English'. *Linguistic Inquiry* 3: 269–320.

1976. 'Subject, theme, and the speaker's empathy: a reexamination of relativization phenomena'. In C. N. Li (ed.) *Subject and Topic*, pp. 419–44. New York: Academic Press.

1987. *Functional Syntax: Anaphora, Discourse, and Empathy*. Chicago University Press.

Kuppevelt, J. van 1995. 'Discourse structure, topicality and questioning'. *Journal of Linguistics* 31: 109–47.

Kuroda, S. Y. 1965. *Generative Grammatical Studies in the Japanese Language*. Dissertation, MIT.

1972. 'The categorical and the thetic judgement: evidence from Japanese syntax'. *Foundations of Language* 9: 153–85.

1977. 'Description of presuppositional phenomena from a non-presuppositionist point of view'. *Lingvisticae Investigationes* 1: 63–162.

Kush, D. 2010. 'The future and epistemic modality in Hindi'. Presentation at LSA 2010, Baltimore, January 2010. www.ling.umd.edu/~kush/Kush_LSA_2010.pdf.

Kuteva, T. 2001. *Auxiliation: An Enquiry into the Nature of Grammaticalization*. Oxford University Press.

Kuzar, R. 2009. 'Sentence patterns in English and Hebrew'. Unpublished ms. Haifa University.

Kytö, M. and Romaine, S. 2005. '*We had like to have been killed by thunder & lightning*: the semantic and pragmatic history of a construction that like to disappeared'. *Journal of Historical Pragmatics* 6: 1–35.

Labov, W. 1972. *Sociolinguistic Patterns*. Philadelphia: University of Pennsylvania Press. Reprinted Oxford: Blackwell, 1978.

   1978. 'Denotational structure'. In D. Farkas, W. M. Jacobsen and K. W. Todrys (eds.) *Papers from the Parasession on the Lexicon*, pp. 220–60. Chicago Linguistics Society.

Lachenicht, L. 1980. 'Aggravating language: a study of abusive and insulting language'. *International Journal of Human Communication* 13: 607–88.

Ladd, R. 1978. *The Structure of Intonational Meaning*. London: Indiana University Press.

   1996. *Intonational Phonology*. Cambridge University Press.

Lakoff, G. 1987. *Women, Fire, and Dangerous Things: What Categories Reveal About the Mind*. University of Chicago Press.

   1993. 'The contemporary theory of metaphor'. In A. Ortony (ed.) *Metaphor and Thought*, pp. 202–51. 2nd edition. Cambridge University Press.

   2008. 'The neural theory of metaphor'. In R. Gibbs (ed.) *The Cambridge Handbook of Metaphor and Thought*, pp. 17–38. Cambridge University Press.

Lakoff, G. and Johnson, M. 1980. *Metaphors We Live By*. University of Chicago Press.

Lakoff, R. 1971. 'If's, And's, and But's about conjunction'. In C. J. Fillmore and D. T. Langendoen (eds.) *Studies in Linguistic Semantics*, pp. 115–50. New York: Holt, Rinehart and Winston, Inc.

   1973. 'The logic of politeness; or minding your p's and q's'. In C. Corum, T. C. Smith-Stark and A. Weiser (eds.) *Papers from the Ninth Regional Meeting of the Chicago Linguistic Society*, pp. 292–305. Chicago Linguistic Society.

   2005. 'Civility and its discontents: or, getting in your face'. In R. Lakoff and S. Ide (eds.) *Broadening the Horizon of Linguistic Politeness*, pp. 23–43. Amsterdam: John Benjamins.

Lakusta, L., Wagner, L., O'Hearn, K. and Landau, B. 2007. 'Conceptual foundations of spatial language: evidence for a goal bias in infants'. *Language Learning and Development* 3: 179–97.

Lambek, J. 1958. 'The mathematics of sentence structure'. *American Mathematical Monthly* 65: 154–69.

Lambrecht, K. 1994. *Information Structure and Sentence Form: Topic, Focus and the Mental Representation of Discourse Referents*. Cambridge University Press.

Land, J. P. N. 1876. 'Brentano's logical innovations'. *Mind* 1: 289–92.

Landau, B. 2010. 'Paths in language and cognition: Universal asymmetries and their cause'. In G. Marotta *et al.* (eds.) *Space in Language*, pp. 73–94. Pisa: University of Pisa Press.

Landau, B. and Jackendoff, R. S. 1993. '"What" and "where" in spatial language and spatial cognition'. *Behavioral and Brain Sciences* 16: 217–38.

Lang, E. 1984. *The Semantics of Coordination*. Amsterdam/Philadelphia: John Benjamins.

    2000. 'Adversative connectors on distinct levels of discourse: a re-examination of Eve Sweetser's three-level approach'. In E. Couper-Kuhlen and B. Kortmann (eds.) *Cause – Condition – Concession – Contrast: Cognitive and Discourse Perspectives*. Berlin/New York: Mouton de Gruyter.

Langacker, R. W. 1987. *Foundations of Cognitive Grammar*, vol. I: *Theoretical Prerequisites*. Stanford, CA: Stanford University Press.

    1990. 'Subjectification'. *Cognitive Linguistics* 1: 5–38.

    1991. *Foundations of Cognitive Grammar*, vol. II: *Descriptive Application*. Stanford, CA: Stanford University Press.

    2006. 'Subjectification, grammaticalization, and conceptual archetypes'. In A. Athanasiadou, C. Canakis and B. Cornillie (eds.) *Subjectification: Various Paths to Subjectivity*, pp. 17–40. Berlin: Mouton de Gruyter.

    2007. 'Constructing the meaning of personal pronouns'. In G. Radden, K.-M. Köpcke and T. Berg (eds.) *Aspects of Meaning Construction*, pp. 171–87. Amsterdam: John Benjamins.

Langdon, R., Davies M. and Coltheart, M. 2002. 'Understanding minds and understanding communicated meanings in schizophrenia'. *Mind and Language* 17: 68–104.

Langendoen, D. T. and Savin, H. 1971. 'The projection problem for presuppositions'. In C. Fillmore and D. T. Langendoen (eds.) *Studies in Linguistic Semantics*, pp. 373–88. New York: Holt, Reinhardt and Winston.

Larson, R. K. and Ludlow, P. 1993. 'Interpreted logical forms'. *Synthese* 95: 305–55. Reprinted in P. Ludlow (ed.) *Readings in the Philosophy of Language*, pp. 993–1039. Cambridge, MA: MIT Press.

Lascarides, A. and Asher, N. 1993. 'Temporal interpretation, discourse relations and commonsense entailment'. *Linguistics and Philosophy* 16: 437–93.

Lasersohn, P. 1999. 'Pragmatic halos'. *Language* 75: 522–51.

    2005. 'Context dependence, disagreement, and predicates of personal taste'. *Linguistics and Philosophy* 28: 643–86.

Lassiter, D. 2008. 'Semantic externalism, language variation, and sociolinguistic accommodation'. *Mind and Language* 23: 607–33.

Lee, C. 1999. 'Contrastive Topic: A locus of the interface evidence from Korean and English'. In K. Turner (ed.) *The Semantics/Pragmatics Interface from Different Points of View*, pp. 317–41. CRiSPI 1. London: Elsevier.

Lee, C., Gordon, M. and Büring, D. (eds.) 2007. *Topic and Focus: Cross-Linguistic Perspectives on Meaning and Intonation*. Dordrecht: Springer.

Leech, G. 1980. *Explorations in Semantics and Pragmatics*. Amsterdam: John Benjamins.

    1983. *Principles of Pragmatics*. London: Longman.

    2007. 'Politeness: is there an East-West divide?'. *Journal of Politeness Research* 3: 167–206.

Lehmann, C. 1995. *Thoughts on Grammaticalization*. Munich: LINCOM EUROPA. 2nd revised edition of *Thoughts on Grammaticalization: A Programmatic Sketch*, 1982. 2002 version is available at www.christianlehmann.eu/.

2008. 'Information structure and grammaticalization'. In E. Seoane and M. J. López-Couso (eds.), in collaboration with T. Fanego, *Theoretical and Empirical Issues in Grammaticalization*, pp. 207–99. Amsterdam: John Benjamins.

Lenzen, W. 1996. 'Necessary conditions for negation operators'. In H. Wansing (ed.) *Negation: A Notion in Focus*, pp. 37–58. Berlin: Walter de Gruyter.

Lerner, G. and Kitzinger, C. 2007. 'Introduction: person-reference in conversation analytic research'. *Discourse Studies* 9: 427–32.

Leslie, A. 1987. 'Pretense and representation: the origins of "theory of mind"'. *Psychological Review* 94: 412–26.

Levelt, W. 1999. 'Perspective taking and ellipsis in spatial descriptions'. In P. Bloom, M. Peterson, L. Nadel and M. Garrett (eds.) *Language and Space*, pp. 77–107. Cambridge, MA: MIT Press.

Levinson, S. C. 1979. 'Activity types and language'. *Linguistics* 17: 365–99.

1983. *Pragmatics*. Cambridge University Press.

1987. 'Minimization and conversational inference'. In J. Verschueren and M. Bertuccelli-Papi (eds.) *The Pragmatic Perspective*, pp. 61–129. Amsterdam: John Benjamins.

1988. 'Putting linguistics on a proper footing: Explorations in Goffman's participation framework'. In P. Drew and A. Wootton (eds.) *Goffman: Exploring the Interaction Order*, pp. 161–227. Oxford: Polity Press.

1995. 'Three levels of meaning'. In F. Palmer (ed.) *Grammar and Meaning*, pp. 90–115. Cambridge University Press.

1997. 'From outer to inner space: linguistic categories and non-linguistic thinking'. In J. Nuyts and E. Pederson (eds.) *Language and Conceptualization*, pp. 13–45. Cambridge University Press.

1999. 'Frames of reference and Molyneux question: cross-linguistic evidence'. In P. Bloom, M. Peterson, L. Nadel and M. Garrett (eds.) *Language and Space*, pp. 109–69. Cambridge, MA: MIT Press.

2000. *Presumptive Meanings*. Cambridge, MA: MIT Press.

2003a. 'Contextualizing "contextualization cues"'. In S. L. Eerdmans, C. L. Prevignano and P. L. Thibault (eds.) *Language and Interaction: Discussions with John J. Gumperz*, pp. 31–40. Amsterdam: John Benjamins.

2003b. 'Language and mind: let's get the issues straight!'. In D. Gentner and S. Goldin-Meadow (eds.) *Language in Mind*, pp. 25–45. Cambridge, MA: MIT Press.

2003c. *Space in Language and Cognition*. Cambridge University Press.

2006a. 'Cognition at the heart of human interaction'. *Discourse Studies* 8: 85–93.

2006b. 'The language of space in Yélî Dnye'. In S. C. Levinson and D. Wilkins (eds.) *Grammars of Space*, pp. 157–205. Cambridge University Press.

Levinson, S. C. and Burenhult, N. 2009. 'Semplates: a new concept in lexical semantics?'. *Language* 85: 153–74.

Levinson, S. C. and Wilkins, D. 2006. 'Towards a semantic typology of spatial description'. In S. C. Levinson and D. Wilkins (eds.) *Grammars of Space*, pp. 512–52. Cambridge University Press.

Lewis, D. 1969. *Convention*. Oxford: Blackwell.

   1970. 'General semantics'. *Synthese* 22: 18–67.

   1979. 'Scorekeeping in a language game'. *Journal of Philosophical Logic* 8: 339–59.

   2003. 'Rhetorical motivations for the emergence of discourse particles, with special reference to English *of course*'. In T. van der Wouden, A. Foolen and P. Van de Craen (eds.) *Particles*, special issue of *Belgian Journal of Linguistics* 16: 79–91.

Li, C. N. and Thompson, S. A. 1976. 'Subject and topic: a new typology of language'. In C. N. Li (ed.) *Subject and Topic*, pp. 457–89. New York: Academic Press.

Lieberman, M. 2000. 'Intuition: A social-cognitive neuroscience approach'. *Psychological Bulletin* 126: 109–37.

Lightfoot, D. 1998. *The Development of Language: Acquisition, Change, and Evolution*. Oxford: Blackwell.

   2003. 'Grammaticalisation: cause or effect?'. In R. Hickey (ed.) *Motives for Language Change*, pp. 99–123. Cambridge University Press.

Locher, M. 2004. *Power and Politeness in Action: Disagreements in Oral Communication*. Berlin/New York: Mouton de Gruyter.

   2006. *Advice Online*: *Advice-giving in an American Internet Health Column*. Pragmatics and Beyond New Series 149. Amsterdam/Philadelphia: John Benjamins.

Locher, M. and Watts, R. 2005. 'Politeness theory and relational work'. *Journal of Politeness Research* 1: 9–33.

López-Couso, M. J. 2010. 'Subjectification and intersubjectification'. In A. H. Jucker and I. Taavitsainen (eds.) *Handbook of Historical Pragmatics*, pp. 127–64. Berlin: de Gruyter.

Luckmann, T. 1995. 'Interaction planning and intersubjective adjustment of perspectives by communicative genres'. In E. Goody (ed.) *Social Intelligence and Interaction*, pp. 175–88. Cambridge University Press.

Lucy, J. 1992. *Language Diversity and Thought*. Cambridge University Press.

Lucy, J. and Gaskins, S. 2003. 'Interaction of language type and referent type in the development of nonverbal communication'. In D. Gentner and S. Goldin-Meadow (eds.) *Language in Mind*, pp. 465–92. Cambridge, MA: MIT Press.

Ludlow, P. 1995. 'Logical form and the hidden-indexical theory: a reply to Schiffer'. *Journal of Philosophy* 92: 102–7.

   1996. 'The adicity of "believes" and the hidden-indexical theory'. *Analysis* 56: 97–101.

Lüdtke, J., Friedrich, C. K., de Filippis, M. and Kaup, B. 2008. 'Event-related potential correlates of negation in a sentence-picture verification paradigm'. *Journal of Cognitive Neuroscience* 20: 1355–70.

Lyons, W. 1995. *Approaches to Intentionality*. Oxford: Clarendon Press.

MacDonald, M. C. and Just, M. A. 1989. 'Changes in activation levels with negation'. *Journal of Experimental Psychology (Learning, Memory, and Cognition)* 15: 633–42.

MacFarlane, J. 2003. 'Epistemic modalities and relative truth'. Ms. University of Berkeley. http://philosophy.berkeley.edu/macfarlane/work.html.

2005. 'Making sense of relative truth'. *Proceedings of the Aristotelian Society* 105: 321–39.

(forthcoming). 'Relativism and knowledge attributions'. In S. Bernecker and D. Pritchard (eds.) *Routledge Companion to Epistemology*. London: Routledge.

MacLaury, R. E. 1997. *Color and Cognition in Mesoamerica: Constructing Categories as Vantages*. Austin: University of Texas Press.

MacWhinney, B. 1987. 'The competition model'. In B. J. MacWhinney (ed.) *Mechanisms of Language Acquisition*, pp. 249–308. Hillsdale, NJ: Erlbaum.

MacWhinney, B., Keenan, J. M. and Reinke, P. 1982. 'The role of arousal in memory for conversation'. *Memory and Cognition* 10: 308–17.

Magri, G. 2009. 'A theory of individual-level predicates based on blind mandatory scalar implicatures'. *Natural Language Semantics* 17: 245–97.

Maier, E. 2009. 'Presupposing acquaintance: A unified semantics for *de dicto, de re* and *de se* belief reports'. *Linguistics and Philosophy* 32: 429–74.

Malle, B. 2004. *How the Mind Explains Behaviour: Folk Explanations, Meaning, and Social Interaction*. Cambridge, MA: MIT Press.

2006. 'Intentionality: morality, and their relationship in human judgment'. *Journal of Cognition and Culture* 6: 87–112.

Malle, B., Moses, L. and Baldwin, D. (eds.) 2001. *Intentions and Intentionality: Foundations of Social Cognition*. Cambridge, MA: MIT Press.

Malotki, E. 1983. *Hopi Time: A Linguistic Analysis of Temporal Concepts in the Hopi Language*. Berlin: Mouton de Gruyter.

2002. *Hopi Tales of Destructions*. Lincoln: University of Nebraska Press.

Malt, B. C., Sloman, S. A. and Gennari, S. P. 2003. 'Speaking versus thinking about objects and actions'. In D. Gentner and S. Goldin-Meadow (eds.) *Language in Mind*, pp. 81–111. Cambridge, MA: MIT Press.

Manes, J. and Wolfson, N. 1981. 'The compliment formula'. In F. Coulmas (ed.) *Conversational Routine: Explorations in Standardized Communication Situations and Prepatterned Speech*, pp. 115–32. The Hague: Mouton de Gruyter.

Mao, L.-M. 1994. 'Beyond politeness theory: "face" revisited and renewed'. *Journal of Pragmatics* 21: 451–86.

Marantz, A. 2005. 'Generative linguistics within the cognitive neuroscience of language'. *The Linguistic Review* 22: 429–45.

Markee, N. 2000. *Conversation Analysis*. Mahwah, NJ: Lawrence Erlbaum.

Markee, N. and Kasper, G. 2004. 'Classroom talks: an introduction'. *Modern Language Journal* 88: 491–500.

Marquez Reiter, R. 2000. *Linguistic Politeness in Britain and Uruguay: A Contrastive Study of Requests and Apologies*. Amsterdam: John Benjamins.

Martin, I. and McDonald, S. 2004. 'An exploration of causes of non-literal language problems in individuals with Asperger syndrome'. *Journal of Autism and Developmental Disorders* 34: 311–28.

Martin, N. M. 1989. *Systems of Logic*. Cambridge University Press.

Marty, A. 1918. *Gesammelte Schriften*, vol. II, Part 1. Halle: Max Niemeyer.

Mastop, R. 2005. *What Can You Do? Imperative Mood in Semantic Theory*. PhD thesis, ILLC, University of Amsterdam.

Mathesius, V. 1928. 'On linguistic characterology with illustrations from Modern English'. In *Actes du Premier Congrès International de Linguistes à La Haye*, pp. 56–63. Reprinted in J. Vachek (ed.) *A Prague School Reader in Linguistics*, pp. 59–67. Bloomington: Indiana University Press.

Matras, Y. 1998. 'Utterance modifiers and universals of grammatical borrowing'. *Linguistics* 36: 281–331.

Matsumoto, Y. 1988. 'Reexamination of the universality of face: Politeness phenomena in Japanese'. *Journal of Pragmatics* 12: 403–26.

1995. 'The conversational condition on Horn scales'. *Linguistics and Philosophy* 18: 21–60.

Mauri, C. 2008a. *Coordination Relations in the Languages of Europe and Beyond*. Berlin/New York: Mouton de Gruyter.

2008b. 'The irreality of alternatives: towards a typology of disjunction'. *Studies in Language* 32: 22–55.

Mauri, C. and Sansò, A. 2009. 'Irrealis and clause linkage'. Paper presented at the 8th Biennial Meeting of the Association of Linguistic Typology, Berkeley, 23–26 July 2009.

Maydon, H. C. (ed.) 1951. *Big Game Shooting in Africa*. London: Seeley Service and Co.

Maynard Smith, J. 1982. *Evolution and the Theory of Games*. Cambridge University Press.

McCawley, J. D. 1975. 'Lexicography and the count–mass distinction'. In *Proceedings of the First Annual Meeting of the Berkeley Linguistics Society*, pp. 314–21. Berkeley Linguistics Society. Reprinted in J. D. McCawley (ed.) *Grammar and Meaning*, pp. 165–73. Tokyo: Taikushan.

1978. 'Conversational implicature and the lexicon'. In P. Cole (ed.) *Syntax and Semantics 9: Pragmatics*, pp. 245–59. New York: Academic Press.

McGinn, C. 2000. *Logical Properties: Identity, Existence, Predication, Truth*. Oxford: Clarendon Press.

McGlone, M. 2001. 'Concepts as metaphors'. In S. Glucksberg (ed.) *Understanding Figurative Language: From Metaphors to Idioms*, pp. 90–107. Oxford University Press.

McGregor, W. B. and Wagner, T. 2006. 'The semantics and pragmatics of irrealis mood in Nyulnyulan languages'. *Oceanic Linguistics* 45: 339–79.

McHoul, A., Rapley, M. and Antaki, C. 2008. 'You gotta light? On the luxury of context for understanding talk in interaction'. *Journal of Pragmatics* 40: 42–54.

McKay, T. and Nelson, M. 2005. 'Propositional attitude reports'. In E. N. Zalta (ed.) *Stanford Encyclopedia of Philosophy*. http://plato.stanford.edu/.

McRae, K., Spivey-Knowlton, M. J. and Tanenhaus, M. K. 1998. 'Modeling thematic fit (and other constraints) within an integration competition framework'. *Journal of Memory and Language* 38: 283–312.

Meier, A. J. 1997. 'Teaching the universals of politeness'. *ELT Journal* 51: 21–8.

Meierkord, C. and Fetzer, A. 2002. 'Introduction: sequence, sequencing, sequential organization and sequentiality'. In A. Fetzer and C. Meierkord (eds.) *Rethinking Sequentiality: Linguistics Meets Conversational Interaction*, pp. 1–33. Amsterdam: John Benjamins.

Méndez-Naya, B. 2008. 'The which is most and right harde to answere. Intensifying *right* and *most* in earlier English'. In R. Dury, M. Gotti and M. Dossena (eds.) *English Historical Linguistics 2006*, Vol. II: *Lexical and Semantic Change. Selected Papers from the Fourteenth International Conference on English Historical Linguistics*, pp. 31–51. Amsterdam: John Benjamins.

Merchant, J. 2010. 'Ellipsis'. In A. Alexiadou, T. Kiss, and M. Butt (eds.) *A Handbook of Contemporary Syntax*. 2nd edition. Berlin: Walter de Gruyter.

Mey, J. (ed.) 1998a. *Concise Encyclopedia of Pragmatics*. Oxford: Elsevier.

  1998b. 'Pragmatics'. In J. Mey (ed.) *Concise Encyclopedia of Pragmatics*, pp. 716–37. Amsterdam: Elsevier.

  2001. *Pragmatics: An Introduction*. Oxford: Blackwell.

  2006a. 'Pragmatic acts'. In K. Brown (ed.) *Encyclopedia of Language and Linguistics*, vol. x, pp. 5–11. 2nd edition. London: Elsevier.

  2006b. 'Pragmatics: an overview'. In K. Brown (ed.) *Encyclopedia of Language and Linguistics*, vol. x, pp. 51–62. Amsterdam: Elsevier.

  2009a. *Concise Encyclopedia of Pragmatics*. 2nd edition. Amsterdam: Elsevier.

  2009b. 'Speech acts in context'. Paper presented at the IPrA 2009 in Melbourne.

  2010. 'Societal pragmatics'. In L. Cummings (ed.) *The Pragmatics Encyclopedia*, pp. 444–6. London: Routledge.

Michaelis, L. 2004. 'Type shifting in construction grammar: an integrated approach to aspectual coercion'. *Cognitive Linguistics* 15: 1–67.

Mill, J. S. 1843. *A System of Logic*. London: Longmans. Reprinted in 1947.

  1867. *An Examination of Sir William Hamilton's Philosophy*. 3rd edition. London: Longman.

  1872. *An Examination of Sir William Hamilton's Philosophy*. 4th edition. London: Longmans, Green, Reader and Dyer.

Miller, J. 1965. 'Living systems: basic concepts'. *Behaviour Science* 10: 193–237.

Millikan, R. 1984. *Language, Thought and Other Biological Categories*. Cambridge, MA: MIT Press.

Mills, S. 2003. *Gender and Politeness*. Cambridge University Press.

2009. 'Impoliteness in a cultural context'. *Journal of Pragmatics* 41: 1047–60.

Minsky, M. 1975. 'A framework for representing knowledge'. In P. Winton (ed.) *The Psychology of Computer Vision*, pp. 211–77. New York: MacGraw-Hill.

Mithun, M. 1988. 'The grammaticization of coordination'. In J. Haiman and S. A. Thompson (eds.) *Clause Combining in Grammar and Discourse*, pp. 331–60. Amsterdam: John Benjamins.

Mo, S., Su, Y., Chan, R. and Liu, J. 2008. 'Comprehension of metaphor and irony in schizophrenia during remission: the role of theory of mind and IQ'. *Psychiatry Research* 157: 21–9.

Molencki, R. 2007. 'The evolution of *since* in medieval English'. In U. Lenker and A. Meurman-Solin (eds.) *Connectives in the History of English*, pp. 97–113. Amsterdam: John Benjamins.

Molnár, V. and Winkler, S. (eds.) 2005. *The Architecture of Focus*. Berlin: Mouton de Gruyter.

Monck, W. H. S. 1881. *Sir William Hamilton*. London: Sampson, Low.

Montague, R. 1974a. *Formal Philosophy: Selected Papers of Richard Montague*. Ed. R. Thomason. New Haven, CT: Yale University Press.

1974b. 'The proper treatment of quantification in ordinary English'. In R. Thomason (ed.) *Formal Philosophy: Selected Papers of Richard Montague*, pp. 247–70. New Haven, CT: Yale University Press.

Montminy, M. 2010. 'Context and communication: a defense of intentionalism'. *Journal of Pragmatics* 42: 2910–18.

Montry, J. 2002. *How To Be Rude! A Training Manual for Mastering the Art of Rudeness*. Incline Village, NV: Stairwell Press.

Moortgat, M. 1998. *Categorial Investigations*. Dordrecht: Foris.

Morgan, J. L. 1978. 'Two types of convention in indirect speech acts'. In P. Cole (ed.) *Syntax and Semantics 9: Pragmatics*, pp. 261–80. New York: Academic Press.

Mori, J. 2003. 'The construction of interculturality: a study of initial encounters between American and Japanese students'. *Research on Language and Social Interaction* 36: 143–84.

Morrill, G. 1994. *Type-Logical Grammar*. Dordrecht: Kluwer.

Morris, C. W. 1938. *Foundations of the Theory of Signs*. International Encyclopedia of Unified Science 1. University of Chicago Press.

MWDEU 1994. *Merriam-Webster's Dictionary of English Usage*. Springfield, MA: Merriam Webster.

Myers, G. 2009. 'Structures of conversation'. In J. Culpeper, F. Katamba, P. Kerswill, R. Wodak and T. McEnery (eds.) *English Language: Description, Variation and Context*, pp. 501–11. Basingstoke: Palgrave Macmillan.

Nauze, F. 2008. *Modality in Typological Perspective*. PhD thesis, ILLC, University of Amsterdam.

Neale, S. 1990. *Descriptions*. Cambridge, MA: MIT Press.

1992. 'Paul Grice and the philosophy of language'. *Linguistics and Philosophy* 15: 509–59.

1993. 'Term limits'. *Philosophical Perspectives* 7: 89–123.

1994. 'Logical Form and LF'. In C. Otero (ed.) *Noam Chomsky: Critical Assessments*, pp. 788–838. London: Routledge.

2000. 'Reply to Stanley and Szabó'. *Mind and Language* 15: 284–94.

2004. 'This, that, and the other'. In A. Bezuidenhout and M. Reimer (eds.) *Descriptions and Beyond*, pp. 68–182. Oxford University Press.

2008. 'Term limits revisited'. *Philosophical Perspectives* 22: 370–442.

Nef, F. 1978. 'Maintenant 1 et maintenant 2: sémantique et pragmatique de *maintenant* temporel et non temporel'. In J. David and R. Martin (eds.) *La Notion d'Aspect*, pp. 145–66. Paris: Klincksieck.

Nelson, C. A. and de Haan, M. 1996. 'Neural correlates of infants' visual responsiveness to facial expressions of emotion'. *Developmental Psychobiology* 29: 577–95.

Németh, T. E. 2008. 'Verbal information transmission without communicative intention'. *Intercultural Pragmatics* 5: 153–76.

Nerlich, B. 2009. 'History of pragmatics'. In J. Mey (ed.) *Concise Encyclopedia of Pragmatics* (2nd edition), pp. 328–35. Amsterdam: Elsevier.

2010. 'History of pragmatics'. In L. Cummings (ed.) *The Pragmatics Encyclopedia*, pp. 192–5. London: Routledge.

Nerlich, B. and Clarke, D. D. 1996. *Language, Action and Context: The Early History of Pragmatics in Europe and America, 1780–1930*. Amsterdam: John Benjamins.

Neumann. J. von and Morgenstern, O. 1944. *Theory of Games and Economic Behavior*. Princeton University Press.

Nevala, M. 2004. *Address in Early English Correspondence: Its Forms and Sociopragmatic Functions*. Mémoires de la Société Néophilologique de Helsinki 64. Helsinki: Société Néophilologique.

Nevalainen, T. and Raumolin-Brunberg, H. 2003. *Historical Sociolinguistics: Language Change in Tudor and Stuart England*. London: Pearson Education.

Nevalainen, T. and Rissanen, M. 2002. 'Fairly pretty or pretty fair? On the development and grammaticalization of English downtoners'. *Language Sciences* 24: 359–80.

Neys, W. de and Schaeken, W. 2007. 'When people are more logical under cognitive load: Dual task impact on scalar implicature'. *Experimental Psychology* 54: 128–33.

Nicolle, S. 1997. 'A relevance theory perspective on grammaticalization'. *Cognitive Linguistics* 9: 1–35.

Nishizaka, A. 1995. 'The interactive constitution of interculturality: how to be a Japanese with words?'. *Human Studies* 18: 301–26.

Noonan, M. 1992. *A Grammar of Lango*. Berlin/New York: Mouton de Gruyter.

Norbury, C. 2005. 'The relationship between theory of mind and metaphor: evidence from children with language impairment and autistic spectrum disorder'. *British Journal of Developmental Psychology* 23: 383–99.

Nöth, W. 1990. *Handbook of Semiotics*. Bloomington/Indianapolis: Indiana University Press.

Nouwen, R. 2007. 'On appositives and dynamic binding'. *Research on Language and Computation* 5: 87–102.

Noveck, I. A. 2001. 'When children are more logical than adults'. *Cognition* 86: 253–82.

Noveck, I. A. and Chevaux, F. 2002. 'The pragmatic development of *and*'. In B. Skarabela (ed.) *Proceedings of the 26th Annual Boston University Conference on Language Development*, pp. 453–63. Somerville, MA: Cascadilla Press.

Noveck, I. A. and Posada, A. 2003. 'Characterizing the time course of an implicature: an evoked potentials study'. *Brain and Language* 85: 203–10.

Noveck, I. A. and Sperber, D. (eds.) 2004. *Experimental Pragmatics*. Basingstoke: Palgrave Macmillan.

Noveck, I. A., Chierchia, G., Chevaux, F., Guelminger, R. and Sylvestre, E. 2002. 'Linguistic-pragmatic factors in interpreting disjunctions'. *Thinking and Reasoning* 8: 297–326.

Nowell-Smith, P. H. 1954. *Ethics*. Harmondsworth: Pelican Books.

Nunberg, G. 1995. 'Transfers of meaning'. *Journal of Semantics* 12: 109–32.

Nunberg, G. and Zaenen, A. 1992. 'Systematic polysemy in lexicology and lexicography'. In H. Tommola, K. Varantola, T. Salmi-Tolonen and J. Schopp (eds.) *EURALEX '92: Proceedings I–II: Papers submitted to the 5th EURALEX International Congress on Lexicography in Tampere, Finland*, pp. 387–98. Tampere: Tampereen yliopisto.

Nurmi, A., Nevala, M. and Palander-Collin, M. (eds.) 2009. *The Language of Daily Life in England (1400–1800)*. Pragmatics and Beyond New Series 183. Amsterdam/Philadelphia: John Benjamins.

Nuyts, J. 2000. 'Intentionality'. In J. Verschueren, J.-O. Östman, J. Blommaert and C. Bulcaen (eds.) *Handbook of Pragmatics: Quintessence*. Amsterdam: John Benjamins (loose-leaf publication).

Nwoye, O. 1992. 'Linguistic politeness and socio-cultural variations of the notion of face'. *Journal of Pragmatics* 18: 309–28.

Ockham, W. 1967–88. *Guillelmi de Ockham Opera Philosophica et Theologica*. Ed. G. Gál and S. Brown, 17 vols. St Bonaventure, NY: The Franciscan Institute, St Bonaventure University.

O'Connor, J. and Arnold, G. 1973. *Intonation of Colloquial English*. Harlow: Longman.

O'Driscoll, J. 1996. 'About face: a defence and elaboration of universal dualism'. *Journal of Pragmatics* 25: 1–32.

2007. 'Brown and Levinson's face: How it can—and can't—help us to understand interaction across cultures'. *Intercultural Pragmatics* 4: 463–92.

O'Hair, S. G. 1969. 'Implications and meaning'. *Theoria* 35: 38–54.

Ohori, T. 2004. 'Coordination in Mentalese'. In M. Haspelmath (ed.) *Coordinating Constructions*, pp. 41–66. Amsterdam/Philadelphia: John Benjamins.

Oleksy, W. (ed.) 1989. *Contrastive Pragmatics*. Pragmatics and Beyond New Series 3. Amsterdam/Philadelphia: John Benjamins.

O'Neill, D. K. 1996. 'Two-year-old children's sensitivity to a parent's knowledge state when making requests'. *Child Development* 67: 659–77.

Onodera, N. O. and Suzuki, R. (eds.) 2007. *Subjectivity, Intersubjectivity and Historical Changes in Japanese*. Special issue of *Journal of Historical Pragmatics* 8 (2).

Origgi, G. and Sperber, D. 2000. 'Evolution, communication and the proper function of language'. In P. Carruthers and A. Chamberlain (eds.) *Evolution and the Human Mind: Modularity, Language and Meta-cognition*, pp. 140–69. Cambridge University Press.

Ortony, A., Schallert, D. L., Reynolds, R. E. and Antos, S. J. 1978. 'Interpreting metaphors and idioms: some effects of context on comprehension'. *Journal of Verbal Learning and Verbal Behavior* 17: 465–77.

Pacherie, E. 2000. 'The content of intentions'. *Mind and Language* 15: 400–32.
    2003. 'Intention'. In L. Nadel (ed.) *Encyclopedia of Cognitive Science*, pp. 599–604. London: Macmillan.
    2006. 'Towards a dynamic theory of intentions'. In S. Pockett, W. Banks and S. Gallagher (eds.) *Does Consciousness Cause Behaviour? An Investigation of the Nature of Volition*, pp. 145–67. Cambridge, MA: MIT Press.
    2007. 'Is collective intentionality really primitive?'. In C. Penco, M. Beaney and M. Vignolo (eds.) *Explaining the Mental: Naturalist and Non-naturalist Approaches to Mental Acts and Processes*, pp. 153–75. Newcastle-on-Tyne: Cambridge Scholars Press.
    2008. 'The phenomenology of action: a conceptual framework'. *Cognition* 107: 179–217.

Pacherie, E. and Dokie, J. 2006. 'From mirror neurons to joint actions'. *Cognitive Systems Research* 7: 101–12.

Padilla Cruz, M. 2009a. 'Towards an alternative relevance-theoretic approach to interjections'. *International Review of Pragmatics* 1: 182–206.
    2009b. 'Might interjections encode concepts?' *Lodz Papers in Pragmatics* 5: 241–70.

Pagin, P. 2004. 'Is assertion social?'. *Journal of Pragmatics* 36: 833–59.
    2006. 'Meaning holism'. In B. Smith and E. Lepore (eds.) *The Oxford Handbook of Philosophy of Language*, pp. 213–32. Oxford University Press.

Pagin, P. and Pelletier, J. 2007. 'Context, content and communication'. In G. Preyer and G. Peter (eds.) *Context-Sensitivity and Semantic Minimalism*, pp. 25–62. Oxford: Clarendon Press.

Pakkala-Weckström, M. 2010. 'Chaucer'. In A. H. Jucker and I. Taavitsainen (eds.) *Handbook of Historical Pragmatics* (Handbooks of Pragmatics 8), pp. 219–45. Berlin: Mouton de Gruyter.

Pandharipande, R. 1997. *Marathi*. London/New York: Routledge.

Panther, K.-U. and Thornburg, L. L. 2003a. 'Introduction. On the nature of conceptual metonymy'. In K.-U. Panther and L. L. Thornburg (eds.) *Metonymy and Pragmatic Inferencing*, pp. 1–20. Amsterdam: John Benjamins.
    2003b. 'Metonymies as natural inference and activation schemas: the case of dependent clauses as independent speech acts'. In K.-U. Panther and L. L. Thornburg (eds.) *Metonymy and Pragmatic Inferencing*, pp. 126–47. Amsterdam: John Benjamins.

Papafragou, A. 2000. *Modality: Issues in the Semantics-Pragmatics Interface*. Amsterdam: Elsevier.

Papafragou, A. and Musolino, J. 2003. 'Scalar implicatures: experiments at the semantics/pragmatics interface'. *Cognition* 86: 253–82.

Papafragou, A. and Tantalou, N. 1998. 'The other side of language: pragmatic competence'. *Journal of Neurolinguistics* 11: 1–10.

2004. 'Children's computation of implicatures'. *Language Acquisition* 12: 71–82.

Paraskevaides, H. A. 1984. *The Use of Synonyms in Homeric Formulaic Diction*. Amsterdam: A. M. Hakkert.

Parmentier, R. J. 1997. 'Charles S. Peirce'. In J. Verschueren, J.-O. Östman, J. Blommaert and C. Bulcaen (eds.) *Handbook of Pragmatics 1997*. Amsterdam: John Benjamins (loose-leaf publication).

Parsons, T. 1968[1937]. *The Structure of Social Action*. New York: Free Press.

Partee, B. 1973. 'Some structural analogies between tenses and pronouns in English'. *Journal of Philosophy* 70: 601–9.

(ed.) 1976. *Montague Grammar*. New York: Academic Press.

1984. 'Nominal and temporal anaphora'. *Linguistics and Philosophy* 7: 243–86.

1999. 'Focus, quantification, and semantics-pragmatics issues'. In P. Bosch and R. van der Sandt (eds.) *Focus: Linguistic, Cognitive, and Computational Perspectives*, pp. 213–31. Cambridge University Press.

Paul, H. 1880. *Prinzipien der Sprachgeschichte*. Tübingen: Niemeyer.

1889. *Principles of the History of Language*. Trans. H. A. Strong. London: Macmillan.

Payne, J. 1985. 'Complex phrases and complex sentences'. In T. Shopen (ed.) *Complex Constructions*, vol. II of *Language Typology and Syntactic Description*, pp. 3–41. Cambridge University Press.

Pearsall, J. (ed.) 1998. *New Oxford Dictionary of English*. Oxford University Press.

Pederson, E., Danziger, E., Wilkins, D. P., Levinson, S. C., Kita, S. and Senft, G. 1998. 'Semantic typology and spatial conceptualization'. *Language* 74: 557–89.

Pelczar, M. W. 2004. 'The indispensability of *Farbung*'. *Synthese* 138: 49–77.

2007. 'Forms and objects of thought'. *Linguistics and Philosophy* 30: 97–122.

Peleg, O. and Eviatar, Z. 2008. 'Hemispheric sensitivities to lexical and contextual constraints: Evidence from ambiguity resolution'. *Brain and Language* 105: 71–82.

2009. 'The disambiguation of homophonic versus heterophonic homographs in the two cerebral hemispheres'. *Brain and Cognition* 70: 154–62.

Peleg, O. and Giora, R. (in press). 'Salient meanings: the whens and where's'. In K. Allan and K. M. Jaszczolt (eds.) *Salience and Defaults in Utterance Processing*. Berlin/New York: Mouton de Gruyter.

Peleg, O., Giora, R., and Fein, O. 2001. 'Salience and context effects: Two are better than one'. *Metaphor and Symbol* 16: 173–92.

2004. 'Contextual strength: The whens and hows of context effects'. In I. Noveck and D. Sperber (eds.), *Experimental Pragmatics*, pp. 172–86. Basingstoke: Palgrave Macmillan.

2008. 'Resisting contextual information: You can't put a salient meaning down'. *Lodz Papers in Pragmatics* 4(1): 13–44.

Pell, M. 2002. 'Surveying emotional prosody in the brain'. In B. Bel and I. Marlien (eds.) *Proceedings of the Speech Prosody 2002 Conference*, pp. 77–82. Denver, CO.

Peregrin, J. 2001. *Meaning and Structure*. Aldershot: Ashgate.

2008. 'Inferentialist approach to semantics'. *Philosophy Compass* 3: 1208–23.

2009. 'Normative pragmatics'. In L. Cummings (ed.) *The Pragmatics Encyclopedia*, pp. 297–330. London: Routledge.

2011. 'The enigma of rules'. *International Journal of Philosophical Studies* 18: 377–94.

Perner, J. and Winner, E. 1985. '"John thinks, that Mary thinks that...". Attribution of second-order belief by 5- to 10-year-old children'. *Journal of Child Experimental Psychology* 39: 437–71.

Perry, J. 1977. 'Frege on demonstratives'. *Philosophical Review* 86: 474–97. Reprinted in P. Ludlow (ed.) *Readings in the Philosophy of Language*, pp. 693–715. Cambridge, MA: MIT Press.

2001. *Reference and Reflexivity*. Stanford, CA: CSLI Publications.

Perry, J. and Croft, D. 1968–1977. 'Dad's Army'. British Broadcasting Corporation (BBC). UK.

Petrilli, S. 2000. 'Charles Morris'. In J. Verschueren, J.-O. Östman, J. Blommaert and C. Bulcaen (eds.) *Handbook of Pragmatics 2000*. Amsterdam: John Benjamins (loose-leaf publication).

Petrus, K. (ed.) 2010. *Meaning and Analysis: New Essays on Grice*. Basingstoke: Palgrave Macmillan.

Pexman, P. M., Ferretti, T. R. and Katz, A. N. 2000. 'Discourse factors that influence on-line reading of metaphor and irony'. *Discourse Processes* 29: 201–22.

Phillips, R. D., Wagner, S. H., Fells, C. A. and Lynch, M. 1990. 'Do infants recognise emotion in facial expressions? Categorical and metaphorical evidence'. *Infant Behaviour and Development* 13: 71–84.

Pierrehumbert, J. 1980. *The Phonology and Phonetics of English Intonation*. Ph.D. dissertation, MIT.

Pierrehumbert, J. and Hirschberg, J. 1990. 'The meaning of intonational contours in the interpretation of discourse'. In P. Cohen, J. Morgan and M. Pollack (eds.) *Intentions in Communication*, pp. 271–311. Cambridge, MA: MIT Press.

Pietroski, P. 2005. 'Meaning before truth'. In G. Preyer and G. Peter (eds.) *Contextualism in Philosophy: Knowledge, Meaning, and Truth*, pp. 255–302. Oxford University Press.

Pilkington, A. 2000. *Poetic Effects: A Relevance Theory Perspective*. Amsterdam: John Benjamins.

Piller, I. 2007. 'Linguistics and intercultural communication'. *Language and Linguistics Compass* 1.3: 208–26.

Pizziconi, B. 2003. 'Re-examining politeness, face and the Japanese language'. *Journal of Pragmatics* 35: 1471–506.

Placencia, M. E. 2008. 'Requests in corner shop transaction in Ecuadorian Andean and Coastal Spanish'. In K. P. Schneider and A. Barron (eds.) *Variational Pragmatics*: *A Focus on Regional Varieties in Pluricentric Languages* (Pragmatics and Beyond New Series 178), pp. 307–32. Amsterdam/Philadelphia: John Benjamins.

Pollard, C. and Sag, I. 1994. *Head-Driven Phrase-Structure Grammar*. University of Chicago Press.

Pomerantz, A. 1984. 'Agreeing and disagreeing with assessments: some features of preferred/ dispreferred turn shapes'. In J. Atkinson and J. Heritage (eds.) *Structures of Social Action*, pp. 57–101. Cambridge University Press.

1988. 'Offering a candidate answer: an information seeking strategy'. *Communication Monographs* 55: 360–73.

Portner, P. 2003. 'The temporal semantics and modal pragmatics of the perfect'. *Linguistics and Philosophy* 26: 459–510.

2007. 'Imperative and modals'. *Natural Language Semantics* 4: 351–83.

Potts, C. 2005. *The Logic of Conventional Implicatures*. Oxford University Press.

2007a. 'Into the conventional-implicature dimension'. *Philosophy Compass* 2: 665–79.

2007b. 'The expressive dimension'. *Theoretical Linguistics* 33: 165–98.

Pouscoulous, N., Noveck, I., Politzer, G. and Bastide, A. 2007. 'A developmental investigation of processing costs in implicature production'. *Language Acquisition* 14: 347–76.

Prandi, M. 2004. *The Building Blocks of Meaning*. Amsterdam/Philadelphia: John Benjamins.

Predelli, S. 1998a. 'I am not here now'. *Analysis* 58: 102–15.

1998b. 'Utterance, interpretation, and the logic of indexicals'. *Mind and Language* 13: 400–14.

Prevignano, C. and di Luzio, A. 2003. 'A discussion with John J. Gumperz'. In S. L. Eerdmans, C. L. Prevignano and P. L. Thibault (eds.) *Language and Interaction*: *Discussions with John J. Gumperz*, pp. 7–30. Amsterdam: John Benjamins.

Prince, E. F. 1978. 'A comparison of WH-clefts and IT-clefts in discourse'. *Language* 54: 883–906.

1981. 'Towards a taxonomy of given/new information'. In P. Cole (ed.) *Radical Pragmatics*, pp. 223–55. New York: Academic Press.

1985. 'Fancy syntax and shared knowledge'. *Journal of Pragmatics* 9: 65–81.

1988. 'Discourse analysis: a part of the study of linguistic competence'. In F. J. Newmeyer and R. H. Robins (eds.) *Linguistics: The Cambridge Survey*, vol. II: *Linguistic Theory: Extensions and Implications*, pp. 164–82. Cambridge University Press.

1992. 'The ZPG letter: subjects, definiteness, and information status'. In S. Thompson and W. Mann (eds.) *Discourse Description: Diverse Analyses of a Fund Raising Text*, pp. 295–325. Amsterdam: John Benjamins.

1998. 'On the limits of syntax, with reference to left-dislocation and topicalization'. In P. W. Culicover and L. McNally (eds.) *Syntax and Semantics 29: The Limits of Syntax*, pp. 281–302. San Diego: Academic Press.

Purver, M., Cann, R. and Kempson, R. 2006. 'Grammars as parsers: the dialogue challenge'. *Research on Language and Computation* 4: 289–326.

Pustejovsky, J. 1995. *The Generative Lexicon*. Cambridge, MA: MIT Press.

Putnam, H. 1975. 'The meaning of meaning'. In H. Putnam, *Philosophical Papers*, vol. ii, pp. 215–71. Cambridge University Press.

Quine, W. V. O. 1956. 'Quantifiers and propositional attitudes'. *Journal of Philosophy* 53: 177–87. Reprinted in A. Marras (ed.) *Intentionality, Mind and Language*, pp. 402–14. Urbana: University of Illinois Press.

1960. *Word and Object*. Cambridge, MA: MIT Press.

1965. *Elementary Logic*. New York: Harper and Row.

1973. *The Roots of Reference*. LaSalle, IL: Open Court.

1981. *Mathematical Logic*. Revised edition. Cambridge, MA: Harvard University Press.

1992. *Pursuit of Truth*. 2nd revised edition. Cambridge, MA: Harvard University Press.

Quirk, R., Greenbaum, S., Leech, G. and Svartvik, J. 1972. *A Grammar of Contemporary English*. London: Longman.

1985. *A Comprehensive Grammar of the English Language*. London: Longman.

Rando, E. and Napoli, D. J. 1978. 'Definites in *there* sentences'. *Language* 54: 300–13.

Ravelli, L. 2003. 'A dynamic perspective: implications for metafunctional interaction and an understanding of Theme'. In A. Simon-Vandenbergen, M. Taverniers and L. Ravelli (eds.) *Grammatical Metaphor*, pp. 187–234. Amsterdam: John Benjamins.

Raymond, G. 2003. 'Grammar and social organization: yes/no interrogatives and the structure of responding'. *American Sociological Review* 68: 939–67.

Raymond, G. and Heritage, J. 2006. 'The epistemics of social relations: owning grandchildren'. *Language in Society* 35: 677–705.

Reboul, A. 1997. 'What (if anything) is accessibility? A relevance-oriented criticism of Ariel's accessibility theory of referring expressions'. In J. H. Connolly, R. M. Vismans, C. S. Butler and R. A. Gatward (eds.) *Discourse and Pragmatics in Functional Grammar*, pp. 91–108. Berlin: Mouton de Gruyter.

Recanati, F. 1986. 'On defining communicative intentions'. *Mind and Language* 1: 213–42.

1987. *Meaning and Force: The Pragmatics of Performative Utterances*. Cambridge University Press.

1989. 'The pragmatics of what is said'. *Mind and Language* 4: 295–329. Reprinted in S. Davis (ed.) 1991, *Pragmatics: A Reader*, pp. 97–120. Oxford University Press.

1993. *Direct Reference: From Language to Thought*. Oxford: Blackwell.

1994. 'Contextualism and anti-contextualism in the philosophy of language'. In S. Tsohatzidis (ed.) *Foundations of Speech Act Theory*, pp. 156–66. London: Routledge.

1995. 'The alleged priority of literal interpretation'. *Cognitive Science* 19: 207–32.

2000. *Oratio Obliqua, Oratio Recta: The Semantics of Metarepresentations*. Cambridge, MA: MIT Press.

2001. 'What is said'. *Synthese* 128: 75–91.

2002. 'Unarticulated constituents'. *Linguistics and Philosophy* 25: 299–345.

2003. 'Embedded implicatures'. *Philosophical Perspectives* 17: 299–332.

2004a. *Literal Meaning*. Cambridge University Press.

2004b. 'Pragmatics and semantics'. In L. Horn and G. Ward (eds.) *The Handbook of Pragmatics*, pp. 442–62. Oxford: Blackwell.

2005. 'Literalism and contextualism: some varieties'. In G. Preyer and G. Peter (eds.) *Contextualism in Philosophy: Knowledge, Meaning, and Truth*, pp. 171–96. Oxford: Clarendon Press.

2007. *Perspectival Thought: A Plea for (Moderate) Relativism*. Oxford University Press.

2008. 'Moderate relativism'. In M. Garcia-Carpintero and M. Kölbel (eds.) *Relative Truth*, pp. 41–62. Oxford University Press.

2010. *Truth-Conditional Pragmatics*. Oxford University Press.

Reddy, M. 1979. 'The conduit metaphor'. In A. Ortony (ed.) *Metaphor and Thought*, pp. 164–201. Cambridge University Press.

Reeder, K. 1978. 'The emergence of illocutionary skills'. *Journal of Child Language* 7: 13–28.

Reichenbach, H. 1947. *Elements of Symbolic Logic*. New York: Free Press.

Reimer, M. 1995. 'Performative utterances: a reply to Bach and Harnish'. *Linguistics and Philosophy* 18: 655–75.

Reinhart, T. 1981. 'Pragmatics and linguistics. An analysis of sentence topics'. *Philosophica* 27: 53–94.

Reinhart, T. and Reuland, E. 1993. 'Reflexivity'. *Linguistic Inquiry* 24: 657–720.

Rescorla, M. 2007. 'Convention'. In E. N. Zalta (ed.) *The Stanford Encyclopedia of Philosophy*. http://plato.stanford.edu/archives/spr2010/entries/convention/.

Reyle, U. 1998. 'A note on enumerations and the semantics of *puis* and *alors*'. *Cahiers de Grammaire* 23: 67–79.

Rhodes, R. 1989. '"We are going to go there": positive politeness in Ojibwa'. *Multilingua* 8: 249–58.

Richard, M. 1990. *Propositional Attitudes: An Essay on Thoughts and How We Ascribe Them*. Cambridge University Press.

1995. 'Defective contexts, accommodation, and normalization'. *Canadian Journal of Philosophy* 25: 551–70.

Rissanen, M., Kytö, M. and Palander-Collin, M. 1993. *Early English in the Computer Age: Explorations Through the Helsinki Corpus*. Topics in English Linguistics 11. Berlin: Mouton de Gruyter.

Rizzolatti, G. and Craighero, L. 2004. 'The mirror-neuron system'. *Annual Review of Neuroscience* 27: 169–92.

Rizzolatti, G. and Fabbri Destro, M. 2007. 'Understanding action and the intentions of others: the basic neural mechanism'. *European Review* 15: 209–22.

Rochemont, M. 1986. *Focus in Generative Grammar*. Amsterdam: John Benjamins.

Romero-Trillo, J. (ed.) 2008. *Pragmatics and Corpus Linguistics: A Mutualistic Entente*. Mouton Series in Pragmatics 2. Berlin: Mouton de Gruyter.

Rooij, R. van 2007. 'Strengthening conditional presuppositions'. *Journal of Semantics* 24: 289–304.

  2009. 'Optimality-theoretic and game-theoretic approaches to implicature'. In E. Zalta (ed.) *Stanford Encyclopedia of Philosophy*. http://plato.stanford.edu/archives/spr2009/entries/implicature-optimality-games/.

Rooth, M. 1985. *Association With Focus*. Ph.D. dissertation, University of Massachusetts at Amherst.

  1992. 'A theory of focus interpretation'. *Natural Language Semantics* 1: 75–116.

Ross, J. R. 1967. *Constraints on Variables in Syntax*. Ph.D. thesis, MIT.

  1970. 'On declarative sentences'. In R. A. Jacobs and P. S. Rosenbaum (eds.) *Readings in English Transformational Grammar*, pp. 222–72. Waltham, MA: Ginn.

  1972. 'The category squish: Endstation Hauptwort'. In P. M. Peranteau, J. N. Levi and G. C. Phares (eds.) *Papers from the Eighth Regional Meeting of the Chicago Linguistic Society*, pp. 316–38. Chicago Linguistic Society.

Rothschild, D. and Segal, G. 2009. 'Indexical predicates'. *Mind and Language* 24: 467–93.

Ruhi, S. 2007. 'Higher-order intentions and self-politeness in evaluations of (im)politeness: the relevance of compliment responses'. *Australian Journal of Linguistics* 27: 107–45.

  2010. 'Face as an indexical category in interaction'. *Journal of Pragmatics* 42: 2131–46.

Russell, Benjamin 2006. 'Against grammatical computation of scalar implicatures'. *Journal of Semantics* 23: 361–82.

  2007. 'Imperatives in conditional conjunction'. *Natural Language Semantics* 15: 131–66.

Russell, Bertrand 1905. 'On denoting'. *Mind* 14: 479–93. Reprinted in B. Russell, *Logic and Knowledge: Essays 1901–1950*, pp. 49–56. London: Allen and Unwin.

  1911. 'Knowledge by acquaintance and knowledge by description'. *Publications of the Aristotelian Society* 11: 108–28. In B. Russell, *Mysticism and Logic and Other Essays*, pp. 209–32. London: Allen and Unwin, 1918.

1918. 'The philosophy of logical atomism'. *The Monist* 28: 495–527. In R. C. Marsh (ed.) *Logic and Knowledge*, pp. 175–282. London: Allen and Unwin, 1956.

1919a. 'Descriptions'. In B. Russell, *Introduction to Mathematical Philosophy*, pp. 167–80. London: Allen and Unwin. Reprinted in A. P. Martinich (ed.) 1990, *The Philosophy of Language* (2nd edition), pp. 213–19. Oxford University Press.

1919b. *Introduction to Mathematical Philosophy*. London: George Allen and Unwin.

Sacks, H. 1986. 'Some considerations of a story told in ordinary conversations'. *Poetics* 15: 127–38.

1992. *Lectures on Conversation*, vol. I. Oxford: Blackwell. (First published 1964.)

Sacks, H., Schegloff, E. A. and Jefferson, G. 1974. 'A simplest systematics for the organization of turn-taking for conversation'. *Language* 50.4: 696–735.

Sadock, J. M. 1974. *Toward a Linguistic Theory of Speech Acts*. New York: Academic Press.

1978. 'On testing for conversational implicature'. In P. Cole (ed.) *Syntax and Semantics 9: Pragmatics*, pp. 281–97. New York: Academic Press.

2004. 'Speech acts'. In L. Horn and G. Ward (eds.) *The Handbook of Pragmatics*, pp. 53–73. Oxford: Blackwell.

Sadock, J. M. and Zwicky, A. M. 1985. 'Speech act distinctions in syntax'. In T. Shopen (ed.) *Language Typology and Syntactic Description*, vol. I: *Clause Structure*, pp. 155–96. Cambridge University Press.

Sag, I. and Liberman, M. 1975. 'The intonational disambiguation of indirect speech acts'. In R. E. Grossman, L. J. San and T. J. Vance (eds.) *Papers from the Eleventh Regional Meeting of the Chicago Linguistics Society*, pp. 487–97. Chicago Linguistics Society.

Salmon, N. 1986. *Frege's Puzzle*. Cambridge, MA: MIT Press.

Samovar, L. A. and Porter, R. 2001. *Intercultural Communication Reader*. New York: Thomas Learning Publications.

Sanders, R. 1987. *Cognitive Foundations of Calculated Speech*. Albany, NY: State University of New York Press.

Sandt, R. van der 1982. *Kontekst en Presuppositie*. Nijmegen: NIS.

1988. *Context and Presupposition*. London: Croom Helm.

1992. 'Presupposition projection as anaphora resolution'. *Journal of Semantics* 9: 333–77.

Sandt, R. van der and Geurts, B. 1991. 'Presupposition, anaphora and lexical content'. Technical report, IBM, Wissenschafliches Zentrum, Institut für Wissensbasierte Systeme.

Sapir, E. 1930. *Totality*. Language Monograph No. 6. Baltimore, MD: Waverly Press (for the Linguistic Society of America).

Sauerland, U. 2004. 'Scalar implicatures in complex sentences'. *Linguistics and Philosophy* 27: 367–31.

Saul, J. 2002a. 'Speaker meaning, what is said and what is implicated'. *Noûs* 36: 228–48.

2002b. 'What is said and psychological reality: Grice's project and relevance theorists' criticisms'. *Linguistics and Philosophy* 25: 347–72.

Saussure, L. de. 1998. 'Portée temporelle de la négation'. *Langues* 1–1: 25–32.

2000. 'Quand le temps ne progresse pas avec le passé simple'. *Cahiers Chronos* 6: 37–48.

2003. *Temps et Pertinence*. Brussels: De Boeck.

Saussure, L. de and Morency, P. (forthcoming). 'Remarques sur l'usage interprétatif épistémique du futur'. *Travaux neuchâtelois de linguistique*.

Saussure, L. de and Sthioul, B. 1999. 'L'imparfait narratif: point de vue (et images du monde)'. *Cahiers de Praxématique* 32: 167–88.

Saxe, R. 2006. 'Uniquely human social cognition'. *Current Opinion in Neurobiology* 16: 235–9.

Sbisà, M. 1991. 'Speech acts, effects and responses'. In J. Searle, H. Parret and J. Verschueren (eds.) *(On) Searle on Conversation*, pp. 101–11. Amsterdam: John Benjamins.

2002. 'Speech acts in context'. *Language and Communication* 22: 421–36.

2006. 'John L. Austin'. In J. Verschueren, J.-O. Östman, J. Blommaert and C. Bulcaen (eds.) *Handbook of Pragmatics 1998*. Amsterdam: John Benjamins (loose-leaf publication).

2010. 'Austin, J. L.'. In L. Cummings (ed.) *The Pragmatics Encyclopedia*, pp. 188–92. London: Routledge.

Schank, R. 1982. *Dynamic Memory: A Theory of Reminding and Learning in Computers and People*. Cambridge University Press.

Schank, R. and Abelson, R. C. 1977. *Scripts, Plans, Goals and Understanding: An Inquiry into Human Knowledge Structures*. Hillsdale, NJ: Lawrence Erlbaum.

Schegloff, E. 1986. 'The routine as achievement'. *Human Studies* 9: 111–51.

1987. 'Between macro and micro: contexts and other connections'. In J. Alexander, B. Giesen, R. Munch and N. Smelser (eds.) *The Micro-Macro Link*, pp. 207–34. Los Angeles: University of California Press.

1991. 'Reflections on talk and social structure'. In D. Boden and D. Zimmerman (eds.) *Talk and Social Structure*, pp. 44–70. Oxford: Polity Press.

1995. 'Discourse as an interactional achievement III: the omnirelevance of action'. *Research on Language and Social Interaction* 28: 185–211.

1996. 'Confirming allusions: toward an empirical account of action'. *American Journal of Sociology* 102: 161–216.

1997. 'Practices and actions: boundary cases of other-initiated repair'. *Discourse Processes* 23: 499–545.

1999. 'Discourse, pragmatics, conversation, analysis'. *Discourse Studies* 1: 405–35.

2005. 'On complainability'. *Social Problems* 52: 449–76.

2006. 'Interaction: the infrastructure for social institutions, the natural ecological niche for language, and the arena in which culture is enacted'.

In N. J. Enfield and S. Levinson (eds.) *Roots of Human Sociality: Culture, Cognition and Interaction*, pp. 70–96. Oxford: Berg.

2007. *Sequence Organization in Interaction*. Cambridge University Press.

Schenkein, J. N. 1972. 'Towards an analysis of natural conversation and the sense of *heheh*'. *Semiotica* 6: 344–77.

Schiffer, S. 1972. *Meaning*. Oxford: Clarendon Press.

1992. 'Belief ascription'. *Journal of Philosophy* 89: 499–521.

1996. 'The hidden-indexical theory's logical-form problem: a rejoinder'. *Analysis* 56: 92–7.

Schiffrin, D. 1987. *Discourse Markers*. Cambridge University Press.

1994. *Approaches to Discourse*. Oxford: Blackwell.

Schlenker, P. 2005. 'The Lazy Frenchman's approach to the subjunctive'. In T. Geerts, I. van Ginneken and H. Jacobs (eds.) *Romance Languages and Linguistic Theory 2003*, pp. 269–309. Amsterdam: John Benjamins.

2008. 'Be articulate: a pragmatic theory of presupposition projection'. *Theoretical Linguistics* 34: 157–212.

Schmerling, S. F. 1976. *Aspects of English Sentence Stress*. Austin: University of Texas Press.

Schmidt, R. 1980. 'Review of Esther Goody (ed.) *Questions and Politeness: Strategies in Social Interaction*'. *Regional English Language Centre (RELC) Journal* 11: 100–14.

Schmidtke-Bode, K. 2009. *A Typology of Purpose Clauses*. Amsterdam/ Philadelphia: John Benjamins.

Schmitt, N. 2004. *Formulaic Sequences: Acquisition, Processing and Use*. Amsterdam/Philadelphia: John Benjamins.

Schneider, K. P. 2008. 'Small talk in England, Ireland, and the USA'. In K. P. Schneider and A. Barron (eds.) *Variatonal Pragmatics: A Focus on Regional Varieties in Pluricentric Languages*, pp. 99–139. Amsterdam/Philadelphia: John Benjamins.

Schneider, K. P. and Barron, A. (eds.) 2008a. *Variational Pragmatics: A Focus on Regional Varieties in Pluricentric Languages*. Pragmatics and Beyond New Series 178. Amsterdam/Philadelphia: John Benjamins.

2008b. 'Where pragmatics and dialectology meet. Introducing variational pragmatics'. In K. P. Schneider and A. Barron (eds.) *Variational Pragmatics: A Focus on Regional Varieties in Pluricentric Languages*, pp. 1–32. Amsterdam/Philadelphia: John Benjamins.

Scholl, B. and Leslie, A. 1999. 'Modularity, development and "theory of mind"'. *Mind and Language* 14: 131–53.

Schubert, L. K. and Pelletier, F. J. 1989. 'Generically speaking, or using Discourse Representation Theory to interpret generics'. In G. Chierchia, B. H. Partee and R. Turner (eds.) *Properties, Types and Meaning*, pp. 193–268. Dordrecht: Kluwer Academic Publishers.

Schulz, K. 2007. *Minimal Models in Semantics and Pragmatics: Free Choice, Exhaustivity, and Conditionals*. PhD thesis, ILLC, University of Amsterdam.

Schwager, M. 2006. *Interpreting Imperatives*. PhD thesis, Frankfurt am Main.

Schwenter, S. A. 2000. 'Viewpoints and polysemy: linking adversative and causal meanings of discourse markers'. In E. Couper-Kuhlen and B. Kortmann (eds.) *Cause – Condition – Concession – Contrast: Cognitive and Discourse Perspectives*, pp. 257–81. Berlin: Mouton de Gruyter.

Scollon, R. and Scollon, S. W. 1995. *Intercultural Communication: A Discourse Approach*. Oxford: Blackwell.

2001. *Intercultural Communication*. 2nd edition. Oxford: Blackwell.

2003. *Discourse in Place: Language in the Material. World*. London and New York: Routledge.

Scott, D. S. 1970. 'Advice on modal logic'. In K. Lambert (ed.) *Philosophical Problems in Logic: Recent Developments*, pp. 143–73. Dordrecht: Reidel.

Searle, J. R. 1969. *Speech Acts: An Essay in the Philosophy of Language*. Cambridge University Press.

1975a. 'A taxonomy of illocutionary acts'. In K. Gunderson (ed.) *Language, Mind and Knowledge*, pp. 344–69. Minneapolis: University of Minnesota Press.

1975b. 'Indirect speech acts'. In P. Cole and J. L. Morgan (eds.) *Syntax and Semantics 3: Speech Acts*, pp. 59–82. New York: Academic Press.

1978. 'Literal meaning'. *Erkenntnis* 13: 207–24.

1979a. *Expression and Meaning: Studies in the Theory of Speech Acts*. Cambridge University Press.

1979b. 'Metaphor'. In J. R. Searle, *Expression and Meaning: Studies in the Theory of Speech Acts*, pp. 76–116. Cambridge University Press.

1983. *Intentionality: An Essay in Philosophy of Mind*. Cambridge University Press.

1990. 'Collective intentions and actions'. In P. Cohen, J. Morgan and M. Pollack (eds.) *Intentions in Communication*, pp. 401–16. Cambridge, MA: MIT Press.

1991. 'Response: Meaning, intentionality, and speech acts'. In E. Lepore and R. van Gulick (eds.) *John Searle and His Critics*, pp. 81–102. Oxford: Blackwell.

1992a. 'How performatives work'. *Linguistics and Philosophy* 12: 535–58.

1992b. *The Rediscovery of the Mind*. Cambridge, MA: MIT Press.

2007. 'What is language: some preliminary remarks'. In I. Kecskes and L. R. Horn (eds.) *Explorations in Pragmatics: Linguistic, Cognitive and Intercultural Aspects*, pp. 7–37. Berlin: Mouton de Gruyter.

Searle, J. R. and Vanderveken, D. 1985. *Foundations of Illocutionary Logic*. Cambridge University Press.

Seddoh, S. 2002. 'How discrete or independent are "affective" prosody and "linguistic" prosody?'. *Aphasiology* 16: 683–92.

Seeley, T. 1989. 'The honey-bee colony as a superorganism'. *American Scientist* 77: 546–53.

Selinker, L. 1972. 'Interlanguage'. *IRAL* 10: 209–31.

Selkirk, E. 1995. 'Sentence prosody: Intonation, stress and phrasing'. In J. Goldsmith (ed.) *Handbook of Phonological Theory*, pp. 550–69. Oxford: Blackwell.

Sellars, W. 1962. 'Truth and correspondence'. *Journal of Philosophy* 59: 29–56.

Seuren, P. A. M. 1985. *Discourse Semantics*. Oxford: Blackwell.

2010. *The Logic of Language*. Oxford University Press.

Seyfarth, R. and Cheney, D. 1992. 'Meaning and mind in monkeys'. *Scientific American* 267/6: 78–86.

Sgall, P., Hajičová, E. and Benešova, E. 1973. *Topic, Focus, and Generative Semantics*. Kronberg: Scriptor Verlag GmbH.

Sgall, P., Hajičová, E. and Panevová, J. 1986. *The Meaning of the Sentence in its Semantic and Pragmatic Aspects*. Dordrecht: Reidel.

Shatz, M. 1978. 'On the development of communicative understandings: an early strategy for interpreting and responding to messages'. *Cognitive Psychology* 10: 271–301.

Shaul, D. L. 2002. *Hopi Traditional Literature*. Albuquerque: University of New Mexico Press.

Siewert, C. 2006. 'Consciousness and intentionality'. In E. N. Zalta (ed.) *Stanford Encyclopedia of Philosophy*. http://plato.stanford.edu/contents.html.

Sigwart, C. 1873. *Logik, I*. Tübingen: H. Laupp. (Page references to translation by H. Dendy. London: Swan Sonnenschein and Co., 1895.)

Simon-Vandenbergen, A.-M. 2007. '*No doubt* and related expressions: a functional account'. In M. Hanney and G. J. Steen (eds.) *Structural-Functional Studies in English Grammar*. Amsterdam: John Benjamins.

Slobin, D. I. 2000. 'Verbalised events: a dynamic approach to linguistic relativity and determinism'. In S. Niemeier and R. Dirven (eds.) *Evidence for Linguistic Relativity*, pp. 107–38. Amsterdam: John Benjamins.

2006. 'What makes manner of motion salient? Explorations in linguistic typology, discourse and cognition'. In M. Hickmann and S. Robert (eds.) *Space in Languages: Linguistic Systems and Cognitive Categories*, pp. 59–81. Amsterdam: John Benjamins.

Slugowski, B. and Turnbull, W. 1988. 'Cruel to be kind and kind to be cruel: sarcasm, banter and social relations'. *Journal of Language and Social Psychology* 7: 101–21.

Small, S. L., Cottrell, G. W. and Tanenhaus, M. K. (eds.) 1988. *Lexical Ambiguity Resolution: Perspectives from Psycholinguistics, Neuropsychology, and Artificial Intelligence*. San Mateo, CA: Morgan Kaufmann.

Smet, H. de and Verstraete, J.-C. 2006. 'Coming to terms with subjectivity'. *Cognitive Linguistics* 17: 365–92.

Smith, B. and Smith, D. W. 1995. 'Introduction'. In B. Smith and D. W. Smith (eds.) *The Cambridge Companion to Husserl*, pp. 1–44. Cambridge University Press.

Smith, C. and Erbaugh, M. 2009. 'Temporal interpretation in Mandarin Chinese'. In R. P. Meier, H. Aristar-Dry and E. Destruel (eds.) *Text, Time, and*

*Context: Selected Papers by Carlotta Smith* (Studies in Linguistics and Philosophy 87), pp. 303–42. Dordrecht: Springer.

Smith, C., Perkins, E. and Fernald, T. 2007. 'Time in Navajo: Direct and indirect interpretation'. *International Journal of American Linguistics* 73: 40–71.

Smith, D. W. 2008. 'Phenomenology'. In E. N. Zalta (ed.) *Stanford Encyclopedia of Philosophy*. http://plato.stanford.edu/contents.html.

Smith, N. 1990. 'Observations on the pragmatics of tense'. *UCL Working Papers in Linguistics* 2: 82–94.

Smith, N. and Tsimpli, I.-M. 1995. *The Mind of a Savant: Language Learning and Modularity*. Oxford: Blackwell.

Smith, N. J. J. 2008. *Vagueness and Degrees of Truth*. Oxford University Press.

Smith, S. and Jucker, A. 2002. 'Discourse markers as turns'. In A. Fetzer and C. Meierkord (eds.) *Rethinking Sequentiality: Linguistics meets Conversational Interaction*, pp. 151–78. Amsterdam: John Benjamins.

Snow, C., Perlmann, R., Gleason, J. and Hooshyar, N. 1990. 'Developmental perspectives on politeness: sources of children's knowledge'. *Journal of Pragmatics* 14: 289–305.

Soames, S. 1987. 'Direct reference, propositional attitudes, and semantic content'. *Philosophical Topics* 15: 44–87. Reprinted in N. Salmon and S. Soames (eds.) *Propositions and Attitudes*, pp. 197–239. Oxford University Press.

1995. 'Beyond singular propositions?'. *Canadian Journal of Philosophy* 25: 515–49.

2002. *Beyond Rigidity: The Unfinished Semantic Agenda of Naming and Necessity*. Oxford University Press.

Solan, L. and Tiersma, P. 2005. *Speaking of Crime: The Language of Criminal Justice*. University of Chicago Press.

Sommers, F. 1982. *The Logic of Natural Language*. Oxford: Clarendon Press.

Spenader, J. 2003. 'Between binding and accommodation'. In P. Kuehlein, H. Rieser and H. Zeevat (eds.) *Perspective on Dialogue in the New Millennium*, pp. 79–110. Amsterdam: John Benjamins.

Spencer-Oatey, H. 2000. 'Rapport management: a framework for analysis'. In H. Spencer-Oatey (ed.) *Culturally speaking: Managing Rapport through Talk Across Cultures*, pp. 11–46. London: Continuum.

2005. '(Im)politeness, face and perceptions of rapport: unpacking their bases and interrelationships'. *Journal of Politeness Research* 1: 95–119.

2007. 'Theories of identity and the analysis of face'. *Journal of Pragmatics* 39: 639–56.

Spencer-Oatey, H. and Ruhi, Ş. 2007. 'Identity, face and (im)politeness'. *Journal of Pragmatics* 39: 635–8.

Sperber, D. 1985. 'Apparently irrational beliefs'. In D. Sperber, *On Anthropological Knowledge*, pp. 35–63. Cambridge University Press.

1996. *Explaining Culture: A Naturalistic Approach*. Oxford: Blackwell.

2002. 'In defense of massive modularity'. In E. Dupoux (ed.) *Language, Brain and Cognitive Development: Essays in Honor of Jacques Mehler*, pp. 47–57. Cambridge, MA: MIT Press.

2007. 'Seedless grapes: nature and culture'. In S. Laurence and E. Margolis (eds.) *Creations of the Mind: Theories of Artifacts and their Representation*, pp. 124–37. Oxford University Press.

Sperber, D. and Wilson, D. 1981. 'Irony and the use–mention distinction'. In P. Cole (ed.) *Radical Pragmatics*, pp. 295–318. New York: Academic Press.

  1986. *Relevance: Communication and Cognition*. Oxford: Blackwell.

  1990. 'Rhetoric and relevance'. In J. Bender and D. Wellbery (eds.) *The Ends of Rhetoric*, pp. 140–55. Palo Alto, CA: Stanford University Press.

  1995a. 'Postface'. In D. Sperber and D. Wilson, *Relevance: Communication and Cognition* (2nd edition), pp. 255–79. Oxford: Blackwell.

  1995b. *Relevance: Communication and Cognition*. Oxford: Blackwell. 2nd edition.

  1998a. 'Irony and relevance'. In R. Carston and S. Uchida (eds.) *Relevance Theory: Applications and Implications*, pp. 283–93. Amsterdam: John Benjamins.

  1998b. 'The mapping between the mental and the public lexicon'. In P. Carruthers and J. Boucher (eds.) *Language and Thought*, pp. 184–200. Cambridge University Press.

  2002. 'Pragmatics, modularity and mindreading'. *Mind and Language* 17: 3–23.

  2005. 'Pragmatics'. *UCL Working Papers in Linguistics* 17: 353–88.

  2008. 'A deflationary account of metaphors'. In R. Gibbs (ed.) *The Cambridge Handbook of Metaphor and Thought*, pp. 84–105. Cambridge University Press.

Spivey-Knowlton, M. and Sedivy, J. 1995. 'Resolving attachment ambiguities with multiple constraints'. *Cognition* 55: 227–67.

Srioutai, J. 2004. 'The Thai c1a: a marker of tense or modality?'. In E. Daskalaki *et al.* (eds.) *Second CamLing Proceedings*, pp. 100–7. University of Cambridge.

Stainton, R. J. 2006. *Words and Thoughts: Subsentences, Ellipsis, and the Philosophy of Language.*Oxford: Clarendon Press.

Stalnaker, R. 1970. 'Pragmatics'. *Synthese* 22: 272–89. Reprinted in R. Stalnaker 1999, *Context and Content*. Oxford University Press.

  1973. 'Presuppositions'. *The Journal of Philosophical Logic* 2: 447–57.

  1974. 'Pragmatic presuppositions'. In M. Munitz and P. Unger (eds.) *Semantics and Philosophy*, pp. 197–214. New York University Press.

  1978. 'Assertion'. In P. Cole (ed.) *Syntax and Semantics* 9: *Pragmatic*, pp. 315–32. New York: Academic Press.

  1999. *Context and Content: Essays on Intentionality in Speech and Thought*. Oxford University Press.

  2004. 'Assertion revisited, on the interpretation of two-dimensional modal semantics'. *Philosophical Studies* 118: 299–322.

Stanley, J. 2000. 'Context and logical form'. *Linguistics and Philosophy* 23: 391–434.

  2002a. 'Making it articulated'. *Mind and Language* 17: 149–68.

2002b. 'Nominal restriction'. In G. Preyer and G. Peter (eds.) *Logical Form and Language*, pp. 365–88. Oxford University Press.

2005. *Knowledge and Practical Interests*. Oxford University Press.

Stanley, J. and Szabó, Z. 2000. 'On quantifier domain restriction'. *Mind and Language* 15: 219–61.

Stassen, L. 2001. 'Noun phrase coordination'. In M. Haspelmath, E. König, W. Österreicher and W. Raible (eds.) *Language Typology and Language Universals: An International Handbook*, pp. 1105–11. Berlin/New York: Walter de Gruyter.

Steedman, M. 1991. 'Structure and intonation'. *Language* 67: 260–96.

2000. 'Information structure and the syntax–phonology interface'. *Linguistic Inquiry* 31: 649–89.

Steensig, J. and Drew, P. 2008. 'Introduction: questioning and affiliation/disaffiliation in interaction'. *Discourse Studies* 10: 5–15.

Stenström, A.-B., Andersen, G. and Hasund, I. K. 2002. *Trends in Teenage Talk: Corpus Compilation, Analysis and Findings*. Studies in Corpus Linguistics 8. Amsterdam/Philadelphia: John Benjamins.

Stern, G. 1968. *Meaning and Change of Meaning*. Bloomington: Indiana University Press. (First published in 1931.)

Stern, J. 2000. *Metaphor in Context*. Cambridge, MA: MIT Press.

Sthioul, B. 2000. 'Aspect et inferences'. *Cahiers de linguistique française* 22: 165–87.

Stivers, T. 2008. 'Stance, alignment, and affiliation during storytelling: when nodding is a token of affiliation'. *Research on Language and Social Interaction* 41: 31–57.

2010. 'An overview of the question-response system in American English conversation'. *Journal of Pragmatics* 42: 2772–81.

Stockwell, R., Schachter P. and Partee, B. 1973. *The Major Structures of English*. New York: Holt, Rinehart and Winston.

Stokke, A. 2009. 'Intention-sensitive semantics'. *Synthese* 175: 383–404.

Strawson, P. 1950. 'On Referring'. *Mind* 59: 320–44. Reprinted in P. Strawson, *Logico-Linguistic Papers*, pp. 1–27. London: Methuen, 1971.

1952. *Introduction to Logical Theory*. Methuen.

1964a. 'Identifying reference and truth values'. *Theoria* 3: 96–118.

1964b. 'Intention and convention in speech acts'. *The Philosophical Review* 73: 439–60.

1971. 'Meaning and truth'. In P. Strawson, *Logico-Linguistic Papers*, pp. 131–46. London: Methuen.

Stubbs, M. 1983. *Discourse Analysis: The Sociolinguistic Analysis of Natural Language*. Oxford: Blackwell.

2001. *Words and Phrases: Corpus Studies of Lexical Semantics*. Oxford: Blackwell.

Sun, J. T.-S. 2007. 'The irrealis category in rGyalrong'. *Language and Linguistics* 8: 797–819.

Suzuki, S. (ed.) 2006. *Emotive Communication in Japanese*. Amsterdam: John Benjamins.

Sweetser, E. E. 1990. *From Etymology to Pragmatics: Metaphorical and Cultural Aspects of Semantic Structure*. Cambridge University Press.

Swinney, D. 1979. 'Lexical access during sentence comprehension: (re)consideration of context effects'. *Journal of Verbal Learning and Verbal Behavior* 18: 645–60.

Szabó, Z. G. 2000. 'Compositionality as supervenience'. *Linguistics and Philosophy* 23: 475–505.

Taavitsainen, I. and Fitzmaurice, S. 2007. 'Historical pragmatics: what it is and how to do it'. In S. M. Fitzmaurice and I. Taavitsainen (eds.) *Methodological Issues in Historical Pragmatics*, pp. 11–36. Berlin: Mouton de Gruyter.

Taavitsainen, I. and Jucker, A. H. 2010. 'Trends and developments in historical pragmatics'. In A. H. Jucker and I. Taavitsainen (eds.) *Handbook of Historical Pragmatics*. (Handbooks of Pragmatics 8), pp. 3–30. Berlin: Mouton de Gruyter.

Taavitsainen, I. and Pahta, P. (eds.) 2004. *Medical and Scientific Writing in Late Medieval English*. Studies in English Language. Cambridge University Press.

Talmy, L. 1985. 'Lexicalization patterns: semantic structure in lexical forms'. In T. Shopen (ed.) *Language Typology and Syntactic Description*, vol. III, pp. 57–149. Cambridge University Press.

  1996. 'The windowing of attention in language'. In M. Shibatani and S. Thompson (eds.) *Grammatical Constructions: Their Form and Meaning*, pp. 235–87. Oxford University Press.

  2000. *Toward A Cognitive Semantics*, vol. I. Cambridge, MA: MIT Press.

  2006. 'The representation of spatial structure in spoken and signed language'. In M. Hickman and S. Robert (eds.) *Space in Languages: Linguistic Systems and Cognitive Categories*, pp. 207–38. Amsterdam: John Benjamins.

Talwar, V. and Gordon, H. M. 2007. 'Lying in the elementary school years: verbal deception and its relation to second-order belief understanding'. *Developmental Psychology* 43: 804–10.

Tanenhaus, M. K., Spivey-Knowlton, M. J., Eberhard, K. M. and Sedivy, J. C. 1995. 'Integration of visual and linguistic information in spoken language comprehension'. *Science* 268: 1632–4.

Tannen, D. 1985. 'Cross-cultural communication'. In T. A. van Dijk (ed.) *Handbook of Discourse Analysis*, vol. IV, pp. 203–15. London: Academic Press.

  1993a. *Gender and Conversational Interaction*. Oxford University Press.

  (ed.) 1993b. *Framing in Discourse*. Oxford University Press.

  2005. 'Interactional sociolinguistics as a resource for intercultural pragmatics'. *Intercultural Pragmatics* 2: 205–8.

Tannen, D. and Kakava, C. 1992. 'Power and solidarity in Modern Greek conversation: disagreeing to agree'. *Journal of Modern Greek Studies* 10: 11–34.

Tartter, V. C., Gomes, H., Dubrovsky, B., Molholm, S. and Vala Stewart, R. 2002. 'Novel metaphors appear anomalous at least momentarily: evidence from N400'. *Brain and Language* 80: 488–509.

Tasmowski-De Ryck, L. 1985. 'L'imparfait avec et sans rupture'. *Langue française* 67: 59–77.

Tendahl, M. and Gibbs, R. 2008. 'Complementary perspectives on metaphor: cognitive linguistics and relevance theory'. *Journal of Pragmatics* 40: 1823–64.

Terkourafi, M. 2001. *Politeness in Cypriot Greek: A Frame-based Approach.* PhD dissertation, University of Cambridge. Available online at: www.ideals.illinois.edu/handle/2142/9573.

2002. 'Politeness and formulaicity: evidence from Cypriot Greek'. *Journal of Greek Linguistics* 3: 179–201.

2003. 'Generalized and particularized implicatures of politeness'. In P. Kühnlein, H. Rieser and H. Zeevat (eds.) *Perspectives on Dialogue in the New Millennium*, pp. 151–66. Amsterdam: John Benjamins.

2004. 'Testing Brown and Levinson's theory in a corpus of conversational data from Cypriot Greek'. *International Journal of the Sociology of Language* 168: 119–34.

2005. 'Beyond the micro-level in politeness research'. *Journal of Politeness Research* 1: 237–62.

2006. 'Review of Watts, Richard, Politeness'. *Journal of Pragmatics* 38: 418–28.

2007. 'Toward a universal notion of face for a universal notion of co-operation'. In I. Kecskes and L. Horn (eds.) *Explorations in Pragmatics: Linguistic, Cognitive and Intercultural Aspects*, pp. 313–44. Berlin: Mouton de Gruyter.

2008. 'Toward a unified theory of politeness, impoliteness, and rudeness'. In D. Bousfield and M. Locher (eds.) *Impoliteness in Language: Studies on its Interplay with Power in Theory and Practice*, pp. 45–74. Berlin: Mouton de Gruyter.

2009a. 'Finding face between Gemeinschaft and Gesellschaft: Greek perceptions of the in-group'. In M. Haugh and F. Bargiela-Chiappini (eds.) *Face, Communication, and Social Interaction*, pp. 269–88. London: Equinox.

2009b. 'On de-limiting context'. In A. Bergs and G. Diewald (eds.) *Context and Constructions*, pp. 17–42. Amsterdam: John Benjamins.

2009c. 'What use is what is said'. In P. De Brabanter and M. Kissine (eds.) *Utterance Interpretation and Cognitive Models*, pp. 27–58. Bingley: Emerald Group Publishing.

2011. 'From Politeness 1 to Politeness 2: Tracking norms of im/politeness across time and space'. *Journal of Politeness Research*, 7: 159–85.

(forthcoming). *From Politeness to Impoliteness: The Frame-based Approach*. Cambridge University Press.

Thomas, J. 1983. 'Cross-cultural pragmatic failure'. *Applied Linguistics* 4(2): 91–112.

Thomason, R. H. 1992. 'Accommodation, meaning, and implicature: inter-disciplinary foundations for pragmatics'. In P. Cohen, J. Morgan and M. E. Pollack (eds.) *Intentions in Communication*, pp. 325–63. Cambridge, MA: MIT Press.

Thompson, G. and Zhou, J. 2000. 'Evaluation and organization in text: the structuring role of evaluative disjuncts'. In S. Hunston and G. Thompson (eds.) *Evaluation in Text: Authorial Stance and the Construction of Discourse*, pp. 121–41. Oxford University Press.

Thompson, S. A. 1990. 'Information flow and dative shift in English discourse'. In J. A. Edmondson, C. Feagin and P. Mühlhäusler (eds.) *Development and Diversity: Language Variation Across Time and Space* (Summer Institute of Linguistics and the University of Texas at Arlington Publications in Linguistics 93), pp. 239–53. Dallas: Summer Institute of Linguistics and University of Texas at Arlington.

Thompson, S. A. and Mulac, A. 1991. 'A quantitative perspective on the grammaticization of epistemic parentheticals in English'. In E. Traugott and B. Heine (eds.) *Approaches to Grammaticalization*, pp. 313–27. Amsterdam/Philadelphia: John Benjamins.

Tindale, C. W. 2010. 'Rhetoric'. In L. Cummings (ed.) *The Pragmatics Encyclopedia*, pp. 403–4. London: Routledge.

Ting-Toomey, S. 1999. *Communicating Across Cultures*. New York/London: The Guilford Press.

Tirassa, M. 1999. 'Communicative competence and the architecture of the mind/brain'. *Brain and Language* 68: 419–41.

Tobler, A. 1921. 'Il ne faut que tu meurs; "du darfst nicht sterben"'. In *Vermischte Beitrage zur französisichen Grammatik*, vol. iii, pp. 78–111. Leipzig: Hirzel, 2nd edition (first published 1882).

Tomasello, M. and Call, J. 1997. *Primate Cognition*. Oxford University Press.

Tomasello, M. and Rakoczy, H. 2003. 'What makes human cognition unique? From individual to shared to collective intentionality'. *Mind and Language* 18: 121–47.

Tomasello, M., Carpenter, M., Call, J., Behne, T. and Moll, H. 2005. 'Understanding and sharing intentions: the origins of cultural cognition'. *Behavioural and Brain Sciences* 28: 675–735.

Torres Cacoullos, R. and Walker, J. A. 2009. 'The present of the English future: grammatical variation and collocations in discourse'. *Language* 85: 321–54.

Tracy, K. 1990. 'The many faces of facework'. In H. Giles and P. Robinson (eds.) *The Handbook of Language and Social Psychology*, pp. 209–26. Chichester: Wiley.

   2008. 'Reasonable hostility: Situation-appropriate face-attack'. *Journal of Politeness Research* 4: 169–91.

Tracy, K. and Tracy, S. 1998. 'Rudeness at 911: reconceptualizing face and face-attack'. *Human Communication Research* 25: 225–51.

Traugott, E. 1982. 'From propositional to textual and expressive meanings: some semantic-pragmatic aspects of grammaticalization'. In W. P. Lehmann and Y. Malkiel (eds.) *Perspectives on Historical Linguistics*, pp. 245–71. Amsterdam: John Benjamins.

1989. 'On the rise of epistemic meanings in English: an example of subjectification in semantic change'. *Language* 65: 31–55.

1995. 'Subjectification in grammaticalization'. In D. Stein and S. Wright (eds.) *Subjectivity and Subjectivisation*, pp. 31–54. Amsterdam/Philadelphia: John Benjamins.

2004. 'Historical pragmatics'. In L. Horn and G. Ward (eds.) *The Handbook of Pragmatics*, pp. 538–61. Oxford: Blackwell.

2008a. '"All that he endeavoured to prove was . . . ": on the emergence of grammatical constructions in dialogic contexts'. In R. Cooper and R. Kempson (eds.) *Language in Flux: Dialogue Coordination, Language Variation, Change and Evolution*, pp. 143–77. London: King's College Publications.

2008b. 'The state of English language studies: a linguistic perspective'. In M. Thormählen (ed.) *English Now: Selected Papers from the 20th IAUPE Conference in Lund 2007*, pp. 199–225. Lund Studies in English.

2010. 'Revisiting subjectification and intersubjectification'. In K. Davidse, L. Vandelanotte and H. Cuyckens (eds.) *Subjectification, Intersubjectification and Grammaticalization*, pp. 29–71. Berlin: Mouton de Gruyter.

Traugott, E. and Dasher, R. B. 2002. *Regularity in Semantic Change*. Cambridge University Press.

Traugott, E. and Heine, B. (eds.) 1991. *Approaches to Grammaticalization*. 2 vols. Amsterdam: John Benjamins.

Traugott, E. and König, E. 1991. 'The semantics-pragmatics of grammaticalization revisited'. In E. Traugott and B. Heine (eds.) *Approaches to Grammaticalization*, vol. I, pp. 189–218. Amsterdam: John Benjamins.

Travis, C. 1975. *Saying and Understanding*. Oxford: Blackwell.

1997. 'Pragmatics'. In B. Hale and C. Wright (eds.) *A Companion to the Philosophy of Language*, pp. 87–107. Oxford: Blackwell.

2006. 'Psychologism'. In E. Lepore and B. C. Smith (eds.) *The Oxford Handbook of Philosophy of Language*, pp. 103–26. Oxford: Clarendon Press.

2008. *Occasion-Sensitivity: Selected Essays*. Oxford University Press.

Trosborg, A. 1995. *Interlanguage Pragmatics: Requests, Complaints and Apologies*. Berlin: Mouton de Gruyter.

Truss, L. 2005. *Talk to the Hand: The Utter Bloody Rudeness of the World Today, or Six Good Reasons to Stay Home and Bolt the Door*. London: Profile.

Tuggy, D. 1993. 'Ambiguity, polysemy and vagueness'. *Cognitive Linguistics* 4: 273–91.

Tuomela, R. 2005. 'We-intentions revisited'. *Philosophical Studies* 125: 327–69.

Tuomela, R. and Miller, K. 1988. 'We-intentions'. *Philosophical Studies* 53: 367–89.

Turner, K. 1996. 'The principal principles of pragmatic inference: Politeness'. *Language Teaching* 29: 1–13.

(ed.) 1999. *The Semantics/Pragmatics Interface from Different Points of View.* Oxford: Elsevier.

Uhlig, G. (ed.) 1883. *Grammatici Graeci.* Leipzig: Teubner.

Underwood, G., Schmitt, N. and Galpin, A. 2004. 'The eyes have it: an eye-movement study into the processing of formulaic sequences'. In N. Schmitt (ed.) *Formulaic Sequences: Acquisition, Processing and Use*, pp. 153–72. Amsterdam/Philadelphia: John Benjamins.

Usami, M. 2002. *Discourse Politeness in Japanese Conversation: Some Implications for a Universal Theory of Politeness.* Tokyo: Hituzi Syobo.

Vallduví, E. 1992. *The Informational Component.* New York: Garland.

Vallduví, E. and Vilkuna, M. 1998. 'On rheme and kontrast'. In P. Cullicover and L. McNally (eds.) *The Limits of Syntax*, pp. 79–108. New York: Academic Press.

Van Lancker, D. 2009. 'Formulaic and novel language in a "dual process" model of language competence'. In R. Corrigan, E. A. Moravcsik, H. Ouali and K. M. Wheatley (eds.) *Formulaic Language*, vol. II: *Acquisition, Loss, Psychological Reality, and Functional Explanations*, pp. 445–70. Amsterdam/Philadelphia: John Benjamins.

Van Lancker, D., Canter, G. J. and Terbeek, D. 1981. 'Disambiguation of ditropic sentences: acoustic and phonetic cues'. *Journal of Speech and Hearing Research* 24: 330–5.

Van linden, A. 2009. *Dynamic, Deontic and Evaluative Adjectives and their Clausal Complement Patterns: A Synchronic-diachronic Account.* Doctoral dissertation, Katholieke Universiteit Leuven.

Van Valin, R. 2006. *Exploring the Syntax-Semantics Interface.* Cambridge University Press.

Vandeloise, C. 2003. 'Containment, support and linguistic relativity'. In H. Cuykens, R. Dirven and J. Taylor (eds.) *Cognitive Approaches to Lexical Semantics*, pp. 393–425. Berlin: Mouton de Gruyter.

2006. 'Are there spatial prepositions?'. In M. Hickman and S. Robert (eds.) *Space in Languages: Linguistic Systems and Cognitive Categories*, pp. 149–54. Amsterdam: John Benjamins.

Vandepitte, S. 1989. 'A pragmatic function of intonation'. *Lingua* 79: 265–97.

Vandewinkel, S. and Davidse, K. 2008. 'The interlocking paths of development to emphasizer adjective *pure*'. *Journal of Historical Pragmatics* 9: 255–87.

Vega Moreno, R. 2007. *Creativity and Convention: The Pragmatics of Everyday Figurative Speech.* Amsterdam: John Benjamins.

Velleman, D. 1997. 'How to share an intention'. *Philosophy and Phenomenological Research* 57: 29–50.

Veltman, F. 1996. 'Defaults in update semantics'. *Journal of Philosophical Logic* 25: 221–61.

Vendler, Z. 1967. *Linguistics in Philosophy.* Ithaca, NY: Cornell University Press.

Verschueren, J. 1999. *Understanding Pragmatics.* Understanding Language Series. London: Arnold.

Verschueren, J., Östman, J.-O., Blommaert, J. and Bulcaen, C. (eds.) 2003. *Handbook of Pragmatics Online*. Amsterdam: John Benjamins.

Verstraete, J.-C. 2005. 'The semantics and pragmatics of composite mood marking: non-Pama-Nyungan languages of northern Australia'. *Linguistic Typology* 9: 223–68.

Vigliocco, G., Meteyard, L., Andrews, M. and Kousta, S. 2009. 'Toward a theory of semantic representation'. *Language and Cognition* 1: 219–47.

Visconti, J. 2006. 'The role of lexical semantics in semantic change'. *Acta Linguistica Hafniensia* 38: 207–34.

Vu, H., Kellas, G. and Paul, S. T. 1998. 'Sources of sentence constraint on lexical ambiguity resolution'. *Memory and Cognition* 26: 979–1001.

Vu, H., Kellas, G., Metcalf, K. and Herman, R. 2000. 'The influence of global discourse on lexical ambiguity resolution'. *Memory and Cognition* 28: 236–52.

Walter, H., Adenzato, M., Ciaramidaro, A., Enrici, I., Pia, L. and Bara, B. 2004. 'Understanding intentions in social interaction: the role of the anterior paracingulate cortex'. *Journal of Cognitive Neuroscience* 16: 1854–63.

Waltereit, R. 2006. 'The rise of discourse particles: a specific type of language change'. In K. Fischer (ed.) *Approaches to Discourse Particles*, pp. 61–76. Oxford: Elsevier.

Waltereit, R. and Detges, U. 2007. 'Different functions, different histories. Modal particles and discourse markers from a diachronic point of view'. In M. Cuenca (ed.) *Contrastive Perspectives on Discourse Markers*, pp. 61–80. Special issue of *Journal of Catalan Linguistics* 6.

Ward, G. 1990. 'The discourse functions of VP preposing'. *Language* 66: 742–63.

Ward, G. and Hirschberg, J. 1988. 'Intonation and propositional attitude: the pragmatics of L* + H L H%'. In J. Powers and K. J. de Jong (eds.) *Proceedings of the Fifth Eastern States Conference on Linguistics*, pp. 512–22. Columbus: Ohio State University Department of Linguistics.

Warner, A. 1990. 'Reworking the history of English auxiliaries'. In S. Adamson, V. Law, N. Vincent and S. Wright (eds.) *Papers from the 5th International Conference of English Historical Linguistics*, pp. 537–58. Amsterdam: John Benjamins.

1993. *English Auxiliaries: Structure and History*. Cambridge University Press.

Watts, R. 1989. 'Relevance and relational work: Linguistic politeness as politic behaviour'. *Multilingua* 8: 131–66.

2003. *Politeness*. Cambridge University Press.

Watts, R., Ide, S. and Ehlich, K. 1992/2005. 'Introduction'. In R. Watts, S. Ide and K. Ehlich (eds.) *Politeness in Language: Studies in its History, Theory and Practice* (2nd edition), pp. 1–17. Berlin: Mouton de Gruyter.

WDS 1942. *Webster's Dictionary of Synonyms*. Springfield, MA: G. C. Merriam Co.

Wearing, C. 2006. 'Metaphor and what is said'. *Mind and Language* 21: 310–32.

Webster, N. 2002. *Webster's Third New International Dictionary of the English Language, Unabridged*. Ed. P. B. Gove. Springfield, MA: Merriam-Webster.

Weiner, M. 2006. 'Are all conversational implicatures cancellable?'. *Analysis* 66: 127–30.

Weinreich, U. 1962. 'Lexicographic definition in descriptive semantics'. In F. W. Householder and S. Saporta (eds.) *Problems in Lexicography*, pp. 25–43. Bloomington: Indiana University Press.

1966. 'Explorations in semantic theory'. In T. A. Sebeok (ed.) *Current Trends in Linguistics 3*. The Hague: Mouton. Reprinted in W. Labov and B. S. Weinreich (eds.) 1980, *Weinreich on Semantics*, pp. 99–201. Philadelphia: University of Pennsylvania Press.

Welman, J. B. 1948. *Preliminary Survey of the Freshwater Fishes of Nigeria*. Lagos: Government Printer.

Westerståhl, D. (forthcoming). 'Compositionality in Kaplan Style Semantics'. In W. Hinzen, E. Machery and M. Werning (eds.) *The Handbook of Compositionality*. Oxford University Press.

Wharton, T. 2003a. 'Interjections, language and the "showing"/"saying" continuum'. *Pragmatics and Cognition* 11: 39–91.

2003b. 'Natural pragmatics and natural codes'. *Mind and Language* 18: 447–77.

2008. 'Gricean intentions and relevance-theoretic intentions'. *Intercultural Pragmatics* 5: 131–52.

2009. *Pragmatics and Non-Verbal Communication*. Cambridge University Press.

Whitehead, A. N. and Russell, B. 1910. *Principia Mathematica*, vol. I. Cambridge University Press.

Wichmann, A. 2002. 'Attitudinal intonation and the inferential process'. In B. Bel and I. Marlien (eds.) *Proceedings of the Speech Prosody Conference*, pp. 11–16. Denver, CO.

Wichmann, A. and Blakemore, D. (eds.) 2006. 'Prosody and pragmatics'. Special issue of *Journal of Pragmatics* 38 (10).

Widdowson, H. 2004. *Text, Context, and Pretext: Critical Issues in Discourse Analysis*. Oxford: Blackwell.

Wierzbicka, A. 1985. 'Different cultures, different languages, different speech acts'. *Journal of Pragmatics* 9: 145–78.

1991. *Cross-cultural Pragmatics: The Semantics of Human Interaction*. Berlin: Mouton de Gruyter.

2006. 'On folk conceptions of mind, agency and morality'. *Journal of Cognition and Culture* 6: 165–79.

Wilkins, D. 2006. 'Towards an Arrernte grammar of space'. In S. Levinson and D. Wilkins (eds.) *Grammars of Space*, pp. 24–62. Cambridge University Press.

Williamson, T. 1994. *Vagueness*. London: Routledge.

2009. 'Reference, inference, and the semantics of pejoratives'. In J. Almog and P. Leonardi (eds.) *Philosophy of David Kaplan*, pp. 137–58. Oxford University Press.

Wilson, D. 1992. 'Reference and relevance'. *UCL Working Papers in Linguistics* 4: 165–91.

2006. 'The pragmatics of verbal irony: echo or pretence?'. *Lingua* 116: 1722–43.

2009a. 'Parallels and differences in the treatment of metaphor in relevance theory and cognitive linguistics'. *Studies in Pragmatics (Journal of the Pragmatics Society of Japan)* 11: 42–60. Revised version 2010, in *UCL Working Papers in Linguistics* 22.

2009b. 'Irony and metarepresentation'. *UCL Working Papers in Linguistics* 21: 183–226.

Wilson, D. and Carston, R. 2006. 'Metaphor, relevance and the "emergent property" issue'. *Mind and Language* 21: 404–33. Revised version 2007, in *The Baltic International Yearbook of Cognition, Logic and Communication*, 3 (A Figure of Speech). http://thebalticyearbook.org/journals/baltic/issue/view/2.

2007. 'A unitary approach to lexical pragmatics: relevance, inference and ad hoc concepts'. In N. Burton-Roberts (ed.) *Pragmatics*, pp. 230–59. Houndmills: Palgrave Macmillan.

Wilson, D. and Sperber, D. 1979. 'Ordered entailments: An alternative to presuppositional theories'. In C.-K. Oh and D. A. Dinneen (eds.) *Syntax and Semantics 11: Presupposition*, pp. 299–323. New York: Academic Press.

1986. 'Inference and implicature'. In C. Travis (ed.) *Meaning and Interpretation*, pp. 45–75. Oxford: Basil Blackwell.

1988. 'Mood and the analysis of non-declarative sentences'. In J. Dancy, J. M. Moravcsik and C. C. W. Taylor (eds.) *Human Agency, Language, Duty and Value: Philosophical Essays in Honour of J. O. Urmson*, pp. 77–101. Stanford University Press.

1992. 'On verbal irony'. *Lingua* 87: 53–76. Reprinted in R. Gibbs and H. Colston (eds.) 2007, *Irony in Language and Thought: A Cognitive Science Reader*, pp. 35–55. Hillsdale, NJ: Lawrence Erlbaum.

1993a. 'Linguistic form and relevance'. *Lingua* 90: 1–25.

1993b. 'Pragmatics and time'. *UCL Working Papers in Linguistics* 5: 277–300.

2002. 'Truthfulness and relevance'. *Mind* 111/442: 583–632.

2004. 'Relevance theory'. In L. Horn and G. Ward (eds.) *The Handbook of Pragmatics*, pp. 607–32. Oxford: Blackwell.

Wilson, D. and Wharton, T. 2006. 'Relevance and prosody'. *Journal of Pragmatics* 38: 1559–79.

Winch, P. 1997. 'Can we understand ourselves?'. *Philosophical Investigations* 20: 193–204.

Winner, E. 1988. *The Point of Words: Children's Understanding of Metaphor and Irony*. Cambridge, MA: Harvard University Press.

Winner, E. and Gardner, H. 1993. 'Metaphor and irony: two levels of understanding'. In A. Ortony (ed.) *Metaphor and Thought*, pp. 425–43. Cambridge University Press.

Winner, E. and Leekam, S. R. 1991. 'Distinguishing irony from deception: understanding the speaker's second-order intention'. *British Journal of Developmental Psychology* 9: 257–70.

Witek, M. 2009. 'Skepticism about reflexive intentions refuted'. *Lodz Papers in Pragmatics* 5: 69–83.

Wittgenstein, L. 1953. *Philosophische Untersuchungen*. Oxford: Blackwell. English translation *Philosophical Investigations*, 1953. Oxford: Blackwell. Reprinted 2003 as *Philosophical Investigations: The German Text, with a Revised English Translation*. 3rd edition. Malden, MA: Blackwell.

1969. *Philosophische Grammatik*. Suhrkamp, Frankfurt. English translation *Philosophical Grammar*. Oxford: Blackwell, 1974.

2001. *Philosophical Investigations*. 3rd edition. Oxford/Malden: Blackwell Publishers Ltd.

Woodfield, A. 1994. 'Intentionality'. In R. E. Asher (ed.) *The Encyclopedia of Language and Linguistics*, vol. IV, pp. 1705–9. Oxford: Pergamon Press.

Woods, J. 2010. 'Inference'. In L. Cummings (ed.) *The Pragmatics Encyclopedia*, pp. 218–20. London: Routledge.

Wray, A. 2002. *Formulaic Language and the Lexicon*. Cambridge University Press.
2008. *Formulaic Language: Pushing the Boundaries*. Oxford University Press.

Xrakovski, V. S. (ed.) 2001. *Typology of Imperative Constructions*. Munich: Lincoln.

Yap, F. H., Matthews, S. and Horie, K. 2004. 'From pronominalizer to pragmatic marker: implications for unidirectionality from a cross-linguistic perspective'. In O. Fischer, M. Norde and H. Perridon (eds.) *Up and Down the Cline: The Nature of Grammaticalization*, pp. 137–68. Amsterdam: John Benjamins.

Yap, F. H., Lam, C. T. and Wang, J. 2008. 'Clausal integration and the emergence of sentence-final particles in Chinese: a comparison of ER YI YI and YE YI YI'. http://www.sfu.ca/gradlings/SFUWPL/ICEAL2/Yap_EtAl.pdf.

Zeevat, H. 1992. 'Presupposition and accommodation in update semantics'. *Journal of Semantics* 9: 379–412.

1997. 'The common ground as a dialogue parameter'. In G. Jäger and A. Benz (eds.) *Proceedings Mundial 1997*, pp. 195–214. Munich: CIS.

2007. 'Exhaustivity, questions and plurals in update semantics'. In M. Aloni, A. Butler and P. Dekker (eds.) *Questions in Dynamic Semantics*, pp. 161–92. Amsterdam: Elsevier.

2009. *Optimal Interpretation as an Alternative to Gricean Pragmatics: Structuring Information in Discourse; the Explicit/Implicit Dimension*. Oslo: OSLA.

Zimmermann, T. E. 2001. 'Free choice disjunction and epistemic possibility'. *Natural Language Semantics* 8: 255–90.

Zipf, G. K. 1949. *Human Behavior and the Principle of Least Effort: An Introduction to Human Ecology*. Cambridge, MA: Addison-Wesley.

Ziv, Y. 1982. 'Getting more mileage out of existentials in English'. *Linguistics* 20: 747–62.

Zwicky, A. and Sadock, J. 1975. 'Ambiguity tests and how to fail them'. In J. P. Kimball (ed.) *Syntax and Semantics 4*, pp. 1–35. New York: Academic Press.

# Index